THE OXFORD HANDBOOK OF

CHILDREN'S RIGHTS LAW

THE OXFORD HANDBOOK OF

CHILDREN'S RIGHTS LAW

Edited by

JONATHAN TODRES

and

SHANI M. KING

OXFORD

UNIVERSITY PRESS

OXFORD
UNIVERSITY PRESS

Oxford University Press is a department of the University of Oxford. It furthers
the University's objective of excellence in research, scholarship, and education
by publishing worldwide. Oxford is a registered trade mark of Oxford University
Press in the UK and certain other countries.

Published in the United States of America by Oxford University Press
198 Madison Avenue, New York, NY 10016, United States of America.

Library of Congress Cataloging-in-Publication Data
Names: Todres, Jonathan, editor. | King, Shani M, editor.
Title: The Oxford handbook of children's rights law / edited by
Jonathan Todres and Shani M. King
Description: New York, New York Oxford University Press, 2020. |
Series: Oxford handbooks | Includes bibliographical references and index.
Identifiers: LCCN 2019025726 | ISBN 9780190097608 (hardback) |
ISBN 9780190097615 (pdf) | ISBN 9780190097622 (epub)
Subjects: LCSH: Children—Legal status, laws, etc. | Children's rights.
Classification: LCC K639 .O98 2020 | DDC 342.08/772–dc23
LC record available at https://lccn.loc.gov/2019025726

1 3 5 7 9 8 6 4 2

Printed by Sheridan Books, Inc., United States of America

TABLE OF CONTENTS

I. HISTORICAL AND THEORETICAL FRAMEWORK

II. PERSPECTIVES AND METHODS

IV. SELECTED INDIVIDUAL AND INSTITUTIONAL ACTORS

V. SELECTED POPULATIONS

VI. CONCLUSION

PREFACE

MARTHA MINOW

To be the subject of a handbook is to arrive at a point when people need and want advice about how to do something.[1] This book on children's rights joins handbooks already in print on children's literature and on children and the law.[2] Like those works, this book addresses a wide range of practical settings and policies as well as conceptual and philosophic themes connected with ideas about and actual needs of children. The turn to children's *rights* reflects and underscores the work of the 1989 UN Convention on the Rights of the Child that by now has all nations except the United States as signatories.[3] Yet even thirty years later, the turn to rights for children remains a subject for debate, development, and challenge of both conceptual and practical dimensions.

This handbook brings particular attention to critical perspectives rooted in the Global South, in children's own practices, and in concerns about identities and power relationships. The authors defend the universal availability of children's rights and highlight many specific contexts and needs reflecting different identities. Mindful of the international children's rights framework, the chapters also emphasize bottom-up perspectives grounded in the lives of children, communities, and movements.

RIGHTS AND PROTECTIONS; INTERESTS AND PARTICIPATION

The familiar contest over whether children are best served by rights or protections gains detailed and fresh analysis in light of concrete issues. Authors here turn to the best interests of the child standards to show how the concept can at times serve as a proxy for rights but also remain open to manipulation, paternalism, and bias.[4] Rights conceived as claims to particular relationships break out of the rights/protection divide.[5] Rights may be rooted in children's evolving capacities.[6] Even more memorable is a conception of children as rights-bearers regardless of their current or future capacities. Rights for children are the common coin of societal respect and also operational claims on the responsibilities of others.[7]

Illuminating discussions of children's participation in politics and in local, national, and international institutions give texture and weight to what the *agency* and *voice* of children can mean.[8] Participation by children requires opportunities in terms of space and flexibility.[9] The authors herein call for and provide explicit attention to the needs of children without adult providers,[10] to children concerned about climate change,[11] and to the predicate of education about children's rights for children's empowerment.[12]

OBJECTS OR SUBJECTS

Implicit in the entire handbook is the struggle to convert children from a status as objects to a status as subjects. A subject observes, an object is observed; a subject acts, while an object is acted upon. Children have been objects of ownership, trafficking, violence, punishment, and deployment into combat.[13] Parents, peers, communities, militia groups, national states, and other actors have treated children as objects in these and other ways. Recognizing children as subjects takes work, especially when some join armed conflicts, enter into marriages, face criminal sanctions, or become victims of violence. Rights discourse, advocacy, and reforms can help people see and treat children as subjects.[14] Being beneficiaries of expansive aspirations and boundless love may not follow inexorably from bearing rights, but rights can help.[15]

Also many of the chapters reveal how children are the objects of adult confusions. Confusions over who is a child and for what purposes arise within and across legal communities.[16] A central confusion is the dilemma over whether and when children benefit if treated as the same as or as different from adults. Rather like the dilemmas arising over gender, race, and disability, in worlds that have made a particular trait matter, children can be both helped and hurt when recognized as diverging from adults.[17] Children are harmed at times if treated as vulnerable, but they can also be harmed when their vulnerabilities are ignored. Denying children the opportunity to earn payment through work can be a violation of rights, but so also can children be exploited and harmed by workplace demands and practices.[18] Marriage of children can be abuse, so children should have the right not to marry, but children who are married also should have the rights to obtain education, health, and social security due any child.[19]

Used by adults to address adult concerns such as the Cold War preoccupations of the United States in the 1950s,[20] children also embody the future of all human beings and hold the potential to draw out the best in others.[21] Adults both use children and gain inspiration from them, as expressed in the claim that we must begin with children if we want world peace[22] and in current efforts to combat climate change.[23] Acknowledging that children may be objects as well as subjects in such initiatives would heighten arguments for their greater participation and for reflections by those who were recently children in campaigns waged in their names.

Negative versus Positive and Individuals versus Communities

Legal and political traditions framed in terms of rights often reflect Western preoccupations with autonomous individuals and with protections against state power.[24] These features of rights discourse can pose conceptual and practical obstacles to positive liberties. Rights *to* education, health, family, and other affirmative goods acknowledge dependency, as do rights *against* violence, discrimination, harassment, and abuse. Authors here explore affirmative rights to health and health care, to education, and to sustainable development.[25] The handbook makes sure not to leave out these rights for migrating children.[26] Whether rights discourse can mobilize resources and whether government action risks harming children are questions thus deserving sustained treatment afforded in handbook chapters. Taken together, the chapters demonstrate that to guard against abusive relationships with adults is to let go of a distinction between affirmative and negative rights.

Context and Concentric Circles

Contexts matter. Contexts matter in acknowledging how positive and negative rights intertwine, in attending to children's needs, and in giving force and meaning to children's rights while also demanding particularized translations.[27] Notable contributions in this book map the concentric circles of contexts for children. From their solitary embodiment to their relationships with family members and peers, from their membership in political communities to their status as immigrants or people without a state, from the variations across regions and nations to the universality of children's rights (at least as seen by particular movements and institutions), children live in ecosystems with sometimes concentric and sometimes overlapping circles of governance.[28] And yet even this understates the experiences of children who share much with their peers but diverge in race, sexual and gender identities, and family composition.[29] A strength of this book is its attention to children from indigenous communities,[30] children affected by the societal and legal divisions of public and private,[31] children marked by social caste and descent-based discrimination,[32] street children and children heading households without adult caregivers,[33] children subject to international adoptions,[34] and children migrating with families or alone across national borders.[35]

The effects of global power arrangements infuse discussions about what is or can be universal in children's rights.[36] Alongside politics are cultures. Rights may seem in tension but may also produce synergies with cultural resources.[37] Just as advocates need to resist an exclusive focus on deficits of individuals by attending also to their potential capabilities,[38] the entire project of building, revising, and implementing children's rights should draw attention to both shortfalls and progress in children's rights.[39]

A Big Bet

Taken together, the many perspectives expressed in this work bring to mind a different definition of a handbook—that is, as a bookmaker's book of bets.[40] For despite the legal and social reforms of the past few decades, the hope that such rights will better the lives of children remains a wager. Will summoning the language, institutions, advocacy, and hopes surrounding rights, make the lives of children better? That is one bet. Another is the debate over what *better* means. Unlike so many other subjects, this one has an unavoidable time sensitivity. Even with disagreements over when childhood begins and ends, there is no debate that it is short. Even a week of deprivation in the life of a child—a week of exclusion from school, a week of sexual assault, a week of military deployment, a week of enforced separation from parents—will have lasting effects. The clock is ticking. This handbook summons talent and effort from across the globe to make rights for children real.

Notes

1. Cambridge Dictionary, https://dictionary.cambridge.org/us/dictionary/english/handbook. See also Merriam-Webster Dictionary, https://www.merriam-webster.com/dictionary/handbook (defining handbook as "a book capable of being conveniently carried as a ready reference").

2. Prior handbooks regarding children address, as well as children's and young people's nursing, early childhood intervention, children's literature, social justice in music education, and children and the law, among many other topics. See Cathy Benedict, Patrick Schmidt, and Gary Spruce, eds., *The Oxford Handbook of Social Justice in Music Education* (New York: Oxford University Press, 2018); Edward Alan Glasper, Gillian McEwing, and Jim Richardson, eds., *The Oxford Handbook of Children's and Young People's Nursing*, 2nd. ed. (New York: Oxford University Press, 2010); Jack P. Shonkoff, ed., *Handbook of Early Childhood Intervention*, 2nd ed. (Cambridge: Cambridge University Press, 2000); Lynne Vallone and Julia Mickenberg, eds., *Oxford Handbook of Children's Literature* (New York: Oxford University Press, 2011). See also Martin D. Ruck, Michele Peterson-Badali, and Michael Freeman, eds., *Handbook of Children's Rights* (New York: Routledge, 2016).

3. UN Convention on the Rights of the Child, G.A. Res. 44/25, 44th Sess., UN Doc. A/RES/44/25 (1989); Rachel Hodgkin and Peter Newell, *Implementation Handbook for the Convention on the Rights of the Child*, 3rd ed. (Geneva: UNICEF, 2007), https://www.unicef.org/publications/files/Implementation_Handbook_for_the_Convention_on_the_Rights_of_the_Child.pdf. On the solitude of the United States in this context, see B. Shaw Drake and Megan Corrarino, "U.S. Stands Alone: Not Signing U.N. Child Rights Treaty Leaves Migrant Children Vulnerable," Huffington Post, October 13, 2015, https://www.huffingtonpost.com/b-shaw-drake/children-migrants-rights_b_8271874.html.

4. See Wouter Vandenhole and Gamze Erdem Türkelli, chapter 10, this volume.

5. See Barbara Bennett Woodhouse, chapter 12, this volume. See also Martha Minow and Mary Lyndon Shanley, "Relational Rights and Responsibilities: Revisioning the Family in Liberal Political Theory and Law," *Hypatia* 11 (Winter): 4–26; reprinted as Martha Minow and Mary Lyndon Shanley, "Relational Rights and Responsibilities: Revisioning the Family in Liberal Political Theory and Law," in *Reconstructing Political Theory: Feminist Perspectives*, ed. Mary Lyndon Shanley and Uma Narayan (University Park: Pennsylvania State University Press, 1998), 84–108. See also Martha Minow, "Interpreting Rights: An Essay for Robert Cover," *Yale Law Journal* 96, no. 8 (1987): 1860–1915; Martha Minow, "Essay Review: Are Rights Right for Children?" *American Bar Foundation Research Journal* 12 (1987): 203–223; Martha Minow, "Rights for the Next Generation: A Feminist Approach to Children's Rights," *Harvard Women's Law Journal* 9 (1986): 1–24; reprinted as Martha Minow, "The Public Duties of Families and Children," in *From Children to Citizens*, vol. 2: *The Role of the Juvenile Court*, ed. Francis X. Hartmann (New York: Springer-Verlag, 1987); translated into Japanese by Hiroshi Oh'e in *The Socio-Legal Studies on Family Law* 10 (September 1994); reprinted in Rosaline Ekman Ladd, *Children's Rights Re-Visioned: Philosophical Readings* (Belmont, CA: WadsworthPublishing Co., 1996).

6. For a nuanced argument in this vein, see Anne Dailey, "Children's Constitutional Rights," *Minnesota Law Review* 95 (2010–2011): 2099–2179. See generally Tom D. Campbell, "The Rights of the Minor: As Person, as Child, as Juvenile, as Future Adult," *International Journal of Law, Policy and the Family* 6, no. 1 (April 1992): 1–23, https://doi.org/10.1093/lawfam/6.1.1; John Tobin, "Justifying Children's Rights," *International Journal of Children's Rights* 21, no. 3 (2013): 395–441, https://doi.org/10.1163/15718182-02103004. Valuable contributions to conceptions of children's rights include Tamar Ezer, "A Positive Right to Protection for Children," *Yale Human Rights and Development Journal* 7, no. 1 (2004), http://digitalcommons.law.yale.edu/yhrdlj/vol7/iss1/1 (argument for protection and dignity); Colleen Sheppard, "Children's Rights to Equality: Protection versus Paternalism," *Annals of Health Law*, no. 1 (1992): 197–211 (advancing claims for both noninterference and for protection and care); David B. Thronson, "Kids Will Be Kids? Reconsidering Conceptions of Children's Rights Underlying Immigration Law," *Ohio State Law Journal* 63 (2002): 979–1016; Sharon Bessel and Tali Gal, "Forming Partnerships: The Human Rights of Children in Need of Care and Protection," *International Journal of Children's Rights* 15 (2008): 1–16; Annette R. Appell, "Children's Voice and Justice: Lawyering for Children in the Twenty-First Century," *Nevada Law Journal* 6 (2006): 692–723; R. J. R. Levesque, "International Children's Rights Grow Up: Implications for American Jurisprudence and Domestic Policy," *California Western International Law Journal* 24 (1994): 193–240.

7. See Michael Freeman, chapter 3 (this volume), text at notes 7–8; versus responsibilities of others, see text at notes 101–109.

8. See Perpetua Kirby and Rebecca Webb, chapter 23, and Gerison Lansdown, chapter 24, this volume.

9. See Karl Hanson and Olga Nieuwenhuys, chapter 5, and Jaap Doek, chapter 13, this volume.

10. See Julia Sloth Nielsen and Katrien Klep, chapter 29, this volume.

11. See Christine Bakker, chapter 22 (this volume), text at notes 78–79.

12. See R. Brian Howe and Katherine Covell, chapter 33, this volume.

13. See Mike Dottridge, chapter 30, and Mark Drumbl, chapter 31, this volume.

14. See Ton Liefaard, chapter 14; Drumbl, chapter 31; and Marta Santos Pais, chapter 15, this volume.

15. See Shani King, *Have I Ever Told You?* (Thomaston, ME: Tilbury House, 2018).

16. See Freeman, chapter 3, text at notes 66–82 and text at notes 146–160; Hanson and Nieuwenhuys, chapter 5, text at notes 22–25.

17. Martha Minow, *Making All the Difference: Inclusion, Exclusion, and American Law* (Ithaca, NY: Cornell University Press, 1990); Christine Littleton, "Reconstructing Sexual Equality," *California Law Review* 75 (1987): 1279–1337.

18. See Manfred Liebel, chapter 17, this volume.

19. See Jessica Dixon Weaver, chapter 9, and Nielsen and Klep, chapter 29, this volume.

20. Cynthia Price Cohen, "The Role of the United States in the Drafting of the Convention on the Rights of the Child," *Emory International Law Review* 20 (Spring 2006): 185–198.

21. See Jo Becker, chapter 2 (this volume), text at note 21.

22. See Hanson and Nieuwenhuys, chapter 5, text at note 9 (quoting Mahatma Gandhi).

23. See Bakker, chapter 22.

24. See Afua Twum-Danso Imoh, chapter 21, this volume.

25. See Ursula Kilkelly, chapter 18, Laura Lundy and Amy Brown, chapter 19, and Aoife Nolan, chapter 20, this volume.

26. See Sarah Paoletti, chapter 32, this volume.

27. Hanson and Nieuwenhuys, chapter 5.

28. Meredith Johnson Harbach, chapter 8 (this volume), text at notes 39–50; Hanson and Nieuwenhuys, chapter 5, text at notes 29–30; Lansdown, chapter 24; David B. Thronson, chapter 11; Paoletti, chapter 32, text at notes 38–54; Tali Gal, chapter 6, this volume.

29. Natsu Taylor Saito and Akilah J. Kinnison, chapter 7, and Berta Esperanza Hernández-Truyol, chapter 26, this volume.

30. Addie C. Rolnick, chapter 27, and Maya Sabatello and Mary Frances Layden, chapter 28, this volume.

31. Harbach, chapter 8, text at notes 45–62; Weaver, chapter 9.

32. See Philip E. Veerman, chapter 25, this volume.

33. Nielsen and Klep, chapter 29.

34. See Twila L. Perry, chapter 16, this volume.

35. Paoletti, chapter 32.

36. See Savitri Goonesekere, chapter 4, this volume, and Freeman, chapter 3, text at notes 13–14.

37. Weaver, chapter 9; regarding rights versus culture binary, see Imoh, chapter 21, text at notes 9–39, and, regarding "synergies," see text at note 77.

38. Goonesekere, chapter 4, text at notes 83–84; Gal, chapter 6, text at notes 32–33.

39. See Jonathan Todres and Shani King, chapter 34, this volume.

40. Merriam-Webster Dictionary, https://www.merriam-webster.com/dictionary/handbook.

Acknowledgments

Jonathan Todres I first want to thank the contributing authors. It has been wonderful reading your work and learning from you. Thank you also to editorial team at Oxford University Press for supporting this project. A book project depends on strong institutional support; my thanks to Dean Wendy Hensel and Georgia State University College of Law. Thank you also to Monica Laredo Ruiz and Susan Heikkila (both GSU College of Law, J.D. 2019) for their truly excellent research and editorial assistance. Finally, I want to thank Alison, Benjamin, and Desmond for their support and for making my life better in countless ways.

Shani M. King For excellent research and editorial assistance I thank Ava Sigman. Thank you to Dean Laura Rosenbury and the University of Florida Fredric G. Levin College of Law for generous research support for this project. Thank you to my wife, Gabriela Ruiz, for her tireless support and to my children, Soraya and Matias, for their daily inspiration. Finally, thank you to Professor Martha Minow for her continued and unwavering support.

List of Contributors

Christine Bakker, who holds a PhD from the European University Institute, Florence, is an international lawyer specializing in human rights law, including children's rights, international environmental law, and climate change. She has published widely in these fields, including, inter alia, *The EU, the US and Global Climate Governance* (Ashgate, 2014), which she co-edited with Francesco Francioni. She also has carried out research for the UNICEF Innocenti Research Centre and previously worked at the European Commission (DG Development). She is currently Adjunct Professor at LUISS University (Rome) and a visiting lecturer at the University of Roma-Tre and the Scuola Superiore di Sant'Anna (Pisa).

Jo Becker is a child rights activist with over twenty years of experience working for human rights and social justice. As the children's rights advocacy director for Human Rights Watch, she has been at the forefront of international efforts to end the use of child soldiers, child labor, and to protect other vulnerable children. She has investigated children's rights in Burma, Ghana, India, Indonesia, Iraq, Morocco, Nepal, Sri Lanka, Uganda, and the United States. An adjunct associate professor of international and public affairs at Columbia University, she has published widely in major international news publications and is the award-winning author of *Campaigning for Justice: Human Rights Advocacy in Practice* (2012) and *Campaigning for Children: Strategies to Advance Children's Rights* (2017), both from Stanford University Press.

Amy Brown studied law at Queen's University Belfast before moving to England to train as a post-primary English teacher. Subsequent experience teaching young people who struggled to establish rapport with teachers prompted an interest in young people's participation rights, both in the classroom and in the wider school context, in particular, their right to be heard and their right to freedom of expression. She is a PhD candidate in the Centre for Children's Rights at Queen's University, where she is exploring young people's right to be heard in schools and how this right is implemented and realized in practice.

Katherine Covell PhD, is Professor Emerita of Psychology and the former Executive Director of the Children's Rights Centre at Cape Breton University. Much of her teaching, research, and writing has been contextualized within the UN Convention on the Rights of the Child. Her primary foci have been education rights and rights to protection from violence. She has published numerous articles, book chapters, and six books on child development and children's rights. As an advocate, she has worked with the Canadian Coalition for the Rights of Children, UNICEF, Save the Children, and the Canadian Government. Covell was lead researcher for the UN Global Study on Violence against Children for North America in 2005. From 2007 to 2014 she represented North America on the International UN NGO Advisory Council on Violence against Children.

Jaap E. Doek is an Emeritus Professor in Family and Juvenile Law at the Vrije Universiteit Amsterdam, and an extraordinary Professor in Children's Rights at the Anton de Kom University of Suriname. He is the special legal advisor of ECPAT and a member of the board of various international NGOs, including the African Child Policy Forum and Child Helpline International. He has been a juvenile court judge in the district courts of Alkmaar and The Hague (1978–1985) and a deputy justice in the court of appeal of Amsterdam (2005–2012). He was a visiting scholar at the law schools of Georgetown University and the University of Michigan (1993) and a visiting professor at the school of law of Northwestern University (1999). He was a member of the UN Committee on the Rights of the Child (1999–2007) and the chairperson of that Committee (2001–2007). Doek has published numerous books and articles on various topics in the area of children's rights and family law in national (Dutch) and international journals.

Mike Dottridge has worked in the human rights field for four decades. He was employed by two human rights NGOs: Amnesty International (1977 to 1995), focusing on sub-Saharan Africa, and Anti-Slavery International, where he was director from 1996 until 2002. Since 1995 he has focused on the rights of adults and children subjected to economic or sexual exploitation, working independently since 2002, undertaking evaluations and institutional learning exercises for both international organizations and NGOs. He is the author of articles and handbooks on human rights in relation to slavery, servitude, forced labor, trafficking of adults and children, and child labor and exploitation. He advised the UN High Commissioner for Human Rights on her Recommended Principles and Guidelines on Human Rights and Human Trafficking (2002) and was a trustee of the UN Fund on Contemporary Forms of Slavery from 2011 until 2016.

Mark A. Drumbl is the Class of 1975 Alumni Professor at Washington & Lee University School of Law, where he also serves as Director of the Transnational Law Institute. He lectures, consults, and publishes widely in the areas of international criminal law, post-conflict justice, war-afflicted youth, and public international law. He is author of *Atrocity, Punishment, and International Law* (Cambridge University Press, 2007) and *Reimagining Child Soldiers in International Law and Policy* (Oxford University Press, 2012), and co-editor of the *Research Handbook on Child Soldiers* (Elgar, 2019). He also has taught at law faculties at the following universities: Oxford, Paris, Melbourne, Monash, Ottawa, Masaryk, and the VU Amsterdam.

Michael Freeman Emeritus Professor of Law at University College London, has published over eighty-five books and hundreds of articles on law and society, the transdisciplinary study of law and legal institutions in such subjects as jurisprudence, theories of law, medical law, legal and medical ethics, rights of children, family law, domestic violence, law and literature, popular culture, law and neuroscience, law and anthropology, sociology, health law, dispute resolution, religion, law and personal life, cricket, and law and countless other applications of social realties to the making, interpretation, and enforcement of law. Freeman is a legal scholar whose primary goals in legal scholarship and pedagogy have been to query how law can be used to improve the lives of the disempowered and to deliver real, not just imagined, social justice. He is Founding Editor of the *International Journal of Children's Rights* and author of *The Rights and Wrongs of Children* (Pinter, 1983). Freeman is a Fellow of the British Academy and a Visiting Research Professor at Liverpool University and Queens University Belfast.

Tali Gal PhD, is Senior Lecturer and Head of the School of Criminology at the University of Haifa. Her scholarship integrates legal, criminological, and psychosocial knowledge and involves restorative justice, children's rights, and therapeutic jurisprudence. She is a member of the Advisory Committee for the Minister of Justice on Juvenile Justice Reform and a former member of the Rotlevi Committee for Evaluating the Implementation of the UN Convention on the Rights of the Child in Israeli Legislation. She is the author of *Child Victims and Restorative Justice: A Needs-Rights Model* (Oxford University Press, 2011) and co-editor (with Benedetta Faedi-Duramy) of *International Perspectives and Empirical Findings on Child Participation* (Oxford University Press, 2015). She has published extensively in peer-reviewed as well as law review journals. Prior to joining academia, Tali was Legal Advisor to the Israel National Council for the Child.

Savitri Goonesekere is Emeritus Professor of Law at the University of Colombo Sri Lanka. She was Vice Chancellor of the same university from 1999 to 2002, served as a member of several regional and international bodies concerned with human rights and gender equality, held fellowships in universities in the United States and the United Kingdom, and acted as a consultant to several UN agencies working on law and human rights projects. She has published widely in the areas of children's rights, gender equality, and law and development and received the Fukokua Asian Culture Academic Prize in 2008. She was a member of the UN CEDAW Committee from 1999 to 2002.

Karl Hanson is Full Professor in Public Law at the University of Geneva in Switzerland and Deputy Director of the University of Geneva's Centre for Children's Rights Studies. He obtained his doctorate in law in 2004 from Ghent University, Belgium, where he worked as a Researcher at the Children's Rights Centre and as a Senior Researcher at the Human Rights Centre. His publications and primary research interests are in the emerging field of interdisciplinary children's rights studies and include theorizations on children's rights and childhood studies, child labor and working children, juvenile justice, and the role of independent national children's rights institutions. He teaches at the University of Geneva in the Master interdisciplinaire en droits de l'enfant (MIDE). He is also Program Director of the Master of Advanced Studies in Children's

Rights (MCR) and Chair of the Steering Committee of the Children's Rights European Academic Network (CREAN). Hanson is also co-editor of the journal *Childhood* (Sage).

Meredith Johnson Harbach is Professor of Law at the University of Richmond School of Law, where she teaches courses in family law, children and the law, reproductive justice, and civil procedure and supervises the Family Law Certificate Program. Her recent scholarship has analyzed and critiqued the state's relationship to families and children through the lens of American child care law and policy. Harbach most recently served as Chair of the AALS Section on Children and the Law and has also served on the Virginia Council on Women, where she was Chair of the Women's Healthcare Initiative. Harbach has also been a Visiting Scholar with the Vulnerability and the Human Condition Initiative at Emory Law School.

Berta Esperanza Hernández-Truyol is an international human rights scholar who utilizes an interdisciplinary and international framework to promote human well-being around the globe. She joined the University of Florida Levin College of Law and was named Levin, Mabie & Levin Professor of Law in 2000. In 2019 she was named the Stephen C. O'Connell Chair. Hernández-Truyol is engaged in initiatives that seek to develop, expand, and transform human rights discourse with a focus on issues of gender, race, ethnicity, culture, sexuality, language, and other vulnerabilities as well as their interconnections. She travels broadly to discuss and teach human rights. She has made presentations and offered courses in countries around the world, including Argentina, Brazil, Colombia, Costa Rica, Cuba, Guatemala, France, Italy, Mexico, Peru, Spain, and Uruguay. Her current research includes an examination of the ongoing migration crises. Among her many publications, she coauthored *Just Trade: A New Covenant Linking Trade and Human Rights* (NYU Press, 2009), which elucidated how embracing the interdependence of trade and human rights promotes human flourishing. She earned her LL.M. in international legal studies from New York University School of Law, her J.D. from Albany Law School of Union University, and her B.A. from Cornell University.

R. Brian Howe PhD, is a professor emeritus (political science) at Cape Breton University. He is the author or coauthor of numerous books, articles, and book chapters on education policy, children's rights, human rights, children's human rights education, child advocacy offices, and human rights commissions. His books include *Empowering Children: Children's Rights Education as a Pathway to Citizenship* (2005), *Education in the Best Interests of the Child* (2013), *Children, Families, and Violence* (2009), and *The Challenge of Children's Rights for Canada* (2001, 2019). The first edition of *The Challenge* (2001) was selected for two national awards, and *Empowering Children* formed the basis for an award in citizenship education by the Canadian Education Association. He was also the co-recipient of a children's rights award (2014) by the Canadian Coalition for the Rights of Children. His current research is on parenting education and children's human rights education.

Ursula Kilkelly is a Professor of Law at the School of Law, University College Cork, where she teaches children's rights on the LL.M. Children's Rights and Family Law. She has published several monographs, edited collections, and peer reviewed articles on a range of children's rights issues, including children's rights in and to health care, juvenile justice and detention, and on the legal implementation and enforcement of children's rights. Her recent book, *International Human Rights of Children* (Springer, 2018), is a collection co-edited with Ton Liefaard. Kilkelly has also undertaken multiple funded research projects on the child's right to health and child-friendly health care with the Council of Europe, the Irish Research Council, the Department of Children and Youth Affairs, and the Ombudsman for Children in Ireland. Her publications are available on Google Scholar, and she can be followed on Twitter @ukilkelly.

Shani M. King is a Professor of Law and Director of the Center on Children and Families at the University of Florida Levin College of Law. Prior to joining the UF Law faculty, he practiced at Legal Services for Children, Inc., in San Francisco, where he litigated cases under the UN Convention against Torture and represented children in immigration, dependency, guardianship, and school discipline proceedings. King is an active writer and scholar in the area of children's rights, with a particular interest in the rights of children and families from traditionally underserved populations—and the public responsibility to protect those rights. His wide-ranging scholarship has been recognized and cited by leading scholars in the field, has been cited and relied upon by courts, and is also frequently relied upon by not-for-profit organizations and practitioners in the field. King has been active in local, regional, and national child welfare and juvenile reform in the United States and has worked with the American Academy of Arts and Sciences, the American Constitution Society, and state and local governmental officials, in addition serving as a reviewer for the *Children and Youth Services Review* as well as the quarterly of the National School of the Judiciary and Public Prosecution in Poland. King received a B.A. from Brown University, a J.D. from Harvard Law School, and an MSt in international human rights law from Oxford University. He is also an award-winning author of children's books—his latest, *Have I Ever Told You?*, was published in 2019 (Tilbury House).

Akilah J. Kinnison is an Assistant Professor of Law at the University of Arizona's James E. Rogers College of Law, where she is part of the faculty of the Indigenous Peoples Law and Policy Program. She teaches critical race theory and public international law. In addition, she works on issues related to the use of international human rights law to address problems in US federal Indian law jurisprudence. She received her J.D. in 2012 and her LL.M. in 2013 from the University of Arizona.

Perpetua Kirby PhD, is a Research Associate at the University of Sussex, where she co-convenes a course on the BA in Child and Youth Studies and is also an independent research consultant. She has spent over twenty years researching children and young people's participation within different sectors, including social care, health, and education. Her research interests are children's agency and participation, democratic schooling, and multimodal creative research approaches. Together with Rebecca Webb, she co-founded TRANSFORM-*i*N EDUCATION (www.transformineducation.org), an initiative aimed at challenging an exclusive emphasis on children's conformity within schools.

Katrien Klep, LLM, is Assistant Professor of Children's Rights at the Department of Child Law at Leiden University. She lectures in the Advanced Master International Children's Rights program on international systems of human rights, economic, social and cultural rights, and research design. In her academic work she has two major research interests: (1) how (human) rights work in practice and (2) the use of qualitative methods in legal research. Her current research on access to (social) justice focuses on complaints procedures in youth care at the municipal level in the Netherlands.

Gerison Lansdown was founding director (1992–2000) of the Children's Rights Alliance for England and has since worked as an international consultant and advocate, publishing and lecturing widely on the subject of children's rights. She has been involved in the development of several General Comments for the UN Committee on the Rights of the Child, including on the right of children to be heard, to play and recreation, and on the rights of children both during adolescence, and in the digital environment. She was actively involved in the drafting of the UN Convention on the Rights of Persons with Disabilities. She is an adjunct professor at Carleton University Canada, has an Honorary Doctorate from Open University and from Carleton University, an Honorary Fellowship from the University of Central Lancashire, is a member of the Open Society Foundation Early Years Advisory Board, and is on the editorial advisory board of the *Canadian Journal of Children's Rights*. She is a former Vice Chair of UNICEF-UK and currently chairs both Child to Child and the ODI Gender and Adolescence: Global Evidence Advisory Board.

Mary Frances Layden is a co-founder of the apparel company love♡bili♡nyc, which promotes disability awareness and empowerment, and the former leader of community engagement at the NYC-based nonprofit organization A Leg To Stand On (ALTSO), which provides free orthopedic care to children with disabilities in developing countries. As a woman with a physical disability, Layden is dedicated to disability advocacy. She holds a bachelor's degree in social work from New York University and a master's degree in developmental psychology from Teachers College, Columbia University. Currently she is an M.A. student at CUNY School of Professional Studies in the disability studies graduate program.

Gertrud Lenzer Dr. phil., is Professor Emerita of Sociology and Children's Studies at The City University of New York. In 1991 she was both the founder internationally of the interdisciplinary field of children's studies as well as the founding chair of the Sociology of Children Section of the American Sociological Association. The UN Convention on the Rights of the Child (CRC) provided the overarching framework for this new interdisciplinary field. Lenzer has published widely in the fields of philosophy and the social sciences, children's rights, and children's studies. She is editor of *Violence* *against Children: Making Human Rights Real* (Routledge, 2018), a study of the pervasiveness of violence against children internationally and in the United States, which includes contributions from leading scholars and child rights advocates. She has been the recipient of honors and such fellowships as the American Council of Learned Societies Fellowship in American Studies, a Rockefeller Fellowship in the Humanities, a Fellowship at the National Humanities Center, a Visiting Fellowship at the Institute for Advanced Study in Princeton, and a Research Fellowship at the Rockefeller Bellagio Center, Italy.

Manfred Liebel, Dr. phil., is Professor Emeritus of sociology at Technical University Berlin and co-founder and patron of the M.A. Childhood Studies and Children's Rights (MACR) at Free University Berlin and the University of Applied Sciences Potsdam. He is also vice chair of the council of the National Coalition Germany for the Implementation of the UN Convention on the Rights of the Child. Liebel is an editorial board member of scientific journals in Germany, Spain, Nicaragua, Ecuador, and Peru. He has served as a consultant to the Movements of Working Children and Adolescents in Latin America and Africa. His research focuses on: international and intercultural studies on childhood and youth, children's rights, child work, social movements, and postcolonial studies. He has published books in German, Spanish, English, French, and Polish. His most recent books include *Children's Rights from Below: Cross-Cultural Perspectives* (2012), *Kinder und Gerechtigkeit. Über Kinderrechte neu nachdenken* (2013), *Janusz Korczak— Pionier der Kinderrechte* (editor, 2013), *Kinder und Gerechtigkeit. Über Kinderrechte neu nachdenken* (2013), *Niñez y Justicia Social* (2013), *Kinderinteressen—Zwischen Paternalismus und Partizipation* (2015), *'Children out of Place' and Human Rights: In Memory of Judith Ennew* (co-editor, 2017), and *Postkoloniale Kindheiten. Zwischen Ausgrenzung und Widerstand* (2017).

Ton Liefaard is Professor of Children's Rights and holds the UNICEF Chair in Children's Rights at Leiden Law School, Leiden University. He is Leiden Law School's Vice Dean for Education and Director of the Master of Law's Programme (LL.M.) on Advanced Studies in International Children's Rights at Leiden University. He teaches and publishes widely on the meaning of the UN Convention on the Rights of the Child and related international, regional, and domestic children's rights standards for specific issues, including juvenile justice, deprivation of liberty of children, children's access to justice, child-friendly justice, and violence against children. He supervises PhD students from across the globe and regularly works as a consultant and researcher for international organizations, including UNICEF, the Council of Europe, and the European Union. He also serves as a substitute Justice of the Court of Appeal in The Hague. He is a member of the editorial boards of the *International Journal of Children's Rights, Youth Justice,* and the *Flemish Journal for Youth and Children's Rights*. Liefaard holds a master's degree and a PhD in law from the Vrije Universiteit Amsterdam.

Laura Lundy is Co-Director of the Centre for Children's Rights and a Professor in the School of Social Sciences, Education and Social Work at Queen's University, Belfast.

She is co-Editor in Chief of the *International Journal of Children's Rights*. Her expertise is in children's right to participate in decision-making, education rights, and implementation of the UN Convention on the Rights of the Child.

Martha Minow is the 300th Anniversary Professor at Harvard University, where she has taught since 1981 and served as Dean of Harvard Law School for eight years. An expert in human rights and advocacy for members of racial and religious minorities, women, children, and persons with disabilities, her books include *When Should Law Forgive?* (forthcoming 2019), *The First Global Prosecutor: Promise and Constraints* (co-editor with Cora True-Frost and Alex Whiting, 2015), *In Brown's Wake: Legacies of America's Educational Landmark* (2010), *Partners, Not Rivals: Privatization and the Public Good* (2002), *Between Vengeance and Forgiveness: Facing History after Genocide and Mass Violence* (1998), and *Not Only For Myself: Identity, Politics, and the Law* (1997). Minow serves on the board of the MacArthur Foundation and the federally funded Legal Services Corporation, serving low-income Americans.

Olga Nieuwenhuys holds degrees in sociology from the University of Paris (Sorbonne) and in non-Western sociology and anthropology from the University of Amsterdam. She obtained her doctorate from the Vrije Universiteit Amsterdam in 1989. She has taught at the University of Amsterdam for more than thirty years, including courses on gender, childhood, and international development as well as more specialized courses on child labor, urban children's participation in development and action research, and theories of development, post-development, and postcolonialism. Nieuwenhuys is author of *Children's Lifeworlds: Gender, Labour and Welfare in the Developing World* (Rouledge, 1994; Social Science Press, 2001) and of numerous academic articles, book chapters, and co-edited volumes. She has been co-editor of the leading Sage journal in childhood studies, *Childhood: A Journal of Global Child Research*, and is on the international advisory board of the journal *Children´s Geographies* and of *Contemporary Education Dialogue*. She is currently working on social justice and reproduction and preparing a revised edition of *Children's Lifeworlds*.

Aoife Nolan has been Professor of International Human Rights Law at Nottingham University School of Law since 2012. She was elected to the Council of Europe's European Committee of Social Rights, Europe's leading economic and social rights monitoring mechanism, in November 2017. In 2018 she served on the Scottish First Minister's Advisory Group on Human Rights Leadership. She has published extensively in the areas of human rights and constitutional law, particularly in relation to economic and social rights, children's rights, and non-state actors. She was founding coordinator of the Economic and Social Rights Academic Network, UK and Ireland (ESRAN-UKI). Nolan has acted as an expert advisor to a wide range of international and national organizations and bodies working on human rights issues, including numerous UN Special Procedures, UN treaty-monitoring bodies, the Council of Europe, multiple NHRIs and NGOs. Her books include *Children's Socio-Economic Rights, Democracy & the Courts* (Hart, 2011), *Applying an International Human Rights Framework to State*

Budget Allocations: Rights and Resources (coauthor with O'Connell, Harvey, Dutschke and Rooney; Routledge, 2014), *Economic and Social Rights after the Global Financial Crisis* (editor; Cambridge University Press, 2014), and *The United Nations Special Procedures System* (co-editor with Freedman and Murphy). She has held visiting positions at numerous academic institutions in Europe, Africa, the United States, and Australia. She is an Academic Expert member at Doughty Street Chambers.

Marta Santos Pais was appointed Special Representative of the Secretary-General on Violence against Children in May 2009. As a high level global independent advocate and bridge-builder, she promotes the prevention and elimination of all forms of violence against children in the home, in schools, in institutional care, in justice institutions, in the workplace, in the community, and in cyberspace. She is strongly committed to mobilizing action and political support to maintain momentum around this agenda and to achieve progress, including through law and policy reforms, information and mobilization campaigns, and sound data and research. She has more than thirty years of experience working on human rights issues, including engagement in United Nations and intergovernmental processes and research institutions. She participated in the drafting of the UN Convention on the Rights of the Child and of its Optional Protocols and of other key international human rights standards. She has authored many human rights and children's rights publications and was a Special Advisor to two major UN studies, on violence against children and on the impact of armed conflict on children, respectively. Before her appointment as UN Special Representative, she was Director of the UNICEF Innocenti Research Centre and, before then, Director of Evaluation, Policy and Planning for UNICEF. She also previously served as the Rapporteur of the Committee on the Rights of the Child and Vice Chair of the Coordinating Committee on Childhood Policies of the Council of Europe.

Sarah Paoletti is a Practice Professor of Law at the University of Pennsylvania Law School, where she founded and directs the Transnational Legal Clinic. From 2003 to 2006 she was a Practitioner-in-Residence in the International Human Rights Law Clinic at American University's Washington College of Law. Prior to entering academia, she was a staff attorney at Friends of Farmworkers, Inc. (now, Justice at Work), a statewide legal services program serving migrant workers in Pennsylvania, and later served on its Board from 2007 to 2016. Paoletti is a founding member of the Board of Directors of Centro de los Derechos del Migrante, Inc., a binational migrant worker rights organization with offices in the US and Mexico. She was a law clerk for the Judge Anthony J. Scirica, U.S. Court of Appeals for the Third Circuit. She received her J.D. from the Washington College of Law American University *summa cum laude* in 1998 and her B.A. from Yale University in 1992. Paoletti has authored numerous articles, amicus briefs, and blog posts addressing the intersection of immigration and refugee law and human rights.

Twila L. Perry is a Professor of Law and the Judge Alexander P. Waugh Sr. Scholar at Rutgers University School of Law in Newark, New Jersey, where she teaches family law, children and the law, torts, and a seminar on race, gender, and tort law. Perry is the author of numerous law journal articles examining the intersection of law with issues of race, gender, culture, and class in the context of family life. Some of the topics have included divorce, the theory of alimony, the legal duties of support and services within marriage, marriage in the African American community, and gentrification. Perry has written extensively on transracial and international adoption and has presented her work on these issues at conferences across the United States as well as internationally.

Addie C. Rolnick is a Professor of Law at the William S. Boyd School of Law at the University of Nevada, Las Vegas. She teaches federal Indian law, criminal law, civil rights, critical race theory, and a practicum in tribal law. Prior to joining UNLV, she was the inaugural Critical Race Studies Law Fellow at UCLA School of Law. Before that, she represented tribal governments as a lawyer and lobbyist with Sonosky, Chambers, Sachse, Endreson & Perry, LLP in Washington, DC. She earned her J.D. and her M.A. in American Indian studies from UCLA and her B.A. from Oberlin College. Rolnick's scholarship investigates the relationships between sovereign power and indigenous/ minority rights in four main areas: equal protection–based challenges to indigenous rights; Native youth and juvenile justice; the role of race and gender in the administration of criminal and juvenile justice; and tribal jurisdiction.

Maya Sabatello LLB, PhD, is an Assistant Professor of Clinical Bioethics and Co-Director of the Precision Medicine: Ethics, Politics, and Culture Project at Columbia University. She is a former litigator with a transdisciplinary background and has extensive experience in national and international policymaking relating to human and disability rights. Sabatello studies how biomedical technologies impact social structures, vulnerable groups, and individual rights. Her scholarship focuses on law, society, medicine, and disability; regulations of reproductive technologies; and genomic dilemmas and policies, especially as these are relevant to children and people with disabilities; and the uses of psychiatric genetics in nonclinical and judicial settings. In addition to peer-reviewed articles, she is the author of *Children's Bioethics* (2009) and co-editor of *Human Rights and Disability Advocacy* (2014).

Natsu Taylor Saito is Distinguished University Professor and Professor of Law at Georgia State University, where she teaches international law, human rights, and the legal history of race in the United States. She is the author of numerous articles on human rights as well as three books, *Settler Colonialism, Race, and the Law: Why Structural Racism Persists* (forthcoming from NYU Press, 2020), *Meeting the Enemy: American Exceptionalism and International Law* (2010), and *From Chinese Exclusion to Guantánamo Bay: Plenary Power and the Prerogative State* (2006). She earned her J.D. from Yale University in 1987.

Julia Sloth-Nielsen is Professor of Law in the Faculty of Law at the University of the Western Cape and Professor of Children's Rights in the Developing World at Leiden University. She teaches and publishes on a wide range of children's rights and family law related issues and has worked extensively on children's rights law reform in the southern and east African region. She served a term as a member of the African Committee of Experts on the Rights of the Child (2011–2016). She enjoys a rating as an internationally acclaimed researcher by the National Research Foundation.

David B. Thronson is Professor of Law and Associate Dean for Academic Affairs at the Michigan State University College of Law. His research focuses on the intersection of family law and immigration law, with particular emphasis on the impact of immigration law on children. He is coauthor (with Stephen H. Legomsky) of the casebook *Immigration and Refugee Law and Policy*.

Jonathan Todres is Distinguished University Professor and Professor of Law at Georgia State University College of Law. His research focuses on children's rights and child well-being. He has authored numerous publications on child trafficking, the implementation of children's rights law, human rights education, and legal and cultural constructs of childhood. He also coauthored *Human Rights in Children's Literature: Imagination and the Narrative of Law* (Oxford University Press, 2016), and *Preventing Child Trafficking: A Public Health Approach* (Johns Hopkins University Press, 2019). Todres serves as a regular advisor to nongovernmental organizations working to address various children's rights issues. He is also a member of the Board on Children, Youth, and Families of the National Academies of Sciences, Engineering, and Medicine. Todres is a past chair of the Section on International Human Rights and the Section on Children and the Law of the Association of American Law Schools. In 2018 he served as a Fulbright Scholar in residence at University College Cork in Ireland. He holds a J.D. from Columbia Law School and a B.A. (international development) from Clark University.

Gamze Erdem Türkelli is a Postdoctoral Fellow of Fundamental Research at the Research Foundation–Flanders (FWO) and a member of the Law and Development Research Group at the University of Antwerp. She received her PhD in Law from the University of Antwerp, focusing on children's rights obligations and responsibility for businesses and development financing institutions under international law. She is a graduate of Bogazici University (Turkey) and holds master's degrees from the University of Paris 1–Pantheon Sorbonne and from Yale University, where she was a Fulbright Fellow. Her research interests include children's rights, transnational human rights obligations, and new and traditional economic actors in development financing and governance, including multi-stakeholder partnerships as well as the links between law and development.

Afua Twum-Danso Imoh is a Lecturer in the Sociology of Childhood at the University of Sheffield. Since obtaining her PhD from the Centre of West African Studies (University of Birmingham), she has managed nine funded research and networking projects focusing on children's lives and well-being in Ghana and Nigeria, among other countries. Her work has been published in a number of edited collections as well as in a range of peer-reviewed journals. She is also the lead co-editor of three edited collections: *Childhoods at the Intersection of the Global and the Local* (Palgrave, 2012),

Children's Lives in an Era of Children's Rights: The Progress of the Convention on the Rights of the Child in Africa (Routledge, 2013), and *Global Childhoods beyond the North-South Divide* (Palgrave, 2019).

Wouter Vandenhole is a human rights and law and development scholar. He holds the chair in human rights law at University of Antwerp. Vandenhole is a member of the Law and Development Research Group and the lead convener of an intensive training program on sustainable development and global justice. His research interests include children's rights, economic, social and cultural rights, and the relationship between human rights law and development. For some years now he has focused on transnational human rights obligations, that is, the human rights obligations of new duty-bearers (in particular companies). More recently, he has started to explore the conceptual implications of sustainable development for human rights law, in particular, questions of distribution. He has co-edited the *Routledge International Handbook of Children's Rights Studies* (Routledge, 2015) and coauthored *Children's Rights: A Commentary on the CRC and Its Protocols* (Elgar, 2019).

Philip E. Veerman, CPsychol., lives in The Hague (the Netherlands), where he works as a health psychologist for children and adolescents. He wrote his PhD thesis on children's rights (*The Rights of the Child and the Changing Image of Childhood*, published by Martinus Nijhoff, 1992) and is the founder of the *International Journal of Children's Rights*. From 1997 to 2002 he served as the President of Defence for Children International (DCI) in Geneva. For seventeen years he lived in Jerusalem, where he served as Executive Director of the Israeli Section of DCI. He participated in the Steering Committee of the Coalition against the Use of Child Soldiers in London and founded the Janusz Korczak Foundation in the Netherlands. He also worked in the field of drug and alcohol addiction. With Damon Barrett, he coauthored the *Commentary on CRC Article 33: Protection from Narcotic Drugs and Psychotropic Substances.* To contact, see www.childrightsfocus.org.

Jessica Dixon Weaver is an Associate Professor at Southern Methodist University Dedman School of Law, where she teaches courses on family law, children and the law, and legal ethics. She received her B.A. from the University of Pennsylvania and her J.D. from the University of Virginia School of Law. Weaver served as founding Director of the W.W. Caruth, Jr. Child Advocacy Clinic and became the first African American female to earn tenure at the law school in 2015. Weaver is an expert in child welfare law and public policy, and her scholarship focuses on theorizing methods for improvement of the legal systems and policies affecting families and children. She also examines intergenerational caregiving for children and the elderly. Her current research explores the historical impact of race and gender on family construction and state regulation of the family. She is the author of two forthcoming books, *Family Law Simulations: Bridge to Practice* (West Academic) and *Adoption Law: Theory, Policy, and Practice* (3rd ed., William Hein). She is the recipient of the 2019–2020 university-wide Gerald J. Ford Senior Research Fellowship and the law school's Robert G. Storey Distinguished Faculty Fellowship.

Rebecca Webb PhD, is a Lecturer in Education at the University of Sussex. She co-leads, and teaches on, a master's degree and professional qualification in early-years education. She is an ethnographic and qualitative researcher with research interests in the areas of citizenship, democratic schooling and children's rights, pedagogy and practice, and creativity in academic writing. She has been a primary teacher, EAL specialist, and local authority education adviser in equality, inclusion, and achievement. Together with Perpetua Kirby she co-founded TRANSFORM-*i*N EDUCATION (www.transformineducation.org), an initiative aimed at challenging an exclusive emphasis on children's conformity within schools.

Barbara Bennett Woodhouse is L. Q. C. Lamar Professor of Law at Emory University Law School. She is author of *Hidden in Plain Sight: The Tragedy of Children's Rights from Ben Franklin to Lionel Tate* (Princeton University Press, 2008) and *The Ecology of Childhood: How Our Changing World Threatens Children's Rights* (forthcoming from NYU Press, 2020). She is also David H. Levin Chair in Family Law (emeritus) at the University of Florida, where she founded the Center on Children and Families. She obtained her law degree from Columbia University and clerked for Associate Justice Sandra Day O'Connor at the U.S. Supreme Court before joining the faculty of University of Pennsylvania, where she co-founded the multidisciplinary Center for Children's Policy Practice and Research. Author of over one hundred articles and book chapters, she utilizes methods from a range of disciplines, including comparative legal and cultural studies, child development, sociology, ethnography and history, to explore the legal and social ecology of childhood. At Emory she founded the Child Rights Project, which engages students in amicus briefs involving the rights and needs of children.

INTRODUCTION

JONATHAN TODRES AND SHANI M. KING

In November 2019, the international community celebrated the thirtieth anniversary of the United Nations Convention on the Rights of the Child, the most comprehensive treaty on children's rights and the most widely ratified human rights treaty in history.

The Convention on the Rights of the Child (CRC) represented a definitive shift in the way that children are viewed and understood—from passive objects subsumed within the family requiring protection to full human beings with a distinct set of rights. The treaty includes the full panoply of children's rights—civil, political, economic, social, and cultural rights. It reaffirms that rights previously recognized in the context of adults—from freedom of expression and protections against torture to rights to health care and an adequate standard of living—are rights held by children. And it also recognizes rights unique to children, such as the right to know and be cared for by one's parents. This comprehensive framework established a legal mandate for securing the rights and well-being of all children.

After thirty years, there is much to celebrate. Since the adoption of the CRC, numerous new international instruments—including three optional protocols to the CRC, new treaties from the International Labor Organization, and regional treaties—have added to the corpus of international children's rights law. At the national level, an increasing number of states parties make reference to children's rights in their constitutions and in their national legislation.[1] There is now evidence of law reform connected to the CRC and improvements in the welfare of children, particularly in the educational and health sectors.[2] There are now more than two hundred independent human rights institutions that exist in over seventy countries.[3] And some states have established coordinating mechanisms at the national, state, and local levels to make—as repeatedly urged by the committee charged with monitoring implementation of the CRC—government work for children.[4] Furthermore, because the CRC is broadly consistent with traditional values across many cultures, it has even proved impactful in legal systems that are linked to local culture or religion.[5]

Notwithstanding the success of the Convention, implementation of the CRC is still a work in progress. Millions of children confront rights violations on a daily basis. We have now reached a state in the evolution of children's rights in which we need more critical evaluation and assessment of the impact of the CRC and the large body of children's rights law and policy that this treaty has inspired. We have moved from conceptualizing and adopting legislation to focusing on implementation and making the content of children's rights meaningful in the lives of all children.

This book provides a critical evaluation and assessment of children's rights law, including the CRC. It includes contributions from leading legal scholars, criminologists, social scientists, child rights practitioners, jurists, and former government officials. Together with the contributing authors, we seek to elucidate the content of children's rights law, explore the complexities of implementation, and identify critical challenges and opportunities for this relatively young field that covers approximately one-third of the world's population and governs every human being's first stages of life.

OVERVIEW: CORE THEMES

This text is written to be useful for scholars and practitioners, but also accessible and relevant to students with interests in international children's rights or human rights more generally. The book tackles significant issues in international children's rights, in their theoretical, historical, cultural, political, and cultural complexity. We touch on key controversies in international children's rights law involving cultural relativism, globalization, power, gender, class, and family relations. The book offers a guide through many of the challenges that need to be confronted if we are to ensure that human rights are understood and practiced in new and creative ways that are fully inclusive of and protective of children.

There is a growing discourse on children's rights, but as with human rights discourses, certain critical themes continue to be overlooked or relegated to the margins. We have tried to use this volume to bring greater attention to these themes, both by encouraging all contributing authors to engage these themes and by including chapters that focus specifically on aspects of these issues. First, in this volume we have sought to incorporate global perspectives and critiques, including both Global South perspectives and chapters that view children's rights through the lens of particular critical perspectives. If rights are to be meaningful in the lives of all children and their communities, we must foster a more inclusive dialogue in which all voices are heard. Second, given the developmental nature of childhood, we believe that multidisciplinary perspectives and other social science insights are vital to deepening understanding of children's rights. Yet frequently perspectives from these other fields are overlooked in studies on children's rights law. This volume reflects the use of multidisciplinary perspectives, such as developmental psychology, anthropology, sociology, and other social science insights. Third, as in other fields, children's rights law at times suffers from overly simplistic binary constructs—for example, the rights versus protection arguments. While these constructs identify important questions, they also gloss over issues and complexities that are relevant to understanding and implementing children's rights. This volume does address questions of rights versus care, but it also aims to go beyond such debates to explore how dignity, equality, and other rights perspectives fit with children. Fourth, this volume also attempts to challenge the distinction between negative liberties and positive rights. All rights require resources—both human and financial—if they are to be secured for all individuals. The right to education requires resources for schools and educational programs, but so too do voting rights, which require resources for elections, civic education, etc. Fifth, we explore how rights can be used to constrain potential oppression by government and other actors. Sixth and finally, we have included the works of selected authors with an eye toward a conception of rights relevant to building and exercising capabilities in this volume. By incorporating these themes and perspectives along with other traditional analyses of children's rights, we hope to provide a volume that both deepens our understanding of children's rights and challenges the field to develop more rigorous research that can foster advances in the rights and well-being of children.

PART I: HISTORICAL AND THEORETICAL FRAMEWORK

This handbook begins with perspectives on the historical and theoretical framework for children's rights. Gertrud Lenzer begins by outlining how in modern, Western history, the concepts of the child and childhood have evolved and how the arc of developments in empiricist philosophy, the Enlightenment, the Romantic poets, and Victorian novels have all contributed to the conceptualization of children as subjects entitled to rights. Next, Jo Becker explores the history of the children's rights movement. In some respects, Becker picks up where Lenzer leaves off, by illustrating how children conceptualized as subjects entitled to rights have become an integral part of the human rights agenda. This agenda has helped drive the development and adoption of international standards for children and has resulted in governments adopting new policies, laws, practices, and community initiatives involving children's rights. Michael Freeman then challenges conventional wisdom by arguing that notwithstanding the aforementioned developments, we still fundamentally fail to take children's rights seriously. He further explains how we should conceptualize children's rights going forward. Freeman also reminds us that "the language of rights" makes visible what is oppressed. And, finally, Savitri Goonesekere walks us through the interrelated and interdependent nature of children's rights. While all rights are interrelated and interdependent, the interconnected nature of rights is particularly relevant for children, given the developmental nature of childhood. Goonesekere suggests that these interconnectivities must be addressed and conflicts resolved in a holistic manner to make children's rights a meaningful recourse for their well-being in families and communities.

PART II: PERSPECTIVES AND METHODS

The authors in this part explore children's rights from various conceptual and methodological perspectives. In the first of these chapters, Karl Hanson and Olga Nieuwenhuys explain that a child-centered approach to children's rights recognizes that children shape, interpret, and practice what their rights are and that they have the right to do so. Hanson and Nieuwenhuys also critique essentialist tendencies that diminish children's engagement with their rights and explain how the concepts of *living rights* and *translations* may help provide children with space to negotiate meanings and to influence interpretations of their rights. In attempting to provide a richer context for children's rights, Tali Gal then argues for an ecological model of children's rights in which children's development—and rights—can only be understood when considering the range of interconnected domains related to their lives. This chapter, Gal explains, is based on developmental psychologist Uri Brofenbrenner's socioecological model, which suggests not only that human behavior and development are shaped by these multiple systems and processes, but also that these various components are interconnected and affect each other in complex ways that must be accounted for.

The authors of the next two chapters in this part apply different theoretical frameworks to the field of children's rights, specifically critical race theory and feminist legal theory. Natsu Saito and Akilah Kinnison use critical race theory, a theoretical framework traditionally used to examine society and culture as they relate to categorizations of race, law, and power, to examine international children's rights. Specifically, they ask what critical race theory can contribute to the realization of children's rights under international law and consider ways in which use of the theory can help ensure that children of color and their communities benefit from internationally recognized children's rights. Then, in the feminist legal theory chapter, Meredith Harbach provides an overview of feminism as a movement and feminist legal theory as a discipline and then considers the ways in which feminist legal theory and children's rights are in conversation. Harbach explores the potential for newer variants of feminist legal theory—vulnerability theory and social justice feminism—to inform new directions in children's rights. In a fitting end to this part, in "Intersectionality and Children's Rights," Jessica Dixon Weaver considers how intersectionality—a theoretical framework that attempts to identify how various systems of subordination or power impact those who are most marginalized in society—can be used to analyze how various laws and treaties that purport to protect children's rights fail to do so when children fall within multiple identities.

PART III: SUBSTANTIVE LEGAL AREAS

Each of the authors in this part focus on a different area of international children's rights law. In some cases, the author focuses on a critical substantive right, such as education or health, and in others the author focuses on an issue affecting children, such as poverty. Wouter Vandenhole and Gamze Türkelli first analyze the application of the best interests of the child standard in international law—a foundational concept of a breadth of law related to children—and suggest the use of a number of safeguards in order to prevent this malleable concept from being used in a paternalistic, biased, or other way that undermines children's rights. David Thronson then explores the multitude of ways in which citizenship can affect the rights of children and argues persuasively that within a modern human rights framework—one that recognizes the humanity and autonomy of children—nationality of children should not determine whether states recognize their rights. Next, Barbara Bennett Woodhouse considers the child's right to family in international human rights law, examining the contours of the right to family, the circumstances when the right is triggered, and the question of who should exercise the right. Ultimately, Woodhouse argues that a child's right to family should be understood as adding to the family's resources, augmenting rather than diminishing protections against government oppression and neglect of the family unit.

In the next chapter, Jaap Doek examines the right to be heard and broader questions about child participation under international children's rights law. Ton Liefaard then examines the international children's rights framework for juvenile justice, the progress made since the adoption of the CRC, and the key implementation challenges in light of the complexity of and controversies inherently related to juvenile justice. Next, Marta Santos Pais explores children's rights law's response to violence against children, an issue that affects children in every country. Santos Pais details the global policy agenda for confronting violence against children and the barriers that must be overcome to make meaningful progress toward a world free of violence against children. Twila Perry then discusses the international legal framework governing international adoption and critiques of the current system. Perry explores philosophical debates about whether and when international adoption is in the best interests of children, utilizing theoretical frameworks such as postcolonial theory, critical race theory, and feminist theory.

Then, in "Economic and Labor Rights of Children," Manfred Libel considers what it means for children to have economic and labor rights. His chapter challenges traditional protection-centered constructs of children's rights. Following that, Ursula Kilkelly explores the child's right to health and health care and makes the case for an integrated approach to children's health—across human rights and development fields—in order to secure every child's health rights.

In tackling the right to education, Laura Lundy and Amy Brown focus not on what these rights are or why they are necessary per se but, rather, the barriers that obstruct the realization of the right to education. In doing so, Lundy and Brown propose their own typology that is based on three themes—relationships, resources, and redress—and they propose to revisit and reclaim the three R's, re-envisioning them in a way that is more useful to both understanding children's rights and making them more real.

In addressing the ever deepening relationship between poverty and child rights, Aoife Nolan explains why child rights is an appropriate lens through which to view child poverty, how the CRC has been interpreted when considering the causes, impacts, and responses to child poverty, and the strengths and weaknesses of the current international child's rights framework in terms of its ability to address the complex global challenge of child poverty.

In the last two chapters of this part, Afua Twum-Danso Imoh and Christine Bakker address the issues of culture and climate change, respectively. Imoh challenges the long dominant dichotomy that situates culture and human rights as antithetical to each other by focusing on sub-Saharan Africa. Bakker, meanwhile, explores how the enjoyment of children's rights is endangered by climate change and whether the remedies that children have at their disposal are effective in holding states accountable for their failure to protect these rights.

Through each of these chapters, readers can explore in-depth not only relevant law but also key issues—in law and its implementation in practice—critical to advancing children's rights and well-being.

PART IV: SELECTED INDIVIDUAL
AND INSTITUTIONAL ACTORS

Individuals and institutions play a critical role in the implementation and realization of children's rights. From children to parents and other caregivers, to professionals who work with children, and to policy makers and international entities, a breadth of key stakeholders in the children's rights enterprise must be part of the development, implementation, and evaluation of children's rights law, policy, and programs. This part offers chapters on three of the essential actors in the children's rights arena. Perpetua Kirby and Rebecca Webb address the role of children as child rights actors. Their chapter considers how Article 12—the right to be heard—of the CRC is realized among very young children, drawing on ethnographic research at primary schools in England. Focusing on an often-overlooked population (young children), Kirby and Webb probe questions around child participation, the role of adults, and whether initiatives for child participation truly work to empower children. Shifting attention from children to state actors, Gerison Lansdown explores the various children's rights institutions, commissioners, and ombudsperson offices that have been created since the adoption of the CRC. Lansdown examines their utility in facilitating the realization of children's rights. Finally, in the last chapter of this part, Philip Veerman reviews the work of the UN Committee on the Rights of the Child—the entity responsible for monitoring states' implementation of the CRC—through a focus on the Committee's engagement on the issue of caste- and descent-based discrimination.

PART V: SELECTED POPULATIONS

Part V of this volume discusses specific populations of children that merit special discussion because of their historical and current vulnerability. Our intention in this section is not to be exhaustive per se but, rather, to focus on populations that are at the forefront of current national and international discussions regarding international children's rights, such as trafficked children and children in armed conflict, as well as populations that receive lesser attention but also present unique challenges and concerns for the protection of international children rights, such as LGBTQ children, indigenous children, children with disabilities, and independent children. In the first chapter of this part, Berta Hernández-Truyol begins with a discussion of LGBTQ children, exploring structural inequalities, global attitudes toward homosexuality, and international and regional protections, as well as recommendations for adopting a new child rights paradigm for LGBTQ youth. Addie Rolnick then investigates how international law has sought to protect the rights of indigenous children through various legal regimes. Rolnick's chapter identifies common themes and potential tensions between the various conceptions of human rights embodied in each regime and considers how international law relates to particular problems faced by indigenous children, such as child removal, poor health, violence and victimization, and over-criminalization.

Maya Sabatello and Mary Frances Layden then explore the state of affairs and legal protections for upholding the rights of children with disabilities and consider some of the prime achievements to date and challenges that persist in the implementation of a child-friendly disability rights agenda. Sabatello and Layden focus in particular on two salient issues for children with disabilities—inclusive education and deinstitutionalization—in exploring the rights of this population of children. Julia Sloth-Nielsen and Katrien Klep then focus on children who find themselves by force, choice, or both, in a situation in which they have to fend for themselves without adult caregivers—or so-called "Independent Children." In exploring the situation of children in street situations and child-headed households, Sloth-Nielsen and Klep tackle the fundamental question in this area: How can we understand the experiences of children who adopt "adult" roles and act at times with maturity and independence from a child-rights perspective?

The last three chapters of this part address populations of children who confront significant rights violations and also are at the forefront of current political debates and dialogues on children's rights. Mike Dottridge discusses what it means to be a trafficked child, the international legal framework regarding trafficked children, and some of the challenges in protecting the human rights of trafficked children. Mark Drumbl then discusses children in armed conflict. Drumbl surveys the international law framework on children in armed conflict—in particular, the law that allocates responsibility for child soldiering—and identifies significant gaps where the law fails to achieve positive outcomes for child soldiers. In the final chapter of this part, Sarah Paoletti discusses refugee and migrant children. Paoletti examines tensions that arise between the rights and realities of children subject to the jurisdiction of a country other than their country of origin.

Collectively, the chapters in this part allow readers to start with a population of children, rather than a substantive area of law, and explore the relevance and effectiveness of international children's rights law to these vulnerable populations of children. In turn, by exploring the lived experience of selected children, these chapters reveal important insights about the content of children's rights law and the effectiveness of its implementation and enforcement mechanisms.

Part VI: Conclusion

Two chapters with a forward-looking focus make up the final part of this handbook. First, Brian Howe and Katherine Covell address passing the baton on to the next generation by exploring the need for and value of educating children about children's rights. Then, in the final chapter, we discuss our view of challenges and opportunities in the field of international children's rights for the twenty-first century.

Notes

1. See generally UNICEF, *25 Years of the Convention on the Rights of the Child: Is the World a Better Place for Children?* (New York: UNICEF, 2014); UNICEF Innocenti Research Centre, *Law Reform and the Implementation of the Convention on the Rights of the Child* (Florence: UNICEF Innocenti Research Centre, 2007).

2. See UNICEF, *Law Reform and Implementation of the Convention on the Rights of the Child*, chaps. 7 and 8. See also Howard Davidson, "Does the U.N Convention on the Rights of the Child Make a Difference?" *Michigan State International Law Review* 22, no. 2 (2014): 514–522.

3. See UNICEF, *Championing Children's Rights: A Global Study of Independent Human Rights Institutions for Children—Summary Report* (Florence: Innocenti Research Centre, 2013).

4. See UNICEF, *Championing Children's Rights*.

5. See UNICEF, *Protecting the World's Children: Impact of the Convention on the Rights of the Child in Diverse Legal Systems* (New York: UNICEF, 2007).

PART I

HISTORICAL AND THEORETICAL FRAMEWORK

....

CHAPTER 1

IMAGES TOWARD THE EMANCIPATION OF CHILDREN IN MODERN WESTERN CULTURE

....

GERTRUD LENZER

Steven Marcus: In Memoriam

> Ideas concerning the rights of children are dependent on the prevailing image of childhood, and when that image changes the ideas about the rights of the child also change.
>
> —Philip E. Veerman[1]

1 INTRODUCTION

....

PHILIPPE Ariès's *Centuries of Childhood. A Social History of Family Life* was published in 1962.[2] This date marks the effectual beginning of the field of the history of childhood.[3] In this study of the history of the family, Ariès refers to the "importance of the child's role in this silent history."[4] According to Ariès: "In medieval society the idea of childhood did not exist; this is not to suggest that children were neglected, forsaken or despised. The idea of childhood is not to be confused with affection for children: it corresponds to an awareness of the particular nature which distinguished the child from the adult, even the young adult. In medieval society this awareness was lacking. That is why, as soon as the child could live without the constant solicitude of his mother, his nanny or his cradle-rocker, he belonged to the adult society."[5]

This 1962 publication was followed by four decades of extensive research and argument by historians who either confirmed or disputed Ariès's theses. As Margaret L. King put it: His "greatest contribution, however, is his insistence on the historicity of childhood: that childhood was not an essential condition, a constant across time, but something that changed."[6] Ariès himself further qualifies: "No doubt the discovery of childhood began in the thirteenth century, and its progress can be traced in the history of art in the fifteenth and sixteenth centuries. But the evidence of its development became more plentiful and significant from the end of the sixteenth and throughout the seventeenth."[7] According to King, "Ariès was right, at least in this regard: the modern concept of the child, the sentimental concept of childhood, of which there were glimpses in Renaissance Italy and Reformation Germany, first crystallized in seventeenth-century England, more or less, and, then, in the eighteenth century in France and more highly urbanized regions of Europe and Americas."[8]

The Arèsian debate about the history of childhood actively engaged numerous historians for a few decades, but today, for most purposes, it has wound down. Yet the question remains: how did both the images of the child and childhood change over the centuries and underlie the emergence of the claims of rights of children across time into the present? It has been argued, in numerous circles related to the academic field of childhood studies in particular, that the child and childhood have been socially constructed. This assumption of the child as a social construct has become a topos—a rhetorical convention so to speak, without the merit of much further historical elaboration and/or discussion. One response to this process is Ian Hacking's question: *A Social Construction of What?*—also the title of his 1999 publication.[9] The historicity of the images of the child and childhood is indubitable. But, as we shall see, these are intimately connected both to changing historical, cultural, social, and economic conditions, to interventions by society and the state, and to the systems of ideas that emerged along with them until the present, with its emphasis on the rights of children as persons with their own inalienable universal human rights. In the course of modern history, as Philip E. Veerman observes, "The perception of the child changed from the *object* of rights in need of protection to the *subject* of rights whose opinion is voiced and asked for."[10]

2 Emergence of the New Concept of the Child and Childhood

The modern history of children and childhood begins in the late seventeenth and into the eighteenth century with such philosophers as John Locke in *Some Thoughts Concerning Education* (1693) and Jean-Jacques Rousseau, who held up the importance of the child and childhood as an ideal in *Émile; or, On Education* (1762). This interest in children was followed by English Romanticism, with such poets as William Blake in *Songs of Innocence and Experience* and William Wordsworth in, for example, *Immortality Ode* and *The Prelude*, which dramatize the surpassing importance of childhood and the child in the sustained development of the powers of the adult's imaginative responsiveness to life. What we witness in such representations is the historical development of conceptual images of childhood as a natural phenomenon which in the course of time has broad repercussions in the general views about the upbringing of children as a social ideal by which the actual historical conditions of children are measured. These conceptions eventually lead to the assertion of the right of children to a childhood consonant with the natural needs of their development. In other words, major changes in epistemological and cultural ideas as developed in philosophy and literature become leading representations of what a proper childhood should be. Such representations help to change social values in upper- and middle-class society and, with it, the entitlements—or natural rights—of children as children to a childhood which is formed in accordance with the proposed natural impulses and tendencies expressed in empiricist philosophy, Rousseau's *Émile*, and the literature of the Romantic period. Not only do these expressive articulations begin to evolve into a child's right to a childhood, with the child coming to be viewed *as a subject* with inherent rights as a human being, but they also antedate as among the earliest instances of future conceptions of the rights of the child as these have developed, for example, in the work of Janucz Korczak and eventually in the UN Convention on the Rights of the Child.

These notions of the right to a childhood serve as guideposts in the reform movements that focus on the living conditions of children of the lower classes and the poor in the developing industrial and capitalist states at the end of the eighteenth and in the course of the nineteenth and early twentieth centuries. In these movements the child is regarded as an *object* of protection, provision, and care that define the duties of society toward children. The reforms concentrate in particular on child labor and the protection of children from cruel treatments by adults. They also involve children as street children and delinquents. In these instances, childhood and children are also regarded as essential to the maintenance of social order and stability. Accompanying these convictions was the establishment of the child-saving institutions of the asylum and houses of refuge. These child-care institutions exemplify the importance of dependent children as future adults.

As the conditions of daily life changed—from an agrarian to an industrialized society—the child became increasingly visible. This was not a social construction, but a veritable change in the social and economic role of the child and children. Children became increasingly visible as a special and distinctive social group and emerged as objects of social and political public deliberations. It was in this connection that the actual conditions of working and poor children confronted the new image of the child that had evolved under the influence of the Enlightenment and Romanticism among the upper and middle classes. The right to a childhood of freedom and play and appropriate child development was the touchstone by which the conditions of laboring and factory children came to be viewed, and reform movements on their behalf were established, and claims to extending a right to childhood to these poor children and their best interests were advanced. With this the right of *all* children to a childhood emerged and informed the work of philanthopists, educators, and policymakers.

3 Nature and the Rights to a Childhood: Locke, Rousseau, and the Romantic Poets

3.1 John Locke: The Empiricist Turn

The development in philosophy of empiricism brought about a change to child-focused development and the entitlements of the child to an upbringing in accordance with the new epistemological holdings of that philosophy. In *An Essay Concerning Human Understanding* (1689),[11] John Locke describes what is commonly referred to as his argument of the mind as a tabula rasa. In book 2, chapter 1 ("Of Ideas in General and Their Original") he states: "Let us then suppose the Mind to be, as we say, white Paper, void of all Characters, without any Ideas; How comes it to be furnished? Whence comes it by that vast store, which the busy and boundless Fancy of Man has painted on it, with an almost endless variety? Whence has it all the materials of Reason and Knowledge? To this I answer, in one word, From Experience: In that, all our Knowledge is founded; and from that it ultimately derives itself."

This theory of empiricism that everything which furnishes the mind comes from the outside world does have an obvious influence on beliefs about the upbringing of children. Childhood as it were from its very beginnings becomes the source of everything we know and feel and reason and hence takes on a special dimension in human development. The importance of the environment, the training from infancy, takes on an increased character and significance. And education is assigned a role different from a vantage point which postulates innate ideas, such as in Descartes, or the depravity of the child, such as in Puritanism. It is therefore—or so it appears—no accident that after publication of his *Essay*, Locke's writing comes to focus on the importance of upbringing and education of the child from infancy forward.

Locke contributed in major ways to a new sense and image of childhood in *Some Thoughts Concerning Education* (1693)[12]—a treatise that immediately went into several republications and was widely translated and published across Europe.[13] And his treatise "became the guide for innumerable middle-class families." Moreover, his influence was far-reaching; in *Émile; or, On Education* (1762), Jean-Jacques Rousseau refers to Locke's essay on numerous occasions, almost as a kind of dialogue.

Locke announces that "the principal aim of my discourse is how a young gentleman should be brought up from his infancy, which in all things will not so perfectly suit the education of *daughters*; though where the difference of sex requires different treatment, twill be no hard matter to distinguish."[14] From its beginning his discourse resembles a child-rearing manual focusing on the best interests of the child. In its early sections, Locke goes into great detail about such matters of health as the sleeping of infants, their clothing, the washing of feet in cold water every day, the need for open air, and the danger of *strait-lacing*[15] (italics in original).

More than an additional thirty sections are devoted to corporal punishment. Locke's general view is against it. He concludes in Section 60: "Frequent beating or chiding is therefore carefully to be avoided: because this sort of correction never produces any good." Or, as he puts it in Section 57: "children (earlier perhaps than we think) are very sensible of praise and commendation. They find a pleasure in being esteem'd and valu'd, especially by their parents and those whom they depend upon. If therefore the father caress and commend them when they do well, shew a cold and neglectful countenance to them upon doing ill, and this accompany'd by a like carriage of the mother and all others that are about them, it will, in a little time, make them sensible of the difference; and this, if constantly observ'd, I doubt not but will of itself work more than threats and blows."

In line with this argument, Locke advocates that reasoning with children is a preferred behavior. In Section 81 he states that "It will perhaps be wonder'd, that I mention reasoning with children; and yet I cannot but think that the true way of dealing with them. They understand it as early as they do language; and, if I misobserve not, they love to be treated as rational creatures, sooner than is imagin'd." A bit later, Locke returns to the custom of beating children: "But, as I said before, beating is the worst, and therefore the last means to be us'd in the correction of children, and that only in cases of extremity, after all gentle ways have been try'd, and prov'd unsuccessful; which, if well observ'd, there will be very seldom any need of blows" (Section 84).

Locke then turns to the need of a tutor and the difficulty of finding the right one. As we shall see, Rousseau also addresses this question. Locke admonishes the father to spare no cost and effort to find one. As far as the learning of the child is concerned, Locke goes on at length to develop the theory that *learning should be play and a game* for the child. Learning how to read "which let him never be driven to, nor chid for; cheat him into it if you can, but make it not a business for him. 'Tis better it be a year later before he can read, than that he should this way get an aversion to learning" (Section 155). He suggests games to help the child learn to read: "It must never be imposed as a task, nor made a trouble to them. There may be dice and play-things, with the letters on them to teach children the alphabet by playing: and twenty other ways may be found, suitable to their particular tempers, to make this kind of learning a sport to them" (Section 148). "Thus children may be cozen'd into a knowledge of the letters; be taught to read, without perceiving it to be anything but a sport, and play themselves into that which others are whipped for. Children should not have anything like work, or serious, laid on them; neither their minds, nor bodies will bear it" (Section 149).

3.2 Jean-Jacques Rousseau: Childhood and Child Development Move Center Stage

According to Rousseau, "the education begins with life, the child is at birth already a disciple, not of the governor, but of nature."[16] It is worthwhile to reiterate that the belief that children had a right to a childhood as it developed in Locke and Rousseau as well as in the nineteenth century was a precondition of the developments of children's rights in the twentieth century. In the modern period in the West, the role of Rousseau, who claimed that we need to look at a child as a child and not as the future man, was decisive. The influence of *Émile* on his contemporaries as well as future thinkers and artists cannot be underestimated. As Allan Bloom states in his introduction to *Émile*, it was "Kant's view that its publication was an event comparable to the French Revolution."[17] Rousseau declared in his preface to *Émile* that "*Childhood is unknown*. Starting from the false idea one has of it, the farther one goes, the more one loses one's way. The wisest men concentrate on what it is important for men to know without considering what children are in a condition to learn. They are always seeking the man in the child without thinking of what he is before being a man" (emphasis added).[18] Or as he also put it: "And childhood is taken to be a pitiable state! It is not seen that the human race would have perished if man had not begun as a child."[19] Moreover, "Humanity has its place in the order of things. The man must be *considered* in the man, and the child in the child."[20] Or, "The truly free man wants only what he can do and does what he pleases. That is my fundamental maxim. It need only be applied to childhood for all the rules of education to flow from it."[21] He added: "Nature wants children to be children before being men." Or at another point—anticipating the Romantic poets—Rousseau admonishes adults to let children be children and be happy.[22] "Respect childhood, and do not hurry to judge it, either for good or for ill.... You are alarmed to see him consume his early years in doing nothing. What? Is it nothing to be happy? Is it nothing to jump, play, and run all day? He will never be so busy in his life."[23]

Rousseau divides childhood into stages: infancy, early childhood, and adolescence before puberty. He says of the last: "This is the third stage of childhood.... I continue to call it *childhood* for want of a term to express it, for this age approaches adolescence without yet being that of puberty."[24] He continues: "we never know how to put ourselves in the place of children; we do not enter into their ideas; we lend them ours, and, always following our own reasonings, with chains of truths we heap up only follies and errors in their heads."[25]

Among the best known advice Rousseau offers to his readers regarding infancy is that bourgeois mothers ought to take care of their own babies rather than send them away to wet nurses.[26] Rousseau also claims that "all children are weaned too soon."[27] This change should be undertaken only at the time of teething. In addition, he devotes entire paragraphs to why children cry and how they should be listened and responded to. The child is in need of something, and the source of the discomfort must be found. "He implores another's help by screams." When one cannot determine the source of a child's needs, "one caresses the child to make him keep quiet, one rocks him, one sings to him to make him go to sleep."[28]

Like Locke, Rousseau also asserts that the general practice of swaddling babies and infants should be discontinued. For the "countries where children are swaddled teem with hunchbacks, cripples.... For fear that bodies be deformed by free movements, we hurry to deform the children by putting them into a press.... Could not so cruel a constraint have an influence on their disposition as well as on their constitution? Their first sentiment is a sentiment of pain and suffering. They find only obstacles to all the movements which they need.... Their first voices, you say, are tears. I can well believe it. You thwart them from their birth. The first gifts they receive from you are chains"[29] It is worth observing that *The Social Contract* published in the same year of 1762 states that "Man is born free, and everywhere he is in chains."

Rousseau created "an imaginary pupil"—Émile. And he further imagined himself as Émile's "governor" from before birth, unlike those tutors that are chosen for a child after "he is already formed." "I shall only remark that, contrary to common opinion, a child's governor ought to be young and even as young as a wise man can be. I would want him to be a child himself if it were possible, to be able to become his pupil's companion and attract his confidence by sharing his enjoyments."[30] But the role of the governor is "less to instruct than to lead. He ought to give no precepts at all: he ought to make them be discovered."[31] "Do not give your pupil any *kind of verbal lessons; he ought to receive them only from experience*" (emphasis added).[32] It is through nature and natural experiences that Émile discovers the world and the sciences and by which he learns. In the course of the text which he at times refers to as a novel, Rousseau leads his pupil through his life and development until, in book 5, he meets Sophie—for "We have promised him a companion." " 'Since our young gentleman,' says Locke, 'is ready to marry, it is time to leave him to his beloved.' And with that he finishes his work. But as I do not have the honor of raising a gentleman," Rousseau continues, "I shall take care not to imitate Locke on this point."[33]

As for the influence of John Locke and Jean-Jacques Rousseau, Julia Grant, in her essay "Parent-Child Relations in Western Europe and North America, 1500–Present," states: "One can never underestimate the impact of French philosopher Jean-Jacques Rousseau or English philosopher John Locke on discourses about parenting not only in the Netherlands, England, Germany, and France, but in the United States, even though it is unlikely that more than a very few people read them. Their ideas seeped into European and American homes through magazines, short treatises, and local pedagogues and ministers."[34]

Once childhood came to be regarded as a supremely important stage in human development, and once the child was recognized as an indisputably important member of the human family, it became implicit that the rights of children should be given special attention and their development allotted explicit special treatment. In fact, such conceptions were already contained in the philosophy of empiricism in which from the moment of birth the development of mind is based on experience from the earliest sensations forward. Indeed, child development with all its possibilities and needs dictated the rights of the child to a responsible attention that ranged from health and education to general well-being and happiness. The future development of the adult human being was thus firmly anchored in the appropriate, kind, and solicitous manner of the child's upbringing.

3.3 The Romantic Poets: The Glorification of Childhood

To this cognitive and metaphysical dimension, the poetry of Romanticism, with William Blake (1757–1827) and William Wordsworth (1770–1850) in the foreground, was added to the celebration of childhood and its innocence, along with the pleasures and sorrows of the lives of children. It is from here as well that the Romantic idealization of childhood emerged and began to dominate its cultural representations. The rights of every child to a childhood became more articulately pronounced and influenced the sentiments of subsequent interpretations of the conditions of children in and by society.

As Peter Coveney observes, "The literary climate in which the Romantic Child developed was prepared in the half-century from Rousseau's *Émile* to Wordsworth's *Prelude*."[35] The poetry of Blake and Wordsworth is, so to speak, modernized and placed as one of the vital centers of conscious interest. In Blake's *Songs of Innocence and Experience* the child is at first regarded as a "little Lamb," a traditional Christian image. But this lamb is raised only to be slaughtered and is transformed into a child chimney sweeper.[36]

> When my mother died I was very young,
> And my father sold me while yet my tongue
> Could scarcely cry 'Weep! Weep! Weep!
> So your chimneys I sweep, & and in soot I sleep.[37]

Here the poet is referring to the practice, among the very poor and destitute, of putting out young children for hard and dangerous labor. It is no accident that the chimney sweeper's street cry, "Sweep, sweep," is at the same time transformed by the poet into "weep, weep."

In the poetry of Wordsworth, the representation of childhood is equally a focus of interest. As he wrote in *Intimations of Immortality* ("Ode"): "Heaven lies about us in our infancy." Wordsworth seems actually to be making original discoveries about children. In such poems as "We are Seven" and "Anecdote for Fathers" he reveals in concrete narratives how different mentally are young children from adults and respects and defends them against adult correction and coercion. In *The Prelude,* the most original and extended autobiographical poem in the English language, he endeavors to depict how his vocation as a poet and as a feeling human being was brought about by his early experiences. In one daring passage he attributes the origin of poetry and the imagination to nothing less than the baby attached to and drinking in both nourishment and love from the mother, as well as the fusion of perception and security and active mental power from the primary and universal symbiosis of our earliest of experiences.

> *Blest the Infant Babe*
> (For with my best conjecture I would trace
> Our Being's earthly progress), blest the Babe,
> Nursed in his Mother's arms, who sinks to sleep
> Rocked on his Mother's breast; who with his soul
> Drinks in the feelings of his Mother's eye!
> For him, in one dear Presence, there exists
> A virtue which irradiates and exalts
> Objects through widest intercourse of sense.
> No outcast he, bewildered and depressed:

Along his infant veins are interfused
The gravitation and the filial bond
Of nature that connect him with the world...
Emphatically such a Being lives,
Frail creature as he is, helpless as frail,
An inmate of this active universe.
For feeling has to him imparted power
That through the growing faculties of sense
Doth like an agent of the one great Mind.
Create, creator and receiver both,
Working but in alliance with the works
Which it beholds.—Such, verily, is the first
Poetic spirit of our human life,
By uniform control of after years,
Through every change of growth and of decay,
Pre-eminent till death.

The Prelude, book 2 (1850)[38]

This section explores how Locke, in his treatise on *Some Thoughts Concerning Education*, and Rousseau, in *Émile*, develop the modern concept of the child as an all-important life stage in human beings and of the importance of childhood as a period of play, free exploration of nature and the world. For Wordsworth also, "The Child is the father of the man." Although he is close to Rousseau and the experience of nature by the child, "for Wordsworth nature would implant the foundations of moral virtue and of beauty; and these in turn would shape the adult life."[39] As Hugh Cunningham affirms: "A romantic sensibility towards childhood dominated the nineteenth and much of the twentieth centuries. It was probably at its height between 1860 and 1930."[40]

4 THE CHILDREN OF THE POOR: SAVING THE CHILDREN

4.1 The Factory Child and Child Employment

The image of a right to a childhood began to be socially effective in the reform movements of the late eighteenth and the nineteenth centuries which aimed to mitigate the cruelties and excessiveness of child labor in England, the leading country of the Industrial Revolution. The idea of childhood articulated by empiricist philosophers and Romantic poets informed the work of English philanthropists and of the Royal Commissions Acts and the Factory Acts.[41] It represented cultural and intellectual landmarks rising to meet the changing economic and social relations of developing capitalism and industrialization as well as the widespread institutionalization of child employment.[42]

Child labor ranged from chimney sweeps and the indentured labor of orphans as unpaid apprentices to the so-called free labor of children of the poor in the collieries, the cotton mills, and industrialized agricultural work. The plight of these children awakened increasingly the literate public's concerns, criticism, and actions.[43] In England such reforming activities, which undertook to report on the conditions of children and young people in these labor-intensive industries, led in turn to legislation limiting the hours of work and the age of children to be employed in the best interests of the child.[44] One of the important Royal Commission's report—also called Blue Books—was *The Condition and Treatment of the Children Employed in the Mines and Collieries of the United Kingdom* (1842), which also contained extensive oral testimony from children.[45]

It was in connection with the Factory Acts of the first half of the nineteenth century in England that the idea of children's rights to a childhood for all children was confirmed. As Cunningham points out in *The Children of the Poor: Representations of Childhood since the Seventeenth Century*[46]: "Out of these beliefs that both the order of nature and the order of England were distorted by the labour of children in factories, there emerged the first articulation of the idea that *all children had rights*, which, ultimately, it fell to the state to protect. A sense of what these rights were had been in existence since the earlier part of the century" (emphasis added).[47] Discussions about the rights of infants and children by numerous authors led Cunningham to conclude, "It was only a small step from this to a conviction that work was in fact an offence against the true nature of childhood."[48] Furthermore, there was "a growing belief that children should not work."[49] Or, as Cunningham puts it, the novelty was not state intervention with the Factory Acts; rather, "The novelty was the first voicing of the assertion that children had a right not to work at all."[50]

Moreover, other contemporaries of the period referred to by Cunningham argued against the very term *work-children*, and he concludes: "This was a decisive moment, perhaps the first occasion in history when there seemed to be something intrinsically unnatural in the labour of children."[51] In addition, "This sensibility and rhetoric was unquestionably informed by an internalized acquaintance with the Romantic poets."[52]

The Industrial Revolution is closely associated with the employment of child labor in Germany, France, and the United States. In 1839 Prussia passed a law controlling the practice of child labor in its industrial regions. It forbade the factory employment of those younger than nine, limited the labor of youths under sixteen to ten hours a day, and outlawed night and Sunday shifts for children.[53] This law went into effect as "Regulative regarding the Employment of Children in Factories."[54] After England, Prussia became "the first continental European state"—and the second country in the world—"to pass a law regulating child labor in factories, mines, and quarries."[55] In France, however, in contrast to England, the conditions of child labor did not arouse widespread public concern; theories of laissez-faire prevailed and worked against the introduction of laws curtailing child labor. The major defenders of child labor were factory owners as well as working-class parents, both groups feeling threatened by the potential loss of income. It was not until 1841 that a child labor law was passed in France, but it was not very effective, and further legislation took until 1874, but even then, implementation proved to be difficult.[56]

By comparison, the federal regulations of child labor in the United States did not occur until much later, with passage of the Fair Labor Standards Act in 1938. Although public interest and organizational efforts started during the 1880s, it was not until 1904 that the National Child Labor Committee (NCLC) was founded and incorporated by an act of Congress in 1907. With a distinguished board of directors representing the "major figures in social welfare at the time," NCLC spearheaded the reform and regulation of child labor. Its mission was "promoting the rights, awareness, dignity, well-being and education of children and youth as they relate to work and working." It was also the National Child Labor Committee that employed (in 1908) Lewis Wickes Hine as a photographer who became famous for his documentation of children and workers laboring in factories. In 1916, NCLC backed the Keating-Owen Act, which "prohibited shipment in interstate commerce of goods manufactured or processed by child labor. The act passed and was signed by President Woodrow Wilson, but was declared unconstitutional in 1918 by the Supreme Court."[57] The US Congress passed two laws in 1918 and 1922, but the Supreme Court again declared both unconstitutional. In 1924 Congress proposed a constitutional amendment prohibiting child labor, but the states failed to ratify it. Finally, in 1938, Congress passed the Fair Labor Standards Act.

4.2 Street Children and the "Delinquent" Child: Saving the Children

In England and the United States, the existence of street children and "street Arabs"—as they were referred to in both countries—led to child-saving movements to improve their life chances in their best interests as well as protect society from such "nuisances." In the nineteenth century, public concern was often preoccupied with street children and the related problem of what was then often called the delinquent child. These children upon whom public attention focused were the children of the poor. The image of the poor and vagrant child and the child's deformed childhood were widely decisive. At the same time, the general tenor of public discussion was not that these children were poor, but that they needed to be rescued and potentially were a danger to society. The conception of childhood of play and innocence was overshadowed by the realities of a perverted childhood. Waifs and stray children and their childhoods were regarded as an aberration of what childhood should be. This conviction appears to be realized in the efforts to save and to "reform" the child. Both images are closely connected. At the same time, the Romantic image of the virtuous and good child was still at work. As Cunningham put it, in England the "young offender ... must be treated with consideration for 'the nature of the child, *as a child*' ... And finally, the offender must 'gradually be restored to the true position of childhood ... he must be placed in a family.' This was not simply sentimentalism, a regret for childhoods which had not been allowed to happen. ... it was also an internalization of the romantic belief that the enjoyment of a proper childhood was the only foundation for a tolerable adult life." Not only in England but in other

European countries as well, "there was an intensified phase of institution building, catering for children of all kinds thought to be in need."[58]

This conviction was particularly relevant in the United States. As David Rothman writes in *The Discovery of the Asylum*, "the admissions policies of child-care institutions were a catalogue of practically every misfortune that could befall a minor. The abject, the vagrant, the delinquent, the child of poverty-stricken or intemperate parents were all proper candidates for one or another asylum or refuge."[59] Although street children were a centuries-old problem, they became a major preoccupation in Paris, London, and New York. They were also institutionalized as delinquent children both for their own improvement and to isolate society from them and them from public society. These children, therefore, were perceived as both victims of and threats to society.[60] But here also, they were as a rule the children of the poor or just poor children.[61]

4.3   Charles Dickens and Victorian Childhood

Coveney introduces Charles Dickens as follows: "The child was at the heart of his interest; at the centre of the Dickens world. There is perhaps no other major English novelist whose achievement was so closely regulated by a feeling for childhood."[62] Dickens must also be viewed, per Coveney, "as heir to the romantic poets."[63] Dickens (1812–1870) is indeed the greatest of Victorian novelists who placed the life of the child near the center of his imagination. The origin of his creative obsession was his own personal experience. At the age of twelve his father was imprisoned for debt (his mother and sister accompanied the father into prison). The young son was left alone on the outside and labored for a number of months in a blacking factory. This traumatic experience was kept secret by the immensely successful novelist throughout his life. But in all his novels there are children, often damaged and desolate, that are refractions of his own childhood. This experience is of utmost importance throughout "the rest of his childhood, and indeed for so many of the multitude of children who haunt his fiction."[64]

All of Dickens's novels were published serially. They were almost universally read in sections of English-speaking society (and in translation as well). The characters in them quickly became a permanent part of the folklore of the modern world—Oliver Twist and Fagin, Scrooge and Tiny Tim, David and Mr. Micawber, along with numerous others, remain familiar and virtually living figures until the present. If works of literature may be said to affect or influence cultural attitudes and sensibilities, then the representation of children in Dickens's popular fiction helped to form parts of the growing sympathetic perception and understanding of them in the modern West.

4.4   Cruelty to Children

It was also toward the end of the nineteenth century that the conception arose that the child needed to be protected from the cruelty of adults. The idea of child abuse emerged in the United States and in England during the same period. The New York Society for the Prevention of Cruelty to Children was founded in 1875; the National Society for the Prevention of Cruelty to Children, in England, in 1889.[65] In these organizations the protection of the child took on another dimension, one in which the role of adults comes under close examination. As the right to a childhood continued to emerge and develop both in law and in thought, society began to realize the importance of the right of children to freedom from physical and emotional abuse by adults. Increasingly, the child and the adult worlds are regarded as separate and may even stand in opposition. The child was now conceived as a human subject entitled to be protected from the unlimited rights of parents and adults as authorities. In other words, child maltreatment deprives the child of the care that one is entitled to receive. With this development, the right of children not to be mistreated begins to be publicly established. The image of childhood is again enlarged and, with it, the right to a childhood free from violence. As Joseph M. Hawes notes: "The nineteenth century saw the growth and expansion of the concept of *parens patriae*—the legal underpinning of the state's authority to assert and enforce children's rights. It also saw the development of a greater sensitivity to children and their needs. Some authorities have argued that this sensitivity arose from a greater romantic sensibility in society in general."[66]

5 THE WHOLE CHILD AS THE FOCUS OF NEW DISCIPLINES AND PROFESSIONS

5.1 Johann Heinrich Pestalozzi and Wilhelm August Froebel

Not only were Locke and Rousseau widely read, but their strategic influence can be traced as the discussion moves forward through Johann Heinrich Pestalozzi (1746–1827), the Swiss pedagogue and educational reformer, and his student Wilhelm August Froebel (1782–1852). In an echo of Rousseau, Pestalozzi writes that "the instruction of the young must in every aspect be directed more toward developing their abilities than toward the enrichment of their knowledge.... To arrive at knowledge slowly, by one's own experience, is better than to learn by rote, in a hurry, facts that other people know, and then, glutted with words, to lose one's own free, observant and inquisitive ability to study."[67] It was Froebel who developed the idea of kindergarten as a component of preschool education. He also became well known for Froebel's Gift, play materials he developed between 1837 and 1850. These play objects consisted of five play gifts. Froebel, like Pestalozzi, was an educational psychologist. His conception of kindergarten spread to the United States, where Elizabeth Peabody founded the first English speaking kindergarten in 1860 in Boston. (Margarete Schurz, Froebel's student, founded the first German-speaking kindergarten in the United States in 1856.) And Pestalozzi and Froebel's "concern for the education of the whole child...found fertile soil in.... most urban American schools." In addition, "Pestalozzi's theory that the child learned from the perception of natural objects rather than from ill-understood words, the object method was widely hailed."[68] In short, his method was founded in the natural world and the senses. Just as Locke had been a proponent of the individuality of each child, Pestalozzi based his educational theory precisely on the uniqueness of the individual self of every child. Froebel, in turn, praised play as "the highest form of child development at this period" of childhood.[69] "The plays of childhood are the germinal leaves of all later life; for the whole man is developed and shown in these, in his tenderest dispositions, in his innermost tendencies."[70]

The influence of Froebel in the United States is further confirmed by the author of many children's books and kindergarten champion Kate Douglas Wiggin (1856–1923) and her writings on children's rights. In *Children's Rights: A Book of Nursery Logic* (1892), she asserts that "once a child is born, one of his inalienable rights, which we too often deny him, is the right to his childhood."[71] She and her sister founded sixty kindergartens for the poor in San Francisco and Oakland, and her writings are replete with descriptions and affirmations of Froebel's philosophy and educational methods. In 1878 she started the first free kindergarten in San Francisco and established with her sister a training school for kindergarten teachers along the lines of Froebel's methods. Here is one of her descriptions of the role of play in early childhood: "We found that in Froebel's plays the mirror is held up to universal life; that the child in playing them grows into unconscious sympathy with the natural, the human, the divine."[72] Or, equally, "the object of the kindergarten is not to make Froebel an *idol*, but an *ideal*. He seems to have found type-forms admirable for awaking the higher senses of the child."[73]

5.2 The New Disciplines of Pedagogy, Psychology and Social Work

The late nineteenth and early twentieth centuries provided the setting for the emergence of new academic disciplines to understand and focus on children and adolescents. The creation of the new disciplines of pedagogy, child and adolescent psychology, as well as social work represents significant alterations in the image of the child. A further major development is also to be recognized in the work of Sigmund Freud and the importance he attributed to the experiences of the infant and the child. In it we find new articulations of childhood experiences for the formation of human beings in adulthood. As Coveney observes: "In this sense, it is not preposterous to suggest that across the century Wordsworth's Prelude and Freud's Essay on Infantile Sexuality may be said to join hands."[74]

This rise in interest in the child as a subject of scholarly and scientific study is of central significance and has far-reaching implications for the twentieth-century conception of childhood. In this connection, the child study movement starting in the 1880s in the United States under the leadership of G. Stanley Hall is of special note.[75] Hall "drew heavily on Froebel for the early years and the metaphor of growth, and on Rousseau for the years of childhood and adolescence."[76] In fact, Hall wanted to "base education on a scientific study of child development"[77] at a moment when the first major publications in child development in Germany and England, based on observations of children and infants, were occurring. His own study "was based on a list of 123 questions asked of kindergarten children in Boston and became so popular that Hall decided to launch a movement in order to gather the data necessary to construct a scientific (and professional) view of the child."[78] The movement "reached its zenith in the 1890s." In England, the movement developed into the Child Study Association established in 1894.[79] The advancement of a *psychological scientific interest in the child as child* represents a major evolutionary turn in the image of the child and a considerable step forward in the conception of the rights of the child. This shift in scientific inquiry was a precursor of and important foundation for the conception of the human rights of the child.

6 The Century of the Child

Ellen Key declared the oncoming twentieth century to be the "Century of the Child."[80] The First World War led to the inception of the Save the Children Society Fund under the leadership of Eglantyne Jebb and articulation of the first children's rights declaration, the Declaration of the Rights of the Child (Geneva Declaration), in 1924. It is clear from the five articles of the Declaration that "mankind owes to the child the best it has to give." The Declaration remains a document aimed at child protection but now including all children—a globalization and internationalization of the image of the child. These rights had come to be understood to serve as protection for all children and not only children of the poor and disadvantaged in Europe and the United States. It is of interest that Janusz Korczak was nonetheless critical of the Geneva Declaration when he observed in *The Child's Right to Respect*: "The Geneva lawmakers confused duties with rights; the tone of the declaration is one of persuasion not insistence; an appeal to goodwill, a plea for kindness."[81]

The pediatrician Dr. Henryk Goldszmit, known by his pen name Janusz Korczak (1878–1942), through his writings, life, and death as director of the Jewish orphanage in Warsaw, is widely recognized as having developed a new image of the child that became central to the UN Convention on the Rights of the Child. In his introduction to the *Legislative History of the Convention on the Rights of the Child*, Adam Lopatka—chairman/rapporteur of the Working Group on a Draft Convention on the Rights of the Child—has described how this new conception of childhood came about:

> In the years between the two world wars, a contemporary concept of childhood was developed. At its core is the conviction that the *child is an autonomous person who has his or her own needs, interests and rights; and that he or she is not only an object of care and concern but also a subject whose interests and rights should be respected.* According to that concept, the child, at a certain stage of his or her development, is

capable of formulating and expressing his/her own opinions which ought to be taken into consideration. The main exponent of this new concept of childhood is Dr. Janusz Korczak—a doctor of medicine, a writer, a philosopher and an educator. He confirmed the loyalty to his vision of childhood in his own life. Although he had the opportunity to save his life, he decided to remain instead with the children he was taking care of until the very end—and died with them in a gas chamber in the Nazi concentration camp of Treblinka in 1942. When the Polish government put forward the first draft convention on the rights of the child in 1978, it wished to popularize Dr. Korczak's concept of childhood throughout the world. (Emphasis added)[82]

Of the numerous publications of Korzcak, *The Child's Right to Respect* (1929) is the most widely known. He wrote that "it is really children who are the real prince of feelings, the poets and thinkers"[83] and that "years of work have confirmed for me more and more clearly that children deserve respect, trust, and kindness."[84] Korczak's educational ideas were also influenced by Pestalozzi. A trip to Zurich "while still a university student in 1901, brought him a closer look at Pestalozzi's educational principles and practices with which he was fascinated since youth." It is relevant that "Korczak's own educational writings bear frequent references to Pestalozzi, while his own 'school' later bore a striking resemblance to Pestalozzi's views. 'We will build a school,' wrote Korczak, 'where children will not be learning dead letters from a life-less page; where, rather, they will learn how people live, why they live, how they can live differently, what they need to learn and do in order to live full of the free spirit.' "[85]

With this statement we come full circle back to Locke, Rousseau, and the inception of the modern image of the child as well as a child-centered conception of childhood that ultimately leads to the UN Convention on the Rights of the Child—the treaty that affirms the civil, political, economic, social, and cultural human rights of the child and of children everywhere. The child is no longer merely an object of rights in need of protection, but a subject of rights who, in Korczak's view, "at a certain stage of his or her development, is capable of formulating and expressing his/her own opinions which ought to be taken into consideration." With this, Korczak anticipates the central articles 12, 13, and 14 of the Convention, which affirm the right of the child to form and express freely his or her own views in all matters affecting the child and "in a manner consistent with the evolving capacities of the child." Korczak's *The Child's Right to Respect* together with the child's participatory rights are among the fundamental rights of the Convention.

As this essay explores the development of the modern images of the child and childhood, it is also important to emphasize the evolution of the idea and historical injunction of the best interests of the child. What all the philosophers, poets, philanthropists, pedagogues, policymakers, educators, and scholars who have been discussed in this chapter share is their commitment to explore and enhance the best interests of the child and of childhood. Although they never address this expressly, the best interests of the child are part of the history of the new conceptions of the child and childhood in the modern period. This commitment reaches over from Locke's and Rousseau's prescriptions for a proper and happy childhood and from the Romantic image of the child to the charitable intentions of saving the children of the poor, as well as street and abused children, to state interventions of the Factory Acts and legislation against child labor of the nineteenth and early twentieth centuries.

It is in the UN Declaration of the Rights of the Child of 1959 that the idea of the best interests of the child is first articulated at the international level. It also reaches back to earlier tenets that childhood and the child should be happy: "The General Assembly Proclaims this Declaration of the Rights of the Child to the end that he may have a happy childhood and enjoy for his own good and for the good of society the rights and the freedoms herein set forth" (General Assembly Resolution 1386 [XIV], Nov. 20, 1959). As announced in the second of the UN Declaration's ten principles, "The child shall enjoy special protection, and shall be given opportunities and facilities, by law and by other means, to enable him to develop physically, mentally, morally, spiritually and socially in a healthy and normal manner and in conditions of freedom and dignity. In the enactment of these laws for this purpose, the best interests of the child shall be *the paramount consideration.*" This wording was to change in the UN Convention on the Rights of the Child of 1989 to read, in Article 3, that "the best interests of the child shall be *a primary consideration*"—a difference in formulation and meanings that became the source of a host of discussions in subsequent years in the children's rights literature (emphasis added).

7 Conclusion

In the course of over two hundred years, the image of the child and the role of childhood went through profound changes, starting with the importance assigned to physical and emotional child-rearing by the parents or a tutor from infancy and forwarded by the discourses of Locke and Rousseau. The educational needs of the infant and adolescent child are to be met by game and play, not stern and rote teaching, and in the case of Rousseau, it is the discovery of nature which provides children with all they are bound to learn. The use of physical punishment is ruled out by Locke, who views the child as a rational being open to reasoning. According to Rousseau, "the truly free man wants only what he can do and does what he pleases. That is my fundamental maxim. It need only be applied to childhood for all the rules of education to flow from it." Since childhood is unknown, according to Rousseau, the rules of education for childhood are those which promote the child as a happy and carefree human being. The rules of early and later education of the child as advanced by Locke and Rousseau find profound repercussions in the philosophies of Pestalozzi, Froebel, and other nineteenth- and twentieth-century pedagogues, such as Janusz Korczak. From Locke forward, the writers discussed in this chapter all served the best interests of the child. The child and childhood were viewed as life stages in which the well-being and happiness of the child were paramount to all other considerations held in the past.

The glorification of the child and childhood as supreme human manifestations by the Romantic poets and its influence were powerful also in the social response to the abject conditions of children of the streets, of child labor, and of abused children who needed to be rescued and afforded happiness and redemption. In the twentieth century, as articulated in the 1959 UN Declaration of the Rights of the Child, the Romantic image of the child and its influence remained among the most powerful set of ideas.

NOTES

1. Philip E. Veerman, *The Rights of the Child and the Changing Image of Childhood* (Norwell, MA: Martinus Nijhoff, 1992), 10.
2. Philippe Ariès, *Centuries of Childhood: A Social History of Family Life*, trans. Robert Baldick (New York: Random House, 1962). Originally published as *L'Enfant et la vie familial sous l'ancien régime* (Paris: Librairie Plon, 1960).
3. "The uniqueness of the west lay in the fact that the time when key ideas about childhood were developing in the eighteenth century coincided with the growing influence of the west over other parts of the globe. If the world is in some degree (but by no means wholly) a legatee of western ideas of childhood, it is because the west exported childhood, and sometimes children, as part and parcel of an age of imperialism." See the excellent study by Hugh Cunningham, Preface to *Children and Childhood in Western Society since 1500*, 2nd ed., repr. (Harlow, UK: Pearson Edition Ltd., 2005), ix. This chapter focuses on the emergence of new images of the child and childhood especially in Western Europe and the United States since the late seventeenth century.
4. Ariès, *Centuries of Childhood*, 10.
5. Ariès, *Centuries of Childhood*, 128.
6. Margaret L. King, "Concepts of Childhood: What We Know and Where We Might Go," *Renaissance Quarterly* 60, no. 2 (2007): 372.
7. Ariès, *Centuries of Childhood*, 47.
8. King, "Concepts of Childhood," 371. King adds: "In terms of their investment in children, bourgeois and professional families of the fifteenth through eighteenth centuries quite nearly resembled our own—which is to say, bourgeois and professional—families today." King, "Concepts of Childhood," 372.
9. Ian Hacking, *A Social Construction of What?* (Cambridge, MA: Harvard University Press, 1999).
10. Veerman, *Rights of the Child*, 396.
11. John Locke, *An Essay Concerning Human Understanding*, ed. Peter N. Nidditch (1689; reprint, Oxford: Clarendon Press, 1975).
12. John Locke, *Some Thoughts Concerning Education* (1693; reprint, Canton, SD: NuVision Publications, 2007).
13. Cunningham, *Children and Childhood in Western Society*, 61.
14. Locke, *Some Thoughts Concerning Education*, section 6.
15. Locke is opposed to the common practice of swaddling of infants.
16. Jean-Jacques Rousseau, *Émile; or, On Education*, trans. Allan Bloom (1762; reprint, New York: Basic Books, 1979), 61.
17. Rousseau, *Émile*, 4.
18. Rousseau, *Émile*, 33–34.
19. Rousseau, *Émile*, 38.
20. Rousseau, *Émile*, 80.

21. Rousseau, *Émile*, 84.

22. Rousseau, *Émile*, 90.

23. Rousseau, *Émile*, 107.

24. Rousseau, *Émile*, 165.

25. Rousseau, *Émile*, 170.

26. Although Rousseau is often credited with having initiated maternal breastfeeding, Edward Shorter points out that in "the 1760s we find the switch to maternal nursing already well underway among the middle classes" but suggests that *Émile* "may serve as a useful landmark in intellectual history." Edward Shorter, *The Making of the Modern Family* (New York: Basic Books, 1975), 182, 183. As far as swaddling was concerned, Shorter claims that it "had begun to lose its hold among the people before 1850." Yet the "decline in swaddling had begun perhaps a century earlier among the middle and upper classes. Their heads filled with the exhortations of Rousseau, propertied Parisians had fairly early started to liberate their infants 'from the tyranny of the *maillot*.' " Shorter, *Making of the Modern Family*, 197–198. There were, however, differences according to countries. In England it was reported that the practice had been abandoned by the 1790s, whereas in Puritan New England "swaddling never seems to have existed." This again was in contrast to Germany, where the binding of children appears to have been common into the 1840s. Shorter, *Making of the Modern Family*, 198–199.

27. Rousseau, *Émile*, 69.

28. Rousseau, *Émile*, 65.

29. Jean-Jacques Rousseau, *Émile; or, on Education*, trans. and ed. Christopher Kelly and Allan Bloom (1762; reprint, Hanover, NH: Dartmouth College Press, 2010), 168. As Cunningham points out: "Evidence of this from America comes from a significant change in the clothes that children wore and the furnishings of the household; whereas in the seventeenth and first half of the eighteenth centuries the aim was to get the child upright at an early age, to progress as rapidly as possible to adulthood, in the period 1750 to 1830 the emphasis was on the child growing up in accordance with the precepts, and on the timescale, of nature. In England there were at least 200 treatises on education published before the end of the century, all in some way influenced by Émile." Cunningham, *Children and Childhood*, 64.

30. Rousseau, *Émile*, 50–51.

31. Rousseau, *Émile*, 52.

32. Rousseau, *Émile*, 95.

33. Rousseau, *Émile*, 357.

34. Julia Grant, "Parent-Child Relations in Western Europe and North America, 1500–Present," in *The Routledge History of Childhood in the Western World*, ed. Paula S. Fass (London: Routledge, 2013), 108.

35. Peter Coveney, *The Image of Childhood* (Harmondsworth, UK: Penguin Books, 1967), 37.

36. The poems, with the exception of *The Prelude*, are reprinted from Russell Noyes, ed., *English Romantic Poetry and Prose* (New York: Oxford University Press, 1956), 198–370.

37. This poem was inspired by agitation in Blake's time to outlaw the conditions of chimney sweeps.

38. Jonathan, M. H. Abrams Wordsworth and Stephen Gill, eds., *William Wordsworth. The Prelude 1799, 1805, 1850: Authoritative Texts, Context and Reception* (New York: W.W. Norton 1979).

39. Cunningham, *Children and Childhood*, 68.

40. Cunningham, *Children and Childhood*, 69.

41. Royal Commissions Acts and Factory Acts were parliamentary inquiries and labor law acts passed by the Parliament of the United Kingdom beginning in 1833.

42. What we call *child labor* was referred to in the nineteenth century as *child employment*. See Steven Marcus, *Engels, Manchester, and the Working Class* (1974; reprint, New York: W.W. Norton, 1985), 216.

43. As opposed to the work of unpaid apprentices, free labor entailed that done by children of the poor, whose parents agreed to the employment of their children.

44. Oz Frankel, *States of Inquiry: Social Investigations and Print Culture in Nineteenth Century Britain and the United States* (Baltimore: Johns Hopkins University Press, 18, 2006), 4–6.

45. Charles Dickens had evidently planned on writing a political pamphlet titled "An Appeal to the People of England on behalf of the Poor Man's Child," but it appears that he published *A Christmas Carol* on December 19, 1843, instead.

46. Hugh Cunningham, *The Children of the Poor: Representations of Childhood since the Seventeenth Century* (Oxford: Basil Blackwell, 1991).

47. Cunningham, *Children of the Poor*, 87.

48. Cunningham, *Children of the Poor*, 89.

49. Cunningham, *Children of the Poor*, 146.

50. Cunningham, *Children and Childhood*, 140.

51. Cunningham, *Children and Childhood*, 89.

52. Cunningham, *Children and Childhood*, 90.

53. Elizabeth Anderson, "Ideas in Action: The Politics of Prussian Child Labor Reform, 1817–1839," *Theory and Society* 42, no. 1 (January): 81–119.

54. Anderson, "Ideas in Action," 108.

55. Anderson, "Ideas in Action," 82.

56. Lee S. Weissbach, "Child Labor Legislation in Nineteenth-Century France," *Journal of Economic History* 37, no. 1 (March 1977): 268–271.

57. C. A. Paul, "National Child Labor Committee, (NCLC)," Social Welfare History Project, Virginia Commonwealth University Libraries, October 4, 2017, https://socialwelfare. library.vcu.edu/organizations/National-Child-Labor-Committee.

58. Cunningham, *Children and Childhood*, 148.

59. David J. Rothman, *The Discovery of the Asylum: Social Order and Disorder in the New Republic*, rev. ed. (1971); reprint, Boston: Little, Brown, 1990), 209.

60. Harry Hendrick argues that children were perceived not only as victims but also as threats as far as social policy was concerned. In fact, he suggests, "it is important for a proper understanding of social policy in relation to children (and adolescents) that we recognize just how much of so-called protective legislation has been concerned with their presence as *threats* rather than their suffering as victims." For Hendrick, the "overlapping" of the "victim" and the "threat" status of children throughout the nineteenth century informs his book. See Harry Hendrick, *Child Welfare: England 1872–1989* (London: Routledge, 2011), 8.

61. Rothman reports that reformers eventually became disenchanted with the houses of refuge and asylum, which had a prison-like character. "The leading exponent and publicist for this critique, as well as one of the first reformers to organize a placing-out program, was Charles Loring Brace." Rothman, *Discovery of the Asylum*, 259. Brace founded the philanthropic Children's Aid Society in 1853 in New York City.

62. Coveney, *Image of Childhood*, 111.

63. Coveney, *Image of Childhood*, 114.

64. Coveney, *Image of Childhood*, 117.

65. For the history of the NSPCC in England, see Cunningham, *Children of the Poor*, 143–146.

66. Joseph M. Hawes, *The Children's Rights Movement: A History of Advocacy and Protection* (Boston: Twayne Publishers, 1991), 25.

67. Friedrich Froebel, *The Education of Man: Aphorisms*, trans. Heinz and Ruth Norden (New York: Philosophical Library, 1951), 35.

68. Dorothy Ross, *G. Stanley Hall: The Psychologist as Prophet* (Chicago: University of Chicago Press, 1972), 115.

69. Friedrich Froebel, *The Education of Man*, trans. W. N. Hailmann (1826 and 1827; unabridged reprint, Mineola, NY: Dover Publications, 2005), 54.

70. Froebel, *Education of Man*, 55.

71. Kate Douglas Wiggin, "The Rights of the Child," in *Children's Rights* (1892; reprint, Gloucester, UK: Dodo Press, 2007), 4. The book also contains three articles by Wiggin's sister, Nora Smith.

72. Wiggin, "Rights of the Child," 22.

73. Wiggin, "Rights of the Child," 23.

74. Coveney, *Image of Childhood*, 34. Or, as Coveney put it elsewhere: "Later eighteenth-century educational theory became largely a gloss on the ideas conveyed so forcefully into the European consciousness through Rousseau's *Emile*. The vital genius of the book inspired the whole progressive school of educational thought in the nineteenth century. If original sin had informed the Christian centuries in their attitude to childhood, it is Rousseau's *Emile* that dominates the eighteenth and nineteenth centuries until Freud." Coveney, *Image of Childhood*, 45–46.

75. Hall founded the *American Journal of Psychology* in 1887 and became the first president of the American Psychological Association in 1892; as president of Clark University he invited Sigmund Freud and Carl Jung to the Clark Conference in 1909.

76. Ross, *G. Stanley Hall*, 120n55.

77. Ross, *G. Stanley Hall*, 124.

78. Ross, *G. Stanley Hall*, 29.

79. Harry Hendrick, *Child Welfare: England 1872–1989* (London: Routledge, 2011), 33–35.

80. Ellen Key, *The Century of the Child* (New York: Putnam, 1909). For excellent biographical essays about Ellen Key, Eglantyne Jebb, and Janusz Korczak, see Veerman, *Rights of the Child*.

81. Janusz Korczak, *When I Am Little Again and The Child's Right to Respect*, trans. E. P. Kulawiec (1925; reprint, Lanham, MD: University Press of America, 1992), 176.

82. Adam Lopatka, "Introduction," in *Legislative History of the Convention of the Rights of the Child*, vol. 1 (New York: United Nations, 2007), xxxviif. According to Lopatka, in 1978 the Polish government introduced its draft for a convention that, in its proposal, closely connects to the Polish government's desire to make a contribution to human rights. As Lopatka put it: "Poland wanted to prove that—as a country at that time belonging to the system of socialist States—it was able to come up with a constructive and badly needed initiative in the field of human rights." Lopatka, "Introduction," xxxviii.

83. Korczak, *When I Am Little Again*, 129.

84. Korczak, *When I Am Little Again*, 171.

85. E. P. Kulawiec, "Foreword," to Korczak, *When I Am Little Again*, xiii.

CHAPTER 2

THE EVOLUTION OF THE CHILDREN'S RIGHTS MOVEMENT

JO BECKER

1 INTRODUCTION

OVER the past century, children's rights have become an integral part of the human rights agenda, with the establishment of a robust body of law and standards. This evolution of children's rights has been driven largely by a global movement of individuals and organizations—national, regional, and international—working to spotlight the abuse and exploitation of children.

These advocates have helped drive the development and adoption of international standards for children and used them to hold governments accountable for their actions. They have pressed national governments for new policies, laws, and practices and developed community initiatives to enhance child protection. Although the movement initially focused on protecting children from abuse and exploitation, increasingly it has stood up for children's rights to express themselves and be heard. In many instances, children themselves have been on the forefront for change, advocating on their own behalf.

2 ADVOCACY TO ESTABLISH CHILDREN'S RIGHTS STANDARDS

The first formal legal protections for children emerged in nineteenth-century Europe as a reaction to the grueling and hazardous working conditions that many children endured.

Children had long worked alongside their family members on farms or in family enterprises, but with the Industrial Revolution, many began working in factories. Children as young as five or six years old labored twelve to sixteen hours a day in deplorable conditions, received little pay, and were subjected to harsh punishment. Social reformers began to advocate for legal restrictions, and beginning in 1802 in Britain, for the first time in Europe, laws were enacted governing child labor.[1] Reformers also established orphanages for abandoned and destitute children and reformatories, or industrial schools, for children found begging or engaged in theft. The purpose of these institutions was not necessarily to nurture the child, but to instill obedience and to protect the child from negative influences.

World War I brought new attention to the vulnerabilities of children. Across Central and Eastern Europe, a British economic blockade contributed to unprecedented deprivation and suffering. Hundreds of thousands of people starved to death, and rates of infant and child mortality were appallingly high. Eglantyne Jebb, a British social reformer, worked to expose the humanitarian crisis and its impact on children.[2] In 1919 she was arrested in London's Trafalgar Square for distributing pamphlets depicting starving children in Austria. She established an emergency relief effort, the Save the Children Fund, to deliver shipments of food and medicine to children affected by the blockade. Over time, Save the Children expanded to include 28 member organizations, providing programs and services for children in more than 120 countries.[3]

Jebb was originally trained as a schoolteacher and believed that protecting the rights of children was essential to creating a better world order. "Every generation of children... offers mankind anew the possibility of rebuilding his ruin of a world," she said.[4] In 1922 she drafted a five-point "Charter for Children," declaring that children must be given the opportunity for development, be protected from exploitation, and receive assistance in times of distress.[5]

In 1924 the League of Nations adopted Jebb's charter as the Declaration of the Rights of the Child. It was nonbinding and did not articulate the responsibilities of states, only the general "duties" of "mankind." Nevertheless, heads of state pledged to incorporate it into national legislation, and French authorities ordered every school to display the text.[6]

In 1948, following World War II, the United Nations adopted the Universal Declaration of Human Rights, setting out fundamental human rights that applied to all people, including the right to life, liberty, dignity, non-discrimination, freedom of expression, education, employment, an adequate standard of living, and freedom from torture and slavery. The Declaration gave special recognition to children as "entitled to special care and assistance."[7] In 1959 the United Nations adopted a new Declaration on the Rights of the Child, outlining ten nonbinding principles. It expanded on the 1924 Declaration by recognizing a child's rights to non-discrimination, a name and nationality, free primary education,[8] and protection from all forms of neglect, cruelty, and exploitation.

In 1978 the government of Poland proposed the first legally binding convention devoted solely to children's rights.[9] It was inspired by a Polish hero Janusz Korczak, a pediatrician and educator regarded by many as the father of children's rights. In 1911 Korczak founded an orphanage for Jewish children in Warsaw and served as its director for over thirty years. He helped the children of the orphanage create their own parliament and their own newspaper. He appeared on a regular radio program, wrote over twenty books, and more than fourteen hundred articles published in some one hundred magazines.[10] He wrote of children as "a diminutive nation" that "had been forgotten in the great historical transformations from the struggle for the abolition of slavery to the struggle for equal rights for women."[11] As an illustration of his unparalleled dedication to children, and a tragic postscript to Korczak's life, in 1942 Nazis raided Korczak's orphanage and removed 190 children to transport them to the Treblinka concentration camp. The Nazis reportedly offered Korczak sanctuary, but he refused to abandon the children. Korczak died with the children at Treblinka.

By proposing a children's convention, Poland sought to honor Korczak and popularize his views of children's rights, including not only the responsibility to protect children from harm but also to respect their individual agency. A draft submitted to the UN Commission on Human Rights included the first provision recognizing a child's right to participation, noting that the child "who is capable of forming his own views [has] the right to express his opinion in matters concerning his own person."[12]

Negotiations on what would become the UN Convention on the Rights of the Child (CRC) took ten years. Negotiations typically took place only one week per year, and as states put forward new proposals, the treaty grew to encompass four times as many substantive articles as the 1959 Declaration.[13] The United States alone proposed seven specific articles, far more than any other country. These pertained to children's rights to freedom of expression (Article 13), freedom of religion (Article 14), freedom of association and assembly (Article 15), and the right to privacy (Article 16). Cynthia Price Cohen, a lawyer involved in the negotiations, believed that the US proposals reflected the political dynamics of the Cold War and "were inspired more by the desire to irritate the Soviet Union than from any grand philosophy regarding children's rights."[14] In fact, during the negotiations a US delegate stated that the United States had no intention of ratifying the CRC.[15]

Nongovernmental organizations (NGOs) played an unprecedented role during the negotiations, forming an NGO ad hoc group on the drafting of the CRC and proposing recommendations for the text before every negotiation session. According to advocates who were part of the process, when government proposals were rejected, the NGO text often emerged as the basis for further negotiations.[16] NGO representatives also participated in working groups of government representatives assigned to negotiate specific provisions.

The CRC, adopted in 1989, was one of the first international treaties to combine civil and political rights with economic, social, and cultural rights. It was also the first binding international agreement that treated children as rights-holders rather than passive objects of care and protection—a significant shift. It affirms children's rights to express their own views, including in judicial and legal proceedings that might affect them, and "to seek, receive and impart information and ideas of all kinds . . . through any media of the child's choice."[17] By 2018 every country, save one—the United States—had ratified the treaty.

After adoption of the CRC, NGOs active during its negotiation renamed their group the NGO Group for the Convention on the Rights of the Child (now Child Rights Connect). The NGO Group shifted its focus toward implementation of the new Convention, in particular, by supporting and encouraging national-level NGOs to provide independent information on government compliance to the UN Committee on the Rights of the Child, the group of experts charged with reviewing states parties' compliance with the Convention. In many countries, NGOs formed national child rights coalitions to advocate nationally for implementation of the Convention and to draft shadow reports for the Committee. As a result, the Committee on the Rights of the Child has some of the most sustained and dynamic engagement with the NGO community of any of the human rights treaty bodies.

Other international treaties also have galvanized the children's rights movement. For example, in the late 1990s Kailash Satyarthi (who shared the Nobel Peace Prize with Malala Yousafzai in 2014) organized a global march against child labor. A primary goal of the march was to influence diplomats who were negotiating a new child labor treaty at the International Labour Organization (ILO). With support from more than 350 organizations around the globe, Satyarthi began the march on January 17, 1998, eventually covering eighty thousand kilometers across 103 countries. A core group of marchers began in the Philippines, flew to Vietnam, and then crossed Asia, while other contingents traveled across the Americas and Africa.[18] Thousands of individuals joined the marchers for short periods along the way. Organizers called it the largest single social intervention in history for the benefit of children.[19]

As planned, the core marchers converged in Geneva on May 30, 1998, just before the International Labour Conference, where delegates from around the world were deliberating over new child labor standards. Children from the Philippines, India, and Brazil led about ten thousand people through the streets of Geneva, shouting "Stop child labour! End it now! Education for all children!" The following day, May 31, 150 children entered the conference assembly hall and for the first time in ILO history, took the platform during the conference's opening plenary. Child marchers gave speeches about the aims of the global march and the significance of the convention being debated; they received a standing ovation from the thousands of government, worker, and employer delegates assembled.[20] According to a senior ILO official, "The voices of those children echoed throughout the debate" on the convention.[21] The following year, in 1999, the conference unanimously adopted the Worst Forms of Child Labour Convention (ILO Convention No. 182), obliging ratifying states to take immediate action to prohibit and eliminate slave-like practices, commercial sexual exploitation, illicit activities, and other work likely to harm the health, safety, or morals of children under the age of eighteen.

The Worst Forms of Child Labour Convention subsequently became the most widely ratified convention in ILO history, securing 182 ratifications by late 2018. It helped spur legislative and other measures that significantly reduced child labor rates. In 2000 the

ILO estimated that 245 million children were engaged in child labor, but by 2016 the number had dropped to 152 million—a decline of over one-third.[22]

Also in the late 1990s, negotiations on an optional protocol to the Convention on the Rights of the Child prompted a global campaign on the issue of child soldiers. Governments had agreed to address an anomaly in the CRC related to the recruitment and use of children in armed conflict. While all other articles established protections for children up to the age of eighteen, Article 38 allowed children as young as fifteen to be recruited to fight in war. Initially, the United States, the United Kingdom, and a handful of other states opposed a standard that would set eighteen as the minimum age for participation in armed conflict, in large part because their armed forces both recruited and deployed under-eighteen soldiers.[23] In response, human rights and humanitarian NGOs formed the Coalition to Stop the Use of Child Soldiers (now Child Soldiers International), which campaigned globally to mobilize political and public opinion in favor of a strong protocol. The Coalition supported dozens of national campaigns that lobbied their national governments, organized regional conferences, and worked closely with like-minded states during the protocol's negotiations. Its efforts were largely responsible for the final result: a protocol setting eighteen as the minimum age for participation in hostilities, for conscription or forced recruitment by government forces, or any recruitment by non-state armed groups.[24]

During the same period, governments negotiated another optional protocol to the CRC dealing with the sale of children, child prostitution, and child pornography.[25] While it did not generate the same level of NGO campaigning as the child soldiers' protocol, both protocols were adopted by the UN General Assembly in 2000. Like the CRC itself, both of these instruments were widely accepted; by 2018 each had been ratified by more than 165 countries.

In 2010 Child Rights Connect began a new campaign for a third optional protocol to the CRC, which would allow children to bring individual complaints to the Committee on the Rights of the Child when states have violated or failed to protect their rights and when domestic remedies have been exhausted.[26] All other UN human rights treaties had such a mechanism; the CRC was the only one that had no individual complaints procedure. Child Rights Connect mobilized NGOs to support the protocol (known as OP3), participated in expert consultations, provided input on the drafting of the protocol text, and lobbied UN diplomatic missions in both Geneva and New York. The protocol was adopted by the General Assembly in late 2011. Child Rights Connect then spearheaded a broader campaign for ratification of the protocol, targeting an initial ten states from all regions.[27] The campaign grew to include nearly one hundred NGOs and utilized trainings, letter-writing initiatives, and other advocacy. By late 2018, fifty-one countries had signed the protocol and thirty-nine had ratified it.

The Committee on the Rights of the Child issued its first decision under the OP3 in early 2018, finding that Denmark had violated the rights of a young girl by ordering her and her mother to be deported to Somalia, where the girl was at risk of female genital mutilation.[28]

3 OTHER THEMATIC CAMPAIGNS

Other children's rights campaigns gained momentum in the 1990s and subsequent decades, focusing on the sexual exploitation of children, violence against children, child marriage, and the right to education. For example, activists in Southeast Asia began a campaign in 1990 to combat the sexual exploitation of children and sex tourism in the region, often involving US soldiers on leave from the large military bases the United States maintained in the Philippines. Originally envisioned to last three years, the End Child Prostitution in Asian Tourism (ECPAT) initiative became a global campaign to combat all forms of sexual exploitation of children. ECPAT (which later changed its acronym to stand for End Child Prostitution and Trafficking) persuaded the government of Sweden to host a global conference in 1996. The conference drew 122 governments and resulted in the Stockholm Declaration and Agenda for Action, which called on all sectors of society to take action against the commercial sexual exploitation of children, and, in particular, urged states to develop national plans of action to combat the problem. ECPAT worked closely with the tourism industry globally to address sexual exploitation in the context of travel and tourism and with law enforcement in various countries and others to address the growing phenomenon of online sexual exploitation of children. By 2018 ECPAT's network included 102 civil society organizations in 93 countries.[29]

In 1999 the Global Campaign for Education began to take shape. Ahead of the World Education Forum in Dakar, Senegal, a group of education activists met in Brussels to discuss how they could pressure governments to make concrete commitments to universal primary education. The activists included representatives from countries across Africa, Latin America, and Asia as well as representatives from ActionAid, Oxfam, Education International, and the Global March against Child Labor. In less than a year, the Global Campaign encompassed thirty-eight national coalitions and eight regional networks.

Like ECPAT, the Global Campaign was initially envisioned as a short-term campaign, but in 2001, members committed to building a longer term international movement around the right to education. The campaign published reports assessing wealthy countries' performance in supporting education and advocated with the United Nations, the World Bank, and other international entities. It organized Global Action Weeks with a different theme each year, to engage education advocates at the local level. In 2005, for example, the theme was "Send my Friend to School." Over five million people participated, making cutouts of "buddies" representing the millions of children who were out of school. The Week of Action has become one of the most recognized campaign movements around the world, engaging as many as twenty million people a year in 120 countries.[30]

The Global Campaign for Education helped catalyze a significant increase in school enrolment; between 2000 and 2014, the number of children in primary school rose by over 110 million globally.[31] Some individual countries made remarkable progress: in just a decade, Burundi increased primary school enrollment from 41 to 94 percent, while Mozambique and Burkino Faso increased primary school enrolment by over 66 percent in twelve years.[32]

In the late 1990s, NGOs also began pushing for a stronger international response to violence against children. According to a 2014 UNICEF survey, four out of every five children between the ages of two and fourteen—an estimated one billion children globally—experience physical punishment in their homes on a regular basis.[33] Children in detention facilities, orphanages, and other institutions are particularly vulnerable to violence. To highlight the issue, NGOs urged the Committee on the Rights of the Child to hold two general days of discussion on violence against children. Following the days of discussion, held in 2000 and 2001, the Committee recommended to the UN General Assembly that it initiate an in-depth UN global study on violence against children. NGOs conducted follow-up advocacy with member states, and in late 2001 the General Assembly formally asked the Secretary-General to undertake the study.

The study, led by Paulo Sérgio Pinheiro of Brazil, explored violence against children in their homes, schools, workplaces, institutions, and communities. It found that violence against children was a serious global problem, taking place in every country of the world, across all social groups.[34] For example, it found that more than 220 million children, both boys and girls, had been subjected to rape or sexual violence; 50,000 children a year were killed as a result of homicide; and only 2.4 percent of the world's children were legally protected from physical punishment in all settings.[35]

After the study was presented to the UN General Assembly in 2006, NGOs advocated for a stronger international response to violence against children and campaigned successfully for the creation of a new UN mandate, a special representative to the Secretary-General on violence against children, which was established in 2007. The study prompted the creation of national and regional action plans to combat violence against children. World Vision, Save the Children, Plan International, and other entities also won the inclusion of a specific target to end violence against children by 2030 as part of the Sustainable Development Goals adopted by UN member states in 2015.

Parallel to the UN study, the Global Initiative to End All Corporal Punishment of Children led efforts to legally prohibit all corporal punishment of children, including in the home. The Global Initiative, which began in 2001, systematically mapped national laws, worked with local NGOs, and used UN treaty bodies, and the Human Right's Council's universal periodic review (UPR) to press states to prohibit corporal punishment. It was remarkably successful, contributing to a dramatic increase in the number of countries banning corporal punishment, from only eleven in 2001 to fifty-three in 2018. During this time period, an additional fifty-seven states pledged to enact a ban, most in the context of the UPR, which every four years examines the human right record of each UN member state.[36]

In 2011 the Elders, a network of global leaders convened by Nelson Mandela, launched Girls Not Brides, a global partnership to end child marriage. The partnership facilitates the sharing of experience and knowledge about ending child marriage among members, develops advocacy resources, and facilitates coordinated activities and advocacy. By late 2018, Girls Not Brides had over a thousand member organizations in ninety-five countries.[37] In a number of countries, members successfully worked for legislative reform.[38] In 2015 and 2016, for example, Chad, Gambia, Guatemala, Malawi, Tanzania, and Zimbabwe each raised their legal age for marriage to eighteen. The partnership also advocated successfully for a target of ending child marriage by 2030 as part of the Sustainable Development Goals.

4 NATIONAL-LEVEL ORGANIZING

Thousands of organizations are working at the national level to protect and promote children's rights. Child Rights International Network (CRIN), for example, has nearly three thousand member groups from over 160 countries.[39] Many of the global networks mentioned previously, such as ECPAT, the Global March to Stop Child Labor, the Global Campaign for Education, and Girls Not Brides, involve hundreds of organizations working at the local or national level to end the sexual exploitation of children, child labor, and child marriage. Others work on juvenile justice, protecting children from violence and armed conflict, and ensuring children's rights to health and education.

A tiny sampling of such organizations include Bachpan Bachao Andolan, which has extracted children from bonded labor and established child-friendly villages in India; groups like Kembatti Mentti Gezzima in Ethiopia and Tostan, based in Senegal, which use community dialogue to transform social norms around female genital mutilation/cutting (FGM/C) and child marriage; Ajedi-Ka in eastern Congo, dedicated to the identification, demobilization, and reintegration of former child soldiers; and Foro Socioeducativo, a coalition advocating for greater investments in education in the Dominican Republic. Thousands of others are engaged in creative and persistent advocacy on behalf of children.

5 MOBILIZATION BY CHILDREN

Children themselves have long advocated on their own behalf, playing a significant role in the children's rights movement. In 1889, for example, children in England went on strike for better education,[40] while in 1903 striking child textile workers marched with Mother Jones from Philadelphia to the New York home of US president Theodore Roosevelt to protest child labor.[41] Sixty years later, in 1963, thousands of children left their classrooms to march through Birmingham, Alabama, as part of the Children's Crusade, helping to turn the tide of public opinion in favor of the US civil rights movement.[42] In South Africa thousands of schoolchildren marched as part of the 1976 Soweto uprising, and thousands more were arrested for protesting apartheid.[43]

More recent examples include a campaign by children in Sierra Leone to win free primary education. After the end of the country's civil war in 2001, fifteen-year-old Chernor Bah and other children formed the Children's Forum Network to have a voice in the country's peace process. They held consultations among children across the country to identify access to free education as a priority. The network advocated for the abolition of school fees, organized public forums and a weekly radio program, and drafted a children's manifesto to influence politicians.[44] Their advocacy helped prompt a free education policy introduced in 2002 and a 2004 Education Act that guaranteed free primary and junior secondary education for every child. Within five years, primary enrolment doubled.[45]

In many countries, girls have mobilized to end child marriage. In Malawi, for example, the Girls Empowerment Network (GENET) has trained girls and young women as advocates for justice and gender equality. In one district in southern Malawi, girls successfully lobbied sixty village chiefs to enact local by-laws to protect children from early marriage and harmful sexual initiation practices. The network also won a change in national law, which had allowed children as young as fifteen to marry. Using the slogan "No to 15; Yes to 18," the network held policy forums and collected letters from girls to the president. In 2015 Malawi's parliament raised the minimum age for marriage to eighteen.[46]

A growing number of children have engaged with the UN's human rights mechanisms. Between 2010 and 2015, for example, Child Rights Connect supported over 150 children from a variety of countries to address the Committee on the Rights of the Child about children's rights violations in their countries.[47]

In the 2010s children in several countries went to court to sue their governments for failing to protect them from the impact of climate change. In 2012, for example, youth in Uganda sued the government for failing to comply with international climate change agreements.[48] In 2015 children in the Netherlands won a suit against the Dutch government, claiming it was in negligent breach of its policies to stop global warming.[49] The court ordered the government to reduce emissions by 25 percent within five years.[50] That same year, twenty-one children from across the United States filed a suit[51] arguing that US government policies on fossil fuel use violated "the youngest generation's constitutional rights to life, liberty, and property" and that the government's failure to reduce carbon emissions discriminated against youth, who would "disproportionately experience the destabilized climate system" in the future.[52] Powerful trade associations representing oil and manufacturing companies joined the US government to argue that the case should be dismissed, but a federal judge ruled that it should proceed to trial.[53]

In 2016 a climate change suit brought by a seven-year-old girl against the Pakistani government was allowed to proceed over state objections.[54] In 2017 a nine-year-old Indian girl filed a similar suit against the Indian government.[55] In Portugal, after unprecedented forest fires linked to climate change claimed over sixty lives, the Global Legal Action Network began working with a group of Portuguese children to initiate litigation against forty-seven European governments in the European Court of Human Rights. A crowdfunding effort raised over 25,000 British pounds to pursue the case.[56]

On February 14, 2018, a mass shooting at Marjory Stoneman Douglas High School in Parkland, Florida, prompted unprecedented organizing against gun violence by US teenagers from the school. Just one day after the attack, which killed seventeen students and staff, seventeen-year-old Cameron Kasky began organizing the Never Again MSD movement, which other Parkland students quickly joined. Within a week of the shooting, the students announced a national march on Washington, and seventeen-year-old Jaclyn Cornin mobilized over one hundred students to travel to the state capital to speak with lawmakers about gun violence. A month after the shooting, an estimated one million students from across the country took part in a national school walk-out, leaving their classes for seventeen minutes in honor of the Parkland victims.[57]

On March 24, the Parkland students organized the March for Our Lives, which drew over two hundred thousand people to a Washington, DC, rally to protest gun violence.[58] Companion marches and demonstrations took place in over eight hundred other locations in all fifty states and on six continents.[59] The Parkland students influenced the Florida state legislature to adopt its first gun control legislation in thirty years,[60] corporate firms such as MetLife, Hertz, and Avis to sever ties with the National Rifle Association,[61] and sporting goods stores to stop selling assault-style rifles and prohibit gun sales to individuals under age twenty-one.[62]

The role of children as effective advocates was powerfully reinforced in 2014, when Malala Yousafzai, then seventeen, became the youngest person in history and the first child to receive the Nobel Peace Prize for her advocacy on behalf of girls' education. Together with her father, she set up the Malala Fund to promote access to education for all girls, and she has become arguably the world's best-known child rights advocate, traveling internationally to meet with girls and heads of state to promote children's rights.

6 Controversies and Criticism

At times, the demands of child advocates have been at odds with more seemingly mainstream children's rights groups. In 2014 in Bolivia, for example, a union of child and adolescent workers, Unatsbo, held demonstrations calling on the government to lower the minimum age of child labor, arguing that they had no choice but to work to help support their families and that a lower age for employment would offer them stronger governmental protections. The government ultimately lowered the age for employment to ten, despite opposition from the International Labour Organization and international human rights groups, which argued that the move was contrary to international law and would perpetuate cycles of poverty.

The controversy in Bolivia highlights a broader tension in the children's rights movement: the balance between child protection and child agency. While many NGOs support measures to protect children from exploitation and abuse, children themselves may wish to make different choices. For example, NGOs in the United States have been split over the issue of child marriage, with some arguing that a strict minimum age of eighteen for marriage is the best course to protect children's rights to education, health, and development, while others argue that children's rights include the right to marry, if they wish.[63] CRIN has sought to initiate a dialogue over accepted minimum age standards and argues that instead of blanket standards, individual age and capacity should be considered on such issues as compulsory education, employment, and marriage.[64]

Like other parts of the human rights movement, the children's rights movement has been perceived as overly dominated by Western norms and international NGOs. For example, some African nations believed that the CRC did not adequately address the economic, social, and cultural realities in Africa and that African countries had been underrepresented during the drafting process.[65] In response, in 1990 they negotiated the African Charter on the Rights and Welfare of the Child. While the charter encompasses many of the rights enshrined in the CRC, it also emphasizes African social and cultural values. Under the African Charter, for example, the aims of education should include "the preservation and strengthening of positive African morals, traditional values and cultures."[66]

The efforts of outside NGOs have sometimes been perceived as counterproductive. In some communities, for example, advocacy against child marriage through reproductive health and sex education projects is perceived as promoting promiscuity.[67] Outside advocacy against FGM/C, similarly, is sometimes seen as an attack on local values and only strengthens the resolve of communities to continue the practice. Increasingly child rights advocates recognize that local organizations are often best placed to address such issues with their own methods and approaches, such as sustained community dialogue.[68]

7 CONCLUSION

The children's rights movement has influenced a robust body of international law protecting the rights of children as well as legal and policy reforms at the national level to uphold and promote children's rights. As a result, states have created and strengthened juvenile justice systems, improved children's access to education and health services, criminalized violence and exploitation of children, stepped up enforcement measures, and created avenues for children to participate in policy debates.

Governments increasingly recognize that protecting children's rights is a prerequisite for their countries' economic and social advancement. The UN's Millennium Development Goals, adopted in 2000, included specific targets for child health and education but otherwise paid little attention to children's rights. In contrast, the UN's Sustainable Development Goals, adopted in 2015, incorporated a much broader set of targets for children, including not only universal education through grade twelve and various health indicators but also goals to end child marriage, FGM/C, child labor, the use of child soldiers, and violence against children.[69]

Key indicators show that the lives of millions of children have improved in recent decades. Since 2000 child labor rates have dropped by one-third,[70] the number of children in primary school has increased by more than 110 million,[71] and the number of countries prohibiting all physical punishment of children has increased nearly five-fold.[72] Girls are nearly one-third less likely to be subjected to FGM than they were three decades ago.[73] Many of these changes would not have happened without advocacy and campaigning by nongovernmental organizations and children themselves.

While much of the progress to date is laudable, children's rights continue to be violated on a daily basis and on a massive scale. This reality will require advocates to continue holding governments and powerful others to account, to keep building and strengthening the children's rights movement, and to look for new and creative ways to ensure children's rights.

NOTES

1. The Health and Morals of Apprentices Act (42 Geo III c.73) was adopted in 1802. In 1819, the Cotton Mills and Factories Act (59 Geo III c.66) was adopted, prohibiting work by children under the age of nine and limiting working hours for children aged nine to sixteen to twelve hours per day.

2. Clare Mulley, *The Woman Who Saved the Children: A Biography of Eglantyne Jebb, Founder of Save the Children* (Oxford: OneWorld Publications: 2009).

3. See the Save the Children website, https://www.savethechildren.net/what-we-do.

4. Mulley, *The Woman Who Saved the Children*, 249.

5. The Declaration of the Rights of the Child, adopted by the League of Nations, September 26, 1924.

6. Geraldine Van Bueren, . *The International Law on the Rights of the Child* (The Hague: Martinus Nijhoff Publishers, 1998), 9.

7. Universal Declaration of Human Rights, Article 25, G.A. Res. 217A (III), UN GAOR, 3rd Sess., UN Doc. A/810 (Dec. 12, 1948).

8. Principle 7 of the Declaration states: "The child is entitled to receive education, which shall be free and compulsory, at least in the elementary stages." UN Declaration of the Rights of the Child, G.A. Res. 1386 (XIV), UN Doc. A/RES/1386 (Nov. 20, 1959).

9. On February 7, 1978, Poland submitted its first draft of a convention on the rights of the child to the Commission on Human Rights. E/CN.4/L.1366/Rev.1.

10. Council of Europe, *Janusz Korczak: The Child's Right to Respect*, (Strasbourg: Council of Europe, 2009), 11, https://rm.coe.int/janusz-korczak-the-child-s-right-to-respect/16807ba985.

11. Cited by Jadwiga Bińczycka in "Janusz Korczak—Champion of Children's Rights," paper presented in Warsaw, September 2010, http://www.januszkorczak.ca/Prof_Binczycka.pdf (accessed Dec. 12, 2019).

12. UN Convention on the Rights of the Child (CRC), art. 7, G.A. Res. 44/25, 1577 UNTS 3 (Nov. 20, 1989).

13. Cynthia Price Cohen, "The Role of the United States in the Drafting of the Convention on the Rights of the Child," *Emory International Law Review* 20 (Spring: 2006): 185–198.

14. Price Cohen, *Role of the United States*, 191.

15. Price Cohen, *Role of the United States*, 188.

16. Price Cohen, *Role of the United States*, 192.

17. CRC, arts. 12 and 13.

18. BBC News, "Asia-Pacific Global March against Child Labor Begins," January 17, 1998, http://news.bbc.co.uk/2/hi/asia-pacific/48267.stm.

19. International Education and Resource Network (iEarn), "From the Global March International Secretariat," http://www.iearn.org.au/clp/archive/update2.htm (accessed Aug. 4, 2019).

20. Melanie Gow, "The Global March against Child Labor Arrives in Geneva," iEarn Fight against Child Labour Project, last modified May 30, 1998, http://www.iearn.org.au/clp/archive/geneva.htm.

21. International Labour Organization, "The End of Child Labour: Millions of Voices, One Common Hope," *World of Work* magazine, December 3, 2007, https://www.ilo.org/global/publications/world-of-work-magazine/articles/WCMS_090028/lang--en/index.htm.

22. International Labour Organization (ILO), *Global Estimates of Child Labour: Results and Trends, 2012–2016* (Geneva: ILO, 2017), 11, https://www.ilo.org/wcmsp5/groups/public/@dgreports/@dcomm/documents/publication/wcms_575541.pdf.

23. See Jo Becker, "Campaigning to Stop the Use of Child Soldiers," in *Campaigning for Justice: Human Rights Advocacy in Practice* (Palo Alto: Stanford University Press, 2013), 11–31.

24. Optional Protocol to the Convention on the Rights of the Child on the Involvement of Children in Armed Conflict, G.A. Res. 54/263, UN Doc. A/RES/54/263 (adopted May 25, 2000; entered into force Feb. 12, 2002). For more information about the Coalition to Stop the Use of Child Soldiers and its campaign, see Becker, *Campaigning for Justice*.

25. Optional Protocol to the Convention on the Rights of the Child on the Sale of Children, Child Prostitution and Child Pornography, G.A. Res. 54/263, UN Doc. A/54/49 (2000; entered into force Jan. 18, 2002).

26. Optional Protocol to the Convention on the Rights of the Child on a Communications Procedure, UN G.A. Res. 66/138, UN Doc. A/RES/66/138 (Dec. 19, 2011; entered into force April 14, 2014).

27. Mary Robinson, "Evaluation of the Work of Child Rights Connect: Final Report of SIDA-Funded Evaluation," December 2015, http://www.childrightsconnect.org/wp-content/uploads/2016/05/GA_2016_7ChildRightsConnect_FinalEvaluationReport-1.pdf.

28. UN Committee on the Rights of the Child, "Views Adopted by the Committee on the Rights of the Child under the Optional Protocol to the Convention on the Rights of the Child on a Communications Procedure in Respect of Communication No. 3/2016," UN Doc. CRC/C/77/D/3/2016 (Jan. 25, 2018), https://www.ohchr.org/_layouts/15/WopiFrame.aspx?sourcedoc=/Documents/HRBodies/CRC/CRC-C-77-DR-3-2016.pdf&action=default&DefaultItemOpen=1.

29. For more on ECPAT, see "About ECPAT," http://www.ecpat.org/about-ecpat.

30. See Jo Becker, "Access to Education," in *Campaigning for Children: Strategies for Advancing Children's Rights* (Palo Alto, CA: Stanford University Press, 2017).

31. UNESCO, *Education for All 2000–2015: Achievements and Challenges* (Paris, UNESCO, 2015), xiii.

32. UNESCO, *Education for All*, 80.

33. UNICEF, *Hidden in Plain Sight: A Statistical Analysis of Violence against Children* (New York: UNICEF, 2014), 96.

34. Paulo Sérgio Pinheiro, *World Report on Violence against Children* (Geneva: United Nations, 2006), http://www.unviolencestudy.org.

35. Pinheiro, *World Report*, 12.

36. See Global Initiative to End All Corporal Punishment of Children, Countdown to Universal Prohibition, https://endcorporalpunishment.org/countdown (accessed Aug. 4, 2019).

37. See the Girls Not Brides website, https://www.girlsnotbrides.org/about-girls-not-brides.

38. Chad, Guatemala, and Malawi raised the legal age for marriage to eighteen in 2015; Gambia, Tanzania, and Zimbabwe did so in 2016.

39. See the Child Rights International Network (CRIN) website, https://home/crin.org.

40. Judith Ennew, "Rethinking Childhood: Perspectives on Child Rights," *Cultural Survival Quarterly* 24, no. 2 (2000): 44–48.

41. Global Nonviolent Action Database, "Philadelphian Mill Children March against Child Labor Exploitation, 1903," http://nvdatabase.swarthmore.edu/content/philadelpian -mill-children-march-against-child-labor-exploitation-1903 (accessed Aug. 4, 2019).

42. Kim Gilmore, "The Birmingham Children's Crusade of 1963," *Biography*, February 14, 2014, https://www.biography.com/news/black-history-birmingham-childrens-crusade -1963-video.

43. South Africa: Overcoming Apartheid, Building Democracy, "Soweto Student Uprising," http://overcomingapartheid.msu.edu/sidebar.php?id=65-258-3 (accessed Aug.4, 2019).

44. Author interview with Chernor Bah, April 20, 2015.

45. UNESCO, Sierre Leone Education Country Status Report (Dakar: UNESCO, 2013).

46. Howard Mlozi, "Information on GENET Malawi's Work in the Fight to End Child Marriage," December 2013. See also Denise Dunning and Joyce Mkandawire, "How Girl Activists Helped to Ban Child Marriage in Malawi," *The Guardian*, February 26, 2015, http://www.theguardian.com/global-development-professionals-network/2015/feb/26/ girl-activists-child-marriage-malawi-let-girls-lead. Though a step forward, the new law does not change Malawi's constitution, which still includes the parental exception for child marriage.

47. Robinson, "Evaluation of the Work of Child Rights Connect".

48. Ephrat Livni, "Kids around the World Are Suing Their Governments for Ruining the Planet," *Quartz*, December 16, 2017, https://qz.com/1156876/juliana-vs-usa-kids-are -suing-over-climate-change.

49. Urgenda Foundation v. the State of the Netherlands, C/09/456689/HA ZA 13–1396 (June 24, 2015).

50. Roger Cox, "A Climate Change Litigation Precedent: *Urgenda Foundation v. the State of the Netherlands*," CIGI Papers No. 79, November 2015, https://www.cigionline.org/sites/ default/files/cigi_paper_79.pdf.

51. Livni, "Kids around the World Are Suing Governments for Ruining the Planet." (citing *Juliana v. United States*).

52. Our Children's Trust, "*Juliana v. United States*: Youth Climate Lawsuit," https://www. ourchildrenstrust.org/juliana-v-us (accessed August 4, 2019).

53. Ephrat, "Kids around the World Are Suing Governments for Ruining the Planet." .

54. Naeem Sahoutara, "Seven-Year-Old Girl Takes on Federal, Sindh Governments," *Express Tribune*, June, 29, 2016, https://tribune.com.pk/story/1133023/seven-year-old-girl-takes -federal-sindh-governments.

55. Our Children's Trust, "Youth Files Climate Case with Indian Environmental Court," press release, March 30, 2017, https://cms.qz.com/wp-content/uploads/2017/12/d5131-2017-03 -30indiaclimatecasepr.pdf.

56. Global Legal Action Network, "Children v Governments of Europe and Climate Change," Crowdjustice   https://www.crowdjustice.com/case/climate-change-echr (accessed Aug. 4, 2019).

57. Arian Campo-Flores, "Gun Violence Protests Drew an Estimated 1 Million Students," *Wall Street Journal*, March 15, 2018, https://www.wsj.com/articles/students-plan-national-school -walkout-to-protest-shootings-1521019801.

58. CBS News, "How Many People Attended March for Our Lives? Crowd in DC Estimated at 200,000," March 25, 2018, https://www.cbsnews.com/news/march-for-our-lives-crowd-size -estimated-200000-people-attended-d-c-march.

59. Rebecca Shabad, Chelsea Bailey, and Phil McCausland, "At March for Our Lives, Survivors Lead Hundreds of Thousands in Calls for Change," NBC News.com, March 24, 2018, https://www.nbcnews.com/news/us-news/march-our-lives-draws-hundreds-thousands -washington-around-nation-n859716.

60. John Cassidy, "Donald Trump Is Just Another NRA Patsy, but He Can't Stop the 'Never Again' Movement," *The New Yorker*, March 12, 2018, https://www.newyorker.com/news/ our-columnists/donald-trump-is-just-another-nra-patsy-but-he-cant-stop-the -never-again-movement.

61. Dean Obeidallah, "The NRA's Worst Nightmare Is Here," CNN.com, February 25, 2018, https://www.cnn.com/2018/02/25/opinions/nra-parkland-shooting-opinion-obeidallah/ index.html.

62. Damian J. Troise, "Retailers Dick's and Walmart Take Harder Line against Guns," Associated Press News.com, February 28, 2018, https://www.apnews.com/2663d23b8d544 2fbb1d92f6845d0f65d.

63. The Economist, "Why America Still Permits Child Marriage," January 3, 2018, https:// www.economist.com/the-economist-explains/2018/01/03/why-america-still-permits -child-marriage.

64. Child Rights International Network (CRIN), "Age Is Arbitrary: Setting Minimum Ages," discussion paper, https://archive.crin.org/sites/default/files/discussion_paper_-_minimum_ ages.pdf (accessed Aug. 4, 2019).

65. See Osifunke Ekundayo, "Does the African Charter on the Rights and Welfare of the Child (ACRWC) Only Underlines and Repeats the Convention on the Rights of the Child (CRC)'s Provisions? Examining the Similarities and the Differences between the ACRWC and the CRC," *International Journal of Humanities and Social Science* 5, no. 7 (July 2015): 143–158.

66. African Charter on the Rights and Welfare of the Child, art. 11(2)(c), OAU Doc. CAB/ LEG/24.9/49 (1990; entered into force Nov. 29, 1999).

67. Annie Bunting, "Stages of Development: Marriage of Girls and Teens as an International Human Rights Issue," *Social and Legal Studies* 14, no. 1 (March 2005): 17–38.

68. See, for example, Haile Gabriel Dagne, *Ethiopia: Social Dynamics of Abandonment of Harmful Practices: Experiences in Four Locations*" (Florence: UNICEF Innocenti Research Centre, 2010).

69. See United Nations, Sustainable Development Goals, https://www.un.org/sustainable development/sustainable-development-goals (accessed Aug. 4, 2019).

70. International Labour Organization, *Global Estimates of Child Labor: Results and Trends 2012–2016* (Geneva: International Labour Organization, 2017). http://www.ilo.org/wcmsp5/ groups/public/@dgreports/@dcomm/documents/publication/wcms_575499.pdf.

71. UNESCO Institute for Statistics and the Global Education Monitoring Report, *Leaving No One Behind: How Far on the War to Universal Primary and Secondary Education?* Policy Paper 27/Fact Sheet 37, July 2016, https://en.unesco.org/gem-report/leaving -no-one-behind-how-far-way-universal-primary-and-secondary-education.

72. Global Initiative to End All Corporal Punishment of Children, Countdown to Universal Prohibition.

73. UNICEF, *Female Genital Mutilation/Cutting: A Global Concern* (New York: UNICEF, 2016).

CHAPTER 3

....

TAKING CHILDREN'S HUMAN RIGHTS SERIOUSLY

....

MICHAEL FREEMAN

1. INTRODUCTION

....

I have long been struck and dismayed by how rarely in books and articles on human rights I encounter propagation of the rights of children. Even those like Ronald Dworkin, who proclaim the need to take rights seriously, are curiously silent, even ambivalent, when it comes to children.[1]

More attention is paid to animal rights, even to the rights of rivers and rocks, than is paid to children's rights. Advocates of children's rights are often relegated to the margins of human rights.

In the few places where serious philosophical discussion of children's rights does take place, the analysis seems intended to demolish the value of rights for children. The work of Onora O'Neill is an early example of this.[2] Work by Michael King[3] and essays in a collection edited by David Archard and Colin Macleod[4] by James Griffin, Harry Brighouse, Samantha Brennan, and Barbara Arneil are further examples of what I suppose I must call, though it pains me to do so, the new orthodoxy.[5] None of these critics is malevolent toward children. A lunatic fringe may defend the corporal punishment of children, but the above mentioned do not. Further, one will find no defenses of child abuse or of the torture or imprisonment without trial of children in this new orthodoxy. Even the critics of children's rights want the best for children, or the best as they see it. But they do not think this can be achieved by a rights agenda, or, as I have put it elsewhere by "taking children's rights seriously."[6]

In *The Alchemy of Race and Rights*, Patricia Williams writes:

> For the historically disempowered, the conferring of rights is symbolic of all the denied aspects of their humanity: rights imply a respect that places one in the

referential range of self and others, that elevates one's status from human body to social being.[7]

Williams writes also of "the right to expect civility from others."[8] As is evident from the title of her book, she is writing not about children—they do not feature in her argument—but about African Americans and women. But what she says is all too pertinent in other contexts too, particularly, I will argue, to children (but also to the learning disabled, the mentally ill, and the elderly).

There are trenchant critiques by critical legal theorists and others of this emphasis on the importance of rights.[9] These can be traced back as far as Marx's famous essay "On the Jewish Question."[10] But as Robert Williams notes in an essay advocating for "taking rights aggressively,"[11] this may reflect blindness to the privileged position from which such critics make their arguments.

It is true that rights may be a disciplinary, or at least potentially disciplinary, practice.[12] The early children's rights movement—which spoke in the language of rights but was concerned exclusively with welfare—can be seen as a vehicle for enlarging state power over both children and their caregivers.[13] But the movement does not have to operate in this way. We must not overlook the importance of having rights where rights are the currency in use. Rights may atomize: communitarians recoil at the horror of this. But, as Patricia Williams notes, "For me, stranger-stranger relations are better than stranger-chattel."[14]

This language is most relevant to children who, for much of history, have been little more than property. The sacrificial son is at the root of two of the world's great religions.[15] This conception of children is present in such classic epics as the *Aeneid*, Shakespeare's plays (*Hamlet*, *The Winter's Tale*), Dickens's *Dombey and Son*, and much else.[16] Throughout history, custody disputes were often, and sometimes still are, fought as unseemly squabbles over possessions.[17] Until recently in England (as elsewhere), it was thought that the parental right of an unimpeachable parent should take priority over considerations of a child's welfare.[18] It was not until the mid-1970s that the right of the so-called unimpeachable parent—or rather, its myth—was finally scotched.

In England, the *Gillick* decision from the mid-1980s is often seen as a watershed.[19] It acknowledged that "parental right yields to the child's right to make his own decisions when he reaches a sufficient understanding and intelligence to be capable of making up his own mind on the matter requiring decision."[20] But the decision shocked and also offended; in response to the decision, a national campaign to "protect the family from interference from officialdom" was established.[21] Popular opinion supported parental rights, and *Gillick* had undermined them. That there was subsequently a retreat from *Gillick* should not surprise,[22] though it did to those imbued with the Whig interpretation of history, those for whom the halting of progress was inexplicable.[23]

That parental rights are alive and well can be seen in the many UK decisions which limit *Gillick*[24] and in cases relating to a child's medical treatment, such as *Re T*,[25] in which parents were effectively allowed to countermand medical opinion and deny a toddler life-saving treatment.[26] A good recent illustration of litigation brought by parents where children appear to be little more than objects is the *Williamson* case,[27] in which parents alleged their human rights were infringed by legislation that took away from schools the liberty to inflict corporal punishment on children. Note there is no reference in *Williamson* to the human rights of the children. The parents in that case were Christians who wanted to ensure their children were educated in conformity with their religious convictions.[28]

Throughout the *Williamson* litigation, the dispute was portrayed as one between the state (its right to ban corporal chastisement in schools) and the parents (and teachers).[29] The children were not represented; their views were not known or sought. Of course, it is possible that, indoctrinated as they were, the children would have agreed with their parents, if asked.[30] But that is not the issue. More significant is the potential impact on children as a minority class. In this case, the courts found against the parents (and teachers).[31] Had they not done so, children would once again have been exposed to sanctioned school beatings, or at least subject to the threat of such beatings ostensibly under the guise of the protection of parental rights. Notably, the state did not argue in *Williamson* that corporal punishment necessarily involved an infringement of any of the children's rights. But, of course it does, as a cursory glance at Article 19 of the United Nations Convention on the Rights of the Child (CRC) reveals.[32]

In relevant part, in the *Williamson* appellate judgment, in an opinion that expressly inserted children into the narrative of the case, Baroness Hale proclaimed:

> My Lords, this is, and always has been, a case about children, their rights and the rights of their parents and teachers. Yet there has been no one here...to speak on behalf of the children.... The battle has been fought on ground selected by the adults.[33]

Her opinion was "for the sake of the children."[34] From Baroness Hale's perspective, instead of focusing only on "whether the beliefs of the parents and teachers qualified for protection,"[35] the lower court should also have considered the rights of children. Had this case been argued from a children's rights perspective, it would have looked very different. The result (the parents and teachers losing) may have been the same. The reasoning, however, would likely have included consideration of and reliance on the rights and humanity of the children themselves.

That you don't have to be a fundamentalist Christian to view children as right-less is superbly illustrated by a 2006 *Guardian* article titled "Six Weeks of Suffering."[36] That the article was written by the founder of Justice for Women, Julie Bindel, is all the more telling. That it was published in a leading liberal newspaper says even more about how children are still perceived. If "Six Weeks of Suffering" had focused on women or Muslims, there would have been a public outcry. Bindel's argument is that school holidays should be cut (in half) because the presence of children in her space—streets, parks, museums, public transport, and restaurants—offends her.[37]

An excerpt illustrates the article's tone:

> I live in an area where kids are routinely taken to proper restaurants for lunch, but I was here before it became Nappy Valley.... There seems to be no escape this summer. [London mayor] Ken Livingstone has made it easier for the little monsters to follow me around London by giving schoolchildren free bus travel throughout the capital. There they are, in the museums when you least expect them.[38]

The article provoked numerous responses,[39] including the following:

> Why, when overt racism and homophobia are no longer accepted, is it permissible to seek to deprive young people of their human rights?[40]

I am reminded of what the court said in *Dred Scott*,[41] an 1857 US Supreme Court case declaring slaves—in this case, referring to those of African descent—"so far inferior, that they had no rights which the white man was bound to respect."[42] This idea of slave-like societal inferiority is explored by Hannah Arendt in *The Origins of Totalitarianism*. There, Arendt comments on the Holocaust, observes that before the Nazis started exterminating the Jews, they deprived them of all legal status. "The point is," she notes, "that a condition of complete rightlessness was created before the right to live was challenged."[43]

The most fundamental of rights is the right to possess rights. Arendt adds:

> Slavery's fundamental offense against human rights was not that it took liberty away...but that it excluded certain category of people ever from the possibility of fighting for freedom.[44]

Those who would deny children human rights—rights such as the participating freedoms in the UN Convention, including freedom of expression, thought, conscience, and religion, association, and peaceful assembly[45]—sometimes argue, as Onora O'Neill did, that a child's "main remedy is to grow up."[46] In other words, unlike slaves or women, for example, there is a finite time limit to children's rightlessness.

But is there really a satisfactory reason to withholding children rights now? After all, many legal systems, including that of the English, impose criminal responsibility on children at a very young age. In England, it's just ten years old.[47] We expect children to obey laws before they are enfranchised. There is thus an argument that the age for voting in elections should be set at the same age as that of criminal responsibility, though this argument is not frequently proffered.[48] In my view, children deprived of the sort of rights envisaged by the CRC will grow up to be rather different adults than ones who are able to enjoy such rights. Indeed, those who enjoy rights during childhood will grow into more fulfilled adults, both to their own benefit and to the benefit of society as a whole.[49]

Utilitarians are not overly sympathetic to rights agendas. From a utilitarian's perspective, rights are an obstacle to the smooth running of government. It is much easier to rule people without rights; decision-making is swifter, cheaper, and more efficient when rights do not get in the way. Notably, American family lawyer Martin Guggenheim's critique of children's rights implicitly endorses utilitarianism.[50] Jeremy Bentham famously remarked that "there is no right which, when the abolition of it is advantageous to society, should not be abolished."[51]

If we reject utilitarianism when it comes to human rights in general, we must ask why those who support human rights do not do so when it comes to children. According to the views of prominent Kantian thinker Onora O'Neill, there is no point or value in talking about children's rights;[52] she and others believe it is misguided to think children's rights achieve something positive for children. In an influential article originally published in 1988 and reproduced many times, O'Neill argues that "taking rights as fundamental in ethical deliberation about children has neither theoretical nor political advantage."[53] In her view, we should instead identify what obligations parents, teachers, and the wider community have toward children.[54] "We can perhaps go *further* to secure the ethical basis of children's positive rights if we do *not* try to base them on claims about fundamental rights," she argues.[55] And, she adds, "in the specific case of children, taking rights as fundamental has political cost rather than advantages."[56] Meanwhile, "a construction made from the agent's perspective may deliver more, though it promises less, since it does not aim at an 'all or nothing' construction of ethical requirements."[57]

Might it deliver more as O'Neill claims? Consider the *Williamson* case, to which I have already drawn attention.[58] How would we identify the parental obligation in this case? From the perspective of the child? It is unlikely that O'Neill intends this. Instead, O'Neill likely envisions basing adult obligations toward children on the lens of the parents, or perhaps even on the lens of Christianity; and, if that is the case, which Christianity? If, as I suspect, it would be the parents' perspective that counts, the obligation could presumably be to raise children in an environment that encourages physical chastisement.[59] It may be added that the parents' perspective would be one in which the package of participatory rights denoted in the CRC would count for little.[60] An emphasis on obligations places parents and other adult authorities at center stage. It marginalizes children. As so often demonstrated by the past, where there is no concern for or interest in children's rights, children appear to be little more than objects of concern. O'Neill's model of childhood is the conventional deficit one.[61]

This conventional deficit view underlies other contemporary philosophical writing about children. To Harry Brighouse, there is "something very strange about thinking of children as bearers of rights."[62] In Brighouse's view, "the further an agent departs from the liberal model of the competent rational person, the less appropriate it seems to be to attribute rights."[63] It hardly needs to be said, but it was once thought inappropriate to attribute rights to women who were thought to fall short of the "liberal model."[64]

Brighouse does not have difficulty seeing children as bearers of welfare rights, but he has problems with agency rights, at least as far as young children are concerned.[65] I do not deny that it is easier to justify welfare rights, and of course, there are likely to be some limitations to agency rights.[66] But welfare rights work better in a rights culture where agency, the right to participate in decisions about oneself, is acknowledged. Children are better protected (from abuse, neglect, etc.) where their agency rights are recognized.[67] Brighouse is critical of those agency rights, which he lists out as freedom of expression, freedom of religion, and the right to enjoy one's own culture.[68] But why should children not have these rights? To take one of his examples, why should the child's right to cultural identity "jeopardize the family as an institution"?[69] Is a small child not entitled to adopt a vegetarian lifestyle or to express an opinion about schooling (perhaps opting into or out of a faith-based school)?

The conventional deficit model is also exemplified by the concern of some critics of children's rights that children make mistakes.[70] Samantha Brennan's main reason for refusing to acknowledge that children have autonomy is because "often children do not choose well or wisely."[71] "Brennan accepts that adults can also fail to make the right decisions. But, as Dworkin told us many years ago, it is fundamental to believing in rights that we accept that there is a right to do what we consider to be the wrong thing to do, to make mistakes, to let others do things we would not do."[72]

We have to accept what Feinberg calls the child's "right to an open future"[73] while also learning how to act autonomously; we can only accomplish this by being allowed try. Hugh LaFollette expresses this consideration well when he writes, "We must train children to become autonomous, and that requires, among other things, that we treat them in some respects as if they already were autonomous."[74]

But should we respect the person, the dignity of the child *now*, or see him or her as a person in being whose *future* dignity is the important consideration? The dilemma can be illustrated by examining case studies. Suppose we are confronted by a thirteen-year-old Jehovah's Witness for whom a life-saving blood transfusion is required but which he refuses on the grounds of religious conscience.[75] Or a sixteen-year-old girl suffering from anorexia nervosa who refuses treatment by doctors.[76] Or an intelligent fifteen-year-old girl who has been diagnosed as needing a heart transplant but who insists she would rather die with her own heart than live with someone else's.[77] These are not fictional scenarios; these cases have all been brought to English courts within the past decade or so. In each case, the courts refused to allow the child to make their own decisions. In doing so, the courts came to decisions that nearly everyone else would make. For most of us are paternalists when it comes to children.

The clearest rule coming out of the English cases is that a child can agree to medical treatment but cannot refuse it if others (parents, a court) believe it to be in his or her best interests.[78] (Of course, a child can only agree to treatment that a doctor is prepared to provide.) *Gillick* was premised on competence marking the difference between children who can make their own decisions and children who cannot,[79] but the above cases demonstrate the fictive nature of that demarcation. Courts, and perhaps doctors too, are reluctant to find a child competent, so they impose more stringent requirements on children than they do on adults. No court would force that Jehovah's Witness to have a blood transfusion were he eighteen.

Those who think the courts are right to take decisions away from children are unashamedly paternalistic. It is important, as authors Margaret Brazier and Caroline Bridge argue, that decision makers satisfy themselves that a choice is "maximally autonomous."[80] But what does this involve? I suggest that it requires us to understand the young person's decision to see how it fits their value system and coheres with their goals. There are some cases where an adolescent is able to make a competent, maximally autonomous choice to refuse life-saving treatment. And, as Penney Lewis observes, though "respecting such a choice [is] difficult... it is preferable to arbitrary discrimination on the basis of age alone."[81]

But are we putting too much faith in the power of rights and rights discourse, particularly when it comes to children? Indeed, has this dependence resulted in bad consequences for children? This critique of rights is not new; it may be said to unite such disparate philosophies as those we associate with the New Right, communitarianism, feminism, and also many on the Left.

Michael King is one to pose the question.[82] Why, he asks, has it become important for advocates of children's rights to move from seeing rights as "dignified statements" to seeing them as "rules designed to regulate relationships."[83] Why is it that those who called for and drafted the CRC thought it was important that the document become accepted as law? This is an important question, though not one that needs to be asked exclusively with reference to children. In answer, law is one of the most significant symbols of legitimacy.[84] When enacted, it is an accomplished fact, one that is difficult to resist; it can change attitudes as well as behavior.[85] For King, however, law is one version of reality, and whether it is experienced as real hinges upon whether it can deliver the goods,[86] that is, improve the welfare and enhance the interests of children.

But if the law—in this instance the CRC, though we can generalize—disappoints, as of course, it has done,[87] are we to explain this, as King does? Are we to believe that failure is the result of the fact that "socially perceived 'problems' over children's suffering and defencelessness are so diffuse and their perceived causes so diverse that it is difficult to see how law could possibly reconstruct the issues according to its lawful/unlawful coding?"[88]

There are a number of answers to this. The reasons why the CRC disappoints are numerous. Its scope is too narrow,[89] its enforcement procedures are weak[90] (I doubt this can be explained within King's theoretical structure), and the CRC itself embodies many compromises.[91] Too many countries have considered rhetoric and symbolism to be sufficient and have paid only lip service to the treaty's obligations.[92] King's explanation is that "once political and economic rights have been reconstructed as legal communications, it is possible, and indeed appropriate, for governments to respond by further legal communications, declaring their policies are 'lawful' within the terms of the Convention."[93] Possible, it certainly is; appropriate, it most certainly is not.

There is another answer. Many—I agree, far from all—of the provisions in the CRC could be reformulated within the binary coding King thinks is not possible.[94] The CRC could be more explicit. Instead of targeting traditional practices harmful to the health of children, as it does in Article 24(3), the CRC could list the harmful practices. The CRC could feature an explicit prohibition of corporal chastisement. Instead this has to be read into Article 19.[95]

Another response to King is to ask what is the appropriate way to create, as he puts it in one of his books, "a better world for children."[96] An interesting answer—by another critic who believes we have invested too much faith in a rights strategy—is by Barbara Arneil.[97] Taking her cue from the well-known work of Carol Gilligan,[98] Arneil argues that an ethics of care that emphasizes responsibilities over rights offers a better way of answering children's needs. Although there is superficial similarity between O'Neill's thesis and Arneil's pro-responsibilities thesis, Arneil's argument is very different.[99]

It is Arneil's view that "rights theories do not see children as children."[100] This is a criticism that one sees voiced increasingly. In effect, Arneil is saying that children's rights are an oxymoron. Arneil's own vision sees the child's development in "holistic terms, going beyond the capacity for rationality."[101] Every child is included, and the "state's role goes beyond both education and social welfare to a fully integrated set of services focused on the child's need for care and the parent's responsibility for care-giving."[102] She envisions the child's growth to independent adulthood as "an organic process that unfolds within the context of a multitude of interdependent relationships both within the family and society at large" and believes this vision embraces children as "full beings."[103]

There are a number of responses to this. Arneil's theory envisions, as so often is the case, the child as the object of concern rather than as a subject or a participant. The emphasis is unashamedly on welfare rather than citizenship. It oversimplifies the distinction between adults and children: does something truly magical occur on an individual's eighteenth birthday? It fails to appreciate the importance of rights where relationships, for whatever reason, are poor or have broken down. Is the abused child to rely on those abusive relationships? How would Arneil respond to the fifteen-year-old who cannot discuss contraception or abortion with her parents, perhaps because she is being sexually abused by a family member? It underestimates the role that a rights agenda can play in forging relationships, and it overlooks the asymmetry of relationships where rights, and therefore power, are on one side only.

If children's rights are human rights, they should have the characteristics of human rights. Thus, the rights should be universal, to be held by children simply because they are children. Race, sex, religion, social position, nationality, and so on, are irrelevant;[104] hence the non-discrimination principle in Article 2 of the CRC.[105] At their basis, as John Rawls puts it, lies a "common good conception of justice."[106] Rawls adds, "These rights are guaranteed and the requirement that a system of law must be such as to impose moral rights and duties is met. Human rights understood in the light of that condition cannot be rejected as peculiar to our Western tradition."[107] Rather, he sees them as "politically neutral."[108] Children's rights could be undermined by cultural relativism.

But it will be noted, different societies have different understandings of childhood. There are different views on such questions as whether children should work, when they should be allowed to marry, and what choices, if any, they should have. Views differ also on such basics as education, punishment, and medical treatment. As Welshman Ncube, a writer and leading thinker on children in Zimbabwe, recognizes, "the normative universality achieved in the definition and formulation of children's rights has to contend with diverse and varied cultural and traditional conceptions of childhood, its role, its rights and obligations."[109] In his work, Ncube describes some aspects of the traditional

African concepts of childhood that are very different from the model found in the Global North. He explains that "in the African cultural context childhood is not perceived and conceptualized in terms of age but in terms of intergenerational obligations of support and reciprocity.[110] In this sense an African 'child' is often always a 'child' in relation to his or her parents who expect and are traditionally entitled to all forms of support in times of need and in old age."[111]

Unfortunately, when culture is discussed in the context of human/children's rights, the tendency is to confine discussion to cultural practices in Africa or other parts of the Global South. The emphasis tends to be on female genital mutilation, child marriage, arranged and forced marriages, and issues like child soldiers.[112] Although these issues are undoubtedly of great concern, we should not ignore cultural practices in the Global North that may also violate the human rights of children.

A valuable way of looking at the debate is suggested by Philip Alston, who urges an analogy drawn from European human rights jurisprudence, a "margin of apprecia-tion."[113] This allows for some flexibility, some direction, but would not allow culture to "be accorded the status of a metanorm which trumps rights."[114] Certain practices will fall outside the margin of acceptability. At its most extreme, slavery is an example of an unacceptable practice that falls outside the margin. But so too do practices similar to slavery, such as imprisonment within brothels and forcing children into prostitution. There can be no space for the so-called cultural defense,[115] nor for female infanticide, female genital mutilation,[116] and many other objectively unacceptable practices often shielded by the cultural defense.

To recognize that children's rights are human rights is to recognize that children are humans, that they are not animals or pieces of property.[117] But this does not mean that we have to overlook the fact that they are also children and, as such, vulnerable. This is one of the reasons why the CRC adopts, as arguably its most important principle, the normative standard that "in all actions concerning children, whether undertaken by public or private social welfare institutions, courts of law, administrative authorities, or legislative bodies, the best interests of the child shall be a primary consideration."[118]

The best interests provision puzzles some, partly because the concept of best interests is itself difficult to grasp. As Robert Mnookin points out, "deciding what is best for a child poses a question no less ultimate than the purposes and values of life itself."[119] And, of course, to return to an issue previously discussed, different cultures will also inevitably operate with different concepts of what is in a child's best interests.[120]

But there is a more important concern for those who wish to proclaim children's rights: There is, they will point out, some incongruity in emphasizing best interests, a concept rooted in paternalism, when the goal is to propagate children's rights, a non-paternalistic ambition. Article 3(1) of the CRC talks of best interests, not best rights.

So, what is the relationship between best interests and rights?[121] The question can be asked generally, but it is easier to pose it in terms of the CRC: Suppose it is not consid-ered—and, of course, the question then arises, by whom—that actualizing a particular right under the CRC is in a child's best interests. Does the emphasis on best interests trump other considerations? Does it afford space to values other than those sanctioned in the CRC? Are there circumstances where a consideration other than the best interests of the child should prevail? For example, can cultural or religious norms override a child's best interests?[122] Take the headscarf controversy, which has arisen in a number of European countries in recent years.[123] Or take the issue of immigration control; decisions here are often taken with considerations other than the child's best interests.[124]

There are answers to this within the CRC itself. The best interests principle must be seen both as informed by and constrained by the rights provided for under the CRC. As John Tobin argues, "a proposed outcome for a child cannot be said to be in his or her best interests where it conflicts with the provisions of the Convention."[125] Writing specifically about a child's health rights, he notes that this "requires a consideration of the other guiding principles under the Convention…The other rights listed under the CRC such as the protection against violence (article 19); the right to an adequate standard of living (article 27); the right to education (article 28); the right to play and leisure (article 31), and protection against all forms of exploitation (articles 32–36) also inform any assessment of the best interests of a child."[126] It is significant that the CRC maintains that the obligation to consider children's best interests requires a child impact assessment and evaluation with respect to all legislation and other forms of policy development to determine the impact of any proposed law, policy, or budgetary allocation on children's rights.[127]

The best interests principle can also be seen to supplement any catalogue of children's rights, such as those provided within the CRC. Stephen Parker is surely right to appreciate that the best interests principle offers guidance where there is a gap in the CRC.[128] For example, the CRC does not specifically focus on street children.[129] Of course, since they are children,[130] it is possible to read nearly every article in the CRC as being applicable to them. But street children have specific problems. For example, they may need greater employment protection laws than other children.[131] No catalogue of rights for children should ever be seen as definitive. The best interests principle may also be valuable where rights conflict. Alston sees it as "a mediating principle which can assist in resolving conflicts between different rights."[132]

One of the rights provided within the CRC, a right unquestionably central to human rights generally, is participation.[133] Further, at the heart of participation rights within the CRC is the normative value of autonomy, the idea that persons have a set of capacities that enables them to make independent decisions regarding appropriate life choices.[134] Kant expressed this by asserting that people are equal and autonomous in the Kingdom of Ends.[135] 'To believe in autonomy is to believe that anyone's autonomy is as morally significant as anyone else's.[136] "To respect a child's autonomy is to treat that child as a person, and as a rights-holder."[137] It is now clear that we can respect children as equal rights–holders "to a much greater extent than we have assumed hitherto."[138] Priscilla Alderson's work on children's consent to surgery offers evidence of this.[139] At the same time, as I have already indicated, the CRC emphasizes that the best interests of children should guide decision-makers. Is there a conflict here, and if so, can it be resolved?

There is, of course, a let-out in Article 12: "the views of the child" are to be given "due weight in accordance with the age and maturity of the child."[140] The CRC gives no indication of how to judge maturity or of what is meant by *maturity*. It is clear, however, that maturity is judged by adults and not by children. What if a child's views—let us assume for a moment the child is considered mature enough (*Gillick* competent, perhaps[141])—conflict with what adults think is in that child's best interests?[142] What is the point, it may be asked, of providing children the opportunity to be heard if, at the end of the day, we do not listen to or we override their views in the name of upholding what we consider to be their best interests?

English courts have, as courts must, come to a conclusion on this, though it cannot really be said that they have grappled with the issue very satisfactorily.[143] For the courts, autonomy ends where the best interests analysis begins. One judge was recently prepared to take a broad view of interests, going beyond the medical to embrace "religious, social, whatever they may be."[144] As far as religious interests are concerned, it might be thought somewhat arrogant for a judge to rule on a seventeen-year-old Jehovah's Witness's religious interests better than the young man himself. As far as social interests are concerned, the judge was at least honest enough to add "whatever they may be."

But we must still ask why courts will not allow a child/young person of seventeen to refuse medical treatment despite being clearly competent—even if the court holds otherwise—but will allow an eighteen-year-old to take the same decision on a more liberal test of competence. There is suspicion that the underlying concern is to protect doctors from litigation[145] or, perhaps, to protect judges from a bad conscience when a child dies. It may be that the court would argue society has an interest in protecting the young, irrespective of competence.[146] It should be observed that there has been no attempt to couch the issue in human rights terms.

When can we impose limits on rights in the name of best interests? One of the best attempts at an answer comes from John Eekelaar, who situates children's rights within dynamic self-determinism.[147] The goal of his argument "is to bring a child to the threshold of childhood with the maximum opportunities to form and pursue life-goals which reflect as closely as possible an autonomous choice."[148] The autonomy is dynamic "because it appreciates that the optimal course for a child cannot always be mapped out at the time of decision, and may need to be revised as the child grows up."[149] It involves "self-determinism because the child itself [*sic*] is given scope to influence the outcomes."[150] Note that Eekelaar says to influence, not determine, the outcome.

Similarly supporting the dynamic self-determinism theory, Virginia Morrow explains that autonomy recognizes "not the straightforward delegation of decision making to children but rather enabling children to make decisions in controlled conditions, the overall intention being to enhance their capacities for mature well founded choice."[151] Further, Jane Fortin notes that there are "respectable jurisprudential arguments for maintaining that a commitment to the concept of children's rights does not prevent interventions to stop children making dangerous short-term choices, thereby protecting their potential for long-term autonomy."[152]

The burden lies on those who wish to deny rights to children. An argument drawn from age alone will not do. Arguments based on competence (or its absence) are often suspect, and we should remember Katherine Hunt Federle's comment that children—unlike women, for example—have been "unable to redefine themselves as competent beings," such that "powerful elites decide which, if any, of the claims made by children they will recognize."[153] Recognition by the elite is critical because there is a distinction between having rights and being allowed to exercise them. There are dangers to dichotomizing this way. Nevertheless, lack of recognition by the elite may explain those few decisions, exercises of autonomy, that we deny children. Some quarter of a century ago, I explained this in terms of what I called "liberal paternalism."[154]

The idea of liberal paternalism is to legitimize interventions in children's lives and to protect children against irrational actions.[155] It is important to realize the potential dangers of doing this. To prevent those dangers, what is regarded as irrational would have to be strictly confined. The subjective values of the would-be protector cannot be allowed to intrude. What is irrational must be defined in terms of a neutral theory capable of accommodating pluralistic visions of the good.[156] We need to understand the experiences and the culture of the children we wish to protect. We must engage with them. The space should be created for a child advocate to assist the child. Merely imposing a decision—for example, medical treatment—achieves nothing in the long-term. On the contrary, doing so may alienate both the child in question and others in comparable situations. We must look at decisions we make, not just in terms of the impact they may have on the young person in the case, but with an understanding of what the decision would say about our concept of childhood. It is difficult to forget the thalassemia victim in *Re S*, who described being compelled to undergo blood transfusions as being "like rape."[157]

We must nevertheless tolerate mistakes; as Dworkin puts it, "someone may have the right to do something that is wrong for him to do."[158] We would not be taking rights seriously if we only respected autonomy when we believed the agent (the child or young person) was doing the right thing (or what we would do).[159] However, we would also be failing to recognize a child's integrity if we allowed her to choose an action—using heroin might be a good example—that could severely and irreversibly damage her. The test of irrationality must be so confined that it justifies intervention only to the extent necessary to obviate the immediate harm or to develop the child's capacities of rational choice by which he or she may have a reasonable chance of avoiding such harms.[160]

The question we should ask ourselves is: what sort of action or conduct would we wish, as children, to be shielded against on the assumption that we would wish to mature to a rationally autonomous adulthood and be capable of deciding on our own system of ends as free and rational beings? It is my view that we would choose principles that would enable children to mature to independent adulthood.[161] One definition of irrationality would be such as to preclude action and conduct which would frustrate such a goal. And, within the constraints of such a definition, we would defend a version of paternalism that I call "liberal paternalism."[162] It should be stressed that this version is a catch-22; because the goal is rational independence, those who exercise constraints must only intervene in such a way as to enable children to develop their full capacities.

I have concentrated in this chapter on some of the more difficult issues relating to children's rights: questions of culture, best interests, and limits to autonomy. On the whole, the critics of children's rights do not consider these issues. If, as they do, you consider children's rights to be misplaced rhetoric, it is not necessary to raise the same issues I have done. These rights are also important for those interested in human rights because, of course, many of the same issues arise, or could arise, there too. But it is necessary to separate children's rights from human rights. As I indicated at the beginning of this chapter, this is all commonly done. Human rights theorists ignore children's rights at their peril; if the world grew up believing in children's rights, the battle to establish human rights would be almost won.

Notes

1. See, in particular, Ronald Dworkin, *Law's Empire* (Cambridge, MA: Harvard University Press, 1986).

2. Onora O'Neill, 1988. "Children's Rights and Children's Lives," *Ethics* 98 (April 1988): 445–463.

3. Michael King, "Against Children's Rights." *Acta Juridica 1996*: 28–50.

4. David Archard and Colin M. Macleod, eds., *The Moral and Political Status of Children* (New York: Oxford University Press, 2002).

5. James Griffin, "Do Children Have Rights?," 19–30; Harry Brighouse, "What Rights (if any) do Children Have?," 31–52; Samantha Brennan, "Children's Choices or Children's Interests: Which Do Their Rights Protect?," 53–69; Barbara Arneil, "Becoming versus Being: A Critical Analysis of the Child in Liberal Theory," 70–94, all in Archard and Macleod, *Moral and Political Status of Children*.

6. Ronald Dworkin, *Taking Rights Seriously* (Cambridge, MA: Harvard University Press, 1979).

7. Patricia J. Williams, *The Alchemy of Race and Rights* (Cambridge, MA: Harvard University Press, 1991), 153.

8. Williams, *Alchemy of Race and Rights*, 165.

9. "Critical Perspectives on Rights," *The Bridge* (Harvard), https://cyber.harvard.edu/bridge/CriticalTheory/rights.htm (accessed Jan. 19, 2019).

10. Karl Marx, "On the Jewish Question," *Deutsch-Französische Jahrbücher* (February 1844; edited by Andy Blunden, Matthew Grant, and Matthew Carmody, 2008/2009), https://www.marxists.org/archive/marx/works/1844/jewish-question (accessed Jan. 19, 2019).

11. Robert A. Williams Jr., "Taking Rights Aggressively: The Perils and Promise of Critical Legal Theory for Peoples of Color," *Law and Inequality* 5 no. 1 (1987): 103–134.

12. See, for example, Wendy Brown, *States of Injury: Power and Freedom in Late Modernity* (Princeton: Princeton University Press, 1995).

13. See Jacques Donzelot, 1978. *The Policing of Families* (New York: Pantheon Books, 1978);Eli Zaretsky, *Capitalism, the Family, and Personal Life* (New York: Harper and Row, 1976). See also, Michael Grossberg, *Governing the Hearth: Law and the Family in Nineteenth-Century America* (Chapel Hill: University of North Carolina Press, 1985), 287–307; Martha Minow, "Interpreting Rights: An Essay for Robert Cover," *Yale Law Journal* 96, no. 8 (1987): 1860–1915.

14. Williams, *Alchemy of Race and Rights*, 148.

15. See Carol Delaney, *Abraham on Trial: The Social Legacy of Biblical Myth* (Princeton: Princeton University Press, 1998).

16. See David Lee Miller, *Dreams of the Burning Child: Sacrificial Sons and the Father's Witness* (Ithaca: Cornell University Press, 2003).

17. The so-called Zulu boy case in England in the 1990s is a clear illustration. See *Re M* [1996] 2 FLR 441.

18. See *Re Thain* [1926] Ch. 676. Forty years later, the same unimpeachable parent ideology prevailed. See *Re C (MA)* [1966] 1 ALL ER 838.

19. See Michael Freeman, "The Best Interests of the Child? Is The Best Interests of the Child in the Best Interests of Children?," *International Journal of Law, Policy and the Family* 11, no. 3 (1997): 360–388, 369 (discussing the holding and impact of *Gillick v. West Norfolk & Wisbech Area Health Authority* [1986] AC 112).

20. *Gillick* [1986] AC 112.

21. Michael Freeman, "Feminism and Child Law," in *Feminist Perspectives on Child Law*, ed. Jo Bridgeman and Daniel Monk (London: Cavendish Publishing, 2000), 36n129 (referencing *The Times*, May 28, 1985) Pre-*Gillick*, concerns were expressed by Ferdinand Mount in *The Subversive Family* (London: Jonathan Cape, 1982.).

22. See Michael Freeman, "Rethinking *Gillick*," *International Journal of Children's Rights* 13, no. 1–2 (2005): 201–217.

23. Herbert Butterfield, *The Whig Interpretation of History* (London: W.W. Norton,1965). Note that *Whig* is perhaps an ethnocentric term applied specifically due to the terminology of this observation's source material; more pertinently to children's rights, see Carole Smith, "Children's Rights: Judicial Ambivalence and Social Resistance," *International Journal of Law, Policy and the Family* 11, no. 1 (1997): 103–139.

24. Freeman, "Rethinking *Gillick*," 201–217.

25. *Re T* [1997] 1 FLR 502.

26. But for a decision the other way, see the famous conjoined twins decision in *Re A* [2001] 1 FLR 1.

27. R (Williamson) v. Secretary of State for Education and Employment [2005] 2 AC 246 (HL) (appeal taken from England).

28. Of course, their understanding of Christ is rather contrary to the majority of canonical Christian interpretation. See Philip Greven, *Spare the Child: The Religious Roots of Punishment and the Psychological Impact of Physical Abuse* (New York: Random House, 1990).

29. *Williamson* [2005] 2 AC.

30. See, for example, *Wisconsin v. Yoder*, 406 U.S. 205 (1972).

31. *Williamson* [2005] 2 AC.

32. UN Convention on the Rights of the Child, art. 19 (1989).

33. *Williamson* [2005] 2 AC at para. 71.

34. *Williamson* [2005] 2 AC at para. 71. For more details regarding Baroness Hale and her role in *Williamson*, See Michael Freeman, "The Human Rights of Children," *Current Legal Problems 2010* 63, no. 1 (2010), 28.

35. *Williamson* [2005] 2 AC at para. 74 (declaring that "the High Court focused mainly on whether the beliefs of the parents and teachers qualified for protection, whether this practice was a manifestation of those beliefs, and whether the ban was an interference with their manifestation.").

36. Julie Bindel, "Six Weeks of Suffering," *The Guardian*, August 18, 2006, https://www.theguardian.com/commentisfree/2006/aug/18/comment.schools. See Freeman, "Human Rights of Children," 2 (discussing the *Guardian* article in greater detail).

37. Bindel, "Six Weeks of Suffering."

38. Bindel, "Six Weeks of Suffering."

39. There were five letters in the August 22, 2006, issue of *The Guardian* responding to Bindel's "Six Weeks of Suffering," https://www.theguardian.com/news/2006/aug/22/mainsection. guardianletters.

40. Raised by Sibyl Ruth of Birmingham in *The Guardian*, August 22, 2006, https://www. theguardian.com/news/2006/aug/22/mainsection.guardianletters.

41. Dred Scott v. Sandford, 60 U.S. 393 (1857).

42. *Dred Scott*, 60 U.S. at 407 (elaborating further to assert that because "the negro" had no rights that white people were "bound to respect…the negro might justly and lawfully be reduced to slavery").

43. Hannah Arendt, *The Origins of Totalitarianism* (New York: Harcourt, 1968), 296; See also Freeman, "Human Rights of Children," 18 (discussing further Arendt's work and its relationship to children's rights).

44. Arendt, *Origins of Totalitarianism*, 294.

45. UN Convention on the Rights of the Child, arts. 13, 14, 30 (1989).

46. O'Neill, "Children's Rights and Children's Lives," 463.

47. See Michael Freeman, 1982. "The Rights of the Child in England," *Columbia Human Rights Law Review* 13, no. 2 (Fall-Winter 1981–1982): 601–674, 607 (explaining "Ten is the age of criminal responsibility..... Youths may be convicted of a criminal offense provided the prosecution can prove that they knew that what they were doing was wrong."). See also Freeman, "Human Rights of Children," 22n169 and accompanying text (providing that the age range effectively was "lowered to 10 by the abolition of the *doli incapax* principle in 1998. Perhaps the worst example of this legal failure comes from the conviction of two 10-year-old boys for their attempted rape of an 8-year-old girl.").

48. Richard Farson, *Birthright* (New York: Macmillan, 1974), 182. See also Michael Freeman, "Whither Children: Protection, Participation, Autonomy?," *Manitoba Law Journal* 22, no. 3 (1994): 307–327, 313 (analyzing *Birthright*, as Farson lists nine rights arguably derived from the right to self-determination, one of which is the "right to political power, including the right to vote. Nothing, [Farson] suggests, indicates that children will 'vote less responsibly than adults.'"

49. See, for example, Michael Freeman, "Upholding the Dignity and Best Interests of Children," *Law and Contemporary Problems* 73, no. 2 (Spring 2010): 211–251, 251.

50. See Martin Guggenheim, *What's Wrong with Children's Rights* (Cambridge, MA: Harvard University Press, 2005), 43. See also Freeman, "Human Rights of Children," 20 (remarking that Guggenheim's theory "offers children but one right, to be raised by parents who are minimally fit and who are unlikely to make significant mistakes in judgement in their rearing of their children…he is a passionate defender of parents" rights, even describing them as "sacred").

51. Jeremy Bentham, *The Works of Jeremy Bentham*, vol. 2. (Boston: Adamant Media Corp., 2001), 501 (stating in full that "there is no right, which ought not to be maintained so long as it is upon the whole advantageous to the society that it should be maintained, so there is no right which, when the abolition of it is advantageous to society, should not be abolished.").

52. Michael Freeman, "Taking Children's Rights More Seriously," *International Journal of Law and the Family* 6, no. 1 (1992): 52–71, 56–57 (critiquing theories O'Neill puts forward in "Children's Rights and Children's Lives": "O'Neill does not question the view that children's

lives are a public concern…. Nor does she query the aim of securing positive rights for children. What she does question is whether children's positive rights are best grounded by appeals to fundamental rights. She claims that 'children's fundamental rights are best grounded by embedding them in a wider account of fundamental obligations, which can also be used to justify positive rights and obligations.'").

53. O'Neill, "Children's Rights and Children's Lives," 25.

54. See O'Neill, "Children's Rights and Children's Lives," 25 (advocating for establishing a series of obligations owed to children by adults based on the adult's relationship to the child. Once those obligations are concrete, they become fundamental as to normative adult behavior without having to deal with the theoretical or political pitfalls associated with establishing rights for children.).

55. O'Neill, "Children's Rights and Children's Lives," 25.

56. O'Neill, "Children's Rights and Children's Lives," 25.

57. O'Neill, "Children's Rights and Children's Lives," 34.

58. *Williamson* [2005] 2 AC; see notes 27 through 36 of this chapter (and accompanying text).

59. Where in *Williamson* the parents fiercely advocated for corporal punishment in schools (see notes 27 through 36 of this chapter), other parents can and do value parenting methods that are perhaps less than desirable by the children and by society as a whole. It is incredibly difficult to first determine what parenting acts violate parental obligations and, second, to go about enforcing those obligations. See Freeman, "Rights of the Child in England," 628–633 (describing the complexities of state supervision of parental obligations).

60. See Michael Freeman and Bernadette J. Saunders, "Can We Conquer Child Abuse if We Don't Outlaw Physical Chastisement of Children?," *International Journal of Children's Rights* 22, no. 4 (2014): 681–709, 698 (explaining that when it comes to "giving children participatory rights," adults tend to undermine the effort by ignoring the status of children as equal human beings. "If one asked what percentage of people in a country favoured the 'smacking' of children, one would almost certainly be told the percentage of adults, because children would not be counted in 'people'. This may be thought particularly incongruous since children are the persons who are 'smacked.' "

61. See Freeman, "Human Rights of Children," 22–23 (explaining further O'Neill's conventional deficit model and its applications).

62. Brighouse, "What Rights (if any) Do Children Have?," 31.

63. Brighouse, "What Rights (if any) Do Children Have?," 31.

64. Brighouse, "What Rights (if any) Do Children Have?," 31 (defining the "liberal model": "The liberal model for the attribution of rights is of a competent rational person, who is better positioned than any other feasible assignee to judge what is in his or her interests, and is therefore guaranteed freedom to act on what she judges to be the best reasons for action.").

65. See Freeman, "Human Rights of Children," 23 (describing further Brighouse's views as to agency and his stance's applications as to children's rights).

66. As I explain when advocating for "liberal paternalism." See, for example, Freeman, "Whither Children," 325–326.

67. See Freeman, "Whither Children," 324 (arguing that it is not enough to put institutions in place to protect children, as that strategy clearly has not worked optimally. By culturally recognizing the rights of children, we give them a better chance at being able to protect themselves.).

68. Brighouse, "What Rights (if any) Do Children Have?," 32.

69. Brighouse, "What Rights (If Any) Do Children Have?," 49.

70. See, for example, Brennan, "Children's Choices or Children's Interests," 59.

71. Brennan, "Children's Choices or Children's Interests," 59.

72. Freeman, "Human Rights of Children," 24–25 (referencing Dworkin, *Taking Rights Seriously*).

73. Joel Feinberg, "The Child's Right to an Open Future," in *Whose Child?*, ed. W. Aiken and H. LaFollette (Lanham, MD: Rowman and Littlefield, 1980), 124–153.

74. Hugh LaFollette, "Circumscribed Autonomy: Children, Care, and Custody," in *Having and Raising Children: Unconventional Families, Hard Choices, and the Social Good*, ed. Uma Narayan and Julia J. Bartkowiak (University Park, PA: Pennsylvania State University Press, 1999), 137–152, 139.

75. *Re L* [1998] 2 FLR 810 (medical treatment: *Gillick* competency).

76. *Re W* [1993] Fam. 64; *Re C* [1997] 2 FLR 180.

77. *Re M* [1999] 2 FLR 1097.

78. Freeman, "Rethinking *Gillick*," 201–217.

79. Gillick v. West Norfolk & Wisbech Area Health Authority [1986] AC 112.

80. Margaret Brazier and Caroline Bridge, "Coercion or Caring: Analysing Adolescent Autonomy," *Legal Studies* 16, no. 1 (March 1996): 84–109, 109.

81. Penney Lewis, "The Medical Treatment of Children," in *Legal Concepts of Childhood*, ed. Julia Fionda (Portland, OR: Hart Publishing Co., 2001), 151–163, 159.

82. Michael King, "Children's Rights as Communication: Reflections on Autopoietic Theory and the United Nations Convention," *Modern Law Review* 57, no. 3 (May 1994): 385–401.

83. King, "Children's Rights as Communication," 385.

84. See Freeman, "Rights of Children in England," 614 ("The law in England still distinguishes between legitimate and illegitimate children and discriminates against illegitimate offspring. In the main, the legal effects of illegitimacy bite only while the illegitimate person is a minor. There is also social stigma attached to illegitimacy, though this is considerably less of a social degradation today than was the case a hundred years ago.").

85. Williams, *Alchemy of Race and Rights*, 163 ("Patricia Williams explained: For the historically disempowered, the conferring of rights is symbolic of all the denied aspects of their humanity: rights imply a respect that places one in the referential range of self and others, that elevates one's status from human body to social being."

86. King, "Children's Rights as Communication," 391.

87. See Freeman, "Human Rights of Children," 33 (discussing problems encountered when attempting to integrate the UNCRC into UK law).

88. King, "Children's Rights as Communication," 394.

89. See Freeman, "Human Rights of Children," 19 (discussing interpretive ambiguities within even the CRC's name).

90. See Freeman, "Human Rights of Children," 33n242 (enforcement procedures are "contained in part II of the UNCRC: see Articles 42–45.").

91. See Freeman, "Human Rights of Children," 35n 255 and accompanying text (pointing to sources "D Johnson, 'Cultural and Regional Pluralism in the Drafting of the UN Convention on the Rights of the Child' in M Freeman and P Veerman (eds), The Ideologies of Children's Rights (Dordrecht, 1992), 95–114").

92. See Freeman, "Human Rights of Children," 44 (concluding: "No international treaty commands as much support. But paying lip-service to its ideals is insufficient, and too many

countries fall down on their obligations under it. Our own record is especially poor, particularly in relation to poverty and to the criminal justice system.").

93. King, "Children's Rights as Communication," 398.

94. King, "Children's Rights as Communication," 390 (explaining the "binary" system: "Since each of these subsystems has its own binary coding which reflects its function within society, it is impossible for them to communicate directly with one another. For a statement to have meaning within one subsystem, it must comply with the procedures for selectivity and reality construction or truth validation of that subsystem. Within law, therefore, non-legal communications about the external world, such as political or scientific statements, must be reconstructed as legal communications in order to make sense as law; that is, they must be reproduced in ways that make them accessible to law's binary code of lawful/unlawful.").

95. See Freeman and Saunders, "Can We Conquer Child Abuse if We Don't Outlaw Physical Chastisement of Children?," 691 (referencing CRC Article 19: "The Convention on the Rights of the Child of 1989 is clear that all forms of violence from a smack to a beating should not be countenanced. In Article 19 it requires "all States Parties to take all appropriate legislative, administrative, social and educational measures to protect the child from all forms of physical or mental violence, injury or abuse…while in the care of parent(s), legal guardian(s) or any other person who has care of the child.").

96. Michael King, *A Better World for Children* (London: Routledge, 1997).

97. See Arneil, "Becoming versus Being," 70–94.

98. See Carol Gilligan, 1982. *In a Different Voice: Psychological Theory and Women's Development* (Cambridge, MA: Harvard University Press, 1982) (emphasizing responsibilities over rights).

99. Compare Gilligan, *In a Different Voice*, to Arneil, "Becoming versus Being," 70–94.

100. Arneil, "Becoming versus Being," 93.

101. Arneil, "Becoming versus Being," 93.

102. Arneil, "Becoming versus Being," 93.

103. Arneil, "Becoming versus Being," 93.

104. See Freeman, "Human Rights of Children,"16 ("Rights are about necessities, not luxuries. They are important because they are inclusive: they are universal, available to all members of the human family. In the past, they have depended on gender and race. Women were non-persons. Black people were kept in subservience by policies which justified 'separate but equal' practices (or worse, by slavery). But, just as concepts of gender inequality have been key to understanding womanhood and women's social status, so 'the concept of generation is key to understanding childhood.' ").

105. UN Convention on the Rights of the Child, art. 2 (1989).

106. John Rawls, "The Law of Peoples," *Critical Inquiry* 20, no. 1 (Autumn 1993): 36–68, 51.

107. Rawls, "Law of Peoples," 58.

108. Rawls, "Law of Peoples," 58.

109. Welshman Ncube, "Prospects and Challenges in Eastern and Southern Africa: The Interplay between International Human Rights Norms and Domestic Law, Tradition and Culture," in *Law, Culture, Tradition and Children's Rights in Eastern and Southern Africa*, ed. Welshman Ncube, (Aldershot, UK: Ashgate, 1998), 5.

110. Welshman Ncube, "The African Cultural Fingerprint? The Changing Concept of Childhood," in Ncube, *Law, Culture, Tradition and Children's Rights*, 11n115.

111. Ncube, "African Cultural Fingerprint?," 18.

112. See Freeman, "Human Rights of Children," 26 (discussing a feminist critique by Fran Olsen in "Children's Rights: Some Feminist Approaches to the United Nations Convention on the Rights of the Child," in *Children, Rights, and the Law*, ed. Philip Alston, Stephen Parker, and John Seymour (Oxford: Clarendon, 1992), 192–220).

113. Philip Alston, "The Best Interests Principle: Towards a Reconciliation of Culture and Human Rights," *International Journal of Law, Policy and the Family* 8, no. 1 (1994), 1–25, 20.

114. Alston, "Best Interests Principle," 20.

115. Compare Doriane Lamblet Coleman, "Individualizing Justice through Multiculturalism: The Liberals' Dilemma," *Columbia Law Review* 96, no. 5 (1996): 1093–1167, 1094 (describing the "cultural defense" and the challenges posed by the model), with Leti Volpp, "Taking 'Culture': Gender, Race, Nation and the Politics of Multiculturalism," *Columbia Law Review* 96, no. 6 (1996): 1573–1617 at 1575 (responding to Coleman's article and expanding further on cultural defense analysis).

116. According to UNICEF, about seventy million women today have been subjected to this practice; see UNICEF, "Female Genital Cutting Must Stop," press release, February 6, 2009, https://www.unicef.org/media/media_47845.html. On its long-term problems see World Health Organization, "Female Genital Mutilation and Obstetric Outcome," *The Lancet* 367(June 3, 2006): 1835–1841.

117. See, Freeman, "Upholding the Dignity and Best Interests of Children," 215 ("Dignity asserts the worth of the person who is imbued with it. We cannot define what a human being is without recourse to an essential characteristic such as dignity. Animals do not have dignity; children, I would argue, do.").

118. UN Convention on the Rights of the Child, art. 3, sec. 1 (1989).

119. Robert Mnookin, "Child Custody Adjudication: Judicial Functions in The Face of Indeterminacy," *Law and Contemporary Problems* 39, no. 3 (1975): 226–93, 260.

120. See, for example, L. J. Thorpe in *Al-Habtoor v. Fotheringham* [2001] 1 FLR 951, 970–971.

121. This is a different question from the relationship between interests and rights. This is not the place to debate the will and interests theories of rights.

122. See, for example, Eva Brems, *Human Rights: Universality and Diversity* (The Hague: Martinus Nijhoff, 2001).

123. Most controversially in France. See Eva Brems, "Above Children's Heads: The Headscarf Controversy in European Schools from the Perspective of Children's Rights," *International Journal of Children's Rights* 14, no. 2 (2006): 119–136.

124. See, for example, Caroline Sawyer, "Not Every Child Matters: The UK's Expulsion of British Citizens," *International Journal of Children's Rights* 14, no. 2 (2006): 157–185.

125. John Tobin, "Beyond the Supermarket Shelf: Using a Rights Based Approach to Address Children's Health Needs," *International Journal of Children's Rights* 14, no. 3 (2006): 275–306, 287.

126. Tobin, "Beyond the Supermarket Shelf," 287.

127. UN Committee on the Rights of the Child, *General Comment No. 5: Article (3)(1): Monitoring Implementation—the Need for Child Impact Assessment and Evaluation*, CRC/GC/2003/5, para. 45.

128. Stephen Parker, "The Best Interests of the Child: Principles and Problems," *International Journal of Law and the Family* 8, no. 1 (April 1994): 26–41, 27.

129. See Judith Ennew, "Why the Convention Is Not about Street Children," in *Revisiting Children's Rights: 10 Years of the UN Convention on the Rights of the Child*, ed. Deirdre Fottrell (The Hague: Kluwer Law International, 2000), 169–182.

130. Provided they are under eighteen years of age: see Article 1.
131. See Freeman, "Human Rights of Children," 7–8 (describing the particular vulnerability of street children).
132. Alston, "Best Interests Principle," 16.
133. See Freeman, "What's Wrong with Children's Rights," 90 (asserting: "As agents, rights-bearers can participate. They can make their own lives, rather than having their lives made for them. And participation is a fundamental human right. It enables us to demand rights; See also, Freeman, 'Human Rights of Children,' " 44; concluding: "A healthy democracy is one in which all its citizens can participate; it is one where authority and tradition can be challenged. The burden lies on those who would deny rights to children. It is often said, but it bears repeating, that you can judge a society by the way it treats its weakest members. The world will be a better place when this is recognized.").
134. See Freeman, "Taking Children's Rights More Seriously," 52 (asserting that "rights should be taken seriously. Rights are important if children are to be treated with equality and as autonomous beings. This means believing that anyone's autonomy is as significant as anyone else's.").
135. See Freeman, "Taking Children's Rights More Seriously," 64 (explaining: "Kant (1785) expressed [the idea of rights theory being based on equality and autonomy] by asserting that persons are equal and autonomous in the kingdom of ends").
136. Freeman, "Taking Children's Rights More Seriously," 64.
137. Freeman, "Whither Children," 323.
138. Freeman, "Whither Children," 323.
139. See P. Alderson, K. Sutcliffe, and K. Curtis, "Children as Partners with Adults in Their Medical Care," Archives of Diseases in Childhood 91 (2006): 300–303; Priscilla Alderson, "The Ethics of Space in Clinical Practice," Clinical Practice 2 (2007): 85–91.
140. UN Convention on the Rights of the Child, art. 12 (1989). See Freeman, "Whither Children," 319 (analyzing the history and application of Article 12).
141. Gillick v. West Norfolk & Wisbech Area Health Authority [1986] AC 112.
142. See generally, Freeman, "Rethinking Gillick," 201–217.
143. Freeman, "Rethinking Gillick," 201–217.
144. Freeman, "Rethinking Gillick," 211 (Referencing Re W, "Johnson J. concluded, in the interests of the patient 'in the widest possible sense—medical, religious, social, whatever they may be' to make the order sought, though he added the proviso 'unless no other form of treatment is available.' ").
145. Freeman, "Rethinking Gillick," 211 (analyzing possible effects of the retreat from Gillick).
146. See UN Convention on the Rights of the Child, art. 19 (1989) (dealing with the need "to protect the child from all forms of physical or mental violence, injury, or abuse…while in the care of parent(s), legal guardian(s)," and other caretakers).
147. John Eekelaar, "The Interests of the Child and the Child's Wishes: The Role of Dynamic Self-Determinism," International Journal of Law and the Family 8, no. 1 (1994): 42–61.
148. Eekelaar, "Interests of the Child and the Child's Wishes," 53.
149. Eekelaar, "Interests of the Child and the Child's Wishes," 48.
150. Eekelaar, "Interests of the Child and the Child's Wishes," 48.
151. Virginia Morrow, " 'We Are People Too': Children's and Young People's Perspectives on Children's Rights and Decision Making in England," International Journal of Children's Rights 7, no. 2 (1999): 149–170, 166.
152. Jane Fortin, "Children's Rights: Are the Courts Now Taking Them More Seriously?," King's College Law Journal 15, no. 2 (2004): 253–272, 259.

153. Katherine Hunt Federle, "Rights Flow Downhill," *International Journal of Children's Rights* 2, no. 2 (1994): 343–368, 344.

154. Michael Freeman, *The Rights and the Wrongs of Children* (London: Frances Pinter, 1983), 54–60.

155. Freeman, "Taking Children's Rights More Seriously," 69 (explaining liberal paternalism: "To take children's rights more seriously requires us to take seriously nurturance and self-determination. It demands of us that we adopt policies, practices, structures and laws which both protect children and their rights.").

156. Freeman, "Taking Children's Rights More Seriously," 67 (noting that "what is to be regarded as 'irrational' must be strictly confined. The subjective values of the would-be protector cannot be allowed to intrude.").

157. *Re S* [1994] 2 FLR 1065.

158. Dworkin, *Taking Rights Seriously*, 188–189.

159. Freeman, "Whither Children," 323 (referencing: "As Dworkin has famously announced, if we take rights seriously we must accept that rights-holders will sometimes do things that we do not think are good for them (or perhaps even for us).").

160. Freeman, "Whither Children," 325.

161. Freeman, "Whither Children," 325.

162. Freeman, "Whither Children," 325–326.

CHAPTER 4

THE INTERRELATED AND INTERDEPENDENT NATURE OF CHILDREN'S RIGHTS

SAVITRI GOONESEKERE

1 INTRODUCTION

THE UN Convention on the Rights of the Child (CRC) has been referred to as one of a third generation of human rights treaties that focus on categories of people whose rights had to be contextualized in terms of their specific experience. The CRC reached near universal ratification in a very short time across diverse regions of the world. Ratification has stimulated, in just three decades, a variety of measures to carry the children's rights agenda forward.[1] A significant body of scholarship and intellectual discourse has developed, providing conceptual clarity on the meaning and scope of these rights.[2] All of these initiatives focus on the dynamics and challenges of implementing children's rights and making them meaningful at the national level. There is a perception that the CRC reflects Western norms and standards because the drafting procedures gave voice mostly to the Global North.[3]

Although the drafting process was dominated by the Global North, a common normative framework was already in the legal systems of many countries of the Global South. Colonialism contributed to English Common law and Roman law–based civil law influencing legal systems and societies in all parts of the globe.[4] It is also true that religion-based law and customary law play a role in regulating the lives of children and adults in countries in the Global South. Some non-Western countries also engaged in the drafting process of the CRC, and this religion-based and customary law tradition is sometimes reflected in their contributions to the text. Indeed, the reference to "kafalah as a generic form of foster care" in the CRC is a North African custom not familiar to Islamic communities in other regions.[5] The CRC was an effort to set universal normative standards by conceptualizing the child as a distinct person, a holder and beneficiary of human rights. It inevitably incorporated new thinking in regard to the child and his or her entitlements and relationships to the state and adults in the family and the community.

As Michael Freeman has written, the language of rights makes visible what has been suppressed.[6] The universality of children's rights reflected in the CRC resonates with the lived experience of abuse of power and authority in diverse societies, which diminishes human potential and well-being. Even if the origin of rights may be related to a particular Western experience of abuse of power, this does not justify a patronizing attitude that denies their universal relevance to all people.

This chapter discusses the interrelated and interdependent nature of children's rights within the context of CRC as a set of universal norms and standards applicable globally in diverse contexts. The near universally ratified treaty recognizes a range of general principles and diverse rights usually clustered as provision (survival and development), protection, and participation rights. Their implementation demands an understanding of and response to the manner in which they connect with one another. Besides, children's rights must be implemented in an environment where the human rights of others in their families and communities also are accommodated. The interrelated and interdependent nature of children's rights makes implementation of children's rights complex, but it is essential to grapple with the way in which rights are related to and interact with other rights, if they are to be implemented effectively.

This chapter examines the approach to the indivisibility of human rights and the interrelated and interdependent nature of children's rights in the normative standards set by the CRC and the International Bill of Rights, the latter comprising the Universal Declaration of Human Rights (UDHR) plus the International Covenant on Economic, Social and Cultural Rights (ICESCR) and the International Covenant on Civil and Political Rights (ICCPR) along with the quasi-jurisprudence of treaty bodies. These documents—the CRC and International Bill of Rights, and the work of treaty bodies have set the norms and standards that most countries have accepted in "bringing human rights home" at the national level, and they are endorsed in the rights-based approach to development.

The manner in which these issues have been discussed and dealt with in the process of implementation at the national level also will be considered here. The interdependence of rights and the challenges of implementation are considered in relation to the rights of women, the human rights of parents, and the community. This chapter suggests that these connectivities must be addressed, and conflicts resolved, using a holistic approach—as emphasized by the CRC Committee—to make children's rights a meaningful recourse for their well-being in families and communities.

2 CHILDHOOD AS A SOCIAL CONSTRUCT AND CHILDREN'S HUMAN RIGHTS

The idea of universal norms in the context of children's rights is often critiqued using the argument that childhood is a social construct and can have no real meaning without cultural legitimacy.

In response to the idea of universal norms, an internal cultural discourse and cross cultural dialogue are advocated as the best ways of working toward the implementation of human rights norms and standards.[7] What are perceived as so-called Western norms on human rights have been distinguished from "Asian values."[8] The CRC's concept of childhood and human rights demanding national recognition and integration of universal norms has been described by one writer as the "fallacy of universal childhood" or the "tyranny of children's rights."[9] The concept of treating children in diverse societies as adults with competence and capacity to exercise rights has been challenged on the premise that in some societies the social construct of childhood considers children as dependent persons with needs that must be fulfilled. This is described as a contradiction that, when embedded in a concept of human rights, undermines the meaning of human rights of autonomous individuals. The concept of universal children's rights has also been described as a Western standard of childhood, thrust upon a Global South that cannot afford to implement them. Generally, then, the CRC has been described as an effort to globalize a Western model of childhood.[10]

These criticisms of the approach of CRC and the concept of universal norms and standards on children's rights are belied by the manner in which governments and civil society across the globe have in fact internalized the children's rights agenda in the decades since the CRC's adoption and with its near universal ratification. The fact that violations of the rights of children occur has not meant that the idea of a "first call for children" under the CRC has been rejected, even by those governments and communities that have performed poorly on implementation. Indeed, the importance of CRC and other human rights treaties and of integrating these universal norms into national development has been recognized and incorporated into the most recent global policy consensus on the UN's Sustainable Development Goals (SDGs).[11]

The CRC has also broadened the definition and the scope of international human rights as they relate to children. The focus is no longer exclusively on traditional individual civil liberties as might have been recognized in the West as the full universe of international human rights. Consequently, the idea that individual civil liberties are rights, and that the state and family can adopt welfare measures at their discretion to address children's basic needs, has been rejected. The child welfare approach to state and family protection of children has been replaced by the idea that an agenda of human rights and children's rights demands recognition of their personhood and dignity as well as the implementation of economic and social rights to health, education, and shelter, and to protection from social and economic exploitation.[12]

The concept of participation rights for children, which has its genesis in values on autonomy, agency, and capacity, is also sometimes viewed as alien to non-Western social constructs of childhood. But the idea that a child's evolving capacity and child participation rights reflect an exclusively Western model of childhood seems somewhat patronizing in a context where non-Western legal systems recognize age thresholds during which children move from a situation of dependence and incapacity to assuming roles and responsibilities. The concept of the age of puberty is an important concept of Islamic law, is also a threshold of capacity recognized in other cultures, and is similar to the age of discretion in common law or tacit emancipation in Roman Dutch law. Sardar Ali points out that there is a lack of awareness of the importance of human agency in Islamic law. Besides, norms of common law and civil law were imposed in many countries across the globe through colonialism. When incorporated into non-Western legal systems and institutions, their impact extended, in many instances, to transforming values of societies in Asia, Africa, and the Pacific.[13]

The CRC rejects a relativist vision of childhood. International and national human rights agendas contribute to norms and standards that can help promote accountability in governance, create a culture of understanding, and counteract the abuse of power in states, communities, and families. When inadequacies in implementation and enforcement promote cynicism and disregard for human rights norms and standards, this, in and of itself, becomes a path to legitimizing violations of human rights, including the rights of children.

3 INTERNATIONAL TREATY NORMS AND THE INVISIBILITY AND INDIVISIBILITY OF CHILDREN'S RIGHTS

The Universal Declaration of Human Rights (UDHR) and the International Covenants (ICESCR and ICCPR) focus on "the inherent dignity and the equal and inalienable right of all members of the human family."[14] Most of the rights enumerated in the UDHR refer to civil liberties. Only four of thirty articles refer to what can be described as economic and social rights.[15] In describing the beneficiaries of rights, the UDHR uses the words "everyone" and "no one" and "rights of men and women." Children are mentioned specifically only in relation to the right to "social protection." There is no specific reference to children's rights even in the article on education—which refers to the right of access to free compulsory elementary education, but subject to parental rights of choice in education.[16]

The ICCPR, in contrast with the ICESCR, is considered by some as incorporating only so-called negative civil and political versus so-called positive economic, social, and cultural rights (notwithstanding the fallacy of this distinction, as both sets of rights involve various kinds of expenditures by the government). Yet the Preamble to the ICCPR broadens the concept of rights in the UDHR significantly by referring to that document's recognition that the idea of freedom with civil and political rights can only be realized when these rights as well as economic and social rights are enjoyed.[17] So the idea of indivisibility of both sets of rights was recognized in the ICCPR itself, even though the general principles in the ICCPR focus exclusively on civil liberties.

Within the ICCPR itself, rights are described as being as the entitlement of "all people," "all individuals," "persons," and "human beings."[18] These words can be interpreted as referring to children, but there are hardly any specific provisions on children's rights. Children are specifically referred to as "juvenile" rights holders in only two subprovisions on administration of criminal justice. There is one reference to a child's right to protection generally, and even then it is in circumstances of dissolution of their parents' marriage. Even the child's right to registration of birth and nationality is not specifically incorporated but instead included in general provisions dealing with the right to protection for minors in the family, society, and the state.[19]

Despite the "missing children" in both of these international instruments, and the implication that children do not have the capacity to be rights holders, national constitutions that have incorporated UDHR and ICCPR standards on human rights have been interpreted by their courts as recognizing children as the holders of all the civil rights enjoyed by adults. Jurisprudence has also interpreted the civil and political rights to life and equality guaranteed by these constitutions as conferring a right of access to education on children themselves. This type of constitutional development has contributed to strengthening the idea of the indivisibility of human rights generally as well as the recognition and indivisibility of the rights of children.[20]

The concept of the indivisibility of human rights is incorporated and developed further in specific provisions of ICESCR. Its preamble recognizes that "the dignity" of the human being cannot be achieved without everyone enjoying "economic and social rights as well as civil and political rights."[21] The ICESCR also uses the language of "all people," "men and women," "everyone," and "all persons" in its references to the holders of rights. While this language can be interpreted as referring to children, the ICESCR also has specific provisions on children's rights to education. Similarly, specific health rights of children, not mentioned in UDHR or ICCPR, are incorporated into the ICESCR.[22]

The concept of the indivisibility of rights was therefore incorporated into the International Bill of Rights long before the Vienna World Conference on Human Rights (1993) became the reference point for this norm. This concept has also been strengthened and developed in later international treaties, such as the Convention on Elimination of all Forms of Discrimination against Women (CEDAW) and the CRC, both of which explicitly recognize the indivisibility of human rights and the equal status and importance of both sets of rights. An optional protocol to the ICESCR adopted in 2008 recognizes not merely the indivisibility and interdependent nature of human rights, but also the legitimacy of an international complaints procedures to claim these rights.[23]

The recognition of economic and social rights and the norm of indivisibility strengthen the obligation of the state to allocate expenditures and other resources for implementing children's rights. Civil liberties and economic and social rights have often been bifurcated on the basis that the latter require financial resources and expenditure. This argument ignores the reality that enforcement of civil liberties, especially through legal and other institutions, requires financial resources. The concept of international complaints procedures to enforce all rights, in protocols, also undermines the argument that only civil liberties are rights capable of enforcement through legal procedures. This approach to the indivisibility of rights and the movement away from identifying human rights as exclusively civil liberties are reflected in the regional conventions on human rights in Europe, Africa, and Latin America.[24]

The CRC has achieved a balanced normative framework by recognizing the dignity and status of the child as a human person and a holder of varied interdependent rights, the content and scope of which can be defined by reference to the reality of growth from infancy and early childhood to adolescence and adulthood. Viewed in this way, the state's duty to protect is not conceptualized as a welfare response to the care needs of the child. Instead, the infant or young child who is beaten, raped, sexually abused, or affected by such harmful customary practices as genital mutilation suffers a violation of the civil liberties of life, personal security, and equal protection of the law. Violations of these rights can now also be linked to violations of economic and social rights, such as the rights of children to education and health.

The lack of capacity of some children to articulate their rights does not diminish the significance of the right to protection from abuse incorporated in the CRC. Nor should these rights be determined or circumscribed by arguing that children lack the competence to exercise the full range of rights of participation, identified with evolving capacity in the CRC.

A third optional protocol adopted by the CRC in 2011 provides for a complaints and inquiry procedure for violations of children's rights, similar to those included in the optional protocols to CEDAW and the ICESCR. The preamble incorporates the concept of the "universality indivisibility interdependence and interrelatedness of all human rights." The CRC concept that a child can be recognized as a holder of rights with the capacity to enforce them, as he or she grows to adulthood through evolving capacity, is reflected in the third optional protocol, which reaffirms the status of children as human beings of evolving capacity who are also holders of rights but may face difficulties in pursuing violation of their rights. These developments challenge a discourse that focuses on incapacity and limitations of personal autonomy as a basis for rejecting the idea of children's human rights.[25] Full enjoyment of all civil liberties granted to adults can no longer be the lens for arguments for or against a concept of children's rights.[26]

Although initial communications under the optional protocol were considered inadmissible, the CRC Committee issued its first opinion in a case in 2018.[27] The case, in which a deportation order against a Somali girl was challenged successfully for violation of rights guaranteed under the CRC, reflects the trend toward recognizing the full range of children's rights. Even the process of getting a complaint to the CRC Committee, which requires exhaustion of domestic remedies first, can help draw attention to children's rights issues and the failure by the state to provide remedies, such as appeal procedures at the national level. This process itself can motivate bringing the national law and procedures into harmony with CRC.

4 Interrelatedness of Children's Rights

4.1 Interpretations of Treaty Bodies

General Comments of the ICESCR Committee have helped establish the concept that there is a state obligation to fulfill minimum core obligations in implementing socioeconomic rights. Later General Comments have interpreted this as a mandatory immediate obligation to "respect, protect and fulfill" economic and social human rights.[28] This standard imposes an obligation to prevent violations by state and non-state actors (a negative obligation) and a positive obligation to implement all rights through appropriate resource allocation. Here, the state obligation goes beyond enabling relief and remedy through judicial procedures, the familiar method of enforcing civil and political rights in a Western liberal tradition. This new concept of promotion, protection, and fulfillment of children's rights in implementation has now been incorporated and developed in specific General Comments of the CRC Committee, including a joint General Comment of the CEDAW and CRC Committees, and reinforces the interrelatedness of children's rights.[29]

The concept of the best interests of the child in English common law was one that traveled to colonized legal regimes across the globe. The discretion given to courts in common law jurisdictions in interpreting the meaning of the concept, and the need for guidelines to ensure some consistency, has been the focus of legislative reform.[30] However, the CRC Committee has adopted a different approach by very clearly indicating in a General Comment that the best interests of the child in CRC Article 3 must be interpreted in light of the substantive provisions on the obligations of state and non-state actors, including the family. This is considered a general principle for interpreting and implementing *all* rights outlined in the CRC. The importance of ensuring that the principle is used in implementing substantive rights, including measures of law, policy, and resource allocation and rules of procedure, also is emphasized in this General Comment.[31]

This approach of the CRC Committee draws attention to the importance of rejecting subjective interpretations of the concept of the best interests of a child and of being attuned to attempts to manipulate it to realize an objective or agenda that has no relationship to the substantive rights of provision, protection, and participation defined in the Convention. The ideas of *culture* and *tradition* cannot be used to justify a concept of best interests of the child that conflicts with the core norms of the CRC. A General Comment on corporal punishment also clarifies that the interpretation of best interests must conform to the entire CRC and cannot be interpreted to justify use of corporal punishment. Similarly, the General Comment on the right to be heard clarifies that best interests cannot be correctly applied if "the components of Article 12 on the right to be heard are not respected." The link between the right of protection from violence in CRC, and the best interests of the girl child, has been made in the Committee's views in the optional protocol case of 2018.[32]

General Comments of the CRC Committee interpreting evolving capacity and participation rights clarify that children's rights to be heard in matters that affect their lives in Article 12 is a core general principle.[33] This norm is applicable to all rights of the child and is not an isolated objective connected only to the participation rights enumerated in Articles 13 to 16. General Comments recognize that in law reform, policy formulation, and resource allocation to implement specific rights, such as the right to health and protection from violence and abuse, a balance must be maintained between those rights and participation or autonomy rights. For instance, the General Comment on health recognizes the need to "understand children's evolving capacities, and the different health priorities during the life cycle."[34] Similarly a link is made between provision or development rights of health and education, protection of dignity and personal security, and such participation rights as the right to be heard in the Committee's approach to corporal punishment as a violation of children's rights.[35]

Two General Comments interpreting participation rights also attempt to clarify the need to understand evolving capacity.[36] General Comment No. 12 on the right to be heard explains the various ways in which the right can be implemented substantively and in judicial and administrative procedures. However, the interpretation is located within a framework that accepts the need to balance autonomy, agency, and evolving capacity, recognizing that lack of capacity must be addressed but with respect for the child's dignity and persona. The phrase "capable of forming his or her views" is not interpreted so as to set minimum age thresholds only in law or policy, but it places an obligation on states to develop methods to assess the child's capacity to form autonomous opinions. This calls for a holistic interdisciplinary approach to legislative reform that facilitates assessing children's maturity and evolving capacity. This approach is further endorsed and elaborated in the Committee's General Comment No. 20 on implementing child rights during adolescence.[37] The Committee clarifies that different levels of maturity must be considered in interpreting the rights of children in this group. It is therefore clear that participation rights must be balanced with protection rights as well as provision or development rights.

This holistic approach is well illustrated in dealing with child labor. The child's right to be protected from economic exploitation and to claim such development rights as health and education according to their ages is emphasized. The CRC Committee reminds states parties that evolving capacity and the right to exercise increasing levels of responsibility do not obviate the state obligation to guarantee protection.[38] Protection and development rights are recognized, as well as "age appropriate" forms of work, as a dimension of evolving capacity.

The quasi-jurisprudence developed by the CRC Committee over the years clearly recognizes the interrelated nature of children's rights and the importance of interpreting specific rights in a manner that reinforces all other rights. The concept of the indivisibility of human rights and the interpretation of the best interests of the child in a manner that rejects relativist approaches also promote a movement away from an overfocus on autonomy, capacity, and participation as the core of children's rights. A civil liberties approach to autonomy and agency can no longer be considered the sine qua non of children's rights. The concept *evolving capacity* can therefore be interpreted in a balanced and nuanced manner to recognize the reality of childhood, as a child grows from infancy to adolescence and adult status.

4.2 Some National Approaches

The Convention on the Rights of the Child has stimulated a range of national interventions, despite the fact that states parties have diverse approaches to the incorporation of international law into their domestic systems. There are two general types of incorporation—monist and dualist—though the practice in many states reflects some combination of the two. In pure monist countries, there is direct incorporation of international law into domestic systems; it does not need to be translated into national law—it is just incorporated and goes into effect automatically. In contrast, in pure dualist countries, which are more common, international law must be translated into domestic law to enter into effect.

Research on child rights and legislative reform reflect different approaches.[39] A 2008 UNICEF Study found that sixty-nine countries (37%) had enacted consolidated children's rights statutes. A 2013 study of twelve countries on legal implementation of CRC in developed countries (including South Africa) found that very few states parties had provided for direct incorporation, some had constitutional provisions, and the more common method was to incorporate specific provisions, like those in CRC Articles 3 and 12 into legislation. A 2007 study of CRC implementation in countries with diverse legal regimes based on common law, Islamic law, and plural legal systems in Africa, found that states parties had adopted a practice of implementing the CRC through children's acts or legislation on specified topics. In this study, a few countries had constitutions with general bills of rights applying to children. And, some countries with plural legal systems, such as South Africa and Uganda, had incorporated specific children's rights derived from the CRC into their constitutions. A common focus on child protection in legislation was noted, while many Latin American countries had incorporated an indivisibility of rights approach in legislation, focusing also on economic social and cultural rights.

The constitutional incorporation of children's rights, either through a bill of rights or as specific constitutional provisions based on CRC, tends to promote accountability in governance and resource allocation as well as responses that recognize connections between rights. Constitutional provisions in many countries also provide an opportunity for constitutional jurisprudence, sometimes through public interest litigation, as in

South Asia. Such jurisprudence in areas such as education, health, and shelter help to create an understanding of the link between equality and development rights, and protection, development and participation rights, as envisaged in the CRC General Comments.[40]

India, for instance, was a country that consistently adopted a permissive attitude toward adult exploitation of child labor, in conflict with the CRC rights of provision, protection and participation. Jurisprudence in the supreme court interpreting the right to life in Article 21 of the Indian Constitution, as well as the right to equality in the constitution, led to a constitutional amendment incorporating a right of access to free compulsory education from ages six through fourteen as part of the right to life. Legislation then provided for compulsory education and commitments on resource allocation. This is a reform child civil rights activists had been advocating for many decades.[41]

When incorporation takes the form of ad hoc efforts at legislation, the holistic perspective and the connections between rights can be ignored. Conflicts and contradictions can emerge. For example, many countries in South Asia set minimum legislative standards for employment. And, in light of the International Labour Organization's (ILO) Convention No. 182 (1999) on the worst forms of child labor, they define hazardous work as work in which children should not be engaged.[42] However, accompanying laws, policies, and resource allocations on access to birth registration and to education, which are critically important and directly related to children's employment, as indicated in General Comments of the CRC Committee, do not receive attention. It is also worth noting that ILO Convention No. 182 was a compromise that diluted the importance of ILO Convention No. 138 (1973) and its Minimum Age Recommendation No. 146, which set a firm agenda of removing children from all forms of exploitation in child labor, especially through access to education. The definition of what is and what is not hazardous in ILO Convention No. 182, while adopting a protective approach to "preventing the worst form of exploitation," does not address the violation of children's provision, protection, and participation rights by state and non-state actors employing children, which undermines some of the protections that this convention provides.

Ad hoc legislative responses in the area of violence against children and juvenile justice can also lead to confusion and contradictions in implementing children's rights. For example, there has been a global campaign to treat child marriage as sexual exploitation and child abuse.[43] National legislation sometimes bans child marriage and sets minimum ages of marriage as a dimension of child protection. The concept of children's evolving capacity and an age of discretion can also motivate policies that incorporate the concept of an age of consent to sexual intercourse into either the state's penal code or criminal law. When the rationale for protection and participation rights of children are not understood, laws on minimum age of marriage can fail to address the issue of sexual activity among adolescents and the need to promote responsible sexual behavior as a child grows from adolescence to adulthood. In a recent case in India, for instance, the supreme court read down a specific provision in the penal code that set an age for sexual consent that was meant to address marital rape in circumstances of child marriage in light of later legislation.[44] The new laws had made eighteen the minimum relevant age for both marriage and sexual consent in relation to the offense of statutory rape. The controversial decision, ignoring the language of the penal code, can be viewed as reinforcing the prohibitions on child marriage. However, the decision also reflects an approach in Indian law that ignores the need to consider the dimension of evolving capacity and a lower age for consensual sex between adolescents.

There has been legislation across the globe focusing on sexual abuse of children that reflects a child protection approach. Now that cybercrime and sexual exploitation of children on the Internet crosses borders, law and policy reform is required to ensure protection for the very young child and against the risk to development rights. The need to hear children and empower them to protect themselves may not receive the same priority.[45]

When policies are not clear in regard to the need to balance child development and protection policies with participation rights, in responding to sexual abuse and early marriage, there is confusion in judicial procedures, law enforcement, education, and health interventions. This can lead to impunity for sexual abuse of a child below the age of consent or, as in the recent Indian case mentioned above, a tendency to consider consensual sexual relations by adolescents above the age of sexual consent as sexual abuse by one of them.

There has been reform in many countries in the area of juvenile justice, promoting legislation to harmonize the UN Standard Minimum Rules for Administration of Juvenile Justice adopted in 1985 (the Beijing Rules), which are also incorporated in the CRC.[46] Issues of public concern with national and public security, violence, and terrorism pose a serious challenge to adhering to these norms and standards. International standards on child combatants and forced conscription in armed conflict have been developed over the years in the Optional Protocol to the CRC, UN Security Council resolutions, and UN policies and programs.[47] However, as noted above and below, an emerging challenge is to address the rights of children to freedom of association and political participation. The technology and social media revolution and developing capacity for political mobilization on issues of societal concern have potentially significant impact on children and their rights.

The importance of recognizing children's participation rights, including the right to be heard, in post-conflict and transitional justice situations has led to a shift away from an exclusive focus on issues of implementing protection and development rights.[48] However, when participation rights are recognized, there can be a public demand for adult responsibilities, resisting the protection and development norms of juvenile justice, when a child engages in the criminal activity.

The lack of public sympathy for a seventeen-year-old who was part of an adult group that committed violent gang rape was clearly demonstrated in the Nirbhaya case in India.[49] The public outcry motivated reforms to the legislation on juvenile justice, reforms that are in conflict with CRC and constitutional guarantees on child rights, as adolescent offenders can now be tried as adults if they commit heinous crimes. Juvenile justice is an area where CRC's balance of protection and participation rights has become difficult to achieve in facing the hard realities of adolescents in conflict with the law. The CRC's General Comments on the subject of juvenile justice and the right to be heard, and comparative experience in handling this problem, can provide assistance in developing interventions that do not undermine and conflict with commitments of states regarding international and national human rights norms and standards.[50]

5 The Interdependence of Children's Rights

Accommodating children's rights in the context of family and community can be complex.

5.1 Parents, Children, and Family

The concept of children being part of a human family and community has been incorporated in the UDHR and later human rights instruments. The UDHR provision that "the family is the natural and fundamental group unit of society, and is entitled to protection by society and the State" is a provision that has been incorporated in national constitutions.[51] The UDHR refers to "duties to the community in which alone the free and full development of personality is possible." Limitations on individual rights by law are permitted "for the purpose of...due recognition and respect for the rights and freedoms of others and meeting the just requirements of public order and the general welfare of democratic society."[52] These same principles are incorporated in the International Covenants.[53]

The CRC follows this approach. The CRC states that individual human rights are entitlements of persons in the "human family." The idea that the individual child can exercise his or her rights best in a family environment of happiness, love, and understanding reinforces the importance of family in the life of a child.[54] The perception that individual human rights and dignity atomize the child in an individualism that has no space for links with family and community is contradicted by these core norms set out in the preamble to the CRC.

Specific provisions in the CRC clarify that the full range of children's human rights must be implemented so as to ensure that the family and community have a role in the child's life but do not become the site for violating or undermining CRC principles.[55] The state obligation to ensure the best interests of the child accommodates the rights and duties of parents and children as well as legal guardians and their legal responsibilities. But the concept of a gradual diminution of parental rights and duties of care as the child grows from childhood through adolescence is incorporated also in the concept of evolving capacity.[56] It is within this framework that Article 18 requires the state to recognize the "common (parental) responsibility, for the upbringing and development of the child."

General Comments of the CRC Committee adhere to the above normative framework and seek to maintain a balance between the recognition of children's human rights and the rights and responsibilities of parents, the state, and non-state actors whose lives and actions impact children.

The CRC Committee's General Comment on Measures of Implementation (2003) recognizes that the task of implementing human rights needs the engagement of "all sections of society" and that this includes creating awareness among parents of children as holders of human rights.[57] Other General Comments reflect the need to balance and recognize the status of parents, the family, and adult state and non-state actors in the same manner in which individual adult human rights must be implemented to accommodate other societal demands.[58]

The provisions of the CRC and the quasi-jurisprudence of the CRC Committee therefore reflect a paradigm shift from past legal and social traditions that interpreted a father's parental responsibility, including his parental power, as rights and duties that ignored the individual status of a child as a human being with entitlements.[59] The change may not always be reflected in law and policy reform and, specifically in national jurisprudence, creating confusion and also contributing to an erosion of the idea of children's rights.

The interdependence and indivisibility of the human rights of adults and the need to harmonize those rights and to balance conflicting interests are recognized in the discourse on human rights. However, in relation to children, most discussions focus on human rights as undermining the status of family, parents, or other non-state actors who feature in children's lives.

Recent scholarship has analyzed national situations and pointed to the disjuncture that has emerged between parental rights and children rights. This experience is reflected in the manner in which the best interests of the child concept continues to be interpreted as a discretionary norm, delinked from the norms and standards set by the CRC on children's rights.[60] It is also demonstrated in law reform and policies on corporal punishment, children's right to be heard, and in the areas of health and political participation.

The failure to recognize this new and different conceptual framework that seeks to balance parental rights and responsibilities in the family with the role of the state and other adult, non-state actors who impact the lives of children is manifest in the continuing controversies over children's autonomy and agency in a rights-based approach.[61]

Many countries across the globe have banned the use of corporal punishment in schools and the home.[62] There has been some political will in recognizing that in this area at least, discipline within family and schools cannot be used as a rationale to deny the rights of children to development (provision), protection from violence, and to be heard. There is some evidence that legislation that promotes a culture of zero tolerance to corporal punishment has had the effect of reducing child mortality and child physical abuse.[63]

Jurisprudence in some countries regarding parental decision-making in the context of children's right to health, particularly when it involves physical restraints, has been problematic. In some cases, the child's best interests has been interpreted so as to give more priority to parental and adult decisions in health and education, even when that has meant the restriction of a child's personal liberty, on the rationale of a parent's duty and responsibility. This approach can effectively deny the child's choice and consent in areas of personal concern. The failure to put in place mechanisms to facilitate the child's expression of concern and consent creates an environment conducive to ignoring the importance of children's participation and an overfocus on protection in defining the best interests of the child.[64]

The CRC Committee has adopted a rights-based approach in its observations on children's right to freedom of religion and practice and on the issue of state support for family and community, and it has emphasized CRC norms on children's rights of participation in this area. The state may be disinclined to interfere with family and community values and practices for political reasons and thereby disregard CRC commitments on child rights of participation. The CRC Committee's views, expressed in regard to the optional protocol case of 2018, clarify that the socially accepted and family-supported practice of female genital mutilation (FGM) constitutes an infringement of the girl child's rights under the CRC to protection from violence and bodily integrity. There is, unfortunately, no discussion in the Committee's opinion of the infringement of the girl's right of personal autonomy and choice and the connected dimension of participation rights under the CRC.[65]

In the precedent-setting *Gillick* case in the United Kingdom, [66] the House of Lords set thresholds and guidelines for determining a child's competence to make decisions that affect his or her personal life and for disregarding parental consent. This was a case in which a parent sought a declaration prohibiting a health authority from giving contraceptives to her daughters under the age of sixteen without parental knowledge and consent. Setting guidelines to determine a child's competence may help in interpreting children's rights in this complex area. The concept of *age of discretion* derives from the common law and equity and is used in some countries to determine age thresholds in ways that facilitate working out the balance between parental and adult rights.[67]

5.2 Children's Rights and Women's Rights

The concept of rights in a civil liberties tradition is especially relevant for the status of children and women in most societies. Childhood and gender are both social constructs, and when combined with the deeply rooted patriarchal idea of a male head of household and family, have worked to deny the human entitlement of both women and children. The English common law concepts of *coverture* and *parent (father) lord* and the civil law concept of *patria potestas* (power of the father) located women, children, and insane persons in a situation where they lacked legal capacity. These ideas were carried to diverse legal systems and societies in a colonial era of empire and conquest. Female-centered family units and female-centered norms and standards where they existed, in some countries of Asia and Africa, were undermined, resulting in the reinforcement of parallel male-centered families and patriarchal norms that also existed in these societies.[68]

The initial concepts and ideologies of the feminist movement in the West, also carried to all parts of the globe, saw the overlap between the low status of women and children in society. Linking women's situation to that of children was identified as the source of laws, policies, and social norms that denied women life chances, dignity, and agency in matters that affected their lives. The initial focus of radical feminists in particular was to consider child care a burden placed on women that limited their lives to the private sphere of family and that excluded them from occupying their rightful place in the public sphere of their societies. In contrast, liberal feminists supported women's choice in regard to family planning and having children, demanding also opportunities to combine this with engagement in the public sphere. This approach was rejected as undermining the feminist women's rights project. When the NGO World Conference on Human Rights took place in Vienna in 1993, feminist groups resisted a suggestion by some delegations from Asia to also include children in a statement on women's rights. An eminent male, child rights activist assembled another group of women and men who drafted a statement on the rights of children and the girl child.[69]

Over the years, some male child rights activists have critiqued the feminist movement as an effort to undermine what these children's right activists see as the need for inclusiveness and gender neutrality in the child rights project.[70] Global development agendas that link women and children in programming on the basis of their combined vulnerability also have been the object of feminist criticism of making connections between women's rights and the children's rights agenda.[71]

Scholarship has tried to address these tensions.[72] Both the complementarity in the agendas and their compatibility have been explored and considered important for implementing both women's rights and children's rights. Empirical evidence has been cited to support this analysis. Also, campaigns on violence against women, sexual abuse, and trafficking in developing countries in Asia and Africa have helped to respond effectively to gender-based exploitation and to the abuse of both women and girls. Linking children and women has invariably contributed to discrimination against both groups in the areas of reproductive health, access to education, and nationality. This approach has been replaced in many countries by legal changes, policy reforms, and allocation of financial resources for implementing changes that recognize the entitlements of both groups. Gender sensitization programs for men and boys, especially on gender-based violence, focus on creating an understanding of the need for their support for a gender equality agenda. Effective campaigns on law and policy reform have originated in emblematic cases of violence and sexual abuse against women and children. There are judicial precedents in countries with received English law where jurisprudence in the courts has used the best interests concept in custody disputes to erode the deeply entrenched preferential status of the father as the so-called natural guardian of his children. The demand for giving women choice in regard to child care and family responsibilities has stimulated changes in laws and policies that have strengthened the reproductive rights of women, creating better opportunities for employment and engagement in public life.

The Vienna World Conference Declaration (1993)[73] adopted an intergenerational approach that calls for implementing the human rights of women and girls. Separate sections on the subject of equality, dignity, and tolerance deal with women's and children's rights and urge universal ratification of the CRC. The girl child is referred to specifically in the section on children's rights. Most importantly, the World Conference emphasized the universality and the indivisibility and interdependence of civil and political rights and economic and social rights,[74] providing conceptual clarity on the interrelated nature of both women's rights and children's rights. It has fertilized interpretations of gender-based discrimination addressed in CEDAW and the CRC.

The CEDAW Committee's General Recommendations clarify the overlap between women's rights and children's rights and the need to address this in law reform, policy formulation, and resource allocation. The quasi-jurisprudence of the CEDAW Committee interpreting equality as substantive equality in impact and outcome, and the state obligation to "respect, protect and fulfill" women's rights, carry forward the concept of the indivisibility and interdependence of the rights of both groups. When equality is not just a civil liberty issue of de jure equality, but of substantive equality in result and outcome, both sets of rights are important. They become a link to children in areas such as reproductive health, access to education, employment rights, and violence against women. The CEDAW Committee recognizes that the impact of that link has to be recognized and addressed if women's rights are to be implemented.[75] The Committee's recent General Recommendation No. 2017 on gender-based violence includes a specific reference to girl children.[76]

The CRC Committee's General Comments also recognize the overlap and the possibility of the women's rights and children's rights agendas reinforcing each other. The indivisibility of rights and the state obligation to "respect, protect and fulfill" is recognized in CRC General Comments.[77] The Third Optional Protocol to the CRC (2011) reiterates and reaffirms the indivisibility and interdependence of human rights. The CRC Committee's views expressed recently in the optional protocol case in 2018 demonstrate how infringements of the rights of girls to protection from violence can be a manifestation of gender-based discrimination under CRC Article 2, thus connecting with the status and rights of women. In this case, an order of deportation against a woman and an accompanying girl child was challenged on the basis that it infringed upon the girl's right to be protected from the proven risk of being subjected to FGM. The CRC Committee, however, failed to address and comment on the discrimination against the girl child embedded in the practice.[78] The CRC Committee has adopted mostly gender-neutral comments that do not focus on the interface between the rights of women and the girl child per se. There are only occasional specific references made to the girl child in the General Comments. The gender neutrality in the General Comment on health is particularly striking, given the unique health issues that girls and boys confront. General Comments on adolescence devote two paragraphs to special issues that must be addressed regarding girls and another two to special issues affecting boys. This is the only CRC General Comment that explicitly deals substantively with girl children's situation.[79]

The joint General Comment of the CRC Committee (General Comment No. 18) and the CEDAW Committee (General Recommendation No. 31) on harmful practices (2014) is unique in addressing the interface between women and children's rights, and the rights of girl children in particular.[80] The concept that gender-based violence results in the infringement of the rights of both women and girls is recognized in this joint General Comment and has been reinforced by CEDAW General Recommendation No. 35, updating the quasi-jurisprudence of its General Recommendation No. 19 (on violence against women). The CRC Committee referred to this joint General Comment in considering the issue of FGM in 2018. The link between the girl's situation and the social pressures on the mother to conform to the practice, despite legislative prohibitions, was referred to, and there was a call for gender-sensitive approaches to decisions on deportation. The CRC Committee, however, rejected the argument of an infringement of CRC Article 2 on the basis of discrimination against the girl child, confining its views to infringements of the girl's rights under Articles 3 and 19 on best interests and child abuse.

This case demonstrates that a joint approach to interpreting the two treaties, useful as it is, needs to be reinforced by a General Comment with the CEDAW Committee on CRC Article 2. Such an initiative will give both the CRC and CEDAW Committees an opportunity to incorporate the developments on the definitions of gender-based discrimination and substantive equality in international human rights law, discussed earlier. There is a need for conceptual clarity in this regard, clarity that harmonizes the approach of the CRC Committee with changes in international human rights norms and standards on gender-based discrimination. Combining CEDAW and CRC standards on gender-based discrimination and substantive equality can help provide guidance on responding to the interface between women's and children's rights.

The recently adopted Sustainable Development Goals[81] have tried to integrate a human rights perspective into the global development agenda based on international law and treaty commitments. This rights-based approach to development can help governments and civil society reinforce standards and norms on substantive equality and the indivisibility of rights in law, policy formulation, and resource allocation at the national level as well as help displace the undermining of women and girls' agency by reinforcing vulnerability in development planning and programs. Most importantly, the new development agenda can contribute to recognizing the overlap between the women's rights and children's rights agendas and the relevance of achieving complementarity in development planning and resource allocation nationally.

The 2030 agenda offers an opportunity to recapture the human rights–based approach that was undermined by the Millennium Development Goals, which delinked national human rights treaty commitments from development. It has been argued that the CRC Committee has recognized the importance of the socioeconomic rights of children but not developed an in-depth rights-specific analysis of state obligations in this area that can facilitate effective monitoring of national implementation.[82] The specific manner in which the CEDAW Committee has addressed the economic and social rights of women and girls, which is also reflected in the 2030 Sustainable Development Goals, can be used even now at the national level to address this gap so that the overlap can be advantageous to both women and girls.

The capabilities approach to development that interprets the foundation of human rights as the right to enjoy opportunities that facilitate a person's capacity to enhance their full human potential has been discussed in relation to adult men and women.[83] The vulnerability approach to children in development planning focuses on survival and development rights and tends to ignore children's agency and participation rights. The capabilities approach resonates with the indivisibility of human rights, and the importance of economic and social rights, sometimes described inappropriately as welfare, connoting discretion in state obligation.[84] The capabilities approach, integrated into the human rights and development discourse, results in cross-fertilization in a way that is in line with the interdependence of women's and children's rights but also the indivisibility of rights. This can help to connect women's rights and children's rights in programming and resource allocation at the national level, reinforcing the complementarity of the CEDAW and the CRC.

The Committee on the Rights of the Child has, in its General Comments, addressed the obligation of the state and the corporate sector to promote and protect children's rights as they engage in development activities within countries.[85] Although the obligation of the state is a primary one, the obligation of protection imposes a duty to ensure that the corporate sector does not undermine children's rights. Women's situation in the workplace, and its impact on children's rights, is specifically highlighted in the CRC's General Comments.[86] Women's and children's rights can both be undermined by development initiatives that consider them as a human capital resource in order to carry forward a market-oriented neo-liberal economic project focusing exclusively on economic growth. In the absence of human rights standards that directly apply to the corporate sector, the state obligation to ensure that the rights of both groups are not undermined in development, in a way that recognizes their agency and participation, can make a contribution to a rights-based capabilities approach to development at the national level. Space for the care of children and the elderly, and shared responsibilities of men and women in the family, can address falling birth rates as well as diminished opportunities for women in the area of work and public life.

The interrelated nature of women's rights and children's rights and the potential for recognizing them as complementary rather than in conflict also requires addressing areas of potential conflict. Feminist critiques of human rights sometimes point to the manner in which this project locates rights in an individualistic male-centered equality framework that ignores the importance of an ethic of care and concern in human relationships. The use of *equity* rather than *equality* is advocated by some feminists as a more appropriate conceptual framework for women's rights. However, the CEDAW Committee has gone beyond focusing on a male comparator in the quasi-jurisprudence on the meaning of equality. It has explained and interpreted the core general articles of the CEDAW Convention and the specific rights in terms of substantive equality, moving beyond de jure equality to address de facto discrimination in impact and outcome. This shift focuses on taking account of and addressing women's experiences and their relationship with others in the family and the community. Consequently, the CEDAW Committee has requested state parties to achieve a standard of substantive equality rather than an open-ended discretionary norm of equity.[87]

Substantive equality strengthens the indivisibility of rights norm in relation to both women and children's rights, moving beyond the male adult or boy comparator in addressing the reality of gender-based discrimination. Substantive equality has room for accommodating women and children's agency while avoiding a focus on their seemingly vulnerable situation. A girl is not perceived as just an incapacitated minor who will become a disempowered adult women affected by women's diminished status.[88] The goal of achieving substantive equality encourages an intergenerational approach to the elimination of discrimination against both women and girls in the family and community. The substantive equality concept also reinforces the capabilities approach to the realization of women and children's rights, thereby having the potential to impact positively on the status especially of the girl child, instead of the gender-neutral approach currently adopted in monitoring national commitments under CRC.

There are some hard areas of conflict where the agenda of women and children's rights can undermine each other. Abortion and infanticide committed by women due to the impact of gender-based discrimination and violence place women's rights and child rights activism on a collision course. However, neither the CRC nor the CEDAW Committee has interpreted reproductive rights in a manner that recognizes the rights of an unborn child. The CEDAW Committee has addressed abortion as a reproductive rights and health issue and has required law and policy reform and resource allocation to ensure essential services for women and girls. It has considered criminalization of abortion or restriction on abortion in cases of sexual violence an infringement of women's rights. The CRC's definition of a child as a human being below the age of majority avoids the issue of abortion, leaving it to individual states to determine for themselves.[89]

Women's rights advocates argue that excluding men is critical in custody cases and in cases of domestic violence and that the CRC concept of a child's right of access to a male parent can prejudice decision-making in courts and in service delivery to women affected by violence. However, as observed earlier, gender-based violence is an area where the activism of women's groups has contributed to law and policy reform on domestic violence and on crimes against women and children, especially girls across the globe. The concept of the best interests of the child has also been used in jurisprudence in the courts and in legislation on domestic violence to exclude a violent male partner, so as not to undermine women's rights through children's rights. Recognizing a male parent's rights as responsibilities in setting standards on employment can also be a positive contribution in ensuring non-discrimination and substantive equality in the workplace.[90]

When a horrendous crime like a brutal gang rape is committed by an adolescent against an adult woman or a girl, public pressure to avoid following the norms on child rights in the area of juvenile justice often arises. For example, as already mentioned, the Indian government established legislation to prioritize women's rights after the Nirbhaya case of 2012, a brutal gang rape involving a seventeen-year-old boy. The change in the law was not recommended by a committee appointed to consider reforms to the law on sexual violence against women and chaired by a former chief justice. Experience in comparative law could have helped policy formulation, balancing the best interests of the child and public safety. Populist demands need to be resisted when they create a conflict between the human rights of groups within a society. A balancing of conflicting interests must be prioritized. In this case, a balance was not achieved. The objective of setting deterrent standards for such a grave crime of violence against women and the concept of victims' rights seem to have motivated a change in the law. This denied the seventeen-year-old defendant access to child rights in the juvenile justice system.[91]

Diversity in age thresholds for the purpose of determining the scope of children's rights is a basic dimension of the concept of children's evolving capacity, as reflected in the agenda of human rights of children as well as in the CRC. With increasing use of social media, children are in a position to engage in activism on issues of concern to them as well as to others in the community in general more extensively than could have perhaps ever been envisaged. This poses challenges in regard to determining and interpreting their participation rights and other rights, such as to protection and development. Should children who engage in political activity that also involves acts of terrorism and brutal acts of violence against women be considered entitled to the status of childhood? Can they claim the full range of children's rights, including in the area of juvenile justice, or should they be considered persons with adult rights and responsibilities? When the concept of evolving capacity of a child cannot be interpreted in a manner where it harmonizes with civic responsibility, the time may have come to review the age threshold for majority. Although eighteen is the preferred age of majority, the CRC recognizes in Article 1 that majority can be attained earlier. The age threshold for the status of majority may be changed in line with current knowledge and realities on child development in a given society after a process of objective and professional review that is a necessary part of responsible law and policy reform on the status of minority and majority. What is not acceptable is to prioritize violence against women and women's rights above all other considerations, in ad hoc legislative and or policy reforms, undermining the rights of the person defined as a child according to norms on children's rights and juvenile justice created by ratification of the CRC.[92]

6   CONCLUSION

The CRC incorporates general principles, defines the scope of children's rights, and has been extensively interpreted in the quasi-jurisprudence of the CRC Committee. With near universal ratification, integration of a human rights–based approach to development in the SDGs and national child rights activism, it has become a legitimate benchmark for implementation in diverse national contexts.

Human rights for children now link to the concept of indivisibility of rights and the capabilities approach. Consequently, children's best interest cannot be interpreted in a discretionary manner focusing exclusively on a single dimension of need, welfare, capacity, or autonomy. Evolving capacity and participation rights must also address implementation issues of child development and protection.

Just as limitations on adults' rights ensure a balance in accommodating conflicting interests, achieving such a balance to accommodate the rights of others whose lives connect with children must not be considered an erosion of children's rights. Implementation of children's rights therefore requires addressing in a holistic manner the interrelated nature of diverse rights and connections to the rights of parents and women.

National experience suggests that the incorporation of children's rights in constitutions or comprehensive penal codes encourages such a holistic approach. Ad hoc legislative initiatives can result in fractured and contradictory policies and resource allocation that prevent effective implementation. General Comments are comprehensive interpretations of the above connections. They need to be used at the national level. A joint General Recommendation/Comment from the CEDAW and CRC Committees on gender-based discrimination can help strengthen the norm of substantive equality and contribute to a shift away from the current gender-neutral approach to children's rights.

Notes

1. Laura Lundy, Ursula Kilkelly, and Bronagh Byrne, "Incorporation of the United Nations Convention on the Rights of the Child in Law: A Comparative Review," *International Journal of Children's Rights* 21, no. 3 (2013): 442–463; Enakshi Ganguly Thukral, *Every Right for Every Child: Governance and Accountability* (New Delhi: Routledge, 2012); UNICEF, *Protecting the World's Children: Impact of the Convention on the Rights of the Child in Diverse Legal Systems* (New York: Cambridge University Press, 2007).
2. The *International Journal of Children Rights* (Brill Nijhoff) is a rich resource in this respect and used in this chapter.
3. John Tobin, "Justifying Children's Rights," *International Journal of Children's Rights* 21, no. 3 (2013): 442–441.
4. UNICEF, Protecting the World's Children.
5. Tobin, "Justifying Children's Rights," 419; UN Convention on the Rights of the Child, art. 20(3), G.A. Res. 44/25, 44th Sess., UN Doc. A/RES/44/25 (1989); Shaheen Sardar Ali, "A Comparative Perspective of the Convention on the Rights of the Child and the Principles of Islamic Law," in UNICEF, *Protecting the World's Children*, 142–208; Smitu Kothar and Sethi Harsh, *Rethinking Human Rights: Challenges for Theory and Action* (New York: New Horizon Press, 1989).
6. Michael Freeman, "Why It Remains Important to Take Children's Rights Seriously," *International Journal of Children's Rights* 15, no 1 (2007): 5–23.

7. Abdullahi An-Naim, "Introduction," in *Human Rights in Cross-Cultural Perspectives: A Quest for Consensus*, ed. Abdullahi An-Naim (Philadelphia: University of Pennsylvania Press, 1992), 1–15.

8. Henry Stiener and Philip Alston, eds., *International Human Rights in Context: Law, Politics, and Morals*, 2nd ed. (Oxford: Oxford University Press, 2000), 539–553, 549; Bangkok Declaration of Government (1993), paras. 7 and 8.

9. Norman Lewis, "Human Rights Law and Democracy in an Unfree World," in *Human Rights Fifty Years On: A Reappraisal*, ed. Tony Evans (Manchester: Manchester University Press, 1998).

10. Lewis, "Human Rights Law," 92–94.

11. UN Commission on Sustainable Development, "Transforming Our World: The 2030 Agenda for Sustainable Development," G.A. Res. 70/1, 70th Sess., UN Doc. A/RES/70/1 (Oct. 21, 2015), preamble, paras. 10, 17, 19, goals 3, 4, 16.2, 16.9 (Oct. 21, 2015).

12. *See* Lundy, Kilkelly, and Byrne, "Incorporation"; UNICEF, *Protecting the World's Children*.

13. Erwin Spiro, *Law of Parent and Child*, 4th ed. (Cape Town: Juta and Co. Ltd, 1985); Sardar Ali, "Comparative Perspective," 148, 179; David Pearl, *A Textbook on Muslim Personal Law* (Kent, UK: Croom Helm Ltd., 1987), 42; UNICEF, *Protecting the World's Children*.

14. Universal Declaration of Human Rights, preamble, para. 1, G.A. Res. 217 (III) A, UN Doc. A/RES/217(III) (Dec. 10, 1948); International Covenant on Civil and Political Rights, preamble, para. 1, 999 UNTS 171 (1966; entered into force March 23, 1976); International Covenant on Economic, Social and Cultural Rights, preamble, para. 1, 993 UNTS 3 (1966;, entered into force Jan. 3, 1976).

15. Universal Declaration of Human Rights, arts. 22, 23, 25, 26.

16. Universal Declaration of Human Rights, arts. 25(2), 26(1) (3).

17. International Covenant on Civil and Political Rights, preamble, para. 3.

18. See generally, International Covenant on Civil and Political Rights, art. 3.

19. International Covenant on Civil and Political Rights, arts. 10(2)(b), 10(3) (juvenile justice), 23(4) (protection of rights as "minor"), 24.

20. J. P. Unni Krishnan & Ors. v. State of Andhra Pradesh & Ors., Supreme Court of India AIR 217 (Feb. 4, 1993); Sheela Barse & ANR v. Union of India & Ors., Supreme Court of India, AIR 1773 (Aug. 5, 1986); Lakshmi Kant Pandey v. Union of India, Supreme Court of India, AIR 469 (Feb. 6, 1984); Savitri Goonesekere, "Child Rights: The Principle of Nondiscrimination," in *Child Rights the Sri Lanka Experience* (Nawala, Sri Lanka: Open University, 1998), 27–38; Dinesha Samararatne, "Judicial Protection of Human Rights," in *Sri Lanka: State of Human Rights* (Colombo, Sri Lanka: Law and Society Trust, 2014), 25–67, 38–43; The Constitution of India, art. 86, amend. 21(a) (1949).

21. International Covenant on Economic, Social and Cultural Rights, preamble, paras. 2, 3.

22. International Covenant on Economic, Social and Cultural Rights, art. 12; Universal Declaration of Human Rights, art. 25.

23. Convention on the Elimination of all Forms of Discrimination against Women, arts. 3, 10, 11, 12, 1249 UNTS 13 (1979; entered into force Sept. 3, 1981); Convention on the Rights of the Child, arts. 4, 24, 26, 27, 28; UN Committee on the Rights of the Child, *General Comment No. 5: General Measures of Implementation of the Convention on the Rights of* the Child, CRC/GC/2003/5 (2003) para. 6; Optional Protocol to the International Covenant on Economic, Social and Cultural Rights, G.A. Res. 63/117, 63rd Sess., UN Doc. A/RES/63/117 (2009).

24. European Social Charter, ETS 163 (1996); American Convention on Human Rights, art. 26 (1969; entered into force July 18, 1978); Additional Protocol to the American Convention on Human Rights in the Area of Economic, Social and Cultural Rights, "Protocol of San Salvador" (1988); African Charter on Human and Peoples' Rights, arts. 15, 16, 17, OAU Doc. CAB/LEG/67/3 rev. 5, 21 ILM. 58 (1982; entered into force Oct. 21, 1986); African Charter on the Rights and Welfare of the Child, OAU Doc. CAB/LEG/24.9/49 (1990); see also, Lundy, Kilkelly, and Byrne, "Incorporation"; UNICEF, *Protecting the World's Children*.

25. Optional Protocol to the Convention on the Rights of the Child on a Communications Procedure, preamble, paras. 4, 5, G.A. Res. 66/138, 66th Sess., UN Doc. A/RES/66/138 (Dec. 19, 2011; entered into force April 14, 2014).

26. Freeman, "Why It Remains Important," 401–404; Freddy Mortier, "Competence in Children: A Philosophical Perspective," In *Understanding Children's Rights: Collected Papers Presented at the Second International Interdisciplinary Course on Children's Rights, Held at the University of Ghent*, ed. Eugeen Verhellen (Ghent: University of Ghent, 1997), 99–114.

27. UN Committee on the Rights of the Child, *I.A.M. v. Denmark, Communication No. 3/2016*, CRC/C/77/D/3/2016 (Jan. 25, 2018) (deportation order against Somali girl challenged successfully for violation of rights guaranteed under CRC); see also, UN Human Rights Office of the High Commissioner's About the Jurisprudence database, juris.ohchr.org/en/search/results?Bodies5&sortOrder=Date (inadmissible communications). Like other complaints mechanisms, the CRC Optional Protocol requires individuals to exhaust domestic remedies before filing a complaint under the Protocol.

28. Committee on Economic, Social and Cultural Rights, *General Comment No. 3: The Nature of States Parties' Obligations*, UN Doc. HRI/Gen/1/Rev. 1 (1990), 45; Committee on Economic, Social and Cultural Rights, *General Comment No. 16: Substantive Issues Arising in the Implementation of the International Covenant on Economic, Social and Cultural Rights*, UN Doc. E/C.12/2005/4 (2005), para. 17.

29. UN Committee on the Rights of the Child, *General Comment No. 16 (2013) on State Obligations Regarding the Impact of the Business Sector*, CRC/C/GC/16 (April 17, 2013), sect. iv; UN Committee on the Elimination of All Forms of Discrimination against Women and UN Committee on the Rights of the Child, *Joint General Recommendation No. 31 of the Committee on the Elimination of Discrimination against Women/General Comment No. 18 of the Committee on the Rights of the Child on Harmful Practices*, CEDAW/C/GC/31-CRC/C/GC/18 (Nov. 14, 2014), sect. 4, para. 10; UN Committee on the Rights of the Child, *General Comment No. 15 (2013) on the Right of the Child to the Enjoyment of the Highest Attainable Standard of Health (art. 24)*, CRC/C/GC/15 (April 17, 2013), sect. iv.

30. UNICEF, *Protecting the World's Children*; Philip Alston, ed., *The Best Interests of the Child* (Oxford: Oxford University Press, 1994); E. Kay Tisdall, Jane Brown, and M. Docherty, "Children's Best Interests versus Public Safety: How Are They Balanced," *International Journal of Children's Rights* 6, no. 4 (1998): 395–405.

31. UN Committee on the Rights of the Child, *General Comment No. 14 (2013) on the Right of the Child to Have His or Her Best Interests Taken as a Primary Consideration (art. 3, para. 1)*, CRC/C/GC/14 (May 29, 2013), paras. 1(A)(4), 32; UN Committee on the Rights of the Child, *General Comment No. 5*, para. 12.

32. U.N. Committee on the Rights of the Child, *General Comment No. 8 (2006): The Right of the Child to Protection from Corporal Punishment and Other Cruel or Degrading Forms of*

Punishment, CRC/C/GC/8 (March 2, 2007), para. 26; UN Committee on the Rights of the Child, *General Comment No. 12 (2009): The Right of the Child to Be Heard*, CRC/C/GC/12 (July 20, 2009), para. 74; UN Committee on the Rights of the Child, *I.A.M. v. Denmark*.

33. UN Committee on the Rights of the Child, *General Comment No. 12*.

34. UN Committee on the Rights of the Child, *General Comment No. 15*, sect. F.

35. UN Committee on the Rights of the Child, *General Comment No. 15*, para. 68; UN Committee on the Rights of the Child, *General Comment No. 8*, paras. 2, 7.

36. CRC, art. 12; UN Committee on the Rights of the Child, *General Comment No. 12*, paras. 1, 20; UN Committee on the Rights of the Child, *General Comment No. 20 (2016) on the Implementation of the Rights of the Child during Adolescence*, CRC/C/GC/20 (Dec. 6, 2016). paras. 5, 19, 39, 84–86.

37. U.N. Committee on the Rights of the Child, *General Comment No. 20*.

38. U.N. Committee on the Rights of the Child, *General Comment No. 20*.

39. Beatrice Akua Duncan, *Global Perspectives on Consolidated Children's Rights Statutes* (New York: UNICEF, 2008), ii, iii, https://www.unicef.org/policyanalysis/files/postscript_Childrens_Codes_formatted_final.pdf; Lundy, Kilkelly, and Byrne, "Incorporation," 442, 451; UNICEF, *Protecting the World's Children*, 5–9.

40. John Tobin, "Increasingly Seen and Heard: The Constitutional Recognition of Children's Rights," *South African Journal on Human Rights* 21 (2005): 86–126; UNICEF, *Protecting the World's Children*; Centre on Housing Rights and Evictions (COHRE), *Litigating Economic Social and Cultural Rights: Achievements, Challenges and Strategies, Featuring 21 Case Studies* (Geneva: COHRE, 2003), https://www.right-to-education.org/sites/right-to-education.org/files/resource-attachments/COHRE_Litigating_Esc_Rights_2003_en.pdf; Child Rights International Network, "CRC in Court," CRIN case law database, https://archive.crin.org/en/home/law/research/crc-court-case-law-database.html.

41. Indian Constitution, Article 21-A (Eighty Sixth Amendment Act 2002); Parliament of India, Right to Free and Compulsory Education Act, Act No. 35 (2009); Shantha Sinha, "Overcoming Barriers for Getting Children Out of Work and Into Schools," in *Every Right for Every Child: Governance and Accountability*, ed. Enakshi Ganguly Thukral (New Delhi: Routledge, 2011), 156–178.

42. Yoshie Noguchi, "ILO Convention No 182 on the Worst Forms of Child Labour and the Convention on the Rights of the Child," *International Journal of Children's Rights* 10, no. 4 (2002): 355–369.

43. UNICEF, *Early Marriage: A Harmful Traditional Practice* (New York: UNICEF, 2005); UN Committee on the Elimination of All Forms of Discrimination against Women and Committee on the Rights of the Child, *Joint General Recommendation No. 31/General Comment No. 18*; Pallavi Gupta, "Child Marriages and the Law: Contemporary Concerns," *Economic and Political Weekly* 47, no. 43 (Oct. 27, 2012): 49–55.

44. Independent Thought v. Union of India, Supreme Court of India, Writ Petition Civil 382 of 2013 (Oct. 11 2017); Criminal Law Amendment Act (2013), Act No. 13 of 2013 (age of consent raised from sixteen in penal code to eighteen years for rape); Prohibition of Child Marriage Act (2006+), No. 6 of 2007 (marriage age for girls, eighteen); Protection of Children from Sexual Offences Act, Parliament of India (2012).

45. Paulo Sérgio Pinheiro, *World Report on Violence against Children* (Geneva: UN Publishing Services, 2006), 312–316.

46. UN Standard Minimum Rules for the Administration of Juvenile Justice ("Beijing Rules"), G.A. Res. 40/33, UN Doc. A/RES/40/33 (Nov. 29, 1985); CRC, art. 40.

47. UN Optional Protocol to the Convention on the Rights of the Child on the Involvement of Children in Armed Conflict, G.A. Res. 54/263, 54th Sess., UN Doc. A/RES/54/263 (2000; entered into force Feb. 12, 2002).

48. Pinheiro, *World Report on Violence*, 306, 320; Daniel Evans, "Forgotten Voices in Forgotten Conflict," *International Journal of Children's Rights* 24, no. 1 (2016): 65–92, 74–80.

49. Juvenile Justice (Care and Protection of Children) Act (2015), § 15(1), No. 2 of 2016, Parliament of India; Gauri Pillai and Upadhyay Shrikrishna, "Juvenile Maturity and Heinous Crimes: A Re-Look at Juvenile Justice Policy in India," *NUJS Law Review* 10, no 1 (2017): 49–82.

50. UN Committee on the Rights of the Child, *General Comment No. 10: Children's Rights in Juvenile Justice*, UN Doc. CRC/C/GC/10 (2007); Tisdall, Brown, and Docherty, "Children's Best Interests."

51. Universal Declaration of Human Rights, preamble, art. 1(3); art. 6, para. 1; art. 12 (family privacy); M. V. Pylee, *Select Constitutions of the World* (New Delhi: Universal Publishing Co., 2006).

52. Universal Declaration of Human Rights, art. 29(1), (2).

53. International Covenant on Economic, Social and Cultural Rights, preamble, para. 2, art. 4 (limitations), art. 10(1) (protection for family); International Covenant on Civil and Political Rights, preamble. para. 2, art. 12(3) (limitations), art. 23 (1) (protection of family).

54. CRC, preamble, paras. (1), 5, 6.

55. CRC, arts. 3(2) 5, 9, 14(2), 19(1).

56. CRC, arts. 5, 14(2).

57. UN Committee on the Rights of the Child, *General Comment No. 5*," para. (1), 66.

58. UN Committee on the Rights of the Child, *General comment No. 8*, paras. 26, 27, 28; UN Committee on the Rights of the Child, *General Comment No. 12*; UN Committee on the Rights of the Child, *General Comment No. 14*, paras. 4, 34, 39, 67; UN Committee on the Rights of the Child, *General Comment No. 13 (2011): The Right of the Child to Freedom from All Forms of Violence*, CRC/C/GC/13 (2011), para. 72(d); UN Committee on the Rights of the Child, *General Comment No. 15*, paras. 20–22, 67, 78; UN Committee on the Rights of the Child, *General Comment No. 20*.

59. Michael Cretney, *Principles of Family Law*, 3rd ed. (London: Sweet and Maxwell, 1979), 429–430; Spiro, *Law of Parent and Child*, 1–3, 257.

60. Tobin, "Justifying Children," 423–432; Esther Erlings, "Is Anything Left of Children's Rights?," *International Journal of Children's Rights* 24, no. 3 (2016): 624–657.

61. Erlings, "Is Anything Left?"; Lewis, "Human Rights Law," 92–94.

62. Bernadette J. Saunders, "Ending the Physical Punishment of Children by Parents in the English Speaking World: The Impact of Language Tradition and Law," *International Journal of Children's Rights* 21, no 2 (2013): 278–304; UN Committee on the Rights of the Child, *General Comment No. 13*.

63. Karen A. Polonko, Lucien X. Lombardo, and Ian M. Bollling, "Law Reform, Child Maltreatment and the UN Convention on the Rights of the Chil,d" *International Journal of Children Rights* 24, no. 1 (2016): 29–64.

64. Erlings, "Is Anything Left?"; Geraldine Van Buueren, "Children's Rights: Balancing Traditional Values and Cultural Plurality," in Verhellen, *Understanding Children's Rights*, 375–385.

65. Sylvie Langlande Doné, "Children and Religion under Article 14 UNCRC: A Critical Analysis," *International Journal of Children's Rights* 16, no. 4 (2008): 475–504; UN Committee on the Rights of the Child, *I.A.M. v. Denmark*.

66. Gillick v. West Norfolk & Wisbech Health Authority [1986] AC 112.

67. Savitri Goonesekere, *Children Law and Justice: A South Asian Perspective* (New Delhi: UNICEF, 1998), 310–348 (chap. 8: Participation Rights).

68. Savitri Goonesekere, *Women's Rights and Children's Rights: The United Nations Conventions as Compatible and Complementary to International Treaties* (Florence: UNICEF Innocenti Research Centre, 1992).

69. Personal experience of author in 1992 as a participant from Sri Lanka.

70. Goonesekere, *Women's Rights and Children's Rights*; Women's Commission for Refugee Women and Children, *Masculinities: Male Roles and Male Involvement in the Promotion of Gender Equality* (New York: Women's Commission for Refugee Women and Children, 2005), https://www.womensrefugeecommission.org/resources/viewDocument/292.

71. Erica Burman, "Beyond 'Women vs. Children' or 'Women and Children': Engendering Childhood and Reformulating Motherhood," *International Journal of Children's Rights* 16, no. 2 (2008): 177–194.

72. Cynthia Price Cohen, "The United Nations Convention on the Rights of the Child: A Feminist Landmark," *William and Mary Journal of Women and Law* 3 (1997): 29–78; Jonathan Todres, "Women's Rights and Children Rights: A Partnership with Benefits for Both," *Cardozo Women's Law Journal* 10 (2004): 603–624; Goonesekere, *Children Law and Justice*; UNICEF, *Protecting the World's Children*; Marsha Freeman, Christine Chinkin, and Beate Rudolf, eds., *The UN Convention on the Elimination of All forms of Discrimination against Women: A Commentary* (Oxford: Oxford University Press, 2012).

73. World Conference on Human Rights Vienna Declaration and Programme of Action, UN Doc. A/CONF.157/23 (June 12, 1993), para. 2.

74. Vienna Declaration and Programme of Action, sect. 1, para. 5 (universality indivisibility and interdependence), para. 18 (women and girls), part II (B), sect. 3 (women rights), sect. 4 (children's rights), sect. 4, para. 49 (girl child).

75. UN Committee on the Elimination of All Forms of Discrimination against Women, *General Recommendation No. 25, on Article 4, Paragraph 1, of the Convention on the Elimination of All Forms of Discrimination against Women, on Temporary Special Measures* (2004), https://tbinternet.ohchr.org/Treaties/CEDAW/Shared%20Documents/1_Global/INT_CEDAW_GEC_3733_E.pdf (accessed Aug. 8, 2019); UN Committee on the Elimination of Discrimination against Women, *General Recommendation No. 24: Article 12 of the Convention (Women and Health)*, A/54/38/Rev.1 (1999); Freeman, Chinkin, and Rudolph, *UN Convention on the Elimination of All forms of Discrimination against Women*. See also the emblematic cases referred to in note 90, below.

76. UN Committee on the Elimination of All Forms of Discrimination against Women, *General Recommendation No. 35 on Gender-Based Violence against Women, Updating General Recommendation No. 19*, CEDAW/C/GC/35 (2017), para. 14.

77. UN Committee on the Rights of the Child, *General Comment No. 15*, para. 71; *General Comment No. 18*, para. 10; *General Comment No. 5*, para. 6.

78. Optional Protocol to the Convention on the Rights of the Child on a Communications Procedure, para 3; UN Committee on the Rights of the Child, *I.A.M. v Denmark*.

79. UN Committee on the Rights of the Child, *General Comment No. 20*, paras. 27–28 (girls); *General Comment No. 16*, para. 54 (women); *General Comment No. 15*, paras. 18, 34, 44, 51 (women).

80. UN Committee on the Elimination of All Forms of Discrimination against Women and Committee on the Rights of the Child, *Joint General Recommendation No. 31/General*

Comment No. 18; UN Committee on the Elimination of All Forms of Discrimination against Women, *General Recommendation No. 35*; UN Committee on the Rights of the Child, *I.A.M. v. Denmark.*

81. Burman, "Beyond 'Women vs. Children' "; UN Commission on Sustainable Development "Transforming Our World," preamble, para. 3, para. 10 (respect for international law UDHR and Human Rights treaties), target 1.2 (poverty women children), target 2.2 (poverty women and children) target 2.2 (women and children and nutrition), targets 4.1, 4.3 (women and girls education), goal 5 (gender equality and employment of women and girls), targets 16.1 and 16.2 (inclusive societies; access to justice, reducing violence, including abuse, trafficking, and torture of children), goal 3 (health only) (in regard to maternal and child mortality and reproductive health in targets 3.1 and 3.2, 3.7).

82. Aoife Nolan, "Economic and Social Rights Budgets and the Convention on the Right of the Child." *International Journal of Children's Rights* 21, no 2 (2013): 248–277.

83. Amartya Sen, *Development as Freedom* (Oxford: Oxford University Press, 1999).

84. Rosalind Dixon and Martha Nussbaum, "Children's Rights and the Capability Approach: The Question of Special Priority," *Cornell Law Review* 97 (May 2012): 541–593; Martha C. Nussbaum, *Women and Human Development: The Capabilities Approach* (Cambridge: Cambridge University Press, 2001).

85. UN Committee on the Rights of the Child, *General Comment No. 16*, paras. 8–11 (introduction and objectives), section iv(B).

86. UN Committee on the Rights of the Child, *General Comment No. 16*, para. 54 (women's rights as parents and children rights).

87. Fiona Robinson, "The Limits of a Rights Based Approach to International Ethics," in Evans, *Human Rights Fifty Years On*, 58–76; Carol Gilligan, *In a Different Voice: Psychological Theory and Women's Development* (Cambridge, MA: Harvard University Press, 1993); Patricia A. Cain, "Feminism and the Limits of Equality," *Georgia Law Review* 24, no. 4 (1990): 803–847; Alda Facio and Martha I. Morgan, "Equity or Equality for Women? Understanding CEDAW's Equality Principles," *IWRAW Asia Pacific Occasional Paper Series* No. 14 (2009); Freeman, Chinkin, and Rudolph, *UN Convention on the Elimination of All forms of Discrimination against Women*, arts. 1, 3.

88. Andrew Byrnes, "Article 1," in Freeman, Chinkin, and Rudolph, *UN Convention on the Elimination of All forms of Discrimination against Women*, 51–70; UN Committee on the Elimination of All Forms of Discrimination against Women, *General Recommendation No. 25*; UN Committee on the Elimination of Discrimination against Women, *General Recommendation No. 28 on the Core Obligations of States Parties under Article 2 of the Convention on the Elimination of All Forms of Discrimination against Women*, CEDAW/C/GC/28 (Dec. 16, 2010).

89. CRC, art 1; Rebecca J. Cook and Verónica Undurraga, "Article 12," in Freeman, Chinkin, and Rudolph, *UN Convention on the Elimination of All forms of Discrimination against Women*, 311–334.

90. Emblematic cases: Vishaka v. Rajastha (1997) 6 SCC 241 (India; rape of social worker campaigning for abolition of child marriages); Mathura rape case (1979) (India; rape of girl, leading to law reform); child prostitution catalyst for reforms on gender-based violence in the penal code of Sri Lanka (1995), discussed in Savitri Goonesekere, ed., *Violence Law and Women's Rights in South Asia* (New Delhi: Sage, 2004); Muktharan Mai gang rape case (Pakistan 2002); and Zainab child rape case (Pakistan 2018), discussed in Goonesekere, *Children Law and Justice*, chapter 5; Frances Raday, "Article 11," in Freeman, Chinkin, and

Rudolph, *UN Convention on the Elimination of All forms of Discrimination against Women*, 279–309.

91. Juvenile Justice (Care and Protection of Children) Act (2015), §§ 5, 15; Gauri and Upadyay, "Juvenile Maturity"; Tisdall, Brown, and Docherty, "Children's Best Interests."

92. A. West, "Children and Political Participation," in Verhellen, *Understanding Children's Rights*, 375–385; Evans, "Forgotten Voices," 65–92; Stuart Haslen, "The Use of Children as Soldiers: The Right to Kill and be Killed," *International Journal of Children's Rights* 6, no. 4 (1998): 445–451; Gauri and Upadyay, "Juvenile Maturity."

PART II

PERSPECTIVES AND METHODS

CHAPTER 5

....

A CHILD-CENTERED
APPROACH TO
CHILDREN'S RIGHTS LAW
Living Rights and Translations

....

KARL HANSON AND OLGA NIEUWENHUYS

1 INTRODUCTION

....

SHORTLY after the adoption of the Convention on the Rights of the Child (CRC) by the UN General Assembly on November 20, 1989, many observers commended the Convention for radically breaking with the then prevailing paternalistic approach to children. Thomas Hammarberg, a Swedish diplomat and human rights defender, wrote in 1990: "More than any earlier international agreement, the Convention recognizes children as human beings of equal value. It marks the end of the age-old idea that children, at least in legal terms, are no more than possessions of their guardians. At the same time, it recognizes children as children. The importance of a happy childhood is accepted for its own sake."[1] One year later, Hammarberg became one of the first ten members of the Committee on the Rights of the Child, a function he exercised between 1991 and 1997. Hammarberg was a strong supporter of Article 12 of the CRC, which asserts the right of a child to express his or her views and was designated by the CRC Committee as one of the Convention's four "general principles."[2] Article 12 has been a source of inspiration and has provided an international normative backup for the idea that children have participation rights and are to be considered as autonomous human beings.[3] Martin Woodhead aptly summarizes the consensus among many authors about the importance of children's participation rights as follows:

> The individual child is no longer to be viewed merely as an object of concern, care and protection, whose life and destiny are shaped and regulated by laws, institutions,

parents and professionals, acting in what they judge to be the child's interests. Henceforth, children are also to be recognised (and supported towards recognising themselves) as active in the process of shaping their lives, learning and future. They have their own view on their best interests, a growing capacity to make decisions, the right to speak and the right to be heard.[4]

The ideas of living rights and translations, we contend, help explore the consequences of recognizing children's right to contribute to conceptualizations of what their rights are.[5] But before discussing living rights and translations, we will first explain how we came to these concepts through a critique of essentialist understandings of children's rights, which we will illustrate in section 1 with a short portrait of the 2014 Nobel Peace Prize recipients, Kailash Satyarthi and Malala Yousafzai. Section 2 builds further on this example to unpack universalism and cultural relativism and looks at the importance of local realities and practices for considering children's rights and autonomy. In section 3, we discuss how the living rights concept recognizes children's rights as a form of embodiment and helps highlight that rights are what they become in everyday practice. In an effort to recognize children as active subjects of rights, we advocate an inclusive approach that accepts a degree of indeterminacy and even contradiction. The notion of translations, as we explore in section 4, explains the importance of this non-essentialist stand. Taking the perspective of children as bodily beings-in-the-world, embodiment acknowledges children's relatedness, that knowledge about children's rights is embedded in specific contexts with their own history, language, and values, and that there are always multiple readings at play in a given situation. We conclude with some examples of how the living rights and translations framework can be mobilized to further explore a child-centered approach to children's rights law.

2 ESSENTIALIST UNDERSTANDINGS
OF CHILDREN'S RIGHTS

The understanding that children, like other human beings, have fundamental rights, which had long been contested, has now become a mainstream idea. However, the overall acceptance of children's rights does not imply the existence of a broad consensus of its meaning or consequences. Academic literature on the UN Convention on the Rights of the Child, for instance, contains both abundant praise for the Convention and its achievements as well as severe criticism.[6] When children's rights are presented in general terms, as is the case on websites and in brochures of international child protection agencies, children's rights are mostly conceived in terms of their essence, or indispensable conceptual characteristics, rather than their concrete, experienced existence. As the portraits of the 2014 Nobel Peace Prize recipients in this section illustrate, at least two forms of essentialism are at work here. The first relies on a paternalist view of

the world and assumes that experts, based on their experience and knowledge stemming from such fields as developmental psychology, social work, human rights law, or
humanitarian advocacy, are better able than the children concerned to understand what
children's rights are. The second form makes children themselves the central spokesper-
sons of their rights but tends to recognize only those children's voices attuned to what
experts contend.

In 2014 the Nobel Peace Prize was awarded to two advocates for children's rights,
sixty-year-old Kailash Satyarthi, a long-standing activist in the fight against child labor
in India, and Malala Yousafzai, a seventeen-year-old campaigner for girls' right to education in Pakistan. In his Nobel lecture held on December 10, 2014, at Oslo City Hall,
Satyarthi offered the archetype of the first form of essentialism to children's rights.[7] He
pointed at one empty chair in the majestic city hall and contended that it was reserved
for the millions of invisible children who are left behind and cannot speak for themselves. The empty chair represents a powerful metaphor of the paternalist claim that
children would remain unprotected without the intervention of authoritative adult representatives for whom saving them from harm is a moral duty. Satyarthi's claim that he
was speaking on behalf of millions of invisible children is emblematic of an approach
that considers children as inherently different from adults and, because of their physical
weakness, immaturity or inexperience, as needing the help of well-meaning and caring
adults to guide and protect them. Besides being a moral duty for individual adults, this
form of essentialism based on paternalism has informed the setting up of separate legal
and institutional arrangements for children, such as specialized juvenile justice and
child protection systems and legislation and policies that aim at the abolishment of child
labor.[8] These kinds of specialized systems and legislation for children are generally seen
as beneficial for children, as they aim to secure children's protection rights. However,
separate regimes have also prohibited children from relying on certain fundamental
rights, such as the legal guarantees prevailing in the adult criminal justice system or the
regulation of labor conditions included in general labor legislation.

Contrary to an essentialist understanding, we do not think that the mere existence
of separate rules and mechanisms for children improves respect for children's rights.
Specialized arrangements can indeed increase children's protection, but they can also
have detrimental consequences for children. This is especially the case with separate
childhood laws having the dual goal of improving the protection of both children and
society. Paternalist arguments may then refer to children's inherent vulnerability and
inexperience to promote change in a desired direction. Satyarthi illustrates this idea
when, in his Nobel lecture, he cites Mahatma Gandhi's claim that if we want peace in this
world, we must begin with children. Here the goal is not the well-being of children, who
are merely the instruments to bring about change, but the future of world peace.[9] The
separate legislation and programs that target the elimination of child labor are not only
paternalistic, as they decide for the children concerned what is best for them; they are
also less concerned with the well-being of children than with such economic issues as
fair competition and a level playing field. Representing the individual child in isolation,

these laws and programs have diverted attention away from social and economic inequalities or discrimination underlying both children's and adults' exploitation. Protectionism, in short, separates children from the general human rights framework and diminishes, paradoxically, their legal status.[10]

But not all essentializing positions are paternalistic or the preserve of adults; a second form of essentialism makes children the almost exclusive representatives of their rights but only in so far as their views agree with those of the paternalists. In his Nobel lecture, Satyarthi, in tune with his paternalist stance, addressed joint recipient Yousafzai as "my dear daughter Malala." Having been the victim at age fifteen of an assassination attempt by the Taliban because of her engagement with girls' right to education, Yousafzai was the youngest Nobel recipient ever. A child herself, Yousafzai is emblematic of the belief that a child is the best natural defender of his or her rights. This is illustrated in her 2014 Nobel lecture, in which, departing from the savior tone of her co-recipient, she claimed that being a child makes her the voice of all children claiming the right to education.[11] Her claim contains the idea that only children can speak for other children and ignores children's diversity and contrasting viewpoints about their right to education. Yousafzai's position reflects schools of thought in childhood research which contend that children are "the most authentic source of knowledge about themselves and their lives."[12] It is important to consider, though, that this authenticity may veil that voice is often entrenched in the agenda of people or organizations that lend legitimacy to and interpret rights claims. In the case of the Malala Fund, a children's rights NGO that Yousafzai and her father Ziauddin Yousafzai founded in 2013 to promote the right of girls to education, a board of directors oversees strategic decisions about the organization's mission, work plan, program, staff, and budget. The board's adult members include senior staff members from private companies (McKinsey & Company, Unilever), private philanthropic foundations (Open Society Institute, Aman Foundation, Obama Foundation), and a UN Sustainable Development Goals Advocate.[13] As critics have remarked, Malala's voice remains mute when it comes to the wider geopolitical context of children's rights violations in war zones.[14]

Observing how children's voices in this example are subordinated to powerful global humanitarian actors helps one understand that the positions held by both Nobel Peace Prize recipients, even if they are informed by a different form of essentialism, are closely related. Where Satyarthi referred to children as harbingers of peace, the Malala Fund sees secondary education for girls as an instrument to transform society. Girls' right to education is, according to the organization's website, "an investment in economic growth, a healthier workforce, lasting peace and the future of our planet." Yousafzai's success in mobilizing powerful people to help advance her cause is possible, in sum, because her rights claims resonate with their values and worldviews. Despite their apparent antagonism, both Satyarthi and Yousafzai share a common moral ground that takes the convergence of children's interests and those of their powerful protectors for granted. When they refer to children's rights, they do so by using only vague and general terms and by providing merely some anecdotal evidence of instances where children's rights are violated. They build on the assumption that is possible to capture the essence of children's rights by making abstractions of their own beliefs about children, the social, economic, political, and institutional contexts in which their interpretations of children's rights are produced, the particular usages of language, and the prevailing ideological and discursive climates.[15]

3 Culture, Rights, and Autonomy

The Nobel Peace Prize recipients' heroic profiles would be meaningless without the powerful enemy confronting them in the form of carefully entertained representations of cultures deemed ignorant or resistant to what they consider enlightened insights about children's rights. Kailash Satyarthi's campaign against child labor acquires its meaning from a carefully constructed representation of India as a caste-based society condemning the children of the lower castes to a life of ignorance and drudgery. Malala Yousafzai's Pakistan is, likewise, typecast as the land where Islam denies girls the right to education. Although there is, of course, some truth in these representations, they tend to gloss over local forms of resistance and to typically portray children as passive victims utterly dependent on outside intervention. We argue that these representations are difficult to reconcile with the recognition of children's ability to understand and exercise rights. But they also incriminate whole cultures of abusing children, implicitly positing Western values as the best guarantors of children's (and human) rights. A critical position toward the values embedded in one's own culture—or cultural relativism—is, however, not only the heuristic device that enables social anthropologists to make sense of other cultures but also, more widely, a condition for acknowledging the equality of all people, irrespective of cultures. This means that all cultures need to be assessed on their own merits and that no culture is superior to another. Children's rights, therefore, cannot be assessed as globally removed from local culture contexts and instead be based on a priori defined criteria because there is no way of establishing such criteria outside the scope of a specific cultural context, of which Western is only one.[16] Attempts at doing so would not only be pointless, but potentially harmful, as they may instill a sense of inferiority in those accused of belonging to the wrong culture and stifle attempts at resolving conflict and coming up with solutions tailored to their specific situations.

In the case of Sierra Leone's child soldiers, for example, anthropologist Susan Shepler argues that humanitarian agencies have worked with a locally unacceptable notion of childhood innocence and misunderstood the importance of intergenerational exchange. Shepler, importantly, adds that these agencies have uncritically worked with Western interpretations of children's rights and childhood innocence that has made child soldiers' reintegration into local society very problematic. This does not mean taking a cultural relativist stance and positing that aspects of cultures that oppress the young should be ignored. Shepler points at the conflictual nature of Sierra Leonean generational relations against which the former child soldiers had rebelled and suggests that by incriminating culture, the humanitarian agencies also overlooked the importance of this issue.[17]

Essentialist understandings of children's rights not only disregard children's local realities and practices; they also risk undermining children's attempts at securing rights that have a bearing on their specific situations. In other words, both the abstract universalism that incriminates cultures and the apparent alternative, cultural relativism, that ignores the oppressive aspects of cultures tend to perceive the young as incapable of meaningful autonomous action and fail to recognize their agency in claiming and practicing their rights.[18] This is precisely what a child-centered approach to children's rights seeks to address. When children forward rights claims that conflict with their protectors' rights claims, they are not only less likely to garner the same level of support as the more consensual children's rights claims put forward by the 2014 Nobel recipients, for example, but may be met with active containment or even violent suppression. This is the case with sizable numbers of children claiming the right to work in dignity, to take up arms to resist oppression, to make a living on the streets, or to marry and form a family.[19] In social domains that have a positive meaning, such as school councils or local policymaking, children's rights advocates champion children's agency and participation rights. However, "in relation to social domains that have a negative connotation, prevalent children's rights norms, practices and discourses tend to take the opposite viewpoint. When children marry, work, engage in armed conflict or commit a criminal offence, dominant claims no longer emphasize children's capacities or participation but prioritize the protection of vulnerable children."[20] Arguments and positions over which there is disagreement not only illustrate the normative and ideological stakes in debates about children's rights, but they can also open up our thinking about child-centered approaches to children's rights. What should adults do when children make use of their agency and right to autonomy to advance claims with which we disagree? This question provides the starting point for thinking about living rights, a notion we will discuss in the next section.

4 LIVING RIGHTS

In this section, we first explain what we mean by *living rights* and, second, highlight why the concept helps bridge different levels of society engagement in defining, legislating, and realizing the rights of children. We also discuss why the concept is particularly relevant to better understanding the social practices that emerge when different social actors interact across these various levels.

To begin with what living rights are, we wish to make three points: first, children's rights exist even before they are translated into law; second, children's rights are complex and unstable; and, third, the notion of living rights is primarily a heuristic device. We contend that the meaning, interpretation, and practice of children's rights constitute a living, dynamic process. Law is always an unstable translation of ideas of right and wrong that exists at a certain moment in a given situation. Law does not exist in a vacuum, but is embodied. By this we mean that these ideas belong to beings in the world who act and think in a specific context in relation to others. In other words, knowledge and understanding of children's rights are both always situated. Children and people in general, while claiming and putting notions of rights into practice, help shape what these rights are—and become—in the social world. This means that children's rights already exist in practice before they are translated into legal principles and are therefore not the mere product of philosophical, political, and legal deliberations of international institutions or states.

There are many examples in the real world of how children's everyday concerns drive children's rights dynamics. Shareen Hertel describes, for instance, how in 1995 US trade unions sought to discourage garment factories in Bangladesh from employing children by threatening a boycott.[21] Bangladeshi activists soon pointed out that the mere threat had already thrown tens of thousands of children out of employment and left them without means of subsistence. But even if the sacked children held protest meetings in front of the factory gates, the criticisms were brushed aside as an attempt to invoke human rights merely to maintain business. It was only after international agencies, such as UNICEF and Save the Children, had succeeded in mobilizing public opinion in favor of defending Bangladeshi children's right to work that the trade unions understood that the boycott would harm very poor and vulnerable children in unacceptable and unpopular ways, and so they decided to use more child-friendly methods.

By positing that children's rights are alive, we also say that they are complex and unstable, and this is our second point. Individuals representing different local and organizational interests and possessing different kinds of knowledge, skills, and power negotiate an imperfect compromise that may then be partially translated into law. An illustration of this is human rights norms that prescribe age limitations for recruitment and participation in hostilities that result from successful humanitarian advocacy efforts.[22] These norms are based on understandings of the rights of the child that actively contest other conceptions that inform different forms of youth agency during armed conflict. Current international law prohibits the participation in hostilities of any person below the age of eighteen,[23] an age that matches the prevailing ideas about children and youth's vulnerability upheld by the humanitarian actors who succeeded in raising previously lower age limitations. However, age eighteen does not necessarily correspond to how, in specific localities and under certain circumstances, young people conceive of their social, economic, and political responsibilities in times of social instability[24] and thereby might choose to actively participate in armed struggle. The age limitations in international law are particularly challenging when conflicts come to an end and questions arise on how to deal with people younger than eighteen who, in practice, have deliberately participated in armed conflicts. Our point, however, is not to suggest that social practice should override international norms, but to highlight that children's rights are not the fixed outcome of a consensus but can be made to carry many, even contradictory, meanings.[25] How should victims and communities take care of underage soldiers when they have committed atrocities for which they cannot be held accountable because of their young age? Also, how can a society pay tribute to its young fighters who have contributed to ending violent oppression by taking up arms but who cannot be officially recognized for the life-threatening risks they might have taken during past struggles?

Our third point is that living rights are a heuristic device facilitating empirical investigation of how coexisting children's rights practices, ideas, and legal codifications influence a given social arena.[26] Since adoption of the CRC in 1989, divergence and competition over the precise meaning or interpretation of what children's rights are or ought to be have continued, despite numerous persons, agencies, and institutions producing prolific policy, advocacy, and research activities. For example, the question of how to respond to young people who are accused of having committed an offense has been answered in various ways, ranging from welfare to justice to restorative-oriented approaches. Each approach relies on children's rights as a starting point but ends up designing quite different arrangements for dealing with young offenders, ranging from welfare measures to criminal sanctions to reparations for damage caused. Even if the restorative model has been receiving the largest support, international children's rights standards do not as such provide a precise outline for youth justice, but merely present a yardstick against which legislation policies and practice in the field of youth justice can be assessed.[27] This is not surprising considering the diversity and sheer size of the fields in which children's rights are played out and the worldviews and biographies of the people involved, the relative positions and power of the entities that participate in the debate, the kind of rights under discussion, the contexts in which such debates and interpretations occur, the practical considerations of agencies working with children, and so on. We consider extant divergence and competition not as limitations that need to be overcome, but the inevitable results of children's rights being alive and providing an opportunity to better understand how children—while making use of notions of rights—shape what these rights are, and become, in the social world. Emphasizing children's agency in living with and through their rights helps bring the interplay between how children understand their rights and the way others translate and make use of rights claims on children's behalf into the limelight.[28]

This brings us to how the idea of living rights helps bridge the different levels of society in which debates on children's rights play out—such as the global and state level, the intermediary level in which national institutions, civil society, and NGOs operate, and finally the local level from where children's rights claims originate. But before discussing what we feel are the sources of children's rights claims, let us begin with the level that is highest and most prominent in the public eye. The highest level entities, implementing the rights of such vulnerable children as street children, working children, displaced and trafficked children, children orphaned by AIDS, and (former) child soldiers, are the United Nations and affiliated agencies, such as the International Labour Organization (ILO), as well as internationally operating NGOs, such as Save the Children, Terre des Hommes, and international trade union organizations. To coordinate efforts, many of these agencies have embraced the so-called child rights approach, which recognizes that children are legal subjects able to forward claims and negotiate social assumptions and constraints. But the consequences of this approach are very unevenly acknowledged and may often be little more than decoration.

International conventions offer an interpretation of the underlying rights principles, but states, though agreeing with the rights principle that inspired the norm, may not accept the way it has been codified. Take the example of Bolivia and Argentina. In Bolivia, a national debate about children's rights and child labor led to a new law in 2014 that makes it legal for children older than ten to work in certain sectors and under specific circumstances. The government and key civil society actors insist that the law is designed to protect child workers and uphold their rights. In Argentina, by contrast, not only was the minimum working age raised from fourteen to sixteen in 2008, in 2013 the country adopted new legislation that punishes those who employ children under sixteen with up to four years of prison.[29]

One of the reasons why interpretations of international law by states may vary is that society is filled with multiple legal orders, including those sanctioned by custom and religious institutions that regulate behavior and set normative standards by which people from different walks of life abide. The Bolivian state's efforts to recognize indigenous rights and their culturally embedded notions of child upbringing account for some of the differences with Argentina. But the role of civil society and particularly of social movements of working children who actively engaged with the new law is equally important.[30] In other words, the diversity of interpretations owes to the diversity of actors involved, which may include government officials and staff of NGOs, such local institutions as churches, schools, and children's homes but also refugee camps in war zones, the children's kith and kin, and finally the children themselves.

Children's rights are always interpreted and implemented in a given context that is dynamic and potentially conflict-ridden. These conflicts may appear to be about who supposedly owns children's rights at the expense of the children themselves, but this again reiterates the assumption that children would be unable to fully understand and practice their rights. Dailey suggests that this assumption is linked to the liberal belief that only adults can make mature, fully informed, autonomous decisions. She proposes the notion of transitional rights to conceptualize the capacities that children do have rather than those they lack. Drawing from psychoanalysis, she contends that children's emotional, relational, and developmental capacities are the necessary ingredients to become a mature, autonomous, rights-bearing adult.[31] Anthropologists, however, are critical of the very idea that rights-bearers must per se be autonomous individuals. Tatek Abebe proposes the notion of interdependent agency to highlight that both children and adults may conceive of their rights as intimately bound up with those of the collectives to which they belong.[32] Children's rights must include children's conceptions and practices of their rights. Or, to quote Brian Tamanaha's conventionalist way of identifying law emptied of any essentialist feature, "Law is whatever people identify and treat through their social practices as 'law' (or recht, or droit and so on)."[33] Children's rights, in other words, are: "all of the many ways in which social actors across the range talk about, advocate for, criticize, study, legally enact, vernacularize, and so on, the idea of human rights in its different forms."[34]

The experience and exercise of rights can therefore not be made conditional upon enlightened outsiders teaching children and their parents about their rights.[35] What happens if there are no such outsiders? Does this mean that children "are unable to exercise agency and creatively address the challenges of keeping their end up in the most daunting situations?"[36] And how do we conceptualize children's ability to make a life out of situations in which many child rights activists would be completely lost?

The notion of living rights implies that children have implicit or explicit understandings of what children's rights mean to them. It makes little sense to posit that children have rights if at the same time we deny that they have the ability and understanding to participate in the production of knowledge about their rights. In other words, children's rights are inalienable: there is no higher authority that confers human rights on some children but not on others or that can take these rights away. All children have the same rights simply because they are children.

Do children need to ask for their rights in terms of rights talk? Or is it sufficient that they act according to what they believe their rights are, without explicitly claiming them? This question amounts to finding out from what point onward a certain conduct or specific terminology can be assumed to correspond to a rights claim and be part of living rights. Do children realize their right to food by stealing when they are hungry? Are children who move from one locality to another, such as refugee children, expressing their right to mobility, even if they remain silent throughout the journey? Also, who decides what kind of actions or expressions are at least needed to be considered as a living right? To start answering these important questions we need to move away from the abstract and take particular situations into account where rights claims can be made and come alive. The boundaries between activities and claims that do not explicitly refer to rights talk but can count as living rights, and those that are not, are not only porous but can also shift according to time and place, and much will depend on the context in which certain actions take place or statements are expressed. Childhood researchers have described how children's notions of rights may vary widely, from inoffensive demands for play spaces and healthy environments to more contentious claims addressed to local authorities and both national governments and international development agencies. These may involve stopping police violence on the streets or deportation, maltreatment, rape, and murder. Claims often take the form of a challenge to how their rights are interpreted. For instance, we and Edward Van Daalen have documented how in Yogyakarta a movement of street people in which children figured prominently organized resistance against police raids and claimed the right to earn a living and lead a dignified life on the streets.[37]

In sum, all social practices that are conventionally identified as rights may be understood as living rights. They are alive through active and creative interpretations, association, and framing of what various actors in a given context bring together to form an unstable understanding of what children's rights are. But even if we claim that children's rights are under construction and that their interpretation is a multifaceted and even a contentious exercise, what is it that makes some interpretations more valid than others? In other words, how do they become entrenched? To study the processes through which children's rights become seen as fixed in particular contexts and settings, we turn to the concept of translations.

5 TRANSLATIONS

In this section, we present the concept of translations to discuss what happens with rights in the encounter of children's and other actors' perspectives, ranging from international agencies, state authorities, cosmopolitan elites, child rights professionals, and grassroots social movements. To ensure their impact on the lives of children, international children's rights are implemented through a vast array of legislative, administrative, and other measures that translate the children's rights discourse to national and subnational legislative and policy systems as well as to the entities and professionals entrusted with their application. In this process different series of translations are performed. If we want to understand the prevalent worldviews and interests that are at play in these processes of translation, the current so-called international children's rights economy needs to accept critical scrutiny of the assumptions that are hidden behind its consensus thinking.[38] According to translation studies, translation does not look for a perfect equivalence between source text and target text, but allows for disparities depending on the purpose of the activity and the intended addressees.[39] The notion of *translation*, therefore, is not limited to the transfer of one idea into another context, but implies an active stance of re-production and change. As a theoretical construct, the concept of translation sustains reflexivity and can make the active re-production of meaning more explicit and open to debate.[40]

Social and legal research on human rights looks into interconnections, movement, and boundary crossing of different forms of legal discourse across governance levels and domains and also examines how norms are "remade as they travel."[41] In her analysis of the transnational circulation of international women's rights, Susanne Zwingel prefers the term *translation* to *norm diffusion* because "translation implies that differently contextualized norms may be translated into another realm, for example, from global to national or local to national, whereas diffusion assumes a one-way influence from global to non-global."[42] Zwingel makes a useful distinction between three forms of norm translation, including "global discourse translation," "impact translation," and "distorted translation," that permit an intelligible analysis of the distinct processes at work in translation activities. Global discourse translation looks at how norm entrepreneurs, such as NGO activists, seek to influence international institutions to create specific norms that are in their field of interests, for instance by organizing international conferences, requesting and performing large surveys and study reports, or lobbying intergovernmental entities or states. An example is how some international lawyers and development experts privilege the idea that labor is only valuable if it is performed by paid adults and dismiss all unpaid domestic and subsistence work as beneficial to children and of no economic value. Paradoxically, this entails that children can only work unpaid, as claiming payment would turn their work into prohibited child labor. The prohibition hides the contribution of children in the Global South to the global economy, children's struggles for rights and emancipation, and their agency in seeking to realize a good life for themselves and their families.[43]

Impact translation examines the kind and degree of impact international norms have on national normative and material settings. Besides the study of technical legal and policy mechanisms, such as the domestication of international children's rights law or the setting up of national independent children's rights institutions like children's ombudsperson offices, this also concerns how international norms can be translated into locally relevant, understandable, and culturally acceptable norms.

Distorted translation considers disconnections between international and domestic norms, such as in situations where international norms have unintentional consequences or where local activism for social justice is disconnected from international human rights norms. Chantal Medaets and Fernanda Bittencourt Ribeiro, for instance, point to the discrepancy between planned national legislation in Brazil to prohibit corporal punishment, proposed, ostensibly, to implement international children's rights norms, and the local moral codes in two Amazonian villages in Brazil that permit corporal punishment due to the fact that local communities consider it necessary to establish parental authority with as little violence as possible, in a way that was ultimately beneficial to children.[44]

Contrary to terms generally used in human rights literature, such as *implementation*, *dissemination*, or *diffusion*, the lens of translation acknowledges a two-way process. For Sally Engle Merry, the notion of translations can hence contribute to reversing the traditional top-down approach to human rights, as it involves a double movement whereby international human rights can be translated down to the local level while local stories can also be translated up internationally into conventional human rights language.[45] In this dynamic two-way process, both sides of the exchange get transformed, a process that Robert Young terms "Caribbean creolization," which "comes close to a foundational idea of postcolonialism: that the one-way process by which translation is customarily conceived can be rethought in terms of cultural interaction, and as a space of re-empowerment."[46] The postcolonial perspective helps replace the routine belief in children's rights as a Western invention with a conceptualization that sees them as the unstable and contingent result of a situated and unequal encounter.[47] Nicolas Argenti, for example, provides an enlightening discussion of how, in many postindependence African countries, frustration about unmet promises has set in motion a huge exodus of, at times, very young people from rural areas and sparked a whole set of uprisings, millenarian movements, and guerrilla wars challenging paternalism and demanding rights for the young.[48] It is against highly conflictual backgrounds that translators or "people in the middle" who "connect transnationally circulating discourses and particular social contexts"[49] must operate. They therefore do not merely translate discourses and practices from the field of international law and international organizations to specific situations in which people are believed to be ignorant about their rights; they also translate specific local grievances to often unaware transnational actors.

Translations are not limited to single instances where translation occurs, such as between international and national law, but often include long chains of translation, for instance, within governmental and nongovernmental organizations between senior staff members at headquarters, international and local staff working at country-level and grassroots organizations or between a national education ministry, regional directors, school principals, individual teachers, and pupils.

In the field of international human rights, large organizations that exercise decisive influence, such as Amnesty International and Human Rights Watch, are more likely than local populations to inaugurate issues that get on the local agenda.[50] Research on international advocacy in children's rights suggests that large children's rights agencies, such as UNICEF, Save the Children, and the ILO, have had a decisive role in getting on the agenda such issues as specific needs and rights of children exposed to emergencies; children's basic needs; the worst forms of child labor; and violence against children.[51] International agencies act not only as translators of human rights claims but also as gatekeepers who select which claims are passed on and which are not, making it difficult for certain demands to even find a suitable translator. John I'Anson, Ann Quennerstedt, and Carol Robinson report that the present economy of children's rights leaves insufficient room for alternative ways of thinking and practicing children's rights and find that children and young people should be more fully included in the translation process.[52] This brings us back to the importance of the notion of living rights. In conceiving translation as a two-way process, there should be, at least conceptually, sufficient space for including children's situated knowledge and understanding of their rights.

Instead of seeing the translation of children's rights as a top-down or a bottom-up activity, we think translation should be considered "a circular process whereby source and target languages constantly engage with one another giving rise to unforeseen complexities that produce a state of constant indeterminacy."[53] Looking at these processes as translations implies that there is room to acknowledge difference. Also, it involves recognizing children's representations of their lives and situations and provides them with space to negotiate meanings and influence interpretations of children's rights. The most emblematic discussion of this idea to date is how working children's organizations struggle to have their interpretations of their rights related to work taken into account by international law-making entities in the field of labor law, in particular by the ILO. Even if their claim to recognize children's right to work in dignity has met with only limited success in international law and policymaking circles, they have succeeded in offering an original alternative account of how children's rights should be interpreted in relation to their work. These discussions have led to the availability of a well-documented body of work that challenges the classic top-down view that all child labor under a certain age should be merely prohibited by offering a bottom-up approach suggesting that the cluster of work-related rights is a complex but fundamental human right that should also be recognized for children.[54]

6 CONCLUSION

The 2014 Nobel Peace Prize ceremony has offered a great occasion to celebrate consensus among the apparently noble "us" who advocate for children's rights versus the outwardly evil "them" who violate those rights. The Oslo City Hall has obviously not been the best place to criticize essentialist approaches to children and childhood or to explore potentially conflicting ideas and understandings of children's rights. However, the moral grounds upon which the prevalent us versus them dichotomy are built are highly problematic:

> as Mouffe puts it, "with the 'evil them' no agonistic debate is possible, they must be eradicated." (2005, 76) Indeed, in spite of an increasing rhetoric of dialogue, the relationship between child rights advocates and local communities always aims at changing the norms and values of the latter, while those of the incomers are assumed to remain unchanged. A more genuine and constructive approach to dialogue, acknowledging the equal legitimacy of antagonistic ontological, epistemological and axiological perspectives (Chateauraynaud, 2011, 162–164), would open the space for producing a more complex account of children's problems and, possibly, for devising more appropriate solutions.[55]

This chapter has argued that children's rights do not exist in a social vacuum but are always necessarily realized in a specific situation or social field in which different forces and different normative beliefs around social justice are at play. It is in this third space or "in-between space"[56] that the exchange of equally legitimate sets of values and norms takes place and new social practices around children's rights emerge. Taken together, living rights and translations offer a conceptual framework that may contribute to improving the study and understanding of the variations of children's rights claims and of the place of children's conceptions and practices of their rights within these discussions.[57] The questions at the center of a child-centered approach to children's rights law can be formulated as follows. What are children's conceptualizations of their rights? How can we have access to children's positions? How do children's interpretations of their rights interact with other, concurring, competing or alternative views on children's rights? How do the notions of living rights and translations interact, and how can they help apprehend, question, and interpret children's rights law?

It has not been our aim to give a direct answer to all these questions, but to provide a framework that can be mobilized to examine these questions in a wide range of cases and in numerous specific situations that matter for the field of children's rights studies. An example of the new insights this approach can produce is offered in a study by Gurchathen Sanghera and his colleagues, who have applied the living rights framework to examine young people's rights claims during the 2014 Scottish independence referendum that had granted sixteen- and seventeen-year-olds the right to vote. Understanding the right to vote as a living right, the authors have gained insights into how various claims-making processes simultaneously challenge, redefine, and transform boundaries of citizenship, whereby "the idea of living rights re-frames the way we think about rights, young people and citizenship."[58] They also found that the language of living rights may prove central to protect the most vulnerable non-citizens in society, such as refugees or asylum seekers, especially at a time of austerity and growing hostility of those considered to be outsiders." The establishment and development of the international children's rights regime indeed coincided with increasing social, political, and scholarly interest for the mobility and migration of children.[59] A globalized economy implies the global circulation not only of goods and capital but also of people, including children, for whom the respect of their rights is particularly challenging in the context of migration. In this context, children's rights to mobility offers an example of how a child-centered approach to children's rights law can contribute to further conceptualizing the social and legal recognition of the right to mobility and migration as a global human right itself.[60] A right to mobility can be understood both as a substantive right to move around freely as well as an instrumental right that may help children realize the rights they would be deprived of without moving. In addition, the right to mobility encompasses the right not to move, which brings into focus how being forced to move may deprive children of the rights they enjoy when staying put. The claim not to be obliged to move from the rural areas to the city, for instance, was one of the ten claims made by movements of working children in the declaration they adopted in 1996 in Kundapur, India.[61] In the current controversy about migration laws that tend to obstruct rather than enable people's mobility, children's rights are increasingly invoked to justify policy interventions in the lives of children and families. These policies work overwhelmingly from an essentialist reading of what is best for children, ignoring children's own ideas about their right to either migrate or be protected against forced migration. We believe that introducing the notions of living rights and translations into the analysis of specific situations such as these not only offers a productive starting point to further conceptualize how children perceive their rights but also to more explicitly include children's conceptualizations of their rights in discussions about childhood and youth policies on local and global scales.

NOTES

1. Thomas Hammarberg, "The UN Convention on the Rights of the Child—And How to Make It Work," *Human Rights Quarterly* 12, no. 1 (February 1990): 99–105.
2. Karl Hanson and Laura Lundy, "Does Exactly What It Says on the Tin? A Critical Analysis and Alternative Conceptualisation of the So-called 'General Principles' of the Convention on the Rights of the Child," *International Journal of Children's Rights* 25, no. 2 (2017): 285–306.
3. Didier Reynaert, Maria Bouverne-de-Bie, and Stijn Vandevelde, "A Review of Children's Rights Literature since the Adoption of the United Nations Convention on the Rights of the Child," *Childhood* 16, no. 4 (2009): 518–534.
4. Martin Woodhead, "Foreword," in *A Handbook of Children and Young People's Participation: Perspectives from Theory and Practice*, ed. Barry Percy-Smith and Nigel Thomas (Oxon: Routledge, 2010), xx.
5. Karl Hanson and Olga Nieuwenhuys, eds., *Reconceptualizing Children's Rights in International Development: Living Rights, Social Justice, Translations* (Cambridge: Cambridge University Press, 2013).
6. Karin Arts, "Twenty-Five Years of the United Nations Convention on the Rights of the Child: Achievements and Challenges," *Netherlands International Law Review* 61, no. 3 (2014): 267–303.

7. Kailash Satyarthi, "Nobel Lecture: Let Us March!," Nobelprize.org, Dec. 10, 2014, http://www.nobelprize.org/nobel_prizes/peace/laureates/2014/satyarthi-lecture.html.

8. Karl Hanson, "Separate Childhood Laws and the Future of Society." *Law, Culture and the Humanities* 12, no. 2 (June 2016): 195–205.

9. *See also*, Laura King, "Future Citizens: Cultural and Political Conceptions of Children in Britain, 1930s–1950s." *Twentieth Century British History* 27, no. 3 (September 2016): 389–411.

10. Hanson, "Separate Childhood Laws," 195–205.

11. Malala Yousafzai, "Nobel Lecture," Nobelprize.org, Dec. 10, 2014, http://www.nobelprize.org/nobel_prizes/peace/laureates/2014/yousafzai-lecture.html.

12. Lesley-Anne Gallacher and Michael Gallagher, "Methodological Immaturity in Childhood Research? Thinking through 'Participatory Methods,'" *Childhood* 15, no. 4 (2008): 499–516, 502; see also, Spyros Spyrou, "The Limits of Children's Voices: From Authenticity to Critical, Reflexive Representation," *Childhood* 18, no. 2 (2011): 151–165.

13. See the Malala Fund website, www.malala.org.

14. Assed Baig, "Malala Yousafzai and the White Saviour Complex," *Huffington Post* blog, last modified Sept. 12, 2013, http://www.huffingtonpost.co.uk/assed-baig/malala-yousafzai-white-saviour_b_3592165.html.

15. Spyrou, "Limits of Children's Voices," 151–165.

16. Olga Nieuwenhuys, "Global Childhood and the Politics of *Contempt*," *Alternatives* 23, no 3 (July–September 1998): 267–289.

17. Susan Shepler, *Childhood Deployed: Remaking Child Soldiers in Sierra Leone* (New York: New York University Press, 2014).

18. Olga Nieuwenhuys, "The Ethics of Children's Rights," *Childhood* 15, no. 1 (2008): 4–11.

19. Hanson and Nieuwenhuys, *Reconceptualizing Children's Rights in International Development*.

20. Karl Hanson, "Children's Participation and Agency When They Don't 'Do the Right Thing.'" *Childhood* 23, no. 4 (2016): 471–475.

21. Shareen Hertel, *Unexpected Power. Conflict and Change among Transnational Activists* (Ithaca: Cornell University Press, 2006).

22. Karl Hanson, "International Children's Rights and Armed Conflict.", *Human Rights & International Legal Discourse* 5, no. 1 (2011): 40–62.

23. UN Optional Protocol to the Convention on the Rights of the Child on the Involvement of Children in Armed Conflict, G.A. Res. 54/263, 54th Sess., UN Doc. A/RES/54/263 (May 25, 2000; entered into force Feb. 12, 2002).

24. See, for instance, the findings by Shepler in Sierra Leone in *Childhood Deployed*.

25. Pamela Reynolds, Olga Nieuwenhuys, and Karl Hanson, "Refractions of Children's Rights in Development Practice: A View from Anthropology," *Childhood* 13, no. 3 (2006): 291–303.

26. See Brian Z. Tamanaha, "A Non-Essentialist Version of Legal Pluralism," *Journal of Law and Society* 27, no. 2 (2000): 296–321.

27. Ursula Kilkelly, "Youth Justice and Children's Rights: Measuring Compliance with International Standards," *Youth Justice* 8, no. 3 (2008): 187–192.

28. Hanson and Nieuwenhuys, *Reconceptualizing Children's Rights in International Development*.

29. Lorenza B. Fontana and Jean Grugel, "Deviant and Over-Compliance: The Domestic Politics of Child Labor in Bolivia and Argentina," *Human Rights Quarterly* 39, no. 3 (2017): 631–656.

30. Manfred Liebel, "Protecting the Rights of Working Children Instead of Banning Child Labour: Bolivia Tries a New Legislative Approach," *International Journal of Children's Rights* 23, no. 3 (2015): 529–547.

31. Anne C. Dailey, "Children's Transitional Rights," *Law, Culture and the Humanities* 12, no. 2 (2016): 178–194.

32. Tatek Abebe, "Interdependent Rights and Agency: The Role of Children in Collective Livelihood Strategies in Rural Ethiopia," in Hanson and Nieuwenhuys, *Reconceptualizing Children's Rights in International Development*, 71–92.

33. Tamanaha, "Non-Essentialist Version," 313.

34. Mark Goodale and Sally Engle Merry, eds., *The Practice of Human Rights: Tracking Law between the Global and the Local* (Cambridge: Cambridge University Press, 2007), 24.

35. Nieuwenhuys, "Ethics of Children's Rights."

36. Edward Van Daalen, Karl Hanson, and Olga Nieuwenhuys, "Children's Rights as Living Rights: The Case of Street Children and a New Law in Yogyakarta, Indonesia." *International Journal of Children's Rights* 24, no. 4 (2016): 803–825, 817.

37. Van Daalen, Hanson, and Nieuwenhuys, "Children's Rights as Living Rights," 803–825.

38. John I'Anson, Ann Quennerstedt, and Carol Robinson, "The International Economy of Children's Rights: Issues in Translation," *International Journal of Children's Rights* 25, no. 1 (2017): 50–67; see also, Reynaert, Bouverne-de-Bie, and Vandevelde "Review of Children's Rights Literature."

39. Karen Zethsen, "Beyond Translation Proper—Extending the Field of Translation Studies," *TTR: Traduction, terminologie, rédaction* 20, no. 1 (2007): 281–308.

40. Richard Freeman, "What Is 'Translation'?" *Evidence & Policy: A Journal of Research, Debate and Practice* 5, no. 4 (November 2009): 429–447.

41. Anna Tsing, "The Global Situation," *Cultural Anthropology* 15, no. 3 (August 2000): 327–360, 347.

42. Susanne Zwingel, "How Do Norms Travel? Theorizing International Women's Rights in Transnational Perspective," *International Studies Quarterly* 56, no. 1 (2012): 115–129, 124.

43. Olga Nieuwenhuys, "Embedding the *Global Womb*: *Global* Child Labour and the New Policy Agenda," *Children's Geographies* 5, nos. 1–2 (February–May 2007): 149–163.

44. Chantal Medaets and Fernanda Bittencourt Ribeiro, "Projet de loi 'anti-fessée'—Enjeux politiques, débats publics et pratiques parentales (Brésil)," in *Des Politiques Institutionnelles aux Représentations de l'Enfance. Perspectives d'Amérique Latine et d'Europe*, ed. Véronique Pache Huber and Charles-Édouard de Suremain et Élise Guillermet (Liège: Presses universitaires de Liège, 2016), 123–142.

45. Sally Engle Merry, "Transnational Human Rights and Local Activism: Mapping the Middle," *American Anthropologist* 108, no. 1 (March 2006): 38–51.

46. Robert J. C. Young, *Postcolonialism: A Very Short Introduction* (Oxford: Oxford University Press, 2003), 142.

47. Olga Nieuwenhuys, "Theorizing Childhood(s): Why We Need Postcolonial Perspectives," *Childhood* 20, no. 1 (2013): 3–8.

48. Nicolas Argenti, "Youth in Africa: A Major Resource for Change," in *Young Africa, Realizing the Rights of Children and Youth*, ed. Alex De Waal and Nicolas Argenti (Trenton, NJ, and Asmara, Eritrea: Africa World Press, 2002), 123–155.

49. Merry, "Transnational Human Rights and Local Activism," 39.

50. Clifford Bob, "Introduction: Fighting for New Rights," in *The International Struggle for New Human Rights*, ed. Clifford Bob (Philadelphia: University of Pennsylvania Press, 2009), 1–13.

51. Karl Hanson, Michele Poretti, and Frédéric Darbellay, "Children's Rights between Normative and Empirical Realms," in *Children's Rights and the Capability Approach: Challenges and Prospects*, ed. Daniel Stoecklin and Jean-Michel Bonvin (Dordrecht, NE: Springer, 2014), 233–252.

52. I'Anson, Quennerstedt, and Robinson, "International Economy of Children's Rights."

53. Hanson and Nieuwenhuys, *Reconceptualizing Children's Rights in International Development*, 19.

54. Karl Hanson and Arne Vandaele, "Translating Working Children's Rights into International Labour Law," in Hanson and Nieuwenhuys, *Reconceptualizing Children's Rightsin International Development*, 250–272.

55. Michele Poretti, Karl Hanson, Frédéric Darbellay, and André Berchtold, "The Rise and Fall of Icons of 'Stolen Childhood' since the Adoption of the UN Convention on the Rights of the Child," *Childhood* 21, no. 1 (2014): 22–28, 35.

56. Goodale and Merry, *Practice of Human Rights*.

57. Hanson and Nieuwenhuys, *Reconceptualizing Children's Rights in International Development*.

58. Gurchathen, Sanghera, Katherine Botterill, Peter Hopkins, and Rowena Arshad, " 'Living Rights', Rights Claims, Performative Citizenship and Young People—The Right to Vote in the Scottish Independence Referendum," *Citizenship Studies* 22, no. 5 (2018): 540–555, 553.

59. Karl Hanson, "A Global Journal of Local and Global Child Research," *Childhood* 25, no. 3 (2018): 269–271.

60. See Tanya Golash-Boza and Cecilia Menjívar, "Causes and Consequences of International Migration: Sociological Evidence for the Right to Mobility," *International Journal of Human Rights* 16, no. 8 (December 2012): 1213–1227.

61. Article 9 of the 1996 Kundapur Declaration is formulated as follows: "We want more initiatives in rural areas so that children do not have to go to the city"; cited in Manfred Liebel, "Do Children Have a Right to Work? Working Children's Movements in the Struggle for Social Justice," in Hanson and Nieuwenhuys, *Reconceptualizing Children's Rights in International Development*, 225–249. For a detailed discussion of the Kundapur Declaration see also, Michel Bonnet, "La 'Déclaration de Kundapur': et si on écoutait les enfants travailleurs?," in *Enfants Travailleurs: Repenser l'Enfance*, ed. Michel Bonnet, Karl Hanson, Marie-France Lange, Olga Nieuwenhuys, Graciela Paillet, and Bernard Schlemmer (Lausanne: Page deux, 2006), 59–100.

CHAPTER 6

....

A SOCIOECOLOGICAL MODEL OF CHILDREN'S RIGHTS

....

TALI GAL

1 INTRODUCTION

....

SINCE the middle of the twentieth century, and even more so since the adoption by almost every country of the UN Convention on the Rights of the Child (CRC), children's rights laws have been enacted almost everywhere. Children's rights legislation covers a range of topics, including education, labor, child protection, and juvenile justice, and is supplemented by international and national policymaking. With this massive regulatory coverage, an urgent need arises for a methodological approach to addressing empirical questions, such as what types of children's rights laws *exist* in different areas, as well as normative questions, such as which children's rights laws *should* exist in certain areas. A related question concerns enforcement, including the extent to which children's rights laws are actually enforced and ways of improving implementation.

The socioecological model elaborated by child developmentalist Urie Brofenbrenner provides such a helpful methodology. Bronfenbrenner's framework is based on an understanding that knowledge about the worlds of children can be understood and organized largely in five concentric circles: the *microsystem*: parents and family; the *mesosystem*: environments outside the family with which children are in direct contact, such as schools and health care providers; the *exosystem*: circles indirectly related to children through their families, such as parents' workplaces and social circles; the *macrosystem*: broader cultural and social values; and finally, the *chronosystem*: changes over time that affect children directly (such as changes in the family structure—a birth of a sibling or divorce) and indirectly (war, global financial crisis).[1]

The socioecological model is a suitable conceptual framework for analyzing children's rights legislation because it captures the interconnections between different environments while also addressing the developmental nature of childhood and thus the constant change in individual characteristics and needs of children. The socioecological perspective zooms out from given rights, jurisdictions, and normative sources to consider a range of different domains in the human ecosystem. As such, it provides a methodology to organize existing and desirable children's rights laws and their enforcement according to concentric circles formed around individual children.

This chapter presents three main propositions: (a) that the needs-rights of children,[2] namely, empirically documented and specified human needs of children that are universally acknowledged as human rights, appear in a range of interconnected domains in children's lives, which can be organized according to Brofenbrenner's socioecological construct; (b) that children's rights laws can, and often do, regulate children's lives across these different domains and thus can, and at times do, address the full range of children's needs-rights; and (c) that because the various domains in children's lives are interconnected, the enforcement of children's rights laws must be targeted at the full range of the domains of the human ecosystem of children.

2 The Socioecological Model

The basic proposition of the socioecological model is that children's development can be understood only when considering the range of systems related to their lives: microsystems, mesosystems, exosystems, macrosystems, and chronosystems.[3] As noted above, the *microsystem* refers to the family, its characteristics, and the dynamics between the children and their family members. The *mesosystem* refers to external environments with which children have direct contact, such as, depending on the situation, schools, welfare services, or health services, the characteristics of these environments, and the dynamics between the children and the representatives of these environments. *Exosystems* are environments that children do not have direct contact with but that significantly affect children's lives, such as parents' social or professional networks, their characteristics, and the dynamics between these environments and the parents. *Macrosystems* comprise the larger factors that affect children as part of the general population, such as social norms, political leadership, and legislative reforms. And, finally, *chronosystems*[4] refer to the temporal characteristics of the different domains, such as the duration and consistency of interactions between children and others as well as historical changes that occur throughout children's development.

The model suggests not only that human behavior and development are shaped by these multiple systems and processes but that these various components are interconnected and affect each other in complex ways, similar to biological ecosystems.[5] For example, how parents interact with their children affects the ways in which children interact with teachers and other adults outside the family. Cultural and social perceptions of gender roles affect the professional environments of women, which in turn affect their role modeling as mothers and the development of their children.

A socioecological approach requires interdisciplinary research, as it assumes connections between the social and natural environments and between the study of human behavior, cultures, and geography.[6] This exploration of the interconnections between social and natural characteristics is what makes the socioecological approach so helpful in explaining how children's rights laws affect and are affected by the natural and social conditions of children's lives. The seemingly natural characteristics of the child (to the extent that anything is purely *natural*), the family, and the immediate environment are interconnected with laws, cultural norms, enforcement measures, education, and status.

Bronfenbrenner's socioecological model has had a formative effect on the study of childhood and beyond. The model was used, for example, to explain child abuse and exploitation, including child trafficking,[7] examining the interrelationships between microsystem (parent-child attachment and marital conflict), macrosystem (cultural values), and chronosystem variables (parents with child abuse histories).[8] Teen dating violence also has been explained from a socioecological perspective, which has suggested that the phenomenon is affected by a range of factors, including individual, interactional, community, and societal.[9] Research on prevention efforts suggests that to be successful, prevention programs need to address the multiple layers of children's and youths' socioecological environments.[10] The socioecological approach has been used similarly to explain youth health,[11] willingness to report misbehavior,[12] and child resilience.[13] Its theoretical influence extends beyond children's lives. The World Health Organization, for example, used the model as a basis for explaining violence against women in its World Report on Violence and Health.[14]

Despite the significant scholarship relying on the socioecological approach to understand children's lives and other social phenomena, seldom has this perspective been used to inform research and practice in the legal arena.[15] One reason for this omission may be that the socioecological model emerged as part of developmental psychology, not legal studies. The field of therapeutic jurisprudence (TJ), however, has been instilling the understanding that psychosocial knowledge is crucial for both legal practice and scholarship.[16] A growing body of knowledge, with regard to childhood in particular, integrates legal and psychosocial scholarship.[17] And, findings from psychosocial research have been inspiring TJ scholars to introduce legal reforms in such fields as criminal law,[18] family law,[19] and torts.[20] Adopting a socioecological perspective as an analytical methodology is a natural next step for TJ and other legal scholars exploring children's rights laws and their enforcement. The socioecological perspective not only utilizes knowledge from psychosocial scholarship; it also organizes such knowledge in a way that highlights the different layers in children's lives and the interconnections between them. Although a comprehensive review of the full range of psychosocial and legal knowledge surrounding children's needs-rights, national and international legislation, and its enforcement is beyond the scope of this chapter, the following sections seek to demonstrate the model and its potential contribution to the field.

3 Understanding Children's Rights as Derived from Their Needs

What are the rights that children have by the fact of being children? And how are we to answer this question? An answer that relies purely on positivistic grounds (a systematic review of laws and regulations) is vulnerable to criticism that it may miss areas of interest for children that local, national, or international laws do not currently protect. For example, the CRC itself, the most comprehensive international document on children's rights, has been criticized for failing to address certain rights, such as those of gay or transgender children.[21] Such a positivistic answer is also open to the criticism that laws and regulations provide only abstract information on children's rights and that they are often culturally insensitive.[22] An answer that relies purely on normative grounds, that is, on moral beliefs regarding the human rights that children should enjoy, is too vague and utopian and, at the same time, lacks cultural relativism.[23]

Aiming to bridge the gap between the rich empirical literature on children's needs and that of children's rights, I developed an integrated needs-rights model in relation to children.[24] The model combines legal norms and international human rights with empirical findings on children's needs derived from the psychosocial literature. The legal and psychosocial frameworks complement each other. The legal framework directs us to the relevant fields of research; the psychosocial framework provides concrete, evidence-based substance for the implementation of children's rights. Once integrated with the legal framework, the psychosocial needs of children benefit from the normative strength of accepted children's rights.[25] For example, CRC Article 12 regarding children's participation invites further examination of empirical findings regarding what participation actually means to children, what level of control over the decision-making they consider important, and what are potentially harmful participatory experiences for children of different ages in different contexts. Findings regarding control as a coping mechanism among children in stressful situations indicate that perceived low controllability (perceiving a certain situation as uncontrollable) is associated with greater stress and that in relatively uncontrollable situations, asserting control might actually increase negative feelings.[26] Interpreting this empirical finding through a human rights lens leads to a conclusion that children should be provided with opportunities to take part in decision-making processes to the maximum extent possible but, at the same time, that adults should avoid creating false expectations among children that their views will affect the outcomes when this is untrue. Other empirical findings regarding children's wishes to take part in discussions about their placement[27] highlight the importance of involving children even in sensitive and potentially painful decision-making processes while acknowledging their pain and sadness. The term *needs-rights*, then, refers to internationally accepted human rights of children that are rigorously anchored in empirical findings regarding their importance for children and at the same time are tuned according to children's specific characteristics.

The needs-rights model offers an explicit integration of legal and psychosocial frameworks. Others have resorted to similar methodologies, albeit with lesser attention to the legal sphere. The capabilities approach, developed by the socioeconomist Amartya Sen,[28] offers such a methodology, according to which all human beings are entitled to hold potential functions that, if the holder desires, can become operational. The focus on potential rather than actual functioning makes the set of capabilities robust against personal, gender, and cultural differences.[29] People must be able to choose whether to realize their capabilities or not, and their choices are likely to vary, but society is expected to guarantee the social basis for achieving these capabilities. Following Sen, the international research conducted by legal philosopher Martha Nussbaum led to a list of ten central capabilities to be incorporated in national and international documents: life; health; bodily integrity; senses, imagination, and thought; emotions; practical reason; affiliation; other species; play; and control over one's environment.[30] The capabilities approach was further developed in relation to children and youth by psychologists Esperanza Ochaíta and Angeles Espinosa,[31] who, based on psychosocial knowledge, proposed a list of "satisfiers" or second-order needs for satisfying children's basic needs, which should be understood as universal rights of children. For them, the universality of these satisfiers grants them the normative status of human rights. The satisfiers for children's basic needs for *physical health* include nutrition, housing, clothing and hygiene, health care, sleep and rest, exterior space, physical exercise, and protection from physical risks. The satisfiers for their basic need for *autonomy* include active participation and stable norms, primary effective bonds, interaction with adults, formal and non-formal education, play and recreation, protection from psychological risks, and acceptance of sexual needs. Naturally, the specific implementation of the satisfiers differs across children's developmental stages, but their existence remains constant throughout childhood. Similarly, Mario Biggeri and colleagues[32] identified fourteen capabilities vital for youth to achieve their full potential: life and physical health, love and care, mental well-being, bodily integrity and safety, social relations, participation, education, freedom from economic and noneconomic exploitation, shelter and environment, leisure activities, respect, time-autonomy, mobility, and religion and identity.[33]

The capabilities approach and the needs-rights model are two examples demonstrating the importance of conducting an empirical, systematic research of children's needs to identify their actual and desired rights. From a legal-philosophy perspective, such an empirical examination provides a crucial moral basis for children's rights: while the will theory of rights[34] establishes that having a right means having the power to demand that others fulfill their duties, the interest theory of rights[35] maintains that people have rights by virtue of the importance of their needs, not as a result of their legal power to assert them. The interest theory of rights has been widely accepted as a more suitable philosophical basis for considering young children, people with disabilities, and incapacitated individuals as rights-holders.[36] The needs-rights model, as well as the capabilities approach and its consequent scholarship, provide integrated frameworks of empirically proven needs of children of different ages, backgrounds, and individual characteristics combined with internationally accepted global norms and principles.[37]

But how are we to organize the enormous body of knowledge concerning the needs-rights of children? The attempts to list the needs-rights of children by Ochaíta and Espinosa[38] and Biggeri and colleagues[39] as well as others[40] are comprehensive and compelling. But they do not capture the different arenas in children's lives in which their needs-rights are germane, nor do they explore the interconnections between them. The socioecological perspective becomes useful here. According to this perspective, to fully understand the rights of children across place, time, and demographic characteristics, it is necessary to examine the various components of the model and the interrelationships between them.

4 The Needs-Rights of Children across Different Socioecological Layers

Figure 6.1 below is a revised version of an earlier publication where I used Bronfenbrenner's socioecological perspective to consider child participation.[41]

The diagram in figure 6.1 attempts to apply the Bronfenbrenner model to organize the full range of needs-rights of children across the multiple socioecological layers surrounding children. At the *microsystem* level of the home and familial context, children have needs-rights related to their health; protection against physical risks; love and care; and gradual development of their autonomy and identity. Moving outward, the *mesosystem* addresses the interconnections between central domains external to the family with which children interact, such as school and welfare or health services.[42] Children's needs-rights in these areas revolve around the type of interactions they have with other children and professionals (safety, respect, gradual autonomy and identity, and social relations) and the services they receive (the right to education and physical health, freedom from economic and noneconomic exploitation).

The *exosystem* refers to domains that are generally not part of children's daily interactions but affect their lives nevertheless. The prime examples of exosystems are parents' workplace environments and social circles.[43] When considering the needs-rights of children in those contexts, related aspects include children's need for appropriate conditions that enable their parents to secure their health, safety, mental well-being, shelter and environment, and leisure time.

The *macrosystem* refers to global components, such as national and international laws, as well as cultural and social norms and the different ways in which they affect the other levels of the ecosystem. Many needs-rights of children have to do with the global environment they grow up in: their health, nutrition, housing, hygiene, health care, exterior space, leisure time, protection against economic and other exploitation, mobility, religion and identity, all of which depend on appropriate national and international norms.

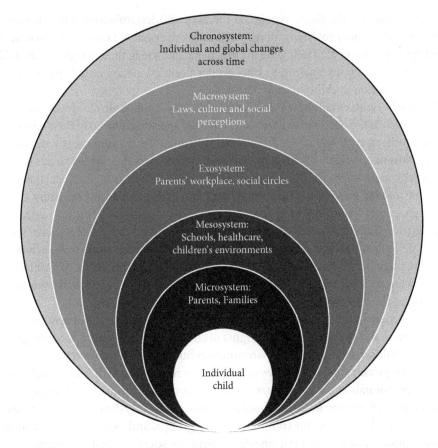

FIGURE 6.1

The *chronosystem* refers to changes and dynamics that occur over time. Some of the changes stem from the individual child. As children grow, the actual content of certain needs-rights changes. Participation and autonomy are as important at age three as at age seventeen, but they manifest differently. The same can be said about the need-right to leisure time, social relations, and education. Other changes and dynamics are external to the individual child. Global, historical changes may have affected the ways we understand certain needs-rights. The earlier international documents on children's rights, the 1924 Declaration of the Rights of the Child (also, Geneva Declaration) and the 1959 UN Declaration of the Rights of the Child, were heavily influenced by the tragedies of the first and the second world wars. They focused on children's rights to protection, to food, to development, and to relief. The initial drafts of the CRC, originating from Poland in 1979, focused on children's social rights and reflected the socialist ideology of Eastern European countries in those years. However, in the decade that followed the initial drafts, the deliberations of the working group tasked with drafting the CRC reflected the debate between the Western and Eastern ideologies in the Cold War era. The final content of the CRC moved far beyond what the Polish representatives envisioned and ultimately reflected the Western political values of self-determination and autonomy as well as social welfare provisions. In recent decades, the right of LGBT children to sexual identity has been accepted following the broader acknowledgment of rights of the LGBT community, and rights relating to transgender populations are only beginning to be debated in relation to children and youths.

The needs-rights of children, then, apply to different domains in children's lives. Some of them, such as the need for love and care, typically apply to children in their own home, whereas others, such as the need for social relations, are relevant mostly outside the home. Most needs-rights of children, however, apply across the various circles but have a different meaning at each of them. For example, children's right to participate in decision-making processes is relevant at home (taking part in family decisions that are age-appropriate, from how to spend the weekend to whether or not to relocate); at school (from individual decisions, such as placement, to schoolwide decisions, such as school policy); at the level of the local municipality (individual decisions, such as out-of-home placement, as well as public decisions, such as neighborhood planning); and finally, at the national and international level (from public policy consultations to youths monitoring the implementation of the CRC).

Each domain in the ecosystem of children's lives is affected by the others and affects them in turn, and the specific needs-rights of children are influenced accordingly. For example, children lacking a safe environment at home are in need (and have a right) to state-based protections, which they can expect to receive through social workers and other professionals at the *mesosystem* level. Children with special needs enjoy needs-rights at the *mesosystem* level, in school as well as in the *exosystem*, where their parents are (or should be) eligible for training, support groups, and extra sick days. Children whose families endure poverty, unemployment, or social exclusion (situations that are often the result of *macrosystem* policies or circumstances) are in need of social rights and services, such as food stamps, adult education, and parenting classes, which the family members receive through the *exosystem* of children's lives. Immigrant and refugee children have special needs-rights implemented at the *exo-* or *mesosystem* levels. As mentioned earlier, most needs-rights apply across the different levels, with different manifestations. Violation of a need-right at one level is likely to affect other levels as well.

The socioecological perspective takes into account the different ways children grow in different places, communities, and cultures. Although the basic needs-rights of children are universal, different contexts require different legal provisions and enforcement mechanisms. One example is the phenomenon of child labor, most common in some regions, particularly in Southeast Asia. While children everywhere need and deserve to be free from economic exploitation and to be safe and healthy, work-related legislation that banned child labor altogether actually increased child labor in India and was counterproductive.[44] A perspective that considers children's ecosystems is more likely to identify legislative policies that can address the needs-rights of children in specific social and cultural contexts, as explained in the following sections.

5 Children's Rights Laws across the Ecosystems of Children's Lives

The socioecological model is not only helpful in organizing our knowledge regarding the needs-rights of children according to the interconnected circles of life; it also demonstrates that laws at all levels affect children and their rights. Some of the laws target the *microsystem*. Although states generally refrain from intervening inside the family, when some needs-rights of children are not met they are considered critical enough to justify intervention. For example, child protection laws set the boundaries between acceptable and unacceptable behaviors of caretakers toward children, the latter justifying state intervention that may even lead to forced separation of the child from the parent. In contrast with the family system, in which intervention is justified only sparingly, *mesosystems* are a typical target of state regulation. For example, school rules and regulations affect children daily, including rules protecting children from violence, rules on participation in school councils, and rules relating to punishment and conflict resolution. For adolescents, the workplace is another arena of involvement and where state laws and regulations protect their rights, such as those related to minimum wage, rest, and safety. Another *mesosystem* includes the places of leisure of children and youth. Laws may protect children's rights in these areas through restrictions relating to their structure (such as safety standards of public playgrounds) or daily operation (such as the requirement that summer camp personnel have no criminal record).

Other laws regulate areas that ostensibly are not directly related to children, but once they are understood as *exosystems* their effect on children's lives becomes clear. Legislation affecting children's *exosystem* includes parental sick leave, maternity leave, and vacation entitlements. All of these affect children's well-being and interests in crucial ways. Health care and social support services also are part of children's rights legislation affecting their *exosystems*. For example, home visits for new mothers and social security benefits for families with children have a considerable influence on the rights of children to appropriate food, health care, parental care, and living conditions. Even laws providing adult education affect the family unit and therefore the children in it.

Some laws, treaties, and declarations target *macrosystems* in addition to the other levels of children's ecosystems. Some international children's rights and human rights laws regulate the duties of states toward children. For example, the CRC encourages states, in Article 17, to disseminate mass media information with social or cultural value for children and to promote international collaboration promoting the production, exchange, and dissemination of such information. Article 24 highlights the importance of national and international efforts to ensure clean water and combat environmental pollution. Other international norms, appearing in such documents as the 1992 Rio Declaration on Environment and Development and the 2002 Johannesburg Declaration on Sustainable Development, relate to sustainable development and climate protection.

These legal instruments affect children's health, safety, mobility, and well-being.[45] The *macrosystem* also highlights the importance of examining cultural and social norms in order to fully understand the needs-rights of children and the need for legal reform in certain areas. Non-legal norms arising from cultural and social constructions affect the ways children grow. For example, traditional gender role perceptions affect female girls' living conditions, aspirations, and opportunities. A study by Umar Serajuddin and Paolo Verme about subjective perceptions of deprivation related to joblessness among Moroccan young people found that although young women are significantly more disadvantaged than young men in terms of employment, young men feel much more deprived than young women.[46] These findings help explain why certain groups are louder than others in their protests (and thus are more likely to have their demands addressed) and highlight the need for special attention to less forceful, yet more disadvantaged, groups, such as girls in the labor market.

A chronological perspective, or the *chronosystem*, concerns the emergence of children's rights legislation across time. For example, since the 1970s, many European countries have enacted and gradually implemented laws banning corporal punishment.[47] The *chronosystem* also helps understand how children's rights laws apply differently to individual children as they age. For example, laws granting legal capacity to children at times define children's legal capacity based on their age or maturity. The same law typically has a different meaning for the same child regarding different points in time. Furthermore, laws granting certain rights become relevant at given ages, such as the right to carry a driver's license, the right to consult with a doctor privately, or the right to public education.

Categorizing children's rights laws according to the domains that they target within the complex ecosystems of children's lives can be instructive. Such categorization can identify moral and practical difficulties, as in the case of legislation targeting the family. It can also be of help in uncovering domains that are over- or underregulated. For example, such categorization may reveal that some states have created mechanisms for children to participate in public consultations on policy issues but have failed to regulate child participation in schools. Some states may have focused legislation on protecting children from violence in schools but not provided sufficient regulatory protection against parental abuse or neglect. Some states may have created extended legislation mandating health and mental health professionals to report child abuse but have failed to establish a similar mandate for reporting by kindergarten, school, or informal education professionals. Some states make school attendance mandatory but fail to address the home domain where health problems or an inadequate standard of living may impose barriers to school attendance.

Another feature of the socioecological model is that it highlights the interconnections between the various domains in children's lives and thus the potential impact on others of legislation targeting one domain. For example, a legislative reform requiring schools (*mesosystem*) to implement a gender-equality curriculum may affect family dynamics (*microsystem*), including role definitions and even family violence. In fact, reformers may knowingly invest in regulating one domain (such as schools), aiming to indirectly affect other domains (such as the home), when more intrusive legislation is less likely to be accepted.

The categorization of children's rights laws according to children's ecosystems can also be helpful in identifying where enforcement, education, and training are most needed and where they can be most effective, as discussed in the next section.

6 Implementing Children's Rights Laws across Children's Ecosystems

As noted above, the socioecological model is helpful in understanding enforcement and implementation as factors that occur, or should occur, across the various interconnected domains of children's lives. Starting at the *microsystem*, parents are powerful socialization agents who may coach children in asserting their rights and implementing them in ways that suit their age and development. In other words, the degree to which children's rights laws are implemented and enforced depends, to a significant extent, on the ability of the child to assert these rights. This ability in turn depends on the child's personal characteristics as well as on the amount of practice, encouragement, and support provided by her or his parents in expressing views and asserting rights. For example, it is reasonable to assume that children who are used to engaging in dialectic decision-making processes with their parents on a daily basis will be more able and more inclined to assume their participatory rights in school and at the local municipality. An ecosystems approach highlights such assumptions and encourages their empirical examination.

At the *mesosystem* level there is a constant need for enforcement of children's rights laws targeted at schools, health care, and other child-related services. Examples of such laws are regulated participation in school councils and placement decisions at schools; laws regulating children's consent and assent before getting medical treatment; and laws requiring equal treatment by a range of service providers. In all these cases, targeted enforcement can be executed by children and youths themselves, by their parents, by peer and employer feedback, and by external state authority review. Naturally the better educated children and parents are about the existence of children's rights laws, the more they can insist on their application. Human rights education in schools, as suggested by Article 29 of the CRC and the 2011 UN Declaration on Human Rights Education and Training, is a critical vehicle for developing rights consciousness among schoolchildren that can enhance their ability to assert their rights. A study by Shulamit Almog and Lotem Perry-Hazan on the education of Ultra-Orthodox girls in Israel demonstrates how the typical education track of such girls prepares them to support their families through employment but lacks any rights consciousness training and experience, thus limiting their ability and motivation to assert the full scope of their human rights.[48]

Similar to parents, teachers too can provide children with opportunities to develop their needs-rights according to their age and developmental stage. The term *scaffolding* has been used as a metaphor to demonstrate the importance of support, guidance, and modeling provided by adults to children in executing their rights.[49] When children learn a new skill—from eating to developing social relations to expressing their views— they need intensive support from the adults around them, whether their parents at the *microsystem* level or teachers and other professionals at the *mesosystem* level. Adults can provide physical and emotional support, guidance, modeling, and protection. As children develop their relevant skills, the adults can gradually loosen their grip, metaphorically or literally, until eventually children are able to practice the right on their own, without scaffolding.[50] *Mesosystem* professionals may provide scaffolding for parents as well. For example, pediatricians can provide parents with information about nonviolent forms of discipline and about the harms of corporal punishment.[51] Such indirect assistance to parents is likely to improve children's right to a safe and nonviolent environment.

Exosystems, such as workplaces and social networks, can act as hubs for educating parents to pursue the full range of rights that the laws offer for the benefit of their children. Employers can provide information and consultation about social support services and how to pursue social benefits. If families are not encouraged to assert their social rights, they might remain poor and undereducated despite legislative efforts to advance equality. For example, a governmental program for adult literacy education may not be known or accessible to parents unless employers support its advertisement and encourage employees to attend the program, possibly while offering benefits for successful completers. Similarly, social networks act as resources for gaining immediate information that can help parents promote the needs-rights of their children at home and beyond. A work-based antipoverty program introduced to parents of school-aged children improved children's academic achievements and their social behavior.[52] When parents are scaffolded by friends and colleagues in carrying out their complex parental roles, children's rights are likely to be better implemented.

The *macrosystem* is a crucial part of the enforcement ecosystem. State policies can promote professional and parental training targeted at the implementation of certain rights. For example, training programs on the implementation of child protection and mandatory reporting laws can help teachers and health care professionals identify children at risk and report child abuse.[53] For such training programs to be effective, they must be adequately funded and specifically tailored to the professional population they target. Public campaigns can educate parents against the use of violence as a disciplinary method and thus promote the implementation of laws banning corporal punishment. Such campaigns have proved effective in countries like Sweden, where the ban against corporal punishment became law in 1979 and was supported with continuous public campaigns.[54] Further enforcement occurs at the *macrosystem* level regarding each of the domains where children's rights laws apply. Governmental agencies are the official authorities responsible for ensuring that children are provided with education as well as health and social services and that at-risk children are effectively protected. Ombudsman offices, now operating in approximately fifty countries, typically are independent governmental agencies charged with the authority to monitor the implementation of children's rights.[55] From a child's ecosystems approach, a children's ombudsman is a powerful instrument of oversight to ensure that the *macrosystem* not only implements its obligations toward children but also regulates enforcement. At the European level, the European Network of Ombudspersons for Children (ENOC) was established in 1997 to encourage children's rights implementation, to share information, and to support the promotion of children's rights and their enforcement.[56]

The *macrosystem* also refers to international and regional treaty systems, which include a range of mechanisms to monitor and enforce international laws. The CRC, for example, established a monitoring body, the UN Committee on the Rights of the Child, to which state parties are required to submit periodic reports.[57] The Council of Europe (CoE), founded in 1949, adopted the European Convention on the Exercise of Children's Rights (1996)[58] as well as treaties on a range of specific children's rights issues, such as the Convention on the Protection of Children against Sexual Exploitation and Sexual Abuse (2010),[59] the European Convention on the Repatriation of Minors,[60] and the Convention on Cybercrime.[61] In Africa, the African Charter on the Rights and Welfare of the Child entered into force in 1999 and addressed, in addition to the principles appearing in the CRC, some specific issues that are unique to Africa. The Charter established the African Committee of Experts that is authorized to collect information about the implementation of the Charter among African states, investigate individual complaints, make suggestions and recommendations, and provide explanations for specific provisions. In the Americas, the Inter-American Children's Institute (IIN) was founded as early as 1927 and became a specialized organ of the Organization of American States in 1949. The IIN includes all Inter-American states, and its mission is to develop public policies for promoting, protecting, and enforcing children's rights, with the CRC as its reference.[62]

7 THE SOCIOECOLOGICAL MODEL: IMPLEMENTATION AND CONTRIBUTION

A socioecological perspective means that to understand the rights of a particular child it is important to explore the societal context, including norms, laws, and demographics, the individual child's attributes and characteristics, and the child's interactions with others. Only a full examination of these various domains can uncover the relevant regulatory regime and its implementation in practice. For example, if we are interested in exploring the child's right to active participation in school settings, investigation of the national and international laws governing free speech and participation rights that apply in the specific country would be only a first step. We would also need to examine the cultural norms and the democratic ethos of the given society as well as barriers to participation for different children within that society. We would also need to consider policies and programs encouraging and supporting schools in advancing children's deliberative capabilities. No less important are the contextual factors relating to societal and demographic characteristics of the individual children and of their families, such as gender, age, ethnicity, race, place of residence, socioeconomic status, religion, and cultural background. These characteristics directly affect the ways in which local, national, and international laws relating to children's freedom of speech are implemented. We would also need to examine factors relating to relevant *personality* features (introversion or extroversion, political or ideological orientation, general temper, and earlier experience with executing free-speech rights). All of these shape children's ability and motivation to assert their participatory rights. We would then need to examine the processes that occur within the school (such as interactions between staff and students, encouragement to express views, and protection measures against violence and bullying) and within the families (parental encouragement to express opinions, child-rearing styles). Only after such an analysis can we understand the ability and motivation of individual children at a given place and time to assert their participation rights, as much as they exist, in school. Such an exploration may lead to practical conclusions regarding the need for improving professional training, educating children and families, or changing the legal requirements relating to child and youth participation.

When applied to children's rights, the socioecological model is helpful for several reasons. First, it organizes knowledge regarding children's needs-rights according to the different ecosystems and highlights their interconnections and mutual effects. The argument presented earlier about the possible association between children's experience in participation in familial decision-making (*microsystem*) and their ability to assert their rights at school (*mesosystem*) demonstrates the model's importance in uncovering interconnections among the various ecosystems of children's lives. Second, the model uncovers the interface between regulation and people, between existing laws and rules, on one hand, and the well-being of children, on the other. Laws relating to child labor, child protection, or freedom of expression have specific outcomes for children in different contexts that the model can uncover. Third, the model can identify areas in need of improvement: those in which regulation is lacking or where enforcement and implementation are weak. Fourth, the model can uncover areas where further research is needed. The example of youth participation presented earlier demonstrates the need to explore and measure whether and how familial practices enhance or diminish children's capacities to assert their rights.

A further use of the model is its ability to identify possible links not only between and across the domains of children's lives but across the different rights and needs as well. For example, focusing on a certain jurisdiction, once we have data on a range of children's rights laws and their implementation, a possible connection may appear between discriminatory practices in certain schools and children's ability to assert their participatory rights. In other words, it is possible to assume that when children are separated into different schools according to gender, ethnicity, or religion, they will exhibit different levels of participation in school councils and in individual decision-making processes in the school setting. Data collection regarding the rights of children in the labor market (such as minimum wage, minimal age, limitations on the length and timing of labor, safety regulations, and rest) may be compared against children's rights in education and, more generally, the enforcement of children's right to development.[63] Similarly, once we have data on national efforts relating to health, nutrition, and risk-behavior education among children and youth, we can compare them with findings regarding youth mortality, mental health, and physical health.[64] Finally, if we focus our attention on national efforts to enact and enforce social rights for refugee children, a connection may be identified between the services and assistance they receive and their protection against sexual exploitation and violence.[65] These are only some examples of possible links that merit empirical studies. The model can help identify these links and provide a research agenda.

8 CONCLUSION

This chapter introduced the socioecological perspective developed by Urie Bronfenbrenner and demonstrated its utility as an analytical and theoretical methodology in the children's rights field. The model identifies the concentric circles, or domains, in which children live their lives. It defines the range of levels affecting each domain (personal characteristics, processes/dynamics, and predetermined demographic circumstances) and highlights the interconnections between the various domains. Organizing knowledge about children's needs-rights, existing legislation and its enforcement according to the model can help researchers and policymakers identify needed reform in ways that address individual, societal, and cultural differences across time and place.

NOTES

1. Urie Bronfenbrenner, "Ecology of the Family as a Context for Human Development: Research Perspectives." *Developmental Psychology* 22, no. 6 (November 1986): 723–742. Within these five concentric circles, Brofenbrenner relates to three dimensions: *Person* refers to the characteristics of a particular child. *Process* refers to processes and dynamics between the child and others, such as parents and teachers. *Context* refers to societal and demographic characteristics, such as gender, social class, nationality, and geographic area.
2. Tali Gal, "Child Victims' Needs: Empirical Findings," in *Child Victims and Restorative Justice: A Needs-Rights Model* (New York: Oxford University Press, 2011), 57–90.
3. See Bronfenbrenner, "Ecology of the Family"; Urie Bronfenbrenner, "Ecological Models of Human Development," in *International Encyclopedia of Education*, 2nd ed., ed. Torsten Husen and T. Neville Postlethwaite (Oxford: Pergamon Press, 1994), 1643–1647; Urie Bronfenbrenner and Pamela A. Morris, "The Ecology of Developmental Processes," in *Handbook of Child Psychology: Theoretical Models of Human Development*, 5th ed., ed. William Damon and Richard M. Lerner (Hoboken, NJ: John Wiley and Sons, 1998), 993–1028.
4. Bronfenbrenner and Morris, "Ecology of Developmental Processes."

5. Nicholas R. G. Stanger, "Moving 'Eco' Back into Socio-Ecological Models: A Proposal to Reorient Ecological Literacy into Human Developmental Models and School Systems," *Human Ecology Review* 18, no. 2 (December 2011): 167–173.

6. John G. Bruhn, "Human Ecology: A Unifying Science?," *Human Ecology* 2, no. 2 (April 1974): 105–125.

7. Paul Rigby and Bill Whyte, "Children's Narrative within a Multi-Centred, Dynamic Ecological Framework of Assessment and Planning for Child Trafficking," *British Journal of Social Work* 45, no. 1 (January 2015): 34–51.

8. Chloe Ling and Sylvia Kwok. , "An Integrated Resilience and Ecological Model of Child Abuse (REC-Model)," *Journal of Child and Family Studies* 26, no. 6 (June 2017): 1655–1663.

9. M. Pippin Whitaker and Tamara Estes Savage, "Social-Ecological Influences on Teen Dating Violence: A Youth Rights and Capabilities Approach to Exploring Context," *Journal of Child & Adolescent Trauma* 7, no. 3 (August 2014): 163–174.

10. Maury Nation, Cindy Crusto, Abraham Wandersman, Karol L. Kumpfer, Diana Seybolt, Erin Morrissey-Kane, and Katrina Davino, "What Works in Prevention: Principles of Effective Prevention Programs," *American Psychologist* 58, no. 6–7 (June–July 2003), 449–456.

11. Katy Atkiss, Matthew Moyer, Mona Desai, and Michele Roland, "Positive Youth Development: Integration of the Developmental Assets Theory and the Socio-Ecological Model," *American Journal of Health Education* 42, no. 3 (May–June 2011): 171–180.

12. Lee Ann Slocum, Finn-Aage Esbensen, and Terrance J. Taylor, "The Code of Silence in Schools: An Assessment of a Socio-Ecological Model of Youth's Willingness to Report School Misbehavior," *Youth & Society* 49, no. 2 (March 2017): 123–149.

13. Michael Ungar, "The Social Ecology of Resilience: Addressing Contextual and Cultural Ambiguity of a Nascent Construct," *American Journal of Orthopsychiatry* 81, no. 1 (January 2011): 1–17.

14. Etienne G. Krug, Linda L. Dahlberg, James A. Mercy, Anthony B. Zwi, and Rafael Lozano, *World Report on Violence and Health* (Geneva: World Health Organization, 2002), 12–14.

15. Catherine Cerulli, Ann Marie White, Nancy Chin, and Neil McLaughlin, "Unlocking Family Court's Potential for Public Health Promotion," *Buffalo Journal of Gender, Law and Social Policy* 22, no. 1 (2013): 49–70.

16. David B. Wexler and Bruce J. Winick, "Therapeutic Jurisprudence as a New Approach to Mental Health Law Policy Analysis and Research," *University of Miami Law Review* 45, no. 5 (May 1991): 979–1004; Bruce J. Winick, "The Jurisprudence of Therapeutic Jurisprudence," *Psychology, Public Policy and Law* 3, no. 1 (March 1997): 184–206.

17. For example, Susan L. Brooks, "Therapeutic Jurisprudence and Preventive Law in Child Welfare Proceedings: A Family Systems Approach," *Psychology, Public Policy, and Law* 5, no. 4 (December 1999): 951–965; see also Tali Gal and Dahlia Schilli-Jerichower, "Mainstreaming Therapeutic Jurisprudence in Family Law: The Israeli Child Protection Law as a Case Study," *Family Court Review* 55, no. 2 (April 2017): 177–194.

18. See, for example, suggestions for law reforms designed to make criminal law more therapeutic for crime victims in Edna Erez, Michael Kilchling, and Jo-Anne M. Wemmers, eds., *Therapeutic Jurisprudence and Victim Participation in Justice: International Perspectives* (Durham, NC: Carolina Academic Press, 2011).

19. Marsha B. Freeman, "Love Means Always Having to Say You're Sorry: Applying the Realities of Therapeutic Jurisprudence to Family Law," *UCLA Women's Law Journal* 17, no. 2 (Spring 2008): 215–242.

20. Daniel W. Shuman, "Therapeutic Jurisprudence and Tort Law: A Limited Subjective Standard of Care," *SMU Law Review* 46, no. 2 (January 1992): 409–432.

21. Michael M. Freeman, "Human Rights, Children's Rights and Judgment: Some Thoughts on Reconciling Universality and Pluralism," *International Journal of Children's Rights* 10, no. 4 (2002): 345–354.

22. Erica Burman, "Local, Global or Globalized? Child Development and International Child Rights Legislation," *Childhood* 3, no. 1 (February 1996): 45–66.

23. Freeman, "Human Rights."

24. Gal, "Child Victims' Needs," 57–90.

25. Gal, "Child Victims' Needs," 193.

26. Christopher A. Thurber and John R. Weisz, " 'You Can Try or You Can Just Give Up': The Impact of Perceived Control and Coping Style on Childhood Homesickness," *Developmental Psychology* 33, no. 3 (May 1997): 508–517.

27. Anne Graham and Robin Fitzgerald, "Taking Account of the 'To and Fro' of Children's Experiences in Family Law," *Children Australia* 31, no. 2 (February 2005): 30–36.

28. Amartya Sen, "Rights and Capabilities," in *Morality and Objectivity*, ed. Ted Honderich (London: Routledge, 1985), 130–148.

29. Mario Biggeri, Renato Libanora, Stefano Mariani, and Leonardo Menchini, "Children Conceptualizing Their Capabilities: Results of a Survey Conducted during the First Children's World Congress on Child Labour," *Journal of Human Development* 7, no. 1 (March 2006): 59–83.

30. Martha Nussbaum, *Women and Human Development: The Capabilities Approach*, 1st ed. (Cambridge: Cambridge University Press, 2000), 76–80.

31. Esperanza Ochaíta and Angeles Espinosa, "Needs of Children and Adolescents as a Basis for the Justification of Their Rights," *International Journal of Children's Rights* 9 (2001): 313–315.

32. Biggeri et al., "Children Conceptualizing Their Capabilities: Results of a Survey Conducted During the First Children's World Congress on Child Labour," *Journal of Human Development* 7, no. 1, (March 2006):59–83.

33. See also Whitaker and Savage, "Social-Ecological Influences," 166–171.

34. H. L. A. Hart, Law, *Liberty and Morality*, 1st ed. (Oxford: Oxford University Press, 1963).

35. Neil MacCormick, *Legal Rights and Social Democracy: Essays in Legal and Political Philosophy* (Oxford: Clarendon, 1982).

36. Hilde Bojer, "Children and Theories of Social Justice," *Feminist Economics* 6, no. 2 (February 2000): 23–39.

37. Burman, "Local, Global or Globalized?"

38. Ochaita and Espinoza, "Needs of Children and Adolescents."

39. Biggeri et al., "Children Conceptualizing Their Capabilities."

40. See, e.g., Len Doyal and Ian Gough, *A Theory of Human Need* (London: Macmillan, 1991).

41. Tali Gal, "An Ecological Model of Child and Youth Participation," *Children and Youth Services Review* 79, no. C (August 2017): 57–64.

42. Bronfenbrenner, "Ecology of the Family," 723–724.

43. Bronfenbrenner, "Ecology of the Family," 727–731.

44. Pearl Boateng, "Interventions on Child Labour in South Asia," K4D Helpdesk Report, May 16, 2017, https://assets.publishing.service.gov.uk/media/5984577fe5274a1707000067/105-Interventions-on-Child-Labour-in-South-Asia.pdf.

45. Stanger, "Moving 'Eco' Back."

46. Umar Serajuddin and Paolo Verme, "Who Is Deprived? Who Feels Deprived? Labor Deprivation, Youth, and Gender in Morocco," *Review of Income and Wealth* 61, no. 1 (March 2015): 140–163.

47. K. D. Bussmann, Claudia Erthal, and Andreas Schroth, "Effects of Banning Corporal Punishment in Europe—A Five-Nation Comparison," in *Global Pathways to Abolishing Physical Punishment: Realizing Children's Rights*, Joan E. Durrant and Anne B. Smith (New York: Routledge, 2011), 299–322.

48. Shulamit Almog and Lotem Perry-Hazan, "The Ability to Claim and the Opportunity to Imagine: Rights Consciousness and the Education of Ultra-Orthodox Girls," *Journal of Law & Education* 40, no. 2 (April 2011): 273–304.

49. See C. Addison Stone, "The Metaphor of Scaffolding: Its Utility for the Field of Learning Disabilities," *Journal of Learning Disabilities* 31, no. 4 (July–August 1998): 344–364; Anne Graham, Jenni Whelan, and Robyn Fitzgerald, "Progressing Participation: Taming the Space between Rhetoric and Reality," *Children Youth and Environments* 16, no. 2 (January 2006): 231–247; Judith Cashmore, "Children's Participation in Family Law Decision-Making: Theoretical Approaches to Understanding Children's Views," *Children and Youth Services Review* 33, no. 4 (April 2011): 515–520.

50. This example also demonstrates the importance of considering the temporal domain—the *chronosystem*—since scaffolding changes over time.

51. Joan Durrant and Ron Ensom, "Physical Punishment of Children: Lessons from 20 Years of Research," *Canadian Medical Association Journal* 184, no. 12 (2012): 1373–1377.

52. Aletha C. Huston, Greg J. Duncan, Robert Granger, Johannes Bos, Vonnie McLoyd, Rashmita Mistry, Danielle Crosby, Christina Gibson, Katherine Magnuson, Jennifer Romich, and Ana Ventura, "Work-Based Antipoverty Programs for Parents Can Enhance the School Performance and Social Behavior of Children," *Child Development* 72, no. 1 (February 2001): 318–336.

53. See, e.g., Russell Hawkins and Christy McCallum, "Mandatory Notification Training for Suspected Child Abuse and Neglect in South Australian Schools," *Child Abuse & Neglect* 25, no. 12 (December 2001): 1603–1625.

54. Bussmann, Erthal, and Schroth, "Effects of Banning Corporal Punishment."

55. Linda C. Reif, "The Ombudsman for Children: Human Rights Protection and Promotion," in *The Ombudsman, Good Governance, and the International Human Rights System* (Leiden: Martinus Nijhoff, 2004), 246.

56. See "ENOC Aims" on the European Network of Ombudspersons for Children website, http://enoc.eu/?page_id=174.

57. John Muncie, "The Globalization of Crime Control—The Case of Youth and Juvenile Justice; Neo-Liberalism, Policy Convergence and International Conventions," *Theoretical Criminology* 9, no. 1 (2005): 35–64. For a critical analysis of the role of the international community as an enforcement mechanism, see Jonathan Todres, "Emerging Limitations on the Rights of the Child: The UN Convention on the Rights of the Child and Its Early Case Law," *Columbia Human Rights Law Review* 30 (January 1998): 159–200.

58. Council of Europe, European Convention on the Exercise of Children's Rights, ETS No. 160, adopted January 25, 1996, https://www.coe.int/en/web/conventions/search-on -treaties/-/conventions/treaty/160.

59. Council of Europe, Council of Europe Convention on the Protection of Children against Sexual Exploitation and Sexual Abuse, CETS 201, adopted October 25, 2007, https://www. coe.int/en/web/conventions/full-list/-/conventions/treaty/201.

60. Council of Europe, European Convention on the Repatriation of Minors, ETS No. 071, adopted May 28, 1970, https://www.coe.int/en/web/conventions/full-list/-/conventions/treaty/071.

61. Council of Europe, Convention on Cybercrime, ETS No. 185, adopted November 23, 2001, https://www.coe.int/en/web/conventions/full-list/-/conventions/treaty/185.

62. See Inter-American Children's Institute, Organization of American States, http://iin.oea.org/en/index.html.

63. See, e.g., Daniel Holgado, Isidro Maya-Jariego, Ignacio Ramos, Jorge Palacio, Oscar Oviedo-Trespalacios, Vanessa Romero-Mendoza, and José Amar, "Impact of Child Labor on Academic Performance: Evidence from the Program 'Edúcame Primero Colombia,'" *International Journal of Educational Development* 34 (2014): 58–66, demonstrating a link between work-school conflict and low academic achievement among Colombian children.

64. Sheridan Bartlett, Roger Hart, David Satterthwaite, Ximena de la Barra, and Alfredo Missair, *Cities for Children: Children's Rights, Poverty and Urban Management* (London: Routledge, 2016).

65. Martin D. Ruck, Daniel P. Keating, Elizabeth M. Saewyc, Felton Earls, and Asher Ben-Arieh, "The United Nations Convention on the Rights of the Child: Its Relevance for Adolescents," *Journal of Research on Adolescence* 26, no. 1 (March 2016): 16–29.

CHAPTER 7

··

CRITICAL RACE THEORY AND CHILDREN'S RIGHTS

··

NATSU TAYLOR SAITO AND
AKILAH J. KINNISON

1 INTRODUCTION

··

WHAT can critical race theory (CRT) contribute to the realization of children's rights in international law? CRT helps us focus on the intersection of race and rights, providing a framework for considering the extent to which structural racism is implicated in any given endeavor. Although initially articulated as a critique of the United States' legal system, a critical race perspective is being brought to other disciplines, including international law. We consider here ways in which CRT can help ensure that children of color and their communities benefit from internationally recognized children's rights and how the growing recognition of these rights can contribute to struggles for racial justice.

2 CRITICAL RACE THEORY: AN OVERVIEW

··

2.1 Origins

Put most simply, critical race theory begins by asking, "What does race have to do with it?"[1] The inquiry considers how and why race plays a role in the issue at hand and uses the insights this generates to formulate strategies for exposing and contesting racial subordination.[2] This approach, long utilized by scholars such as the brilliant sociologist

W. E. B. Du Bois, was introduced to the legal academy as a conscious framework in the late 1980s by professors committed to incorporating the struggle against racism into their analysis of US law and legal institutions.[3] Kimberlé Crenshaw explains the origin of the term as follows: "We would signify the specific political and intellectual location of the project through 'critical,' the substantive focus through 'race,' and the desire to develop a coherent account of race and law through the term 'theory.' "[4]

Many early critical race scholars ("race crits") had been involved in the civil rights movement but were convinced by the retrenchment of the 1970s that liberal reforms would not suffice.[5] Many appreciated, and helped develop, the more radical view of the critical legal studies (CLS) movement that law is neither objective nor neutral but inherently political. They nonetheless recognized that CLS did not adequately theorize the role played by race in the legal system or appreciate the extent to which legal remedies remained essential to contesting racism.[6] As Angela Harris observes,

> CRT inherits from CLS a commitment to being "critical," which in this sense means also to be "radical"—to locate problems not at the surface of doctrine but in the deep structure of American law and culture.... At the same time, CRT inherits from traditional civil rights scholarship a commitment to a vision of liberation from racism through right reason. Despite the difficulty of separating legal reasoning and institutions from their racist roots, CRT's ultimate vision is redemptive, not deconstructive. Justice remains possible, and it is the property of whites and nonwhites alike.[7]

The genealogy of critical race theory in the legal academy can be traced not only to CLS but also to the movements that brought African American studies and ethnic studies more generally into colleges and universities. In turn, CRT provided inspiration to such movements as critical race feminism,[8] LatCrit,[9] Asian American legal scholarship,[10] and Third World Approaches to International Law (TWAIL)[11] and made it possible for a diverse range of approaches to race to thrive within the legal academy.

Conceptual frameworks inspired by critical race theory are now being utilized across a range of other disciplines, including education, psychology, cultural studies, political science, and philosophy.[12] Three decades into the venture, there are differing definitions of the term critical race theory, varied perspectives on the movement's origins, and critiques from within and without the field,[13] indicating not only that race and racism remain core concerns in the pursuit of social justice but also that CRT as a movement retains its vitality. Reflecting on the evolution of critical race theory, Crenshaw notes that "CRT is not so much an intellectual unit filled with natural stuff—theories, themes, practices, and the like—but one that is dynamically constituted by a series of contestations and convergences pertaining to the ways that racial power is understood and articulated in the post-civil rights era."[14] As such, it has much to offer to the field of children's rights.

2.2 Basic Principles

With no pretense of being comprehensive, this section summarizes some of the basic principles of critical race theory we consider most relevant to theorizing and realizing children's rights. These tenets provide both methodological and substantive guidance. Developed in the context of the historical experiences of people of color in the United States, these tenets are readily adapted to other contexts in which communities are systematically subordinated on the basis of race, ethnicity, national origin, or indigeneity.

Critical race theory begins from the premise that law and science are neither objective nor neutral but, rather, that they rationalize and reinforce the status quo. In the United States and throughout much of the rest of the world, this means reinforcing racial disparities. Recognizing that all analyses arise from particular perspectives, critical race scholars have made, in Mari Matsuda's words, "a deliberate choice to see the world from the standpoint of the oppressed."[15] Narrative is often used both to highlight the fact that scholarship is never simply objective or empirical and to emphasize the importance of listening to and conveying the perspectives of those "at the bottom."[16] Critical race theory consciously embraces a commitment not only to understand the perspectives of those who are racially subordinated but also to change the dynamics of power and privilege that maintain their subordination. In other words, academic work and institutions should be serving the people.[17]

From this methodological foundation widespread consensus has been reached on numerous substantive principles. In considering the impact of racism on children's rights, the following tenets seem particularly relevant.

2.2.1 *"Race" Is a Powerful Social Construct, Not a Biological Reality*

In the United States, as in other countries, such as South Africa, racial categories have been created and enforced by law; they can create classifications that appear inconsistent or illogical but serve to maintain white privilege.[18] Building on Kendall Thomas's insight that "race" is best understood as a verb rather than a noun, CRT recognizes that racial identity is both imposed and "performative."[19]

2.2.2 *Identities Are Complex, Dynamic, and Intersectional[20]*

Race is but one dimension of a person's actual or perceived identity, and racism does not function independently, but in concert with other social forces, including sexism, homophobia, xenophobia, and presumptions based on language, religion, and national origin. This results in experiences that are uniquely intersectional, not simply the result of accumulated independent oppressions. CRT "recenters" the inquiry from the mainstream experience to the "cultural borderlands," where differences attributed to race, gender, sexual orientation, age, class, and any of a number of other socially constructed classifications constitute cumulatively interactive dimensions of identity.[21]

2.2.3 *Unconscious Racism Is Pervasive and Often More Destructive Than Intentional Bias*

CRT has incorporated and built upon the argument advanced by Charles Lawrence that the harm caused by racism goes far beyond individual bias or prejudice. Lawrence characterizes racism as a "societal illness" that should be approached as a problem of epidemiology, noting that "the ubiquity of conscious and unconscious racism [is] evidence of the continued vitality of racist ideology."[22]

2.2.4 *Racism Is Structural and Has Always Been Ordinary, Not Exceptional, in American Society*[23]

CRT understands racial domination and subordination as neither aberrational nor simply vestiges of the past, but integral to the foundations of the country. Because racism is so thoroughly institutionalized, it is presumptively normative. Thus, for example, Cheryl Harris explains, in "Whiteness as Property," how indigenous peoples' lands that were occupied and appropriated by Euro-American settlers did not constitute property until claimed by those identified as white.[24] Despite the racism evident in this proposition, the property relations that rest on this foundation remain unquestioned in the dominant American narrative.

2.2.5 *Colorblindness Can Perpetuate Structural Racism*

Promoting colorblindness as a solution to racial disparity presumes that racism is overt and intentional.[25] However, if racism can be unconscious and racial disparities perpetuated without intent, a refusal to see color simply allows the problem to persist. For this reason, critical race theory recognizes that formal equality and efforts to combat racism based on prevailing interpretations of the Constitution's guarantee of equal protection have limited utility and may even be counterproductive.[26] Instead, CRT emphasizes that all uses of race are not equivalent and that social and historical context is always critical to understanding racial inequity.

2.2.6 *Assimilationism Contributes to Racial Subordination*

From a critical race perspective, people of color should not be prohibited from assimilating into mainstream society, but neither should they be required to assimilate. Assimilation depends not only on the willingness and ability of subordinated peoples to conform to mainstream expectations but the willingness of those in power to incorporate them, and historically this has been precluded by racism. CRT understands assimilationism to be detrimental to people of color because it presumes their cultures to be inferior to that of the Euro-American majority, and it recognizes that coerced assimilation can be and has been used for genocidal purposes.[27]

2.2.7 *Racial Realism Forces Us to Reject the Standard Narrative of "Progress"*

Devon Carbado observes that "CRT rejects the standard racial progress narrative...that characterizes the history of race relations in the United States [as] a history of linear uplift and improvement."[28] In 1992 Derrick Bell insisted that the struggle for racial justice had to begin with "racial realism," that is, the acknowledgment that full equality would never be achieved by Black people in America; that even as victories were achieved, "racial patterns [would] adapt in ways that maintain white dominance."[29] While many critical race scholars remain more optimistic than this, Bell's thesis of "interest convergence," that "[t]he interest of blacks in achieving racial equality will be accommodated only when it converges with the interests of whites"[30] is widely accepted.

2.3 Critical Race Theory and International Law

As a conceptual framework, critical race theory provides insights relevant to the realization of international human rights, including those pertaining specifically to children. It can help us understand how international law can further the recognition and implementation of fundamental rights while simultaneously constraining the exercise of such rights. Before addressing provisions of international law that explicitly address racial discrimination, it is helpful to note some general observations about race and international law made by legal theorists who approach the subject from a critical race perspective. These scholars have explained in considerable detail how our contemporary international legal order emerged from, and remains rooted in, a Euro-derivative network of agreements intended to facilitate the colonization of Africa, Asia, the Pacific, and the Americas.[31]

In this process, race itself emerged as a malleable and contingent construct. As Antony Anghie explains, it incorporated the notion of more and less "civilized" peoples and provided the "dynamic of difference" relied upon by colonizing powers to justify their "civilizing mission."[32] In other words, race as we know it today was born in the colonial encounter and matured to serve the evolving needs of colonial appropriation and exploitation.[33] Although the number of new states recognized and admitted to the United Nations in the 1960s and 1970s was dramatic, this did not result in a reformulation of the basic tenets of international law. Only those states willing to abide by the rules established by the colonial powers were deemed sufficiently civilized to gain international recognition, and the legacy of colonialism is further reflected in the fact that their territories were largely defined by boundaries arbitrarily imposed upon them by European powers.[34] As Makau Mutua observes, "the right to self-determination was exercised not by the victims of colonization but by their victimizers, the elites who control the international state system."[35] In the meantime, settler states were intent on precluding their own decolonization, insisting on the narrowest possible interpretation of the right to self-determination, ensuring that the UN General Assembly's 1960 Declaration on the Granting of Independence to Colonial Countries and Peoples would not be applied to them, delaying adoption of the UN Declaration on the Rights of Indigenous Peoples by some twenty years.[36]

Racism persists, in part, because the colonial relationships that gave birth to the core tenets of international law live on. In the aftermath of World War II, as formal decolonization became inevitable, those who benefited from colonialism recognized that it needed to be rendered invisible. On this point, there was a convergence of interests: external colonial powers did not want to be accountable for centuries of exploitation and expropriation; newly independent states did not want their sovereignty or territorial boundaries to be questioned; settler states did not want their ongoing occupation of indigenous lands subjected to legal scrutiny. The result is that international law has never squarely confronted the legacies of colonialism.[37] Applying a critical race perspective, we can see that while international instruments have proscribed racial discrimination, and numerous monitoring bodies and experts have studied and denounced racial attacks as well as systemic disparities, the international legal system has yet to address the deepest and most structurally embedded sources of racialized privilege and subordination.

3 RACE AND INTERNATIONAL HUMAN RIGHTS LAW

3.1 Prohibitions on Racial Discrimination

Modern human rights protections grow out of the experiences of World War II, the consequent recognition of genocide as both a crime and a violation of a *jus cogens* norm, and the movements for decolonization that swept through Africa and Asia. One result is that prohibitions on racial discrimination are an integral part of this body of law and are often articulated in a manner consistent with the perspectives of critical race scholars. For instance, there is a focus on human dignity, acknowledgment that racism need not be overt to have discriminatory effect, and recognition that pervasive racial disparities will require structural solutions. There is also an important recognition of the right to self-determination, addressing many of the problems with assimilationism and the narrative of continual progress identified by CRT, especially when considered in conjunction with the legal definition of genocide.

Central to the purposes of the UN, as articulated in its 1945 Charter, are "develop[ing] friendly relations among nations based on respect for the principle of equal rights and self-determination of peoples" and "achiev[ing] international cooperation in...promoting and encouraging respect for human rights and for fundamental freedoms for all without distinction as to race, sex, language, or religion."[38] In 1948 the UN General Assembly adopted its first human rights treaty, the International Convention on the Prevention and Punishment of the Crime of Genocide (Genocide Convention). The Genocide Convention defines genocide as the commission of certain acts "with intent to destroy, in whole or in part, a national, ethnical, racial or religious group, *as such*."[39] Thus, in its very first human rights treaty, the UN addresses the rights of racial and ethnic groups and does so by prohibiting not merely violence against members of those groups but, rather, actions designed to destroy the identity of the group itself. This is consistent with critical race theory's insistence that contesting racism requires us to look beyond the harms inflicted on individuals to consider systemic injustices against peoples.[40] Just as the individual racist is not the primary concern of CRT, neither is its analysis limited to the individual target of discrimination.

The day after adopting the Genocide Convention, the General Assembly approved the Universal Declaration of Human Rights (UDHR). The UDHR is a declaration rather than a legally binding treaty but is widely recognized as articulating fundamental principles of modern customary human rights law. As stated in its first article, "All human beings are born free and equal in dignity and rights," and it enshrines the principle of non-discrimination in Article 2, stating that "[e]veryone is entitled to all the rights and freedoms set forth in this Declaration, without distinction of any kind, such as race."[41] Article 2 further provides that no distinction is to be made based on the "political, jurisdictional or international status of the country or territory to which a person belongs," thereby providing human rights protections to peoples in various states of continued colonization. Thus, from the very beginnings of the modern human rights system, racial equality and protection of peoples on the basis of race has played a central role.

The Genocide Convention remained the UN system's primary human rights treaty for nearly a generation.[42] Then, in 1966, the General Assembly promulgated three treaties that now form the core of modern human rights protections, beginning with a convention specifically addressing racial discrimination as well as treaties addressing civil and political rights and economic, social, and cultural rights.

Adopted in March 1966, the International Convention on the Elimination of All Forms of Racial Discrimination (ICERD) begins by grounding the treaty in the UN's objective of promoting the "dignity and equality inherent in all human beings," with a nod to the condemnation of "colonialism and all practices of segregation and discrimination associated therewith."[43] It then commits states parties to "pursue by all appropriate means and without delay a policy of eliminating racial discrimination in all its forms."[44]

ICERD recognizes, as critical race theorists advocate, that racism need not be conscious or intentional and that solutions should be structural. Article 1 defines racial discrimination broadly to include any "distinction, exclusion, restriction or preference based on race, colour, descent, or national or ethnic origin which has the *purpose or effect* of nullifying or impairing the recognition, enjoyment or exercise, on an equal footing, of human rights and fundamental freedoms."[45] The treaty obligates states parties to "condemn racial discrimination and undertake to pursue by all appropriate means and without delay a policy of eliminating racial discrimination in all its forms," to commit to refrain from state or state-sponsored racial discrimination, and to review laws and regulations that "have the *effect* of creating or perpetuating racial discrimination."[46] Thus, an inquiry into whether a practice is contrary to the Convention need not address its subjective rationale but can focus solely on its disparate impact. The Committee on the Elimination of Racial Discrimination (CERD), responsible for monitoring implementation of the treaty, emphasizes that a "distinction is contrary to the Convention if it has either the purpose or the effect of impairing particular rights and freedoms."[47]

Consistent with a critical race perspective, ICERD recognizes that equality under the law extends beyond formal equality. In defining racial discrimination for purposes of the treaty, Article 1 specifies that racial discrimination does not include "[s]pecial measures taken for the sole purpose of securing adequate advancement of certain racial or ethnic groups or individuals requiring such protection as may be necessary in order to ensure such groups or individuals equal enjoyment or exercise of human rights and fundamental freedoms." These "special measures" are also termed "affirmative measures," "positive action," or, as in the United States, "affirmative action." Interpreting this provision, CERD notes that non-discrimination is not equivalent to "uniform treatment";

"[t]o treat in an equal manner persons or groups whose situations are objectively different will constitute discrimination in effect, as will the unequal treatment of persons whose situations are objectively the same."[48]

ICERD contains a general prohibition against racial discrimination (Article 2) and highlights particular state obligations, including ensuring freedom from apartheid and segregation (Article 3) and condemning racist propaganda (Article 4).

In addition, Article 5 requires states to guarantee "equality before the law," with specific reference to equality in the enjoyment of particular rights that include treatment before tribunals; security of person; the right to vote, marry, or own property; the right to access public places and services; and economic, social, and cultural rights, including rights to work, housing, union membership, health, and education. In interpreting the treaty, CERD has specifically invoked the concept of intersectionality, noting that "[t]he 'grounds' of discrimination are extended in practice by the notion of 'intersectionality' whereby the Committee addresses situations of double or multiple discrimination— such as discrimination on grounds of gender or religion—when discrimination on such a ground appears to exist in combination with a ground or grounds listed in article 1 of the Convention."[49]

Shortly after adopting ICERD, the General Assembly promulgated two overarching human rights treaties, the International Covenant on Civil and Political Rights (ICCPR) and the International Covenant on Economic, Social and Cultural Rights (ICESCR).[50] Both treaties begin by recognizing the "inherent dignity" of all humans and referencing the recognition of dignity and equal rights in the UN Charter and the UDHR. Their common Article 1 provides: "All peoples have the right to self-determination. By virtue of that right they freely pursue their economic, social and cultural development." In their second article, each commits states parties to protecting the rights recognized in the treaties "without distinction of any kind," including distinction based on race. The ICCPR also recognizes the right to a group identity independent of state citizenship, providing in Article 27 that persons belonging to "ethnic, religious or linguistic minorities...shall not be denied the right, *in community* with other members of their group, to enjoy their own culture, to profess and practice their own religion, or to use their own language."[51]

Non-discrimination provisions are integral also to international instruments specifically addressing children's rights, most notably the Convention on the Rights of the Child (CRC), adopted by the General Assembly in 1989.[52] The CRC's preamble recalls the emphasis on inherent dignity and equality without regard to race found in the UN Charter, UN Declaration of Human Rights, ICCPR, and ICESCR. Further, it takes "due account of the importance of the traditions and cultural values of each people for the protection and harmonious development of the child." Non-discrimination is one of the CRC's four core principles, and its Article 2 obligates states parties to protect the rights in the treaty "without discrimination of any kind, irrespective of the child's or his or her parent's or legal guardian's race, colour, sex, language, religion, political or other opinion, national, ethnic or social origin, property, disability, birth or other status."

Several CRC provisions also directly protect cultural identity. Article 8 enshrines a child's right "to preserve his or her identity, including nationality," Article 17 highlights the linguistic needs of indigenous children and children belonging to minority groups, and Article 29 provides that education should develop respect for the child's cultural identity, language, and values. Article 30, echoing Article 27 of the ICCPR, provides that an indigenous child or a child belonging to an ethnic, religious, or linguistic minority "shall not be denied the right, in community with other members of his or her group, to enjoy his or her own culture, to profess and practice his or her own religion, or to use his or her own language."

3.2 Limitations of Anti-Discrimination Provisions

As the provisions of the foundational human rights treaties illustrate, the international legal system takes seriously its commitment to prohibit racial discrimination.[53] Many of the non-discrimination provisions found in international human rights instruments are consistent with CRT tenets, but applying a critical race perspective allows us to see that these instruments often fail to look beyond formal equality, choosing instead to promote assimilationist objectives and reflecting the presumptions of colonial narratives of progress and civilization. Perhaps most importantly, international human rights law tends to focus on individual rights rather than the rights of communities and cultures. This approach at best ignores, and at worst reinforces, continuing legacies of colonialism.

ICERD's preamble, for instance, says that states parties are "[a]larmed by manifestations of racial discrimination still in evidence in *some* areas of the world."[54] This appears to leave open the possibility that, in 1966, there were areas of the world where racial discrimination did not exist and implies as well that such discrimination will almost inevitably be eliminated. The language of Article 2(1)(c) has similar implications, as it commits states parties to take effective measures to correct laws and policies that create or perpetuate racial discrimination "wherever it exists." In fact, in 1972 CERD found the need to issue a General Recommendation reiterating the requirement that all states parties submit reports under the treaty because it was receiving "some reports . . . which expressed or implied the belief that the [required] information . . . need not be supplied by States parties on whose territories racial discrimination does not exist."[55]

ICERD Article 2 also provides that one way to eradicate racial discrimination is "to encourage, where appropriate, integrationist multiracial organizations and movements and other means of eliminating barriers between races, and to discourage anything which tends to strengthen racial division." When the Convention was adopted, South African apartheid was of particular concern, and this language should be read in light of this context as well as Article 3, which explicitly condemns segregation and apartheid. Certainly the mandate to eliminate racial barriers was needed, but Article 2's endorsement of integration as the primary remedy for segregation and apartheid is troubling, as it appears to assume the continuation of the state as currently constructed and to support the incorporation of racially subordinated groups—the majority, not the minority, in countries such as South Africa—into the extant body politic. It thus fails to recognize that while in some circumstances an integrationist approach may be entirely appropriate, in others it may reinforce oppressive regimes imposed by colonial powers.

International treaty-monitoring bodies have resisted fully addressing the continuing effects of colonialism. CERD, for instance, interprets the right to self-determination as having: (1) an "internal" aspect consisting of "the rights of all peoples to pursue freely their economic, social and cultural development" and (2) an "external" aspect that "implies that all peoples have the right to determine freely their political status and their place in the international community based upon the principle of equal rights and exemplified by the liberation of peoples from colonialism and by the prohibition to sub-ject peoples to alien subjugation, domination and exploitation."[56] Disregarding, for all practical purposes, the external aspect of the right to self-determination, CERD reminds states of their responsibilities to protect "individual rights without discrimination" and to encourage them, "within their respective constitutional frameworks," to consider "vesting" individuals with the right to engage in activities relevant to their identity as members of ethnic or linguistic groups.[57] CERD then reiterates that it is not authorizing or encouraging any action that would interfere with the territorial integrity or sover-eignty of a state.[58] It is, in effect, attempting to limit self-determination to rights that can be exercised within colonially constructed state formations.

A similar approach has been taken by the UN Human Rights Committee (HRC), the body responsible for monitoring implementation of the ICCPR. As noted above, Article 27 of the ICCPR provides that persons belonging to ethnic, religious, or linguistic minorities shall not be denied the right "in community" with others in their group to enjoy their culture, religion, and language. In its General Comment No. 23, the HRC emphasizes that Article 27 articulates "a right which is conferred on individuals belong-ing to minority groups" rather than a communal right, and it warns against confusing this with the right of all peoples to self-determination proclaimed in Article 1.[59] The HRC's interpretation reinforces the notion that self-determination is simply a right of states to be free from the domination of other states and, as interpreted and applied, may have little to do with peoples per se.[60] This means that indigenous peoples in settler colo-nial states, those under the jurisdiction of former colonial powers, and those who have been involuntarily incorporated into postcolonial states remain subject to the racial discrimination and oppression intrinsic to colonial rule. By refusing to address this legacy, the HRC imposes significant limitations on the potential of the ICCPR or other treaties prohibiting racial discrimination to address structural racism.

3.3   A Critical Race Perspective on Children's Rights

Critical race theory's focus on intersectionality invites us to ask what race has to do with children's rights and also what children's rights have to do with non-discrimination pro-visions. It encourages us to examine ways in which facially race-neutral international children's rights laws impact children of color and also invites us to look at the implications that children's rights can or should have on non-discrimination norms and other civil, political, or socioeconomic rights. When this analysis is undertaken with an eye toward protecting future generations, a CRT perspective allows us to understand that many of the rights we normally view through an adult-rights lens are, in fact, children's rights— rights necessary not only for children's individual well-being but also for the survival of their communities and cultures.

Considering the strengths and limitations of the Convention on the Rights of the Child from a CRT perspective reveals that the CRC has some of the same deficiencies identified above with respect to the three core human rights treaties. This is not surprising, as the CRC, for the most part, translates rights already recognized with respect to adults into the framework of children's rights while adding some elements specific to the unique concerns of children. Although it includes anti-discrimination provisions and references to the right to culture, including culture in community with others, it echoes the focus on the individual and reinforces the notion that the primary function of human rights law is to protect a vulnerable population without fundamentally altering the power balances found within states. The CRC relies, in other words, on an individual and minority rights framework that has limited ability to meaningfully address structural racism.

Taking an intersectional approach to children's rights, as is sometimes done in the context of indigenous children, means reading rights broadly with future generations in mind. The Genocide Convention has particular relevance for children's rights because it recognizes that future generations are essential to the perpetuation of peoples. The Genocide Convention criminalizes the killing members of a "national, ethnical, racial or religious group" with the intent to destroy the existence of the group as such.[61] But it also criminalizes four other types of action committed with such intent: inflicting physical or mental harm, deliberately imposing living conditions intended to lead to physical destruction, preventing births within the group, and forcibly removing children from the group.[62] The UN's very first human rights treaty, therefore, enshrines the principle that future generations must be protected, and protected in ways that go beyond the mere physical survival of individuals. It seeks to ensure that those future generations of children remain in their communities, in healthy living conditions, and under circumstances that allow for the transmission of their cultures, languages, religions, and worldviews.

Critical race theory suggests that the CRC should be interpreted and applied in light of the implications its provisions have for future generations and with the understanding that racial subordination, assimilationism, and the suppression of indigenous rights inevitably have detrimental effects on children. The potential for this mode of analysis can be seen in the approach taken by the Committee on the Rights of the Child in interpreting the CRC's provisions in the specific context of indigenous children. The CRC's Article 30 is very similar to ICCPR Article 27, protecting rights to culture, language, and religion, including in community with others. The CRC, however, specifically mentions indigenous children, and the Committee has interpreted this provision to establish a right that is both individual and collective, "an important recognition of the collective traditions and values in indigenous cultures."[63] In addition, the Committee states that "the best interests of the child is conceived both as a collective and individual right, and that the application of this right to indigenous children as a group requires consideration of how the right relates to collective cultural rights."[64] The Committee opines that Article 12's mandate to give weight to the views of the child has a communal aspect, noting that the right of expression not only extends to the individual child but also allows "children as a group to be involved in consultation on matters involving them."[65]

Other treaty-monitoring bodies have also been more inclined to protect collective rights in the unique context of indigenous peoples, and the analysis applied to indigenous children's rights provides a good model for taking a critical race approach to children's rights more generally.[66] Even in the indigenous context, however, the right to self-determination is consistently subordinated to the principles of state sovereignty and territorial integrity, principles that prioritize the maintenance of the state over the rights of peoples to freely determine their own political status.[67] Outside of the indigenous context, other peoples of color are often relegated to a minority-rights framework that is largely individualistic and assimilationist.

4 AN INTERSECTIONAL APPROACH TO RACE AND CHILDREN'S RIGHTS

A critical race perspective on children's rights can lead to a more robust analysis of the effects that violations of children's rights have on the larger community. For instance, in the US criminal justice system children may be treated as adults. Children can be charged as adults and, upon conviction, given longer prison sentences conceived with the adult penal system in mind.[68] Children can be charged and convicted of felonies, which in some states means they lose their right to vote for the rest of their lives. It is estimated that on any given day some ten thousand juveniles are being held in adult prisons and jails in the United States, where they do not receive the rehabilitation and educational services often available in juvenile facilities and, of course, face other dangers related to being a child in an adult prison, including the increased risk of physical and sexual abuse.[69]

From an international human rights perspective, treating children as adults for the purposes of the criminal justice system or placing them in adult prisons violates their rights. Article 37 of the CRC provides that the "arrest, detention, or imprisonment of a child...shall be used only as a measure of last resort and for the shortest appropriate period of time."[70] It further states that "[e]very child deprived of liberty shall be treated with humanity and respect for the inherent dignity of the human person, and in a manner which takes into account the needs of persons of his or her age." Incarcerated children "shall be separated from adults unless it is considered in the child's best interest not to do so."[71]

From a critical race perspective, the inquiry broadens to also ask how this violation of human rights intersects with the child's race. Children from certain racial or ethnic groups in the United States face higher rates of arrest, are subject to higher incarceration rates, and are more likely to be treated as adults. African American youth receive adult prison sentences at a rate nine times that of white youth.[72] In New Jersey, nearly 90 percent of children prosecuted as adults from July 2011 through May 2016 were African American or Hispanic.[73] A 2009 study found that 84 percent of children in Florida receiving a sentence of life without parole in non-homicide cases were African American.[74] Despite federal studies showing that American Indian children are particularly vulnerable and traumatized, they are placed in adult federal prisons much more often than children of other racial groups because of the unique characteristics of federal jurisdiction on Native lands.[75]

Examining the role that race plays in this violation of children's rights, CRT takes us beyond the question of discriminatory intent that is the focus of US domestic law and also beyond the statistical disparities considered unacceptable in international law. It urges us not only to confront the fact that children of color are disproportionately treated as adults within criminal justice systems but also to ask how denying children of color their child status perpetuates systems of oppression.[76] What connections exist between these practices and historic policies of treating children as property, selling children through slavery, and forcibly removing children from their families in order to strip them of their culture? What effect does this have on the future of communities of color? How does perceiving these children as adults devalue lives of color and relate to other human rights abuses, such as higher rates of extrajudicial killings? What can this tell us about the relationship between international law's prohibition of racial discrimination and its provisions designed to protect culture? How does the treatment of children of color in the criminal judicial system implicate the right to self-determination?

An intersectional approach to race and children's rights can also expand our understanding of human rights issues that are often framed in an adult-centered context but have clear intergenerational consequences. The protection of indigenous land rights, for instance, illustrates this point.

International law recognizes that indigenous peoples have distinct land rights requiring protection in ways that are different from those of nonindigenous property owners. Further, it has acknowledged that the failure to protect indigenous land tenure can violate the right to equal protection. In 2006 CERD issued its first decision against the United States under its Early Warning and Urgent Action procedure. In that decision, CERD addressed allegations that the United States violated the rights of the Western Shoshone to their traditional lands, rights the US claimed were extinguished by the "gradual encroachment" of nonindigenous settlers.[77] The Western Shoshone lands at issue had been claimed by the federal government, leased to nonindigenous ranchers, and, most significantly, opened up to massive open-pit gold mining operations, potential nuclear waste storage, and other destructive activities.[78]

CERD viewed the issue as one not just of land title, but of racial discrimination. Stating that "past and new actions taken by the State party on Western Shoshone ancestral lands leads to a situation where, today, the obligations of the State party under the Convention are not respected," CERD highlighted the state's "obligation to guarantee the right of everyone to equality before the law in the enjoyment of civil, political, economic, social and cultural rights, without discrimination based on race, colour, or national or ethnic origin." CERD urged the US to "pay particular attention to the right to health and cultural rights of the Western Shoshone people, which may be infringed upon by activities threatening their environment and/or disregarding the spiritual and cultural significance they give to their ancestral lands." Among other recommendations, CERD also directed the United States to engage in immediate consultation with the Western Shoshone.[79]

Examining discriminatory land recognition policies from a children's rights perspective provides insights into the intergenerational aspects of self-determination. As CERD recognized, failure to protect land title is more than a property rights issue; it also implicates rights related to culture, environment, and health. Environmental devastation and its attendant health consequences clearly impact future generations. Further, indigenous peoples are land-based and, therefore, depend on their ancestral lands to transmit culture to future generations. Cases like that of the Western Shoshone could be seen as violating several provisions of the CRC, including Article 24's rights to health, which specifically mentions environmental pollution, and Article 30's protection of indigenous children's rights to enjoy their culture in community.

Bringing a children's rights perspective to a case that has generally been framed only in terms of racial discrimination and indigenous rights enriches the analysis and adds weight to the underlying claims by allowing us to see how the state's policies and practices affect children today and well into the future. Incorporating the impact that racial discrimination has on children into a critical race analysis encourages us to think about the long-term implications of the laws and policies we may be contesting. How should children of color be consulted regarding policies affecting their communities? What do violations of indigenous property rights mean for the right of children to have their culture transmitted? What children's rights are implicated by policies that prioritize extractive industries over environmental preservation? How does failure to incorporate children into analyses of discriminatory policies undermine the right to self-determination for all peoples?

5 CONCLUSION

A critical race perspective complements the commitment of children's rights advocates to see issues from the perspective of the child and to actively endeavor to address injustices. It tells us that identities are multidimensional and intersecting, emphasizing the particularly significant impact that racial subordination has on children while not imposing on them an essentialized understanding of race. It appreciates the power of unconscious or invisible racism, identifies deeply rooted causes of systemic disparities, and proposes structural solutions. Critical race theory resists the role that colorblindness and assimilationism have played in perpetuating racial subordination, and it supports the right of all children to grow up in communities that are self-determining and, therefore, their right to maintain and pass on their cultures, histories, identities, and worldviews. This approach encourages us to analyze how currently recognized children's rights, most notably those articulated in the CRC, are interpreted in the context of children of color and their communities and how the growing recognition of these rights can contribute to struggles for racial justice. More generally, by viewing international human rights instruments from the perspectives of children of color, CRT can help us see that, in very concrete ways, the political and socioeconomic rights enshrined in those treaties *are* children's rights.

NOTES

1. Dorothy Brown, "Introduction to Critical Race Theory," in *Critical Race Theory: Cases, Materials, and Problems* (St. Paul, MN: West Academic, 2014), 1–3, 1.
2. For basic texts see Richard Delgado and Jean Stefancic, eds., *Critical Race Theory: The Cutting* 3rd ed. (Philadelphia: Temple University Press, 2013); Kimberlé Crenshaw, Neil Gotanda, Gary Peller, and Kendall Thomas, eds., *Critical Race Theory: The Key Writings That Formed the Movement* (New York: New Press, 1995).
3. Derrick A. Bell, "Who's Afraid of Critical Race Theory?," *University of Illinois Law Review* 1995 (February 1995): 893–910, 898.
4. Kimberlé Williams Crenshaw, "The First Decade: Critical Reflections, or 'A Foot in the Closing Door.' " *UCLA Law Review* 49, no.5 (June 2002): 1343–1372, 1361.
5. Richard Delgado, "Brewer's Plea: Critical Thoughts on Common Cause," *Vanderbilt Law Review* 44, no.1 (January 1991): 1–14, 6. See, generally, Kimberlé Williams Crenshaw, "Race, Reform, and Retrenchment: Transformation and Legitimation in Antidiscrimination Law," *Harvard Law Review* 101, no.7 (May 1988): 1331–1387.
6. Cheryl I. Harris, "Critical Race Studies: An Introduction," *UCLA Law Review* 49 (June 2002): 1215–1235, 1220; Athena D. Mutua, "The Rise, Development and Future Directions of Critical Race Theory and Related Scholarship," *Denver University Law Review* 84, no. 2 (2006): 329–394.
7. Angela P. Harris, "Foreword: The Jurisprudence of Reconstruction," *California Law Review* 82 (July 1994): 741–785, 743.
8. See Adrien Katherine Wing, ed., *Critical Race Feminism: A Reader*, 2nd ed. (New York: New York University Press, 2003).
9. See Tayyab Mahmud, Athena Mutua, and Francico Valdes, "LatCrit Praxis@XX: Toward Equal Justice in Law, Education and Society," *Chicago-Kent Law Review* 90, no. 2 (2015): 361–427.
10. See Robert S. Chang, "Toward an Asian American Legal Scholarship: Critical Race Theory, Post-Structuralism, and Narrative Space," *Asian Law Journal* 1 (1994): 1–83.
11. See Makau Mutua and Antony Anghie, "What Is TWAIL?," *American Society of International law Proceedings* 94 (2000): 31–40, 38; James Thuo Gathii, Henry J. Richardson III, and Karen Knop, "Introduction to Symposium on Theorizing TWAIL Activism," *AJIL Unbound* 110 (2000): 18–19. See also Ediberto Román, "A Race Approach to International

Law (RAIL): Is There a Need for Yet Another Critique of International Law?," *U.C. Davis Law Review* 33 (2000): 1519–1545.

12. See Kimberlé Crenshaw, "Twenty Years of Critical Race Theory: Looking Back to Move Forward," *Connecticut Law Review* 43 (2011): 1253–1352, 1256; Devon W. Carbado, "Critical What What?" *Connecticut Law Review* 43 (2011): 1593–1643, 1620–1623.

13. See Darren Lenard Hutchinson, "Critical Race Histories: In and Out," *American University Law Review* 53 (2003): 1187–1215.

14. Crenshaw, "Twenty Years of Critical Race Theory," 1260.

15. Mari J. Matsuda, "When the First Quail Calls: Multiple Consciousness as Jurisprudential Method," *Women's Rights Law Reporter* 14 (1992): 297–300, 299.

16. Mari J. Matsuda, "Looking to the Bottom: Critical Legal Studies and Reparations," *Harvard Civil Rights–Civil Liberties Law Review* 22 (1987): 323–399, 324; see Derrick A. Bell, *Faces at the Bottom of the Well: The Permanence of Racism* (New York: Basic Books, 1992).

17. See Mutua, "Rise, Development and Future Directions," 354; Harris "Foreword," 753.

18. See Michael Omi and Howard Winant, *Racial Formation in the United States*, 3rd ed. (New York: Routledge, 2015); Ian Haney López, *White by Law: The Legal Construction of Race*, rev. ed. (New York: New York University Press, 2006).

19. See Charles R. Lawrence III, "If He Hollers Let Him Go: Regulating Racist Speech on Campus," *Duke Law Journal* 1990, no. 3 (June 1990): 431–483, 443n52 (quoting Thomas's comments at the Frontiers of Legal Thought Conference, Duke Law School (1990); Carbado, "Critical What What?," 1609.

20. Kimberlé Crenshaw, "Mapping the Margins: Intersectionality, Identity Politics, and Violence against Women of Color," *Stanford Law Review* 43, no. 6 (July 1991): 1241–1299.

21. John O. Calmore, "Critical Race Theory, Archie Shepp, and Fire Music: Securing an Authentic Intellectual Life in a Multicultural World," *Southern California Law Review* 65, no. 5 (July 1992): 2129–2230, 2138.

22. Charles R. Lawrence III, "Local Kine Implicit Bias: Unconscious Racism Revisited (Yet Again)." *University of Hawai'i Law Review* 37 (2015): 457–500, 458. See also Lawrence, Charles R. Lawrence III, "The Id, the Ego, and Equal Protection: Reckoning with Unconscious Racism," *Stanford Law Review* 39, no. 2 (January 1987): 317–388.

23. Richard Delgado, "Introduction," in *Critical Race Theory: The Cutting Edge*, ed. Richard Delgado (Philadelphia: Temple University Press, 1995), xiii–xvi, xiv.

24. Cheryl I. Harris, "Whiteness as Property," *Harvard Law Review* 106, no. 8 (June 1993): 1709–1791; see also Robert A. Williams Jr., *Like a Loaded Weapon: The Rehnquist Court, Indian Rights, and the Legal History of Racism in America* (Minneapolis: University of Minnesota Press, 2005).

25. Eduardo Bonilla-Silva, *Racism without Racists: Color-Blind Racism and the Persistence of Racial Inequality in America*, 5th ed. (Lanham, MD: Rowman and Littlefield, 2018); Neil Gotanda, "A Critique of 'Our Constitution Is Color-Blind,'" *Stanford Law Review* 44, no. 1 (July 1991): 1–68.

26. Darren Lenard Hutchinson, "'Unexplainable on Grounds Other Than Race': The Inversion of Privilege and Subordination in Equal Protection Jurisprudence," *University of Illinois Law Review* 2003, no. 3 (2003): 615–700.

27. Alex M. Johnson Jr., "Bid Whist, Tonk, and *United States v. Fordice*: Why Integrationism Fails African-Americans Again," *California Law Review* 81, no. 6 (December 1993): 1401–1470; George A. Martinez, "Latinos, Assimilation and the Law: A Philosophical Perspective," *Chicano-Latino Law Review* 20, no.1 (1999): 1–34; Gary Peller, "Race Consciousness," *Duke Law Journal* 1990, no. 4 (September 1990): 758–847.

28. Carbado, "Critical What What?," 1607.

29. Derrick Bell, "Racial Realism," *Connecticut Law Review* 24, no. 2 (Winter 1992): 363–379, 373.

30. Derrick A. Bell Jr., "*Brown v. Board of Education* and the Interest-Convergence Dilemma," *Harvard Law Review* 93, no. 3 (January 1980): 518–533, 523.

31. Antony Anghie, *Imperialism, Sovereignty and the Making of International Law* (Cambridge: Cambridge University Press, 2005).

32. Angie, *Imperialism, Sovereignty*, 40, 207; see Tayyab Mahmud, "Colonialism and Modern Constructions of Race: A Preliminary Inquiry," *University of Miami Law Review* 53 (1999): 1219–1246.

33. See Patrick Wolfe, *Traces of History: Elementary Structures of Race* (London: Verso, 2016); Ronald Sanders, *Lost Tribes and Promised Lands: The Origins of American Racism* (New York: Little, Brown, 1978).

34. See Anghie, *Imperialism, Sovereignty*, 196–207; Makau Wa Mutua, "Why Redraw the Map of Africa: A Moral and Legal Inquiry," *Michigan Journal of International Law* 16, no. 4 (1995): 1113–1176, 1134; Tayyab Mahmud, "Colonial Cartographies, Postcolonial Borders, and Enduring Failures of International Law: The Unending Wars along the Afghanistan-Pakistan Frontier," *Brooklyn Journal of International Law* 36, no. 1 (December 2010): 1–74.

35. Mutua "Why Redraw the Map of Africa," 1116.

36. See Kristen A. Carpenter and Angela R. Riley, "Indigenous Peoples and the Jurisgenerative Moment in Human Rights," *California Law Review*: 102, no. 1 (February 2014): 173–234.

37. See Tayyab Mahmud, "International Law and the 'Race-ed' Colonial Encounter," *Proceedings of the Annual Meeting of the American Society of International Law* 91 (1997): 408–428, 414–420; Henry J. Richardson III, "The Danger of the New Legal Colonialism," *American Society of International Law Proceedings* 104 (2010): 393–398.

38. Charter of the United Nations, arts. 1(2), (3), 1 UNTS XVI (1945; entered into force October 24, 1945).

39. International Convention on the Prevention and Punishment of the Crime of Genocide (Genocide Convention), art. 2, 78 UNTS 277 (1948; entered into force Jan. 12, 1951) (emphasis added).

40. While the definition of peoples in international contexts is contested, it generally refers to those who identify as a people based not only on common ancestry but also common culture and traditions, history, worldviews, and/or social institutions. See Bernard Nietschmann, "The Fourth World: Nations versus States," in *Reordering the World: Geopolitical Perspectives on the Twenty-first Century*, 1st ed., ed. George J. Demko and William B. Wood (Boulder, CO: Westview, 1994), 225–242, 226; Howard J. Vogel, "Reframing Rights from the Ground Up: The Contribution of the New U.N. Law of Self-Determination to Recovering the Principle of Sociability on the Way to a Relational Theory of International Human Rights," *Temple International and Comparative Law Journal* 20 (2006): 443–497, 447.

41. Universal Declaration of Human Rights, arts. 1, 2, G.A. Res. 217 (III) A, UN Doc. A/RES/217(III) (Dec. 10, 1948).

42. In the interim the UN General Assembly articulated the need to bring about a speedy and unconditional end to colonialism. 1960 Declaration on the Granting of Independence to Colonial Countries and Peoples, G.A. Res. 1514 (XV), UN Doc A/4684 (Dec. 14, 1960). This was quickly followed by a resolution attempting to limit decolonization to territories "geographically separate" as well as "distinct ethnically and/or culturally" from the "administering" state. G.A. Res. 1541 (XV), UN Doc A/4684 (Dec. 15, 1960).

43. International Convention on the Elimination of All Forms of Racial Discrimination (ICERD), preamble, 660 UNTS 195 (1965; entered into force January 4, 1969).

44. ICERD, art. 2(1).

45. ICERD, art. 1(1) (emphasis added).

46. ICERD, art. 2(1) (emphasis added).

47. Committee on the Elimination of Racial Discrimination (CERD), *General Recommendation No. 14: Definition of Discrimination (art. 1, para 1)*, A/48/18 (1993).

48. CERD, *General Recommendation No. 14*, para. 8.

49. CERD, *General Recommendation No. 32: The Meaning and Scope of Special Measures in the International Convention on the Elimination of All Forms of Discrimination*, CERD/C/GC/32 (2009), para. 7.

50. International Covenant on Civil and Political Rights (ICCPR), 999 UNTS 171 (1966; entered into force March 23, 1976); International Covenant on Economic, Social and Cultural Rights (ICESCR), 993 UNTS 3 (1966; entered into force January 3, 1976).

51. ICCPR, art. 27 (emphasis added).

52. UN Convention on the Rights of the Child, 1577 UNTS 3 (1989; entered into force Sept. 2, 1990).

53. See Theodore M. Shaw, "The Race Convention and Civil Rights in the United States," *New York City Law Review* 3, no. 1 (May 1998): 19–38.

54. ICERD, preamble (emphasis added).

55. CERD, *General Recommendation No. 2: Concerning States Parties' Obligations*, UN Doc. A/8718 (1972).

56. CERD, *General Recommendation No. 21: The Right to Self-Determination* UN Doc. A/51/18 (1996), para. 4.

57. CERD, *General Recommendation No. 21*, para. 5.

58. CERD, *General Recommendation No. 21*, para. 6.

59. Human Rights Committee, *General Comment No. 23: The Rights of Minorities (Art. 27)*, CCPR/C/21/Rev.1/Add.5 (1994), paras. 1, 2.

60. CERD, *General Recommendation No. 21*, para. 3.2 (noting that Article 27 "does not prejudice the sovereignty and territorial integrity of a State party").

61. Genocide Convention, art. 2.

62. Genocide Convention, art. 2.

63. Committee on the Rights of the Child, *General Comment No. 11: Indigenous Children and Their Rights under the Convention*, CRC/C/GC/11 (2009), para. 16.

64. Committee on the Rights of the Child, *General Comment No. 11*, para. 30.

65. Committee on the Rights of the Child, *General Comment No. 11*, para. 37.

66. See, e.g., CERD, *General Recommendation No. 23: Indigenous Peoples*, UN Doc. A/52/18 (1997), annex V, 121.

67. See, e.g., CERD, *General Recommendation 21*.

68. See Cynthia Soohoo, "You Have the Right to Remain a Child: The Right to Juvenile Treatment for Youth in Conflict with the Law," *Columbia Human Rights Law Review* 48, no. 3 (2017): 1–74; Liz Ryan, "Youth in the Adult Criminal Justice System," *Cardozo Law Review* 35, no. 3 (February 2014): 1167–1184.

69. Wendy Sawyer "Youth Confinement: The Whole Pie," Prison Policy Initiative press release, February 27, 2018, https://www.prisonpolicy.org/reports/youth2018.html; Jessica Lahey, "The Steep Costs of Keeping Juveniles in Adult Prisons," *The Atlantic*, January 8, 2016, https://www.theatlantic.com/education/archive/2016/01/the-cost-of-keeping-juveniles -in-adult-prisons/423201.

70. Although the United States has not yet become a party, acceptance of the CRC by all of the other UN member states allows us to consider it representative of the international human rights perspective.

71. We note that the Juvenile Justice and Delinquency Prevention Act, 88 Stat. 1109 (1974), does require children to be separated from adults when they are placed in adult facilities.

72. Ryan, "Youth," 1174.

73. Sarah Gonzales, "Kids in Prison: Getting Tried as an Adult Depends on Skin Color," WNYC News, October 10, 2016, https://www.wnyc.org/story/black-kids-more-likely-be -tried-adults-cant-be-explained.

74. Jennifer L. Eberhardt and Aneeta Rattan, "The Race Factor in Trying Juveniles as Adults," *New York Times*, June 5, 2012, https://www.nytimes.com/roomfordebate/2012/06/05/ when-to-punish-a-young-offender-and-when-to-rehabilitate/the-race-factor-in-trying -juveniles-as-adults.

75. See Addie C. Rolnick, , "Native Youth & Juvenile Justice in South Dakota," *South Dakota Law Review* 62, no. 3 (2017): 705–727, 715; Addie C. Rolnick, "Untangling the Web: Juvenile Justice in Indian Country," *NYU Journal of Legislation and Public Policy* 19, no. 1 (2017): 49–140, 51.

76. See Vincent M. Southerland, "Youth Matters: The Need to Treat Children Like Children," *Journal of Civil Rights & Economic Development* 27, no. 4 (2015): 765–788; Annette Ruth Appell, "Accommodating Childhood," *Cardozo Journal of Law and Gender* 19, no. 3 (July 2013): 715–779.

77. See Julie Ann Fishel, "The Western Shoshone Struggle: Opening Doors for Indigenous Rights," *Intercultural Human Rights Law Review* 2 (2006): 41–91, 46–47. See also *Dann v. United States*, Case 11.140, Inter-Am. C.H.R., Report No. 75/02, OEA/Ser.L/V/II.117, doc. 1 rev. 1 (2002); *United States v. Dann*, 470 U.S. 39 (1985).

78. Fishel, "Western Shoshone Struggle," 44–45.

79. CERD, *Decision 1 (68): Early Warning and Urgent Action Procedure*, UN Doc. CERD/C/ USA/DEC/1 (April 11, 2006), para. 9.

CHAPTER 8

FEMINIST LEGAL THEORY AND CHILDREN'S RIGHTS

MEREDITH JOHNSON HARBACH

1 INTRODUCTION

ACROSS the long arc of law's history, the fates of women and children frequently have been tied together, primarily through shared legal and social subordination. Historically, both have suffered legal disabilities—their legal and social identities subsumed under the cover of the patriarch. And conversely, as old rules gradually have been supplanted by modern law, significant reforms have resulted in improved circumstances for many women and children, both inside and outside of families.

Given this shared subordination, it would be reasonable to assume that the goals of feminist legal theory (FLT) and children's rights dovetail. The reality is more complicated. Feminist theory has at times expressed a deep ambivalence toward childhood, focused on challenging women's positions vis-à-vis children[1] and essentializing childhood even while seeking to complicate and contextualize our understanding of women's experiences.[2] Thus, while there are values and goals shared by both movements,[3] there are also tensions.

This chapter is a selective genealogy of FLT from its early expressions in the late twentieth century to today. I begin with a brief overview of feminism's development as a social and political movement and FLT as a discipline, highlighting some of the FLT camps that have emerged. I then examine selected feminist theoretical critiques and methods, focusing on areas implicating children's rights and interests. Finally, I explore some areas of potential tension between FLT and children's rights before turning to recent developments in FLT that might suggest new directions—or at least a pivot—for children's rights advocates.

2 Overview: Feminism and FLT

Because of the diverse and rich variants of feminist theory, it is difficult to generalize about what feminism is, what its aims are, or what it does. Despite these variations, however, feminism as a discipline focuses on gender and the ways in which gendered stereotypes, norms, and assumptions lead to inequality. Here I provide a brief history of feminist movements and FLT.

2.1 Feminist Waves

The genesis and evolution of FLT has intersected, but not evolved in lock-step, with the three waves of feminism as a social movement. The first wave developed in the late nineteenth and early twentieth centuries, focusing on expanding women's basic legal and citizenship rights, including the right to vote, hold property, and work outside the home. The second wave emerged in a time of dramatic social transformation in the 1960s and 1970s and extended through the early 1990s. Activism during the second wave focused on sex equality in the workplace and public life and sexual violence against women. Both first- and second-wave feminisms generally have subscribed to a set of core elements of feminist activism: a commitment to sex equality, a belief that women's status has been socially constructed (gender), and self-conscious identification with women as a social group.[4] Feminism's third wave refers to the generation of feminists that has emerged since the 1990s and who broadly identify as subscribing to a broader, more inclusive, and nonjudgmental feminism that accounts for and includes the diversity of women's experiences. Third-wave feminists see themselves as critiquing social justice issues through a feminist lens rather than focusing discretely on women's issues.[5]

Internationally, too, coalitions have been working to advance women's rights and interests since feminism's first wave, advocating for equal political, economic, and social rights as well as peace and liberation.[6] Early human rights instruments included formal equality rights for women but did not fully address or vindicate women's interests.[7] The Commission on the Status of Women, established in 1946, spearheaded the development and adoption of the 1979 Convention on the Elimination of All Forms of Discrimination against Women (CEDAW).[8] During the second half of the twentieth century, a series of UN-sponsored summits provided opportunities for feminist activists to come together across borders to discuss common goals of promoting gender equality.[9] In 1984 Development Alternatives with Women for a New Era (DAWN) became the first international network of feminist scholar-activists offering a Global South–based critique of the international feminist movement, which was still primarily associated with white, middle-class women from the Global North.[10] Since then, transnational feminist movements have flourished, especially beginning in the 1990s alongside the rise of globalization and the advent of new information technologies.[11]

While each of the successive waves has built on the theorizing and successes of its predecessors, the transition from second- to third-wave feminism has been fraught, perceived by some as creating a generational rift between feminists, both in the US and internationally.[12] But differences among feminists are nothing new. FLT has long been marked by internal debate and difference.

2.2 The Emergence and Evolution of FLT

As second-wave feminism developed in the 1970s, feminist activists began looking to law as a site of subjugation and the potential for liberation. The concept of FLT, or feminist jurisprudence, first emerged in the US toward the end of the 1970s[13] and by the early 1990s gained prominence as a theoretical critique in international law.[14] In the US, three broad phases of FLT emerged and developed in the late twentieth century: the equality phase (1970s), the difference phase (1980s), and the intersectional or complex identities phase (1990s–present).[15] Collectively, FLT scholars challenge the subordination of women as a class and seek to use law and policy to transform social institutions and eradicate inequality.[16] At times their paths to achieving these goals diverge dramatically.[17]

2.3 Convergences and Divisions

2.3.1 *Sameness versus Difference*

A persistent divide in FLT concerns the question of gender difference. The 1970s equality phase saw the rise of liberal feminism, with a focus on *formal equality*—equal access to public life and work and equal treatment for men and women.[18] In general, liberal feminists have focused on sameness; their primary commitment is to gender neutrality. They tend to be wary of acknowledging gender differences, for fear these would be used as justifications for paternalistic treatment that would treat women less favorably than men. These goals naturally lead to a focus on anti-discrimination strategies, seeking to undo gender-based assumptions that are either incorporated into law or tolerated by it.[19] In some respects, this focus on sameness and formal equality has led to a distancing of women's interests from those of children. Grouping women and children together can imply that both are subautonomous and in need of paternalistic protection. And a focus on children's interests risks essentializing all women as mothers.[20]

If liberal feminists emphasized sameness and formal equality, by the 1980s cultural or difference feminists were critiquing liberal feminism and shifting the focus to differences between men and women. These feminists highlight differences between men's and women's lived experiences. They call for renewed attention to the special contributions of women and imagine a world in which those contributions are valued equally with other social contributions that traditionally have been gendered male.[21] Consequently, cultural feminists have embraced recognition of women's special roles in parenting and caregiving more generally. Cultural feminism views formal equality and negative rights as insufficient to achieve justice. Instead, in a world in which both men and women lead gendered lives, affirmatively different treatment may be required to achieve *substantive equality* with men. The law and social institutions should evolve to reflect, accommodate, and support these realities. Feminist theorists on the international stage similarly have critiqued the differences between formal and substantive equality. They have argued that formal equality models privilege male experiences[22] and have called for international instruments and norms to acknowledge women's differences so as to pursue substantive equality.[23]

2.3.2 *Women's Interests: Essentialized or Intersectional?*

Second-wave feminists often relied on essentialized claims about women's universal experiences. By the end of the twentieth century, many were warning against rigid categories and sweeping generalizations.[24] Intersectional/post-identities feminism arose in response to liberal feminism's generalizations.[25] The primary claim is that gender subordination and hierarchy cannot be analyzed in a vacuum. Instead, gender interacts with a number of other social identities, including race, class, sexual orientation, age, disability, and immigration status. The intersection of multiple social identities leads to unique and different experiences of subordination among women.[26] It is thus impossible to generalize about the experiences of all women and important to recognize that differently situated women will experience privilege and subordination differently. Intersectional feminism has been especially critical of older feminist schools that focused primarily, if not exclusively, on white, middle-class women's experiences to the disadvantage of women of color and working-class women, whose interests frequently have been obscured or overlooked.

Postmodern/poststructuralist feminists continue the intersectional approach by blurring gender identities and challenging feminist activists to move beyond the masculine/feminine gender binary to make space for multiple, fluid gender and sexual identities.[27] For many, law is part of the problem, reinforcing dominant gender categories and heteronormative policies rather than challenging and problematizing them.[28] Internationally, feminist schools have taken similarly varied approaches to gender justice and eradicating patriarchy, incorporating other critical theoretical perspectives, such as critical race theory and postcolonial theory, among others.[29]

2.3.3 *Transnational Feminisms: Global Intersectionality, Global Focus*

Transnational feminisms take the intersectional and post-identity critiques among feminists global, with a focus on intersections of class, culture, and space (both geographical and metaphorical). Global North feminist models have tended to presume a white, middle-class subject located in the Global North and imagine them as saviors of their disadvantaged "sisters."[30] Transnational feminists critique Global North feminisms as too dominant in setting the benchmark for assessing women's situations.[31] They ask, instead, how excluded perspectives from the Global South might "radically reshape feminist politics."[32]

Like other feminisms, transnational feminist movements' core concerns are women's rights and gender equality, but these are linked to broader global, regional, national, local, and "glocal" struggles.[33] They "organize through a sense of shared struggle against all forms of patriarchal power and control, violence, and exploitation as they are manifested in neoliberalism, militarism, and religious fundamentalisms across North-South divides and state borders."[34] These activists have developed shared values and goals across differences and seek to work in solidarity to change structural inequalities and pursue social justice.[35] Like intersectional feminists in the US, transnational feminists emphasize political, racial, and cultural differences and the importance of intersectional perspectives on feminist projects.[36] These activists move beyond gender subordination to also critique oppression of women *and* men, not only because of gender but also because of "geographic location, race, ethnicity, indigeneity, class, caste, religion, age, ability, and sexuality."[37]

In the context of international human rights law, transnational feminists critique the influence of Global North feminisms, which have often essentialized and universalized culture rather than recognize cultural differences and focused on Global North priorities (e.g., violence against women) to the detriment of other priorities for women of the Global South (e.g., living wages).[38] Postcolonial critiques of human rights law, for example, question whether universal gender equality ought to always trump culture.[39] Transnational feminist critics also point toward the ways in which US interests and prioritizes have shaped human rights law, which may obscure other global priorities and lead to blind spots, ultimately reflecting and reinforcing existing power differentials.[40] More broadly, transnational feminists critique the ways in which feminist projects have been co-opted via their assimilation within global policymaking institutions and neoliberal agendas, homogenizing and obscuring the needs of women in particular societies.[41]

3 FLT Methods

FLT methods can be understood broadly as approaches that seek to uncover aspects of law that more traditional methods miss or ignore. Unlike more traditional legal methods, which prioritize predictability, certainty, and stability, FLT methods have tended to prefer flexibility and an ability to uncover missing or submerged perspectives.[42] Child rights advocates deploy methods in similar ways to advance children's interests.

3.1 Feminist Critiques of the Theoretical Status Quo

In an early FLT text, Martha Fineman observed that "the task of feminists concerned with the law and legal institutions must be to create and explicate feminist methods and theories that explicitly challenge and compete with the existing totalizing nature of grand legal theory."[43] A central project for FLT scholars is to challenge the received wisdom and gendered background assumptions undergirding our legal and political systems. Here, I examine feminist critiques of public-private dichotomies, private dependency, and rights hegemony that grow out of liberal theoretical assumptions.

3.1.1 *Public/Private Divides*

FLT theorists have long critiqued the understanding, once legally sanctioned, that our social and political lives are naturally divided into separate spheres—with women and children naturally occupying the private sphere of home, family, and domesticity and men naturally situated in the public sphere of market, politics, and civic participation.[44] This assumed demarcation had two primary effects: first, women and children were excluded from participation in the public sphere; second, decisions and actions made within the family were coded as private and thus outside the purview or regulatory reach of the state. This second norm continues to find expression in the family privacy doctrine: The family and family decision-making are considered private—involving private matters, taking place in the private home, and are a matter of private responsibility.[45] Consequently, the family becomes a "black box,"[46]—obscured within the private sphere where state interference is unjustified and undesirable.[47]

FLT has blurred the line between public and private, demonstrating how "the personal is political," and asserted that state abdication from so-called private family life is theoretically flawed and practically dangerous. Feminists have disrupted assumptions about the fitness of women for public life, successfully challenging women's exclusion from paid work, professions, and civic responsibilities. They also have urged that in order to liberate women to fully participate in all social spheres, the construction of the family itself must evolve.[48] On the international stage, feminists have worked similarly to integrate women into the public sphere and break down perceived or erected barriers between public and private, both domestically and within international law.[49] Transnational feminists, too, have wrestled with public/private distinctions, instead invoking "women's rights as human rights" and "democracy in the country and in the home."[50]

Separate spheres ideology was legally manifest in the doctrine of coverture and, in some ways, continues to be expressed in the family privacy doctrine. Coverture and family privacy, for example, protected husbands' and fathers' prerogatives to batter and sexually assault their wives and abuse their children with legal impunity.[51] Like domestic law, international law historically viewed family matters, influenced by culture and religion, as private rather than public matters and therefore outside the purview of law or the state.[52]

Feminists have worked to dismantle the wall of family privacy that has served primarily as cover for patriarchal domination and abuse. This breach of the public-private divide has benefited not only women, but also children. As *pater familias* has given way to *parens patriae*, the state has come to see a legitimate (if limited) role in engagement with children and families to ensure protection from harm. So domestic violence, child abuse, and neglect are no longer shielded from state scrutiny by the shroud of family privacy.

3.1.2 *Private Dependency*

Separate spheres ideology relegated children and dependency to the realm of the private family rather than recognize any direct relationship between families and the state.[53]

Likewise, liberal theory has worked to situate social responsibility for families and children within private families, thus privatizing dependency.

The conventional liberal theoretical view underlying many Global North legal systems sees individuals and families as self-reliant and capable of providing for themselves and their members.[54] Because the family is essentially self-sufficient and private, liberal theory does not generally recognize an affirmative state obligation to provide support to children, caregivers, and families. By contrast, FLT theorists seek to uncover the family as a public institution—both publicly constituted and of significant public concern. They have demonstrated the mutual interdependence of family and the state. The state relies on families for critical social reproduction work via child-rearing and providing care for dependents. And families need state support in performing this work.[55] In order to achieve substantive equality and justice for women, these feminists argue that we must not only reform dynamics within the family but also look to the broader, public work that the family does for society and reimagine the state's relationship to that work.[56]

Liberal theory's focus on autonomy and private dependency has been augmented by neoliberalism. FLT theorists have explored in detail the shortcomings of neoliberalism and assumptions about private dependency, observing the ways in which the ascendance of neoliberalism has led to retrenchment from the gains made during feminism's second wave.[57] As women become full participants in the workforce, and less dependent in marriage, the family in isolation is less able to bear the responsibilities for dependency that inevitably arise within families. What is more, in a world of rising income inequality and poverty, far too many families are unable to adequately care for their children, and the pressures of combining caregiving and market work only exacerbate these challenges.[58]

Now that social and legal expectations about family, work, and responsibility have been unsettled, some in FLT call for a reimagining of the relationships among state, market, and families. They argue that to be coherent and just, liberal theory must be revised to account for universal vulnerability, inevitable dependency, and caretaking.[59] Pushing back against neoliberalism, they argue that the state must support families in their child development work,[60] buffer families from the most extreme consequences of the market,[61] and, more generally, enable individuals to combine family and market work over time in ways that enable them to achieve self-sufficiency and flourish.[62]

3.1.3 *Rights Hegemony*

Because liberal theory prioritizes individual autonomy and liberty, the ideal state orientation is one of restraint. The state's central role is to protect against unwarranted interferences with liberty, primarily through the enforcement of negative rights. As discussed above, liberal feminists' moves to secure formal equality rights for women typically pursued these goals via negative rights and anti-discrimination policy.

By contrast, FLT theorists pursuing substantive equality critique the liberal theoretical bent that reifies autonomy and liberty as the transcendent social values. Instead, they focus on the limits of rights, especially negative rights, in achieving true equality of opportunity and justice. Negative rights may promote individual agency and liberty, but they cannot incorporate the broader circumstances in which rights might or might not be exercised or vindicated.[63] Negative rights preventing discrimination, for example, may protect against overtly unfair treatment but cannot ensure a just distribution of assets and equal opportunity to achieve and thrive. And the pursuit of equal rights cannot account for the many ways in which individuals are differently situated and therefore experience the law's formally neutral approach in starkly different ways. Thus negative rights, standing alone, cannot guarantee social justice.[64]

At the international level, feminist critics question the adequacy of human rights approaches for advancing women's interests globally or for achieving equality.[65] Traditional human rights norms and strategies have tended to rely heavily on courts and law reform, which traditionally are most useful in enforcing and implementing negative rights.[66] But courts and lawyers are not equipped to respond to systemic social and structural equality problems, frequently stemming from income inequality. Nor are they empowered to make the political decisions that would shift allocation of resources toward a more just distribution.[67] As summarized by Wendy Brown, "if rights secure the possibility of living without fear of express state coercion, they do not thereby decrease the overall power and reach of the state nor do they enhance the collective power of the citizenry to determine the contours and content of social, economic, and political justice."[68]

3.2 Foregrounding Experiences

At least since the 1960s and the emergence of feminism's second wave, the use of personal narrative and consciousness-raising has been central to the feminist project. Early consciousness-raising groups in which women shared their subjective experiences became the basis for understanding shared experiences and the myriad ways in which the personal was political.[69] Consciousness-raising—sharing and interpreting experiences in order to integrate experience into theory and adapt theory to more accurately reflect experience—is a distinctly FLT approach to analyzing and critiquing law.[70] Thus, there has long been broad agreement that "legal scholarship is not feminist unless it is grounded in women's experience, an experience which produces a feminist point of view."[71] Third-wave feminists use personal narrative to demonstrate the intersectional nature of women's experiences, giving voice to a variety of experiences and stories as opposed to essentializing about women's universal experiences vis-à-vis sexism and patriarchy.[72] Others use personal narrative but also revisit historical developments to better understand how subordination was created and has been perpetuated.[73]

Consciousness-raising and sharing stories is tied to another classic FLT method: asking the "woman question" to disrupt assumptions about the subject of law as a reasonable man, liberal subject, or *homo-economicus*.[74] FLT theorists begin analysis of law's operation and effects by asking how *women* might experience it. Thus, they situate women's experiences at the center of legal analysis and demonstrate how even seemingly neutral norms or rules can have deeply gendered implications.[75]

Children's rights scholars have worked similarly to pose the child question, using children's stories to illustrate their unique experiences of law and articulating a child-centered foundation for recognizing children's rights and interests.[76] Internationally, implementation of children's human rights norms has led to the development of independent agencies that monitor the ways in which state law and policymaking may impact children's particular interests and well-being, placing children's experiences squarely at the forefront of analysis. Since the beginning of the twenty-first century, for example, a number of countries have established children's commissioners or ombudspersons to, among other things, promote higher priority of children within all levels of government and to assess and influence the impact of law, policy, and practice on the well-being of children.[77]

3.3 Integrating Theory and Practice

While much of the FLT project is decidedly theoretical, a prominent FLT goal is to not only theorize a different role for law but also to change the lived realities of women. Many see FLT as a necessary mediator between theory and practice, seeking to change the way we understand the law's function, and then to transform law and policy to address subordination and inequality.[78] FLT has enjoyed a number of successes in law reform. For example, liberal feminists have successfully eliminated gender-based classifications in law across a range of domains in the public sphere and continue this work in efforts around equal pay.[79] Cultural feminists have secured increased state recognition of and support for caregiving and have highlighted employment discrimination based on actual or presumed family responsibilities.[80] Postmodern feminists have achieved positive employment law reform through successful gender-stereotyping challenges.[81] At the transnational level, too, feminists are building coalitions that seek to produce knowledge, develop policy, and implement change on the ground.[82]

Likewise, the children's rights movement seeks not only theoretical insight but also material, practical, and particular improvement of children's status in the world. At the international human rights level, child rights advocates have succeeded in securing broad acceptance of the primary human rights instrument concerning children's rights: The UN Convention on the Rights of the Child (CRC) is the most ratified human rights treaty.[83] The CRC recognizes and elevates children's interests through both formal and substantive human rights norms. It recognizes a broad range of civil and political rights, such as the right to freedom of expression, thought, religion, and association,[84] which ensure, if not full equality with adults, approximate rights to those enjoyed by adults. The CRC also includes anti-discrimination guarantees similar to the sorts of anti-discrimination laws feminists have successfully implemented.[85] But, in its recognition of economic, social, and cultural (ESC) rights, the Convention also recognizes that without sufficient access to basic resources and at times special provisions, children will not enjoy equality of opportunity necessary to vindicate their formal legal rights.[86] Since the Convention's adoption, nations across the world have changed laws and adopted policies to protect children and ensure that they thrive, enacting constitutional and legislative reforms across a range of issues.[87]

3.4 Understanding Law through Complex Identities

FLT has brought the theoretical insights from intersectionality theory to an analysis of law. Moving beyond the woman question, beginning in the 1990s FLT theorists began to explore the intersectional nature of subordination.[88] The recognition that women's experiences are not monolithic requires a commitment by FLT theorists to account for these differences when analyzing law and to understand that not all women will experience subordination or discrimination in the same way; some may feel it more acutely, while others may not experience it as all. Thus, to understand the interconnectedness of subordination through law, Mari Matsuda urges that we "ask the other question," looking for obvious and less obvious intersections of domination across a variety of identity markers.[89] Put another way, rather than simply ask the women question, an intersectional perspective requires that we ask "*which* women?"[90]

An intersectional understanding of children's rights requires that we similarly ask "*which* child?"[91] Like women, children's lived experiences are not monoliths but are instead mediated by intersecting markers of social difference combined with the larger social contexts in which particular children are embedded. In addition to social difference, taking an anti-essentialist approach is especially important in the context of children because of the individualized, developmental nature of maturity and capacity. So, for example, gender inequality does not begin in adulthood, but instead at birth (or before), when gender is assigned and gendered norms and expectations first attach. And although all children are affected by gendered norms and expectations, girls are more likely to be subordinated.[92] Yet girls' unique experiences of subordination can be obscured by a traditional children's rights discourse that uses universalized categories of children or youth and a women's rights discourse preoccupied with the experiences of adults.[93] Thus, the intersection of gender and age can exacerbate girls' experiences of oppression.[94] And a lack of attention to intersectional oppression can lead to suboptimal policy on the ground, for example, adolescent health programming that implements gender-neutral policy, excluding girls' specific health problems, or juvenile detention centers that are unequipped to provide for the needs of detained girls.[95]

An understanding of children's identities and experiences as plural and intersectional necessarily affects how we understand the nature of children's legal rights and how they are implemented.[96] Children's rights scholarship has begun to critique essentialized framings of human rights that sometimes overlook children's intersectional identities and experiences.[97] For example, the CRC explicitly guarantees equal treatment for both boys and girls and uses gender-neutral language.[98] Yet while the treaty specifically addresses concerns predominantly affecting boys, such as military service,[99] it does not specifically respond to others that predominantly affect girls, such as child marriage.[100] Children's rights advocates have similarly critiqued constructions of the Global South girl-child in human rights discourse as stereotyping and essentializing as victims of regressive, repressive, and highly patriarchal societies.[101] By contrast, the intersectional lens demands that we avoid essentialized claims about childhood and children while adapting law and policy agendas to address the particular needs of particular children as embedded in broader social and cultural contexts.[102]

4 Tensions, Accords, and New Directions

4.1 Privacy, Redux: Parents' Rights versus Children's Rights

FLT has a complicated relationship with both privacy and children. As discussed above, certain aspects of family privacy have been deeply problematic for FLT theorists. Yet family privacy also can serve a salutary purpose. Shielding family life and decisions from undue state interference protects against authoritarianism and promotes values of pluralism and liberty, enabling parents to pursue their vision of the good life for themselves and their children.[103]

In the United States, parents frequently come out the winners in conflicts of interest among parents, children, and the state, in large part because of their constitutionally recognized right to the care, custody, and control of their children.[104] These rights and interests have been important for feminist goals in some domains, such as child welfare, in which the state disproportionately surveilles and polices mothers, especially poor mothers and mothers of color.[105] Robust parental rights in the face of state interference in this context can serve a protective function against state overreach that can break up families and override mothers' prerogatives, all without appreciably improving children's situations or outcomes.

Yet on the other hand, some critical theorists have argued that the muscular, liberally informed version of parental rights, such as those enshrined in the US Constitution, in fact confers far too much power and control on parents over their children, essentially relegating children's status to that of parental property.[106] Upholding parental rights as sacrosanct can harm children and society and tends to undercut the state's protective function and responsibility to promote healthy child development and education.[107]

Other scholars of feminism, children, and the family reject binary thinking around parental rights versus children's interests. Instead, they urge that in most cases their interests overlap rather than being zero-sum.[108] Both parents and children need autonomy and relationships. One solution to this dilemma in the child welfare context is to focus primarily on ensuring children's safety by providing support for their families rather than by casting parents' and children's rights as necessarily oppositional. In the end, pitting parents' and families' ability for self-determination against their ability to make claims for support on the state is a false choice.[109] Instead, providing parents and families with adequate resources and supporting their child development work will in fact empower them to exercise agency and pursue their desired aims.

The perceived clash between parents' and children's rights has been a primary obstacle to ratification of the CRC by the United States. Yet the CRC recognizes the values of family privacy and pluralism alongside the primacy of children's rights, recognizing the importance of the parent-child relationship and protecting children and parents from state overreach.[110] The CRC also recognizes that providing support and assistance to parents will ultimately benefit children and obligates states to assist parents, encouraging a partnership between families and the state to provide for their children.[111] Beyond direct assistance to parents, the CRC also commits states to establish, monitor, and oversee the institutions, such as childcare facilities and schools, that provide services directly to children and support parents' ability to, for example, balance market work and family care.[112]

In sum, many contemporary advocates of FLT and children's rights seek theories and interventions that can further the interests of both women and children.[113]

4.2 New Directions in FLT and Children's Rights

The status and stakes of FLT continue to be contested: Nearly two decades into the twenty-first century, some see FLT as languishing, whereas other critical legal scholars have advocated (not without controversy) taking a break from feminism and critique the "governance feminism" that has gained a foothold in traditional legal and political power structures.[114] While critical policy challenges remain, large-scale theorizing with women or gender ideology as its foundation has moved toward applied theory and practical legal strategies.[115]

Similar to other critical legal theorists,[116] newer feminisms are coming to recognize the limitations of identity or even status-based categories in achieving substantive equality. These difficulties are compounded by the complexities of women's multiple identities, which make it difficult to challenge women's subordination along discrete categorical lines. Focusing on identities has discouraged some activists from working to find common ground; consequently, at times discrete minorities' claims and concerns remain obscured.[117] And despite the reality of formal equality achievements for women, gender subordination persists, now frequently manifesting in more subtle ways.[118] Thus, moving beyond the centrality of the woman question, FLT has evolved to focus more broadly on gender, intersectionality, and on critiquing the larger social institutions generated and regulated by the state.[119]

These newer threads move away from liberal theory's focus on individual liberty and autonomy and instead call for more universal, structural approaches to seeking equality.[120] They turn their focus to providing equal access to the background conditions and resources necessary for human resilience and flourishing.[121] What these newer projects share with FLT is their conviction that patriarchy is a primary driver of inequality and subordination. They depart, however, from an exclusive focus on women and gender subordination in favor of a more expansive critique of our laws and institutions that is contextual and considers how inequality manifests across a range of social identities as well as social and institutional domains. More broadly, they see the limits of law as currently configured and recognize the limitations of rights-based frameworks in achieving true, substantive equality and justice. Instead, they seek to broaden the focus beyond law's rights-based, anti-discrimination focus and look to larger dynamics of power, privilege, and disadvantage.[122]

This broader, structural approach to achieving justice and improving conditions on the ground illustrates the interrelated and interdependent nature of rights.[123] Formal recognition of civil and political rights means little without these basic background conditions. Equitable access to the basic resources and services necessary for human development are essential to ensuring equal opportunity and more just outcomes. ESC rights aim to secure these essential elements for well-being—things like food, water, housing, health care, education, and an adequate standard of living, for example.[124] Yet ESC rights are largely aspirational[125] and have tended to suffer from relative neglect in the human rights agenda.[126] If civil and political rights (which tend to be negative liberty rights) can be difficult to implement, ESC rights (positive rights to state assistance) are even more challenging.[127] States' obligations to fully realize and implement ESC rights are further qualified by the concession of "progressive realization," meaning that states are obligated to implement these rights only "to the maximum extent of their available resources" and over time.[128] More specifically, the CRC and other children's rights instruments provide relatively weak protection for ESC rights, and research suggests that judicial intervention to protect the socioeconomic rights of children may be limited in efficacy.[129]

Child rights theory and advocacy are similarly exploring new terrain. On a theoretical level, children's rights scholars are taking the discipline in new directions. The field of critical children's rights studies opens up opportunities for alternative ideas in children's rights.[130] Rather than adopting a universal, top-down approach to children's rights, newer work in children's rights advocates a bottom-up approach.[131] In contrast to the tradition of universalist appeals in children's rights, these scholars seek to understand children's rights in context, intersecting with the full panoply of identity markers and the broader socioeconomic contexts in which children are situated.[132] As FLT has acknowledged in the context of women's equality, these scholars recognize that there is a difference between rights recognition and the ability to exercise them. Moreover, these scholars observe that broader structural factors materially affect whether we realize social justice or dignity for children.[133] They move away from a liberal, individualistic understanding of rights and, like FLT, toward a relational understanding of rights.[134] More broadly, they critique the tendency in children's rights fields to focus on legal mechanisms[135] and instead recognize the limits of law in achieving the social change, arguing that law reform must be incorporated into broader, structural strategies.[136]

Some newer advocacy and policymaking for children is taking a similar, bottom-up approach to achieving justice for children and society. Consider work around early childhood development. Newer research confirms that early childhood (the period from birth to age five) is a critical period in human development with dramatic effects on children's future prospects. Yet socioeconomic and structural barriers have led to stark inequality during early childhood, contributing to a growing opportunity gap among children. Inequality that begins in childhood persists well into adulthood and threatens to reproduce and exacerbate existing inequalities at a broad, societal level.[137] Thus, early childhood plays a critical role more broadly in perpetuating or mitigating inequality, and achieving social justice.

The UN Committee on the Rights of the Child (CRC Committee) appreciates children's universal need for early childhood opportunities. The CRC Committee further recognizes that a number of specific rights are implicated during early childhood, including the right to life, survival, and development, as well as the right to non-discrimination and the best interests of the child.[138] Yet the CRC Committee does not approach child development as a context in which the best strategy is to assert the existence and violation of children's rights and to seek legal enforcement. Instead, the CRC Committee urges states parties to develop comprehensive strategies and policies, including program standards and professional training for caregivers, access to services for children, provision of a basic standard of living, health care, early childhood education, and an integrated approach to providing support and services to legal guardians and caregivers.[139]

Few, if any, of these initiatives involve legal enforcement mechanisms, such as anti-discrimination claims and judicial enforcement, although some would involve the state in a regulatory role while others would require legislative enactment. Instead, proposed law reform efforts are incorporated into a broader, structural strategy. Critically, as the CRC Committee recognizes, equality of opportunity in early childhood is about resources. Consequently, the CRC Committee has urged states parties to "increase their human and financial resource allocations for early childhood development services and programmes."[140]

Thus, achieving greater equality in early childhood requires more than simply enforcing human rights law; instead, a broader strategy is needed that raises awareness, generates political will, and helps to change the structures of power, privilege, and disadvantage that determine the quality of early childhood. It requires collaborative, interdisciplinary work across a range of areas of expertise and professions alongside professional and family caregivers. It is deeply contextual and intersectional, recognizing that children's experiences of early childhood are dramatically impacted by their particular identities as well as by the broader socioeconomic and cultural contexts in which they are embedded. It recognizes the need to support parents and guardians. It moves beyond rights-based framing and advocates for early childhood development through prisms of development and even economic growth,[141] noting, for example, that investments in early childhood development promote economic growth as well as expand equal opportunity and address poverty.[142]

The newer work of FLT and critical children's rights studies expand the scope of our inquiry to broader, more structural challenges. They explain that the paper promises of rights may do little without the material, structural, and institutional wherewithal to pursue them. These new frameworks look to the ways in which we are socially embedded within larger institutions of families, communities, markets, and corporations. As such, they shift our gaze from the vindication of individual rights to broader claims for state support. Ultimately, they may lead to a more fulsome and equitable realization of the social contract.

5 CONCLUSION

Despite rumors of (and even calls for) its demise, FLT is alive and well in the twenty-first century, although sometimes assuming less familiar forms than the more traditional stances of the second wave. In a political and economic climate in which neoliberalism increasingly dominates, part of FLT's current work is to question the background assumptions animating the state's current orientation toward women, children, families, and the market and to move beyond rights-based paradigms to focus more broadly on structural and institutional inequalities while making broader claims for more robust state responsibilities. If contemporary social conditions have made clear that, despite the gains of formal equality, women have not achieved full, substantive equality with men, the status of the world's children surely leads to the same conclusion. Our recognition of the work that remains to be done, and perhaps the limitations of a purely rights-based framework in achieving our goals, may lead us to look beyond the law in our quest for equality and justice for all children.

NOTES

1. Erica Burman, "Beyond 'Women vs. Children' or 'WomenandChildren': Engendering Childhood and Reformulating Motherhood," *International Journal of Children's Rights* 16, no. 2 (2008): 177–194.
2. Katrien De Graeve, "Children's Rights from a Gender Studies Perspective: Gender, Intersectionality and Ethics of Care," in *Routledge International Handbook of Children's Rights Studies*, ed. Wouter Vandenhole, Ellen Desmet, Didier Reynaert, and Sarah Lembrechts (London: Routledge, 2015), 150–152.
3. Jonathan Todres, "Children's Rights and Women's Rights: Interrelated and Interdependent," in *Handbook of Children's Rights: Global and Multidisciplinary Perspectives*, ed. Martin D. Ruck, Michele Peterson-Badali, and Michael Freeman (New York: Routledge, 2017), 21–35.
4. Ellen Marrus and Laura Oren, "Introduction: Feminist Jurisprudence and Child-Centered Jurisprudence: Historical Origins and Current Developments," *Houston Law Review* 46, no. 3 (2009): 671–702.
5. Kathleen K. Janus, "Finding Common Feminist Ground: The Role of the Next Generation in Shaping Feminist Legal Theory," *Duke Journal of Gender Law & Policy* 20, no. 2 (Spring 2013): 255–285, 257–259.
6. Rawwida Baksh and Wendy Harcourt, "Introduction: Rethinking Knowledge, Power, and Social Change," in *The Oxford Handbook of Transnational Feminist Movements*, ed. Rawwida Baksh and Wendy Harcourt (New York: Oxford University Press, 2015), 1–50.

7. Christine Chinkin, "Feminism, Approach to International Law," in *Max Planck Encyclopedia of International Law* (Oxford: Oxford University Press, 2010), para. 9; Mary S. Dairiam, "CEDAW, Gender and Culture," in Baksh and Harcourt, *Oxford Handbook of Transnational Feminist Movements*, 367–393.

8. Dairiam, "CEDAW."

9. Baksh and Harcourt, "Introduction: Rethinking Knowledge."

10. Peggy Antrobus, "DAWN, the Third World Feminist Network: Upturning Hierarchies," in Baksh and Harcourt, *Oxford Handbook of Transnational Feminist Movements*, 159–187.

11. Baksh and Harcourt, "Introduction: Rethinking Knowledge."

12. Alexandra Garita, "Moving toward Sexual and Reproductive Justice: A Transnational and Multigenerational Feminix Remix," in Baksh and Harcourt, *Oxford Handbook of Transnational Feminist Movements*, 271–294; Janus, "Finding Common Feminist Ground."

13. Patricia A. Cain, "Feminist Jurisprudence: Grounding the Theories," *Berkeley Women's Law Journal* 4, no. 2 (1989): 191–214, 193 (first recorded use of "feminist jurisprudence" occurred in 1978).

14. Chinkin, "Feminism, Approach to International Law."

15. Martha. E. Chamallas, *Introduction to Feminist Legal Theory*, 3rd ed. (New York: Wolters Kluwer Law & Business, 2013).

16. Patricia Cain, "Feminist Legal Scholarship," *Iowa Law Review* 77, no. 1 (October 1991): 19–40; Martha A. Fineman, "Gender and Law: Feminist Legal Theory's Role in New Legal Realism," *Wisconsin Law Review* 2005, no. 2 (2005): 405–431.

17. For a comprehensive treatment of the history and evolution of feminist legal theory in the US, *see* Chamallas, *Introduction to Feminist Legal Theory*.

18. Martha Chamallas, "Past as Prologue: Old and New Feminisms," *Michigan Journal of Gender and Law* 17, no. 1 (2010): 157–174.

19. Fineman, "Gender and Law."

20. Gerda Neyer and Laura Bernardi, "Feminist Perspectives on Motherhood and Reproduction," *Historical Social Research* 36, no. 2 (2011): 162–176.

21. Chamallas, "Past as Prologue."

22. Dairiam, "CEDAW."

23. Rebecca J. Cook and Susannah Howard, "Accommodating Women's Differences under the Women's Anti-Discrimination Convention," *Emory Law Journal* 56 (2007): 1039–1091; Sandra Fredman and Beth Goldblatt, "*Gender Equality and Human Rights*, UN Women Discussion Paper Series (2014), http://www.austlii.edu.au/au/journals/UTSLRS/2014/8.pdf.

24. Chamallas, "Past as Prologue;" Rosalind Dixon, "Feminist Disagreement (Comparatively) Recast," *Harvard Journal of Law and Gender* 31, no. 2 (Summer 2008): 277–321.

25. Kimberlé Crenshaw, "Demarginalizing the Intersection of Race and Sex: A Black Feminist Critique of Antidiscrimination Doctrine, Feminist Theory and Antiracist Politics," *University of Chicago Legal Forum* 140, no. 1 (1989): 139–167.

26. Chamallas, "Past as Prologue."

27. Baksh and Harcourt, "Introduction: Rethinking Knowledge;" Chamallas, "Past as Prologue."

28. Chamallas, "Past as Prologue."

29. Chinkin, "Feminism, Approach to International Law."

30. Asha Nadkarni, "Transnational Feminism," in *Oxford Bibliographies in Literary and Critical Theory*, ed. Eugene O'Brien (New York: Oxford University Press, 2017).

31. Chamallas, "Past as Prologue."

32. Nadkarni, "Transnational Feminism."

33. "Glocal" describes "how transnational feminist movements often work simultaneously at the global and local levels, where global solidarity informs and contributes to local possibilities for social change." Baksh and Harcourt, "Introduction: Rethinking Knowledge," 12.

34. Baksh and Harcourt, "Introduction: Rethinking Knowledge," 9.

35. Baksh and Harcourt, "Introduction: Rethinking Knowledge."

36. Linda Carty and Chandra T. Mohanty, "Mapping Transnational Feminist Engagements: Neoliberalism and the Politics of Solidarity," in Baksh and Harcourt, *Oxford Handbook of Transnational Feminist Movements*, 82–115.

37. Baksh and Harcourt, "Introduction: Rethinking Knowledge," 3.

38. Rachel Rebouché, "Reproducing Rights: The Intersection of Reproductive Justice and Human Rights," *U.C. Irvine Law Review* 7 (2017): 579–610.

39. Rebouché, "Reproducing Rights."

40. Rebouché, "Reproducing Rights."

41. Maitrayee Mukhopadhyay, "Gendered Citizenship in the Postcolony: The Challenge for Transnational Feminist Politics," in Baksh and Harcourt, *Oxford Handbook of Transnational Feminist Movements*, 607–626; Baksh and Harcourt, "Introduction: Rethinking Knowledge."

42. Katharine T. Bartlett, "Feminist Legal Methods," *Harvard Law Review* 103 (1990): 829–888.

43. Martha A. Fineman, "Introduction," in *At the Boundaries of Law: Feminism and Legal Theory*, ed. Martha Albertson Fineman and Nancy Sweet Thomadsen (London: Routledge, 2014), xi–xvi, xiii.

44. Marrus and Oren, "Introduction: Feminist Jurisprudence."

45. Maxine Eichner, *Supportive State: Families, Government, and America's Political Ideals* (Oxford: Oxford University Press, 2010); Meredith J. Harbach, "Childcare Market Failure," *Utah Law Review* 2015, no. 3 (2015): 659–719.

46. Jennifer S. Hendricks, "Renegotiating the Social Contract," *Michigan Law Review* 110, no. 6 (2012): 1083–1100, 1084.

47. Martha A. Fineman, "The Vulnerable Subject: Anchoring Equality in the Human Condition," *Yale Journal of Law and Feminism* 20, no. 1 (2008): 1–23.

48. Fineman, "Gender and Law."

49. Chinkin, "Feminism, Approach to International Law"; Virginia Vargas, "Feminism and Democratic Struggles in Latin America," in Baksh and Harcourt, *Oxford Handbook of Transnational Feminist Movements*, 534–552.

50. Baksh and Harcourt, "Introduction: Rethinking Knowledge," 2.

51. Of course, enslaved women and children in the United States were not governed by the common law or coverture but, instead, by the law of slavery, which generally refused to recognize legal statuses like marriage and conferred no legal—or other—autonomy on non-free people. Marrus and Oren, "Introduction: Feminist Jurisprudence," 674–677.

52. Chinkin, "Feminism, Approach to International Law."

53. Hendricks, "Renegotiating the Social Contract."

54. Eichner, *Supportive State.*

55. Clare Huntington, *Failure to Flourish: How Law Undermines Family Relationships* (New York: Oxford University Press, 2014).

56. Fineman, "Gender and Law."

57. Rebecca J. Hall, "Feminist Strategies to End Violence against Women" in Baksh and Harcourt, *Oxford Handbook of Transnational Feminist Movements*, 394–417.

58. Income inequality is rising across most of the globe as well as within countries. Facundo Alvaredo, Lucas Chancel, Thomas Piketty, Emmanuel Saez, and Gabriel Zucman, *World Inequality Report 2018: Executive Summary*, World Inequality Lab Report, https://wir2018. wid.world/files/download/wir2018-summary-english.pdf (accessed Aug. 12, 2019). Although they represent only one-third of the global population, children constitute more than one-half of individuals living in poverty, and thirteen percent of the world's children are very poor. Katharina Fenx and Kristofer Hamel, *More than Half of the World's Poor are Children*, Brookings, https://www.brookings.edu/blog/future-development/2019/06/20/more-than -half-of-the-worlds-poor-are-children/ (accessed Oct. 25, 2019).

59. Martha A. Fineman, *The Autonomy Myth: A Theory of Dependency* (New York: The New Press, 2004).

60. Shahrashoub Razavi, "Care and Social Reproduction: Some Reflections on Concepts, Policies and Politics from a Development Perspective," in Baksh and Harcourt, *Oxford Handbook of Transnational Feminist Movements*, 440–441.

61. Maxine Eichner, "The Privatized American Family," *Notre Dame Law Review* 93, no. 1 (2017): 213–266.

62. Fineman, "Gender and Law;" Huntington, *Failure to Flourish*.

63. Wendy Brown, " 'The Most We Can Hope For...': Human Rights and the Politics of Fatalism." *South Atlantic Quarterly* 103, nos. 2–3 (2004): 451–463; Rebouché, "Reproducing Rights."

64. Martha A. Fineman, "Equality across Legal Cultures: The Role for International Human Rights," *Thomas Jefferson Law Review* 27, no. 1 (Fall 2004): 1–13.

65. Rebouché, "Reproducing Rights."

66. Rebouché, "Reproducing Rights."

67. Brown, "Most We Can Hope For"; Rebouché, "Reproducing Rights."

68. Brown, "Most We Can Hope For," 459.

69. Chamallas, *Introduction to Feminist Legal Theory*.

70. Bartlett, "Feminist Legal Methods."

71. Cain, "Feminist Legal Scholarship," 20.

72. Janus, "Finding Common Feminist Ground," 266–268.

73. Kristin Kalsem and Verna L. Williams, "Social Justice Feminism," *UCLA Women's Law Journal* 18, no. 1 (Fall 2010): 131–193.

74. Bartlett, "Feminist Legal Methods," 837–849; Chinkin, "Feminism, Approach to International Law," para. 5.

75. Chamallas, *Introduction to Feminist Legal Theory*.

76. Barbara B. Woodhouse, *Hidden in Plain Sight: The Tragedy of Children's Rights from Ben Franklin to Lionel Tate* (Princeton, NJ: Princeton University Press, 2010) (using children's stories and narratives to advance human rights education achieves similar goals). See Jonathan Todres and Sarah Higinbotham, *Human Rights in Children's Literature: Imagination and the Narrative of Law* (New York: Oxford University Press, 2016).

77. Nigel Thomas, "The Role and Impact of Independent Children's Rights Institutions in the UK and Europe," *Journal of Social Welfare and Family Law* 33, no. 3 (September 2011): 279–288.

78. Fineman, "Gender and Law;" Kalsem and Williams, "Social Justice Feminism."

79. Chamallas, "Past as Prologue."

80. Chamallas, "Past as Prologue."

81. Price Waterhouse v. Hopkins, 490 U.S. 228 (1989); Chamallas, "Past as Prologue."

82. Baksh and Harcourt, "Introduction: Rethinking Knowledge."

83. U.N News, "Hailing Somalia's Ratification, UN Renews Call for Universalization of Child Rights Treaty," October 2, 2015, https://news.un.org/en/story/2015/10/511312-hailing -somalias-ratification-un-renews-call-universalization-child-rights; Human Rights Watch, "25th Anniversary of the Convention on the Rights of the Child: Questions and Answers," November 17, 2014, https://www.hrw.org/news/2014/11/17/25th-anniversary-convention -rights-child.

84. UN Convention on the Rights of the Child (CRC), G.A. Res. 44/25, 44th Sess., UN Doc. A/RES/44/25 (1989).

85. CRC, arts. 2, 30.

86. CRC, art. 19 (protecting children from abuse and neglect); CRC, art. 24 (highest attainable standard of health); CRC, art. 27 (adequate standard of living); CRC, art. 28 (education); CRC, art. 32 (protection from economic exploitation).

87. UNICEF, *25 Years of the Convention on the Rights of the Child: Is the World a Better Place for Children?*, November 2014, https://www.unicef.org/publications/files/CRC_at_25_ Anniversary_Publication_compilation_5Nov2014.pdf.

88. Fineman, "Gender and Law," 430–431; Kalsem and Williams, "Social Justice Feminism," 131, 175–184.

89. Mari Matsuda, "Beside My Sister, Facing the Enemy: Legal Theory out of Coalition," *Stanford Law Review* 43 (1990): 1189–1192.

90. Burman, "Beyond 'Women vs. Children,'" 191.

91. Burman, "Beyond 'Women vs. Children,'" 191.

92. De Graeve, "Children's Rights."

93. De Graeve, "Children's Rights;" Nura Taefi, "The Synthesis of Age and Gender: Intersectionality, International Human Rights Law and the Marginalisation of the Girl-Child," *International Journal of Children's Rights* 17, no. 3 (2009): 345–376.

94. Taefi, "Synthesis of Age."

95. Taefi, "Synthesis of Age."

96. De Graeve, "Children's Rights."

97. Burman, "Beyond 'Women vs. Children'"; De Graeve, "Children's Rights"; Taefi, "Synthesis of Age;" Jonathan Todres, "Women's Rights and Children's Rights: A Partnership with Benefits for Both," *Cardozo Women's Law Journal* 10, no. 3 (2004): 604–694.

98. Rachael L. Johnson, "Feminist Influences on the United Nations Human Rights Treaty Bodies," *Human Rights Quarterly* 28, no. 1 (February 2006): 148–185.

99. CRC, art. 38.

100. Taefi, "Synthesis of Age."

101. Yasmin Jiwani and Helene Berman, "Introduction," in *In the Best Interests of the Girl Child, Phase II Report*, ed. Yasmin Jiwani and Helene Berman, Status of Women Canada, January 2002, 1–13, http://www.unb.edu/fredericton/arts/centres/mmfc/_resources/ pdfs/girlchild_e.pdf.

102. Burman, "Beyond 'Women vs. Children.'"

103. Annette Appell, "The Pre-Political Child of Child-Centered Jurisprudence," *Houston Law Review* 46, no. 3 (2009): 703–758.

104. Troxel v. Granville, 530 U.S. 57 (2000).

105. Dorothy Roberts, "Prison, Foster Care, and the Systematic Punishment of Black Mothers," *UCLA Law Review* 59, no. 6 (2012): 1464–1515.

106. Barbara B. Woodhouse, " 'Who Owns the Child?': Meyer and Pierce and the Child as Property," *William and Mary Law Review* 33, no. 4 (Summer 1992): 995–1122.

107. Martha A. Fineman and George Shepherd, "Homeschooling: Choosing Parental Rights over Children's Interests," *University of Baltimore Law Review* 46, no. 1 (Fall 2016): 57–106.

108. Barbara B. Woodhouse, "The Family Supportive Nature of the U.N. Convention on the Rights of the Child," in *The U.N. Convention on the Rights of the Child: An Analysis of Treaty Provisions and Implications of U.S. Ratification,* ed. Jonathan Todres, Mark E. Wojcik, and Cris R. Revaz (Ardsley, NY: Transnational Publishers, 2006), 37–50.

109. Naomi Cahn, "Placing Children in Context: Parents, Foster Care, and Poverty," in *What Is Right for Children?: The Competing Paradigms of Religion and Human Rights,* ed. Martha Albertson Fineman and Karen Worthington (New York: Routledge, 2009), 145–168.

110. CRC, arts. 4, 8, 14(2), 18; Woodhouse, "Family Supportive Nature."

111. CRC, art. 18; Woodhouse, "Family Supportive Nature."

112. CRC, arts. 3(3), 18(2), 19(2).

113. Marrus and Oren, "Introduction: Feminist Jurisprudence."

114. Janet Halley, *Split Decisions: How and Why to Take a Break from Feminism* (Princeton, NJ: Princeton University Press, 2008); Janet Halley, "Preface: Introducing Governance Feminism," in Janet Halley, Prabha Kotiswaran, Rachel Rebouché, and Hila Shamir, *Governance Feminism: An Introduction* (Minneapolis: University of Minnesota Press, 2018), ix–xii. Halley's urging to take a break from feminism is focused squarely on feminism as a hegemonic theory about the nature of sexuality. Halley, *How and Why.* Reception to Halley's exhortation within the feminist legal community was largely negative. Chamallas, *Introduction to Feminist Legal Theory.*

115. Martha Chamallas, "Backlash, Covering, and the State of Feminist Legal Theory," *Issues in Legal Scholarship* 9, no 2 (2011): 8.

116. John A. Powell, "Post-Racialism or Targeted Universalism," *Denver University Law Review* 86 (2008): 785–806.

117. Garita, "Moving toward Sexual and Reproductive Justice."

118. Janus, "Finding Common Feminist Ground."

119. Angela P. Harris, "What Ever Happened to Feminist Legal Theory?" *Issues in Legal Scholarship* 9, no. 2 (2011): 2–7.

120. Chamallas, "Past as Prologue."

121. Martha A. Fineman, "Equality and Difference—The Restrained State," *Alabama Law Review* 66, no. 3 (2015): 609–626.

122. Brown, " 'The Most We Can Hope For' "; Martha. A. Fineman, "Beyond Identites: The Limits of an Antidiscrimination Approach to Equality," *Boston University Law Review* 92, no. 6 (December 2012): 1713–1770; Janus, "Finding Common Feminist Ground."

123. Jonthan Todres, "Rights Relationships and the Experience of Children Orphaned by AIDS," *U.C. Davis Law Review* 41, no. 2 (December 2007): 417–476.

124. International Covenant on Economic, Social and Cultural Rights (ICESCR), 993 UNTS 3 (Dec. 16, 1966; entered into force Jan. 3, 1976).

125. Brown, " 'The Most We Can Hope For' "; Woodhouse, "Family Supportive Nature."

126. UN Office of the High Commissioner for Human Rights, "Fact Sheet No. 33: Frequently Asked Questions on Economic, Social and Cultural Rights," December 2008, http://www.refworld.org/docid/499176e62.html (accessed Aug. 13, 2019).

127. Rebouché, "Reproducing Rights."

128. ICESCR, art. 2(1); CRC, art. 4.

129. Aoife Nolan, *Children's Socio-Economic Rights, Democracy and the Courts* (Oxford, UK: Hart Publishing, 2011); Wouter Vandenhole, "Children's Rights from a Legal Perspective: Children's Rights Law," in *Routledge International Handbook of Children's Rights Studies*, ed. Wouter Vandenhole, Ellen Desmet, Didier Reynaert, and Sara Lembrechts (London: Routledge, 2015), 27–42.

130. Didier Reynaert, Maria Bouverne-De Bie, and Stijn Vandevelde, "Between 'Believers' and 'Opponents': Critical Discussions on Children's Rights," *International Journal of Children's Rights* 20, no. 2 (2012): 155–168, 165–166.

131. Manfred Liebel, *Children's Rights from Below: Cross-Cultural Perspectives* (London: Palgrave Macmillan, 2012).

132. Ellen Desmet, Sara Lembrechts, Didier Reynaert, and Wouter Vandenhole, "Conclusions: Towards a Field of Critical Children's Rights Studies," in Vandenhole et al., *Routledge International Handbook of Children's Rights Studies*, 412–429.

133. Desmet, "Conclusions: Towards a Field."

134. Desmet, "Conclusions: Towards a Field."

135. Liebel, *Children's Rights from Below.*

136. Vandenhole, "Children's Rights from a Legal Perspective."

137. Saguaro Seminar, Harvard Kennedy School, *Closing the Opportunity Gap*, 2016, http://www.theopportunitygap.com/wp-content/uploads/2015/08/2016-Working-Group-Report.pdf#page=74.

138. UN Committee on the Rights of the Child, *General Comment No. 7: Implementing Child Rights in Early Childhood*, CRC/C/GC/7/Rev.1 (2005).

139. UN Committee on the Rights of the Child, *General Comment No. 7*.

140. UN Committee on the Rights of the Child, UN Children's Fund, and Bernard van Leer Foundation, *A Guide to General Comment 7: "Implementing Child Rights in Early Childhood"* (The Hague: Bernard van Leer Foundation, 2006), 26, https://www.unicef.org/earlychildhood/files/Guide_to_GC7.pdf.

141. Saguaro Seminar, *Closing the Opportunity Gap*.

142. UNICEF, "Early Childhood Development: For Every Child, Early Moments Matter," https://www.unicef.org/early-childhood-development (accessed Aug. 13, 2019).

CHAPTER 9

....

INTERSECTIONALITY
AND CHILDREN'S RIGHTS

....

JESSICA DIXON WEAVER

1 INTRODUCTION

....

INTERSECTIONALITY is a theoretical framework that illustrates how social identities, such as race, gender, and class, overlap and how interlocking systems of power impose a specific type of oppression and discrimination on those who sit at the crossroads.[1] The term was first introduced by critical race feminist Kimberlé Crenshaw, who made an anti-essentialist argument that women cannot be defined by one single identity, but rather, that their identity is shaped by multiple characteristics and experiences.[2] Crenshaw "has defined intersectionality as a way of conceptualizing a problem in a way that captures the dynamics of the interplay between two or more axes of subordination."[3] She and other scholars have expanded on the understanding and analysis of intersectionality, and it has been used within the law and other disciplines to further understand the complexities of living with multiple cultural characteristics and the cumulative harm experienced by certain individuals and groups.[4]

Within the context of international children's rights, intersectionality has been used to examine the experiences of children, their subordination by law, and the ways in which these different identities come together to exacerbate discrimination and limitations placed on children because of their minority status.[5] Intersectionality can be used to analyze how various laws and treaties that purport to protect children's rights fail to do so in specific situations where children fall within multiple identities. It can also be used to support the construction of laws intended to support the most vulnerable children at distinct points of marginalization. This chapter will analyze how intersectionality operates in international children's rights documents and law and whether intersectionality offers tangible solutions for children in the context of international human rights law.

Specifically, this chapter will focus on child marriage as a case study to explore intersectionality as a useful tool for both interpreting the law and hypothesizing legal changes to better protect children. Child marriage is globally viewed as "an egregious violation of every child's right to reach her or his full potential."[6] Within the realm of child marriage, several overlapping or interlocking identities of children present different types of bias. For example, the identity of a child as a refugee, female, person of color, Muslim, and child bride creates five layers of oppression that are not simply addressed by one or two provisions of international law. There is no overarching treaty or convention that currently addresses this combination of characteristics that cause more entrenched harms to children within this intersectional identity. However, the combination of applicable domestic or international laws could theoretically account for a variety of ways by which the child who has entered marriage early has been oppressed. The Universal Declaration of Human Rights (UDHR), Convention on the Rights of the Child (CRC), the Convention on Consent to Marriage, Minimum Age for Marriage, and Registration of Marriages (Convention on Consent to Marriage), and the Convention on the Elimination of All Forms of Discrimination Against Women (CEDAW) are the most relevant international instruments that address the rights of children and women as individuals within both the family unit and the greater society. While each source contains articles that seemingly provide legal protection for girl children who are forced to marry, the ability of these sources to prevent child marriage will be examined along with selected state legislation and proposed laws set forth to address some of these intersections.

2 Intersectionality and Children's Right to be Free from Forced Marriage

Child marriage is a marital union entered into by an individual before reaching a certain age, specified by the CRC Committee and other international organizations as minors below the age of eighteen. A forced marriage is marriage where one party does not or is not able to consent and often involves an element of duress.[7] The UDHR recognizes the right to free and full consent to marriage for men and women of full age.[8] Both the Convention on Consent to Marriage and CEDAW contain language that places restrictions on child marriage.[9] However, neither states a minimum age for marriage.[10] They set forth that state parties to the Convention "shall specify a minimum age for marriage." Article 2 of the Convention on Consent to Marriage sets forth an exception that many countries have, "where a competent authority has granted a dispensation as to age, for serious reasons, in the interest of the intending spouses."[11] This exception typically includes parental and/or judicial consent, with pregnancy or cultural tradition qualifying as a serious reason for underage marriage. Thus, despite these international treaties and other national and state laws prohibiting child marriage, the number of female children who are conscripted into marriage is extremely large worldwide.[12]

According to the United Nations Children's Fund (UNICEF), more than 700 million women worldwide were married before the age of eighteen, with 250 million marrying before the age of fifteen.[13] Fifteen million children a year enter child marriages, and the projections are that if there is no reduction in the practice of child marriage by 2050, there will be 1.2 billion women who first married under the age of eighteen.[14] Boys also are married as children, but girls are disproportionately affected.[15] In contrast to the 720 million girls who married before age of eighteen, 156 million boys were married before reaching the age of eighteen.[16] Girls enter child marriages at more than four and a half times the rate as boys. The ages for child marriage vary from as young as seven or eight to seventeen.[17] Several factors influence the likelihood of child marriage, including poverty, traditional cultural or religious practices, gender inequality, social status, and physical insecurity due to conflict or natural disasters.[18] Parental desire to marry off a young female child is complex. In certain instances it is done to keep a girl child alive, prevent her from being subjected to sexual assault or trafficking, and offer her protection in a climate where single women are vulnerable to exploitation and slavery.[19] In other instances, it is incentivized by economic gain or survival, release of parental duties, and patriarchal prestige.[20]

Child marriage is a global issue but is most common in South Asia and Sub-Saharan Africa.[21] Marriage shortly after puberty is also common among those living traditional lifestyles in the Middle East, North Africa, and other parts of Asia.[22] Nationality and poverty are perhaps the most dominant intersectional identities influencing whether a young girl will become a child bride. In Central and West Africa, early marriage affects 40 percent and 49 percent of girls under nineteen, respectively. Many of these young brides are second or third wives in Islamic polygamous households. Where nationality, poverty, and religion overlap, the risk of child marriage is higher. Niger has the highest rate of child marriage—77 percent of women aged twenty to forty-nine were married before age eighteen.[23] The high rate of early marriage can be attributed to the combination of extreme poverty, tradition, and religious encouragement.[24] Parents receive a bride price for young girls, and when wealthy men offer substantial sums of money to purchase girls, poor families are hard pressed to say no.[25]

More than 40 percent of all child brides live in South Asia, and one in three women child brides are in India.[26] A recent study on child marriage in the Middle East and North Africa notes that gender roles and rights are institutionalized by patriarchal readings of the Islam religion, the dominant practice in these regions.[27] This impacts women's participation in political and religious leadership, which has implications for child marriage prevention.[28] Early marriage reduces a girl's ability to be independent. "Limited mobility, household responsibilities, pregnancy and raising children, and other social restrictions prevent married girls from taking advantage of education or work opportunities."[29]

Child marriage is likely more widespread than the above percentages because so many of the unions are unregistered and unofficial.[30] Under certain circumstances child marriage renders the identity of some girls invisible. In countries where there is no formal record of the marriage,[31] the female party to the marriage is typically still subsumed under the nuclear family of her father, making it more challenging to address this form of marginalization. Until children are born of the marriage, there would be no indication that there even was a legal joining together of two people.[32] Child marriage is also illegal in many countries where it is practiced.[33] There are very few if any parents willing to admit that they violated the law by forcing their child to marry.[34]

There are also many countries that provide for legal exceptions to the minimum age requirement of eighteen, including parental consent and pregnancy.[35] Furthermore, in many countries the minimum age is below eighteen, with children as young as twelve being able to marry legally. For example, there is no minimum legal age to marry in 40 percent of the United States.[36] In many of these cases, the children are girls marrying men that are ten to thirty years older than them.

While it is true that child marriage as a cultural custom is extremely difficult to eliminate, it is viewed as a human rights violation pursuant to CEDAW and by many countries, UNICEF, and international nongovernmental organizations (NGOs). The health risks and devastating consequences of child marriage are well documented. Many child brides are not physically ready for pregnancy, leading to a high maternal death rate and significant risks for the baby as well.[37] Girls who marry early are more likely to contract HIV/AIDS, suffer domestic violence, and drop out of school.[38] Child brides also suffer mentally and emotionally, often showing signs symptomatic of sexual abuse and post-traumatic stress disorder, including severe depression and feelings of helplessness and hopelessness.[39] As human rights advocates strategize to change the law and public policies surrounding child marriage, intersectionality is useful in understanding the compounded risks young girls face when they lose proximity to and support from their family and community. For example, in Yemen, according to the personal status law, a wife is required to be obedient to her husband and obtain his consent to leave the home to travel abroad (Article 40). Similarly, in Egypt and Morocco men have control over women's mobility, thereby restricting a woman's ability to move freely within and outside of the household. Without freedom, the intersectional identity of a minor female from a certain culture poses health and safety risks because of the practice of early marriage.

There are several intersectional identities that intensify the chances that a girl will become a child bride. Socioeconomic status is a prime factor. In every region of the world poor girls are most at risk of child marriage.[40] In India and the Dominican Republic, the wealthiest women marry about four years later than the poorest women.[41] Acute poverty in Yemen has led poor families to resort to tourist marriages, defined as "temporary, formal union[s] between a Yemini woman and a man from an Arabian Gulf country."[42] Families believe that these marriages will provide financial stability to the girl, lift her out of dire circumstances, and help her acquire citizenship in a more stable country.[43] Geography can also play a role in whether a girl is more likely to become an early bride. Girls who live in rural areas are more likely to become child brides than their urban counterparts.[44]

Violent conflict within or outside of a country can increase the prevalence of child marriage. A 2013 survey taken in Yemen showed the prevalence of respondents married before the ages of fifteen and eighteen had increased since the start of conflict. The growing number of Syrian refugee girls being married in Jordan, Lebanon, Iraq, and Turkey reveal the impact of conflict on child marriage.[45] Although child marriage was a significant practice before the war, it rose from 13 percent between 2002 and 2011 to 17.3 percent in 2014.[46] Among refugees in Lebanon, it may be as high as 23 percent.[47] In Jordan, child marriage among Syrian refugees increased from 15 percent in 2014 to 36 percent in 2018.[48] Syrian refugee families report that the displacement of family life caused by the conflict has increased their reliance on child marriage as a way to cope with the financial and protection challenges they face.[49] Driving factors include feeling insecure about the honor or reputation of their daughter, worsening economic conditions, and disrupted education for young adolescent women.[50] Sexual harassment and rape threaten to destroy *al Sutra*, the protection of a woman's honor and reputation. In addition, there have been changes in marriage practices, such as shorter engagement periods, lower bride prices, and a reduced age in marriage. Nine of the top ten countries with the highest rates of child marriage are considered fragile states or those with insecure environments, such as war, civil conflict, or natural disasters.[51]

Religion and traditional practices within certain religions play a large role in child marriages. They weave yet another identity that presents discriminatory gender issues as well as social norms that provide community support for girls to enter marriage early. Although no one religion embraces child marriage, the perception that many people have is that child marriage is a part of Islamic principles.[52] One of the misinterpretations of Islamic law is that the prophet Mohammed married a nine-year-old; however, this has been proved to be false by a religious scholar.[53] According to this expert, Mohammed married his wife when she was seventeen or eighteen, and the National Taskforce to End Child Marriage in Sudan is advocating that this age frame be adopted.[54] The law and social norm of Islamic families is within the Qu'ran, creating a difficult task to separate religion from family affairs.[55] The complication of the overlay of traditional attitudes toward child marriage is that it is still acceptable in Islam and is necessary to avoid social sanctions, like shame and stigma.[56] Some Orthodox Jews, conservative Christians, and certain Mormon sects (such as the Fundamentalist Church of Jesus Christ of Latter Day Saints) also embrace early marriages.

Another problem related to the intersection of ethnic identity and nationality in some countries is statelessness.[57] When an ethnic minority is denied national status during civil conflict, young women who are members of the group face additional forms of discrimination because of the combination of gender inequality and patriarchal institutions.[58] For example, a young Muslim girl who was an ethnic Rohingya and one of eight children was smuggled to another country by her parents in order to protect her from potential sexual violence in Burma.[59] She was prohibited from attaining Burmese statehood, which meant that she could not obtain identification documents or legal status, attend school, receive state health care, or seek employment.[60] During her harrowing sea trip to Malaysia, she was apprehended and detained by traffickers.[61] A Rohingya man she never met took pity on her and paid a little more than two thousand dollars to secure her release.[62] Once the girl's family learned of the man's deed, they told him he could take her as his bride.[63] Even though she had escaped being the victim of rape in Burma, she was forced to marry because she had no nation under which she could claim protection. As Sheila Menz has reported, "Stateless women and girls are vulnerable not only to exploitation and abuse on account of their lack of legal status; their femaleness also contributes to further marginalization and insecurity. These two discriminatory regimes interact and compound on themselves to perpetuate the cycle of statelessness and early/forced marriage for generations."[64]

3   The Utility of International and State Laws against Child Marriage

Although international law comprises international agreements and customary law, it is difficult to enforce children's rights consistently across the world. In many instances, countries agree to self-regulate in that they submit reports periodically to account for how they are complying with treaty obligations. The regulating arm of the United Nations, the International Court of Justice (ICJ), does not regulate member states. The ICJ settles disputes between member states or issues advisory, nonbinding opinions on legal questions. Moreover, states opt into participation within the ICJ. Therefore, there is no penalty or punishment to incentivize bad actors to change. Countries are essentially expected to operate in good faith. For example, both the Convention on Consent to Marriage and CEDAW contain articles that set forth that marriage of a child or person under a specific minimum age is illegal. However, it is up the states to determine what that minimum age is. So even though 158 countries have set the minimum age that women can marry at eighteen, 146 countries allow for girls under the age of eighteen to marry with parental consent.[65] Since religious traditions and culture are slow to change, early marriage practices continue in rather large numbers where historically the wife is a young girl whose parents arrange the marriage.

The CRC is the most comprehensive treaty that addresses the range of social, economic, civil, political, and cultural issues that children face around the globe. Having been ratified by every UN member state except the United States, it serves as a model human rights treaty that provides protection, autonomy, and dignity for every child. It is viewed as a gender-neutral document that addresses both male and female children as individuals, and it prohibits discrimination in all forms. However, with all of its comprehensiveness, it does not cover certain key concerns for children in the twenty-first century.[66] Unfortunately, the CRC does not have a provision that directly addresses child marriage.[67] Since child marriage disproportionately affects girls rather than boys, there has been criticism that the CRC missed an opportunity to legally address an intersectional harm unique to females.[68] At the same time, the CRC does have a distinct article that addresses human rights violations that disproportionately affect boys, such as Article 38, which deals with child soldiers.[69] This unequal treatment of gender within the CRC amplifies how intersectionality can have both positive and negative effects depending on the cross section of identity.

There are many categories that children migrate into that create new and different vulnerabilities for them. When a child is without parents due to war, death, or health issues, the CRC states clearly what the responsibility of a nation-state is with respect to the care and protection of an unaccompanied child.[70] However, without commensurate domestic laws that support the CRC's general command for support of the child, Article 9 (separation from parents), Article 10 (family reunification), and Article 11 (illicit transfer and non-return of children abroad) can ring hollow for a parentless child in another country seeking asylum. Alternative care is provided for in Article 20, which sets forth that a child is entitled to special protection and assistance by a state if the child is temporarily or permanently deprived of his or her family environment.[71] However, when a minor is married, this status can prevent the child from utilizing laws that protect minors and their rights to be reunited with their families.[72] Article 22 also establishes the role that states parties must take when dealing with refugee children, whether unaccompanied or accompanied by parents.[73] Appropriate protection and humanitarian assistance must be provided, and states parties must also cooperate with the United Nations, NGOs, and other competent intergovernmental organizations in order to assist the child, trace the parents, and reunify the child with his or her family.[74]

Female children in search of a specific article that provides protection from forced marriage will not find an article in the CRC that addresses this involuntarily acquired status, though there are general statements in Article 24(3) regarding the abolishment of traditional practices prejudicial to the health of children, and Article 19 (protection against interfamilial violence), Article 36 (protection from exploitation), and Article 37 (prohibiting unlawful deprivation of liberty) address problems specifically relevant to girls. There are certain intersectional identities that are highlighted by the gaps within the CRC. Poor female Muslim children under the age of eighteen who are also refugees are at risk of becoming child brides with their parents' consent. Article 14(2) directs states parties to "respect the rights and duties of parents...to provide direction to the child in the exercise of his or her right [to freedom of religion] in a manner consistent with the evolving capacities of the child."[75] This provision of the CRC gives deference to the rights of parents to control certain aspects of their children's lives, especially in the area of religions, education, and cultural heritage.[76] The younger a girl is, the more an argument can be made that "the CRC explicitly protects the right of a father to instruct his daughter on how to be a good Muslim (or...a good Mormon) and to honor and obey the father's pious decision to marry off his daughter."[77] As many scholars have noted, the CRC is a great foundation for international children's rights, but it is imperative that national or domestic law follow behind it to pass legislation with teeth that will meet children where they are and provide a process for government institutions and the judiciary seeking to protect the rights of the child.[78]

Despite the lack of a direct statement prohibiting child marriage, there are articles of the CRC that advocates have used to support the push for a ban on child marriage. Article 2 provides that the rights present in the CRC should be allocated without discrimination of any kind, including on account of a child's or a parent's race, color, sex, language, religion, political, national, ethnic or social origin, property, disability birth or other status. Article 2 can be read with Article 24(3), which sets forth that "States Parties shall take all effective and appropriate measures with a view to abolishing traditional practices prejudicial to the health of children."[79] Since child marriage has been shown to be detrimental to children's health, if a child's religion, nationality, ethnicity, or other status includes the traditional practice of child marriage, a member state can use the CRC to support domestic changes in the law. Other relevant articles include Article 6 (the right to life, survival, and development), Article 19 (the right to be protected from all forms of physical and mental violence, injury, or abuse), Article 28 (right to education), Article 36 (protection from exploitation), and Article 37 (prohibiting unlawful deprivation of liberty). Article 14(3) could be used to limit traditional customs that encourage child marriages in that it allows for limitations when necessary to protect health or morals or the fundamental rights and freedoms of others. Article 27 places some responsibility on CRC states parties to take appropriate measures, in accordance with national conditions and within their means, to assist parents with providing a standard of living for their children that is adequate for their physical, mental, spiritual, moral, and social development. Ideally this might assist some poor families in countries that have the capacity for a larger safety net.

CEDAW is a core international human rights treaty that addresses gender violence. Even though CEDAW requires states parties to condemn discrimination against women in all its forms and to adopt legislative measures to end it, the treaty itself does not mention gender violence.[80] The CEDAW Committee has issued general recommendations regarding gender violence and the obligation of states to respond to gender violence. General Recommendation No. 12 requires states to maintain statistics on gender violence, and Recommendation No. 19 clearly identifies gender violence as a form of gender discrimination, "linking violence to historic gender roles in which women are subordinated to men."[81] General Recommendation No. 19 addresses how specific practices, such as family violence, forced marriage and female genital mutilation, keep women in subordinate roles and contribute to low levels of political participation, education, skills, and work opportunities.[82] As it pertains to child marriage specifically, CEDAW Article 16 (2) states that "betrothal and the marriage of a child shall have no legal effect, and all necessary action, including legislation, shall be taken to specify a minimum age for marriage and to make the registration of marriages in an official registry compulsory."[83] Although a specific age is not mentioned in Article 16, CEDAW General Recommendation No. 21 calls on countries to legislate the minimum marriage age at eighteen.[84]

The UN Sustainable Development Goals (SDG) set a goal of eliminating child marriage by 2030. Even though the practice of child marriage has declined 15 percent over the past decade, a substantial acceleration would be required to eliminate the practice by that year.[85] The largest decline has been in India, where a girl's risk of marrying in childhood has declined by more than a third.[86] Population growth in sub-Saharan Africa threatens to increase the number of child brides in the future, primarily because progress to reduce child marriage in this region has been the slowest.[87] As discussed below, the recent statistics regarding the declines in child marriage in South Asia illustrate how some countries have recognized that an intersectional approach to the problem can help to change the problem. South Asia has achieved this decline by using international human rights norms as interpretive tools to fill the gaps in domestic laws and clarify ambiguities in local laws.[88]

India presents one example of how the CRC and CEDAW have been helpful in transcending the intersectional subordination of young girls forced into child marriage. A human rights NGO, the Forum for Fact-Finding Documentation and Advocacy (FFDA) filed a public interest case seeking strict implementation of the Child Marriage Restraint Act of 1929 (CMRA), citing several international conventions, including CEDAW and the CRC.[89] The CMRA, subsequently amended in 1949 and 1978, increased the age of marriage for girls from fourteen to fifteen and finally to eighteen.[90] For men, the age for legal marriage went from eighteen to twenty-one. The FFDA reminded the government that being a party to these treaties meant that it had committed the country to protecting and ensuring child rights and had also agreed to hold itself accountable before the international community for this commitment.[91] The judiciary's decision to embrace international law was a catalyst for legislative action that was used at the local level to protect children from child marriage. The FFDA asked the Indian Supreme Court to direct states to require police to prevent child marriage from taking place, hold government officials who fail to prevent child marriage accountable, and ensure that the CMRA is implemented.[92] Since the Indian Supreme Court had previously ruled that its constitution and any ambiguity in national law must be interpreted in accordance with India's international obligations, the CRC and CEDAW were cited in the case that prompted passage of the Prohibition of Child Marriage Prevention Bill.[93] This bill, enacted in 2006, allegedly goes further to enforce the CMRA, widely viewed a dead letter. The bill set forth punishments in order to prevent child marriage, along with options to void a child marriage if there was fraud, deceit, or enticement for the purpose of trafficking or immoral purposes. A major criticism of this bill is that it tasked the minor with complaining about the child marriage; because the child bride was often under the control of her husband, this law did not afford her much assistance.

Various laws in many countries in Africa have contributed to the reduction of child marriage. Interestingly, the development and formation of the African Charter on the Rights of the Welfare of the Child (the Charter) is in itself an example of intersectionality with regard to children's rights. Although African countries were among the first nations to ratify the CRC, they played a marginal role in the overall framing of it.[94] They set out to establish a regional response to address gaps in the CRC and the absence of sociopolitical concerns of African nations from the dominant agenda of children's rights.[95] Adopted in 1990 by the Organization of African Unity (OAU; now the African Union or AU), the Charter reiterates to the world that an African conception of children's rights already existed before the CRC. Thus, child participation and protection was not foreign, imposed upon, or adopted from the Northern Hemisphere.[96] The Charter addressed issues that were unique to the African diaspora, such as apartheid (at the time), the impact of armed conflict and use of child soldiers, and gender equality related to female children and harmful traditional practices.[97] Within the African culture and value system, the Charter also provides for the role of the extended family in matters of child care and the responsibility of children to their parents, communities, and society relative to their age and ability.[98] The Charter set the legal norm for the minimum age of marriage at eighteen.[99]

In fact, a majority of African constitutions explicitly refer to a variety of children's rights.[100] South Africa is an international leader in constitutionalizing justiciable children's rights rooted in human rights law.[101] Article 28 establishes specific rights for children, including the right to family and parental or appropriate alternative care when removed from the family environment.[102] It also establishes the right not to be required or permitted to perform work or provide services that are inappropriate for a person of that child's age or that place at risk the child's well-being, education, physical or mental health or spiritual, moral, or social development.[103] It can be argued that a child bride is forced to perform services that place her physical and mental well-being at risk.

Even within the United States, there has been a push for state changes in the law regarding child marriage.[104] Approximately 170,000 children under eighteen were married in the US between 2000 and 2010.[105] Several states, such as Texas, New York, and Connecticut, have passed laws limiting child marriage or increasing the age to sixteen or seventeen.[106] Delaware is the first state to ban child marriage altogether.[107] Similar to the situations in other countries around the globe, state opposition to ending child marriage comes from members of some religious communities.[108] For example, former New Jersey governor Chris Christie objected to an outright ban of child marriage because "it would violate the cultures and traditions of some communities in New Jersey based on religious traditions."[109] Resistance to new laws restricting or banning child marriage have come from both liberal and conservative groups advocating for teens to marry with parental or judicial consent as an act of individual autonomy or to prevent abortions, respectively.[110] The majority of child brides in the US are white, poor, and live in southern or western rural, religiously conservative towns.[111] Gender, poverty, regional customs, and religion are intersectional identities similar to other children around the globe entering child marriage. The Violence Against Women Reauthorization Act of 2013 set forth a federal requirement that the US secretary of state must establish and implement a multi-year, multi-sectoral strategy aimed at ending child marriage.

In February 2018, the US House of Representatives introduced House Bill 5034, the International Violence Against Women Act of 2018. In Section 2 of the bill, Finding 15 explicitly identifies child and forced marriage as a harmful practice that deprives girls of their dignity and violence as well as increases their vulnerability to gender-based violence.[112] The bill is effectively a policy statement that presents a strategic plan requiring significant funding to address violence against women and girls around the world "as a matter of basic human rights and to promote gender equality, economic growth and improved public health."[113] Per the bill, five to twenty low-income countries with significant levels of violence against women and girls will be selected, and there will be coordinated efforts to promote a wide array of protective programs, including public awareness programs to change social norms and attitudes about harmful traditional practices, including child marriage.[114] If adopted, House Bill 5034 will help close the financial and service gap for some of the countries that are in need of ways to expand their outreach to young girls, their families, local school systems, and governments.

4 At the Intersection of Cultural Norms and Practices: Challenging the Nucleus of Child Marriage

While legal reform on the international, national, and local levels is important, widespread cultural change is needed in order to eradicate child marriage. South African Archbishop Desmond Tutu offered insight into what is necessary to eradicate child marriage, stating that real change needed to happen at the grassroots level and that a human rights movement is needed.[115] As a member of The Elders, an organization of global world leaders brought together by Nelson Mandela in 2007, Tutu visited India, Ethiopia, and other countries in order to learn the causes of child marriage and its harmful impact on human rights and development.[116] In an effort to encourage local attempts to end child marriage, The Elders met with political and business leaders, UN and NGO representatives, media representatives, and communities affected by child marriage.[117] In 2011 The Elders created Girls Not Brides: The Global Partnership to End Child Marriage.[118] Tutu notes that although the laws in all of the countries where child marriage is common provide that the minimum age of marriage for girls is eighteen, what happens on the ground is different from what is authorized by statute.[119] He acknowledged that these traditions were patriarchal:

> Maybe because I am a man, I have spent much of my life ignorant of the scale and awfulness of child marriage. But, in recent years, I have talked to many girls and women who have educated me. It wasn't until my retirement that I realized that one in three women in the developing world is married before the age of 18, or understood what they risk as a result.[120]

Tutu has stated that the biggest challenge in ending child marriage is to change the mindset in villages, towns, and homes. Ultimately, communities have to organize as a collective to break the painful bondage of traditions. In Ethiopia, there were coalitions built between the cultural and religious leaders and the youth.[121] When Tutu visited Zambia in 2014, he commended the innovative work of the nation's first lady, a group of government ministers, traditional chiefs, religious leaders, diplomats, young activists, international donors, UN agencies, and civil society organizations to end child marriage.[122] Forty-two percent of the girls in Zambia are married before their eighteenth birthday, placing the country among the top twenty countries with the highest prevalence of child marriage.[123] The Zambian government launched a campaign to end child marriage, and the traditional leaders saw the need to amend the traditions that were holding girls and the larger community back.[124] Part of the meetings included personal stories of girls who had been married as children as well as stories of girls who courageously resisted child marriage and found allies to help them prevent it from happening.[125] One young girl, Mirriam, told how her parents promised her into marriage when she was twelve and how before she left school in preparation to become a wife, she wrote her teacher, who alerted the local Young Men's Christian Association (YMCA) office of the situation.[126] The YMCA was able to work with the Victim Support Unit of the local Zambian police to prevent the marriage, which allowed Mirriam to return to school.[127]

The efforts in Ethiopia and the campaign in Zambia are examples of how the intersectionality framework can pull people together to make a difference across many nations. A religiously affiliated, nonprofit organization working with a local educator and the police were able to intervene in the private life of Mirriam to change her life outcome. Each organization served a different role and purpose in Mirriam's life, but all were committed to protecting her vulnerable identity and place in society. The intersections that created Mirriam's unique vulnerability—her age, gender, nationality, family network, and local traditions—were overcome by another set of intentionally created intersections. The collaborative partnerships initiated by the government campaign to end child marriage formed networks among civil society organizations and a commitment by the Ministry of Justice to synchronize customary and statutory laws to avoid loopholes and inconsistencies.[128] So rather than have a statutory law that establishes the minimum age of marriage as eighteen and a customary law that allows for parents to promise a young girl to an adult man for marriage, the community and the legal standard match in both practice and enforcement.

The alternative to child marriage is education. Girls with secondary or higher education are three times less likely to marry as children compared to girls with no education.[129] On average, every additional year of schooling reduces the risk of marriage before age eighteen by six percentage points.[130] The rationale is that a girl can be more beneficial to her family and her future children by gaining knowledge and a set of skills that will help her earn a living as well as give her useful information to pass down to her children. However, sending a girl to school until she is eighteen does not help the economic situation of a family right away. While it is assured to eventually lift that child, her family, and eventually the locality out of poverty, it takes time to get to that place. Without adequate financial support from the government and other institutions, the daily realities for poor families will not change. Schools are also not always available to certain rural towns, leaving very little choice for girls except for a long commute to the nearest school, which could be several miles away.

The distance between home and school presents another intersectional conflict for female children who have reached puberty. The trek to and from school leaves a young girl vulnerable to physical or sexual attacks; in many instances these attacks can result in a pregnancy.[131] Due to religious or cultural nonacceptance of out-of-wedlock children, fathers typically arrange a marriage with a young man who can pay the dowry.[132] Sometimes it is the man who raped the young girl who is forced to marry her.[133] Faced with being pregnant and disowned by her family, most young girls do not have any other choice but to acquiesce to early marriage.[134]

Even the availability of school toilets and access to sanitary napkins or towels can affect a girl's susceptibility to early marriage.[135] For example, in Amhara province in Ethiopia over half of all schoolgirls missed school during menstruation.[136] In Uganda, schoolgirls who begin menstruating are forced into child marriages by parents who are too poor to purchase sanitary pads.[137] Lack of menstrual hygiene support is noted as a strong factor for schoolgirls' dropout rate.[138] UNICEF estimates that sixty percent of girls in Uganda miss class because of a lack of separate toilets and washing facilities that would help them manage their periods.[139] So even though Ugandan law bans child marriage, four in ten girls are wed before eighteen, and one in ten weds before fifteen.[140] As noted earlier in this chapter, staying in school could reduce these girls' chances of becoming a child bride. It is a circular issue, with one predicament leading to the next. This same issue has been noted in Kenya, Tanzania, and Nepal.[141] The restrictions that are imposed on young girls by menstruation highlight the intersectionality of caste, gender, age, space, and material practice.[142] The combination of these, coupled with a patriarchal culture, stigmatizes and demeans the dignity of young girls. Although the government in Uganda promised funding for feminine hygiene products, it was a crowdfunding campaign, #Pads4girlsUg, launched by a university lecturer that spurred an outpouring of support for schoolgirls negatively affected by this intersectional dilemma.

Finally, it should be noted that children, not just adults, are speaking up and advocating for themselves. A legal case that made a difference in Zimbabwe was the case of Loveness Mudzuru and Ruvimbo Tsopodzi, two former child brides who were forced to wed at age sixteen. Child marriage in Zimbabwe is illegal unless the parents consent to it, which their parents did. The girls sued the government, alleging that the law allowing for child marriage with parental consent was unconstitutional and clashed with the nation's marriage act. They argued that it was a form of child abuse, which trapped girls in lives of poverty and suffering. They called on the court to bring the law in line with Zimbabwe's 2013 Constitution as well as regional and international treaties banning child marriage. The Constitutional Court of Zimbabwe ruled in their favor and recognized eighteen as the age for legal marriage, including customary law unions. The court also struck down a section of the marriage act that allowed girls to marry at sixteen but boys at eighteen. The voice of the youth should not be underestimated in the quest to reduce child marriage.

5 Intersectionality and Children's Right to Family Integrity

For well over the past decade, there has been a global crisis of refugees from war-torn countries or places where people are experiencing extreme violence, internal conflict, or persecution.[143] In 2015 children constituted ten million of the world's twenty-one million refugees who had been forcibly displaced from their own countries.[144] Another seventeen million children were internally displaced in 2015 due to conflict and violence.[145] Of course, not all of these children are without parents or family. According to the Office of the United Nations High Commissioner for Refugees (UNHCR), 173,800 are unaccompanied.[146] These refugee children are among the most vulnerable children in the world.[147] Refugee children face numerous challenges, and there is some crossover between their situation and the issue of child marriage. Incidents of early marriage are alarmingly high among refugee children.[148] It is the dual nature of children being minors and refugees that make them particularly vulnerable to these particular human rights violations. One example of intersectionality with regard to child refugees and child marriage is the geography of where they are displaced. Three out of five child migrants live in Africa and Asia.[149] These two continents have the highest incidence of child marriage. Children who are female refugees living in African or Asia may have a higher chance of becoming a child bride, depending on which country within the continent they live.

While the CRC does offer general protection and services for children who are separated from their parents, refugee children fall through the cracks of certain articles that do not account for the ways in which perpetrators use gender to underscore weaknesses among children. Refugee children from Central America are often fleeing gang violence, and those from countries like Syria, Afghanistan, and South Sudan are attempting to escape the effects of civil conflict and war. Child marriage may sometimes be the forced result of a rape and subsequent pregnancy of a minor refugee girl. Typically, after a child marries a man who is much older, physical abuse and rape follow the nuptials. Children from conflict war zones are faced with a choice of physical harm, death, or forced recruitment as a child soldier. They can also be vulnerable to physical and sexual abuse within the armed forces because of their minor status (size, maturity, capacity for self-defense). Later, male children can become the rapist and force girls under eighteen to marry. It is an awful cycle of interlocking identities that brings focus to the various ways that the intersectionality framework applies to international children's rights.

6 Conclusion

In reviewing the countries that support the end of child marriage and have achieved a reduction in the institution, this chapter notes several themes regarding the interplay of the established law, the judicial system, and both national and community leaders. A common theme that runs through the children's rights issues addressed in this chapter is the disturbing degree to which violence and poverty are such key aspects of the institution of child marriage. On the one hand, prevention of violence (i.e., sexual assault) and economic survival are primary reasons parents agree to marry off young daughters to much older adult men. The consequence of children's lack of autonomy in exercising their right to be free from forced marriage is often domestic violence and poverty. They are sexually and physically assaulted within their marriage, and because they are economically dependent on their husband, they remain poor and unable to do anything other than household and parenting tasks.

Another common global theme within the examination of child marriage and intersectionality is the extent to which written laws establishing a minimum age for marriage remain dead without substantial coalition-building to address gaps in prevention and enforcement. Many countries have laws on the books that make underage marriage illegal, but unwritten customary laws or local traditions encourage child marriage. Other countries have had no written laws preventing child marriage or legal exceptions allowing it. Recognizing the various intersections that influence which children are most at risk for child marriage brings to light the actors necessary to create change. An important observation is the degree to which change requires the collaboration of young girls, older female activists, government leaders, and men in power at both the government and customary law levels. The disruption of social norms, whether religious or cultural, has significantly impacted how the law has been activated outside the pages of books and within the actual community. This is the meaning of a grassroots human rights movement, and it is crucial to the global goal of ending child marriage.

Two large factors in the global prevalence of child marriage are patriarchal cultural systems and the female child's status as property. In countries where the emphasis has been on grassroots or community changes, women and female children have been necessary advocates who voice the detrimental effects of underage marriage on a girl's health and ability to lift herself and her children out of poverty. In conservative religions where a woman's role as wife is defined by childbearing and homemaking, a female child bride is regulated to the role of mother much earlier and at greater risk to herself and her child.[150] Viewing female children as more valuable to the family than a dowry is the task set before many nations that wish to curb the tide of child marriage. Beyond providing income for a poor family, female children must also be valued as contributing members of their nuclear family, even if they are raped or engage in sexual activity outside of the bounds of marriage. The honor of a woman and her family should extend beyond the gendered role of virgin, and the stigma or punishment for a female's family (as opposed to the male) only serves to perpetuate traditions grounded in male control and the protection of a man's societal reputation.

Another interesting observation is the extent to which each separate inquiry into different aspects of children's rights leads to a new overlay of identity that connects one to the other. The fact that a young girl of a certain ethnicity or nationality is more susceptible to child marriage when she is a refugee or when she lives in a country that is ravaged by war is a compounded violation of international human rights. In that same war-torn country, a young boy can be conscripted into the armed forces and compelled to rape a young girl, kill her parents, and force her to marry him, making her his prisoner and a continued victim of violence. These are cyclical intersections that will require much more resources and efforts outside of the campaigns begun in countries like India and Zambia. The crisis of civil wars and long-standing international conflicts cannot be solved overnight, and how countries respond to refugees and families seeking asylum remains an ongoing question beyond the scope of this chapter.

There is no magic bullet or easy answer. Illuminating the intersections should bring a new level of analysis to international children's rights by delving deeper into the facets of children's lives that come together in complex ways. While international children's rights law can set a standard for what nation-states should implement at the domestic level, much of the change that needs to occur is greater than law. As Bishop Desmond Tutu, UNICEF, and other international NGOs have noted, there must be a strong push by community leaders to change the culture and societal expectation of the role of girls and women. At the heart of intersectionality is a multifaceted identity. At once many young girls are female, poor, raised in the Muslim, Jewish, or Christian faith to be obedient, desirous of a larger future that includes access to a full education, and in need of a stable home and community environment free of violence. It is impossible to compartmentalize these various facets of a girl's life because they intersect and influence one another. Acceptance and recognition of multiple layers of identity is the door that intersectionality opens, but equal treatment and compassion require an urgent, systematic interruption of the internal core of entire groups of people mired in economic quicksand and family traditions. Convincing predominantly male leaders and families to forego dowries and customs is complex, but the narratives of child bride experiences resonate with those willing to listen. With any hope, children will lead us.

Notes

1. Merriam-Webster Dictionary, "Intersectionality," https://www.merriam-webster.com/dictionary/intersectionality.
2. Kimberlé Crenshaw, "Demarginalizing the Intersection of Race and Sex: A Black Feminist Critique of Antidiscrimination Doctrine, Feminist Theory, and Antiracist Politics," *University of Chicago Legal Forum* 1989, no. 1 (1989): 139–167, 139–140.
3. Rangita de Silva de Alwis, "Mining the Intersections: Advancing the Right of Women and Children with Disabilities within an Interrelated Web of Human Rights," *Pacific Rim Law & Policy Journal Association* 18, no. 1 (2009): 293–322, 301 (citing UN Expert Group Meeting on Gender and Racial Discrimination, *Gender-Related Aspects of Race Discrimination*, UN Doc. EGM.GRD/2000/WP.1 (2000)).
4. Kimberlé Crenshaw, "Mapping the Margins: Intersectionality, Identity Politics and Violence against Women of Color," *Stanford Law Review* 43, no. 6 (1991): 1241–1299; Patricia Hill Collins, "Learning from the Outsider Within: The Sociological Significance of Black Feminist Thought," *Social Problems* 33, no. 6 (1986): S14; Devon W. Carbodo and Mitu Gulati, "The Fifth Black Woman," *Journal of Contemporary Legal Issues* 11 (2001): 701–729; Darren Lenard Hutchison, "Identity Crisis: 'Intersectionality,' 'Multidimensionality,' and

the Development of an Adequate Theory of Subordination," *Michigan Journal of Race and Law* 6, no. 2(2001): 285–317; Sumi Cho, Kimberlé Crenshaw, and Leslie McCall, "Toward a Field of Intersectionality Studies: Theory, Applications and Praxis," *Signs* 38, no. 4 (2013): 785–810.

5. Sherrie L. Russell-Brown, "Bridging the 'Divide' between Feminism and Child Protection Using the Discourse of International Human Rights," *Southern California Review of Law and Women's Studies* 13, no.1 (2003): 163–168; de Silva de Alwis, "Mining the Intersections," 293; Thomas A. Mayes, "Understanding Intersectionality between the Law, Gender, Sexuality and Children," *Children's Legal Rights Journal* 36, no. 2 (2016): 90–106; Aurelie Roche-Mair, "Challenges to the Protection of Children's Human Rights and the Perpetuated Marginalization of Children in Transitional Justice," *Georgetown Journal of International Law* 49, no. 1 (2017): 135–161.

6. United Nations Children's Fund (UNICEF), "Child Marriage: Latest Trends and Future Prospects," 2018, https://www.unicef.org/protection/files/Child_Marriage_data_brief_20June(3).pdf (accessed Aug. 13, 2019).

7. Ann Laquer Estin and Barbara Stark, *Global Issues in Family Law* (St. Paul, MN: West Academic Publishing, 2007), 34.

8. Universal Declaration of Human Rights, art. 16, G.A. Res. 217 (III) A, UN Doc. A/RES/217(III) (Dec. 10, 1948).

9. Convention on Consent to Marriage, Minimum Age for Marriage and Registration of Marriages, arts. 1–3, 521 UNTS 231 (1962); Convention on the Elimination of All Forms of Discrimination against Women (CEDAW), arts. 1, 5, 9, and 16, 1249 UNTS 13 (1979).

10. Lynne Marie Kohm, "A Brief Assessment on the 25-Year Effect of the Convention on the Rights of the Child," *Cardozo Journal of International & Compliance Law* 23 (2015): 323–351, 336.

11. Convention on Consent to Marriage, art. 2.

12. Kohm, "Brief Assessment," 337.

13. UNICEF, "Ending Child Marriage: Progress and Prospects," 2014, https://www.unicef.org/media/files/Child_Marriage_Report_7_17_LR..pdf (accessed Aug. 13, 2019).

14. Girls Not Brides (Global Partnership to End Child Marriage), "Addressing Child Marriage through Education: What the Evidence Shows," https://www.girlsnotbrides.org/wp-content/uploads/2018/01/Addressing-child-marriage-through-education-what-the-evidence-shows-knowledge-summary.pdf (accessed Aug. 13, 2019).

15. UNICEF, "Ending Child Marriage" (156 million boys are married before the age of eighteen, which is 4.6 times lower than the number of girls who are married).

16. UNICEF, "Ending Child Marriage."

17. Sara Dillon, *International Children's Rights* (Durham, NC: Carolina Academic Press 2010), 77.

18. UNICEF, "Ending Child Marriage."

19. UNICEF, "Ending Child Marriage."

20. UNICEF, "Ending Child Marriage."

21. UNICEF, "Ending Child Marriage."

22. Dillon, *International Children's Rights*, 77.

23. UNICEF, "Ending Child Marriage."

24. Fergal Keane, "Big Money for Niger's Child Brides," BBC News.com, May 29, 2014, https://www.bbc.com/news/world-africa-27619295.

25. Keane, "Big Money for Niger's Child Brides."

26. UNICEF, "Ending Child Marriage."

27. UNICEF, "Child Marriage in the Middle East and North Africa," 2017, 31, https://www. unicef.org/mena/media/1786/file/MENA-ChildMarriageInMENA-Report.pdf.pdf.

28. UNICEF, "Child Marriage: Latest Trends."

29. Saranga Jain and Kathleen Kurz, "New Insights on Preventing Child Marriage: A Global Analysis of Factors and Programs," April 2007, 8, https://www.icrw.org/wp-content/ uploads/2016/10/New-Insights-on-Preventing-Child-Marriage.pdf.

30. Dillon, *International Children's Rights*, 77.

31. Minzee Kim, "When Do Laws Matter? National Minimum-Age-of-Marriage Laws, Child Rights, and Adolescent Fertility, 1989–2007," *Law and Society Review* 47, no. 3 (2013): 589–619, 592 (noting that the reason the CRC requires states to register all births is to identify underage marriages even when there is no formal state record of the marriage).

32. Kim, "When Do Laws Matter?"

33. Kim, "When Do Laws Matter?"

34. Kim, "When Do Laws Matter?"

35. Kim, "When Do Laws Matter?," 593.

36. Bethany Blankley, "Analysis: Child Marriage Is Legal in 49 States," Watchdog.org, May 25, 2018, https://www.watchdog.org/national/analysis-child-marriage-is-legal-in-u-s-states/ article_fbefbf04-5d0e-11e8-b6e6-cb9d5643bc13.html.

37. Camellia Burris, "Why Domestic Institutions Are Failing Child Brides: A Comparative Analysis of India's and the United States' Legal Approaches to the Institution of Child Marriage," *Tulane Journal of International and Comparative Law* 23, no. 1 (2014): 151–176, 152.

38. UNICEF, "Ending Child Marriage."

39. Mara Steinhaus and Neetu John, "A Life Not Chosen: Early Marriage and Mental Health," International Center for Research on Women research brief, https://www.icrw.org/ wp-content/uploads/2018/08/ICRW_EICMResearchBrief_v5_WebReady.pdf (accessed Aug. 13, 2019).

40. UNICEF, "Ending Child Marriage."

41. UNICEF, "Ending Child Marriage."

42. UNICEF, "Child Marriage in the Middle East and North Africa," 2017, 54, https://www. unicef.org/mena/media/1786/file/MENA-ChildMarriageInMENA-Report.pdf.pdf.

43. UNICEF, "Ending Child Marriage."

44. UNICEF, "Ending Child Marriage."

45. UNICEF, "Child Marriage: Latest Trends."

46. Rima Mourtada, Jennifer Schlecht, and Jocelyn DeJong, "A Qualitative Study Exploring Child Marriage Practices among Syrian Conflict-Affected Populations in Lebanon," *Conflict and Health* 11, no. S1 (November 2017): 27.

47. Mourtada, Schlects, and DeJong, "A Qualitative Study Exploring Child Marriage Practices."

48. Al Jazeera.com, "Child Marriage on the Rise among Syrian Refugee Girls in Jordan," April 18, 2018, https://www.aljazeera.com/news/2018/04/child-marriage-rise-syrian-refugee-girls -180418084029464.html.

49. Al Jazeera.com, "Child Marriage on the Rise."

50. Al Jazeera, "Child Marriage on the Rise."

51. UNICEF, "Child Marriage: Latest Trends."

52. UNICEF, "Ending Child Marriage."

53. UNICEF, "Child Marriage in the Middle East and North Africa," 2017, 51, https://www. unicef.org/mena/media/1786/file/MENA-ChildMarriageInMENA-Report.pdf.pdf.

54. UNICEF, "Child Marriage in the Middle East and North Africa," 2017, 51, https://www. unicef.org/mena/media/1786/file/MENA-ChildMarriageInMENA-Report.pdf.pdf.

55. UNICEF, "Ending Child Marriage."

56. UNICEF, "Ending Child Marriage."

57. Sheila Menz, "Statelessness and Child Marriage as Intersectional Phenomena: Instability, Inequality, and the Role of the International Community," *California Law Review* 104, no. 2 (2013): 497–544.

58. Menz, "Statelessness and Child Marriage," 503–504 (citing Thompson Reuters Foundation, "Rohingya Women and Children Brave the Seas to Flee Myanmar," July 17, 2013, http:// www.trust.org/item/20130711095259-lup2a.

59. Menz, "Statelessness and Child Marriage," 499.

60. Menz, "Statelessness and Child Marriage."

61. Menz, "Statelessness and Child Marriage."

62. Menz, "Statelessness and Child Marriage," 500.

63. Menz, "Statelessness and Child Marriage."

64. Menz, "Statelessness and Child Marriage," 504.

65. UNICEF, "Child marriage, Adolescent Pregnancy and Family Formation in Central and West Africa," 2015, https://www.unicef.org/wcaro/english/Child_Mariage_Adolescent_ Pregnancy_and_Family_Formation_in_WCA.pdf.

66. Jonathan Todres, "Emerging Limitations on the Rights of the Child: The U.N. Convention on the Rights of the Child and Its Early Case Law," *Columbia Human Rights Law Review* 30, no. 1 (1998): 159–200; Lynne Marie Kohm, "Suffer the Little Children: How the United Nations Convention on the Rights of the Child Has Not Supported Children," *New York International Law Review* 22 (2009): 57–98 (arguing that because the CRC is premised on a rights rather than a best-interest standard framework, it is ineffective at protecting children); Brian K. Gran, "An International Framework of Children's Rights," *Annual Review of Law and Social Science* 13 (2017): 79–100 (noting that compliance with CRC reporting requirements is lax and that the new individual complaints procedure provides weak accountability to nation-states).

67. Ladan Askari, "The Convention on the Rights of the Child: The Necessity of Adding a Provision to Ban Child Marriage," *ILSA Journal of International and Comparative Law* 5, no. 1 (1998): 123–138, 124.

68. Askari, "Convention on the Rights."

69. Askari, "Convention on the Rights."

70. UN Convention on the Rights of the Child (CRC), arts. 9, 10, 11, G.A. Res. 44/25, 44th Sess., UN Doc. A/RES/44/25 (1989).

71. CRC, art. 20.

72. Medha Makhlouf, "Theorizing the Immigrant Child: The Case of Married Minors," *Brooklyn Law Review* 85 (2016): 1603–1650, 1625–1626.

73. CRC, art. 22.

74. CRC, art. 22.

75. Elizabeth Warner, "Behind the Wedding Veil: Child Marriage as a Form of Trafficking in Girls," *American University Journal of Gender, Social Policy and the Law* 12 (2004): 233–272, 252.

76. Warner, "Behind the Wedding Veil," 252.

77. Warner, "Behind the Wedding Veil," 252.

78. de Silva de Alwis, "Mining the Intersections," 293.

79. CRC, art. 24.

80. CRC, art. 24.

81. CRC, art. 24.

82. CRC, arts. 24, 11.

83. CEDAW, art. 16(2).

84. Kim, "When Do Laws Matter?," 591.

85. UNICEF, "Child Marriage: Latest Trends."

86. UNICEF, "Child Marriage: Latest Trends."

87. UNICEF, "Child Marriage: Latest Trends."

88. de Silva de Alwis, "Mining the Intersections," 313.

89. Forum for Fact Finding Documentation and Advocacy (FFDA) v. Union of India, Supreme Court of India, W.P. (Civ.) No. 212 of 2003 (Apr. 25, 2003).

90. Jaya Sagade, *Child Marriage in India: Socio-legal and Human Rights Dimensions* (New York: Oxford University Press, 2005), 44.

91. Sagade, *Child Marriage in India*, 44.

92. Sagade, *Child Marriage in India*, 44.

93. de Silva de Alwis, "Mining the Intersections," 313–314.

94. Julia Sloth-Neilsen, "Modern African Childhoods: Does Law Matter?," *Law and Childhood Studies* 14 (2012): 117–132.

95. Sloth-Neilsen, "Modern African Childhoods."

96. Sloth-Neilsen, "Modern African Childhoods."

97. Sloth-Neilsen, "Modern African Childhoods"; Julia Sloth-Neilson and Benyam D. Mezmur, "Surveying the Research Landscape to Promote Children's Legal Right in an African Context," *African Human Rights Law Journal* 7 (2007): 330–353.

98. Sloth-Neilsen, "Modern African Childhoods," 7; Sloth-Nielson and Mezmur, "Surveying the Research Landscape."

99. Sloth-Neilsen, "Modern African Childhoods," 7; Sloth-Nielson and Mezmur, "Surveying the Research Landscape."

100. Sloth-Neilsen, "Modern African Childhoods," 7; Sloth-Nielson and Mezmur, "Surveying the Research Landscape."

101. Sloth-Neilsen, "Modern African Childhoods," 7; Sloth-Nielson and Mezmur, "Surveying the Research Landscape."

102. Constitution of the Republic of South Africa, Chap. 28 (1)(b) (1996).

103. Constitution of the Republic of South Africa, Chap. 28 (1)(f)(i) and (ii) (1996).

104. Sebastien Malo, "New Jersey Law Gives Momentum to U.S. Efforts to Ban Child Marriage," Thomson Reuters Foundation, June 22, 2018, https://www.reuters.com/article/us-usa-marriage-children/new-jersey-law-gives-momentum-to-u-s-efforts-to-ban-child-marriage-idUSKBN1JI2X9; Violence Against Women Act, Public Law No. 113–114 (2013).

105. Malo, "New Jersey Law Gives Momentum"; Violence Against Women Act.

106. Anjali Tsui, "In Fight over Child Marriage Laws, States Resist Call for Total Ban," *Frontline*, July 6, 2017, https://www.pbs.org/wgbh/frontline/article/in-fight-over-child-marriage-laws-states-resist-calls-for-a-total-ban.

107. Anjali Tsui, "Delaware Becomes First State to Ban Child Marriage," *Frontline*, May 9, 2018, https://www.pbs.org/wgbh/frontline/article/delaware-becomes-first-state-to-ban-child-marriage.

108. Malo, "New Jersey Law" (noting that Orthodox Jews in New Jersey assert that the new law banning child marriage fails to respect religious diversity).

109. Tsui, "In Fight over Child Marriage Laws."

110. Tsui, "In Fight over Child Marriage Laws."

111. Tsui, "In Fight over Child Marriage Laws."

112. International Violence against Women Act of 2018, H.R. 5034, 115th Cong. sect. 2(15) (2018).

113. International Violence against Women Act of 2018, sect. 3.

114. International Violence against Women Act of 2018, sects. 101, 102.

115. Archbishop Desmond Tutu, "Child Marriage Harms Our Human Family," Girls Not Brides blog, November 21, 2016, https://www.girlsnotbrides.org/desmond-tutu-child -marriage-harms-human-family.

116. Marianne Schnall, "Ending Child Marriage: Insights from Desmond Tutu and Mary Robinson," *Huffington Post*, December 6, 2017, https://www.huffingtonpost.com/ marianne-schnall/desmond-tutu-and-mary-rob_b_1254218.html.

117. Schnall, "Ending Child Marriage."

118. Lisa Rein, "Tutu Promotes Campaign to End Child Marriage," *Washington Post*, October 10, 2012, https://www.washingtonpost.com/politics/decision2012/tutu-promotes -campaign-to-end-child-marriage/2012/10/10/545a0146-130e-11e2-a16b-2c110031514a_ story.html.

119. Rein, "Tutu Promotes Campaign."

120. Archbishop Desmond Tutu, "Child Marriage."

121. Archbishop Desmond Tutu, "Child Marriage."

122. Girls Not Brides, "Desmond Tutu: 'We Can End Child Marriage in Zambia if All Work Together,'" press release, September 18, 2014, https://www.girlsnotbrides.org/press -release-desmond-tutu-can-end-child-marriage-zambia-work-together.

123. Girls Not Brides, "Zambian Government Steps Up Efforts to End Child Marriage in Zambia," July 28, 2013, https://www.girlsnotbrides.org/zambian-government-steps-efforts -end-child-marriage-zambia.

124. Girls Not Brides, "Zambian Government Steps Up Efforts."

125. Girls Not Brides, "Desmond Tutu and Mabel Van Oranje Visit Zambia to Encourage End Child Marriage Efforts," October 1, 2014, https://www.girlsnotbrides.org/photos -desmond-tutu-mabel-van-oranje-visit-zambia-support-end-child-marriage-efforts (noting the story of Chipasa, married at fifteen, divorced, and now an ambassador for the national campaign to end child marriage).

126. Girls Not Brides, "Desmond Tutu and Mabel Van Oranje Visit Zambia."

127. Girls Not Brides, "Desmond Tutu and Mabel Van Oranje Visit Zambia."

128. Girls Not Brides, "Zambian Government Steps Up Efforts."

129. Girls Not Brides, "Addressing Child Marriage through Education," 2.

130. Quentin Wodon, Chata Male, Ada Nayihouba, Adenike Onagoruwa, Aboudrahyme Savadogo, Ali Yedan, Jeff Edmeades, Aslihan Kes, Neetu John, Lydia Murithi, Mara Steinhaus and Suzanne Petroni, "Economic Impacts of Child Marriage: Global Synthesis Report," June 27, 2017, https://www.alnap.org/system/files/content/resource/files/main/ eicm-global-conference-edition-june-27-final.pdf.

131. Grace Bantebya, Florence Kyoheirwe Muhanguzi, and Carol Watson, "Adolescent Girls in the Balance: Changes and Continuity in Social Norms and Practices around Child Marriage and Education in Uganda," Overseas Development Institute Country Report, September 2014, https://www.odi.org/sites/odi.org.uk/files/odi-assets/publications-opinion -files/9180.pdf.

132. Bantebya, Muhanguzi, and Watson, "Adolescent Girls in the Balance."

133. Bantebya, Muhanguzi, and Watson, "Adolescent Girls in the Balance."

134. Bantebya, Muhanguzi, and Watson, "Adolescent Girls in the Balance."

135. Girls Not Brides, "Addressing Child Marriage through Education," 8–9.

136. Girls Not Brides, "Addressing Child Marriage through Education," 9.

137. Emma Batha, "Ugandan Girls Forced into Child Marriage Because They Can't Afford Sanitary Pads," Reuters.com, October 23, 2017, https://af.reuters.com/article/kenyaNews/idAFL5N1KQ2L6.

138. Batha, "Ugandan Girls."

139. Batha, "Ugandan Girls Forced into Child Marriage."

140. Batha, "Ugandan Girls Forced into Child Marriage."

141. Sarah Jewitt and Harriet Ryley, "It's a Girl Thing: Menstruation, School Attendance, Spatial Mobility and Wider Gender Inequalities in Kenya," *Geoforum* 56 (2014): 137–147; Marni Sommer, "Where the Education System and Women's Body Collide: The Social and Health Impact of Girls' Menstruation and Schooling in Tanzania," *Journal of Adolescence* 33 (2010): 521–529; Andrea J. Nightingale, "Bounding Difference: Intersectionality and the Material Production of Gender, Caste, Class and Environment in Nepal," *Geoforum* 42 (2010): 153–162.

142. Nightingale, "Bounding Difference," 156.

143. Joanne Kelsey and Krista Zimmerman, "The Refugee Children's Progress Report: Grading U.S. Refugee Policy from 2015–2017, Save the Children Refugee Children's Progress Report, 2017, 8, https://www.savethechildren.org/content/dam/usa/reports/advocacy/refugee-children-progress-report.PDF.

144. UNICEF, "Child Migration," December 2018, https://data.unicef.org/topic/child-migration-and-displacement/migration.

145. UNICEF, "Child Migration."

146. United Nations High Commissioner for Refugees (UNHCR), "Global Trends: Forced Displacement in 2017," 2018, https://www.unhcr.org/5b27be547.pdf (accessed Aug. 14, 2019).

147. Kelsey and Zimmerman, "Refugee Children's Progress Report," 8.

148. Kelsey and Zimmerman, "Refugee Children's Progress Report," 10.

149. UNICEF, "Child Migration."

150. Kaplan Yehiel, "A Father's Consent to the Marriage of His Minor Daughter: Feminism and Multiculturalism in Jewish Law," *Southern California Review of Law and Social Justice* 18 (2009): 393–460.

PART III

SUBSTANTIVE LEGAL AREAS

CHAPTER 10

THE BEST INTERESTS OF THE CHILD

WOUTER VANDENHOLE AND GAMZE ERDEM TÜRKELLI

1 INTRODUCTION

M. is a thirteen-year-old boy who has traveled to Europe from his conflict-ridden home country unaccompanied by his parents and is seeking asylum in Country X. Should M. be given asylum and stay in Country X, or should he be sent back to his home country to rejoin his family? What is in M's best interests?

C. is a nine-year-old girl. She lives with her mother and four siblings in dire conditions. Her mother has been out of employment for more than three years, and her father is often absent. C.'s teachers notified social services, based on her worsening school performance and home situation. After making recommendations and deploying short-term financial assistance, social services recommended that C. and her siblings be placed into care on the basis that their parents are unable to provide for the children (irregular school attendance, lack of home hygiene, incomplete vaccinations, lack of dialogue between home and school). The state has also prohibited the mother from any contact with the children. She is contesting the decision. A family court will decide. Is it in C.'s and her siblings' best interests to be placed into care or to stay with their mother?

These two examples illustrate how difficult it often is to assess and define a child's best interests.

The best interests of the child principle is now a pillar of children's rights law, recognized as one of the four general or fundamental principles guiding the realization and implementation of the UN Convention on the Rights of the Child (CRC) and children's rights more generally.[1] Even more importantly, best interests has risen to the status of "a mainstreaming principle" crosscutting in all children's rights interventions.[2]

2 Best Interests in Children's Rights Law

The three decades following adoption of the CRC have seen best interests become entrenched as a prominent children's rights principle. Yet, as a concept and a legal doctrine, the best interests principle far predates the CRC. Common law family courts, particularly in the United States, have been developing the doctrine for over two centuries.[3] Internationally, best interests was recognized as the main principle in providing education and guidance to the child in the 1959 Declaration of the Rights of the Child.[4] Notwithstanding its long history, best interests is an elusive principle with no universal definition or description. In fact, even the CRC contains several differently worded references to best interests. The CRC's general provision on best interests in Article 3(1) states, "In all actions concerning children, . . . the best interests of the child shall be a primary consideration." This best interests formulation is also found in other international treaties. For example, Article 4 of the African Charter on the Rights and Welfare of the Child (ACRWC) repeats this language while expressing a stronger obligation: "In all actions concerning the child undertaken by any person or authority the best interests of the child shall be the primary consideration." This general obligation is balanced with an obligation to allow for and give due weight to the views of a child capable of communicating these views in all proceedings (judicial or administrative) affecting the child.[5] Similarly, the Convention on the Rights of Persons with Disabilities (CRPD) notes that the best interests of children with disabilities shall be a primary consideration (Article 7). And, the EU Charter of Fundamental Rights provides that "the child's best interests must be a primary consideration [in all actions relating to children]" taken by public authorities and private institutions (Article 24(2)).

The exact wording of Article 3 (i.e., best interests of the child being "a primary consideration") is not accidental. In fact, the *travaux préparatoires* indicate that the 1980 Working Group text had referred to best interests as "the paramount consideration."[6] This phrasing was changed as several states considered "paramount" to be "too broad" due to concerns that in some cases, the competing interests of other parties may be at least as important as or more important than children's best interests with respect to individual rights, such as the rights of mothers in emergency childbirth or societal or justice considerations,[7] for instance, in child offender cases. In addition, the formulation of children's best interests being *the* primary consideration was rejected in favor of the less decisive wording of *a* primary consideration due to similarly strong objections.[8] According to the CRC Committee, the current formulation of the best interests of the child as a primary consideration in the CRC means that when balancing different interests, states parties have to be willing to prioritize children's interests as a rule, especially in cases of actions with patent effects on the children in question.[9]

The other references in the CRC to best interests are linked mostly to family life: the CRC refers to the "best interests of the child" again in Article 9 on children separated from their parents, Article 10 on family reunification, Article 18 on parental responsibilities, Article 20 on children deprived of a family environment, and Article 21 on adoption. Best interests references are also found in Article 37(c) on separation from adults in detention and Article 40(2)(b)(iii) on procedural guarantees for children in conflict with the law.

With respect to child-rearing by parents and parental figures, in a formulation that seems deferential to parents and legal guardians, CRC's Article 18(1) provides that "[t]he best interests of the child will be . . . [the] basic concern" of parents or legal guardians (if applicable). The ACRWC, on the other hand, seems to accord less deference to caregivers on this point: Article 20(1)(a) of the African Charter sets out the parental (primary caregiver's) duty to "ensure that the best interests of the child are their basic concern at all times." The ACRWC also allows for children's best interests and evolving capacities to be taken into account in the parent's (or legal guardians') duty "to provide guidance and direction" in the exercise of the freedom of thought, conscience of religion (Article 9(2)).

The CRC also recognizes that being raised by parents may not always be the most beneficial for a given child and that separation from parents may be considered if in the child's best interests (Articles 9(1) and 9(3)). Article 23(4) of the CRPD contains a similar provision. And, under Article 20(1), the CRC foresees special state protection and assistance, including to children whose best interests dictate they not be allowed to remain in their family environment or children who are deprived of a family environment. Similarly, the Hague Convention on Parental Responsibility and Protection of Children (1996) confirms a child's best interests as a primary consideration (Preamble) in all civil measures of protection and requires a best interests assessment in all state decisions to enact or implement measures of protection, including placement in alternative care.[10] When states parties recognize or permit adoption services, the CRC articulates a stronger obligation of protection in that a child's best interest must be "the paramount consideration" (Article 21). The ACRWC also requires a consideration of the best interests in situations of separation from parents but provides a more nuanced and culturally sensitive articulation in providing that alternative family care situations and best interests should be balanced with continuity in the child's upbringing and due consideration of the "child's ethnic, religious or linguistic background" (Article 25(3)). It should be clear from this overview that even when best interests is explicitly the primary consideration in implementing children's rights, this consideration is always contextualized, in which it may be balanced with competing interests.

In addition to the CRC, the Optional Protocol on the Sale of Children, Child Prostitution and Child Pornography (OPSC) pronounces an obligation to ensure that best interests is "a primary consideration" for children victims in their treatment by criminal justice systems.[11] According to the Optional Protocol on a Communications Procedure (OPC), which governs complaints to the CRC Committee, the Committee's work is to be guided by the best interests principle with a "regard for the rights and views of the child" to ensure that children are not manipulated.[12]

In 2013 the CRC Committee adopted General Comment No. 14 on the best interests of the child, which further refines and redefines best interests in a threefold fashion: as "a substantive right," "a fundamental, interpretative legal principle," and a "rule of procedure."[13] With General Comment No. 14, the CRC Committee construes best interests as a substantive and actionable right, creating a "self-executing" obligation on states parties that can be invoked in decisions involving individual children, groups of children, or children in general.[14] Furthermore, best interests is deemed a fundamental principle that guides the interpretation of legal provisions toward the choice that "most effectively serves the child's best interests."[15] Finally, as a rule of procedure, best interests dictates that in all matters affecting children, an evaluation of possible impacts on children should be an integral part of the decision-making process with an explicit assessment of how and why the final decision is respectful of the child's or children's best interests.[16] The implication is that states parties have an obligation to "clarify the best interests of all children, including those in vulnerable situations" when implementing their human rights commitments,[17] meaning that the interests of one child or a group of children may also need to be balanced against those of another child or group of children.

3   APPLICATION OF THE BEST INTERESTS PRINCIPLE

Challenges around best interests can be traced to the vagueness of the norm and the lack of an authoritative definition. The CRC Committee defines best interests as a "dynamic concept that requires an assessment appropriate to the specific context," leading to the need for a flexible case-by-case approach in determining its content.[18] This flexibility has been considered a possible asset, for instance, in opening up judicial systems to cultural diversity in matters of family law.[19] Conversely, as Jean Zermatten notes, in the absence of an authoritative definition, best interests is fraught with difficulty as no one knows for a fact the best interests of a given child or children.[20]

One critique of the inclusion of a best interests norm in the CRC and the requisite balancing exercise inherent in Article 3 is that it can give rise to paternalistic implementation, thereby jeopardizing hard-won progress in furthering children's interests through children's rights.[21] The CRC Committee is cognizant of this danger and has noted that the flexibility needed in determining best interests has allowed for manipulation and abuse by states, parents, and professionals alike.[22]

The best interests principle has been manipulated and abused to justify cultural imperialist policies, such as the former practice of placing indigenous children outside the care of their parents and communities. The Australian National Inquiry into the Separation of Aboriginal and Torres Strait Islander Children from Their Families found that the notion of best interests, articulated as the child's welfare, was often employed after the fact as a justification for the forcible removal of indigenous children.[23] In fact, that forcible removal was based on multiple objectives: removing the influence of

Aboriginal communities, acculturating children into Anglo-Australian values, and educating children to prevent their becoming "a burden to society."[24] In Canada, during a period called the Sixties Scoop, thousands of First Nations children were similarly taken away from their families and communities and placed in the care of households with parents of Caucasian descent or taken into state institutions as permanent wards, justified by claims that such removal and placement served their best interests.[25] Marlee Kline has argued that the application of the best interests principle in Canada's child welfare adjudication has allowed "facts and arguments [to be] constructed and organized so as to give credence and legitimacy to the removal of First Nations children from their families and communities," thereby rendering the removal "unproblematic" by "constructing the child conceptually as separate from her culture."[26]

In addition to balancing competing interests, one view is that the determination of best interests is a delicate, sometimes fraught balancing act between dependency and autonomy, "between nurturing and supporting the emerging autonomy of children and adolescents and protecting them so that they have the opportunity to develop to their fullest potential."[27] Although best interests is now a well-established legal concept, its implementation takes place in different contexts, including policymaking and social work where best interests may be conceptualized through non-legal perspectives, such as child development theories. For instance, one exploration in New Zealand concluded that children's best interests were often equated by social work practitioners with children's psychological and emotional needs, conceptualized by using attachment theory.[28] Gerison Lansdown identifies four areas of protection that are frequently utilized to determine a child's best interests: from physical and emotional harm; in personal decision-making; from harmful social or economic factors; and from exploitation and abuse.[29] Such a strong emphasis on children's needs and protection may be detrimental if it overshadows children's agency and autonomy. Acting in a child's best interests may necessitate looking beyond special protection for children and acknowledging that children have valid insights, solutions, and roles as agents in their own right.[30]

The need to balance protection and autonomy is apparent in the tension between the movement to abolish child labor and the right to work claims of working children, especially in Latin America and Africa. Arguments about the protection of children from economic exploitation are often made in children's best interests. Yet working children's organizations, such as the Union of Child and Adolescent Workers of Bolivia (UNATsBO),[31] have demanded better wages and working conditions as well as the protection of their right to work, all of which were being jeopardized by abolitionist attitudes toward child labor, pushing working children into spaces unregulated by law.[32] As an alternative to the abolitionist attitudes, Karl Hanson and Arne Vandaele argue that children's participation rights may allow a more "emancipatory perspective" by permitting working children to influence norms around work and child labor.[33] In fact, the CRC Committee has taken the view that best interests under Article 3 and the children's right to express their views under Article 12 are complementary, the former setting an objective and the latter providing the methodology for achieving the best interests.[34]

The vagueness of best interests, coupled with the lack of an authoritative definition, also gives rise to difficulties in operationalizing best interests in different policy fields. Operationalizing the three facets of best interests—as a right, an interpretive principle, and a rule of procedure—is a complex endeavor in the absence of clear criteria and one that may require issue specific guidance. UN High Commissioner for Refugees (UNHCR) Guidelines on Determining the Best Interests of the Child is one attempt at articulating building blocks for best interests *in concreto*. The guidelines associate best interests with the general well-being of a child[35] and link up this idea of well-being with the UNHCR's work through two processes: a continuous best interests assessment in all actions concerning a child and a formal best interests determination in special cases of unaccompanied or separated children with procedural requirements to guarantee child participation without discrimination and with due consideration for the views of the child.[36] While there is no systematic follow-up on their implementation, the UNHCR guidelines bar the use of a law enforcement approach to children's asylum claims as well as such tools as detention or age assessments without due justification.[37] In the next section we look extensively at some of the case law on the best interests of the child.

4   Impact of the Best Interests Principle

The best interests of the child has been given particular prominence in the case law of the European Court of Human Rights (European Court) and has had a significant impact on the interpretation and application of the European Convention of Human Rights (ECHR). There are two main reasons for this. First, the European Court often uses the best interests of the child as a proxy for children's rights more generally, in particular in the areas of juvenile justice and migration. While best interests are not necessarily synonymous with children's rights, this approach allows the Court to read substantive CRC provisions into the ECHR. Second, the Court has held that the best interests of the child may override the rights and interests of parents, as an exception to the typical balancing-of-interests exercise that the Court undertakes to assess the proportionality of a given interference, as will be illustrated below in the context of placement decisions. Other human rights bodies have engaged much less with the best interests principle, hence our focus on the European Court of Human Rights.

4.1   Defining the Best Interests of the Child

The European Court has identified two limbs to the best interests of the child: first is that ties with the family must be maintained (except where the family proved particularly unfit, as will be discussed further below). Family ties can be severed by the state only in very exceptional circumstances; everything must be done to preserve personal relations and to rebuild the family. The second limb is to ensure that the child develops in a sound environment. Therefore, no measures are allowed that harm the child's health and development.[38] Both limbs are firmly embedded in the CRC, and the latter has been echoed by the African Committee of Experts on the Rights and Welfare of the Child. The African Committee has argued that the best interests principle "aims at safeguarding the realization of children's rights effectively and contributing to their holistic development."[39] The child's development "will depend on a variety of individual circumstances, in particular his age and level of maturity, the presence or absence of his parents and his environment and experiences ... [and thus] those best interests must be assessed in each individual case."[40]

Defining the best interests of the child becomes tricky if the best interests must be determined in the context of a *conflict* between the parents. As a matter of principle, the Court has held that it "is in the child's best interests to maintain contact with both parents, in so far as practicable, on an equal footing, save for lawful limitations justified by considerations regarding the child's best interests."[41] One such example is where a child has been abducted by one of the parents. The Hague Convention on International Abduction favors "restoration of the status quo by means of a decision ordering the child's immediate return,"[42] and the European Court has accepted that "the objectives of prevention [of international child abduction] and immediate return correspond to a specific conception of 'the best interests of the child.' "[43] More precisely, when examining a request for a child's return in pursuance of the Hague Convention, the concept of best interests of the child must be evaluated in the light of the exceptions provided for by that Convention.[44]

Under the European Court's jurisprudence, the child's best interests must be understood in the specific context in which it arises. Hence, it "cannot be understood in an identical manner irrespective of whether the court is examining a request for a child's return in pursuance of the Hague Convention or ruling on the merits of an application for custody or parental authority."[45] Some examples of this case-by-case approach include that joint custody for both parents against the will of the mother should not prima facie be assumed to contravene the child's interest.[46] In some instances, the Court has been more affirmative in defining the best interests of the child; in disputes about paternity, for example, it has declared that the child has the "right to have uncertainty as to her personal identity eliminated without unnecessary delay."[47] And, in instances of surrogacy, the Court has argued that it is not in the best interests to deprive the child of legal ties with the intended parent who is also the biological father of the child.[48] Whereas this case-by-case approach helps avoid legal inflexibility, it turns out to be rather unpredictable and may give rise to bias. The Court should therefore justify more explicitly the way in which it defines and determines the child's best interests in each case.

In migration cases,[49] in determining a child's best interest, the European Court has considered two questions, that is, the adaptability of the child (by looking into the ties a child has with the country of origin and the country of residence or destination as well as the age of the child) and the existence of an effective family bond.[50] In parental expulsion cases,[51] the Court has generally considered young children to be of an adaptable age and therefore concluded that the expulsion of a parent did not violate that parent's right to a family life.[52] However, older age does not exclude adaptability.[53] The second element in migration cases to decide whether a migration measure is in the best interests of the child is the existence of an effective family bond. Here European Court case law lacks clarity. As Ciara Smyth has argued, it is "difficult to draw any firm conclusions about what impact the child's ties to and dependency on the parent has on the Court's decision-making in expulsion cases."[54] In entry cases, there has often been a "focus on a dereliction of parental, often motherly, duty,"[55] but occasionally, the Court has taken all aspects of family life into consideration to determine whether a child should be allowed to rejoin his or her parents after they have moved to another country.[56]

The European Court has often viewed the best interests of the child as a proxy for children's rights. In a case in which the state refused to restore the lapsed residence permit of a minor due to a two-year stay abroad, the Court argued that very serious reasons were required to refuse family reunification to an underage settled migrant who has lawfully spent a major part of her childhood and youth in the host country.[57] It submitted that the child's interest included her own right to respect for private and family life.[58] Likewise, when detaining an underage migrant, his or her best interests must be examined, and the latter are to be understood in light of Article 37 of the CRC, which makes deprivation of liberty a measure of last resort.[59] In the context of juvenile justice more generally, beyond deprivation of liberty, the Court has argued that taking the best interests into account includes an obligation to facilitate the child's reintegration.[60]

Regrettably, the European Court has only rarely paid attention to the views of the child in question in the attempt to define what was in her or his best interests.[61] This is unlike the CRC Committee, which insists that the best interests of the child cannot be defined without taking the child's views into account and giving them due weight.

4.2 State Obligations

Having explained how the European Court understands the best interests of the child, we turn our attention to state obligations. The Court seems to have moved from *defining* the best interests of the child per se to emphasizing the *process* domestic courts have to go through in addressing best interests. This can be seen very clearly, for example, in the case law on parental child abduction. In its early case law, the Court had submitted that the best interests of the child lay in her "prompt return to her habitual environment."[62] Some judges dissented, however, including on the question of how to deal with elapsed time between the abduction and the implementation of the return order.[63] This led the Grand Chamber of the Court to assert that the requested courts must conduct an "in-depth examination of the entire family situation and . . . factual, emotional, psychological, material and medical [factors], and [make] a balanced and reasonable assessment of the respective interests of each person, with a constant concern for determining what the best solution would be for the abducted child in the context of an application for his return to his country of origin [reference omitted]."[64] And if the child has settled in her or his new environment, the judge must not order the return after a one-year period. Furthermore, guidance on whether the child can be considered to have settled is to be found in case law on the expulsion of foreigners: the judge must take into account a child's best interest and well-being and "in particular the seriousness of the difficulties which he or she is likely to encounter in the country of destination and the solidity of social, cultural and family ties with the host country and with the country of destination."[65] In a subsequent 2013 judgement and the leading case on the issue since, the Grand Chamber again adopted a procedural approach, emphasizing that the requested court must take the exceptions (in the Hague Convention) to the child's immediate return genuinely into account, and its decision must be sufficiently reasoned on this point. The exceptions must be evaluated in light of Article 8 of the ECHR, which guarantees respect for private and family life.[66]

A similar procedural approach can be found in the European Court case law on visitation and access rights for a noncustodial parent, where the Court has argued that the child's best interests are to be assessed on the basis of expert advice (independent psychological report) and involvement (of the noncustodial parent) in the decision-making process on whether or not to grant access rights.[67] Likewise, in a paternity suit, legal guarantees for the procedural protection of the child's interests must be provided for,[68] and judges need to take into account the best interests of the child.[69] The Court also emphasized the need to adopt a case-by-case approach in a recent case in which a (former) husband, who had taken care of the child for more than five years, lost all contact rights after it had been established that he was not the biological father of the child. The Court heavily criticized the inflexibility of the legal provisions governing contact rights,[70] adding:

> The Court is not convinced that the best interests of children in the sphere of contact rights can be truly determined by a general legal presumption. Having regard to the great variety of family situations possibly concerned, the Court considers that a fair balancing of the rights of all persons involved necessitates an examination of the particular circumstances of each case [reference omitted]. Accordingly, Article 8 of the Convention can be interpreted as imposing on member States an obligation to examine on a case-by-case basis whether it is in the child's best interests to maintain contact with a person, whether biologically related or not, who has taken care of him or her for a sufficiently long period of time.[71]

Both the need for a case-by-case determination of the child's best interests and the emphasis on procedural obligations on the state were reaffirmed by the CRC Committee's very first decision under its complaints procedures; the case involved a deportation order in Denmark challenged by a mother on the account that her daughter would be subjected to female genital mutilation if returned to Somalia.[72] The Committee found that Denmark had failed to establish the best interests of the child in question from a procedural perspective, as the assessment by Danish authorities of whether the child would be subjected to irreparable harm had been made "without assessing the specific and personal context in which the [mother] and her daughter would be deported."[73]

The case-by-case and procedural approaches are welcome developments as long as the best interests concept is not stripped of a more generalized and substantive meaning based on notions of family bonds, development, and needs, among others.

A challenge to an abstract and generalized definition of the best interests of the child was launched by Judge Nussberger in a dissenting opinion in a case on paternal affiliation. The domestic courts had judged that the best interests of the child lay in the establishment of its real biological affiliation rather than in the maintenance of the paternal affiliation with the husband of his mother. The European Court concluded that the domestic courts had not exceeded their margin of appreciation.[74] In his dissenting opinion, Judge Nussberger introduced a distinction between the subjective and objective definition of best interests, dismissing an objective one. This distinction makes clear once more that the views of the child are crucial in defining the best interests. Subjectively defined, the child did not want to re-establish ties with the presumed biological father. The abstract and generalized definition of the best interests, that is, to know the truth about one's origins, failed to take into account the child's individualized concrete circumstances.[75] In this case the child lost his social and legal father and was forced to accept, during his adolescence, his presumed biological father as his new legal father.[76]

Nonetheless, in some areas, the Court remains more prescriptive on the substantive (as opposed to procedural) obligations incumbent on states. For example, in a case about contact rights for a father with a hearing impairment, the Court argued that the domestic courts "should have envisaged additional measures, more adapted to the specific circumstances of the case."[77] The Court argued that they should have looked into steps that could have been taken "to remove existing barriers and to facilitate contact between the child and the non-custodial parent."[78] Likewise, the Court emphasized that a state should not force children to return to their father after a long stay with their maternal family "without considering a proper transition and preparatory measures aimed at assisting the boys and their estranged father in rebuilding their relationship."[79] According to the Court, placement into care is permissible only to protect a child confronted with an immediate danger[80] and, thus, cannot be based exclusively on material need. Moreover, the Court emphasized that the state has the positive obligation to take measures to facilitate the reunion of the family as soon as possible. From the perspective of family life, the latter obligation becomes more forceful as time progresses but must also be balanced against the duty to consider other aspects of the best interests of the child.[81]

4.2.1 *Weight Given to the Best Interests of the Child*

Typically, in the context of relative rights, such as the right to respect for private and family life or the right to property—which can be restricted provided there is a legal basis, a legitimate aim, and proportionality between the restriction and the legitimate aim being pursued—interests will be weighed against each other as part of the proportionality test. The European Court has often argued that the best interests of the child may trump the parents' interests, contrary to the usual approach under the proportionality test of striking a balance between rights and interests without prioritization. Whereas this key idea of trumping or overriding parents' interests has been applied consistently, the language used has been variable, without clarification or justification; the Court sometimes submits that the best interests of the child are paramount,[82] at other times that they must be given significant weight[83] or must prevail and be given decisive weight.[84] In balancing the best interests of the child with the rights of parents, Article 8 of the ECHR "requires that the domestic authorities strike a fair balance between the interests of the child and those of the parents and that, in the balancing process, primary importance should be attached to the best interests of the child, which, depending on their nature and seriousness, may override those of the parents."[85] "In particular, a parent cannot be entitled under Article 8 to have such measures taken as would harm the child's health and development."[86] In other words, and as an exception to the general proportionality test which requires a weighing of interests, the best interests of the child may be rather absolute and override the interests of parents. This position was echoed in a case on the property rights of minors, where a real estate swap agreement had been concluded:

> There is a broad consensus, including in international law, in support of the idea that in all decisions concerning children, their best interests are of paramount importance. Whilst alone they cannot be decisive, such interests certainly must be afforded significant weight [reference omitted]. Indeed, the [CRC] gives the child the right to have his or her best interests assessed and taken into account as a primary consideration in all actions or decisions that concern him or her, both in the public and private sphere, which expresses one of the fundamental values of that Convention.[87]

Here again, the mixed use of language (paramount importance, significant weight, a primary consideration) can lead to confusion, but the basic message is clear: the interests of children weigh heavier than those of adults.

In the specific context of migration though, where the best interests must be balanced with the state's interest in immigration control or national security, the former may be outweighed by the latter.[88] In first-entry cases,[89] the weight of the child's best interests plays a role in assessing the obstacles to establishing family life in the country of origin test—that is, the Court examines whether sufficient weight has been given to the child's interests in examining obstacles to family life in the country of origin.[90] For expulsions, the child's best interests are taken into account in the exceptional circumstances test, that is, whether exceptional circumstances apply rendering the expulsion in violation of family life.[91] In Smyth's analysis of best interests in the context of migration, "the best interests of the child were ascribed more or less weight depending on the run of other factors. Drifting in the slip-stream of other factors (whether positive or negative for the applicant), the best interests of the child had no *inherent* weight."[92] However, in a 2014 Grand Chamber judgment in the area of migration, the Court held that whereas the "best interests of the child alone cannot be decisive, such interests certainly must be afforded significant weight."[93] This Grand Chamber judgment seems to generalize an approach that was previously specific to one "factual matrix," that is, where parents are divorced or separated and where an access arrangement exists in respect of the parent susceptible to deportation or seeking regularization,[94] and suggests that in migration cases generally, the best interests of the child must now also be given more weight than the general interest.

4.3 Best Interests as a Substantive Right

The African Commission has found a violation of the best interests principle independently of any other substantive provision. It has, moreover, read a protection obligation into the provision and thereby given it indirect horizontal effect (that is, it applies in the horizontal relation between individuals but via the state obligation to protect, hence, indirectly). In one case, Talibés children attending Qur'an schools were made to beg for more hours than the hours designated to studying, and the Commission held that this practice violated those children's best interests.[95] The CRC Committee has similarly concluded that best interests as a substantive right requires states parties to base their decisions concerning the return of migrant or asylum-seeker children to their country of origin on the child's best interests, which should "ensure—within a procedure with proper safeguards—that the child, upon return, will be safe and provided with proper care and enjoyment of rights."[96]

5 Insights on Best Interests

Given its open-ended nature, the best interests of the child will always remain an elusive concept and amenable to manipulation, bias, and paternalism. Nonetheless, it may be legally operational and in line with the spirit and philosophy of children's rights under certain conditions. We agree with the CRC Committee and the European Court of Human Rights that we should reject an abstract and general definition of best interests. Instead, best interests must be determined on a case-by-case basis based on the individual circumstances of each child. While this may open the door to abuses of discretion, bias, and paternalism, we argue for a case-by-case best interests test with the following safeguards.

First, the best interests of the child cannot be defined without giving the child the opportunity to express her or his views or taking these views duly into account. This is an important safeguard against paternalism. Second, to enhance objectivity and shield against discretion and bias, the best interests of the child needs to be defined with reference to (other) human rights of the child. As Smyth has suggested,

The rights of the child that are relevant to a particular context function as general signposts for identifying what is in the best interests of the child in that context. Furthermore, the rights of the child that are relevant to a particular context circumscribe what can be said to be in the best interests of the child in that context.[97]

This second safeguard is particularly important in the application of best interests in the context of treaties that are not (primarily) about children's rights, such as general human rights treaties or treaties in the domain of private international law: "once relied on in the interpretation of other conventions, such as the ECHR, it serves to bring the full gamut of relevant rights in the CRC to bear in both an enabling and constraining way. Accordingly, the task of identifying the child's interests...becomes one of identifying relevant rights of the child."[98] As explained above, the European Court has used the best interests of the child as proxy for children's rights in the context of juvenile justice, deprivation of liberty, and migration. Courts should do this in all cases concerning children.

Third, building on Smyth's distinction between two alternative readings of "primary" in the weighing of interests, we submit that the best interests of the child must be considered chronologically prior to other interests but also be seen as hierarchically higher—without taking an absolutist approach.[99] Considering the best interests of the child chronologically prior to other considerations ensures that "the best interests of the child are not (accidently or willingly) subsumed into the interests of other actors."[100] By being placed hierarchically higher, "the best interests of the child can only be displaced by other rights-based considerations."[101] An absolutist approach is not warranted though. Such an approach may easily become a source of administrative formalism on the part of child protection services, a formalism that may degenerate under the pretext of a "bienveillance paternaliste de l'Etat."[102]

Applied to the two examples with which we started this chapter, this would mean, in M.'s case, that the unaccompanied minor's views must be solicited and taken into account. In addition, a difficult trade-off will need to be found between family life and other children's rights, such as life, development, and fulfilment of socioeconomic rights. In that balancing exercise, the general interest should not prevail. For instance, if return to his family would clearly expose M. to the dangers of armed conflict, threatening his right to life or physical integrity, the receiving state would then be required to provide shelter to M. and extend to him the facilities and services available to unaccompanied children in that state. In the case of the C. and her siblings, age and maturity will play a role in how the children are heard and to determining the weight given to their views. By putting the best interests of these children chronologically prior and hierarchically higher, and in line with the established consensus that material poverty alone can never justify a placement into care, it seems obvious in the latter case that the children's best interests are best served by allowing children to stay with the family, provided that the state takes other measures to support the family and alleviate their plight.

Notes

1. The terminology of *general principles* originally served as the expression of signposts to guide states parties in their periodic reporting to the CRC Committee. Over time, the so-called general principles came to denote fundamental principles of children's rights after being thus acknowledged by the CRC Committee in General Comment No. 5. UN Committee on the Rights of the Child, *General Comment No. 5: General Measures of Implementation of the Convention on the Rights of the Child*, CRC/GC/2003/5 (2003). (The so-called general principles are expressed in Article 2 on non-discrimination, Article 3 on best interests, Article 6 on survival and development, and Article 12 on the right to express views freely).

2. Arne Tostensen, Hugo Stokke, Sven Trygged, and Kate Halvorsen, "Supporting Child Rights: Synthesis of Lessons Learned in Four Countries," Joint Evaluation 2011:1, February 2011, 78, https://www.oecd.org/countries/sudan/48350333.pdf.

3. Lynn Marie Kohm, "Tracing the Foundations of the Best Interest of the Child Standard in American Jurisprudence," *Journal of Law and Family Studies* 10, no. 2 (2008): 337–375.

4. UN Declaration of the Rights of the Child, art. 7, G.A. Res. 1386 (XIV), 14th Sess., A/RES/14/1386 (1959).

5. UN Convention on the Rights of the Child, art. 12, G.A. Res. 44/25, 44th Sess., UN doc. A/RES/44/25 (1989).

6. Sharon Detrick, *The United Nations Convention on the Rights of the Child: A Guide to the "Travaux Préparatoires"* (Dordrecht, NE: Nijhoff, 1992), 131.

7. Detrick, *Travaux Préparatoires*, 133 and 137.

8. Detrick, *Travaux Préparatoires*, 138. Prior to the CRC, the Convention on the Elimination of all forms of Discrimination against Women (CEDAW), while not using the term *best interests*, referred to the interests of children as being "primordial" in their upbringing and development (Article 5(b)) and "paramount" in the context of parental rights and responsibilities as well in the context of care for children outside of the family unit (Article 16(d) and (f)).

9. UN Committee on the Rights of the Child, *General Comment No. 14 (2013) on the Right of the Child to Have His or Her Best Interests Taken as a Primary Consideration (Art. 3, Para. 1)*, CRC/C/GC/14 (2013).

10. The Hague Convention on Jurisdiction, Applicable Law, Recognition, Enforcement and Co-Operation in Respect of Parental Responsibility and Measures for the Protection of Children, arts. 8(1), 8(3), 9(1), 10, 22, 23, 38, 33 (1996; entered into force Jan. 1, 2002).

11. Optional Protocol to the Convention on the Rights of the Child on the Sale of Children, Child Prostitution and Child Pornography (OPSC), art. 8(3), G.A. Res. 54/263, 54th Sess., UN Doc. A/RES/54/263 (2000; entered into force Jan. 18, 2002).

12. Optional Protocol to the Convention on the Rights of the Child on a Communications Procedure (OP3), arts. 2, 3(2), G.A. Res. 66/138, 66th Sess., UN Doc. A/RES/66/138 (2011; entered into force April 14, 2014).

13. UN Committee on the Rights of the Child, *General Comment No. 14*, para. 6.

14. UN Committee on the Rights of the Child, *General Comment No. 14*, para. 6(a).

15. UN Committee on the Rights of the Child, *General Comment No. 14*, para. 6(b).

16. UN Committee on the Rights of the Child, *General Comment No. 14*, para. 6(c).

17. UN Committee on the Rights of the Child, *General Comment No. 14*, para. 33.

18. UN Committee on the Rights of the Child, *General Comment No. 14*, paras. 1 and 32.

19. Caroline Simon, "The 'Best Interests of the Child' in a Multicultural Context: A Case Study," *Journal of Legal Pluralism and Unofficial Law* 47, no. 2 (2015): 175–189.

20. Jean Zermatten,"Best Interests of the Child," in *Child-Friendly Justice: A Quarter Century of the UN Convention on the Rights of the Child*, ed. Said Mahmoudi, Pernilla Leviner, Anna Kaldal, and Katrin Lainpelto (Leiden: Brill Nijhoff, 2015), 30–42.

21. John Tobin, "Judging the Judges: Are They Adopting the Rights Approach in Matters Involving Children?", *Melbourne University Law Review* 33, no. 2 (2009): 580–625.

22. UN Committee on the Rights of the Child, *General Comment No. 14*, para. 34.

23. Australia Human Rights and Equal Opportunity Commission and Meridith Wilkie, *Bringing Them Home: Report of the National Inquiry into the Separation of Aboriginal and Torres Strait Islander Children from Their Families* (Sydney: Human Rights and Equal Opportunity Commission, 1997).

24. Australia Human Rights and Equal Opportunity Commission and Wilkie, *Bringing Them Home*.

25. Brown v. Canada (Attorney General), 2017 ONSC 251 (Ont. Superior Ct. of Justice 2017). paras. 67, 69.

26. Marlee Kline, "Child Welfare Law, 'Best Interests of the Child' Ideology, and First Nations," *Osgoode Hall Law Journal* 30, no. 2 (1992): 375–425, 396.

27. Jonathan Todres and Sarah Higinbotham, "Reading, Rights, and the Best Interests of the Child," in *Human Rights in Children's Literature*, ed. Jonathan Todres and Sarah Higinbotham (New York: Oxford University Press, 2016), 197–212, 202.

28. Although the study was based on a small sample, it included interviews with practitioners as well as other stakeholders, such as biological and foster parents in addition to some young persons, thereby allowing for the drawing out of the rationale behind practitioner decisions and interventions. Emily Keddell, "Interpreting Children's Best Interests: Needs, Attachment and Decision-Making," *Journal of Social Work* 17, no. 3 (2017): 411–429, 332.

29. Gerison Lansdown, *The Evolving Capacities of the Child* (Florence: UNICEF, 2005), 32.

30. Lansdown, *Evolving Capacities*, 33.

31. Sara Sahriari, "Children in Bolivia Fight for Their Right to Work," *Deutsche Welle Online*, December 4, 2013, http://p.dw.com/p/18Ehh.

32. Manfred Liebel, "Do Children Have a Right to Work? Working Children's Movements in the Struggle for Social Justice," in *Reconceptualizing Children's Rights in International Development: Living Rights, Social Justice, Translations*, ed. Karl Hanson and Olga Nieuwenhuys (Cambridge: Cambridge University Press, 2013), 225–249, 236.

33. Karl Hanson and Arne Vandaele, "Translating Working Children's Rights into International Labour Law," in Hanson and Nieuwenhuys, *Reconceptualizing Children's Rights in International Development*, 250–272, 250, 259.

34. UN Committee on the Rights of the Child, *General Comment No. 12 (2009): The Right of the Child to Be Heard*, CRC/C/GC/12 (2009), para. 74.

35. United Nations High Commissioner for Refugees (UNHCR), "UNHCR Guidelines on Determining the Best Interests of the Child," May 2008, 14, https://www.unhcr.org/4566b16b2.pdf.

36. UNHCR, "UNHCR Guidelines," 22–24.

37. UNHCR, "A Framework for the Protection of Children", June 26, 2012, 27, https://www.refworld.org/docid/4fe875682.html.

38. Neulinger and Shuruk v. Switzerland, Application No. 41615/07, Eur. Ct. H.R. (July 6, 2010), para. 136.

39. The Centre for Human Rights (University of Pretoria) and La Rencontre Africaine pour la Defense des Droits de l'Homme (Senegal) v. Government of Senegal, Decision No. 003/Com/001/2012; African Committee of Experts on the Rights and Welfare of the Child (ACERWC, April 15, 2014), para. 34.
40. *Neulinger and Shuruk* , para. 138; Soares De Melo v. Portugal, Application No. 72850/14, Eur. Ct. H.R. (Feb. 16, 2016), para. 93.
41. Kacper Nowakowski v. Poland, Application No. 32407/13, Eur. Ct. H.R. (Jan. 10, 2017), para. 81.
42. X. v. Latvia, Application No. 27853/09, Eur. Ct. H.R. (Nov. 26, 2011), para. 97.
43. *X.*, para. 95.
44. *X.*, para. 101.
45. *X.*, 100.
46. Zaunegger v. Germany, Application No. 22028/04, Eur. Ct. H.R. (Dec. 3, 2009), para. 59.
47. Mikulic v. Croatia, Application No. 53176/99, Eur. Ct. H.R. (Feb. 7, 2002), para. 65.
48. Mennesson v. France, Application No. 65192/11, Eur. Ct. H.R. (June 26, 2004).
49. Migration cases are cases in which the complaint primarily relates to a decision or policy in the broad area of migration (entry, stay or removal from the territory).
50. Ciara Smyth, "The Best Interests of the Child in the Expulsion and First-Entry Jurisprudence of the European Court of Human Rights: How Principled Is the Court's Use of the Principle?," *European Journal of Migration and Law* 17, no. 1 (2015): 70–103, 75.
51. Parental expulsion cases are cases in which there is a complaint regarding the expulsion of a foreigner, often due to irregular stay on the territory or the commission of criminal offences.
52. Üner v. the Netherlands, Application No. 46410/99, Eur. Ct. H.R. (Oct. 18, 2006).
53. Smyth, "Best Interests of the Child," 77 (For an overview of the cases and criticism of "conflating (young) age with adaptability," see 76).
54. Smyth, "Best Interests of the Child," 82.
55. Smyth, "Best Interests of the Child," 83.
56. Smyth, "Best Interests of the Child," 84; Berisha v. Switzerland, Appliation No. 948/12, Eur. Ct. H.R. (July 30, 2013); Sen v. the Netherlands, Application No. 31465/96, Eur. Ct. H.R. (Dec. 21, 2001).
57. Osman v. Denmark, Application No. 38058/09, Eur. Ct. H.R. (June 14, 2011), para. 65.
58. *Osman*, para. 73.
59. Rahimi v. Greece, Application No. 8687/08, Eur. Ct. H.R. (Sept. 5, 2011), para. 108.
60. Maslov v. Austria, Application No. 1638/03, Eur. Ct. H.R. (March 22, 2007).
61. See, for example, *Osman*; N. TS. and Others v. Georgia, Application No. 71776/12, Eur. Ct. H.R. (Feb. 2, 2016), paras. 81–82.
62. Maumousseau and Washington v. France, Application No. 39388/05, Eur. Ct. H.R. (Dec. 6, 2007), para. 75.
63. See *Maumousseau and Washington*, dissenting opinion.
64. *Neulinger and Shuruk*, para. 139.
65. *Neulinger and Shuruk*, para. 146.
66. *X.*, para. 106.
67. Elsholz v. Germany, Application No. 25735/94, Eur. Ct. H.R. (July 13, 2000), paras. 52–53.
68. A.M.M. v. Romania, Application No. 2151/10, Eur. Ct. H.R. (Feb. 14, 2012), para. 56.
69. *A.M.M.*, para. 64.
70. Nazarenko v. Russia, Application No. 39438/13, Eur. Ct. H.R. (July 16, 2015), para. 65.

71. *Nazarenko*, para. 66.
72. UN Committee on the Rights of the Child, *I.A.M. v. Denmark: Views Adopted by the Committee on the Rights of the Child under the Optional Protocol to the Convention on the Rights of the Child on a Communications Procedure in Respect of Communication No. 3/2016*, CRC/C/77/D/3/2016 (2018).
73. UN Committee on the Rights of the Child, *I.A.M. v. Denmark*, paras. 11.8(a) and 11.9.
74. Mandet v. France, Application No. 30955/12, Eur. Ct. H.R. (Jan. 14, 2016), para. 59.
75. *Mandet*, dissenting opinion, paras. 8–10.
76. *Mandet*, dissenting opinion para. 2.
77. *Kacper Nowakowski*, para. 93.
78. *Kacper Nowakowski*, para. 95.
79. *N. TS. and Others*, para. 83.
80. *Soares De Melo*, para. 91.
81. Achim v. Romania, Application No. 45959/11, Eur. Ct. H.R. (Oct. 24, 2017), para. 113.
82. *Neulinger and Shuruk*.
83. Jeunesse v. The Netherlands, Application No. 12738/10, Eur. Ct. H.R. (Oct. 3, 2014).
84. *Mandet*, para. 57.
85. *Nazarenko*, para. 63; *Neulinger and Shuruk*, para. 135; *X.*, para. 96.
86. Sahin v. Germany, Application No. 30943/96, Eur. Ct. H.R. (July 8, 2003), para. 66.
87. S.L. and J.L. v. Croatia, Application No. 13712/11, Eur. Ct. H.R. (May 7, 2015), para. 62.
88. Smyth, "Best Interests of the Child," 72.
89. That is, cases whereby a nonnational enters a country for the first time in the context of family reunification.
90. Smyth, "Best Interests of the Child," 93.
91. Smyth, "Best Interests of the Child," 94.
92. Smyth, "Best Interests of the Child," 97.
93. *Jeunesse*, para. 120.
94. Smyth, "Best Interests of the Child," 97; see Rodrigues Da Silva and Hoogkamer v. The Netherlands, Application No. 50435/99, Eur. Ct. H.R. (Jan. 1, 2006).
95. *Centre for Human Rights (University of Pretoria) and La Rencontre Africaine pour la Defense des Droits de l'Homme (Senegal)*, para. 36.
96. UN Committee on the Rights of the Child, *I.A.M. v. Denmark*, para. 11(8).
97. Smyth, "Best Interests of the Child," 86.
98. Smyth, "Best Interests of the Child," 87.
99. Smyth, "Best Interests of the Child," 99.
100. Smyth, "Best Interests of the Child," 100.
101. Smyth, "Best Interests of the Child," 101.
102. *Soares De Melo*, dissenting opinion Sajo (Here, the case of Aboriginal survivors of the Sixties Scoop in Canada is particularly instructive.).

CHAPTER 11

....

CITIZENSHIP AND RIGHTS OF CHILDREN

....

DAVID B. THRONSON

1 INTRODUCTION

....

THE citizenship of a child should not matter nearly as much as it does. Children, simply as children, have significant claims to care and protection. For example, the UN Convention on the Rights of the Child (CRC) requires states parties, without regard to nationality, to "respect and ensure the rights set forth in the present Convention to each child within their jurisdiction."[1] It further bars discrimination of any kind "irrespective of the child's or his or her parent's or legal guardian's ... national, ... birth or other status."[2] Within a modern human rights framework that recognizes the humanity and autonomy of children, nationality should not be a key factor in a child's development.

But nationality is appropriately recognized as an integral part of a child's identity and plays a critical role in a child's life. At perhaps the most basic level, this is because citizenship impacts where a child can live. This, in turn, influences cultural and linguistic background, education, economic and environment exposures, and virtually all aspects of daily life. Citizenship, at its foundation, provides children with the ability to claim the protection of their state. Yet when states fail to protect children and drive them into forced migration, citizenship still affects children as it influences migration options.

Further, a child's citizenship often affects not just where the child lives but also with whom the child lives. Family, like country, is a critical factor in the development of a child's identity and the advancement of the child's well-being. Citizenship can unite families and provide for stability and security. It can provide for migration options. But it also can work to separate families, dividing parents and children. As families extend across borders and face complex migration challenges, a child's citizenship can take on added significance in the quest for family unity.

This chapter first examines children's right to citizenship and the pervasive roles that citizenship can have in securing other rights for children. It also looks at the ongoing crisis of statelessness that undermines these rights. It then delves deeper into the role that citizenship plays in both voluntary and forced migration of children, and child-specific protections found in both universal and regional human rights frameworks. Finally, it examines the role of children's citizenship in promoting family unity.

2 THE PERSISTENCE OF STATELESSNESS

A child's right to a nationality, to citizenship somewhere, is widely and unequivocally recognized. Indeed, many human rights instruments specifically articulate rights related to nationality especially for children. For example, the International Covenant on Civil and Political Rights (ICCPR) long ago noted that "[e]very child has the right to acquire a nationality."[3] This is accompanied by the corollary rights to have a name and to be registered immediately after birth.[4] Unsurprisingly, this seemingly uncontroversial idea is echoed in the CRC, which requires that the "child shall be registered immediately after birth and shall have the right from birth to a name, the right to acquire a nationality."[5] Moreover, states have an obligation to ensure implementation of these rights, "in particular where the child would otherwise be stateless."[6] Recognition of these rights is also found in Article 29 of the International Convention on the Protection of the Rights of All Migrant Workers and Members of Their Families.[7]

As elsewhere, flat pronouncements of rights do not easily guarantee that rights are honored, and severe problems establishing nationality for children persist. The "exact number of stateless people is not known, but UNHCR estimates that there are at least 10 million people globally—of which approximately one third are children."[8] At least "70,000 new stateless children are born every year in the 20 countries hosting the world's largest stateless populations."[9]

By definition, a stateless person is "a person who is not considered as a national by any State under the operation of its law. In simple terms, this means that a stateless person does not have a nationality of any country. Some people are born stateless, but others become stateless."[10] Statelessness occurs for a variety of reasons, "including discrimination against particular ethnic or religious groups, or on the basis of gender; the emergence of new States and transfers of territory between existing States; and gaps in nationality laws."[11]

Despite the human rights promise that children be protected without regard to citizenship, it remains true that citizenship plays a significant role in mediating children's opportunities and protections. In formal and de facto forms, the consequences of statelessness "are damning for children. Without a legal identity or the right to one, children can be denied essential services including health care, social protection, and education. They may be restricted in their future movements and unable or unwilling to seek protection when they need it."[12]

Statelessness for children:

> is a story of lack of opportunity, of lack of human rights protection and of lack of participation. [Stateless children] face challenges in all areas of life, including:

accessing education and healthcare,...obtaining a birth certificate.... Obtaining a passport or being issued any form of identity documentation is extremely difficult, such that many stateless persons have no proof that they exist and no means by which to identify themselves in their day-to-day interactions with the state or with private entities. International travel is almost inconceivable, unless by illicit—and dangerous—means. Free movement within the state of residence, even if it is where the person was born and has all of his or her ties, can also be difficult....Where a stateless person wants to assert their rights, or where they have become a victim of crime or exploitation, their statelessness can also stand in the way of accessing justice.[13]

The inability to obtain citizenship has serious consequences for children.

Beyond stateless children who formally lack citizenship, many others who are de facto stateless face similar complications and challenges. Some children are effectively stateless, such as "children whose irregular migration renders them *de facto stateless*— stateless in the sense that despite having a nationality, they cannot turn to the state in which they live for protection or assistance."[14] In other instances, because children's rights are so deeply (and in many instances improperly) interwoven with parents' rights, even children with formal citizenship are themselves marginalized when their parents lack regular immigration status. As a result, "citizen children in mixed status families are denied the full social benefits of citizenship as a variety of formal and informal barriers assimilate them to the status of noncitizen."[15]

While "this intensifying problem is not exclusively linked to migration and displacement, children and families who move between countries are more susceptible to it and more profoundly affected by it."[16] Citizenship is often linked to place and is significantly intertwined with migration.

3 CHILDREN, CITIZENSHIP, AND MIGRATION

Citizenship impacts the most fundamental aspects of children's lives, often including where and with whom they can live. When children find themselves outside their countries of nationality, their nationality and migration status can have outsized influence on both of these issues.

3.1 Citizenship and Children as Migrants

Children are a substantial, if not evenly distributed, portion of the population of international migrants. They migrate with families, yet in significant numbers they are unaccompanied by adults. They sometimes move by choice but far too often are forced to migrate. Children and adolescents who migrate by choice "tend to be underrepresented amongst international migrants: globally, 14 per cent of all migrants were under the age of 20 years, compared to a proportion of 34 per cent of the total population."[17]

Unfortunately, children's underrepresentation in total migration does not hold true in the context of forced migration. In the decade from 2005 to 2015, the number of child refugees under the mandate of the UN High Commissioner for Refugees (UNHCR) increased from four million to nine million.[18] As of 2016, "28 million or 1 in 80 children in the world were living in forced displacement—this includes 12 million child refugees and child asylum seekers, and 16 million children living in internal displacement due to conflict and violence."[19] In 2016 children below the age of eighteen constituted 51 percent of the world's refugee population.[20] This level of forced migration demonstrates that many children are not safe at home, and a child's nationality does not guarantee that he or she will be protected in or by their country of citizenship or birth. This lack of protection from countries of nationality places millions of children in the posture of seeking protection outside their countries of nationality. In such settings, citizenship still plays a role in where a child can live and grow.

3.1.1 *Children under the Refugee Convention*

The principal document framing parameters for the legal treatment of refugees, the Convention Relating to the Status of Refugees (Refugee Convention), and its 1967 Protocol, make scant reference to children in particular.[21] The few specific references to children in the Refugee Convention reflect international law's focus on adults and marginalized vision of children at the time the treaty was adopted. Of the two direct references to children within the Refugee Convention, one guarantees parents "freedom to practice their religion and freedom as regards the religious education of their children,"[22] and the other provides for a parent's employment authorization when "[h]e has one or more children possessing the nationality of the country of residence."[23] The Refugee Convention does specify that "Contracting States shall accord to refugees the same treatment as is accorded to nationals with respect to elementary education," a provision of high relevance to children.[24] But strikingly, the heart of the Refugee Convention, the obligation of states not to return refugees to places where they fear persecution on account of a protected ground, makes no special provisions for children.[25] Children may indeed assert claims under the Refugee Convention, but its text does not distinguish such claims from those of adults. This means that normative and legal frameworks, both substantive and procedural, are built with adult perspectives and capabilities in mind and are not tailored to the peculiar experiences of children.[26]

The application of the Refugee Convention has shifted over time, influenced substantially by the CRC, to better recognize children as autonomous beings and not just passive objects under the control of their parents.[27] In contrast to the limited vision of children in the Refugee Convention, the CRC's central notion is the idea of children as persons, as the subjects of rights. Children have rights not because they are sufficiently like adults who have rights, and not because of their particular development stage or vulnerabilities. Rather, children are simply human beings who deserve the dignity and respect required by human rights law.[28] Even when children lack the capacity to exercise these rights autonomously, they are still individual, rights-holding persons.[29]

Central to the CRC are two critical approaches: (1) that in "all actions concerning children...the best interests of the child shall be a primary consideration"[30] and (2) that children have the right to participate in decisions that affect their lives in a manner consistent with their age and maturity.[31] The CRC therefore turns children "from family possessions into individual agents, from objects into subjects."[32] For migration purposes, these approaches are vital. Too often it is simply assumed that adults in children's lives can and will make decisions about children's movements and that whatever is in the best interests of the adult is also in the best interests of the child. Under the CRC approach, the child's participation and consideration of the child's interests prevent such blithe assumptions.[33]

Critically, under the CRC, the principle that children possess the rights reserved to all persons is coupled with an understanding that they may require assistance to effectuate those rights. Children often are more physically and emotionally vulnerable than adults. Given these inequalities, differential treatment may be required to effectuate their rights. The CRC makes clear, though, that children's more limited autonomy vis-à-vis adults does not undercut their status as rights holders and, furthermore, that their possible need for alternative mechanisms and protections is not an excuse to fail to recognize their rights. This approach is brought directly to bear on migrant children in Article 22 of the CRC, which provides that

> States Parties shall take appropriate measures to ensure that a child who is seeking refugee status or who is considered a refugee in accordance with applicable international or domestic law and procedures shall, whether unaccompanied or accompanied by his or her parents or by any other person, receive appropriate protection and humanitarian assistance in the enjoyment of applicable rights set forth in the present Convention and in other international human rights or humanitarian instruments to which the said States are Parties.[34]

The approach of the CRC, through this provision, is incorporated into the application of the Refugee Convention when children are involved.[35]

The influence of the CRC is seen in the 2009 UNHCR guidelines that bring a child-centered perspective into the refugee adjudication process. The guidelines provide that "the refugee definition 'must be interpreted in an age and gender-sensitive manner, taking into account the particular motives for, and forms and manifestations of, persecution experienced by children.' "[36] The guidelines also note that children "may not be able to articulate their claims to refugee status in the same way as adults and, therefore, may require special assistance to do so."[37]

3.1.2 Citizenship and Forced Migration of Children under Regional Human Rights Frameworks

Regional human rights frameworks also contain certain child-specific protections but also protections that are available to children—and have been interpreted through a child specific lens—that are particularly relevant here. For example, the American

Declaration of the Rights and Duties of Man (American Declaration) declares that "all children have the right to special protection, care and aid."[38] Further, for all persons it guarantees the right "to seek and receive asylum in foreign territory, in accordance with the laws of each country and with their international agreements."[39] Similarly, the American Convention on Human Rights guarantees the right of every person "to leave any country freely, including his own," and "to seek and be granted asylum in a foreign territory."[40] The American Convention also prohibits the collective expulsion of aliens.[41] Invoking the framework of the CRC, the Inter-American Commission on Human Rights has declared that these provisions "should be considered in the context of the broader international and Inter-American human rights systems to include the incorporation of the principle of the best interests of the child."[42]

In another example, the African Charter on the Rights and Welfare of the Child expressly sets forth the rights of children to nationality, birth registration, and a name.[43] Perhaps "the greatest obstacle to the effective realization of the right to a nationality in Africa is the lack of functional and universal civil registration systems."[44] Children "born to vulnerable parents such as those who are nomadic, with disabilities, refugees, asylum seekers, or undocumented immigrants or parents belonging to a certain (targeted or threatened) ethnic group should a fortiori benefit from special protection measures including their registration at birth."[45] States parties to the African Charter "shall take all appropriate measures to ensure that a child who is seeking refugee status or who is considered a refugee in accordance with applicable international or domestic law shall, whether unaccompanied or accompanied by parents, legal guardians or close relatives, receive appropriate protection and humanitarian assistance in the enjoyment of the rights set out in this Charter and other international human rights and humanitarian instruments to which the States are Parties."[46] Under international human rights law—including regional instruments—when children are forced to migrate outside their country of citizenship, they are able to assert their rights to international protection just as adults would. Moreover, child migrants are entitled to special assistance as required to make their participation in the process fair and meaningful.

3.2 Children, Family Unity, and Migration

Children are too often forced to migrate unaccompanied by caring adults, but a hallmark of international migration is that, in addition to individual movements, families move together or struggle to reunite after separation across borders. Indeed, the view that children are integral parts of a family remains a starting point for analysis of rights in many jurisdictions, even where the influence of the CRC is strong.[47] And, as discussed below, a child's citizenship can play a key role here as well.

International human rights instruments almost universally emphasize the importance of family. The Universal Declaration of Human Rights declares that the "family is the natural and fundamental group unit of society and is entitled to protection by society and the State."[48] The CRC, the ICCPR, and the American Convention on Human

Rights echo this language.[49] Articles 5 and 6 of the American Declaration provide that every person has "the right to the protection of the law against abusive attacks upon his…private and family life" and "the right to establish a family, the basic element of society, and to receive protection thereof."[50] Article 7 of the American Declaration states that "all children have the right to special protection, care and aid," and Article 9 provides that "every person has the right to the inviolability of his home."[51] In fact, virtually all major international human rights instruments stress the importance of family.[52]

Yet this emphasis on family, which is also found in the CRC, should not detract from the central notion of the CRC, that is, positing children as individuals and rights holders. Under a child-centered approach, parents, families, and communities are trustees, charged with assisting children in the assertion and realization of their rights.[53] Truly adopting a child-centered approach, however, can be at odds with other state concerns in the context of migration, especially when children and parents do not share the same citizenship. Most obviously, there can be evident conflicts between family unity and migration control, such as when the immigration regime in a country calls for the deportation of a noncitizen parent but not the parent's citizen child. More subtly, asymmetries in the treatment of adults and children in various immigration regimes often relegate children to less favored status, devaluing their citizenship, as children's citizenship is less likely to transfer to parents than vice versa. This can have dire consequences for a child's claim to family unity.

For example, children's interests can easily be submerged in the enforcement of migration laws against adults. Under international human rights law, "applications by a child or his or her parents to enter or leave a State Party for the purpose of family reunification shall be dealt with by States Parties in a positive, humane and expeditious manner."[54] Further, a "child whose parents reside in different States shall have the right to maintain on a regular basis, save in exceptional circumstances personal relations and direct contacts with both parents."[55] This does not mean that a child's right to family unity will not at times conflict with the state's legitimate interests in making decisions about the entry or stay of nonnationals, but interference with family life cannot be arbitrary or unlawful.[56] Significantly, "[s]eparating a family by deporting or removing a family member from a State party's territory, or otherwise refusing to allow a family member to enter or remain in the territory, may amount to arbitrary or unlawful interference with family life."[57]

In analyzing the appropriateness of states exercising their power to control matters of entry and stay against protections for family unity, the key is balance. In *Stewart v. Canada* (1996), the UN Human Rights Committee found that a state's right to deport a noncitizen, even for a legitimate state reason, must be balanced against due consideration of the deportee's family connections and any hardship to family that the expulsion may cause.[58] The European Court of Human Rights (European Court) also has emphasized balance.

It is for the Contracting States to maintain public order, in particular by exercising their right, as a matter of well-established international law and subject to their treaty obligations, to control the entry and residence of aliens and notably to order the expulsion of aliens convicted of criminal offences. However, their decisions in this field must, in so far as they may interfere with a right protected under paragraph 1 of Article 8 (art. 8-1) [right to private and family life], be necessary in a democratic society, that is to say, justified by a pressing social need and proportionate to the legitimate aim pursued.[59]

While the nonnational's right to remain is not unqualified, neither is the state's right to expel.[60] In this context, a child's citizenship and rights as a citizen in a particular country should be an important factor in any decision by that country to expel a parent. Significantly, this is not simply a parent taking advantage of a child's citizenship status but, rather, a way to implement "measures directed at enabling parents to fulfil their duties with regard to child development."[61]

In seeking to balance family with migration control, the European Court and the UN Human Rights Committee both "considered a variety of elements in balancing a deportee's rights to remain in a host country and a state's interest to protect its citizenry and other individuals under its jurisdiction."[62] The relevant elements were the age at which the noncitizen immigrated to the host state, the noncitizen's length of residence in the host state, the noncitizen's family ties in the host state, the extent of hardship the noncitizen's deportation poses for the family in the host state, the extent of the noncitizen's links to the country of origin, the noncitizen's ability to speak the principal language(s) of the country of origin, and the nature and severity of any criminal offenses committed by the noncitizen.[63] While reviewing a claim that US immigration law violated protections for family and children under the American Declaration, the Committee noted that "[b]oth the Inter-American Commission and the European Court have recognized that under international law the best interest of a deportee's citizen children must be duly considered in any removal proceeding."[64] Thus, when a child's citizenship allows the child to remain in a country from which a parent will potentially be deported, the interests and voice of the child should be part of any decision regarding the parent.

To ensure that a child's interests remain a primary consideration and are not rendered meaningless, states must reconsider assumptions about the primacy of immigration law and recognize that "the sacrifice inherent in the restriction of family life and the impact on the life and development of the child is not outweighed by the advantages obtained by forcing the parent to leave the territory because of an immigration-related offence."[65] States also must not assume that children's status will follow parents' status and therefore must "provide avenues for status regularization for migrants in an irregular situation residing with their children, particularly when a child has been born or has lived in the country of destination for an extended period of time, or when return to the parent's country of origin would be against the child's best interests."[66] Even where the expulsion of parents is based on criminal activity, "their children's rights, including the right to have their best interests be a primary consideration and their right to be heard and have their views taken seriously, should be ensured, also taking into account the principle of proportionality and other human rights principles and standards."[67]

Generally, when deportation threatens "the rupture of the family unit by the expulsion of one or both parents based on a breach of immigration laws," the resulting negative impact on the child "is disproportionate" to the state's interests in expelling a parent.[68] As such, a child's citizenship status should serve as a powerful force against the deportation of a parent for purely immigration status–related reasons.[69]

Unfortunately, the requirement of balance is often honored in the breach. For example, under US immigration law, persons facing deportation have "no opportunity to present a humanitarian defense to deportation or to have their rights to family duly considered before deportation," placing the United States in violation of the American Declaration's Articles 5, 6, and 7 "by failing to hear their humanitarian defense and duly consider their right to family and the best interest of their children on an individualized basis in their removal proceedings."[70] The United States fails to "take due consideration of the best interest of the non-citizens' children and a deportee's rights to family, in accordance with international law."[71]

In addition to situations where the possible expulsion of the parents of noncitizens is at stake, the lack of pathways to regularize immigration status often prevents children's citizenship from contributing to the parent's appeal for lawful status. The United States is a prime example. When parents succeed in obtaining lawful immigration status in the United States, usually they are empowered to extend that benefit to their children. But when children achieve lawful immigration status, they almost always are prevented from providing immigration benefits to a parent.[72] As a practical matter, immigration law's frameworks for family immigration subordinate children's status to that of their parents.[73] So when children gain citizenship or are granted asylum, no corresponding immigration or citizenship benefit is granted to their parents. This leaves the parent vulnerable and places children at risk of either losing the ability to stay in the care of their parents or forgoing the immigration or citizenship benefits to which they are entitled. The asymmetry built into the system is not inherent in the underlying relationship involved, as the same parent-child relationship results in different outcomes when the holder of lawful immigration status is the parent and not the child.[74]

4 Conclusion

Citizenship plays a larger and more critical role in the life of children than it should. When children lack citizenship, they are incredibly vulnerable to exploitation. And the ideal that children are nurtured and protected regardless of citizenship quickly breaks down when children are outside their country of nationality. In the migration context, a child's citizenship can be largely determinative of where and with whom a child lives. In the life of a child, these are tremendously consequential determinations.

Asserting and valuing a child's citizenship and related rights is not always convenient, especially in the context of migration. Advancing the interests of children makes demands on society and the state. They can be at odds with the strict application of states' migration controls. The vindication of migration laws may compromise family unity, and attaining family unity often can be achieved only in violation of migration controls. But it is important that children's citizenship is taken into account and not subordinated to the citizenship of adults in children's lives. A child-centered approach to issues of citizenship and nationality is needed. Children's citizenship should not define their rights and opportunities, and certainly their parent's citizenship should not either.

Notes

1. UN Convention on the Rights of the Child (CRC), G.A. Res. 44/25, 44th Sess., UN Doc. A/RES/44/25 (1989), art. 2(1).
2. CRC, art. 2(1).
3. International Covenant on Civil and Political Rights (ICCPR), 999 UNTS 171 (1966; entered into force March 23, 1976), art. 24(3).
4. ICCPR, art. 24(2).
5. CRC, art. 7(1).
6. CRC, art. 7(2).
7. International Convention on the Protection of the Rights of All Migrant Workers and Members of Their Families, G.A. Res. 45/158, UN Doc. A/RES/45/158/Annex (1990).
8. UN High Commissioner for Refugees (UNHCR), "Statelessness around the World," http://www.unhcr.org/en-us/statelessness-around-the-world.html (accessed Aug. 15, 2019).
9. Emily Garin, Jan Beise, Lucia Hug, and Danzhen You, "Uprooted: The Growing Crisis for Refugee and Migrant Children," September 2016, 41, https://www.unicef.org/videoaudio/PDFs/Uprooted.pdf.
10. UNHCR, "Ending Statelessness," http://www.unhcr.org/en-us/stateless-people.html (accessed Aug. 15, 2019). See Convention Relating to the Status of Stateless Persons, 360 UNTS 117 (1954; entered into force June 6, 1960).
11. UNHCR, "Ending Statelessness."
12. Garin et al., "Uprooted," 40.
13. Institute on Statelessness and Inclusion, "Impact of Statelessness," https://web.archive.org/web/20190412153537/http:/www.institutesi.org/world/impact.php
14. Jacqueline Bhabha, *Children without a State: A Global Human Rights Challenge* (Cambridge, MA: MIT Press, 2011), xiii.
15. David B. Thronson, "You Can't Get Here From Here: Toward a More Child-Centered Immigration Law," *Virginia Journal of Social Policy and the Law* 14, no. 1 (2006): 58–86, 61.
16. Garin et al., "Uprooted," 41.
17. UN Department of Economic and Social Affairs, Population Division, *International Migration Report 2017: Highlights*, U.N. Doc. ST/ESA/SER.A/404 (2017), 17.
18. United Nations Children's Fund (UNICEF), "Children on the Move: Key Facts & Figures," data brief, February 2018, 2, https://data.unicef.org/wp-content/uploads/2018/02/Data-brief-children-on-the-move-key-facts-and-figures-1.pdf.
19. UNICEF, "Children on the Move," 2.
20. UNHCR, "Global Trends: Forced Displacement in 2016," June 19, 2017, http://www.unhcr.org/5943e8a34.pdf.

21. Convention Relating to the Status of Refugees (Refugee Convention), 189 UNTS 137 (1951; entered into force April 22, 1954); Protocol Relating to the Status of Refugees, 606 UNTS 267 (1967; entered into force Oct. 4, 1967).

22. Refugee Convention, art. 4.

23. Refugee Convention, art. 17(2).

24. Refugee Convention, art. 22(1).

25. Refugee Convention, art. 33 ("No Contracting State shall expel or return ('refouler') a refugee in any manner whatsoever to the frontiers of territories where his life or freedom would be threatened on account of his race, religion, nationality, membership of a particular social group or political opinion.").

26. See David B. Thronson, "The Legal Treatment of Immigrant Children in the United States," in *Protecting Migrant Children: In Search of Best Practice*, ed. Mary Crock and Lenni Benson (Northampton, MA: Elgar Publishing, 2018), 259–260.

27. The Refugee Convention "has been treated in recent years as a 'framework' document that can be read to evolve over time. The UN High Commissioner for Refugees (UNHCR) and the United Nations General Assembly have encouraged and supported a child-focused approach to refugee law, affirming the protection needs of refugee children on a great many occasions." See Mary Crock and Phoebe Yule, "Children and the Convention Relating to the Status of Refugees," in Crook and Benson, *Protecting Migrant Children*, 97–113, 97. However, the "first such affirmation was not until 1988, when UNHCR released its Guidelines on Refugee Children." Crock and Yule, "Children and the Convention Relating to the Status of Refugees," 97 n4.

28. Martha Minow, "Whatever Happened to Children's Rights?," *Minnesota Law Review* 80, no. 2 (1995): 267–298.

29. Barbara Bennett Woodhouse, "Keynote Address, Symposium on Legal Reform and Children's Human Rights," *St. John's Journal of Legal Commentary* 14, no. 3 (2000): 331–346.

30. CRC, art. 3(1).

31. CRC, art. 12.

32. Jacqueline Bhabha and Wendy Young, "Not Adults in Miniature: Unaccompanied Child Asylum Seekers and the New U.S. Guidelines," *International Journal of Refugee Law* 11, no. 1 (1999): 84–125, 93.

33. Any "assumption that children's immigration status must derive from that of their parents rather than vice versa recalls an earlier set of gendered assumptions—that women traveled with or followed their husbands, but not vice versa." Jacqueline Bhabha, "The 'Mere Fortuity' of Birth? Are Children Citizens?," *Differences* 15, no. 2 (2004): 91–117, 96.

34. CRC, art. 22.

35. Article 22 "works to draw in the CRC as an aid in interpreting the Refugee Convention." Crock and Yule, "Children and the Convention Relating to the Status of Refugees," 99.

36. UNHCR, "Guidelines on International Protection: Child Asylum Claims under Articles 1(A)2 and 1(F) of the 1951 Convention and/or 1967 Protocol Relating to the Status of Refugees," UN Doc. HCR/GIP/09/08 (Dec. 22, 2009), 4 (quoting UN Committee on the Rights of the Child, *General Comment No. 6 (2005): Treatment of Unaccompanied and Separated Children Outside Their Country of Origin*, CRC/GC/2005/6 (2005)).

37. UNHCR, "Guidelines on International Protection," 3.

38. American Declaration of the Rights and Duties of Man, art. 7, OAS. Res. 30 (1948).

39. American Declaration of the Rights and Duties of Man, art. 27.

40. American Convention on Human Rights, 1144 UNTS 123 (Nov. 22, 1969; entered into force July 18, 1978), arts. 22(2) and (7).

41. American Convention on Human Rights, art. 22(9).

42. Inter-American Commission on Human Rights, *Refugees and Migrants in the United States: Families and Unaccompanied Children*, OAS/Ser.L/V/II. 155 Doc. 16 (July 24, 2015), 46.

43. African Charter on the Rights and Welfare of the Child, art. 6, OAU Doc. CAB/LEG/24.9/49 (1990).

44. African Committee of Experts on the Rights and Welfare of the Child (ACERWC), *General Comment on Article 6 of the African Charter on the Rights and Welfare of the Child*, ACERWC/GC/02 (2014), sect. 1.1(7).

45. ACERWC, *General Comment on Article 6*, sect. 1.2.2.1, 51.

46. African Charter on the Rights and Welfare of the Child, art. 23(1).

47. See Jonathan Todres, "Independent Children and the Legal Construction of Childhood," *Southern California Interdisciplinary Law Journal* 23, no. 2 (2014): 261–304, 261 (noting that "the prevailing construct of childhood...envisions children foremost as part of a family").

48. Universal Declaration of Human Rights, art. 16(3), G.A. Res. 217 (III), UN Doc. A/810 (1948).

49. CRC, preamble ("The family, as the fundamental group of society and the natural environment for the growth and well-being of all its members and particularly children, should be afforded the necessary protection and assistance so that it can fully assume its responsibilities within the community."); ICCPR, art. 23(1) ("The family is the natural and fundamental group unit of society and is entitled to protection by society and the State."); American Convention on Human Rights, art. 17(1) ("The family is the natural and fundamental group unit of society and is entitled to protection by society and the state.").

50. American Declaration of the Rights and Duties of Man, art. 26.

51. American Declaration of the Rights and Duties of Man, art. 26.

52. See, e.g., African [Banjul] Charter on Human and Peoples' Rights, OAU Doc. CAB/LEG/67/3, 21 ILM 58 (1982; entered into force Oct. 21, 1986), art. 18(a) ("The family shall be the natural unit and basis of society. It shall be protected by the State which shall take care of its physical health and moral."); European Convention for the Protection of Human Rights and Fundamental Freedoms, 213 UNTS 222 (1950; entered into force Dec. 3, 1953), art. 8 ("Everyone has the right to respect for his private and family life . . ."); International Covenant on Economic, Social and Cultural Rights, 993 UNTS 3 (1966; entered into force Jan. 3, 1976), art. 10(1) ("The widest possible protection and assistance should be accorded to the family, which is the natural and fundamental group unit of society.").

53. Bhabha and Young, "Not Adults in Miniature," 93.

54. CRC, art. 10(1).

55. CRC, art. 10(2).

56. See Committee on the Protection of the Rights of All Migrant Workers and Members of Their Families, *General Comment No. 2: On the Rights of Migrant Workers in an Irregular Situation and Members of Their Families*, UN Doc. CMW/C/GC/2 (2013).

57. UN Committee on the Protection of the Rights of All Migrant Workers and Members of Their Families. *Joint General Comment No. 4 (2017) of the Committee on the Protection of the Rights of All Migrant Workers and Members of Their Families and No. 23 (2017) of the Committee on the Rights of the Child on State Obligations Regarding the Human Rights of*

Children in the Context of International Migration in Countries of Origin, Transit, Destination and Return, UN Doc. CMW/C/GC/4-CRC/C/GC/23 (2017), para. 28; see also UN Human Rights Committee, *Communication No. 2009/2010*, UN Doc. CCPR/C/111/D/2009/2010 (2014); UN Human Rights Committee, *Communication No. 2243/2013*, UN Doc. CCPR/C/112/D/2243/2013* (2014); UN Human Rights Committee, *Communication No. 1875/2009*, UN Doc. CCPR/C/113/D/1875/2009 (2015); UN Human Rights Committee, *Communication No. 1937/2010*, UN Doc. CCPR/C/113/D/1937/2010 (2015); UN Human Rights Committee, *Communication No. 2081/2011*, UN Doc. CCPR/C/117/D/2081/2011 (2016).

58. UN Human Rights Committee, *Stewart v. Canada*, UN Doc. CCPR/C/58/D/538/1993 (Nov. 1, 1996).

59. C. v. Belgium, 541 Eur. Ct. H.R. 627 (1996), para. 31; see also Beldjoudi v. France, No. 12083/86, Eur. Ct. H.R. 86 (1992), para. 74.

60. Wayne Smith, Hugo Armendariz et al. v. United States, Case 12.562, Inter-American Commission on Human Rights Report No. 81/10 (2010), para. 58 ("[T]he European Court and the U.N. Human Right Committee's decisions in this area demonstrate that a deportee's establishment of a family or private ties to a host country does not establish an immutable right of a non-citizen to remain in the host country.... The Commission finds that a balancing test is the only mechanism to reach a fair decision between the competing individual human rights and the needs asserted by the State.").

61. UN Committee on the Protection of the Rights of All Migrant Workers and Members of Their Families, *Joint General Comment No. 4*, para. 31.

62. UN Committee on the Protection of the Rights of All Migrant Workers and Members of Their Families, *Joint General Comment No. 4*, para. 54.

63. UN Committee on the Protection of the Rights of All Migrant Workers and Members of Their Families, *Joint General Comment No. 4*.

64. UN Committee on the Protection of the Rights of All Migrant Workers and Members of Their Families, *Joint General Comment No. 4*, para. 57; *see also* Andrea Mortlock v. United States, Case 12.534, Inter-American Commission on Human Rights Report No. 63/08 (2008), para. 78 ("[I]mmigration policy must guarantee to all an individual decision with the guarantees of due process: it must respect the right to life, physical and mental integrity, family, and the right of children to obtain special means of protection.").

65. UN Committee on the Protection of the Rights of All Migrant Workers and Members of Their Families, *Joint General Comment No. 4*, para. 29.

66. UN Committee on the Protection of the Rights of All Migrant Workers and Members of Their Families, *Joint General Comment No. 4*, para. 29.

67. UN Committee on the Protection of the Rights of All Migrant Workers and Members of Their Families, *Joint General Comment No. 4*, para. 29.

68. UN Committee on the Protection of the Rights of All Migrant Workers and Members of Their Families, *Joint General Comment No. 4*, para. 29 (citing Inter-American Court of Human Rights, *Rights and Guarantees of Children in the Context of Migration and/or in Need of International Protection*, Advisory Opinion OC-21/14 (2014), para. 280).

69. UN Committee on the Protection of the Rights of All Migrant Workers and Members of Their Families, *Joint General Comment No. 4*, para. 32 (noting that "preservation of the family unit should be taken into account when assessing the best interests of the child in decisions on family reunification").

70. *Smith and Armendariz et al.*, paras. 59–60.

71. *Smith and Armendariz et al.*, para. 57.

72. See, e.g., Thronson, "You Can't Get Here From Here" (discussing manner in which children's immigration status is subordinated to that of parents).

73. See David B. Thronson, "Choiceless Choices: Deportation and the Parent–Child Relationship," *Nevada Law Journal* 6, no. 3 (2006): 1165–1214, 1182 ("To the extent that the framework for family-sponsored and derivative immigration tends to achieve family integrity, it does so by ceding control over a child's status to parents and by denying opportunities for children to achieve legal status as children without their parents.").

74. See Bhabha, " 'Mere Fortuity' of Birth?"

CHAPTER 12

THE CHILD'S RIGHT
TO FAMILY

BARBARA BENNETT WOODHOUSE

1 INTRODUCTION

THE child's right to family is made explicit in the UN Convention on the Rights of the Child (CRC), and it is implicit in the general protections of the family in numerous other human rights documents.[1] Separating children from their families has been a hallmark of oppression throughout human history. It was a central feature of slavery.[2] It was employed during the Holocaust by the Nazis, by the Khmer Rouge in Cambodia, and by the military junta in Argentina.[3] Indigenous children were separated from their families in Canada, the United States, and Australia as a means of promoting assimilation.[4] In the aftermath of wars and natural disasters, or because of poverty, children have been needlessly separated from their families of origin.[5] Despite universal recognition of a right to family integrity, children from racial, religious, and ethnic minorities continue to suffer disproportionate rates of removal from their families due to poverty and culturally biased interpretations of the best interest of the child.[6]

The child's right to family raises many complex issues, including who counts as family, the circumstances in which the right is triggered, who should exercise the right, and how to integrate children's voices, experiences, and perspectives in defining the right to family. As cases discussed in this chapter will show, human rights law leaves a large margin of appreciation to states in interpreting the contours of the right according to their own national laws and values.[7] The child's right to family is also closely connected in international human rights law with the family rights and duties of parents and guardians and the duties of the state to respect family integrity and to support the family in its critical role as the natural environment for children's growth and well-being. Rather than undercutting parental rights, children's rights should be understood as adding to the family's resources in advocating for greater supports for families and resisting government oppression.[8]

Contemporary threats to implementation of children's rights to family come from many directions, including lack of cultural sensitivity in defining family, the impact of reproductive technology on definitions of family, discrimination against LGBTQ families, lack of support for minority children and children with disabilities. Violent assaults on the child's right to family are still occurring, in the trafficking of children for labor, sex work, and adoption and the kidnapping of children by militias and terrorists. One current issue that stands out above the rest is the impact of mass migrations of displaced families and unaccompanied minors and the rise of anti-immigrant sentiment, resulting in the separation of children from their families on a scale not seen since World War II.

2 Human Rights Charters Articulating Children's Rights to Family

Children's rights are a relatively recent outgrowth of the human rights revolution. Traditionally, the right to preserve and enjoy a family relationship was viewed as the right of a parent or other adult, with children as the objects rather than the holders of rights.[9] Although many vulnerable children and their families remain marginalized, the legal focus has shifted to recognize that children are not mere objects but also possessors of this fundamental human right. There are many national constitutions that explicitly or by interpretation protect children's rights to family.[10] This chapter, however, will focus on human rights documents and decisions interpreting children's rights to family as human rights.

The Declaration of the Rights of the Child (1959) was the first document explicitly to recognize children's right to grow up in the care of their parents as a human right. Principle 6 provides, in relevant part: "The child, for the full and harmonious development of his personality, needs love and understanding. He shall, wherever possible, grow up in the care and under the responsibility of his parents, and, in any case, in an atmosphere of affection and or moral and material security; a child of tender years shall not, save in exceptional circumstances, be separated from his mother."[11]

This concept of children's rights to grow up in a family was further amplified in 1989 by the UN Convention on the Rights of the Child (CRC) and appears in numerous sections of this treaty.[12]

The CRC preamble repeats the language of the 1959 Declaration regarding the importance to children of growing up in a family environment and makes explicit the duty of the state to protect and assist the family. Paragraph five of the Preamble reads: "Convinced that the family, as the fundamental group of society and the natural environment for the growth and well-being of all its members and particularly children, should be afforded the necessary protection and assistance so that it can fully assume its responsibilities within the community."

Article 7(1) recognizes the child's right from birth to a name and "as far as possible the right to know and be cared for by his or her parents."

Article 8 requires states parties "to respect the right of the child to preserve his or her identity, including nationality, name and family relations as recognized by law without unlawful interference" and establishes the duty of the state to assist children who have been deprived of some or all elements of identity in re-establishing their identity.

Article 9(1) is perhaps the strongest statement concerning family, providing that "States Parties shall ensure that a child shall not be separated from his or her parents against their will, except when competent authorities subject to judicial review determine, in accordance with applicable laws and procedures, that such separation is necessary for the best interests of the child."

Other CRC articles reinforcing the importance of children's family relationships include Article 10 (family reunification), Article 16 (protecting child from arbitrary or unlawful state interference in his or her family), Article 18 (affirming child's rights to relationship with both parents and the duties of states to assist parents in their child-rearing responsibilities), Article 20 (providing special protections to children deprived of their family environment), Article 21 (regulating adoption), and Article 22 (recognizing rights of child refugees to remain with or be reunified with their families).

The CRC repeatedly reaffirms the paramount role of parents and families in protecting the best interests of the child and in guiding children's exercise of their rights. It places primary responsibility on the family but commits the state to assisting parents in need. It depicts parents as guardians of the child's rights and as responsible for directing and guiding children as they gain greater cognitive capacity in exercising their rights. For example: Article 5 requires states to "respect the responsibilities, rights and duties of parents or, where applicable, the members of the extended family or community as provided by local custom, legal guardians or others persons legally responsible for the child, to provide, in a manner consistent with the evolving capacities of the child, appropriate direction and guidance in the exercise by the child of the rights recognized in the present convention."

Article 14, which requires states to respect children's freedom of thought, conscience, and religion, also establishes that states "shall respect the rights and duties of the parents and, when applicable, legal guardians, to provide direction to the child in the exercise of his or her rights in a manner consistent with the evolving capacities of the child."

Article 20 requires that a child deprived of his or her family environment is entitled to alternative care, with a preference for family-like environments over institutional care.

Article 21, governing the creation of families through adoption, requires that the adoption occur only after an investigation of the child's status with respect to parents, relatives, and legal guardians and that surrenders be based on informed consent. It also authorizes placement of a child in intercountry adoption only when there is no suitable manner for the child to be cared for in his or her own country of origin.

Article 27 recognizes the right of every child to an adequate standard of living and emphasizes the primary responsibilities of parents to provide for their children's needs. It also commits the state to take appropriate measures to assist parents in need, especially with respect to nutrition, clothing, and housing.

While the CRC is the most comprehensive articulation of children's human rights, regional charters also contribute to an understanding of children's rights in a regional context. The preamble to the Declaration of the Rights and Welfare of the African Child (1979) asserts that "the welfare of the African child is inextricably bound up with that of its parents and other members of its family, especially the mother."[13] The 1990 African Charter on the Rights and Welfare of the Child (African Charter), in its preamble recognizes that "the child occupies a unique and privileged position in African society and that for the full and harmonious development of his personality, the child should grow up in a family environment in an atmosphere of happiness, love and understanding."[14] The African Charter's provisions recognize essentially the same rights articulated in the CRC but with greater specificity to the African context and often with greater detail. For example, the African Charter's discussions of education, harmful social and cultural practices, the rights of refugee children, protection against apartheid, and the rights of children of imprisoned mothers are more detailed and context specific.[15] The African Charter, like the CRC, stresses the obligations of governments to support and respect the rights and duties of parents.

Article 18 of the African Charter states that "the family shall be the natural unit and basis of society. It shall enjoy the protection and support of the State for its establishment and development" and adds that no child shall be deprived of maintenance (child support) by reference to the parents' marital status.

Article 19(1) provides that "every child shall be entitled to the enjoyment of parental care and protection and shall, wherever possible, have the right to reside with his or her parents. No child shall be separated from his parents against his will, except when judicial authorities determine that it is in the child's best interest." Section (2) recognizes the right of a child separated from one or both parents to maintain personal relations and direct contact with both.

Article 20 recognizes parents' primary responsibility for the upbringing and development of the child, to make children's best interest their basic concern, to secure, within their abilities, adequate conditions of living, and to ensure that discipline is administered with humanity and in a manner consistent with the inherent dignity of the child.

And, Article 31, setting forth "the responsibilities of the child," is a unique and striking feature of the African Charter. It emphasizes the child's responsibilities toward family and society, including "to work for the cohesion of the family, to respect his parents and elders at all times, to assist them in case of need, and to preserve and strengthen African cultural values in the child's relations with other members of society."

The European Union and Council of Europe have established an integrated system of human rights. The European Commission is guided in its activities by the principles set out in the CRC, which has been ratified by all its member countries. In addition, Europe's regional human rights treaty, the Convention for the Protection of Human Rights and

Fundamental Freedoms (1950), also known as the European Charter of Human Rights (ECHR), provides important protections, plus a forum in which violations of children's rights can be adjudicated.[16] This forum, the European Court of Human Rights (European Court), is located in Strasbourg and has handed down a number of important family rights decisions, to be discussed later in this chapter.

Article 8 of the ECHR states: "Everyone has the right to respect for his or her private and family life, home and communications." It incorporates a limiting clause: "There shall be no interference by a public authority with the exercise of this right except such as is in accordance with the law and is necessary in a democratic society in the interests of national security, public safety or the economic well-being of the country, for the prevention of disorder or crime, for the protection of health or morals, or for the protection of the rights and freedoms of others."

Article 24(3) states: "Every child shall have the right to maintain on a regular basis a personal relationship and direct contact with both his or her parents, unless that is contrary to his or her interests." The same article also protects children's rights to protection and to express their views and makes children's best interests a primary consideration in all actions by government or private institutions.

The 2008 Treaty on European Union (Lisbon Treaty) in its Article 3(3) establishes as one objective of the Union the promotion of the rights of the child, including the right of the child to maintain regular contact with parents as set forth in ECHR Article 24(3).[17] Implementation of this objective is fleshed out in the EU Guidelines for the Promotion and Protection of the Rights of the Child (EU Guidelines) (revised 2017).[18] The EU Guidelines articulate a policy of "mainstreaming" of children's rights, defined as "systematically integrating the rights of the child in all policies and actions and programmes of the EU," both internally and externally. Children's right to family can be found in various provisions discussed in the EU Guidelines, including the recognition that children have a right to be directed and guided in the exercise of their rights by their parents.[19]

The Arab League's Charter on Human Rights (revised 2004) in Article 33 states that the family is the natural and fundamental group unit of society.[20] It requires states parties to take all necessary legislative, administrative, and judicial measures to guarantee the protection, survival, development, and well-being of the child in an atmosphere of freedom and dignity. It provides that states shall ensure, in all cases, that the child's best interests are the basic criterion for all measures taken in his regard, whether the child is at risk of delinquency or is a juvenile offender.

The American Convention on Human Rights, promulgated by the Organization of American States (OAS), provides in Article 17: "The family is the natural and fundamental group unit of society and is entitled to protection by society and the state" and that "the law shall recognize equal rights for children born out of wedlock and those born in wedlock."[21]

Various multilateral conventions also address the child's right to family. Among these are The Hague Convention on the Civil Aspects of International Child Abduction,[22] which provides for return of children who have been unlawfully removed from a parent, and The Hague Convention on the Protection of Children and Co-operation in Respect of Intercountry Adoption, which provides safeguards against unlawful removal of children from their families of origin for placement in an intercountry adoption.[23]

3 PERSPECTIVES ON AND CRITIQUES OF THE CHILD'S RIGHT TO FAMILY

The right to family has only recently been recognized as a right of the child, but it has a long history in the guise of parental rights to custody and control of children. It is among the most ancient rights, dating back to Roman times and before. At least in the common law and code systems of Europe, the right to family historically took the form of a right of adults rather than a right of children. Children were seen as quasi-property of the parent or head of household rather than as individuals with their own rights.[24] Under most formalized legal systems, adults were assigned a priori rights at birth to custody and control of children. Family might be defined broadly as including different degrees of kinship or community, but the right was perceived as a right belonging to the adults, not to the child. The existence of a legal bond between parent and child might depend on marital status, as in systems that treated unmarried fathers as having neither rights nor obligations toward their offspring. Custody rights might be assigned according to a parent's gender, as in the patriarchal common law system where children were essentially the legal property of their fathers. It might be assigned according to beliefs about which parent was the natural or superior caregiver, as in the so-called tender-years presumption that favored the mother. Custody and control might be awarded to a relative or a nonrelative guardian when the biological family members were deemed unfit or unavailable.[25]

Various forces have combined to challenge the law's adult-centric perspective. One such force was the emergence of a human rights jurisprudence focusing on human dignity and human flourishing rather than on property rights. Another force was the gradual recognition of children's rights as human rights.[26] While children's rights movements date back to the nineteenth century, children and women are still relative newcomers to human rights jurisprudence. Finally, science has played an important role in shaping our conception of children's right to family. As stated by the US National Institute of Medicine and National Research Council, "The scientific evidence on the significant developmental impacts of early experiences, caregiving relationships, and environmental threats is incontrovertible. . . . The science of early development is also clear about the specific importance of parenting and of regular caregiving relationships more generally."[27] Scientists have documented with increasing specificity, utilizing neuroscience as well as traditional psychological research, the fundamental role played by children's access to loving and caring adults. We now understand that these attachments are essential to children's psychological, physical, and cognitive development. The forces outlined above have combined so that the right to family could be revealed not as a right pertaining only to adults but as a relational right pertaining to all human beings and flowing in both directions between children and their families.

In discussing perspectives and critiques, this section will focus primarily on the CRC as the most fully developed charter of children's rights. It is especially important because of its influence on the drafting of regional charters and also due to the fact that judges and scholars look to the CRC as well as other charters to give content to the right to family. Looking at the CRC, we can see that the child's right to family is not isolated in one or two articles but pervades the entire CRC scheme. Beginning with the CRC's preamble, family is explicitly recognized as the fundamental social unit and the natural environment for the growth of children. In the substantive articles of the CRC, the right to family reappears again and again, in its many different aspects. We see it in the rights to name, identity, family relations, and parental care, in the right to be protected from arbitrary and unlawful separation from one's parents and family, and in the right to family reunification. Protection from intrusion into the family is explicitly singled out as an element of the child's privacy rights.[28]

It is noteworthy that numerous articles of the CRC explicitly affirm the rights of parents, sometimes referring only to parents and sometimes referring to family, extended family, relatives, legal guardians, and the community.[29] This is not only because of the fact that attachments between family members flow in both directions but also because children need adults to guide and protect them. The CRC recognizes and protects parents' rights to raise their children as integral to children's flourishing and to children's enjoyment of the rights protected by the CRC. Many of the child's rights involve choices that call for a level of maturity and autonomy that children acquire only gradually, as they develop, and that very young children may lack entirely. Parents' role as guardian and trustee of the child's rights is evident in provisions that call for parents to guide and direct the child in the exercise of his or her rights. As the child's cognitive and emotional capacities evolve, parents are asked to give appropriate regard to the child's developing autonomy. This role as guardian and guide along the path to autonomy is familiar to parents the world over and is featured in virtually every legal system. It rests on the inescapable fact that childhood is not a static thing but, rather, a process of evolution.[30] Although the pace and details of children's growth to maturity may vary, the scope of autonomy and responsibility given to children must increase as they mature if they are to be ready for adult responsibilities when they reach the age of majority.

The CRC is not without its critics. One criticism touching on the child's right to family is that the CRC attempts to be too "universal" and fails to account for regional and cultural differences.[31] The CRC's apparent assumption that family means nuclear family has been criticized as ignoring the diversity of family forms and also as failing to reflect more expansive conceptions of relationship between children and their elders and connections to other members of the child's community beyond the immediate family. This criticism is valid. While the CRC adopts as its default setting the notion that parents are the primary holders of rights and responsibilities for child-rearing, it also recognizes "where appropriate" the role of others in the family and community in guiding the child's exercise of his or her rights. The African Charter, as noted above, draws a larger circle of relationships consistent with customary African cultures. It also is more expansive in referring not only to children's rights but also to children's "duties" to respect "elders" and "other members of society." As the African Charter and the CRC itself suggest, in interpreting what is meant by *family*, any children's rights charter should incorporate deference to the family culture and tradition of the child's social community.

Some of the harshest opposition to children's rights comes from the United States, the only UN member state that has refused to ratify the CRC.[32] While the CRC has widespread support in the US from mainstream organizations, it is staunchly opposed by many on the far right.[33] At the core of US opposition is the widespread belief that attributing rights to children would undermine the constitutional rights of parents to control the upbringing of their children. Supporters of the CRC and other children's rights initiatives point out that rights need not be a zero-sum game. In the vast majority of contexts, children's rights supplement and complement the rights of parents.[34] Defenders of the CRC point to the many family-supportive provisions highlighted above and analogize the rights of the child to a trust fund established on behalf of the child and placed under the guidance of their parents acting as trustees.[35] Thus, children's rights should be understood as supportive of family integrity. They add to the store of resources available to the family, augmenting rather than diminishing protections against government oppression and neglect.

Another element present in the CRC, as well as other human rights charters, that strikes US critics as alien to their system is the very notion of welfare rights or positive rights. Accustomed to seeing rights through the lens of the Bill of Rights of the US Constitution, which focuses on protecting individuals from the state, conservative critics reject the concept of a charter that obligates government to take positive action rather than refrain from action.[36] Yet one of the most crucial and integral elements of the child's right to family in the CRC is its recognition of the positive right of the child to state policies that support and assist children and their families. The internal reasoning of the CRC makes sense from a child-developmental perspective. Negative rights to be free of state coercion or state intervention mean little to a child whose family lacks the means to survive. Instead of undermining family autonomy, the CRC envisions a relationship of solidarity between family and state, both committed to the best interests of the child.

The CRC, like other human rights instruments, also envisions human rights as indivisible and interrelated.[37] All of the child's rights are mutually reinforcing, and deprivation of any right risks undermining all of the others. Given the pivotal role of family in children's lives, the CRC includes numerous provisions emphasizing governments' obligations, in light of their available resources, to provide positive protection and material support to the family. This is understood as an essential step toward fully realizing the rights of the child.

4 Progress and Obstacles in Assuring the Child's Right to Family

The past thirty years have seen great progress in recognition of the child's right to family. At the same time, formidable obstacles stand in the way of implementation of children's rights. One of these impediments is the slow pace of incorporation of the CRC's principles into domestic laws of states parties. The CRC until very recently did not include any enforcement mechanism. Despite its near universal ratification, in many jurisdictions, especially those in which treaties are not self-executing, the CRC does not provide an independent ground for asserting a claim. Its most powerful effect has been in introducing a more holistic view of family rights into judicial systems, laws, and policies at the regional, national, and local levels.[38]

While the child's right to family may not be cited as the primary ground of a court judgment, it often goes hand in hand with other provisions of national or regional law to support and influence the contours of court judgments. Often the language utilized by courts and policymakers invokes specific rights established in the CRC without necessarily citing that document. Because so many influential judgments on the child's right to family come from decisions on ECHR Article 8 (right to respect for family life) from the European Court of Human Rights (European Court), this chapter will focus on exploring these decisions. The following are only a few examples of important decisions of the European Court touching on the child's right to family. These cases are rarely simple and often raise debate about how courts interpret children's rights and how well they balance competing rights, but the judgments all represent progress in that they explicitly recognize that the right to family belongs to children as well as to adults.

4.1 Right to Reunification

The European Court has issued many judgments that uphold the child's right to reunification after being separated from family. *Sen v. Netherlands* (Dec. 21, 2001) concerned the application of a Turkish couple who had emigrated to the Netherlands to be reunified with a child who had been left behind in Turkey. The Dutch authorities had denied the application, citing concerns about controlling immigration. Citing Article 8, the European Court held that the Netherlands had failed to strike a fair balance between its interests and those of the child. In weighing the balance of interests, the court notes that many members of the family have been resident for years in Netherlands and that the only route to reunification, should the Netherlands close its doors to this child, would mean displacing the rest of the family. In *Osman v. Denmark* (June 14, 2011), a Somali child of fifteen, who had been living with her parents in Denmark since age seven, was sent by her parents to care for her aunt in Somalia. When she tried to return two years later, Denmark cited a law that only children under the age of fifteen could apply for family reunification. Noting that the child had been a settled migrant who spent most of her childhood in Denmark, the European Court held that there had been a violation of the child's right to respect for family life. In cases like these, the child is recognized as an integral member of a family unit as well as an individual with a history of his or her own.

4.2 Right to Identity

In *Mikulic v. Croatia* (Feb. 7, 2002), a child born out of wedlock sought a DNA test to determine her paternity, but the Croatian courts failed to enforce orders requiring her putative father to submit to testing. The European Court held that this failure constituted a violation of Article 8 (right to respect for private and family life) of the ECHR. The Court identified the child's right to identity as a protected right under Article 8, triggering the Article 6 and Article 13 rights to fair procedures and a remedy. In cases like this, the Court is giving greater weight to the right of children to know their identity than to the right of a parent who seeks to avoid responsibility.

The case of *Odievre v. France* (Feb. 13, 2003, Grand Chamber) involved the right of a child who had been abandoned by her mother at birth, placed in state care, and later adopted in a full adoption to learn her biological mother's identity. French law protected the right of the mother to remain anonymous, although non-identifying information was provided and identifying information was available if the mother consented. The European Court held that, in light of the child's long-established ties with her adoptive family and lack of established ties to her biological mother, France had struck an appropriate balance between the interests of all affected parties.

A similar case involving the Italian scheme for anonymous birth reached a different conclusion. In *Godelli v. Italy* (Sept. 25, 2012) the applicant was seeking identifying information about her birth mother who had abandoned her at birth. The European Court found a violation of Article 8, pointing to the fact that the Italian legislative scheme did not provide for release of non-identifying information or any opportunity to gain the mother's consent.

4.3 Defining Family

The European Court has also been presented with cases in which the very definition of family was at issue. In *Paradiso and Campanelli v. Italy* (Jan. 24, 2017, Grand Chamber), an infant born in Russia following a gestational surrogacy contract between a Russian woman and an Italian couple was placed in the care of social services by Italian authorities when it transpired that the child had no biological relationship with the Italian couple. The child's Russian birth certificate identified the Italian couple as her parents. However, Italian law defined the legal child-parent relationship according to biology or lawful adoption. In light of the absence of a biological connection, the short duration of the relationship and the lack of emotional bonds, the Grand Chamber of the European Court deferred to Italy's authority to apply its rules in deciding her parentage. Thus biology, psychological bonds, and passage of time all played a role in assessing the existence of a family relationship.

In *Mandet v. France* (Jan. 14, 2016), a mother, her husband, and her child complained that their family rights were violated by the quashing of the husband's recognition of paternity at the request of the child's biological father. The Court noted that, although the child considered the husband to be his father, his primary interest lay in knowing the truth about his origins. It did not dismiss his right to define his own family, noting that he would not be prevented from remaining with the person he regarded as his father. This judgment indicates that a child can have a right to a biological identity that is independent of, yet coexists with, his right to define his own family.

Zaiet v. Romania (March 24, 2015) concerned the annulment of an adoption over thirty years after it had been approved and many years after the adoptive mother's death at the insistence of relatives who challenged the child's right to an inheritance. The adoptive child protested that she had lived with her adoptive mother from age nine and that their relationship had been one of affection, responsibility, and mutual support. The European Court held that the annulment of the adoption was not supported by evidence and that it constituted an interference in the right to respect for family life and contravened the principle that the best interests of the child should be paramount in adoption. This judgment reinforces the importance of the child's lived experience in defining family bonds.

In *Mustafa and Armağan Akin v. Turkey*, a custody order by the Turkish court was challenged as violating a father and his son's rights under Article 8 of the ECHR. The custody order provided that the son and his sister could not have contact. The practical effect of the custody order was to prevent the siblings from having contact with each other and to prevent the father from having contact with his two children at the same time. The European Court held that the decision of the Turkish court constituted a violation of the right to respect for family life because it not only prevented the brother and sister from seeing each other but also made it impossible for their father to enjoy the company of both children at the same time. This judgment illustrates the interconnectedness of family relationships. While the marital unit may have been dissolved, the ties among and between siblings and parents remained intact and deserved protection.

In *S.H. v. Italy* (Oct. 13, 2015), the European Court considered whether the removal of three children from a mother struggling with mental health problems followed by a judicial declaration of adoptability constituted a violation of Article 8. The Court concluded that the Italian child welfare authorities had failed to take sufficient positive steps to keep the family intact, resulting in the placement of the children in three separate foster homes. The Court awarded damages to the parents but did not address the status of the children's foster placements. Cases like this illustrate the positive rights of children and families in need to state support. They stop short, however, of ordering that children's current family relationships with foster or adoptive parents be ruptured in order to vindicate the parent's rights.

These judgments, taken together, show how the definition of family and the recognition of rights to respect for family are more nuanced and child-centered than under a traditional parental rights model. While giving great weight to biological connection and to legal parenthood, the judgments also give weight to the mutual bonds that develop between children and those who care for them. In this sense, they incorporate a child's eye view of family, a perspective that has been missing from family law in many jurisdictions. They also reveal that the child's right to family is much broader than the binary right of contact between parent and child familiar from traditional laws on child custody. It extends to protect relationships between networks of family members, including siblings.

The remedies provided by the European Court also respect the child's own experience of family attachments. The Court takes into account the passage of time and the strength of children's affective attachments. While the Court may award monetary damages to the parent whose Article 8 rights have been violated, a finding of a violation does not automatically result in return of the child to the victorious adult if such a move would involve separating the child from a foster or adoptive family with which the child has developed deep relationships over an extended period of time. This approach stands in sharp contrast to the procedures typical in US constitutional law whereby the remedy for violation of the parent's constitutional rights in adoption is often return of the child, even if it involves separation of the child from the only family he or she has ever known.

4.4 Mainstreaming of Children's Rights

Progress in implementation of children's right to family also comes in the form of regional, national, and global mainstreaming of rights. As noted above, the child's right to family is integral to and inseparable from all of the child's rights. While mainstreaming is concerned primarily with political and administrative action, it works in synchrony with courts and legislatures. For example, the EU Guidelines for the Promotion and Protection of the Rights of the Child (revised 2017) expand upon the earlier Lisbon Treaty in promoting the integration of children's rights across every area of the EU's activities, internal and external. "This child rights approach is holistic and places emphasis on supporting the strengths and resources of the child him/herself and all social systems of which the child is a part: family, school, community, institutions, religious and cultural systems."[39] As the EU Guidelines recognize, certain children are especially vulnerable as a result of separation from family, due to war, migration, or state action. "By implementing a system-strengthening approach, States address the full spectrum of the rights of the child as a system-approach would aim to protect all the rights of all children including—and especially—the most vulnerable and marginalized, such as internally displaced or migrant and refugee children, including unaccompanied children, children with disabilities or those belonging to a minority group."[40] At the global level, children's rights to family are an integral part of the Sustainable Development Goals of the United Nations.[41] On the subnational level, resolutions adopting the CRC, establishing rights-regarding communities, and creating youth parliaments serve to promote the spread and entrenchment of children's rights, including their right to family at regional, state, provincial, and municipal levels.[42]

5 KEY CHALLENGES GOING FORWARD

Children's rights are a prime example of the power of soft law in the form of a moral commitment. However, our challenges going forward lie in the transformation of its principles into hard law in the form of norms accepted as binding at the national and international level. If the family is the basic unit of society, the rule of law is the basic unit of civilization. As we approach the third decade of the twenty-first century, numerous challenges remain, including improving cultural sensitivity in defining family, addressing the impact of reproductive technology on definitions of family, assuring respect for LGBTQ families, protecting the family rights of minority children and children with disabilities, and integrating children's voices, experiences, and perspectives into the balancing of rights. Ongoing challenges involve the threats posed by human trafficking and kidnapping of children by militias. However, at this writing, one threat to children's right to family and to its place in the rule of law stands out above all the rest. This challenge is the catastrophic effect of mass migrations that separate children from their families and undermine support for family rights.

In the past decade, large regions of the world have been engulfed in armed conflict and economic dislocation, driven in part by climate change and by increasing levels of inequality. Each year hundreds of thousands of children and their families are forced to flee from their homes, made uninhabitable by war and poverty. In 2017, according to the United Nations Human Rights Commission, 68.5 million people were displaced either internally or across national borders because of persecution, armed conflict, violence, or human rights violations.[43] As of 2013, over a million refugee children had fled war-torn Syria.[44] While some remained in the immediate area, very large numbers sought safety and opportunity by migrating to the developed nations of Europe and North America. In Europe, 650,000 applications for asylum were filed during 2017, primarily by refugees from Syria and Iraq.[45] Many of these people arrived by ship, and their documentation was processed at ports of arrival or at border crossings. The picture in the US was somewhat different. Many displaced persons were fleeing chaos and violence in the Northern Triangle of Central America. They arrived in Mexico on foot and crossed the porous border with Mexico by swimming the Rio Grande or by paying smugglers to transport them. In fiscal year 2016, about 85,000 migrants arriving in the US formally sought refugee status.[46] Their numbers were dwarfed by those who entered as clandestine migrants. In the same fiscal year, the US Border Patrol apprehended 563,204 persons illegally crossing the border.[47]

By 2018 the populist backlash against immigration had reached a crisis point in both the United States and many parts of Europe. Anti-immigrant leaders had been elected in both.[48] In the United States, Donald Trump was elected on an anti-immigrant platform in November 2016 and inaugurated as president in January 2017. In the British Isles, England, Scotland, Wales and Northern Ireland were preparing to leave the European Union as a result of the anti-immigrant sentiment behind the Brexit vote. In Italy, the March 2018 general election resulted in the ouster of the center-left Democratic Party and formation of a new coalition government dominated by two populist and anti-immigrant parties (the Five Star Movement and the Northern League). In Germany, Chancellor Angela Merkel was facing rising opposition from anti-immigrant forces within her own increasingly divided coalition government. In France, President Emmanuel Macron was following a hard line against allowing migrants from Africa and the Middle East to enter at French ports or border crossings.

During the spring of 2018, headlines on both sides of the Atlantic were dominated by shocking stories of family tragedy. Under Donald Trump, the US government had implemented a policy of separating migrant parents from their children as soon as they crossed the border. The authorities arrested the parents for the misdemeanor crime of illegal border crossing, reclassified the children as unaccompanied minors, and placed them in detention centers and foster homes, often for long periods of time and in distant locations. The US government explicitly stated that the purpose of these policies was to deter migration. It became clear that forced separation of parents and children was being used, cynically and illegally, as a means to deter and punish parents for seeking security and safety for their children. To their credit, ordinary US citizens were horrified. The airwaves and Internet were flooded with images of sobbing children being torn from their parents' arms to be warehoused in pens hastily constructed in empty Walmart stores and military installations. A massive outcry caused President Trump to revoke the policy of separating families, but the policy of removal had been implemented without proper record-keeping or any plans for family reunification. Ordered by a federal court to speedily reunify the children with their parents, the federal government had to concede it was unable to meet deadlines because it had failed to document which children belonged with which parents and in some cases had destroyed records linking parents and children.[49] As Judge Sabraw pointed out in his order granting a preliminary injunction, a chain of custody must be documented when the authorities remove property, such as money, important documents, or automobiles, from a suspect, but children, far more precious than property, were being taken from parents without documentation and without a plan for return.[50] As many US advocates for children observed, there was an uncanny similarity between removal of these migrant children from their families and a long and continuing history of unnecessary removal of poor children, children of color, and indigenous children from their families of origin.[51]

Meanwhile, on the other side of the Atlantic, Italians had become frustrated with the EU agreement (Dublin Accords) that required refugees and asylum seekers to file their cases in the member state where they first set foot on EU soil. Because of Mediterranean geography and the closing by France and Spain of their ports of entry, the burden of receiving migrants fell most heavily on Greece and Italy. Greece reached an agreement with the EU to stanch the flow of migrants headed west and north from Africa and the Middle East by maintaining migrant camps on its soil. Migrant flows from Libya to Italy surged, then seemed to ebb, but popular fears of immigrants did not recede.

In June 2018 Italian vice premier and minister of the interior Matteo Salvini, leader of the Northern League, instructed Italian ports to turn away rescue vessels seeking to disembark refugees rescued from Mediterranean waters. Inevitably, some of the flimsy rubber rafts filled with migrants foundered, and the headlines were filled with images of small children's lifeless bodies floating ashore. The children's mothers had dressed them in red so they would more easily be spotted by rescuers. Many Italians, shaken by these images, marched in red T-shirts in solidarity with the dead children. The Italian coalition threatened to come apart, with the defense minister, interior minister, judiciary, and coalition premier sharply divided. When an Italian Coast Guard ship was blocked from docking in an Italian port to discharge survivors rescued from the Mediterranean waters, the political crisis reached a head. It was temporarily defused when President Sergio Mattarella intervened, but we can expect that similar crises, in Italy and elsewhere, will become the norm.[52]

The populist response to these mass migrations, especially in developed nations, threatens children's right to family on a scale not seen since World War II. In the name of controlling migration governments are closing their borders and denying children's rights to family preservation as well as to family reunification. Courts and policymakers are becoming less open to placing family rights on par or above state concerns about the costs, both social and economic, of protecting refugees and migrants. We see the impact on children in camps of refugees, where family members who have been separated from one another as well as children unaccompanied by any adult family member are trapped on the borders between countries where they cannot survive and countries that do not want them. We see it when families are forcibly separated by authorities, when policies turn against family reunification, and when migrant children die needless deaths because there are no safe havens for families. International human rights laws that protect children from being separated from their families and give families special protection in times of crisis are being ignored and swept aside.

Sadly, much of the backlash against migrant families in wealthier nations has been driven by misconceptions. Many of these beliefs are the result of disinformation marketed by politicians seeking to stir up popular resentment. Due to technology, baseless non-facts can spread like wildfire through social media. In one study of popular beliefs among native-born citizens in France, Germany, Italy, the UK, the US, and Sweden, researchers from Harvard University found that citizens grossly overestimated the numbers of migrants, both in absolute numbers and as a percentage of the population, and grossly overestimated the numbers of migrants who commit crimes, their rates of unemployment, and the financial costs to taxpayers of providing refuge. When provided with accurate information, native-born citizens were much more likely to approve of humane immigration policies.[53]

6 CONCLUSION

Much progress has been made in entrenching children's right to family in international and national law.[54] Family rights, once framed as a right of adults to possession and control of children, are now almost universally recognized as rights of the child to relationships with parents and other family members. The CRC has been most influential in its role as a framework for thinking about children's rights to family, and it has stimulated legislatures and judicial bodies at the national and regional levels to greater protections of children's family connections. The decisions of the European Court of Human Rights show how the child's right to family, as an independent human right, has taken shape and gained acceptance in the period between 1989 and the present. Yet great challenges remain to family integrity. The current backlash in wealthier nations against migrants fleeing war, violence, and poverty has become a global test of our commitment to preserving children's rights to know and be cared for by their families.

NOTES

1. UN Convention on the Rights of the Child (CRC), G.A. Res. 44/25, 44th Sess. UN Doc. A/RES/44/25 (1989).
2. Peggy Cooper Davis, *Neglected Stories: The Constitution and Family Values* (New York: Hill and Wang, 1997).
3. Uki Goñi, "40 Years Later, the Mothers of Argentina's Disappeared Refuse to Be Silent," *The Guardian*, April 28, 2017, https://www.theguardian.com/world/2017/apr/28/mothers-plaza-de-mayo-argentina-anniversary; Zachery Zimmer, John Knodel, Kiry Sovan Kim, and Sina Puck, "The Impact of Past Conflicts and Social Disruption in Cambodia on the Current Generation of Older Adults," University of Michigan Population Studies Center Report No. 05-582, September 2005, http://globalag.igc.org/armedconflict/countryreports/asiapacific/Cambodia.pdf.
4. Nick Evershed and Lorena Allam, "Indigenous Children's Removal on the Rise 21 Years after Bringing Them Home: Government Data Shows the Group Remains Overrepresented in All Parts of the Child Protection System," *The Guardian*, May 25, 2018, https://www.the-guardian.com/australia-news/2018/may/25/australia-fails-to-curb-childrens-removal-from-indigenous-families-figures-show.
5. Marilyn Irving Holt, *The Orphan Trains: Placing Out in America* (Lincoln: University of Nebraska Press, 1992); Shani M. King, "Challenging Monohumanism: An Argument for Changing the Way We Think About Intercountry Adoption," *Michigan Journal of International Law* 30 (2009): 413–470.
6. Dorothy E. Roberts, *Shattered Bonds: The Color of Child Welfare* (New York: Basic Books, 2002).
7. See sections 4.1 through 4.3.
8. Barbara Bennett Woodhouse, "The Family Supportive Nature of the U.N. Convention on the Rights of the Child," in *The United Nations Convention on the Rights of the Child: An Analysis of Treaty Provisions and Implications of U.S. Ratification*, ed. Jonathan Todres, Mark E. Wojcik, and Cris Revaz (Ardsley, NY: Transnational Publishers, 2006), 37–46.

9. Barbara Bennett Woodhouse, "The Child's Right to a Parent: Charting the Path from Mere Interest to Constitutional Right," in *Family Law in Britain and America in the New Century*, ed. John Eekelaar (Leiden: Brill-Nijhoff, 2016), 127–142.

10. Warren Binford, "Comparative Constitutional Rights of Children," in *Max Planck Encyclopedia of Constitutional Law*, June 9, 2016, http://ssrn.com/abstract=2792513; Barbara Bennett Woodhouse, "The Constitutionalization of Children's Rights: Incorporating Emerging Rights into the Constitutional Framework," *University of Pennsylvania Journal of Constitutional Law* 2 (1999): 1–52.

11. U.N. Declaration of the Rights of the Child, art. 7, G.A. Res. 1386 (XIV), 14th Sess., A/RES/14/1386 (1959).

12. CRC, arts. 5, 7, 8, 9, 10, 14, 16, 18, 20, 21, 22, 27.

13. Organization of African Unity, Declaration on the Rights and Welfare of the African Child, AHG/St. 4(XVI) Rev. 1 (1979).

14. Organization of African Unity, African Charter on the Rights and Welfare of the Child (African Charter), OAU Doc. CAB/LEG/24.9/49 (1990).

15. African Charter, arts. 11, 21, 23, 26, 30.

16. European Convention for the Protection of Human Rights and Fundamental Freedoms, adopted November 4, 1950, www.echr.coe.int/Documents/Convention_ENG.pdf (states parties include all forty-seven member states of the Council of Europe, including Albania, Andorra, Armenia, Austria, Azerbaijan, Belgium, Bosnia Herzegovina, Bulgaria, Croatia, Cyprus, Czech Republic, Denmark, Estonia, Finland, France, Georgia, Germany, Greece, Hungary, Iceland, Ireland, Italy, Latvia, Lichtenstein, Lithuania, Luxembourg, Malta, Moldova, Monaco, Montenegro, Netherlands, Norway, Poland, Portugal, Romania, Russian Federation, San Marino, Serbia, Slovak Republic, Slovenia, Spain, Sweden, Switzerland, Macedonia, Turkey, Ukraine, and United Kingdom).

17. European Union, "Consolidated Version of the Treaty on European Union and the Treaty on the Functioning of the European Union," 2012/C 326/01, *Official Journal of the European Union* 55 (Oct. 26, 2012), https://eur-lex.europa.eu/LexUriServ/LexUriServ.do?uri=OJ:C:2012:326:FULL:EN:PDF (states parties are the twenty-seven members of the European Union, including Austria, Belgium, Bulgaria, Croatia, Cyprus, Czech Republic, Denmark, Estonia, Finland, France, Germany, Greece, Hungary, Ireland, Italy, Latvia, Lithuania, Luxembourg, Malta, Netherlands, Poland, Portugal, Romania, Slovak Republic, Slovenia, Spain, Sweden and United Kingdom).

18. European Union (EU), "EU Guidelines for the Promotion and Protection of the Rights of the Child," 2017, https://eeas.europa.eu/sites/eeas/files/eu_guidelines_rights_of_child_2017.pdf (accessed Aug. 16, 2019).

19. EU, "EU Guidelines," 9.

20. League of Arab States, Arab Charter on Human Rights (adopted May 22, 2004; entered into force March 15, 2008), http://hrlibrary.umn.edu/instree/loas2005.html (parties include Algeria, Bahrain, Iraq, Jordan, Kuwait, Lebanon, Libya, Palestine, Qatar, Saudi Arabia, Syria, the UAE, and Yemen).

21. The American Convention on Human Rights, OAS Treaty Series No. 36 (adopted Nov. 22, 1969; entered into force April 17, 1978), http://www.oas.org/dil/treaties_B-32_American_Convention_on_Human_Rights_sign.htm (parties include Argentina, Barbados, Bolivia, Chile, Columbia, Costa Rica, Dominica, Ecuador, El Salvador, Grenada, Guatemala, Haiti, Honduras, Jamaica, Mexico, Nicaragua, Panama, Paraguay, Peru, Dominican Republic, Suriname, Trinidad & Tobago, United States, Uruguay and Venezuela).

22. Hauge Convention on the Civil Aspects of International Child Abduction (signed Oct. 25, 1980), https://www.hcch.net/en/instruments/conventions/full-text/?cid=24.

23. The Hague Convention on the Protection of Children and Co-operation in Respect of Intercountry Adoption (signed May 29, 1993), https://www.hcch.net/en/instruments/conventions/full-text/?cid=69.

24. Barbara Bennett Woodhouse, "Who Owns the Child? *Meyer* and *Pierce* and the Child as Property," *William & Mary Law Review* 33 (1992): 995–1122.

25. For historical perspectives see Masha Antokolskaia, *Harmonisation of Family Law in Europe: A Historical Perspective; A Tale of Two Millennia* (Antwerp: Intersentia, 2006); Michael Grossberg, *Governing the Hearth: Law and the Family in Nineteenth Century America* (Chapel Hill: University of North Carolina Press, 1985); Joanna Grossman and Lawrence M. Friedman, *Inside the Castle: Law and the Family in 20th Century America* (Princeton: Princeton University Press, 2011); Stephen Cretney, *Family Law in the Twentieth Century: A History* (Oxford: Oxford University Press, 2010).

26. Michael Freeman and Philip Vreeman, *The Ideologies of Children's Rights* (Norwell, MA: Kluwer Academic Press, 1992); Woodhouse, "Children's Right to a Parent."

27. National Research Council and Institute of Medicine of the National Academies, *From Neurons to Neighborhoods: The Science of Early Childhood Development* (Washington, DC: National Academies Press, 2000), 10. See also Institute of Medicine and National Research Council of the National Academies, *From Neurons to Neighborhoods: An Update* (Washington, DC: National Academies Press, 2012); Alan L. Stroufe, Byron Egeland, Elizabeth A. Carlson, and W. Andrew Collins, *The Development of the Person: The Minnesota Study of Risk and Adaptation from Birth to Adulthood* (New York: Guilford Press, 2009).

28. Barbara Bennett Woodhouse, "The Family Supportive Nature of the U.N. Convention on the Rights of the Child," in Todres, Wojcik, and Revaz, *The United Nations Convention on the Rights of the Child: An Analysis.*

29. Parents' rights are singled out in CRC Articles 7(1), 9(1), 18. Other articles, including Articles 5, 14, 20, 21, and 22, refer as well to family, relatives, the community, and legal guardians.

30. National Research Council and Institute of Medicine of the National Academies, *From Neurons to Neighborhoods.*

31. Michael Freeman, "Cultural Pluralism and the Rights of the Child," in *The Changing Family: Family Forms and Family Law*, ed. John Eekelaar and Thandabantu Nhlapo (Oxford, UK: Hart Publishing, 1998), 289–305; Michael Freeman, "Children, Culture and Rights," *The Family in Law* 5 (2011): 15–33.

32. Jonathan Todres, "Analyzing the Opposition to the Ratification of the U.N. Convention on the Rights of the Child," in Todres, Wojcik, and Revaz, *United Nations Convention on the Rights of the Child: An Analysis*, 19–32; Howard Davidson, "Does the U.N. Convention on the Rights of the Child Make a Difference?," *Michigan State International Law Review* 22, no. 2 (2014): 447–530 (see the discussion on pages 500–507).

33. Martha Middleton, "ABA Adds Its Voice to Calls for the US to Ratify the Convention on the Rights of the Child," *ABA Journal*, March 1, 2016, http://www.abajournal.com/magazine/article/aba_adds_its_voice_to_calls_for_the_us_to_ratify_the_convention_on_the_righ.

34. Davidson, "Does the CRC Make a Difference?"

35. Davidson, "Does the CRC Make a Difference?"; Woodhouse, "Family Supportive Nature."

36. Tamar Ezer, "A Positive Right to Protection for Children," *Yale Human Rights & Development Law Journal* 7 (2004): 1–50 (discussing distinction between positive and negative rights in context of children, pages 4–10); Barbara Bennett Woodhouse, "Re-Visioning Rights for Children," in *Rethinking Childhood*, ed. Peter B. Pufall and Richard P. Unsworth (Piscataway, NJ: Rutgers University Press), 229–243; Jeremy Waldron, "Introduction," in *Theories of Rights*, ed. Jeremy Waldron (Oxford: Oxford University Press, 1984), 1–20.

37. UN General Assembly, *Indivisibility and Interdependence of Economic, Social, Cultural, Civil and Political Rights*, G.A. Res. 44/130, UN Doc. A/Res/44/130 (1989); Jonathan Todres, "The Importance of Realizing 'Other Rights' to Prevent Sex Trafficking," *Cardozo Journal of Law and Gender* 12, no. 3 (Summer 2006): 885–907.

38. Davidson, "Does the CRC Make a Difference?" (discussing influence of soft law); Barbara Bennett Woodhouse, *Hidden in Plain Sight: The Tragedy of Children's Rights from Ben Franklin to Lionel Tate* (Princeton: Princeton University Press, 2008), 30–32 (describing norms of CRC as promoting change at statutory and constitutional levels).

39. EU, "EU Guidelines," 9.

40. EU, "EU Guidelines," 18.

41. The UN Sustainable Development Goals implicate a wide range of factors contributing to child and family well-being, including reduction of poverty and hunger, improvement in gender equality, health care and education. Goal 16 (peace and justice) directly affects the right to family by urging full implementation of the right to registration at birth. See United Nations, "Goal 16: Promote Just, Peaceful and Inclusive Societies," https://www.un.org/sustainabledevelopment/peace-justice (accessed Aug. 16, 2019).

42. Jane Williams, "The Rights of Children and Young Persons (Wales) Measure 2011 in the Context of the International Obligations of the UK," in *The United Nations Convention on the Rights of the Child in Wales*, ed. Jane Williams (Cardiff, Wales: University of Cardiff Press, 2013), 49–63.

43. The 2016 global figure of 68.5 million displaced persons included 25.4 million refugees, 40 million internally displaced persons, and 3.1 million asylum seekers. They came from the Central African Republic as well as Cameroon, the Republics of Congo, Chad, and South Sudan in Africa, the Northern Triangle of Central America, Iraq, Jordan, Syria, and Yemen in the Middle East, from Myanmar in Asia and from the Ukraine in the former Soviet Union. UNHCR, "Refugee Statistics: Global Trends At-a-Glance," https:www.unrefugees.org/refugee-facts/statistics.

44. UNHCR, "The Future of Syria: Refugee Children in Crisis," http://unhcr.org/FutureOfSyria (accessed Aug. 16, 2019); Barbara Bibbo, "Syria's Refugee Children: Futures Lost to the War," Al Jazeera, April 11, 2018, https://www.aljazeera.com/news/2018/04/syria-refugee-children-futures-lost-war-180411151533233.html.

45. Eurostat, "Statistics Explained: Asylum Statistics," http://ec.europa.eu/eurostat/statistics-explained/index.php/Asylum_statistics#Number_of_asylum_applicants:_drop_in_2017 (accessed Aug. 16, 2019).

46. Phillip Connor, "U.S. Admits Record Number of Muslim Refugees in 2016," Pew Research Center, October 5, 2016, http://www.pewresearch.org/fact-tank/2016/10/05/u-s-admits-record-number-of-muslim-refugees-in-2016.

47. US Customs and Border Protection, "Southwest Border Migration FY2018," last modified 10 December 10, 2018, https://www.cbp.gov/newsroom/stats/sw-border-migration/fy-2018 (apprehensions/inadmissibles FY 2013 to FY 2018 accurate as of July 2, 2018).

48. Barbara Bennett Woodhouse, *The Ecology of Childhood: How Our Changing World Threatens Children's Rights* (New York: New York University Press, forthcoming 2020).

49. Camila Domonoske and Richard Gonzales, "What We Know: Family Separation and 'Zero Tolerance' at the Border," National Public Radio, June 19, 2018, https://www.npr.org/2018/06/19/621065383/what-we-know-family-separation-and-zero-tolerance-at-the-border?t=1531586703422; Maria Sacchetti, "Trump Administration Seeks More Time to Reunite Some Migrant Families Split at Border," *Washington Post*, July 6, 2018, https://www.washingtonpost.com/local/immigration/trump-administration-seeks-to-extend-deadline-for-reuniting-some-migrant-families-split-at-border/2018/07/06/b3260a02-8131-11e8-b658-4f4d2a1aeef1_story.html?noredirect=on%26utm_term=.231d60cc8356.

50. Ms. L. et al. v. U.S. Immigration and Customs Enforcement et al., Case No. 18cv0428 DMS (MDD) (S.D. Cal. June 26, 2018), 14–15 (order granting plaintiffs' motion for a class-wide preliminary injunction).

51. MSNBC, "Professor Dorothy Roberts Talks U.S. Family Policy with MSNBC's Ali Veshi," June 28, 2018, https://www.youtube.com/watch?v=5zQcRdBliN0.

52. Marzio Breda, "Migranti, la spinta di Martarella perche' il governo trovi una linea univoca," *Corriere della Sera*, July 13, 2018, https://www.corriere.it/politica/18_luglio_13/spinta-colle-perche-governo-riesca-trovare-linea-univoca-3c94edac-86dd-11e8-83d7-334832af0f98.shtml. The Italian president, like the Queen of England, usually stands somewhat aloof from politics but can intervene in a crisis when the political system appears to be breaking down.

53. Alberto Alesina, Armando Miano, and Stefanie Stantcheva, "Immigration and Redistribution," NBER Working Paper 24733 (June 2018; revised October 2018), https://www.nber.org/papers/w24733; Alberto Alesina, "La Forza dei Numeri sull'Emergenza Migranti," *Corriere della Sera*, July 8, 2018, https://www.corriere.it/opinioni/18_luglio_09/forza-numerisull-emergenza-migranti-576ebeec-82e0-11e8-8c19-eee67e3476a0.shtml.

54. Ursula Kilkelly, "Protecting Children's Rights under the ECHR: The Role of Positive Obligations," *Northern Ireland Legal Quarterly* 61, no. 3 (2010): 245–261; European Union Agency for Fundamental Rights and Council of Europe, *Handbook on European Law Relating to the Rights of the Child* (Luxembourg: Publications Office of the European Union, 2017).

CHAPTER 13

....

CHILD PARTICIPATION

....

JAAP E. DOEK

1 INTRODUCTION

....

ACCORDING to Article 31 of the UN Convention on the Rights of the Child (CRC), states parties recognize, respect, and promote the right of the child to participate fully in cultural and artistic life, while Article 23(1) requires states parties to facilitate active participation of children with disabilities. In its General Comments on these articles, the Committee on the Rights of the Child (CRC Committee) provides some explanation of the meaning of these provisions but does not, for example, recommend that the right to participation mentioned in Article 31 be expanded to all other areas covered by the CRC.[1] In light of this limited recognition of the right to participation, it is remarkable that child participation has emerged as an activity that should be considered an integral part of the interpretation and implementation of all CRC provisions and by some experts qualifies as part of the core of the CRC. There is no article in the CRC that requires recognition of the right to participation—other than Article 31—and the fact that child participation is increasingly presented as a right of the child is surprising. It prompts the question what exactly the content of that right is and whether or not it is justiciable.

This chapter is an exploration of the emergence of the child's right to participation in the monitoring activities of the CRC Committee and a discussion of the content and/or meaning of this right. Here I also discuss the practice on the ground, that is, how the right to participation actually manifests in different settings in which a child grows up, such as the family, the school, the local community, health care, and the legal system. The first part of this chapter addresses the question of whether participation is a right and what that should mean for the implementation of the CRC. My conclusions in this section are primarily based on the views of the CRC Committee in its Concluding Observations, recommendations after Days of General Discussion, and General Comments. The second part provides information on how child participation is and can be implemented. In this section I rely, in part, on illustrative examples from research. The chapter ends with recommendations for further development of the participation of the child.

2 CHILD PARTICIPATION: A RIGHT?

2.1 Adoption of the CRC to 2006, the Day of General Discussion

The CRC entered into force on September 2, 1990. During the first ten years of its implementation, the participation of children was not given much attention in the CRC Committee's Concluding Observations, with some rare exceptions. For instance, in 1998, the Committee recommended that Bolivia make further efforts to ensure the implementation of "respect for the views of the child especially his or her right to participation in the family, at school, within other institutions and in society in general."[2] This mention of "the right to participation" came without a clear explanation of the basis of this right, except for the suggestion that it has something to do with CRC Articles 12, 13, and 15.[3] However, the limited attention to child participation is understandable because the CRC does not contain an article that explicitly recognizes the right of the child to participation and the related obligation of states parties to respect, protect, and fulfill this right.

In 1999 the CRC Committee celebrated the tenth anniversary of the CRC with a two-day meeting focused on various children's rights topics, including child participation. At that meeting, children from Albania, Belgium, Mali, Mexico, the Netherlands, the Philippines, and the United Kingdom expressed their views on participation, proposed establishment of a world parliament for children, and recommended including children among the members of the CRC Committee. During the closing plenary session some children complained that the language of the recommendations presented at the session had been extremely hard to follow and that some key proposals had not been included. Responses to these complaints led to some rather emotional reactions by the children. In her closing statement, the High Commissioner for Human Rights emphasized that encouraging child participation would require adult and children alike to learn how to interact.[4]

The CRC Committee stated in its report on the two-day meeting that it will consider, as a priority, a comprehensive general comment on child participation as envisaged in the Convention (and more particularly in Articles 12 through 17),[5] bearing in mind that participation includes, but is not limited to, consultation and proactive initiatives by children themselves. The CRC Committee observed that states parties should give adequate attention to the requirements of Articles 12 through 17, which should include inter alia ensuring that schools, as well as other bodies providing services for children, establish permanent ways of consulting with children in all decisions concerning their functioning, the content of the curriculum and other activities, including increased consideration of the creation of structures and/or mechanisms to facilitate the expression by children of their views, in particular with regard to the formulation of public policies from local up to national level.[6] It should be noted that the CRC Committee did not in its conclusions presented in its report on the two-day meeting use the term *right to participation*.

In light of the views of the CRC Committee expressed in its Concluding Observations and during commemoration of the CRC's tenth anniversary, the status of child participation in the context of the UN Convention on the Rights of the Child at the beginning of the twenty-first century could be summarized as follows:

- The CRC Committee did raise the issue of child participation, not primarily as a right, but as an activity envisaged in the CRC and made specific reference to Articles 12, 13, and 15 and also, more generally, to Articles 12 through 17.
- The content of the concept of child participation was not well elaborated in the views expressed by the Committee. It includes (at least) consultation with children in all decisions made in the family, in schools, in services for children, and at the local up to the national level regarding formulation of public policies as well as pro-active initiatives by children themselves. In terms of child-initiated activities, it was not clear what the CRC Committee envisioned, but one could assume that it could be linked to Article 15 on the right to freedom of association and peaceful assembly.

After this tenth anniversary, and perhaps as a spin-off of some conclusions, the CRC Committee paid more attention to the matter of child participation in its Concluding Observations under the right of the child to be heard (Article 12). However, the attention was not a regular part of the Concluding Observations for all states parties. A frequently used phrase in the recommendations was to promote and facilitate respect for the views of children and their participation in all matters affecting them.[7] The term *right* was rarely used. By way of example: the Committee recommended that Zambia increase awareness of the "participatory rights" of children and that Italy place particular emphasis on the right of every child to participate in the family, at school, within other institutions and bodies and society at large.[8] At the same time, no specific recommendation was made on child participation for quite a number of countries, such as China, Ghana, Ireland, Latvia, Mexico, and Saudi Arabia (all in 2006).[9] Altogether we may conclude that in its Concluding Observations well into 2006 the CRC Committee did not present the participation of children as a right; nor did it indicate that it was as such a core element of the CRC.

2.2 Day of General Discussion 2006 and General Comment No. 12 (2009)

2.2.1 *The Day of General Discussion 2006*

In 2006 the concept, and thus the presentation, of the participation of children changed considerably as a result of the Day of General Discussion devoted to the Right of the

Child to Be Heard. More than sixty written submissions were received by the CRC Committee prior to the Day of General Discussion, highlighting the role of child participation at the community level. In addition, informal meetings took place for the preparation of a General Comment on Article 12, during which a lot of attention was given to child participation as a possible core element of the General Comment. However, the recommendations presented as a result of this Day of General Discussion (DoGD) are remarkable, inter alia, because the Committee gave a deeper meaning to Article 12 and recognized a right that is not expressly stated in the CRC[10]

In the preamble to its report of the DoGD, the Committee states that recognizing the right of the child to express views and to participate in various activities is beneficial for the child, for the family, for the community, the school, the state, and for democracy. To speak, to participate, and to have their views taken into account describe the sequence of the enjoyment of the right to participate from a functional point of view. The Committee continues: "The new and deeper meaning of this right is that it should establish a new social contract."[11]—one in which children are recognized as rights-holders who have the right to participate in all matters affecting them, a right that can be considered as the symbol for their recognition as rights-holders. The CRC Committee asserts—without any explanation—that there is a right to participation and even claims that this right should establish a new social contract. The reference to the commitment to the right of the child to participate expressed by states parties at the Special Session of the UN General Assembly and the Resolution "A World Fit for Children" is not convincing. It appears in the Declaration of this document in which states declare that they are upholding their commitment to specified principles and objectives, such as respect for the right of children to express themselves and to participate in all matters affecting them. However, this nonbinding declaration is not more concretely elaborated under paragraph 32 with the heading "Partnerships and Participation."[12] After some general observations, such as the need to combat certain traditional and cultural attitudes which fail to recognize the child to participate in society, the report of the DoGD continues with many recommendations for the implementation of the child's right to participate at home, in school, and in the community.

In short, in 2006 the CRC Committee recognized a right of the child to participate in all matters affecting her or him, a right that is not explicitly enshrined in the CRC. This recognition of the right to participation is linked to Article 12. The question of what this recognition more precisely entails is left unanswered, except that it requires a variety of activities of states parties and other stakeholders. The Committee welcomes the contributions by nongovernmental organizations in promoting awareness-raising regarding the right of the child to participate fully in accordance with Article 12. This includes the right of the child to have his or her views given due weight in accordance with the age and maturity of the child. If children participate, for example, in a local discussion on the location of playgrounds it seems to be problematic to give due weight to the views of every child in accordance with age and maturity. Thus, participation in full compliance with Article 12 creates problems especially when a group of children participates.

In its report on the DoGD, the Committee reaffirms its intention to develop a General Comment on Article 12 (something that was not completed until three years later).[13]

2.2.2 *General Comment No. 12 on Article 12 of the CRC and Child Participation*

Although Article 12 was and still is used in arguing that (the right to) participation is embedded in the CRC, the core content of General Comment No. 12 on Article 12 is not child participation, but the right to be heard.[14] A few key points from General Comment No. 12 are important to note here.

- General Comment No. 12 is a careful legal analysis and interpretation of Article 12 with a clear focus on the right of the child to express her or his views and the right to have these views given due weight in accordance with age and maturity of the child. It is not a formal interpretation of participation rights; nor is it guidance for implementing the right to participation.[15]
- The right of children to express their views is dependent on the child's capability to form his or her own views. The CRC Committee is of the view that very young children can have this capability, though they may express their views in nonverbal ways (e.g., drawings, play). States cannot begin with the assumption that a child is incapable of forming his or her views.[16]
- Giving due weight to the views of the child in accordance with the age and maturity of the child is a challenge. In the context of Article 12, the CRC Committee defines maturity as the capacity of a child to express her or his views in a reasonable and independent manner. In order to give due weight to the views of the child, these views have to be assessed on a case-by-case basis.[17]
- The phrase "all matters affecting the child" is interpreted by the CRC Committee in a very broad manner such that it covers issues not explicitly mentioned in the CRC. This goes against the intention of the drafters of the CRC. The drafting history shows that "matters" are clearly meant to be those that are directly pertinent to the life of the child concerned.[18]
- The CRC Committee expressed as its view that the right to express views is applicable not only to the individual child, as was the intention of Article 12, but also to groups of children. This view is elaborated in a kind of confusing way; for example, the Committee states that the CRC stipulates that states parties must assure the right of the child to be heard according to the age and maturity of the child.[19] However, age and maturity are not criteria for the right to be heard, but for assessing the weight that should be given to the views of the child. So the rest of the reasoning is missing this point. In other words, you do not need to assess the age and maturity of all children of a group before allowing them to express their views. The Committee's recommendation that states parties should exert all efforts to listen to or seek the views of those children speaking collectively is relevant but arguably would be better framed in the context of Article 13.[20] Article 13 creates not

only the (negative) obligation to refrain from interference of the right to freedom of expression but also the (positive) obligation to promote, encourage, and support the exercise of this right—including, for example, by inviting children to give their opinion or views on measures the government intends to take for the prevention of child abuse, bullying, or the criminalization of certain forms of online sexual abuse or exploitation of children. The online environment provides significant opportunities for strengthening and expanding participation of children and their communication with local or national governments and/or authorities.

- The CRC Committee does not adequately address a key issue when allowing or inviting children to express their views collectively: how much weight should be given to these collective views in accordance with the age and maturity of each child (or all children)?

- Article 12(2) clearly pertains to the individual child in any kind of legal or administrative proceedings. An important element of the CRC Committee's interpretation is the need to provide the child with feedback. This includes not only information for the child about the outcome of the process but also an explanation of the weight given to the views of the child.[21]

- Part C of General Comment No. 12 (para 89 e.a.) deals with the implementation of Article 12 in the different settings in which the child grows up, develops, and learns, such as the family, alternative care, health care, education, recreation, sports, cultural activities, the workplace, situations of violence, and immigration and asylum proceedings. In these paragraphs, the term *participation* is used quite frequently, but terms like *consultation, contributing views*, or just the *right to be heard* are utilized as well. There is, however, no explicit mention of the right of the child to participation per se.

In conclusion, the CRC Committee does not explicitly recognize participation as a right of the child in its General Comment No. 12. However, we may conclude that the child's right to express his or her views creates an opportunity to participate or "take part or become involved" in decision-making processes in different settings as well as in policy development and implementation. The CRC Committee clearly encourages states parties to promote or even ensure the involvement of children in all matters affecting the child in the broadest sense of the word.[22] That the Committee is of the view that Article 12 is also applicable to groups of children creates some confusion here. It does so by linking the right to express views with age and maturity while not paying attention to the matter of giving due weight to the views of groups of children. It would be more appropriate to deal with groups of children and their views in the context of Articles 13 and 15.

Contrary to the enthusiastic recognition of the child's right to participation in the report of the CRC Committee on the Day of General Discussion 2006, the CRC Committee carefully avoids the right to participation in its General Comment No. 12 (2009), though the Committee did recognize the importance of children's participation. I think we may conclude that the Committee does not want to present participation as a right of the child, a conclusion which would be consistent with the text of the CRC, as it does not contain a right of the child to participate in all matters affecting her or him. A recognition of participation as a right of the child would go far beyond its mandate and may not serve the interests of children. Of note, the Committee's presentation of participation as a right of the child lacks attention to the justiciability or enforceability of this right. In addition, to present Articles 12, 13, 14, 15 and sometimes also 17 as the participatory rights of the CRC may contribute to misunderstandings of the rights of the child. The importance of these articles is the recognition of the child as holder of fundamental civil and political rights. They provide at the same time a variety of opportunities for children (and adolescents) to participate in all sectors of social, economic, political, and other developments at the local and national level. The use of these opportunities should be encouraged, promoted, and supported by not only the states parties but also by NGOs, professional associations, the business world, and UN agencies.

3 Participation of Children and Adolescents: Some Examples

In its General Comment No. 12, the CRC Committee elaborates on the implementation of Article 12 of the CRC for different settings and circumstances in which children may exercise their right to express their own views and thus participate in decision-making or other processes. This section highlights illustrative examples in settings and circumstances that are particularly relevant to the child's right to express her or his views and details some of the challenges in the implementation of this right.

3.1 The Family

Article 5 of the CRC recognizes the crucial role of the family in the development of respect for and understanding of children's rights and their implementation. It requires states parties to "respect the responsibilities, rights and duties of parents...to provide the child, in a manner consistent with the evolving capacities of the child, appropriate direction and guidance" in exercising the rights recognized in the CRC.[23] This means, among other things, that parents should provide their children with a meaningful opportunity to express their views on all matters affecting them. It may result in lively communication between parents and children on a range of issues relevant to the daily life of the child as well as participation of the child in decision-making processes related to family matters (e.g., holidays, timing, and location) and may result in participation of the child in such matters as choice of education or medical treatment.[24] Allowing children to give input on decisions affecting them does not mean they will have the final say. Nonetheless, an important element of participation is parents explaining to their children how their input was taken into account—in particular when their views were not, or only partly, followed.

It is fair to assume that child participation in the family setting differs considerably from country to country and depends on culture.[25] A study carried out in South Africa in 2006 found that children engage in discussions with female caregivers more easily than with male caregivers. This study also found that boys had more influence in the decision-making process than girls. There was some room for negotiations related to household chores in terms of who would do which chores. Child participation increased with age and was greatest in decisions on education.[26] However, research on the practice of child participation in the family setting is rather scarce.

The "shall respect" obligation of states parties in CRC Article 5 means not only that they should avoid interfering in how and when parents provide direction and guidance but also that states should provide parents with information on children's rights and opportunities to participate in parenting classes with a view to strengthening parents' capacities to support the child as a rights holder. This is clearly expressed in Article 18 of the CRC, which provides that both parents have "common responsibilities for the upbringing and development of the child" and requires states parties to render appropriate assistance in the performance of their child-rearing responsibilities *for the purpose of guaranteeing and promoting the rights recognized in the CRC*. To wit, when a parent makes a decision involving a child, that parent must give due consideration to any views and wishes expressed by the child, bearing in mind the child's age, maturity, and stage of development[27]; in deciding questions related to the child's personal affairs, the parent is to take progressively greater account of the child's viewpoints and wishes, in parallel with the child's advancing age, maturity, and development.[28]

3.2 Education

In light of the CRC Committee's interpretation of Article 12, child participation in education can take place at the individual or group level.

In making decisions for an individual child—for example, on transition to the next level, on the choice of tracks or streams in the curriculum, on disciplinary measures—the teacher or school board is to provide the student with a meaningful opportunity to express her or his views. This includes providing the student with information about the decision that will be taken and the reason for that decision in order to allow the student to prepare his or her views and in order to allow for the possibility to be heard in the company of a parent or another well-trusted adult. The child's views must be given due weight in accordance with the age and maturity of the child. When the decision is made it should contain a motivation understandable to the child, including information on the degree to which the views of the child have been taken into account.

Article 12's requirements that the child be capable of forming a view and that due weight be given to these views consistent with the age and maturity of the child provide school personnel with a wide margin of discretion. For instance, decisions regarding younger children might be discussed primarily with the child's parents if the child has limited capacity to understand the situation. However, the views of the CRC Committee in this regard are clear: "even the youngest children are entitled to express their views"— in other words, the right of the child to be consulted in matters affecting him or her should be implemented from the earliest stage.[29]

Finally, the issue of child participation in schools raises an important question: should every decision taken by the school related to an individual child be subject to judicial or administrative review?[30] The CRC does not provide specific provisions requiring such review; instead it leaves it up to the states to decide. In doing so, states may take into consideration, inter alia, the position of very young children and the role of parents in asking for a review and which types of decisions will be subject to judicial or administrative review. If the decision itself constitutes a violation of the child's rights, the child and his or her parent(s) have the right to an effective remedy.[31] Although this right is not explicitly recognized in the CRC, the CRC Committee is of the view that the child is entitled to such a remedy.[32]

The participation of children as a group in school and/or educational matters is relatively well developed in a number of countries—for example, via student councils, student representatives on the local school board, publication of a student bulletin or newspaper, and student associations.[33] Despite the presence of these structures, the practice of participation in school matters seems to be weak. Student representatives on school councils have varied experiences: some children feel respected and listened to, while others feel neglected and intimidated by adults.[34] To link this part of participation to Article 12, as the CRC Committee does, requires due weight be given to the views of these or other student groups taking into account not just the age (which typically range from twelve to sixteen), but also the maturity of the students. That is quite difficult, and as noted before, it is not necessary to link collective participation to Article 12. The "collective" participation in school matters is an opportunity created by Articles 13 and 15 of the CRC. The right to freedom of expression (Article 13) is both directly and indirectly linked to education, and the right to peaceful assembly (Article 15) allows for meetings in support of certain views of students. Both articles open the door to lobbying and campaigning in school with a view toward ensuring that adequate weight be given to the views of students.

Participation of children in schools should be a kind of natural element of education that is rights-based and child-friendly. When education is child-centered, it encourages participation, creativity, and self-esteem, reflects and realizes the rights of every child, is gender-sensitive, provides education linked to the reality of children's lives, and is flexible and responsive to diversity.[35] As Laura Lundy argues, the right to education is much more than access to school. It is participating in a learning environment in which the rights of the child are to be respected and implemented.[36] As stated by the CRC Committee: "Children do not lose their human rights by virtue of passing through the school gates."[37]

3.3 Health Care

Participation of children in health care is very much limited to individual cases. Even without Article 12, doctors should listen to the child in order to understand what health issues the child has and to be able to administer effective medical care to their patients. However, Article 12 is not just about listening to the child because it helps facilitate treatment; it explicitly recognizes the *right* of the child to express her or his views. This implies that doctors have to provide the child with information about medical care options and the (side) effects of each of the possibilities.[38] The views of the child on the available options must be given due weight by the doctor in accordance with Article 12.

The importance of listening to children is undisputed in the world of health care. However, there are at least two important aspects of the implementation of Article 12 that health care professionals have to deal with in their interactions with children: confidentiality and consent. The CRC Committee discusses these issues in its General Comment No. 12 as well as in two other General Comments focusing on the implementation of children's rights during adolescence.[39] The CRC Committee does not define adolescence but states that it focuses on children between age ten and eighteen.[40] These three General Comments may raise questions on the applicability of some recommendations made on health care of adolescents for children below the age of ten.

With respect to confidentiality, the CRC Committee asserts that states parties need to introduce legislation to ensure that children have access to confidential medical counseling and advice without the consent of a parent or guardian, irrespective of the child's age.[41] The Committee does not provide further information on how young children, without parental involvement, can get access to confidential counseling and advice. A similar recommendation regarding adolescents makes more sense and is linked to their possibility to give informed consent.[42]

With respect to consent, one of the most challenging aspects of implementing Article 12 is how and to what extent the views of the child in a decision-making process on his or her health care (e.g., medication, vaccination, surgery) are given due weight. In practice, it depends on the opinion of adults on the maturity and the evolving capacities of the child as well as on the nature of the medical treatment the child has to undergo. Another factor is the requirement that in all actions the best interests of the child must be a primary consideration (Article 3). Thus, if the child expresses the view that he or she does not want a proposed treatment, while doctors and parents are of the view that following the view of the child is not in her or his best interests, the best interests of the child can trump the child's views. A key unresolved question is when does the view of the child become the decisive factor? Should that be a matter for medical professionals to decide given the risk of discriminatory practices in light of their extreme discretion in these circumstances? Keep in mind that the CRC Committee underscores that Article 12 does not contain an age limit with regard to the right to express views, nor with regard to the right to have these views given due weight. A traditional rule in most, if not all, countries is that medical treatment of a child cannot take place without the consent of the parents (except in limited circumstances, such as emergencies). However, in light of the evolving capacities of the child and the factor of (increasing) maturity, the consent of the child may become more important. To resolve uncertainties around consent, some countries have introduced an age at which the views of the child are decisive. This means that medical treatment of a child at or above that age cannot be carried out without the consent of the child. The CRC Committee has welcomed this kind of legislation and encouraged states parties to introduce a fixed age at which the consent of the child can be dispositive, though it did not make any recommendation on what would be an appropriate age for this consent.[43] In practice, different rules for consent of the child for medical treatment exist: a fixed (minimum) age at which the child's consent is necessary without the requirement to assess the capacity of the child; the same rule but with the condition that the child understands the risks and benefits of the treatment (assessed by the doctor(s)); the same rule but with the possibility that, if the child can demonstrate capacity and understanding below that age, the child's consent will be decisive; a gradual increase of the weight to be given to the child's views and a decreasing weight to be given to the role of the parents. For example, the law may provide that a medical treatment of a child twelve years of age or older requires the consent of the child next to the consent of the parents, with the possibility that the doctor decides to perform a medical treatment without the consent of the parents if the child clearly wants the treatment and shows that this view is well informed. Furthermore, the law can provide that the child aged sixteen or older is the only person whose consent is necessary.[44]

The matter of consent is of course also an issue in conducting medical research and leads to rather extensive discussions around the question of when a child is competent to consent to and participate in medical research. The MacArthur Competent Assessment Tool for Clinical Research indicates that children above the age of 11.2 years are competent to give consent and that children below 9.6 are not, while the competence of children in between these ages could be assessed with the Competence Assessment Tool.[45]

The setting of a minimum age range for the consent of the child in health care decisions is helpful because it provides clarity for the child, the parents, and the doctors and other medical professionals. But it remains important, and is often explicitly stated in the law, that the child below a minimum age should be listened to and be allowed to express his or her views (if she or he is capable of forming them), and these views should be given due weight in accordance with the age and maturity of the child.

3.4 In Legal Proceedings

The participation of the child in legal proceedings is guaranteed in paragraph 2 of Article 12, which states that "the child shall in particular be provided with the opportunity to be heard in any judicial and administrative proceedings affecting the child."[46] This hearing can be direct or via a representative of the child or an appropriate body. It means that the child is a participant in all proceedings affecting her or him—this includes custody and visitation, adoption, child protection (including placement in alternative care), asylum, cases of conflict with the law, and maltreatment in which the child is a victim as well as disputes related to education, health care, and housing. The right to be heard should be implemented not only in formal proceedings but also in cases of alternative dispute resolution, mediation, family conferencing, and arbitration.[47]

Child participation in legal proceedings has received a lot of attention not only from child rights activists, researchers, NGOs, and UN agencies, in particular UNICEF, but also from national legislators and courts and from international and regional courts and bodies. It is beyond the scope of this chapter to address all the aspects of participation in legal proceedings, but several key issues are highlighted below.

- It is the view of the CRC Committee that states parties have the obligation to assess the capacity of the child to form her or his own views.[48] This means that in court proceedings, the judge has to make that assessment of the capability of every child who is part of the proceeding. However, the CRC Committee also observes that the maturity of the child should be considered when determining the individual capacity of the child. In the context of Article 12, maturity means the capacity of the child to express his or her views on issues in a reasonable and independent manner.[49] In my view, this means that the court is not obliged to hear very young children. However, courts have to assess the capacity of all children. While the CRC Committee does not provide guidance on how that should be done, it probably means hiring a specialist for this assessment because most judges are likely not trained to work with children. In practice, due to resource constraints, many courts and judges do not have specialists who conduct this assessment. My recommendation for all states parties is to set a minimum age at which the child must be provided an opportunity to be heard. Below that age, a child can be heard if the judge is of the view that the child has the capacity and wants to express her or his views. If such a child submits a request to be heard, the judge should in principle grant that request. If a judge rejects such a request, the judge should explain that decision in a language that the child understands. States should provide an opportunity for the child to challenge the decision on his or her request to be heard. Research shows that children at or above the legal minimum age are indeed heard, while that is less the case for children below that age.[50] In addition, judges are more likely to refer directly or indirectly to the views of the child in their judgments if the child is at or above the minimum age set by law making it mandatory for the judge to hear the child.[51]
- Participation of children alleged to have "infringed the penal law" (CRC Article 40) in the juvenile justice system must be allowed. These children have the right to be heard from the beginning of the juvenile justice proceedings and are entitled to legal and other assistance and have the right to appeal a decision made during this process.
- In all proceedings that affect the child, he or she must be treated in a manner that takes into account her or his age, maturity, and specific vulnerability. The CRC

does not contain express provisions with concrete and specific steps that must be taken by states to ensure this occurs. However, a lot of attention is given to what is known as the development of a child-friendly justice system. Rules and recommendations have been developed regarding the preparation of the child for a hearing by a court, the provision of legal counsel and appropriate psychological assistance, the use of language appropriate to the child's age and level of understanding, the avoidance of direct contact, confrontation, or interaction between the child and an alleged perpetrator as much as possible, and the importance of informing the child about the decision that was made, its consequences, and the possibility of appeal or the filing of a complaint to an independent body, such as a children's ombudsperson.[52] Special attention has been given to the child-sensitive treatment of children victims and witnesses in criminal law matters.[53] A study by the European Union showed that child victims or witnesses of crime greatly appreciated the support they received, particularly when provided continuously throughout the proceedings, but did not always feel sufficiently protected due to unfriendly and disrespectful behavior of professionals, such as defense lawyers, judges, and police officers.[54] Cross-cutting principles, such as dignity, non-discrimination, best interests of the child, protection, and participation must be respected. The Guidelines of the Council of Europe (2010) cover issues like the right to be informed, the right to effective assistance, the right to privacy and safety, the right to be protected from hardship during the process, and the right to a remedy. These and other measures are meant to facilitate active and meaningful participation of the child in the proceedings. However, the nature of the proceedings may also affect the level of participation. For instance, one study found that effective participation of juvenile defendants was not possible in adversarial juvenile justice systems.[55]

- A major challenge for judges and other decision makers is their obligation to give due weight to the views of the child in accordance with the age and maturity of the child. Maturity refers to the ability to understand and assess the implications of a particular matter.[56] This seems to suggest that the better the child understands the implications of a matter, the more weight should be given to her or his views. It means that giving weight to the views of the child requires a case-by-case assessment of the maturity of the child. How and by whom that assessment should be made is not clear. I assume, on the basis of my experience as a judge, that it is usually the judge who makes that assessment in light of the judge's meeting and interview with the child, other available information (e.g., from the social worker in the case), and, if necessary, in consultation with a psychologist. Article 12 does not require feedback to the child on the decision made. However, the CRC Committee set a new and specific standard by encouraging states parties to introduce legislative measures requiring decision makers in judicial or administrative proceedings to explain the extent of the consideration given to the views of the child and the consequences for the child.[57] Judgments and rulings of courts affecting children should be duly motivated by and explained to them in language they can understand, particularly those decisions in which the child's views and opinions have not been followed.[58] If that explanation cannot be given in the judgment (e.g., for technical legal reasons), it should be given orally and, as much as possible, by the person who made the decision. In some countries (Netherlands and United Kingdom) there is an emerging practice of producing child-friendly judgments.[59]

3.5 In the Community and Society

In General Comment No. 12, the CRC Committee makes various and very specific recommendations on the participation of children in activities in community and society. For instance, states parties should seek the views of children on all aspects of health provision, including what services are needed, how and where they are best provided, discriminatory barriers to accessing services, and the quality and attitudes of professionals. Information on these aspects could be obtained via, for example, feedback systems for children using services or research and consultative processes.[60] States parties should consult children at the local and national level on all aspects of education policy, such as school curricula, teaching methods, school structures, standards, and budgeting.[61] Similar recommendations are made for play, recreation and sports, child labor, situations of violence, and migration and asylum.[62]

The CRC Committee sets a higher standard of obligation for states parties with respect to adolescents than simply seeking their views. The CRC Committee requires that states parties "should ensure that adolescents are involved in the development, implementation and monitoring of all relevant legislation, policies, services and programs affecting their lives, at school and at the community, local, national and international levels."[63]

With regard to these collective forms of child participation, the CRC Committee welcomes the growing number of local youth parliaments, municipal children's councils, and ad hoc consultations with children while noting that they only allow for a relatively small number of children to engage in their local communities. The CRC Committee recommends that children should be supported and encouraged to form their own child-led organizations and initiatives, which will create space for meaningful participation and representation. The CRC Committee notes that participation opportunities are established in many countries on the district, regional, and federal level while appreciating the significant contribution of UNICEF and NGOs in awareness-raising on children's right to be heard and their participation in all domains of their lives.[64]

The importance of involving children (and adolescents) at the local, national, and international level in matters affecting them is not disputed. An overwhelming body of publications confirms it and provides guidance on such issues as how to organize the participation of children in local and national politics.[65] There are studies on the importance of face-to-face participation of children and adolescents with policymakers[66] and the positive impact of youth councils at the local level.[67] However, there is still a long way to go to achieve effective public participation of children in all states parties to the CRC, and we need more research that measures the actual impact, in term of real changes in law or policy, of this form of participation. In further discussing and researching public participation of children, attention should be given to the following issues.

Articles 12, 13, 14, 15, and 17 of the CRC do not establish an express right to (public) participation and do not establish a legal obligation of states parties to the CRC to ensure involvement of adolescents. The reference to the right to express your views and have them given due weight (Article 12) is rather problematic in the context of public partici-pation. It would require that the weight given to the views of children in the public arena of legislation and policy depends on a case-by-case examination of the views of the child.[68] In practice, the weight of the views of children in public participation most likely depends on various social and political factors, such as the support for the views of chil-dren from civil society organizations and the political will to take these views into account. Finally, the promotion of child participation in accordance with Article 12 implies that participation becomes dependent on the capability of the child to form his or her own views.

I support Meda Couzens's approach to understanding where to situate public partici-pation of children in international human rights law.[69] She starts with reference to Article 21(1) of the Universal Declaration of Human Rights, stating that everyone has the right to take part in the government of his or her country, directly or through freely cho-sen representatives. This right was included in Article 25(a) of the ICCPR and in regional human rights treaties.[70] Couzens's interpretation of these texts suggests that the exist-ence of a general right to participate in public affairs is also applicable to children. However, the UN Human Rights Committee is of the view that Article 25(a) of the ICCPR does not guarantee a right to public participation beyond the electoral rights protected in Article 25(b) and (c). In other words, the right to participate in public affairs can only be enjoyed by persons with the right to vote. So where does that leave children? Possible answers to this question follow.

First, the interpretation of the Human Rights Committee is at least questionable in light of the Vienna Convention on the Law of Treaties. The relevant texts do not suggest that the right to public participation is or can be limited. In particular, limiting this right to persons with electoral rights is not required by the ICCPR or regional human rights treaties. Thus, it could be argued that others without the right to vote, including chil-dren, have the right to public participation.

Second, if the interpretation of the Human rights Committee is to prevail, then one answer would be to give every citizen of a country the right to vote. Measures to dero-gate from the obligation to ensure the right to vote to every citizen are possible only in very specific circumstances (Article 4(1) of the ICCPR). A measure that excludes a whole category of citizens from the right to vote amounts to discrimination. However, the Human Rights Committee is of the view that a restriction based on age is reasonable.[71] I disagree with this opinion, inter alia, because since they were given more than twenty years ago, the rights of the child as enshrined in the CRC have been recognized by 196 states and implemented with a strong emphasis on participation of children in legislation, policy development and implementation, and other facets of public life. The right to vote of every citizen includes every child. The exercise of this right faces some practical problems, such as the need to authorize parent(s) or legal guardian(s) to vote on behalf of the child and the question of when the child should be deemed competent to exercise her or his voting right independently. There seems to be growing support, so far mainly in Europe, for lowering the voting age to sixteen,[72] while some suggest that the voting age could be linked to the minimum age of criminal responsibility.[73] Finally, and despite the questionable interpretation of the Human Rights Committee, states can guarantee in their national laws a right to direct participation for citizens that do not have the right to vote, including children and in quite a number of countries, other excluded or marginalized groups.

4 Concluding Remarks and Recommendations

The participation of children is a very important tool for promoting respect for and implementation of the rights of the child and for the empowerment of the child inter alia as a defender of the human rights of children. In discussing participation of children, a distinction should be made between the individual and collective level.

At the individual level, whenever a decision concerning an individual child has to be made, the child has the right to express her or his own views and is thus a participant in the decision-making process. That applies to decisions made in the context of the family, school, health care, alternative and institutional care, and in the context of legal proceedings. The rule that the views of the child shall be given due weight in accordance with the age and maturity of the child is clearly meant for decisions to be made for an individual child. To extend the applicability of Article 12(1) to groups of children makes application of the rule requiring that due weight be given to the views of the child problematic, as it is unclear how one would assess the age and maturity of a diverse group of children. More generally, because the CRC does not explicitly recognize a general right of the child to participation, the term *right to participation* should be avoided because it potentially undermines respect for the rights enshrined in the CRC to produce a right not recognized in the CRC.

At the collective level, the participation of a group of children, organized or non-organized, in any kind of discussion or decision-making in matters affecting a certain group of children (e.g., students, children with disabilities, indigenous children, asylum-seeking children, children in institutions of alternative care, children in detention centers) should not be based on Article 12. The drafting of Article 12 shows that it was meant for the individual child and not a group of children. We do not need Article 12 as a legal foundation of participation of children in policymaking or other areas. Basing the participation of children in policymaking and other public areas on

Article 12(1) means that this participation is limited to children capable of forming their own views. Public participation should be open for children who are not (yet) capable of forming their views but like to be informed on public issues and thus want to be involved by, for instance, attending meetings of local councils or of political parties. The rights enshrined in Articles 13 and 15 provide a variety of opportunities to participate in a wide range of activities. The right to freedom of expression implies an engagement in social, political, or other matters, including those that do not affect children, with a full use of the right to seek, receive, and impart information and ideas of all kinds (see also Article 17 on the role of mass media). Children can strengthen their participation by establishing associations with the goal of achieving changes in the law or in policies at the national or regional level, whether it is in education, health care, or juvenile justice.

Further strengthening of the participation of children, particularly in the public arena, could be achieved by basing it on the recognized right of every citizen, without any discrimination, to take part in the conduct of public affairs, directly or through freely chosen representatives and the right to vote. I hope that child rights activists, including children defending their rights, will campaign for the formal recognition of the right of children to participate in the conduct of public affairs even when they cannot exercise their right to vote. Furthermore, the most powerful tool for effective participation is the right to vote. Child citizens of countries that have ratified the ICCPR do have the right to vote. They are not excluded by Article 25 of the ICCPR; however, the exercise of this right can be and is de facto in most countries restricted by age (usually under eighteen). Thus, campaigning should first focus on lowering the voting age and as a long-term goal on ensuring that every child can exercise her or his right to vote via a representative or directly by him- or herself.

A variety of research has been conducted on participation of children in both individual decision- making processes and on the participation of groups of children. Most of these studies are limited to experiences in a country or in specific situations, such as education or juvenile justice. Attention has also been given to the perception of participation by children and parents, showing some interesting differences.[74] However, there is no global picture of the extent, quality, and impact of child participation either at the individual or the collective level. Much more research is needed to assess the benefits of child participation and best practices for addressing the main obstacles for meaningful and effective participation of children.

NOTES

1. UN Committee on the Rights of the Child (CRC Committee), *General Comment No. 9: The Rights of Children with Disabilities*, CRC/C/GC/9 (2007); CRC Committee, *General Comment No. 17: Article 31: The Right of the Child to Rest, Leisure, Play, Recreational Activities, Cultural Life and the Arts*, CRC/C/GC/17 (2013).
2. CRC Committee, *Concluding Observations on the Second Report of Bolivia*, UN Doc. CRC/C/15/Add.95 (Oct. 26, 1998), para. 18.

3. See CRC Committee, *Concluding Observations on the First Report of Germany*, UN Doc. CRC/C/15/Add.42 (Nov. 27, 1995), paras. 17 and 29.

4. CRC Committee, *Tenth Anniversary of the Convention on the Rights of the Child Commemorative Meeting: Achievements and Challenges* (excerpted from UN Doc. CRC/C/87, Annex IV, 22nd Sess. (Sept. 30–Oct. 1, 1999), paras. 280, 285, 288 and 289), https://www.ohchr.org/Documents/HRBodies/CRC/Discussions/Recommendations/Recommendations1999.pdf.

5. This General Comment was never issued.

6. CRC Committee, *Tenth Anniversary*, para. 291 under (w).

7. See, e.g., CRC Committee, *Concluding Observations for Estonia*, UN Doc. CRC/C/15/Add.196 (March 17, 2003), para. 27; CRC Committee, *Concluding Observations: Georgia*, UN Doc. CRC/C/15/Add.222 (March 27, 2003), para. 25; CRC Committee, *Concluding Observations: Morocco*, UN Doc. CRC/C/15/Add.211 (July 10, 2003), para. 31(b); CRC Committee, *Concluding Observations: Pakistan*, UN Doc. CRC/C/15/Add.217 (Oct. 27, 2003), para. 37(a); CRC Committee, *Concluding Observations: Peru*, UN Doc. CRC/C/PER/CO/3 (March 14, 2006), para. 32; CRC Committee, *Concluding Observations: Republic of Korea*, UN Doc. CRC/C/15/Add.197 (March 18, 2003), para. 35; CRC Committee, *Concluding Observations: Vietnam*, UN Doc. CRC/C/15/Add.200 (March 18, 2003), para. 30(c).

8. See, e.g., CRC Committee, *Concluding Observations: Zambia,* UN Doc. CRC/C/15/Add.206 (July 2, 2003), para. 27; CRC Committee, *Concluding Observations: Italy*, UN Doc. CRC/C/Add.198 (March 18, 2003), para. 26(b).

9. See, e.g., CRC Committee, *Concluding Observations: China*, UN Doc. CRC/C/CHN/CO/2 (Nov. 27, 2005), paras. 37–40; CRC Committee, *Concluding Observations: Ghana*, UN Doc. CRC/C/GHA/CO/2 (June 8, 2006), paras. 30 and 31; CRC Committee, *Concluding Observations: Ireland*, UN Doc. CRC/C/IRL/CO/2 (Nov. 1, 2006), para. 25; CRC Committee, *Concluding Observations: Latvia*, UN Doc. CRC/C/LVA/CO/2 (June 28, 2006); CRC Committee, *Concluding Observations: Mexico*, UN Doc. CRC/C/MEX/CO/3 (June 8, 2006) CRC Committee, *Concluding Observations: Saudi Arabia*, UN Doc. CRC/C/SAU/CO/2 (March 17, 2006), para. 37.

10. CRC Committee, *Report on the Day of General Discussion on the Right of the Child to Be Heard*, 43rd Sess., Geneva (Sept. 29, 2006), http://www2.ohchr.org/English/bodies/crc/docs/discussion/Final_Recommendations_after_DGD.doc.

11. CRC Committee, *Report on the Day of General Discussion*, Preamble.

12. UN General Assembly, *Resolution S-27/2 A World Fit For Children*, UN Doc. A/RES/S-27/2 (2002) (Declaration para. 7, subpara. 9, and para. 32).

13. For an explanation of why it took so long before the Committee could agree on the text, see Nigel Cantwell, "Are Children's Rights Still Human?," in *The Human Rights of Children: From Visions to Implementation*, ed. Antonella Invernizzi and Jane Williams (New York: Routledge, 2016), 37–59, 56.

14. CRC Committee, *General Comment No. 12: The Right of the Child to Be Heard*, UN Doc. CRC/C/GC/12 (2009).

15. See Tali Gal and Benedetta Faedi Duramy, eds., *International Perspectives and Empirical Findings on Child Participation: From Social Exclusion to Child-Inclusive Policies* (Oxford: Oxford University Press, 2015), 7–8.

16. CRC Committee, *General Comment No. 12*, para. 20. Although this generous interpretation of "capable of forming his or her own views" is amended by a statement in para. 29 that research has shown that information, experience, social and cultural expectations, and levels of support contribute to the child's capacities to form a view.

17. CRC Committee, *General Comment No.12*, paras. 28–30.

18. See Cantwell, "Are Children's Rights Still Human?," 55.

19. See CRC Committee, *General Comment No. 12*, para. 9.

20. See CRC Committee, *General Comment No. 12*, para. 10; Cantwell, "Are Children's Rights Still Human?," 55.

21. See CRC Committee, *General Comment No. 12*, para. 45.

22. See, e.g., CRC Committee, *General Comment No. 20: The Implementation of the Rights of the Child during Adolescence*, UN Doc. CRC/C/GC/20 (2016), para. 23 ("States should ensure that adolescents are involved in the development, implementation and monitoring of all relevant legislation, policies, services and programmes affecting their lives at school and at the community, local, national and international levels.").

23. UN Convention on the Rights of the Child (CRC), G.A. Res. 44/25, 44th Sess., UN Doc. A/RES/44/25 (1989), art. 5. In addition to recognizing parents' critical role, Article 5 also acknowledges the relevance of "members of the extended family or community as provided by local custom, legal guardians or other persons legally responsible for the child." This clause underscores not only the importance of providing the child with direction and guidance in the exercise of his or her rights but also the recognition of the role the family and the community could and should play.

24. See, e.g., Smiljka Tomanovic, "Negotiating Children's Participation and Autonomy within Families," *International Journal of Children's Rights* 11 (January 2003): 51–71.

25. CRC Committee, *General Comment No. 12*, para. 93. See also Afua Twum-Danso, "The Construction of Childhood and the Socialization of Children in Ghana," in *A Handbook of Children and Young People's Participation*, ed. Barry Percy-Smith and Nigel Thomas (London: Routledge 2010), 133–140.

26. See Gerison Lansdown, *Every Child's Right to Be Heard: A Resource Guide on the U.N. Committee on the Rights of the Child General Comment No.12* (London: Save the Children, 2011), 2.

27. South African Children's Act 2005, Act. 38, Sect. 31, http://www.justice.gov.za/legislation/acts/2005-038%20childrensact.pdf.

28. Swedish Code of Parenthood and Guardianship, *Concerning the Exercise of Custody*, Chapter 6, Sect. 11, http://ceflonline.net/wp-content/uploads/Sweden-Parental-Responsibilities-Legislation.pdf (accessed Aug. 17, 2019).

29. CRC Committee, *General Comment No. 7: Implementing Child Rights in Early Childhood*, UN Doc. CRC/C/GC/7/Rev.1 (2006), para. 14.

30. Gerison Lansdown is of the view that in all circumstances the decision must be subject to judicial or administrative review if the child wishes to challenge it. See Lansdown, *Every Child's Right to Be Heard*, 100.

31. Universal Declaration of Human Rights G.A. Res. 217 (III) A, UN Doc. A/RES/217(III) (Dec. 10, 1948), art. 8; International Covenant on Civil and Political Rights (ICCPR), 999 UNTS 171 (1966;entered into force March 23, 1976), art. 2(3).

32. See CRC Committee, *General Comment No. 5: General Measures of Implementation of the Convention on the Rights of the Child (arts. 4, 42 and 44, para.6)*, UN Doc. CRC/GC/2003/5 (2003), paras. 24, 60. See also Nevena Vuckovic Sahovic, Jaap E. Doek, and Jean Zermatten, *The Rights of the Child in International Law* (Berne: Stampfli Publishers, 2012), 391–409.

33. See legislative provisions in this regard in Sweden, Denmark, and The Netherlands and for participation of children organizing themselves into ministries in Mali, Cameroon, Guinea, and Guinee Bissau; Lansdown, *Every Child's Right to Be Heard*, 105 and 107.

34. Ann Quennerstedt, "The Construction of Children's Rights in Education—A Research Synthesis," *International Journal of Children's Rights* 19 (January 2011): 661–678, 671.

35. See Lansdown, *Every Child's Right to Be Heard*, 101; CRC Committee, *General Comment No. 1: The Aims of Education*, U.N. Doc. CRC/GC2001/1 (2001), paras. 5–14.

36. Laura Lundy, " 'Voice' Is Not Enough: Conceptualizing Article 12 of the United Nations Convention on the Rights of the Child," *British Educational Research Journal* 33, no. 6 (January 2007): 927, 942.

37. CRC Committee, *General Comment No. 1*, para. 8

38. For practical Guidelines for listening to children in healthcare, see Lansdown, *Every Child's Right to Be Heard*, 93.

39. CRC Committee, *General Comment No. 4: Adolescent Health and Development in the Context of the Convention on the Rights of the Child*, CRC/GC/2003/4 (2003); CRC Committee, *General Comment No. 20*. General Comment No. 4 focuses on health and development while the scope of General Comment No. 20 is broader.

40. CRC Committee, *General Comment No. 20*, para. 5. We assume that the recommendations made in General Comment No. 4 are applicable to the same age group.

41. CRC Committee, *General Comment No. 20*, para. 101.

42. CRC Committee, *General Comment No. 20*, para. 29.

43. CRC Committee, *General Comment No. 20*, para. 102.

44. See also Lansdown, *Every Child's Right to Be Heard*, 69.

45. Irma Hein, *Children's Competence to Consent to Medical Treatment and Research* (Amsterdam: Amsterdam University Press, 2015); Jozef H. H. M. Dorscheidt and Irma M. Heins, "Medical Research Involving Children—Giving Weight to Children's Views," *International Journal of Children's Rights* 26 (March 2018): 93–116.

46. On direct and indirect hearing the child, see, e.g., Claire Fenton-Glynn, "The Child's Voice in Adoption Proceedings: A European Perspective," *International Journal of Children's Rights* 22 (January 2024): 135–163, 157–160.

47. CRC Committee, *General Comment No. 12*, para. 32.

48. CRC Committee, *General Comment No. 12*, para. 20.

49. CRC Committee, *General Comment No. 12*, para. 30.

50. Anne-Mette Magnussen and Marit Skivenes, "The Child's Opinion and Position in Care Proceedings," *International Journal of Children's Rights* 23 (June 2015): 705–723.

51. Taria Poso and Rosi Enroos, "The Representation of Children's Views in Finnish Court Decisions Regarding Care Orders," *International Journal of Children's Rights* 25 (2017): 736–753.

52. See, e.g., Committee of Ministers of the Council of Europe, *Guidelines of the Committee of Ministers of the Council of Europe on Child-Friendly Justice* (Strasbourg: Council of Europe, 2010).

53. UN Economic and Social Council, *Guidelines on Justice in Matters Involving Child Victims and Witnesses of Crime*, UN Doc. E/RES/2005/20 (July 22, 2005).

54. European Union Agency for Fundamental Rights (FRA), *Child-Friendly Justice: Perspectives and Experiences of children Involved in Judicial Proceedings as Victims, Witnesses or Parties in Nine EU Member States* (Luxembourg: Publications Office of the European Union, 2015).

55. Stephanie Rap. *The Participation of Juvenile Defendants in Youth Court* (Utrecht: Pallas Publications, 2013).

56. CRC Committee, *General Comment No. 12*, para. 30. The confusing part of this paragraph is that the Committee links maturity to the capacity to express views. The condition in Article 12, para. 1, "capable of forming his or her own views," is not linked to maturity, and the Committee is thus of the view that states should assume that a child, also the very young ones, are capable of forming views. CRC Committee, *General Comment No. 12*, para. 20.

57. CRC Committee, *General Comment No. 12*, para. 33.

58. Committee of Ministers, *Guidelines of the Committee of Ministers of the Council of Europe on Child-Friendly Justice*.

59. See, e.g., Lancashire County Council v. M & Ors (Rev 1), 2016 EWFC 9 (Feb. 4, 2016), www.bailii.org/ew/cases/EWFC/HCJ/2016/9.html. And, for two 2017 district court decisions in the Netherlands see ECLI:NL:RBROT:2017:911 and ECLI:NL:RBMNE:2017:1541.

60. CRC Committee, *General Comment No. 12*, para. 104.

61. CRC Committee, *General Comment No. 12*, para. 111.

62. CRC Committee, *General Comment No. 12*, paras. 115, 117, 118 and 123.

63. CRC Committee, *General Comment No. 20*, para. 23.

64. CRC Committee, *General Comment No.12*, paras. 127–130.

65. See, e.g., United Nations Children's Fund (UNICEF), *Child Participation in Local Governance. A UNICEF Guidance Note* (New York: UNICEF, 2017); Council of Europe Children's Rights Division and Youth Department. *Child Participation Assessment Tool* (Strasbourg: Council of Europe, 2016); UNICEF, A *Handbook on Child Participation in Parliament* (Geneva: Inter-Parliamentary Union, 2011); Save the Children, "The European Union and Child Participation," December 2011, https://www.savethechildren.net/sites/default/files/libraries/Child-Participation-Position-Paper-FINAL.pdf.

66. Chelsea Marshall, Bronagh Byrne, and Laura Lundy, "Face to Face: Children and Young People's Right to Participate in Public Decision-Making," in Gal and Duramy, *International Perspectives and Empirical Findings on Child Participation*, 357–380.

67. Catherine Forde and Shirley Martin, "Children and Young People's Right to Participate: National and Local Youth Councils in Ireland," *International Journal of Children's Rights* 24, no. 1 (April 2016): 135–154.

68. CRC Committee, *General Comment No. 12*, para. 29.

69. Meda Couzens, "Exploring Participation as a Vehicle for Child Participation in Governance: A View from South Africa," *International Journal of Children* Rights 20, no. 4 (July 2012): 674–704.

70. American Convention on Human Rights, O.A.S.T.S. No. 36, 1144 UNTS 123 (entered into force July 18, 1978), art. 23; African Charter on Human and Peoples Rights, OAU Doc. CAB/LEG/67/3 rev. 5, 21 ILM 58(entered into force Oct. 21, 1986), art. 13, para. 1.

71. UN Human Rights Committee, *CCPR General Comment No. 25: The Right to Participate in Public Affairs, Voting Rights and the Right of Equal Access to Public Service*, CCPR/C/21/Rev.1/Add.7 (July 12, 1996), para. 4.

72. See, e.g., CRC Committee, *Concluding Observations on The Combined Third and Fourth Periodic Report of Austria, Adopted by the Committee at Its Sixty-First Session (17 September—5 October 2012)*, UN Doc. CRC/C/AUT/CO/3–4 (2012), para. 3; CRC Committee, *Concluding Observations of the CRC Committee on the Fifth Periodic Report of the United Kingdom of Great Britain and Northern Ireland*, UN Doc. CRC/C/GBR/CO/5 (2016), paras. 32 and 33; CRC Committee, *General Comment No. 20*, para. 24; Council of Europe. *Motion for Resolution: Expansion of Democracy by Lowering the Voting Age*, Doc. 11895 (May 4, 2009).

73. See Mark Henaghan, "Article 12 of the UN Convention on the Rights of Children: Where Have We Come From, Where Are We Now and Where to from Here?," *International Journal of Children's Rights* 25 (August 2017): 537–552, 549. This article focuses on the situation in New Zealand. The minimum age of criminal responsibility (MACR) is ten, and thus Henaghan is in favor of setting the voting age at ten. Perhaps this is a reason, instead, for the government to increase the MACR.

74. See, e.g., Hanita Kosher, "What Children and Parents Think about Children's Right to Participation," *International Journal of Children's Rights* 26, no. 2 (May 2018): 295–328.

CHAPTER 14

....

JUVENILE JUSTICE

....

TON LIEFAARD

1 INTRODUCTION

INTERNATIONAL instruments and jurisprudence regulating children's rights in the context of juvenile justice recognize that state intervention—and consequently limitations of human rights and fundamental freedoms of an individual child—can be justified when that child is in conflict with the law.[1] The justification lies in the protection of the interests of others and/or society as a whole, which encompasses the rehabilitation and reintegration of the child and which gives juvenile justice a fundamentally different orientation than adult criminal justice. International children's rights, as laid down in the almost universally ratified UN Convention on the Rights of the Child (CRC),[2] aim to protect the rights and interests of the individual child by stipulating that states parties are under the obligation to

> recognize the right of every child alleged as, accused of, or recognized as having infringed the penal law to be treated in a manner consistent with the promotion of the child's sense of dignity and worth, which reinforces the child's respect for the human rights and fundamental freedoms of others and which takes into account the child's age and the desirability of promoting the child's reintegration and the child's assuming a constructive role in society.   (Article 40(1))

This international children's rights approach has resulted in an extensive and comprehensive legal framework, developed at the international and regional level, consisting of specific rules with regard to the treatment of children in conflict with the law. These rules revolve around each individual child's entitlement to be treated fairly and with respect for his[3] inherent dignity and in a child-specific manner. This essentially calls for a criminal justice system specifically designed for and tailored to the needs and deeds of children (Article 40(3)) and finds support in a growing body of scientific research on child development, including brain development.[4] In a landmark case, *Roper v.*

Simmons,[5] in which the death penalty was ruled unconstitutional as applied to minors, the US Supreme Court held that children are less culpable than adults due to their "susceptibility to immature and irresponsible behavior." The Court in *Roper* observed that "it would be misguided to equate the failings of a minor with those of an adult, for a greater possibility exists that a minor's character deficiencies will be reformed."[6]

Specific attention for children in conflict with the law predates the CRC, to earlier recognition in domestic juvenile criminal justice systems, which began to emerge at the beginning of the twentieth century, mostly in Western Europe and the United States.[7] This also explains why the first international instrument on children's rights, the Declaration of Geneva, adopted by the League of Nations in 1924, explicitly refers to the delinquent child as a child that "must be reclaimed."[8]

This chapter sheds light on the international children's rights framework for juvenile justice and elaborates on its implications for juvenile justice systems at the domestic level. Without disregarding the importance of prevention of juvenile delinquency and the interaction between the juvenile justice system and other systems that are relevant for children and their families, such as the welfare system, the child protection system, or the (mental) health care system, this chapter focuses on the juvenile justice system only. It begins, like international children's rights standards do, by recognizing that—across the globe—children are involved in criminal justice systems, and that is likely to remain the case. After elaborating on the international legal framework and its key instruments, and the development of the international agenda with regard to juvenile justice, the chapter addresses some of the main implications of international children's rights for domestic juvenile justice systems, more specifically the establishment of a child-specific criminal justice system and the safeguarding of fair treatment, including the right to participate effectively in justice proceedings. The chapter subsequently addresses some of the key challenges with regard to the implementation of children's rights at the domestic level, in light of the particular complexity of and controversies related to juvenile justice. The chapter concludes by suggesting that despite the many challenges, much has been achieved, which makes the future of children's rights implementation in the context of juvenile justice a hopeful one.

2 International Children's Rights and Juvenile Justice at the International Level

2.1 Standard-Setting at the International Level

The CRC forms the core of a comprehensive international legal framework that has particular meaning for juvenile justice. Article 40 of the CRC builds on and essentially codifies the 1985 UN Standard Minimum Rules for the Administration of Juvenile

Justice (Beijing Rules),[9] which were the first relevant set of juvenile justice standards developed at the international level and provide rules regarding a wide variety of aspects of juvenile justice, including the minimum age of criminal responsibility, investigation and prosecution, adjudication and disposition, and (non-)institutional treatment. The CRC provision proclaims the establishment of a specific justice system for children and sets the objectives of juvenile justice (paras. 3 and 1, respectively). It also provides that children in conflict with the law are entitled to be treated fairly by granting them fair trial rights (para. 2.). In addition to CRC Article 40, CRC Article 37(b) prohibits torture and other forms of cruel, inhuman, or degrading treatment or punishment (para. a) and compels states parties to use deprivation of liberty only as a last resort and for the shortest appropriate period of time. CRC Article 37(c) and (d) regulate the treatment of children deprived of liberty and provide procedural safeguards. Together with the CRC's general principles,[10] CRC Articles 40 and 37 have served as a catalyst for further standard setting at the international and regional level.

At the international level, two additional instruments were adopted by the UN General Assembly in 1990: the UN Rules for the Protection of Juveniles Deprived of their Liberty (also known as the Havana Rules)[11] and the UN Guidelines for the Prevention of Juvenile Delinquency (the Riyadh Guidelines).[12] The Havana Rules "are intended to establish minimum standards...for the protection of juveniles deprived of their liberty in all forms, consistent with human rights and fundamental freedoms, and with a view to counteracting the detrimental effects of all types of detention and to fostering integration in society."[13] To this end, they provide detailed rules, including rules on admission, conditions, contact with the outside world, disciplinary measures, inspection and complaint procedures, and reintegration. The Riyadh Guidelines aim to guide UN member states on how to set up a successful strategy on the prevention of juvenile delinquency that is grounded in human rights and child-centered, that is: a strategy that "[y]oung persons should have an active role and partnership within society and should not be considered as mere objects of socialization and control."[14] Like the Beijing Rules, the Havana Rules and the Riyadh Guidelines are not legally binding. However, the CRC Committee has been consistent in its call upon states parties to integrate these international standards in a "national and comprehensive national juvenile justice policy."[15] It has also used the Beijing Rules and the Havana Rules for the interpretation of the obligations of states parties under the CRC[16] and calls upon states to "fully implement" the Havana Rules.[17] This finds support in the way regional human rights courts and domestic courts include such sources of soft international law, as the Beijing Rules and the Havana Rules in their case law as a basis of interpretation.[18] Consequently, it can be argued that both the CRC and the UN resolutions ought to be seen as components of a comprehensive children's rights framework regulating juvenile justice.

General human rights instruments that are particularly relevant for criminal justice and target children like all other human beings complement the children's rights framework.[19] This is particularly true for the provisions of the 1966 International Covenant on Civil and Political Rights (ICCPR)[20] on fair trial (Articles 14 and 15), on treatment and punishment of individuals (Articles 6 and 7), and on deprivation of liberty (Articles 9 and 10) that have informed the drafters of the CRC and formed the basis for CRC Articles 40 and 37.[21] In addition, ICCPR Article 24 recognizes that a child is entitled to a higher level of protection "as... required by his status as a minor, on the part of the family, society and the State," a notion that underlies the CRC as well and justifies a child-specific focus in the context of juvenile justice. Other general instruments, such as the 1985 Convention against Torture (CAT),[22] the 1965 International Convention on the Elimination of All Forms of Racial Discrimination,[23] the 2015 UN Standard Minimum Rules for the Treatment of Prisoners (the Nelson Mandela Rules),[24] and the 1990 UN Standard Minimum Rules for Non-custodial Measures (the Tokyo Rules)[25] also are relevant for children in conflict with the law.

2.2 Standard-Setting at the Regional Level

In different regions, various specific instruments and case law add to the international legal framework relevant for juvenile justice. The European and the Inter-American regions report the most prominent developments in this regard. Again, such general human rights instruments as the American Convention on Human Rights (ACHR) and the European Convention on Human Rights bear relevance for children and occasionally refer to children.[26] The Inter-American Court of Human Rights and the Inter-American Commission on Human Rights (Inter-American Commission) have developed a growing body of judgments and decisions, respectively, with specific relevance for juvenile justice, including cases involving the deprivation of liberty and arrest and the detention and ill treatment of children by the police.[27] An important example is the landmark case *Villangrán Morales v. Guatemala* (also known as the "Street Children" case), in which the Court held that the state had inadequately protected the "street children" against "a systematic practice of aggression... carried out by members of the State security forces, which included threats, persecution, torture, forced disappearance and homicide."[28] In having applied or tolerated "the prevailing pattern of violence against 'street children' in Guatemala," which "culminated in the death of the minors,"[29] the state had disregarded its obligations under ACHR Article 19, which grants "[e]very minor child the right to measures of protection as required by his condition as a minor on the part of his family, society, and the state." The Court found that "[b]oth the [ACHR] and the [CRC] form part of a very comprehensive international *corpus juris* for the protection of the child that should help... establish the content and scope of [Article 19 of the ACHR]."[30] It emphasized the need to safeguard "non-discrimination, special assistance for children deprived of their family environment, the guarantee of survival and development of the child, the right to an adequate standard of living, and the social rehabilitation of all children who are abandoned or exploited."[31] As Monica Feria-Tinta observes, "[i]n the CRC, the Inter-American System has found an important tool that has contributed to better state the law in the Americas,"[32] which points at the Court's leading role in integrating international and regional children's rights standards; a role in which the Court was joined later by the Inter-American Commission, which additionally considered the views of the CRC Committee expressed in its General Comments and Concluding Observations as relevant reference material for interpretation purposes.[33]

At the European level, the Committee of Ministers of the Council of Europe has issued recommendations and guidelines that are relevant for the juvenile justice systems of the forty-seven member states. The most important ones are the 2003 Recommendation concerning new ways of dealing with juvenile delinquency and the role of juvenile justice,[34] the 2008 European Rules for juvenile offenders subject to sanctions or measures[35] (European Rules for Juvenile Offenders), and the 2010 Guidelines on child-friendly justice (the Guidelines).[36] While the 2003 Recommendation provides recommendations on how to respond to juvenile delinquency in light of contemporary juvenile justice and scientific insights, the European Rules for juvenile offenders set specific rules for the protection of the rights and interests of juvenile offenders subjected to custodial and non-custodial interventions. The Guidelines provide guidance to Council of Europe member states on how to enable children to participate effectively in justice proceedings, including juvenile justice proceedings. The Guidelines have emerged from the case law of the European Court of Human Rights (European Court) and the CRC Committee's General Comment No. 10, in which a child's right to effective participation has been recognized as part of the right to a fair trial.[37] Since their adoption, the Guidelines have informed the European Court's case law in matters related to justice proceedings, including juvenile justice,[38] and legislation developed by the European Union, specifically on the protection of children in conflict with the law.[39] The Guidelines serve as an example for similar standard-setting initiatives in other parts of the world and by certain professional organizations.[40] In addition to case law on effective participation, the European Court has developed juvenile justice case law, specifically on the right to legal assistance during police interrogations,[41] the use of pre-trial detention,[42] and on the conditions of detention.[43] The Court has, thus, incorporated international children's rights standards, including soft law instruments, in its jurisprudence under the European Convention on Human Rights.[44] In addition, it has drawn upon the reports and standards of the European Committee on the Prevention of Torture, which target the protection of children deprived of their liberty across the Council of Europe.[45]

2.3 A Comprehensive International Legal Framework and the Emerging Global Interest in Juvenile Justice

These regional developments show that the different standard-setting initiatives at the international and regional level are interconnected. As a result, the world has witnessed the emergence of a comprehensive international legal framework of human and children's rights standards relevant to juvenile justice. At the same time, it is fair to say that, so far, not all parts of the world have been reached. Thus, there remain questions as to what extent this international legal framework on juvenile justice represents a universal movement and the extent to which there is support at the national level in all countries, notwithstanding the CRC Committee's admonition that a juvenile justice system that is compliant with the CRC and related international standards "will provide States parties with possibilities to respond to children in conflict with the law in an effective manner serving not only the best interests of children, but also of the short- and long-term interests of the society at large."[46]

The development of the international children's rights framework relevant for juvenile justice, which started with the adoption of the 1985 Beijing Rules and the CRC, forms part of an emerging and global interest in this particular field that has manifested itself at the international, regional, and domestic level. It has paved the way for law reform in many domestic jurisdictions[47] and for a growing body of jurisprudence, internationally and domestically.[48] In addition, it has raised significant awareness around the importance of children's rights protection in this particular field and has contributed to our understanding of the implementation of children's rights and related challenges. Over the years, numerous reports have been produced by intergovernmental agencies, bodies, and representatives[49] as well as civil society organizations and coalitions.[50] These reports not only show the gaps and challenges with regard to implementation; they also provide guidance and support on how to safeguard the generally vulnerable position of children in conflict with the law.

3 Implications of International Children's Rights for Juvenile Justice

International children's rights have many implications for juvenile justice systems at the domestic level.[51] There are two assumptions underlying CRC Article 40.[52] First, children in conflict with the law are entitled to be treated in a child-specific manner. Second, each child is entitled to be treated fairly and with respect for his inherent dignity. This section elaborates on these "limbs" of the CRC framework and addresses some of their main implications.

3.1 A Specific Justice System for Children

The call for a specific justice system for children can be found in CRC Article 40(3), which provides that "States Parties shall seek to promote the establishment of laws, procedures, authorities and institutions specifically applicable to children alleged as, accused of, or recognized as having infringed the penal law." The CRC itself does not provide much further guidance on this call for specificity, unlike, for example, ACHR Article 5(5), which proclaims the establishment of "specialized tribunals" for minors.

Article 40 does, however, require the establishment of a minimum age of criminal responsibility and "measures dealing with [children in conflict with the law] without resorting to judicial proceedings," which refers to "diversion" (see the following section). More guidance can be found in the Beijing Rules, CRC Committee General Comment No. 10, and CRC Article 40(1), which elaborate on the specific objectives of juvenile justice (section 3.1.1) and underscore the significance of specialization (section 3.1.2).

3.1.1 *The Objectives of the Juvenile Justice System—Pedagogical Orientation*

According to CRC Article 40(1), children subjected to criminal justice proceedings must be treated in a manner that takes into account the age of the child and that focuses on the child's reintegration in society. According to the CRC Committee, this means that the juvenile justice system ought to recognize that "children differ from adults in their physical and psychological development, and their emotional and educational needs," which "constitute the basis for the lesser culpability of children in conflict with the law."[53] It also means that children should be treated differently from adults and that state intervention should give primary consideration to the individual interests of the child offender and his future role in society. This call for a specific approach for children reflects a pedagogical or educational orientation, which makes the juvenile justice system fundamentally different from the adult criminal justice system.

CRC Article 40(1) also refers to the "the promotion of child's sense of dignity and worth, which reinforces the child's respect for the human rights and fundamental freedoms of others." This provision should be understood in light of the aims of education as laid down in CRC Article 29 and shows that prevention (i.e., the prevention of recidivism) is a key focus point of juvenile justice.[54] That is not to say that the juvenile justice system should not recognize the more general objectives of criminal justice, including retribution, deterrence, protection of society, and the restoration and reparation for victims and communities (see also CRC Article 39). The CRC Committee underscores, however, that "the protection of the best interests of the child means, for instance, that the traditional objectives of criminal justice, such as retribution, must give way to rehabilitation and restorative justice objectives in dealing with child offenders," which "can be done in concert with attention to effective public safety."[55]

The pedagogical orientation and strong focus on education and reintegration also imply that the potential negative impact of a justice intervention on the child's short- and long-term interests should be acknowledged, which essentially comes down to a call for the use of juvenile justice interventions as an *ultimum remedium*. This is directly linked with the prevention of juvenile delinquency,[56] the prevention of discrimination in the context of juvenile justice,[57] the exclusion of status offenses from prosecution,[58] and the setting of a minimum age of criminal responsibility (MACR). According to CRC Article 40(3)(a), "State Parties shall seek to promote…establishment of a minimum age below which children shall be presumed not to have the capacity to infringe the penal law." As Jaap Doek observes, the MACR is about the age at which a child can be prosecuted and held criminally accountable for committing an offense.[59] The main purpose of the MACR is to recognize that there is a certain group of children who should not be prosecuted because of the irrefutable presumption that they are not mature enough to be held criminally accountable. At the same time, it is important to recognize that children underneath the MACR may be involved in criminal offences, which raises the question of how to respond to these children in an effective, rights-based manner.[60]

The call for states parties to use diversion "[w]henever appropriate and desirable"[61]— instead of resorting to formal judicial proceedings—should also be understood as part of the pedagogical orientation of a child-specific criminal justice system. Diversion serves multiple objectives, including avoiding the exposure of children to the negative impact of formal judicial proceedings, such as stigmatization, which could jeopardize reintegration. In addition, diversion serves the objective of effectuating a quick response to criminal behavior, since it aims to keep the child from going through lengthy court proceedings, which is considered important for the effectiveness of justice interventions.[62] The CRC provides states with the discretion to decide "on the exact nature and content of the measures" when using diversion.[63] The CRC Committee elaborates further in its General Comment No. 10 on the meaning of diversion and the importance of sharing good practices and highlights the importance of a full respect for the human rights of the child and legal safeguards.[64] Among others, this means that diversion should be used only when there is "compelling evidence" and that the child "freely and voluntarily admits responsibility."[65] The CRC Committee notes that "it is clear that a variety of community based programmes have been developed, such as community service, supervision and guidance by, for example, social workers or probation officers, family conferencing and other forms of restorative justice including restitution to and compensation of victims."[66]

CRC Article 40(1)'s reference to the age of the child also underscores the need for a child-specific focus, refers to differences between children in terms of their developmental stage, and can be seen as a directive to treat children in accordance with their age and maturity.[67] This has implications for their individual accountability (and therefore links to the MACR), the determination of the appropriate intervention, and the effective participation of children, including by ensuring their right to information, for example, on charges and dispositions. The age of the child also plays a role in relation to other critical issues for children, such as the involvement of parents or legal guardians[68] and the deprivation their liberty.[69]

3.1.2   *Specificity and Specialization*

One may wonder whether the call for a specific juvenile justice system presupposes that a state should separate its justice system for children entirely from the adult system. CRC Article 40(3), as well as CRC Committee's interpretation, suggests that specificity and specialization matters more than strict separation.[70] The safeguarding of specific treatment or punishment for children can be realized through the inclusion of child-specific elements in existing legislation, procedures, and policies and through specialization of the authorities and institutions involved. Therefore, it seems not necessary to draw up separate legislation for children, even though many countries have developed separate legislation regulating juvenile justice, which certainly contributes to greater child-specificity in the focus of the justice system.[71] States will meet the requirements of CRC Article 40(3) if they include special juvenile justice provisions in existing substantive and procedural legislation regulating the criminal procedure and penal law, like many European countries have done in various ways.[72] In general, states' willingness, efforts, and need to adopt special juvenile justice acts depend on their already existing legal frameworks.[73]

In addition to legislation, specific implementation measures for children are required to make the existing justice infrastructure and its actors more sensitive to children and to children's rights. According to the CRC Committee, states parties should "develop and implement a comprehensive juvenile justice policy."[74] This policy should also embrace the proclaimed general principles of the CRC, Articles 2, 3, 6 and 12,[75] and encompass other relevant provisions, such as CRC Article 39, on the recovery and reintegration of victims. Specialization of authorities and institutions, including police, law enforcement, judicial authorities, lawyers, probation services, and institutions, should be part of this policy as well.[76]

Although the international legal framework does not seem to force states to separate children in conflict with the law entirely from adults, a stricter approach may be required concerning the use of deprivation of liberty. Article 37(c) of the CRC provides that children should be separated from adults if they are deprived of their liberty. This provision builds on ICCPR Article 10,[77] which calls for strict separation or segregation of children in pre-trial detention or imprisoned from adults. The rationale behind this requirement is that children must be protected against the negative influence of adult detainees or prisoners, including violence and abuse and criminal contamination.[78] In fact, the best interests of the child standard, which should be the paramount consideration in this situation, requires separation, thereby ruling out administrative justifications for mixing children and adults.[79]

The separation requirement should, however, also be understood in light of the objectives of juvenile justice, which assumes a child-specific approach with a clear pedagogical orientation. In other words, it is not enough to build a separate institution for children. Such institutions should be regulated and equipped in such a way that they safeguard a specific and specialized approach for children, including education and reintegration programs, which may, if appropriate, also include mental health treatment or drug rehabilitation. In the context of deprivation of liberty, it has been argued that education, specific treatment if appropriate, and reintegration programs are essential elements of the child's legal status under Article 37(c) of the CRC. In other words, children who are deprived of liberty are entitled to be supported in their reintegration, an obligation of the state that is inherent to the decision to deprive a child of his liberty, regardless of the justification for it.[80]

It can be concluded that specificity and specialization are key in light of the objectives of juvenile justice. Moreover, an over emphasis on separation runs the risk of disregarding that children have the same entitlements as adults revolving around the requirement of fair treatment. Treating children in conflict with the law with fairness and with respect for their inherent dignity can be considered fundamental in light of the need for the system to reinforce the child's respect for the human rights and fundamental freedoms of others and the role that this plays in their reintegration.[81] Understandably, the CRC Committee raises the question: "If the key actors in juvenile justice, such as police officers, prosecutors, judges and probation officers, do not fully respect and protect [the child's right to be treated fairly], how can they expect that with such poor examples the child will respect the human rights and fundamental freedom of others?"[82] The right of the child to a fair trial starts with the assumption that children have the same fair trial rights but that—also in this regard—child specificity matters, both in terms of specific entitlements and specific implementation.

3.2 Fair Trial—Child-Friendly Justice

3.2.1 Children's Right to a Fair Trial—Equal and Specific Rights

The starting point of human rights law is that there should be no distinction between adults and children as far as the right to a fair trial (or due process) is concerned. "All persons shall be equal before the courts and tribunals," according to ICCPR Article 14(1), which served as the foundation of Article 40(2) of the CRC, together with ICCPR Article 15, embodying the principle of legality, including the prohibition of retroactive justice and sentencing.[83] Consequently, Article 40 of the CRC repeats fundamental fair trial rights, in particular: the presumption of innocence,[84] the right not to incriminate oneself,[85] the right to prompt information on the charges in a language one understands,[86] the right to be tried before a competent, independent, and impartial authority or judicial body,[87] the right to cross-examine witnesses,[88] and the right to free assistance of an interpreter.[89]

Specifically for children, CRC Article 40(2) lists additional fair trial rights or formulates certain rights in such a way that they have more specific meaning for children. First, a child alleged as or accused of having infringed the penal law is entitled to have the criminal trial determined "without delay by a competent, independent and impartial authority or judicial body."[90] The use of the wording "without delay"— rather than "without undue delay" or "within reasonable time"[91]—assumes that children are entitled to a trial that is speedier.[92] According to the CRC Committee, this assumption is based on the "[international] consensus that for children in conflict with the law the time between the commission of the offence and the final response to this act should be as short as possible."[93] Another child-specific element of CRC Article 40(2) is the right of the child to have his privacy "fully respected at all stages of the proceedings."[94] According to the CRC Committee, this implies that trial in juvenile court should "as a rule"[95] be held behind closed doors—*in camera*. The child's right to privacy also relates to criminal records. The CRC Committee recommends that states develop legislation which provides that the criminal records of a child be erased once he reaches the age of eighteen and should not thereafter be used against the same offender in adult proceedings.[96]

Furthermore, CRC Article 40(2) explicitly refers to the child's parents or legal guardians, who can be present during hearings to provide general psychological and emotional assistance to the child. Parents can also play a role in relation to information on the charges, which the child should receive "as soon as possible"[97] and in a child-friendly manner.[98] The reference to parents (or legal guardians) fits in the more general recognition in the CRC of the child-parent/family relationship, also in light of the child's evolving capacities.[99] CRC Article 37(c) provides that the child who is deprived of liberty has the right to maintain contact with his family, unless this is not regarded as being in the best interests of the child. Article 40(2) of the CRC contains the same best interests clause, which underscores the importance of recognizing that parental involvement is not always in the child's interests and can therefore be limited or even excluded.[100]

Finally, it is important to mention the child's right to legal or other appropriate assistance.[101] The European Court of Human Rights has recognized that, as part of the right to a fair trial, an arrested child has the right to legal counsel during the initial police interrogations, including the right to have a lawyer *present* during these interrogations free of charge.[102] The CRC Committee has taken the position that legal or other appropriate assistance should be free of charge and recommends that "adequate legal assistance" be provided "as much as possible."[103] There is a potential tension between the legal protection offered to children, particularly in the earliest stages of the criminal justice process, and the importance of responding diligently and in a pedagogically effective manner.[104] A lawyer may not be available, for practical reasons, which could result in police custody or detention until the lawyer arrives. In addition, lawyers may not be sufficiently specialized to understand that in the first stages there may be other options, including diversion, which may affect the defense strategy and, for example, the level of cooperation and the usage of the right to remain silent.[105] This underscores the need for specialized lawyers. Non-legal assistance, for example by a social worker, also may support good outcomes, and it is important to note that the CRC leaves room for providing mere non-legal assistance.[106] It can be assumed that the quality of the assistance matters the most.[107] At the same time, the importance of legal assistance, particularly during the first stages, should not be underestimated.[108] One may also wonder why children in conflict with the law do not have the mandatory right to legal assistance.[109] Children deprived of their liberty have the right to legal *and* other appropriate assistance.[110]

3.2.2 *Right to Effective Participation—Child-Friendly Justice*

The right of the child to effective participation as part of the right to a fair trial was first recognized by the European Court of Human Rights in the landmark case *T. & V. v. UK* (Bulger case).[111] In this case, the European Court observed, with explicit reference to CRC Article 40, that "it is essential that a child charged with an offence is dealt with in a manner which takes full account of his age, level of maturity and intellectual and emotional capacities, and that steps are taken to promote his ability to understand and participate in the proceedings."[112] In this particular case, the Court ultimately concluded that the two young boys were unable to participate effectively, since it is was "highly unlikely" that they would have felt "sufficiently uninhibited, in the tense courtroom and under public scrutiny, to have consulted with [their lawyers] during the trial or, indeed, that, given [their] immaturity and [their] disturbed emotional state, [they] would have been capable outside the courtroom of cooperation with [their] lawyers and giving them information for the purposes of [their] defence."[113] In *S.C. v U.K.*, the European Court ruled that " 'effective participation'...presupposes that the accused has a broad understanding of the nature of the trial process and of what is at stake for him or her, including the significance of any penalty which may be imposed" and that Article 6's right to a fair trial does not require that a child on trial should "understand or be capable of understanding every point of law or evidential detail."[114] This case law, in which the court essentially highlighted specific aspects of effective participation, was later embraced by the CRC Committee in its General Comment No. 10[115] and paved the way for the development of the concept of "child-friendly justice."[116] According to the CRC Committee, the right to effective participation has implications for each stage of the juvenile justice process[117] and revolves around Rule 14 of the Beijng Rules, which provides that proceedings "shall be conducted in an atmosphere of understanding, which shall allow the juvenile to participate therein and to express herself or himself freely."[118] The CRC Committee observes that the child "needs to comprehend the charges, and possible consequences and penalties, in order to direct the legal representative, to challenge witnesses, to provide an account of events, and to make appropriate decisions about evidence, testimony and the measure(s) to be imposed." In addition, it notes that "[t]aking into account the child's age and maturity may also require modified courtroom procedures and practices," that "a child cannot be heard effectively where the environment is intimidating, hostile, insensitive or inappropriate for her or his age," and that "[p]articular attention needs to be paid to the provision and delivery of child-friendly information, adequate support for self-advocacy, appropriately trained staff, design of court rooms, clothing of judges and lawyers."[119] In other words, juvenile justice proceedings must be both "accessible and child-appropriate,"[120] which according to the CRC Committee, also means that "[t]he court and other hearings of a child in conflict with the law should be conducted behind closed doors."[121] These CRC Committee recommendations find support in research on effective participation of children in youth court proceedings[122] and also are supported by children themselves.[123]

The Guidelines on child-friendly justice adopted by the Council of Europe in 2010 build on the child's right to be heard and the recognition of the right to effective participation and provide specific guidance to member states on how to make justice systems more child-friendly.[124] States should consider the position of the child before, during, and after justice proceedings and safeguard access to information; ensure the protection of private and family life as well as access to legal counsel and representation; avoid undue delay; and ensure the provision of an appropriate environment in and around judicial proceedings (including after disposition) and child-specific training for professionals.[125]

In conclusion, the international children's rights framework recognizes that children in conflict with the law have the right to be treated fairly, which includes the right to participate effectively in justice proceedings and comes with child-specific implications.

As previously mentioned, there may be a tension between safeguarding the right to a fair trial and the pedagogical orientation of juvenile justice. A good understanding of the specific context in which the balancing exercise has to take place seems to be a prerequisite for an effective implementation of children's rights. Interdisciplinary research aiming to achieve a better understanding of the meaning of children's rights in the context of juvenile justice could assist in supporting states to live up to their obligations under international law.[126] Attempts to develop regional standards, such as the Guidelines on child-friendly justice, assist states in this regard. It is also worth noting that the Guidelines were drafted with input from children and that there has been research on their implementation,[127] research which should be supported and be used to carefully evaluate the meaning of child-friendly justice for children in conflict with the law and juvenile justice professionals.[128]

4 IMPLEMENTATION OF CHILDREN'S RIGHTS: REFORM AND PERSISTENT CHALLENGES

4.1 Juvenile Justice Reform

Over the past three decades, juvenile justice reform has taken place across the globe, and the influence of international children's rights on this reform cannot be denied.[129] As noted above, many states have developed or adjusted legislation on juvenile justice in order to integrate children's rights standards. A growing body of regional and domestic jurisprudence is safeguarding a higher level of protection of children in conflict with the law (see section 2). Countries report institutional reform, such as the establishment of specialized juvenile justice tribunals or specialized services for children in conflict with the law.[130] There is also a growing interest in the use of diversion—in some countries with a significant reduction of the number of children in the formal juvenile justice system as a result[131]—and in multidisciplinary approaches toward juvenile delinquency. Much more than before, juvenile justice reform can benefit from recent scientific insights in child development, brain development, effective juvenile justice interventions, and requirements for the effective participation of children in justice proceedings.[132] And these insights confirm key juvenile justice principles, which have been embraced by international children's rights standards, such as the recognition that children are less culpable than adults, the acknowledgment that a fair, tailored, and child-specific pedagogical approach toward children in conflict with the law is more likely to have positive outcomes for both the child and society, and the need to protect children against the negative impact of the juvenile justice system and to support them in navigating through that system.[133]

4.2 Implementation of International Children's Rights: A Serious Challenge in Different Ways

At the same time, the implementation of international children's rights in the context of juvenile justice remains a serious challenge.[134] The rights of children in conflict with the law are often not or not fully respected with negative consequences for their short- and long-term interests.[135] As the CRC Committee observes, this is likely to have a negative impact on society's interests as well.[136] Among others, there are persistent concerns about the widespread use of deprivation of their liberty and the way children deprived of liberty are being treated. Contrary to what international children's rights stipulate, deprivation of liberty is not used with the utmost restraint and for the shortest appropriate period of time.[137] It has been reported that many children languish in pre-trial detention for months or even years[138] and that states have difficulties in implementing adequate alternatives for arrest, detention, or imprisonment.[139] In addition, children deprived of liberty may not have access to basic services, such as sanitation, mental health care, or education; are not separated from adults and have little or no means of maintaining contact with family; run the risk of being subjected to various forms of violence, including disciplinary measures, such as solitary confinement; and have no access to justice. Many institutions in which children in conflict with the law are placed lack independent oversight. As a consequence, these children find themselves in a situation that makes them particularly vulnerable and dependent on the state and that puts them in serious jeopardy of having their rights disregarded or denied.[140]

Another issue of significant concern is the widespread occurrence of violence in the juvenile justice system. Since the 2006 UN violence study, which placed the issue of violence against children on the international agenda, different studies have reported on the various forms of violence committed against children in conflict with the law, that is: peer-to-peer violence, self-harm or suicide, or violence committed against children by state actors, such as police officials, security forces, or staff of institutions.[141] In 2012 the UN Special Representative on Violence against Children expressed her concern about the wide range of acts of violence against children throughout the juvenile justice system, from the first contact with law enforcement until the disposition of sentences. She concluded that an important strategy for the prevention of violence would be "preventing children from becoming involved with the juvenile justice system."[142] In 2015 the UN Special Rapporteur on Torture expressed his grave concerns about torture and other forms of ill-treatment against children deprived of their liberty who are more vulnerable than adults and require a higher level of protection.[143] Many states have difficulties or simply fail in protecting children against violence, a stark contrast to one of the cornerstones of international children's rights expressed in this oft-cited slogan: "All violence is preventable, and no violence is justifiable."[144]

The issues of deprivation of liberty and violence in the juvenile justice system show that the rights of children in conflict with the law are not always respected or adequately protected. This relates to a number of crosscutting challenges affecting children's rights implementation in the context of juvenile justice.[145] A first challenge referred to in this regard could be called *stigmatization*. Children in and around the juvenile justice system, mainly adolescents, often belong to the most stigmatized groups of society, that is: children belonging to minorities, children in street situations,[146] immigrant children, girls,[147] and children in need of mental health or alternative care. Not only do these children suffer from racial discrimination, exclusion, or biases in their arrest, prosecution, sentencing, and treatment by law enforcement;[148] they also may have special needs that do not get adequate attention, which affects their health and well-being.[149] For these children, being in conflict with the law means they run the risk of being stigmatized even more.[150]

Second, juvenile justice is an area of *controversy* and heavily discussed and debated, despite the growing body of scientific knowledge on juvenile delinquency (and its decline[151]), adolescent development, and effective justice interventions. The way juvenile justice operates and is being regulated is significantly influenced by concerns, opinions, perceptions, and stigmas around juvenile delinquency and public safety. Juvenile justice is affected by "zero tolerance" or "tough on crime" approaches,[152] and used by politicians for political gain.[153] In addition, misconceptions persist regarding the incidence and prevalence of juvenile delinquency, its impact on public safety, and effective strategies to prevent or respond to juvenile delinquency.[154] A nuanced, evidence-based, children's rights–based construct of children in conflict with the law can be seriously challenged by the politicized nature of the debate around juvenile justice and the continuous pressure to address children's accountability when they commit a criminal offense, particularly when this offense is a serious one. Although one has to acknowledge that children do commit serious offenses,[155] which may justify and even call for an intervention to protect public interests and/or interests of victims, the reality of stigmatization and controversy highlights a serious challenge for the implementation of children's rights and therefore requires states' full attention.[156] For example, it has implications for sentencing policies and practices and can explain the use of harsh sentences resulting in institutionalization of children for long periods of time. The specific concerns expressed by the CRC Committee about juvenile justice systems that allow for (or mandate) a waiver or transfer of children to the adult criminal justice system should be understood also in light of the stigmatizing and controversial nature of juvenile justice. Although this practice can, according to the CRC Committee, be regarded as discriminatory because it excludes certain children from the protection of children's rights, it is widely used.[157]

A third crosscutting challenge for the implementation of international children's rights, providing universal standards for juvenile justice, relates to the *differences* among juvenile justice systems across the globe,[158] differences in terms of their functioning, legal tradition, and meaning for fundamental juvenile justice concepts, such as accountability, pedagogical orientation, effective participation, proportionality,[159] and in terms of the context in which juvenile delinquency manifests itself. Explanations for these differences can be found, among others, in the historical background of legal systems,[160] in the availability of financial and human resources, and in social factors related to juvenile delinquency, including poverty, social exclusion, and stigmatization.[161] Effective implementation of international children's rights requires the taking into account of the context in which a domestic justice system operates, which comes with a certain level of *discretion* under international children's rights law. At the same time, the international children's rights framework aims to protect all children in conflict with the law on the basis of principles that are assumed to have *universal meaning* and can be summarized as establishing children's entitlements to be treated fairly and in a child-specific manner (see section 3). Recognizing differences and discretion while upholding universal rights and principles makes implementation of children's rights in the context of juvenile justice not only a challenging endeavor but also a complex one.[162] Two examples are provided below.

A first example concerns sentencing of children. Sentencing practices and approaches toward sentencing vary dramatically across the globe.[163] The CRC has embraced this reality by granting states broad discretion on the matter, though it also provides for minimum standards—prohibiting capital punishment and corporal punishment as a sentence, among others[164]—and a framework for sentencing revolving around the pedagogical orientation of juvenile justice (see section 3). With regard to imprisonment as a sentence for children, the CRC stipulates that it must be used as a last resort and for the shortest appropriate period of time,[165] which seems to rule out mandatory or minimum sentences[166] and calls for the use of alternatives.[167] CRC Article 40(4) refers to the principle of proportionality, the application of which in the context of sentencing requires a tailored approach that takes into account "the circumstances and the gravity of the offence, but also…the age, lesser culpability, circumstances and needs of the child, as well as…the various and particularly long-term needs of the society."[168] At the same time, it must be noted that CRC Article 37(a) allows for the use of life imprisonment as long as there is the possibility of parole. This is clearly one of weakest provisions in the CRC, which, as a result of a political compromise,[169] shows the lack of willingness to accept that long custodial sentences cannot cohere with the pedagogical orientation of CRC Article 40(1) and with Article 37(b)'s requirement that deprivation of liberty shall be used only for the shortest appropriate period of time.[170]

International children's rights further oblige states to develop a legislative framework within which tailored decisions can be made and legal uncertainty and inequality prevented. This framework should also include procedural safeguards, such as the right to habeas corpus,[171] and support the pedagogical orientation of juvenile justice, meaning that in the case of children, considerations of public safety and sanctions "must always be outweighed by the need to safeguard the well-being and the best interests of the child and to promote his/her reintegration," even in case of severe offenses.[172] Tailored decision-making, however, implies that there will always be a certain risk for legal uncertainty, inequality, or even bias, which explains why the CRC Committee underscores the importance of respecting the CRC's general principles, in particular CRC Article 2, prohibiting discrimination.[173] Decisions on the use of alternatives to imprisonment depend, among other things, on the availability of human and financial resources, domestic legislation that encourages the use of alternatives, and the willingness of decision makers to apply alternatives. Whether decision makers utilize such alternatives depends in part on their knowledge of and sensitivity to children's rights, which suggests that juvenile justice policies should also include targeted training of decision makers.[174]

A second example illustrating the complexity of children's rights implementation concerns the minimum age of criminal responsibility (MACR). The CRC Committee provides that states should set a MACR.[175] It does not, however, provide what the MACR should be, and there is no consensus among states from which age children can and should be held accountable.[176] As was recognized by the drafters of the Beijing Rules, "the minimum age of criminal responsibility differs widely owing to history and culture" and "[t]he modern approach would be to consider whether a child can live up to the moral and psychological components of criminal responsibility; that is whether a child, by virtue of her or his individual discernment and understanding, can be held responsible for essentially antisocial behaviour."[177] Consequently, Rule 4.1 of the Beijing Rules provides that the MACR "shall not be fixed at too low an age level, bearing in mind the facts of emotional, mental and intellectual maturity." Despite the lack of international consensus, the CRC Committee has decided to recommend using a MACR of at least twelve years "as the absolute minimum age."[178] An age limit below that, according to the CRC Committee, would not be "internationally acceptable," and it is recommended that the minimum age be raised "to a higher level."[179] As a consequence, states parties should not lower their age to twelve, and the CRC Committee seems to suggest that a MACR of fourteen or sixteen should be favored instead. It is interesting to see that there are states that have raised their age to a higher level (i.e., not necessarily to the age of twelve yet) and that some are in the process of doing so, in part due to the recommendations made by the CRC Committee.[180] A small number of states, however, have lowered their MACR, and some states are considering doing so in the future.[181] This shows, on the one hand, the support for the international standard carried out by the CRC Committee,[182] which aims to shield younger children from prosecution and to guarantee older children the fair and child-specific treatment to which they are entitled.[183] At the same, the lowering or attempts to lower the MACR in some countries suggests that the implementation of children's rights in the context of juvenile justice systems can easily be pushed back in times of hostile political headwinds.[184]

5 Conclusion

Juvenile justice is clearly a children's rights issue. The comprehensive international legal framework obliges states, as the primary duty bearers, to protect the rights and interests of each child in conflict with the law, in a system that is, above all, focused on the protection of the interests of society and others. States have a lot discretion, which calls for legislation at the domestic level and investment in the quality of its application, for which specialized professionals who are sensitive to children's rights are key.[185] Moreover, juvenile justice reform requires coordination and leadership as well as an approach that makes children visible and places them at the heart of the system, building on the recognition that children in conflict with the law are above all children with children's rights. It is clear that the juvenile system is a rather difficult context in which children's rights must find their way. The implementation gap may justify the conclusion that children's rights in juvenile justice will always remain a utopian dream. Drawing this conclusion, however, would disregard the enormous progress made in the past thirty years and the efforts and investments of many. Therefore, it is important to remain hopeful and to continue to work on the diverse challenges children's rights implementation face in the specific context of juvenile justice.

ACKNOWLEDGMENT

The author wishes to thank Chris Sandelowsky, LL.M., for her assistance.

NOTES

1. This chapter refers to the child in conflict with the law as a child (i.e., in principle, a person under the age of eighteen; CRC Article 1) who is alleged as, accused of, or recognized as having infringed the domestic penal law.
2. UN Convention on the Rights of the Child (CRC), G.A. Res. 44/25, 44th Sess., UN Doc. A/RES/44/25 (1989).
3. Where this chapter refers to *he, she* is meant as well, unless stated otherwise.
4. See, e.g., Elizabeth Scott and Laurence Steinberg, *Rethinking Juvenile Justice* (Cambridge, MA: Harvard University Press, 2008).
5. Roper v. Simmons, 543 U.S. 551 (2005).
6. *Roper.*
7. Jean Trépanier, "Children's Rights in Juvenile Justice: A Historical Glance," in *The UN Children's Rights Convention: Theory Meets Practice*, ed. André Alen, Henry Bosly, Maria De Bie, Johan Vande Lanotte, Fiona Ang, Isabelle Delens-Ravier, Marie Delplace, Charlotte Herman, Didier Reynaert, Valentina Staelens,Riet Steel, and Mieke Verheyde (Mortsel, BE: Intersentia, 2007), 509–530.
8. Geneva Declaration of the Rights of the Child, adopted by the League of Nations on September 26, 1924.
9. UN Standard Minimum Rules for the Administration of Juvenile Justice (Bejing Rules), G.A. Res. 40/33, 40th Sess., UN Doc. A/RES/40/33 (1985); Sharon Detrick, *A Commentary on the United Nations Convention on the Rights of the Child* (The Hague: Kluwer Law International, 1999), 681.
10. CRC, arts. 2, 3(1), 6, and 12; UN Committee on the Rights of the Child (CRC Committee), *General Comment No. 5: General Measures of Implementation of the Convention on the Rights of the Child (arts. 4, 42 and 44, para. 6)*, UN Doc. CRC/GC/2003/5 (2003), para. 12.
11. UN Rules for the Protection of Juveniles Deprived of Their Liberty (Havana Rules), G.A. Res. 45/113, 45th Sess., UN Doc. A/RES/45/113 (1990).
12. United Nations Office of the High Commissioner for Human Rights (OHCHR), "Guidelines for the Prevention of Juvenile Delinquency" (The Riyadh Guidelines), G.A. Res. 45/112, 45th Sess., UN Doc. A/RES/45/112 (Dec. 14, 1990).

13. Havana Rules, Rule 3.
14. Riyadh Guidelines, Guideline I.3.
15. CRC Committee, "General Comment No. 10: Children's Rights in Juvenile Justice," UN Doc. CRC/C/GC/10 (2007), paras. 4, 8 and 17.
16. CRC Committee, "General Comment No. 10," paras. 32, 46, 66 and 89.
17. CRC Committee, "General Comment No. 10," para. 88.
18. See, e.g., European Union Agency for Fundamental Rights and Council of Europe, *Handbook on European Law Relating to the Rights of the Child* (Luxembourg: Publications Office of the European Union, 2017); Ganguly E. Thukral and A. Kumar Asthana, "Children's Rights in Litigation: Use of the CRC in Indian Courts," in *Litigating the Rights of the Child: The U.N. Convention on the Rights of the Child in Domestic and International Jurisprudence*, ed. Ton Liefaard and Jaap Doek ed. Ton Liefaard and Jaap Doek. (The Hague: Springer Netherlands, 2015), 39 and 41; Ann Skelton, "Child Justice in South Africa: Application of International Instruments in the Constitutional Court," *International Journal of Children's Rights* 26, no.3 (August 2018): 391–442; Monica Feria-Tinta, "The CRC as a Litigation Tool before the Inter-American System of Protection of Human Rights," in Liefaard and Doek, *Litigating the Rights of the Child*, 238.
19. See also CRC, art. 41.
20. International Covenant on Civil and Political Rights (ICCPR), G.A. Res. 2200A (XXI), 21st Sess., UN Doc. A/6316 (1966).
21. Detrick, *Commentary on the United Nations Convention on the Rights of the Child*, 622, 629, and 682.
22. Convention against Torture and Other Cruel, Inhuman or Degrading Treatment or Punishment, G.A. Res. 39/46, 39th Sess., UN Doc. A/RES/39/46 (1984).
23. International Convention on the Elimination of All Forms of Racial Discrimination, G.A. Res. 2106 (XX), 20th Sess., UN Doc. A/6014 (1965).
24. The Nelson Mandela Rules are a revised version of the 1955 UN Standard Minimum Rules for the Treatment of Prisoners, GA Res. 663 C (XXIV), A/RES/663 C (XXIV) (1957), and ECOSOC Res. 2076 (LXII) (1977).
25. UN Convention on the Rights of the Child (CRC), G.A. Res. 45/110, 68th Sess., A/ RES/45/110 (1990).
26. See, e.g., American Convention on Human Rights (ACHR), 36 O.A.S.T.S. (Nov 22, 1969; entered into force July, 18, 1979), arts. 5(5) and 19; and European Convention on Human Rights, European Convention for the Protection of Human Rights and Fundamental Freedoms, 213 UNTS 221 (Nov. 4, 1950; entered into force Sept. 3, 1953), arts. 5 and 6.
27. Feria-Tinta, "CRC as a Litigation Tool"; Inter-American Commission on Human Rights, "Juvenile Justice and Human Rights in the Americas," OEA/Ser.L./V/II (July 13, 2011), http://www.cidh.org/countryrep/JusticiaJuvenileng/jjsummary.eng.htm. See also Bernardine Dohrn, "Something's Happening Here: Children and Human Rights Jurisprudence in Two International Courts," *Nevada Law Journal* 6, no. 3 (2006): 749–773.
28. Case of the "Street Children" (Villagran-Morales et al.) v. Guatemala, Inter-American Court of Human Rights (Nov. 19, 1999), para. 189.
29. *Villagran-Morales et al.*, paras. 190–191.
30. *Villagran-Morales et al.*, para. 194.
31. *Villagran-Morales et al.*, para. 196 (with reference to CRC arts. 2, 3(2), 6, 20, 27, and 37 (para. 195)). The Court also referred to the Riyadh Guidelines and Beijing Rules, para. 197.
32. Feria-Tinta, "CRC as a Litigation Tool," 247.

33. Feria-Tinta, "CRC as a Litigation Tool," 239 (with reference to Inter-American Commission on Human Rights, *Children and Their Rights*, para. 53).

34. Council of Europe Committee of Ministers, "Recommendation Rec(2003)20:Concerning New Ways of Dealing with Juvenile Delinquency and the Role of Juvenile Justice" (Sept. 24, 2003).

35. Council of Europe Committee of Ministers, "Recommendation Rec(2008)11 on the European Rules for Juvenile Offenders Subject to Sanctions or Measures" (Nov. 5, 2008), https://www.unicef.org/tdad/councilofeuropejjreco8(1).pdf.

36. Committee of Minsters of the Council of Europe, "Guidelines of the Committee of Ministers of the Council of Europe on Child-Friendly Justice" (Nov. 17, 2010), 13, www.coe.int/childjustice.

37. See Ursula Kilkelly, "CRC in Litigation under the ECHR," in Liefaard and Doek, *Litigating the Rights of the Child*; and Ton Liefaard and Ursula Kilkelly, "Child-Friendly Justice: Past, Present and Future," in *Juvenile Justice in Europe: Past, Present and Future*, ed. Barry Goldson (New York: Routledge, 2018).

38. Liefaard and Kilkelly, "Child-Friendly Justice." See, e.g., Blokhin v. Russia, Application No. 47152/06, Eur. Ct. H. R., GC (March 23, 2016), paras. 170 and 203.

39. The European Parliament and Council, "Directive (EU) 2016/800 of the European Parliament and of the Council of 11 May 2016 on procedural safeguards for children who are suspects or accused persons in criminal proceedings," https://eur-lex.europa.eu/legal-content/EN/TXT/?uri=CELEX%3A32016L0800. See also Stephanie Rap and Daniella Zlotnik, "The Right to Legal and Other Appropriate Assistance for Child Suspects and Accused," *European Journal of Crime, Criminal Law, and Criminal Justice* 26, no. 2 (May 2018): 110–131.

40. The African Committee of Experts on the Rights and Welfare of the Child and the African Union et al, "Guidelines on Action for Children in the Justice System in Africa" (2011), and "The Munyonyo Declaration on Child Justice in Africa" (final version Jan. 24, 2012), http://www.kampalaconference.info (accessed Aug. 19, 2019). See also the International Association of Youth and Family Judges and Magistrates (AYFJM), "Guidelines on Children in Contract with the Justice System" (adopted Oct. 21, 2016; ratified April 26, 2017), http://www.aimjf.org/storage/www.aimjf.org/Documentation_EN/AIMJF/Guidelines_-_ENG_-_Ratified_17.04.26.pdf (developed on the basis of the child-friendly justice guidelines and their equivalents in Africa and Latin America). The IAYFJM guidelines use the term "child focussed justice" (see page 11), which the IAYFJM deemed more appropriate in relation to the context of juvenile justice.

41. See Salduz v. Turkey, Application No. 36391/02, Eur. Ct. H.R. 27 (November 2008); Panovits v. Cyprus, Application No. 4268/04, Eur. Ct. H.R 11 (December 2008).

42. See, e.g., Güveç v. Turkey, Application No. 70337/01, Eur. Ct. H.R. (Jan. 20, 2009), and Korneykova v. Ukraine, Application No. 39884/05, Eur. Ct. H.R. (Jan. 19, 2012).

43. See, e.g., *Güveç*; and Nart v. Turkey, Application No. 20817/04, Eur. Ct. H.R. (May 6, 2008); see also *Blokhin*.

44. European Union Agency for Fundamental Rights and Council of Europe, *Handbook on European Law Relating to the Rights of the Child*.

45. European Committee for the Prevention of Torture and Inhuman or Degrading Treatment or Punishment (CPT), "24th General Report of the CPT," CPT/Inf 2015 1 (January 2015).

46. CRC Committee, "General Comment No. 10," para. 3.

47. See, e.g., Julia L. Sloth-Nielsen, "The Influence of International Law on South Africa's Juvenile Justice Reform Process," LLD thesis, University of the Western Cape, 2001; UNICEF Innocenti Research Centre, *Law Reform and the Implementation of the Convention on the Rights of the Child* (Florence: UNICEF Innocenti Research Centre, 2007); Laura Lundy, Ursula Kilkelly, Bronagh Bryne, and Jason Kang, "The UN Convention on the Rights of the Child: A Study of Legal Implementation in 12 Countries," Centre for Children's Rights School of Education, Queen's University Belfast (November 2012), http://www.qub.ac.uk/research-centres/CentreforChildrensRights/filestore/Filetoupload,453628,en.pdf#search=The%20UN%20Convention%20on%20the%20Rights%20of%20the%20Child%3A%20A%20Study%20of%20Legal%20Implementation%20in%2012%20Countries; Raoul Wallenberg Institute, "A Measure of Last Resort? The Current Status of Juvenile Justice in ASEAN Member States" (April 2015), https://rwi.lu.se/app/uploads/2015/04/Juvenile-Justice-Report.pdf; Franklin Zimring, Maximo Langer, and David Tanenhaus, *Juvenile Justice in Global Perspective* (New York: NYU Press, 2015).

48. See, e.g., Liefaard and Doek, *Litigating the Rights of the Child*, and Skelton, "Child Justice in South Africa."

49. These groups include the Human Rights Council, the Office of the High Commissioner for Human Rights (OHCHR), the UN Office on Drugs and Crime (UNODC), the UN Special Representative on Violence against Children, UNICEF, the Inter-American Commission on Human Rights, the Council of Europe.

50. See, for example, the former Inter-Agency Panel on Juvenile Justice, International Juvenile Justice Observatory (IJJO), Defence for Children International, Penal Reform International (PRI), and Human Rights Watch.

51. This paragraph is partly based on Ton Liefaard, "Juvenile Justice from a Children's Rights Perspective," in *The Routledge International Handbook of Children's Rights Studies*, ed. Wouter Vandenhole, Ellen Desmet, Didier Reynaert, and Sara Lembrechts (London: Routledge, 2015).

52. Liefaard, "Juvenile Justice from a Children's Rights Perspective."

53. CRC Committee, "General Comment No. 10," para. 10.

54. See CRC art. 29(1)(b) and CRC Committee, "General Comment No. 10."

55. CRC Committee, "General Comment No. 10," para. 10.

56. CRC Committee, "General Comment No. 10," paras. 16 and 17. See also Riyadh Guidelines and Council of Europe Committee of Ministers, "Recommendation Rec(2003) 20."

57. CRC Committee, "General Comment No. 10," paras. 6–8.

58. CRC Committee, "General Comment No. 10," para. 8; see also Riyadh Guidelines, Guideline VI.56, and CRC Committee, "General Comment No. 21: Children in Street Situations," UN Doc. CRC/C/GC/21 (2017).

59. Jaap Doek, "Juvenile Justice: International Rights and Standards," in *Criminals. The Development of Child Delinquency and Effective Interventions*, ed. N. Wim Slot, Machteld Hoeve, and Rolf Loeber (London: Routledge, 2008), 236.

60. For more on the controversies around the MACR see Liefaard, "Juvenile Justice from a Children's Rights Perspective."

61. CRC, art. 40(3)(b). The UN Committee on the Rights of the Child underscores that diversion should not be reserved for first offenders only; recidivist and even serious offenders should also have access to appropriate diversion programs. CRC Committee, "General Comment No. 10," paras. 23 and 25.

62. CRC Committee, "General Comment No. 10," para. 25. Diversion also is considered as potentially more cost-effective. See Frieder Dünkel, "Diversion: A Meaningful and Successful Alternative to Punishment in European Juvenile Justice System," in *Reforming Juvenile Justice*, ed. Josine Junger-Tas and Frieder Dunkel (New York: Springer-Verlag. 2009), 147.

63. CRC Committee, "General Comment No. 10," para. 27.

64. CRC Committee, "General Comment No. 10," paras. 24–26.

65. CRC Committee, "General Comment No. 10," para. 27.

66. CRC Committee, "General Comment No. 10," para. 27. See also United Nations Children's Fund (UNICEF), "Diversion Not Detention: A Study in Diversion and Other Alternative Measures for Children in Conflict with the Law in East Asia and the Pacific" (March 2018), https://www.unicef.org/eap/reports/diversion-not-detention; and UN Special Representative of the Secretary-General on Violence against Children, "Promoting Restorative Justice for Children," Office of the SRSG on Violence against Children (2013), https://sustainable development.un.org/index.php?page=view&type=400&nr=2599&menu=1515.

67. Note that CRC, art. 40(1), does not refer to *maturity*, but arguably this can be read into the text of the convention, also in light of other provisions referring to the developmental dynamics regarding children; see, e.g., CRC, arts. 5 and 12.

68. See CRC, arts. 18 and 5.

69. CRC, art. 37(c); see also Havana Rules, Rule 11a (calling for the establishment of a minimum age of deprivation of liberty). See also Council of Europe, "Commentary to the European Rules for Juvenile Offenders Subject to Sanctions or Measures," CM(2008)128 (2008), addendum 1, 47, https://www.unicef.org/tdad/councilofeuropejjreco8commentary(1).pdf.

70. Liefaard, "Juvenile Justice from a Children's Rights Perspective."

71. UNICEF Innocenti Research Centre, *Law Reform and Implementation*.

72. Ineke Pruin, "The Scope of Juvenile Justice Systems in Europe," in *Juvenile Justice Systems in Europe—Current Situation and Reform Developments*, ed. Frieder Dünkel, Joanna Grzywa, Phillip Horsfield, and Ineke Pruin, 2nd ed. (Mönchengladbach, DE: Forum-Verlag, 2011), 1523–1525.

73. Liefaard, "Juvenile Justice from a Children's Rights Perspective." See also Lundy et al., " UN Convention on The Rights of the Child," and UNICEF Innocenti Research Centre, *Law Reform and Implementation*.

74. CRC Committee, "General Comment No. 10," para. 4.

75. CRC Committee, "General Comment No. 5," para. 12.

76. CRC Committee, "General Comment No. 10," para. 92; see also, e.g., Beijing Rules 12.1.

77. Detrick, *Commentary on the United Nations Convention of the Rights of the Child*, 633.

78. Ton Liefaard, *Deprivation of Liberty of Children in Light of International Human Rights Law and Standards* (Cambridge, UK: Intersentia, 2008).

79. This exception should be understood in light of CRC Article 3(1) as one of the key concepts of international children's rights law and one of the CRC's general principles (identified as such by the CRC Committee). This exception has also been included because of the fact that the stricter approach under ICCPR Article 10 (i.e., separation/segregation without any exceptions) has resulted in quite a number of reservations. Liefaard, *Deprivation of Liberty of Children*.

80. See Liefaard, *Deprivation of Liberty of Children*.

81. CRC Committee, "General Comment No. 10," para. 13.

82. CRC Committee, "General Comment No. 10," para. 13.

83. Detrick, *Commentary on the United Nations Convention of the Rights of the Child*. See also ECHR, arts. 6 and 7, and ACHR, arts. 8 and 9.

84. CRC, art. 40(2)(b)(i).

85. CRC, art. 40(2)(b)(iv).

86. CRC, art. 40(2)(b)(ii).

87. CRC, art. 40(2)(b)(iii). There is also the right to appeal—see CRC, art. 40(2)(b)(v), and ICCPR, art. 14(5).

88. CRC, art. 40(2)(b)(iv).

89. CRC, art. 40(2)(b)(iv).

90. CRC, art. 40(2)(b)(iii).

91. Compare ICCPR, art. 14(2)(c), and ECHR, art. 6(1).

92. CRC Committee, "General Comment No. 10," para. 51.

93. CRC Committee, "General Comment No. 10," para. 51.

94. CRC, art. 40(2)(b)(vii); see also CRC, art. 16.

95. CRC Committee, "General Comment No. 10," para. 65.

96. CRC Committee, "General Comment No. 10," para. 67.

97. CRC Committee, "General Comment No. 10," para. 47.

98. See CRC Committee, "General Comment No. 10," para. 47. See also Committee of Ministers of the Council of Europe, "Guidelines of the Committee of Ministers of the Council of Europe on Child-Friendly Justice."

99. See CRC, arts. 18 and 5; see also the CRC's preamble.

100. See also Beijing Rules 15.2 and 18.2.

101. CRC, art. 40(2)(b)(iii).

102. See *Salduz*; *Panovits*. This right has recently been incorporated in European Union legislation. See Rap and Zlotnik, "Right to Legal and Other Appropriate Assistance for Child Suspects and Accused."

103. CRC Committee, "General Comment No. 10," para. 49.

104. T. Liefaard and Yannick Van den Brink, "Juveniles' Right to Counsel during Police Interrogations: An Interdisciplinary Analysis of a Youth-Specific Approach, with a Particular Focus on the Netherlands," *Erasmus Law Review*, 7 no. 4 (2014): 206–218.

105. CRC Article 40(3)(b) underscores that in case of diversion the human rights of and legal safeguards for children must be fully respected; see also CRC Committee, "General Comment No. 10," paras. 22 and 27.

106. CRC Committee, "General Comment No. 10," para. 50.

107. Geraldine Van Bueren, *A Commentary on the United Nations Convention on the Rights of the Child, Article 40: Child Criminal Justice* (Leiden: Martinus Nijhoff Publishers 2006), 19.

108. CRC Committee, "General Comment No. 10," para. 49.

109. Liefaard and Van den Brink, "Juveniles' Right to Counsel." Mandatory legal assistance, which excludes children from waiving this right, was included by the European Commission in its proposal for the EU directive on procedural safeguards for children suspected or accused in criminal proceedings; see https://eur-lex.europa.eu/legal-content/EN/TXT/?uri=CELEX%3A52013PC0822. The adopted text of the EU directive leaves room for EU member states not to provide for legal counsel if this is regarded disproportionate. See also Rap and Zlotnik, "Right to Legal and Other Appropriate Assistance for Child Suspects and Accused."

110. CRC, art. 37(d).

111. T. v. the United Kingdom, Application No. 24724/94, Eur. Ct. H.R. (Dec. 16, 1999); see also V. v. the United Kingdom, Application No. 24888/94, Eur. Ct. H.R. (Dec. 16, 1999). See also Kilkelly, "CRC in Litigation under the ECHR," and Liefaard and Kilkelly, "Child-Friendly Justice."

112. *T.*, para. 84.

113. *T.*, para. 88.

114. S.C. v. the United Kingdom, Application No. 60958/00, Eur. Ct. H.R. (June 15, 2004), , para. 29. This court also pointed at the significance of legal representation in this regard.

115. CRC Committee, "General Comment No. 10," para. 46 (with reference to CRC Article 12(2)). See also CRC Committee, "General Comment No. 12: The Right of the Child to be Heard," UN Doc. CRC/C/GC/12 (2009).

116. Kilkelly, "CRC in litigation under the ECHR." See also Liefaard and Kilkelly, "Child-Friendly Justice."

117. CRC Committee, "General Comment No. 10," para. 12.

118. CRC Committee, "General Comment No. 10," para. 46.

119. CRC Committee, "General Comment No. 12," para. 34.

120. CRC Committee, "General Comment No. 12," para. 34.

121. CRC Committee, "General Comment No. 12," paras. 60–61.

122. Stephanie Rap, "The Participation of Juvenile Defendants in the Youth Court: A Comparative Study of Juvenile Justice Procedures in Europe," PhD diss. (Utrecht University, 2013); Stephanie Rap, "A Children's Rights Perspective on the Participation of Juvenile Defendants in the Youth Court," *International Journal of Children's Rights* 24, no. 1 (2016): 93–112. See also Aoife Daly and Stephanie Rap, "Children's Participation in the Justice System," in *International Human Rights of Children*, ed. Ursula Kilkelly and Ton Liefaard (Singapore: Springer, 2018), 299–319.

123. See Liefaard and Kilkelly, "Child-Friendly Justice"

124. According to the guidelines: " '[C]hild-friendly justice' refers to justice systems which guarantee the respect and the effective implementation of all children's rights at the highest attainable level, bearing in mind the principles listed below and giving due consideration to the child's level of maturity and understanding and the circumstances of the case. It is, in particular, justice that is accessible, age appropriate, speedy, diligent, adapted to and focused on the needs and rights of the child, respecting the rights of the child including the rights to due process, to participate in and to understand the proceedings, to respect for private and family life and to integrity and dignity." See Committee of Ministers of the Council of Europe, "Guidelines of the Committee of Ministers of the Council of Europe on Child-Friendly Justice," II(c).

125. For more on the drafting and the added value of the guidelines see Liefaard and Kilkelly, "Child-Friendly Justice"; and Council of Europe Directorate General on Human Rights and Legal Affairs, Group of Specialists on Child-Friendly Justice, "Listening to Children about Justice: Report of the Council of Europe's Consultation with Children on Child-Friendly Justice" (Oct. 5, 2010). See also Directorate-General for Justice and Consumers (European Commission), "Children's Involvement in Criminal, Civil and Administrative Judicial Proceedings in the 28 Member States of the EU," policy brief (July 7, 2015).

126. See, e.g., Rap, "Participation of Juvenile Defendants in the Youth Court."

127. See European Commission, "Summary of Contextual Overviews on Children's Involvement in Criminal Justice Proceedings in the 28 Member States of the European Union" (April 16, 2014); Liefaard and Kilkelly, "Child-Friendly Justice"; European

Commission, "Children's Involvement in Criminal, Civil and Administrative Judicial Proceedings in the 28 Member States of the EU."

128. See, e.g., M.J. Bernuz Beneitez and E. Dumortier, "Why Children Obey the Law: Rethinking Juvenile Justice and Children's Rights in Europe through Procedural Justice," *Youth Justice* 18, no. 1 (2018): 34–51.

129. UNICEF Innocenti Research Centre, *Law Reform and Implementation*. See also UNICEF Innocenti Research Centre, *Juvenile Justice Innocenti Digest No. 3* (Florence, UNICEF International Child Development Centre, 1998); Zimring, Langer, and Tanenhaus, *Juvenile Justice in Global Perspective*; Barry Goldson and John Muncie, "Towards a Global 'Child-Friendly' Juvenile Justice?," *International Journal of Law Crime and Justice* 40, no. 1 (January 2012): 47–64.

130. See, e.g., specific studies on China, South Africa, and Latin-America in Zimring, Langer and Tanenhaus, *Juvenile Justice in Global Perspective*.

131. See, e.g., Georgia. See UNICEF Innocenti Research Centre, *Juvenile Justice Innocenti Digest no. 3*; UNICEF, "Diversion not Detention"; Raoul Wallenberg Institute, "Measure of Last Resort?"

132. See Scott, Elizabeth S. and Steinberg, Laurence, *Rethinking Juvenile Justice*; see also Scott, Elizabeth, Thomas Grisso, Marsha Levick, and Laurence Steinberg. 2016. "Juvenile Sentencing Reform in a Constitutional Framework." *Temple Law Review* 88: 675–716.

133. Rap, "Participation of Juvenile Defendants in the Youth Court."

134. See, e.g., Raoul Wallenberg Institute, "A Measure of Last Resort?"

135. See, e.g., OHCHR, "Joint Report of the Office of the High Commissioner for Human Rights, the United Nations Office on Drugs and Crime and the Special Representative of the Secretary-General on Violence against Children on Prevention of and Responses to Violence against Children within the Juvenile Justice System," UN Doc. A/HRC/21/25 (June 27, 2012).

136. CRC Committee, "General Comment No. 10," para. 3.

137. CRC, art. 37 (b).

138. CRC Committee, "General Comment No. 10," para. 80.

139. See CRC, art. 40(4) (mentions "care, guidance and supervision orders; counselling; probation; foster care; education and vocational training programmes and other alternatives to institutional care" as alternative dispositions).

140. United Nations Secretary-General, "Report of the Independent Expert for the United Nations Study on Violence against Children," UN Doc. A/61/299 (Aug. 29, 2006). See also OHCHR, "Joint Report on Violence against Children"; Barry Goldson and Ursula Kilkelly, "International Human Rights Standards and Child Imprisonment: Potentialities and Limitations," *International Journal of Children's Rights* 21, no. 2 (January 2013): 345–371; Center for Human Rights and Humanitarian Law, *Protecting Children against Torture in Detention: Global Solutions for a Global Problem* (Washington, DC: American University Washington College of Law, 2017); OHCHR, "Children Deprived of Liberty: The United Nations Global Study," http://www.ohchr.org/EN/HRBodies/CRC/StudyChildrenDeprivedLiberty/Pages/Index.aspx (accessed Aug. 20, 2019).

141. See, e.g., United Nations Secretary-General, "Report of the Independent Expert for the United Nations Study on Violence against Children"; OHCHR, "Joint Report on Violence against Children"; Ton Liefaard, "Report on Violence in Institutions for Juvenile Offenders," PC-CP\docs 2014\PC-CP(2014)13e rev2, European Council (Nov. 7, 2014). See also the case law of the Inter-American Court referred to in section 2.

142. OHCHR, "Joint Report on Violence against Children," para. 66.

143. Center for Human Rights and Humanitarian Law, *Protecting Children against Torture in Detention*.

144. United Nations Secretary-General, "Report of the Independent Expert for the United Nations Study on Violence against Children."

145. See, e.g., OHCHR, "Joint Report on Violence against Children," para. 9.

146. See, e.g., CRC Committee, "General Comment No. 21."

147. A group of children currently receiving the attention of the international community is made up of children associated with violent extremism; see, e.g., UN Office on Drugs and Crime, "Handbook on Children Recruited and Exploited by Terrorist and Violent Extremist Groups: The Role of the Justice System," (2017), https://www.unodc.org/documents/justice-and-prison-reform/Child-Victims/Handbook_on_Children_Recruited_and_Exploited_by_Terrorist_and_Violent_Extremist_Groups_the_Role_of_the_Justice_System.E.pdf.

148. See, e.g., Nancy Dowd, *Reimagining Equality: A New Deal for Children of Color* (New York: NYU Press, 2018). See also OHCHR, "Joint Report on Violence against Children."

149. See, e.g., Liefaard, "Report on Violence in Institutions for Juvenile Offenders."

150. See, e.g., Office of the Special Representative of the Secretary-General on Violence against Children, "Safeguarding the Rights of Girls in the Criminal Justice System," (2007), https://violenceagainstchildren.un.org/sites/violenceagainstchildren.un.org/files/document_files/safeguarding_the_rights_of_girls_in_the_criminal_justice_system_1.pdf.

151. See, e.g., Leslie McAra and Susan McVie, "Transformations in Youth Crime and Justice across Europe: Evidencing the Case for Diversion," in Goldson, *Juvenile Justice in Europe*, 74–104.

152. Roger Smith, *Youth Justice: Ideas, Policy, Practice*, 3rd ed. (New York: Routledge, 2013). See also Michael Cavadino and James Dignan, *Penal Systems: A Comparative Approach* (London: Sage, 2005).

153. David Downes and Rod Morgan, "Waiting for Ingleby: The Minimum Age of Criminal Responsibility—A Red Line Issue?," in *Policing: Politics, Culture, and Control*, ed. Tim Newburn and Jill Peay (Oxford, UK: Hart Publishing, 2011), 245–264. See also John Muncie, *Youth & Crime*, 4th ed. (London: Sage Publications, 2015). And see Wendy O'Brien and Kate Fitz-Gibbon, "Can Human Rights Standards Counter Australia's Punitive Youth Justice Practices?," *International Journal of Children's Rights* 26, no. 2 (2018): 197–227.

154. See CRC Committee, "General Comment No. 10," para. 96.

155. Nessa Lynch, "Towards a Principled Legal Response to Children Who Kill," *Youth Justice* 18 no. 3 (2018): 211–229.

156. CRC Committee, "General Comment No. 10," para. 96. It also implicates the role of media.

157. CRC Committee, "General Comment No. 10." para. 38.

158. Cavadino and Dignan, *Penal Systems*. See also Don Cipriani, *Children's Rights and the Minimum Age of Criminal Responsibility: A Global Perspective* (Farnham, UK: Ashgate, 2009). See also Rap, "Participation of Juvenile Defendants in the Youth Court."; Goldson and Muncie, "Towards a Global 'Child-Friendly' Juvenile Justice?"; Zimring, Langer, and Tanenhaus, *Juvenile Justice in Global Perspective*.

159. A simplified distinction can be made between *welfare* systems, which focus primarily on care, protection, and treatment of children in conflict with the law and less on rights and freedoms, and *justice* systems, which focus primarily on competence and accountability of children but also include attention for rights and freedoms and proportionality; see Muncie, *Youth & Crime*. See also Jenneke Christiaens, *It's for Your Own Good: Researching Youth Justice Practices* (Brussels: Vubpress, 2015); Raymond Arthur, *The Moral Foundations of The Youth Justice System* (New York: Routledge, 2017). It can be argued that the CRC essentially combines elements of both models.

160. See, e.g., Cipriani, *Children's Rights and the Minimum Age of Criminal Responsibility.*

161. See, e.g., Leslie McAra and Susan McVie, "Understanding Youth Violence: The Mediating Effects of Gender, Poverty and Vulnerability," *Journal of Criminal Justice* 45 (February 2016): 71–77; and Barry Goldson, "Reading the Present and Mapping the Future(s) of Juvenile Justice in Europe: Complexities and Challenges," in Goldson, *Juvenile Justice in Europe*, 209–253.

162. See also, e.g., Goldson and Muncie, "Towards a Global 'Child-Friendly' Juvenile Justice?"

163. Frieder Dünkel, "Sanctions Systems and Trends in the Development of Sentencing Practices," in *Juvenile Justice Systems in Europe: Current Situation, Reform Developments, and Good Practices* (Mönchengladbach, DE: Forum Verlag Godesberg, 2018). See also Zimring, Langer, and Tanenhaus, *Juvenile Justice in Global Perspective.*

164. CRC, art. 37(a) CRC Committee, "General Comment No. 10," para. 71 (with reference to CRC Committee, "General Comment No. 8").

165. CRC, art. 37(b).

166. See, e.g., Centre for Child Law v. Minister of Justice, 2009 (6) SA 632 (CC).

167. CRC, art. 40(4).

168. CRC Committee, "General Comment No. 10," para. 71.

169. Detrick, *Commentary on the United Nations Rights of the Child.*

170. CRC Committee, "General Comment No. 10," para. 77.

171. See, e.g., CRC, art. 37(d).

172. CRC Committee, "General Comment No. 10,", para. 71.

173. CRC Committee, "General Comment No. 10," para. 6.

174. CRC Committee, "General Comment No. 10"; compare Y. N. van den Brink, "Voorlopige hechtenis in hetnederlandse jeugdstrafrecht: wet en praktijk in het licht van internationale en Europese kinder—en mensenrechten," PhD diss., Leiden University, 2018.

175. Despite the rather weakly formulated provision, the UN Committee on the Rights of the Child understands it as an obligation for states parties to set a MACR. See CRC Committee, "General Comment No. 10," para. 31.

176. Cipriani, *Children's Rights and the Minimum Age of Criminal Responsibility.*

177. Commentary to Beijing Rules 4.1.

178. CRC Committee, "General Comment No. 10," 32.

179. CRC Committee, "General Comment No. 10," para. 32.

180. Youth Justice Board, "Cross-National comparison of Youth Justice" (2008), https://dera.ioe.ac.uk/7996/1/Cross_national_final.pdf (accessed Aug. 20, 2019). See also Maria Lourijsen and Ton Liefaard, "Raising the Minimum Age of Criminal Responsibility," Leiden Law Blog (Mar. 21, 2018), https://leidenlawblog.nl/articles/outline-on-raising-the-minimum-age-of-criminal-responsibility.

181. Child Rights International Network (CRIN), "Juvenile Justice: Stop Making Children Criminals," CRIN Policy Paper (Jan. 29, 2013), https://archive.crin.org/en/library/

publications/juvenile-justice-stop-making-children-criminals.html. See also Jacqui Gallinetti, "Getting to Know the Child Justice Act," Child Justice Alliance/Children's Rights Project, Community Law Centre, University of the Western Cape (2009); Klarise Anne C. Estorninos, "Batang Bata Ka Pa: An Analysis of the Philippine Minimum Age of Criminal Responsibility in Light of International Standards," *Ateneo Law Journal* 62, no. 1 (2017): 259–273.

182. Chris Cunneen, "Arguments for Raising the Minimum Age of Criminal Responsibility," Comparative Youth Penalty Project Research Report, University of New South Wales, Sydney (2017), https://www.cypp.unsw.edu.au/node/146; Frieder Dünkel, "Juvenile Justice Systems in Europe: Current Situation and Reform Developments."

183. Liefaard, "Juvenile Justice from a Children's Rights Perspective."

184. See Cipriani, *Children's Rights and the Minimum Age of Criminal Responsibility*. See also Liefaard, "Juvenile Justice from a Children's Rights Perspective"; CRIN, "Stop Making Children Criminals"; Downes and Morgan, "Waiting for Ingleby"; Inter-American Commission on Human Rights, "Juvenile Justice and Human Rights in The Americas," OEA/Ser.L/V/II (July 13, 2011).

185. See also CRC Committee, "General Comment No. 10."

....

CHAPTER 15

PLACING CHILDREN'S FREEDOM FROM VIOLENCE AT THE HEART OF THE POLICY AGENDA

....

MARTA SANTOS PAIS

1 INTRODUCTION

....

THE right of every child to freedom from violence is a fundamental thrust of the UN Convention on the Rights of the Child (CRC)[1] and its Optional Protocols.[2] Since its adoption, the CRC has mobilized nations across regions behind a common mission: to spare no effort to translate its provisions into a tangible reality for children—all children, everywhere and at all times.

The CRC is the most widely ratified human rights treaty in history and is in force in 196 states. Thanks to its rich process of implementation, decisive strides have been made toward the realization of children's rights. This includes the adoption of significant international standards and national laws to protect children from neglect, abuse, and exploitation; the promotion of child-sensitive policies and child-friendly services; the setting up of independent national institutions for the protection of children's rights and the promotion of awareness-raising and advocacy initiatives; and certainly also, the increase of the capacity and ethical standards of professionals working with and for children. More broadly, the CRC marked a paradigm shift in the way children are envisaged by society: not as passive beneficiaries of services or adults in the making, but as citizens of today and real partners in the consolidation of social progress.

The right of all children to live free from violence lies at the heart of the CRC. Indeed, the Convention explicitly prohibits torture, cruel, inhuman or degrading treatment or punishment; bans the use of the death penalty and life imprisonment for children; and makes imperative the protection of children from harmful practices as well as from sexual abuse, from being sold or trafficked, and from any other form of exploitation. It prohibits school violence and any form of school discipline contrary to the child's human dignity, and it safeguards children from the hidden manifestations of violence within the home or behind the walls of child protection institutions.[3]

Sadly, in striking contrast with these binding international standards, violence against children remains pervasive, concealed, and socially condoned. In many nations, incidents of such violence are still perceived as a social taboo, as a needed form of discipline, or as an entirely private matter that needs to be kept within closed circles. Incidents of violence against children are seldom reported, and official statistics do not fully capture the true scale and extent of this phenomenon.

This persistence of violence was the reason why at the dawn of this century the United Nations Committee on the Rights of the Child (CRC Committee) asked that the UN conduct a study on violence against children.[4] The resulting study[5] was presented to the UN General Assembly in 2006. It provided, for the first time, a comprehensive picture of children's exposure to violence: within the family, in schools, in care and justice institutions, in work settings, and within the community at large. Recognizing that "No violence against children is justifiable; all violence against children is preventable," the study presented a set of recommendations to overcome the invisibility and social acceptance of violence against children and to safeguard every child from its serious and long-lasting consequences.[6]

To translate the findings of the UN Study into action, in 2009 the United Nations established a new position—the Special Representative of the UN Secretary-General on Violence against Children—which I have been honored to hold for the past ten years.[7] The UN Special Representative is a global independent advocate for the prevention and elimination of all forms of violence against children.[8] Acting as a bridge-builder and a catalyst of actions in all regions, and across sectors and settings where violence against children may occur, the Special Representative mobilizes action and political support to maintain momentum around this agenda and to generate steady progress in children's protection from violence.

Thanks to the implementation of the recommendations of the UN Study, over the past decade violence against children has evolved from a largely hidden and neglected phenomenon into a priority concern on the global policy agenda. Adoption of the 2030 Agenda for Sustainable Development[9] in September 2015 marked an historic breakthrough. The 2030 Agenda has an ambitious vision: to build a world free from fear and from violence, in which every child grows up free from violence, abuse, and exploitation; it addresses violence against children as a crosscutting concern and includes a distinct target on ending all forms of violence against children in Sustainable Development Goal (SDG) target 16.2. Ensuring children's protection from violence is an imperative for all nations. But it must not remain simply an ideal: it needs to be translated into a tangible change for every child. The countdown to 2030 has started, and the clock is ticking. There is no time for complacency.

2   VIOLENCE AGAINST CHILDREN:
A GLOBAL CONCERN

Violence knows no geographic, cultural, or social borders. Around the world millions of boys and girls of all ages continue to be exposed to appalling levels of violence, in their neighborhoods, in their schools, in institutions aimed at their care and protection as well as within the home.[10] "Every five minutes a child dies as a consequence of violence. Every year, at least one billion children—half of the world's children—are affected by violence. They are intentionally targeted in politically driven processes, manipulated by organized crime, forced to flee violence in their communities, sold and exploited for economic gain, groomed online, disciplined by violent means, sexually assaulted in the privacy of their homes, neglected in institutions, abused in detention centers, bullied in schools, and stigmatized and tortured as a result of superstitious beliefs or harmful practices."[11] Online abuse has also become a growing concern. According to data from the Internet Watch Foundation,[12] in 2017 there was a 37 percent increase in confirmed cases of child sexual abuse materials uncovered; the majority of the victims were girls, while 55 percent of the victims were ten or younger, and 33 percent were cases of particular severity, including rape and sexual torture of children.

2.1 Violence: A Beginning in Early Childhood

As highlighted by UNICEF's recent report "A Familiar Face,"[13] shouting, yelling, or screaming are common forms of discipline for one-year-olds; close to three hundred million children between the ages of two and four experience psychological aggression and/or physical punishment by their caregivers at home; and 176 million children under five years of age witness domestic violence. These figures are deeply distressing.

Violence can alter the developing brain's structure and function, with a detrimental impact on children's language skills and cognitive development while compromising children's health and education. And, as longitudinal studies show, children exposed to violence in early years are also more likely to be victims of violence later in life and become perpetrators themselves; use violence as adults against domestic partners and their own children; and be at increased risk of engaging in violent and criminal behavior.

We must break this vicious and devastating cycle of violence. Violence prevention must start in early childhood.[14] That is also when investment can achieve a very high return. Scientific evidence shows that the human brain develops wider and faster during its first one thousand days than at any other stage of life and that it is during this crucial developmental period that the foundation for a person's future well-being is laid.[15] A nurturing and caring environment helps to secure children's health, nutrition, early learning, and sense of belonging. It promotes their self-esteem and improves their ability to handle stress and adversity.

Investing in early childhood and ending violence in children's lives are first and foremost a question of children's rights. But in addition, they make economic sense. Lack of investment in early years may hold children back even before they reach school age, paving the way to a life of disadvantage. Such a poor start in life can lead to a loss of about a quarter of average adult income per year. And countries may forfeit as much as two times their expenditure on GDP on health and education. Recognizing the importance of this area, SDG target 4.2 of the 2030 Agenda commits states to ensuring that all children have access to inclusive and quality early childhood education and care so that they may acquire the knowledge and skills to fulfill their potential, pursue opportunities, and participate fully in society as productive citizens.

2.2 Violence: A Continuum in Children's Lives

Violence starts early in life, but as children grow it often becomes part of a continuum. School and peer violence illustrate this well. Schools have a unique potential to generate an environment where attitudes condoning violence can be changed and nonviolent behavior can be learned. But for many children, school can become an ordeal rather than an opportunity.[16] Playground fighting, verbal abuse, intimidation, humiliation, corporal punishment, sexual abuse, gang violence, or other forms of cruel and humiliating treatment at the hands of teachers and other school staff are some common expressions of this phenomenon.

Peer violence is another traumatizing experience. Indeed, bullying and cyberbullying are among children's top concerns.[17] Whether verbal, psychological, or physical, either in schools or in the cyberspace, bullying is often part of a continuum, a torment that generates a deep sense of fear, loneliness, and hopelessness in children's lives. In this regard, the findings from an online survey we have conducted in cooperation with UNICEF, involving more than one hundred thousand children and young people around the world, are quite telling:

- nine in every ten respondents considered that bullying is a major problem;
- two-thirds reported having been victims;
- one-third believed it was normal and therefore did not tell anybody,
- while many did not know whom to tell or felt afraid to do so.[18]

With children's growing access to the Internet and the wide use of smartphones, cyberbullying has become a particularly pressing risk. Spreading rumors and posting false information, hurtful messages, and embarrassing comments or photos or being excluded from online networks can affect children deeply. Anonymity is an aggravating factor, but in addition, harassment may strike at any time, with harmful messages or materials spreading faster and further to an ever-growing audience and magnifying the risks and impact for child victims. As children sometimes describe the experience: you feel lonely and abandoned in a hopeless shipwreck.

2.3   Violence: A Pressing Risk within and across Borders

Violence takes place within countries as well as across borders. Over the past five years, the number of those forced to leave their communities has grown by more than fifty percent. In fact, every minute, thirty-one people are forced to flee their home as a result of violence, persecution, or conflict. In 2017 more than forty-four thousand people were forcibly displaced every day.[19] This situation has a serious impact on children.

While constituting less than one-third of the world's population, children represent more than half of the refugee population; at least three million children are stateless, and in 2017 alone more than forty-five thousand asylum claims were lodged by unaccompanied or separated children.[20] All these children are at high risk of abuse and exploitation.[21]

A child's decision to leave home can be driven by the desire to develop skills and talents, improve their education and employment opportunities, or join their family. But more often than not, it has become an escape strategy: to secure safety and protection; to reach a safe haven from political instability, conflict, natural disasters, violence and exploitation. And children face turmoil and distress at every step of the way. In their home countries, children may experience horrific scenes: the killing of their parents, the rape of their sisters, and the forced disappearance of their friends. They are exposed to street crime and community violence, to systematic threats and extortion, and to the harassment of gang members who mobilize support within the school or in their neighborhood. At times, children are manipulated by elements of organized crime and forced to take part in criminal activity, including acting as watchers in places where drugs or arms are trafficked or where smugglers congregate. When they refuse to cooperate, they may pay a heavy price and put their lives at risk.

Girls face particularly serious risks of abuse and exploitation. Some may be lured by traffickers with false promises of safety, an education, or a future job. Others may be fleeing sexual abuse or the threat of a forced marriage; some may have been sold into marriage by their desperate families, both to avoid the risk of rape and with the hope that the girl will acquire the citizenship of her husband.

Traumatic journeys through unfamiliar terrain, psychological manipulation, physical harassment, sexual abuse, extortion, trafficking, or neglect outside transit centers or in transit with no clear destination constitute a daily life shrouded in fear and uncertainty. Children on the move often fail to enjoy the protection to which they are entitled. Many endure forced separation from their families and placement in overcrowded facilities, mixed together with unrelated adults where they face high risk of abuse. Several end up placed in hot spots with fast-tracking proceedings and strong risks of fast-return procedures, where their best interests will hardly be considered, while others end up in detention centers, allegedly for their own protection. Deprivation of liberty is never in the child's best interests, and alternatives must be promoted to ensure children's safety and well-being.

Time and time again children on the move experience fear, anxiety, panic, depression, sleep disorders, mental health problems, increased risk of self-harm, and an aggravated sense of hopelessness, all of which has a severe impact on their development and well-being. These children have been left very far behind. For them, the ambitious vision of the CRC and of the 2030 Agenda is a very distant ideal.

It is urgent to transform the continuum of violence that shapes their life into a continuum of protection of their fundamental rights. It is against this background that two global compacts on migration and refugees were adopted at the end of 2018.[22] It is now incumbent upon each state to ensure their effective implementation in line with the CRC and always guided by the best interests of the child.

3 Children's Protection from Violence: A Core Dimension of States' Accountability for Children's Rights

The CRC made it a legal and ethical imperative to safeguard the right of every child to freedom from all forms of violence.[23] Indeed, children must be envisaged as a zone of peace. To underscore this crucial commitment, the CRC provides detailed attention to a non-exhaustive list of manifestations of violence across different settings: significant provisions prohibit the use of the death penalty and life imprisonment and ban any act of torture, cruel, inhuman or degrading treatment, or punishment;[24] others address protection of children from harmful practices[25] as well as from sexual abuse, sale, trafficking, and any other form of exploitation;[26] still others focus on school violence and any form of school discipline contrary to the child's human dignity;[27] on the protection from armed conflict;[28] and special attention is given to manifestations of violence within the privacy of the family or behind the walls of care institutions.[29]

Alongside this ambitious vision of effective and comprehensive protection of children from all forms of violence, the CRC offers important guidance to support states in their implementation efforts. This explains the steady attention given by the CRC Committee to this important concern, both in its review of reports by states parties and in the thematic discussions held,[30] as well as through its important jurisprudence. Violence has in fact been a constant concern in the CRC Committee's General Comments,[31] certainly those concerning corporal punishment, harmful practices, and the right to freedom from violence but also those addressing a wide range of topics, including children's bests interests, the aims of education, health, adolescence, street situations, or international migration.

While all provisions are interrelated and mutually supportive, Article 19 is particularly paradigmatic. First, it recognizes a legal obligation of purpose: states must ensure children's freedom from all forms of violence, including physical, mental, or sexual violence; injury, abuse, neglect or negligent treatment; maltreatment or exploitation.

Second, it sets an obligation of conduct: to address the multidimensional nature of violence, states must adopt all appropriate legislative, administrative, social, and educational measures, including protective measures to provide support for the child and those who have the care of the child. Such a comprehensive strategy is critical to ensure the prevention, identification, reporting, referral, investigation, and treatment of, and follow-up on, incidents of violence, and, when appropriate, it may include judicial involvement.[32]

Legislative measures are indispensable. They help to ensure conformity of the national legal framework with the principles and provisions of the CRC, including by explicitly banning all violence in all contexts; by establishing protective measures for child victims and witnesses; and by investigating incidents and fighting impunity.[33] Legislation is also key to the prevention and condemnation of unacceptable behavior, the legitimization of actions taken by services and institutions, and the provision of support to children's care and upbringing through nonviolent means. Expressions such as "punishment in moderation," "reasonable chastisement," and "treatment without excessive harshness" should therefore be avoided in legal provisions, since they lack precision and clarity and leave room for discretionary and subjective interpretation contrary to the best interests and human dignity of the child.

And not less importantly, legislation helps child victims feel they matter. Children must feel supported and confident to report incidents and to seek support, redress, and genuine recovery and reintegration. As the CRC highlights,[34] this process must take place in an environment which fosters the health, self-respect, and dignity of the child.

Legislation is essential but certainly not insufficient to safeguard children's safety and protection. As noted by the CRC Committee,[35] administrative measures are crucial to define roles and responsibilities of all relevant actors and at all levels of the administration; social measures are necessary to reduce risks and prevent violence through basic and targeted services for children, their families, and other caregivers; and educational measures are essential to supporting changes in attitudes, traditions, customs, and behavioral practices which condone or promote violence against children.

The imperative to safeguard children's freedom from violence has also been a key concern for regional human rights standards and institutions. For example, Article 16 of the African Charter on the Rights and Welfare of the Child includes provisions similar to those of Article 19 of the CRC. The African Committee on the Rights and Welfare of the Child has given strong attention to this topic: in its 2011 statement on violence against children[36] it called for the firm engagement of African states, at the highest level, to support the eradication of all forms of violence against children; through its 2018 General Comment 5,[37] it highlighted the obligation of states parties to adopt legislation prohibiting all corporal punishment of children in all settings, including the home, schools, and penal institutions, and as a sentence for a crime; it also stressed that the perpetuation of harmful cultural practices cannot be defended on the basis of custom, tradition, religion, or culture and that such harmful practices must be eliminated.

In Europe the case law from the European Court of Human Rights and the European Committee of Social Rights considered the corporal punishment of children as contrary to Article 3 of the European Convention on Human Rights[38] and to Article 17 of the European Social Charter[39] (revised), respectively. Moreover, the Parliamentary Assembly adopted a Recommendation calling for Europe to become a "corporal punishment-free zone." An important campaign was also launched: "Raise your hand against smacking,"[40] which aims to increase awareness, promote the abolition of corporal punishment, and encourage positive, nonviolent parenting.

In the Americas, the Inter-American Commission on Human Rights issued in 2009 an important report on corporal punishment and the human rights of children and adolescents.[41] As noted then, "meeting the obligation of respecting and upholding human rights assumed by States in the protection of children and adolescents against corporal punishment requires measures of many different kinds, the goal of which must be the absolute eradication of the practice. In that regard, a consensus can be seen to exist within the international community regarding the urgency of legally prohibiting corporal punishment against children. This legal ban, however, must be accompanied by measures of other kinds—judicial, educational, financial, etc.—that, taken together, serve to eradicate the use of this form of punishment in the everyday lives of all children and adolescents."[42] The Inter-American Commission stressed that the use of corporal punishment as a way of disciplining children and adolescents, whether imposed by state agents or when a state permits or tolerates it, constitutes a form of violence against children that wounds their dignity and hence their human rights. Organization of American States member states are thus obliged to guarantee children and adolescents special protection against the use of corporal punishment and to promote alternative disciplinary measures that are participatory, positive, and not violent in such a way that the human dignity of children is respected.

4 Children's Protection from Violence Must Be at the Heart of the Policy Agenda

Violence against children is a pervasive and silent emergency, but it is not an inevitable outcome. With the implementation of the CRC and of the 2030 Agenda, children's freedom from violence can be placed at the heart of the policy agenda of every nation. This will help to prevent the risk of neglect, abuse, and exploitation in children's lives, provide effective and long-term support to victims, investigate and follow cases, and fight impunity.

The roots of violence against children are multifaceted, and preventing and eliminating it require a multisectoral and integrated approach. Indeed, violence goes hand in hand with vulnerability and deprivation, with high risks of poor health, poor school performance, and, at times, long-term welfare dependency. Children exposed to violence— at home, in schools, in the community, at work, in care and justice institutions, or online—are at greater risk of enduring cumulative acts of violence and engaging in aggressive and violent behavior later in life.

Violence leaves long-lasting scars on children's lives and often has irreversible consequences affecting their development and well-being. It also weakens the very foundation of social progress, generating huge costs for society—according to some estimates, the global costs of violence against children could be as high as US\$7 trillion per year or 8 percent of global GDP.[43] In addition, violence slows economic development and erodes states' human and social capital.[44]

While half of those living in extreme poverty are children, and half of the world's children are affected by violence every year, budget allocations to address children's protection are often inadequate. Unlike other dimensions of child well-being, spending to address violence against children is not systematically monitored, and there is no international methodology for tracking and recording allocations, whether from official development assistance, domestic resources, or other financial flows. Yet through enhanced cooperation, and with serious investment in proven strategies for prevention, violence can become a thing of the distant past.

The 2030 Agenda is global and universal and has the unique potential to bring positive results to all parts of the world. But more importantly, it concerns all children. It is critical to invest in children to achieve inclusive, equitable, and sustainable development for present and future generations. The value and success of the 2030 Agenda will be measured by the strategic action taken and tangible progress made in implementation on the ground, especially for those furthest behind, those who are the least visible and most forgotten children and who often are also the most at risk of violence, abuse, and exploitation.

It is therefore essential to promote the adoption and implementation of a comprehensive and cohesive nationally owned sustainable development strategy that is supported by predictable resources; informed by solid evidence and robust, reliable, and disaggregated data; and reviewed through an open, inclusive, and periodic assessment of progress, using internationally agreed upon benchmarks.

The experience gained from ten years of implementation of the recommendations of the UN Study on Violence against Children provides a solid basis to build upon. An increasing number of states have promoted awareness and social mobilization initiatives on this topic and adopted legislation and national plans of action to prevent and respond to violence, along with mechanisms to collect and analyze data to inform planning, policy, and budgetary decisions as well as monitor and evaluate. States conduct regular reviews to assess progress in the implementation of the 2030 Agenda. Through these voluntary national reviews submitted to the United Nations High-Level Political Forum,[45] increasing attention is being given to the protection of children from violence as a key component of sustainable development. As highlighted by the ministerial declaration adopted in 2018, "developing the human capital required to build sustainable and resilient societies must begin with investing in all children, adolescents and youth, safeguarding their rights and ensuring that from early childhood they grow up in a safe environment, free from all forms of violence, including neglect, abuse and exploitation, and through the elimination of all harmful practices."[46]

Translating the 2030 Agenda into national action is well under way,[47] though much more needs to be done to mainstream the goals and targets into national development plans, strategies, and actions that are nationally owned to further the realization of children's rights. Regional organizations and institutions have become crucial players in these efforts. In some cases, such as the Association of Southeast Asian Nations (ASEAN)[48] and the Council of Europe,[49] regional intergovernmental organizations have already adopted new regional policy plans on violence against children aligned with the 2030 Agenda. In others, such as the South Asia Initiative to End Violence against Children and the High-Level Authorities on Human Rights of the Southern Common Market (MERCOSUR), similar efforts are being promoted. In many cases, analytical studies have also been conducted to review progress, as was, for instance, the case of the studies conducted by the League of Arab States[50] or the study to follow-up implementation of the UN Study on Violence against Children in the Caribbean.[51] These steps are now translating into the strengthening of national legal standards and public policies, the promotion of better research and monitoring tools, and the emergence of evidenced-based campaigns to support, stimulate, and monitor progress in the protection of children from violence.

4.1 From the Periphery of the Debate to the Center of the Policy Agenda

Around the world, significant efforts have been made to place violence against children high in the public debate and on the policy agenda. First, close to one hundred countries today have a strong national agenda on violence against children—examples include recently adopted strategies in Cambodia, Canada, Chile, France, Indonesia, Lao People's Democratic Republic, Malawi, Mexico, Nigeria, Panama, Paraguay, the Philippines, and Tanzania.[52]

As called for by the first recommendation of the UN Study, the comprehensive policy or strategy framework to prevent and respond to violence against children needs to be evidenced-based; integrated into national planning processes, with realistic and time-bound targets; adequately funded and coordinated by an agency with the capacity to involve multiple sectors; and critical to spearheading action to end violence in children's lives. The advances in this recommendation since 2006, when only forty-seven countries had such a policy framework, are commendable and show the commitment across regions to elevate this concern to the highest levels.

Second, the number of states with a comprehensive legal prohibition of all forms of violence has more than tripled since the UN Study was adopted.[53] Sweden broke new ground with its 1979 law. But today, more than fifty states have adopted similar provisions, sometimes in their constitutions, to ban the use of violence as a form of discipline, correction, or punishment. Most recently a comprehensive legal ban was enacted in such countries as Benin, Ireland, Lithuania, Mongolia, Montenegro, Nepal, Paraguay, Peru, Slovenia, and Vietnam.

As a core recommendation of the UN Study, legislation is key to expressing state accountability for children's rights. Legislation provides a sound normative foundation to safeguard children's dignity and physical integrity at all times and conveys an unequivocal message to society condemning any form of violence against children while also encouraging the upbringing and education of children through nonviolent means. Strong legislation provides clear guidance to state officials, teachers, and other public professionals as well as to families and common citizens about what is acceptable and what is nonnegotiable and provides the necessary means to fight impunity. Of greater importance, child victims feel they matter! They can enjoy protection from neglect, abuse, and exploitation and can gain access to effective tools of redress and to genuine recovery and reintegration.

In addition, legal reform opens avenues for wide public information and social mobilization initiatives, helping to engage key actors and institutions to promote change in attitudes and behavior that condone violence against children. In all regions we have witnessed crucial processes promoted by parliamentarians, religious leaders, local authorities, professional associations, and families themselves to support this important process of social change.

Linked with a stronger national policy and legal framework, we have seen the bolstering of national child protection systems and services, with more and more professionals being trained in early detection, prevention, and response to violence, as well as promising programs opening avenues to help children and their families gain access to counseling, medical services, legal advice, and representation to seek redress, recovery, and reintegration.

Third, the past two decades have witnessed an incremental development of different measurement activities aimed at shedding light on this issue and filling existing data gaps, including through the inclusion of violence-related questions in several international multipurpose survey programs, such as the UNICEF-supported Multiple Indicator Cluster Surveys (MICS) as well as dedicated national surveys on violence against children.[54]

A crucial recommendation put forward by the UN Study, consolidating national data systems and research is essential to capture the prevalence of violence, break its invisibility, challenge its social acceptance, understand its causes, and enhance protection for children at risk. A growing number of countries in Africa and Asia are gathering data to assess the prevalence of violence in children's lives to inform evidenced-based policy and budgetary decisions for violence prevention and response. In 2018 alone, four comprehensive data surveys were launched in the Lao People's Democratic Republic, Rwanda, Uganda, and Zambia, helping to inform evidence-based advocacy and policy action for violence prevention and elimination.[55]

Similarly, evidence has been steadily strengthened with valuable studies and guidance issued on a number of topics and particular areas of concern. In this regard, children's protection from bullying has gained a special relevance, with two significant reports of the United Nations Secretary-General presented to the General Assembly[56] and a study conducted on this topic, "Ending the Torment: Tackling Bullying from Schoolyard to Cyberspace."[57]

Children's protection from different manifestations of violence was also given much attention, for example, within the justice system,[58] including through restorative justice;[59] promotion of a gender-sensitive approach to criminal justice;[60] protection from armed violence and organized crime in the community;[61] online abuse;[62] and sexual exploitation in travel and tourism.[63] At the same time, the past years were marked by the development of standardized tools to support national implementation efforts, such as INSPIRE, a package of evidence-based strategies to prevent and address violence,[64] and the Luxembourg Terminology Guidelines to enhance conceptual clarity and action for the protection of children from sexual exploitation and abuse.[65]

The positive change achieved so far is the result of the sustained commitment and collective efforts of an ever-growing number of governments, organizations, institutions, and individuals around the world, including children themselves. But alongside these significant developments, many challenges remain.

4.2 Overcoming Challenges and Seizing Strategic Opportunities to Safeguard Children

4.2.1 *Breaking the Invisibility of Violence against Children*

Despite significant progress in raising awareness of the extent and impact of violence on children's lives, a particularly pervasive challenge is that much of it still remains hidden, especially when it occurs in the privacy of the home and behind the closed doors of institutions.

The true extent of violence and its impact on children's health, education, self-esteem, and resilience is masked when violence remains socially condoned and accepted—be it as a form of discipline, correction, or punishment. In fact, it is often not fully appreciated that almost ninety percent of situations of violence in children's lives occur in non-conflict situations.[66]

Violence is a silent and corrosive emergency. It shapes children's daily existence, generating fear, anxiety and depression, and mistrust in their relationships with others. Children feel frightened to tell their stories and to seek help. In fact, most of the time they do not know where to turn or whom to call. And even if they do seek help, only a small fraction receive the services to which they are entitled.[67]

Changing attitudes that condone or normalize violence and overcoming a degree of fatalism that ending violence in all its forms is unachievable remain imperative and urgent. There are many positive examples to draw upon to show how the process of changing attitudes can be promoted and the abandonment of harmful practices supported. In Africa, addressing such deeply rooted social conventions as child and forced marriage, female genital cutting, sexual initiation ceremonies, attacks against children with albinism, and other harmful practices has been high on the agenda and has gained a special relevance when supported by engagement with the communities concerned and action at the local level. This is particularly so when the leadership and determination of traditional and community leaders is supported by efforts to mobilize the abandonment of such practices.[68]

In Malawi, for example, incremental progress is being achieved through a combination of recent constitutional and legislative developments to raise the minimum age of marriage to eighteen and community-based social mobilization processes to promote children's rights. In one single district, efforts led by a female traditional chief heralded a landmark initiative that resulted in the annulment of 850 child marriages and the banning of sexual initiation of girls, leading to the return of those who got married to school.[69]

Dealing with such deeply rooted social conventions implicates many different levels. This can be seen from the community to national level, all the way to regional commitments, as evidenced by the work promoted by the African Union (AU) and the African Committee of Experts on the Rights and Welfare of the Child (ACERWC) to launch a region-wide campaign to end child marriage, supported by strategic follow-up action in twenty-four countries.

But sustained awareness, advocacy, and policy dialogue has also led to placing these concerns on the global policy agenda. This is well illustrated by the important mobilization to prevent the marginalization, neglect, and serious attacks against persons with albinism, which has led to the proclamation by the UN General Assembly of International Albinism Awareness Day,[70] and by the establishment of a new mandate of the Human Rights Council to address violations of human rights against persons with albinism[71] and to stimulate debate and policy reforms to strengthen the protection of these particularly vulnerable children.

4.2.2 Reactive and Fragmented Responses and Actions

Violence in children's lives is a multifaceted problem and can be effectively addressed only through a comprehensive multisector and multidisciplinary approach. Although it is well known that no single sector or service in isolation can effectively prevent and respond to all the risks children face, actions still tend to be reactive, fragmented, and pursued in administrative and programmatic silos. The UN Study found that strategies to address violence against children were all too often poorly coordinated, not informed by data and evidence, and with inadequate or nonexistent communication across government departments and between central and local authorities and professionals. This continues to be an area where much remains to be done.

Similarly, enforcement of legislation remains a challenge. Where clear and comprehensive laws are in place, legal provisions are often not known, understood, or used by professionals, families, and communities. And for children, recourse to the law seems like entering an impenetrable labyrinth. It is imperative to simplify the language used, to promote accessible and child-friendly materials, and to bring policies and laws close to professionals and the people whom they were developed to protect.

4.2.3 Weak Monitoring and Evaluation of Progress

While incremental progress has been made in the consolidation of data and research, information on violence against children remains scarce and fragmented across and within countries. Most importantly, it often neglects children left furthest behind, including those with disabilities, placed in care and criminal justice institutions, those who are socially excluded or who belong to minorities or indigenous groups. This is a grave concern, considering the global scale and severity of the problem.

Information is crucial to regularly monitor progress and assess impact. Yet there is still a serious lack of comprehensive and disaggregated data at the national level to expose the reality of children's lives, to identify those at greatest risk, to capture the root causes, and to provide sound evidence of what works to help achieve positive change. It is urgent to improve the collection, analysis, dissemination, and use of data on violence against children; to harmonize measurement tools to produce estimates that are reliable, comprehensive, and internationally comparable in order to accurately document the widespread nature of violence; to support government planning and budgeting for child protection services; and to inform the development of effective laws, policies, and prevention efforts worldwide.[72] Together with initiatives to develop robust, credible, and accurate data and research, it is vital to integrate information across sectors, disciplines, and data sources, keeping the human dignity and best interests of the child as central concerns in the assessment of the cumulative impact of different manifestations of violence over the child's life cycle.

Children's perceptions, views, and experiences are crucial for understanding the hidden face of violence and helping address its root causes. However, their involvement in data collection and analysis confronts significant challenges and dilemmas, including the lack of clear ethical standards to balance the need to protect children from harm with their right to express their views and influence decisions.

Data and research are not politically neutral. They provide transparency to policy-making and make possible public scrutiny of states' actions for and achievements in the protection of children from violence. This is an area where the leadership and commitment of governments may be most meaningfully expressed by placing the best interests of the child above the temptation to preserve a positive political image.

The need for action has never been more urgent in light of the 2030 Agenda for Sustainable Development and its SDG target 16.2 to end all forms of violence against children. To achieve progress in this area, many countries need support to enhance their national statistical and research capacity with the tools and methodologies necessary to do it right. Furthermore, it is essential to address new and emerging threats to children, to be vigilant in monitoring developments and agile in adjusting our responses.

The opportunities and risks associated with information and communication technologies (ICTs) illustrate this well.[73] Indeed, mobile phones, computers, and access to the Internet are very present in children's lives: children use ICTs in ever growing numbers, navigate the online world for longer hours, and start at an increasingly younger age. ICTs offer children new and exciting means of enhancing knowledge and skills, experiencing creative research and cultural activities, and engaging in play, socialization, and entertainment. And they open avenues for children to learn about their rights and about ways of securing their protection.

But alongside this potential, there are also associated risks. Children can be exposed to harmful information or abusive material, groomed by potential predators, and subjected to cyberbullying, exploitation and abuse, including through the production and distribution of child abuse images or live web streaming and through sexting or sextortion. Although a small proportion of children may be affected, online abuse can have devastating consequences for children—including fear, depression, anxiety, low self-esteem, eating and sleeping disorders, suicidal ideation, and feelings of shame and guilt.

For marginalized children who may not have access to the Internet at home or in school, who may lack advice and guidance from caregivers and who often explore the cyber universe on their own, the opportunity to become an empowered digital citizen will be limited, and these children will also be more likely to encounter cyber violence and harassment.

At the same time, in many countries technology has advanced faster than the state's capacity to respond, and countries still largely lack laws, policies, mechanisms, and institutions to protect children from these serious risks and to empower them to be the first line of prevention. To address this phenomenon, it is critical to promote a multifaceted, safe, inclusive, and empowering digital agenda that supports children's potential and effectively detects and addresses abuse. An agenda that avoids solutions driven by fear or censorship and which ensures the optimal balance between preserving children's natural curiosity, creativity, sense of innovation, and freedom to explore and learn online with their effective protection from harm. In this regard, important initiatives provide a sound basis to build upon. The Model National Response to Child Sexual Exploitation and Abuse, promoted by the WePROTECT Global Alliance and endorsed by an increasing number of countries, is one valuable example in this field.[74]

4.3 Promoting the Agency of Children

The inclusion for the first time on the international development agenda of a distinct target (SDG target 16.2) calling for the elimination of all forms of violence by 2030 marked a turning point in global efforts on safeguarding children's freedom from violence. This is a universal agenda and requires all of our collective efforts.

SDG target 16.2 is crucial but should not be seen in isolation. In fact, the sustainable development agenda addresses violence against children across different goals and targets, and they are all closely interrelated—including the promotion of healthy lives and of quality, safe, and nonviolent education; the elimination of child marriage and female mutilation and of forced and child labor; the promotion of safe public spaces and of peaceful and inclusive societies with accountable and transparent institutions and access to justice for all.

Implementation of the entire 2030 Agenda and progress toward SDG target 16.2 and the violence-related targets will give tremendous impetus to our common endeavor to end all forms of violence against children, in all settings.

To achieve this goal, it is urgent that states adopt and implement a comprehensive, integrated, multidisciplinary, time-bound strategy to prevent and respond to all forms of violence against children. Such a strategy must be supported by predictable resources informed by solid evidence and robust, reliable, and disaggregated data that are well-coordinated and periodically reviewed through an open, inclusive, and transparent process. In addition, it must be promoted with all stakeholders—including children themselves.

The UN Study was the first UN report drafted in collaboration with children and young people. Their involvement has remained crucial to the implementation of its recommendations, including in advocacy, expert discussions, and the development of thematic reports. Similarly, thousands of children were actively involved in the shaping of the 2030 Agenda.[75] The elimination of violence was at the top of their concerns. Indeed, across regions, their message was clear and unambiguous: "Violence is a major obstacle to child development and it urgently needs to be brought to an end!" Children's commitment has not weakened, and they remain eager to influence the important process of review and follow-up.

Children cannot be ignored as not-yet persons or adults in the making; they are citizens of today and crucial partners in the process of social change we are committed to promote.

Joining hands with young people and listening to their views and experiences is crucial to gain a better understanding of the hidden face of violence and, more importantly, to become better equipped to prevent this phenomenon. Children help us develop tools to provide advice and report incidents of violence as well as to put in place long-lasting reintegration strategies for child victims. Their support is crucial to monitor progress and impact.

Children's views and experiences also help us realize the importance of addressing cultural attitudes that compromise progress in the fight against violence. Their insights and experiences are essential to mobilizing community and opinion leaders and in promoting a strong system of legal protection.

Children are key actors in expressing solidarity and support to their peers who suffer violence. They promote awareness and understanding of the impact of violence, including through social media where they have unique experience and expertise, in engaging in the sensitization of communities and in practicing respect for each other, acting as a model of tolerance and nonviolence. But participation has a cost, and it will not happen if children are not empowered and effectively protected. As children tell me time and time again, "For participation to happen, we need security and justice; security to be protected from the risk of harassment and reprisals; justice to ensure that impunity is fought whenever violence takes place!"

For this ambition to become a reality, it is urgent to promote the development in all countries of safe, child-sensitive, and accessible counseling, complaints procedures, and reporting mechanisms. And countries must also establish and support institutions that children can genuinely trust, and before whom they can tell their stories, without fear or publicity, punishment, or reprisal.

Children want to join hands in the building of a world free from fear and from violence, a world of the size of their dreams! Violence can be prevented and eliminated, but this cannot be a dream pursued by a few; it needs to become a priority for all.

5 Conclusion

With the implementation of the Convention on the Rights of the Child, the world has made tremendous strides toward the realization of children's rights. But the vision of the CRC will not be fully realized unless children's rights become one of the sustaining pillars of society and are embraced as a core value of the dialogue between generations.

As we look ahead, it is crucial to sustain and consolidate further the gains that have been made, grasp the lessons learned, and move boldly together to address emerging challenges to transform into reality the momentum gained with the adoption of the 2030 Agenda for Sustainable Development. It is high time to close the gap between the commitments to prevent and address violence against children and the action that can turn this goal into a reality for each and every child. It is high time to genuinely address the root causes of violence and to promote a culture of respect for children's rights and of zero tolerance of violence. It is high time to mobilize and ignite the passion of all those who can actively engage in the creation of circles of nonviolence in children's homes, schools, and communities.

To achieve lasting progress, hope must replace despair and confidence must supplant distrust. Talent must be placed at the service of the violence-free society we all aspire to build. And it is imperative to move with a deep sense of urgency. In the countdown to 2030, everybody counts, and everybody is needed. The transformative power of leaders from all walks of life, together with the determination of people to stand up for children, alongside children's own agency, experience, and resilience, provide a unique opportunity to widen the global movement to free all children from violence. UN actors, governments, regional intergovernmental organizations, civil society organizations, religious communities, professional networks, the private sector, and individuals are joining in this global mobilization effort to widen circles of nonviolence around children's lives.

2019 marked the thirtieth anniversary of the CRC. Also in 2019, the UN General Assembly hosted its first Heads of State Summit to review the implementation of the 2030 Agenda for Sustainable Development, including SDG target 16.2 on ending all forms of violence against children. This is a unique milestone that we cannot miss.[76] Guided by the human rights imperative of freeing children from violence, by the evidence gathered in recent years of what works, by children's inspiring efforts and resilience, and by the ambitious vision and historic opportunity offered by the 2030 Agenda, we can promote a quantum leap in violence prevention and response efforts and build a world as big as children's dream.

In the countdown to 2030, every citizen can be an agent of change. And this can inspire others to bring about the change we need. With our hands joined together, the sum of all forces will be zero: zero violence for all children. And zero will become humankind's favorite number.

Notes

1. UN Convention on the Rights of the Child (CRC), G.A. Res. 44/25, 44th Sess., UN doc. A/RES/44/25 (1989).
2. Optional Protocol to the Convention on the Rights of the Child on the Sale of Children, Child Prostitution and Child Pornography, G.A. Res. 54/263, 54th Sess., UN Doc. A/RES/54/263 (2000); Optional Protocol to the Convention on the Rights of the Child on the Involvement of Children in Armed Conflict, G.A. Res. 54/263, 54th Sess., UN Doc. A/RES/54/263 (2000); Optional Protocol to the Convention on the Rights of the Child on a Communications Procedure, G.A. Res. 66/138, 66th Sess., UN Doc. A/RES/66/138 (2011).
3. See CRC, arts. 19, 24, 28, 32–37, and 39.
4. UN Special Representative of the Secretary-General on Violence against Children (SRSG on Violence against Children), "UN Study on Violence against Children" (2006), https://violenceagainstchildren.un.org/content/un-study-violence-against-children.
5. UN General Assembly, "Report of the Independent Expert for the United Nations Study on Violence against Children," UN Doc. A/61/299 (2006).
6. UN General Assembly, "Report of the Independent Expert," para. 91
7. See the SRSG on Violence against Children home page, https://violenceagainstchildren.un.org.
8. UN General Assembly, "Rights of the Child," G.A. Res. 62/141, 62nd Sess., UN Doc. A/Res/62/141 (2018).
9. UN General Assembly, "Transforming Our World: The 2030 Agenda for Sustainable Development," G.A. Res. 70/1, 70th Sess., UN Doc. A/Res/70/1 (2015).
10. UN Human Rights Council, "Annual Report of the Special Representative of the Secretary-General on Violence against Children," A/HRC/37/48 (2018), 3–5.
11. UN Human Rights Council, "Annual Report (2018)," para 15.
12. Internet Watch Foundation (IWF), "IWF Global Figures Show Online Child Sexual Abuse Imagery Up by a Third" (April 18, 2018), https://www.iwf.org.uk/news/iwf-global-figures-show-online-child-sexual-abuse-imagery-up-by-a-third.
13. United Nations Children's Fund (UNICEF), "A Familiar Face: Violence in the Lives of Children and Adolescents" (November 2017), https://data.unicef.org/wp-content/uploads/2017/10/EVAC-Booklet-FINAL-10_31_17-high-res.pdf.
14. SRSG on Violence against Children, "Violence Prevention Must Start in Early Childhood," https://violenceagainstchildren.un.org/news/violence-prevention-must-start-early-childhood (accessed Aug. 21, 2019).
15. UN General Assembly, "Annual Report of the Special Representative of the Secretary-General on Violence against Children," UN Doc. A/73/276 (July 30, 2018), 15–16.
16. SRSG on Violence against Children, "Tackling Violence in Schools: A Global Perspective Bridging the Gap between Standards and Practice" (2012), vii, https://violenceagainstchildren.un.org/sites/violenceagainstchildren.un.org/files/documents/publications/10._tackling_violence_in_schools_a_global_perspective.pdf.
17. SRSG on Violence against Children, "Ending the Torment: Tackling Bullying from the Schoolyard to Cyberspace" (2016), v–vii, https://violenceagainstchildren.un.org/sites/violenceagainstchildren.un.org/files/documents/publications/tackling_bullying_from_schoolyard_to_cyberspace_low_res_fa.pdf.
18. SRSG on Violence against Children, "Ending the Torment," v.

19. See UN High Commissioner for Refugees, "Trends at a Glance," https://www.unhcr.org/globaltrends2017 (accessed Aug. 21, 2019).

20. UN High Commissioner for Refugees, "Trends at a Glance."

21. UN General Assembly, "Annual Report of the Special Representative of the Secretary-General on Violence against Children," U.N. Doc. A/72/275 (Aug. 2, 2017), 8–10.

22. UN General Assembly, "Intergovernmental Conference to Adopt the Global Compact for Safe, Orderly and Regular Migration: Draft Outcome Document of the Conference," UN Doc. A/CONF.231/3 (July 30, 2018); see also UN General Assembly, "Report of the United Nations High Commissioner for Refugees: Part II Global Impact on Refugees," UN Doc. A/73/12 (2018).

23. UN Office of the High Commissioner for Human Rights (OHCHR), "Manual on Human Rights Reporting Under Six Major International Human Rights Instruments," UN Doc. HR/PUB/91/1 (Rev.1) (1997), 408, 447–448.

24. CRC, art. 37(a).

25. CRC, art. 24.3.

26. CRC, arts. 32–36.

27. Convention on the Rights of the Child, art. 28.2.

28. CRC, art. 38.

29. CRC, art. 19.

30. Including those held on violence against children, online abuse, the impact of armed conflict, and economic exploitation.

31. See OHCHR, CRC General Comments, UN Treaty Body Database, http://tbinternet.ohchr.org/_layouts/treatybodyexternal/TBSearch.aspx?Lang=en&TreatyID=5&DocTypeID=11 (accessed Aug. 21, 2019).

32. CRC, art. 19.2.

33. UN Committee on the Rights of the Child (CRC Committee), *General Comment No. 13 (2011): The Right of the Child to Freedom from All Forms of Violence*, CRC/C/GC/13 (2011), paras. 41–42.

34. CRC, art. 39.

35. CRC Committee, *General Comment No. 13*.

36. Global Initiative to End All Corporal Punishment of Children, "African Charter on the Rights and Welfare of the Child (ACRWC)" (last modified November 2018), https://endcorporalpunishment.org/human-rights-law/regional-human-rights-instruments/acrwc.

37. African Committee of Experts on the Rights and Welfare of the Child, "General Comment no 5 on State Party Obligations under the African Charter on the Rights and Welfare of the Child (Article 1) and Systems Strengthening for Child Protection" (2018), https://violenceagainstchildren.un.org/sites/violenceagainstchildren.un.org/files/regions/acerwc_general_comment_no._5_-2018.pdf.

38. See, for example, A. v. The United Kingdom, Application No. 100/1997/884/1096, Eur. Ct. H.R. (Sept. 23, 1998).

39. Council of Europe. "The European Social Charter," http://www.coe.int/t/dghl/monitoring/socialcharter/ECSR/ECSRdefault_en.asp (accessed Aug. 21, 2019).

40. Council of Europe/Human Rights Europe, "Raise Your Hand against Smacking" (Jan. 29, 2012), http://www.humanrightseurope.org/2012/01/raise-your-hand-against-smacking.

41. Inter-American Commission on Human Rights Rapporteurship on the Rights of the Child, "Report on Corporal Punishment and Human Rights of Children and Adolescents,"

OEA/Ser.L/V/II.135, Doc. 14 (Aug. 5, 2009), http://www.cidh.oas.org/Ninez/CastigoCorporal 2009/CASTIGO%20CORPORAL%20ENGLISH%20FINAL.pdf.

42. Inter-American Commission on Human Rights Rapporteurship on the Rights of the Child, "Report on Corporal Punishment," 34.

43. Paola Pereznieto, Andres Montes, Lara Langston, and Solveig Routier, "The Costs and Economic Impact of Violence against Children," Child Fund Alliance briefing paper, https://www.odi.org/sites/odi.org.uk/files/odi-assets/publications-opinion-files/9178.pdf (accessed Aug. 21, 2019).

44. UN Human Rights Council, "Annual Report (2018)," 3.

45. The High-Level Political Forum is the main United Nations platform on sustainable development, and it has a central role in the follow-up and review of the 2030 Agenda for Sustainable Development at the global level.

46. UN Economic and Social Council, "Ministerial Declaration of the High-Level Segment of the 2018 Session of the Economic and Social Council on the Annual Theme 'From Global to Local: Supporting Sustainable and Resilient Societies in Urban and Rural Communities'" and "Ministerial Declaration of the 2018 High-Level Political Forum on Sustainable Development, Convened under the Auspices of the Economic and Social Council, on the Theme 'Transformation Towards Sustainable and Resilient Societies,'" UN Doc. E/HLS/2018/1 (Aug. 1, 2018), para. 17.

47. UN Human Rights Council, Report of the Special Representative of the Secretary-General on Violence against Children UN Doc. A/HRC/40/50 (Jan. 9, 2019), 9–10.

48. The ASEAN Secretariat, "ASEAN Regional Plan of Action on the Elimination of Violence against Children" (March 2016), https://violenceagainstchildren.un.org/sites/violenceagainstchildren.un.org/files/documents/political_declarations/east_asia_and_pacific/asean_regional_plan_of_action_on_elimination_of_violence_against_children.pdf.

49. Council of Europe, "Council of Europe Strategy for the Rights of the Child (2016–2021)" (March 2016), https://violenceagainstchildren.un.org/sites/violenceagainstchildren.un.org/files/documents/political_declarations/coe2016_2021.pdf.

50. Secretariat General of the League of Arab States (LAS), Women, Family and Childhood Department—Social Affairs Sector, "The Comparative Arab Report on Implementing the Recommendations of the UN Secretary-General's Study on Violence against Children: Second Report, 2010–2012" (2013), https://violenceagainstchildren.un.org/sites/violenceagainstchildren.un.org/files/documents/political_declarations/las_report_final_2012.pdf.

51. Nadine Perrault, "Study on the Follow-Up to the Implementation of the UN Study on Violence against Children for the Caribbean" (September 2013), http://www.movimientoporlainfancia.org/wp-content/uploads/2013/05/Estudio-II-FINAL.pdf.

52. UN General Assembly, "Annual Report of the Special Representative (2018)," paras. 46–61.

53. UN Human Rights Council, "Report of the Special Representative (2019)," para 57.

54. Together for Girls, "Violence against Children Surveys," https://www.togetherforgirls.org/violence-children-surveys (accessed Aug. 21, 2019).

55. Together for Girls, "Violence against Children Surveys."

56. UN General Assembly, "Protecting Children from Bullying: Report of the Secretary-General," UN Doc. A/71/213 (July 26, 2016); see also UN General Assembly, "Protecting Children from Bullying: Report of the Secretary-General," U.N. Doc. A/73/265 (July 30, 2018).

57. SRSG on Violence against Children, "Ending the Torment."

58. SRSG on Violence against Children, "Prevention of and Responses to Violence against Children within the Juvenile Justice System" (2012), https://violenceagainstchildren.un. org/sites/violenceagainstchildren.un.org/files/documents/publications/8._prevention_of _and_responses_to_violence_against_children_within_the_juvenile_justice_system.pdf.

59. SRSG on Violence against Children, "Promoting Restorative Justice for Children" (2013), https://violenceagainstchildren.un.org/sites/violenceagainstchildren.un.org/files/ documents/publications/7._promoting_restorative_justice.pdf.

60. SRSG on Violence against Children, "Safeguarding the Rights of Girls in the Criminal Justice System: Preventing Violence, Stigmatization, and Deprivation of Liberty" (2015), https://violenceagainstchildren.un.org/sites/violenceagainstchildren.un.org/files/ document_files/safeguarding_the_rights_of_girls_in_the_criminal_justice_system_1.pdf.

61. SRSG on Violence against Children, "Protecting Children Affected by Armed Violence in the Community" (2016), https://violenceagainstchildren.un.org/sites/violenceagainstchildren. un.org/files/documents/publications/2._protecting_children_affected_by_armed _violence_in_the_community.pdf.

62. SRSG on Violence against Children, "Releasing Children's Potential and Minimizing Risks: ICTs, the Internet and Violence against Children" (2014), https://violenceagainstchildren. un.org/sites/violenceagainstchildren.un.org/files/documents/publications/6._releasing _childrens_potential_and_minimizing_risks_icts_fa_low_res.pdf.

63. Angela Hawke and Alison Raphael, "Offenders on the Move: Global Study on Sexual Exploitation of Children in Travel and Tourism 2016" (May 2016), http://cf.cdn.unwto.org/ sites/all/files/docpdf/globalstudy.pdf.

64. World Health Organization (WHO), "INSPIRE: Seven Strategies for Ending Violence against Children" (2016), https://apps.who.int/iris/bitstream/handle/10665/207717/9789241565356 -eng.pdf;jsessionid=F29A8B5D8BB5081D6DD9014F4ABF845A?sequence=1.

65. Terminology and Semantics Interagency Working Group on Sexual Exploitation of Children, "Terminology Guidelines for the Protection of Children from Sexual Exploitation and Sexual Abuse" (June 2016), http://luxembourgguidelines.org/english-version.

66. Geneva Declaration on Armed Violence and Development, "Global Burden of Armed Violence 2015: Every Body Counts" (May 8, 2015), http://www.genevadeclaration.org/ measurability/global-burden-of-armed-violence/global-burden-of-armed-violence-2015. html; see also UN Office on Drugs and Crime, "The Global Study on Homicide 2013: Trends, Context, and Data" (Aug. 8, 2014), https://www.unodc.org/documents /data-and-analysis/statistics/GSH2013/2014_GLOBAL_HOMICIDE_BOOK_web.pdf.

67. Steven A. Sumner, "Prevalence of Sexual Violence against Children and Use of Social Services—Seven Countries, 2007–2013," *Morbidity and Mortality Weekly Report* 64, no. 21 (June 2015): 565–569.

68. SRSG on Violence against Children, "Protecting Children from Harmful Practices in Plural Legal Systems with a Special Emphasis on Africa" (2012), https://violenceagainstchildren. un.org/sites/violenceagainstchildren.un.org/files/documents/publications/5._protecting _children_from_harmful_practices_low_res.pdf.

69. Human Rights Council, "Annual Report of the Special Representative of the Secretary -General on Violence against Children," UN Doc. A/HRC/34/45 (Jan. 3, 2017).

70. UN General Assembly, "International Albinism Awareness Day," G.A. Res. 69/170, 69th Sess., UN Doc. A/RES/69/170 (Feb. 12, 2015).

71. UN Human Rights Council, "Independent Expert on the Enjoyment of Human Rights by Persons with Albinism," UN Doc. A/HRC/RES/28/6 (April 10, 2015).

72. UN General Assembly, "Annual Report of the Special Representative of the Secretary -General on Violence against Children," UN Doc. A/67/230 (Aug. 2, 2012), 8–9.

73. SRSG on Violence against Children, "Releasing Children's Potential."

74. We Protect Global Alliance, "Preventing and Tackling Child Sexual Exploitation and Abuse (CSEA): A Model National Response" (November 2016), https://www.weprotect.org/the-model-national-response.

75. PLAN International, Save the Children, and SRSG on Violence against Children, "Why Children's Protection from Violence Must be at the Heart of the Post-2015 Development Agenda: A Review of Consultations with Children on the Post-2015 Development Agenda" (2014), v, https://violenceagainstchildren.un.org/news/why-children%E2%80%99s-protection -violence-should-be-heart-post-2015-development-agenda-review-0.

76. UN Human Rights Council, "Report of the Special Representative (2019)," 4.

CHAPTER 16

CONTINUING DILEMMAS OF INTERNATIONAL ADOPTION

TWILA L. PERRY

1 INTRODUCTION

INTERNATIONAL adoptions began primarily as a humanitarian response by North Americans to the problem of European children orphaned by World War II. After the war, when Europe was rebuilt and its economic condition stabilized, the problem of orphaned children was resolved.[1] Since that time, birth rates have fallen in the Western world, abortion and contraception have become more widely available,[2] and the stigma against women having children outside of marriage has declined.[3] The result has been fewer white women surrendering babies for adoption.[4] These factors led to a decline in the number of highly sought after children available for adoption in the West.[5] Also, beginning in the 1990s, after the fall of communism in the Soviet Union, social, political, and economic upheavals resulted in conditions that pressured many families in Russia and Eastern Europe to place their children in orphanages or for adoption.[6] A few widely publicized cases in the United States in which courts returned children to their biological parents after substantial periods with adoptive parents led to the perception among some people that international adoption was less risky than domestic adoption.[7] There has also been the perception on the part of some prospective adoptive parents that international adoptions were less complicated and could be processed more quickly.[8]

As a result of such developments, over the years there was a dramatic increase in adoptions by people in Western countries of children from Global South countries and from Eastern Europe and Russia.[9] Between 1990 and 2003, international adoptions into the United States rose from 7,093 to 21,364.[10] While the US has always had the largest group of international adopters, a parallel trend was in evidence in other Global North countries as well.[11] However, after the peak year of 2004, international adoptions began a decline that continues today. The numbers of international adoptions rise and fall in response to demographic changes, changes in social, political, and economic circumstances within nations, and changes in the political relationships between nations.

While many have viewed international adoption as a primary solution for children in need of homes, the practice has also generated significant controversy. There are debates about whether the existing legal structure for international adoption is sufficient to protect children from child trafficking, child buying, and other abuses. There are debates about whether international adoption is in the best interests of children who need homes or whether it results in children becoming alienated from the heritage and culture of their country of birth. Another point of contention is whether adoptive parents are able to meet the needs of internationally adopted children, some of whom have spent most or all of their lives in institutional care. There is significant disagreement as to the extent to which there should be efforts to place children in need of homes into caretaking arrangements in their countries of origin before they are placed for international adoption.

There are other complex issues. Even if all possible procedural safeguards were put into place to protect children from such abuses as trafficking and child buying, the question would remain as to whether the adoption of children of color from Global South countries represents further exploitation of a resource of countries that may have already experienced a history of colonialism and exploitation at the hands of the West. Also, the fact that many international adoptions consist of a transfer of children from some of the world's most disadvantaged women to some of the most advantaged raises troubling issues for women who advocate a feminist approach to public policy, including global issues.

This chapter begins by offering a brief background on adoption. It then describes the relevant human rights and children's rights framework that governs international adoption. Following this, using the example of the adoption of children from foreign countries into the United States, the chapter provides a brief description of the processes involved in pursuing an international adoption. It then examines some of the critiques of the international legal framework. This is followed by a discussion of the decline in international adoptions since 2004 and some of the reasons for that decline. The chapter then briefly summarizes some of the recommendations that have been offered by groups and individuals through the years in the hope of improving the existing system's ability to further the best interests of internationally adopted children.

The chapter then turns to some issues concerning international adoption not easily addressed simply by implementing various practical recommendations. These complex issues arise from the continuing problems of poverty, racism, and patriarchy in the world, including the effect of histories of colonialism and imperialism between some Western nations and many of the countries from which internationally adopted children have come. The chapter notes the importance for scholarship and public policy analysis to find ways to more directly address some of these concerns, which have been expressed in such theoretical scholarship as postcolonial theory, critical race theory, and feminist theory.

2 ADOPTION

Adoption is the legal transfer of a child from his or her biological parent or parents to another adult. The parent who has surrendered a child for adoption no longer has any legal rights or responsibilities with respect to that child—those rights and responsibilities are entirely assumed by the adoptive parents. The adopted child is entitled to all of the same legal privileges and benefits as a biological child of the adoptive parents.[12]

The touchstone principle in adoption has long been the best interests of the child.[13] That principle embodies the idea that decisions concerning the placement of children, whether in custody disputes, foster care, or adoption, should be based on the best interests of each individual child rather than the best interests of adults or the interests of the state or other institutions. Although the best interests rule has been criticized by some as being subjective and indeterminate,[14] it remains the widely accepted principle for child-placement decisions.

Much of the literature on adoption stresses the value of children growing up in a family context in which there is permanence rather than in an institution such as an orphanage or in foster care. There is general agreement among experts that orphanages or other institutional settings are not settings in which children are most likely to thrive and may even be harmful to the child.[15] While foster care places children in a family setting on a temporary basis while the child's birth family addresses problems necessitating the temporary separation, foster care is still regarded as seriously limited in its ability to meet the important needs of children for permanence and a loving family that the child understands is committed to them for life.[16]

3 INTERNATIONAL ADOPTION: THE HUMAN RIGHTS AND CHILDREN'S RIGHTS FRAMEWORK

3.1 The Legal Framework for International Adoption

The legal framework for international adoption is very complex and difficult to summarize. It involves international law as well as the laws of the countries sending children for adoption and the countries receiving them. It is important for any person planning to undertake an international adoption to understand that it is a multistep process that incorporates ideas rooted in principles of international human rights and international children's rights and that it is a process that must comply with the laws of a number of different governmental authorities. The discussion below offers a brief introduction to the general international legal framework.

The laws governing international adoptions are derived from the broader context of the concept of human rights. The 1948 Universal Declaration of Human Rights reflects the principle that all human beings are to be treated equally and with respect. In addition, there are nine core treaties: the International Covenant on Civil and Political Rights, the International Covenant on Economic, Social and Cultural Rights, the Convention against Torture and Other Cruel, Inhuman or Degrading Treatment or Punishment, the International Convention on the Elimination of All Forms of Racial Discrimination, the Convention on the Elimination of All Forms of Discrimination against Women, the Convention on the Rights of the Child, the International Convention on the Protection of the Rights of all Migrant Workers and Members of Their Families, the International Convention for the Protection of All Persons from Enforced Disappearance, and the Convention on the Rights of Persons with Disabilities.[17]

That the UN Convention on the Rights of the Child (CRC) is recognized as one of the major international conventions is an indication that the international community sees the rights of children as being an important issue. Adopted in 1989, the CRC is a core component of the legal framework governing international adoption.

Article 21 of the CRC,[18] which specifically addresses the issue of adoption, embodies a number of important principles. First, it specifically adopts the best interests of the child principle. Article 21 also recognizes the "subsidiarity principle," which embodies the idea that, whenever possible, a child should be raised by his or her birth family or extended family. If that is not possible, under the subsidiary principle, other suitable forms of care in the country of origin should be considered, and only after such consideration should international adoption be considered if it is in the child's best interests.

Article 21 further recognizes the need of children for legal protections when they are sought after for adoption. Thus, it requires a child who is to be adopted internationally to have the same protections as a child who is adopted within a country. This means informed consent of the child's parents and appropriate documentation that the child is, indeed, legally free for adoption. The CRC also seeks to protect children by requiring that there be no improper financial gain for those involved in the adoption transaction. Article 21 seeks to promote agreements and arrangements between the countries to the Convention to ensure that the placement of children is arranged by competent authorities.

Article 20 of the CRC also is an important provision. It stipulates that a child who is temporarily or permanently in need of care is entitled to protection and assistance from the state, which must ensure alternative care for the child. Article 20 further states that the care provided by the state must be delivered in a way that respects the child's ethnic, religious, cultural, and linguistic background.[19] Suitable alternative care by the state may exclude the possibility of adoption within selected countries that do not recognize adoption as legally defined and generally understood in the West but may include related structures of child care and custody. Article 20 allows for that flexibility as long as the state ensures appropriate care arrangements for the child.

The other key international convention governing international adoption is the Hague Convention on Protection of Children and Cooperation in Respect of Intercountry Adoption (1993), usually referred to in discussions about international adoption as the Hague Convention. The Hague Convention responded to the call of the CRC for countries to enter into multilateral agreements to implement the principles set forth in the CRC.[20]

The Hague Convention, like the CRC, explicitly embraces the principle of the best interests of the child. The Hague Convention also explicitly adopts the subsidiarity principle, though the CRC expresses a stronger preference for adoption within the child's country of origin.[21] Thus, while both the Hague Convention and the CRC prefer in-country adoption to intercountry adoption, the Hague Convention favors intercountry adoption if a suitable adoptive family cannot be found within the country of origin,[22] while the CRC provides that alternative care arrangements for a child in need of care can include foster care, adoption, or other suitable institutions for the care of children within the child's country of origin.[23] The Hague Convention adopts safeguards and procedures that give life to the principles and norms of Article 21 of the CRC.[24]

Thus, the Hague Convention sets in place safeguards and procedures designed to ensure that international adoptions take place in the best interests of the children adopted and with respect for the child's fundamental rights. It provides that states should establish safeguards to prevent the abduction, sale, and trafficking of children and to protect birth families from exploitation. It further provides that states should prevent improper financial gain and corruption and regulate both individuals and agencies involved in adoption by adopting and enforcing accreditation processes.[25] The Hague Convention requires that states ensure that a child is adoptable and that informed consent has been obtained from the birth parents and the child. States must preserve information about the child and his or her parents,[26] evaluate the prospective adoptive parents, and match the child with a family that will be suitable.[27]

The Hague Convention mandates that states establish a central authority as a source of information and a point of contact for international adoptions as well as a system of automatic recognition by member states of adoptions made in accordance with the Convention's rules.

3.2 The Process of International Adoption: The United States as an Illustration

US citizens seeking to adopt children through an international adoption must fulfill the requirements of the foreign country from which they are adopting the child, US immigration law, and the legal requirements of the prospective adoptive parents' state of residence. The adoption involves multiple steps, which include: selecting an adoption service provider (ASP), obtaining approval to adopt, being matched with a child, adopting or obtaining legal custody of the child in the child's country of origin, applying for a visa for the child to move to the United States, and traveling back to the United States with the child.[28] These steps vary significantly and are difficult to describe in detail because the requirements of specific countries from which the child is being adopted differ. The requirements and the steps also differ depending on whether the country from which the child is being adopted is or is not a party to the Hague Convention.[29] The Hague Convention imposes requirements that must be met by the country from which a child is being adopted. It also imposes requirements that must be met in the receiving country. The Hague Convention entered into force in the United States in 2008.

Every adoption service provider facilitating the international adoption of children into the United States must be licensed in the state in which it operates. If the adoption is from a Hague Convention country, the ASP must also be accredited by one of the US State Department's designated accreditation agencies. And, if the adoption is from a Hague country, the adoption services contract must provide information concerning policies, fees, and the history of the ASP's relationship with in-country providers. The home study required for a Hague country is more in-depth than that which might be done for adoption from a non-Hague country, and a Hague country adoption requires that the prospective adoptive parents undergo ten hours of pre-adoption training. In an adoption from a Hague country, the child's medical records are prepared by an approved authority and provided to the prospective adoptive parents. The prospective adoptive parents are then given two weeks to review these records. Also, in an adoption from a Hague country, the adoption records are preserved for seventy-five years. Thus, a Hague country requires more information to be provided to prospective adoptive parents, sets in place structures designed to facilitate the ability of the adoptive parents to meet the child's needs, and requires the preservation of records that would be important for an adoptive child should the child someday seek information about his or her pre-adoption background.[30]

Some countries require prospective adoptive parents to travel to and be evaluated in the child's country, while others accept a US-authorized home study. There are different kinds of visas required in order for the adoptive parents to bring the child into the United States, depending on whether or not the adoption is from a Hague country. Also, some countries do not allow full and final adoption inside the country of origin. Instead, the prospective adoptive parents are granted guardianship, and the final adoption takes place in the adopting parents' state of residence after they return to the United States with the child.[31] The wide variety in the procedures for international adoption depending on the varied requirements of the different governmental structures involved can mean that individuals seeking international adoption must be prepared to undertake what can be a complicated and sometimes lengthy process.

3.3 Criticisms of the Current International Legal Framework

Both the CRC and the Hague Convention have been praised and criticized by those with varying values and perspectives concerning the issues the conventions address. While both critics and supporters of either or both conventions view themselves as seeking to promote children's best interests, they do not always agree as to what the best interests of children are in the context of international adoption or how those interests are most effectively furthered.

Both the CRC and the Hague Convention have been criticized by some for their adoption of the subsidiarity principle. Those critics argue that the subsidiarity principle conflicts with the best interests of the child principle because it may keep in institutions children who might otherwise have the chance to be adopted by families in other countries.[32] They argue that a child's most basic human right is to grow up with a family and that this may require international adoption.[33] Supporters of the subsidiarity principle see that principle as protecting what they view as a right of children to grow up within the experience of their culture of origin. Some critics of international adoption argue that while the Hague Convention rightly embraces the subsidiary principle, it falls short by placing less emphasis than the CRC on a child's right to be raised in the context of his or her family and culture.[34] Some critics of the CRC also argue that that Convention poses a danger of undermining the sovereignty of nations who become a party to it because it could impose obligations that conflict with the values of the member country with respect to a range of child-related issues that implicate parental rights, such as the access of teenagers to reproductive health services, the rights of same-sex parents, or the right of parents with respect to administering corporal punishment.[35] Concerns about potential conflicting values between the United States and other countries around these kinds of issues have been expressed by some critics in the United States, which is yet to ratify the CRC.[36] It is clear that differing and deeply held cultural and political values continue to complicate international adoption.

Some critics of the Hague Convention argue that its specific substantive requirements, such as requiring the use of accredited agencies and requiring parental education, medical records, and in-depth home studies, discourage international adoption because the requirements can result in higher costs and longer timelines for prospective adoptive parents. Others argue that the Hague Convention's stricter requirements are necessary and that they provide more protection for both children and adoptive parents. For example, agencies must spend additional money in order to become accredited. These costs are ultimately passed on to the adopting families. Some argue that these additional costs discourage families from adopting internationally or force families to adopt from non-Hague countries, where there may be fewer protections in place for children. Others believe that these additional costs are necessary because they help to ensure that adoption intermediaries are qualified and accountable.

The Hague Convention has been criticized also for a lack of penalties or sanctions for violations of its requirements.[37] However, there is disagreement as to the extent of noncompliance with Hague requirements, and there is disagreement concerning the extent of specific abusive practices, such as child abduction, sale, and trafficking. Some argue that the Hague Convention does not do enough to acknowledge and address these issues, while others argue that undue focus has been placed on the incidents that have been uncovered.[38] There is also disagreement as to what level of fees is appropriate for agencies facilitating international adoptions and the degree to which fees should be regulated. Non-Hague countries are not regulated with respect to fees. The Hague

Convention states that the fees paid to adoption agencies in Hague countries are to be reasonable, but it does not set a cap on them.[39]

It is clear, then, that international adoption is governed by a complex web of international conventions and the laws of the countries involved in the adoption of each individual child. While there is widespread agreement that the goal of adoption regulation is to promote children's best interests, there is less agreement about the extent to which the existing framework serves that end or as to which aspects of existing regulations need to be changed. Such disagreements are difficult to resolve because they often reflect varying conceptions of the best interests of children in a context that involves many complex and interrelated issues of politics, economics, and culture.

4 The Decline of International Adoption

4.1 Reasons for the Decline

After the increase in international adoptions between 1990 and 2003, the number of international adoptions began to decline, in recent years, precipitously. Adults in the United States have led the world in international adoptions,[40] and the decline in adoptions by this group has been dramatic—nearly 70 percent, from 19,498 in 2007 to 5,987 in 2014.[41] In 2016, 5,372 immigrant visas, which are required for any child who is being adopted from a foreign country, were issued to children adopted or planned to be adopted from abroad by Americans.[42] This number is a modest decline from the 5,648 visas issued in 2015, but it represents a dramatic decline in international adoptions from the 22,884 that took place in 2004, the peak year.[43] The latest figure is also the lowest figure since 1981, when there were 4,868 international adoptions by US families.[44] There has been a similar decline in other receiving countries as well.[45]

A number of reasons have been given for the dramatic decline in international adoptions. Some countries are encouraging domestic adoptions of their children rather than placing the children internationally.[46] Some have suspended intercountry adoptions because of concerns about corruption[47] by various intermediaries, including ASPs.[48] Alleged abuses include baby selling, kidnapping, and falsifying children's status as relinquished or abandoned and then processing them through the traditional adoption system.[49] The US banned adoption from some countries, including Cambodia, Vietnam, and Nepal, because of evidence of baby peddling and document fraud.[50] Guatemala ended overseas adoptions because of concerns about various kinds of malfeasance.[51]

In 2010 a widely publicized incident took place in which an American woman adopted a boy from Russia and later sent him back, putting him on an airplane to Moscow with a note stating that she did not want him anymore.[52] Although this incident did not result in Russia ending adoptions to the US, a few years later, in 2012, Russia banned the adoption of Russian children into the United States in retaliation for the Magnitsky Act, which imposed sanctions on Russia because of human rights abuses.[53]

Another reason that has been cited for the decline in international adoptions, especially in the US, is that adoptive parents have not been complying with post-adoption reporting obligations required by many countries that permit intercountry adoptions [54] These post-adoption reports may be required for several years—sometimes until the child reaches the age of majority. Some reports may require substantial detail, addressing the child's development and the child's progress in adjusting to the adoptive family and the new country.[55] The Intercountry Adoption Act of 2000 requires the US State Department to issue an annual report on intercountry adoption,[56] and the 2016 State Department Annual Report noted that failure by adoptive parents to file these reports can damage the sending country's view of the US, which can affect the willingness of a country to continue sending children.[57]

4.2 The "Rehoming" Issue

A concern related to the problem of compliance by adoptive parents with post-adoption reporting obligations involves the issue of the unregulated transfer of children after adoption, known as UCTs—unregulated custody transfers. The issue has received increased attention in recent years. UCTs are often referred to as the *rehoming* of adopted children. UCTs pose serious danger to the welfare of the affected children and strengthen the arguments of critics and opponents of international adoption.

The issue of UCTs gained wide media exposure as a result of an investigative report conducted by Reuters in 2013[58] and was noted in the 2016 State Department Annual Report.[59] The Reuters report described situations in which adoptive parents who feel that the adoption has failed, transfer the children to other adults or families without any state involvement in the process. Most of the children who have been the subject of UCTs are from failed international adoptions, though some children have been placed who were originally adopted domestically.[60]

The rehoming problem has arisen as a result of the fact that many of the children who are adopted internationally, especially from Eastern Europe and Russia, have spent a significant part of their lives in institutions prior to being adopted. These circumstances place these children at extreme risk for a variety of problems, including developmental disorders, especially with respect to attachment, self-regulation, aggression, and peer relationships.[61] Also, some children who have resided in institutions have had inadequate medical care, may have been subject to malnutrition and exposure to infectious diseases, and usually have had few opportunities for intellectual and linguistic stimulation. Some children may have been subjected to various kinds of abuse.[62]

In rehoming, so-called new parents are often found through groups on the Internet where parents who no longer want their adoptive children offer them for transfer. Children have been transferred by the adoptive parents simply by signing a power of attorney with the adults to whom they are transferring the child. There is no investigation of the individuals to whom the children have been transferred. Although the precise extent of the rehoming problem is not clear, the analysis by Reuters of five years of postings on one Internet message board revealed that, on average, a child was advertised for rehoming once a week. The Reuters report also described several reported cases of alleged physical and sexual abuse,[63] though it is unclear how often this has occurred. The 2016 State Department Annual Report specifically noted that countries often mention the issue of rehoming in connection with their concerns about the noncompliance of adoptive parents with post-adoption reporting requirements.[64] In a statement to the media, the State Department's director of the adoption division said she could not overstate the damage these factors do to international adoption.[65]

In the United States, all fifty states have adopted the Interstate Compact on the Placement of Children,[66] an interstate contract providing a legal framework and imposing legal requirements when custody of a child is transferred across state lines. The goal is to protect the child—to ensure the safety and the appropriateness of a child's placement.[67] Unfortunately, there often are only small or no penalties for violation of the compact.[68] Since the publication of the Reuters investigative report, several states, including Wisconsin, Arkansas, Maine, and Colorado, have passed statutes directed at rehoming within the same state. These state laws criminalize rehoming and/or provide penalties for advertising children or advertising potential homes for such placements.[69] However, in many states, there are no laws specifically directed at the rehoming of children within the same state.

The rehoming issue is an important and troubling one that is receiving more and more attention. The practice presents a serious problem for the welfare of the individual children affected and raises justifiable concerns in sending countries about the safety of children who may be sent to the US. Unless the problem is effectively addressed, it will pose an increasing problem for the whole institution of international adoption and may become another important factor in its decline.

5   Practical Recommendations

Through the years, recommendations for improvements in the laws and processes governing international adoption have come from many sources, including child welfare organizations, adoption advocacy groups, adoptive parents, legal scholars, and others.

A common recommendation is that existing international laws be strengthened and more strictly enforced. There have also been calls for more laws and more severe penalties to address the problems in international adoption in which children become available as a result of bad acts, such as fraud, kidnapping, baby selling, and falsification of eligibility for adoption by adoption intermediaries at various stages of the process. Not surprisingly, there have been calls for laws to be passed in more states in the US to protect children who have been internationally adopted from the devastating practice of rehoming. All of these recommendations appear to be sound, with the potential to increase the protection of children who may be adopted internationally.

The chaos and resulting harm that can result when nations do not comply with existing laws governing intercountry adoption is illustrated by what happened after the devastating earthquake in Haiti in 2010. Under a program known as Humanitarian Parole, more than one thousand children were admitted into the US within the period of a few months.[70] Unfortunately, children were sometimes released for transfer without documentation, with no determination of the status of the relationships with their own parents, and without any screening of the prospective adoptive parents in the US. Some Haitian orphanages, including some not licensed to do adoptions, were practically emptied. Many problems resulted, including some children ending up in foster care or even in juvenile facilities pending determination of their legal status.[71] As a result, it has been recommended that countries develop protocols in advance to deal with such issues as war or weather or environmental disasters that may result in child dislocation. UNICEF and some other organizations have recommended that family tracing should be the first priority in such circumstances, and international adoption should only be considered if tracing efforts fail and other in-country alternatives are not available.[72]

It has been noted that many international adoptions run the risk of creating problems of adjustment in older children who must adapt to a new culture and language and that they sometimes create problems of identity for children of various ages who are of a different ethnic group from that of their parents.[73] Adoption providers facilitating adoptions from Hague countries are already required to provide prospective adoptive parents with at least ten hours of preparation and training before they travel to adopt the child or the child is placed with them. The regulations list the specific topics the training is to address. The issues include information about the conditions in the country from which the child is being adopted that might affect the child's physical and/or emotional development as well as some of the personal and emotional issues, including cultural or racial issues, their adopted child might experience.[74] This training should also be required for adoption from non-Hague countries. There are also calls for the increased provision of post-adoption services to be made available to families who are experiencing trouble with the children they have adopted domestically or internationally. While there are public and private nonprofit organizations that provide post-adoption resources and services,[75] a recent report by a prominent adoption organization described a dearth of publicly funded post-adoption services and noted the need to increase these services for all kinds of adoptive families.[76] The report noted the Hague Convention requirement that its members promote the development of adoption and counseling and post-adoption services.[77]

While it is critical for the safeguards for children adopted internationally to be increased, the reality is that there are millions of children in need of care who will, for various reasons, never be adopted. Even if every parent who wanted to adopt internationally was able to do so, there would still be many children in the world in need of care in terms of adequate food, shelter, clothing, and adults committed to caring for their emotional needs. Thus, there is still a need to improve systems for foster care and institutional care in the countries from which many internationally adopted children come. There is also an urgent need in those countries to expand kinship care, in which children are placed with relatives rather than strangers. And, of course, family preservation efforts must be expanded so that as few children as possible are ever separated from their families, cultures, and countries of birth. It has been suggested that this could be accomplished by fees from the individuals and families who adopt children internationally as well as by requiring contributions from the governments of the countries to whom children are sent.[78] These recommendations seem clearly applicable to sending countries in the Global South, some of which have had complex and troubling colonial and/or neocolonial relationships with the US and other countries in the Global North. But implementation of some of these recommendations would further the best interests of children in other sending countries as well.

6 BEYOND PRACTICAL RECOMMENDATIONS AND LEGAL DOCTRINES: CRITICAL LEGAL PERSPECTIVES

International adoptions have been subject to controversy and criticism beyond issues concerning the effectiveness of the existing processes and legal framework.[79] It is very likely that even if many of the safeguards often recommended were put into place, international adoption would still remain a controversial practice. In recent years, international adoption has also begun to be examined through the lens of recent movements in legal and other scholarship that look beyond critiques of formal legal structures to examine the effect on international adoption of more subtle underlying issues involving racial, ethnic, and cultural hierarchies and past and present structures of subordination. These scholarship movements include critical race theory, postcolonial theory, and feminist theory and are applicable primarily to the adoption of children of color from Global South countries.

While there is no one definition of critical race theory, it can be described generally as an approach that seeks to look behind formal or doctrinal approaches to the law to raise questions about the limitations of the law to address the realities of racism. It often seeks to examine ways in which even formal legal equality is not sufficient to address subtle questions of racial and cultural hegemony, subordination, and power relationships.[80] Postcolonial theory is a heterogeneous area of inquiry that examines the continuing economic, social, political, and cultural consequences of colonialism after colonies achieve independence.[81] While there is also no one generally accepted definition of feminist theory, there does seem to be general agreement that feminist theory is based on the assumption that gender is a central category of analysis, that gender equality and freedom and dignity for women is a goal, and that fundamental social change is needed in order for this goal to be achieved.[82]

6.1 Critical Race Theory and Postcolonial Theory

Because international adoption often involves the adoption of children from Global South countries by people from Western nations, the history of the relationship between different countries and the relevance of that relationship to the issue of international adoption is an important, complex, and sometimes painful part of the analysis of international adoption. With respect to this issue, there is substantial overlap in the analysis from the perspectives of critical race theory and postcolonial theory.

A number of countries from which children of color come have a history of colonialism–military and/or economic domination by Western nations at some point in their histories. Obviously, colonial relationships exist to serve the interests of the colonizing countries; the result is generally exploitation of the people and the resources of the country that is being dominated. However, colonialism is not only military and economic—it also has a cultural component which often finds expression in the belief that the subjugated country is comprised of an inferior people. While the era of actual colonialism may be over in much of the world, many of the racist and ethnocentric rationales for it linger. This can cause resentment in the country from which the children have been taken. It can also complicate the relationship of the adoptive child and the adoptive parents as the child grows older and increasingly understands the historical, political, and economic context within which his or her adoption has taken place.[83]

As troubling as it may be for many people to admit, a conception of poor, third-world countries as subordinate nations fits very comfortably with the practice of international adoption. This kind of view translates quite easily into the idea that Western adoptive parents are simply saving unfortunate third-world children by bringing them out of primitive, impoverished, and disease-ridden countries into the more affluent life that the West can offer. It permits a discourse that allows Westerners to take the high ground and portray their international adoptions as simple acts of humanitarianism and altruism.[84]

Admittedly, there is a humanitarian aspect to many international adoptions. Obviously, there are children adopted from poor countries who would face a very bleak life or even death in their home countries. However, the analysis of international adoption should go farther than a simple altruism narrative. Indeed, an appropriate question might not be what Westerners are giving to the children of impoverished nations, but what they are taking from those nations and the families whose children are adopted.[85]

In some countries, the availability of children for adoption is affected by issues that sit at the intersection of racism and patriarchy. The question here is how the factors of racism and patriarchy function within the countries from which children are often adopted. This presents issues related to, but separate from those discussed below, concerning the relationship of feminist theory to the reality of the social and economic inequality that often exists in international adoptions between the women adopting children and the birth mothers who have surrendered them.

Racism and patriarchy can intersect and function in the context of international adoption in different ways in different countries. In some countries patriarchy may be the dominant factor. In Asian countries, such as Korea, adoption historically has only been considered as a means to perpetuate family lines in families without a male heir.[86] Because adoption has been unpopular as a general practice, it has been difficult to place children for adoption within the country.[87]

In China the availability of many baby girls for adoption is also largely a function of patriarchy. The Chinese tradition of favoring male children, combined with the policy of limiting families to one child, resulted in many families choosing to keep a male child and putting female infants in orphanages or, in some instances, even putting them to death.[88] Adoption by foreigners has sometimes been a fortunate alternative to these fates. In Vietnam, children fathered by foreigners, often by American soldiers, have not been easily accepted by the society.[89] Where the children have obviously been fathered by black men, racial prejudice can compound the factors of foreign blood and birth outside of marriage, placing on these children a triple burden.[90]

That international adoption implicates the kind of issues discussed above is not an argument for abolition of the practice. However, these issues do support the view that it is important for both the policies and the discourse concerning international adoption to be respectful of the countries and the cultures from which the children come. The issues foregrounded by these scholarship movements also support arguments for efforts to better prepare adoptive parents for the complications that can be a reality as they raise a child from a different culture, race or ethnicity. They also support arguments supporting the subsidiarity principle and family preservation programs in the children's countries of origin.

6.2 Feminist Legal Theory

One aspect of international adoption that has been neglected in many discussions of academics is the fact that international adoption often results in the transfer of children from some of the most disadvantaged women in the world to some of the most advantaged. International adoption raises many issues that should be of interest to feminist scholars and others whose work concerns issues of poverty, the economic status of women, the nature of mothering, and the relationships between women of different classes, ethnic backgrounds, and races and nations.[91]

Looking at the issues from both sides is complicated. Many women experience a powerful desire to become mothers. Not all women can conceive children biologically, and not all women choose to. It is also probably true that some women who place their children for adoption do not, in any sense, see their choice as dictated by anything other than their own free will. Adoption is an institution with ancient roots, and it is likely that even in a more humane and egalitarian world than the one that currently exists, there would still be some women who would choose to surrender their children for adoption.[92]

There is a challenge, however, for feminism to begin to analyze adoption as more than an individual transaction in which one or two adults legally become the parents of a particular child. Just as feminists view marriage as an institution warranting an analysis that goes beyond individual couples, adoption must be approached with a similarly broad perspective. Adoption, like marriage, involves issues of hierarchy and power; unlike marriage, however, adoption involves these issues among women.[93]

The imbalance in the circumstances of the two women usually involved in international adoptions presents a troubling dilemma: in a sense, the access of affluent, often white, Western women to children of color for adoption is often dependent on the continued desperate circumstances of women in the Global South.[94]

This analysis implicates many issues that have been at the core of feminist analysis. For example, feminist theory is generally critical of the market-focused law and economics approach to the law,[95] yet there is little critique of applying a model of supply and demand to the adoption context. Women scholars often strongly oppose the use of wealth as an important factor in custody disputes between parents because of the disproportional harm that approach has on women.[96] However, there needs to be more discussion of the role of unequal distribution of resources in the pattern of international adoption in which the children of poor women are adopted by women who are more economically privileged. An important tool of feminist method has been the use of the personal narrative,[97] especially around issues of motherhood. There are numerous narratives of adoptive mothers.[98] There is a need for more focus on the stories of women who have given children up for adoption or who have been separated from their children for other reasons relevant to their being in a disadvantaged status by virtue of race, class, or geography.

7 CONCLUSION: THE FUTURE OF INTERNATIONAL ADOPTION

Although the number of international adoptions has declined in recent years, international adoption remains an important issue. There are still many children who need homes, and in many countries there are still adults who have a strong desire to parent. But, as this chapter has shown, there are complex issues that still need to be addressed.

The face of international adoption is also changing in ways some people might find surprising. As previously noted, the US has been the largest country of international adopters. However, in recent years, children from the US have been placed for adoption in several other countries, including Canada, Ireland, Mexico, Austria, Great Britain, the Netherlands, and Switzerland.[99] This is a clear departure from the paradigm of a child being transferred from a troubled Global South country or unstable Eastern European nation to a country presumed to offer a higher standard of living to its citizens. It also appears that a substantial number of the children who are being adopted from the United States into Europe are children of mixed-race backgrounds.[100] It will be interesting to see whether this pattern continues, and if so, how it affects the analysis of and discourse surrounding international adoption.

Also, whereas in the past, children of color adopted by Westerners were often from Asia and Latin and South America, in recent years, as a result of difficulties in adopting children from those countries, there has been an increase in the adoption of children from Africa, including sub-Saharan Africa.[101] Given the racial and color hierarchies that continue to exist in the world, it merits monitoring whether these adoptions will pose complications that differ in complexity or intensity from those for children from Asia and Latin and South America in terms of the children's adjustment to and acceptance in the countries into which they have been adopted.

The nature and structure of international adoption continues to evolve in response to economic, political, and cultural changes in countries around the world. It is clear that there will continue to be issues concerning international adoption that will be intensely debated by people and groups with many different perspectives. What offers hope for the future is that these people and groups share the common goal of furthering the rights of all children in the world to grow up in contexts in which they are protected and loved.

Notes

1. Howard Altstein and Rita J. Simon, *Intercountry Adoption: A Multinational Perspective* (New York, Greenwood Publishing Group, 1991), 1.
2. Altstein and Simon, *Intercountry Adoption*, 8.
3. Rickie Solinger, *Wake Up Little Susie: Single Pregnancy and Race before Roe v. Wade* (New York: Routledge, 1992), 224–228.
4. Tamar Lewin, "Fewer Children Up for Adoption, Study Finds," *New York Times*, February 27, 1992, www.nytimes.com/1992/02/27/us/fewer-children-up-for-adoption-study-finds.html.
5. Howard and Altstein, *Intercountry Adoption*, 8–11.
6. Maria Kuznetsove, "Adjustment of Families with Children Adopted from Eastern Europe," PhD diss., Virginia Commonwealth University, 2011.
7. Susan Frelich Appleton and Kelly D. Weisberg, *Adoption and Assisted Reproduction: Families under Construction* (New York: Wolters Kluwer Law and Business, 2009), 229.
8. Joan Hollinger, "International Adoption: A Frontier without Borders," in *Families by Law: An Adoption Reader*, ed. Joan Hollinger and Naomi Cahn (New York: New York University Press, 2004), 215.
9. Twila L. Perry, "Transracial and International Adoption: Mothers, Hierarchy, Race and Feminist Legal Theory," *Yale Journal of Law & Feminism* 10, no. 1 (1998): 130.
10. David M. Smolin, "Child Laundering and the Hague Convention: The Future and Past of Intercountry Adoption," *University of Louisville Law Journal* 48 (2010): 441–498.
11. Smolin, "Child Laundering," 463; UN Department of Economic and Social Affairs, Population Division, "Child Adoption: Trends and Policies," UN Doc. ST/ESA/SER.A/292 (2009), 74–75.
12. Douglass E. Abrams and Sarah H. Ramsay, *Children and the Law: Doctrine, Policy and Practice*, 4th ed. (St. Paul, MN: West Academic Publishing, 2010).
13. The best interests principle is accepted in US as well as international law. Homer C. Clark, *The Law of Domestic Relations in the United States* (St. Paul, MN: West Academic

Publishing, 1968); UNICEF Innocenti Research Centre, *The Best Interests of the Child in Intercountry Adoption* (Florence: UNICEF Innocenti Research Centre, 2014).

14. Robert H. Mnookin, "Child Custody Adjudication in the Face of Indeterminacy," *Law and Contemporary Problems* 43 (1975): 226.

15. Robert H. Mnookin, "Foster Care–In Whose Best Interest?," *Harvard Law Review* 43 (1973): 599–638.

16. Save the Children, *The Risk of Harm to Young Children in Institutional Care* (London: Save the Children, 2009).

17. UN Office of the High Commissioner for Human Rights, "The Core International Human Rights Instruments and Their Monitoring Bodies," https://www.ohchr,org/en/professionalinterest/pages/coreinstruments.aspx (accessed Aug. 22, 2019).

18. UN Convention on the Rights of the Child (CRC), G.A. Res. 44/25, 44th Sess. UN Doc. A/RES/44/25 (1989).

19. CRC, art. 20.

20. Smolin, "Child Laundering," 458.

21. David M. Smolin and Elizabeth Bartholet, "The Debate," in *Intercountry Adoption: Policies, Practices and Outcomes*, ed. Judith L. Gibbons and Karen Smith Rotabi (New York: Routledge, 2012), 233–254.

22. The Hague Convention on the Protection of Children and Co-Operation in Respect of Intercountry Adoption (Hague Convention), 32 ILM. 1134 (entered into force May 1, 1995).

23. CRC, art. 20.

24. Hague Conference on Private International Law, "Outline: Hague Intercountry Adoption Convention," https://assets.hcch.net/docs/e5960426-2d1b-4fe3-9384-f8849d51663d.pdf (accessed Aug. 22, 2019).

25. Hague Convention.

26. Hague Convention.

27. Hague Convention.

28. US Department of State, Bureau of Consular Affairs, "Adoption Process," https://travel.state.gov/content/travel/en/Intercountry-Adoption/Adoption-Process.html (accessed Aug. 22, 2019).

29. US Department of State, Office of Children's Issues, "Intercountry Adoption from A to Z," https://travel.state.gov/content/dam/aa/pdfs/Intercountry_Adoption_From_A_Z.pdf (accessed Aug. 22, 20119).

30. US Department of State, Bureau of Consular Affairs, "Adoption Process."

31. US Department of State, Office of Children's Issues, "Intercountry Adoption from A to Z."

32. Elizabeth Bartholet, "International Adoption: The Human Rights Position," *Global Policy* 91, no. 1 (January 2010): 91–100.

33. Bartholet, "International Adoption."

34. Shani Mahiri King, "Challenging MonoHumanism: An Argument for Changing the Way We Think about Intercountry Adoption," *Michigan Journal of International Law* 30 (2009): 466–469, 413.

35. Amy Rothschild, "Is America Holding Out on Protecting Children's Rights?," *The Atlantic*, May 17, 2017.

36. Rothschild, "Is America Holding Out?"

37. Erica Briscoe, "The Hague Convention on Protection of Children and Co-operations in Respect of Intercountry Adoption: Are Its Benefits Overshadowed by Its Shortcomings?," *Journal American Academy of Matrimonial Lawyers* 22 (2009): 437–449.

38. Smolin, "Child Laundering," 443.

39. Final Rule, Hague Convention on Intercountry Adoption, Intercountry Adoption Act of 2000, Accreditation of Agencies, Approval of Persons, 71 Fed. Reg. 8142 (Feb. 15, 2006) (codified at 22 CFR pts. 96, 97, 98).

40. Miriam Jordan, "Overseas Adoptions by Americans Continue to Decline," *New York Times*, April 13, 2017.

41. National Council for Adoption, *Adoption by the Numbers* (Alexandrea, VA: National Council for Adoption, 2017).

42. US Department of State, Bureau of Consular Affairs, "2016 Annual Report on Intercountry Adoption," https://travel.state.gov/content/dam/NEWadoptionassets/pdfs/AnnualReportonIntercountryAdoptions6.8.17.pdf (accessed Aug. 22, 2019).

43. Jordan, "Overseas Adoptions by Americans."

44. Jordan, "Overseas Adoptions by Americans."

45. Smolin, "Child Laundering," 471.

46. Jordan, "Overseas Adoptions by Americans."

47. Jordan, "Overseas Adoptions by Americans."

48. US Department of State, "2016 Annual Report on Intercountry Adoption."

49. Smolin, "Child Laundering," 455.

50. Jordan, "Overseas Adoptions by Americans."

51. Jordan, "Overseas Adoptions by Americans."

52. Damian Cave, "In Tenn., Reminders of a Boy Returned to Russia," *New York Times*, April 10, 2010.

53. Amanda Taub, "When the Kremlin Says 'Adoptions,' It Means 'Sanctions.'" *New York Times*, July 10, 2017, https://www.nytimes.com/2017/07/10/world/americas/kremlin-adoptions-sanctions-russia.html.

54. US Department of State, Bureau of Consular Affairs, "Post Adoption," https://travel.state.gov/content/travel/en/Intercountry-Adoption/post-adoption.html (accessed Aug. 22, 2019).

55. US Department of State, Bureau of Consular Affairs, "Post Adoption."

56. Intercountry Adoption Act of 2000, 42 U.S.C. §§ 14901–44 (2000).

57. US Department of State, "2016 Annual Report on Intercountry Adoption."

58. Megan Twohey, "Americans Use the Internet to Abandon Children Adopted from Overseas," Reuters, September 9, 2013.

59. US Department of State, "2016 Annual Report on Intercountry Adoption."

60. Twohey. "Americans Use the Internet to Abandon Children."

61. Karen Purvis, Shanna k. Mittie, David R. Cross, and Kelly L. Reed, "Parents' Reports of Their International Adoption Experience," in *Adoption Factbook V*, ed. Elisa A. Rosman, Charles E. Johnson, and Nicole M. Callahan (Baltimore, MD: National Council for Adoption, 2011), 357–364.

62. Purvis et al., "Parents' Reports," 357 (citing various sources, including, C. H. Zeanah, "Disturbance of Attachment in Young Children Adopted from Institutions," *Journal of Developmental and Behavioral Pediatrics* 21 (2000): 230–236; M. Rutter and the English and Romanian Adoptees Study Team, "Developmental Catchup and Deficit Following Adoption after Severe Global Early Deprivation," *Journal of Child Psychology and Psychiatry* 35 (1998): 465–476).

63. Twohey, "Americans Use the Internet to Abandon Children."

64. US Department of State, "2016 Annual Report on Intercountry Adoption."

65. Jordan, "Overseas Adoptions by Americans."

66. American Public Human Services Administration, "Text of Interstate Compact on the Placement of Children (ICPC)," https://aphsa.org/AAICPC/AAICPC/text_icpc.aspx (accessed Aug. 22, 2019).

67. American Public Human Services Administration, ICPC.

68. Twohey, "Americans Use the Internet to Abandon Children."

69. Yunqi Zhang, "Is Criminalizing Re-Homing the Best Solution? A Look into Safe Adoption Policy," *Columbia Social Work Review* 7 (2016): 26–34.

70. Megan Lindsey, "Examining Intercountry Adoption after the Earthquake in Haiti," in Rosman, Johnson, and Callahan, *Adoption Factbook V*, 345–350.

71. Ginger Thompson, "After Haitian Quake, the Chaos of U.S. Adoptions," *New York Times*, August 3, 2010, https://www.nytimes.com/2010/08/04/world/americas/04adoption.html.

72. United Nations Children's Fund (UNICEF), "Intercountry Adoption," https://www.unicef.org/media/intercountry-adoption (accessed Aug. 22, 2019).

73. Christopher Bagley, Loretta Young, and Anne Scully, *International and Transracial Adoptions: A Mental Health Perspective* (Aldershot, UK: Avebury, 1994), 136.

74. US Department of State, Bureau of Consular Services, "How to Adopt," https://travel.state.gov/content/travel/en/Intercountry-Adoption/Adoption-Process/how-to-adopt.html (accessed Aug. 22, 2019).

75. US Department of State, Bureau of Consular Services, "Post Adoption."

76. Susan Livingston Smith, "Supporting and Preserving Adoptive Families: Profiles of Publicly Funded Adoption Services," report for the Donaldson Institute for adoption (April 2014), https://www.adoptioninstitute.org/wp-content/uploads/2014/04/Supporting-and-Preserving-Families.pdf.

77. Smith, "Supporting and Preserving Adoptive Families," 5.

78. King, "Challenging Monohumanism," 464–465.

79. Bagley, Young, and Scully, *International and Transracial Adoptions*, 136.

80. Kimberly Crenshaw, Neil Gotanda, Gary Peller, and Kendall Thomas, "Introduction," in *Critical Race Theory: The Key Writings That Formed the Movement*, ed. Kimberly Crenshaw, Neil Gotanda, Gary Peller, and Kendall Thomas (New York: The New Press, 1996), xii–xiii.

81. Ben Ashcroft, Gareth Griffiths, and Helen Tiffin, eds., *The Post-Colonial Studies Reader* (New York: Routledge, 1995).

82. Deborah L. Rhode, "Feminist Critical Theories," *Stanford Law Review.* 42 (1990): 617–619.

83. Perry, "Transracial and International Adoption."

84. Perry, "Transracial and International Adoption," 135.

85. Perry, "Transracial and International Adoption," 135.

86. Bagley, Young, and Scully, *International and Transracial Adoptions*, 177.

87. Perry, "Transracial and International Adoption," 136.

88. Bagley, Young, and Scully, *International and Transracial Adoptions*, 188–190.

89. Bagley, Young, and Scully, *International and Transracial Adoptions*, 208.

90. David Gonzalez, "For Afro-Amerasians, Tangled Emotions," *New York Times*, November 6, 1992.

91. Perry, "Transracial and International Adoption," 101.

92. Perry, "Transracial and International Adoption," 108–109.

93. Perry, "Transracial and International Adoption," 106.

94. Perry, "Transracial and International Adoption," 105.

95. Tamar Frankel and Helen H. Miller, "The Inapplicability of Market Theory to Adoptions," *Boston University Law Review* 67 (1987): 99.

96. Lenore Weitzman, *The Divorce Revolution: The Unexpected Social and Economic Consequences for Women and Children in America* (New York: Free Press, 1985), 240–243.

97. Carol Sanger, "M is for the Many Things," *Southern California Law Review* 1 (1992): 15–28.

98. Elizabeth Bartholet, "Where Do Black Children Belong? The Politics of Race Matching in Adoption," *University of Pennsylvania Law Review* 139 (1991): 1164–1174.

99. US Department of State, "2016 Annual Report on Intercountry Adoption."

100. Sophie Brown, "Overseas Adoptions Rise—For Black American Children," CNN, September 17, 2013, http://www.cnn.com/2013/09/16/world/international-adoption-us -children-adopted-abroad/index.html.

101. US Department of State, "2016 Annual Report on Intercountry Adoption."

CHAPTER 17

....

ECONOMIC AND LABOR RIGHTS OF CHILDREN

....

MANFRED LIEBEL

1 INTRODUCTION

ECONOMIC and labor rights have so far received little attention in children's rights studies. When reference is made to the UN Convention on the Rights of the Child (CRC),[1] it is usually assumed that it encompasses all categories of human rights, including economic rights. One needs to be careful, though, as when dealing with children, economic rights are often conflated with social rights. For example, a review by the Child Rights International Network on the questions "What are children's economic rights? Why are they important?"[2] points out that these are the rights that serve to combat child poverty. The list reads as follows: "the right to benefit from social security" (Article 26), "the right to a standard of living adequate for his or her physical, mental, spiritual, moral and social development" (Article 27), and "the right to be protected from work that threatens his or her health, education or development" (Article 32). In one of the rare legal analyses of children's social and economic rights, without distinguishing between the two categories of rights, an apodictic statement is that "social and economic rights of children include rights to health care and adequate nutrition, to education, to housing, to freedom from economic exploitation."[3] There is almost no literature on children's rights concerning the question of whether children have or ought to have labor rights, except in those contributions dealing with the movements of working children and their demands for the "right to work in dignity."[4]

The question of whether children have economic and labor rights, and what practical meaning they have, is in fact not easy to answer, and a possible answer depends on what is meant by such rights. With regard to international law, it is necessary to clarify the relationship between different areas of law and legal concepts. With regard to children, this relates in particular to the relationship between human rights in general and children's rights in particular, with respect to economic and social rights, human and labor rights, and legal and moral rights. In this chapter I intend to clarify not only whether or which economic and/or labor rights children have but, also, whether these correspond to their best interests, what they mean for the children, and whether they can actually use them. I then focus on working children and their associations, that is, which economic and labor rights they consider necessary and how they have been or could be taken up in international law and in national legislation. Finally, I discuss the obstacles in international law and what practical difficulties are to be overcome on the ground in order to realize and bring to life the economic and labor rights of children.

2 What Are Economic and Labor Rights?

In international law, *economic rights* are those codified in the International Covenant on Economic, Social and Cultural Rights (ICESCR), adopted by the UN General Assembly in 1966 and entered into force in 1976.[5] These rights were first formulated in the Universal Declaration of Human Rights of 1948. International *labor rights* are those defined in the conventions of the International Labor Organization (ILO), a specialized agency of the United Nations. The most important of these conventions[6] are summarized in the ILO Declaration on Fundamental Principles and Rights at Work (ILO Principles), adopted by the International Labor Conference in 1998.[7]

In Articles 7 and 8 of the ICESCR, economic rights are described in the following way:

- Everyone has the right to work, to free choice of employment, to just and favorable conditions of work, and to protection against unemployment.
- Everyone, without any discrimination, has the right to equal pay for equal work.
- Everyone who works has the right to just and favorable remuneration ensuring that they and their families have an existence worthy of human dignity and supplemented, if necessary, by other means of social protection.
- Everyone has the right to form and to join trade unions for the protection of one's interests.
- Everyone has the right to rest and leisure, including reasonable limitation of working hours and periodic holidays with pay.

In Article 10 of the ICESCR, children are referred to as "dependent" persons, and in paragraph 3, it specifically states that

- Special measures of protection and assistance should be taken on behalf of all children and young persons without any discrimination for reasons of parentage or other conditions. Children and young persons should be protected from economic and social exploitation. Their employment in work harmful to their morals or health or dangerous to life or likely to hamper their normal development should be punishable by law. States should also set age limits below which the paid employment of child labor should be prohibited and punishable by law.

In the ILO Declaration on Fundamental Principles and Rights at Work, the following fundamental rights are emphasized:

- freedom of association and the effective recognition of the right to collective bargaining;
- elimination of all forms of forced or compulsory labor;
- effective abolition of child labor;
- elimination of discrimination in respect of employment and occupation.[8]

Economic rights and labor rights differ in the sense that economic rights are intended for all people, while labor rights are only for those who are employed. As all human rights, economic rights are based on the principles of freedom and dignity. They can be distinguished from other human rights but cannot be seen as detached from them. For example, the social rights enshrined in the ICESCR include the rights to food, health, housing, social security, and education. Without the acknowledgment and realization of these rights, neither the rights of work nor life would be possible. On the other hand, economic and labor rights also help make social rights a reality.

Economic rights, as well as social and cultural rights, are commonly referred to as the second generation of human rights in comparison to civil and political rights, the so-called first generation of human rights.[9] While civil and political rights are intended to protect individuals from state restrictions on their freedom and personal integrity, economic and social rights are aimed at taking action or facilitating one's own actions to improve their living and working conditions and those of others in terms of human dignity. Social and economic rights were conceptualized because it was recognized that living in dignity requires not only guarantees of freedom but also the guarantee of certain living and working conditions and that individual freedoms themselves require social framing. This reminds us that human rights do not fall from heaven but are the result of aspirations and struggles aimed at better livelihoods.[10] This, of course, also applies to the labor rights that resulted from the struggle of workers' organizations for better working conditions (which is why they are also referred to as "workers' rights"). And notwithstanding the false dichotomy between these civil and political rights, on the one hand, and economic and social rights, on the other, it is important to remember that political rights as well as economic and social rights require resources and state action to secure them.

As far as economic and labor rights are concerned, it should be remembered that they refer to an economy and to employment relationships that have emerged with the capitalist mode of production. They target regulations that apply within this mode of production but do not contain a vision that goes beyond it. This poses a challenge to the further development of human rights, in particular social and cultural rights, as well as the new generation of ecological or environmental rights, including the rights of future generations.[11] Therefore, every political and personal decision must take into account that these rights transcend national boundaries and present-day generations and that realization of these rights may endanger certain livelihoods but also create the conditions for a better life. This is a challenge not only for states but also for citizens to rethink their way of life and the associated consumption of vital resources. This, as well, has considerable consequences for the question of to what extent economic and labor rights apply or should apply to children. First, I will discuss whether and which economic and labor rights, according to international law, children have and the problems associated with them. Then I will discuss which political and legal alternatives are feasible and necessary to protect these rights.

3 Do children Have Economic and Labor Rights?

Looking at the economic and labor rights enshrined in international law it is easy to detect the arguably contradictory statements made concerning children. According to the wording of the ICESCR, economic rights apply to everyone and are therefore applicable to all people regardless of their age. The ILO fundamental principles, such as "freedom of association" and "elimination of discrimination in respect of employment and occupation," also fail to incorporate any mention of age and, therefore, implicitly apply to all working people. Nevertheless, both the ICESCR and the ILO principles contain provisions that are incompatible with this logic. When it is argued that the statements concerning children are not contradictory, but complementary, in my view it is based on a Eurocentric-imperial understanding of childhood and a protectionist understanding of children's rights that, above all, ignores children's participation rights as enshrined in the CRC.

With regard to children, the ICESCR requires minimum ages as a prerequisite for the legal exercise of "paid employment" (though without specifying them).[12] And the fundamental right of the "effective abolition of child labor" in the ILO Fundamental Principles can logically only be understood as a right to be exercised exclusively by adults, since children are affected by it but are not thought of as a legal subject of that right.[13] While it may be argued that this is also a right of children, because they eventually benefit from protection, in my view, this argument is based on a paternalistic concept of protection that excludes the participation of children in their protection. Because they are based on the ILO conventions, the ILO Fundamental Principles reflect the Minimum Age Convention No. 138,[14] which stipulates minimum age requirements for employment. Although these provisions are intended to meet and protect the particular needs of children, they constitute a serious restriction of economic rights and raise the question whether or not, in contrast to protecting the rights of children, this is in reality an age-specific form of discrimination and whether the claimed child protection function is actually reversed. For children below the minimum age, for instance, it is impossible to use "rights *at* work," thus preventing working children from referring to rights in the context of their work. Thus, the establishment of minimum ages is also in contradiction to the provision to ensure "special measures of protection and assistance...on behalf of *all children and young persons*" (emphasis added),[15] since these measures can apply only for working children above the minimum age.

The same logical contradiction is reproduced in the CRC. Article 32 reads in relevant part:

1. States Parties recognize the right of the child to be protected from economic exploitation and from performing any work that is likely to be hazardous or to interfere with the child's education, or to be harmful to the child's health or physical, mental, spiritual, moral or social development.

2. States Parties shall take legislative, administrative, social and educational measures to ensure the implementation of the present article. To this end, and having regard to the relevant provisions of other international instruments, States Parties shall in particular:

   (a) Provide for a minimum age or minimum ages for admission to employment;

   (b) Provide for appropriate regulation of the hours and conditions of employment;

   (c) Provide for appropriate penalties or other sanctions to ensure the effective enforcement of the present article.

While the CRC does not refer to child labor as the relevant ILO conventions do, the requirement to set one minimum age or more for admission to employment contradicts the proclaimed right of all children to be protected against economic exploitation or hazardous work. Despite what may be the best intentions, there is a logical short circuit in assuming that the exclusion from work also serves to protect the children involved, and to tie this exclusion to a certain age is based on the problematic assumption that employment below this age automatically harms the children or that the prohibition makes employment impossible. Studies show that the general setting of minimum ages and corresponding prohibitions in practice do not have this consequence because they do not eliminate the real reasons that cause children to take up work. Therefore, they do not result in the intended protection, but increase the risk of working under even worse conditions.[16]

At the least, CRC Article 32 remains ambiguous and raises another question: whether the promised protection of children from exploitation and hazardous work is credible. To be credible, it should have positive consequences for the working children. The protection against economic exploitation and hazardous work promised in the CRC certainly can be understood as an economic or labor right of children. However, if this protection for children is to be achieved only by excluding them from work, it falls short and can even cause additional risks for the children. In order to avoid this potential harm, the children who, for whatever reason, start or continue to work have to be entitled to rights in the places of work and to have the means of protection. This could be done, for example, by informing working children about the risks associated with various forms of employment and supporting their organizing themselves in the workplace, allowing them to take part in decisions on the conditions of their work, and in securing support from adults who share responsibility for the children. If the workplace cannot counteract unreasonable risks due to the nature of the work, a measure of protection could be to provide the children in those work settings with alternative legal work opportunities that ensure their human dignity and enable them to exercise their other rights as well.

Since the CRC came into force, the protection of children can no longer be done solely at the discretion of adult authorities; it must be conceived of as the right of children. This means that children can no longer be treated as mere objects of action but must be involved in shaping relevant policies and be able to participate in them. It also means that children's views must be taken into account when identifying the risks from which children are to be protected. A policy aimed at eliminating child labor, which it seeks to achieve through children's exclusion from work, does not live up to this claim, especially when children have no means of expressing their own views. If the right established in Article 12 of the CRC to give due weight to children's views is taken seriously, children, working or not, must have the opportunity to express their views. This does not necessarily mean that the children alone decide whether to work, but the decisions have to be made in dialogue with the affected children, and their views must be taken into account. Thus, the right of children to form their own associations, established in Article 15 of the CRC, can be understood essentially as an economic right that facilitates the forming of relationships at work and collective bargaining, and must now be incorporated into relevant international human rights instruments.

4   WHAT DO ECONOMIC AND LABOR RIGHTS MEAN FOR CHILDREN?

With regard to the rights of working children, Karl Hanson and Arne Vandaele speak of a "difference dilemma."[17] This is to say that working children can be considered both as workers and as children. As workers, they are entitled to the same economic and labor rights as adults. On the other hand, as children, they also need special rights because of their specific development needs, their relative powerlessness, and their greater vulnerability. This is the purpose of the CRC, which enshrines both rights that correspond to those of adults and specific rights that are different from those of adults. The difference dilemma arises when children, with reference to their particular situation, are deprived of rights that adults possess or when children's rights are associated with the restriction of universal human rights.

With regard to economic and labor rights, the question arises as to whether other rights, which are considered essential for adults besides the right to be protected from exploitation and hazardous work, should also be granted to children. This applies in particular to the following rights, which can be found in formulations in the ICESCR, in some ILO conventions, and in the ILO Fundamental Principles:

- the right to work and to free choice of employment;
- the right to just and favorable conditions of work;
- the right to protection against unemployment;
- the right to equal pay for equal work, without any discrimination;
- the right to form and to join trade unions for the protection of his or her interests, including the right to collective bargaining;
- the right to rest and leisure, including reasonable limitation of working hours and periodic holidays with pay.

According to widespread opinion, these rights are not relevant to children, and many of are the opinion that granting such rights to children would in fact harm them.[18] This opinion is based on a particular childhood pattern that has emerged with bourgeois society in Europe and is now a worldwide and internationally relevant pattern; it has guided, for example, the developmental policy of governments and some Global North–based NGOs as well as corresponding international agreements. According to this pattern, the lives of the children should be completely "free from work," with that time replaced by compulsory school attendance. Children who do not (yet) attend school are deplored as "children without childhood" and often discriminated against as "backward" or "underdeveloped."[19] Nonetheless, despite legal prohibitions, millions of children continue to work, and they often do not only work but also study in schools or other learning arrangements. The reasons and motives are as varied as the conditions under which this work is carried out.

That work continues to belong, perhaps even increasingly, to the lives of many children and that it is part of their childhood makes it seem appropriate to grant all adult economic and labor rights to children as well. It will be illustrated below why, unlike labor prohibitions, this would help protect working children from exploitation, preserve their human dignity, and improve their working and living conditions. This would also contribute to making social rights enshrined in the CRC real, such as the rights to health (Article 24), social security (Article 26), adequate standard of living (Article 27), education (Articles 28 and 29), and rest and leisure (Article 31). In short, if working children are not without legal protections and support at work and can influence the conditions of their work, they can also better defend their social rights.

It should also be borne in mind that the right to form independent associations and to promote common interests in an organized manner, that is, rights that belong to economic and labor rights, is also, as a general matter, established in the CRC. Article 15 states as follows:

1. States Parties recognize the rights of the child to freedom of association and to freedom of peaceful assembly.
2. No restrictions may be placed on the exercise of these rights other than those imposed in conformity with the law and which are necessary in a democratic society in the interests of national security or public safety, public order (ordre public), the protection of public health or morals or the protection of the rights and freedoms of others.

Although these rights are not formulated as economic or labor rights, they do and should have this meaning for children who work or want to work.[20] Working children in many regions of the Global South have long since made use of these rights by establishing their own social movements and organizations and by insisting on their independence. They are rarely referred to as unions, but they perform inter alia trade union tasks. The main reason they have not been part of the trade union movement is that the trade unions refuse to accept working persons below the age of sixteen as equal members.[21] Exclusion from so-called adult trade unions, of course, leaves working children to their own devices in terms of organizing and starting their own organizations/unions.

The refusal to grant children full economic and labor rights is the consistent view advocated by unions and by the International Labor Organization. It is expressed, for instance, in the ILO conventions against child labor and the corresponding action programs for the complete eradication of all forms of child labor. Unions and the ILO have shown a stubborn refusal to recognize working children and their organizations as partners and to enable them to participate in decisions that affect their situation as working children.[22]

One of the conventions that the ILO regards as a particularly important part of its framework is ILO Convention No. 138, which provides minimum ages for employment. According to this convention, the minimum age "shall not be less than the age of completion of compulsory schooling and, in any case, shall not be less than 15 years" and in exceptional cases, which must be explicitly justified by governments, 14 years (Article 2). "The minimum age for admission to any type of employment or work, which, by its nature, or the circumstances in which it is carried out, is likely to jeopardize the health, safety or morals of young persons, shall not be less than 18 years" (Article 3). ILO Convention No. 138 does not refer to either human or children's rights per se but, instead, stipulates legal measures designed to prevent children from working beyond defined age limits. Although the conditions under which children work vary greatly, the convention assumes that age alone should be the determinant as to whether work is per se harmful to children and should therefore be prevented by all means of law. In this, as in the numerous previous conventions against child labor,[23] it becomes apparent that one of the main motivations is to ward off wage competition that might result from children working. While humanitarian motives often are being cited, it has not been proven to date that the convention has contributed significantly to improving the situation of working children.[24] On the contrary, various studies have shown that excluding children from work simply because of their young age has counterproductive effects and has in fact worsened the situation of many working children, including their families.[25] There is also empirical evidence that other rights of children can be and indeed are violated through child labor eradication policies, which unduly undermine survival and liveli-hood strategies as well as access to education, and the like.[26] It is for these reasons that some children's rights experts have argued for recognizing the "unwritten rights" of children "to work and do so in fair conditions and for fair wages."[27]

Despite academics' and experts' acknowledgment of the difficulties in the field, holistic evaluation of child protection by child labor eradication policy and programs has never been carried out.[28] Although the ILO's Global Reports on Child Labor, published since 2002, speak of a worldwide decline in child labor, they note that in many areas the con-ditions under which children work have worsened. From report to report, it is stressed that the envisaged abolition of child labor by 2025 can only be achieved if the pace is accelerated considerably.[29] In this context, the participation of working children's organizations, refused so far by ILO, represents not only a right in itself, enshrined in the CRC, but it also represents an indispensable channel through which children can outline their problems and identify rights violations and a channel through with policy-makers can, and indeed should, gain information on actual outcomes of current policies and practices.[30]

5 Why Children Must Have the Right to Work

The right to work and to free choice of employment is an essential economic right. It is not only enshrined in international law but is also found in the constitutions and labor laws of many countries. However, it is still rarely granted to children by law and, if so, only to certain children. Only a few national laws recognize this right of children. The Children and Adolescents Code of Peru (Código de los Niños y Adolescentes, Ley N° 28330), adopted in 2004, grants adolescents the right to work from the age of twelve. According to Article 22 of this law, "The State recognizes the right of adolescents to work, with the restrictions imposed by this Code, as long as there is no economic exploitation and their work does not pose any risk or danger, affects their educational process or is harmful to their health or their physical, mental, spiritual, moral or social development." As such, a formulation of the Children and Adolescents Code (Decreto Ley N° 26102) of 1992 was adopted almost literally.[31] Another example is Bolivia's Child and Adolescent Code (Código Niña, Niño y Adolescente, Ley N° 548), which came into force in 2014. According to this law, children would have had the right, under certain conditions and depending on the form of work, to obtain a work permit from the age of ten or twelve.[32] Both laws were enacted at the instigation and with the cooperation of working children's organizations. Their implementation, however, has faced difficulties, mainly due to a lack of government commitment and resources. In addition, the ILO continues to press for the minimum age for employment to be raised to fifteen. In Bolivia, in December 2018, the ILO succeeded in spurring modification of the law such that permission to work now applies only to adolescents from the age of fourteen. Working children under this age are no longer granted any special protection rights.

The right to work, on the other hand, in the opinion of its advocates, serves as protection against economic exploitation and, as a subjective right of the children, goes beyond CRC Article 32. This right is understood in various ways. In some constitutions, it obliges the state to ensure that all citizens able and entitled to work get paid employment. In other cases, it corresponds to the right to free choice of employment or freedom to choose a profession. From the point of view of the working children's organizations, this right does not mean, as it is often misunderstood to mean, that any person has the right to demand a child's work or that children have to be guaranteed contracted employment.[33] As opposed to the right to employment, the right to work as claimed by working children is correctly understood as an individual child's right to freely decide whether, where, how, and for how long he or she works. It goes beyond mere access to employment of some kind, whether in the official or informal economy. The raison d'être of the claim of the right to work is to broaden children's scope for decision-making and to strengthen their social status as acting subjects. It challenges the dominant legal conception that children's rights are first and foremost the rights exercised by adults, and it sets up a framework which fosters children's best interests.[34] Likewise, it opposes a narrow conception of child protection, which relies on measures of exclusion and prohibitions to prevent children's exposure to exploitation.

In contrast to the right to be protected from economic exploitation—codified in CRC Article 32—the right to work is a claim put forward by *children* themselves. The demand is a result of working children's experiences and the fact that legislation and policy measures devised to protect them from exploitation have contributed rarely if ever to ameliorate their situation.[35] Quite to the contrary, the prohibition of child labor contained in ILO Convention No. 138 was translated into laws and according measures that often have made the situation of working children more complicated and difficult.[36]

Even ILO Convention No. 182, which aims specifically at combating the "worst forms of child labor," turned out to be an instrument that contributed to the problems that working children face instead of constituting a solution to these problems. The problem is not to identify harmful forms of child labor, but how they are defined and how they are to be combated. Some of the action programs of the International Programme on the Elimination of Child Labor (IPEC), which was launched by ILO in 1992, were initiated without taking into account the particular living conditions of the children and their families. Decisions were made as to what should be considered the worst forms of child labor without consulting children and their families. Although it is certainly helpful to specify which work is harmful to children, the definition of the worst forms of child labor includes prostitution and drug trafficking, activities that are not children's work, but crimes against children. Furthermore, in many cases, this convention was used as a justification to displace working children from their places of work without offering alternative solutions.[37] Such solutions require improving the living conditions of families and bringing about structural changes in the economy and society responsible for the exploitation of children. Working children sometimes express this idea with the words "Poverty must be banned instead of our work" or "Not work is a problem for us, but the conditions under which we have to work."

The laws and policies designed to protect working children fail to take into consideration the reasons which motivate children to take up work, and they fail to consider children's views and perceptions. Children are seen merely as victims and objects in need of help as opposed to individuals with thoughts about their situation and ideas about how to solve their problems.

These laws and policies also reflect a striking neglect of the specific sociocultural contexts in which children grow up as well as existing concepts of childhood and work in which children's work is not seen as an anomaly, but as a contribution to shared responsibilities and something to be appreciated. Of course, there is indeed the risk that in situations of extreme poverty children are only seen in terms of their labor force potential, and little attention is paid to their rights and needs. Nevertheless, in view of working children's experiences with child labor bans, and insights we have gained on the unintended impacts of such bans, one has to ask whether these risks can be adequately addressed if children's work is only defined as intrinsically negative. Instead, a combination of an honest assessment of children's working conditions and a recognition of the value and potential benefits of work, especially for, but not restricted to, children, seems to be a more promising approach to improving the situation of working children. One cannot ignore that often children like to help their families and are proud of contributing to the family's needs and income.[38]

The claim for the right to work corresponds to the demand of working children for better social recognition of their work and its contributions not only to their own and their families' lives but also to the production and reproduction of society in general. The children who demand the right to work have experience with work and exploitation as well as with the inadequacy of many measures taken for their protection. These children demand solutions that take into account their living conditions and experiences. They want to be respected as persons who have an interest in and are capable of contributing to solving the problems they and their communities face. In this sense, they consider the right to work as an instrument of empowerment in which they take command of their own situation.[39]

Because children do not yet have complete access to political rights, they are often excluded from the most important avenues for political participation and, thus, can neither vote, otherwise contribute to legislation, nor interpret and or administer the law. Therefore, there is a special significance in children's perspectives and demands formulated and voiced collectively through their social movements and organizations. Children demand of adults, who compared to children undoubtedly are in a more privileged situation, to be more inclusive in regard to their needs and perspectives. Or, as Pamela Reynolds, Olga Nieuwenhuys, and Karl Hanson state, "some danger lies in our use of rights to abstract and universalize at the expense of efforts to imagine the stake we have in mutual comprehensibility and to be responsive to other forms of life, especially those under construction by the young."[40]

The formulation of rights by children finds legitimacy in that through such claims they seek answers to urgent needs and demand that the social realities they face be improved. The rights they demand are closely related to their concrete life experiences and are claimed because children consider them to be relevant and appropriate solutions to their claims. Due to the fact that these claims are voiced by children themselves (in this case working children) and based on their specific experiences, the right to work can be best understood as a *living right* or *right from below*.[41]

6 CHILDREN'S RIGHT TO WORK AS A LIVING ECONOMIC RIGHT

The right to work is not only an economic right that demands participation for children on equal terms in society, but it is also a tool for protecting working children from exploitation. Protection does not solely mean the general and strict avoidance of hazardous situations ("protection from …") but also how those situations are handled through the agency and activities of those directly affected ("protection by …"). There are certainly risks in this approach. One could ask whether children are always in the position to judge the inherent dangers in specific forms of work, that is, if they are able to recognize their "best interests" or to differentiate between their short- and long-term interests (despite the temptations that earning money can constitute) or whether they have the necessary power to stand up against unreasonable working conditions and thereby achieve the necessary changes.

Although there is some risk involved in this approach, it would be erroneous to think that a conception of protection of children focused on the general avoidance of risk does not expose children to other potential dangers or harms. Not only can it reinforce the dependency of children at the expense of freedom and participation rights, and preclude them from developing the necessary competencies for taking appropriate actions when facing possibly harmful situations, it is also blind and inflexible toward the specific living conditions of children and the culture-specific positioning of children in the respective society.[42] It throws the baby out with the bathwater by making it impossible to identify the contexts of children's work, the meanings of work for children, and the active roles children could play in their own protection. Furthermore, in the sense of a self-fulfilling prophecy, the avoidance concept itself ex ante contributes to putting the child in a state of helplessness, which serves as evidence of the need for protection.[43]

On the other hand, if the right to work is granted to children, this would allow them to better protect themselves against risks and to improve their situation through legal means. For example, regulations could specify the conditions for work accessible to children, such as maximum working hours, parallel school attendance, or protection and participation rights in the workplace. In addition, children willing to work could be provided with employment opportunities that comply not only with these regulations but also with children's ideas about working. These employment opportunities could be imagined in the context of public institutions or with regard to new forms of a solidarity economy[44] and nonprofit economic activity. This, in turn, could contribute to the reduction of child poverty. Such initiatives also apply to younger children, as they can be part of collectives where they share responsibility with older children and are accompanied and supported by adult educators or workers.

Like all human rights, the right to work can claim validity before any formal codification in national laws or international conventions. It receives its legitimacy by being increasingly articulated and, in an organized manner, by children themselves. For instance, the "twelve rights" formulated in the founding document of the African Movement of Working Children and Youth[45] partly correspond to some of the articles in the CRC, but they are not explicitly contained in any official legal document. This document not only requires the right "to learn to read and write" or the right "to be listened to" but, also, the right to "a light and appropriate work" or the right "not to have to migrate (to remain in our villages)." In contrast to national and international legal documents, these twelve rights are characterized by the fact that they relate specifically to the life and interests of the working children who formulated them and to the lives and interests of the working children represented by this movement. In all countries where this movement is represented, the young members evaluate on a regular basis the extent to which their twelve rights are being put into practice, and they discuss the role played by responsible adults and governments in supporting their goals.

The right to work is especially relevant to the implementation of other children's rights. The fundamental new beginning that the CRC promises by granting children the right to dignity and a self-determined social identity will not reach its full potential as long as children remain dependent on the benevolence of adults. When children can legally become economically active and have their own income at their disposal, they can better expect to gain the necessary independence and social importance to enforce their own rights in society.

In declarations and statements issued by children's movements, the right to work does not relate to *any* kind of work; instead, these materials repeatedly emphasize "work in dignity," "light" work or "not too hard work," and "work appropriate to the child's skills."[46] At first glance, this could be understood in a manner that means children can claim only a limited right to "child-specific" work that may be connected to a particular age. Judging by the context, however, one can conclude that rather than age being the main criterion, respect for human dignity is. As understood by children's movements, the right to work aims at obtaining the "best possible" work and actively opposing any kind of exploitation and degradation in the workplace. It thus contains a utopian surplus, which points beyond the wage labor dominant in capitalist society. Moreover, children want to decide for themselves whether prospective work meets their specific criteria or not.

7 CONCLUSION

Children's economic and labor rights are de facto restricted, often considered as unnecessary or even rejected, but they certainly make sense and are necessary for children. This is especially true for working children, as their economic and labor rights serve to protect them and to improve their working and living conditions. Nevertheless, these rights also make sense for children as a whole because they can help strengthen their position in society, foster their emancipation, and expand their options for action.

The demand for economic and labor rights, and the engagement of movements of working children, challenge widespread ideas about childhood as a life stage of becoming, of preparation, as well as the inferior state of being cared for. By understanding children's rights as subjective or agency rights, the demand for these rights, particularly the right to work, also requires rethinking the subordinated status of children as a social group and addressing its implicit injustice. It contests widespread concepts of protection, which primarily involve regulations that impose bans and exclusion. This means recognizing working children and their organizations as equal partners in the struggle for fairer living and working conditions. This is a challenge both to trade unions, which have to unlearn their view of working children as victims and unwelcome competitors, and to social movements and NGOs, which have to accept that working children should not be merely the objects of supportive measures. Children whose economic and labor rights have been recognized and who are supported in realizing these rights could play a much greater role in the process of social transformation toward a more just world than they have been able to do so far.

NOTES

1. UN Convention on the Rights of Child (CRC), G.A. Res. 44/25, 44th Sess., UN Doc. A/RES/44/25 (1989).
2. Child Rights International Network, "Economic Rights," https://archive.crin.org/en/home/rights/themes/economic-rights.html (accessed Aug. 23, 2019).
3. Virginia A. Leary, "The Social and Economic Rights of the Child," *Law & Policy* 17, no. 4 (October 1995): 353–375, 353. On the confusion between economic and social rights see Terence Daintith, "The Constitutional Protection of Economic Rights," *International Journal of Constitutional Law* 2, no. 1 (2004): 56–90, 57–59.
4. Karl Hanson and Arne Vandaele, "Working Children and International Labour Law: A Critical Analysis," *International Journal of Children's Rights* 11, no. 1 (2003): 73–146; Manfred Liebel, *A Will of Their Own: Cross-Cultural Perspectives on Working Children* (London: Zed Books, 2004); Karl Hanson and Arne Vandaele, "Translating Working Children's Rights into International Labour Law," in *Reconceptualizing Children's Rights in International Development: Living Rights, Social Justice, Translations*, ed. Karl Hanson and Olga Nieuwenhuys *Cambridge: Cambridge University Press, 2013), 250–274; Manfred Liebel, "Do Children Have a Right to Work? Working Children's Movements in the Struggle for

Social Justice," in Hanson and Nieuwenhuys, *Reconceptualizing Children's Rights in International Development*, 225–249; Manfred Liebel, Philip Meade, and Iven Saadi, "Working Children as Subjects of Rights: Explaining Children's Right to Work," in *Handbook of Children's Rights: Global and Multidisciplinary Perspectives*, ed. Martin D. Ruck, Michelle Peterson-Badali, and Michael Freeman (New York: Routledge, 2017), 437–453.

5. International Covenant on Economic, Social and Cultural Rights (ICESCR), G.A. Res. 2200A (XXI) (1966).

6. International Labour Office, *The International Labour Organization's Fundamental Conventions* (Geneva: International Labour Office, 2002). The following conventions have been identified as "fundamental" and are at times referred to as the "core labour standards": Freedom of Association and Protection of the Right to Organise Convention, 1948 (No. 87), Right to Organise and Collective Bargaining Convention, 1949 (No. 98), Forced Labour Convention, 1930 (No. 29), Abolition of Forced Labour Convention, 1957 (No. 105), Minimum Age Convention, 1973 (No. 138), Worst Forms of Child Labour Convention, 1999 (No. 182), Equal Remuneration Convention, 1951 (No. 100), Discrimination (Employment and Occupation) Convention, 1958 (No. 111).

7. International Labour Organization (ILO), "Declaration on Fundamental Principles and Rights at Work and Its Follow-up" ("Fundamental Principles"), in *The International Labour Organization's Fundamental Conventions*, ed. ILO (Geneva: International Labour Office, 1998/2002), 73–75; see also International Labour Office, *Rules of the Game: A Brief Introduction to International Labour Standards* (Geneva: International Labour Office, 2014).

8. ILO, *The International Labour Organization's Fundamental Conventions*, ed. ILO (Geneva: International Labour Office, 2002), 74.

9. ICESCR.

10. See Neil Stammers, *Human Rights and Social Movements* (London: Pluto Press, 2009).

11. See UNESCO Office of International Standards and Legal Affairs, "Declaration on the Responsibilities of the Present Generations towards Future Generations" (Nov. 12, 1997) http://portal.unesco.org/en/ev.php-URL_ID=13178&URL_DO=DO_TOPIC&URL_SECTION=201.html.

12. ICESCR, art. 10(3).

13. ILO, "Fundamental Principles."

14. ILO Convention (No. 138) Concerning Minimum Age for Admission to Employment, 1015 UNTS 297 (1973; entered into force June 19, 1976).

15. ICESCR, art. 10(3).

16. See, for example, International Working Group on Child Labour, *Working Children: Reconsidering the Debates, Report of International Working Group on Child Labour*, ed. Jim McKechnie and Sandy Hobbs (Amsterdam: Defence for Children International, 1998); Martin Woodhead, *Children's Perspectives on Their Working Lives: A Participatory Study in Bangladesh, Ethiopia, the Philippines, Guatemala, El Salvador and Nicaragua* (Stockholm: Rädda Barnen and Save the Children, 1998); Prashant Bharadwaj, Leah K. Lakdawala, and Nicholas Li, "Perverse Consequences of Well-Intentioned Regulation: Evidence from India's Child Labor Ban," NBER Working Paper No. 19602 (October 2013).

17. Hanson and Vandaele, "Working Children"; Hanson and Vandaele, "Translating Working Children's Rights."

18. This view is represented in nearly all publications of the ILO and many publications of NGOs. It is also reflected in the fact that these rights with regard to children are not mentioned at all.

19. See Manfred Liebel, "Children without Childhood? Against the Postcolonial Capture of Childhoods in the Global South," In *"Children Out of Place" and Human Rights: In Memory of Judith Ennew*, ed. Antonella Invernizzi, Manfred Liebel, Brian Milne, and Rebecca Budde (New York: Springer, 2017), 79–97.

20. They correspond to the rights enshrined in ILO Conventions No. 87 of 1948, "Freedom of Association and Protection of the Right to Organize," and ILO Convention No. 98 of 1949, "Right to Organize and Collective Bargaining," which are basic to the ILO Fundamental Principles.

21. This is regulated in the statutes of trade unions. See, e.g., Florian Lian, "Explain Classes of Person Who Cannot Join Trade Union," https://de.scribd.com/doc/75978749/Explain-Classes-of-Person-Who-Cannot-Join-Trade-Union (accessed Aug. 23, 2019). The main reason is that employment of children is seen as illegal child labor, but also relevant is an adultist attitude that does not recognize the political agency and participation of children.

22. International Working Group on Child Labour (IWGCL), "Have We Asked the Children?," IWGCL working paper (February 1997), http://www.concernedforworkingchildren.org/wp-content/uploads/Have-we-The-Children-discussion-paper_IWGCL-1.pdf; Jo Boyden, Birgitta Ling, and William Myers, *What Works for Working Children* (Stockholm: Rädda Barnen, Save the Children, and UNICEF, 1998); Antonella Invernizzi and Brian Milne, "Are Children Entitled to Contribute to International Policy Making? A Critical View of Children's Participation in the International Campaign for the Elimination of Child Labour," *International Journal of Children's Rights* 10, no. 4 (2002): 403–431; Judith, Ennew, William Myers, and Dominique Pierre Plateau, "Defining Child Labor as if Human Rights Really Matter," in *Child Labor and Human Rights*, ed. Burns H. Weston (Boulder, CO: Lynne Rienner, 2005), 27–54; Sharon Bessell, "Influencing International Child Labour Policy: The Potential and Limits of Children-Centred Research," *Children and Youth Services Review* 33 (2011): 564–568; Nandana Reddy, "The International Movement of Working Children" (February 2013), http://www.concernedforworkingchildren.org/wp-content/uploads/International-Movement_Nandana-Reddy_March-7_Paper.pdf.

23. See Marianne Dahlén, "The Negotiable Child: The ILO Child Labour Campaign 1919–1973," LLD diss., Uppsala University, 2007, http://uu.diva-portal.org/smash/get/diva2:169702/FULLTEXT01.pdf.

24. This was one of the main reasons why the ILO launched the International Programme on the Elimination of Child Labor (IPEC) in 1992 and on June 17, 1999, adopted "ILO Convention 182 concerning the Prohibition and Immediate Action for the Elimination of the Worst Forms of Child Labour," 2133 UNTS 161). Nevertheless, Convention No. 182 did not replace ILO Convention No. 138 but is understood only as its complement.

25. See, for example, Beatrice Hungerland, Manfred Liebel, Brian Milne, and Anne Wihstutz, eds., *Working to Be Someone: Child Focused Research and Practice with Working Children* (London: Jessica Kingsley Publishers, 2007); Michael Bourdillon, Ben White, and William Myers, "Re-Assessing Minimum-Age Standards for Children's Work," *International Journal of Sociology and Social Policy* 29, nos. 3–4 (2009): 106–117; Bharadwaj, Lakdawala, and Li, "Perverse Consequences."

26. For an overview see Michael Bourdillon, Deborah Levison, William Myers, and Ben White, *Rights and Wrongs of Children's Work* (Brunswick, NJ: Rutgers University Press, 2010).

27. Judith Ennew, "Outside Childhood: Street Children's Rights," in *The New Handbook of Children's Rights: Comparative Policy and Practice*, ed. Bob Franklin (London: Routledge, 2002), 201–215, 399.

28. Michael Bourdillon and William Myers, "Introduction," in *Child Protection in Development*, ed. Michael Bourdillon and William Myers (London: Routledge and INTRAC, 2013).

29. ILO, "A Future without Child Labour: Global Report under the Follow-Up to the ILO Declaration on Fundamental Principles and Rights at Work" (2002), https://www.ilo.org/wcmsp5/groups/public/---dgreports/---dcomm/---publ/documents/publication/wcms_publ_9221124169_en.pdf; ILO, "The End of Child Labour: Within Reach; Global Report on Child Labour under the Follow-Up to the ILO Declaration on Fundamental Principles and Rights at Work" (2006), https://www.ilo.org/public/english/standards/relm/ilc/ilc95/pdf/rep-i-b.pdf; ILO, "Accelerating Action against Child Labour: Global Report on Child Labour under the Follow-Up to the ILO Declaration on Fundamental Principles and Rights at Work" (2010), https://www.ilo.org/wcmsp5/groups/public/@dgreports/@dcomm/documents/publication/wcms_126752.pdf; ILO, "Global Estimates of Child Labour: Results and Trends, 2012–2016" (2017), https://www.ilo.org/wcmsp5/groups/public/@dgreports/@dcomm/documents/publication/wcms_575499.pdf.

30. Judith Ennew, Yuli Hastadewi, and Dominique Pierre Plateau, "Seen, Heard—and Forgotten? Participation of Children and Young People in Southeast, East Asia and Pacific in Events and Forums Leading to and Following Up on the United Nations General Assembly Special Session for Children, 2002," *Children, Youth and Environments* 17, no. 1 (2007): 33–42.

31. See Liebel, "Do Children Have a Right to Work?," 242–243.

32. See Manfred Liebel, "Protecting the Rights of Working Children instead of Banning Child Labour: Bolivia Tries a New Legislative Approach," *International Journal of Children's Rights* 23, no. 3 (2015): 491–509.

33. In some national constitutions or the constitutions of some German federal states, the right to work is defined as the obligation of the state to achieve full employment so that everyone who wishes to may work. In the Finnish constitution of 1999, for example, it says in section 18.2: "The public authorities shall promote employment and work towards guaranteeing for everyone the right to work." For further information, see Terence Daintith, "The Constitutional Protection of Economic Rights," *International Journal of Constitutional Law* 2, no. 1 (2004): 56–90, 76–80.

34. See Manfred Liebel, Karl Hanson, Iven Saadi, and Wouter Vandenhole, *Children's Rights from Below: Cross-Cultural Perspectives* (Basingstoke, UK: Palgrave Macmillan, 2012).

35. See Liebel, "Do Children Have a Right to Work?"

36. For a review see Bourdillon et al., *Rights and Wrongs*.

37. According to my personal observations as a street worker and participant of working children's meetings, this happened particularly in Latin-American countries, such as Colombia, Ecuador, Peru, Mexico, and Nicaragua.

38. Ina Gankam Tambo, *Child Domestic Work in Nigeria: Conditions of Socialisation and Measures of Intervention* (Münster, DE: Waxmann, 2014); Martha Areli Ramírez Sánchez, " 'Helping at Home': The Concept of Childhood and Work among the Nahuas of Tlaxcala, Mexico," in Hungerland et al., *Working to Be Someone*, 87–95; Tobias Samuelsson, *Children's Work in Sweden: A Part of Childhood, a Path to Adulthood* (Linköping: Linköping University, 2008); Woodhead, *Children's Perspectives on Their Working Lives*.

39. *See* Liebel, Meade, and Saadi, "Working Children."

40. Pamela Reynolds, Olga Nieuwenhuys, and Karl Hanson, "Refractions of Children's Rights in Development Practice: A View from Anthropology," *Childhood* 13, no. 3 (2006): 291–302, 300–301.

41. On the concepts of "living rights" and "rights from below" *see* Karl Hanson and Olga Nieuwenhuys, eds., *Reconceptualizing Children's Rights in International Development: Living Rights, Social Justice, Translations* (Cambridge: Cambridge University Press, 2013); Liebel et al., *Children's Rights from Below*.

42. Gerison Lansdown, "The Evolving Capacities of the Child," UNICEF Innocenti Research Centre report (2005), https://www.unicef-irc.org/publications/pdf/evolving-eng.pdf; Manfred Liebel, "From Evolving 'Capacities' to Evolving 'Capabilities': Contextualizing Children's Rights," in *Children's Rights and the Capability Approach: Changes and Prospects*, ed. Daniel Stoecklin and Jean-Michel Bonvin (New York: Springer, 2014), 67–84.

43. *See* Liebel et al., *Children's Rights from Below*, 100–101.

44. A solidarity economy comprises income-generating activities aimed primarily at meeting the needs of the workers in mutual support, not at gaining the highest profit. Various movements of working children have realized solidarity economies on a small scale, and some export their goods to European fair-trade organizations (i.e., the Italy-based organization Little Hands, http://www.littlehands.it).

45. This document is presented in detail and explained in the following publications: ENDA, ed., "Voice of African Children: Work, Strength and Organisation of Working Children and Youth," Occasional Papers no. 217 (2001); and Manfred Liebel, "Children's Work, Education, and Agency: The African Movement of Working Children and Youth (AMWCY)," in *African Children at Work: Working and Learning in Growing Up for Life*, ed. Gerd Spittler and Michael Bourdillon (Zurich: LIT, 2012), 303–332.

46. *See* Liebel, "Do Children Have a Right to Work?"

CHAPTER 18

....

THE HEALTH RIGHTS
OF CHILDREN

....

URSULA KILKELLY

1 INTRODUCTION

....

THE UN Convention on the Rights of the Child (CRC)[1] codified the rights of the child in international law, bringing together civil and political rights and economic, social, and cultural rights for the first time. While some of the rights in the Convention are newly recognized, many of its provisions are adapted from other human rights treaties to address the specific needs and circumstances of children. One such provision is Article 24, which recognizes the right of the child to enjoy the highest attainable standard of health and to access facilities for the treatment of disease and rehabilitation of health. The human right to health first appeared in the Universal Declaration of Human Rights in 1948, before being recognized as a substantive legal right in the International Covenant on Economic Social and Cultural Rights (ICESCR) in 1966.[2] Its inclusion in the CRC is the first time a child-specific composite right to health and to health care has been enshrined in binding international law.

Article 24 of the CRC requires states to ensure that no child is deprived of the right of access to health care services, and it requires states to pursue full implementation of the right, including by taking measures that address infant and child mortality; ensure the necessary provision of medical assistance to all children; combat disease and malnutrition; ensure appropriate pre- and post-natal care for mothers; make health education available to all; and develop preventive health care, guidance for parents, and family planning education and services. The focus in Article 24 is thus on the child's most basic health care needs and on treating illness, preventing disease, and health care promotion. Its recognition of the right of the child to the highest attainable standard of health and to health care services necessary to meet that standard marks Article 24 as one of the most important of the CRC's substantive provisions.

In addition to being fundamental in its own right, good health is recognized to be essential to the realization of children's other rights. In this sense, children who enjoy access to health care enjoy a multiplier effect, as this enables them to enjoy their right to education and to play, for instance, while children who do not may suffer the outcomes associated with poor health, including developmental delay and disadvantage that spills over into other areas of their lives.[3] Despite its importance, however, the codification of the right of the child to health in binding international law appears to have had limited effect on the status of the right to health. At present, no dedicated international children's rights organizations are campaigning specifically on the child's right to health, and indications are that the UN Committee on the Rights of the Child (CRC Committee), the body that monitors implementation of the Convention, has not considered the right a particular priority. For example, despite its importance, the right to health was not included as one of the Convention's general principles when the Committee established this approach in 1991.[4] Moreover, it took the Committee nearly twenty years to adopt General Comment No. 15, its guidance for states parties on the implementation of the child's right to health.[5]

That is not to say that child health is not a priority at the national or international level or that advances have not been made in children's health. The World Health Organisation reports substantial gains across a range of indicators in child health during the lifetime of the Convention on the Rights of the Child. And the focus on child health in the Sustainable Development Goals (SDGs) indicates a very substantial international commitment to improving child health outcomes. What is concerning, however, is the apparent disconnect between children's rights and international development discourse around the child's health. For children's rights, an important question arises as to what difference it has made to children to have health care defined as a right, one that states have a legally binding duty to implement. Moreover, when children's health care is so fundamentally important, why does it not enjoy a higher profile among children's human rights?

This chapter aims to examine the child's right to health and health care, under Article 24 of the CRC against this backdrop. To begin, the chapter explores the terms of Article 24, seeking to understand the terms of the provision in its own right, while reflecting on the relevance of associated CRC provisions. The chapter then goes on to consider the jurisprudence of the CRC Committee with a view to examining the importance of Article 24 to the Committee's work of monitoring implementation of the CRC. The next section looks briefly at the work of other international organizations committed to the advancement of children's health and health care, with a particular emphasis on the SDGs, considering the extent to which this work is based on or informed by Article 24. The chapter concludes by identifying some steps that might be taken to ensure a more progressive, rights-based future for the child's right to health. It makes the case for a more integrated approach—across human rights and development fields—for the child's right to health.

A word, before the chapter begins, on nomenclature. It is clear from the language of Article 24 of the CRC that the provision covers both health and health care as the right of the child. While it is acknowledged that these are distinct rights, it must be acknowledged that the highest attainable standard of health can only be achieved by ensuring access to health care. For this reason, health and health care are used interchangeably in this chapter, and the right to health is intended to include the right to health care.

2 THE CRC: A CHILD'S RIGHT TO HEALTH

The origins of international law on the right to health can be traced to the Constitution of the World Health Organization of 1946[6] and, shortly thereafter, the Universal Declaration of Human Rights in 1948.[7] It is thus firmly rooted in a human rights approach even though it was not until 1966 that the right to health was enshrined in binding international law.[8] This took place via the ICESCR, Article 12 of which guarantees to "everyone" the right to enjoy the highest attainable standard of physical and mental health. Specific to children, Article 12(2) of the ICESCR provides that states are required to take steps to achieve the full realization of this right, including those necessary, inter alia, for "the provision for the reduction of the stillbirth-rate and of infant mortality and for the healthy development of the child." In 2000 the UN Committee on Economic, Social and Cultural Rights, the committee charged with overseeing implementation of the ICESCR, adopted a General Comment on the right to health where it expanded on the duty to protect, respect, and fulfill the right without discrimination.[9] According to the General Comment, the right to health has four components—availability, accessibility, affordability and quality.[10] Unusually, perhaps, given that treaty bodies normally confine their commentaries to their own instruments, the commentary of the Committee on Economic, Social and Cultural Rights on the child's right to health relies heavily on the CRC in highlighting the duty to ensure that in all policies and programs on the right to health, the child's best interests are a primary consideration.[11] Specific mention is made also of the need to provide a safe and supportive environment for adolescents, one that enables them to participate in decisions affecting their health, and an environment in which they have access to information and counseling that helps them negotiate health-behavior choices.[12] In its General Comment, the Committee on Economic, Social and Cultural Rights stretched beyond the terms of Article 12 by addressing some of the challenges faced by adolescent young people in enjoying the right to the highest attainable standard of health. This is evident from the fact that Article 12 neither addresses the particular health needs of young people nor makes any reference to health care decision-making. The General Comment sets out the legal obligations on states in Article 12 of the ICESCR, namely, the obligation to respect, protect, and fulfill health rights, noting in particular, the duty of states to "adopt appropriate legislative, administrative, budgetary, judicial, promotional and other measures towards the full realization of the right to health."[13] Given that health care rights are normally subject to the concept of progressive (rather than immediate) realization, like other socio-economic rights, this explicit articulation that Article 12 imposes a legal duty to realize the right to health care is very welcome. In particular, the Committee's articulation of states' broader human rights obligations is a welcome reminder that the right to health is a fundamental right, which the state has a duty to respect, protect, and fulfill.[14] This approach thus underlines both the fundamental nature of the right to health to the rights holder and the responsibility of the state in this context. Significantly, as is explained below, the approach of the Committee on Economic, Social and Cultural Rights to its General Comment appears to have influenced the approach of the CRC Committee when it developed General Comment No. 15 (on the child's right to health) in 2013.[15]

In 1989, adoption of the CRC by the United Nations General Assembly gave explicit recognition of the child's right to health in international law.[16] Article 24(1) of the CRC recognizes the child's right to "the highest attainable standard of health and to facilities for the treatment of illness and the rehabilitation of health" and provides that states shall "strive to ensure that no child is deprived of his or her right of access to such health care services." Thereafter, in Article 24(2), the provision focuses on basic state responsibilities, including addressing infant and child mortality; developing a primary health care system; combating disease and malnutrition; and providing pre- and post-natal care for mothers and health promotion. The emphasis on the fundamental needs of children is accentuated by the final paragraph, Article 24(4), which requires states to "promote and encourage international co-operation with a view to achieving progressively the full realization of the right recognized in the present article," with particular account being taken of the "needs of developing countries." Separately, Article 24(3) of the CRC requires states to take "all effective measures" to abolish traditional practices prejudicial to the health of children, but it stops short of naming various forms of mutilation or cutting carried out for religious, cultural, or social reasons.[17]

Although Article 24 is the most important provision in the CRC concerning the child's right to health, it is not the only provision relevant to this issue. The Convention's general principles (discussed further below)—under Articles 2, 3, 6, and 12—also resonate loudly in the health care setting. Article 2, which requires states to ensure CRC rights to all children without discrimination of any kind, highlights the continuing challenge of achieving equity in the implementation of health care rights. Article 3, which requires the best interests of the child to be a primary consideration in all actions concerning children, reinforces the notion that health care must meet the needs of individual children[18] and that the child's best interests must be at the center of all health care decision-making. The CRC Committee has recognized the importance of ensuring that the child's best interests inform treatment options for children, superseding economic considerations "where feasible."[19] It also proposes the best interests principle as a valuable means by which conflicts of interest might be resolved between parents and health care professionals in decision-making about the child's health care.[20] According to the CRC Committee, the application of Article 3 to health care also includes "the allocation of resources, and the development and implementation of policies and interventions that affect the underlying determinants of a child's health."[21]

Finally, Article 12, which requires that children capable of forming their views shall be assured the right to express those views in all matters affecting them, and to have these views be given due weight in line with their age and maturity, plays an important role in ensuring that health care decision-making is Convention compliant. It is relevant in at least two areas—on an individual basis, where the child has the right to participate in decisions made about his/her health, and, more generally, where it requires that children's views are taken into account in health care policy and the planning, delivery, and improvement of health care services.[22] According to the CRC Committee, the Convention requires that children are included in health care decision-making in line with the child's evolving capacity.[23] It is especially important, given how continuously a child grows and develops during childhood, that the parent's role to support the child's exercise of his/her rights should diminish as the child's matures.[24]

It is well established that children's rights under the CRC and more generally are indivisible and interdependent. From the perspective of health care, it is important to highlight the extent to which the fulfillment of Article 24 acts to scaffold other substantive CRC rights and vice versa. Children in poor health, or who are deprived of timely or effective health care or treatment for disease, struggle to enjoy their rights under multiple CRC provisions, such as Article 6 (the right to life, survival and development), Article 27 (the right to an adequate standard of living), Article 28 (the right to education), and Article 12 (the right to have a say). At the same time, children who are deprived of certain other socio-economic rights, like the right to an adequate standard of living (Article 27) and the right to social security (Article 26), or the right to protection from harm (Article 19) or exploitation (Articles 33 and 34), can suffer poor health outcomes, thereby making it difficult to distinguish where one right begins and the other ends. Thus, the child's right to health should enjoy a particularly elevated status under the Convention, as a right that provides a solid platform from which the implementation of other rights can be achieved. In this regard, it is clearly important that both health and health care have been recognized under the CRC as a right and an entitlement of every child. It is important too that the Convention's approach to child health reflects the indivisibility of children's rights, by taking a holistic approach that views child health as an integral part of a child's development and well-being and positions child health in the context of the family and the community. The CRC frames child health as a universal right, recognizing its importance to the child in all circumstances and in its emphasis on universal and basic health care.

In terms of regional children's rights instruments, two instruments stand out as important to this discussion. First, it is interesting to note that the African Charter on the Rights and Welfare of the Child (African Charter), the only regional children's rights charter, which was adopted in 1990 and came into force in 1999, contains a very similar provision to Article 24 of the CRC. In particular, Article 14 of the African Charter recognizes the right of the child "to enjoy the best attainable state of physical, mental and spiritual health" and goes on to elaborate on the measures that states must take in the implementation of this right. In particular, Article 14 provides that African states must ensure that children have access to adequate nutrition and safe drinking water; must combat disease and malnutrition within the framework of primary health care; and must provide preventive health care both for mothers and babies. Article 14 emphasizes the importance of developing primary health care and integrating basic health care programs into national development plans. It requires states to ensure that "all sectors of the society, in particular, parents, children, community leaders and community workers are informed and supported in the use of basic knowledge of child health and nutrition, the advantages of breastfeeding, hygiene and environmental sanitation and the prevention of domestic and other accidents."[25] The African Committee of Experts on the Rights and Welfare of the Child has not to date adopted a General Comment in the area of health care.[26] This would appear a remarkable gap given the stark challenges, highlighted below, facing implementation of the right to health for children in the African region.

The CRC has also influenced the development of child-specific instruments, including on healthcare, as in the "Council of Europe Guidelines on Child-Friendly Healthcare" (European Guidelines).[27] Adopted in 2011, the European Guidelines propose an integrated approach to the development of the children's health care by placing children at the heart of health care decision-making and service delivery. They articulate a children's rights–based approach to children's health and health care by marrying the children's rights approach to health care with approaches from public and social health care, producing an integrated blueprint for states parties. Although non-binding in nature, the European Guidelines represent an important statement of political consensus as to how children's rights to and in health care can be protected and promoted.

In summary, then, the child's right to health care is firmly established in international law as a legal right. Building on the ICESCR and other instruments, Article 24 of the CRC is an important provision that recognizes health as a specific and fundamental right of the child. It emphasizes the basic elements of health care—primary health care, health promotion, and the prevention of disease—and advocates international co-operation in the implementation of the health rights of children. In this regard, the Convention appears to have had a positive impact on the regional development of a human rights approach to child health through the adoption of both Article 14 of the African Charter and the European Guidelines. There are many gaps, however—the absence of a framework for health care decision-making, the lack of an age of consent to medical treatment, and the failure to address medical research, to name just three important right to health issues.[28] Ultimately, however, the terms of the Convention are just a starting point; the approach of the CRC Committee to monitoring their implementation plays a substantial role in bringing about the Convention's impact on the area. This will be discussed in the section that follows.

3 CONTRIBUTION OF THE COMMITTEE ON THE RIGHTS OF THE CHILD: A MORE CRITICAL VIEW

The CRC Committee has a mandate under Article 43 to monitor implementation of the Convention. It does this in a number of ways, including in its assessment of implementation at the national level through the state party reporting process and, second and related, through the adoption of its General Comments, which act as position statements on various aspects of the Convention. The reporting process enables the CRC Committee to address country specific issues with the Convention's implementation, and its Concluding Observations, the formal statement adopted after the process has concluded, highlight both gaps and progress made in the implementation of the Convention. Concluding Observations also contain recommendations as to how better implementation can be achieved. An analysis of the CRC Committee's Concluding Observations from the perspective of the right to health is beyond the scope of this chapter—though some analysis is presented below. Suffice to say, although the CRC Committee clearly scrutinizes the implementation of Article 24 as part of the reporting process, it does not pay any particular attention to health care issues as part of this process. Arguably, one reason for this is the position of Article 24 in the guidelines on state reporting. In 1991, when these guidelines were first adopted, the right to health was grouped with other provisions—including Article 6 on the right to life, survival and development; children with disabilities under Article 23; Article 27 on the adequate standard of living; and social security and child care services under Articles 26 and 18(3).[29] As well as being bundled with a range of other provisions under the heading "Basic Health and Welfare," the right to health was further diminished in status by not being included among the four "general principles" that the CRC Committee identified as: the right to life, survival and development (Article 6); the right to enjoy Convention rights without discrimination (Article 2); the best interests principle (Article 3), and the right to have a say in decision-making (Article 12).[30] The connection between Article 6 and Article 24 perhaps mitigates the absence of the latter right from this elevated group of provisions, which the CRC Committee has identified as overarching principles that must inform the interpretation and application of the entire Convention.[31] Whatever the merits of its approach, which has proven effective in raising the profile of these provisions, it is controversial nonetheless that the CRC Committee decided to elevate these rights above the Convention's other provisions.[32] Furthermore, it is clear that this has led to the diminution in profile if not in substance of some of the Convention's other fundamental rights. The right to health is undeniably one of the rights that has lost out in this process.

More generally, as highlighted above, it is important that Article 24 is supplemented significantly by other Convention provisions. In particular, Article 6, which recognizes the right of the child to life, requires states to secure the right to survival and development to the maximum extent possible. Taken together, Articles 6 and 24 make clear that children are entitled to a standard of health that is commensurate with their healthy development, including all of its physical, mental, moral, spiritual, and social dimensions.[33] The CRC Committee has implicitly linked Articles 6 and 24 to the body of evidence on social determinants of health,[34] highlighting that the "many risks and protective factors that underlie the life, survival, growth and development of the child need to be systematically identified in order to design and implement evidence-informed interventions that address a wide range of determinants during the life course."[35] According to the Committee, these determinants include: individual factors, such as age, sex, educational attainment, and socioeconomic status; determinants that work in the child's immediate environment, such as families, peers, and teachers, notably in terms of the violence that threatens the life and survival of children; and structural determinants, such as policies, systems, values and norms.[36] The Committee also highlights that "the health and health-related behaviours of parents" have a major impact on children's health.[37] Taking Article 6 and Article 24 together is an approach that enables the Committee to adopt a holistic interpretation of the child's health care rights under the Convention, insofar as they are linked to the goal of child development while also contextualized in their wider familial and social context.

The second area of CRC Committee activity that can be used to measure its commitment to the implementation of Article 24 is its approach to the adoption of General Comments. As noted above, these are position statements that the Committee (and indeed all UN treaty bodies) adopts to guide states parties on the implementation and application of Convention provisions in specific areas. Although the Committee has addressed health issues in many of its General Comments,[38] it took the Committee more than 20 years to adopt General Comment No. 15 on the right to the highest attainable standard of health in Article 24.[39] Many of the General Comments follow a general day of discussion on the topic in question and are part of an international campaign by either the non-governmental community or bodies like the United Nations. The case of the child's right to protection from violence is one such example.[40] Although different factors—the professional interests of Committee members, the focus of international advocacy, or contemporary themes in children's rights—can determine in what order General Comments are adopted by the Committee, it is clear nonetheless that the Committee's decision to adopt a General Comment on a particular subject or Convention provision is an indicator of the issue's importance from a children's rights perspective. In this regard, the Committee frequently highlights, in its General Comments, its motivation to publish its views on a subject by concerns that arise through the monitoring process, including the gaps in measures of implementation,[41] or alternatively by a pressing need to articulate its authoritative views on such matters.[42] Given the importance of the child's health rights, it is unclear why it took the Committee so long to articulate, through a General Comment, the priority that should be attached to the implementation of Article 24. Just as the Committee's decision to issue a General Comment on a certain topic can be traced to the strength of international children's rights advocacy (e.g., against corporal punishment),[43] it is likely that the absence of an international campaign advocating for a child rights approach to health care is at least partly responsible for the delay.

To date, the CRC Committee has adopted 24 General Comments on various aspects of the Convention. References to Article 24 of the CRC are contained in almost all of them, and the right to health is highlighted with particular importance in General Comment No. 21 on children in street situations,[44] General Comment No. 9 on children with disabilities,[45] General Comment No. 11 on indigenous children,[46] and General Comment No. 3 on children affected by HIV/AIDS.[47] Throughout these instruments, respect for the right to health is recognized as an important aspect of a holistic and rights-based approach to children. While the relevance of the child's right to health to the application of the CRC's general principles, like Article 3[48] (best interests of the child) and Article 12[49] (right to be heard), has been discussed above, the Committee has also recognized the relevance of the right to health in General Comments that reflect other cross-cutting themes affecting implementation of the CRC. Of particular importance in this context is the General Comment on the impact of the business sector on children's rights,[50] which addresses the implications of commercial activity—for example, environmental harm as a by-product of commerce or the marketing of junk food—on the protection of children's health care rights. This General Comment takes a particularly wide view of the risks to children's health for which states have responsibility, with reference to the privatization of health care services, the regulation of global business corporations, and the informal economy.

There are two General Comments that deal specifically with health rights under the CRC; the first deals with the health of adolescents, while the other is a more comprehensive General Comment dealing with Article 24. Each will now be examined in turn.

Just a few years following its establishment, the CRC Committee adopted a General Comment on adolescent health and development, addressing the application of Article 24 and associated provisions to older children.[51] Here the Committee adopted an expansive approach to the interpretation of Article 24 in a way that highlighted the measures necessary to combat the particular health challenges faced by this group. More specifically, the Committee pointed out that it "understands the concepts of 'health and development' more broadly than being strictly limited to the provisions defined in Articles 6 (right to life, survival and development) and 24 (right to health) of the Convention."[52] According to the Committee,

> [o]ne of the aims of this General Comment is precisely to identify the main human rights that need to be promoted and protected in order to ensure that adolescents do enjoy the highest attainable standard of health, develop in a well-balanced manner, and are adequately prepared to enter adulthood and assume a constructive role in their communities and in society at large.[53]

To this end, the Committee continued: "this General Comment should be read in conjunction with the Convention and its two Optional Protocols on the sale of children, child prostitution and child pornography, and on the involvement of children in armed conflict, as well as other relevant international human rights norms and standards."[54] Accordingly, the General Comment went on to address broad themes relevant to ensuring that older children mature into healthy adults, not by expressly drawing on the terms of Article 24 or the Convention per se, but, rather, by relying on the indivisible nature of its provisions to articulate a general obligation on states to eliminate and respond to unhealthy behavior and other serious health risks (like obesity, sexually transmitted diseases, and mental health) of adolescence. A further comprehensive General Comment on the rights of adolescents, adopted in 2016, also addresses the particular health care needs of these young people, including with regard to sexual health and the contemporary challenges of adolescence, such as body image, bullying, and depression.[55] Here the Committee recommended that states engage with young people with a view to adapting health care services that are accessible to them to meet their particular needs.

Despite concerns about its delay, General Comment No. 15 on the right of the child to the enjoyment of the highest attainable standard of health is a comprehensive and detailed instrument in which the Committee takes a noticeably broad and progressive approach to the application and interpretation of Article 24. In addition to detailing state obligations with respect to matters addressed in Article 24—such as the prevention of illness, disease, and accidents, prioritizing access to primary health care, and health care promotion—the General Comment notably applies the Convention to areas not explicitly referenced in Article 24 (e.g., mental health). It also contains significant detail on the health care systems and policies that are essential to the delivery of many aspects of Article 24 in practice, seeking to influence state approaches in this regard. In many areas, the General Comment supplements the details of Article 24, including by identifying the types of health care programs—like vaccination—that are considered essential to the highest attainable standard of health for children.[56] On nutrition, the General Comment attaches considerable importance to breastfeeding within the context of the provision of adequate nutritious foods (Article 24(2)(e)) with relatively little focus on malnutrition and scant reference to food security.[57] Obesity is also given surprisingly little attention in the General Comment, given the scale of the global epidemic,[58] and the focus of the General Comment here—on "fast food" and the need to limit the marketing of foods high in salt and sugar to children—belies both the complexity and the enormity of this challenge to children's attainment of an adequate standard of health. It is also regrettable that the Committee does not address Article 24(3) on traditional practices at all in the General Comment, while only a passing reference is made to eliminating the practice of female genital mutilation in the General Comment on adolescent health.[59] In the absence of explicit prohibition of female genital mutilation, a clear violation of the child's right to health, parents' rights, and religious/cultural rights, often presented as competing considerations in this context, have been allowed to trump those of the child in this area.[60] The Committee's weak leadership on this important children's rights issue can thus be said to have a very real impact on the extent to which children's rights are protected in practice.[61]

Overall, however, the General Comment does reasonably well to flesh out the state obligation to fulfill, protect, and promote the child's right to health under the Convention, including recommending that states adopt "measurable indicators" to assist them in monitoring and evaluating progress in the implementation of children's right to health.[62] Although adopted too early to allow reference to the SDGs, adopted by the international community in 2015, it is welcome that the General Comment references the targets set by international organizations, such as the World Health Organization's recommended minimum health expenditure per capita and prioritization of children's health in budgetary allocations.[63] Welcome too is the use of other international standard-setting instruments, such as the World Health Assembly's 2012 resolution on mental health disorders.[64] The SDGs are considered next here, along with the standard setting work of other international bodies, such as the World Health Organization, the United Nations Development Programme, and the Council of Europe. This serves to consider the CRC within its wider international context.

4 The Child's Right to Health in the Context of International Development

The CRC Committee is not the only international body working to advance the health rights of children—several other bodies have contributed to standard-setting and implementation of the child's right to health care in different ways. In fact, it is relevant that other bodies—notably the World Health Organization—have a primary and perhaps pre-eminent role in the recognition and monitoring of children's health at an international level, both for children and for the world's population in general.

4.1 The World Health Organization

As noted in the introduction to the chapter, the World Health Organization (WHO) led the way in the recognition of the right to health at an international level, a leadership role it has played since the 1940s when it assumed responsibility as the director and coordinating authority of international health within the UN system. The WHO has a range of programs and projects that aim to address specific health issues, including responding to global pandemics and disease and tracking and monitoring the health of the world's population. The WHO undertakes standard-setting work, providing guidance to states as to how best to tackle problems of child health and development, while serving an important public function in researching, collecting, and analyzing qualitative and quantitative data on global health. Child health is an obviously important focus for the organization. Despite being a UN body, however, WHO's work is not rights-based, and neither its guidance materials nor its other resources draw on or are informed by the CRC with respect to child or maternal health. This highlights the apparent disconnect between the global health agenda pursued by the world's leading health organization and the rights focus of human rights treaty monitoring bodies like the CRC Committee, which is explored further below.

4.2 UNDP and the Sustainable Development Goals

The SDGs are a global call to action for the eradication of poverty, climate action, and the pursuit of economic development and prosperity.[65] Adopted in 2015 as a successor to the Millennium Development Goals, and in force since 2016, the SDGs are a set of 17 interconnected targets to be achieved by 2030 under the guidance of the UN Development Programme (UNDP).[66] Clearly, all the Goals are relevant to children and child development, and several directly address aspects of children's health and development, including SDG 2 on zero hunger, which targets child malnutrition, and SDG 3 on good health and well-being, which targets various aspects of child health, mortality, and disease prevention. Other goals, such as SDG 1, no poverty, resonate particularly strongly for children on whom poverty has the heaviest impact. It is disappointing, therefore, that the SDGs do not use rights language and that the Goals themselves are not articulated in the terms of human rights that are internationally agreed upon by the member states of the United Nations. All the Goals are relevant to children's rights insofar as they articulate objectives that are conducive to and consistent with the ideals of the CRC.[67] At the same time, certain CRC provisions are of particular importance to the SDGs, especially Article 6, which recognizes the right of the child to life, survival, and development, Article 27 on the right to the highest attainable standard of living, and Article 28 on the right to education. In this regard, even obvious linkages between children's rights and the SDGs are absent; it is not surprising, then, that notwithstanding that the special vulnerability of children to climate change, the targets relating to SDG 13 (addressing "urgent action to combat climate change and its impact") hardly raise any child-related aspects at all, never mind any concern for children's rights.[68] More generally, it is concerning that the SDGs hardly reference the CRC[69] and contain no substantive engagement with its provisions. Although UNICEF published a document on the relationship between children's rights and the SDGs in 2016 to support its advocacy work,[70] the disconnect between the SDGs and the CRC is, at the very least, a missed opportunity to articulate these SDGs as legal rights and to strengthen their implementation with clearly measurable targets. It also reveals a chasm between the UN's development work, on the one hand, and its human rights work, on the other. It is positive that the SDGs include targets on birth registration and on ending violence against children, and admittedly, this is a welcome highlight of the common ground among those setting international priorities. This is reinforced by the inclusion of four other targets (in SDG 16) that are relevant to adults and children alike—that is, the call for action to significantly "reduce all forms of violence and related death rates everywhere"; to promote "the rule of law at the national and international levels and ensure equal access to justice for all"; to develop "effective, accountable and transparent institutions at all levels"; and to ensure "responsive, inclusive, participatory and representative decision-making at all levels."[71] Although not as precise as some of the other numerically precise targets, this alignment of general objectives between international human rights law and the global development agenda is important.

It is arguable, maybe even self-evident, that the success of target-focused development organizations and campaigns, like UNDP and the SDGs, do not need the language of rights to achieve results that have a positive impact on children's lives. The extent of the progress made in the past decade is indeed undeniable, as is further illustrated below. What is less evident of course is whether even greater progress might have been achieved had a joined-up approach been adopted between the human rights and the development communities. The failure to frame goals associated with human development as rights also reduces them to political claims or, worse, charitable requests, and the absence of human rights from the SDGs serves to hollow out the legal entitlement on which human rights treaty law is based.

To strengthen the coherence further between the development and human rights frameworks, it is significant that in March 2017 the UN Human Rights Council adopted a resolution on children's rights in the implementation of Agenda 2030 (the formal name for the SDGs) calling on states "to promote, protect, respect and fulfil the rights of the child and to mainstream them into all legislation, policies, programmes and budgets, as appropriate, aimed at implementing the 2030 Agenda."[72] The Council also encouraged states "to promote a child rights-based approach in the implementation of the 2030 Agenda."[73] It remains to be seen whether this will represent the sea change in approach required to ensure that Agenda 2030 advances implementation of the CRC in the promotion of child health and development as a right of the child.

5 Progress in the Implementation of Children's Health

Notwithstanding the progress that is still left to make, it is important to consider that success has been achieved in meeting some of the targets set by the Millennium Development Goals. For instance, there has been a 56 percent reduction in the under five mortality rate from 1990 to 2016 worldwide (however, the under-five mortality rate in the WHO African Region is almost eight times higher than that in the WHO European Region).[74] In addition, vaccinations are now preventing more deaths than ever before (the measles vaccine has averted nearly 15.6 million deaths since 1990, and over 6.2 million malaria deaths have been averted between 2000 and 2015, primarily of children under five years of age in sub-Saharan Africa).[75] Nonetheless, there continues to be a huge gulf between the right to health and health care, as recognized by the CRC, and its effective enjoyment by children around the world. Geography and socio-economic factors play a substantial role in the fulfilment of the child's right to health, and this continues to be frustrated by health care systems that are inaccessible, expensive, inequitable, or poor in quality.[76] Child survival rates are improving, but preventable premature death continues to be a serious problem, especially for neonates who die due to pre-term birth complications, pneumonia, birth asphyxia, diarrhea, and malaria.[77]

Poverty, famine, and drought continue to be hugely significant barriers to the realization of children's health. The impact of conflict and migration clearly pose challenges to children's ability to access timely, life-saving medical treatment. And, the destruction of health care facilities during war means that current-day conflicts will have generation-long effects.[78] Thus, equal enjoyment of the right to health remains a huge challenge.[79]

6 A Rights Approach
to Child Health

The CRC recognized without doubt that the child's right to health is a fundamental legal right that states parties have a duty to implement. As this chapter explains, Article 24 of the Convention identifies the child's basic health care needs, reflecting the importance of tackling mortality and avoidable disease, poor sanitation, and poor nutrition for children. Although the CRC Committee has addressed child health across multiple General Comments, it did not adopt a substantive General Comment on Article 24 until 2013, and its failure to identify Article 24 as a "general principle" means that it has struggled for attention among a long list of competing substantive rights in the treaty monitoring process. Although the weaving of the child's health care rights through many of the General Comments has reinforced their indivisibility and interdependence with other CRC rights, the long delay in the adoption of a General Comment dedicated to the child's right to health resulted in a vacuum in rights based health care advocacy at an international level. This is one explanation for the absence of a rights approach in international standard-setting on child health.

The SDGs represent an important milestone in the international community's commitment to the achievement of better health and development objectives for children. But while the child-specific nature of a number of the SDGs is very welcome, the absence of a rights-based approach represents a missed opportunity to reinforce child health as a rights issue. More seriously, it suggests that there is a disconnect within the international community, between the human rights treaty bodies that hold a child rights mandate and development and health organisations, like the WHO and UNDP, that hold a health care mandate. Although the General Comment on Article 24 was adopted in 2013, that is, prior to the adoption of the SDGs, the fact that the latter were under development makes the absence of any reference to the SDGs surprising. Although the references to the SDGs by the CRC Committee in its monitoring work under the Convention is very welcome,[80] the fact that the General Comment did not connect the child's right to health with the international development agenda demonstrates a lack of coherence to the standard-setting work of the international community in this area.

Philip Alston's analysis of the Millennium Development Goals—the forerunner of the SDGs—from a human rights perspective highlights that this issue is not new.[81] But although his plea to the human rights community to embrace the SDGs appears to have influenced the approach of the CRC Committee, there has been little reciprocity. In particular, there is limited if any literature in the development arena addressing the detachment between the global human rights and development agendas. Although the absence of a rights approach appears to have become entrenched in the approach to the SDGs, it is a positive development that the CRC Committee has in recent times sought to remind states of their obligations to implement the child's right to health. References to the

SDGs made by the CRC Committee in its Concluding Observations are a welcome reminder of the advantages of an integrated approach in this area. In some instances, these linkages are extensive,[82] and such an approach demonstrates the value in a co-ordinated, strategic approach that combines the legal strength of the human rights duty with the political weight of the SDGs. But for the approach to be truly holistic, the global development agenda must also draw on and speak in the language of human rights. For example, targets set on child health, development, and protection from violence could very usefully be set against CRC Articles 24, 6, and 19. Although it is too late for this iteration of the SDGs to embed rights language in the approach, it is not too late for the reporting on progress to be made to align with obligations under the CRC. For example, references to the CRC could be made in the regular progress reporting of SDG implementation, an approach that would have the added value of bringing the CRC to the national level, where SDGs are becoming embedded in government policy.

Only when the approach is reciprocal in nature, where children's goals are pursued as a matter of rights for children, will states be persuaded to pursue their commitments under the SDGs as a matter of obligation. What this chapter demonstrates is that the child health area—standard-setting and implementation—appears to exist almost entirely separate from international children's rights law. The fact is that the opportunity to combine the potential of both approaches, where state delivery on the targets set by the SDGs is pursued as a matter of right for children, remains the only way in which both approaches can be maximized.

7 CONCLUSION

This chapter has sought to analyze progress in the implementation of the child's right to health in international law. It analyzed Article 24 of the CRC and considered the approach by the CRC Committee to the interpretation and application of this provision. In particular, it noted the significance of the Committee's delayed adoption of a General Comment on Article 24 and its failure to adopt Article 24 as a "general principle," and it questioned whether this same weak international child rights advocacy contributed to the absence of child rights from the SDGs. The fact that they identify critical milestones to be reached in the pursuit of child health, but do so without reference to the child's right to health (or indeed to other human rights duties), has been highlighted with some concern. Notwithstanding the progress made in child health, the absence of a rights based approach to the SDGs is considered a missed opportunity to ensure a coherent international approach to child health. Although the CRC Committee has begun to remedy this deficit by making extensive linkages between the SDGs and Article 24 as part of the monitoring process, the full value of a co-ordinated approach will only be realized through the reciprocal nature of this approach by bodies like WHO and the UNDP.

NOTES

1. UN Convention on the Rights of the Child, G.A. Res. 44/25, 44th Sess., UN Doc. A/RES/44/25 (1989).

2. International Covenant on Economic, Social and Cultural Rights (ICESCR), 993 UNTS 3 (1966; entered into force Jan. 3, 1976).

3. Council of Europe, "Council of Europe Guidelines on Child-Friendly Health Care" (Sept. 21, 2011); see https://rm.coe.int/168046ccef.

4. UN Committee on the Rights of the Child (CRC Committee), "General Guidelines Regarding the Form and Content of Initial Reports to Be Submitted by States Parties under Article 44, Paragraph 1(a) of the Convention, UN Doc. CRC/C/5/1991 (1991).

5. CRC Committee, *General Comment No. 15 on the Right of the Child to the Enjoyment of the Highest Attainable Standard of Health*, UN Doc. CRC/C/GC/15/2013 (2013).

6. The Preamble of the WHO Constitution recognized that "the enjoyment of the highest attainable standard of health is one of the fundamental rights of every human." The Constitution was adopted by the International Health Conference held in New York from June 19 to July 22, 1946, signed on July 22, 1946, by the representatives of sixty-one states (Official Records of the World Health Organization, no. 2, p. 100), and entered into force on April 7, 1948.

7. Although the Universal Declaration did not contain a stand-alone provision on the right to health, it is significant nonetheless that Article 25(1) recognizes that "Everyone has the right to a standard of living adequate for the health and well-being of himself and of his family, including food, clothing, housing and medical care." Adopted and proclaimed by UN General Assembly Resolution 217 A (III) of December 10, 1948.

8. John Tobin, *The Right to Health in International Law* (Oxford: Oxford University Press, 2012).

9. UN Committee on Economic, Social and Cultural Rights, *General Comment No 14: The Right to the Highest Attainable Standard of Health*, UN Doc. E/C.12/2000/4 (Aug. 11, 2000).

10. UN Committee on Economic, Social and Cultural Rights, *General Comment No 14*, para. 12.

11. UN Committee on Economic, Social and Cultural Rights, *General Comment No 14*, para. 22.

12. UN Committee on Economic, Social and Cultural Rights, *General Comment No 14*, para. 23.

13. UN Committee on Economic, Social and Cultural Rights, *General Comment No 14*, para. 33.

14. See further Aoife Nolan, "Children's Economic and Social Rights," in *International Human Rights of Children*, ed. Ursula Kilkelly and Ton Liefaard (Singapore: Springer, 2018).

15. CRC Committee, *General Comment No. 15.*

16. The CRC was adopted by the General Assembly of the United Nations by its Resolution 44/25, November 20, 1989.

17. Jane Fortin, *Children's Rights and the Developing Law*, 3rd ed. (Cambridge: Cambridge University Press, 2009).

18. CRC Committee, *General Comment No. 15*, para. 12.

19. CRC Committee, *General Comment No. 15*, para. 13.

20. CRC Committee, *General Comment No. 15.*

21. CRC Committee, *General Comment No. 15*, para. 13.

22. CRC Committee, *General Comment No. 12 (2012): The Rights of the Child to Be Heard*, UN Doc. CRC/C/GC/12/2009 (July 21, 2009), para. 20.

23. CRC Committee, *General Comment No. 12.*

24. CRC Committee, *General Comment No. 12*, paras. 20–21.

25. African Charter on the Rights and Welfare of the Child, OAU Doc. CAB/LEG/24.9/49 (1990; entered into force Nov. 29, 1999), art. 14.

26. The work of the Committee can be viewed at http://www.acerwc.africa/general-comments.

27. Council of Europe, "Council of Europe Guidelines on Child-Friendly Health Care."

28. These are identified and analyzed in Ursula Kilkelly, "Health and Children's Rights," in *The Routledge International Handbook of Children's Rights Studies*, ed. Wouter Vandenhole, Ellen Desmet, Didier Reynaert, and Sara Lembrechts (London: Routledge, 2015), 216–233.

29. CRC Committee, "General Guidelines Regarding the Form and Content of Initial Reports," 5–6.

30. CRC Committee, *General Comment No. 5: Articles 4, 42, and 44(6): General Measures of Implementation of the Convention on the Rights of the Child*, UN Doc. CRC/GC/2003/5 (2003), para. 12. See also CRC Committee, "General Guidelines Regarding the Form and Content of Initial Reports."

31. CRC Committee, *General Comment No. 5*, para. 22.

32. Karl Hanson and Laura Lundy, "Does Exactly What It Says on the Tin? A Critical Analysis and Alternative Reconceptualization of the So-Called 'General Principles' of the Convention on the Rights of the Child," *International Journal of Children's Rights* 25, no. 2 (2017): 285–306.

33. CRC Committee, *General Comment No. 15*, para. 16.

34. Commission on the Social Determinants of Health, *Closing the Gap in a Generation: Health Equity through Action on the Social Determinants of Health. Final Report of the Commission on Social Determinants of Health* (Geneva, World Health Organization, 2008).

35. CRC Committee, *General Comment No. 15*, para. 16.

36. CRC Committee, *General Comment No. 15*, para. 17.

37. CRC Committee, *General Comment No. 15*, para. 18.

38. See, for example, CRC Committee, *General Comment No. 3: HIV/AIDS and the Rights of the Child*, CRC/GC/2003/3 (2003), and *General Comment No. 4: Adolescent Health and Development in the context of the Convention on the Rights of the Child*, CRC/GC/2003/4 (2003).

39. CRC Committee, *General Comment No. 15*.

40. See CRC Committee, *General Comment No. 8: Articles 12, 28(2), and 37, inter alia: The Right of the Child to Protection from Corporal Punishment and Other Cruel or Degrading Forms of Punishment*, UN Doc. CRC/C/GC/8/2006 (2006), and *General Comment No. 13: The Right of the Child to Freedom from all Forms of Violence*, UN Doc. CRC/C/GC13/2011 (2011). These General Comments coincided with the UN Study on the Violence against Children and the subsequent appointment by the Secretary General of the Special Representative on Violence against Children. See further Jonathan Todres, "Violence, Exploitation and the Rights of the Child," in Kilkelly and Liefaard, *International Human Rights of Children*.

41. See, for example, CRC Committee, *General Comment No. 11: Indigenous Children and Their Rights under the Convention*, UN Doc. CRC/C/GC/11/2011 (2011), para. 5.

42. See, for example, CRC Committee, *General Comment No. 9: The Rights of Children with Disabilities*, UN Doc. CRC/C/GC/9/2009 (2009), paras. 1–6.

43. CRC Committee, *General Comment No. 8.*
44. CRC Committee, *General Comment No. 21: Children in Street Situations*, UN Doc. CRC/C/GC/21 (2017).
45. CRC. Committee, *General Comment No. 9.*
46. CRC Committee, *General Comment No. 11.*
47. CRC Committee. *General Comment No. 3.*
48. CRC Committee, *General Comment No. 14 on the Right of the Child to Have His or Her Best Interests Taken as a Primary Consideration (Art. 3, para 1)*, UN Doc. CRC/C/GC/14 (2013).
49. CRC Committee, *General Comment No. 12.*
50. CRC Committee, *General Comment No. 16: On State Obligations regarding the Impact of the Business Sector on Children's Rights*, UN Doc. CRC/C/GC/16 (2013).
51. CRC Committee, *General Comment No. 4.*
52. CRC Committee, *General Comment No. 4*, para. 4.
53. CRC Committee, *General Comment No. 4.*
54. CRC Committee, *General Comment No. 4.*
55. CRC Committee, *General Comment No. 20 on the Implementation of the Rights of the Child during Adolescence*, UN Doc. CRC/C/GC/20 (2016).
56. See, for instance, CRC Committee, *General Comment No. 15*, para. 41.
57. CRC Committee, *General Comment No. 15*, para. 49.
58. CRC Committee, *General Comment No. 15*, para. 47.
59. CRC Committee, *General Comment No. 4*, para. 3.
60. Debra, L. DeLaet, "Genital Autonomy, Children's Rights and Competing Rights Claims in International Human Rights Law," *International Journal of Children's Rights* 20, no. 4 (2012): 554–583. See also Committee on the Elimination of Discrimination against Women and the Committee on the Rights of the Child, *Joint General Recommendation No. 31 of the Committee on the Elimination of Discrimination against Women/General Comment No. 18 of the Committee on the Rights of the Child on Harmful Practices*, UN Doc. CEDAW/C/GC/31-CRC/C/GC/18 (2014).
61. Importantly, the UN has provided leadership inter alia by adopting a resolution in 2012. See UN General Assembly, "Intensifying Global Efforts for the Elimination of Female Genital Mutilations," U.N. Doc A/RES/67/146 (2012).
62. UN General Assembly, "Intensifying Global Efforts," para. 107.
63. UN General Assembly, "Intensifying Global Efforts," para. 106.
64. World Health Organization, "The Global Burden of Mental Disorders and the Need for a Comprehensive, Coordinated Response from Health and Social Sectors at the Country Level," Resolution WHA65.4 (adopted May 25, 2012), para. 39.
65. UN General Assembly, "Transforming Our World: The 2030 Agenda for Sustainable Development," UN Doc. A/RES/70/1 (2015).
66. See UN Development Programme, "Sustainable Development Goals," http://www.undp.org/content/undp/en/home/sustainable-development-goals.html (accessed Aug. 24, 2019).
67. Karin Arts, "Children's Rights and the Sustainable Development Goals," in Kilkelly and Liefaard, *International Human Rights of Children.*
68. Arts, "Children's Rights and the Sustainable Development Goals."
69. Admittedly, there is one such reference to the CRC, in paragraph 67, in the context of the role of the private sector.
70. United Nations Children's Fund (UNICEF), *Mapping the Global Goals for Sustainable Development and the Convention on the Rights of the Child* (New York: UNICEF, 2016).

71. UN General Assembly, "Transforming Our World," 25.

72. UN Human Rights Council, "Resolution on the Rights of the Child: Protection of the Rights of the Child in the Implementation of the 2030 Agenda for Sustainable Development," UN Doc. A/HRC/34/L.25 (2017), para. 4.

73. UN Human Rights Council, "Resolution on the Rights of the Child," para. 6.

74. World Health Organization, "Global Health Observatory (GHO) Data," http://www.who.int/gho/child_health/en (accessed Aug. 24, 2019).

75. UN Development Programme, "Sustainable Development Goals: Goal 3 Targets," http://www.undp.org/content/undp/en/home/sustainable-development-goals/goal-3-good-health-and-well-being/targets (accessed Aug. 24, 2019).

76. Bronwyn Harris, Jane Goudge, John E. Ataguba, Diane McIntyre, Nonhlanhla Nxumalo, Siybonga Jikwana, and Matthew Chersich, "Inequities in Access to Health Care in South Africa," *Journal of Public Health Policy* 32 (2011): 102–123; Manfred Huber, Anderson Stanciole, Jeni Brenner, and Kristian Wahlbeck, *Equality in and Equality of Access to Healthcare Services* (Brussels: European Commission, 2008).

77. World Health Organization, "Children: Reducing Mortality," fact sheet (Sept. 19, 2018), http://www.who.int/news-room/fact-sheets/detail/children-reducing-mortality.

78. Save the Children, "A Devastating Toll: The Impact of Three Years of War on the Health of Syria's Children" (2014), https://www.savethechildren.org/content/dam/global/reports/emergency-humanitarian-response/devastating-toll-14.pdf

79. Michael Marmot, Sharon Friel, Ruth Bell, Tanja A. J. Houweling, and Sebastian Taylor, "Closing the Gap in a Generation: Health Equity through Action on the Social Determinants of Health," *The Lancet* 372 (2008): 1661–1669; Jay G. Berry, Sheila Bloom, Susan Foley, and Judith S. Palfrey, "Health Inequity in Children and Youth with Chronic Health Conditions," *Pediatrics* 126, Supp. 3 (2010): 111–119.

80. See, for example, CRC Committee, "Concluding Observations on the Combined Fifth and Sixth Periodic Reports of Seychelles," UN Doc. CRC/C/SYC/CO/5-6 (2018), para. 30; CRC Committee, "Concluding Observations on the Combined Fifth and Sixth Periodic Reports of Ecuador," UN Doc. CRC/C/ECU/CO/5-6 (2017), paras. 18 and 33.

81. Philip Alston, "Ships Passing in the Night: The Current State of the Human Rights and Development Debate seen through the Lens of the Millennium Development Goals," *Human Rights Quarterly* 27, no. 3 (2005): 755–829.

82. See, for example, CRC Committee, "Concluding Observations on the Second Periodic Report of Lesotho," UN Doc. CRC/C/LSO/CO/2 (2018); CRC Committee, "Concluding Observations on the Combined Fifth and Sixth Periodic Reports of Spain," UN Doc. CRC/C/ESP/CO/5-6 (2018); CRC Committee, "Concluding Observations on the Combined Fifth and Sixth Periodic Reports of Guatemala," UN Doc. CRC/C/GTM/CO/5-6 (2018).

CHAPTER 19

REVISITING THE THREE 'R'S IN ORDER TO REALIZE CHILDREN'S EDUCATIONAL RIGHTS

Relationships, Resources, and Redress

LAURA LUNDY AND AMY BROWN

1 INTRODUCTION

EDUCATION rights are included in almost all international human rights instruments and are a core feature of those that are specific to children.[1] Even the earliest international statement of children's rights was dominated by education, with the Geneva Declaration on the Rights of the Child providing the prototype for the set of rights to follow: "The child must be given the means requisite for its normal development, both materially and spiritually ... the child that is backward must be helped; ... The child must be put in a position to earn a livelihood.... The child must be brought up in the consciousness that its talents must be devoted to the service of fellow men."[2]

The Universal Declaration on Human Rights (1948), the International Declaration on the Rights of the Child (1959), and the International Covenant on Economic, Social and Cultural Rights (1966) echoed these statements, and their reformulations have, in turn, been incorporated into and expanded upon within the UN Convention on the Rights of the Child (CRC). The CRC contains not one, but two articles specific to education: Article 28 focuses primarily on the right of access to education at all levels and introduces a new obligation to ensure that discipline is carried out in accordance with the child's dignity (Article 28 (1)(d)), and Article 29 sets out ambitious goals for education. The Committee on the Rights of the Child (CRC Committee) has captured the latter as follows: "Education must also be aimed at ensuring that life skills are learnt by every child…such as the ability to make well balanced decisions, to resolve conflicts in a non violent manner; and to develop a healthy lifestyle, good social relationships and responsibility, critical thinking, creative talents and other abilities which give children the tools needed to pursue their options in life."[3]

Moreover, while Articles 28 and 29 are dedicated to education, education is addressed in five additional provisions; there is specific mention of health education and education about drugs as well as references to the education of children with disabilities, child workers, and those in detention.[4] Moreover, Article 6, which includes the child's right to development, is clearly significant both in itself and as a crosscutting principle of the Convention. Thus, the widely cited notion that all human rights are interrelated and interdependent, contestable in many instances, proves itself to be largely true in the case of education; almost every provision of the CRC is directly or indirectly relevant to and/or dependent on a child's education and/or development.

The rights that pertain to education are many and diverse, so much so that a rich body of work by both academics and practitioners has attempted to capture them in a series of models and conceptualizations. The best known of these are Eugène Verhellen's typology of rights in, to, and through education[5] and Katarina Tomasveski's 4-A framework which addresses the rights-based qualities of education, namely, that it should be available, accessible, adaptable, and acceptable.[6] More recently, UNESCO has developed a right to education framework propagating access, quality, and respect;[7] this has been adapted by scholars in a range of ways, such as adding "relations" in education in order to transcend the "rights to" and "rights in" conceptualization of education rights, which focus on access and content,[8] and incorporating parents' rights, which are often omitted in these conceptualizations yet clearly are integral to any discussion of children's human rights and children's education.[9]

While all of these are helpful to those attempting to understand the span of rights that are relevant in the context of education, we suggest that the major challenge in the context of education and human rights does not, for the most part, concern understanding what they are or indeed why they are necessary. Education rights are neither complex nor, in most instances, contentious with states parties. They have featured in international human rights instruments without exception, and the relevant provisions have been adopted by states with minimal reservations.[10] Moreover, diverse as they are, the remit of human rights in education can be captured and explained with relative simplicity: states should be doing all that they can to make sure that children receive the highest levels of education, develop to the best of their ability in contexts where they are safe and protected, be treated equally, and are taught about human rights and respect for themselves, their families, and others and that their views are sought and taken seriously.

Most of this is not contentious—at least on the face of it. Yet there is no country in the world where every child is receiving education that meets this descriptor.[11] We suggest that the major challenge in the context of education rights does not, for the most part, lie in understanding what needs to be done (the content of education rights) but in the doing of it (their realization). That is not to say that some of the human rights challenges faced by children, their parents, and educators are not problematic. Schools are often the child's (or the family's) first interface with the state, a reality that provides rich soil for dispute, for example, when a family's values do not align with broader social norms or when a child's autonomy rights conflict with parental values and guidance.[12] However, even in instances where rights conflict, and therefore need to be unpacked and articulated, the response and resolution of these often resides in the implementation of the rights framework, the pathways and obstacles to the so-called realization of rights.

With this is mind, this chapter focuses not on the core content of education rights (though it will be discussed as it arises), but on the challenges and opportunities that underpin their implementation. For this we have devised a new typology based on three key Rs—relationships, resources and redress. We are conscious that *the three Rs* has been a commonly used catchphrase, employed by educators to categorize the traditional content of education, that is, reading, writing, and arithmetic. It is also used frequently when children are being educated about their rights. In this instance, the Rs stand for rights, respect, and responsibility, with emphasis placed on the latter two Rs, respect and responsibility. Important as these are, the three Rs can be problematic in practice: for example, where children's rights are presented as contingent upon them showing respect and responsibility, excluding the fact that adults should be taught to respect children and ultimately are responsible for children's rights—not children themselves.[13] So, in this chapter we propose to revisit and reclaim the three Rs, re-envisioning them in a way that we think may be more useful to both understanding children's education rights and how they can be made real.

2 Relationships

The literature on educational relationships abounds with discussion of student-teacher relationships from the perspective of student voice and children's right to be heard and consulted under Article 12 of the CRC, which affords children the right to have their views given due weight in accordance with their age and maturity on all matters affecting them. Research on children's rights, however, tends to be normative and to direct focus on evaluation of standards away from the lived meanings and contextualization of children.[14] While this research and its ensuing discussions are vital to the accountability of rights broadly, and education rights specifically, they omit educational relationships which bear great significance when considering a child's education, namely, the relationships between and among children and young people as well as individual and collective relationships with adults and within the wider community. Education rights pertaining to such relationships are codified in Article 29 of the CRC, an oft-overlooked and underestimated article that enhances all other rights within the CRC by setting out not only content but also the purpose and quality of education, its intrinsic value, and instrumentalist function.[15] Article 29 provides that a child's education must be directed to development of the personality, talent, and mental and physical abilities of the child to their fullest potential, to respect for human rights, to respect for the child's parents, cultural identity, language and values, and to the preparation of the child for responsible life in a free society as well as respect for the natural environment.

Part of the significance of Article 29, according to the CRC Committee, lies in recognition of education, which reconciles diverse values through dialogue and respect—perhaps a cornerstone for establishing the relationships necessary for realization of children's education rights. In its General Comment on the aims of education, the CRC Committee has explicitly stated that the aims of education are to "promote, support and protect the core value of the convention: the human dignity innate in every child and his or her equal and inalienable rights" and emphasizes the need for education, in the broadest sense, to be "child-centered, child-friendly and empowering."[16] Educational processes must be based on the principles and values the Convention itself articulates, stressing that education rights are not limited to curriculum content, but include such life skills as making well-balanced decisions, resolving conflict and developing good social relationships and responsibility[17]—skills that are developed in relationship with others. Thus, for the realization of children's education rights to occur authentically, there is a need to focus on the relationships through which rights are negotiated and navigated and on the processes by which these relationships are nurtured and conducted.

The links between the enjoyment of the right to education and a child's treatment in education are well documented.[18] Yet for effective integration of human rights values of respect, dignity, and equality into the daily realities of children at school, it is crucial that those who teach and promote these values are themselves convinced of their import in the broader picture of relationships in education.[19] That would include not only teaching and learning methods but also approaches to policies, such as discipline, bullying, pastoral care, and child protection,[20] not to mention school mission statements, regulations and codes of conduct, budgeting, and recruitment.[21] Of course, the reality of children's rights in schools reflects both an age and power differential; this perhaps reproduces a prevailing outlook that children must be controlled in order to maintain order and *respect for others*[22]—a far reaching attitude that obstructs serious consideration of the respect owed to children and which perhaps encapsulates conceptualizations of respect as pseudonyms for obedience and conformity. This comes despite international human rights–based approaches to inclusive education and raises the issue that implementation, or realization, of fundamental equality in the school environment may require a drastic transformation of the school institution and, above all, the nature of human relationships among and between the individuals involved: students, teachers, and parents.[23]

Alison Cook-Sather and Laura Lundy took this approach in an examination of a rights-respecting pedagogy, beginning with the foundation of a rights-based approach—respect for the worth of the individual.[24] This foundation is fundamental to the effective and meaningful promotion of children's participation, which reflects the inherent dignity of the child.[25] Realization of this idea involves a profound reevaluation of the status of children in society as a whole as well as in the classroom;[26] this includes the nature of child-adult relationships, peer-to-peer relationships, and student-teacher relationships specifically. While we acknowledge that there are teachers whose pedagogical philosophy is based on their inherent respect for children, a review of both children's rights in education and the literature on student voice highlights that integral to the successful implementation of both is the concept of respect for the child. This resonates with other indications that children are limited and defined by their low status in educational hierarchies and are excluded from dialogue around discipline and school conduct.[27] Indeed, a study by Laura Lundy, Karen Orr, and Chelsea Marshall identified concern among young people across the world about how they were treated by their teachers and their capacity for enunciating respect for and dignity of the child.[28]

Given that it is the influence of families and role models, peers, schooling, and media that shapes children's understanding of rights, it is vital that school cultures work to foster children's appreciation and understanding of their rights, not that they do not have rights or that their rights are restricted;[29] this must include implicit (or hidden) lessons as well as explicit rights education material. This sentiment is stated by the CRC Committee in its General Comment on Article 29 on the aims of education:[30] there is a need to see rights within their social and cultural framework. Children's rights, rather than being externally prescribed, are embedded in the social fabric of communities, such as schools. Their rights, therefore, are not isolated from children's relational context, but exist in the ethical framework prescribed in Article 29; children's rights in the realities of children's lives are much richer than a legal instrument and its implementation—not only about rules, but about relationships and processes.[31] It is perhaps apt, then, to draw a distinction in the realization of children's education rights between vertical orientation of the international treaty, whereby duties are placed on the state to respect the human rights of individuals, and the horizontal realization of a rights culture, which emerges and occurs in human relationships, that is, between private individuals. While the rich body of work to date has invested considerable energy in capturing the vertical orientation of rights, it is the context of the horizontal relation that is often central to the realization of children's rights in education and where educating children on their rights is so vital; perhaps this is what Eleanor Roosevelt meant when she suggested that rights must gain legitimacy at ground level as the basis for achieving acceptance.[32] This is all the more so when considering that schools are often a child's first interface with the state. Children who not only learn about, but *experience* their rights are those who understand not only the "what" of their basic rights but also the social responsibilities that correspond with such rights.[33]

In such a culture where children experience their rights at local level, as well as being educated about them, children also learn to respect others because they are taught that each human being has value (or dignity) on account of being human, and that commands not only respect but also the ability to assert this right on behalf of oneself and on behalf of others.[34] This practice reflects the Committee's observation that children learn about human rights by watching their implementation in practice, including at school and in the community.[35] Moreover, this process begins very young: the CRC Committee has emphasized that very young children have a right to an education that respects their evolving capacities, as this is "crucial for the realization of their rights, and especially significant during early childhood, because of the rapid transformations in children's physical, cognitive, social and emotional functioning, from earliest infancy to the beginnings of schooling."[36]

Indeed, all children, irrespective of age, are much more likely to learn democratic behaviors and values if they are reflected in the formal curriculum and the hidden curriculum, including in mission statements, codes of conduct, and democratic classroom interactions that are rights respecting.[37] This aspect of education rights and relationships also captures the relationships that occur from peer to peer and provides a convincing rights basis on which to tackle bullying and difference—a vital issue because a child's education rights may be just as undermined by discrimination and bullying by peers as by adult duty bearers.[38]

This approach to learning about human rights by watching and experiencing their implementation in practice is perhaps especially salient because in learning about their rights by example, children critically scrutinize the implementation and realization of those rights in their own lived experiences.[39] This might be understood as the *process* through which education rights are promoted and to which the CRC Committee explicitly attaches importance: efforts which promote the enjoyment of other rights must be reinforced by the values which underpin the education process, not only in curriculum content, but pedagogical method and education environment.[40] In other words, gatekeepers of education must practice what they teach by modeling values not only in curriculum content but also in implicit content and community practices.[41] Children must be educated in a way that respects the inherent dignity of the child and enables them to fully participate in school life; this lifelong process begins with rights values in the daily lives and lived experiences of children.[42]

Ultimately, the core principles of both children's rights and educational relationships call for respect and shared responsibility—a partnership—that traditional hierarchies and power imbalances structured into educational institutions do not allow or support[43] because the same hierarchies and power structures give adults exclusive control over time, space, activities, and even, to some extent, bodies.[44] That is, relationships and control of these relationships is conducted vertically using the two-dimensional power hierarchy. What is also required for the effective realization of children's education rights is a horizontal implementation accounting for the multidimensional nature of educational relationships between both adults and young people and among adults and young people separately. As recently as 2009, the CRC Committee expressed its concern at the continuing autocratic and disrespectful practices which characterize the realities of many of the world's classrooms and explained this partly by the long-standing practices and attitudes toward both rights and, it is contended, children themselves.[45] The effective realization of rights lies in many ways with the sentinels of educational relationships: teachers. The crux of the matter of implementation resides in how we treat children in global classrooms.

2.1 Case example: Children's Relationships with Teachers in Schools

A 2013 appellate case in Fiji showcased the centrality of dignity to classroom relation-ships, where a ten-year-old boy was rebuked for talking in class. He was ordered to go to the front of the class and remove his trousers; another child was instructed to remove his boxer shorts, stripping the boy to his underwear. The court found that this was degrad-ing treatment under Article 37(1) of the CRC, as it constituted an assault on the boy's dignity and physical integrity.[46]

3 RESOURCES

Education, a right with a distinct, albeit not exclusively, socioeconomic character, requires resources in order to be fully realized. These resources are often a very significant portion of every country's overall public expenditure, with most allocating between five and eight percent of their budget to education.[47] Like all socioeconomic rights in the CRC, educa-tion rights come with an overarching qualification—that it will be delivered using the "maximum extent of [the state's] available resources" (Article 4). Moreover, Article 28 incorporates some additional limits on the financial expectations placed on states parties. The only absolute obligation is to ensure that primary education is "free" and "available to all"; for secondary and vocational and higher education, the obligations are significantly less ambitious in terms of the states' obligations in relation to the financing of education. CRC Article 28(1) requires states parties to: "Encourage the development of different forms of secondary education, including general and vocational education, make them available and accessible to every child, *and take appropriate measures such as the introduc-tion of free education and offering financial assistance in case of need*" (emphasis added).

Even when a state meets its goal of providing free access to schooling across seven to twelve years of a child's life, there are always some children for whom a lack of resources will present a challenge to the enjoyment of their rights, not least working children who can miss out on their education in order to contribute to their family's income. Moreover, the additional and sometimes hidden costs of schooling can place children in poorer communities at a disadvantage. The CRC Committee has expressed its concern about additional fees and charges for materials, such as books, uniforms, and even teachers' salaries.[48] For example, it recently expressed its concern about the indirect costs of mandatory education in Spain, including textbooks, transport, and school meals, all of which can "make it difficult for children in marginalized situations to access education."[49] Moreover, additional costs can also come in the guise of pressure for the payment of after-school tuition, called "shadow education,"[50] which places some fami-lies in poverty and skews educational advantages.

While the child rights position entails that children should not be discriminated against, the reality is that the costs of educating children are not uniform. They will be cheapest when the child fits into a set of norms—that is, speaks the language of tuition and learns in a typical way at a reasonable pace. In most instances, the most significantly affected group comprises children with disabilities, especially those who require significant adaptations or present challenging behaviors. Underfunded schools respond in various ways, often by excluding the child.[51] The CRC has been recognized to be weak in this respect, incorporating a series of financial get-out clauses in the text of Article 23 (on children with disabilities), and, while the UN Convention on Persons with Disabilities goes further, it still leaves states with significant leeway that allows them to factor in the resources available.[52]

Resources are of course not unlimited, and in some countries they are very limited indeed. One response to this in some settings has been to resort to privately financed schools. While this appears to be an option of choice for many resource-challenged nations, the dangers from a human rights perspective are apparent not just in terms of equality of access but also in the nature and quality of the education provided. Successive special rapporteurs on the right to education have focused on this, with Kishore Singh's final report in 2015 providing a scathing attack on what he described as the "baleful effects" of commercialization: "Education as a public function of States is being eroded by market-driven approaches and the rapid growth of private providers, with scant control by public authorities. Privatization negatively affects the right to education both as an entitlement and as empowerment. It breeds exclusion and marginalization, with crippling effects on the fundamental principle of equality of opportunity in education. It also entails disinvestment in public education."[53]

Ensuring that all children have free places in state schools is, of course, only one part of the picture. A major lesson in the wake of the now-replaced UN Millennium Development Goals (MDGs) is that getting children into classrooms is not a guarantee of the right to education and is a key reason why the current UN Sustainable Development Goals (SDGs) include an additional focus on both quality and equality in education.[54] Many children attend school in classes that are too large, in buildings that are unsafe and without the books and other materials that that they need to learn. Moreover, a further crucial aspect of quality relates to teachers and the resources for their training and their salaries. For example, a 2017 report of the UN secretary-general indicates that many children are not taught by trained teachers and that the majority of schools in Sub-Saharan Africa, for example, do not have access to electricity or potable water.[55] The CRC Committee has also consistently expressed its concern about poor levels of funding for educational resources and for teacher training and employment and conditions in particular.[56]

Monitoring expenditure to ensure that it is both sufficient and effective is a crucial dimension to the realization of children's rights. Children's rights in public budgeting was the focus of a recent general comment by the CRC Committee.[57] This General Comment specifically calls for the visibility of spending in terms of children and their rights. One of the common challenges in this context—that it is hard to separate spending on children from spending on their parents—does not usually apply in education since education is usually in a discrete ministerial department with a separate budget, making it easy to identify overall spending on children. What is sometimes less clear is how this is then allocated to particular regions at a subnational level and whether it is being spent efficiently and effectively. For example, in its Concluding Observations on Sri Lanka, the Committee urged the state "to take measures to promote, in all autonomous communities, a comprehensive assessment of the budget needs of children with a view to redistributing the resources for the implementation of children's rights, particularly regarding increased investment in education."[58]

A crucial dimension of ensuring transparency and accountability is also ensuring that children are offered meaningful involvement in budget decision-making.[59] A study of children's views that informed General Comment No. 19 suggests that children are willing and able to contribute to these decisions, and many have concerns in their own contexts about waste and corruption as well as a failure to provide equality of opportunity to all children in relation to education.[60] Children across the world, including very young schoolchildren, identified a range of areas that needed investment, including school buildings, teacher salaries, books, and transportation to school.[61] Examples of good practice in participatory budgeting do exist, though they tend to focus on older children and operate at a municipal rather than national level of budgetary decision-making.[62]

3.1 Case Example: Children's Participation in Resource Allocation for Schools

In Zimbabwe, the Child Participation in School Governance project supported children in more than 159 schools participate in school budgeting. Children participated as school council representatives on the schools' general purpose and finance committees and were involved in local-level budget tracking, monitoring, and evaluation.[63]

4 REDRESS

Rights are important because those who hold them are able to exercise agency and make autonomous decisions, negotiate with others, and transform relationships: rights bearers can *participate*, itself a human right which enables the agent to demand rights and secure recognition of these rights.[64] Where rights exist, redress is possible, but there must be mechanisms for complaint, as otherwise there is no legal accountability.[65] Rights without remedies are of symbolic importance only, yet, where there is no knowledge or awareness of rights, there cannot be remedies or redress; as such, there is a fundamental need for education *for* rights as well as education *through* rights.[66] Of course, we acknowledge that sustainable rights respecting practice must include education on both children's rights issues and opportunities for children to participate in legal advocacy.[67] The Children's Rights International Network has highlighted the need for children to know *how* to assert their rights.[68] Interestingly, however, in its first General Comment on the aims of education, the CRC Committee does not make reference to mechanisms of redress if and when children and young people's rights are infringed by states parties and duty holders.[69] Given that systems and structures for redress reflect both the reality of implementation and commitment to rights and individual dignity, this perhaps reflects the broad challenges to education rights in practice. That said, children's rights can be advanced through civic action and civil protest and not only through litigation, especially considering that the majority of countries in the world do not grant direct access to judicial remedies until the age of eighteen.[70]

Consequently, we argue that redress in this context must be distinguished from litigation: actual cases taken to court to seek a remedy for a breach of children's rights, a process that more closely aligns to the *vertical* implementation of children and young people's education rights. Education is one of the most frequently litigated areas of human rights in both national and international courts.[71] There have been landmark cases in constitutional courts and in international human rights courts, such as the European Court of Human Rights.[72] It is of note that these forms of redress often challenge behaviors inimical to positive *relationships*, such as corporal punishment and discriminatory treatment by teachers, as well as inadequate *resources* in education generally. Yet, as important as these legal actions are for the realization of children's education rights, it remains rare for legal proceedings to be initiated by children themselves. Parents and/or public interest lawyers commence these cases, and children are often not a party to the proceedings; a child rights-based approach would, conversely, enable children to see the challenges facing them as breaches of human rights and to seek redress themselves.

The challenge for children is that the implementation and realization of their rights frequently depend on adults; often reified, children are treated as objects requiring a series of interventions rather than as the legal subjects of rights: interventions based on meanings assigned to the construct of childhood rather than on the individual person to whom it refers.[73] The accountability that accompanies this status as rights holders is thus diluted, seemingly on the assumption that because children cannot (or, more specifically, face greater challenges to) claim their rights, their denial is thereby justified. Arguably, this challenge has emerged from a vertical orientation of the realization of children's rights and does not take account of alternative, ground-level horizontal realization. While redress remains a significant omission with regard to the CRC Committee's comments on Article 29, they explicitly address it in relation to the right to be heard and consulted under Article 12.[74] As Article 12 forms one of the main pillars of the CRC, and recognizing that rights contained in the CRC are interdependent and indivisible, respect for the right of children to have their voices heard within education settings, especially when their rights are breached, is fundamental to the realization of their education rights. It is through this lens that we consider *horizontal* forms of redress below.

Legislation, policy, and the stated desire to implement rights are often insufficient to uphold children's education rights because inadequate resources, an incapacity to implement policy due to insufficient awareness and training on both rights and redress for infringement of such rights, and low levels of information often render implementation ineffective.[75] Furthermore, for rights to have weight and value, effective remedies must be available to redress violations, a requirement that is implicit in the CRC.[76] In the case of children and young people's education rights, the status of children creates real difficulties in pursuing redress for breaches of states' obligations. Therefore, there is an expectation on the part of the CRC Committee that states parties pay attention to ensuring effective procedures available to children, including complaints procedures and, where rights have been breached, appropriate reparation, recovery, and rehabilitation.[77]

States assume obligations to implement international law on ratifying a treaty; Article 4 of the CRC obliges states parties to take "all appropriate legislative, administrative and other measures" to realize the rights stipulated in the Convention. While the state takes on obligations, the implementation of the CRC in the lived experience of children and young people necessitates the engagement of all sectors of society and also of children themselves.[78] The realization of rights requires recognition of children's capacities and status as holders of human rights worthy of respect as well as their protection, provision, and participation. This is apposite to the widespread paternalism of human rights approaches which views the need for protection as synonymous with passive victims[79] and, indeed, with some educational views of children's learning as passive acceptance of adults' ideas and knowledge.[80] These paternalistic views center children's rights on their vulnerability, which of course carries the risk that children and young people become defined by their vulnerabilities,[81] views which permeate interactions with children and legitimate their control.[82] We suggest that remedies to rights infringements must take account of children's evolving capacities and competence; this demands nurturing relationships and respect in education to effect horizontal (that is, relational) realization of a rights culture which extends to remedies and redress where young people themselves have access to tools for resolution. In line with the CRC Committee's emphasis on the rights of all children to be heard if they are capable of expressing a view, specific efforts should be used to ensure that young children and children with disabilities are not excluded from the opportunity to seek redress and/or be heard when decisions are being made that affect them, a process that will often require appropriate information and the support of adults who are skilled in communicating with them.[83]

Children's views must not only be given due weight, but decision makers and duty bearers should also inform children of decisions that affect them, explaining how decisions were reached and how the views of children and young persons were considered. One example would be the decision to exclude or isolate a child in the implementation of a school discipline policy or the case of other punitive measures, such as detentions. A child rights approach would result in the views of children being heard and taken seriously and also would uphold respect for children's rights to receive information and ideas under Articles 13 and 17. Providing this feedback to children may prompt young persons to make alternative proposals or to file an appeal or complaint, all part of the process of realizing their rights. Thus, remedies and procedures for complaints must exist to address non-implementation; in fact, the CRC Committee suggests that children should have access to a person of comparable role to an ombudsman in schools in order to voice their complaints.[84] Children should know who this person is, how to access him or her, and that using these procedures will not expose them to risk of punitive reprisals. It is important that any complaint made by a young person is addressed promptly. This requires clear and unambiguous internal complaints procedures and a robust and impartial grievance policy, a move that will also require fresh perspectives on the place of young people in education and on their capacity to pursue redress and remedies through appropriate channels. These channels include the appointment of a designated, objective ombudsman to implement said policies and procedures impartially and the consultation of young people and adults in doing so.

Human rights education, then, must play a central role in the redress of rights infringements and not only in terms of the education provided to children; education staff and other duty holders must also be provided the requisite education in line with Article 42 of the CRC. This is particularly the case considering that the role of duty bearers is to build the capacity of children and young people to demand their rights.[85] Indeed, the CRC Committee has emphasized the centrality of rights education not only for children, education staff, and other duty holders living in peaceful societies but also for those "living in situations of conflict or emergency"[86]—all the more relevant with current events and refugee crises. Felisa Tibbits terms this aspect of education as "transformational," where individuals are enabled not only to recognize rights violations but also to commit to their prevention or redress,[87] perhaps in part because children come to see beings as having worth and value simply on account of their existence and not their backgrounds, achievements, or characteristics.[88] This is significant because, as discussed above, rights do not exist only between students and teachers but also among students and their peers and between young people and their communities. Katherine Covell and colleagues point to evidence of child-initiated efforts to actively redress rights infringements of other children among children in rights-respecting schools, which demonstrates a horizontal implementation of children's rights without time-consuming and costly recourse to legal redress.[89] With regard to adult duty bearers, education for and through rights will address the CRC Committee's mandate for upholding the values inherent in Article 29 by constructing a values framework for all educational practices.[90] This would also address both the lack of awareness around rights education and of knowledge of rights and the consequent suspicion around rights as a threat to adult authority or adult competence.[91]

4.1 Case Example: Children Demand Their Rights

In 2018 student survivors of a mass shooting in Florida that killed fourteen students and three staff[92] mobilized other child survivors of other gun violence and school shootings as well as public support from across the United States. As a direct result of these protests and the public outcry, two further actions were prompted: a school walkout for seventeen minutes to honor those who died and a march on the Florida legislature to demand tighter gun controls. Consequently, the state of Florida passed its first piece of legislation for gun control in twenty years.[93] Remarkably, a number of schools planned to penalize students for walking out of school as part of this peaceful protest, and others sought to prescribe acceptable alternative protests, such as tying ribbons to school fences or moments of silence. This is a clear example of peaceful efforts at advocacy on the part of young people being limited by adults in authority, based largely on the fact that the protestors were children, and being viewed as a threat to the control that adults hold over educational spaces.[94]

5 CONCLUSION

In spite of the near universal acceptance of education rights across the world, global evidence repeatedly reminds us that many children in all countries struggle to enjoy their rights to education, irrespective of how these are categorized or classified.[95] In this chapter, we suggest that a more fruitful focus may be on implementation of the rights and, in particular, on ensuring respectful *relationships*, adequate and accountable *resources*, and accessible means of *redress* when rights are breached. These are, of course, often important for the realization of all children's rights. Michael Freeman has argued that the symbolic and theoretical politics of rights are irrelevant in the lived experiences of children and young people for whom these questions and challenges revolve around issues of distributive justice.[96] He suggests that there is little to be gained in creating improved legal frameworks for children's rights unless resource allocation and redress are addressed.[97] We agree but add *relationships* to the list, recognizing that all three are, of course, interconnected. Moreover, establishing and maintaining respectful relationships is easier where teachers are valued and work in clean and safe classrooms with the materials they need to offer children a quality education. Likewise, systems of redress are not resource-neutral. Yet, where they do exist, they can expose where there is a lack of resources and thus enable public money to be allocated where it is needed so that all children can learn in contexts that enable them to develop to the best of their ability.

As discussed, it is the *doing*, or the implementation of education rights, that is problematic, and it is to this salient point that we return. Freeman argued for the *demanding* of rights, which necessitates human agency.[98] In particular, it is the agency of children and young people upon which rests the transformation of hierarchical relationships that have the potential to transform education across the globe. In recognition of this, and in recognition of the centrality of such relationships in providing future rights respecting societies, resources and redress must support and nurture the respect upon which such relationships exist. This includes the acceptance and recognition that children and young people possess the agency with which to make these transformations as well as the trust to enable and support them to do so: that is, a horizontal understanding and implementation of respect for and recognition of young people's capacities for seeking redress. Educational relationships are a microcosm of the interaction between the child and the state where foundational understandings of citizenship and democratic values are learned.[99] As such, the cornerstone of rights respecting values begin at school, and it is therefore imperative that the continuing construction of such relationships is built on a judicious and steadfast foundation.

In conclusion, the significance of education rights cannot be underestimated. While they enjoy a high profile in international human rights advocacy and practice, their significance is not always fully understood or embraced in research and scholarship. Not only are education rights the route for children to enjoy all of their other rights—a recognized passport to the realization of children's human rights more generally—they are fundamental to the human rights project more generally. The most significant precursor of rights-respecting societies is that rights-holders not only know their rights but also embrace and embody the underpinning values of equality, dignity, and respect. For most people, the first interface between the home and society, between the public and the private, is school. Ensuring children's rights in, to, and through education through a focus on the three Rs of relationships, resources, and redress may therefore provide a way of securing a culture of respect not just for children, but for global society as a whole.

Notes

1. Laura Lundy, Karen Orr, and Harry Shier, "Children's Education Rights: Global Perspectives," in *Handbook of Children's Rights: Global and Multidisciplinary Perspectives*, ed. Martin Ruck, Michele Petersen-Badali, and Michael Freeman (London: Routledge, 2016), 364–380.
2. Declaration of the Rights of the Child/Geneva Declaration on the Rights of the Child (1924), http://www.un-documents.net/gdrc1924.htm.
3. UN Committee on the Rights of the Child (CRC Committee), *General Comment No. 1 (2001), Article 29 (1): The Aims of Education*, CRC/GC/2001/1 (2001), para. 9.
4. UN Convention on the Rights of the Child (CRC), G.A. Res. 44/25, 44th Sess., UN Doc. A/RES/44/25 (1989), arts. 23, 24, 32, 33, and 40.
5. Eugène Verhellen, "Children's Rights and Education: A Three Track Legally Binding Imperative," *School Psychology International* 14, no. 3 (August 1993): 199–208.
6. Katarina Tomasevski, *Human Rights Obligations in Education: The 4-A Scheme* (Netherlands: Wolf Legal Publishers, 2006).
7. UNESCO, *A Human Rights Based Approach to Education for All: A Framework for the Realization of Children's Right to Education and Rights within Education* (New York: UNICEF, 2007).
8. Ann Quennerstedt, "Education and Children's Rights," in *The Routledge International Handbook of Children's Rights Studies*, ed. Wouter Vandenhole, Ellen Desmet, Didier Reynaert, and Sara Lembrechts (New York: Routledge, 2015), 201–215.
9. Patricia O'Lynn and Laura Lundy, "The Education Rights of Children," in *International Human Rights of Children*, ed. Ursula Kilkelly and Ton Liefaard (Singapore: Springer, 2019), 259–276.

10. Lundy, Orr, and Shier, "Children's Education Rights."
11. Lundy, Orr, and Shier, "Children's Education Rights."
12. Laura Lundy, "Family Values in the Classroom? Reconciling Parental Wishes and Children's Rights in State Schools," *International Journal of Law, Policy and the Family* 19, no. 3 (December 2005): 346–372.
13. R. Brian Howe and Katherine Covell, *Empowering Children: Children's Rights Education as a Pathway to Citizenship* (Toronto: University of Toronto Press, 2005).
14. Deborah Harcourt and Solveig Hägglund, "Turning the UNCRC Upside Down: A Bottom-Up Perspective on Children's Rights," *International Journal of Early Years Education* 21, no. 4 (July 2013): 286–299.
15. Laura Lundy and John Tobin, "Article 29: The Aims of Education," in *The UN Convention on the Rights of the Child: A Commentary*, ed. John Tobin (Oxford: Oxford University Press, 2019).
16. CRC Committee, *General Comment No. 1*, paras. 1 and 2.
17. CRC Committee, *General Comment No. 1*, para. 9.
18. Tomasevski, *Human Rights Obligations in Education*.
19. CRC Committee, *General Comment No. 1*.
20. Lundy and Tobin, "Article 29."
21. Katherine Covell, R. Brian Howe, and Justin McNeil, "Implementing Children's Human Rights Education in Schools," *Improving Schools* 13, no. 2 (August 2010): 117–132.
22. O'Lynn and Lundy, "Education Rights of Children."
23. Lundy, Orr, and Shier, "Children's Education Rights;" O'Lynn and Lundy, "Education Rights of Children."
24. Laura Lundy and Alison Cook-Sather, "Children's Rights and Student Voice: Their Intersections and Implications for Curriculum and Pedagogy," in *The SAGE Handbook of Curriculum, Pedagogy and Assessment*, ed. Dominic Wyse, Louise Hayward, and Jessica Pandya (London: SAGE, 2016), 263–277.
25. Lundy and Cook-Sather, "Children's Rights and Student Voice."
26. Gerison Lansdown, "Promoting Children's Participation in Democratic Decision-Making" (February 2001), https://www.unicef-irc.org/publications/pdf/insight6.pdf.
27. See John I'Anson and Julie Allan, "Children's Rights in Practice: A Study of Change within a Primary School," *International Journal of Children's Spirituality* 11, no. 2 (August 2006): 265–279; see also Johanna Geldenhuys and Hannelie Doubell, "South African Children's Voice on School Discipline: A Case Study," *International Journal of Children's Rights* 19, no. 2 (2011): 321–337.
28. Laura Lundy, Karen Orr, and Chelsea Marshall, "Towards Better Investment in the Rights of the Child: The Views of Children," report by the Centre for Children's Rights, Queen's University Belfast (2015), https://www.qub.ac.uk/research-centres/CentreforChildrensRights/filestore/Filetoupload,496273,en.pdf.
29. Jonathan Todres and Sarah Higinbotham, *Human Rights in Children's Literature: Imagination and the Narrative of Law* (New York: Oxford University Press, 2016).
30. CRC Committee, *General Comment No. 1*.
31. Virginia Morrow and Kirrily Pells, "Integrating Children's Human Rights and Child Poverty Debates: Examples from *Young Lives* in Ethiopia and India," *Sociology* 46, no. 5 (October 2012): 906–920.
32. Morrow and Pells, "Integrating Children's Human Rights."
33. Lundy, Orr, and Shier, "Children's Education Rights."

34. Lundy, Orr, and Shier, "Children's Education Rights."

35. CRC Committee, *General Comment No. 1*.

36. CRC Committee, *General Comment No. 7: The Right of the Child to Rest, Leisure, Play, Recreational Activities, Cultural Life and the Arts (art. 31)*, CRC/C/GC/7 (2013), para. 17.

37. Lundy, "Family Values in the Classroom?"

38. Lundy, Orr, and Shier, "Children's Education Rights."

39. CRC Committee, *General Comment No. 12 (2009): The Right of the Child to Be Heard*, CRC/C/GC/12 (2009).

40. CRC Committee, *General Comment No. 1*.

41. Tony Shallcross, Callie Loubser, Cheryl Le Roux, Rob O'Donoghue, and Justin Lupele, "Promoting Sustainable Development through Whole School Approaches: An International, Intercultural Teacher Education Research and Development Project," *Journal of Education for Teaching* 32, no. 3 (September 2006): 283–301, 286.

42. CRC Committee, *General Comment No. 1*.

43. Quennerstedt, "Education and Children's Rights."

44. Ann Quennerstedt and Mikael Quennerstedt, "Researching Children's Rights in Education: Sociology of Childhood Encountering Educational Theory," *British Journal of Sociology of Education* 35, no. 1 (January 2014): 115–132.

45. CRC Committee, *General Comment No. 12: The Right of the Child to Be Heard*, CRC/C/GC/12 (2009), para. 105.

46. Chief Executive Officer for Education v. Gibbons, Civil Appeal No. ABU0002.2012, [2013] FJCA 98 [Fiji Court of Appeals] (Oct. 3 2013).

47. Organisation for Economic Co-operation and Development (OECD), "Public Spending on Education," OECDiLibrary, https://www.oecd-ilibrary.org/education/public-spending-on-education/indicator/english_f99b45d0-en (accessed Aug. 24, 2019).

48. Laura Lundy, "Children's Rights and Educational Policy in Europe: The Implementation of the United Nations Convention on the Rights of the Child," *Oxford Review of Education* 38, no. 4 (August 2012): 393–411.

49. CRC Committee, "Concluding Observations on the Combined Fifth and Sixth Periodic Reports of Spain," CRC/C/ESP/CO/5-6 (2018), para. 39.

50. Mark Bray and Ora Kio, "Behind the Façade of Fee-Free Education: Shadow Education and Its Implications for Social Justice," *Oxford Review of Education* 39, no. 4 (August 2013): 480–497.

51. See, for example, Amanda L. Sullivan, Ethan R. Van Norman, and David A. Klingbeil, "Exclusionary Discipline of Students with Disabilities: Student and School Characteristics Predicting Suspension," *Remedial and Special Education* 35, no. 4 (February 2014): 199–210.

52. Bronagh Byrne, "Minding the Gap? Children with Disabilities and the United Nations Convention on the Rights of Persons with Disabilities," *Law and Childhood Studies: Current Legal Issues* 14 (2012): 419–437.

53. UN Human Rights Council, "Report of the Special Rapporteur on the Right to Education Kishore Singh," A/HRC/29/30 (2015), para. 111.

54. Elaine Unterhalter, "Measuring Education for the Millennium Development Goals: Reflections on Targets, Indicators, and a Post-2015 Framework," *Journal of Human Development and Capabilities* 15, nos. 2–3 (March 2014): 176–187.

55. UNESCO, *Global Education Monitoring Report: Accountability in Education Meeting Our Commitments* (Paris: UNESCO, 2017).

56. Geldenhuys and Doubell, "South African Children's Voice."

57. CRC Committee, *General Comment No. 19 on Public Budgeting for the Realization of Children's Rights (art. 4)*, CRC/C/GC/19 (2016), para. 17.

58. UN Human Rights Committee, "Concluding Observations of the Human Rights Committee: Sri Lanka," CRC/C/LKA/CO/5–6 (2018).

59. CRC Committee, "Concluding Observations: Spain."

60. Lundy, Orr, and Shier, "Children's Education Rights."

61. Geldenhuys and Doubell, "South African Children's Voice."

62. Lundy, Orr, and Marshall, "Towards Better Investment."

63. Lundy, "Family Values in the Classroom?"; Howe and Covell, *Empowering Children*.

64. Michael Freeman, "Why It Remains Important to Take Children's Rights Seriously," *International Journal of Children's Rights* 15, no. 1 (2007): 5–23.

65. Michael Freeman, "Taking Children's Rights More Seriously," *International Journal of Law and the Family* 6, no. 1 (April 1992): 52–71.

66. Freeman, "Taking Children's Rights More Seriously"; see also UN Declaration on Human Rights Education and Training, G.A. Res. 66/137, 66th Sess., UN Doc. A/RES/66/137 (2011).

67. Children's Rights International Network (CRIN), "Strategic Litigation Case Studies: The Stories behind Children's Rights Cases," https://archive.crin.org/en/home/law/strategic-litigation/strategic-litigation-case-studies.html (accessed Aug. 24, 2019).

68. CRIN, "Recommendations on Access to Justice for Children," https://archive.crin.org/sites/default/files/crin_access_to_justice_recommendations.pdf (accessed Aug. 24, 2019).

69. CRC Committee, *General Comment No. 1*.

70. Sonja Grover, "Rights Education and Children's Collective Self-Advocacy through Public Interest Litigation," *Human Rights Education Review* 1, no. 1 (June 2018): 64–83.

71. O'Lynn and Lundy, "Education Rights of Children."

72. Klaus D. Beiter, *The Protection of the Right to Education by International Law: Including a Systematic Analysis of Article 13 of the International Covenant on Economic, Social, and Cultural Rights* (Leiden: Martinus Nijhoff, 2006).

73. Freeman, "Why It Remains Important to Take Children's Rights Seriously."

74. CRC Committee, *General Comment No. 12*.

75. Laura Lundy, Ursula Kilkelly, and Bronagh Byrne, "Incorporation of the United Nations Convention on the Rights of the Child in Law: A Comparative Review," *International Journal of Children's Rights* 21, no. 3 (2013): 442–463.

76. CRC Committee, *General Comment No. 5: General Measures of Implementation of the Convention on the Rights of the Child*, CRC/GC/2003/5 (2003).

77. CRC Committee, *General Comment No. 5*.

78. CRC Committee, *General Comment No. 5*.

79. Edward van Daalen, Karl Hanson, and Olga Nieuwenhuys, "Children's Rights as Living Rights: The Case of Street Children and a New Law in Yogyakarta, Indonesia," *International Journal of Children's Rights* 24, no. 4 (December 2016): 803–825.

80. Ann Quennerstedt, "The Construction of Children's Rights in Education—A Research Synthesis," *International Journal for Children's Rights* 19, no. 4 (2011): 661–678.

81. John Tobin, "Understanding Children's Rights: A Vision beyond Vulnerability," *Nordic Journal of International Law* 84, no. 2 (2015): 155–182.

82. Quennerstedt, "Education and Children's Rights."

83. CRC Committee, *General Comment No. 7*.

84. CRC Committee, *General Comment No. 7*, para. 46.

85. Howe and Covell, *Empowering Children*.

86. CRC Committee, *General Comment No. 1*, para. 16.

87. Felisa Tibbits, "Understanding What We Do: Emerging Models for Human Rights Education," *International Review of Education* 48, nos. 3–4 (July 2002): 159–171.

88. Katherine Covell, "School Engagement and Rights-Respecting Schools," *Cambridge Journal of Education* 40, no. 1 (March 2010): 39–51.

89. Covell, Howe, and McNeil, "Implementing Children's Human Rights Education in Schools."

90. CRC Committee, *General Comment No. 1*.

91. Howe and Covell, *Empowering Children*.

92. Nick Allen, "March for Our Lives: Parkland Survivor Emma Gonzalez Leads Rallies to Demand Tighter US Gun Controls," *The Telegraph*, March 25, 2018, https://www.telegraph.co.uk/news/2018/03/24/massive-crowds-rally-across-us-urge-tighter-gun-controls.

93. Amanda Holpuch, "Six Victories for the Gun Control Movement since the Parkland Massacre," *The Guardian*, March 26, 2018, https://www.theguardian.com/us-news/2018/mar/26/gun-control-movement-march-for-our-lives-stoneman-douglas-parkland-builds-momentum.

94. Grover, "Rights Education."

95. Lundy, Orr, and Shier, "Children's Education Rights."

96. Freeman, "Why It Remains Important to Take Children's Rights Seriously."

97. Freeman, "Why It Remains Important to Take Children's Rights Seriously."

98. Freeman, "Why It Remains Important to Take Children's Rights Seriously."

99. See Lundy, "Family Values in the Classroom?"; see also Lundy and Tobin, "Article 29."

CHAPTER 20

....

POVERTY AND
CHILDREN'S RIGHTS

AOIFE NOLAN

1 INTRODUCTION

....

AN October 2016 report from the World Bank Group and UNICEF estimated that, in 2013, 19.5 percent of children in developing countries lived in extreme poverty, defined as living on less than $1.90 a day.[1] Not only did the report make clear the appalling living conditions experienced by children in many countries, it also demonstrated that children as a social group are disproportionately affected by poverty, with children more than twice as likely as adults to be living in households experiencing extreme poverty. Recent overviews of poverty in wealthy countries also reveal a grim picture, with a 2017 UNICEF Innocenti Centre report finding that one in five children in forty-one high-income countries lived in relative income poverty, with one in eight facing food insecurity.[2]

Findings like these have resulted in ever-more strident calls for action to address child poverty. A range of key policy and child rights actors have argued for greater investment in children in response to child poverty—whether expressed in terms of investment in child rights,[3] equity for children,[4] or social and economic development for children.[5] Intergovernmental organizations (IGOs), such as the International Labour Organization, have emphasized the importance of social protection to reducing and preventing child poverty.[6] This groundswell of activity has been in part motivated and in part complemented by the growing global recognition of the severe impact on children's living conditions resulting from the financial and economic crises that began in 2007–2008 and the fiscal austerity measures implemented in their wake by a large number of states.[7]

This overlaps with one of the most notable developments in terms of anti-child-poverty work over the past twenty years, namely, a significant increase in the use of children's rights in defining, measuring, and developing responses to child poverty. While many such efforts, including those employed by UNICEF,[8] have focused on the UN Convention on the Rights of the Child (CRC), others, such as the 2017 African Agenda for Children 2040 and the 2013 EU Commission Recommendation on Investing in Children: Breaking the Cycle of Disadvantage, have also referred to the child rights contained in regional child rights instruments.[9] Even anti-poverty actors such as the World Bank, whose "agnosticism" on human rights is well known, have taken steps to incorporate a child rights element in their anti-poverty work.[10]

While definitions, methods of identification, and measures of child poverty vary significantly,[11] there is a growing recognition that an exclusively monetary or income-based concept of poverty fails to capture the reality of the multifaceted nature of poverty (which, in turn, requires a multidimensional approach to the conceptualization and measure of such). Such a multidimensional understanding of poverty has been embraced by the United Nations,[12] UN human rights treaty monitoring bodies,[13] and other authoritative human rights actors.[14] Consistent with that approach, the definition of poverty employed in this chapter is provided by the UN Committee on Economic, Social and Cultural Rights. That body describes poverty as "a human condition characterized by the sustained or chronic deprivation of the resources, capabilities, choices, security and power necessary for the enjoyment of an adequate standard of living and other civil, cultural, economic, political and social rights."[15]

This chapter addresses the ever-deepening relationship between child poverty and child rights. In doing so, it takes as its central focus the best known and most important child rights instrument, the CRC. The chapter opens with a justification of why, given the range of different approaches available to and adopted by anti-poverty practitioners and scholars, child rights is an appropriate lens through which to consider child poverty. It then moves on to the relationship between the CRC and child poverty, concentrating both on the Convention itself and on how that instrument has been interpreted by the UN Committee on the Rights of the Child (CRC Committee) when considering causes, impacts, and responses to child poverty. This includes an especial focus on the CRC Committee's approach to the right to an adequate standard of living. In doing so, the chapter provides a critical analysis of the strengths and weaknesses of the current international child rights framework in terms of its ability to address the complex, social global challenge of child poverty. It concludes with a discussion of a key contemporary development in terms of child poverty that presents both risks and opportunities in child rights terms: the post-2015 Sustainable Development Agenda.

2   CHILD RIGHTS ANTI-POVERTY WORK:
PART OF A BROADER PICTURE

Child rights is certainly not the only possible analytical framework for the identification, diagnosis, and development of responses to child poverty. Concepts such as capabilities,[16] basic needs,[17] and well-being[18] have been employed frequently in this context. However, while well-being and the capability approaches in particular have been highly significant in relation to conceptualising poverty and designing anti-poverty initiatives in recent years, this has not necessarily been at the expense of child rights; there is a growing tendency for child rights, capabilities, and well-being frameworks to be employed in tandem in both scholarship and policy work centered on child poverty and social justice (though this remains a far from uniform or inevitable practice).[19]

Such simultaneous engagement with different "lenses" in anti-poverty work is unsurprising given clear overlaps between the concerns and concepts shared by scholar and policymaker proponents of these different approaches—for instance, the achievement of poverty reduction, the advancement of human development and human flourishing, and the protection of human dignity—as well as the close relationship between these approaches explored in detail in the work of those championing them. For instance, the capability approach can be seen as providing a theoretical account of children's rights.[20] Alternatively, child rights can be viewed as justification for the identification of specific capabilities as part of the capability approach in a child-related context, or the realization of child rights can be seen as providing such capabilities.[21] Simultaneously (or alternatively), children's rights can be viewed as corresponding to domains that can be used to measure child well-being.[22] In turn, well-being can also be seen as a way of fleshing out different elements of the CRC, such as the best interests principle.[23] The realization of children's rights can be viewed as contributing to children's well-being[24] and expanding their capability(ies)—and vice versa. This is by no means an exhaustive account of how these different frameworks may interplay in relation to child poverty, but it makes clear that insights from the capability approach, with its focus on "freedom" and "functionings," and the well-being approach's accommodation of multidimensionality have much to offer child rights work in the anti-poverty context.

It is also important to acknowledge that the use of a child rights–based approach to anti-poverty work is far from unproblematic—a fact that those who would argue for its use must acknowledge and address. At a general level, there are a number of powerful critiques of the human rights–based approach, including claims that the individual-focused, public sphere–centric, culturally biased orientation of the international human rights framework results in the prioritization of the rights claims of some groups over those of others, while completely excluding the claims of some of the poorest.[25] Indeed, given the relatively recent acceptance of the notion of the child as rights-bearer and the traditional privileging of civil and political rights over economic and social rights within the human rights framework, using human rights as the perspective from which to analyze or design poverty-related issues or responses might seem to pose certain obstacles to addressing child poverty; if human rights fail to recognize and reflect adequately the lived experience and challenges faced by poor children in terms of their standard of living, health, and education, then such a framework seems of limited utility in terms of shaping and evaluating anti-poverty initiatives intended to address those issues. It should be noted, however, that those arguing in favor of a rights-based approach to poverty do not generally engage in such privileging of civil and political rights.[26] Furthermore, human rights have traditionally been, and continue to be, primarily directed at states. This has resulted in the human rights framework frequently failing to capture non-state actors whose activities may be at least as influential as those of states in contributing to or exacerbating child poverty (for instance, such international financial institutions (IFIs) as the International Monetary Fund, such IGOs as the World Trade Organisation, and powerful transnational corporations).[27]

Looking specifically at the issue of child rights and poverty, the rights framework set out in the CRC has been accused of being Eurocentric,[28] individualistic, and limited in terms of its recognition of the varying characteristics and experiences of different groups of children.[29] From a poverty perspective, the CRC's dominant approach of locating children in the context of families/households when it comes to the right to an adequate standard of living (Article 27) and the right to benefit from social security (Article 26)—key rights in terms of poverty reduction—serves to reinforce the perception that family- and household-oriented measures will necessarily serve to address child poverty. This is despite the fact that there are inevitably children who will not benefit from measures focused on adults (for instance, children living in child-headed households). The CRC Committee has more recently made clear that Article 27(3) (which outlines the state's role in assisting parents and others responsible for the child to implement the right to an adequate standard of living) is not limited to measures to assist parents and others responsible for the child; its 2017 General Comment No. 21 on children in a street situation states that "[t]he obligation to provide material assistance and support programmes in case of need should be interpreted as also meaning assistance provided directly to children."[30] Statements such as this, as well as the application of the child's right to be heard under Article 12 with regard to the design, implementation, and review of anti-poverty measures,[31] including budget decision-making,[32] make it clear that that the Convention envisages children themselves as being at the heart of policy and other measures directed toward the amelioration and/or eradication of child poverty.

The Convention also appears to address some of the concerns expressed with regard to the general human rights framework, particularly through its inclusion of both economic and social rights and civil and political rights (albeit that, as Article 4 makes clear, to some degree, the different categories of rights impose different obligations on states parties).[33] The wide-ranging nature of the rights provided for in the CRC would seem to make it a particularly suitable tool to use in combating child poverty. Furthermore, while the CRC does not impose binding legal obligations on non-state actors, its provisions explicitly recognize duties and responsibilities imposed on agents such as parents and others responsible for the child in ensuring that their economic and social rights needs are met.[34] In practice, the CRC Committee has been more proactive than many other UN treaty monitoring bodies in engaging with the issue of non-state actor responsibility, albeit not in a poverty context specifically.[35]

Ultimately the CRC provides an (admittedly imperfect) framework of child rights premised on an underpinning of legal obligations that are binding under international human rights law. This is not the case for the well-being or capability approaches. The rights set out in the CRC cover a wider range of issues than most major national and international indices of well-being,[36] and the high level of ratification of the CRC[37] means that its contents can be treated as the subject of greater consensus than the capabilities identified as part of different versions of the capability approach. These factors constitute strong arguments in favor of the use of child rights in child poverty work—even in situations in which the dominant paradigm employed is not that of child rights.

3 Child Poverty and Child Rights—Making the Connection through the CRC

3.1 Poverty in the CRC: Nowhere but Everywhere?

It is trite at this point to note that the word *poverty* does not appear in the Convention.[38] It is also trite to note that child poverty constitutes a violation of a wide range of children's rights under the CRC.[39] Living in childhood poverty frequently either results from or causes a failure to secure children's economic and social rights, such as the right to an adequate standard of living, to benefit from social security, to the highest attainable standard of health, and to education. However, it has a significant impact on their civil and political rights as well, with, for example, the UN Special Rapporteur on Extreme Poverty and Human Rights highlighting that poor children are disproportionately affected by maltreatment and neglect, with poverty serving as a risk factor for child abuse and child marriage.[40] Poverty—whether absolute or relative—also has clear implications for children's enjoyment of their participation rights in a range of different contexts, including education and cultural or social life.

That said, child poverty has been most often treated as principally engaging children's economic and social rights; indeed, one commentator has gone so far as to describe children's economic and social rights as a concrete set of responses to specific facets of child poverty.[41] The strong linkage between addressing child poverty and ensuring enjoyment of economic and social rights under the Convention is reflected, inter alia, in the CRC Committee's state reporting guidelines, where the request for information on "[s]tandard of living and measures taken, including material assistance and support programmes with regard to nutrition, clothing and housing, to ensure children's physical, mental, spiritual, moral and social development, and *to reduce poverty* and inequality (art. 27, paras. 1–3)" is located in the cluster on "Disability, basic health and welfare (arts. 6, 18, para. 3, 23, 24, 26, 27, paras. 1–3, and 33)."[42] It is thus unsurprising that Article 27 on the child's right to a standard of living adequate for their physical, mental, spiritual, moral and social development has historically been the key focus of the Committee's treatment of poverty—both in its General Comments and its Concluding Observations.[43] This is consistent with the approach of the Committee on Economic, Social and Cultural Rights, which has made use of the right to an adequate standard of living set out in

Article 11 of the International Covenant on Economic, Social and Cultural Rights (ICESCR) as a "catch-all" provision with regard to addressing poverty issues.[44]

3.2 Addressing Poverty through the Right to an Adequate Standard of Living

One way in which the CRC Committee has engaged with poverty via Article 27 has been by making the link between child "development" for the purposes of Article 27 and poverty. For instance, in its 2010 Concluding Observations on Sudan, the CRC Committee expressed concern that "the living conditions of children and their families in situations of extreme poverty massively impede the holistic development of children's capacities, as envisaged by Article 27, paragraph 2, of the Convention."[45] Elsewhere it has highlighted the "severe negative effects of poverty on the development of children" in the context of ensuring the right adequate standard of living.[46] The preoccupation with the impact on "development" in terms of Article 27 by poverty or material deprivation is evident also from the CRC Committee's General Comments, with the Committee commenting that "[g]rowing up in relative poverty undermines children's well-being, social inclusion and self-esteem and reduces opportunities for learning and development."[47]

In its General Comment No. 20 on the rights of adolescents, the CRC Committee addressed head-on the relationship between an "adequate standard of living" and poverty, stating that "[t]he impact of poverty has profound implications during adolescence, sometimes leading to extreme stress and insecurity and to social and political exclusion."[48] In the same General Comment, the CRC Committee reminded states of the right of every child to a suitable standard of living for physical, mental, spiritual, moral development and "urged" them to introduce social protection floors that provide adolescents and their families with basic income security, protection against economic shocks and prolonged economic crises, and access to social services.[49] In its next General Comment No.21 on children in street situations, again when discussing the right to an adequate standard of living, the Committee outlined a range of measures that states should take to address the structural causes of poverty and income inequalities so as to reduce pressure on and strengthen precarious families.[50] These measures include "introducing tax and expenditure policies that reduce economic inequalities; expanding fair-wage employment and other opportunities for income generation; introducing pro-poor policies for rural and urban development; eliminating corruption; introducing child-focused policies and budgeting; strengthening child-centred poverty alleviation programmes in areas known for high levels of migration; and offering adequate social security and social protection."[51] In doing so, the Committee emphasized that mechanisms and services making material support available to parents, caregivers, and directly to children should be designed and implemented on the basis of a child rights approach.[52]

The CRC Committee's use of Article 27 to address issues of poverty is further demonstrated by its frequent recommendations to states to "provide material assistance and support to economically disadvantaged families" in its Concluding Observations on "standard of living."[53] In the recommendations emerging from its Day of General Discussion on children without parental care, the Committee (having referred to Article 27) urged states parties to take all necessary measures to raise the standard of living among families living in poverty, inter alia, through implementing poverty reduction strategies and community development, including the participation of children.[54] Other poverty-related measures that the Committee has repeatedly recommended in relation to giving effect to Article 27 in the context of its Concluding Observations include: the taking of targeted measures protecting children from the harmful impact of poverty on their development, health and education;[55] ensuring access to clean water, adequate sanitation, food and shelter[56] as well as education, social, and health services;[57] the allocation of adequate human, technical, and financial resources to provide support to families;[58] the provision and strengthening of infrastructure and/or multisectoral coordination;[59] the establishment of a social protection framework or social security system;[60] the elimination of regional disparities in terms of child poverty and rights enjoyment;[61] and the collection of data and monitoring of trends in poverty.[62] States have also been asked to develop and advance specific national initiatives, such as cash transfer schemes,[63] the introduction of universal child benefits,[64] the establishment of social protection floors,[65] the analysis and development of policies to eliminate "pockets of poverty";[66] to implement legislation focused on social protection, social welfare, and ending child poverty;[67] and to operationalize national plans of action for children and development programs.[68]

In urging states parties to implement poverty and development strategies and plans, the CRC Committee has stressed that these should be child rights–informed, centric, and compliant.[69] It has also been concerned to ensure that such measures are not "top-down" in nature, making clear (as mentioned above) that states should encourage the participation of both children and parents in the development of poverty-alleviation strategies.[70] Furthermore, the Committee has emphasized the importance of states parties engaging NGOs in dialogue, and civil society in general in the development of social policies in order better to understand the reasons for exclusion and to stimulate new ideas to raise the standard of living of vulnerable groups of children.[71] This extends to holding targeted consultations with families, children, and children's rights civil society organizations on the issue of child poverty.[72]

The CRC Committee has not limited itself to a consideration of the *responses* to poverty. An important root *cause* of poverty—disability—was addressed by the Committee in its General Comment No. 9 on the rights of children with disabilities. Here, the Committee stated that "poverty [is] both a cause and a consequence of disability" and reiterated that children with disabilities and their families have the right to an adequate standard of living.[73] The Committee stressed the wide-ranging state measures needed to give effect to that right, including the allocation of adequate budgetary resources and ensuring that children with disabilities have access to social protection and poverty reduction programs in order to address the question of such children living in poverty.[74] This emphasis on children with disabilities and poverty is unsurprising given the strong linkage between disability and poverty[75] More broadly, the Committee's Concluding Observations include recommendations on a wide range of other root causes of poverty, focusing on the inequitable distribution of resources resulting in poverty,[76] including land,[77] as well as tax benefits and social transfers.[78] In a notable development, 2016 saw the Committee criticize specific national changes to tax credits and social benefits that impacted negatively on child poverty.[79]

The right to an adequate standard of living has also played an important role in terms of the CRC Committee's consideration of child poverty in "crisis" contexts. Following the financial and economic crises of the late 2000s, the CRC Committee placed particular emphasis on states taking the steps necessary to alleviate the effects of the economic crisis on children.[80] The same is true with regard to the food and fuel crises experienced by many countries in the second half of the 2000s.[81]

3.3 From Article 27 to General Comment No. 19: The Role of Budgets and Resources in Addressing Poverty

We can see clearly from all of this that the CRC Committee has developed an extensive practice with regard to poverty under the Convention, most notably through its approach to Article 27. Much of this work is relatively recent due to a past tendency on the part of the CRC Committee to neither consistently nor extensively apply Article 27 in either its General Comments or its Concluding Observations.[82] However, the past few years have reflected a change in approach, with more regular and effective engagement with regard to both Article 27 generally and its poverty-related components specifically. Beyond Article 27, though as noted above, the CRC contains economic and social rights provisions, the Committee had historically neglected to engage with the obligations imposed by those rights beyond those related to health and education. Among other things, this resulted in a failure to provide crucial guidance to states parties, child rights advocates, and others on the content and scope of CRC Article 4, that is, the key umbrella provision outlining the obligations imposed by economic and social rights under the Convention, which provides that "[w]ith regard to economic, social and cultural rights, States Parties shall undertake such measures to the maximum extent of their available resources and, where needed, within the framework of international co-operation."[83]

While the CRC Committee's 2016 General Comment No. 19 on public budgeting for the realization of children's rights is a significant advance in this area,[84] teasing out a range of different obligations imposed by Article 4, there is still frequent misunderstanding and misapplication in child rights–oriented anti-poverty work of the duties derived from that provision, and of the economic and social rights under the Convention. It is hard to resist the conclusion that at least part of this is due to the fact that much of the discussion around child rights and poverty has been led by sociologists and economists rather than by lawyers. Indeed, even among child rights lawyers, the area of economic and social rights is relatively neglected—a fact that further contributes to the quality of engagements around child rights and child poverty from an economic and social rights perspective.[85]

General Comment No. 19 is also a major addition in terms of progressing the CRC Committee's engagement with the legal, policy, and institutional reforms that are key to ameliorating poverty, in particular those related to budgetary inputs, outputs, processes, and outcomes. The General Comment "identifies States parties' obligations and makes recommendations on how to realize all the rights under the Convention, especially those of children in vulnerable situations, through effective, efficient, equitable, transparent and sustainable public budget decision-making."[86] Children living in poverty are specifically identified as one such group.[87] By addressing the relationship between rights realization and public revenue mobilization, budget allocation, and state expenditures, the Committee has provided crucial guidance to those seeking to address child poverty issues that are attributable to macro-economic and fiscal structures, processes, and policies.

A final notable element of General Comment No. 19 from a poverty perspective is its focus beyond the national, perhaps most evidently in its treatment of the obligation of international cooperation,[88] with the CRC Committee stressing the "obligation of States parties to also foster implementation of the Convention through international cooperation."[89] The Committee's exhortations that, first, states parties should demonstrate that, where necessary, they have made every effort to seek and implement international cooperation to realize the rights of the child and that, second, they should collaborate with other states' efforts to mobilize the maximum available resources for children's rights both have important implications for transnational anti-poverty efforts directed toward developing economies.[90] They are also consistent with recent developments in terms of clarifying the scope of the obligation of international cooperation under international human rights law more generally.[91] This recognition that child rights do not just have implications for state action in the national context builds on the Committee's earlier statement that

> in their promotion of international cooperation and technical assistance, all United Nations and United Nations–related agencies should be guided by the Convention and should mainstream children's rights throughout their activities. They should seek to ensure within their influence that international cooperation is targeted at supporting States to fulfil their obligations under the Convention. Similarly the World Bank Group, the International Monetary Fund and World Trade Organization should ensure that their activities related to international cooperation and economic development give primary consideration to the best interests of children and promote full implementation of the Convention.[92]

Where a state's anti-poverty efforts involve engagement with international development, finance, or trade organizations, it must take all reasonable actions and measures to ensure that such organizations act in accordance with the CRC in their decision-making and operations, as well as when entering into agreements or establishing guidelines relevant to the business sector.[93] Indeed, it is crucial to note that states retain their obligations in the field of development cooperation and must ensure that cooperation policies and programs are designed and implemented in compliance with the CRC.[94] This clearly applies to anti-poverty work also.

This discussion of the CRC Committee's focus on supranational action and poverty would not be complete without mentioning a factor that may be both a positive and a negative in child poverty terms: namely, sovereign debt. While the Committee recognizes in its General Comment No. 19 that sustainable debt management by states, on behalf of creditors and lenders, "can contribute to mobilizing resources for the rights of the child," it also acknowledges that "long-term unsustainable debt can be a barrier to a State's ability to mobilize resources for children's rights, and may lead to taxes and user fees that impact negatively on children," thereby detrimentally affecting efforts to address child poverty.[95] The Committee's proposed solution is that child rights impact assessments should be carried out also in relation to debt agreements—an approach that is consistent with that being pursued by the leading UN actor working in this area, the UN Independent Expert on foreign debt and human rights.[96]

The CRC Committee's growing attention to economic policy and child rights–related financing at both the domestic and the supranational levels is to be strongly welcomed from an anti-poverty perspective. In carrying out this work, the Committee has demonstrated a willingness to grapple with mechanisms and institutions that have a central role in terms of ameliorating poverty but which thus far have received far less attention in human rights law practice and scholarship than should be the case. There is, however, a key issue on the horizon that is set to dominate global efforts around child poverty over the next decade or so: the 2030 Agenda for Sustainable Development, including its Sustainable Development Goals (SDGs).[97]

4   Conclusion: A Brave New Dawn? Child Poverty, the SDGs, and Child Rights

Since 2015 the SDGs have been a growing focus for anti-child poverty discourse and practice. SDG 1, the ending of poverty in all its forms everywhere, includes a specific target to "reduce at least by half the proportion of men, women and *children* of all ages living in poverty in all its dimensions according to national definitions,"[98] while the hunger, education and health-related goals include targets focused on addressing different aspects of child poverty.[99] The SDGs also include state undertakings to address specific potential outcomes of child poverty, such as child labor and trafficking,[100] child marriage,[101] and violence against children.[102]

Child rights and the CRC are certainly not integrated into and across the SDGs in a consistent, comprehensive way.[103] However, positively from a child rights perspective, the 2030 Agenda is explicitly grounded in the Universal Declaration of Human Rights and international human rights treaties,[104] including the CRC.[105] Beyond the explicit textual reference to the CRC in the 2030 Agenda, much has been made of the overlap between the SDGs and provisions of the CRC by prominent actors in the anti-poverty field, for instance through exercises mapping the SDGs in child rights terms (including in the area of poverty),[106] as well as through emphasizing the integration of SDGs into work around the implementation of child rights[107] and the realization of child rights as an essential condition for achieving long-term development goals.[108] In its own work, the CRC Committee has begun to refer to SDG target 1.2 (on reducing child poverty) and SDG target 1.3 (on implementing nationally appropriate social protection systems and measures) in relation to recommending specific measures to strengthen social protection and address child poverty when considering state progress with regard to Article 27.[109]

The SDGs serve as a crucial contemporary impetus and framework for discussions around child poverty. They should, if implemented effectively, result in actions and the mobilization of institutions and resources that will contribute to outcomes which advance children's rights enjoyment in a range of areas. However, Agenda 2030 and its associated implementation processes also pose a range of challenges from a child rights perspective. First, while the SDGs and associated targets strongly echo language and elements of different provisions of the CRC, this is undermined by the narrowness of the indicators that are set to be used to monitor implementation, as well as by growing evidence that the implementation mechanisms will be neither child rights–sensitive nor compliant.[110] More broadly, there are serious grounds for concern about the elision of child rights (particularly child economic and social rights) and the SDG agendas in such a way as to undermine the former. While there has been some acknowledgment of the risks that such an elision poses to human rights by some UN actors,[111] the "synergies" between the SDGs and economic and social rights have been promoted by other UN actors in a way that has been insufficiently clear about the differences between SDGs and human rights (including children's rights),[112] as well as inadequately critical of the failure thus far to adequately incorporate child rights into the SDG implementation, monitoring, and accountability processes.[113] Positively, there is evidence of an effort to ensure that an element of child participation is included in the work of the United Nations High-Level Panel Forum on Sustainable Development (HLPF), the UN platform on sustainable development that has the central role in the follow-up and review of the 2030 Agenda at the global level. However, it remains unclear to what extent the body charged with responsibility for managing this effort, the UN Major Group for Children and Youth (MGCYP),[114] will be able to successfully ensure child participation throughout the HLPF's work "on all matters affecting the child," as required by CRC Article 12. Issues of concern include the ongoing lack of clarity with regard to the parameters of the role of the Major Groups[115] and other stakeholders in terms of contributing to HLPF processes, whether through reporting or otherwise.[116] Furthermore, given that the MGCYP's scope applies to people under thirty, not only children under eighteen, it is unclear the extent to which the participation of different age groups of children will be prioritized and ensured within the MGCYP itself.

In addition, the SDGs threaten to perpetuate many of the factors that currently give rise to or exacerbate child poverty. This creates the risk that they may potentially contribute to the undermining a range of children's rights. For instance, given the challenge that non-state actors and corporations pose to efforts to address child poverty and the ongoing failure of human rights law to capture or address human rights harms caused by such actors comprehensively and effectively,[117] the central role envisaged for the Global Partnership for Sustainable Development (which includes non-state business and IFI actors) is worrying from a rights perspective. Furthermore, the SDGs (and their associated financing model)[118] have been rightly criticized for doing little to change "the broader policy ecosystem that perpetuates poverty and increases inequality."[119] Thus, while child rights have a significant potential role to play in SDG-related anti-poverty efforts, there is limited evidence of those rights having an impact at more than a rhetorical level. And there is a serious risk that the approach in evidence thus far in SDG implementation may serve to undermine child rights–oriented anti-poverty progress that has already been achieved. Ultimately, the SDGs are not binding in the sense that rights are. There is thus a serious risk that states and others who are challenged by the budgets of obligation and accountability imposed by child rights will embrace the language and processes of the SDGS (together with their limited accountability mechanisms) in such a way as to sideline child rights in future anti-poverty work. In turn, this would result in the conceptualization of anti-poverty work as a matter of non-enforceable development goals rather than legally binding rights.

This chapter has highlighted the significant progress that has been made in terms of moving forward the relationship between child poverty and child rights in both theory and in law. Given that, critical engagement on the part of anti-poverty, child rights scholars and practitioners is crucial to ensure that the SDGs and the challenges they pose do not function to undermine that relationship and progress in practice.

NOTES

1. United Nations Children's Fund (UNICEF) and World Bank Group, "Ending Extreme Poverty: A Focus on Children," briefing note (October 2016), https://www.unicef.org/publications/index_92826.html. The data were based on feedback from eighty-nine countries representing just over 84 percent of the developing world's population.
2. Chris Brazier, "Building the Future: Children and the Sustainable Development Goals in Rich Countries," *Innocenti Report Card 14* (2017), https://www.unicef-irc.org/publications/pdf/RC14_eng.pdf; see also Bea Cantillon, Yekaterina Chzhen, Sudhanshu Handa, and Brian Nolan, *Children of Austerity: Impact of the Great Recession on Child Poverty in Rich Countries* (Oxford: UNICEF and Oxford University Press, 2017).
3. See, e.g., UN Committee on the Rights of the Child (CRC Committee), *General Comment No. 19 on Public Budgeting for the Realization of Children's Rights (art. 4)*, UN Doc. CRC/C/GC/19 (2016); Office of the UN High Commissioner for Human Rights (OHCHR), "Towards Better Investment in the Rights of the Child," UN Doc. A/HRC/28/33 (2014); UN Human Rights Council, "Rights of the Child: Towards Better Investment in the Rights of the Child," UN Doc. A/HRC/RES/28/19 (April 7, 2015).

4. See, e.g., UNICEF, "The State of the World's Children 2016: A Fair Chance for Every Child," (June 2016), https://www.unicef.org/publications/index_91711.html.

5. Isabel Ortiz, Jingqing Chai, and Matthew Cummins, "Identifying Fiscal Space: Options for Social and Economic Development for Children and Poor Households in 184 Countries," UNICEF Working Paper (2011).

6. International Labour Organization (ILO), "World Social Protection Report 2017–19: Universal Social Protection to Achieve the Sustainable Development Goals," ILO flagship report (Nov. 29, 2017), https://www.ilo.org/global/publications/books/WCMS_604882/lang--en/index.htm (For more on this point generally, see pps. 11–22.).

7. For more on the adoption of austerity measures after 2007–2008, see UNICEF Office of Research, "Children of the Recession: The Impact of the Economic Crisis on Child Well-Being in Rich Countries," *Innocenti Report Card 12* (October 2014), https://www.unicef-irc.org/publications/733-children-of-the-recession-the-impact-of-the-economic-crisis-on-child-well-being-in.html; Isabel Ortiz Jingqing Chai, and Matthew Cummins, "Austerity Measures Threaten Children and Poor Households: Recent Evidence in Public Expenditures from 128 Countries," UNICEF Division of Policy and Strategy Working Paper (Sept. 29, 2011; last revised Nov. 4, 2013), 1107.

8. See, e.g., UNICEF, "Poverty Reduction Begins with Children" (March 2000), https://www.unicef.org/publications/files/pub_poverty_reduction_en.pdf.

9. See the reference to children's rights in multiple anti-poverty–related aspirations outlined in "Africa's Agenda for Children 2040: Fostering an Africa Fit for Children," adopted by the African Committee of Experts on the Rights and Welfare of Children and approved by the African Union Executive Council of Ministers in July 2017. See also EU Commission, "Investing in Children: Breaking the Cycle of Disadvantage," EU Commission Recommendation, 2013/112/EU (Feb. 20, 2013), which recommended that EU member states "[a]ddress child poverty and social exclusion from a children's rights approach, in particular by referring to the relevant provisions of the Treaty on the European Union, the Charter of Fundamental Rights of the European Union and the UN Convention on the Rights of the Child, making sure that these rights are respected, protected and fulfilled."

10. For a critical analysis of the World Bank's approach to human rights in terms of its functionings, see UN Human Rights Council, "Report of the Special Rapporteur on Extreme Poverty and Human Rights," A/70/274 (2015).

11. For useful discussions of different approaches see Alberto Minujin, Enrique Delamonica, Alejandra Davdiziuk, and Edward Gonzalez, "The Definition of Child Poverty: A Discussion of Concepts and Measurements," *Childhood* 18, no. 2 (October 2006): 481–500; Alberto Minujin and Shailen Nandy, eds., *Global Child Poverty and Well-Being: Measurements, Concepts, Policy and Action* (Bristol, UK: Policy Press, 2012); Gerry Redmond, "Poverty and Social Exclusion," in *Handbook of Child Well-Being: Theories, Methods and Policies in Global Perspective*, ed. Asher Ben-Arieh, Ferran Casas, Ivar Frønes, and Jill E. Korbin (Amsterdam: Springer, 2014), 1387–1426.

12. See, e.g., UN General Assembly, Resolution 61/146 on the Rights of the Child, para. 46, G.A. Res. 61/146, 61st Sess., UN Doc. A/RES/61/146 (Dec. 19, 2006).

13. See, e.g., UN Committee on Economic Social and Cultural Rights, "Statement on Poverty and the International Covenant on Economic Social and Cultural Rights," UN Doc. E/C.12/2001/10 (2001).

14. See, e.g., the definition of "extreme poverty" employed by the UN Special Rapporteur on Extreme Poverty and Human Rights inOHCHR, "Guiding Principles on Extreme

Poverty and Human Rights," 2, https://www.ohchr.org/Documents/Publications/OHCHR_ExtremePovertyandHumanRights_EN.pdf (accessed Aug. 25, 2019).

15. UN Committee on Economic Social and Cultural Rights, "Statement on Poverty."

16. For a useful overview of the most prominent accounts of the capability approach(es) see Martha Nussbaum, *Creating Capabilities: The Human Development Approach* (Cambridge, MA: Harvard University Press, 2013).

17. For a discussion of the basic needs, approach, see the World Bank, "Monitoring Global Poverty: Report of the Commission on Global Poverty," World Bank Report No. 110040 (Oct. 18, 2016), 124–133.

18. See, e.g., UNICEF Innocenti Research Centre, "Child Poverty in Perspective: An Overview of Child Well-Being in Rich Countries," *Innocenti Report Card 7* (2007). It should be noted, however, that understandings of child well-being vary significantly. For more see June Statham and Elaine Chase, "Childhood Wellbeing: A Brief Overview," Childhood Wellbeing Research Centre Briefing Paper 1 (August 2010), http://www.cwrc.ac.uk/documents/CWRC_Briefing_paper.pdf.

19. For examples of work addressing the relationship between children's rights and the capability approach in the context of social justice and child poverty see, e.g., Mario Biggeri and Ravi Karkara, "Transforming Children's Rights into Real Freedom: A Dialogue between Children's Rights and the Capability Approach from a Life Cycle Perspective," in *Children's Rights and the Capability Approach: Challenges and Prospects*, ed. Daniel Stoecklin and Jean-Michael Bonvin (Amsterdam: Springer, 2014), 19–41. For an example of work addressing the relationship between child well-being and the capability approach in this context, see, e.g., Mario Biggeri and Santosh Merhotra, "Child Poverty as Capability Deprivation: How to Choose Domains of Child Well-being and Poverty," In *Children and the Capability Approach*, ed. Mario Biggeri, Jérôme Ballet, and Flavio Comim (New York: Palgrave Macmillan, 2011), 46–75. For an example of work addressing the relationship between child well-being and child rights in the same context, see Organisation for Economic Co-operation and Development, "Doing Better for Children" (2009), https://read.oecd-ilibrary.org/social-issues-migration-health/doing-better-for-children_9789264059344-en#page1.

20. Rosalind Dixon and Martha Nussbaum, "Children's Rights and a Capabilities Approach: The Question of Special Priority," *Cornell Law Review* 97, no. 3 (2012): 549–593.

21. For more see Noam Peleg, "Reconceptualising the Child's Right to Development: Children and the Capability Approach," *International Journal of Children's Rights* 21, no. 3 (2013): 523–542.

22. For an example of the use of the capability approach to measure child well-being (as well as a consideration of the use of CRC rights in determining domains of well-being), see Biggeri and Merhotra, "Child Poverty."

23. See Laura Camfield, Natalia Streuli, and Martin Woodhead, "What's the Use of 'Well-Being' in Contexts of Child Poverty? Approaches to Research, Monitoring and Children's Participation," *International Journal of Children's Rights* 17, no. 1 (2009): 65–109.

24. Jaap Doek, "Child Well-Being: Children's Rights Perspective," in Ben-Arieh et al., *Handbook of Child Well-Being*, 187–217.

25. For instance, the individualist focus of the human rights framework often fails to take into account group or collective rights and does not properly acknowledge the strong link between the individual and the community in which they are based. Jonathan Ensor, "Linking Rights and Culture: Implications for Rights-Based Approaches," in *Reinventing*

Development? Translating Rights-Based Approaches from Theory into Practice, ed. Paul Gready and Jonathan Ensor (London: Zed Books, 2005), 254–277; For a comprehensive analysis of objections about the Western orientation of international human rights law and a discussion of non-Western rights discourses, see Eva Brems, *Human Rights: Universality and Diversity* (The Hague: Martinus Nijhoff, 2001).

26. See, e.g., the holistic approach to human rights demonstrated in UN Human Rights Council, "Extreme Poverty and Human Rights," UN Doc. A/HRC/RES/35/19 (June 22, 2017), the preamble of which emphasizes "that respect for all human rights—civil, political, economic, social and cultural rights—which are universal, indivisible and interdependent and interrelated, is of crucial importance for all policies and programmes to effectively fight extreme poverty at the local and national levels."

27. For authoritative accounts of the application of international human rights standards to non-state actors, see, e.g., Jan Hessbruegge, "Human Rights Violations Arising from Conduct of Non-State Actors," *Buffalo Human Rights Law Review* 21 (March 2005): 21–88; John H. Know, "Horizontal Human Rights Law," *American Journal of International Law* 102, no. 1 (2008): 1–27; UN Committee on Economic, Social and Cultural Rights, *General Comment 24 on State Obligations under the ICESCR in the Context of Business Activities*, UN Doc. E/C.12/GC/24 (2017).

28. For a critique of the cultural bias of the UN CRC see Vanessa Pupavac, "The Infantilisation of the South and the UN Convention on the Rights of the Child," *Human Rights Law Review* 3, no. 2 (1998): 3–8.

29. For a discussion of the limited image of "the child" reflected in the CRC see Michael Freeman, "The Future of Children's Rights," *Children and Society* 14, no. 4 (September 2000): 277–293, 282–285.

30. U.N. Committee on the Rights of the Child. 2017. *General Comment No. 21 (2017) on Children in Street Situations*, UN Doc. CRC/C/GC/21 (2017), para. 49. While the Committee flagged the "particular relevance" of this aspect of 27(3) for children in street situations "with non-existent or abusive family connections," it is clear that this obligation of direct provision to the child may go beyond this to include situations such as those in which children are living in situations with family or others legally responsible for them who may not be in a position to provide nutrition, clothing, and housing due to parental incapacity resulting from severe disability or chronic illness, for example.

31. This is made clear in General Comment No. 12 and the Committee's statement that the views expressed by children "should be considered in decision-making, policymaking and preparation of laws and/or measures as well as their evaluation." CRC Committee, *General Comment No. 12: The Right of the Child to Be Heard*, UN Doc. CRC/C/GC/12 (2009), para. 12.

32. CRC Committee, *General Comment No. 19*, paras. 52–56.

33. See, e.g., UN Convention on the Rights of the Child (CRC), G.A. Res. 44/25, 44th Sess., UN Doc. A/RES/44/25 (1989), art. 4. The obligations imposed by this article are fleshed out in detail in the Committee's General Comment No. 5 on general measures of implementation and General Comment No. 19 on public budgeting for the realization of children's rights. For a critical analysis of the Committee's approach to Article 4, see Aoife Nolan, "Children's Economic and Social Rights," in *International Law on the Rights of the Child*, ed. Ton Liefaard, Ursula Kilkelly, and Stephen Hoadley (Amsterdam: Springer, 2018), 239–258.

34. See, e.g., CRC, art. 27.

35. See CRC Committee, *General Comment No. 16 on State Obligations regarding the Impact of the Business Sector on Children's Rights*, UN Doc. CRC/C/GC/16 (2013), which was the first authoritative interpretation of any UN treaty–monitoring body of the non-state, actor-related responsibilities and obligations under a UN human rights treaty.

36. Laura Lundy, "United Nations Convention on the Rights of the Child and Child Well-Being," in Ben-Arieh et al., *Handbook of Child Well-Being*, 2439–2462.

37. The only UN member state not to have ratified the CRC is the United States.

38. For more on this point and the connection between poverty and CRC rights see Aoife Nolan, "Rising to the Challenge of Child Poverty: The Role of the Courts," in *Freedom from Poverty as a Human Right: Law's Duty to the Poor*, vol. 4, ed. Geraldine Van Bueren (Paris: UNESCO, 2010).

39. UNICEF has highlighted that "[c]hildren living in poverty face deprivations of many of their rights: survival, health and nutrition, education, participation, and protection from harm, exploitation and discrimination." UNICEF, "The State of the World's Children 2005: Childhood under Threat" (December 2004), 15.

40. UN Human Rights Council, "Report of the Special Rapporteur on Extreme Poverty and Human Rights on the Enjoyment of Civil and Political Rights by Persons Living in Poverty," UN Doc. A/72/502 (Oct. 4, 2017).

41. Geraldine Van Bueren, "Combating Child Poverty: Human Rights Approaches," *Human Rights Quarterly* 21, no. 3 (August 1999): 680–706, 681.

42. CRC Committee, "Treaty-Specific Guidelines regarding the Form and Content of Periodic Reports to be Submitted by States Parties under Article 44, Paragraph 1(b), of the Convention on the Rights of the Child," UN Doc. CRC/C/58/Rev.2 (2010), para. 36.

43. For more detail see Aoife Nolan, "Article 27: The Right to a Standard of Living Adequate for the Child's Development," in *The UN Convention on the Rights of the Child: A Commentary*, ed. John Tobin (Oxford: Oxford University Press, 2019).

44. For instance, post-2012, austerity measures (and other measures taken in response to the crisis) that have impacted negatively on poverty levels have been dealt with by the Committee on Economic, Social and Cultural Rights in terms of the right to an adequate standard of living under Article 11 (and, to a lesser extent, under Article 9 on the right to social security and the right to protection for the family set out in Article 10). See, e.g., UN Committee on Economic, Social and Cultural Rights, "Concluding Observations on the Fourth Report of Iceland, Adopted by the Committee at Its Forty-Ninth Session," UN Doc. E/C.12/ISL/CO/4 (2012), para. 16; UN Committee on Economic, Social and Cultural Rights, "Concluding Observations on the Fourth Periodic Report of Portugal," E/C.12/PRT/CO/4 (2014), para. 14; UN Committee on Economic, Social and Cultural Rights, "Consideration of Reports Submitted by States Parties under Articles 16 and 17 of the Covenant, UN Doc. E/C.12/PRT/CO/5 (2012), paras. 16–17.

45. For statements in a similar vein see e.g., CRC Committee, "Consideration of Reports Submitted by States Parties under Article 44 of the Convention, Concluding Observations: Georgia," UN Doc. CRC/C/GEO/CO/3 (2008), para. 55.

46. CRC Committee, "Consideration of Reports Submitted by States Parties under Article 44 of the Convention, Concluding Observations: Dominican Republic," CRC/C/DOM/CO/2 (2008), para. 69. For further examples of the CRC Committee commenting on the negative impact of poverty/economic hardship/etc., on child development in the context of Article 27 see CRC Committee, "Consideration of Reports Submitted by States Parties

under Article 44 of the Convention, Concluding Observations: Venezuela," UN Doc. CRC/C/VEN/CO/2 (2007), para. 65; CRC Committee, "Consideration of Reports Submitted by States Parties under Article 44 of the Convention, Concluding Observations: Norway," UN Doc. CRC/C/MNG/CO/3–4 (2010), para. 46; CRC Committee, "Consideration of Reports Submitted by States Parties under Article 44 of the Convention, Concluding Observations: Tajikistan," UN Doc. CRC/C/TJK/CO/2 (2010), para. 58; CRC Committee, "Consideration of Reports Submitted by States Parties under Article 44 of the Convention, Concluding Observations: Pakistan," UN Doc. CRC/C/PAK/CO/4 (2009), para. 77; CRC Committee, "Concluding Observations on the Fifth Periodic Report of the United Kingdom of Great Britain and Northern Ireland," UN Doc. CRC/C/GBR/CO/4 (2008), para. 65; CRC Committee, "Consideration of Reports Submitted by States Parties under Article 44 of the Convention, Concluding Observations: Australia," UN Doc. CRC/C/15/Add.268 (2005), para. 57; CRC Committee, "Consideration of Reports Submitted by States Parties under Article 44 of the Convention, Concluding Observations: Sri Lanka," CRC/C/LKA/CO/3–4 (2010), para. 60.

47. CRC Committee, *General Comment No. 7: Implementing Child Rights in Early Childhood*, UN Doc. CRC/C/GC/7/Rev.1 (2005). para. 26.

48. CRC Committee, *General Comment No. 20: The Implementation of the Rights of the Child during Adolescence*, UN Doc. CRC/GC/C/20 (2016), para. 66.

49. CRC Committee, *General Comment No. 20*, para. 67.

50. CRC Committee, *General Comment No. 21*, para. 51.

51. CRC Committee, *General Comment No. 21*, para. 51.

52. CRC Committee, *General Comment No. 21*, para. 51.

53. See, e.g., CRC Committee, "Concluding Observations on the Combined Second to Fourth Periodic Reports of Guyana, Adopted by the Committee at its Sixty-Second Session (14 January–1 February 2013)," UN Doc. CRC/C/GUY/CO/2–4 (2013), para. 56; CRC Committee, "Consideration of Reports Submitted by States Parties under Article 44 of the Convention, Concluding Observations: Belize," UN Doc. CRC/C/15/Add.252 (2005), para. 59; CRC Committee, "Consideration of Reports Submitted by States Parties under Article 44 of the Convention, Concluding Observations: Croatia," UN Doc. CRC/C/15/Add.243 (2004), para. 56; CRC Committee, "Consideration of Reports Submitted by States Parties under Article 44 of the Convention, Concluding Observations: Germany," UN Doc. CRC/C/15/Add.226 (2004), para. 51.

54. CRC Committee, "Day of General Discussion: Children without Parental Care," UN Doc. CRC/C/153 (2005), para. 659.

55. See, e.g., CRC Committee, "Concluding Observations: Norway," para. 47; CRC Committee, "Concluding Observations: Tajikistan," para. 59; CRC Committee, "Concluding Observations: Pakistan," para. 77; CRC Committee, "Consideration of Reports Submitted by States Parties under Article 44 of the Convention, Concluding Observations: Djibouti, UN Doc. CRC/C/DJI/CO/2 (2008), para. 61.

56. See, e.g., CRC Committee, "Consideration of Reports Submitted by States Parties under Article 44 of the Convention, Concluding Observations: Democratic Republic of the Congo," UN Doc. CRC/C/COD/CO/2 (2009), para. 64; CRC Committee, "Consideration of Reports Submitted by States Parties under Article 44 of the Convention, Concluding Observations: Grenada," UN Doc. CRC/C/GRD/CO/2 (2010), para. 50.

57. See, e.g., CRC Committee, "Consideration of Reports Submitted by States Parties under Article 44 of the Convention, Concluding Observations: Indonesia," UN Doc. CRC/C/IDN/CO/3-4 (2014), para. 58.

58. See, e.g., CRC Committee, "Consideration of Reports Submitted by States Parties under Article 44 of the Convention, Concluding Observations: Mauritania," UN Doc. CRC/C/MRT/CO/2 (2009), para. 64; CRC Committee, "Consideration of Reports Submitted by States Parties under Article 44 of the Convention, Concluding Observations: Bhutan," UN Doc. CRC/C/BTN/CO/2 (2008), para. 57; CRC Committee, "Consideration of Reports Submitted by States Parties under Article 44 of the Convention, Concluding Observations: Eritrea," UN Doc. CRC/C/ERI/CO/3 (2008), para. 65.

59. See, e.g., CRC Committee, "Consideration of Reports Submitted by States Parties under Article 44 of the Convention, Concluding Observations: Bulgaria," UN Doc. CRC/C/BGR/CO/2 (2008), para. 54; CRC Committee, "Consideration of Reports Submitted by States Parties under Article 44 of the Convention, Concluding Observations: Cameroon," UN Doc. CRC/C/CMR/CO/2 (2010), para. 64; CRC Committee, "Consideration of Reports Submitted by States Parties under Article 44 of the Convention, Concluding Observations: Bolivia," UN Doc. CRC/C/BOL/CO/4 (2009), para. 62.

60. See, e.g., CRC Committee, "Consideration of Reports Submitted by States Parties under Article 44 of the Convention, Concluding Observations: Kenya," UN Doc. CRC/C/KEN/CO/2 (2007), para. 56; CRC Committee, "Consideration of Reports Submitted by States Parties under Article 44 of the Convention, Concluding Observations: Togo," UN Doc. CRC/C/TGO/CO/3-4 (2012), para. 62.

61. See, e.g., CRC Committee, "Concluding Observations: Germany," para. 51; CRC Committee, "Concluding Observations: Croatia," para. 56.

62. See, e.g., CRC Committee, "Consideration of Reports Submitted by States Parties under Article 44 of the Convention, Concluding Observations: Seychelles," UN Doc. CRC/C/SYC/CO/2-4 (2012), para. 58; CRC Committee, "Consideration of Reports Submitted by States Parties under Article 44 of the Convention, Concluding Observations: Malawi," UN Doc. CRC/C/MWI/CO/2 (2009), para. 61.

63. See, e.g., CRC Committee, "Consideration of Reports Submitted by States Parties under Article 44 of the Convention, Concluding Observations: Liberia," UN Doc. CRC/C/LBR/CO/2-4 (2012), para. 71; CRC Committee, "Consideration of Reports Submitted by States Parties under Article 44 of the Convention, Concluding Observations: Mozambique," UN Doc. CRC/C/MOZ/CO/2.(2009), para. 69.

64. CRC Committee, "Concluding Observations: Bhutan," para. 37; CRC Committee, "Concluding Observations: Cameroon," para. 37.

65. CRC Committee, "Consideration of Reports Submitted by States Parties under Article 44 of the Convention, Concluding Observations: Suriname," UN Doc. CRC/C/SUR/CO/3-4 (2016), para. 33.

66. CRC Committee, "Concluding Observations: Seychelles," para. 58.

67. See, e.g., CRC Committee, "Consideration of Reports Submitted by States Parties under Article 44 of the Convention, Concluding Observations: France," UN Doc. CRC/C/FRA/CO/4 (2009), para. 79; CRC Committee, "Concluding Observations on the Fifth Periodic Report of the United Kingdom of Great Britain and Northern Ireland," para. 65.

68. See, e.g., CRC Committee, "Consideration of Reports Submitted by States Parties under Article 44 of the Convention, Concluding Observations: Portugal," UN Doc. CRC/C/PRT/CO/304 (2014), para. 51; CRC Committee, "Consideration of Reports Submitted by

States Parties under Article 44 of the Convention, Concluding Observations: Ukraine," UN Doc. CRC/C/UKR/CO/3-4 (2012), para. 65; CRC Committee, "Concluding Observations: Mauritania," para. 64; CRC Committee, "Consideration of Reports Submitted by States Parties under Article 44 of the Convention, Concluding Observations: Oman," UN Doc. CRC/C/OMN/CO/2 (2006), para. 54.

69. See, e.g., CRC Committee, "Consideration of Reports Submitted by States Parties under Article 44 of the Convention, Concluding Observations: Burkina Faso," UN Doc. CRC/C/BFA/CO/3-4 (2010), para. 63; CRC Committee, "Concluding Observations: Cameroon," para. 64; CRC Committee, "Concluding Observations: Eritrea," para. 64.

70. See, e.g.,CRC Committee, "Consideration of Reports Submitted by States Parties under Article 44 of the Convention, Concluding Observations: Serbia," UN Doc. CRC/C/SRB/CO/1 (2008), para. 59; CRC Committee, "Consideration of Reports Submitted by States Parties under Article 44 of the Convention, Concluding Observations: Philippines," UN Doc. CRC/C/PHL/CO/3-4 (2009), para. 64; CRC Committee, "Consideration of Reports Submitted by States Parties under Article 44 of the Convention, Concluding Observations: Greece," UN Doc. CRC/C/GRC/CO/2-3 (2012), para. 59.

71. CRC Committee, "Consideration of Reports Submitted by States Parties under Article 44 of the Convention, Concluding Observations: Hungary," UN Doc. CRC/C/HUN/CO/2 (2006), para. 47.

72. See, e.g., CRC Committee, "Concluding Observations on the Second to Fourth Periodic Reports of Republic of Congo," UN Doc. CRC/C/COG/CO/2-4 (2024), para. 65; CRC Committee, "Concluding Observations on the Combined Second to Fourth Periodic Reports of Sao Tome and Principe," UN Doc. CRC/C/STP/CO/2-4 (2013), para. 39.

73. CRC Committee, *General Comment No. 9 (2006): The Rights of Children with Disabilities*, UN Doc. CRC/C/GC/9 (2007), para. 3.

74. CRC Committee, *General Comment No. 9*, para. 3.

75. See UNICEF, *The State of the World's Children: Children with Disabilities* (New York: UNICEF, 2013).

76. See, e.g., CRC Committee, "Concluding Observations: Democratic Republic of the Congo," para. 64.

77. CRC Committee, "Consideration of Reports Submitted by States Parties under Article 44 of the Convention, Concluding Observations: Timor Leste," UN Doc. CRC/C/TLS/CO/1 (2008), para. 61.

78. CRC Committee, "Concluding Observations: Canada," paras. 67–68.

79. See e.g., CRC Committee, "Concluding Observations on the Sixth Periodic Report of the United Kingdom of Great Britain and Northern Ireland," UN Doc. CRC/C/GBR/CO/5 (2016), para. 70.

80. See, e.g., CRC Committee, "Concluding Observations: Tajikistan," para. 59; CRC Committee, "Consideration of Reports Submitted by States Parties under Article 44 of the Convention, Concluding Observations: Sweden," UN Doc. CRC/C/SWE/CO/4 (2009), para. 53; CRC Committee, "Concluding Observations: Spain," para. 37.

81. See, e.g., CRC Committee, "Concluding Observations: Pakistan," para. 77; CRC Committee, "Concluding Observations: Djibouti," para. 61.

82. Nolan, "Article 27."

83. For a critique of the CRC Committee's historic non-engagement with Article 4, see Aoife Nolan, "Economic and Social Rights, Budgets and the Convention on the Rights of the Child," *International Journal of Children's Rights* 21, no. 2 (2014): 248–277.

84. For more see Nolan, "Economic and Social Rights."

85. For examples of notable exceptions with regard to academic engagement with child economic and social rights obligations in a poverty-related context see John Tobin, "Article 4," in Tobin, *U.N. Convention on the Rights of the Child: A Commentary*; Wouter Vandenhole, "Economic, Social and Cultural Rights in the CRC: Is There a Legal Obligation to Cooperate Internationally for Development?," *International Journal of Children's Rights* 17, no. 1 (2009): 23–63.

86. CRC Committee, *General Comment No. 19*, para. 1.

87. CRC Committee, *General Comment No. 19*, para. 3.

88. This obligation is set out in Article 4 and is referred to in a number of other provisions in the CRC (Articles 17(b), 22(2), 23(4), 24(4), 28(3), and 45). For more on this obligation see Vandenhole, "Economic, Social and Cultural Rights"; Nolan, "Economic and Social Rights."

89. CRC Committee, *General Comment No. 19*, para. 65.

90. CRC Committee, *General Comment No. 19*, paras. 36 and 37.

91. See, e.g., Maastricht Principles on Extraterritorial Obligations of States in the Area of Economic, Social and Cultural Rights (2013), https://www.etoconsortium.org/nc/en/main-navigation/library/maastricht-principles/?tx_drblob_pi1%5BdownloadUid%5D=23; Committee on Economic, Social and Cultural Rights *General Comment No. 24 on State Obligations under the International Covenant on Economic, Social and Cultural Rights in the Context of Business Activities*, UN Doc. E/C.12/GC/24 (2017).

92. CRC Committee, *General Comment No. 5 (2003): General Measures of Implementation of the Convention on the Rights of the Child*, UN Doc. CRC/GC/2003/5 (2003), para. 64.

93. CRC Committee, *General Comment No. 16*, para. 48.

94. CRC Committee, *General Comment No. 16*, para. 47.

95. CRC Committee, *General Comment No. 16*, para. 78.

96. See, e.g., UN Human Rights Council, "Report of the Independent Expert on the Effects of Foreign Debt and Other Related International Financial Obligations of States on the Full Enjoyment of All Human Rights, Particularly Economic, Social and Cultural Rights," UN Doc. A/HRC/37/54 (2017).

97. UN General Assembly, "Transforming Our World: The 2030 Agenda for Sustainable Development," UN Doc. A/RES/70/1 (2015).

98. UN General Assembly, "2030 Agenda," Target 1.2 (emphasis added).

99. See UN General Assembly, "2030 Agenda," Targets 2.2, 3.2, 4.1, and 4.2.

100. UN General Assembly, "2030 Agenda," Target 8.7.

101. UN General Assembly, "2030 Agenda," Target 5.3.

102. UN General Assembly, "2030 Agenda," Target 16.2.

103. This is largely unsurprising given the historic failure of development goals and processes to integrate rights standards and implementation processes meaningfully. While the SDGs are a significant improvement on the Millennium Development Goals in terms of their recognition of rights instruments and issues, they are far from child "rights-proofed" in terms of language and implementation processes.

104. See UN General Assembly, "2030 Agenda," paras. 10 and 18.

105. The CRC is also explicitly cited as a key standard to be taken into account in fostering "a dynamic and well-functioning business sector." UN General Assembly, "2030 Agenda," para. 67.

106. UNICEF, *Mapping the Global Goals for Sustainable Development and the Convention on the Rights of the Child* (New York: UNICEF, 2016), 4–6.

107. See, e.g., European Union, *EU Guidelines for the Promotion and Protection of the Rights of the Child* (Brussels: EU, 2017), 5.

108. UNICEF, *Innocenti Report Card 14*, 4.

109. With regard to SDG 1.2, see, e.g., CRC Committee ,"Concluding Observations on the Sixth Periodic Report of the United Kingdom of Great Britain and Northern Ireland," para. 71. With regard to SDG 1.3, see, e.g., CRC Committee, "Concluding Observations on the Fifth Periodic Report of Romania," UN Doc. CRC/C/ROU/CO/5 (2017), para. 37; CRC Committee, "Concluding Observations on the Combined Rourth and Fifth Periodic Report of Lebanon," UN Doc. CRC/C/LBN/CO/4–5 (2017), para. 33.

110. For more on this see Aoife Nolan and Simon McGrath, "Submission to OHCHR Call for Inputs on the Protection of the Rights of the Child and 2030 Agenda for Sustainable Development," http://www.ohchr.org/Documents/Issues/Children/2030/UniversityNottingham.pdf (accessed Aug. 26, 2019).

111. See, e.g., Office of the UN High Commissioner for Human Rights (OHCHR), "Report of the UN Expert on Extreme Poverty and Human Rights," UN Doc. A/HRC/32/31 (2016).

112. See, e.g., UN Secretary-General, "Economic, Social and Cultural Rights and the Sustainable Development Goals: A Convergent Agenda," UN Doc. A/HRC34/25 (2016).

113. See, e.g., OHCHR, "Rights of the Child: The Protection of the Rights of the Child in the Implementation of the 2030 Agenda," UN Doc. A/HRC/34/L.25 (2017).

114. The UNMGCY self-describes as the "UN General Assembly–mandated official, formal and self-organised space for children and youth (under 30) to contribute to and engage in certain intergovernmental and allied policy processes at the UN." UN Major Group for Children and Youth, "Who Are We?" https://www.unmgcy.org/about (accessed Aug. 26, 2019).

115. The 178 governments at the first UN Conference on Environment and Development in 1992 (the Earth Summit) adopted Agenda 21, which formalized nine sectors of society as the main channels through which broad participation would be facilitated in UN activities related to sustainable development (https://sustainabledevelopment.un.org/content/documents/10132EGM-Summary_Comments_11May_final.pdf). These nine sectors are known as "Major Groups."

116. Summary Expert Group Meeting, "HLPF 2016: Shaping the reporting by Major Groups and Other Stakeholders on Their Contribution to the Implementation of the 2030 Sustainable Development Agenda" (April 19, 2016), https://sustainabledevelopment.un.org/content/documents/10132EGM-Summary_Comments_11May_final.pdf.

117. For more on this point see Aiofe Nolan, "Not Fit for Purpose? Human Rights in Times of Financial and Economic Crisis," *European Human Rights Law Review* 4 (2015): 358–369.

118. UN General Assembly, "The Addis Ababa Agenda of the Third International Conference on Financing for Development," UN Doc. A/69/L.82 (2015).

119. Center for Economic and Social Rights, "Two Years On: Can Human Rights Save the 2030 Agenda?" (Feb. 15, 2008), http://www.cesr.org/two-years-can-human-rights-rescue-2030-agenda.

CHAPTER 21

SITUATING THE RIGHTS VERSUS CULTURE BINARY WITHIN THE CONTEXT OF COLONIAL HISTORY IN SUB-SAHARAN AFRICA

AFUA TWUM-DANSO IMOH

1 INTRODUCTION

THE observation that human rights and culture are positioned as logically opposed and antithetical has long framed debates within academic, policy, and practitioner discourses.[1] With their focus on the individual, human rights were said to infringe on collective identity and the cultural norms of societies in diverse contexts. In turn, cultures, and their attendant beliefs and practices, were seen to present severe obstacles to the realization of human rights.

On the specific issue of children's rights, these tensions between individual-focused rights and collective-centered cultures have been played out to great effect.[2] In particular, much of the discussion around children's rights seeks to show how its implementation in parts of the Global South has been obstructed by long-held and deep-seated traditions that have been passed from generation to generation. Such norms are seen to still guide the worldview of a community in how it raises and socializes its children—leading to the prevalence of practices that are perceived to be violations of the very concept of rights. Notable examples are child marriage, female genital cutting, and ritual servitude. In some contexts, these concepts—human rights and culture—are perceived and discussed as if they are mutually exclusive. A choice, it is argued, has to be made between the two.[3]

The framing of these two concepts in this way has led to the creation of a dichotomy that has long dominated debates around human rights/children's rights versus culture. This, in turn, has led to discussions that are often polarizing and, hence, restricted in their ability to foster and facilitate meaningful dialogue and the development of interventions that can have a significant impact on the lives of real children living in their social, cultural, and economic contexts.

While in recent years academic debates on the issue have undergone a shift that recognizes that culture and rights are not necessarily mutually exclusive, discussions on this issue remain polarized, at least in policy and practice discourses.[4] This is problematic because the reality of people's lives demonstrates the complexities that frame their worldview and that proceed to shape the decisions they make and the actions they take, not only in relation to themselves but also in relation to their families. These lived realities experienced by individuals within a locale, further highlighted by the campaigns of increasingly vocal marginalized groups,[5] have underscored the critical need to problematize the dichotomy that exists between rights and culture. Added to these voices that underpin such campaigns are more theoretical arguments that critique this binary approach as ahistorical and essentializing for both the concepts of rights and culture, as it fails to recognize the dynamic nature of both.[6] Further, such an approach focusing on binaries has been accused of creating a sharp divide "between the West and the rest of the world" that "just does not exist."[7]

These critiques that have increasingly led to the problematization of this dichotomy can be attributed in part to the intensification of globalization processes in recent decades. However, alongside this consideration must be an examination of the historical context of a society and its implications for that society's relationship to the concept of culture and the concept of rights. Therefore, by focusing on the individuality of human rights versus the principles of collectivity that underpin the social system of many societies, this chapter will explore the role of one historical event—colonial rule and its attendant missionary activities—in shaping a society's relationship to both the cultures that underpin its communities as well as the dominant notion of human rights. To achieve this aim, the chapter will first provide an analysis of the centrality of individuality to the concept of human rights by situating it within a discussion of the vision of the human person developed in Western Europe and North America during the Enlightenment. In order to highlight how this has been seen as an obstacle to the realization of rights in other parts of the world, the chapter then illustrates how different societies have produced different visions of the human being with a specific focus on contexts within sub-Saharan Africa. While acknowledging the ways that these different conceptions of a human being remain in evidence, the section that follows proceeds to problematize the binary created that separates these cultures and global human rights principles. In particular, this is done by situating formerly colonized territories in sub-Saharan Africa within the context of their colonial history, especially as it relates to childhood and child rearing. Although placing an emphasis on this historical backdrop is critical, the chapter also illustrates that any new norms and values exported through colonial rule have not led to a wholesale replacement of cultural norms and the importance of community well-being, at least in relation to childhood constructions and the well-being of children. Instead, both old and new norms that have filtered through exist in an unstable relationship which reflects the instability characterized by colonialism and its legacy on these societies. What this means, then, is that framing the concept of rights and culture in binary terms is limiting and prevents a holistic under-standing of the complexities of children's everyday lives on the continent. Therefore, the paper concludes by suggesting the adoption of a framework which centers its analysis of studies of childhood in sub-Saharan Africa along a continuum. While at one end of the continuum is evidence of how children's lives are disconnected from global human rights discourses, at the other end are examples that illustrate the existence of greater synergy between children's experiences and dominate rights principles. In between these two extremes is a myriad of other positions and standpoints in relation to both culture and global human rights.

In addition to reviewing existing literature, this chapter draws on data collected in 2005 and 2006 as part of a research study on the implementation of the Convention on the Rights of the Child (CRC) in two communities in Accra, the capital of Ghana, the first country to ratify the Convention. Although data were collected from adults and children, only data from the 376 participating children, collected through participant observation, focus group discussions, participatory activities, and questionnaire admin-istration, are presented.

2 Individuality versus Collectivism: Creation of a Binary between the West and the Rest

The notion of individuality lies at the very heart of human rights doctrine, as the new vision of a human being that emerged in Western Europe and North America during the course of the eighteenth century recognized the individual as the core unit of society.[8] The emergence of this vision of what constituted a human being at this time is important as these ideas—about both rights and individuality—originated within *particular* circumstances in a *certain* geographical location at a *specific* moment in historical time. Specifically, this historical period, beginning in the early eighteenth century, was marked by social and economic upheavals and transformations that characterized, and accompanied, the modernization and industrialization of Western European and North American societies from the eighteenth century onward. These transformations were driven by developments viewed as distancing these societies from their primitive premodern pasts and transforming them into technologically advanced and rational societies. Key to this process were: the American War of Independence (1775–1783), the French Revolution (1789–1799), the development and spread of Enlightenment ideas and thinking, which were facilitated by the works of such philosophers as John Locke and

Jean Jacques Rousseau; the publication of the book *Rights of Man* by English philosopher Thomas Paine (1791) and its emphasis on the individual; and the shift within these societies from an agrarian mode of production to a capitalist economy and its consequences for individuals.[9] That the vision of a human being produced at this time had a bias toward white men[10] is important to emphasize, as it highlights the narrow scope of who exactly was included in this vision within this historical period.

Not only was this concept of what it is to be human centered on people as autonomous beings, but it also foregrounded the notion that these individuals bear rights simply because of their humanity.[11] Hence, the concept of human rights is bound up with the notion of the human being as an individual and autonomous actor. As Rhoda Howard states:

> Human rights are private, individual and autonomous. They are private because they inhere in the human person him- or-herself immediated by social relations. They are consequently individual: an isolated human being can, in principle, exercise them. In addition, they are autonomous because again, in principle, no authority other than the individual is required to make human rights claims.[12]

These developments provided the backdrop for the production of a new vision of a human being, which centered on the individual as the core unit of society. The focus on autonomy and individuality of the human being, in turn, informed the construction of rights as inalienable, universal, and protective of the individual, who has claims not only against the state but also against the community and family.[13] This concept of rights was further consolidated in the twentieth century as a result of the First and Second World Wars, which were initiated in Western Europe but ultimately impacted and involved large swaths of the world—due either to a lack of choice, as in the case of colonized territories, or because of the desire to support close allies.

Although individualism and autonomy were crucial to the vision of the human being and the concept of human rights that emerged, as the concept evolved to take into account children's needs and freedoms, the emphasis placed on autonomy—which is intricately tied to notions of self-governance, independence, and decision-making—was loosened. This was largely due to perceptions of children as immature, incompetent, and in need of protection by more competent and responsible others—whether they be parents, relatives, or the state. Such a positioning of children in many societies led children's rights advocates, from the earliest days, to set conditions or limitations on the extent to which the notion of autonomy was integrated into the concept of children's rights.[14] This includes the emphasis placed on the role of parental or state control in the realization of children's rights. As Kristina Bentley asserts,

> One of the aspects of parental control over their children is that parents are regarded as being best placed to make decisions for their children about their physical well-being. So parents are usually regarded as being competent to decide and administer things like choices about their children's food, clothing, shelter, and to a large degree their medical treatment. The underlying assumption is that while all

people are deemed to physically own themselves (a classical liberal assumption giving rise to a whole range of human rights), children are not fit or competent to determine what is in their best interests, and so parents exercise these rights of ownership on their behalf until they can.[15]

Hence, while the concept of individualism is core to both the concepts of human and children's rights, the primacy given to the freedom of autonomy differs, and this is ultimately due, in many societies, to differential conceptualizations of childhood as opposed to adulthood.

Focusing on the principle of individuality, it has been observed that the primacy attached to this concept within human and children's rights discourses is reflected in many of the discourses and policies of the UN, as part of what Rachel Burr calls an "overemphasis on the individualistic conceptions of rights in its development of human rights procedures."[16] International instruments, such as the 1948 Universal Declaration of Human Rights and the 1989 Convention on the Rights of the Child—both adopted by the United Nations—have been pointed to as embodying the very concept of rights as individual. This is evidenced in several ways. For example, both, in their aim to convey that human rights are inalienable and universal, focus on the entitlements of each individual regardless of such critical variables as geographical location, gender, race, and religion. In relation to the Convention, Burr claims:

> The CRC is grounded in a modern Western of the self. It is 'I' who have 'rights', it is the 'individual' child who needs protection and support. It is this modern Western sense of self that is referred to and made universally applicable in the internationalized discourses on children's rights.[17]

While the primacy of the individual runs throughout the text of both treaties, it is made especially explicit in certain sections. The following articles in the Universal Declaration are instructive:

> No one shall be subjected to arbitrary interference with his privacy, family, home or correspondence, nor to attacks upon his honour and reputation. Everyone has the right to protection of the law against such interference or attacks (Article 12).

> Everyone has the right to freedom of thought, conscience and religion; this right includes freedom to change his religion or belief, and freedom, either alone or in the community with others and in public or private, to manifest his religion or belief in teaching, practice, worship and observance (Article 18).[18]

Within the CRC the emphasis placed on the individual emerges in much of the wording of the Preamble:

> Recognizing that the child for the full and harmonious development of his or her personality, should grow up in a family environment, in an atmosphere of happiness, love and understanding (para. 6).

> Considering that the child should be fully prepared to live an individual life in society and brought up in the spirit of the ideals proclaimed in the Charter of the United Nations, and in particular in the spirit of peace, dignity, tolerance, freedom, equality and solidarity (para. 7).

These principles are further reflected in the operative provisions of the treaty:

> The child shall be registered immediately after birth and shall have the right from birth to a name, the right to acquire a nationality, as far as possible, the right to know and be cared for by his or her parents (Article 7(1)).

> States Parties shall assure to the child who is capable of forming his or her own views the right to express those views freely in all matters affecting the child, the views of the child being given due weight in accordance with the age and maturity of the child (Article 12(1)).[19]

This focus on individuality that is evident in both treaties does not mean that these treaties do not recognize the importance of the collective or the community. The fact that they do is apparent in a number of articles; for instance, Article 8(1) of the CRC recognizes the human right not only to an identity but also to family relations. However, despite an acknowledgment of the importance of community and culture, the individual remains the core unit of focus.

This individual focus that is core to the human rights idea has been central to arguments put forward about its inapplicability to other parts of the world—notably in Africa and Asia—where societies have developed along different trajectories and have produced different visions of what it is to be a human being.[20]

These different visions of humanity have been well documented in anthropological literature, especially during the twentieth century. In sub-Saharan Africa, for instance, the evidence illustrates that while there were differences in the organization of societies, many—be they matrilineal or patrilineal, highly stratified or more egalitarian—were underpinned by notions of interdependency, sharing, mutual support and aid, collective responsibility, cooperation, and reciprocal obligations.[21] Such values, which were seen to be intrinsic to human society within these contexts,[22] were among those that tied members of a group into what Meyer Fortes described as a "web of kinship."[23] These underlying principles informed the way goods, resources, wealth, and assets were produced, distributed, and shared.[24] A notable example relates to the arrangements made in many societies in the region for the caring and rearing of children. Specifically, within these contexts, children were valued as assets or resources, and as a result, they were expected to be shared.[25] In West Africa, for example, children were born and reared in social, economic, and political contexts where it was believed that children belonged to the entire lineage, not to their biological parents.[26] This created a situation whereby social parenthood[27] emerged as prevalent, not only in times of crises but also as part of everyday child-rearing practices. Hence, in societies where communalism was foregrounded historically, "members of a community are expected to demonstrate a concern for the well-being of others, to do what they can to advance the common good and generally to participate in the life of the community."[28] To offer an example, Kwame Gyeke refers to the traditional belief system among the Akan peoples of Ghana and Côte d'Ivoire that takes, as its departure point, the idea that humans are communal and social by nature. This worldview further informs the vision of the human being that is produced within their context.

> This means that the human person cannot and should not live in isolation from other persons. It also means that social relationships are essential for every human person, for no one is self-sufficient and therefore, no one can, in isolation, function adequately in the social context. The individual requires the relationships of others and the cooperation of others for most of his or her pursuits.[29]

Josiah Cobbah supports this point when he states

> For the African, a philosophy of existence can be summed up as "I am because we are, and because we are therefore I am."[30]

Hence, he insists on recognizing the human being as a cultural being—an argument he believes is relevant also to modern Western societies. This positioning of the individual within the context of the group led to a situation whereby the rights and well-being of the kinship group were prioritized over those of the individual.[31]

The implications of this belief system for the notion of individuality are noteworthy. First, subsuming the concept of the individual within the needs of the collective may lead to the denial of individual rights if doing so will better serve the interest of the community.[32] Janice Windborne, for instance, refers to Elizabeth Zechenter, who argued that such sacrifices are "consistently made by the least powerful for the benefit of the most powerful members of the group."[33] To elucidate this point, it is worth noting two practices. The first, child pawning, also known as debt bondage, found in parts of West Africa well into the twentieth century, involved the transfer of a child from the home of his or her caregivers to that of a third party to be held as collateral for loans usually incurred by a male relative, such as a father or uncle. The labor of these bonded children served as interest paid on loans and was used to pay off the debt owed.[34] The second practice, *trokosi*, is a form of ritual servitude which can still be found in parts of the Volta Region of Ghana. Although there are various entry routes for, invariably, a girl to become a *trokosi*, one of the primary reasons was due to the belief that as an individual within a family had committed a transgression against a god, it was required for one person within that grouping to bear the brunt of the punishment. This involved such girls going to live and work for a fetish priest in their shrine for a number of years.[35] The choice of a girl as the sacrificial lamb to pay the penance for the transgression of her family is due to the belief of the priests that only a virgin can appease the gods for the crime committed.

Second, while rights principles presume that individual entitlements are inalienable and not based on the fulfillment of any condition, many societies south of the Sahara underscore the importance of reciprocal obligations which require an individual to fulfill certain conditions in order to qualify for any stipulated rights. This notion of reciprocity has been well documented as a key feature of social relations in a number of African societies, both in the past and present.[36] In particular, it has been argued that the value of reciprocity gives community members confidence in being able to access support and assistance in times of need.[37] With regard to the dynamics of reciprocity within adult-child relationships, Ghana presents an interesting example. Within this context, research has shown that by giving birth to a child and then proceeding to take care of him or her, parents are issuing a contract, which they expect to be fulfilled by the child, through the undertaking of expected responsibilities and behaviors.[38] In fact, these reciprocal obligations are seen as lifelong, persisting even after the death of parents, with children expected to continue making sacrifices in the name of parents during the course of their lifetime.[39]

Thus, due to different conceptions of what it means to be human, informed by the social organization of a given society, it has been widely accepted that understandings of rights and entitlements within these contexts, even in the present day, may be in stark contrast to dominant human rights principles centered on the individual. The continuation of so-called cultural practices which require certain individuals within the group, normally the least powerful, to make sacrifices for the so-called good of the collective,[40] underscores the continuing priority placed on the group vis-à-vis the individual and its attendant ramifications.

3 SITUATING THE RIGHTS VERSUS CULTURE BINARY WITHIN THE CONTEXT OF COLONIAL HISTORY

Despite the fact that different societies have historically conceptualized the human being in diverse ways, in recent decades there is evidence that an analysis that focuses on these constructs as though they are static and, thus, can still be found in contemporary societies in an almost intact form is misleading. Rhoda Howard has argued, for instance, that people across the African continent are becoming increasingly motivated by "individual, not collective (whether family or societal), advancement."[41] Howard further states that not only are many Africans increasingly thinking of themselves as "individuals with varying wants and needs, but also national economic policies are based more and more on individual acquisition of wealth."[42] Thus, the primacy attached to the individual may not only be a feature of what it means to be a human in Western European and North American societies, as it is evident also in contemporary conceptions of a human being in contexts across sub-Saharan Africa.

Although some have claimed that this notion of the individual was always recognized in some African societies,[43] it is important to explore the impact of historical developments on a society's relationship to the concepts of both culture and rights. This approach is especially pertinent in sub-Saharan Africa, where almost all countries were formally colonized by a small group of Western European countries in the years after the Berlin Conference of 1884–1886. This event, which initiated the so-called scramble for Africa, led to the establishment of branches of European governments in territories at some distance from the seat of power of these countries.[44] These new colonial state structures oversaw the formation of institutions and the introduction of laws and policies, which not only sought to exploit these territories economically but also imposed new ideas, behaviors, and practices as part of a broader civilization agenda. As a result, laws were introduced relating to the payment of compulsory taxes, crime and policing, local administration, hygiene, education, marriage, and social welfare.[45] Questions remain about the overall impact of colonial rule on subjugated peoples. However, the evidence indicates that some transformations were realized within sections of the indigenous population in various territories.

First, the legislative framework introduced by the colonial state in a number of territories sought to "civilize" indigenous people by reproducing legal systems dominant in European societies in these territories.[46] For example, while customary law was acknowledged by the British, English Common Law became the ultimate source of authority in British colonial West Africa.[47] As a result, while the British colonial state committed, or turned a blind eye to, numerous human rights violations in the process of establishing and maintaining their colonies,[48] at the same time they initiated the process of prohibiting certain indigenous practices which they deemed to be in violation of human rights, such as child pawning.[49] Furthermore, employment policies adopted by the British colonial civil service, which recruited Africans in more junior ranks, promoted the idea of a monogamous nuclear family household through, among other things, the type of housing and benefits offered as well as the pension policy applied.[50]

Second, a key element of the historical transformations stimulated by the colonial state in all territories was the introduction of cash into economies that had previously used other forms of currency.[51] While the initial use of the new money was limited, colonial governments in territories across the continent found ways to create a demand for this new currency by, for example, imposing a range of taxes on individuals and households, the forced sale of livestock, and the enforced cultivation of cash crops.[52] The resulting outcome for many territories on the continent was the emergence of the concepts, and the reality, of individualized wealth[53] and private property[54] as well as the realization that this new currency could become a substitute for customary obligation.[55]

The increasing reliance on cash led to a dependency on the market to meet the needs of the household. This resulted in the migration of economically active men from rural areas to urban centers in search of wage employment to be able to meet various needs and demands which now required cash as a form of payment.[56] In the process, social relations were affected in a number of societies. For instance, by moving to urban areas and engaging in a form of wage labor, young men were able to pay for marriage-related costs themselves instead of relying on their elders. This offered them more autonomy in the choice of marriage partners.[57] As individual men increasingly assumed sole responsibility for paying the required bride price, which was key to the initiation of marriage in many societies, they assumed sole responsibility for, and rights over, not just their wife but also any children produced as a consequence of that union. In particular, the costs of raising those children, which increasingly came to consist of school fees,[58] became the responsibility of biological fathers to bear as opposed to the wider kinship group. The implication of these developments in some societies was that children born within such a marriage began to be seen as the sole responsibility of their biological father, which, it has been argued, was critical to forging and strengthening closer bonds within the nuclear family unit.

The efforts made by colonial state authorities were further promoted by non-state actors, such as missionaries, who were operating across the continent before the formalization of European colonial rule. Although there were differences in the approach of different missionary groups based on their denomination, all had arrived in sub-Saharan Africa with the goal of transmitting what they considered to be proper ideas about personhood, marriage, family, and child-rearing to what they considered to be primitive peoples.[59] This emerges in the account provided by Jean Allman focusing on Ghana.

> All mission groups active in Asante in the early 20th century encouraged their members to marry under government ordinance, which limited a husband to one wife, made divorce much more difficult, and entitled a wife to one-third of her husband's estate and children to one-third of their father's estate.[60]

Schooling, which was largely driven by missionary groups, was a principal component of the process of converting and civilizing primitive heathens. As noted above, schools provided missionaries the opportunity to impart, in a systematic way, proper values to children, an effort that sought to counter the perceived negative influence of family and culture. Boarding schools, in particular, provided an effective environment to ensure the transmission and consolidation of the ideas and values of missionaries while reducing engagement with the familial grouping of the child. The impact of this was that children attending these schools were taught to perceive their culture and families as inferior, ultimately leading in some communities to tensions and conflicts between the generations.[61]

The resulting outcome of this colonial history in these territories has been well documented. Writing of transformations in Benin, Erdmute Alber observed that

> A European family image in which children belong above all to their parents has not only been disseminated by churches and missionaries during the colonial period but also written into national law and the younger generation's reception of it is increasingly positive.[62]

In neighboring Nigeria too, Elisha Renne, writing of the southwestern part of the country noted that

> Individuals such as Baba Francis [her key informant around whom this article is centred] who worked as migrant labourers on farms in the South West and who returned to the town as Christians or Muslims, brought new ways of thinking about

wage labour, about kinship and dependency, about training children, and about education, particularly from books such as the Bible and school health text books.[63]

Hence, while economic interests were the driving force behind the scramble for colonies and the subjugation of indigenous societies, the impact of colonial rule had ramifications that were felt much more broadly, including in the private sphere of the family.

With specific regard to how these historical developments fostered a rise in individualism, there is evidence that illustrates that Christianity transmitted new ideas about individuality as well as the nuclear family.[64] Katherine Smythe, in her study of the Fipa of Tanzania, for example, asserts that

> Catholic missionaries contributed to the dismantling of Fipa elders' participation in their grandchildren's upbringing, introducing instead more nuclear ideas of family and more individualized ways of measuring growth.[65]

Furthermore, the introduction of schooling was especially critical in the process of individualization within these contexts. As Howard has argued, "as literacy spreads, knowledge can be, and is acquired privately."[66] This has the potential to facilitate the breakdown of the cohesion of the group.[67] Therefore, no longer did children and young people have to rely on the knowledge of their elders for their own learning and development. The spread of school-based education and its reliance on books meant that they were now able to gain knowledge independently, which may also have led to the development of world views that contrasted with those of previous generations. Thus, colonialization and the widespread evangelization of missionary groups were critical drivers of many of the social and cultural changes witnessed among certain sectors of populations across sub-Saharan Africa in recent decades.

4 A DUALISTIC APPROACH TO HUMAN RIGHTS AND CULTURE: A LEGACY OF COLONIALISM

This recognition of increasingly individualized behavior among certain groups has not displaced the importance placed on culture and community well-being and welfare. Instead, these coexist and influence the lives of individuals to varying degrees. This emerges clearly in Ming-Chang Tsai and Dan-Bright Dzorgbo's recent study on reciprocity in Ghana. Specifically, they found that despite some evidence to suggest that some individuals had retreated from social exchanges key to the notion of reciprocal obligations, the country remains "a society of intense reciprocal exchange networks and relationships," which was evidenced by the small number of self-reliant families included in their sample.[68] Another good example of this relates to a 2016 investigation by the BBC in Malawi, which revealed details of an age-old practice in parts of the country known as sexual cleansing. As part of this ritual, girls and women are required to engage in sexual intercourse with a man after one of the following events: their first menstruation, the death of their husband, or an abortion. The focus in the investigation was on young girls being required to have sex, upon the onset of their first menstruation, with men in their communities appointed for that very task—known as hyenas.[69] In the aftermath of the publication of this news story, there emerged, on social media, mixed reactions from Malawians themselves about the persistence of this ritual. Although some views emerged as strongly in opposition and challenged the pertinence of this practice in contemporary Malawian society, others demonstrated their support for it and, in fact, showed defiance in the face of global condemnation.[70] Hence, the reality of people's lives continues to highlight the key role culture and social norms play in regulating their everyday experiences and social relationships as well as the way they perceive themselves and the world around them. However, and this is the key point underpinning this chapter, these social norms are now required to share space within a society's belief system with other norms that have filtered into these societies, often from other contexts, and are now additionally being used to frame how individuals view the world.

These examples in particular demonstrate the existence of dynamics that operate at both local and national levels and illustrate that far from culture and human rights being mutually exclusive, they are, in fact, mutually implicated. They exist in tandem in the everyday lives of individuals living in diverse contexts. This coexistence of rights and culture has implications for attitudes toward the concepts of human and children's rights in formerly colonized territories in sub-Saharan Africa. Specifically, they show that the relationship to human and children's rights within these contexts can be identified along a continuum. While at one end of the continuum are those who, for instance, practice sexual cleansing in Malawi, at the other end can be found, also in Malawi, those who are actively opposed to, horrified by, and condemn the practice in no uncertain terms. Importantly, in between these polarized positions a variety of standpoints can be identified that support or oppose one of these positions at different levels of intensity. These varying positions along this continuum indicate that there is a need to adopt a more dualistic approach, which acknowledges that formerly colonized societies have relationships to both the concept of rights as well as to the cultures that have long guided the transmission of norms from one generation to the next in their society.

This dual approach is recognized in treaties adopted by the Organisation of African Unity, now known as the African Union. For example, a comparison between the African Charter on the Rights and Welfare of the Child and the CRC reveals that both place a priority on the individuality of children's rights. At the same time, both also recognize the importance of the family, the community, and the need for children to respect parents. While these are evident in, for instance, Article 3(2), Article 5, and Article 29(1)(c) of the CRC, in the Charter they can be identified, most notably, in Article 10, Article 18, and Article 31. The point of difference is that the African Charter incorporates these elements to a greater degree of intensity than the Convention. Hence, for example, the CRC stipulates in Article 29(1)(c) that

> States Parties agree that the education of the child shall be directed to:...(c) The development of respect for the child's parents, his or her own cultural identity, language and values, for the national values of the country in which the child is living, the country from which he or she may originate, and for civilizations different from his or her own.

In its turn, Article 31(a) of the Charter states

> Every child shall have responsibilities towards his family and society, the State and other legally recognized communities and the international community. The child, subject to his age and ability, and such limitations as may be contained in the present Charter, shall have the duty to work for the cohesion of the family, to respect his parents, superiors and elders at all times and to assist them in case of need.

These extracts from the two treaties show that there is a basic agreement between them about the importance of the community or the collective for the rights-bearing individual. However, the language of the Charter places a stronger emphasis than the CRC on the responsibilities of the child toward his or her parents and family more generally. For example, while the CRC makes a brief mention of the importance of "the development of respect for the child's parents," the Charter expands this duty of respect to cover not only parents but also "superiors and elders," and this is to be done "at all times." Additionally, the Charter goes further and outlines other expected responsibilities of this child toward his or her family and society as a whole and uses the language of duty to set these out. Therefore, embedded within the Charter is a recognition of both the importance of the individuality of rights and the continuing priority that the notion of communalism or the collective has in the lives of rights-bearing individuals on the continent.

Beyond these treaties, the views of many children across societies in sub-Saharan Africa also reveal the duality in their approach to talking about their rights.[71] In my own study on the implementation of the CRC in Ghana, the views expressed by both school-going and out-of-school children illustrated how the desire for schooling was not only due to the expectations arising from their responsibility to their communities but also because of the individual benefits they believed education could offer—a bright future for themselves or the potential to become someone in their own right. These ideas are reflected in the following comments by child participants:

- Children should go to school, so you can have a bright future (FGD with Nima school children III, Tuesday December 13, 2005).
- Children have the right to education, so they can get work in future (FGD with Ga Mashie school children I, Friday Feb. 26, 2006).

- Education [is the most important right]—you must be educated to become somebody because then your parents cannot force you to…(FGD with Nima school children Children I, October to December 2005).
- Education [is the most important right]—so you can take care of yourself in future…(FGD with Nima school children I, October to December 2005).
- To be educated—if you don't go to school your future won't go well (FGD with Nima school children I, October to December 2005).
- School is number one because if you do not go to school today it will worry you in future because you won't be able to get jobs (FGD with Nima out-of-school children II, Thursday Jan. 19, 2006).
- Parents must take their children to school and provide them with everything they need to stay in school. If a child is sent to school, he will grow up to become a responsible person and will take care of his parents (FGD with Nima out-of-school children I, Tuesday Feb. 14, 2006).
- Children have the right to education. Without education the child cannot develop, and the country will not develop (FGD with Ga Mashie school children IV, Tuesday Feb. 28, 2006).
- [Children have the] right to go to school so you can get a job when you grow up and look after your mother and father (FGD with Ga Mashie out-of-school children II, Feb. 10, 2006).
- Children have the right to go to school and when you grow up get money to look after your mother and father (FGD with out-of-school children organized by the Sempe Mantse We, Friday Feb. 10, 2006).

The rationale for highlighting the importance of the right to education is based on the benefits children believe will accrue to either themselves, their families/communities, or, in the case of some children, both. What emerges, both at the level of a regional charter such as the African Charter on the Rights and Welfare of the Child and in individual children's responses in Ghana and elsewhere, is that within the context of sub-Saharan Africa, there is an understanding of the individuality of human and children's rights. However, this is often accompanied by an insistence on the importance of culture as well as community welfare and well-being in the life of a rights-bearing individual—whether a child or an adult.

5 IMPLICATIONS OF A DUALISTIC APPROACH FOR CHILDREN'S RIGHTS DISCOURSES

This acknowledgment of the importance placed on both the individual and the group is an indication that contemporary sub-Saharan Africa is caught between two legacies. The first relates to norms that have been transmitted from generation to generation since the precolonial period. The second involves values that have been imbibed because of a more recent historical event—colonialism and its attendant missionary engagement. These two legacies intersect at a crossroads and create a situation whereby, within particular contexts across the continent, the relationship between these societies and human rights principles are varied, fluid, and inconsistent. Howard supports this point when she asserts that "people are quite adept at being cultural accomodationists; they are able implicitly to choose which aspects of a 'new' culture they wish to adopt and which aspects of the 'old' they wish to retain."[72] For example, as the data from the child participants in the study above show, education in the context of Ghana is a key priority for both school-going and out-of-school children and their families. However, at the same time, in another study I conducted in this context the findings highlighted the extent to which the physical punishment of children remains socially acceptable to both adults and children who, in large numbers, strongly oppose efforts to prohibit the practice.[73] Hence, the relationship of this society to some rights varies from its relationship to others. These variances also differ according to social group based on such variables as socioeconomic background, education level, and geographical location.

The unstable relationship between communities in this context and the dominant notion of human and children's rights is reflective of the "the unstable and contingent result of a situated encounter" that Olga Nieuwenhuys[74] argues must be recognized in studies focusing on childhoods within formerly colonized territories. This is also consistent with Marie-Bénédicte Dembour's[75] insistence on framing this relationship between rights and culture, not as a middle ground, as I have done elsewhere,[76] but as an unstable pendulum which swings from one extreme to the other. Such a framing is an indication of the extent to which the relationship to rights found within communities in sub-Saharan Africa is located along a continuum, with diverse groups interacting with the notion of rights to varying degrees. That there is such a variation in how groups within a particular locale interact with the global human rights discourse can arguably be attributed to the colonial legacy with which former colonial territories still must grapple. Therefore, binary thinking between rights and culture, and between individuality and collectivity, ignores the historical dynamics of social norms, colonial rule, and missionary engagement. This failure to consider these elements and their interactions with each other ultimately provides an analysis which is not only limited but also disconnected from the contemporary realities of children's everyday lives which must be understood as historically situated.[77]

6 CONCLUSION

Thus, by situating the understanding of, and relationship to, human and children's rights within a historical context, it becomes apparent that the construction of a binary—be it between rights and culture or between individuality and communalism—is not reflective of the situated realities of the lives of children and adults within these contexts, which are shaped by the legacy of colonialism as well as the legacy of cultural and social norms. Instead, it would be more pertinent within this context to understand the relationship local communities have to human rights as framed by a continuum.[78] While at one end of the continuum are actions that indicate the existence of a stark binary between rights and culture, at the other are those that reflect a synergy between the two. Between these two extremes are actions that demonstrate the various ways global rights and the cultures of a community interact in the lives of ordinary people with varying levels of intensity. Key to understanding this interaction are the fluidity, variability, and inconsistencies underpinning this relationship—a reflection of societies caught between multiple legacies that sometimes contradict and, at other times, reinforce each other.

Notes

1. Sally Merry, "Changing, Rights, Changing Culture"; Jane Cowan, Marie-Bénédicte Dembour, and Richard Wilson, "Introduction"; and Marie-Bénédicte Dembour, "Following the Movement of a Pendulum: Between Universalism and Relativism," all in *Culture and Rights: Anthropological Perspectives*, ed. Jane K. Cowan, Marie-Bénédicte Dembour, and Richard Wilson (Cambridge: Cambridge University Press, 2001); Janice Windborne, "New Laws, Old Values: Indigenous Resistance to Children's Rights in Ghana," *Atlantic Journal of Communication* 14, no. 3 (September 2006): 156–172; Karen Engle, "Culture and Human Rights: The Asian Values Debate in Context," *N.Y.U. Journal of International Law and Politics* 32 (2000): 291–333; Jane Cowan, "Culture and Rights after *Culture and Rights*," *American Anthropologist* 108, no. 1 (March 2006): 9–24; Rhoda Howard, "Dignity, Community and Human Rights," in *Human Rights in Cross-Cultural Perspectives: A Quest for Consensus*, ed. Abdullahi Ahmed An-Na'im (Philadephia: University of Pennsylvania Press, 1992); Rhoda Howard, "Evaluating Human Rights in Africa: Some Problems of Implicit Comparisons," *Human Rights Quarterly* 6, no. 2 (1984): 160–179; Rhoda Howard, *Human Rights in Commonwealth Africa* (Totowa, NJ: Rowman and Littlefield, 1986).

2. Stuart C. Aitken, "Global Crisis of Childhood: Rights, Justice and the Unchildlike Child," *Area* 33, no. 2 (June 2001): 119–127; Thoko Kaime, "The Struggle for Context in the Protection of Children's Rights: Understanding the Core Concepts of the African Children's Charter," *Journal of Legal Pluralism and Unofficial Law* 58 (2008): 33–68; Olga Nieuwenhuys, "The Ethics of Children's Rights," *Childhood* 15, no. 1 (2008): 4–11; Jo Boyden, "Childhood and the Policy Makers: A Comparative Perspective on the Globalization of Childhood," In *Constructing and Reconstructing Childhood: Contemporary Issues in the Sociological Study of Childhood*, ed. Allison James and Alan Prout (London: Routledge, 1997), 185–219; Erica Burman, "Local, Global or Globalized? Child Development and International Child Rights Legislation," *Childhood* 3 (February 1996): 45–66; Rachel Burr, *Vietnam's Children in a Changing World* (New Brunswick, NJ: Rutgers University Press, 2006); Rachel Burr, "Global and Local Approaches to Children's Rights in Vietnam," *Childhood* 9 (February 2002): 49–61; Karen Valentin and Lotte Meinert, "The Adult North and the Young South: Reflections on the Civilizing Mission of Children's Rights," *Anthropology Today* 25, no. 1 (May 2009): 23–28; Vanessa Pupavac, "Misanthropy without Borders: The International Children's Rights Regime," *Disasters* 25, no. 2 (December 2001): 95–112.

3. Cowan, Dembour, and Wilson, "Introduction"; Thoko Kaime, " 'Vernacularising' the Convention on the Rights of the Child: Rights and Culture as Analytic Tools," *International Journal of Children's Rights* 18, no. 4 (2010): 637–653.

4. Engle, "Culture and Human Rights."

5. Sally Merry, "Anthropology, Law and Transnational Processes," *Annual Review of Anthropology* 21 (1992): 357–379; Cowan, Dembour, and Wilson, "Introduction"; Steven Archibald and Paul Richards, "Converts to Human Rights? Popular Debate about War and Justice in Rural Central Sierra Leone," *Africa* 7, no. 3 (August 2002): 339–367.

6. Nieuwenhuys, "Ethics of Children's Rights"; Kaime, " 'Vernacularising' "; Merry, "Changing, Rights, Changing Culture."

7. Dembour, "Following the Movement of a Pendulum," 59.

8. Windborne, "New Laws, Old Values"; Burr, *Vietnam's Children*; Howard, "Dignity, Community and Human Rights"; Jack Donnelly, "The Relative Universality of Human Rights," *Human Rights Quarterly* 29, no. 2 (May 2007): 281–306; Kaime, " 'Vernacularising' "; Oritsegbubemi Anthony Oyowe, "An African Conception to Human Rights? Comments on the Challenges of Relativism," *Human Rights Review* 15 (2014): 329–347.

9. Howard, "Dignity, Community and Human Rights"; Louise du Toit, "In the Name of What? Defusing the Rights-Culture Debate by Revisiting the Universals of Both Rights and Culture," *Politikon: South African Journal of Political Studies* 4, no. 1 (January 2013): 15–34; Merry, "Changing Rights and Culture"; Cowan, Dembour, and Wilson, "Introduction"; Nieuwenhuys, "Ethics of Children's Rights"; Windborne, "New Laws, Old Values"; Dembour, "Following the Movement of a Pendulum"; Bonny Ibhawoh, "Cultural Relativism and Human Rights: Reconsidering the Africanist Discourse," *Netherlands Quarterly of Human Rights* 19, no. 1 (March 2001): 43–62.

10. du Toit, "In the Name of What?"

11. Jack Donnelly, "Human Rights and Human Dignity: An Analytic Critique of Non-Western Conceptions of Human Rights," *American Political Science Review* 76, no. 2 (June 1982): 303–316.; Donnelly, "Relative Universality of Human Rights"; Burr, *Vietnam's Children*; Howard, "Dignity, Community and Human rights"; Kaime, " 'Vernacularising' "; Ibhawoh, "Cultural Relativism and Human Rights."

12. Howard, "Dignity, Community and Human rights," 82.

13. Merry, "Changing, Rights, Changing Culture"; Howard, "Dignity, Community and Human Rights."

14. See Pupavac, "Misanthropy without Borders"; Debra DeLaet, "Genital Autonomy, Children's Rights, and Competing Rights Claims in International Human Rights Law," *International Journal of Children's Rights* 20 (2012): 554–583; Kristina Bentley, "Can There Be Any Universal Children's Rights?," *International Journal of Human Rights* 9, no. 1 (March 2005): 107–123.

15. Bentley, "Can There Be Any Universal Children's Rights?," 120.

16. Burr, *Vietnam's Children*, 17.

17. Burr, "Global and Local Approaches," 51.

18. Universal Declaration of Human Rights, G.A. Res. 217 (III) A, UN Doc. A/ES/217 (III) (Dec. 10, 1948).

19. UN Convention on the Rights of the Child (CRC), G.A. Res.44/25, 44th Sess., UNDoc. A/RES/44/25 (1989).

20. Burr, *Vietnam's Children*; Engle, "Culture and Human Rights"; Josiah Cobbah, "African Values and the Human Rights Debate: An African Perspective," *Human Rights Quarterly* 9,

no. 3 (August 1987): 309–331. Owoye, "An African Conception to Human Rights?"; Ibhawoh, "Cultural Relativism and Human Rights"; Chi-Chi Undie and Chimaraoke Izugbara, "Unpacking Rights in Indigenous African Societies: Indigenous Culture and the Question of Sexual and Reproductive Rights in Africa," *BMC International Health and Human Rights* 11 no. 3 (December 2011): S2; Howard, *Human Rights in Commonwealth Africa.*

21. Meyer Fortes, *The Web of Kinship among the Tallensi: The Second Part of an Analysis of the Social Structure of a Trans-Volta Tribe* (London: International African Institute and Oxford University Press, 1949); Enid Schildkrout, "Age and Gender in Hausa Society: Socio-Economic Roles of Children in Urban Kano," in *Sex and Age as Principles of Social Differentiation,* ed. J. S. La Fontaine (New York: Academic Press, 1978); Esther Goody, *Context of Kinship: An Essay in the Family Sociology of the Gonja of Northern Ghana* (London: Cambridge University Press, 1973); Jack Goody, "Futures of the Family in Rural Africa," *Population and Development Review* 15 (1989): 119–144; Christine Oppong, *Growing Up in Dagbon* (Accra: Ghana Publishing Corp., 1973) Kwame Gyeke, *African Cultural Values: An Introduction* (Accra: Sankofa Publishing, 1996); Erdmute Alber, Tabea Haberlin, and Jeanett Martin, "Changing Webs of Kinship: Spotlights on West Africa," *Africa Spectrum* 45, no. 3 (2010): 43–67; Bart Rwezaura, "The Concept of the Child's Best Interests in the Changing Economic and Social Contexts of Sub Saharan Africa," in *The Best Interests of the Child: Reconciling Culture and Human Rights,* ed. Philip Alston (Oxford, UK: Clarendon Press, 1994).

22. Gyeke, *African Cultural Values.*

23. Fortes, *Web of Kinship.*

24. Rwezaura, "Concept of the Child's Best Interests"; Erdmute Alber, "Grandparents as Foster Parents: Transformations in Foster Relations between Grandparents and Grandchildren in Northern Benin," *Africa* 74 no. 1 (February 2004): 28–46.

25. Alber, "Grandparents as Foster Parents."

26. Erdmute Alber, "Denying Biological Parenthood: Fosterage in Northern Benin," *Ethnos* 68, no. 4 (2003): 486–506; A. Bame Nsamenang, *Human Development in Cultural Context: A Third World Perspective* (Newbury Park, CA: Sage Publications, 1992).

27. Esther Goody, *Parenthood and Social Reproduction: Fostering and Occupational Roles in West Africa* (Cambridge and New York: Cambridgshire University Press, 1982).

28. Gyeke, *African Cultural Values,* 35.

29. Gyeke, *African Cultural Values,* 36–37.

30. Cobbah, "African Values and the Human Rights Debate," 320.

31. Olusola Ojo, "Understanding Human Rights in Africa," in *Human Rights in a Pluralist World: Individuals and Collectivities,* ed. Jan Berting, Peter Baehr, J. Herman Burgers, Cees Flinterman, Barbara de Klerk, Rob Kroes, Cornelis A. van Minnen, and Koo VanderWal (Wesport, CT: Meckler, 1990); Cobbah, "African Values and the Human Rights Debate"; Ibhawoh, "Cultural Relativism and Human Rights."

32. Rwezaura, "Concept of the Child's Best Interests"; Windborne, "New Laws, Old Values."

33. Windborne, "New Laws, Old Values," 160. See also Elizabeth M. Zechenter, "In the Name of Culture: Cultural Relativism and the Abuse of the Individual," *Journal of Anthropological Research* 53, no. 3 (Autumn 1997): 319–347.

34. Jessica Cammaert, " 'I Want to Follow Kwaku': The Construction of Self and Home by Unfree Children in the Gold Coast c.1941," *Journal of African History* 56 (November 2015): 373–378. Cati Coe, "How Debt Became Care: Child Pawning and Its Transformation in

Akuapem, the Gold Coast, 1874–1929," *Africa* 82, no. 2 (May 2012): 287–311; Elisha Renne, "Childhood Memories and Contemporary Parenting in Ekiti, Nigeria," *Africa* 75, no. 1 (February 2005): 63–82.

35. Sandra Greene, "Modern 'Trokosi' and the 1807 Abolition in Ghana: Connecting Past and Present," *William and Mary Quarterly* 66, no. 44 (October 2009): 959–974.

36. Albert K. Awedoba, *Culture and Development in Africa with Special References to Ghana* (Accra: Institute of African Studies, University of Ghana–Legon, 2002); Afua Twum-Danso, "Reciprocity, Respect and Responsibility: The 3Rs Underlying Parent-Child Relationships in Ghana and the Implications for Children's Rights," *International Journal of Children's Rights* 17, no. 3 (January 2009): 415–432; Ming-Chang Tsai and Dan-Bright S. Dzorgbo, "Familial Reciprocity and Subjective Well-Being in Ghana," *Journal of Marriage and Family* 74, no. 1 (January 2012): 215–228; Lauren Maclean, "Exhaustion and Exclusion in the African Village: The Non-State Social Welfare of Informal Reciprocity in Rural Ghana and Cote d'Ivoire," *Studies in Comparative International Development* 46, no. 1 (March 2011): 118–136.

37. Maclean, "Exhaustion and Exclusion in the African Village"; Tsai and Dzorgbo, "Familial Reciprocity."

38. Twum-Danso, "Reciprocity, Respect and Responsibility."

39. Awedoba, *Culture and Development in Africa*.

40. Rwezaura, "Concept of the Child's Best Interests"; Windborne, "New Laws, Old Values."

41. Howard, *Human Rights in Commonwealth Africa*, 18.

42. Howard, "Evaluating Human Rights in Africa," 176.

43. Gyeke, *African Cultural Values*; Undie and Izugbara, "Unpacking Rights in Indigenous African Societies."

44. Cobbah, "African Values and the Human Rights Debate"; Merry, "Anthropology, Law and Transnational Processes"; Merry, "Changing, Rights, Changing Culture"; Howard, *Human Rights in Commonwealth Africa*; Afua Twum-Danso Imoh, "From the Singular to the Plural: Exploring Diversities in Contemporary Childhoods in Sub-Saharan Africa," *Childhood* 23, no. 16 (August 2016): 455–468.

45. Merry, "Anthropology, Law and Transnational Processes"; Merry, "Changing, Rights, Changing Culture"; Renne, "Childhood Memories and Contemporary Parenting"; Rwezaura, "Concept of the Child's Best Interests"; Jean Allman. "Fathering, Mothering and Making Sense of 'Ntamoba.' " *Africa* 67, no. 2 (1997): 296–321.

46. Ibhawoh, "Cultural Relativism and Human Rights"; Cobbah, "African Values and the Human Rights Debate"; Merry, "Anthropology, Law and Transnational Processes"; Merry, "Changing, Rights, Changing Culture"; Howard, *Human Rights in Commonwealth Africa*.

47. Cobbah, "African Values and the Human Rights Debate."

48. Ibahwoh, "Cultural Relativism and Human Rights"; Howard, *Human Rights in Commonwealth Africa*.

49. Ibhawoh, "Cultural Relativism and Human Rights"; Merry, "Anthropology, Law and Transnational Processes"; Merry, "Changing, Rights, Changing Culture"; Howard, *Human Rights in Commonwealth Africa*; Renne, "Childhood Memories and Contemporary Parenting."

50. Eleanor Fapohunda, "The Nuclear Household Model in Nigerian Public and Private Sector Policy: Colonial Legacy and Socio-Political Implications," *Development and Change* 19, no. 2 (April 1987): 281–294.

51. Alber, Haberlin, and Martin, "Changing Webs of Kinship"; Kenneth Little, "The Study of 'Social Change' in British West Africa," *Africa: Journal of the International African Institute*

23, no. 4 (October 1953):4–284; Allman, "Fathering, Mothering"; Rwezaura, "Concept of the Child's Best Interests"; Merry, "Anthropology, Law and Transnational Processes."

52. Rwezaura, "Concept of the Child's Best Interests"; Merry, "Anthropology, Law and Transnational Processes."

53. Alber, Haberlin, and Martin, "Changing Webs of Kinship."

54. Merry, "Anthropology, Law and Transnational Processes."

55. Little, "Study of 'Social Change' "; Rwezuara, "Concept of the Child's Best Interests."

56. Little, "Study of 'Social Change' "; Rwezaura, "Concept of the Child's Best Interests"; Merry, "Anthropology, Law and Transnational Processes."

57. See, for example, Rwezaura, "Concept of the Child's Best Interests."

58. Rwezaura, "Concept of the Child's Best Interests"; Jean Allman and Victoria B. Tashjian, *I Will Not Eat Stone: A Women's History of Colonial Asante* (Portsmouth, NH: Heinemann; Oxford, UK: James Currey; Cape Town, SA: David Philip, 2000); Allman, "Fathering, Mothering."

59. Allman, "Fathering, Mothering"; Valentin and Meinert, "Adult North and the Young South"; Rwezaura, "Concept of the Child's Best Interests"; Katherine Smythe, "Fipa Childhood: White Fathers' Missionaries and Social Change in Nkansi, Ufipa, 1910–1980," PhD diss., University of Wisconsin 1997.

60. Smythe, "Fipa Childhood," 307.

61. Unokanma Okonjo, *The Impact of Urbanization on the Ibo Family Structure* (Gottingen: Verlag U. Breger, 1970); Smythe, "Fipa Childhood"; Howard, *Human Rights in Commonwealth Africa.*

62. Alber, "Grandparents as Foster Parents," 37.

63. Renne, "Childhood Memories and Contemporary Parenting," 78.

64. Rwezuara, "Concept of the Child's Best Interests"; Smythe, "Fipa Childhood"; Howard, *Human Rights in Commonwealth Africa.*

65. Smythe, "Fipa Childhood," 115.

66. Howard, "Dignity, Community and Human Rights," 93.

67. See also Windborne, "New Laws, Old Values"; Howard, *Human Rights in Commonwealth Africa.*

68. Tsai and Dzorgbo, "Familial Reciprocity," 222.

69. Ed Butler, "The Man Hired to Have Sex with Children," BBC News, July 21, 2016, http://www.bbc.co.uk/news/magazine-36843769.

70. Mphatso Nkhoma, "Nsanje People Defiant to Continue Sexual Ritual as Gender Activists Not Amused with Aniva's 2-Year Jail Term," *Nyasa Times*, Nov. 23, 2016, https://www.nyasatimes.com/nsanje-people-defiant-continue-sexual-ritual-gender-activists-not-amused-anivas-2-year-jail-term/.

71. See Kristen Cheney, *Pillars of the Nation: Child Citizens and Ugandan National Development* (Chicago: University of Chicago Press, 2007); Kaime, " 'Vernacularising' "; Afua Twum-Danso Imoh, "Terminating Childhood: Dissonance and Synergy between Global Children's Rights Norms and Local Discourses about the Transition from Childhood to Adulthood in Ghana," *Human Rights Quarterly* vol. 41 no. 1 (2019): 160–182.

72. Howard, *Human Rights in Commonwealth Africa*, 23.

73. Afua Twum-Danso Imoh, "Children's Perceptions of Physical Punishment in Ghana and the Implications for Children's Rights," *Childhood: A Journal of Global Child Research* 20, no. 4 (January 2013): 472–486; Afua Twum-Danso Imoh, " 'This Is How We Do It Here': The Persistence of Cultural Practices in the Face of Globalized Ideals; The Case of Physical

Punishment of Children in Ghana," in *Childhoods at the Intersection of the Local and Global*, ed. Afua Twum-Danso Imoh and Robert Ame (Basingstoke, UK: Palgrave, 2012), 131–142.

74. Olga Nieuwenhuys, "Editorial: Theorizing Childhood(s): Why We Need Postcolonial Perspectives," *Childhood* 20, no. 1 (February 2013): 3–8.

75. Dembour, "Following the Movement of a Pendulum."

76. Afua Twum-Danso Imoh, "Searching for a Middleground in Children's Rights in Ghana," *Journal of Human Rights* 10, no. 3 (September 2011): 376–392.

77. Nieuwenhuys, "Editorial"; Burman, "Local, Global or Globalized?"; Roy Huijsmans, "Decentring the History of the Idea of Children's Rights," *International Journal of Children's Rights* 24 (2016): 924–929; Sarada Balagopalan, "Constructing Indigenous Childhoods: Colonialism, Vocational Education and the Working Child," *Childhood* 9, no. 1 (February 2002): 19–34; Twum-Danso Imoh, "From the Singular to the Plural."

78. See also Twum-Danso Imoh, "Terminating Childhood."

CHAPTER 22

CLIMATE CHANGE AND CHILDREN'S RIGHTS

CHRISTINE BAKKER

1 INTRODUCTION

> We, the young, have started to move.... United we will rise until we see
> climate justice. We demand the world's decision-makers take responsibility
> and solve this crisis.[1]

THIS striking declaration from schoolchildren across the world who are staging school
strikes and protests not only highlights their awareness of the threats posed by climate
change to their current and future lives but also their determination to act. A better
example of children exercising their participatory rights, as guaranteed by the Convention
on the Rights of the Child (CRC),[2] can hardly be imagined.

The relationship between climate change and children's rights has been explicitly
recognized in the 2015 Paris Agreement on Climate Change, which acknowledges that
Parties should, when taking action to address climate change,

> (R)espect, promote and consider their respective obligations on human rights,...,
> the rights of... children,... as well as... intergenerational equity.[3]

This statement confirms the recognition at the global level that climate change
adversely affects the enjoyment of human rights. The human rights of children[4] are
especially at risk from climate change and its consequences, both directly and indirectly. Indeed, children's right to life is directly affected when they die in hurricanes or
floods caused by climate change. Their right to education is indirectly affected when
children cannot frequent schools as a result of climate-induced migration. In fact, children are uniquely situated to have their human rights violated by climate change for at

least two primary reasons. First, the particular vulnerability of children increases their risk to be affected by the effects of climate change. Second, since climate change causes intergenerational harm, children suffer disproportionally. Consider that the right of children to take part in decisions that are of concern to their lives, both at present and in their future adult lives, is at stake. And consider further that the adverse effects of climate change on children's future economic, social, and cultural rights require specific attention of states when promoting sustainable development, which politically may be difficult to protect to the extent that they are based on the future interests of children: here again, children suffer a risk of current harm and future harm, to the latter of which they are uniquely vulnerable.

Through the adoption and ratification of such international agreements as the 2015 Paris Agreement on Climate Change (Paris Agreement) and CRC, states have committed to respect and fulfill children's rights and also to protect them from threats posed by environmental disasters and climate change. In recent years, the recognition of the links between climate change and children's rights has led to the the publication of several studies and analyses within the UN system.[5] Moreover, children and nongovernmental organizations (NGOs) are increasingly calling on their governments to comply with their obligations under international law, including bringing cases before national courts.

This chapter aims to consider how the enjoyment of children's rights can be endangered by climate change, to critically discuss whether the remedies available to children to hold states accountable for their failure to protect these rights are effective, and to consider how existing limitations could be overcome. To this end, the chapter first examines *which* human rights of children included in the CRC may be adversely affected by climate change and whether children currently have the right to a healthy or adequate environment under human rights law. It then assesses *how* the enjoyment of these rights may be threatened by climate change and how the obligations of states associated with these rights should be interpreted in accordance with the Paris Agreement. This is followed by an analysis of the *impact* of these international legal norms in practice, focusing on children's access to justice before (1) the Committee on the Rights of the Child, (2) regional human rights courts, and (3) national courts, presenting some ongoing climate cases. From this background, the chapter concludes with a discussion of some of the key challenges to the way forward, suggesting that states should adopt a fully integrated approach toward climate adaptation, sustainable development, and their due diligence obligations under the CRC. Moreover, it argues that regional human rights courts should progressively move toward a broader interpretation of the so-called victim requirement when violations occur as a result of a state's failure to effectively address climate change. While the analysis is focused primarily on children's access to justice from a legal perspective, the concluding section of the chapter briefly considers through which other means children, by making use of their participatory rights, can play a role in shaping climate policies and measures that directly concern them.

2 RELEVANT CHILDREN'S RIGHTS (HUMAN RIGHTS) LAW

Provisions of human rights law that are relevant to the protection of children from climate change can be found in the CRC, in specific regional human rights instruments, in particular the African Charter on the Rights and Welfare of the Child, and in international and regional human rights instruments of a general nature.[6] This overview focuses on the relevant provisions in the CRC, inasmuch as it is the most widely ratified and the most specific international human rights convention in the field. This section will first provide a brief overview of *which* children's rights may be adversely affected by climate change (section 2.1). Also the current status of the right to a healthy or adequate environment will be considered (section 2.2) as well as the link between climate change and children's rights as recognized in the Paris Agreement (section 2.3).

2.1 Relevant Provisions in the CRC

The CRC covers a broad range of human rights, combining civil, political, economic, social, and cultural rights. Even though the enjoyment of all the rights of the CRC could, in one way or another, be negatively influenced by climate change, some rights are particularly at risk.[7] Before examining in more detail (section 3) in what way these rights are actually endangered by climate change, this section aims to provide a brief overview of the provisions of the CRC that are the most relevant for this analysis.

In this regard, it should be mentioned that the Committee on the Rights of the Child (CRC Committee) has highlighted the general principles of the CRC that were to help governments in the interpretation of the CRC as a whole and thereby guide its implementation.[8] These principles are the right to non-discrimination (Article 2), the best interests of the child (Article 3), children's right to life, survival, and development (Article 6), and children's right to express their opinions and be heard (Article 12). Given their central role in the implementation of the CRC, these principles also need to be considered when analyzing how children's rights can be affected by climate change and what are the relevant obligations of states to respect, protect, and fulfill these rights.

Moreover, as outlined by UNICEF, in addition to the general principles the CRC covers the following categories of rights: survival and development rights, protection rights, and participatory rights.[9] In each of these categories, some of the rights identified are the most vulnerable to climate change.

Indeed, children's right to life, the most fundamental of the CRC's survival and development rights can be directly at risk from climate change–related extreme weather events. Also, children's right to the highest attainable standard of health (Article 24) and to an adequate standard of living (Article 27) are at risk from climate change, since rising sea levels, extreme drought, and other permanent effects of this phenomenon may lead to unhealthy living conditions, including shortages of clean water and food. Other relevant provisions in this category concern children's right to education (Articles 28 and 29), which can be affected when schools are destroyed, for example, by severe floods or other climate-related catastrophes. Specific articles address the needs of child refugees (Article 22) and children of minority or indigenous groups (Article 30), who are often particularly vulnerable to the effects of climate disasters.

The protection rights of the CRC include the right to protection from all forms of child abuse, including the right to special protection in times of war (Article 38). It has been argued that the effects of climate change, such as extreme drought, can exacerbate conditions that may lead to armed conflict and that they may "induce stress on livelihoods and communities that can potentially result in children being at risk of exploitation and violence, for example increased child labor, abduction, recruitment into fighting forces, sexual violence, and labor migration."[10] Natural disasters also may heighten the risk of children being subjected to trafficking.[11]

Finally, among children's participation rights, the right to express opinions and be heard (Article 12) and the right to information (Article 17) are especially relevant. These rights are meant to help children bring about the realization of all their rights and to prepare them for an active role in society. In the context of climate change these participation rights are crucial, since they aim to ensure that children can express themselves and be informed about climate policies and measures that directly concern them. In this regard, also the participation of today's children in preventing environmental harm for their future adult lives—and even for future generations—needs to be considered.

2.2 The Right to a Healthy or Adequate Environment

The enjoyment of several children's rights is, to a large extent, dependent on a healthy or adequate environment and can therefore also be qualified as environmental or environment-related child rights. This would apply especially to children's right to life, to health, to adequate food, and to clean water.[12] For example, scarcity of clean water for drinking and sanitation leads to illnesses like diarrhea, which in turn is one of the main causes of child mortality. Studies have shown that water contamination through toxic discharges from industries accounts for a high percentage of child deaths worldwide.[13] Also other forms of environmental degradation, such as ground contamination and air pollution, have devastating effects on children's health, especially those already affected by poverty and malnutrition.

These linkages support the view that a human right to an adequate environment needs to be recognized at the international level. Despite the fact that both the UN Sustainable Development Goals (SDGs) and the Paris Agreement, both adopted in 2015, acknowledge the relationship between human rights and the environment, the human right to a healthy or adequate environment is not explicitly recognized at the international level.

However, the right to an adequate or healthy environment has been recognized in several human rights instruments adopted at the regional level in the Inter-American context, Africa, the Association of Southeast Asian Nations (ASEAN), and the Arab League.[14] For example, Article 24 of the African Charter on Human and People's Rights provides that "(a)ll peoples shall have the right to a general satisfactory environment favourable to their development." In the Inter-American System of Human Rights, this right is included in the Protocol of San Salvador (1988), which states in its Article 11(1): "Everyone shall have the right to live in a healthy environment and to have access to basic public services." At the European level, the main regional human rights instrument, the European Convention on Human Rights, which covers primarily civil and political rights, does not include a right to a healthy environment. However, the more recently adopted European Union Charter on Fundamental Rights provides that the improvement of the quality of the environment must be ensured in accordance with the principle of sustainable development. This increasing recognition of a human right to a healthy environment at the regional level could be seen as a first step toward its global acceptance, though the number of cases in which the right to a healthy environment has been invoked is still rather limited. Nevertheless, it has been used to support claims based on other human rights, in particular the right to health. This will be further discussed below (see section 4).

2.3 The Paris Agreement on Climate Change

The Paris Agreement was adopted in December 2015 to succeed and replace the Kyoto Protocol, giving an important new impetus to international efforts to address climate change.[15] While under the Kyoto regime only thirty-seven rich countries (industrialized states and economies in transition) committed themselves to reduce their greenhouse gas (GHG) emissions, all 196 parties to the Paris Agreement agreed to such emission reductions and to other climate policies as laid down in their Nationally Determined Contributions (NDCs). Although the commitments to reduce carbon emissions under the Kyoto Protocol were legally binding, under the Paris Agreement, such commitments are voluntary and thus cannot be legally enforced. This approach was adopted as a concession to the US, China, and others whose economies account for the highest shares of global carbon emissions. The subsequent withdrawal of the United States, announced by US president Donald Trump in June 2017, will reduce the total emission cuts agreed to in Paris by an additional 20 percent—from a level that already fell short of the effort required to keep the rise in global temperatures below two degrees Celsius compared to preindustrial levels.[16] The negative impact of US withdrawal will be offset, in part, by the significant efforts being made by such US states as California, US cities, and the private sector. Despite this serious setback, the Paris

Agreement nonetheless provides the most ambitious and comprehensive framework for international efforts to address climate change.

In this regard, it should be noted that the Paris Agreement—as its predecessors—foresees two types of climate policies, adaptation policies, which aim to adapt to consequences of climate change that already manifest themselves, and mitigation policies, which aim at reducing or slowing down climate change itself through, inter alia, GHG emission reductions. Especially the first type, adaptation policies, often address concerns that are also the subject of efforts aimed at ensuring the enjoyment of children's rights, as will be shown in the following sections of this chapter.

Indeed, the recognition of the linkage between climate change and states' obligations to respect and promote human rights has been formulated in the Paris Agreement more explicitly than in previous agreements:

> Parties should, when taking action to address climate change, respect, promote and consider their respective obligations on human rights, the right to health, the rights of indigenous peoples, local communities, migrants, children, persons with disabilities and people in vulnerable situations and the right to development, as well as gender equality, empowerment of women and intergenerational equity.[17]

Since this paragraph is included in the preamble of the agreement, it does not have any legally binding force.[18] Nevertheless, references to this statement can be found in a resolution of the UN Human Rights Council,[19] a report by the Office of the High Commissioner for Human Rights (OHCHR),[20] and in a report by the Committee on the Rights of the Child.[21] Indeed, the explicit recognition of the relationship between climate change and human rights in the Paris Agreement is significant. It calls on states to ensure that the policies and measures they adopt to address climate change "respect, promote and consider" the state's obligations under human rights law, including the rights of children. This provision not only recalls that states must comply with their due diligence obligations under human rights law to prevent the impacts of climate change from adversely affecting children rights. It also urges them to ensure that their policies and actions aiming to address climate change do not affect either substantive or procedural human rights of children.

3 ASSESSMENT OF THE LAW, INCLUDING RELEVANT PERSPECTIVES AND CRITIQUES

Based on the overview provided above, this section will consider, first, how the identified rights of children can be negatively affected by climate change; second, it will examine how the obligations of states associated with these rights should be interpreted in accordance with the Paris Agreement, considering both the above mentioned preambular provision on human rights and the substantive provisions of the Paris Agreement.

3.1 The Convention on the Rights of the Child (CRC)

3.1.1 *Guiding Principles*

The guiding principles of the CRC are directly relevant for the question how states should interpret the obligations set out in the Convention in relation to the threats posed by climate change. In this regard, children's right to non-discrimination (Article 2) requires states to ensure that the policies adopted in response to climate change duly take account of the rights and vulnerabilities of all children, including those of indigenous children or children of minority groups.[22]

The focus on the best interests of the child (Article 3) has given rise to much debate, in part, because the term *best interests* is not defined in the CRC.[23] In general terms, it could be argued that the best interests of children are negatively affected when the effects of climate change lead to an increased risk of disease and of natural hazards disrupting education and impacting child protection.[24] This principle concerns "*all actions concerning children*, whether undertaken by public or private welfare institutions, courts of law, administrative authorities or legislative bodies," in which these best interests "shall be a primary consideration."[25] Therefore, states must ensure that in policies affecting climate, which can generally be considered to fall within the above mentioned term "actions concerning children," the best interests of the child are taken into account.

The general principle contained in Article 6 (children's right to life, survival, and development) implies that for states, when adopting and implementing climate policies and measures, these rights must be a primary consideration. This also entails the states' duty to take measures to prevent the loss of children's life as a result of climate-related natural disasters. In addition, the general principle of CRC Article 12 (the right to express opinions and be heard) requires that children who are capable of forming their own views be given the opportunity to express these views with regard to all actions taken to address climate change that concern them and that these views be given due weight. This point will be further addressed below, when discussing children's participatory rights.

At this point, it should be recalled that the obligations of states related to civil and political rights, including children's right to life and their right to express their opinions, differ from the obligations related to economic, social, and cultural rights. For this second category of rights, states are required to respect, protect, and fulfill them progressively, and to the "maximum extent of their available resources."[26] A concern may arise that a natural disaster could destroy infrastructure, thereby leaving a state with fewer resources, which would then technically reduce the state's obligations under economic, social, and cultural rights law. However, this concern should not be overblown because, as confirmed by the CRC Committee, the term "available resources" must be considered to cover both the state's national budget and the resources it receives through international (development) cooperation.[27] Such international support is also foreseen through climate financing, as explicitly confirmed in Article 9 of the Paris Agreement.

3.1.2 *Survival and Development Rights*

Children's rights to life, survival, and development (CRC Article 6) may be directly at risk from climate change related disasters, such as floods or extreme weather conditions. Other, more indirect risks to these rights include increased probabilities of diseases and hunger, both as a result of disasters, and risks of more structural changes in the living environment that are caused or exacerbated by global warming, such as drought. The CRC requires that all states parties " ensure to the maximum extent possible the survival and development of the child."[28] This implies that in their climate-related policies, states must take highly ambitious measures aiming to protect children's lives from the risks posed by climate change. At a minimum, states should therefore comply with their internationally agreed upon targets in terms of GHG emission reductions, in particular their nationally determined contribution (NDC) adopted in the context of the Paris Agreement. Moreover, in accordance with Article 4(3) of the Paris Agreement, states should adopt more progressive emission-reduction targets in their next NDC, to be adopted every five years.

Regarding children's right to the highest attainable standard of health (CRC Article 24), specific health effects of climate change include the following:

(i) A global increase of temperatures will lead to changing disease patterns, especially the spreading of tropical diseases to wider areas. Children are the most vulnerable to diseases and they suffer the highest death rates. Also diseases transferred by parasites, such as malaria, will spread as a result of rising temperatures. At present, according to the World Health Organization, malaria kills over 400,000 people every year, mainly African children under 5 years old.[29]

(ii) Increasingly variable rainfall patterns are likely to affect the supply of fresh water. A lack of safe water can compromise hygiene and increase the risk of diarrhoeal disease, which kills over 500,000 children aged under 5 years, every year.[30]

The right to health-sustaining conditions, including nutritious food and clean water, is a related right (CRC Article 24(2c)). Examples of violations under this right that are caused by climate change are: (1) water supplies may be affected by rising sea levels; this can result in salt water contaminating fresh water, including aquifers that provide water for domestic and agricultural purposes, potentially reducing the availability of clean drinking water for children; (2) the rising temperatures will result in changes in agricultural production, both through the increase in diseases affecting crops and through drought and desertification, which may lead to shortages in food supply and ultimately to hunger.

The main state obligations included in the CRC related to children's rights to health and health-sustaining conditions are to take appropriate measures: to diminish infant and child mortality, to provide medical care and assistance, and to combat disease and malnutrition through, inter alia, the provision of adequate nutritious foods and clean drinking water, taking into consideration the dangers and risks of environmental pollution.[31] In relation to climate change–related risks to children's health, states should take the actual and foreseeable effects of rising temperatures and rising sea levels on changing living conditions and disease patterns into account from the planning stage of their health policies. This falls within the ambit of climate adaptation efforts foreseen in Article 7 of the Paris Agreement, which confirms that adaptation also contributes to, and is directly related to, sustainable development. Moreover, states should engage in international cooperation, as envisaged by Article 7(6) of the Paris Agreement, to promote the sharing of information, best practices, and scientific research.

The right to an adequate standard of living (CRC Article 27) is at risk from climate change as well. Rising sea levels, flooding, and hurricanes may destroy housing and create unsafe living conditions for children.[32] The CRC requires states parties "to take appropriate measures . . . to implement this right and . . . in case of need, provide material assistance and support programmes, particularly with regard to nutrition, clothing and housing."[33] Such measures would also fall within the scope of adaptation policies foreseen in Article 7 of the Paris Agreement.

Moreover, climate-related developments may also have a negative impact on children's right to education (CRC Articles 28, 29). Children may be kept from attending school when the effects of climate change negatively affect the living conditions of their families and their parents require them to work to support the family. Moreover, children's access to education can be reduced when schools are destroyed by floods, hurricanes, or by other disasters. Another aspect of this right is that the education of the child shall be directed to, inte alia, "(t)he preparation of the child for responsible life in a free society"[34] and "(t)he development of respect for the natural environment."[35] Therefore, children also need to be educated about the risks of climate change, about their responsibilities, and about their possibilities to contribute to changing behavior and policies aimed at responding to such risks. The enhancement of climate change education, training, and public awareness is envisaged also in Article 12 of the Paris Agreement, while capacity-building efforts for developing countries are also directed toward, inter alia, climate education.

Finally, the right to indigenous culture and language needs to be mentioned. Children of indigenous origin, or those belonging to an ethnic, religious, or linguistic minority or group, "shall not be denied the right, in community with other members of his or her group, to enjoy his or her own culture."[36] Indigenous populations often live in climate-sensitive ecosystems and have cultural traditions that are closely connected to their living environment. Effects of climate change, such as the loss of land and species, may negatively influence the right of children of indigenous populations to their cultural identity.[37] In this regard, Article 7(5) of the Paris Agreement acknowledges that climate adaptation should be guided by knowledge of indigenous peoples.

3.1.3 *Protection Rights*

The risk that climate change–related developments may trigger armed conflicts for access to water and agricultural resources is high and has led to the displacement of environmental refugees. The CRC provides that states parties shall "take all feasible measures to ensure protection and care of children who are affected by an armed conflict."[38] Another indirect risk is that children may be recruited as child soldiers or otherwise be used to actively participate in the hostilities of an armed conflict.[39] The Paris Agreement does not explicitly refer to either the relationship between climate change and armed conflict or to climate refugees. However, it could be argued that the references to countries and people in "vulnerable situations" could apply also to these situations. [40]

Moreover, children whose families are affected by climate change may be exposed to higher risks of violence, physical abuse, child labor, trafficking, and exploitation.[41] For example, girls' security and bodily integrity can be threatened by climate change–related displacement. Indeed, "(e)vacuation to shelters lacking safe facilities for girls has been documented to heighten risks of all forms of sexual harassment and violence, including human trafficking."[42]

States have clear obligations under the CRC to protect children from such abuses,[43] but the linkages with climate change, as referred to above, have not yet been sufficiently recognized.

3.1.4 *Participation Rights*

CRC Article 12(1) provides that

> States Parties shall assure to the child who is capable of forming his or her own views the right to express those views freely in all matters affecting the child, the views of the child being given due weight in accordance with the age and maturity of the child.

Climate change clearly falls within the scope of "all matters affecting" children. Indeed, the children of today, and those of the next generations, will bear the social, economic, and environmental consequences of inadequate climate change decision-making. Therefore, the above mentioned right should be interpreted to cover also the right of children to express their views on how they, their families, their communities, their governments, and even the international community should respond to climate change and its consequences. Also, based on CRC Article 17, children's right to access to reliable information about the risks related to the effects of climate change on their living environment, on the one hand, and about the policies and measures adopted to respond to them, on the other, should be guaranteed. The Paris Agreement refers more generally to enhancing "public participation" (Article 12) and to "participatory approaches" in the context of adaptation policies and capacity building (Article 7).

As this examination has shown, a number of children's rights, as recognized by the CRC, are either directly or indirectly at risk from climate change and its effects. Children's survival and development rights may be directly affected by these phenomena, while their protection rights are more indirectly at risk. Children's participatory rights give them a voice in all matters affecting them, and climate change clearly falls within the scope of this right. Moreover, it follows from the above assessment that, when considering the threats of climate change to the enjoyment of children's rights, the obligations of states under the CRC correspond, to a large extent, to the terms of the Paris Agreement.

4 Impact of the Law—Progress and Obstacles

This section will consider what remedies children have at their disposal to enforce their rights and to hold states accountable for failing to comply with their international human rights obligations. It first considers children's access to justice before the CRC Committee since the recent entry into force of the Optional Protocol to the CRC on a Communications Procedure (section 4.1). It then examines children's access to justice before regional human rights courts, which is limited given the lack of jurisdiction these courts have over cases regarding climate change or environmental harm, unless a direct link can be established with violations of human rights (section 4.2). Finally, it briefly discusses recent climate cases brought by children before national courts (section 4.3).

4.1 Children's Access to the Complaints Procedure before the CRC Committee

With the adoption of the third Optional Protocol to the CRC on a Communications Procedure in 2011 and its entry into force in 2014, children now have the possibility to file a complaint about a violation of their rights with the CRC Committee. The violation must concern one or more rights set forth in the CRC or in one of its substantive optional protocols.[44] This option is available to children who wish to lodge a complaint against a state that has ratified both the CRC and the third optional protocol.[45] To date, only forty-six states have ratified, or acceded to, the Protocol on a Communications Procedure. Before presenting a complaint to the Committee, available domestic remedies, which can include both judicial remedies and nonjudicial complaint procedures, must first be exhausted.[46] Within one year after the outcome of the last domestic proceeding, children can file complaints either individually or as a group, either by themselves or with the support from a representative. Also NGOs, including children's rights organizations, can file a complaint on behalf of one or more personally identified children, provided they have the consent of the child/children or "can justify acting on their behalf without such consent."[47]

It is not inconceivable that children, with the help of legal representatives or NGOs, would introduce a communication against one or more states parties to the CRC for their failure to adopt sufficient measures to protect their rights from the adverse effects of climate change. Reasons why this has not happened yet include the recent entry into force of the optional protocol opening up this possibility, the limited number of states that have ratified it, the relatively recent awareness of the linkages between climate change and children's rights, and uncertainty about the admissibility of such a complaint. This admissibility will depend on how strictly the CRC Committee will apply the victim requirement (i.e., that the children on behalf of whom the communication is filed can be considered to be victims of the alleged violation).[48] The CRC Committee's Rules of Procedures[49] do not provide detailed guidance on the criteria to apply in this regard, and the practice is still extremely rare. A commentary to the optional protocol by Child Rights International Network (CRIN) suggests, based on examples from other UN treaty bodies, including the Human Rights Committee, that the CRC Committee will strictly interpret this requirement.[50] If this is so, it will be harder for children to provide evidence that a government's failure to address climate change has resulted in a violation of their individual rights under the CRC (since such failure could be considered to violate, if at all, the rights of *all* children in a certain country or area, and it will probably be impossible to present a complaint on behalf of a large group of "unidentified" children).

However, the CRC Committee has taken a particular interest in the linkages between children's rights and the environment, announcing that it "will consider adequate steps to provide more robust guidance on children's rights in the environmental context, including in due course the drafting of a General Comment."[51]

4.2 Legal Obstacles to Climate-Related Cases before Regional Human Rights Courts

From the outset it can be affirmed that children's access to justice in climate-related cases before regional human rights courts is extremely limited. The limitations concern several fundamental legal principles, such as the principle of causality, the victim requirement, and the foreseeability of an infringement of a human right (section 4.2.2). First, the question of children's standing, that is, their right to bring a case before these courts, will be considered.

4.2.1 *Children's Standing before Regional Human Rights Courts and Commissions*

Regarding the issue of standing, each court or commission has its own procedures.

As for the European Convention on Human Rights (ECHR), according to its Article 34, any person, group of persons, or nongovernmental organization can bring a case before the European Court of Human Rights (European Court), which does not exclude a minor or a group of minors (through his or her legal representative), when the other conditions are met; these conditions are: (1) being a victim of a violation (2) by a State Party to the ECHR (3) of a right included in the Convention. An NGO, such as a children's rights organization, has standing before the court only when the NGO itself claims to have been a victim of a violation. Neither NGOs nor individual persons can launch an *action populares*, or a public interest case, claiming that the rights of unidentified persons or those of an entire population group are being violated by a state party.

In the Inter-American system, individuals, including minors, who want to introduce a complaint about a violation by a state of a right set forth in the American Convention on Human Rights have to present their claim to the Inter-American Commission for Human Rights (Inter-American Commission). If admissible, this Commission will consider the merits of the claim and usually make recommendations to the state. Only if the state fails to abide by these recommendations, or if the Inter-American Commission decides that the case is of particular importance or legal interest, will the case be referred to the Inter-American Court of Human Rights (Inter-American Court). Claims can also be brought by other individuals or organizations on behalf of the victim(s) of an alleged violation. However, as in the European system, the possibility of lodging public interest claims is not explicitly foreseen.

In the African system, cases alleging violation of rights set forth in the African Charter on Human and Peoples' Rights may be presented either to the African Commission on Human and People's Rights (African Commission) or to the African Court of Human and People's Rights (African Court). Admissibility of cases before the African Court is dependent on the explicit acceptance by the respondent state of the optional jurisdiction of the Court. The African human rights system has adopted a liberal approach to standing, meaning that a communication may be lodged by anyone—including minors—and not only by the direct representatives of a victim or a victim's immediate relatives.[52] Therefore, the African system offers the broadest scope for public interest claims introduced by NGOs, and this has been regularly used in practice.

Also, the African Committee of Experts on the Rights and Welfare of the Child (ACERWC) has been established to monitor implementation of the African Charter on the Rights and Welfare of Children. This Committee, operational since 2001, can hear complaints from "any individual or group of natural or legal persons, including children," states parties to the relevant charter, and intergovernmental and nongovernmental organizations. To date, ten individual complaints have been introduced, of which four are finalized; six were introduced by NGOs, including human rights and children's rights organizations.[53]

In terms of their legal standing, children are formally allowed to present a case before these regional human rights bodies. However, in practice it is difficult for children to lodge such a case. First, they need to know about the existence of this remedy; then they need to find the support of a lawyer or an NGO with the necessary resources to embark on this path, which also requires the exhaustion of domestic remedies, a process that often takes several years.

4.2.2 Other Legal Obstacles

Several other legal obstacles have significantly limited the possibilities for bringing climate change–related cases before regional human rights courts and commissions, namely, the principle of causality, the victim requirement, and the foreseeability of an infringement of a human right. These obstacles are especially related to claims based on a violation of the right to life. The main points of the relevant case law of the different regional human rights monitoring bodies can be summarized as follows,[54] focusing on the European, Inter-American, and African systems of human rights.[55] Since all rights included in regional (and international) human rights conventions also apply to children, this case law is directly relevant to them. Moreover, it may provide interpretative examples for corresponding rights under the CRC, when they are relied upon, for example, in complaints before the CRC Committee.

4.2.2.1 THE EUROPEAN COURT OF HUMAN RIGHTS

The European Convention on Human Rights (ECHR) does not include a right to either a healthy environment or health. Therefore, the most obvious basis for a climate-related claim would be the right to life (ECHR Article 2). Although no case has been brought before this body with specific reference to climate change, the European Court of Human Rights (European Court) has developed consistent case law recognizing that state's obligations to protect the right to life also apply with respect to environmental disasters or pollution. These obligations are both substantive (ranging from such preventive measures as adoption of adequate environmental legislation to protection when environmental harm occurs) and procedural (such as the duty to inform people about environmental risks).[56] These obligations apply not only to environmentally hazardous state activities but also to activities by private actors. The extent of the positive obligations depends on such factors as the harmfulness of the dangerous activities and the foreseeability of the risks to life.[57]

How would this case law then apply to a possible claim alleging the failure of a state to protect children's right to life from the threats posed by climate change? On the one hand, it clearly confirms that states have far-reaching due diligence obligations with respect to environmental threats. However, while high levels of CO_2 and other GHG emissions obviously contribute to global warming, establishing measurable causality between the emissions of a specific factory—or even of all emissions on the territory of one particular state—and the overall phenomenon of climate change is quite difficult. Indeed, the causality between highly polluting industrial activities within one state and the loss of life resulting from the effects of climate change may be seen as too speculative to hold this state responsible for these deaths or for failing to take the necessary measures to prevent such deaths. Therefore, it is far from certain that the causality requirement, or the criterion of the foreseeability of the risks to life, can be fulfilled.

The European Court has also upheld some environment-related claims based on the right to a private and family life (ECHR Article 8).[58] In these cases, the Court has held that this right also covers the right not to be exposed to toxic waste, pollution, or natural disasters that endanger the enjoyment of a healthy living environment.

Finally, it is interesting to note that a group of seven Portuguese children, ages five to eighteen, is preparing, with the support of barristers from a London-based law firm, a complaint to be lodged before the European Court against the forty-seven member states of the Council of Europe.[59] Their claim will be based on the violation of several rights under the ECHR, in particular, the children's right to life. They will be arguing that the Court should base its conclusions on the GHG emission cuts of each of the states parties to the ECHR. This initiative will undoubtedly face the legal obstacles mentioned above, in particular the causality and foreseeability criteria, as well as the victim requirement. Another admissibility criterion that may be problematic is the requirement of prior exhaustion of local remedies. Nevertheless, the initiative itself is absolutely commendable and serves, at the very least, to draw public attention to the linkages between climate change and children's rights, on the one hand, and to the possibilities for children to claim recognition of their rights, also through judicial mechanisms at the regional level, on the other.

It should be noted that another case was brought before the General Court of the European Union in May 2018 by ten families, including their young children, and the Swedish Sami Youth Association Sáminuorra against the European Parliament and the European Council.[60] The claims in this case, referred to as "the people's climate case," include, inter alia, a violation of their fundamental rights of life, health, occupation, and property caused by the EU's failure to adopt adequate CO_2 reduction policies. The decision on the admissibility of the case was still pending at the time of this writing.

4.2.2.2 THE INTER-AMERICAN SYSTEM OF HUMAN RIGHTS

The Inter-American Commission on Human Rights (Inter-American Commission) and the Inter-American Court of Human Rights (Inter-American Court) and have long been at the forefront of environmental rights jurisprudence.[61] Although these cases primarily concern violations of the land and property rights of indigenous peoples resulting from the granting of, inter alia, logging concessions by the state, these violations were also considered to threaten their rights to life and to health. The Inter-American case law also recognizes the rights of indigenous peoples to environmental conditions where they can live in accordance with their cultural traditions as well as the procedural obligations of states related to environmental threats.[62] Here a direct link with the rights of indigenous children can be seen, which are addressed in CRC Article 30.[63]

However, to hold a state accountable for a violation of the right to life, the Inter-American Court requires that "the authorities knew or should have known about the existence of a situation that posed (i) *an immediate and certain risk to the life of* (ii) *an individual or of a group of individuals.*"[64] Even though it could be argued that sufficient scientific data and analyses are available to establish that climate change is causing severe risks to life on earth, it is much more challenging to ascertain the immediacy and certainty of the risks for the life of identified people. According to the Inter-American Court, the conditions of immediacy and certainty will be met only when authorities do not take the necessary measures available to them that could reasonably be expected to prevent or avoid such risk.

The causality between GHG emissions of one state and the effects of climate change for individual groups of people were addressed in the first climate case ever brought before a human rights body, referred to as the Inuit case. The Inuit Circumpolar Conference (ICC) filed its petition in 2005 claiming that the human rights of the Inuit people, a population group living in the Arctic region, were violated as a result of GHG emissions from the United States. Since the US has not ratified the American Convention on Human Rights, the petitioners relied on the American Declaration on the Rights and Duties of Man.[65] The claimants held that (1) climate change has damaged the arctic environment to such an extent that it threatens human life and that (2) as harvested species are becoming scarcer, the Inuit's access to these foods is diminishing due to difficulties in travel and changes in game location. The Inter-American Commission rejected the admissibility of the petition without providing any reasons, but a special hearing was held to investigate the relationship between global warming and human rights. However, the conclusions of this hearing have not been made public. Similar arguments have been advanced in another petition submitted to the Commission in 2013 by the Arctic Athabaskan Council, alleging that Canada's failure to adequately regulate black carbon emissions has resulted in violations of this population's rights to life, to health and culture. At this writing, the petition is still pending.[66]

4.2.2.3 THE AFRICAN SYSTEM OF HUMAN RIGHTS

According to Article 18 of the African Charter on Human and Peoples' Rights, the state "shall ensure...the protection of the rights of...the child as stipulated in international declarations and conventions." This also implies an obligation of its states parties to protect the rights included in the CRC and in the African Charter on the Rights and Welfare of the Child. The African Court of Human and Peoples' Rights (African Court) became operational in 2006. In its 2016 judgment in the *Ogiek* case,[67] the Court found a violation by Kenya of several human rights of the indigenous Ogiek population, who had been expelled without consultation from their ancestral lands, including their right to culture and the right to food as derived from the right to natural resources. With this judgment, the African Court further developed the environmental case law of the African Commission. In 2001, this Commission delivered a landmark decision in the Ogoniland case[68] concerning a claim alleging that the Nigerian government was directly involved in oil production operations causing serious environmental and health problems. That the African Commission upheld the claim for violation of the right to a general satisfactory environment, together with violations of the rights to life and health, is an interesting example. It could be argued that human rights instruments that protect all these rights, such as the African Charter, provide a more solid basis for climate change–related claims than the more traditional European and American Conventions on Human Rights.[69]

As shown above, several limitations persist for children—and their representatives—to lodge claims before regional human rights courts concerning environmental harm and the failure of their government to adequately address climate change. Nevertheless, these limitations may be reduced gradually, if these courts continue to recognize the environmental dimensions of other rights, such as the right to health, the rights of indigenous peoples, and the right to a private and family life. This will ultimately also benefit children's access to justice at the regional level, where such access is not sufficiently ensured in the domestic context.

4.3 Claims by Children before National Courts

At the national level, children's legal standing and the admissibility criteria for cases brought by minors greatly differ among states. In fact, "legislation and procedures concerning the...participation of children in proceedings, including...administrative and civil proceedings, are often not adapted to children's rights and needs or may even be discriminatory towards children based on their age and gender."[70] Therefore, rather than present a comprehensive overview of state laws regarding children bringing legal claims on their own behalf, which is beyond the scope of this chapter, I will briefly present a few recent examples of cases brought—or prepared—by children before national courts in which children claim a violation of their rights caused by the state's failure to adopt sufficiently effective laws and measures to address climate change. Doing this should begin to paint a picture of the role of national in children's ability to protect their rights in this area.

The first case, *Juliana v. United States*, was brought before the U.S. District Court in Oregon (9th Circuit) by twenty-one children, ages nine to twenty, supported by the NGO Our Children's Trust. In a lawsuit against the United States, the president, and other federal defendants, the children alleged that inadequate climate change mitigation measures constitute a violation of their constitutional rights to life, liberty, and property, among others. In November 2016, a district court judge ruled—over the objections of government and energy-industry lawyers—that the Oregon suit could proceed, granting standing to the young plaintiffs. It was the first procedural victory for Our Children's Trust, which is bringing similar actions across the United States. The trial in Oregon was initially set to begin in October 2018, but after repeated attempts by the government to gain interlocutory appeal at the 9th Circuit and at the US Supreme Court, the district court's decisions denying the US government's dispositive motions must first be reviewed by the 9th Circuit before the trial can start.[71]

Another interesting example is the case *Minors Oposa v. Secretary of the Department of Environmental and Natural Resources* (1994), in which the Supreme Court of the Philippines ruled on behalf of a class representing children that the state had an intergenerational responsibility to maintain a clean environment.[72]

These, and other climate-related lawsuits that have recently been launched against states or companies, were arguably also inspired by the first successful case brought by an NGO against a state, *Urgenda v. The Netherlands* (2015).[73] In this case, the court of first instance in The Hague ruled that the Netherlands had not sufficiently complied with its international obligations to curb GHG emissions and ordered the state to ensure that the Dutch emissions in the year 2020 will be at least 25 percent lower than those in 1990. This judgment was confirmed on appeal.[74] A similar case has been brought before a national court in Belgium by an organization of concerned citizens arguing that Belgian law requires the Belgian government's approach to reducing greenhouse gas emissions to be more aggressive. After several pre-trial rulings on procedural matters raised by the Flemish region, the trial is set to proceed throughout 2019, and a final judgment is expected in the fall 2020.[75]

5 CONCLUSION: KEY CHALLENGES AND POSSIBILITIES FOR THE WAY FORWARD

Considering the progress and obstacles discussed in the preceding analysis, a few key challenges can be identified for three main actors: (1) states, (2) regional human rights courts and monitoring bodies, and (3) possibilities for action by children themselves with the support of children's rights NGOs. The main, overall challenge for all these actors—and for the private sector and civil society at large—is to keep the average increase in global temperatures below the internationally agreed upon threshold of two degrees, striving for 1.5 degrees Celsius above preindustrial levels, as foreseen in the Paris Agreement. More specific challenges geared toward ensuring the full enjoyment of children's rights are the following.

5.1 Challenges for States

As indicated in this chapter, in recent years international efforts to address two interconnected major global concerns, namely, climate change and sustainable development, explicitly recognized the need for a coordinated, rights-based approach. This chapter has also shown that many of the obligations of states included in the CRC correspond to a large extent to commitments of states laid down in the Paris Agreement. This is particularly true for the provisions of the Paris Agreement on climate adaptation measures.

Therefore, a key challenge for states is to adopt an integrated approach when formulating and implementing climate policies, together with their efforts to respect, protect, and ensure children's rights. For developing countries, this integrated policy approach should also incorporate its actions aimed at sustainable development. International development cooperation, including climate financing, should fully support such an integrated approach. Rather than bureaucratic integration, the challenge for states is to achieve a genuinely coordinated effort aiming not only at normative consistency but also at a more rational allocation of human and financial resources. This will require, inter alia, increasing awareness among government agencies, and the public at large, about the linkages between climate change and children's rights through training and information campaigns; creating inter-ministerial cooperation channels between those ministries responsible for climate policies and those responsible for human and children's rights to coordinate efforts from the planning stage of adaptation and mitigation policies; and bringing these linkages to the attention of national parliamentarians who can urge their governments to ensure more efficient uses of public resources by ensuring genuinely coordinated efforts in these interrelated fields.[76]

5.2 Challenges for Regional Human Rights Courts and Monitoring Bodies

The examination in this chapter also demonstrates that children and their representatives face many obstacles to their access to justice before regional human rights courts, which significantly limit the possibilities to lodge climate-related complaints. While some of these obstacles are of a general nature, others are specific to children. In particular, children often lack knowledge about their rights and about the available remedies; they generally depend on adults to make use of such remedies; in many countries, children do not have legal standing before national courts and therefore are unable to exhaust domestic remedies before taking a case to a regional court; often it is socially and culturally unacceptable for children to lodge complaints against adults—including their own government.

The general obstacles include the requirements of causality (e.g., between the failure of a state to take preventive measures to mitigate climate change and the death of children in a hurricane or flood) and foreseeability (e.g., of the loss of life or negative health consequences as a result of the failure to take preventive measures). Another requirement that has hampered claims attempting to hold a state accountable for its failure to protect human rights from climate-related natural disasters is the victim requirement. This requirement entails that a state can be held accountable for a violation of, for example, the right to life only if there is a direct relationship between the failure of the state to take preventive measures and the death of an individual identified victim. It has been convincingly argued, in particular by Francesco Francioni, that it would be desirable for regional human rights courts to adopt

> a more imaginative and courageous jurisprudence which takes into consideration the collective dimension of human rights affected by environmental degradation and adapts the language and technique of human rights discourse to the enhanced risk posed by global environmental crises to society and, indeed, to humanity as a whole.[77]

This proposition is especially relevant to environmental crises caused by climate change, since they typically cause harm to whole populations and not only to individual, identified victims. It could indeed be argued that if the existing normative framework is insufficient to respond to new challenges, the norms themselves need to be progressively adjusted to the changing global context and threats through the appropriate means of interpretation by the competent judicial bodies.[78] As Riccardo Pavoni argues with regard to the strictly individual victim requirement, the European Court of Human rights "should be more receptive to well-founded claims calling attention to serious shortcomings in the environmental law and practice of respondent States which potentially affect the well-being of entire communities of people."[79]

In the Inter-American system, where the victim requirement is less strictly applied in the admissibility phase, it is relied upon also during the consideration of the merits, including in environment-related cases.[80] Nevertheless, the Inter-American Court and Commission have already confirmed the obligations of states to protect fundamental, individual rights in a more collective dimension, especially in connection with the rights of indigenous peoples. A similar approach is emerging in the case law of the African system of human rights, which also seems to adopt a broader interpretation of the victim requirement. This tendency in the Inter-American and African case law may well be related to a more general openness in these regions to the acceptance and legal protection of collective rights in addition to the more "traditional" individual human rights. Considering the increasing threats posed by climate change, and the share of the Global North in worldwide CO_2 emissions, it would arguably serve global justice if this approach were also to be progressively accepted at the European level.[81]

Indeed, a broader interpretation of the victim requirement that takes account of the collective dimension of human rights, on the one hand, and of environmental harm, on the other, would make it easier for citizens to win cases before regional human rights courts and to hold their governments to account. Cases that are now declared inadmissible because the claimant cannot prove the direct connection between a government's omission to take preventive action and the immediate and foreseeable threat to his or her life as an individual would arguably have a greater chance if the threats of such an omission to the life (and health) of a whole group of people would be considered.

5.3   Possibilities for Children with the Support of Children's Rights NGOs

The chapter has discussed the possibilities for children themselves to hold their governments to account for their failure to sufficiently address climate change, by examining their access to justice before national, regional, and international courts or monitoring bodies. With the entry into force of the Optional Protocol to the CRC on a Communications Procedure, children and their representatives can lodge an individual complaint against their state, based on any of the rights outlined in section 3, above. NGOs, including children's rights organizations, could play an active role in supporting such claims, which would be extremely beneficial for raising both public and political awareness about the connections between climate change and the rights of the child. Such complaints can also be brought before the African Committee of Experts on the Rights and Welfare of the Child. Similarly, children could bring additional cases before national courts in their own country, claiming violations of their rights to life, to health, and to a healthy environment as enshrined in their national constitutions and laws.[82]

5.4 Conclusion

To conclude, efforts should continue to be made to overcome the obstacles identified in this chapter since access to justice is one of the cornerstones of children's human rights. However, whereas litigation is primarily reactive, children also have other, more proactive possibilities to influence law and policy related to climate change. In particular, based on their participatory rights in the CRC, children should be empowered to be informed, to be heard, and to express their views on the risks posed by climate change as well as on the policies and measures adopted to respond to them. States must ensure that children can make use of these participatory rights, inter alia, by (1) preparing children for and including them in the design and implementation of climate policies and climate vulnerability assessments, giving due weight to children's views according to their age and maturity, and by (2) providing adequate education on climate change, aiming not only at the transfer of knowledge but also at the development of skills that will equip children to confront climate-related challenges, taking into account each child's particular local context and, as appropriate, traditional knowledge.[83]

Also these nonjudicial vehicles for children's participation are not yet sufficiently developed; here, too, formal and material obstacles need to be overcome. Raising awareness, promoting coordinated responses, and empowering young people are crucial steps on the path toward changing attitudes and policies and, ultimately, toward saving our planet. The coordinated protests by schoolchildren mentioned at the beginning of this chapter are vital and extremely encouraging in this regard.

NOTES

1. Damian Carrington, "Youth Climate Strikers: 'We Are Going to Change the Fate of Humanity,'" open letter by students of the global day of protests (excerpt), *The Guardian*, March 1, 2019, https://www.theguardian.com/environment/2019/mar/01/youth-climate-strikers-we-are-going-to-change-the-fate-of-humanity.
2. UN Convention on the Rights of the Child (CRC), G.A. Res. 44/25, 44th Sess. UN Doc. A/RES/44/25 (1989).
3. Paris Agreement on Climate Change, UN Doc. FCCP/CP/2015/L.9/Rev.1 (2012), preamble (para. 11).
4. The term "child" is used in accordance with the CRC Article 1: "every human being below the age of eighteen years unless under the law applicable to the child, majority is attained earlier."
5. United Nations Children's Fund (UNICEF), "The Challenges of Climate Change: Children on the Front Line" (April 2014), https://www.unicef.org/publications/index_74647.html; Human Rights Council, "Analytical Study on the Relationship between Climate Change and the Full and Effective Enjoyment of the Rights of the Child," UN Doc. A/HRC /35/13 (May 4, 2017).
6. This section draws on my analysis in an earlier publication. See Christine Bakker, "Children's Rights Challenged by Climate Change: Is a Reconceptualization Required?," in *International Law for Common Goods: Normative Perspectives on Human Rights,*

Culture and Nature, ed. Federico Lenzerini and Ana Filipa Vrdoljak (Portland, OR: Hart Publishing, 2014).

7. Joy Guillemot and Jazmin Burgess, "Child Rights at Risk," in UNICEF, "Challenges of Climate Change," 47–51.

8. UN Committee on the Rights of the Child (CRC Committee), "General Guidelines regarding Form and Content of Initial Reports to Be Submitted by States Parties under Article 44, Paragraph 1(a) of the Convention," U.N. Doc. CRC/C/5 (Oct. 30, 1991).

9. UNICEF, "Rights under the Convention on the Rights of the Child" (Aug. 7, 2014), https://www.unicef.org/crc/index_30177.html.

10. Guillemot and Burgess, "Child Rights at Risk," 49.

11. Provisions of the CRC that aim to protect children from these abuses include Article 19 (protection from all forms of violence), Article 32 (child labor), Article 35 (abduction, sale, and trafficking), Article 38 (war and armed conflict) as well as the Optional Protocol on Children in Armed Conflict (OPAC).

12. CRC, arts. 6, 24, 27.

13. United Nations Human Rights Council, Report of the Special Rapporteur on the Implications for Human Rights of the Environmentally Sound Management and Disposal of Hazardous Substances substances and Wastes," U.N. Doc. A/HRC/33/41 (2016).

14. Organization of African Unity (OAU), African Charter on Human and People's Rights, CAB/LEG/67/3 rev. 5, 21 ILM. 58 (1982), art. 24; Organization of American States (OAS), Additional Protocol to the American Convention on Human Rights in the Area of Economic, Social and Cultural Rights (Protocol of San Salvador), A-52 (Nov. 16, 1999), art. 11; Association of Southeast Asian Nations (ASEAN), ASEAN Human Rights Declaration (2012), art. 28(f); League of Arab States, Arab Charter on Human Rights (1994), art. 38.

15. These efforts started with the UN Framework Convention on Climate Change (UNFCCC) adopted in 1992, which still constitutes the main legal framework for international climate action. Both the Kyoto Protocol (adopted in 1997; entered into force in 2005) and the Paris Agreement were adopted to implement the general commitments already included in the UNFCCC.

16. The United States is the second largest emitter of GHG, after China, and accounts for about one-fifth of global carbon emissions.

17. See Carrington, "Youth Climate Strikers."

18. For more details on the legally binding nature of the Paris Agreement, see Christine Bakker, "The Paris Agreement on Climate Change: Balancing 'Legal Force' and 'Geographical Scope,' " *Italian Yearbook of International Law*, 143–158.

19. Human Rights Council, "Human Rights and Climate Change," UN Doc. A/HRC/32/L.34 (June 28, 2016), Preamble.

20. Human Rights Council, "Report of the Office of the United Nations High Commissioner for Human Rights—Analytical Study on the Relationship between Climate Change and the Full Enjoyment of the Rights of the Child," UN Doc. A/HRC/35/13 (May 4, 2017), paras. 30, 34.

21. CRC Committee, "Report of the 2016 Day of General Discussion on Children's Rights and the Environment" (3017), 25.

22. Guillemot and Burgess, "Child Rights at Risk."

23. Joachim Wolf, "The Concept of the 'Best Interest' in Terms of the UN Convention on the Rights of the Child," in *The Ideologies of Children's Rights*, ed. Michael Freeman and Philip Veerman (Dordrecht, NE: Martinus Nijhoff, 1992), 125–133.

24. Guillemot and Burgess, "Child Rights at Risk."

25. CRC, art. 3(1) (emphasis added).

26. See CRC, art. 4.

27. CRC Committee, *General Comment No. 5: General Measures of Implementation of the Convention on the Rights of the Child (arts. 4, 42 and 44, para. 6)*, CRC/GC/2003/527 (2003), para 1.

28. CRC, art. 6(2).

29. World Health Organization, "Climate Change and Health," factsheet (Feb. 1, 2018), https://www.who.int/news-room/fact-sheets/detail/climate-change-and-health.

30. World Health Organization, "Climate Change and Health."

31. See CRC, art. 24(2)(c).

32. Guillemot and Burgess, "Child Rights at Risk," 48–49.

33. CRC, art. 27(3).

34. CRC, art. 29(1)(d).

35. CRC, art. 29(1)(e).

36. CRC, art 30.

37. Guillemot and Burgess, "Child Rights at Risk," 48–49.

38. CRC, art. 38(4); see also Office of the High Commissioner for Human Rights (OHCHR), "Optional Protocol to the CRC on the Involvement of Children in Armed Conflict," UN Doc. A/RES/54/263 (May 25, 2000; entered into force Feb. 12, 2002).

39. CRC, arts. 38(2) and (3); see also "Optional Protocol on Children in Armed Conflict."

40. Paris Agreement, arts. 7(5) and 7(9)(c) (adaptation), art. 9(4) (climate financing), art. 11(1) (capacity building)

41. Human Rights Council, "Analytical Study,", para. 19.

42. Human Rights Council, "Analytical Study," para. 22.

43. CRC, arts. 35 (obligation to prevent the abduction, sale, or traffic of children) and 19 (obligation to prevent all forms of violence against children, including sexual abuse).

44. OHCHR, "Optional Protocol to the CRC on Children in Armed Conflict" and "Optional Protocol to the CRC on the Sale of Children, Child Prostitution and Child Pornography," UN Doc. A/RES/54/263 (May 25, 2000; entered into force Jan. 18, 2002).

45. If the complaint concerns a right set forth in one of the substantive optional protocols, the responding state also must have ratified the relevant protocol.

46. OHCHR, "Optional Protocol to the CRC on a Communications Procedure," UN Doc. A/RES/66/138 (Dec. 19, 2011; entered into force April 14 2014), art. 7(e).

47. OHCHR, "Optional Protocol to the CRC on a Communications Procedure," art. 5.

48. OHCHR, "Optional Protocol to the CRC on a Communications Procedure," art. 5.

49. CRC Committee, "Rules of Procedure under the Optional Protocol to the Convention on the Rights of the Child on a Communications Procedure," UN Doc. CRC/C/62/3 (2013).

50. Child Rights International Network (CRIN), CRC "Complaints Mechanism Toolkit: Annex I, Annotated Optional Protocol" (March 12, 2014), https://archive.crin.org/en/guides/legal/crc-complaints-mechanism-toolkit.html.

51. CRC Committee, "Report of the 2016 Day of General Discussion on Children's Rights and the Environment," http://www.ohchr.org/Documents/HRBodies/CRC/Discussions/2016/DGDoutcomereport-May2017.pdf (accessed Aug. 27, 2019).

52. International Federation for Human Rights (FIDH), "Admissibility of Complaints before the African Court: A Practical Guide" (June 6, 2016), https://www.fidh.org/en/region/Africa/admissibility-of-complaints-before-the-african-court-fidh-publishes-a.

53. See African Committee of Experts on the Rights and Welfare of the Child (ACERWC), Table of Communications, , https://www.acerwc.africa/table-of-communications/ (accessed Aug. 27, 2019).

54. A more detailed analysis is provided in Christine Bakker, "Climate Change and the Right to Life: Limits and Potentialities of the Human Rights Protection System," in *Climate Change and Human Rights: An International Law Perspective*, ed. Ottavio Quirico and Mouloud Boumghar (London: Routledge, 2016), 71–88.

55. To my knowledge, to date no specific case law has been developed in relation to the right to a healthy environment in the ASEAN and Arab human rights systems.

56. L.C.B. v. the United Kingdom [1998] Eur. Ct. H.R. 108 (June 9, 1998) (*L.C.B*); Paul and Audrey Edwards v. the United Kingdom [2002] Eur. Ct. H.R. 303 (March 14, 2002); Öneryıldız v. Turkey (*Öneryildiz*) [2004] Eur. Ct. H.R. 657 (GC) (Nov. 30, 2004); Budayeva and Others v. Russia, Application Nos. 15339/02, 21166/02, 20058/02, 11673/02, 15343/02, Eur. Ct. H.R. (Sept. 29, 2008) (*Budayeva*); Özel and Others v. Turkey [2015] Eur. Ct. H.R. 1024 (Nov. 17, 2015).

57. *Öneryıldız*, para. 73; *L.C.B.*, paras. 37–41 (emphasis added).

58. *Lopez Astra v. Spain*, judgment of 9.12.1994, *Guerra a.o. v. Italy*, judgment of 19.2.1998, *Fadeyeva v. Russia*, judgment of 9.6.2005, *Giacomelli v. Italy*, judgment of 2.11.2006, *Tatar v. Romania*, judgment of 22.1.2009, *Dubetska a.o. v Ukrain*, judgment of 10.2.2011.

59. Megan Darby, "Portuguese Kids Hit Climate Lawsuit Crowdfunding Milestone," *Climate Home News*, October 19, 2017, http://www.climatechangenews.com/2017/10/19/portuguese-kids-hit-climate-lawsuit-crowdfunding-milestone.

60. See the People's Climate Case website, https://peoplesclimatecase.caneurope.org.

61. The most important cases are Yanomani Indians v. Brazil, No. 7615, Inter-Am. Comm'n H.R. (March 3, 1985); The Mayagna (Sumo) Awas Tigny Community. v. Nicaragua, Inter-Am. Ct. H.R. (Aug. 31, 2001); Yakye Axa Indigenous Community v. Paraguay, Inter-Am. Ct. H.R. (June 17, 2005); Maya Indigenous Community of the Toledo District v. Belize, Inter-Am. Comm'n H.R. (Oct. 12, 2004); Kichwa Peoples of Sarayaku v. Ecuador, Inter-Am. Ct. H.R. (June 27, 2012).

    For a comprehensive overview of these cases see Cathrin Zengerlin, *Greening International Jurisprudence: Environmental NGOs before International Courts, Tribunals, and Compliance Committees* (Dordrecht, NE: Martinus Nijho, 2013), 109–112.

62. See also Riccardo Pavoni, "Environmental Jurisprudence of the European and Inter-American Courts of Human Rights: Comparative Insights," in *The Environmental Dimension of Human Rights*, ed. Ben Boer (Oxford: Oxford University Press, 2015).

63. Article 30 states: "In those States in which ethnic, religious or linguistic minorities or persons of indigenous origin exist, a child belonging to such a minority or who is indigenous shall not be denied the right, in community with other members of his or her group, to enjoy his or her own culture."

64. European Court of Human Rights, Guide on Article 2 of the European Convention on Human Rights: Right to Life (August 31, 2019), https://www.echr.coe.int/Documents/Guide_Art_2_ENG.pdf, 9.

65. Indeed, claims can also be presented to the Inter-American Commission on Human Rights against states that have not ratified the American Convention but, as members of the Organization of American States (OAS), should protect the rights covered by the American Declaration on Human Rights (Canada, Cuba, and the US).

66. See Veronica de la Rosa Jaimes, "The Arctic Athabaskan Petition: Where Accelerated Arctic Warming Meets Human Rights," *California Western International Law Journal* 45, no. 2 (2015): 213–260.

67. African Commission on Human and Peoples' Rights v. Kenya, Application No. 006/2012, African Ct. H.P.R. (May 26, 2017).

68. Social and Economic Rights Action Center and the Center for Economic and Social Rights v. Nigeria, African Comm'n H.P.R. (May 27, 2002).

69. However, the relative contribution to climate change by African States is significantly smaller than that of the industrialized states in the other regions, thereby adding another limitation to the prospects for effective claims.

70. OHCHR, "Access to Justice for children," UN Doc. A/HRC/25/35. (Dec. 16, 2013), para. 14.

71. Juliana v. United States, Docket No. 18-36082 (9th Cir. 2015). See the US Climate Change Litigation database, Sabin Center for Climate Change Law, Columbia Law School, http://climatecasechart.com/case/juliana-v-united-states (accessed Aug. 27, 2019). Oral arguments were held on June 4, 2019.

72. Minors Oposa v. Secretary of the Department of Environment and National Resources, 33 ILM 173 (1994), cited in Human Rights Council, "Analytical Study," para. 47.

73. Urgenda Foundation v. State of the Netherlands [2015] HAZA C/09/00456689 (June 24, 2015); *aff'd*, Dist. Ct. of the Hague and Hague Ct. App. (Oct. 9, 2018). .

74. State of the Netherlands v. Urgenda Foundation, Case no. 200.178.245/01, Hague Ct. App. (Oct. 9, 2018), (English translation available at https://uitspraken.rechtspraak.nl/inziendocument?id=ECLI:NL:GHDHA:2018:2610).

75. See the L'Affaire Climat website, https://affaire-climat.be/fr/the-case (accessed Aug. 27, 2019).

76. See Human Rights Council, "Analytical Study," paras. 41–43.

77. Francesco Francioni, "International Human Rights in an Environmental Horizon," *European Journal of International Law* 21 (2010): 55.

78. See also Bakker, "Climate Change and the Right to Life," 71–88.

79. Riccardo Pavoni, "Public Interest Environmental Litigation and the European Court of Human Rights: No Love at First Sight," in Vrdoljak and Lenzerini, *International Law for Common Goods*, 331–359, 333.

80. Pavoni, "Environmental Jurisprudence," 92–97.

81. This is obviously also true for the North American continent, but discussing the general reluctance in the US to adhere to regional human rights conventions and to accept international oversight over implementation of human rights would go beyond the scope of this chapter.

82. For example, the *Urgenda* case in the Netherlands was based on Article 21 of the Dutch Constitution, which reads: "The State is entrusted with the care to keep the land fit for human occupation and to preserve and improve the environment."

83. Human Rights Council, "Analytical Study," paras. 60, 61.

PART IV

....

SELECTED INDIVIDUAL AND INSTITUTIONAL ACTORS

....

CHAPTER 23

TAKING PART, JOINING IN, AND BEING HEARD?

Ethnographic Explorations of Children's Participation

PERPETUA KIRBY AND REBECCA WEBB

1 INTRODUCTION

THIS chapter explores how Article 12 and the voice of the child are implemented. It does so with specific reference to two separate research studies conducted by the authors in which children at different primary schools in England are able to articulate, embody, and practice aspects of Article 12 of the UN Convention of the Rights of the Child (CRC) as everyday aspects of taking part in school life and in learning in the classroom. Article 12 recognizes children's right to express their views freely in all matters affecting them. A focus on Article 12 means giving due consideration to the ways in which children are able to participate: to be listened to; to make their voices heard; and to be given opportunities to contribute to decisions affecting them individually as well as democratic decision-making about matters that concern them relationally and socially within compulsory schooling. The CRC establishes that children's views should be given "due weight in accordance with the age and maturity of the child."[1] Developmental psychology, concerned with demarcating stages at which children are deemed able to participate, dominated understandings of children's competence for much of the twentieth century. Nonetheless, we argue that this framing of the child silences many (the youngest and most vulnerable, for example) and privileges those with access to greater knowledge and social networks of power. Within our sociological framing, children are understood as experts of their own lives and competent to navigate their own social worlds, including those within school.[2]

The research presented here draws from two different studies and data gathered within three primary schools between 2010 and 2018, a period of governmental and educational change within the United Kingdom. These studies highlight the importance of what children communicate through moment-to-moment encounters, stressing the significance of this to broadening our understandings of children's participation. They also pay close attention to how children from different backgrounds (including social groupings according to gender, ethnicity, class, and dis/ability) are positioned variously so that rights can be realized more easily for some than for others.

In the context of exploring the implementation of Article 12, section 2 begins by contextualizing two studies undertaken within different governmental climates within the UK. This includes both an era when there is an assumed discourse of children's rights participation in schools and one where there is not, highlighting the broader significance of the findings for schools within various diverse contexts operating within the expectations and under auspices of the CRC. The chapter introduces Article 12 as a commitment to giving due attention to children's experiences within schools and as necessarily political. This means addressing questions of who holds the power to make decisions, and how, in which particular schooling contexts and times. More than this, it involves the potentiality of children to transform rather than simply to conform at school, which we discuss in terms of children's subjectivities and agency. Each of us outlines her localized fieldwork contexts as well as the research methodology of educational ethnography underpinning these research studies. Ethnography relies upon spending extended periods of time within the research context using both observations and interviews to make sense of the richness and complexity of day-to-day life and the way in which beliefs and policies are translated into practices. The data examples from these studies reinforce the value of paying attention to the particular of children's everyday lives. Typically, ethnography relies upon identifying ethnographic researchers as integrated within the dynamic workings of the sites they explore; researchers do not set out to objectively measure and generate distance but rather to acknowledge their own participation, which is captured through the use of the first person.

Section 3 shines a light on excerpts of data, drawn from both studies, illustrating common themes that locate children, and school staff, in tension with aspects of the participatory ideals of Article 12. These examples focus on three themes: the first is about the ways in which inclusive practices require children to be able to fit into existing ways of doings things; the second explores how some dominant discourses (including developmental psychological norms) can prevent ways of reading children as active participants; and the third considers how moralizing scripts can limit what children are able to say and do. The examples also highlight spaces and moments where children may assert their own subjectivities and exhibit agency for transformation.

The concluding section identifies opportunities within everyday practices of schooling, as well as within wider educational discourses, to interrogate where and how children's participation may flourish in order that children can be taken seriously as citizens who matter.

2 THE TWO STUDIES

2.1 An English Context

Webb began her study in 2010, when a Conservative–Liberal Democrat government came to power in the UK. The new government aimed to set the coalition apart from the previous New Labour government but, also, to showcase a concern with issues of society as different from previous Conservative administrations. It meant the signaling of a move away from the view that the state should play a major role in shaping how society was to be organized and by what values. Instead, there was to be a focus on local communities working together. In educational terms, this was not inconsistent with the ideals of Article 12 or, indeed, of the school in which Webb conducted her study, which had embraced the Rights Respecting Schools Initiative (RRSI). The RRSI was an award developed by the UK arm of the United Nations Children's Fund (UNICEF). The RRSI was implemented during the New Labour government and was indicative of an era in which integrated ideas of listening to children were used to inform wider governmental discourses. For example, listening to children and young people was enshrined by New Labour within the Children Act of 2004, requiring all public services, including schools, to evaluate whether they enabled children to make a "positive contribution," which included expectations of children engaging in decision-making.[3] Notions of the value of engaging children in wider societal discussion waned during the life of the coalition government quite quickly.[4] Notwithstanding the fact that the RRSI was indicative of the New Labour period in the UK, it was only a relatively small initiative with limited resources, which most schools did not participate in as they were under no statutory obligation to do so. It still endures, nevertheless, in some areas of England in 2018 as a commitment to putting children at the epicenter of school policies and practices.

Increasingly, the rhetoric of the public service participation came to be replaced by that of austerity within a Conservative administration. This governmental discourse generated its own popular logic of rolling back of the state, which also included, paradoxically, renewed central government control of educational policy that challenged ideas of children's participation. Led by the Secretary of State for Education, Michael Gove, this translated into assumptions about a functional model of teacher authority, discipline, and control. This was pervasive by the time Kirby began to collect her data within her two research sites, where there were few explicit demonstrations of a commitment to children's participation. The functional model included an emphasis on teachers imparting knowledge to children (rather than responding to children's interests) and demanding high standards of pupil behavior.[5] These moves were understood as prerequisites for improvements in individual pupil attainment, seen as important to erode structural societal inequalities between pupils.[6] They emphasized a commitment to a performance-focused educational culture, also evident in the inspection and rating of schools, and ranking by test results.

2.2 Article 12

This chapter adopts a broad understanding of Article 12 as a commitment to paying attention to children's experiences. This extends beyond simply asking children their views about decisions, particularly those defined by adults as significant. It means considering the many different ways children express themselves and the possibilities for children to transform what they can do and be. This includes their adoption and adaptation of available subject positions; their common concerns;[7] and their challenging of the status quo to require things to be done differently that may challenge a traditional locus of power between pupil and teacher in ways that can be deemed political.

Article 12 has played an important role in emphasizing children's competence to participate in policymaking and organizational administration in ways celebrated by many researchers working within educational contexts since the early 2000s.[8] In her study, Webb encountered various adults in different roles who spoke positively and energetically about the ethos of the RRSI to promote children's participation.

Many researchers are critical of assumptions of participation that they read as ignoring some of the dynamic workings of power as political, within-schooling contexts.[9] These researchers, from varying global contexts, suggest that assumptions of participatory practices focus on adultist arenas and agendas, uncritical ideas of sameness and difference, and Western practices that mirror representative political structures demanding ways of acting and excluding certain children in relation to wider familial and institutional networks of relationships. Within the current UK schooling context, such a critique might be applied to assumptions, for example, of a school council, involving small groups of pupils (often elected) taking part in improving their experiences of schools that offer only partial perspectives around limited agendas.[10] Sevasti-Melissa Nolas is critical of a too-straightforward reading of ideas of children's participation, constructed in terms of children's entitlement and self-determination, seldom referring to their civil and political participatory rights.[11] This reading can result in the resonance of a mere depoliticized voice in decisions affecting the child (such as that within the school council). Similarly critical, Kirsi Kallio and Jouni Häkli examine research into children's everyday lives rooted in an understanding of their political relevance.[12] This includes considering children's agency as political struggle and children's "potential to adopt and negotiate the subject positions offered to them,"[13] including the tactics they use to avoid available identities presented to them by more powerful adults, as illustrated in the data example below in which Jake resists being the good, still child, desiring instead to explore his environment through movement.

2.3 Subjectivity and Agency

Although connected through the shared foci on participation, schooling, and children, our research studies pose different questions. Webb asks about ways in which the RRSI enables children, ages seven to eleven, to enact their own subjectivities as part of an overarching school ethos of rights. Kirby focuses on younger children, ages four to six, asking about their opportunities for agency in the classroom. Agency is understood as children acting purposively to achieve outcomes of educational relevance. It is not therefore an internal capacity, but the interplay between individual desires and the power to affect change.[14] This understanding shifts attention toward the everyday processes that are unfolding, relational and temporal, examining the many elements that come into play that extend or limit children's agency to transform themselves and their school contexts. This includes agency to achieve new political subjectivities, changing what it is possible to think, do, and be. In both studies, children's subjectivities are understood as "shifting, multi-faceted and contradictory."[15] They are constituted through their relationships to power, including those with adults within the institution of the school.

2.4 Two Local Contexts

Both studies took place within primary schools where children are between the ages of four and eleven. Webb spent a large part of the academic year conducting fieldwork for three days each week to capture change as it emerged and evolved[16] while also engaging with the ways in which the RRSI discourse shaped everyday practices. She found that many adults (some parents, visitors, and school staff) described opportunities afforded by the RRSI as productive of a "happy," "carefree," and "joyful" school. Indeed the head teacher described being "privileged to be part of shaping young people." The head teacher saw the RRSI as a "set of core beliefs and core values." Around the school, Webb noticed brightly colored UNICEF posters with images of contented, multi-ethnic children in a range of contexts (exemplifying "the right to play," "the right to be healthy," "the right to freedom and safety") as well as RRSI leaflets in public spaces. There were various different styles of a RRSI charter informing children of their "right to be heard," their "right to work," and their "responsibility to listen." In regular newsletters for families, there were reminders of how support could be provided to reinforce the "language of children's rights." The head teacher explained how he got rid of all surveillance systems, including cameras, suggesting these as visible manifestations of adult control incompatible with his rights-focused value system. He was proud that children were welcome in any area of the school, including in the staffroom. The children were required to know when break times began and ended: no bell-ringing delineated the school day. Also, there were no specific rules about how to move around the building and no strictures on where, or where not, to run, including no requirement to line up. Indeed, the extensive outdoor space of the school was designed to enable children to move around freely and energetically, to make decisions about what to do and how to play during break times. Older children were trained to lead and make decisions about how to set up and monitor the outdoor space during break times, especially for younger children, to facilitate their engagement and participation. Nonetheless, another senior manager responsible for the monitoring of the RRSI was careful to explain to Webb that the commitment to the RRSI "was not political, you know," suggesting *politics* as a dirty word conveying an array of connotations and negative associations within wider society.[17]

Webb identified discourse of the UNICEF RRSI literature as silent on the idea that Article 12 is political, insofar as it assumes that it is primarily a technical and managerial process of following guidance and implementing it correctly to change behaviors. Certainly participants in Webb's research school were careful not to position the RRSI as political in any way. Achieving an RRSI award is broken into two levels which depend on demonstrating that the guidance has been followed. It masks difficulties within fundamental assertions of children's rights, neither embracing the possibilities for children transforming their subject positions nor addressing tensions created by competing school discourses that may challenge participation. Webb witnessed these tensions within her own research location, despite the enthusiasm and dedication of many school staff toward ideas of children's participation and the ideals of the RRSI. It is these tensions and difficulties that are taken up in the ethnographic vignettes within section 3.

Kirby's research was conducted over the course of an academic year (2015 to 2016) within two schools. She focused primarily on one class of children within an urban English primary school, rated as good by the governmental Office for Standards in Education (Ofsted). She began the research when the children, aged four and five, were ending their reception year (in England, the first compulsory year of schooling) and followed them through year one, when they turned five and six. The transition into year one becomes more formal, with its work- rather than play-based pedagogy, including an emphasis on listening and writing. The research included a focus on the whole class of children as well as in-depth attention to the experiences of six carefully selected children whom Kirby shadowed a day at a time. She also spent a week in another school, undertaking a rapid ethnography in a year one class in a teaching school rated outstanding by Ofsted with a publicly expressed commitment to children's agency.

Kirby showed how teaching staff had expectations that children should always be on-task. Within the performance-focused classroom, discourses and practices emphasized a normative pupil body as silent and still. Children sat in neat lines on the carpet for long periods of the day, expected to be listening to teacher instruction. The message to children was heard in the class teacher's instruction: "Remember good sitting and listening means good learning." Children were highly competent at knowing what was expected of them. The children repeatedly told Kirby that they did not like sitting and listening for a long time, finding it physically uncomfortable on the carpet and difficult listening to things they already knew or did not understand. One school had an expressed commitment to children's agency, including that of children's inclusion in school governance. Kirby identified, however, how in many ways the two schools were more similar than different, both requiring children to be on-task.

In the vignettes below, Kirby illustrates children's competence in understanding what is expected of them and agency in conforming and performing "good" and "clever" child-subject positions, including the demand that they listen and identify "correct" answers. This helped make classroom life more livable, though it was unhelpful for dealing with the new and unexpected. Kirby illustrates how the children, with little formal space to express their own interests or opinions, find moments to pursue desires and ways of knowing not provided for within the on-task classroom. Pursuing desires, children transform the pupil subject beyond being simply good and clever as well as transform existing social orders within the school. What is easily missed, or else dismissed, in these frequently fleeting moments where children pursue their desires is their critique of school conditions as discussed below in the vignette involving Jake.

2.5 Ethnographic Methodology

Ethnography has offered both of us the opportunity for rich, qualitative description of lived everyday experiences within our respective research contexts, focusing on the mundanity of everyday micro practices while also paying attention to how practices correspond to external processes, including wider policies, and how individuals and schools adjust to them.[18]

Ethnography plays an important role in identifying issues children themselves find important in their social lives. It does not attempt, however, to reveal an authentic child, but, rather, "a rendering of what childhood might be like."[19] We invite children, and other school subjects, to make meaning of their experiences. The aim is not simply to understand what something means to the children but also to probe the breadth of meaning-making. Philip Jackson's review of schooling cautions that pupil attitudes to the classroom are "more complex"[20] than might be gleaned by merely asking children whether they like school, assuming an acceptance that school is doing good and that "many who like school also worry about it."[21] Lisa Mezzai's advice is to attend not only to those voices that are easily understood, translatable, and heard but also those that are errant and silent, "both irrelevant and impossibly full."[22] It is these voices we draw attention to in our data vignettes below, alongside those of adults, as these inform and relate to those of the children.

Fieldwork was conducted in a variety of spaces around the schools: some official, such as classrooms and the assembly hall; others, less formal, such as corridors, play areas, and meeting rooms. On occasion, we were participant-observers joining in with a range of school activities, such as working with groups of children on learning tasks, conducting "playground duty," and generally helping with ancillary tasks. At other times, we had the leisure and privilege of observing what was going on, documenting this with copious field notes, fiercely scribbled at the time, and refined away from the field soon after. The aim was to scrutinize everyday occurrences of school life, acknowledging that they could be understood in many different ways, all and none of which can be seen as true.[23] Like Cath Laws, they aimed to achieve ways of reading the school in new ways to see things that previously they may have taken for granted.[24]

3 Ethnographic Vignettes

The ethnographic vignettes presented below explore different ways in which Article 12 can be considered within the two research studies focused on here. For both of us, this means paying attention to ways in which ideas of children's participation become compromised through a range of competing schooling discourses. These discourses often undermine and limit the possibilities for children to assert some participatory political power to challenge the ways things are done, even where adults have an expressed commitment to the ideas of children's rights and agency.

3.1 Getting Inclusion "Done"?

In the two examples below, the children, James and Jake, central to each vignette, offer a critique of a dominant discourse of inclusion, which depends on their socialization to "slot in" to existing school practices in ways that do not challenge a distribution of participatory power between pupil and teacher. Webb identifies the terms on which inclusion is acknowledged and celebrated within the discourse of the school as well as the pain and challenge of marrying this to the wider schooling logics of an annual school show" that is performed for parents, families, and well-wishers the same way year after year. What makes this show different on the occasion under study is the inclusion of James, a child with special needs, as the lead. This fulfils the Level 2 requirements of an RRSI to demonstrate that "The school has an inclusive and participatory ethos based on the CRC." Kirby illustrates how Jake, at the time a lower achieving child, finds ways to include himself more sensorially in a math lesson in which he is expected to sit still while waiting his turn. We see how Jack's desire for understanding the world is embodied through direct engagement rather than by sitting still.

3.1.1 *Stressy Spring-Time Show*

You wouldn't believe it—that it's spring. Everyone says that. The weather's atrocious. There's still snow on the ground—you know, the slushy stuff that gets in everywhere. The children haven't been outside for days, and now everyone is in the school hall because there's so much to sort out for the Spring Show. James is to be the narrator. He's the prince. It will be his job to ride his wooden hobbyhorse on and off the stage (seamlessly linking each scene of the show which each of the junior classes has rehearsed). He's doing a great job. He's remembered his lines and he's coming on and going off the stage at the right moments and then his crown falls down over his face and it's funny. It's really funny. And Everyone laughs and some children point. James lifts his crown and looks at Everyone laughing and pointing at him, and he laughs at himself and at Everyone laughing at him. James laughs more, and slaps his sides and looks around. It's such a Good Show. The hall is full of laughing children being IMPOSSIBLE. Mrs D. tries to manage James ("Calm down, James, now!" she commands). James lies with his face on the floor. (James' teacher has had to leave the hall because she is so stressed). But she comes back. She's cross: doesn't Mrs D. know the first thing about managing a child such as James with Special Needs? (Webb's field notes, March 2012).

James is the lead in the show. This is the beautiful safe space, which he often finds "horrible," where he can feel confident enough to laugh at himself and his whole self is not risked. Yet on his little wooden hobbyhorse, he must move along a tightrope. He is required—at one and the same time—to both stick out and blend in. This is not a comfortable or straightforward position for anyone. Sara Ahmed suggests that "comfort" is about a "sinking feeling": bodies that *"can sink into spaces that extend their shape"* (emphasis in the original).[25] James may sink in to this rehearsal for a time, but this cannot last. He is confused by those around him: the sounds; the instructions; the laughter; the raised voices. James's version of sinking in is to sink to the floor face down (blending in only to stick out all the more). James has been invited to be different. But this should not feel so difficult to execute—surely—for the very point of the participatory discourse of the RRSI is to give voice to those who can all too easily be excluded, "acknowledging 'difference' as the norm, rather than the aberration."[26] This is clearly challenging in terms of what has been planned for the show. The demands of this require the adults not only to manage themselves but also to oversee the children in managing themselves appropriately. They must do this, likewise, on the evening of the actual performance, even as the school community demonstrates its commitment to participation: to demonstrating "the competency" and "voice" of "all children" (including that of James). The episode ends with one teacher shouting so that the hall of excited children falls silent. There is a reinstatement of the norm with the teacher as the "engineer of behaviour."[27] The teacher steps up to her place to control the children, such that: "school and schooling is experienced as something 'done' to the children by adults."[28] This makes huge demands of both James and the teacher, in particular, to perform a range of contradictory subjectivities in full public gaze.

3.1.2 *Against the Grain*

One autumn morning, some children from the lowest attaining math group are engaged in measuring dry porridge using recycled plastic food pots to see which has the largest capacity. This activity links well to their fairy tale learning journey. Each child must wait their turn to scoop out the porridge from a large gray washing-up bowl and to create a bar chart of the results on a whiteboard. This is a rare opportunity to engage with something real and textual. Jack cannot resist the desire to put his hand in the bowl. Prevented from doing so by a verbal reprimand, he rocks his chair, touches my camera and Nikita's pen, talks with his pen in his mouth, and eats some spilled grains. Jack's desire to know is mediated through the desire to touch, taste, and explore the materiality of his environment. His body is in search of sensory engagement, just like Goldilocks: "to experience the coarseness of matter, to know its grain intimately."[29] Finally, Jack receives a warning for repeatedly trying to tidy up porridge grains. "You need to listen and not be playing with the porridge," he is told.

This measuring activity offers the potential for adults and children to not know together, as they cannot know without measuring, but there is no opportunity for the children to play and inquire with the resources, only to measure as instructed. Without time and a more enriching material environment, the children do not practice porridge-making, and the teacher, busy being on-task, does not reimagine how to use available resources. The value of real-life math for children's understanding compared with school math has previously been highlighted.[30] The narrow focus of this activity is scripted by the curriculum, which requires that "pupils should be taught to: measure and begin to record...capacity and volume,"[31] working with "concrete objects and measuring tools."[32] The on-task classroom does not recognize cooking, a more traditionally feminine pursuit, for its numerous social, cognitive, and imaginative possibilities (to calculate, evaluate, improvise, remember, and match).[33] Jackson's exploration of the classroom identifies patience as the quintessential virtue, where children must "learn to suffer in silence" and "bear with equanimity" the "continued delay, denial, and interruption of their personal wishes and desires,"[34] pleasing the teacher by vocalizing satisfactions and "keeping silent about many of the discomforts engendered by classroom life."[35] Children like Jack are heard as noise more than voice, operating in ways that err from the available script, which is to be still and silent. His actions insinuate a critique of the classroom conditions that allow for such narrow means of making meaning of the world.

3.2 Being "Seen" and "Heard"

The following vignettes focus on how it is difficult for some children who present challenging behaviors, including one child framed as having developmental deficits, to be seen and heard in ways that promote alternative affirming subjectivities. Webb introduces Maya, who gets frustrated within the classroom, leading to outbursts of anger. In the extract below, Maya is participating in an exemplary fashion in terms of the RRSI discourse, but the teacher becomes caught in the normalizing discourse of Maya as deviant. Similarly, Kirby describes how she too gets caught up within a normalizing discourse such that she overlooks Timor as a participant within her participatory research group discussion.

3.2.1 *Anger Management*

Maya has been trained to lead a range of games within the playground and to include different children, some of her own age and some younger. She is playing a ball game with a group of other children, organising them and ensuring that the rules of turn taking are adhered to. The teacher is delighted to see her participating so enthusiastically, especially given her "anger management issues." I speculate aloud alongside the teacher about what it might feel like to be this child within an environment in which most children are clearly very different to her because they find it easier to collaborate with other children than Maya does. I also remark that I haven't seen her angry in the playground. The teacher reminds me that she is angry and that she does have anger management problems that "will need to get fixed." (Webb's field notes, February 2012).

The dominant presentation of Maya as having anger-management issues acts as a block to any alternative way of conceptualizing her within the moment of this encounter, even as she takes part and leads within the terms of the participatory discourse of the RRSI. In the adult exchange, Maya's subjectivity seems to be in need of some permanent fixing before she herself can be taken seriously as a participatory subject on an ongoing basis. The developmental psychological assumptions dominant within education underpin the reading of the RRSI literature, which tends to fix children with characteristics they cannot easily escape. For Maya this makes it difficult for her to be regarded as anything but angry (even when she is not). She must be ever vigilant in order to establish her status as a "proper child"[36] under constant apprehension of the threat of becoming a bad subject.

3.2.2 *The "On-Task" Researcher*

Kirby's intention was to support all children's participation in her study, similar to both research schools' proud inclusion of diverse groups of pupils. It was not until some months after leaving the field, when transcribing a group interview, that she became aware of having excluded Timor, a black child, from joining her group discussion. When he arrived late, she asked him to return to the classroom, believing him to be in the wrong place. On listening repeatedly to the audio recording, she heard other children telling her that he is supposed to be in their group. At the time of the interview, Kirby did not know Timor well. She had observed staff finding him difficult because he challenged their authority, including speaking critically about the classroom. By not hearing the children at the time, Kirby had enlisted in the narrative of Timor as troublemaker. She did not give him and the others the time to explain, anxious instead to get back on-task with the group activity. Participation demands a focus on the mechanisms by which we listen to children, including an awareness of how we silence or distort their voices. Even within a highly participatory context, such as Kirby's group work, designed to engage and to listen, some children remain unseen and unheard beyond the discursive constraints of normalization. The group discussion was already proving difficult to facilitate, as Kirby's expectation that children listen to each other was being resisted, with the children beginning to use the research activities to pursue desires that were not about being on-task. This involved much humor, speaking over each other, and plenty of movement, such as getting up from the table. Kirby used visual and playful research methods, and so, over time, she became positioned as a type of play worker with a "low personal rule frame."[37] The children powerfully and competently identified a large crack in the dominant culture and did not see her sessions as a place to be on-task.

3.3 Moral Regulation: Speaking the Right Script

The following examples identify how children actively seek out ways to do the right thing in terms of what they believe adults expect of them. A dominant discourse of moral conformity thwarts the impetus for children to speak out beyond ventriloquizing a status quo of assumed power. Webb notices that some of the children politely try to figure out what she seems to require of them when asking about a display of UNICEF posters and RRSI school charters. Kirby suggests that being on-task is a schooling in moral rectitude, one in which the moral admonition echoes "the old-time pedagogues [who] used to say 'Stand up straight!' "[38] Children understand what is expected and put in the "ethical labour"[39] in order to create a good impression.

3.4 What Is it You Want Me to Say?

In the exchange below, a group of nine- and ten-year-old pupils, as part of an activity to qualify for Level 2 of the award, have met to tell Webb what the RRSI means to them. They have congregated in an empty entrance hall during a quiet period of the school day.

> WEBB: So, all these new posters that have gone up—the UNICEF ones about "Rights"—Children's Rights—what's that about, then?
> SILENCE—the group of children look at each other.
> WEBB (AGAIN):   What's it about—this stuff? (turning and pointing)
> SILENCE . . . then . . . Oscar: Helping each other?
> SILENCE and long pause . . . Webb: Anyone want to say anymore?
> MIA: Making sure that someone is okay if they are upset or not feeling very well . . . SILENCE
> WEBB (smiling encouragingly):   Do you think that that stuff (pointing again and nodding in direction of all the displays)—being considerate, helping, for example, would happen if you weren't a rights-respecting school?
> RACHAEL: I think they probably would. 'Cos every school needs to do that because they are vital things 'cos if they [children] are hurt you need to do that . . . PAUSE
> WEBB: What does the RRSI stuff do then—the charters, the posters? Why are they up?
> OSCAR: To help us remember . . . the . . . the things on it.
> DAN: You might feel guilty 'cos it's on a poster.
>
> (Interview transcript, March 2012)

There is a great deal of hesitation and a certain amount of embarrassment on the part of the children in this exchange. Webb has a presentiment of having asked something rather stupid. The children look as though she has, or as though they are desperately trying to work out what it is that she is expecting of them. What emerges is a sense, in what they say, of a moral institutional responsibility for children to help each other. Several children articulate a function of the posters as a moral "aide memoire." The message of the posters is moral discourse, presented in the form of secularized rights, echoing a long trajectory of Christian discourse within English primary schooling.[40] This does not rely upon overt forms of teacherly control. Rather, the messages conveyed by the posters require the internalization of forms of self-governance, which become about what each child internalizes as physiologically "normal"[41] to discipline and order.

3.5 Moral Rectitude

Anna is one of the conforming good children, often seen sitting upright with a finger on her mouth. She works diligently and quietly, is currently achieving highly, but what she avoids is expressing something of herself beyond being "good" and "clever." When Kirby asks her to draw a sound that she often hears in the classroom, she draws the teacher "telling us what to do," because "I like work," and when asked to make a sound using her voice or an array of objects, Anna makes a breathing sound:

KIRBY: It's like a heavy breathing noise. Tell us about that noise, Anna.
ANNA: Children breathing.
KIRBY: Children breathing. So tell me, when do you hear that?
ANNA: On the carpet.
KIRBY: Okay.
ANNA: All the time.
KIRBY: And what does it feel like hearing that noise?
ANNA: Breathing. [Another child imitates heavy breathing noises.]
KIRBY: Breathing. And is there any other noise when children are breathing on the carpet? [Anna shakes her head; while she does so, another child in the group breathes loudly and then makes a dying sound.]

(Group interview transcript, July 2016)

Anna is repeatedly unwilling to expand on her views, sometimes saying simply, "I don't know." She is not humorous or playful like some of the other children, who can use spaces, such as this research group away from the classroom, to question, subvert, or make fun of the on-task culture (heard in the dying noise above). Anna's reticence to express a view keeps her out of trouble where there are no clues to answer Kirby's questions. While Anna is fulfilling the right not to express a view (consistent with Article 12), which must be entirely respected, it also demands that as adults we try to understand what may be preventing her from participating. Anna's compliant practice of working hard, sitting still and upright, and saying nothing constitutes a good child subjectivity. Submitting to the discipline of the classroom involves a degree of agency, through navigating the different ways to perform, inhabit, and experience the norms of the good child. It is limited agency, however, with Anna unable to come freely "into presence."[42] This would mean inserting something of her uniqueness into this particular social space at this moment to have the opportunity to explore different ways of being Anna. The form of ethical labor demonstrated by Anna is evocative of pious subjectivities,[43] including those that are core to the English education system which emerged out of a pastoral pedagogy with a spiritual discipline equipping individuals to "comport themselves as reflective subjects."[44]

4 DISCUSSION

Article 12 expresses a political commitment entitling children to participate in transformational processes. The extent to which schools can make such a commitment is framed by governing policy structures and messages. An explicit commitment to the CRC, evident within one research school, created a sensibility of challenging overt coercive disciplining. Even with these best intentions, there remained similar effects on the children as those to be found in the other research schools with no stated commitment to the CRC. In both contexts, Article 12 became reduced to enforcing children's conformity, socializing them into existing social orders on many occasions, rather than providing opportunities for transformation. Nonetheless, Article 12 remains important, and schools need to hold on to what it asks of all school subjects, whether as adults or children, to underscore the political commitment to valuing participation and foregrounding children's experiences. What is needed is for Article 12 to be taken seriously as offering political possibilities and for adults to engage in discussions about how this might be sustained within the everyday life of the school.

How well the CRC is implemented is about children's daily existence and how they experience school. The observational and interview data examples in this chapter demonstrate the power of ethnography to highlight children's desires and concerns. Children are shown to be busy making meaning throughout the school day, beyond "institutionally defined moments,"[45] such as the example school councils mentioned earlier. Children engage in surprising and imaginative ways, mining available cracks, and communicating their interests, feelings, and critiques, even when they are expected to be silent and still. Children forge new subjectivities: the collaborative rather than angry child or the desiring rather than good/clever child. In moments both irrelevant and full, children speak something of their experiences. At times, their pursuit of desires is enacted collectively. Webb, for example, writes separately about the ways in which a group of children transgressed their gendered subjectivities when discussing the school "toilet charter."[46] More often, desires are pursued independently, raising common concerns about opportunities for them to come together to express what they collectively view as important. Kirby identified children's diverse ways of making meaning, including humor and their deployment of movement and sound, which exposed the limitations of their current on-task order that favored children learning primarily when silent and still. The children are not demanding better school conditions, but their actions offer a critique of current educational policies and practices: decisions made without engaging with children's experiences of schooling.

Children cannot alone transform their lives or their school. The CRC acknowledges the importance of them doing so within supportive relationships with adults. The research presented here suggests that this requires adults to have reflective opportunities, similar to those offered by ethnographic methodologies and approaches, to engage with their own observational data and children's voices (or silences). Missing are the chances to make explicit the tensions between the need for both conformity and transformation: where it is possible to explore what might be done differently and what needs to remain the same in the school day. This includes opportunities for spaces to engage critically with pedagogy and practice, and to return to the values underpinning these, when deciding how to engage children. Currently there are too few spaces and limited vocabularies for adults (as well as children) to be vulnerable, to engage in reflection and in collective problematization. Webb found that inevitable tensions arose between ensuring children's conformity to wider school discourses while supporting children's participatory rights. These were aired as staff frustrations and not as opportunities for self-reflection and collective problem-solving. Kirby identified numerous rewards and sanctions employed by staff in their attempts to enforce children to remain on-task, rather than schools aiming to identify why children were not more energized and participative in their learning.

To open up transformational participatory spaces, the data vignettes draw attention to the following questions, important to make evident the tensions between conformity and transformation and to identify possibilities for action. These questions emerge sequentially from the vignettes above.

- Does the inclusion of difference require challenging the way things have (long) been done? What might be gained and lost?
- How do we look beyond children's challenging behaviors to acknowledge moments of participation?
- How can we tease out the ways in which participatory spaces may also demand children's conformity?
- What desires and concerns do children speak in their silences and (errant) actions? How can adults be alert to these?

5 CONCLUSION

Through ethnographic approaches used in two research studies in English primary schools, this chapter has explored how Article 12 can be understood as a commitment to giving due attention to children's experiences within schools. Participation is taken to include children's agency to act purposefully, including achieving new political subjectivities. The studies, undertaken in different political climates, highlight how the implementation of Article 12 in schools is connected to wider governmental priorities, and yet, Article 12 demands that children's participation must not be overridden by different policy agendas. By attending to micro moments of the rhythm of everyday school life, we illustrate how participation is often subsumed within powerful dominant schooling discourses of conformity. This is apparent even within the less coercive ethos of an RRSI school, which aims to redistribute power between adults and children. For adults, who must work within current and dominant educational discourses, as well as the CRC, there are inevitable tensions between supporting children's participation and their conformity. What is lacking are opportunities and spaces for adults to reflect on how to make decisions about where children's participation might take precedence, recognizing that participation will always be contingent on competing priorities for children's education. Nonetheless, the efforts to advance the participation of children must be concerned with attending to, and taking seriously, the brief moments of children's revelations of the ways they think, feel, and experience their worlds in school in order for them to be taken seriously as political subjects.

NOTES

1. UN Convention on the Rights of the Child (CRC), G.A. Res. 44/25, 44th Sess., UN Doc. A/RES/44/25 (1989).
2. Jo Moran-Ellis, "Children as Social Actors, Agency, and Social Competence: Sociological Reflections for Early childhood," *Neue Praxis* 43, no. 4 (2013): 303–318.
3. Office for Standards in Education, Children's Services and Skills (Ofsted), Every Child Matters: Framework for the Inspection of Children's Services (London: Ofsted, 2005), 3.
4. Bernard Barker "Frozen Pendulum?" Journal of Educational Administration and History 44, no.1 (February 2012): 65–88.
5. Michael Gove, "Education Secretary, on Why There Has Never Been a Better Time to be a Teacher," speech given at the Policy Exchange, London, September 5, 2013, https://www.gov.uk/government/speeches/michael-gove-speaks-about-the-importance-of-teaching; Ofsted, "School Inspection Handbook: Handbook for Inspecting Schools in England under Section 5 of the Education Act 2005" (December 2017) (includes amendments made by the Education Act 2011).
6. Michael Gove, "The Secretary of State Talks about the Making of an 'Educational Underclass,' " speech given at Durand Academy, London, Sept. 1, 2011, https://www.gov.uk/government/speeches/michael-gove-to-the-durand-academy
7. S-M. Nolas, C. Varvantakis, and V. Aruldoss, "Political Activism across the Life Course," Contemporary Social Science 12, nos.1–2 (2017): 1–12, 1.
8. Katherine Covell, "School Engagement and Rights-Respecting Schools," Cambridge Journal of Education 40, no. 1 (March 2010): 39–51; Isabelle De Coster, Olga Borodankova, Ana Sofia De Almeida Coutinho, and Paolini Giuli, Citizenship Education in Europe (Brussels: Education, Audiovisual and Culture Executive Agency, 2012); Dympna Devine, "Children's Citizenship and the Structuring of Adult-Child Relations in the Primary School," Childhood 9, no. 3 (August 2002): 303–320; David Hicks and Cathie Holden, The Challenge of Global Education: Key Principles and Effective Practice (London: Routledge Falmer, 2007); R. Brian Howe and Katherine Covell, Empowering Children: Children's Rights Education as a Pathway to Citizenship (Toronto: University of Toronto Press, 2007); Audrey Osler and Hugh Starkey, Teachers and Human Rights Education (Stoke-on-Trent, UK: Trentham, 2010); Judy Sebba and Carol Robinson, Evaluation of UNICEF UK's Rights Respecting Schools Award (London: UNICEF, 2010).
9. Sarada Balagopalan, *Inhabiting Childhood: Children, Labour and Schooling in Postcolonial India* (Basingstoke, UK: Palgrave Macmillan, 2014); Tuula Gordon, Janet Holland, and Elina Lahelma, *Making Spaces: Citizenship and Difference in Schools* (Basingstoke, UK: Macmillan, 2000); Cath Laws, *Poststructuralism at Work with Marginalised Children* (n.p.: Bentham Books, 2011); Ruth Lister, "Citizenship: Towards a Feminist Synthesis,"

Feminist Review 57, no. 1 (September 1997): 28–48; Eve Mayes, Shukria Bakhshi, Victoria Wasner, Alison Cook-Sather, Madina Mohammad, Daniel C. Bishop, Susan Groundwater-Smith et al., "What Can a Conception of Power Do? Theories and Images of Power in Student Voice Work," *International Journal of Student Voice* 2, no.1 (2017), https://ijsv.psu.edu/?article=what-can-a-conception-of-power-do-theories-and-images-of-power-in-student-voice-work; Peter Moss, "Listening to Young Children—Beyond Rights to Ethics," in *Let's Talk about Listening to Children: Towards a Shared Understanding for Early Years Education in Scotland*, (Glasgow: Learning and Teaching Scotland, 2006), 17–23; Jessica Pyckett, "Making Citizens Governable? The Crick Report as Governmental Technology," *Journal of Education Policy* 22, no.3 (April 2007): 301–319; Rebecca Webb, "Negotiating the '3Rs': Deconstructing the Politics of 'Rights, Respect and Responsibility' in One English Primary School," in *Education as Social Construction: Contributions to Theory, Research and Practice*, ed. Thalia Dragonas, Kenneth Gergen, Sheila McNamee, and Eleftheria Tseliou (Chagrin Falls, OH: Taos Institute Publications, 2015), 283–297.

10. Webb, "Negotiating the '3Rs.' "

11. Sevasti-Melissa Nolas, "Children's Participation, Childhood Publics and Social Change: A Review," *Children & Society* 29, no. 2 (March 2015): 157–167.

12. Kirsi P. Kallio and Jouni Häkli, "Are There Politics in Childhood?," *Space and Polity* 15, no.1 (April 2011): 21–34.

13. Kallio and Häkli, "Are There Politics in Childhood?," 28.

14. Moran-Ellis, "Children as Social Actors," 303–318.

15. Jane Kenway, Leonie Willis, Sue Blackmore, and Jill Rennie, "Making 'Hope Practical' Rather Than 'Despair Convincing': Feminist Post-Structuralism, Gender Reform and Educational Change," *British Journal of Sociology of Education* 15 (1994): 187–210, 189.

16. Martin Hammersley and Paul Atkinson, *Ethnography: Principles in Practice.* (Oxfordshire, UK: Routledge, 2007).

17. Colin Hay, *Why We Hate Politics* (Cambridge, UK: Polity Press, 2007).

18. Pat Thomson and Christine Hall, *Place-Based Methods for Researching Schools* (New York: Bloomsbury, 2017), 17.

19. Alison James, "Learning to Be Friends: Participant Observation, Amongst English School Children (The Midlands, England)," in *Being There: Fieldwork in Anthropology*, ed. C. W. Watson (London: Pluto Press, 1999), 98–120, 101.

20. Philip. W. Jackson, *Life in Classrooms* (New York: Holt, Rinehart and Winston, 1968), 61.

21. Jackson, *Life in Classrooms*, 58.

22. Lisa A. Mazzei, "An Impossibly Full Voice," in *Voice in Qualitative Inquiry: Challenging Conventional, Interpretive, and Critical Conceptions in Qualitative Research*, ed. Alecia Y. Jackson and Lisa A. Mazzei (London: Routledge, 2009), 45–62, 50.

23. Laws, *Poststructuralism at Work with Marginalised Children*, 15.

24. Cath Laws, Poststructuralism at Work with Marginalised Children, (Bentham Books (ebook), 2011).

25. Sara Ahmed, *On Being Included: Racism and Diversity in Institutional Life* (Durham, ND: Duke University Press, 2012), 40.

26. Devine, "Children's Citizenship and the Structuring of Adult-Child Relations in the Primary School," 304.

27. Miche, *Discipline and Punish: The Birth of the Prison*, trans. Alan Sheridan (1977; reprint, New York: Vintage Books, 1979).

28. Devine, "Children's Citizenship and the Structuring of Adult-Child Relations in the Primary School," 312.

29. Michel De Certeau, Luce Giard, and Pierre Mayol, *The Practice of Everyday Life, Volume 2: Living and Cooking*, trans.Timothy J. Tomaskit (Minneapolis: University of Minnesota Press, 1998), 186.

30. Charles Desforges and Anne Cockburn, *Understanding the Mathematics Teacher: A Study of Practice in First Schools* (London: Falmer Press, 1987).

31. Department for Education, "The National Curriculum in England: Key Stages 1 and 2 Framework Document" (September 2013), 105, https://assets.publishing.service.gov.uk/government/uploads/system/uploads/attachment_data/file/425601/PRIMARY_national_curriculum.pdf.

32. Department for Education, *National Curriculum in England*, 101.

33. De Certeau, Giard, and Mayol, *Practice of Everyday Life*.

34. Jackson, *Life in Classrooms*, 18.

35. Jackson, *Life in Classrooms*, 66.

36. Maggie MacLure, Liz Jones, Rachel Holmes, and Christina Macrae, "Becoming a Problem: Behaviour and Reputation in the Early Years Classroom," *British Educational Research Journal* 38, no. 3 (2012): 447–471, 447.

37. Andrew Pollard, *The Social World of the Primary School* (New York: Holt, Rinehart and Winston, 1985), 173.

38. Adriana Cavarero, *Inclination: A Critique of Rectitude* (Redwood City, CA: Stanford University Press, 2016), 62.

39. Ian Hunter, *Rethinking the School: Subjectivity, Bureaucracy, Criticism* (St. Leonards, AU: Allen and Unwin, 1994), 56.

40. Michael. A. Elliott, "Human Rights and the Triumph of the Individual in World Culture," *Cultural Sociology* 1, no. 3 (November 2007): 343–363.

41. Thomas. S. Popkewitz, *Struggling for the Soul: The Politics of Schooling and the Construction of the Teacher* (New York: Teachers College Press, Columbia University, 1998).

42. Gert J. J. Biesta, *The Beautiful Risk of Education* (Boulder, CO: Paradigm Publishers, 2014), 143.

43. Saba Mahmood, *Politics of Piety: The Islamic Revival and the Feminist Subject* (Princeton, NJ: Princeton University Press, 2005).

44. Hunter, *Rethinking the School*, 60.

45. Nolas, "Children's Participation, Childhood Publics and Social Change," 161.

46. Rebecca Webb, "Being Yourself: Everyday Ways of *Doing* and Being *Gender* in a 'Rights-Respecting' Primary School," *Gender and Education* 31, no. 2 (2017): 258–273.

CHAPTER 24

NATIONAL HUMAN RIGHTS INSTITUTIONS FOR CHILDREN

GERISON LANSDOWN

1 INTRODUCTION

THE adoption and the rapid near universal ratification of the UN Convention on the Rights of the Child (CRC) paved the way for a discourse not only on the implications of recognition of children as subjects of human rights but also on how to hold governments accountable in the implementation of the measures necessary to ensure their realization. During the same period, the 1993 World Conference on Human Rights affirmed the importance of institutions to protect human rights, advise governments, address violations, and raise awareness.[1] Furthermore, in 1993, the UN General Assembly endorsed the Paris Principles, elaborating on the core responsibilities of institutions established to promote and protect human rights.[2] It was in the context of these developments that the rapid introduction of independent human rights institutions for children began to take place over the subsequent thirty years. These developments were reinforced by the UN Committee on the Rights of the Child (CRC Committee), which has acted as a strong advocate for the establishment of independent human rights institutions, regularly recommending their establishment in their Concluding Observations to states parties.[3] The CRC Committee reinforced this commitment in its General Comment No. 2 (2002), in which all states parties were encouraged "to establish an independent institution for the promotion and monitoring of the implementation of the Convention."[4] The General Comment provides guidance on the role and formation of human rights institutions, building on the Paris Principles and adapting them to the child rights framework introduced by the CRC.[5] The Committee considers these independent human rights institutions to be a core element of states' commitment to the practical implementation of the CRC.[6]

The case for powerful and effective bodies to act as advocates and watchdogs, both with and on behalf of children, is unquestionable. Children in all but a few countries lack the right to vote (and even in those few countries; the lowest voting age is sixteen) as well as any access to the powerful lobbies that typically influence governments. They rarely have access to any of the systems that exist for complaints or redress through which to remedy rights violations, an issue regularly raised as a matter of concern by the CRC Committee.[7] While the optional protocol on a communications procedure does afford a remedy once all domestic avenues for complaint have been exhausted, by 2018 it only had thirty-nine ratifications and is therefore available for only a limited number of children. In the absence of other opportunities, the Committee has specifically identified a role for independent national human rights institutions in ensuring that children can easily access complaints mechanisms and advisory services.[8] Furthermore, children are more affected than other population groups by the actions or inactions of governments: high-level users of public services, including early years care, education, health, sexual and reproductive health care, and youth services, children are also disproportionately vulnerable to the impact of poverty, poor housing, environmental pollution, and violence. And, as our understanding of brain development during childhood evolves, it has become ever more apparent that early experiences have a profound and lasting impact on life chances.[9] Very young children are intensely sensitive to their immediate environment, and acute stress and deprivation during that period can lead to permanent damage to their ability to learn and develop. It is also increasingly evident that continuing brain development throughout adolescence means that failure to provide adequately for children's emotional security, health, education, skills, resilience, and their understanding of rights has profound implications for their social, economic, and political development.[10] Accordingly, there is a developmental as well as a powerful principled case for protecting and promoting children's rights. The costs of failing children are high, and effective mechanisms that seek to hold governments to account and place pressure on them to take all possible measures to ensure the realization of their rights, have a critical role to play in seeking to mitigate such failure.

The arguments for effective independent advocacy for children are encapsulated in the CRC General Comment No. 2.[11] Indeed, the CRC Committee has made it clear that the establishment of independent human rights institutions for children (IHRICs) is a necessary corollary to effective government structures for children. Placing a strong emphasis on the centrality of independence, the Committee insists that such institutions must be completely free to determine their own agenda and activities.[12]

The first ever ombudsman for children was set up in Norway in 1981, but it is since the adoption of the CRC that the development of independent human rights institutions has accelerated. By 2012 there were well over two hundred such bodies in more than seventy countries around the world.[13] They adopt many different forms and names—children's commissioners within wider human right institutions, stand-alone children's ombudsmen, children's right commissioners, and children's advocates. They operate at both national and subnational levels, with significantly varied mandates, degrees of independence, levels of funding, and legislative powers. However, they all have a broad responsibility to advocate for the human rights of children, monitor the actions of governments, and serve as a conduit for the voices of children to reach those in power. The overarching role of all human rights institutions for children should be to promote a holistic approach to the realization of children's rights as elaborated in the CRC, informed also by the four general principles identified by the CRC Committee—non-discrimination, best interests, optimum development, and the right of the child to be heard. The extent to which these institutions are successful in achieving those goals depends on their capacity to act independently, build a reputation for rigor and integrity, and establish relationships of trust and respect with key policymakers. They work through a combination of reporting, mediating, advocating, awareness raising, and educating.

Given the importance of their role, the rapid growth in the numbers of institutions, the experience now of up to thirty years of their operation in practice, and the ongoing as well as evolving threats to the realization of children's rights, it is apposite to review the evidence of their work to date and reflect on their effectiveness and what changes might be necessary to improve and strengthen their role. In so doing, it is important to understand the political and cultural context in which these developments are taking place. Inevitably, perhaps, the contrast between the political rhetoric of commitment to children's rights and the reality on the ground is considerable. It has been argued that the speed of ratification of the CRC represented an assumption on the part of many governments that children's rights, unlike the claims to human rights of other groups, were soft-edged and less demanding of shifts in the preexisting balances of power.

However, the reality proves otherwise, and accordingly, the children's rights institutions have and continue to face multiple challenges. Many of the rights embodied in the CRC involve perceived or real threats to existing normative values—for example, on issues of equal rights for girls and boys, the right of children to make choices in respect of religion, and recognition of the right of all children to be listened to and taken seriously. Children's rights can also challenge controversial political issues, such as ending segregated schooling for children with disabilities in mainstream schools and reorienting youth justice systems away from punishment and detention toward diversion and rehabilitation. Furthermore, in many countries the very process of recognizing the rights of a child is seen by some individuals to undermine parental authority and constitute unwarranted state interference in family life. Given this perception that the CRC, and thereby institutions that seek to promote its implementation, constitute a threat to the role of parents in providing guidance and discipline to their children, it is important to investigate this claim and its implications for the work of IHRICs. In fact, far from seeking to displace or undermine the centrality of the family in children's lives, the CRC strongly emphasizes that the family is the key source of care, provision, and protection of a child, with primary responsibility for the upbringing of the child, and that this must be recognized and supported by the state. However, it also acknowledges that the child is an individual subject of rights who cannot be reduced to the status of the property of parents. The CRC thereby introduces a triangular relationship between the state, the child, and the family. The role of human rights institutions for children in this regard is to support and mobilize parents and other caregivers to advocate for states to fulfill their responsibilities to children, including through provision of material assistance and programs and, if necessary, by intervening to challenge unwarranted interference in family life where so doing is contrary to the best interests of the child.[14] At the same time, IHRICs also have responsibility to promote and protect the rights of children within the family and to press for a legislative and policy environment, backed up by training and awareness, which prohibits parents from acting in ways that serve to violate or abuse the rights of children.

These fears of the threat to family life, together with continuing failure to recognize children as subjects of rights, constitute pervasive and real barriers to the realization of children rights. The threats to the realization of children's rights are currently at risk of being further compounded by the widespread growth of populism and authoritarianism in the second decade of the twenty-first century. These trends are evident, for example, in Russia and the United States as well as in many countries in Europe, the Middle East, Asia, and Latin America. Hostility to asylum seekers and refugees, as well as xenophobia, racism, and Islamophobia, are increasing, as are attacks on the institutions of democracy—the judiciary, the free press, and freedoms of expression and assembly.[15] And it is usually children, as the most vulnerable members of any given society, who are most at risk from the uncertainties and instabilities these challenges pose and who therefore are in greatest need of such protection of their rights. The imperative for independent institutions to uphold and protect human rights takes on additional force in this political environment.

2 Issues Affecting Effectiveness of IHRICs

2.1 Legislative Mandate

The Paris Principles, adopted by the UN General Assembly in 1993, elaborated the core features required by all human rights institutions. They include the need for them to be vested with competence to protect human rights, the responsibility to promote harmonization of legislation to relevant human rights instruments, and responsibilities to provide opinions, recommendations, proposals, and reports on relevant matters. Human rights institutions must also be able to publish independent opinions and reports, to contribute to reports that states submit to UN treaty bodies, and to promote, teach, and publicize human rights.[16]

These features, in general, are equally applicable to IHRICs. Indeed, the European Network of Ombudsmen for Children (ENOC) requires compliance with the Paris Principles as a basis for membership in their network. However, the different legal status of children, and the need to take account of their best interests, evolving capacities, and right to express views and have them taken seriously, does require an additional degree of adaptation in the design and orientation of the institutions serving them. For example, ENOC recommends that the focus on children should be explicit and that the design and development of the institution should take full account of the special status of children. In particular, it recommends that the legislation establishing the IHRIC be linked specifically to implementation of the CRC and address economic, social, and cultural rights as well as civil and political rights, in addition to including provisions setting out specific functions, powers, and duties relating to children that are linked to the Convention.[17] CRC General Comment No. 2 builds on the Paris Principles to construct a model more specifically tailored for children. It emphasizes the importance of reaching out directly to children, involving them on advisory bodies, and using consultative mechanisms to ensure that the work of the institution is informed by children themselves.[18] It also extends the recommended range of activities to enable them to fulfill their role in promoting the implementation of children's rights. For example, CRC General Comment No. 2 proposes that IHRICs should ensure that national economic policy takes account of the rights of children, that IHRICs should promote respect for the views of children and ensure that their views are heard on matters affecting their human rights, and that they should advocate for and facilitate meaningful participation by children's rights NGOs, including those led by children themselves.[19]

In summary then, the mandate and commitment of an IHRIC should include powers to influence policymakers and practitioners to take greater account of the human rights of children, provide children with effective means of redress when their rights are violated, promote respect for the views of children, raise awareness and understanding, and monitor compliance with the human rights of children. It is the specific combination of powers, characteristics, and activities not available to any other organization or group of organizations that enable IHRICs to play a unique role in the promotion of children's rights.

However, analysis of existing IHRICs reveals that many of the features that are vital to their ability to function effectively in advancing the rights of children are not yet in place. A 2010 ENOC survey of its thirty-seven members found that of the twenty-seven respondents, thirteen reported weaknesses in the establishing legislation that limited the effectiveness of the institution and that they were keen to address.[20] Institutions in France, Croatia, Belgium, Finland, Azerbaijan, Ireland, and all four institutions in the United Kingdom identified weaknesses in their mandate. Some have commissioned expert evaluations of the legislation, while others have submitted proposals to their government or parliament. Several members have raised concerns in their reports to the CRC Committee, resulting in some cases to specific recommendations for strengthened legislation.[21] In the case of Ireland in 2006, for example, the CRC Committee recommended "that the State party, together with the Ombudsman for Children, review and propose amendments to the specific provisions which limit the scope of the Ombudsman's Office investigative powers with a view to eliminating possible gaps which may result in a violation of children's rights."[22] However, this concern was again expressed by the Committee in 2013 (indicating that it had not yet been resolved) when it recommended that the "State party consider amending the provisions of the Ombudsman for Children Act of 2002 which preclude the OCO from investigating complaints from children in a refugee, asylum-seeking and/or irregular migration situation."[23] In short, there is a clear understanding of the necessary mandate for effective protection of children's rights. The challenge now is to ensure that all states establish IHRICs with a mandate that covers the requirements necessary to ensure the IHRIC's effectiveness.

2.2 Independence

Independence is perhaps the most critical defining characteristic of IHRICs. It enables them to transcend political parties and maintain a rigorous focus on children's rights regardless of other political developments.[24] It is the primary source of their legitimacy and authority.[25] Of course, their independence is inevitably in tension with their status as a publicly funded body receiving its finances through government. Furthermore, independence is a matter of perception as much as actual formal status and powers.

Multiple factors contribute to the capacity of an institution to function as an independent body able to hold power to account on behalf of children. First, the IHRIC needs to be seen as independent by the constituency it is serving. While that obviously includes children, it also needs to be recognized as such by all marginalized communities, other NGOs working in the field, media, parents, and professionals working with children. It needs to be trusted by representatives from all sides of the political spectrum and not be perceived as aligned with any particular interest group. Factors likely to strengthen perceptions of independence include pluralistic representation within the institution, including gender balance and recruitment from all communities, a physical location not affiliated with any other institutions or within government buildings, a clear and explicit mandate, and professional practice that is consistently impartial.[26] The process of recruitment and appointment for a children's commissioner or ombudsman also is relevant to the status and respect afforded to the IHRIC.

The institution must also have a legal basis that establishes its status as an independent body. Independence is significantly enhanced if it is established through and accountable to parliament (as opposed to having to report to a particular government department) and therefore less vulnerable to pressures imposed by the prevailing government at the time. This foundation is strengthened if it is embedded in the constitution and thereby guaranteed greater sustainability and recognition as an integral pillar of the state system. In practice, this tends to happen only when the constitution is being more widely redrafted, as in South Africa in 1994.[27] Almost all IHRICs have been established by laws, many of which do explicitly afford them an independent mandate, but few to date are mandated within the constitution. The ENOC survey mentioned above found that all but one institution confirmed that they are free to act and speak out on any matter concerning children's human rights.[28] However, meaningful independence is further determined by the financial autonomy of the institution in terms of both the sufficiency of their budgets to carry out their mandated functions and the degree of unrestricted freedom over how it is spent. While state funding is crucial in providing legitimacy for an institution, it can also serve as a lever through which to control its work. The CRC Committee repeatedly raises concern over the inadequacy of secure funds provided to IHRICs as well as the need for genuine independence.[29] Some IHRICs bolster inadequate government funding through support from private or international donors. However, this can bring its own challenges. It may serve to compromise independence and sustainability over the long term and lead to a perception that the institution is influenced by a foreign agenda. In Morocco, for example, a post to recruit a staff member in the Consultative Council for Human Rights specializing in child rights was initially funded by UNICEF, but in the longer term the cost was incorporated into the council's budget.[30]

Of course, the very nature of an institution's independence can serve to undermine its sustainability. Many governments are uncomfortable with highly critical findings and respond by cutting the available resources, restricting the mandate, or even closing the institution down. A 2012 UNICEF survey of IHRICs found that governmental concerns over costs, a desire to integrate different human rights institutions, and political considerations have led to threats to a number of institutions in Ghana, Madrid, Croatia, France, and England. However, in all but the case of France, where the institution was incorporated into a broad-based human rights institution, mobilization by child rights advocates meant they were able to successfully withstand proposed changes.[31] In all these examples the reputation of the institution in garnering the active support of the wider community, including child rights NGOs, media, and other civil society organizations, was critical to their capacity to challenge potential closure.[32]

2.3 Structure

There has been ongoing debate concerning the pros and cons of different organizational structures for creating institutions to promote and protect children's rights.[33] In countries where an institution exists, the current models fall into three categories, with roughly a third being stand-alone institutions, a third being bodies integrated into generic human rights institutions but with a legislated child-specific mandate, and a third being institutions that lack a mandate in legislation.[34] As discussed above, a legislative base and explicit mandate with attendant powers to undertake the role as elaborated by the CRC Committee is essential. Therefore, the preferred structures for these institutions fall into the integrated or stand-alone model categories.

The benefits of a stand-alone body are that it is able to reach out very explicitly to children, with an identifiable commissioner or ombudsman and child-friendly and accessible office environments, websites, and publicity materials. Its separate mandate potentially affords greater opportunities for active engagement of children and the ability to build strong partnerships with key stakeholders involved with the rights of children, including within the private sector. The evidence indicates that it is largely only stand-alone institutions that include a specific mandate requiring accessibility to and involvement of children.[35] Accordingly, it is primarily these institutions that engage in activities to promote systematic and direct contact with children. Finally, a dedicated children's institution offers the space to give a higher profile to children's rights and to report to parliament exclusively on issues affecting them. Visibility is particularly important given the traditional failure to recognize children as subjects of human rights and to subsume their interests within those of the family. Evidence from existing IHRICs indicates that it is stand-alone bodies that are most likely to engage in systematic and direct contact with children.[36] Furthermore, in institutions responsible for promoting the human rights of everyone, there is a danger that other interests will be prioritized over those of children.

On the other hand, integrated institutions allow for greater cross-sectoral advocacy and monitoring, for example, where the joint engagement of commissioners for both disability and children could be called on to challenge the institutionalization of children with disabilities or to bring the commissioners for women and for children together to campaign around the exploitation of girls in domestic labor.[37] It can also be argued that promoting human rights from within an integrated body strengthens legitimacy and authority and raises the profile and status of the work. Many broad-based human rights institutions have mandates established in constitutions, with consequent positive implications for their status, which is rarely the case for specialized children's rights institutions.[38] At a more pragmatic level, a broad-based institution can be more cost-effective with pooled administration and infrastructure.

Overall, the evidence does not point strongly in favor of either approach. Ultimately, the effectiveness of the institution depends less on the overarching structure and more on a strong mandate with appropriate powers, level of resourcing, and both capacity and commitment to be dedicated to, focus on, and reach out directly to children.

2.4 Complaints and Investigations

Access to effective remedies for rights violations is fundamental to the realization of human rights. Unfortunately, while the majority of IHRICs have powers to investigate complaints, it remains far from universal. In the ENOC survey, six of the twenty-seven respondents stated that they were unable to investigate individual complaints: Denmark, England, Finland, Norway, Scotland, and Sweden. As testimony to the significance it attaches to this aspect of the work of IHRICs, CRC General Comment No. 2 goes further than the Paris Principles and argues that individual complaints mechanisms should be embedded in the mandates of all IHRICs.[39] It raises this issue with regularity when examining periodic reports by states parties.

For those that are able to undertake complaints, the 2012 UNICEF survey found that the specific mandates vary significantly, with some prescribing who is eligible to make a complaint and what issues can be the subject of a complaint.[40] Some IHRICs can compel the production of evidence or summon witnesses, while others must rely to a greater degree on goodwill to obtain evidence.[41] Illustrative examples of actions by IHRICs include complaints relating to individual children, such as a case of violence against a child by his uncle that led to the uncle's arrest and prosecution after an investigation by the Jamaican Office of the Children's Advocate.[42] IHRICs can also investigate cases relating to groups of children, such as the National Commission for the Protection of Child Rights in India undertaking investigations into an illegal children's home, missing children, and child labor;[43] and the Defensoria Del Pueblo in Peru intervening after relevant authorities failed to act on reports of sexual abuse of children by a teacher.[44] Overall, the cases brought to IHRICs address a very broad spectrum of issues, including sexual violence, child abuse, detention of children, lack of access to education, inadequate health services, bullying, custody, child support, child participation, discrimination against unaccompanied asylum seekers, and support for children with disabilities.[45]

Some institutions have sought to evaluate the satisfaction levels of the complaints services provided. For example, in 2016 in Northern Ireland, the Children's Commissioner Office dealt with a total of 314 cases, of which 219 were closed with successful resolutions. Evaluations from clients showed that 100 percent of those within remit were happy or very happy with the service provided. The types of cases they had supported included a young person's school expulsion, which they successfully got overturned and expunged from the academic records, and a case in which they provided assistance to a parent to lodge a complaint with the child's school, which ultimately resulted in the child being able to complete an education.[46] However, it is not evident that many IHRICs have undertaken a systematic evaluation of their effectiveness in ensuring either the accessibility of the complaints procedures or the outcomes associated with them.

Although IHRICs can make recommendations as a result of an investigation, they do not have powers of enforcement comparable with courts. The potential, therefore, for action being taken on their findings will necessarily depend on the quality of their research, their perceived independence, and the reputation of the institution. On the positive side, individual complaints can serve to highlight patterns of more systemic rights violations and strengthen the advocacy of the IHRIC. They can also provide the evidence needed to undertake broad-based institutional investigations, such as into mental health services for children or conditions in penal institutions. For example, in Hungary an individual case was reported of children in a particular family being abused over many years. Criminal proceedings were launched against the parents, and the children were placed with foster parents. The commissioner conducted a comprehensive inquiry into the activities of the authorities concerned and discovered not only serious mistakes by child protection authorities but also wider system deficiencies that needed to be addressed.[47]

One area of real concern is that the vast majority of complaints are lodged by parents rather than children. In 2016 in Latvia, for example, the ombudsman's office received 1,022 complaints—a 15 percent increase over the previous year—but less than 5 percent were lodged by children.[48] This pattern is widely replicated across other institutions, and many IHRICs themselves observe that they have failed as yet to make complaints systems genuinely accessible to children. This is a matter of concern in particular for those children who, lacking parental care or being detained in the juvenile justice system, are especially vulnerable to violations and, therefore, in need of accessible, safe, and child-sensitive complaints mechanisms.[49] The ENOC survey highlighted that many institutions experience difficulties in reaching out to more marginalized children, relying instead on concerned professionals to bring issues of concern to their attention. However, even where children are living with parents there can be conflicts as to their best interests and between the views of parents and children, meaning that, without independent access, children's real concerns may be rendered invisible. It is not evident whether the barriers to children derive from a lack of awareness of the systems, a lack of knowledge as to when and how to use them, or a lack of confidence that they will be treated with seriousness, safety, and respect. Clearly this is an issue deserving of further attention and research with children themselves in order to explore how to reach out more effectively, build trust, and encourage more proactive engagement from children.

2.5 Participation

The commitment to child participation in the work of IHRICs needs to apply both to the ways in which they conduct their activities and to the nature of the work they undertake. This dual emphasis on the active engagement of children is viewed by the CRC Committee as foundational to IHRICs' legitimacy and effective functioning.[50] Accordingly, a number of institutions have it written into their mandate that they will establish systems or structures for consulting with children as well as promote the rights of children to express their views on all matters of concern to them, in accordance with CRC Article 12.

The mechanisms adopted by IHRICs to ensure that they involve children tend to fall into two categories. One approach is to establish permanent advisory groups or boards that meet on a regular basis, in person or online, to enable the commissioner, for example, to maintain contact with children's general perspectives; undertake advocacy, monitoring, and peer education; identify priorities; and advise on communications while also offering opportunities for those young people to acquire knowledge and skills. The Cyprus commissioner maintains a standing group of thirteen- to seventeen-year-olds who are carefully selected to reflect diversity and special interests.[51] The office in Serbia has established a young advisors panel consisting of thirty children between the ages of thirteen and seventeen that is gender-balanced, represents of all parts of Serbia, provides for an equal number of primary school students and secondary school students, and ensures representation of children with disabilities, children belonging to national minority, and children in care.[52] In El Salvador the Procuraduría para la Defensa de los Derechos Humanos has established a juvenile dissemination unit involving around three hundred young people aged fifteen to twenty-five who are based in the office and are actively engaged in both human rights promotion and monitoring compliance with the CRC.

The other main approach is to undertake consultations on a more ad hoc basis to elicit children's views, either generically to inform the direction of the institution or with specific groups of children, for example, in order to help design a piece of research or to find out about their experiences and challenges and to help inform advocacy and policy proposals. Considerable investment has been made by many institutions to involve children in helping in this way. The Norwegian ombudsman holds expert meetings and establishes expert groups so that children and young people with a range of different experiences can be heard and their opinions and experiences taken into consideration when the authorities make decisions that impact the group of children in question. The experts' primary task is to advise the ombudsman on the kind of recommendations that should be made to better help children and young people who find themselves in a similar situation. The ombudsman distinguishes between expert meetings and expert groups. Expert meetings are relatively short, one-off meetings with a group of children and young people. Expert groups are made up of children and young people with experience in a particular area who work for a period of time on important issues together with the ombudsman's staff.

In Scotland in 2010, the Children and Young People's Commissioner undertook a consultation with children in order to inform the Commissioner's strategic work plan 2011–2015.[53] The process involved such activities as interactive workshops for children on their rights, opportunities to submit ideas for the future, and opportunities to describe positive experiences and to vote on what issues the commissioner should prioritize; 74,059 children and young people took part in the online element of the consultation alone. The children identified four priorities: being safe and secure, being treated fairly, being respected, and being included. The process not only provided real insight to guide the direction of the commissioner's work; it also served to raise awareness, promote active engagement, and increase dialogue about human rights.

Many IHRICs are also engaged in proactive work to promote awareness of Article 12 as well advocating and providing opportunities for children to be heard in other settings, whether in the home, school, health care facilities, child protection offices, and within justice systems and the context of wider civic engagement. An interesting illustration of this work can be found in Sweden, where the ombudsman has met with and listened to six hundred children and young people who arrived in Sweden unaccompanied or as part of a family. These meetings led to a comprehensive report published in 2016 and in 2017 to a high-level meeting focusing on children in migration organized by the ombudsman together with the Children's Welfare Foundation of Sweden and the Swedish Parliament.[54] The meetings with children provided a number of highlights and illustrations, which provided insight into the experiences children face and demonstrated the value of children being able to speak out, be listened to, and be met with respect.[55] At a more local level, in Wales in 2016, young people brought the issue of transportation to the attention of the children's commissioner. In Wales many children, especially those in rural areas, are dependent on public transportation and spend a disproportionate amount of wages on fares. In 2016 discounted bus travel for young people aged sixteen to eighteen was scheduled to come to an end. The commissioner requested a Children's Rights Impact Assessment (CRIA) for this decision; there was no CRIA in place when the decision was made, and the CRIA that was created subsequent to the commissioner's request reflected the fact that the scheme was only ever planned to run until March 2017. The commissioner wrote to the cabinet secretary for economy and infrastructure to raise concerns about this scheme ending and the lack of consideration for children's rights and experiences. The scheme was reinstated for a transitionary period while alternative options were explored. The Welsh government agreed to review options for future provision.

The work of IHRICs in this regard not only has intrinsic value in ensuring that children's voices are heard and taken seriously, but it also provides demonstration models of good practice in children's participation that can be emulated by other bodies. However, the 2017 UNICEF survey of IHRICs found that a number of institutions continue to fail to involve children in any meaningful way.[56] This undoubtedly derives from a combination of factors—failure to recognize the relevance and importance of children's perspectives, lack of confidence and capacity in working directly with children, and political and cultural environments that lack a history of civic engagement.

2.6 Accessibility and Outreach

An IHRIC has limited value if it is not accessible to children and particularly to those from marginalized communities whose rights are most at risk and who are therefore in greatest need of their services. Interestingly, few institutions actually have any formal mandates requiring them to make themselves accessible to children.[57] Where such requirements do exist, they tend to be in common law countries, such as Australia, Canada, Jamaica, New Zealand, and the United Kingdom. Furthermore, both the ENOC survey and the 2012 UNICEF study found low levels of awareness among children of the existence of the IHRIC in their country. In the former it was observed that, "although the majority of respondents answered 'yes' to the question asking if children 'generally knew about the institution,' it was clear that their replies rested more on hope than certainty. The six who had formally evaluated children's knowledge found that, despite their best efforts, many children were ignorant of their existence."[58] The latter study found that few assessments had been conducted to ascertain levels of awareness and that those that had pointed to limited visibility. For example, an evaluation in Wales found that of seven- to sixteen-year-olds, only between 3 and 16 percent (depending on age) had heard of the children's commissioner.[59]

Many institutions do make significant efforts to overcome these failures. Some have decentralized offices which appear to make a significant and immediate impact on the number of complaints. In Latin America, for example, many IHRICs have local *defensorías* that enable rural and indigenous communities to access their help.

In Peru, there are 840 local Defensorías del Niño y del Adolescente, which dealt with more than 130,000 cases in 2010.[60] Others engage in dedicated outreach programs to take their work out to local schools and communities. In 2016 staff working for the commissioner for children and young people in Northern Ireland, for example, delivered thirty workshops to more than seven hundred children and young people in school, youth clubs, and community settings. Workshops focused largely on raising awareness of the UNCRC and the role of the commissioner. Awareness-raising sessions were also held with one hundred parents and over four hundred health, social care, and education professionals.[61] Evaluations demonstrated the following: 83 percent of participants reported an increased understanding of children's rights; 98 percent reported an increased understanding of the commissioner's role; and 89 percent reported that they had an increased understanding of their own role in relation to promoting and protecting children's rights. In Latvia in 2016, the ombudsman launched a program of action to raise awareness of the office and its services. The program involved organizing lessons for children on what the ombudsman was for and how the office could help. The office created a billboard asking "Who Is Ombudsman?" which was installed in different institutions, such as juvenile prisons, boarding schools, children's homes, crisis centers, state social care centers, and psycho-neurological hospitals in order to reach out to the most marginalized children.[62] The provincial advocate for children in Ontario makes monthly visits to special schools for children with disabilities to hear their experiences of accessing services, as they face barriers in communication which make face-to-face contact more effective.[63]

However, significant challenges remain to be addressed, particularly for children in institutional care, where barriers relating to lack of accessibility, trust, safety, and information are widespread. Given the resources available to most IHRICs, it is unrealistic for them to be directly available to the broad range of children who may be living in institutions as well as in other vulnerable communities. One approach might be to support the development of systems comparable to that which exist in the Netherlands, where all youth care and juvenile justice institutions are required by law to establish a youth council.[64] This body comprises a panel of young volunteers from within the institution who have a role in identifying residents' problems, soliciting suggestions, and ensuring that these issues are raised with management and are properly addressed. In turn, the issues being raised can be communicated to the commissioner within the country to raise awareness of the types of concerns and to alert him or her to any potential need for investigation.

Finally, it can be difficult for IHRICs to visit children in private closed settings, such as those living in homes as domestic servants or employed in factories as workers. The UNICEF survey in 2012 found that few countries provide the legislative powers to enable investigations into such settings.[65] A notable exception is the ombudsman for Mauritius, who is authorized for investigative purposes to enter premises where a child is present or may be in employment.[66] Similarly, the Defensor del Pueblo in Colombia can visit any public or private entity to investigate a complaint or prevent a human rights violation.[67]

3 CONCLUSION

The rapid growth in IHRICs has taken place alongside the near universal ratification of the CRC and the parallel international focus on the importance of human rights institutions during the 1990s. This process has been significantly supported by the work of the CRC Committee, which has placed a high priority on the provision of guidance and encouragement to states to invest in such institutions, as well as UNICEF country offices that have strongly supported the process at a national level around the world. Overall, there is no doubt that IHRICS have served to raise the awareness and profile of children's rights, achieved many concrete changes in the realization of those rights, and developed and promoted innovative approaches regarding the engagement of children alongside undertaking advocacy to ensure that children's voices are heard on all matters of concern to them. IHRICs have also had to undertake their work in a period when challenges to human rights, democracy, justice, and the rule of law are being widely challenged and in many cases undermined. Many have had to fight hard to retain their budgets, powers, independence, and in some cases, their very existence. And there is significant variation in their practice, influenced by a number of variables, including mandate, resourcing, geopolitics, and local politics as well as individual leadership.

However, despite the challenges, it is essential to keep pressing to improve and strengthen the valuable work that IHRICs do. There is now a broad consensus as to the underpinning legislation required to establish an effective institution. Those that lack the necessary powers to conduct their work effectively need to build networks of partners to support them in advocating for the changes they need, together with sufficient budgets to fulfill a meaningful role. Investigations into individual complaints need to be used systematically to identify wider rights violations and to inform subsequent advocacy. Far more work needs to be done to ensure that all children are aware of the institutions, what they do, why they exist, and how they can help them. It is not acceptable simply to admit the difficulties in making contact with younger children or those who are hard to reach. These are precisely the children that an IHRIC should be prioritizing. Good practices in outreach have been put in place by a number of IHRICs, and these can be replicated or adapted by others. Use of social media but also mainstream media, poster displays, and advertising in locations children use—including schools—can be exploited, as can the creation of local offices and regular outreach programs. Efforts should be made to ensure that children's rights and the role of the IHRICs are incorporated into the national curriculum in all schools. Children themselves need to be recognized as an invaluable resource of expertise on how best to communicate and reach out to them.

There is also the potential for most IHRICs to explore a far more radical engagement of children, including through more innovative uses of social media, engagement on management bodies, support for national movements of school students, and involvement of children directly as researchers, advisers, advocates, peer educators, and policy analysts. A number of institutions have used wide-ranging consultations with children to shape and inform priorities for action. This approach should be universal. Of course, an IHRIC will sometimes need to be reactive to current events, legislation passing through parliament, or immediate crises, but empowering children, including those who are most excluded, to drive the agenda will serve to promote a virtuous circle. Listening to children provides insight into the issues most pressing in their lives. Responding to their concerns and priorities will enable the IHRIC to prioritize the most relevant issues. And finally, seeing their concerns are being responded to will strengthen children's confidence that they can make a difference, build self-esteem, promote a sense of self efficacy, and strengthen confidence in democratic and accountable institutions. A journey has been started. A great deal has been learned. Now is the time to consolidate and fully translate into practice the recognition embodied in the CRC that children are entitled to be treated as subjects of rights whose dignity and active participation must be respected.

NOTES

1. Gerison Lansdown, "Independent Institutions Protecting Children's Rights," *Innocenti Digest* 8 (June 2001), https://www.unicef-irc.org/publications/301-independent-institutions-protecting-childrens-rights.html.

2. UN General Assembly, "National Institutions for the Promotion and Protection of Human Rights," G.A. Res. 48/134, 85th Sess., UN Doc. A/RES/48/134 (1993).

3. Rachel Hodgkin and Peter Newell, *Implementation Handbook on the UN Convention on the Rights of the Child* (New York: UNICEF, 2008), 66.

4. UN Committee on the Rights of the Child (CRC Committee), *General Comment No. 2: The Role of Independent Human Rights Institutions in the Promotion and Protection of the Rights of the Child*, CRC/GC/2002/2 (2002).

5. UN General Assembly, "Principles Relating to the Status of National Institutions" (Paris Principles), G.A. Res. 48/134, 48th Sess., UN Doc A/Res/48/134 (1993).

6. Vanessa Sedletzki, "Championing Children's Rights: A Global Study of Independent Human Rights Institutions for Children," UNICEF Office of Research–Innocenti report (2012), https://www.unicef-irc.org/publications/669-championing-childrens-rights-a-global-study-of-independent-human-rights-institutions.html.

7. Hodgkin and Newell, *Implementation Handbook*, 67.

8. CRC Committee, "Day of General Discussion on the Right of the Child to be Heard," 43rd Sess. (2006); see https://archive.crin.org/en/library/events/committee-rights-child-43rd-session.html.

9. Center on the Developing Child, Harvard University. "The Science of Early Childhood Development," INBRIEF series (March 2007), https://46y5eh11fhgw3ve3ytpwxt9r-wpengine.netdna-ssl.com/wp-content/uploads/2007/03/InBrief-The-Science-of-Early-Childhood-Development2.pdf.

10. Human Rights Council, "Report of the Special Rapporteur on the Right of Everyone to the Enjoyment of the Highest Attainable Standard of Physical and Mental Health, UN Doc. A/HRC/29/33 (April 2, 2015).

11. CRC Committee, *General Comment No. 2*, 5.

12. CRC Committee, *General Comment No. 5: General Measures of Implementation of the Convention on the Rights of the Child (arts 4 and 44. Para 6.)*, CRC/GC/2003/5 (2003).

13. Sedletzki, "Championing Children's Rights."

14. Jaap E. Doek, "Independent Human Rights Institutions for Children," Innocenti Research Center Working Paper No. 2008–06 (December 2008), https://www.unicef-irc.org/research/independent-human-rights-institutions-for-children.

15. Kenneth Roth, "The Dangerous Rise of Populism," *Human Rights Watch World Report 2017* (2017), 1–14, https://www.hrw.org/world-report/2017/country-chapters/dangerous-rise-of-populism.

16. UN General Assembly, "National Institutions for the Promotion and Protection of Human Rights," G.A. Res. 48/134, 85th Sess., UN Doc. A/RES/48/134 (1993).

17. European Network of Ombudsmen for Children (ENOC), "Organization of ENOC: Independent Children's Rights Institutions (ICRI's)," http://enoc.eu/?page_id=8 (accessed Aug. 30, 2019).

18. CRC Committee, *General Comment No. 2*, paras. 15–16.

19. CRC Committee, *General Comment No. 2*, paras. 19(f), (j), and (k).

20. Rachel Hodgkin and Peter Newell, "The Role and Mandate of Children's Ombudspersons in Europe: Safeguarding and Promoting Children's Rights and Ensuring Children's Views Are Taken Seriously," *ENOC Survey 2010* (December 2010), http://enoc.eu/wp-content/uploads/2015/02/201012-ENOC-Malta-survey-Role-of-Ombudspersons-for-Children.pdf.

21. Hodgkin and Newell, "Role and Mandate of Children's Ombudspersons," 6.

22. CRC Committee, "Concluding Observations: Ireland," UN Doc. CRC/C/IRL/CO/2 (2006), paras. 13–15.

23. CRC Committee, "Concluding Observations: Ireland," paras. 19–20.

24. Sedletzki, "Championing Children's Rights," 16.

25. Sedletzki, "Championing Children's Rights," 16.

26. Sedletzki, "Championing Children's Rights," 16.

27. South African Human Rights Commission, "Overview," https://www.sahrc.org.za/index.php/about-us/about-the-sahrc (accessed Aug. 30, 2019).

28. Hodgkin and Newell, "Role and Mandate of Children's Ombudspersons."

29. CRC Committee, "Concluding Observations: Cameroon," CRC/C/CMR.CO/3–5 (2017); CRC Committee, "Concluding Observations Georgia," CRC/C/GEO/CO/4 (2017); CRC Committee, "Concluding Observations Serbia," CRC/C/SRB/CO/2–3 (2017).

30. Interview with UNICEF country office reported in Sedletzki, "Championing Children's Rights," 17.

31. Sedletzki, "Championing Children's Rights," 19.

32. Sedletzki, "Championing Children's Rights," 19.

33. Lansdown, "Independent Institutions," 9–10.

34. Sedletzki, "Championing Children's Rights," 15.

35. Sedletzki, "Championing Children's Rights," 15.

36. Sedletzki, "Championing Children's Rights," 15.

37. Richard Carver, "One NHRI or Many? How Many Institutions Does It Take to Protect Human Rights? Lessons from the European Experience," *Journal of Human Rights Practice* 3, no. 1 (2011): 1–24.

38. Sedletzki, "Championing Children's Rights," 15.

39. CRC Committee, *General Comment No. 2*, para. 13.

40. Sedletzki, "Championing Children's Rights," 25.

41. Sedletzki, "Championing Children's Rights," 25.

42. Office of the Children's Advocate–Jamaica, "Annual Report 2007/08 Fiscal Year," https://www.slideshare.net/rodjemalcolm/oca-report-07-08 (accessed Aug. 30, 2019).

43. National Commission for Protection of Child Rights (NCPCR), "NCPCR Inquiry Report on Rajkiya Samprekshan Grih Kishori, Ghaziabad on Matter of 6 Missing Girls, on the Illegal Children Home Exposed in Ghaziabad, and the Child Laborers in Ghaziabad" (2012), http://www.ncpcr.gov.in/showfile.php?lid=106 (accessed Aug. 30, 2019).

44. Defensoría del Pueblo de Peru, "Decimotercer Informe Annual de la Defensoría del Pueblo, Enero–Diciembre 2009" (May 2010), 167–168, http://www.theioi.org/ioi-members/caribbean-latin-america/peru/defensora-del-pueblo.

45. Sedletzki, "Championing Children's Rights," 23.

46. United Nations Children's Fund (UNICEF), *Independent Human Rights Institutions for Children Strengthening Tools and Support in Europe and Central Asia* (Geneva: UNICEF, forthcoming).

47. See Hungarian Office of the Commissioner for Fundamental Rights, https://www.ajbh.hu/en/web/ajbh-en/main_page (accessed Aug. 30, 2019).

48. Ombudsman of the Republic of Latvia, "Summary of Annual Report 2016" (2017). https://www.state.gov/wp-content/uploads/2019/01/Latvia-2.pdf.

49. Child Rights International Network, "U.N. Guidelines for the Prevention of Juvenile Delinquency (the Riyadh Guidelines)," https://archive.crin.org/en/library/legal-database/un-guidelines-prevention-juvenile-delinquency-riyadh-guidelines (adopted and proclaimed by G.A. Res. 45/112 (Dec.14, 1990)); CRC Committee, *General Comment No. 10: Children's Rights in Juvenile Justice*, CRC/C/GC/10 (2007), para. 89; UN General Assembly, "Guidelines for the Alternative Care of Children," G.A. Res. 64/142, 64th Sess., UN Doc. A/64/434 (2010), para. 130.

50. CRC Committee, *General Comment No. 2*, paras. 15–18 and 19 (j) and (k).

51. Hodgkin and Newell, "Role and Mandate of Children's Ombudspersons," 29.

52. Republic of Serbia Protector of Citizens and Protector of Citizens Ombudsman, "Regular Annual Report of the Protector of Citizens for 2017" (March 15, 2018), https://www.ombudsman.rs/attachments/article/5671/Regular%20Annual%20Report%20of%20the%20Protector%20of%20Citizens%20for%202017.pdf.

53. Children and Young People's Commissioner Scotland, "A RIGHT Blether" (2012), https://dera.ioe.ac.uk/15892/1/A_Right_Wee_Blether_final.pdf.

54. Ombudsman for Children in Sweden, "Everything We Left Behind: Voices of Children and Young People on the Move," Ombudsman for Sweden Annual Report 2017, https://www.barnombudsmannen.se/globalassets/dokument-for-nedladdning/english/publications/we-left-everything-behind-stras.pdf (accessed Aug. 30, 2019).

55. Ombudsman for Children in Sweden, "Everything We Left Behind."

56. UNICEF, *Independent Human Rights Institutions for Children*.

57. Sedletzki, "Championing Children's Rights," 20.

58. Hodgkin and Newell, "Role and Mandate of Children's Ombudspersons," 29.

59. Joanne Hillman, Mathew Taylor, Toby Pearson, Josey Cook, Nigel Thomas, Anne Crowley, and Rhodri Pugh-Dungey et al., "Evaluating the Children's Commissioner for Wales: Report of a Participatory Research Study." *International Journal of Children's Rights* 18, no. 1 (January 2010): 19–52.

60. Directorio de Defensorías del Niño y del Adolescente Registradas, Ministry of Women and Social Development Website, http://mimp.gob.pe/webs/mimp/dgnna/dna/directorio/arequipa.pdf (accessed Aug. 30, 2019).

61. Commissioner for Children and Young People for Northern Ireland, "Annual Report and Accounts for the Year Ended 31 March 2017," (2017), https://www.niccy.org/media/2930/niccy-annual-report-16-17-final-laid-1-nov-17.pdf (accessed Aug. 30, 2019).

62. Ombudsman of the Republic of Latvia, "Summary of Annual Report 2016."

63. Provincial Advocate for Children and Youth, "Report to the Legislature 2010–2011," 19, https://cwrp.ca/publications/provincial-advocate-children-youth-report-legislature-201011.

64. CRC Committee, "Concluding Observations: The Netherlands," CRC/C/NLD/4 (2014).

65. Sedletzki, "Championing Children's Rights," 23.

66. "(2) For the purposes of an investigation under this Act, the Ombudsperson for Children may...(b) enter premises where—(i) a child is present, either temporarily or permanently, including an educational or health institution and a place of detention, in order to study the environment of such a place and assess its suitability; (ii) a child may be in employment; (iii) there is reasonable ground to believe that the moral and physical safety of a child may be in danger;...(d) enter any licensed premises where the Ombudsperson for Children suspects that alcohol and tobacco may be handled, consumed or purchased by children;...." Ombudsperson for Children Act, Act 41 of 2003 (Nov. 20, 2003), art. 7.

67. Defensor del Pueblo Colombia, Ley No. 24 of 1992 (December 1992), art. 28.

CHAPTER 25

EXAMINING THE UN COMMITTEE ON THE RIGHTS OF THE CHILD THROUGH THE LENS OF CASTE- AND DESCENT-BASED DISCRIMINATION

PHILIP E. VEERMAN

1 INTRODUCTION: THE IMPORTANCE OF THE CRC COMMITTEE

LYNNE Marie Kohm[1] wrote in a critical assessment of the effect of twenty-five years of the Convention on the Rights of the Child (CRC) that the lack of scholarly debate about the actual merits of the CRC has been troubling. Kohm concludes that the CRC has not protected children from some of the most heinous atrocities.[2] She poses the question whether twenty-five years is not enough time "for the CRC to work its magic" in order to protect children from basic harms. And she puts forward another rhetorical question if the romanticism over the Convention itself possibly overshadowed its failure.[3] It is interesting that Kohm comes to such strong conclusions without analyzing in her article the work of the UN Committee on the Rights of the Child (CRC Committee), as the work and the recommendations of the CRC Committee are a key part of successful implementation of the CRC. No romanticism or magic there, just hard work.

The CRC came into force in September 1990. Cynthia Price Cohen and Susan Kilbourne have written "only the [CRC] has followed the Universal Declaration's comprehensive model by establishing a full panoply of rights for children which includes civil-political rights, economic-social-cultural rights, and humanitarian rights."[4] Since the CRC is broad, the CRC Committee is tasked with the implementation of rights in many fields.

The Committee, now a body of eighteen independent experts, started its work in February 1991 with nine members. The members of the CRC Committee are independent human rights experts serving in their personal capacity. The CRC Committee monitors the implementation of the CRC itself and the implementation of three optional protocols (OPs): the Optional Protocol to the CRC on the Involvement of Children in Armed Conflict, the Optional Protocol to the CRC on the Sale of Children, Child Prostitution and Child Pornography and the Optional Protocol to the CRC on a Communications Procedure, the last of which allows individual children to submit complaints. In addition, the CRC Committee drafts General Comments, which provide interpretation and analysis of specific articles of the CRC or deal with thematic issues related to the rights of the child.

The process that the CRC Committee engages in to monitor implementation of the Convention begins with a review of an initial state report by the state party and then a subsequent review, every five years, of a periodic state report submitted by the state party. Each time the CRC Committee considers a report of a state party, it also receives alternative reports as well as testimony from NGOs working in that country or, in some cases, from intergovernmental organizations (IGOs). The CRC Committee's review process has created an important role for nongovernmental organizations (NGOs), which help to inform the CRC Committee as to the situation in the country being reviewed. The reports are discussed in a constructive dialogue with a delegation of the state party, after which the CRC Committee formulates its Concluding Observations, that is, the state party's to-do list for the next five years. Although some states parties are late in reporting (sometimes several years), governments do pay attention to the Concluding Observations. Lisa Payne[5] reviewed the impact of the Concluding Observations of 1995, 2003, and 2008 on Great Britain and Northern Ireland: "At a conference organised by the Children's Rights Alliance for England in November 2008, the head of the UK delegation to the UN Committee not only acknowledged how challenging the CRC reporting process had been, but also described the Concluding Observations as 'a useful, positive framework for the future'. Government officials have confirmed that they will be drafting action plans based on the Committee's recommendations—a considerable step forward for the UK in the 20th year of the Convention." The CRC Committee seems to be taken seriously in the above case, but how much political will and political possibilities the government has to use the Concluding Observations as "a useful and positive framework for the future" depends on many variables (the economic situation of the country being one of them). In 2015 the Children's Rights Alliance for England (CRAE) concluded,[6] after the UK submitted another state report in 2014, that UK government policies and budget for issues related to children were still failing to prioritize children. Therefore, it is not so easy to judge what impact the recommendations of the CRC Committee and the CRC itself had.

Through an examination of the procedures and the jurisprudence of the CRC Committee, specifically with respect to caste- and descent-based discrimination, this chapter considers whether the work of the CRC Committee helps to strengthen the implementation of the CRC. More broadly, this review helps us reflect on whether, on balance, the CRC is an effective international human rights instrument.

2   A Nepalese Father, His Daughter, and the History of Article 2 of the CRC

A Nepalese father (untouchable Dalit) requested a psychological assessment of his eight-year-old daughter as part of an asylum application considered by a Dutch court. The girl, as well as her parents (her mother was from the higher Chetri-caste), was seen several times. The parents had experienced violence against them after they got married in Nepal. The girl's lawyer added the psychological evaluation, which included an assessment of the best interests of the child,[7] in her plea to the court to accept the asylum request of the girl and her mother. As the psychologist for the girl, I advised the court that returning the girl to Nepal was not an option. However, the Dutch court rejected the request for asylum in the Netherlands—the court virtually ignored the best interests issue.[8] Furthermore, in this case the court concluded that the parents' story that they would be in danger in Nepal was not credible. Unfortunately, this shocking conclusion reflected a fundamental failure to understand the nature of caste discrimination. While at the time this case was shocking to me, after reflecting more broadly—having worked on children's rights for decades, including as president of Defence for Children International in Geneva (1997–2002), and on such important issues as juvenile justice and the sexual exploitation of children—I cannot recall many instances where caste- and descent-based discrimination were identified as an issue meriting significant attention. The first time I read about a form of caste-based discrimination in the context of children's rights was in the CRC Committee's Concluding Observations on Yemen in 1996. Only later would caste discrimination come up in the CRC Committee's Concluding Observations[9] on Micronesia (1998), India (2000), Bangladesh (2001), Pakistan (2003) and Japan (2004). And, notwithstanding dedicating my life to children's rights, it was only recently that I came to fully appreciate what major issues caste discrimination and decent-based discrimination are.

The CRC Committee has to monitor the implementation of the CRC, a document that is the result of many years of negotiations in the UN and which offers a critical—albeit imperfect—framework. If the text of the CRC had been stronger at some points it would have been easier for the CRC Committee to challenge different countries on some important issues, such as caste discrimination. Some history is necessary to give this some context.

The origins of CRC Article 2 on non-discrimination go back to the principle of non-discrimination in the UN Declaration on the Rights of the Child. Thirteen years were needed (from 1946 to 1959) to agree on a text of the UN Declaration on the Rights of the Child. In 1959, Israel's attorney general, Haim Cohn, a member of the UN

Commission on Human Rights, submitted an amendment to the anti-discrimination principle of the Draft Declaration on the Rights of the Child,[10] which included the term *caste*: "The child shall enjoy all the rights set forth in this Declaration without distinction or discrimination on account of race, colour, sex, language, caste, religion, political or other opinion, national or social origin, property, birth or other status, whether of himself or of either of his parents. All children, whether born in or out of wedlock, shall enjoy these rights." However, when on April 1, 1959, Commission members met in New York, Mr. A. K. Mitra, a Commission member from India, noted[11] "that the word caste appeared to apply to one country only and therefore it should not appear in a document which was international in scope." The Commission could rest assured, he stated, that the Indian government "was doing everything in its power to eliminate all discrimination due to the existence of caste... if there did exist elsewhere cases of discrimination due to the existence of caste, his delegation would have no objection to the retention of the word in the text." And, unfortunately, Sir Samuel Hoare, assistant undersecretary of state at the Home Office[12]—the British member of the Commission—supported Mr. Mitra. The interventions by Mr. Mitra of India and Sir Samuel Hoare of the UK effectively excluded caste discrimination from the UN Declaration on the Rights of the Child.

The UN Declaration became one of the bases for the current CRC. In fact, when Poland proposed the creation of a UN convention on children's rights, it used the Declaration as the basis for it. The legislative history of the CRC[13] revealed no mention of caste discrimination and children.

The relevance, therefore, of the non-discrimination provision in the CRC for "untouchable children" is that the lack of any specific references in the CRC to caste discrimination (as in the UN Declaration) makes the task of the CRC Committee considerably more difficult and less effective with respect to discrimination on the basis of caste. Consider the effect of this history on state-based legislation as well, which is often modeled on the CRC and therefore fails to include a specific prohibition based on caste. For instance, the delegation of Mauritania remarked in Geneva in the dialogue with the CRC Committee that "Mauritania had adopted an anti-discrimination law which incorporated the provisions of the Convention, prohibited discrimination on all grounds defined by the Convention, and also addressed the effect of discrimination."[14] In the case study of Mauritania (see section 4.3 herein) we will see that caste still exists in Mauritania and that the CRC Committee's work would have been easier had the word *caste* been mentioned explicitly in the text of the Convention.

3 CASTE- AND DESCENT-BASED DISCRIMINATION: *250 MILLION PEOPLE*

Rita Izsák-Ndiaye, who served from 2011–2017 as UN Special Rapporteur on Minority Issues, highlighted caste discrimination and its consequences in her reports to the UN:

"Discrimination based on caste and analogous systems of inherited status refers to a form of discrimination based on descent. Because one's caste can be determinative of one's occupation, it is also referred to as 'discrimination based on work and descent' and defined as 'any distinction, exclusion, restriction or preference based on inherited status such as caste, including present or ancestral occupation, family, community or social origin, name, birthplace, place of residence, dialect and accent that has the purpose or effect of nullifying or impairing the recognition, enjoyment, or exercise, on an equal footing, of human rights and fundamental freedoms in the political, economic, social, cultural or any other field of public life.... [I]ndividuals placed at the bottom of the system may face exclusion and discrimination in a wide range of areas."[15]

The concept of a caste system is primarily associated with the South Asian region. Izsák-Ndiaye explained that the existence of the caste system in that region "is linked to the religiously sanctioned social structure of Hinduism, which identified four original and endogamous groups, or castes, called varnas."[16] She continued that "the term caste has broadened in meaning, transcending religious affiliation. Caste and caste-like systems may be based on either a religious or a secular background and can be found within diverse religious and/or ethnic groups in all geographical regions, including within diaspora communities."[17]

There are additional definitions of caste systems, depending, in part, on the specific cultural context. Lynn Bennett,[18] for instance, has discussed caste systems in the context of Nepalese women and has defined caste in the context of "ritual purity and pollution." This leads to intergroup behavior where some groups are singled out because they are not considered pure enough to eat with or marry. Hira Singh has viewed the caste phenomenon in an economic context and has stressed the importance of access to land, which some groups in society are denied.[19]

In the aforementioned report, Izsák-Ndiaye, now the former special rapporteur on minority issues, described the disturbing characteristics of caste systems as "a set of collective behaviours and norms stemming from the belief that contact with individuals from lower castes is 'polluting'... inter-caste interactions are limited and in some cases de facto prohibited. Manifestations of enforced endogamy include limitations or prohibitions on inter-caste marriages, commensality... and sharing common goods or services. Attempts to challenge these prohibitions are often severely punished through violence against caste-affected individuals and retaliation against their communities."[20]

According Rita Izsák-Ndiaye, these practices result in a process of dehumanization where lower castes are looked upon as filthy, unworthy, and impure. This degrading people mechanism has led to "an externalized and internalized social norm that eventually legitimatizes mistreatment and abuses against affected communities, perpetuating discrimination and patterns of human rights violations against them."[21]

In Islamic Mauritania, as in Hindu-dominated countries, there are similar processes of discrimination. The Special Rapporteur on minority issues has used the word *caste discrimination* outside the context of Hinduism, as does the CRC Committee in its Concluding Observations on Mauritania. I prefer—even though the Special Rapporteur and the CRC Committee call it caste discrimination—to refer to this discrimination as *descent-based discrimination*, a broader, more inclusive term.

Thinking about discrimination in this way, as descent-based, one may consider various types of discrimination that might be included in a more robust definition of discrimination under the CRC. Living in certain neighborhoods, for example, can lead to discrimination that has been characterized as both caste- and descent-based discrimination. The Burakumin in Japan are an example. According to Minority Rights Group International, the Burakumin are "not an ethnic minority, but rather a caste- or descent-based group. They therefore share with other Japanese the same language, religion, customs and physical appearances."[22] Discrimination against the Burakumin communities started in the feudal period in Japanese history. They were "associated with impure or tainted occupations stigmatized by death, such as butchers and leather workers."[23] Similarly, in Nigeria, social interaction and marriage with a group called Osu (meaning outcast)[24] is discouraged. And in Yemen, 10 percent of the population is believed to be Al-Akhdam (servants) or Muhamasheen (marginalized ones)—set apart "by their African features, they form a kind of hereditary caste at the very bottom of Yemen's social ladder."[25]

Thus, although the aforementioned Mr. Mitra (the UN Commission on Human Rights member from India) stated in 1959 that "the word caste appeared to apply to one country only,"[26] caste-like systems—again, why I prefer the broader term *descent-based discrimination*—were then present in many other countries and still are. Micronesia, Japan, Yemen, Nigeria, Ghana, India, Nepal, and Mauritania (to mention a few) all have some sort of caste system in place that has an enormous influence on the lives of children in those countries. It is certainly not limited to India.

In her 2016 report to the Human Rights Council, Izsák-Ndiaye estimated that "over 250 million people suffer from caste-based discrimination worldwide."[27] A Human Rights Watch report from 2001 estimates that 250 million people are affected by caste discrimination, "a staggering number by any account," they conclude. Human Rights Watch has noted that people who suffer caste-based discrimination "have inherited a life of burdens and few rights, a life of continuous discrimination, a life without dignity. What wrongs have they committed? The world may have changed around them, but not for them. They are ruled by traditions which are hundreds, and sometimes even thousands of years old, traditions that cannot be justified today."[28]

Caste- and descent-based discrimination is a salient human rights issue in Bangladesh, India, Japan, Madagascar, Mauritania, Nepal, Nigeria, Pakistan, Senegal, Sri Lanka, Yemen, Somalia, and countries with large Indian and Bangladeshi populations, such as the United Kingdom. To estimate how many children (defined by the CRC as those under age eighteen) are included within the 250 million people identified by the Special Rapporteur as suffering from caste- or descent-based discrimination is not easy. While the world population is aging, in many places around the world in which descent-based discrimination exists, there are still large percentages of children. In Africa, for example, 41 percent of the population is under age fifteen and 19 percent of the population is between the ages of fifteen and twenty-four.[29] Still, it is hard to determine what percentage of the aforementioned 250 million are under age eighteen because inter alia there are "striking differences among regions in the proportion of adolescent populations"[30] and because UN agencies[31] do not systematically collect data with the criterion "under 18's." It could be a question for the CRC Committee to ask relevant UN agencies to determine how many children in the world suffer from caste- and decent-based discrimination.

Despite the significant numbers of individuals—including children—who suffer caste- or descent-based discrimination, with numerous interest groups lobbying the United Nations system, marginalized groups can face significant challenges drawing attention to violations of their rights. Clifford Bob has written about the challenges Dalit rights groups have faced in promoting an obvious human rights issue.[32] According to Clifford, the often-unchallenged claim that caste is already covered in the broad language of human rights conventions has meant that the untouchables have been "relatively unnoticed on the international stage."[33] French sociologist Martin Aranguren[34] has described how Dalit rights organizations started to work the UN system from 1996 to get recognition. A turning point was the publication in 1999 of a Human Rights Watch report on caste discrimination.[35]

4 THE CRC COMMITTEE AND CASTE- AND DESCENT-BASED DISCRIMINATION IN THREE COUNTRIES

The CRC Committee (like other UN treaty bodies) has from the beginning addressed caste discrimination in its dialogue with the states parties and in its Concluding Observations. States parties to the CRC could now be asked to include in both their initial[36] and periodic reports[37] how they implemented the general principles of the CRC (such as the right to non-discrimination), the right to education, and special protection measures in the context of Dalit children.

4.1 India

The New York Review of Books expressed it well: "India, the world's largest democracy, also happens to be the world's most hierarchical society."[38] As the groundbreaking Human Rights Watch report *Broken People*,[39] published in 1999, stated:

> More than one-sixth of India's population, some 160 million people, live a precarious existence, shunned by much of society because of their rank as untouchables or Dalits—literally meaning broken people—to be at the bottom of India's caste system. Dalits are discriminated against, denied access to land, forced to work in degrading

conditions, and routinely abused at the hands of the police and of higher-caste groups that enjoy the state's protection. In what has been called India's "hidden apartheid", entire villages in many Indian States remain completely segregated by caste. National legislation and constitutional protections serve only to mask the social realities of discrimination and violence faced by those living below the "pollution line"... "Untouchables" may not cross the line dividing their part of the village from that occupied by higher castes. They may not use the same wells, visit the same temples, drink from the same cups in tea stalls, or lay claim to land that is legally theirs.[40]

An Alternative Report by Children from India to the CRC Committee noted: "In our villages, many children face discrimination because they belong to certain castes.... In many schools, children from backward castes are made to clean the classrooms and toilets, and not children from other castes,"[41] A 2014 article in the *Hindustan Times* also described what caste discrimination means for children: "[f]rom being forced to eat mid-day meals in marked out plates to being asked to sit in the back rows of their classrooms, Dalit schoolchildren across rural Madhya Pradesh face dozens of grim abuses.... Some of the other outrageous discriminations include stopping Dalit children from drinking water from common facilities in schools."[42]

The Indian Constitution (1950) recognized liberty, justice, and equality for all Indian citizens. India ratified the CRC in December 1992, and its first state report[43] was submitted in March 1997. The CRC Committee, in its first Concluding Observations,[44] issued in 2000, found that "given such a diverse and multicultural society, the Committee further notes that the existence of traditional customs (i.e. the caste system), and societal attitudes (e.g. towards tribal groups) is an obstacle to efforts to combat discrimination, and compounds, *inter alia*, poverty, illiteracy, child labour, child sexual exploitation, and children living and/or working on the streets." The CRC Committee further commented,

> In the light of article 2 of the Convention, the Committee is concerned at the existence of caste-based discrimination... despite these practices being prohibited under the law.... In accordance with article 17 of the Constitution and article 2 of the Convention, the Committee recommends that the State party takes steps to ensure states to abolish the discriminatory practice of "untouchability", prevent caste- and tribe-motivated abuse, and prosecute State and private actors who are responsible for such practices or abuses. Moreover, in compliance with article 46 of the Constitution, the State party is encouraged to implement, *inter alia*, affirmative measures to advance and protect these groups.... The Committee encourages the State party to continue its efforts to carry out comprehensive public education campaigns to prevent and combat caste-based discrimination.[45]

In 2004 the CRC Committee stated again:[46]

> The Committee is deeply concerned at persistent and significant social discrimination against children belonging to Scheduled Castes and Tribes and other tribal groups,

reflected, inter alia, by the many violations of the 1989 Scheduled Castes and Scheduled Tribes (Prevention of Atrocities) Act, the low number of such violations dealt with by the courts, and the fact that a majority of the States have failed to set up the special courts provided for under this Act....The Committee recommends that the State party, in accordance with article 17 of its Constitution and article 2 of the Convention, take all necessary steps to abolish the discriminatory practice of 'untouchability', prevent caste- and tribe-motivated abuse, and prosecute State and private actors who are responsible for such practices or abuses.

The CRC Committee continued to address inadequate education provisions and the caste issue: "The Committee recommends that the State party...strengthen its efforts to progressively ensure that that all girls and boys, in urban, rural and least developed areas and children belonging to Scheduled Castes and Tribes, have equal access to educational opportunities."[47] Despite criticism of the CRC Committee, the spokesman for the government of India, according to an observer from the India Alliance for Child Rights, who was present at the dialogue of the CRC Committee and a delegation from India, "stuck to the rhetoric that the Indian Constitution does not allow any form of discrimination on the basis of caste and religion."[48]

For many children in India, the social reality of 1935, described by Mulk Raj Anand in his novel *Untouchable* (about a sweeper boy, a hereditary latrine cleaner[49]), continues to be their current reality. To change the reality of children of Dalits in India a lot more has to be done, and "a comprehensive approach which addresses all the barriers to access simultaneously"[50] is necessary. For the CRC Committee it is *frappez, frappez toujours*, or as the Roman writer Ovid has said, "dripping water hollows out stone, not through force but through persistence." In short, one report of Concluding Observations from Geneva will not change an aspect of Indian society that has been part of that society since 400 C.E. Nonetheless, (together with reports of other Treaty Bodies) it might help move the government in the right direction. The CRC Committee must consistently and unwaveringly advocate for better protection of children who suffer from caste discrimination in India. Over time, it can slowly help effectuate change.

4.2 Nepal

Nepal[51] ratified the CRC in 1990. In 2015 BBC News reported on Nepal's new Constitution:

> many members of traditionally marginalised groups fear that the constitution will still work against them as it's been rushed through by established parties which— including the Maoists—are dominated by high-caste, mostly male, leaders. One grievance is that a smaller percentage of the Parliament will now be elected by proportional representation—45%, compared with 58% under the previous post-war interim constitution. The proportional representation system has helped more members of indigenous and low-caste groups, historically repressed and marginalised, get elected.[52]

Bhakta Bishwakarma, the national president of the Nepal National Dalit Social Welfare Organization (NNDSWO), has remarked that his organization "acknowledged that the government has taken strides over the past years to ensure Dalit rights through legislative measures." However, he has expressed the need for "a national action plan to eliminate caste discrimination and an effective coordinating mechanism to oversee its implementation. There is also a need for state led public campaigns and institutional reform."[53]

An estimated five million Dalits live in Nepal.[54] Bennett[55] explains that the highest castes in Nepal avoid being touched by the lower "service castes." People belonging to the two highest castes have avoided inviting people from lower castes, and certainly *untouchables*, into their homes for centuries, a practice that continues to this day.[56]

Despite the importance of this issue in Nepal, the CRC Committee's 1996 Concluding Observations on Nepal's initial report[57] contained few references to caste. One was under the heading "data collection."[58] There is a paragraph in the 1996 Concluding Observations that mentions caste as it relates to "exploitation."[59] In that paragraph the government of Nepal is advised to take concrete measures "including awareness campaigns to change negative attitudes, to protect children belonging to the lowest castes from any form of exploitation."[60] In the CRC Committee's Concluding Observations in 2005, responding to Nepal's second report, caste is taken more seriously: "While noting that discrimination is prohibited under the Constitution and other relevant legislation, as well as the various efforts undertaken by the State party to eliminate discrimination, the Committee reiterates its deep concerns about the widely prevailing de facto discrimination against girls and children belonging to the most vulnerable groups such as the Dalit community, children belonging to indigenous or ethnic minority groups, refugee and asylum-seeking children, street children, children with disabilities and children living in rural areas.... The Committee notes with grave concern that as a consequence of prevailing discriminatory attitudes, children belonging to vulnerable groups are particularly likely to fall victim to abuse and exploitation."[61]

As the CRC Committee noted, caste discrimination in Nepal causes harm in childhood, which can have long-lasting effects. As in India, children who are considered to be untouchables have to sit in the back of the class. Teachers often tell Dalit children it is their duty to clean the toilets. One man[62] from a special untouchable community (the Dom people of Nepal) reported that teachers did not want to rate his work and noted that "I faced other humiliations and discrimination. At meals, while all the other students ate together in the dining area, I was segregated—I was made to sit in a far off distance on a grassy ground.... What's more, I would be served last."

A front-page article in the Nepalese newspaper *Republica*[63] shows how the caste issue is still part of Nepalese society; the article tells a story of non-Dalit students who refused to eat their lunch because a Dalit woman prepared it.

As if the day-to-day reality of some Dalit children is not hard enough, there is also discrimination against so-called subcastes within the Dalit community.[64] Dalits in Nepal are a heterogeneous group. One of the lowest subcastes of the Dalits is the Badis. Amy Waldman[65] reports on the Badis: "Caste has become destiny for many communities, defining their profession through generations. But few people have inherited so vexed a destiny as the Badis of Nepal. Their profession is prostitution, passed down from one generation to the next.... While many Badi women have left the sex trade, others keep falling into it, driven by hunger, a lack of alternatives and the stigma of being a Badi."

The CRC Committee reported in its 2016 Concluding Observations, "There is persistent de facto discrimination against Dalits, on the basis of their caste, resulting in them living in marginalized communities with hindrances in access to education, and public places, including water sources and places of worship."[66] The CRC Committee has recommended that the Nepalese government "[s]trengthen its efforts to combat discrimination against, and stigmatization and social exclusion of, Dalit children and, in so doing, establish targeted programmes, including awareness-raising programmes, to facilitate their integration into other communities and ensure the enforcement of non-discriminatory access to education and to public places."[67] The CRC Committee also recommended affirmative action of "targeted support measures."[68] Whether the government of Nepal implements these recommendations depends on the political will to change Nepalese society, the political space the government has to make the changes, and whether Dalits are able to organize themselves more effectively.

4.3 Mauritania

Mauritania ratified the CRC on 16 May 1991. Mauritania registered reservations regarding "articles or provisions which may be contrary to the beliefs and values of Islam, the religion of the Mauritania People and State."[69] On October 4, 2001, the CRC Committee reviewed Mauritania for the first time. On May 28, 2009, the CRC Committee examined Mauritania for the second time.[70]

The CRC Committee used strong language in its 2001 Concluding Observations.[71] In particular, the Committee recommended that the general principles of the Convention, specifically, the provisions of Articles 2, 3, 6 and 12, "be appropriately integrated in all relevant legislation concerning children."[72] The Committee then stated, "The Committee is concerned by the persistence of discrimination in the State Party."[73] Again in 2009 the CRC Committee urged Mauritania to take "all necessary measures to eradicate slavery" and recommended, "The State party make combating discrimination against vulnerable groups a national priority."[74]

In its Concluding Observations on Mauritania in 2009, the CRC Committee noted "as positive that the principle of non-discrimination is incorporated in the Constitution. The Committee is however concerned that de facto discrimination against girls and certain groups of children persists, particularly with regards to children living in slavery or of slave descent, children living in poverty and orphans."[75]

Alexander Stille,[76] reviewing a book on Mauritania, wrote that "the one thing most people know about Mauritania—if they know anything at all—is that it was the last country on earth to abolish slavery in 1981. Slavery was not actually made a crime until 2007, suggesting that it was still widely practiced.... Less well known is that the same year that Mauritania declared its intention to abolish slavery (encoded in the law the following year), it also announced that it would become a sharia nation, making Koranic percepts the law of the land." Stille explains, "Slavery had an important place in Mauritania's nomadic life.... The system was sanctioned by religious authorities and reinforced by a pervasive caste system.... Near the bottom of the totem pole were the Haratrin, former slaves who had been granted their freedom, and below them, at the very bottom, the slaves."[77]

The International Dalit Solidarity Network has noted in its report "Discrimination Based on Descent in Africa" that "although slavery has been outlawed in Mauritania, it has from one source been estimated that around 90,000 Haratin exist as slaves and other estimates would add another 300,000 part-time and ex-slaves."[78]

In 2015 three NGOs presented interesting background information in their submissions for the Universal Periodic Review of Mauritania (a parallel process to the review by treaty bodies such as the CRC Committee involving a review of the human rights records of all UN member states): "The Mauritanian population (just over 3.5 million people) is composed of various different ethnic groups. The Arabic-speaking Beidan, also known as White Moors, are dominant in the country's government, military, judiciary, and ownership of business, land and other resources. Historically the Beidan raided and enslaved black Africans from sub-Saharan ethnic groups, and over time those slaves were assimilated into Moor culture. The slave-descended population now constitutes a distinct Arabic-speaking group called the Haratine (people of slave descent, also known as Black Moors).... Most now live separately from their traditional masters, but many remain in slavery to this day.... The Haratine continue to suffer discrimination, marginalisation and exclusion because they belong to the 'slave' class. Many remain affected by slavery today; these people live under the direct control of their masters/mistresses, are treated as property, and receive no payment for their work. Slave status is passed down from mother to child, so children born to a mother in slavery will be 'inherited' by children of the master.... It is commonly held by the Mauritanian authorities that slavery no longer exists because it was abolished and criminalised by the government. However, Mauritanian anti-slavery organisations estimate that up to 500,000 Haratine may still be enslaved or living under some form of control by their former masters."[79] The three NGO's continue to explain: "Notwithstanding several recommendations during Mauritania's previous [Universal Periodic Review] to promote children's rights in line with the provisions of the Convention on the Rights of the Child, many children are denied the majority of their rights (including access to education), given that no action is taken to help children out of slavery. Indeed, children in slavery are also considered the masters' property and, like other slaves, can be rented out, loaned, given as gifts in marriage or inherited by the masters' children."[80]

In an attachment to a Human Rights Watch report, the minister of justice of Mauritania claims his country "confronted resolutely through legislation criminalizing the practice of enslavement."[81] However, Anti-Slavery International, Minority Rights Group International, and SOS-Esclaves, in their joint submission for the Universal

Periodic Review, underlined that "the Mauritanian government's arrest of anti-slavery campaigners.... exposes its real hostility to genuine efforts to end the slavery system."[82]

In 2005 Mauritania ratified the African Charter for the Rights and Welfare of the Child (ACRWC), the regional human rights treaty complementing the CRC. The African Charter (which entered into force in 1999) has in its Article 44 a built-in communications (complaints) procedure[83] (contrary to the CRC, where a third special Optional Protocol had to be created to open the option for children to bring communications or complaints to the CRC Committee[84]). It is interesting to compare the work of the African Committee of Experts on the Rights and Welfare of the Child (ACERWC), the regional counterpart of the CRC Committee.[85] Interesting is that, after a very slow start, the ACERWC has found creative ways to work with and to complement efforts of the CRC Committee.

In 2016 Mauritania submitted its initial report to the ACERWC. In this report, the Mauritanian government wrote that under the Mauritanian Constitution, everyone is equal and cannot be discriminated against on the basis of sex, social origin, and race or ethnic background.[86]

On December 15, 2017, ACERWC published its decision on behalf of two young men[87] who had complained against the Mauritanian government through ACERWC's communications procedure. The two men and the NGO's assisting them[88] claimed they were forced into slavery as children and were abused and deprived of their education for eleven years.[89]

The ACERWC concluded that Mauritania was in violation of its obligations,[90] and the ACERWC[91] recommended that the government of Mauritania "ensure that all members of the El Hassin family are prosecuted for the enslavement [of the boys] and the violation of their rights to equality, survival and development, education, leisure, recreation and cultural activities, protection against child abuse and torture, and protection against child labor, and ensure that they receive sentences commensurate to the crimes committed pursuant to the laws of Mauritania."[92] The ACERWC further recommended that Mauritania "give due regard to the issue of slavery or slavery like practices and make the elimination of slavery … one of its priorities."[93]

The Mauritanian courts seem (as reported by the Child Rights International Network)[94] to have taken the issue of slavery slightly more seriously since 2017. International attention to the issue seems key to any progress, but there is still a very long way to go. It also seems that the interventions of the ACERWC and the Concluding Obervations of the CRC Committee have reinforced each other. But other international human rights voices[95] can also reinforce the call for change. This is needed because those in the country speaking out against discrimination based on caste or ethnicity often end up in jail.

The government of Mauritania can no longer deny that there is slavery, and the government is urged to take children out of slavery and slavery-like practices. Nevertheless, in 2018 Mauritania was still in the top ten of the Global Slavery Index. The Global Slavery Index researchers noted, "Despite improvements to legislation in 2015, which … allows third parties to bring cases on behalf of slavery victims and establishes special tribunals to investigate slavery crimes, progress in Mauritania remains slow."[96]

5 Caste Discrimination Makes Implementation of Other Rights Harder

Children of disadvantaged castes are among the most vulnerable children. For example, children born in these castes "are more likely to face infections (e.g. malaria), have iron deficient diet and limited availability of iron supplements which ultimately can lead to anaemia."[97] And "[c]aste is an independent determinant of childhood anemia in India even after accounting for other social advantages including adult education and household wealth."[98] In such instances, being born into a disadvantaged caste leads to further barriers in the realization of the right to "the enjoyment of the highest attainable standard of health" (Article 24 of the CRC). In short, being born into a lower caste in Nepal, India, or elsewhere makes the realization of other rights more difficult.

In Bangladesh, "[p]overty and caste discrimination within schools from both teachers and students are key reasons why Dalit families choose for their children to work rather than attend school," according to an International Dalit Solidarity Network (IDSN) submission to the CRC Committee.[99] In India the dropout rate is relatively higher among the young persons of the Dalit caste,[100] raising questions about the implementation of CRC Article 28(e), which demands that states parties "take measures to encourage regular attendance at schools and the reduction of drop-out rates."[101]

With the caste system in place, it seems as if there is little chance, for example, of Articles 24 and 28(e) of the CRC being effectively implemented for all children.

6 Assessing Progress, Looking Forward

The CRC Committee's primary means of enforcing the CRC is through the reporting process and dissemination of its Concluding Observations. Nigel Rodley remarked that most state reports to treaty bodies (not just to the CRC Committee) are "self-congratulatory, focussing on the provisions of the State's Constitutions and laws that are, in their views, consistent with the obligations."[102] The CRC Committee is like a psychiatrist or psychologist seeing different patients. There are some heavy cases in the caseload with very serious problems, and although the symptoms are quite serious, some of these patients seem not to suffer from the serious symptoms and show only limited willingness to change. Besides, this treatment is delivered only once every five years. These patients, in the course of the five years, have—like with cognitive behavioral therapy—to do a lot of homework[103] before the next session. Like with patients, some states parties are not prepared to do serious homework but will not admit that. Some patients do not have serious problems, but many patients have not only one big problem (like caste discrimination), they also have several significant problems to address—in other words there is a kind of comorbidity. In the same way that a patient can have several serious problems—such as, for instance, a personality problem and depression—states parties may have several significant issues that need to be addressed. And often a compounding factor is that there is not a lot of willingness to be introspective on the part of the state party. But even in these circumstances, after several rounds of Periodic Reports and Concluding Observations, the main problems of each state party are on the table. In other words, the reporting process and the Committee's assessments offer a regular evaluation, the results of which are public and available to all. This is not an insignificant achievement. Concluding Observations and recommendations by the Committee have developed over the past twenty years to become less general and more targeted, specific, and directive to guide, advise, and push governments to make progress. However, there is still major room for improvement. Civil society organizations may advocate for the Committee becoming more concrete and specific in its recommendations, concluded Eva Clarhäll.[104]

6.1 Religious Rules and Beliefs

David Keane writes, "Vedas, the secret books of the Hindus, have been in existence since 1500 BC, which makes the caste system at least 3500 years old . . . and it is the first and the oldest known form of systematic discrimination on the basis of birth, which in modern times has been labelled racial discrimination."[105]

Thus, religious beliefs and rules existing for thousands of years are in part responsible for maintaining caste discrimination, despite constitutions and laws against discrimination and ratifications of conventions like the CRC. And since Concluding Observations are directed at states parties, the issue of religious beliefs is difficult for the CRC Committee to address, as religious beliefs and rules are often promulgated and enforced by non-state actors.

To its credit, the Indian government has recognized that certain religious beliefs present an obstacle that needs to be addressed: "Many discriminatory practices are sought to be justified on grounds of religion, custom or social policy. Some of them are inherited from the feudal, colonial past."[106] Nonetheless, despite the prominent role of religious beliefs in descent-based discrimination, it is only in exceptional cases that the CRC Committee discusses religious beliefs. Relating to Nepal, for example, it made the exception by stating, "The Committee also reiterates its previous concern regarding the disparities in legislation, in particular, in local, customary and religious laws, which result in uneven and discriminatory protection and promotion of children's rights."[107]

Caste discrimination has survived enormous changes in society. Dalit children had to sit separately in schools under the Nepalese monarchy (which ended in 2008), under the rule of the Maoist Centre (communist party of Nepal), and even today.

In 2004 the CRC Committee took on India and noted, "Political, religious and community leaders should be mobilized to support efforts to eradicate harmful traditional practices and attitudes which still discriminate against girls."[108] Even India's prime minister, Narendra Modi, himself coming from a disadvantaged caste, claims that manual scavengers realized it is their "duty to work for the happiness of the entire society and the Gods."[109]

Religious beliefs do not always have to be an obstacle to eliminating descent-based discrimination, as some of the statements of the CRC Committee as well as of various NGOs, such as Girls Not Brides,[110] has shown. This NGO, for example, works with and has mobilized religious leaders against child marriage. Nonetheless, the governments themselves must act upon recommendations by the CRC Committee and fulfill their obligations under the CRC while also navigating sometimes very influential religious forces that resist dismantling of the caste system. Communication between religious leaders and the children's rights community is rare[111] and should be encouraged. In March 2017 the Office of the UN High Commissioner for Human Rights launched the Faith for Rights framework at a workshop of experts held in Beirut, where the High Commissioner looked for support for human rights within faith communities.[112]

6.2   Dalit Children Learn to Be Subservient and Not to Have Horizontal Relationships

Anita Cheria, working with the Dalit community, explained to me how caste discrimination affects children: "Children are dependent on adults for their physical and emotional needs. For children facing caste discrimination their vulnerability increases multiple times by the single factor that they depend on adults who also are vulnerable. Two aspects normalized in the lives of caste discriminated children are violence and subservience. It is common that they are called to clean toilets in school, being last in line for food or studying in schools with very poor facilities and see their parents facing violence for any assertion from wearing slippers or asking for fair wages." This status of all the time being systematically discriminated against, Cheria[113] has pointed out, becomes internalized. The American child psychiatrist Robert Coles has observed "how one's background affects, even strongly determines, one's moral preoccupation, is an issue not sufficiently explored among children."[114] This conclusion applies to caste- and descent-based discrimination, and research is needed.

While there are multiple childhoods as anthropologist Sarada Balagopalan has explained,[115] we tend to look at the "ideal one" and ignore others. When one releases the concept of childhood from its normative moorings, both the impact of discrimination and the importance of combating it can be seen more clearly. Thus, while the CRC promotes horizontal relationships, such as to take the opinion of children into account (Article 12), it is also important to consider that many children grow up in societies where vertical relations shape many aspects of their lives.

6.3 Researchers Are Not Used to Including Caste Discrimination

In 2009 Save the Children published a five-country study on the impact of the CRC Committee's Concluding Observations.[116] This study, conducted by Laura Theytaz-Bergman, included Nepal, about which it concluded: "major political changes have occurred in Nepal following the peace process in 2006, which ended the 12-year-long armed conflict....NGO's note that there is currently a chance to bring children's rights into the Constitution itself. There is also an opportunity to implement some of the recommendations made by the Committee during the consideration of the State party reports."[117] It is interesting that in summarizing the conclusions and recommendations of the CRC Committee vis-à-vis Nepal, the caste issue was not addressed; instead, the researcher focused on such issues as juvenile justice, data collection, and corporal punishment. This reflects the historical pattern of not addressing descent- or caste-based discrimination. In this report, any mention of caste- or descent-based discrimination was opaque, such as "where legislative changes clashed with a deeper set of traditional attitudes, legislative changes were harder to achieve as was the case in Yemen in increasing the age of criminal responsibility and in Nepal in outlawing traditional practices that were harmful to the health of children."[118] When pressed on this, study author Theytaz-Bergman wrote to me "that caste was not looked upon in this study, as the methodology focused on the general measures of implementation and their impact on health, protection and education. General Comment No. 5 on General Measures of Implementation was used to analyse reporting trends. The recommendations in the Concluding Observations on caste were covered under non-discrimination, i.e. general principles."

6.4 Evaluation of the CRC Committee's Work on Caste Discrimination

The Concluding Observations on the three states parties reviewed in this chapter provided a basis for recommendations to states parties to address inequality created by caste- and descent-based discrimination with affirmative action. While explicit discussion of untouchables or Dalits has historically been the exception rather than the rule, things are beginning to change.

Notwithstanding the CRC Committee's early reticence in dealing with descent-based discrimination, the Committee now regularly references recommendations by other treaty bodies and sometimes uses their recommendations in developing its Concluding

Observations. Since several international human rights treaty bodies (in particular, the Committee on the Elimination of Racial Discrimination (CERD)) have taken a strong position on caste discrimination, the CRC Committee should be encouraged to at least take the same position as that of other treaty bodies which have looked closely at this issue. In this way, the different treaty bodies may reinforce each other in advancing efforts to press governments to better secure human rights.

In an encouraging sign, the CRC Committee now regularly addresses caste discrimination where relevant. Selected examples follow. With reference, inter alia, to CERD's concerns regarding the persistent, de facto caste-based discrimination against Dalit in education, employment, marriage, access to public places including water sources and places of worship (CERD/C/64/CO/5), the CRC Committee expresses serious concerns about the harmful effects of this prevailing form of discrimination on the physical, psychological and emotional well-being of the Dalit children in the state party.[119] "In line with the Committee on the Elimination of Racial Discrimination (CERD/C/304/ Add.13) the Committee stresses the importance of the equal enjoyment by members of these groups of the rights in the Convention, including access to health care, education, work, and public places and services, such as wells."[120]

Also, as more recently the CRC Committee has produced joint General Comments with the Committee on the Protection of the Rights of All Migrant Workers and Members of Their Families (CMW) and the Committee on the Elimination of Discrimination against Women (CEDAW), it would seem like an appropriate step for the CRC Committee to address caste discrimination in a joint General Comment with CERD.

While the CRC Committee's discussion of caste discrimination is a positive step, the CRC Committee's recommendations are not as strong or as extensive as General Recommendation 24 by the CERD Committee concerning Article 1, Paragraph 1 of the CERD Convention 2002, which provides that CERD is "Strongly reaffirming that discrimination based on 'descent' includes discrimination against members of communities based on forms of social stratification such as caste and analogous systems of inherited status which nullify or impair their equal enjoyment of human rights."[121]

Moreover, the CRC Committee does not appear to have asked state parties to include members from lower castes in their delegations. It is of course the prerogative of the state party to send whomever they see fit, but this would seem a logical step in the fight against caste-based and descent-based discrimination.

The CRC Committee has indeed become less vague in its recommendations. For instance, in 2016 the CRC Committee recommended to the Nepalese government that it "strengthen its efforts to combat discrimination against, and stigmatization and social exclusion of, Dalit children and, in so doing, establish targeted programmes, including awareness-raising programmes, to facilitate their integration into other communities and ensure the enforcement of non-discriminatory access to education and to public places."[122]

To some, the remarks of the CRC Committee on the topic of caste in their Concluding Observations may seem like drops in the ocean. Still, for the Dalit community these remarks are of enormous importance and can help them in their fight to change society. One of their NGOs, the International Dalit Solidarity Network (IDSN), publishes on its website which treaty bodies have addressed the issue of caste discrimination. Such information gives them strength to continue the struggle.

7 Conclusion: The CRC as an Instrument to Change Inequality

People build walls. A recent promotor of this philosophy is US president Donald Trump, who wants to build a "beautiful wall" between the United States and Mexico. The caste system is an example of psychological walls (a phenomenon described by Varnik Volkan[123]) between groups with different large-group identities. G. C. Pal[124] argues (after studying one of India's federal states) "that a society, which culturally accepts caste and gender hierarchy and allows this culture to permeate in public institutions, accentuates the vulnerability of women from lower caste to structural, systematic and symbolic atrocities." I argued in this chapter that it also accentuates the vulnerability of children of lower castes.

Yet, while a caste system and other similar forms of discrimination erect psychological walls, the view that all children deserve our respect and that we should protect the vulnerable[125] offers an alternative vision. Human rights, including children's rights, are based on the idea that all human beings are equal. There is a fundamental tension in a society if a state party has ratified international human rights treaties, such as the CRC, that promote universal values but have inequality and hierarchy as basic features. The main idea of human rights, as articulated in Article 1 of the Universal Declaration of Human Rights that "all human beings are born free and equal in dignity and rights," is harder to implement when inequality is woven into the society. Even when positive steps are taken—as in Nepal, with the adoption in September 2018 of the Act Relating to Children, which explicitly prohibits corporal punishment of children in all settings (this law was certified by the president of Nepal on Sept. 18, 2018, and has therefore come into effect)[126]—there is still something so fundamentally wrong woven into the fabric of society that the effect of these positive changes seems to be cosmetic. Essential repairs of the building are carried out (with prohibiting corporal punishment), but repair of the foundation is still needed.

The foundation that the CRC offers can provide the building blocks for a more just and equal society. The main international children's rights organ, the CRC Committee— in its role as monitor of CRC implementation—can be an important source for identifying and comparing both positive and harmful approaches to children among different states parties. In this regard, the work of the CRC Committee can be of great importance in overcoming caste- and descent-based discrimination. We should not expect too much of the constructive dialogue method of the CRC Committee (and other international human rights treaty bodies). The CRC Committee is not an international court, and its recommendations in the Concluding Observations are not legally binding. However, civil society groups in the country under review can use these recommendations for further lobbying and action. With each set of Concluding Observations, a government has its homework for the next five years, but like many children, they need to be reminded that they still have to undertake the tasks to ensure positive outcomes. No magic, but it is the drop that eventually erodes the stone.

ACKNOWLEDGMENT

I would like to thank Mrs. and Mr. Tilak X. (family name withheld for privacy reasons) for our meetings. They made me realize how we neglect the caste- and descent-based issue in the children's rights field.

NOTES

1. Lynne Marie Kohm, "A Brief Assessment of the 25-Year Effect of the Convention on the Rights of the Child," *Cardozo Journal of International and Comparative Law* 23, no. 2 (Winter 2015): 323–351, 325.
2. Kohm, "Brief Assessment," 351.
3. Kohm, "Brief Assessment," 351.
4. Cynthia Price Cohen and Susan Kilbourne. "Jurisprudence of the Committee on the Rights of the Child: A Guide for Research and Analysis," *Michigan Journal of International Law* 19, no. 3 (1998): 633–654, 634.
5. Lisa Payne, "Twenty Years On: The Implementation of the UN Convention on the Rights of the Child in the United Kingdom," *Children and Society* 23, no. 2 (2009): 149–155, 154.
6. Children's Rights Alliance for England (CRAE), "UK Implementation of the UN Convention on the Rights of the Child: Civil Society Alternative Report 2015 to the UN Committee–England (2015), http://www.crae.org.uk/media/78665/crae_civil_society_report_to_un_web.pdf (accessed Aug. 30, 2019).
7. Carla Van Os, "Best Interests of the Child Assessments for Recently Arrived Refugee Children: Behavioural and Children's Rights Perspectives on Decision-Making in Migration Law," PhD thesis, University of Groningen, 2018).
8. A colleague in Sweden found that in such cases children's rights issues were marginalized. See Anna Lundberg, "The Best Interests of the Child Principle in Swedish Asylum Cases: The Marginalization of Children's Rights," *Journal of Human Rights Practice* 3, no. 1 (March 2011): 49–70.
9. UN Committee on the Rights of the Child (CRC Committee), "Concluding Observations: Yemen," CRC/C/15/Add. 47 (1996); CRC Committee, "Concluding Observations: Micronesia," CRC/C/15/Add.86 (1998); CRC Committee, "Concluding Observations: India," CRC/C/15/Add.115 (2000); CRC Committee, "Concluding Observations: Bangladesh," CRC/C/15/Add.221 (2003); CRC Committee, "Concluding Observations: Pakistan," CRC/C/15/Add.217 (2003); CRC Committee, "Concluding Observations: Japan," CRC/C/15/Add.231 (2004).

10. UN Commission on Human Rights, "Draft Declaration on the Rights of the Child: Amendments to Draft Declaration on the Rights of the Child by Israel," 15th Sess., item 8, UN Doc. E/CN.4/L.525 (March 31, 1959), found in UN Commission on Human Rights, "Report of the Fifteenth Session, 16 March–10 April 1959," UN Doc. E/CN.4/789 (1959), 18. I would like to thank the Dag Hammarskjöld Library in New York for helping locate the document of March 31, 1959.

11. UN Commission on Human Rights, "Meeting 1 April 1959," E/CN.4/SR.630 (1959).

12. The National Archives, "Home Office: United Nations Organisations (UNO Symbol Series) Files." http://discovery.nationalarchives.gov.uk/details/r/C9138 (accessed Aug. 30, 2019).

13. UN Office of the High Commissioner for Human Rights (OHCHR), *Legislative History of the Convention on the Rights of the Child*, vols. 1 and 2 (Geneva: OHCHR, 2007), 314–334; see also Sharon Detrick, *The United Nations Convention on the Rights of the Child: A Guide to the "Travaux Préparatoires"* (Dordrecht, NL: Martinus Nijhoff, 1992). Nigel Cantwell, founder of Defence for Children International, participated in the drafting process. He confirmed that the issue of caste did not come up.

14. OHCHR, "Committee on the Rights of the Child Examines the Situation of Children in Mauritania," press release, Sept. 18, 2018, https://www.ohchr.org>DisplayNews> Committee on the Rights of the Child examines the situation of children in Mauritania.

15. UN Human Rights Council, "Report of the Special Rapporteur on Minority Issues," UN Doc. A/HRC/31/56 (2016), paras. 25, 26.

16. UN Human Rights Council, "Report of the Special Rapporteur," para. 26.

17. UN Human Rights Council, "Report of the Special Rapporteur," para. 27.

18. Lynn Bennett, *Dangerous Wives and Sacred Sisters: Social and Symbolic Roles of High-Caste Women in Nepal* (New York: Columbia University Press, 1983), 8. Bennett defined caste as "certain groups in a hierarchy of ritual purity and pollution and [as a status that] prescribes intergroup behavior in certain spheres, particularly marriage and commensality."

19. Hira Singh, "The Real World of Caste in India," *Journal of Peasant Studies* 35, no. 1 (2008): 119–132. Singh adds that the status of a caste in the caste system is not only based on purity and pollution but "is determined above all by its access to land, which also carrie[s] with it political power and social honour."

20. UN Human Rights Council, "Report of the Special Rapporteur," para. 28(d).

21. UN Human Rights Council, "Report of the Special Rapporteur," para. 29.

22. Minority Rights Group International, "Burakumin (Buraku People)," https://minority-rights.org/minorities/burakumin-buraku-people (accessed Aug. 31, 2019).

23. Minority Rights Group International, "Burakumin (Buraku People)."

24. See the website for the Nigeria-based Initiative for the Eradication of Traditional and Cultural Stigmatization in Our Society (IFETACSIOS), http://www.ifetacsios.com (accessed Aug. 31, 2019).

25. Robert F. Worth, "Languishing at the Bottom of Yemen's Ladder," *New York Times*, Feb. 27, 2008, https://www.nytimes.com/2008/02/27/world/middleeast/27yemen.html; see also Huda Seif, Alternative Report to the Joint 15th and 16th Periodic Report of the State Party Yemen to the Committee on the Elimination of Racial Discrimination (CERD)," Alternative World/Partnership for Equitable Development and Social Justice and International Dalit Solidarity Network (IDSN) (July 2006), https://tbinternet.ohchr.org/Treaties/CERD/Shared%20Documents/YEM/INT_CERD_NGO_YEM_69_10354_E.pdf.

26. Philip E. Veerman, *The Rights of the Child and the Changing Image of Childhood* (Dordrecht: Martinus Nijhoff, 1992), 169. See also UN Commission on Human Rights, "Meetings," E/CN.4/SR.630 (1959).

27. UN Human Rights Council, "Report of the Special Rapporteur," para. 31.

28. Human Rights Watch, "Caste Discrimination: A Global Concern," *Human Rights Watch* 13, no. 3(G) (2001): 36, https://www.hrw.org/reports/2001/globalcaste/caste0801.pdf.

29. UN Department for Economic and Social Affairs, "World Population Prospects, the 2015 Revision," https://esa.un.org/unpd/wpp/publications/files/key_findings_wpp_2015.pdf (accessed Aug. 31, 2019).

30. UNICEF Data, "Adolescent Demographics: Some 1.2 Billion Adolescents Aged 10–19 Years Today Make up 16 Per Cent of the World's Population" (April 2016), https://data.unicef.org/topic/adolescents/demographics.

31. I received on September 17, 2018 the following from Bela Hovy of the Population Division of the UN Department of Economic and Social Affairs (UN DESA), which included the following: "The Population Division of UN/DESA prepares estimates and projections for national populations by age and sex (https://population.un.org/wpp/) as well as estimates by migratory status (http://www.un.org/en/development/desa/population/migration/data/estimates2/estimates17.shtml). However, we do not produce estimates by the criteria you are interested in." It is strange that while the CRC defines children as below the age of eighteen (see CRC, art. 1), this is not a criterion for collecting data in some UN agencies.

32. Clifford Bob, "Dalit Rights Are Human Rights, Caste Discrimination, International Activism, and the Construction of a New Human Rights Issue," *Human Rights Quarterly* 29, no. 1 (February 2007): 167–193.

33. Clifford Bob, *The International Struggle for New Human Rights* (Philadelphia: University of Pennsylvania Press, 2009), 31–32.

34. Martin Aranguren, "Power Politics, Professionalism, and Patron–Client Relationships in Human Rights Advocacy: How Dalit Rights Became Human Rights," *Globalizations* 8, no. 1 (2001): 341–346.

35. Human Rights Watch, *Broken People: Caste Violence against India's Untouchables* (New York: Human Rights Watch, 1999).

36. CRC Committee, "General Guidelines Regarding the Form and Content of Intitial Reports to Be Submitted by States Parties under Article 44, Paragraph 1 (a) of the Convention," CRC/C/5 (Oct. 30, 1991).

37. CRC Committee, "General Guidelines regarding the Form and Content of the Periodic Reports to be submitted by States Parties under Article 44, Paragraph 1 (b) of the Convention," CRC/C/58/Rev.1 (Nov. 29, 2005). A newer version is CRC Committee, "Treaty-Specific Guidelines regarding the Form and Content of Periodic Reports to Be Submitted by States Parties under Article 44, Paragraph 1 (b), of the Convention on the Rights of the Child," CRC/C/58/Rev.3 (March 3, 2015).

38. Pankaj Mishra, "God's Oppressed Children," *New York Review of Books*, Dec. 21, 2017, https://www.nybooks.com/articles/2017/12/21/dalits-gods-oppressed-children/.

39. Quoted material from Human Rights Watch, *Broken People* (summary), https://www.hrw.org/report>1999>1999/01.01>broken-people (accessed Aug. 31, 2019).

40. Human Rights Watch, *Broken People* (summary).

41. "Children's Alternative Report to UNCRC [Committee]–India (February 2012; updated May 2013), https://tbinternet.ohchr.org/Treaties/CRC/Shared%20Documents/Ind/INT_CRC_ICO_Ind_15693_E.pdf.

42. Sravani Sarkar, "Children Bear the Brunt of Caste Abuses in Rural MP," *Hindustan Times*, Dec. 5, 2014, https://www.hindustantimes.com/bhopal/children-bear-the-brunt-of-caste-abuses-in-rural-mp/story-kx7ViJFX8jjxuybmBBNLAO.html. The survey, used in the article, was carried out by Dalit Adhikar Abhiyan, an umbrella organization working for scheduled caste rights; it covered about 62,500 people in 30 villages of 10 districts across the state. In all, 412 Dalit families and 61 panchayat representatives and government servants of Scheduled Castes category were covered in the survey, which was funded by Action Aid and conducted between January and August 2014.

43. CRC Committee, "Initial Reports of States Parties Due in 1995: India," UN Doc. CRC/C/28/Add.10 (1997).

44. CRC Committee, "Concluding Observations of the Committee on the Rights of the Child: India," CRC/C/15/Add.115 (2000), para. 9.

45. CRC Committee, "Concluding Observations: India," paras. 30–31.

46. CRC Committee, "Consideration of Reports Submitted by States Parties under Article 44 of the Convention Concluding Observations: India," CRC/C/Add.228 (Feb. 26, 2004), paras. 27–28.

47. CRC Committee, "Consideration of Reports: India," para. 65(b).

48. International Dalit Solidarity Network, "UN Experts Slam India's Child Rights Policies," National Campaign on Dalit Human Rights press release, June 4, 2014, https://idsn.org/un-experts-slam-indias-child-rights-policies-ncdhr-press-release.

49. Mulk Raj Anand, *Untouchable* (Delhi: Penguin Books India, 1935).

50. Eimar Barr, Susan Durston, Rob Jenkins, Eriko Onoda, and Anjali Pradhan, "Dalits in India and Nepal: Policy Options for Improving Social Inclusion in Education," UNICEF Division of Policy and Planning Working Paper (June 2007), iii.

51. International Dalit Solidarity Network, "Nepal," http://idsn.org/countries/nepal (accessed Aug. 31, 2019).

52. Charles Haviland, "Why Is Nepal's New Constitution Controversial?" BBC News, Sept. 19, 2015, https://www.bbc.com/news/world-asia-34280015.

53. International Dalit Solidarity Network, "2015 Annual Report," 25, https://idsn.org/wp-content/uploads/2016/03/IDSN_AR2015_Interactive.pdf.

54. "Estimates of the number of Dalits in Nepal vary greatly. According to the official 2011 census, they constitute 13.6 per cent of the total population (or appr. 3.6 million people), but researchers and Dalit organizations assess that this number could be above 20 per cent— or as many as five million people." International Dalit Solidarity Network, "Nepal."

55. Bennett described the Nepalese caste hierarchy. On top are the Brahmans and the Ksatriya, from which groups priests and warriors were recruited. A middle group the *Matwali* follow. On the bottom of this hierarchy is the lowest caste, "those from whom water cannot be accepted." This last group can be subdivided in the Sudra, who still can be touched, and "the group from whom water cannot be accepted but also not be touched, the untouchables." Bennett, *Dangerous Wives and Sacred Sisters*, 10.

56. Personal communication with Inge Bracke, a Belgian social worker and country director in Nepal of Child Protection Centers and Services (CPCS) International.

57. CRC Committee, "Concluding Observations of the Committee on the Rights of the Child: Nepal," CRC/C/15/Add.57 (June 7, 1996), para. 14.

58. "The Committee is concerned at the insufficient attention paid to systematic and comprehensive data collection, identification of appropriate indicators, as well as to a monitoring mechanism for all areas covered by the Convention and in relation to all groups of chil-

dren, including children belonging to minorities, to lower castes, children of very poor families, children in rural areas, disabled children, children placed in institutions, children victims of sale, trafficking and prostitution and children living and/or working on the streets." CRC Committee, "Concluding Observations: Nepal," para. 14.

59. "In the light of article 2 of the Convention, the Committee also recommends that the State party take all necessary measures to reduce the drop-out rate of girls in rural and urban areas and to prevent their involvement in child labour or prostitution, and to reinforce the access to basic services (health, education and social care) for children in rural areas and for disabled children throughout the country. The Government should in particular take concrete measures, including awareness campaigns to change negative attitudes, to protect children belonging to the lowest castes from any form of exploitation." CRC Committee, "Concluding Observations: Nepal," para. 32.

60. CRC Committee, "Concluding Observations: Nepal," para. 32.

61. CRC Committee, "Consideration of Reports Submitted by States Parties under Article 44 of the Convention Concluding Observations: Nepal," CRC/C/15/Add.261 (Sept. 21, 2005), para 35.

62. See Dorje's Dooing, "Caste Out" (Feb. 4, 2015), http://www.dorjegurung.com/blog/2015/02/caste-out.

63. K. C. Govinda, "Students Padlock School after Dalit Woman Cooks Their Lunch," *myRepública*, Feb. 10, 2018, https://myrepublica.nagariknetwork.com/news/students-padlock-school-after-dalit-woman-cooks-their-lunch.

64. One of the Dalit groups, for many generations trapped in a bonded-labor system, *the Kamaiya*, succeeded in freeing themselves. Their road toward a life without discrimination is not easy. See Anita Cheria, Edwin Nanda, Kumar Kandangwa, and Khemraj Upadhyaya, *Liberation Is Not Enough: The Kamaiya Movement in Nepal* (Kathmandu: Action Aid International Nepal, 2005). There are also *the Haliyas*, which include those in the village who do not have enough arable land to provide for their families and are in need of money. "Weaknesses in the rehabilitation process has left former Kamaiya bonded labourers vulnerable to entering into new forms of exploitative working practices including bonded labour." Birendra Giri, "The Bonded Labour System in Nepal: Musahar and Tharu Communities' Assessments of the Haliya and Kamaiya Labour Contracts," *Journal of Alternative Perspectives in the Social Sciences* 4, no. 2 (May 2012): 518–525; see also Anti-Slavery International, "Information on Nepal: Compliance with ILO Convention No.29 on Forced Labour (ratified in 2002)" (July 2009), https://idsn.org/wp-content/uploads/user_folder/pdf/New_files/Nepal/Forced_and_bonded_labour_in_Nepal__-__ASI_July_2009.pdf.

65. Amy Waldman, "Caste System Binds Nepalese Prostitutes," *New York Times*, April 11, 2004, https://www.nytimes.com/2004/04/11/international/asia/caste-system-binds-nepalese-prostitutes.html.

66. CRC Committee, "Concluding Observations on the Combined Third to Fifth Periodic Reports of Nepal," CRC/C/NPL/CO/3–5 (2016), para. 20(b).

67. CRC Committee, "Third to Fifth Periodic Reports of Nepal," para 21(c).

68. CRC Committee, "Third to Fifth Periodic Reports of Nepal," para. 67(b): The CRC Committee recommended to "[p]rovide culturally and linguistically adapted awareness-raising campaigns and targeted support measures in Dalit, minority … to ensure meaningful access to education, health and social services."

69. UN Convention on the Rights of the Child (CRC), G.A. Res. 44/25, 44th Sess., UN Doc. A/RES/44/25 (1989).

70. International Baby Foods Action Network (IBFAN), Report on the 51st Session/52nd Pre-Session of the Committee on the Rights of the Child 25 May-19 June 2009, Geneva GIFA/IBFAN, 2009, 6–9 (II Countries Reviews, para 3 Mauritania 28 May 2009).

71. CRC Committee, "Concluding Observations of the Committee on the Rights of the Child: Mauritania," CRC/C/15/Add.159 (Nov. 6, 2001).

72. CRC Committee, "Concluding Observations: Mauritania," para. 24(a).

73. CRC. Committee, "Concluding Observations: Mauritania," para. 25.

74. CRC Committee, "Consideration of Reports Submitted by States Parties under Article 44 of the Convention Concluding Observations: Mauritania," CRC/C/MRT/CO/2 (June 17, 2009), paras. 30, 37.

75. CRC Committee, "Consideration of Reports: Mauritania," para. 29.

76. Alexander Stille, "The Last Slaves in Mauritania," *New York Review of Books*, Nov. 23, 2017, https://www.nybooks.com/articles/2017/11/23/last-slaves-in-mauritania. The book being reviewed was Zekeria Ould Ahmed Salem, *Prêcher Dans le Desert: Islam Politique et Changement Social en Mauritanie* [Preaching in the Desert: Political Islam and Social Change in Mauritania] (Paris: Karthala, 2013).

77. Stille, "Last Slaves in Mauritania," 328–329. "At the top were the *marabouts*—the religious caste like the Brahmin in Hinduism—and the *guerriers*, the warrior caste, both consisting of major slave owners who considered manual labor dishonorable. Below these were castes often linked with specific professions such as the *griots* (musicians and entertainers), and *artisans* such as the forgerons (metalworkers)." See also Unrepresented Nations and Peoples Organization (UNPO) and Fondation SAHEL, "Submission to the United Nations Committee on the Rights of the Child: Islamic Republic of Mauritania." https://unpo.org/article/21008

78. International Dalit Solidarity Network, "Discrimination Based on Descent in Africa," , para. 3.1.1, https://idsn.org/wp-content/uploads/user_folder/pdf/Old_files/africa/pdf/Africafull.pdf (accessed Aug. 31, 2019).

79. Anti-Slavery International, Minority Rights Group International, and SOS-Esclaves, "Joint Submission for the Universal Periodic Review of Mauritania, 23rd Session, October–November 2015," http://www.antislavery.org/ . . . /1_upr_submission_on_mauritania_2015 (accessed Aug. 31, 2019).
    In this submission it was also pointed out that "[t]here are also other black ethnic groups in the country who were never enslaved by the Beidan, such as the Wolof, Soninke and Pular; these groups are known collectively as Black Mauritanians; these groups also have a tradition of slavery, but it is rarely practised now, though some related discriminatory practices remain."

80. Anti-Slavery International, Minority Rights Group International, and SOS-Esclaves, "Joint Submission," 9.

81. Brahim Ould Daddah (minister of justice): "The necessary care has been taken with the issue of slavery. The phenomenon of slavery has been confronted resolutely through legislation criminalizing the practice of enslavement, penalizing perpetrators and upholding the rights of victims. The authorities continue to fight the effects of this phenomenon, to limit its consequences and combat its social, economic and cultural impact on Mauritanian society as a whole. The road map to combat modern forms of slavery and the institutions founded under it, such as the Joint Ministerial Committee to Combat Slavery and the Technical Committee and the Solidarity Agency, are all shining examples of a clear strategy and ambitious programs to heal the wounds caused by enslavement practices." Human Rights Watch, "Ethnicity, Discrimination, and Other Red Lines: Repression of Human Rights Defenders in Mauritania"

(Feb. 12, 2018), appendix I, https://docplayer.net/79046058-V-appendix-i-letter-to-minister-of-justice-brahim-daddah-and-minister-of-interior-ahmedou-ould-abdallah.html.

82. Anti-Slavery International, Minority Rights Group International, and SOS-Esclaves, "Joint Submission," 12. The Initiative for the Resurgence of the Abolitionist Movement is connected to Biram Ould Dah Ould Abeid, a Haratin who tried to become president. He has been jailed several times....

83. African Charter for the Rights and Welfare of the Child, OAU Doc. CAB/LEG/24.9/49 (1990), art. 44, para. 1. "The Committee may receive communication, from any person, group or non-governmental organization recognized by the Organization of African Unity, by a Member State, or the United Nations relating to any matter covered by this Charter."

84. UN General-Assembly, Optional Protocol to the Convention on the Rights of the Child on a Communications Procedure, G.A. Res. 66/138, 66th Sess., UN Doc. A/RES/66/138 (Dec. 19, 2011; entered into force April 14, 2014).

85. Philip Veerman, "An African and International Perspective on Children's Rights: Interview with Dr. Benyam Dawit Mezmur, Chairperson of the African Children's Rights Committee (ACERWC) and for Two Years (2015–2017) the Chair of the UN CRC Committee," *International Journal of Children's Rights* 25, nos. 3–4 (November 2017): 672–697.

86. "Rapport initial sur les mesures d'application des dispositions de la Charte Africaine des Droits et Bien-être de l'Enfant prises par la Mauritanie," paras. 66 and 67 (pps. 47 and 48), https://acerwc.africa/wp-content/uploads/2018/04/Initial-Report-Mauritania-French.pdf (accessed Aug. 31, 2019).

87. African Committee of Experts on the Rights and Welfare of the Child (ACERWC), "Decision on the Communication Submitted by Minority Rights Group International and SOS-Esclaves on Behalf of Said Ould Salem and Yarg Ould Salem against the Government of the Republic of Mauritania, Decision No. 003/2017 (Dec. 15, 2017) on Communication No. 007/Com/003/2015, https://acerwc.africa/wp-content/uploads/2018/13/ACERWC%20Decision%20FinaL%20ON%20Mauritania.pdf (accessed Aug. 31, 2019).

88. ACERWC, Decision on the Communication Submitted by Minority Rights Group International and SOS-Esclaves."

89. ACERWC, "The Committee Issues a Decision on the Communication against Mauritania," press release, Jan. 26, 2018.

90. African Charter, arts. 1, 3, 4, 5, 11, 12, 15, 16, and 21.

91. ACERWC, "Decision on the Communication Submitted by Minority Rights Group International and SOS-Esclaves, para. 98(A) (p. 28).

92. ACERWC, "Decision on the Communication Submitted by Minority Rights Group International and SOS-Esclaves,"para 98(A) (p. 28).

93. ACERWC, "Decision on the Communication Submitted by Minority Rights Group International and SOS-Esclaves," para 98(I) (p. 29).

94. "A court in Mauritania has sentenced two people to prison for holding several people, including children, in slavery. They received sentences of ten years and 20 years in prison respectively—thought to be the toughest for the crime in the country to-date, though slavery was outlawed in 1981 and only criminalised in 2015. A court in the northwestern town of Nouadhibou gave a 20-year prison sentence to Hamoudi Ould Saleck who, along with his now-deceased father, was accused of 'reducing to slavery' a family, two of whom were children. A woman, Revea Mint Mohamed, was also jailed for ten years for keeping

three slaves—one of them was a 29-year-old who had been enslaved since she was a small girl. Both cases had been brought by former slaves." Child Rights International Network (CRIN), "The Week in Children's Rights—1576" (April 4, 2018), https://archive.crin.org/en/home/what-we-do/crinmail/week-childrens-rights-1576.html.

95. See, e.g., UN Human Rights Council, "Report of the Special Rapporteur on Contemporary Forms of Slavery, Including its Causes and Consequences, Gulnara Shahinian: Follow-up Mission to Mauritania," UN Doc. A/HRC/27/53/add.1 (Aug. 26, 2014).

96. Walk Free Foundation, "Global Slavery Index 2018," 29, https://www.globalslaveryindex.org/resources/downloads (accessed Aug. 31, 2019); see also Anti-Slavery International, "Thematic Report on Slavery in Mauritania for the UN Human Rights Committee, 107th Session, 11–28 March 2013" (Dec. 27, 2012), https://www.ecoi.net/en/file/local/1066447/1930_1371813094_anti-slaveryinternational-mauritania-hrc107.pdf.

97. Priyua Vart, Ajay Jaglan, and Kashif Shafique, "Caste-Based Social Inequalities and Childhood Anemia in India: Results from the National Family Health Survey (NFHS) 2005–2006,"*BMC Public Health* 15 (June 2015): 537, 1–2.

98. Vart, Jaglan, and Shafique, "Caste-Based Social Inequalities."

99. International Dalit Solidarity Network, "Dalit Children in Bangladesh: Alternative NGO Report" (August 2015), https://tbinternet.ohchr.org/Treaties/CRC/Shared%20Documents/BGD/INT_CRC_NGO_BGD_21453_E.pdf (accessed Aug. 31, 2019).

100. National Campaign on Dalit Human Rights, "Equity Watch 2015: Access to Justice for Dalits in India," 28, https://idsn.org Access to Justice – Equity Watch 2015 report – NCDHR (accessed Aug. 31, 2019).

101. CRC, art. 28(e).

102. Nigel S. Rodley, "The Role and Impact of Treaty Bodies." in *The Oxford Handbook of International Human Rights Law*, ed. Dinah Shelton (Oxford: Oxford University Press 2013), 621–648.

103. David Dozoïs, "Understanding and Enhancing the Effects of Homework in Cognitive-Behavioral Therapy," *Clinical Psychology: Science Practice* 17 (2010): 157–161.

104. Eva Clarhäll (consultant for Save the Children), "Monitoring Implementation of the UN Convention on the Rights of the Child: A Review of Concluding Observations by the UN CRC Committee regarding General Measures of Implementation," https://resource-centre.savethechildren.net>node>pdf Monitoring implementation of the UN Convention on the Rights of the Child (accessed Aug. 31, 2019).

105. David Keane, Caste-Based Discrimination in International Human Rights Law (Aldershot, UK: Ashgate Publishing, 2007), 267.

106. CRC Committee, "Initial Reports: India," para. 81.

107. CRC Committee, "Concluding Observations: Nepal," 17.

108. CRC Committee, "Concluding Observations: India," 30.

109. As quoted in: Pankaj."God's Oppressed People."

110. Julie Rialet, "Can Religious Leaders Be Our Best Allies to End Child Marriage?" Girls Not Brides website (July 21, 2017), https://www.girlsnotbrides.org/can-religious-leaders-best-allies-end-child-marriage.

111. Philip Veerman and Caroline Sand, "Religion and Children's Rights," *International Journal of Children's Rights* 7 (1999): 385–393.

112. OHCHR, "Beirut Declaration and Its 18 Commitments on 'Faith for Rights,'" https://www.ohchr.org/EN/Issues/FreedomReligion/Pages/FaithForRights.aspx.

113. Personal communication from Anita Cheria, who works for CIVIDEP, an organization for workers' rights in the Bengaluru area of India.

114. Robert Coles, *The Moral Life of Children* (Boston: Atlantic Monthly Press, 1986), 16.

115. Sarada Balagopalan, "Introduction: Children's Lives and the Indian Context," *Childhood* 18, no. 3 (2011): 292–297.

116. Laura Theytaz-Bergman, "What Happened? A Study on the Impact of the Convention on the Rights of the Child in Five Countries: Estonia, Nepal, Peru, Uganda and Yemen" (2009), https://resourcecentre.savethechildren.net/node/2910/pdf/2910.pdf (accessed Aug. 31, 2019).

117. Theytaz-Bergman, "What Happened?," 26–28.

118. Theytaz-Bergman, "What Happened?," 39.

119. CRC Committee, "Concluding Observations: Nepal," 36.

120. CRC Committee, "Concluding Observations: India," para. 31.

121. UN Committee on the Elimination of Racial Discrimination, "General Recommendation 29: Discrimination Based on Descent (Sixty-first session, 2002)," UN Doc. A/57/18 at 111 (2002), para. 1.

122. UN Committee on the Elimination of Racial Discrimination, "General Recommendation 29,", para. 1.

123. Vamik D. Volkan, "Large-Group Identity, International Relations and Psychoanalysis," *International Forum of Psychoanalysis* 18, no. 4 (2009): 206–213.

124. G. C. Pal, "Caste-Gender Intersectionality and Atrocities in Haryana: Emerging Patterns and State Responses," *Journal of Social Inclusion Studies* 4, no. 1 (June 2018): 30–50, 30.

125. Janusz Korczak, *Selected Works*, edited by Martin Wolins (Warsaw: National Science Foundation, 1967); see also, Philip Veerman, "Janusz Korczak and the Rights of the Child," *Concern: Journal of National Children's Bureau* 62 (Spring 1987): 7–9.

126. Global Initiative to End All Corporal Punishment of Children, "Nepal Prohibits All Corporal Punishment of Children" (Oct. 2, 2018), https://endcorporalpunishment.org/nepal-prohibits-all-corporal-punishment-of-children.

PART V

SELECTED POPULATIONS

CHAPTER 26

EMBRACING OUR LGBTQ YOUTH

A Child Rights Paradigm

BERTA ESPERANZA HERNÁNDEZ-TRUYOL

"All young people, regardless of sexual orientation or identity, deserve a safe and supportive environment in which to achieve their full potential."

—Harvey Milk[1]

"[K]ids are walking 'round the hallway plagued by pain in their heart a world so hateful some would rather die than be who they are."

—Macklemore and Ryan Lewis[2]

"With ignorance comes fear—from fear comes bigotry. Education is the key to acceptance."

—Kathleen Patel[3]

1 INTRODUCTION

LGBT[4] persons—youth, adults, couples, and families—live and thrive in every corner of the world. Myriad social factors—including history, culture, religion, and legal structures—influence attitudes toward and reactions to LGBT persons.[5] Prevalent opinions on sexuality affect all LGBT persons but have a most marked impact on LGBT youth.

Recent studies shed light on global outlooks toward sexual and gender minorities (SGMs). These are important observations, as they expose the climate in which LGBT youth come of age. The studies confirm that although global attitudes toward SGM have improved, "the force of negation still exerts great power all over the planet, played out in violence, negation or discrimination in policy and law, forced surgeries and numerous other violations."[6] Even in states that show a high level of acceptance of sexual minorities, LGBT youth, adults, couples, and/or families encounter rejection and discrimination.[7] For example, "It is probably fair to say that in no country in the world can people of the same sex who are romantically or sexually attracted to each other feel safe enough to hold hands in the public space day or night in their own countries (although there are enclaves where at times it is safe)."[8] Rejection, derision, intolerance, violence, and discrimination affect daily lives, health, social status, status within the family, and the educational climate within which LGBT youth develop.

International human rights law protects LGBT youth against these affronts to dignity and full personhood. The law protects individuals against discrimination based on sexuality.[9] It also affords SGM the rights to security, life, education, freedom of worship, privacy, and to form a family. Yet, notwithstanding international legal safeguards, LGBT persons, in general, and LGBT youth, in particular, often enjoy universal rights in the breach. Consequently, the environment for LGBT youth in society, schools, places of worship, and even at home, can be one of insecurity, marginalization, and hostility.

This chapter begins (Part I) with a discussion of the problems that LGBT youth directly confront at home, at school, and in society as a whole, such as intimidation, rejection by family and society, sexual violence, harassment, poverty, and homelessness. This part critically reviews the structural inequalities[10] that exist with respect to legal frameworks for families, mainly same-sex couples, and the consequences that these inequalities cause for their children. Focusing on LGBT youth,[11] Part III engages recent studies on global attitudes toward homosexuality. Part IV then presents international and regional legal protections of SGM. It also describes national laws, some of which provide rights protection to LGBT individuals but sometimes penalize homosexuality.

The chapter concludes (section in Part V) with a discussion of why a dramatic shift is needed in the framework of analysis of LGBT youth rights,[12] and it proposes adopting a child rights paradigm to ensure that LGBT youth achieve full personhood and dignity.

2 ISSUES AND PROBLEMS AFFECTING LGBT YOUTH

Before addressing some of the specific issues and problems that concern LGBT youth, it is imperative to emphasize that LGBT youth are multidimensional.[13] LGBT youth are diverse with regard to race, ethnicity, religion, culture, education, ability, economic and social position, health, and so on. It is crucial not to homogenize LGBT youth because demographics affect experience. Analysis of LGBT youths' experience of social, educational, and familial climate must be mindful of demographic differences and aggravating factors. In addition, there are gendered dimensions to some LGBT youth experiences. Sexual minority boys are more likely than heterosexual boys to experience sexual victimization by youth; heterosexual girls experience such victimization more than LGB girls. On the other hand, LGB girls have a disproportionately high representation in correctional residential placements.

Notwithstanding LGBT youth's diversity, however, they confront certain aggressions and challenges simply for being LGBT. LGBT youth face discrimination, bullying, harassment, and persecution by both adults and other youth simply because of their sexual orientation or gender expression. This aggression toward LGBT youth often places LGBT youth at an increased risk of depression, suicide, homelessness, and substance abuse.[14]

Significantly, LGBT youth are coming out of the closet—self-identifying as LGBT—at a much younger age than the historic norm. In 2003 the average coming-out age was sixteen; in the 1980s, it was twenty for men and twenty-two for women.[15] In 2013 the average age was 13.4 years—some youth come out as young as age seven.[16]

Such self-recognition occurs in a world that has laws and policies that are hostile to or lack legal protections for LGBT persons. Beyond the law are social, cultural, and religious norms that often enable and perpetuate the repudiation of, opposition to, and discrimination and violence against LGBT persons. These norms that exist in the family, schools, religion, and society structure the hostile environment in which LGBT youth develop. When the environments in which LGBT youth exist are unaccepting, they engender homelessness, poverty, and sexual violence that negatively affect and contribute to the marginability[17] of LGBT youth.

The child rights framework is meant to protect LGBT youth against discrimination and to guarantee the rights to health, safety, security, and education. However, while the protections exist on paper, the reality for LGBT youth is one of vulnerability and exposure to physical and psychological violence. This section explores the challenges that LGBT youth confront in two settings where they spend most of their time—the family and the schools—and the consequences of such challenges.

2.1 The Family

2.1.1 In General—Rejection and Its Consequences

Family rejection of LGBT youth correlates to negative health and social consequences. Rejection of and discrimination against LGBT youth by their family have severe negative repercussions at the personal, social, and psychological levels and are the main causes of LGBT youth homelessness.[18]

Negative health consequences of family rejection also include high rates of attempted death by suicide as well as higher rates of depression, illegal drug use, alcohol abuse, and unprotected sexual activity, with the consequent risk of sexually transmitted infections and unintended adolescent pregnancies, as compared with youth whose families embrace them.[19] On the other hand, family acceptance of LGBT youth generates positive results regarding self-esteem, mental health, and general health.[20]

Non-embracing environments also place LGBT youth at risk of family violence and ejection from the home. Family rejection of LGBT youth results in an overrepresentation of youth in custodial care—be it foster care or juvenile detention—as well as in the homeless population. In addition, once in such compromised circumstances, LGBT youth are vulnerable to additional victimization. LGBT youth of color's multidimensional vulnerabilities aggravate LGBT youth's already dire outcomes. LGBT youth of color face exacerbated outcomes due to the reality that they are victimized not only for their sexual orientation or gender expression but also for their race, culture, or ethnicity.

2.1.2 *Efforts to Change the Sexual Identity*

In the United States and elsewhere, there are efforts to change sexual identity through conversion therapy, a so-called treatment developed during the time when the medical and psychological communities considered homosexuality to be a disease. Conversion therapy, which can include electroshock procedures and self-punishment by stretching a rubber band against the wrist when one feels attracted to someone of the same sex, can cause nausea, vomiting, or paralysis. There is no evidence that these measures, rejected by every mainstream medical and mental health organization in the United States as well as by the leading international organizations, change an individual's sexual orientation.[21] However, unaccepting families seek these treatments, sometimes offered by clergy who are not subject to the professional bans on such treatments, to try to change the sexuality of their children.[22]

There is ample evidence that these treatments hurt LGBT youth. Conversion therapy aggravates the stigma that the youth feels, decreases the possibility of obtaining different therapy at other times in their life, and deteriorates the relationship they have with their family.[23] Young people who have undergone such therapies experience negative effects, including an increased tendency to die by suicide as well as increased feelings of guilt, anxiety, depression, increased illegal drug use, and an increased risk of homelessness.[24]

Some jurisdictions, such as the state of California, have adopted laws that prohibit the use of conversion therapy to change the sexual orientation of minors.[25] Not surprisingly, anti-LGBT groups vehemently resist the prohibition against conversion therapy. Significantly, the laws cover only licensed therapists. Religious entities do not need state licensing for counseling and, thus, can continue to utilize conversion therapy even if licensed professionals are prohibited by law from adopting such methods.

Religion, race, and ethnic origin are additional factors that influence families' reactions toward LGBT youth. Cultural and religious rejections of homosexuality are often the cause of negative family reaction toward LGBT youth. For example, studies have shown that very religious families are much more willing than nonreligious families to repudiate their children for being LGBT.[26]

2.1.3 *Consequences of Family Rejection: Homelessness, Poverty, and Sexual Violence*

LGBT youth experience high levels of homelessness because of their sexuality.[27] Family rejection is the greatest cause of LGBT youth homelessness and poverty.[28]

Although only 5–7 percent of youth identify as LGBT, 40 percent of homeless youth are LGBT.[29] This population experiences homelessness at a tender age and suffers more victimization than other groups. For example, in New York the average age for when

LGBT youth become homeless is 14.4 years for lesbian and gay youth and 13.5 years for transgender youth.[30]

Homeless LGBT youth are victims of sexual harassment almost twice as often as non-LGBT homeless youth. Once they become homeless, LGBT youth experience acts of violence and discrimination at higher levels than the population of heterosexual homeless young people. Homeless LGBT youth are in a precarious state of health;[31] due to victimization, risky sexual behavior, substance abuse, and mental health issues, LGBT youth suffer higher rates of HIV infection.[32]

Homeless LGBT youth endure abuse and sexual assault in the streets and even in shelters that are specifically marketed as safe havens for LGBT youth. One study reports that, while homeless, every four out of ten LGBT youth experience assault or sexual exploitation.[33] Compared to heterosexual homeless youth, almost twice as many report sexual victimization, such as persons offering them money, food, drugs, or shelter in exchange for sexual acts.[34] Multidimensionality of LGBT youth—diversity of age, race, ethnicity, and religion—may also be an aggravating factor with respect to sexual violence.[35]

LGBT youth, like all young people, have the right to family life in which their parents care for them. When there is family rejection, neglect, and abuse, the consequences are dire and result in the denial of LGBT youth their rights to family, security, health, and education. Family rejection, neglect, and abuse are clearly and unambiguously not in the best interests of LGBT youth.

For one, family rejection, abuse, and neglect are among the top five reasons for homelessness, which, in turn, results in the myriad negative outcomes previously discussed.[36] In addition, family rejection, abuse, and neglect lead to depression, drug and alcohol abuse, irresponsible sexual activity, STDs, unwanted pregnancies and death by suicide.[37] On the other hand, family acceptance fulfills the best interests of LGBT youth, as in such environments their mental and physical health is good, their self-esteem is high, and they thrive in social and familial setups.[38]

2.1.4 *Structural Inequalities*

Family structure affects all youth. International law recognizes the family as the basic unit in society. Yet although diverse family structures exist, legally, socially, and economically there is a gendered[39] presumption of heterosexuality in the so-called traditional family. Legal concepts that govern family structure—parental authority, the duties/obligations to children (including education, health, well-being, development), and family responsibilities—have evolved within such a paradigm. Consequently, LGBT families exist outside the framework and fail to receive the same treatment or protection as heterosexual families. The difference in treatment of LGBT couples affects their children.

Because recognition of family units presumes marriage, and because most countries in the world do not recognize marriage between individuals of the same sex, children of same-sex couples whose families are relegated to subordinated status suffer privations. The US acknowledges that marriage protects children and families and has accepted that the prohibition of marriage between persons of the same sex hurts same-sex couples and their children.[40] The recognition of marriage between persons of the same sex grants multiple benefits to children, including recognition that the relationship of their parents should receive the same respect and have the same integrity, dignity, and importance as other families in the community.[41] Excluding same-sex couples from the benefits of marriage—such as the legal validity, stability, and the predictability of relationships facilitated by marriage—creates a stigma for the children of same-sex couples and makes their children believe that their families are inferior and less valuable. Children of same-sex couples deserve equal legal protections, economic resources, family stability, and social legitimacy.

Notwithstanding the social, legal, political, and religious prejudices that advocate against the validity, legitimacy, and acceptance of same-sex couples and their children, studies show that children raised by LGBT couples are as happy, well adapted to their environment, and healthy as children raised by heterosexual couples.[42] Children from LGBT families demonstrate the same level of progress in schools as children raised in traditional families.[43] One study concluded that children in the US living with parents of the same sex have the same positive results regarding school achievement, cognitive development, social development, and mental health as children living with one mother and one father.[44]

LGBT families face discrimination and harassment in their communities, and their children can be harassed, subjected to teasing and intimidated regardless of whether the children are heterosexual or LGBT. These harmful actions reflect social, religious, and cultural biases.

Notwithstanding such adverse environments, the sexuality of LGBT parents does not result in a negative psychological, developmental, or emotional impact on their children.[45] Rather, children of LGBT families thrive.[46]

Archaic and discriminatory interpretations of laws create social stigmas for families and create obstacles to the establishment of stable homes, economic security, health, and well-being. Inequalities resulting from second-rate legal treatment interfere with achieving the best interest and fulfilling the needs of children within LGBT families and cause them harm.

For example, notwithstanding the reality that many children need permanent homes and that children in LGBT homes flourish, many places around the world prohibit LGBT people from adopting or being foster families, which deprive these children of homes. Similarly, while a child born to a heterosexual couple enjoys the security of being the legal child of both parents, a baby born to an LGBT couple potentially lacks a legal relationship to the non-birth parent.[47] This lack of legal sanction places the family in a limbo of legal uncertainties. Denying the child the security of having two legal parents may result in undesired family separation at home or while traveling. In addition, denying parents a legal relationship with the child, including parental rights and responsibilities, can result in the denial of medical treatment, even emergency services, to a child if the parent is not legally permitted to make decisions for the child. Further, if the couple ends the relationship, the nonbiological parent may lose custody and even the right to visit the child, which may cause great emotional and psychological trauma to both the adult and the child. While this scenario remains a possibility in many jurisdictions, in the United States a recent decision, *Pavan v. Smith*, bodes well for LGBT parents. In *Pavan*, the Supreme Court held that it was unconstitutional to deprive same-sex couples the right to be listed on their children's birth certificates.[48] This decision solidifies the parental rights of the nonbiological parents.

The impacts of structural bias in the family are also economic. Many government benefits are available only by meeting the traditional definition of family. Such benefits include tax benefits; inheritance rights; state aid to access food, shelter, and clothing; social security; medical decisions; and family visits. Jurisdictions that do not recognize LGBT relationships deny children the protections that accompany parental status.

These structural problems fly in the face of human rights norms that prohibit discrimination, mandate equality, and prioritize the best interest of the child. The laws were created with so-called traditional families in mind and fail to reflect the realities of LGBT families. LGBT families are vulnerable to social, political, economic, and religious forces that diminish their status and, therefore, can harm their children, whether LGBT or heterosexual. The child rights paradigm provides a framework and a methodology to promote LGBT equality.

2.2 Schools

Schools are a critical component of, and presumably provide a positive environment for, all children's—including LGBT youth's—physical, emotional, social, and educational development. Until the late 1990s, there was a dearth of information about LGBT youth's school experiences. Studies of the population either did not focus on or did not include LGBT youth.

In 1999 the Gay, Lesbian and Straight Education Network (GLSEN) conducted its first biennial investigation on the problems faced by LGBT students in the US.[49] Although literature on LGBT youth is sparse, other global studies[50] confirm GLSEN's observations: the "physical, emotional, and social health" challenges for LGBT youth "are primarily related to social stigma and negative societal responses, particularly in schools."[51] Indeed, the hostility against LGBT youth in schools "may disproportionately direct LGBTQ youth of color into the school-to-prison pipeline."[52] For example, one of the few quantitative investigations into LGBT students and the school sanctions reveals that LGBT youth—in particular girls who are gender-nonconforming—receive juvenile convictions up to three times more than their non-LGBT counterparts."[53] LGBT students experience intimidation, bullying, harassment, persecution, and discrimination in schools not only by their peers but also by the very school personnel whose responsibility it is to keep them safe.

2.2.1 *Intimidation, Bullying, Harassment, and Persecution*

"Homophobic bullying is a global problem. Homophobic bullying occurs in all countries regardless of beliefs or cultures."[54] Studies confirm the ubiquity of the victimization of LGBT students; they are subject to offensive and hostile language as well as intimidation, harassment, persecution, and violent attacks in schools. The abuse creates a hostile environment and has a negative impact on both school performance and the prosperity of LGBT students.[55] The studies reveal that more than half of LGBT students feel unsafe because of their sexual orientation and that almost half feel unsafe because of their gender expression.[56]

Middle school years appear to be a particularly risky time for LGBT students. LGBT middle school students, more so than high school students, report hearing homophobic comments and negative statements about gender expression as well as report more victimization.[57] LGBT students in public schools, religious schools, and schools in rural areas also experience more discrimination and victimization and have less access than their heterosexual counterparts to supportive resources.[58]

Hostility in schools goes beyond physical victimization; it includes anti-LGBT comments, including using the word *gay* negatively, and negative comments about gender expression and transgender people. Many students report hearing teachers or other school personnel making homophobic comments and negative comments about gender expression.[59]

The majority of LGBT students worldwide have experienced verbal harassment, insults, or threats, and almost half have experienced physical harassment due to their sexual orientation or gender expression.[60] Physical attacks include pushing, kicking, and wounding with a weapon.[61] Almost half of LGBT students have suffered cyberbullying—electronic intimidation and harassment through text messages or social media.[62]

School personnel inaction aggravates the impact of harassment, insults, and threats toward LGBT youth. While harassment is pervasive, its reporting is not because students either think that school personnel will not intervene or fear that, if they report the harassment, the already hostile school climate would become worse. In addition, a majority of students who did report assaults said that school personnel failed to take any action on their behalf.

Harassment of LGBT youth occurs even where it is legally prohibited. For example, in the US, even though the laws in twenty states and the District of Columbia (the nation's capital) specifically prohibit intimidation based on sexual orientation or gender expression, harassment persists.[63] It is therefore not surprising that it also occurs in the thirty states that offer no protection to LGBT students, the two states that have laws against harassment but *prohibit* school districts from specifically *protecting LGBT youth*, and the seven states that *restrict* the *inclusion of LGBT* topics in school.[64]

Attacks, bullying, intimidation, and harassment of LGBT students cause serious academic, physical, and emotional damage.[65] This treatment of LGBT youth in school has the effect of denying LGBT youth the rights to be free from discrimination, to education, safety, health, and life.[66]

2.2.2 *Discrimination*

In addition to harassment and bullying, LGBT youth confront discrimination in society as well as in schools by students, administrative staff, and teachers. One study documents that a majority of LGBT students face discriminatory policies and practices in their schools.[67] LGBT students are subject to disciplinary action for showing affection in public, while the same conduct by non-LGBT students is not subject to sanction. Students also report bans on discussing or writing about LGBT issues in their schoolwork,[68] and some report disciplinary actions simply for self-identifying as LGBT.

Some schools prohibit students from taking a person of the same sex to school dances.[69] Notwithstanding successful legal challenges to such practices,[70] schools continue to ban it, even preferring to cancel dances before allowing same-sex couples to attend.[71]

Other schools have dress codes based on traditional gender norms—social constructs based on a binary conceptualization of gender—which has the effect of discriminating based on sex, gender identity and expression. For example, some schools forbid girls from wearing a tuxedo for their school photos. LGBT students also have reported bans on wearing clothing or items with messages of support for LGBT people.[72]

Some of the discriminatory school policies target transgender students. Such policies include forbidding trans students from using their preferred name and requiring them to use a specified bathroom or locker room and to wear clothes that correspond to their legal sex.[73] These realities constitute discrimination and denial of equality based on sexuality, discrimination that is proscribed by human rights norms.

2.2.3 *Consequences of Harassment and Discrimination*

Harassment and discrimination in school have negative educational consequences. The negative impacts include increased absences, avoidance of spaces separated by gender, such as bathrooms and dressing rooms, lower academic performance, decrease participation in both curricular and extracurricular activities, and dropping out of school or deciding not to continue their studies.[74]

Discrimination and harassment in the school environment reflect the discrimination and harassment suffered by LGBT youth in society and place LGBT youth at serious risk of having health problems, including death by suicide, drug use, homelessness, and a worsening of their grades.[75] It also results in higher levels of anxiety, depression, and death by suicide.[76] The negative consequences caused by a hostile school environment, just like those caused by a hostile social environment, constitute violations of students' human rights to equality and non-discrimination, security, education, life, and mental and physical health. International and regional frameworks protect all of these rights.

2.2.4 *Alleviating Factors*

One factor that improves the educational, physical, and psychosocial outcomes for LGBT youth, including lowering the risk of death by suicide, is a positive school environment.[77]

Notwithstanding this reality—and, in some instances, legal mandates—schools often fail to provide necessary resources or support. For example, gay/straight associations (GSAs) are official school clubs that support LGBT issues. Studies establish that GSAs are not only a great support for LGBT students, but they also help to create a culture of inclusion in which the harassment and intimidation of LGBT youth diminishes.[78] Where GSAs exist, LGBT students hear the term *gay* used as a negative expression, homophobic terms, or derogatory terms about gender much less frequently. Also, where GSAs exist, school personnel are more likely to intervene when hearing a homophobic term. In the same spirit, with GSAs students feel less insecure, experience fewer instances of harassment and discrimination, and feel more like a part of their school community.[79] Yet schools often seek to prohibit the formation of such clubs, institute policies that make participation difficult (such as parental permission not required for other clubs), deny funding, or refuse to publicize GSA events.[80]

Beyond GSAs, factors that enhance the school environment and promote LGBT student well-being include: supportive staff and teachers; policies that prohibit bullying, harassment, and discrimination, and promote inclusion; and inclusion of LGBT persons and themes in the curriculum.[81] In order to have supportive staff, it is often necessary to provide training resources for engaging with and being supportive of LGBT youth, such as educator's guides to relating to LGBT youth, LGBT-inclusive curriculum, and training on bullying, bias, and diversity.[82] In order to comply with human rights mandates and allow all students to reach their full potential, the school must create an environment that is one of inclusion, equality, and safety for LGBT students.

3 Global Attitudes

Global trends indicate greater social and legal acceptance of different sexualities. In fact, a 1981–2014, 141-country research project reveals that "the most accepting countries are becoming more accepting"[83] and that "most countries experienced some increase in acceptance."[84] Yet parts of the world still reject and deride LGBT persons. The same research reveals that countries with lower acceptance of sexual diversity are becoming less accepting.[85]

Many unaccepting states have national laws that allow discrimination against LGBT persons or even criminalize homosexuality, leaving the LGBT population exposed to discrimination, harm, and even criminal prosecution simply because of their sexuality. In a troubling trend, a 2018 survey in the US found that the move toward acceptance had ceased and that "the . . . pendulum . . . swung in the opposite direction."[86] The survey unveiled a significant increase both in discomfort around LGBT persons and in LGBT "reporting discrimination because of sexual orientation or gender identity."[87]

Studies also reveal geographic and cultural divides. Generally, the US, Canada, the European Union, and much of Latin America are accepting of homosexuality.

However, states that are predominantly Muslim, African states (particularly in sub-Saharan Africa), sectors of Asia, and Russia are unaccepting. Israel, Poland, and Bolivia show divisions in opinion.[88]

One significant factor in shaping attitudes positively toward LGBT persons is familiarity. Persons who know a sexual or gender minority (SGM) are more accepting; knowing someone results in more "expansive or inclusive" attitudes.[89] For example, across the globe, almost three-quarters of persons who know someone who identifies as an SGM agree that non-discrimination protections should extend to people who so identify. On the other hand, less than one-half of persons who do *not* know an SGM-identifying person believe sexual orientation deserves protection, and barely half think gender minorities deserve protection.[90]

Another factor affecting attitudes toward LGBT is criminalization of same-sex activity. In states that do not criminalize homosexuality, almost two-thirds of persons surveyed believe that non-discrimination laws should apply to everyone; in criminalizing states, less than half of those surveyed believe that non-discrimination laws should apply.[91]

Knowing someone who is LGBT results in positive attitudes not only with respect to rejecting discrimination and criminalization but also to embracing work protections and accepting neighbors involved in same-sex romantic and sexual relationships.[92] In states that criminalize homosexuality, one-third of the persons interviewed stated that they would try to change their LGBT neighbors' sexual orientation.[93]

Religion, gender, and age are additional factors influencing attitudes toward homosexuality. States in which people self-identify as religious generally are less accepting of homosexuality.[94] However, approximately half of the persons interviewed reported that they could both be accepting of SGM persons and respect their religion,[95] a figure that rises to over two-thirds for respondents who know someone who identifies as SGM.[96]

Religion, as a factor affecting attitudes toward the LGBT community, works both with respect to others' perceptions of the LGBT community as well as a person's self-image.

Studies have generally shown that, although the reasons are not clear, religion serves to insulate persons from suicidal thoughts and conduct.[97] However, a recent study suggests that religion has the opposite effect for LGBT youth. A study of college-enrolled young adults revealed that "among people who regarded religion as very important, sexual minority status was more strongly associated with suicide ideation and attempt."[98]

Another factor that has an impact in attitudes toward homosexuality is gender. Although in most states men and women do not have significantly different opinions on LGBT issues, women were "considerably" more accepting than men where a gender gap existed.[99] Interestingly, gender and religiosity interact; self-identification as male appears to be a determinant in increased suicidal thinking among sexual minority religious youth.[100]

Acceptance of homosexuality also varies by age group, with younger respondents being more accepting than older respondents.[101] Beyond age, gender, and religiosity, development appears to be a factor influencing a country's acceptance of homosexuality.[102]

The more developed states tend to be more accepting while the less developed states tend to be less accepting. All these factors play a role in attitudes and environment for LGBT youth, who are subject not only to societal mindsets but to familial ones as well.

4 LEGAL FRAMEWORKS

International and regional frameworks provide the foundation for a child rights paradigm that protects and respects LGBT youth rights. These documents promise to all persons, including youth, the protections enumerated. They can be utilized to protect LGBT youth from harm and to blunt state laws that contravene child rights norms.

4.1 International Framework

The Convention on the Rights of the Child (CRC)[103] is the premier international document that focuses on children and their rights. The CRC, which focuses on all children, creates an environment that promotes LGBT youth thriving. The preamble reiterates that the family is a fundamental unit of society and that young people have the right to be free from violence, and it establishes that young people have the right always to have their interests considered first. This is significant for LGBT youth who, as has been discussed in section 2, are often humiliated, bullied, and marginalized in school, in society, at places of worship, and, sadly, even in their homes because of their sexuality or gender expression.

LGBT youth benefit from CRC's protection of the best interests of the child standard (Article 3). The best interests mandate of the CRC effectively centers LGBT youth interests in contexts of conflicts at school, at home, and at places of worship by specifying that "States Parties shall ensure that the institutions, services and facilities responsible for the care or protection of children shall conform with the standards established by competent authorities, particularly in the areas of safety, health, in the number and suitability of their staff, as well as competent supervision."[104] The CRC protects all youth from discrimination by association, thus protecting the children of LGBT parents (Article 2) and affords all youth freedom of expression, thought, conscience, religion, association, and peaceful gathering (Articles 13, 14, 15)—rights LGBT youth often experience in the breach. The CRC's provision ensuring freedom from arbitrary interference in private life or family (Article 16) affords protection to LGBT youth in having a safe home. The requirement that the state protect children from harm and exploitation (Article 19) should protect LGBT youth from those who deride them—in public or private settings. The rights to health (Article 24), social security (Article 26), an adequate standard of living (Article 27), alternative care (Article 20), education (Article 29), culture (Article 30), and freedom from exploitation, whether economic (Article 32) or sexual (Article 34), protect LGBT youth notwithstanding sexuality. Yet LGBT youth often enjoy these rights in the breach in all their environments—home, school, place of worship, and society at large.

Beyond the CRC, which focuses specifically on children, myriad international documents protect the human rights of all persons—including children. The Universal Declaration of Human Rights (UDHR),[105] the International Covenant on Civil and Political Rights (ICCPR),[106] and the International Covenant on Economic, Social and Cultural Rights (ICESCR)[107] all mandate equality and prohibit discrimination based on sex, a mark of identity that includes sexuality.[108] These international documents protect LGBT persons, including youth, against discrimination based on sexuality.

Moreover, international law offers all persons, notwithstanding their sexual orientation or gender identity, a plethora of rights that protect LGBT youth from circumstances that harm them. For example, beyond proscribing discrimination and ensuring equality, the ICCPR protects the rights to life (Article 6), personal security (Article 9), privacy (Article 17), freedom of expression (Article 19), freedom of thought, conscience, and religion (Article 18), free association (Article 22), peaceful assembly (Article 21), and all other civil and political rights.[109] Similarly, the ICESCR protects the rights to work (Article 6), equal working conditions (Article 7), physical and mental health (Article 12), education (Article 13), and even the status of the family as "the natural and fundamental element of society" (Article 10). All countries that have ratified these documents must respect, protect, and give effect to these human rights with regard to LGBT youth.

The Convention on the Elimination of All Forms of Discrimination Against Women (CEDAW),[110] addresses the universal problem of inequality and discrimination against women in the public and private spheres. This broad document specifically prohibits discrimination in education (Article 10), employment (Article 11), health (Article 12), political life (Article 7), family life (Article 16), and before the law (Article 15).

CEDAW recognizes that to achieve gender equality the traditional roles of men and women in society and in the family need to change. The treaty requires states to adopt legislation to change the culture of inequality, including laws that change culture and the customs that effect or contribute to discrimination, inequality, and gendered hierarchies. In fact, CEDAW was used to draft a new law in Saudi Arabia that would fight employment discrimination by allowing female lawyers to try family law cases in court without the accompaniment of a male guardian; female attorneys are now on the rise in Saudi Arabia.[111]

CEDAW's nondiscrimination mandates, broadly interpreted, can affect significant protections to all persons whose gender identity is female, regardless of biological sex or sexuality.[112] In fact, one of the goals elaborated within the CEDAW is "achieving the elimination of prejudices and customary and all other practices which are based on the idea of the inferiority or the superiority of either of the sexes or on stereotyped roles for men and women" (Article 5). Article 5 can be construed to protect those who identify as female, regardless of their sex at birth, because it aims to eliminate the stereotyped roles of the sexes. Such construal has the potential to protect vulnerable LGBT youth and their families who suffer discrimination based on gendered culture and tradition tropes. In addition, the CEDAW Committee included sexual orientation and gender identity in

General Recommendation No. 27, on older women and protection of their human rights, and in General Recommendation No. 28, on the core obligations of states parties under Article 2 of CEDAW—both of which make explicit that discrimination on the basis of sexual orientation and gender identity is inextricably linked with discrimination against women on the basis of sex or gender and that it must be prohibited and addressed under states' CEDAW obligations.[113]

The Yogyakarta Principles and the Yogyakarta Principles Plus 10 (YP+10)[114] elucidate the application of human rights norms to sexual minorities. These principles recognize that if a person identifies as an SGM, or even if a person is perceived to be an SGM, their rights are more likely to be violated. Such violations are in derogation of the protections inherent in the ICCPR, ICESCR, CEDAW, and the CRC. The YP+10 supplement the original twenty-nine Yogyakarta Principles. The principles that specifically address children are: the right to protection from medical abuses (Principle 18), the right to bodily and mental integrity (Principle 32), and the right to education (Principle 16). Hugely significant in light of protecting LGBT youth, the YP+10 enumerate further state obligations, including the right to found a family, which acknowledges SGM rights to family life in a world that largely has not only failed to recognize but has also excluded their families from the framework of family life. With respect to such rights, the Yogyakarta Principles recognize the duty of states to "[p]rotect children from discrimination, violence or other harm due to the sexual orientation, gender identity, gender expression or sex characteristics of their parents, guardians, or other family members" (Principle 24: additional obligations related to the right to found a family).

Other documents show some ambivalence toward the recognition of the legal status of LGBT persons. As early as 2011, the UN Human Rights Council pronounced that attacks against LGBT persons "constitute a form of gender-based violence, driven by a desire to punish those seen as defying gender norms."[115] And, while in 2014 the UN approved a resolution on sexual orientation and gender identity,[116] in June of that same year, Egypt proposed a resolution entitled "Protection of the Family," which without specifically excluding LGBT families, did not include text recognizing different family compositions. Actions such as the Egyptian-sponsored resolution expose the vulnerability of LGBT families and youth because they are not specifically included within the definition of a traditional family and therefore may not enjoy the same protections that traditional families have under the human rights regime.

The UN's independent expert on sexual orientation and gender identity confirmed LGBT vulnerability:

> Even though human rights are inherent to everyone and involve protection for all persons without exception, regrettably persons with an actual or perceived sexual orientation and/or gender identity diverging from a particular societal concept are at times targeted for violence and discrimination, and violations are pervasive in numerous settings. Killings, rapes, mutilations, torture, cruel, inhuman and degrading treatment, arbitrary detentions, abductions, harassment, physical and

mental assaults, bullying suffered from a young age, pressures leading to suicide, and discriminatory gestures and measures—aggravated by incitement to hatred—in relation to sexual orientation and gender identity, are widespread on several fronts.[117]

Former UN secretary-general Ban Ki Moon supported the equality of LGBT persons and condemned anti-LGBT violence.[118] Similarly, the UN General Assembly has reiterated that governments have the obligation to investigate and prosecute those responsible for violence, including those targeted because of their sexual orientation or gender identity.[119]

Specifically, with respect to LGBT youth, a 2010 UN General Assembly report on the right to education establishes that this includes the right to sexual education. In turn, sexual education must be inclusive of sexual orientation and gender identity.[120] Such education would protect LGBT youth as they learn about sexuality in an accepting context and others learn about LGBT sexuality in affirming ways. Nonetheless, the report notes that, with few exceptions, such inclusiveness is nonexistent in many regions, such as Latin America. Thus, notwithstanding the plethora of existing rights, LGBT youth (and families) regularly experience the denial of those rights.

4.2 Regional Framework

Regional instruments also contain protections against discrimination based on sex. In the European system, Article 1 of Protocol No. 12 to the Convention for the Protection of Human Rights and Fundamental Freedoms[121] (ECHR) prohibits sex-based discrimination. In *Vejdeland and Others v. Sweden*, the European Court of Human Rights (European Court) unambiguously stated that "sexual orientation should be treated in the same way as categories such as race, ethnicity and religion" in evaluating hate crime laws.[122] In that case, the European Court ruled that the free speech guarantees of the ECHR do not extend to homophobic speech in school settings.[123] Moreover, the protection of privacy has been interpreted to include sexuality.[124]

In *International Center for the Legal Protection of Human Rights v. Croatia*,[125] the European Committee of Social Rights (European Committee) provided that states parties to the European Social Charter are required to provide sexual education to young people on a non-discriminatory basis. States parties' educational programs cannot reinforce negative stereotypes or prejudices regarding sexual orientation. The European Committee concluded that biased educational materials with respect to non-heterosexuals effected a violation of rights of the young people who were presented with biased materials.

Significantly, in 2010 the Committee of Ministers of the Council of Europe (COE) issued a recommendation "on measures to combat discrimination on grounds of sexual orientation or gender identity."[126] In an appendix, it recognized the ways in which LGBT populations experienced discrimination, such as hate crimes and hate speech, in employment, education, health, housing, and sports as well as in the context of the right to seek asylum. It also noted existing rights structures that protect against such discriminatory treatment, including the right to life, security, and protection from violence, freedom of association, freedom of expression and peaceful assembly, and the rights to respect for private and family life, employment, education, and health. The recommendation emphasizes the need for education free from discrimination, violence, bullying, and social exclusion for LGBT youth. More specifically focusing on LGBT children, the Commissioner for Human Rights of the COE published a comment emphasizing that "[l]ike all children, LGBTI children are entitled to enjoy human rights and require a safe environment in order to participate fully in society."[127]

Similarly, in the Americas, all pertinent regional instruments prohibit discrimination. The Charter of the Organization of American States[128] incorporates proscriptions against sex discrimination and specifically notes the right of persons, without discrimination, "to material well-being and to their spiritual development, in conditions of freedom, dignity, equality of opportunity and economic security."[129]

Article 2 of the American Declaration of the Rights and Duties of Man[130] states that all persons are equal under the law "without distinction of...sex." The first article of the American Convention on Human Rights (ACHR)[131] and Article 3 of the Protocol of San Salvador[132] prohibit states parties from discriminating on the basis, inter alia, of sex. These protections extend to LGBT youth.

The Inter-American Commission on Human Rights (IACHR) noted that LGBT persons encounter "high levels of cruelty and heightened levels of violence based on both the perception of sexual orientation and gender identity/expression." The Commission was particularly concerned about the young age of trans women victims.[133] The IACHR also observed an intersectional gendered dimension: lesbians are at a high risk because of "misogyny and gender inequality in society."[134]

In *Atala Rifo v. Chile*,[135] the Inter-American Court of Human Rights found that Chile violated the rights to equality and non-discrimination of Karen Atala, a lesbian mother and judge, when it stripped her of parental custody due to her sexual orientation. In 2017 the Court recognized, in an advisory opinion on gender identity and equality and on non-discrimination with respect to same-sex couples,[136] the express protection of human dignity in the Inter-American Convention and advised member states to "recognize and guarantee all the rights that are derived from a family bond between people of the same sex."[137] The Court based its conclusion on the principle of individual autonomy and maintained that private and family life constitute protected spheres. The Court thus acknowledged the right of individuals to be free from abusive and arbitrary state or third-party interference with their liberty.[138] In addition, the opinion, acknowledging that discrimination against LGBT persons often is based on religion,[139] concluded that such beliefs cannot be grounds to deny human dignity.

In sum, international and regional systems provide LGBT youth protections against attitudes and aggressions they confront simply because of their sexuality. The child rights paradigm provides a framework and a methodology to disrupt and eliminate these violations of personhood.

4.2.1 *State Framework*

Notwithstanding legal protections at the international and regional levels, state laws often lack protections for LGBT persons. Around the world, many national and municipal laws criminalize homosexuality. In seventy-two countries, any expression of homosexuality is illegal, even among adults.[140] In forty-five of these countries, the laws extend to women as well as men.[141] Thirteen UN member states allowed the imposition of the death penalty for same-sex sexual contact, though only four of the thirteen actually implement this punishment. In two of the four countries, the implementation of the death penalty is at the level of provinces, and in two countries, non-state actors that control sections of a state's territory in northern Iraq and northern Syria implement it.[142]

In sixteen countries the age of consent to sexual intercourse is different for heterosexual couples and homosexual couples. In these cases, the age of consent for LGBT persons tends to be higher than that for heterosexual persons, which may result in the criminalization of sexual behavior between LGBT youth, even though contact would have been legal if it had been between heterosexuals.[143]

Nineteen countries have "morality" or "homosexual propaganda" laws that target and criminalize the promotion of particular values and condemn LGBT persons as a class.[144] The purpose of these laws is (presumably) to protect public morality, especially with respect to children. The effect is to prohibit the dissemination of information on gender identity as well as the promotion of same-sex sexual behavior. Such prohibition impedes education and dissemination of information that can serve to protect LGBT youth. Moreover, these laws violate the rights to equality and non-discrimination of LGBT youth. Such laws also violate the rights of LGBT youth to privacy, family life, security, information, speech, and life.

Some countries have laws that protect LGBT persons. In seventy-two countries (including Taiwan and Kosovo), employment discrimination based on sexual orientation is prohibited.[145] The constitutions of only nine countries include the prohibition of discrimination based on sexual orientation.[146] Nevertheless, in most states around the world, employers legally can discriminate against LGBT persons in derogation of international and regional norms.

There are forty-three countries that regard sexual orientation as an aggravating factor in their laws concerning hate crimes.[147] And, thirty-six countries prohibit incitement to hatred based on sexual orientation.[148] Outside these seventy-nine states, there is no additional penalty for hate crimes targeting LGBT persons.

Because this chapter focuses on LGBT youth, some of whose families may be LGBT couples, it is important to note the overwhelming lack of access to formal family structures available to LGBT persons. Only twenty-four countries in the world allow same-sex couples to marry.[149] In addition, twenty-eight countries (including Taiwan) provide recognition to some form of partnership between same-sex couples.[150]

Focusing specifically on children, there are merely twenty-six countries that allow same-sex couples to adopt together[151] and twenty-seven that allow a second parent to adopt.[152] Consequently, there are many LGBT families raising children (who can be

LGBT or heterosexual) where it is possible that the law does not recognize the relationship of one of the mothers or one of the fathers with their children.

Moreover, as discussed throughout, culture concretizes and perpetuates the subordinated position of LGBT persons in civil society, exacerbating and encouraging unequal treatment in law.[153] Plainly, notwithstanding broad international legal protections, the global reality is one in which life for LGBT persons is not only second-class but also less safe due to state laws. In countries around the world, the LGBT population is subject to discrimination, harassment, and inequality, including the criminalization of conduct and status based simply on sexual orientation or gender identity—categories protected in international law.

5 CONCLUSION

International and regional conventions establish the human rights to non-discrimination, equality, health, life, security, privacy, and education. In all parts of the world, LGBT youth suffer discrimination, harassment, bullying, and violence in the educational, religious, social, and even family spheres due simply to their sexuality or gender identity. This reality is a reflection of the social, cultural, political, and economic realities faced by LGBT people, couples, and their children.

Despite the progress in legal protections for LGBT persons, there are many jurisdictions where LGBT status is subject to criminalization. Laws that criminalize LGBT sexuality, as well as cultures and traditions that deny LGBT persons equality and full personhood, are at odds with human rights norms that prohibit discrimination, stigma, and violence. A significant factor in decreasing criminalization, stigma, and rejection is familiarity. Educational programs that can promote familiarity increase acceptance.

Harassment, bullying, isolation, homelessness, and discrimination in schools, in the nuclear family, in places of worship, and in the community manifest the lack of respect for, and the denial of rights to, LGBT youth and their families. These abuses violate established human rights: the rights to life, safety, education, family, privacy, and health. Denial of rights results in a myriad of grave harms to LGBT youth.

No child should experience such a tragic and violent—physical, social, educational, emotional, and familial—existence. In addition to the loss of the innocence of youth, there is a permanent loss of human dignity. The adoption and implementation of a children's rights paradigm based on the existing human rights framework, with all the protections it entails, would be a positive way to eradicate the inequalities and the different treatment that our LGBT youths experience.

NOTES

1. Philip Ross, "Harvey Milk Day Quotes 2015: 11 Inspiring Sayings That Still Ring True Today," *International Business Times*, May 21, 2015, https://www.ibtimes.com/harvey-milk-day-quotes-2015-11-inspiring-sayings-still-ring-true-today-1933666.

2. Macklemore and Ryan Lewis, "Same Love (featuring Mary Lambert)," Vagalume.com, https://www.vagalume.com.br/macklemore/same-love.html (accessed Sept. 1, 2019).

3. Kathleen Patel, *The Bullying Epidemic—The Guide to Arm You for the Fight* (Los Gatos, CA: Smashwords, 2011).

4. This chapter uses LGBT throughout. However, when specific research either uses a different acronym or studies a limited population, the chapter uses the acronym utilized by the researchers.

5. Andrew R. Flores and Andrew Park, "Polarized Progress: Social Acceptance of LGBT People in 141 Countries, 1981 to 2014," Williams Institute report (March 2018), https://williamsinstitute.law.ucla.edu/wp-content/uploads/Polarized-Progress-April-2018.pdf.

6. Aengus Carroll and George Robotham. 2017, "Minorities Report 2017: Attitudes to Sexual and Gender Minorities around the World," International Lesbian, Gay, Bisexual, Trans and Intersex Association (ILGA) report (October 2017), https://ilga.org/downloads/ILGA_RIWI_Minorities_Report_2017_Attitudes_to_sexual_and_gender_minorities.pdf.

7. See the discussion of studies of global attitudes toward homosexuality in section 3 of this chapter.

8. Carroll and Robotham, "Minorities Report 2017."

9. UN Human Rights Committee, "*Toonen v. Australia*, Communication No. 488/1992, UN Doc. CCPR/C/50/D/488/1992 (1994).

10. See Aage Sorensen, "The Structural Basis of Social Inequality," *American Journal of Sociology* 101, no. 5 (1996): 1334–1335. Originating in sociology, the idea of structural inequality posits that "social structure is somehow relevant for the creation of inequality....Inequality is generated by structural relations, and advantages and disadvantages are attached to positions in social structure."

11. Víctor Luis Gutiérrez Castillo, Jonatán Cruz Ángeles, and Manuel Ródenas Pérez, *Corpus Jurídico de la Familia Homoparental: Perspectiva Europea, Estatal, y Autonómica* (Madrid: Transexualia: Asociación Española de personas Transexuales, 2014). In order to assess the situation of LGBT youth, it is necessary to consider the state of families of this population regardless of whether the parents are heterosexual or homosexual.

12. The topic of protecting children's rights in general and LGBT youth in particular is getting much attention. See Anne C. Dailey and Laura A. Rosenbury, "The New Law of the Child," *Yale Law Journal* 127, no. 6 (March 2018): 1148–1741 (proposing "a new tripartite framework of relationships, rights, and responsibilities that aims to transform how law treats children and their interactions with others"); see also Tamar Ezer, "A Positive Right to Protection for Children," *Yale Human Rights and Development Law Journal* 7, no. 1 (2004): 1–50 (arguing for "a positive right to protection for children, rooted in dignity"); see also Human Rights Campaign Foundation and All Children-All Families, "Caring for LGBTQ Children and Youth: A Guide for Child Welfare Providers," 2, https://assets2.hrc.org/files/assets/resources/HRC_Caring_For_LGBTQ_Children_Youth.pdf?_g a=2.235468168.881000841.1524679242–687397318.1524679242 (accessed Sept. 1, 2019) (noting that "LGBTQ youth are disproportionately represented in the child welfare system and often face discrimination and mistreatment in out-of-home care" and that "every child and every youth who is unable to live with his or her parents is entitled to a safe, loving and affirming foster care placement" regardless of sexuality).

13. Berta E. Hernández-Truyol, "Latina Multidimensionality and LatCrit Possibilities: Culture, Gender, and Sex," *University of Miami Law Review* 53 (1999): 811–829.

14. See Soon Kyu Choi, Bianca Wilson, Jama Shelton, and Gary Gates, "Serving Our Youth 2015: The Needs and Experiences of Lesbian, Gay, Bisexual, Transgender, and Questioning Youth Experiencing Homelessness," Williams Institute report (June 2015), https://williamsinstitute.law.ucla.edu/wp-content/uploads/Serving-Our-Youth-June-2015.pdf; Joseph G. Kosciw, Emily A. Greytak, Noreen M. Giga, Christian Villenas, and David J. Danischewski, "The 2015 National School Climate Survey: The Experiences of Lesbian, Gay, Bisexual, Transgender, and Queer Youth in Our Nation's Schools," GLSEN report (2016), https://files.eric.ed.gov/fulltext/ED574780.pdf.

15. Jason Ciancotto and Sean Cahill, *Education Policy: Issues Affecting Lesbian, Gay, Bisexual and Transgender Youth* (New York: National Gay and Lesbian Task Force Policy Institute, 2003).

16. Caitlin Ryan, *A Practitioner's Research Guide: Helping Families to Support Their LGBT Children* (Rockville, MD: Substance Abuse and Mental Health Services Administration 2014); see Center for American Progress, "Gay and Transgender Youth Homelessness by the Numbers" (June 21, 2010), https://www.americanprogress.org/issues/lgbt/news/2010/06/21/7980/gay-and-transgender-youth-homelessness-by-the-numbers (some youth identify as LGBT as early as age five).

17. Berta E. Hernández-Truyol, "Globalizing Women's Health and Safety: Migration, Work, and Labor," *Santa Clara Journal of International Law* 15 (2017): 48–76, 48, 51 (defining "Marginableness...[as] fill[ing] a linguistic void existing in the current conversations about...[populations] who are both vulnerable and marginalized").

18. See Choi et al., "Serving Our Youth 2015"; Kosciw et al., "2015 National School Climate Survey."

19. Center for American Progress, "Gay and Transgender Youth Homelessness."

20. Elizabeth Landau, "For LGBT Teens, Acceptance Is Critical," CNN, Dec. 6, 2010, http://www.cnn.com/2010/HEALTH/12/06/lgbt.teens.punishment. problems/index.html.

21. American Psychological Association, "Report of the American Psychological Association Task Force on Appropriate Therapeutic Responses to Sexual Orientation" (2009), http://www.apa.org/pi/lgbt/resources/therapeutic-response.pdf (accessed Sept. 1, 2019).

22. Tanya Erzen, *Straight to Jesus: Sexual and Christian Conversions in the Ex-Gay Movement* (Los Angeles: University of California Press, 2006).

23. Pickup v. Brown, 740 F.3d 1208, 1221 (9th Cir. 2014).

24. Caitlin Ryan, David Huebner, Rafael M. Diaz, and Jorge Sanchez, "Family Rejection as Predictor of Negative Health Outcomes in White and Latino Lesbian, Gay, and Bisexual Young Adults," *Pediatrics* 123, no. 1 (January 2009): 346–352; Human Rights Campaign, "Policy and Position Statements on Conversion Therapy," https://www.hrc.org/resources/policy-and-position-statements-on-conversion-therapy (accessed Sept. 1, 2019).

25. California State Assembly, "Unlawful Business Practices: Sexual Orientation Change Efforts," AB 2943 (2017–2018), http://leginfo.legislature.ca.gov/faces/billTextClient.xhtml?bill_id=201720180AB2943&search_keywords=conversion+therapy (accessed Sept. 1, 2019).

26. Alex Morris, "The Forsaken: A Rising Number of Homeless Gay Teens Are Being Cast Out by Religious Families," *Rolling Stone*, Sept. 3, 2014,rollingstone.com/culture/culture-news/the-forsaken-a-rising-number-of-homeless-gay-teens-are-being-cast-out-by-religious-families-46746.

27. Andrew Cray, Katie Miller, and Laura E. Durso, "Seeking Shelter: The Experiences and Unmet Needs of LGBT Homeless Youth," Center for American Progress report

(September 2013), https://www.americanprogress.org/wp-content/uploads/2013/09/LGBTHomelessYouth.pdf.

28. Laura E. Durso and Gary J. Gates. 2012, "Serving Our Youth: Findings from a National Survey of Service Providers Working with Lesbian, Gay, Bisexual, and Transgender Youth who are Homeless or At Risk of Becoming Homeless," Williams Institute report (2012), https://williamsinstitute.law.ucla.edu/wp-content/uploads/Durso-Gates-LGBT-Homeless-Youth-Survey-July-2012.pdf (accessed Sept. 1, 2019).

29. Morris, "The Forsaken"; Center for American Progress, "Gay and Transgender Youth Homelessness."

30. Center for American Progress, "Gay and Transgender Youth Homelessness."

31. Nusrat Ventimiglia, "LGBT Selective Victimization: Unprotected Youth on the Streets," *Journal of Law in Society*. 13, no. 2 (2012): 439–453; Bryan N. Cochran, Angela J. Stewart, Joshua A. Ginzler, and Ana Mari Cauce, "Challenges Faced by Homeless Sexual Minorities: Comparison of Gay, Lesbian, Bisexual, and Transgender Homeless Adolescents with Their Heterosexual Counterparts," *American Journal of Public Health* 92, no. 5 (2002): 773–777.

32. Child Trends, "Homelessness among LGBT Youth: A National Concern" Nov. 28, 2013), https://www.childtrends.org/homelessness-among-lgbt-youth-a-national-concern.

33. Durso and Gates, "Serving our Youth," 10.

34. Center for American Progress, "Gay and Transgender Youth Homelessness."

35. National Sexual Violence Resource Center (NSVRC) and Pennsylvania Coalition against Rape (PCAR), "Sexual Violence & Individuals Who Identify as LGBTQ," NSVRC and PCAR Research Brief (2012), 3, http://nsvrc.org/sites/default/files/Publications_NSVRC_Research-Brief_Sexual-Violence-LGBTQ.pdf (accessed Sept. 1, 2019) ("Respondents who identified as transgender or gender non-conforming during grades K-12 reported significant rates of harassment (78%), physical assault (35%), and sexual violence (12%). Respondents who identified as American Indian, Asian, Black, and multiracial experienced higher rates of sexual violence than K-12 students of other races.").

36. Durso and Gates, "Serving our Youth," 4.

37. Center for American Progress, "Gay and Transgender Youth Homelessness."

38. Landau, "For LGBT Teens, Acceptance Is Critical."

39. Berta E. Hernandez-Truyol, "The Gender Bend: Culture, Sex, and Sexuality—A LatCritical Human Rights Map of Latina/o Border Crossings," *Indiana Law Journal* 83, no. 4 (2008): 1283–1331.

40. United States v. Windsor, 133 S. Ct. 2675, 2696 (2013).

41. Obergefell v. Hodges, 135 S. Ct. 2584, 2600 (2015). This discussion should not be read as an endorsement of marriage. Rather, it is an observation on disparate treatment. Critiques of marriage as an institution abound. See Franke, Katherine, *Wedlocked: The Perils of Marriage Equality* (New York: New York University Press, 2015).

42. Gary J. Gates, "Marriage and Family: LGBT Individuals and Same-Sex Couples," *The Future of Children* 25, no. 2 (2015): 67–82.

43. Michael J. Rosenfeld, "Nontraditional Families and Childhood Progress through School," *Demography* 47, no. 3 (2010): 755–775.

44. Wendy D. Manning, Marshal Neal Fettro, and Esther Lamidi, "Child Well-Being in Same-Sex Parent Families: Review of Research Prepared for American Sociological Association Amicus Brief," *Population Research and Policy Review* 33, no. 4 (2014): 485–502.

45. Alicia Crowl, Soyeon Ahn, and Jean Baker, "A Meta-Analysis of Developmental Outcomes for Children of Same-Sex and Heterosexual Parents," *Journal of GLBT Family Studies* 4, no. 3 (2008): 385–407.

46. Gates, "Marriage and Family," 67–82; Rosenfeld, "Nontraditional Families," 755–775; Manning, Marshal, and Lamidi, "Child Well-Being," 485–502; Crowl, Ahn, and Baker, "Meta-Analysis," 385–407.

47. Gary White, "State Still Not Recognizing Same-Sex Spouse on Birth Certificates." *The Ledger*, March 10, 2016, https://www.theledger.com/news/20160310/state-still-not-recognizing-same-sex-spouse-on-birth-certificates.

48. See Pavan v. Smith, 137 S. Ct. 2075 (2017).

49. Kosciw et al., "2015 National School Climate Survey."

50. See Oren Pizmony-Levy and Joseph G. Kosciw, "School Climate and the Experience of LGBT Students: A Comparison of the United States and Israel," *Journal of LGBT Youth* 13, nos. 1–2 (2016): 46–66; Nils Muižnieks, "LGBTI Children Have the Right to Safety and Equality," Human Rights Comment (Feb. 10, 2014), https://www.coe.int/en/web/commissioner/-/lgbti-children-have-the-right-to-safety-and-equality; UNESCO, "Education Sector Responses to Homophobic Bullying," Good Policy and Practice in HIV and Health Education Booklet 8 (2012), http://unesdoc.unesco.org/images/0021/002164/216493e.pdf (accessed Sept. 1, 2019) (using reports from more than twenty countries around the world).

51. Ryan et al., "Family Rejection," 346.

52. Bianca Wilson, Sid P. Jordan, Ilan H. Meyer, Andrew R. Flores, Lara Stemple, and Jody L. Herman, "Disproportionality and Disparities among Sexual Minority Youth in Custody," *Journal of Youth and Adolescence* 46, no. 7 (July 2017): 1547–1561; see also Sarah E. Redfield and Jason P. Nance, "The American Bar Association Task Force on Reversing the School-to-Prison Pipeline: Report, Recommendations and Preliminary Report" (February 2016), https://scholarship.law.ufl.edu/cgi/viewcontent.cgi?referer=https://search.yahoo.com/&httpsredir=1&article=1765&context=facultypub:

    students of color [African American, Hispanic, Asian and Native American], with disabilities, or LGBTQ—are disproportionately over—or incorrectly categorized in special education, are disciplined more harshly, including referral to law enforcement for minimal misbehavior, achieve at lower levels, and eventually drop or are pushed out of school, often into juvenile justice facilities and prisons—a pattern now commonly referred to as the School-to-Prison Pipeline (StPP) (p. 7).

    See also Advancement Project, Equality Federation Institute, and Gay Straight Alliance Network, "Power in Partnerships: Building Connections at the Intersections of Racial Justice and LGBTQ Movements to End the School-to-Prison Pipeline," https://b.3cdn.net/advancement/85066c4a18d249e72b_r23m68j37.pdf (accessed Sept. 1, 2019). (noting that "[u]nfortunately, there is a dearth of large-scale quantitative research to show this phenomenon for LGBTQ people, due in part to the sensitivity of collecting this data. Nevertheless, the outcomes and experiences for this community remain pressing.").

53. Kathryn E. W. Himmelstein and Hannah Brückner, "Criminal-Justice and School Sanctions against Nonheterosexual Youth: A National Longitudinal Study," *Pediatrics* 127, no. 1 (January 2011): 49–57 (providing that "nonheterosexual adolescents had between 1.25 and 3 times greater odds than their heterosexual peers of experiencing sanction").

54. UNESCO, "Education Sector Responses to Homophobic Bullying," 7.

55. Kosciw et al., "2015 National School Climate Survey," 11–25, 35–39; Pizmony-Levy and Kosciw, "School Climate," 46, 56; Muižnieks, "LGBTI Children"; UNESCO, "Education Sector Responses to Homophobic Bullying," 1–22.

56. Kosciw et al., "2015 National School Climate Survey," xvi; UNESCO, "Education Sector Responses to Homophobic Bullying," 13, 19.

57. Kosciw et al., "2015 National School Climate Survey," xxiii–xxiv.

58. Kosciw et al., "2015 National School Climate Survey," xxiv.

59. Kosciw et al., "2015 National School Climate Survey," 16–17; UNESCO, "Education Sector Responses to Homophobic Bullying," 16–19.

60. Kosciw et al., "2015 National School Climate Survey," 19–22; UNESCO, "Education Sector Responses to Homophobic Bullying," 17–19, 22.

61. Kosciw et al., "2015 National School Climate Survey," xvi, 21–24; UNESCO, "Education Sector Responses to Homophobic Bullying," 13, 16–20, 22.

62. Kosciw et al., "2015 National School Climate Survey," xvi, 21, 24, 126; UNESCO, "Education Sector Responses to Homophobic Bullying," 16.

63. Kosciw et al., "2015 National School Climate Survey," xvii; Human Rights Campaign. "State Maps of Laws & Policies: School Anti- Bullying Maps," (last modified Jan. 15, 2019), https://www.hrc.org/state-maps/anti-bullying.

64. Human Rights Campaign, "State Maps."

65. Andrew Cray, "3 Barriers That Stand between LGBT Youth and Healthier Futures," Center for American Progress (May 29, 2013), https://www.americanprogress.org/issues/lgbt/news/2013/05/29/64583/3-barriers-that-stand-between-lgbt-youth-and-healthier-futures.

66. UNESCO, "Education Sector Responses to Homophobic Bullying," 20–23; Muižnieks, "LGBTI Children."

67. Kosciw, "2015 National School Climate Survey," xvi, 18–22.

68. See Human Rights Campaign, "State Maps" (noting that seven states "restrict the inclusion of LGBT topics in schools").

69. Kosciw, "2015 National School Climate Survey," 36–37.

70. See Constance McMillen v. Itawamba County School District, No. 1:10-cv-00061-GHD-JAD (N.D. Miss 2010).

71. Samantha Allen, "LGBT Prom Revolution in Texas," *The Daily Beast*, May 3, 2017, https://www.thedailybeast.com/in-texas-you-shall-go-to-the-lgbt-prom.

72. Kosciw, "2015 National School Climate Survey," 36–38.

73. Kosciw, "2015 National School Climate Survey," 38–39.

74. Kosciw, "2015 National School Climate Survey," xvi; UNESCO, "Education Sector Responses to Homophobic Bullying," 13, 19–21.

75. Corinne Munoz-Plaza, Sandra Crouse Quinn, and Kathleen A. Rounds, "Lesbian, Gay, Bisexual and Transgender Students: Perceived Social Support in the High School Environment," *High School Journal* 85, no. 4 (April–May 2002): 52–63.

76. Farah Qureshi, "School Climates, Suicide and Gay and Lesbian Students: Research on LGBT and Youth Education," Journalist's Resource, Shorenstein Center on Media, Politics and Public Policy (Jan. 15, 2015), https://journalistsresource.org/studies/society/gender-society/school-climate-suicide-gay-lesbian-lgbtq-youth (accessed Sept. 1, 2019).

77. Mark L. Hatzenbuehler, Michelle Birkett, Aimee Van Wagenen, and Ilan H. Meyer, "Protective School Climates and Reduced Risk for Suicide Ideation in Sexual Minority Youths," *American Journal of Public Health* 104 (February 2014): 279–286.

78. Kosciw, "2015 National School Climate Survey," 54, 62–65.

79. Kosciw, "2015 National School Climate Survey," 62–65.

80. Kosciw, "2015 National School Climate Survey," 36.

81. Kosciw, "2015 National School Climate Survey," xxiv–xxv.

82. GLSEN. "Inclusion and Respect: GLSEN Resources for Educators," https://www.glsen.org/educate/resources (accessed Sept. 1, 2019).

83. Flores and Park, "Polarized Progress," 16.

84. Flores and Park, "Polarized Progress," 15.

85. Flores and Park, "Polarized Progress," 16–18.

86. The Harris Poll, "Accelerating Acceptance 2018: A Survey of American Acceptance and Attitudes toward LGBTQ Americans," Harris Poll conducted for GLAAD, https://www.glaad.org/publications/accelerating-acceptance-2018 (accessed Sept. 1, 2019).

87. Harris Poll, "Accelerating Acceptance 2018."

88. Pew Research Center, *The Global Divide on Homosexuality: Greater Acceptance in More Secular and Affluent Communities*" (June 4, 2013; updated May 27, 2014), https://www.pewresearch.org/global/2013/06/04/the-global-divide-on-homosexuality; see Carroll and Robotham, "Minorities Report 2017" (finding that the most accepting are Oceania (61% SO; 62% GI) and the Americas (60% SO; 63% GI); Europe's overall acceptance is 53% for SO and 54% for GI, with figures shifting geographically; Western Europe is as accepting as Oceania and the Americas (60% SO; 61% GI), but Eastern Europe, which includes Russia and Ukraine, is less accepting (47% SO; 49% SI); Africa is less accepting (43% SO; 55% GI), and Asia is least accepting (42% SO; 47% GI)). See also Tom W. Smith, "Cross-National Differences in Attitudes toward Homosexuality," GSS Cross-National Report No. 31 (April 2011), https://williamsinstitute.law.ucla.edu/wp-content/uploads/Smith-CrossNational-NORC-May-2011.pdf (noting that most accepting countries are predominantly Western European countries; least accepting were Latin American (except Uruguay) countries in the socialist orbit, and East Asian countries. Although from other data African countries seem to have a low level of acceptance, the 2011 study only included South Africa).

89. Carroll and Robotham, "Minorities Report 2017," 6.

90. Carroll and Robotham, "Minorities Report 2017," 22–23.

91. Carroll and Robotham, "Minorities Report 2017," 24 (60% versus 46%). In this study, of the seventy-seven countries surveyed, twenty-five criminalized homosexuality. There are large differences in attitudes even among criminalizing states.

92. Carroll and Robotham, "Minorities Report 2017," 46.

93. Carroll and Robotham, "Minorities Report 2017," 50 (32% would try to change female neighbors, and 29% would try to change male neighbors).

94. Pew Research Center, *Global Divide*; Carroll and Robotham, "Minorities Report 2017," 60; Flores and Park, "Polarized Progress," 5, 17.

95. Carroll and Robotham, "Minorities Report 2017," 60.

96. Carroll and Robotham, "Minorities Report 2017," 63–64.

97. Megan C. Lytle, John R. Blosnich, Susan M. De Luca, and Chris Brownson, "Association of Religiosity with Sexual Minority Suicide Ideation and Attempt," *American Journal of Preventive Medicine* 54, no. 5 (May 2018): 644–651, 645.

98. Lytle et al., "Association of Religiosity," 650.

99. Pew Research Center, *Global Divide*, 5.

100. Lytle et al., "Association of Religiosity," 646.

101. Pew Research Center, *Global Divide*, 5–7.

102. Smith, "Cross-National Differences."

103. UN Convention on the Rights of the Child (CRC), G.A. Res. 44/25, 44th Sess., UN Doc. A/RES/44/25 (1989).
104. CRC, art. 3(3).
105. Universal Declaration of Human Rights, G.A. Res. 217 (III) A, UN Doc. A/RES/217(III) (Dec. 10, 1948).
106. International Covenant on Civil and Political Rights (ICCPR), 999 UNTS 171 (1966; entered into force Mar. 23, 1976).
107. International Covenant on Economic, Social and Culteral Rights (ICESCR), 993 UNTS 3 (1966; entered into force Jan. 3, 1976).
108. Human Rights Committee, Toonen v. Australia, Communication No. 488/1992, UN Doc. CCPR/C/50/D/488/1992 (1994).
109. UN Human Rights Council, *Report of the United Nations High Commissioner for Human Rights*, A/HRC/29/23 (May 4, 2015).
110. UN Convention on the Elimination of All Forms of Discrimination against Women (CEDAW), G.A. Res. 34/180 (Dec. 18, 1979).
111. International Center for Research on Women, "Recognizing Rights Promoting Progress: *The* Global Impact of CEDAW" (2010), 9, https://www.icrw.org/publications/recognizing-rights-promoting-progress.
112. Berta E. Hernández-Truyol, "Unsex CEDAW? No! Super-Sex it!," *Columbia Journal of Gender and Law* 20, no. 2: 1(2011): 95–223.
113. Grace Poore, "Amazing Responses by CEDAW to Address LGBT Discrimination in Singapore," OutRight Action International (July 27, 2011), https://iglhrc.wordpress.com/2011/07/27/amazing-responses-by-cedaw-to-address-lgbt-discrimination-in-singapore (accessed Sept. 1, 2019).
114. The Yogyakarta Principles (Nov. 10, 2017), http://www.yogyakartaprinciples.org (accessed Sept. 1, 2019).
115. UN Human Rights Council, "Discriminatory Laws and Practices and Acts of Violence against Individuals Based on Their Sexual Orientation and Gender Identity," Annual Report of the United Nations High Commissioner for Human Rights, UN Doc. A/HRC/19/41 (Nov. 17, 2011).
116. UN Human Rights Council, "Human Rights, Sexual Orientation, and Gender Identity," Human Rights Council Res. 27/32, A/HRC/RES/27/32 (Feb. 10, 2014).
117. UN Human Rights Council, "Report of the Independent Expert on Protection against Violence and Discrimination Based on Sexual Orientation and Gender Identity," UN Doc. A/HRC/35/36 (April 19, 2017).
118. Office of the UN High Commissioner for Human Rights, "Combatting Discrimination Based on Sexual Orientation and Gender Identity," https://www.ohchr.org/en/issues/discrimination/pages/lgbt.aspx (accessed Sept. 1, 2019).
119. International Service for Human Rights (ISHR), "U.N. General Assembly: Rights Groups Welcome Condemnation of Killing of LGBT Persons" (Nov. 20, 2014), https://www.ishr.ch/news/un-general-assembly-rights-groups-welcome-condemnation-killing-lgbt-persons.
120. UN General Assembly, "Report of the United Nations Special Rapporteur on the Right to Education," UN Doc. A/65/162 (July 23, 2010).
121. Council of Europe Convention for the Protection of Human Rights and Fundamental Freedoms, European Treaty Series No. 5, 4.XI.1950 (Nov. 4, 1950).
122. Vejdeland and Others v. Sweden, Application No. 1813/07, Eur. Ct. H.R. (Sept. 5, 2012), 1,9.

123. *Vejdeland*, 1, 10–11.
124. Dudgeon v. United Kingdom, Application no. 7525/76, Eur. Ct. H.R. (Oct. 22, 1981).
125. International Center for the Legal Protection of Human Rights v. Croatia, Complaint No. 45/2007, Eur. Comm. S.R. (March 30, 2009).
126. Council of Europe Committee of Ministers, "Recommendation (2010)5, Recommendation to Member States on Measures to Combat Discrimination on Grounds of Sexual Orientation or Gender Identity," CM/Rec(2010)5 (March 31, 2010).
127. Muižnieks, "LGBTI Children."
128. OAS Department of International Law, Charter of the Organization of American States (A-41), adopted at the Ninth International Conference of American States (signed April 30, 1948; amended June 10, 1993), http://oas.org/juridico/english/charter.html.
129. OAS Department of International Law, Charter of the Organization of American States, art. 45.
130. Inter-American Commission on Human Rights, American Declaration of the Rights and Duties of Man, adopted by the Ninth International Conference of American States (April 1948), https://www.cidh.oas.org/Basicos/English/Basic2.American%20Declaration.htm.
131. OAS Department of International Law, American Convention on Human Rights ("Pact of San Jose"), B-32 (Nov. 22, 1969), https://www.oas.org/dil/treaties_B-32_American_Convention_on_Human_Rights_sign.htm.
132. OAS Department of International Law, Additional Protocol to the American Convention on Human Rights in the Area of Economic, Social and Cultural Rights ("Protocol of San Salvador") (Nov. 17, 1988), http://www.oas.org/juridico/english/treaties/a-52.html.
133. Inter-American Commission on Human Rights, "An Overview of Violence against LGBTI Persons: A Registry Documenting Acts of Violence between January 1, 2013 and March 31, 2014," ANNEX–Press Release 153/14, (Dec. 17, 2014), http://oas.org/en/iachr/lgtbi/docs/Annex- Registry-Violence-LGBTI.pdf.
134. Inter-American Commission on Human Rights, "Overview of Violence," 4.
135. Atala Rifo v. Chile, No. 12.502, Inter-Am. Ct. H.R. (Feb. 24, 2012).
136. Inter-American Court of Human Rights (Inter-American Court), Advisory Opinion OC-24/17, Series A No. 24 (Nov. 24, 2017), http://www.masterdirittiumanisapienza.it/sites/default/files/Inter-american%20Court%20of%20Human%20Rights%20-%20Advisory%20Opinion%20OC-24%3A17.pdf.
137. Inter-American Court, "Advisory Opinion OC-24/17," paras. 200–218, 80–84.
138. Inter-American Court, "Advisory Opinion OC-24/17," para. 86, 44.
139. Inter-American Court, Advisory Opinion OC-24/17, para. 40, 26.
140. Aengus Carroll and Lucas R. Mendos, "State-Sponsored Homophobia: A World Survey of Sexual Orientation Laws; Criminalisation, Protection and Recognition," 12th ed. (May 2017), 37–40, https://ilga.org/downloads/2017/ILGA_State_Sponsored_Homophobia_2017_WEB.pdf.
141. Carroll and Mendos, "State-Sponsored Homophobia," 37–40.
142. Carroll and Mendos, "State-Sponsored Homophobia," 40. See CBS News, "Inside look at ISIS' Brutal Persecution of Gays," Dec. 2, 2015, http://www.cbsnews.com/news/isis-persecution-gay-men-murder-lgbt-muslim-society. Although Daesh is not a state, there is evidence that the group practices the persecution of people because of their sexual orientation or gender identity. Persecution includes the imposition of the death penalty when they are convicted in their courts simply because they are homosexual.
143. Carroll and Mendos, "State-Sponsored Homophobia," 26–36.

144. Carroll and Mendos, "State-Sponsored Homophobia," 41–42.

145. Carroll and Mendos, "State-Sponsored Homophobia," 48–53.

146. Carroll and Mendos, "State-Sponsored Homophobia," 46–47.

147. Carroll and Mendos, "State-Sponsored Homophobia," 60–63.

148. Carroll and Mendos, "State-Sponsored Homophobia," 63–66.

149. Carroll and Mendos, "State-Sponsored Homophobia," 68–69. The ILGA report lists only twenty-two countries. However, after publication of the report, both Germany (see *The Local*, "Germany Legalizes Gay Marriage in Historic Vote," June 30, 2017) https://www.thelocal.de/20170630/germanz) and Malta (see Reuters, "Maltese Parliament Legalizes Same-sex Marriage," July 12, 2017, https://www.reuters.com/article/us-malta-gaymarriage-idUSKBN19X2KM) legalized marriage between people of the same sex, bringing the total number of states to twenty-four.

150. Carroll and Mendos, "State-Sponsored Homophobia 2017," 70–72.

151. Carroll and Mendos, "State-Sponsored Homophobia 2017," 73–74.

152. Carroll and Mendos, "State-Sponsored Homophobia 2017," 75–77. There is overlap in these two categories.

153. Berta E. Hernández-Truyol, "Glocalizing Law and Culture: Toward a Cross-Constitutive Paradigm," *Albany Law Review* 67 (2003): 617–627.

CHAPTER 27

....

INDIGENOUS CHILDREN

....

ADDIE C. ROLNICK

1 INTRODUCTION

....

INDIGENOUS children are simultaneously citizens of colonial states—often minority citizens and often residing in rural areas—and members of self-governing indigenous peoples. This dual status means that indigenous children may be doubly vulnerable to denials of human rights because those denials may occur at the individual and the group level. It can also complicate legal efforts to secure and enforce important rights. This chapter investigates how international law has sought to protect the rights of indigenous children through various legal regimes. It identifies common themes and potential tensions between the various conceptions of human rights embodied in each regime and considers how international law relates to particular problems faced by indigenous children, such as child removal, health, violence and victimization, and over-criminalization. Although indigenous children have been the subject of concern at the international level for at least the past two decades,[1] it can be difficult to trace the concrete impact of changes in international law (as opposed to domestic legal regimes) on indigenous children's lives. This is, therefore, a chapter about its potential.

2 WHO IS INDIGENOUS?

....

International law recognizes and protects indigenous peoples, but the various instruments that do so do not contain a single definition of indigeneity. During the consultation and drafting process for the UN Declaration on the Rights of Indigenous Peoples (the Declaration), the working group relied on a working definition of indigeneity originally developed by Special Rapporteur José R. Martínez Cobo for a study on discrimination against indigenous peoples undertaken in the early 1980s, which led to the formation of the working group:

> Indigenous communities, peoples and nations are those which, having a historical continuity with pre-invasion and pre-colonial societies that developed on their territories, consider themselves distinct from other sectors of the societies now prevailing in those territories, or parts of them. They form at present non-dominant sectors of society and are determined to preserve, develop and transmit to future generations their ancestral territories, and their ethnic identity, as the basis of their continued existence as peoples, in accordance with their own cultural patterns, social institutions and legal systems.[2]

In her summary of the process leading to the Declaration, Chair and Special Rapporteur Erica-Irene Daes noted that indigeneity could not be "defined precisely or applied all-inclusively."[3] Indigenous representatives have stressed the right to self-identification and resisted adopting a static definition at the international level.[4] At the same time, a broadly shared understanding is important because some UN member states have inaccurately asserted that there are no indigenous peoples within their territory.[5]

Daes highlighted several basic criteria drawn from the Martínez Cobo report. The first criterion is historical continuity, in the sense that indigenous peoples include the present-day "descendants of the peoples who inhabited the present territory of a country, wholly or partially, at the time when persons of different culture or ethnic origin arrived there from other parts of the world, overcame them and, by conquest, settlement or other means, reduced them to a non-dominant or colonized status."[6] Second, part of the process of colonization involved occupation of the indigenous peoples' ancestral lands.[7] Third, indigenous peoples "possess distinctive cultural characteristics that distinguish them from the prevailing society in which they live."[8] Fourth, indigenous peoples generally "constitute a non-dominant part of the population of countries in which they live."[9] Daes also emphasized the importance of "self-identification and group consciousness,"[10] an approach consistent with the views of other international bodies that self-identification as indigenous, rather than recognition by the state, is all that is required to exert rights under international law.[11]

While indigenous persons may also be racial and cultural minorities, the defining elements of indigenous status concern relationship to land and experience of colonization. International law also recognizes a separate category of tribal peoples, defined as peoples "whose social, culture and economic conditions distinguish them from other sections of the national community, and whose status is regulated wholly or partially by their own customs or traditions or by special laws or regulations."[12] According to Daes, there is "no satisfactory reasoning for distinguishing between 'indigenous' and 'tribal' peoples in the practice or precedents of the UN."[13]

In the case of an individual child, the most important factors in determining whether a child is indigenous is whether the child identifies as a member of a group that self-identifies as indigenous and whether there is some indication that the group considers the child a member.[14] Although membership in the group and indigenous status may be easily identifiable through such means as formal government recognition of the group or tribal citizenship documents to confirm individual membership, it is important to note that neither formal indices of belonging nor formal government recognition of the group are necessary under international law.[15] Furthermore, a child may be indigenous and also a member of a racial minority, and a child may be a member of more than one indigenous group. None of these multiple identities should diminish the child's status as indigenous. As explained below, identifying indigenous children is a critical step because indigenous status triggers the indigenous group's involvement in securing and supporting the child's rights and development.

3   INTERNATIONAL LAW PROTECTIONS FOR INDIGENOUS CHILDREN

The international legal framework for protecting indigenous children lies at the intersection of four major rights-recognizing instruments, none of which was written or adopted with the primary purpose of protecting indigenous children. Two of these, the UN Declaration on the Rights of Indigenous Peoples and the International Labour Organisation (ILO) Convention No. 169 (Indigenous and Tribal Peoples Convention), focus on the rights of indigenous peoples generally. A third, the UN Convention on the Rights of the Child (CRC), protects the rights of children generally. The fourth, the International Convention on the Elimination of All Forms of Racial Discrimination, protects against racial discrimination. Where they exist, specific international law protections for indigenous children fall into three broad categories: (1) recognition that indigenous children may be particularly vulnerable to discrimination and denials of human rights, and related requirements that states take special care to protect them,[16] (2) recognition that indigenous children have unique interests that may require special protections beyond those that ensure basic human rights for all children,[17] and (3) recognition of the collective rights of indigenous groups regarding matters affecting children and attempts to reconcile collective and individual rights within regimes that are otherwise focused on individuals.[18]

3.1 Declaration on the Rights of Indigenous Peoples

The UN Declaration on the Rights of Indigenous Peoples (the Declaration) addresses the group and individual rights of indigenous peoples and individuals.[19] It "[affirms] the equality of indigenous peoples and individuals to all other peoples and individuals, paired with their right to be different."[20] It further states that indigenous peoples "are free and equal to all other peoples and individuals and have the right to be free from any kind of discrimination, in the exercise of their rights, in particular that based on their indigenous origin."[21] The Declaration was adopted in 2007 by 144 countries, and the four countries that voted against it—Canada, the United States, New Zealand, and Australia—have since signed on.[22] These states delayed adoption for several years out of concern that the Declaration would create stronger protections for indigenous peoples than had been incorporated into their domestic legal systems, particularly with regard to decolonization.[23] A declaration is nonbinding, but to the extent that the Declaration incorporates international common law norms, those norms are binding on all states regardless of adoption.[24]

Conceptually, the Declaration provides an important alternative to local legal regimes in which the rights of indigenous groups, often focused on being physically separate and culturally and linguistically distinct, can seem in tension with the value of individual equality seen elsewhere in international law and in the law of many democratic countries.[25] For children, one important theme in the Declaration is the idea that a child's rights and interests rely on and include a connection to family, to community, and (via community) to land. The Declaration refers directly to children in only five articles,[26] but the collective rights enshrined in the Declaration can have a significant impact on children's rights.

The Declaration emphasizes indigenous peoples' right to maintain their own cultures and languages and recognizes the threat of genocide via forced cultural assimilation. Article 8 protects the right "not to be subjected to forced assimilation or destruction of their culture."[27] This recognition is especially significant for indigenous children, who in several states have been the target of government-sponsored efforts to forcibly assimilate indigenous peoples. State efforts to forcibly remove and reprogram indigenous children through their child welfare, adoption, and education systems have been well-documented in Canada, the United States, and Australia. In each of these states, the national governments sponsored or supported campaigns to remove indigenous children from their communities and integrate them into white society by erasing cultural, physical, and identity markers of indigeneity. This often-brutal erasure was accomplished by sending children to specialized schools or placing them with white families via foster care or adoption.[28] The Declaration acknowledges that child removal, adoption, and education have been used by states as tools to eradicate indigenous peoples. Article 7, which protects against genocide, includes a specific protection against the forcible removal of children.[29]

The Declaration also protects land rights and the centrality of territory to identity and culture. The drafters recognized that, for indigenous peoples, the ability to fully enjoy the rights protected by other documents, "in particular the right to enjoy one's culture, may consist of a way of life which is closely associated with territory and use of its resources. This may particularly be true of members of indigenous communities constituting a minority."[30] To that end, the Declaration recognizes indigenous peoples' right "to the lands, territories and resources which they have traditionally owned, occupied or otherwise used or acquired" and the right to "maintain and strengthen their distinctive spiritual relationship" with their "lands, territories, waters and coastal seas and other resources."[31] Article 10 ensures that they "shall not be forcibly removed from their lands or territories" without free, prior, and informed consent of the peoples.[32] Article 29 protects the right to environmental conservation and protection of traditional territories.[33] As the Declaration recognizes, the ability to protect land and water is a critical piece of ensuring the future well-being of indigenous children, who will inherit and continue to depend on and care for the land and water.[34]

In addition to its focus on land rights, the Declaration recognizes that indigenous peoples have collective political rights, including the right to self-determination.[35] This guarantee of self-determination is significant. The International Covenant on Civil and Political Rights (ICCPR) guarantees all "peoples" the right to self-determination while guaranteeing all "minority" groups the "right, in community with the other members of their group, to enjoy their own culture, to profess and practise their own religion, or to use their own language."[36] The Declaration clarifies that indigenous peoples are "peoples" under public international law, even if they may also be minorities in the sense that they are distinct, but numerically and politically non-dominant, in the present-day states in which they live. The right to self-determination, guaranteed in Article 3, is further described in Article 4 as including "the right to autonomy or self-government in matters relating to their internal and local affairs."[37] This includes the right to autonomy in many matters that affect children, such as education, religion, medicine, land tenure, and customary law.[38] In this respect, international law reflects recent trends in the domestic law of some states, which has tended to recognize the strongest protection for indigenous peoples when it comes to control over children.[39]

The Declaration also protects indigenous peoples' rights to be consulted on issues affecting them and to participate in decision-making on those issues;[40] their authority over internal matters, including education, law, political structure, and media;[41] and their rights to maintain, practice, and protect distinct culture, religion, language, and philosophy.[42] Together, these provisions secure the collective rights of indigenous communities, including extended families, to maintain contact with and exercise decision-making power over the fate of indigenous children. Specifically, the Declaration recognizes "the right of indigenous families and communities to retain shared responsibility for the upbringing, training, education and well-being of their children."[43] Article 14 recognizes the right of indigenous children to "all levels and forms of education of the State without discrimination" and to have access to an education in their own language and culture.[44] The same article protects the right of indigenous communities to establish and control their own educational system,[45] recognizing that education of children is also a collective right and establishing a group right separate and distinct from the role of the larger nation-state to provide and control children's education. Education is more often understood as an individual right, but as Lorie Graham has argued, indigenous rights law "seeks to achieve what all human rights law seeks to achieve, redressing wrongs and preventing future ones."[46] Like other human rights, the right to education for indigenous peoples "cannot be looked at in isolation; it must be tied to other human rights norms, such as the right to self-determination and cultural integrity, in order for it to be fully recognized and implemented."[47]

The Declaration recognizes that, among indigenous peoples, children and youth may be especially vulnerable to certain harms. Article 17 requires that states take "specific measures to protect indigenous children from economic exploitation and from performing any work that is likely to be hazardous or to interfere with the child's education, or to be harmful to the child's health or physical, mental, spiritual, moral or social development, taking into account their special vulnerability and the importance of education for their empowerment."[48] Article 21 prohibits discrimination in social and economic conditions and requires countries to pay particular attention to the needs of indigenous "elders, women, youth, children, and persons with disabilities."[49] Article 22 likewise recognizes the special needs of these populations.[50] Finally, the Declaration requires states, working with indigenous communities, to ensure that indigenous women and children are free from violence.[51]

Despite its significance in strengthening and institutionalizing international recognition and protection of indigenous rights, and the involvement of indigenous peoples in its drafting, the Declaration has shortcomings. For example, it guarantees the right to self-determination and identifies indigenous peoples in part by their experience of colonization, but it does not refer to indigenous peoples as sovereign nor guarantee them a right to decolonization.[52] Articles 3 and 4 can be understood as limiting indigenous self-determination rights to internal affairs, while the self-determination rights of "peoples" also extend to external affairs, including the right to political self-determination.[53] Article 46 of the Declaration cautions that it should not be "construed as authorizing or encouraging any action which would dismember or impair, totally or in part, the territorial integrity or political unity of sovereign and independent states."[54] As Martin Scheinen noted in 2004, indigenous peoples clearly qualify as peoples, but

> [i]n the same breath, it must however be emphasized that in most cases the ultimate form of exercising the right of self-determination, unilateral secession, is not available to indigenous peoples. For this reason, they usually have to satisfy themselves with other arrangements that allow for their exercise of the right of self-determination, including autonomy and land management regimes based on the role of freely chosen political structures of the indigenous people itself.[55]

This framing, in which indigenous people within settler states are guaranteed a limited right of self-determination that does not clearly extend to independence or even territorial sovereignty, was a compromise likely necessary to garner the support of settler states, whose existence would potentially be threatened by the independence of indigenous peoples within their borders.[56] According to Daes, any distinction between "indigenous peoples" and "peoples," the latter of which is entitled to independence under the UN's foundational treaties, is "due to the efforts of governments to limit the global effects of indigenous rights and build a high conceptual wall between 'indigenous' 'peoples' and 'non-governing territories'" such that the distinguishing feature of indigeneity has been the inability "to exercise the right of self-determination through participation in the construction of a contemporary nation-state."[57] On the other hand, the content of the right to self-determination for indigenous peoples is still being determined, and some scholars argue that it includes more than internal self-determination.[58] The Preamble to the Declaration provides that nothing in it "may be used to deny any peoples their right to self-determination, exercised in conformity with international law."[59] What is clear is that authority over internal affairs, including children's matters, is the *minimum* degree of self-determination to which indigenous groups are entitled.

3.2 ILO Convention No. 169

The International Labour Organisation's Indigenous and Tribal Peoples Convention (ILO Convention No. 169), adopted in 1989, is the only international convention dedicated to recognizing indigenous peoples' rights, and prior to 2007, when the Declaration was adopted, it was the only such international law instrument. Whereas an earlier version of the ILO Convention was focused on protecting and integrating indigenous peoples into the states in which they live, the 1989 revision shifted the goal from integration to self-determination.[60] ILO Convention No. 169 recognized some of the collective rights eventually enshrined in the Declaration on the Rights of Indigenous Peoples, though it placed greater emphasis on cultural and consultation rights and lesser on political and land rights. Article 6 requires states to consult with indigenous peoples and ensure that they can freely participate in decision-making "to at least the same extent as other sectors of the population."[61] Article 7 states that indigenous peoples have the right to "decide their own priorities" regarding development that affects their lands, cultures, and lives and requires governments to "protect and preserve" the environment.[62]

In contrast to the Declaration, the ILO Convention is clearly binding upon the ratifying states. However, it has been ratified by only twenty-three countries,[63] a number that Trevor Buck has called "disappointing" and attributed to "a general tendency of states to avoid subscribing to international instruments that recognize subgroups within their territories, which might undermine national unity."[64] The ILO Convention has a broader reach, however, in that it provided an early model for interpreting the effect of other instruments on indigenous peoples. It helped move indigenous peoples "from object to subject" in international law.[65]

Articles 26 through 30, which concern education, are the only articles that specifically mention indigenous children. These articles require states to provide indigenous children with equal access to and specialized resources for education.[66] States are urged to ensure the involvement of indigenous persons in creating education programs and to ensure that children are taught to read and write in indigenous languages.[67] The dual nature of indigenous children's citizenship is recognized in Article 29, which states that the purpose of education is to enable children to participate fully in both their indigenous community and the national community to which they belong.[68]

These two instruments provide a foundation for understanding how indigenous rights are different from individual rights and even from the group rights of national minorities.[69] As members of collectives, indigenous children have rights that other children do not, including rights to land, rights to consultation and consent, and rights to self-determination and self-governance.[70] In implementing individual rights regimes, such as that set forth in the Convention on the Rights of the Child, states and international bodies must also protect the right of indigenous groups to control traditional state functions, such as education, and must specially ensure the right of indigenous children to benefit from group rights to culture and language.

3.3   Convention on the Rights of the Child

The Convention on the Rights of the Child (CRC), adopted by the General Assembly in 1989, sets forth "special safeguards and care" needed to protect children's basic human rights, including connection to family.[71] The CRC protects the rights of all children and prohibits discrimination "of any kind, irrespective of the child's or his or her parents' or legal guardian's race, colour, sex, language, religion, political or other opinion, national, ethnic or social origin, property, disability, birth or other status."[72] Indigenous children are mentioned in only three articles, but at the time it was drafted, the Convention was the "only provision of an international human rights instrument to explicitly recognize indigenous children as rights-holders."[73]

Article 30 specifically provides that indigenous children "shall not be denied the right, in community with other members of his or her group, to enjoy his or her own culture, to profess and practise his or her own religion or to use his or her own language."[74] In General Comment No. 11, issued after the 2007 Declaration, the Committee on the Rights of the Child (CRC Committee) recognized that the rights protected by Article 30 of the Convention are "both individual and collective rights" and that they "may be closely associated with the use of traditional territory and the use of its resources."[75] The CRC Committee further recognized that indigenous children's physical and mental health may be dependent on their connection to land.[76] Thus, although the Convention does not specifically mention land rights of indigenous children, such rights may be protected through the CRC Committee's interpretation of Article 30. This is important because the CRC has been ratified by, and is therefore binding on, all UN member states except the US.[77] The CRC Committee also clarified that Article 30 establishes a right of indigenous children to culture, language, and religion and requires states to take positive measures to ensure it.[78] The CRC Committee further affirmed that indigenous groups have a right to be consulted on matters involving their children.[79]

Article 17(d) of the CRC expands further on language rights by obligating states to "[e]ncourage the mass media to have particular regard to the linguistic needs of the child who belongs to a minority group or is indigenous" in order to ensure that these children, like all children, have access to diverse sources of information.[80] Article 29(1) sets forth the tenets of education for all children, including that it help develop respect for that child's cultural and linguistic identity and that it foster "understanding, peace, tolerance, equality of the sexes, and friendship among all peoples, ethnic, national and religious groups and persons of indigenous origin." The primary significance of these sections is in the explicit recognition of indigenous children as requiring protection and respect along with all other children. They do not, however, establish specific rights or special protections for indigenous children.

3.4 Convention on the Elimination of All Forms of Racial Discrimination

The International Convention on the Elimination of All Forms of Racial Discrimination (CERD), adopted by the General Assembly in 1965, prohibits member states from engaging in discrimination on the basis of race, color, or ethnic background and obligates states to reform or nullify laws that have a discriminatory purpose or effect.[81] The Committee on the Elimination of Racial Discrimination (CERD Committee) affirmed in 1997 that discrimination against indigenous peoples falls under the scope of the Convention and called upon states to respect indigenous peoples' "distinct culture, history, language and way of life" as well as their rights to land, while ensuring that they are free from discrimination and enjoy equal rights.[82] The CERD Committee's interpretation is significant for its recognition that denial of the collective rights of indigenous peoples can constitute racial discrimination; this is groundbreaking because racism is most often understood narrowly in terms of its effect on individual rights.[83]

In its General Recommendation No. 23, the CERD Committee also clarified that, as to indigenous peoples, "no decisions directly relating to their rights and interests [should be] taken without their informed consent."[84] Article 5 further requires states parties to guarantee equality in a range of areas, including the administration of justice, civil rights, freedom from violence, and political participation. Because indigenous peoples have been racialized in many states, the CERD provides an important source of protection against racial discrimination.[85] Like the ILO Convention No. 169 and the CRC, the application of CERD represents a binding obligation on the 179 member states that have ratified it, including the United States.[86]

3.5 Advisory Bodies, Treaty Bodies, and Special Rapporteurs

The advisory bodies, treaty bodies, and special rapporteurs charged with implementing and enforcing these instruments have focused to varying degrees on the situation of indigenous children. This section discusses the findings of the three entities tasked with focusing on indigenous issues—the United Nations Permanent Forum on Indigenous Issues (the Permanent Forum), the Special Rapporteur on the situation of human rights and fundamental freedoms of indigenous peoples (Special Rapporteur), and the Expert Mechanism on the Rights of Indigenous Peoples (Expert Mechanism)—as well as the Committee on the Rights of the Child (CRC Committee), the Committee on the Elimination of Racial Discrimination (CERD Committee), the Human Rights Committee, and the Committee on Economic, Social, and Cultural Rights.

The Permanent Forum was established in 2000 to address issues related to economic and social development, culture, environment, education, health, and human rights. Its members are appointed by either the member states or the Permanent Forum's governing body in consultation with indigenous organizations. Each annual forum session focuses on a specific theme; children and youth were the focus of the 2003 session.[87] In its report on the 2003 session, the Permanent Forum called on the UN to develop indicators to collect data, report annually, and develop country-specific analyses of the situation of, and problems faced by, indigenous youth, including education, health, culture, extreme poverty, mortality, incarceration, and labor.[88]

The Special Rapporteur was established by the Committee on Human Rights (which monitors implementation of the ICCPR) in 2001. Part of the Special Rapporteur's mandate is to report on the situation of indigenous peoples in specific countries and in specific cases.[89] Much of the work of the Special Rapporteur has to date focused on land and natural resources,[90] which are important to children but not directly focused on them. However, protection of indigenous persons—including women and children—from state and private violence has been another area of focus.[91] In Australia and Canada, the Special Rapporteur has expressed particular concerns about the treatment of indigenous children, especially in the areas of education and justice.[92]

The Expert Mechanism was established by the Human Rights Council in 2007 to provide it with expertise on the rights of indigenous peoples as established in the Declaration.[93] The Expert Mechanism produced a report on indigenous children's right to health in 2016.[94] The report identified indigenous children as having high rates of infant mortality, malnutrition, malnourishment, and vulnerability to violence as well as mental health problems stemming from intergenerational trauma.[95] Relying primarily on the Declaration and the International Covenant on Economic, Social, and Cultural Rights (ICESCR), the report calls on states to "respect" indigenous peoples' access to health care, refrain from polluting lands that affect their health, "protect" indigenous peoples from discrimination in health care and from the actions of polluting companies, and "fulfill" the right to health, including by establishing separate health plans and enacting special measures.[96] The report identified education, child removal, and mental health as key issues affecting the health of indigenous children.[97]

The Expert Mechanism also produced a 2014 report on access to justice, which identified overrepresentation of indigenous youth as a significant problem.

> Although the available data is limited, several studies show that indigenous children and youth are disproportionately represented in criminal justice systems. As the Committee on the Rights of the Child has pointed out, disproportionately high rates of incarceration of indigenous children "may be attributed to systematic discrimination from within the justice system and/or society." In Australia, for example, indigenous youth aged 10–17 are 15 times more likely than non-indigenous youth to be under community-based supervision and almost 25 times as likely to be in detention. In New Zealand, Māori youth appear in court at a rate more than double the rate for all young people.[98]

Citing Article 12 (respect for children's views) and Article 40 (incarceration as a last resort) of the CRC, the report recommended that traditional indigenous justice systems be used to keep indigenous youth from being incarcerated.[99]

Other treaty bodies also have focused on issues critical to indigenous children. The CRC Committee held a Day of General Discussion on indigenous children in 2003, the same year the Permanent Forum held its annual session devoted to indigenous children.[100] The CRC Committee recognized that indigenous children "are disproportionately affected by specific challenges such as institutionalization, urbanization, drug and alcohol abuse, trafficking, armed conflict, sexual exploitation and child labour and yet are not specifically taken into consideration in the development and implementation of policies and programmes for children."[101] It identified several specific areas of concern, including juvenile justice, family environment, health, and education.[102] With regard to juvenile justice, the Committee recommended that states respect traditional and customary law for dealing with offenses committed by indigenous children.[103] It further recommended that states and international bodies focus specifically on those children, collect data, and work closely with indigenous groups to formulate strategies, create institutional mechanisms for rights protection, and ensure that these efforts are funded.[104]

A 2012 CRC Committee report on the status of the CRC highlighted the vulnerability of indigenous youth and included recommendations for safeguarding their rights in specific areas.[105] Citing evolving international law on indigenous rights, the report highlighted the dual nature of indigenous children's rights (individual and collective), such that "[t]he rights of indigenous children are underpinned not only by the principles of the Convention on the Rights of the Child but also by the principles of self-identification, and respect for cultural identity, as espoused under the Declaration [on the Rights of Indigenous Peoples]."[106] It emphasized indigenous children's rights to cultural identity and to be free from discrimination.[107] It included specific findings regarding health disparities among indigenous children on several continents and on the various ways in which indigenous youth face violence, including armed conflict, trafficking, removal from home, and incarceration.[108]

Like its predecessor reports, this one called for more data collection, particularly data that can be disaggregated by ethnicity, sex, and age.[109] Although calls for more data are important, they do not address the difficulties that are sometimes presented by such data collection, including how to define indigenous children, how to distinguish them from children in other categories, and how to identify them at the point of data collection.[110] Without further work to operationalize data collection and address the issues already identified by existing data, calls for further research will have limited impact.

In its periodic reviews of Australia, Canada, and the United States, the CERD Committee has focused on police violence, racial disparities in criminal and juvenile justice, and violence against indigenous women and girls.[111] These are all critical sites of inequality for indigenous youth, yet they have received less sustained attention from the bodies that monitor indigenous rights and children's rights, demonstrating the continuing vitality of CERD as a tool of indigenous children's rights.

Honing in on indigenous children as a specific group, the CERD Committee, in its 2014 periodic review of the United States, expressed concern over the continued removal of indigenous children by state child welfare systems.[112] The Committee called on the US to halt their removal and to effectively implement and enforce the Indian Child

Welfare Act of 1978. In its 2017 periodic reviews of Australia and Canada, the CERD Committee expressed concern over the precarious state of indigenous children, including their overrepresentation in the criminal justice system and their forcible removal from their families and communities.[113] In the case of Australia, the CERD Committee criticized the ill treatment suffered by indigenous children and the conditions in which they were being held in both the states and territories, especially the Northern Territory. The CERD Committee also expressed concern with the high probability of abuse faced by indigenous children who have been removed from their families and placed in alternative care systems. In Canada's case, the CERD Committee expressed alarm that despite its previous recommendations, Canada had continued its disparate treatment of indigenous children, underfunding child and family services for indigenous children as compared to children in other communities. While the extent to which these, and other states parties, actually heed the CERD Committee's counsel is uncertain, the Committee issued the highest number of recommendations concerning indigenous rights of any treaty-monitoring body, including the CRC Committee, in the decade following adoption of the Declaration.[114]

In addition to the documents described here, which address indigenous peoples or children specifically, indigenous children's rights are also protected by—though not specifically mentioned in—broader rights documents, such as the Universal Declaration of Human Rights,[115] the International Covenant on Civil and Political Rights (ICCPR),[116] and the International Covenant on Economic, Social and Cultural Rights (ICESPR).[117] For example, the Human Rights Committee in 2003 invoked Articles 10 (humanity and dignity) and 24 (special protection for children), which together require "treatment appropriate to his age and legal status," to find that Australia violated the ICCPR in a case involving a mentally disabled Aboriginal offender who was first incarcerated as a juvenile. Specifically, the young man's "extended confinement to an isolated cell without any possibility of communication, combined with his exposure to artificial light for prolonged periods and the removal of his clothes and blanket, was not commensurate with his status as a juvenile in a particularly vulnerable position because of his disability and his status as an Aboriginal."[118]

4 The Potential Power of International Indigenous Children's Rights

Despite the mandates of each of these regimes, available information strongly suggests that indigenous children continue to fare poorly in many of the primary areas of concern to children's rights advocates. For example, periodic reports have noted that indigenous children fall at the bottom of lists of health indicators, including infant mortality, disease rates, suicides, and addiction.[119] Recent investigations by treaty bodies indicate that the practice of removing indigenous children from their homes at high rates has not fully ceased.[120] Indigenous children, particularly girls, remain vulnerable to violence and exploitation[121] and are over-represented in the juvenile and criminal justice systems in many nations.[122] When international law does focus on indigenous children, it is often to simply note their poor outcomes or precarious status and to call on states to pay closer attention to their plight and to collect more data. These documentary actions are properly understood as only the very first steps in a campaign to actually improve the lives of indigenous children.

Yet increased attention and visibility are significant. In settler states, the physical and legal erasure of indigenous peoples has been key to the legitimation of state sovereignty.[123] For individual children, a consequence of the project of elimination is the persistent invisibility of those indigenous people who continue to live within settler states.[124] Where indigenous children constitute a numerical minority, even collecting data can be difficult because indigenous children are statistically and conceptually invisible amid the state's total population of children. As a result, they are often left out of reports on the status of children and excluded from reforms intended to benefit all children. Children themselves are also aware of this invisibility, and it can affect everything from psychological well-being to educational outcomes.[125] More attention at the international level means these children are more visible, which in turn impacts all other aspects of their well-being.

Arguably, the most significant development in international law on indigenous children's rights, however, is the idea that individual and collective well-being are related. The Declaration clarified the importance of collective rights, and various international bodies have relied on it to refine their understanding of children's rights and the obligation of states to protect them. When interpreted in light of international indigenous rights law, all international children's law requires states to support indigenous self-governance over children's issues and to consult with indigenous communities to eliminate discrimination and improve children's well-being. Perhaps the clearest example of this appears in the elaboration on the best interests of the child standard contained in the CRC. In light of the Declaration, the CRC Committee clarified that "the best interests of the child is conceived both as a collective and an individual right, and [] the application of this right to indigenous children as a group requires consideration of how the right relates to collective cultural rights."[126] Where there is a distinction between the best interests of an individual child and the collective cultural rights of a group, the Committee noted that the best interest of the individual child must prevail, but "considering the collective cultural rights of the child is part of determining the child's best interests."[127] This link between individual and collective well-being is a critical step for indigenous children because international human rights law has traditionally focused on individual rights and framed indigenous rights as group rights to have control *over* children. "[G]roup rights are no longer the antithesis of international human rights law, if they ever were."[128]

This international effort to recognize the relationship between collective and individual rights is incomplete. Although the CRC Committee acknowledges that individual rights require consideration of collective rights, the interpretation above appears to contemplate the two as in tension, as evidenced by the provision requiring that individual rights trump group rights in the event the two are not aligned. As Trevor Buck has observed, the CRC Committee's approach "discounts the collective rights of the Indigenous People and of the child as subordinate to the individual rights of the child," does not consider the impact of indigenous jurisprudence or customary law on children's rights, and "fails to provide recognition that collective rights can stand alongside and in parity with individual rights."[129] In contrast, domestic jurisprudence in the US[130] and Canada[131] frames the best interests of individual indigenous children as mutually interdependent with collective rights. The idea that indigenous children's rights are enhanced, not threatened, by the exercise of collective rights, while advanced in the scholarly literature,[132] seems to be difficult for the CRC Committee to comprehend. Patrick Thornberry has written, on one hand, that "the CRC can be seen as elaborating the essential communal dimensions of human rights more thoroughly than the ICCPR," but on the other hand, that "the CRC appears to address culture as instrumental—as a means to deliver up rights of the child," and problems therefore arise "where culture is a thicker, more encompassing concept that reaches out to frame and condition notions of individual and collective identity."[133] Acknowledging the existence of collective rights to children is important, but the CRC Committee must also recognize the individual child's right to maintain a connection to the group. In other words, individual children's rights and collective indigenous rights are interrelated.

5 Conclusion

International law has the potential to offer expansive protections for indigenous children's rights, both as individuals and as members of groups. This potential has grown steadily over the past four decades, largely due to the involvement of indigenous peoples at the international level.[134] Because of this involvement, international instruments, particularly the Declaration on the Rights of Indigenous Peoples, reflect the way indigenous peoples understand their status and rights to a greater extent than many domestic laws do.[135] The greatest barrier to vindication of these rights is at the level of implementation and enforcement. Of particular significance to this volume, children's rights scholarship has only recently begun to attend to the specific needs of indigenous children. Greater attention to indigenous children, including the way that group and individual rights interact, may help children's rights advocates better understand and protect the full range of indigenous children's rights.

Acknowledgment

For comments and criticisms, I thank Kim Hai Pearson, Julian Aguon, and the editors of this volume. For research and citation assistance, I thank Lena Rieke, Rezalia Watson, Alexis Wendl, and the Weiner-Rogers Law Library.

Notes

1. Cynthia Price Cohen, "Development of the Rights of the Indigenous Child under International Law." *St. Thomas University Law Review* 9, no. 1 (Fall 1996): 231–250.
2. José R.Martínez Cobo, "Study of the Problem of Discrimination against Indigenous Populations," vol. 5, E/CN.4/Sub.2/1986/7/Add.4: 29, para. 379.
3. Erica-Irene Daes, "An Overview of the History of Indigenous Peoples: Self-Determination and the United Nations," *Cambridge Review of International Affairs* 21, no. 1 (March 2008): 7–26, 9.
4. UN Department of Economic and Social Affairs, "The Concept of Indigenous Peoples," PFII/2004/WS.1/3, 2–3.
5. Daes, "Overview of the History of Indigenous Peoples," 9.
6. Daes, "Overview of the History of Indigenous Peoples," 9. The Declaration differs from some domestic legal regimes by not conditioning rights "on proof of pre- contact or pre-non-native sovereign assertions" or "on a non-Indigenous event (such as European contact with Indigenous peoples or the assertion of foreign sovereignty . . .)"; John Borrows,"Revitalizing Canada's Indigenous Constitution: Two Challenges," in *UNDRIP Implementation, Braiding International, Domestic and Indigenous Laws*, Centre for International Governance Innovation (CIGI) special report (2017), 21, https://www.cigionline.org/sites/default/files/documents/UNDRIP%20Implementation%20Special%20Report%20WEB.pdf.
7. Daes, "History of Indigenous Peoples," 9.
8. Daes, "History of Indigenous Peoples," 9.
9. Daes, "History of Indigenous Peoples," 9–10.
10. Daes, "History of Indigenous Peoples," 10. The International Labour Organization's Convention No. 169 also recognizes "self-identification as indigenous or tribal" as a fundamental criterion. International Labour Organization (ILO), "Convention No. 169: Indigenous and Tribal Peoples Convention" (adopted June 27 1989), art. 1.
11. UN Committee on the Rights of the Child (CRC Committee), *General Comment No. 11: Indigenous Children and Their Rights under the Convention*, UN Doc. CRC/C/GC/11 (2009); Martínez Cobo, "Discrimination against Indigenous Peoples," 28–29.
12. ILO, "Convention No. 169," art. 1.1(a).
13. Daes, "History of Indigenous Peoples," 10. For an example of a decision by the Inter-American Court of Human Rights distinguishing between the collective rights of indigenous and tribal peoples but recognizing the collective property rights of a tribal group, see *Saramaka People v. Suriname*, IHRL 3046 (IACHR 2007).
14. UN Declaration on the Rights of Indigenous Peoples, UN Doc. A/RES/61/295 (2007), art. 33; UN Department of Economic and Social Affairs, "The Concept of Indigenous Peoples," PFII/2004/WS.1/3, 2 (2004), para. 2; Martínez Cobo, "Study of the Problem of Discrimination against Indigenous Populations," para. 381.
15. ILO, "Convention No. 169," arts. 1, 2; Daes, "History of Indigenous Peoples," 10. While it does not define indigeneity, the Declaration on the Rights of Indigenous Peoples provides that membership and group political status are solely matters for indigenous groups to determine. UN Declaration on the Rights of Indigenous Peoples, arts. 3, 33.
16. UN Declaration on the Rights of Indigenous Peoples, arts. 7, 17, 21, 22.
17. UN Declaration on the Rights of Indigenous Peoples, arts. 11, 29; UN Convention on the Rights of the Child (CRC), G.A. Res. 44/25, 44th Sess., UN Doc. A/RES/44/25 (1989), arts. 17, 30; ILO, "Convention No. 169," arts. 26–30.

18. UN Declaration on the Rights of Indigenous Peoples, arts. 4, 14.

19. UN Declaration on the Rights of Indigenous Peoples, art. 1. A declaration is a nonbinding instrument of international law, but some scholars have argued that the Declaration simply enshrines preexisting international customary law, which would make the rights contained in it binding regardless of the status of the instrument or a particular country's ratification of a treaty. Trevor Buck, *International Child Law*, 3rd ed. (New York: Routledge, 2014), 437–444.

20. UN General Assembly, "Report of the Special Rapporteur of the Human Rights Council on the Rights of Indigenous Peoples," A/72/186 (July 21, 2017), 4; UN Declaration on the Rights of Indigenous Peoples, preamble, art. 1, art. 7(2).

21. UN Declaration on the Rights of Indigenous Peoples, art. 2.

22. UN General Assembly, "Report of the Special Rapporteur," 6. The 2017 report also indicates that most of the eleven countries abstaining from the 2007 vote have adopted the Declaration.

23. Karen Engle, "On Fragile Architecture: The UN Declaration on the Rights of Indigenous Peoples in the Context of Human Rights," *European Journal of International Law* 22, no. 1 (2011): 141–163, 145. African states expressed similar concerns about the right to self-determination and the specter of cession.

24. Megan Davis, "To Bind or Not to Bind: The United Nations *Declaration on the Rights of Indigenous Peoples* Five Years On," *Australian International Law Journal* 19, no. 3 (2012): 17–48, 22–23; UN Human Rights Council, "Report of the Special Rapporteur of the Human Rights Council on the Rights of Indigenous Peoples," A/HRC/9/9 (2008), 13 paras. 40–41; Engle, "On Fragile Architecture," 145n9; Buck, *International Child Law*, 320. A slightly different argument is that the Declaration embodies inherent principles of human rights and therefore needs no specific enactment of international or domestic law to make its principles binding on all states. James (Sa'ke'j) Youngblood Henderson, "The Art of Braiding Indigenous Peoples' Inherent Human Rights into the Law of Nation-States," in CIGI, *UNDRIP Implementation*, 10–15.

25. S. James Anaya, "Indigenous Law and Its Contribution to Global Pluralism," *Indigenous Law Journal* 1, no. 6 (2007): 3–12; James Anaya, "Keynote Address: Indigenous Peoples and Their Mark on the International Legal System," *American Indian Law Review* 31, no. 2 (2007): 257–272.

26. These mentions occur in Articles 7 (child removal as genocide), 14 (education), 17 (labor and economic exploitation), 21 (freedom from economic and social discrimination), and 22 (special measures necessary to protect women, elders, children, and disabled people). Earlier drafts included even fewer mentions; a provision about children in armed conflict was removed, and the references to children's labor and economic and social discrimination were added. Cohen, "Development of the Rights of Indigenous Children," 247.

27. UN Declaration on the Rights of Indigenous Peoples, art. 8.

28. Margaret Connell Szasz, *Education and the American Indian: The Road to Self-Determination since 1928*, 3rd ed. (Albuquerque: University of New Mexico Press, 1999); Ann Murray Haag, "The Indian Boarding School Era and Its Continuing Impact on Tribal Families and the Provision of Government Services," *Tulsa Law Review* 43, no. 1 (2007): 149–168; Brian D. Gallagher, "Indian Child Welfare Act of 1978: The Congressional Foray into the Adoption Process," *Northern Illinois University Law Review* 15, no. 1 (1994): 81–106; Truth and Reconciliation Commission of Canada, "Honouring the Truth, Reconciling for the Future: Final Report" (2015); Australia Human Rights and Equal Opportunity

Commission, "Bringing Them Home: Report of the National Inquiry into the Separation of Aboriginal and Torres Strait Islander Children from Their Families (1997); Lewis Meriam, *The Problem of Indian Administration* (Washington, DC: Institute for Government Research, 1928), 3–14.

29. UN Declaration on the Rights of Indigenous Peoples, art. 7, sec. 2.

30. CRC Committee. "Day of General Discussion on the Rights of Indigenous Children: Recommendations" (Oct. 3, 2003), 2, https://www2.ohchr.org/english/bodies/crc/docs/discussion/indigenouschildren.pdf.

31. UN Declaration on the Rights of Indigenous Peoples, arts. 25, 26(1).

32. UN Declaration on the Rights of Indigenous Peoples, art. 10.

33. UN Declaration on the Rights of Indigenous Peoples, art. 29.

34. UN Declaration on the Rights of Indigenous Peoples, art. 25.

35. UN Declaration on the Rights of Indigenous Peoples, art. 3.

36. International Covenant on Civil and Political Rights (ICCPR), arts. 1, 27, 999 UNTS 171 (1966; entered into force March 23, 1976).

37. UN Declaration on the Rights of Indigenous Peoples, art. 4.

38. UN Declaration on the Rights of Indigenous Peoples, arts. 12 (religion), 14 (education), 24 (medicine and health), 33 (membership), 26–27 (land tenure), 34 (customary law).

39. For example, US law recognizes that tribes have sovereign authority over child welfare, adoption, domestic relations, and inheritance rights. Within tribal territory, their authority is exclusive. Indian Child Welfare Act, 25 U.S.C. § 1911(a) (2012); Fisher v. District Court, 424 U.S. 382, 389 (1976); Santa Clara Pueblo v. Martinez, 436 U.S. 49, 55–56 (1978). Unlike in other matters, their authority over children extends beyond territorial boundaries. Indian Child Welfare Act, 25 U.S.C. § 1911(b); John v. Baker, 982 P.2d 738, 744–759 (Alaska 1999). Canadian courts have held that the national government breached its fiduciary duty by permitting First Nations children to be adopted by non-Native families without consulting indigenous communities. Brown v. Canada (Attorney General), No. CV-09-372025-CP (2017).

40. UN Declaration on the Rights of Indigenous Peoples, arts. 18, 19. Article 19 requires states to obtain the "free, prior and informed consent" of indigenous peoples "through their own representative institutions" before adopting measures that will affect them.

41. UN Declaration on the Rights of Indigenous Peoples, arts. 4, 14, 34, 27, 20, 16, 5.

42. UN Declaration on the Rights of Indigenous Peoples, arts. 11, 12, 14, 13.

43. UN Declaration on the Rights of Indigenous Peoples, preamble.

44. UN Declaration on the Rights of Indigenous Peoples, art. 14, sections 2–3.

45. U.N. Declaration on the Rights of Indigenous Peoples, art. 14(1).

46. Lori M. Graham, "Reconciling Collective and Individual Rights: Indigenous Education and International Human Rights Law," *U.C.L.A. Journal of International Law and Foreign Affairs* 15 (2010): 83–109, 109.

47. Graham, "Reconciling Collective and Individual Rights," 109.

48. UN Declaration on the Rights of Indigenous Peoples, art. 17(2).

49. UN Declaration on the Rights of Indigenous Peoples, art. 21(2).

50. UN Declaration on the Rights of Indigenous Peoples, art. 22(1).

51. UN Declaration on the Rights of Indigenous Peoples, art. 22(2).

52. Under customary international law, "all peoples have the right to freely to determine, without external interference, their political status and to pursue their economic, social and cultural development." United Nations General Assembly, "Declaration on Principles

of International Law Concerning Friendly Relations and Co-operation among States in Accordance with the Charter of the United Nations," G.A. Res. 2625 (XXV), UN Doc. A/8082 (Oct. 24, 1970), 123; Maivân C. Lâm, *At the Edge of The State: Indigenous Peoples and Self Determination* (Ardsley, NY: Transnational Publishers, 2000); Julian Aguon, "The Commerce of Recognition (Buy One Ethos, Get One Free): Toward Curing the Harm of the United States' International Wrongful Acts in the Hawaiian Islands," *'Ohia: A Periodic Publication of Ka Huli Ao Center for Excellence in Native Hawaiian Law* (2012), 35–37.

53. Aguon, "Commerce of Recognition," 37, 49–50.

54. UN Declaration on the Rights of Indigenous Peoples, art. 46(1).

55. Martin Scheinen, "Indigenous Peoples' Land Rights under the International Covenant on Civil and Political Rights," Aboriginal Policy Research Consortium International Paper No. 195 (2004), 2.

56. Eve Tuck and K. Wayne Yang, "Decolonization Is Not a Metaphor." *Decolonization: Indigeneity, Education & Society* 1, no. 1 (2012): 1–40; J. Kēhaulani Kauanui, " 'A Structure, Not an Event': Settler Colonialism and Enduring Indigeneity," *Lateral* 5, no. 1 (Spring 2016). Patrick Thornberry views such state concern as manufactured: "[Secession] is not a burning issue for many indigenous peoples, though State resistance to claims of self-determination often raises secession as a spectre." Patrick Thornberry, *Indigenous Peoples and Human Rights* (Manchester: Manchester University Press, 2002), 216.

57. Daes, "History of Indigenous Peoples," 11.

58. Maivân Clech Lâm, "Remembering the Country of Their Birth: Indigenous Peoples and Territoriality," *Journal of International Affairs* 57, no. 2 (2004): 129–150; Aguon, "Commerce of Recognition," 50.

59. UN Declaration on the Rights of Indigenous Peoples, preamble.

60. Athanasios Yupsanis, "ILO Convention No. 169 Concerning Indigenous and Tribal Peoples in Independent Countries 1989–2009: An Overview," *Nordic Journal of International Law* 79, no. 3 (2010): 433–456.

61. ILO, "Convention No. 169," art. 6. The Convention also recognizes that states must coordinate with and seek input from indigenous peoples when developing rights-protecting regimes and education programs (arts. 2, 27).

62. ILO, "Convention No. 169," art. 7.

63. Buck, *International Child Law*, 435 (stating that the twenty-two countries have ratified it). Luxembourg ratified it in 2018. ILO, "Ratifications of C169 and Tribal Peoples Convention, 1989 (No. 169)" (entered into force Sept. 5, 1991), http://www.ilo.org/dyn/normlex/en/f?p =1000:11300:0::NO:11300:P11300_INSTRUMENT_ID:312314.

64. Buck, *International Child Law*, 435.

65. Russell Lawrence Barsh, "Indigenous Peoples in the 1990s: From Object to Subject of International Law," *Harvard Human Rights Journal* 7 (1994): 33–86.

66. ILO, "Convention No. 169," arts. 26, 27.

67. ILO, "Convention No. 169," art. 27.

68. ILO, "Convention No. 169," art. 29.

69. Some commentators characterize indigenous rights as unlike any other international rights. James Anaya, *Indigenous Peoples in International Law*, 2nd ed. (New York: Oxford University Press, 2004). Others have argued that efforts to distinguish indigenous groups from national minorities in terms of international rights are shortsighted and do not reflect international law norms. Will Kymlicka, "Review: Theorizing Indigenous Rights," *University of Toronto Law Journal* 49, no. 2 (1999): 281–293; Will Kymlicka, *Multicultural Citizenship* (Oxford, UK: Clarendon Press, 1995).

70. UN Declaration on the Rights of Indigenous Peoples, arts. 3, 4, 10, 18, 19, 25.
71. CRC, preamble.
72. CRC, art. 2.
73. CRC Committee, "Day of General Discussion," preamble.
74. CRC, art. 30.
75. CRC Committee, *General Comment No. 11*, 4.
76. CRC Committee, *General Comment No. 11*, 8.
77. CRC, "Status as at: 07-09-2018 05:00:30 EDT: Convention on the Rights of the Child," https://treaties.un.org/pages/ViewDetails.aspx?src=IND&mtdsg_no=IV-11&chapter=4&lang=en.
78. CRC Committee, *General Comment No. 11*, 4.
79. CRC Committee, *General Comment No. 11*, 5. The Committee further stated that states are obligated to work with indigenous communities to address issues relating to children (5, 14–18).
80. CRC, art. 17.
81. UN General Assembly, International Convention on the Elimination of All Forms of Racial Discrimination, G.A. Res. 2106 (XX), (Dec. 21, 1965; entered into force Jan. 4, 1969). The Convention is aimed at protecting equality, civil rights, and access to participatory political rights. However, it also protects "the right to nationality," religious freedom, and cultural rights. International Convention on the Elimination of All Forms of Racial Discrimination, art. 5.
82. Committee on the Elimination of Racial Discrimination (CERD Committee), "General Recommendation No. 23 on the Rights of Indigenous Peoples," UN Doc. A/52/18 (1997), annex V: 122.
83. According to Patrick Thornberry, "there is so much material in the *oeuvre* of [the CERD Committee] on indigenous peoples to suggest that the Committee has engaged in a process of normative expansion—bearing in mind that the term 'indigenous' appears nowhere in the Convention." Thornberry, *Indigenous Peoples and Human Rights*, 223.
84. CERD Committee, "General Recommendation No. 23." In a precursor to the free, prior, and informed consent provision in the Declaration, General Recommendation No. 23 called on states to return any lands taken without "free and informed consent" and to provide restitution only when return is "for factual reasons not possible." (para. 5).
85. For further discussion of the racialization of indigenous peoples see Addie C. Rolnick, "The Promise of Mancari: Indian Political Rights as Racial Remedy," *N.Y.U. Law Review* 86, no. 4 (2011): 958–1045; Patrick Wolfe, "Settler Colonialism and the Elimination of the Native," *Journal of Genocide Research* 8, no. 4 (2006): 387–409; Yael Ben-Zvi, "Where Did Red Go? Henry Louis Morgan's Evolutionary Inheritance and U.S. Racial Imagination," *The New Centennial Review* 7, no. 2 (2007): 201–229.
86. UN Permanent Forum on Indigenous Issues, "Status as at: 07-09-2018 05:00:30 EDT: International Convention on the Elimination of All Forms of Racial Discrimination." https://treaties.un.org/Pages/ViewDetails.aspx?src=IND&mtdsg_no=IV-2&chapter=4&clang=_en.
87. UN Permanent Forum on Indigenous Issues, "Report on the Second Session," E/C.19/2003/22 (2003), 3.
88. UN Permanent Forum on Indigenous Issues, "Report on the Second Session," 4.
89. The Special Rapporteur's mandate was renewed in 2004 by the Commission on Human Rights and in 2007 by the Human Rights Council.
90. UN General Assembly, "Report of the Special Rapporteur on the Rights of Indigenous Peoples on Her Mission to the United States of America," A/HRC/36/46/Add.1 (2017); UN General Assembly, "Informe de la Relatora Especial sobre los derechos de los pueblos

indígenas relativo a su misión al Brasil," A/HRC/33/42/Add.1 (2016); UN General Assembly, "Report of the Special Rapporteur on the Rights of Indigenous Peoples on Her Visit to Honduras," A/HRC/33/42/Add.2 (2016); UN General Assembly, "Report of the Special Rapporteur on the Rights of Indigenous Peoples on the Human Rights Situation of the Sami People in the Sampi Region of Norway, Sweden and Finland," A/HRC/33/42/Add.3 (2016); UN General Assembly, "Report of the Special Rapporteur on the Rights of Indigenous Peoples on Her Visit to Canada," A/HRC/27/52/Add.2 (2014); UN General Assembly, "Report of the Special Rapporteur on the Rights of Indigenous Peoples on Her Visit to Panama," A/HRC/27/52/Add.1 (2014); UN General Assembly, "Report of the Special Rapporteur on the Rights of Indigenous Peoples: Consultation on the Situation of Indigenous Peoples in Asia," A/HRC/24/41/Add.3 (2013).

91. UN General Assembly, "Report of the Special Rapporteur...on Her Mission to the United States of America"; "Informe de la Relatora Especial"; "Report of the Special Rapporteur...on Her Visit to Honduras."

92. UN General Assembly, "Report of the Special Rapporteur on the Rights of Indigenous Peoples on Her Visit to Australia," A/HRC/36/46/Add.2 (2017); "Report of the Special Rapporteur on...Her Visit to Canada."

93. Its mandate was revised in 2016 following the World Conference of Indigenous Peoples to avoid duplication with the other mandates and enhance cooperation between them. UN Human Rights Council, "Resolution No. 30–11: Review of the Mandate of the Expert Mechanism on the Rights of Indigenous Peoples," A/HRC/RES/30/11 (2015).

94. UN Human Rights Council, "The Right to Health and Indigenous Peoples, with a Focus on Indigenous Youth," Draft Study of the Expert Mechanism on the Rights of Indigenous Peoples, A/HRC/EMRIP/2016/CRP.1 (2016).

95. UN Human Rights Council, "Right to Health," 13–14.

96. UN Human Rights Council, "Right to Health," 9–11. Although the Council noted that health rights are also protected by Article 24 of the CRC and Article 5 of the Convention on the Elimination of All Forms of Racial Discrimination, as well as other international instruments, it relied primarily on the Declaration on the Rights of Indigenous Peoples and the ICESCR. UN Human Rights Council, "Right to Health," 4–5.

97. UN Human Rights Council, "Right to Health," 14–15. Notably, the Expert Mechanism found that "indigenous children are still removed from their homes at significantly higher rates than their non-indigenous counterparts," despite the CRC Committee's focus on maintaining the integrity of the family.

98. UN Human Rights Council, "Access to Justice in the Promotion and Protection of the Rights of Indigenous Peoples: Restorative Justice, Indigenous Juridical Systems and Access to Justice for Indigenous Women, Children and Youth, and Persons with Disabilities," Study by the Expert Mechanism on the Rights of Indigenous Peoples, A/HRC/27/65 (2014), 12.

99. Expert Mechanism, "Access to Justice," 13.

100. CRC Committee, "Day of General Discussion on the Rights of Indigenous Children."

101. CRC Committee, "Day of General Discussion," 1.

102. CRC Committee, "Day of General Discussion," 3–4.

103. CRC Committee, "Day of General Discussion," 3.

104. CRC Committee, "Day of General Discussion," 2.

105. UN General Assembly, , "Status of the Convention on the Rights of the Child," Report of the Secretary-General, UN Doc. A/67/225 (2012), 4–17.

106. UN General Assembly, "Status of the Convention," 4–5.

107. UN General Assembly, "Status of the Convention," 5–7.

108. UN General Assembly, "Status of the Convention," 11–15.

109. UN General Assembly, "Status of the Convention," 7.

110. CRC Committee, *General Comment No. 11*, 6.

111. CERD, "Concluding Observations on the Eighteenth to Twentieth Periodic Reports of Australia," CERD/C/AUS/CO/18–20 (2017); CERD, "Concluding Observations on the Combined Seventh to Ninth Periodic Reports of the United States of America," CERD/C/USA/CO/7–9 (2014); CERD, "Consideration of Reports Submitted by States Parties under Article 9 of the Convention: Twenty-First to Twenty-Third Periodic Reports of States Parties Due in 2015, Canada," CERD/C/CAN/21–23 (2016).

112. CERD, "Concluding Observations: United States of America," 11.

113. Committee on the Elimination of Racial Discrimination, "Concluding Observations: Australia," 6–7; CERD, "Consideration of Reports Submitted by States Parties . . . Canada," 23–25.

114. Human Rights Council, "Ten Years of the Implementation of the United Nations Declaration on the Rights of Indigenous Peoples: Good Practices and Lessons Learned—2007–2017," UN Doc. A/HRC/EMRIP/2017/CRP.2 (2017), 4.

115. UN General Assembly, "Universal Declaration of Human Rights," G.A. Res. 217 (III), UN Doc. A/RES/217(III) (1948).

116. International Covenant on Civil and Political Rights (ICCPR), 999 UNTS 171 (1966; entered into force March 23, 1976).

117. International Covenant on Economic, Social and Cultural Rights (ICESCR), 993 UNTS 3 (1966; entered into force Jan. 3, 1976). Applying the ICCPR and the ICESCR to indigenous rights often requires framing indigenous rights as minority rights, a move that contributed to international law's failure to adequately protect indigenous rights and led eventually to the UN Declaration on the Rights of Indigenous Peoples. Thornberry, *Indigenous Peoples and Human Rights*, 116–198.

118. UN Human Rights Committee, "Communication No. 1184/2003, *Brough v. Australia*," CCPR/C/86/D/1184/2003 (2006).

119. For example, see Carrington C. J. Shepherd, Jianghong Li, Matthew N. Cooper, Katrina D. Hopkins, and Brad M. Farrant, "The Impact of Racial Discrimination on the Health of Australian Indigenous Children Aged 5–10 Years: Analysis of National Longitudinal Data." *Journal for Equity in Health* 16, no. 116 (July 2017): 5–6 (mental health and physical health); Australian Institute of Health and Welfare, "The Health and Welfare of Australia's Aboriginal and Torres Strait Islander Peoples," Cat. No. IHW 47 (2015) (physical health and psychological distress); Janet Smylie and Paul Adomako, *Indigenous Children's Health Report* (Toronto: Centre for Research on Inner City Health, 2009) (infant mortality, suicide, mental and physical health); Addie C. Rolnick, "Untangling the Web, Juvenile Justice in Indian Country," *N.Y.U. Journal of Legislation & Public Policy* 19, no. 1 (2016): 78–79 (mental health, drug and alcohol use, suicide).

120. See notes 97, 112. Chris Cuneen, "Surveillance, Stigma, Removal: Indigenous Child Welfare and Juvenile Justice in the Age of Neoliberalism," *Australian Indigenous Law Review* 19, no. 1 (2016): 32–45; Aliza Organick, "Holding Back the Tide: The Existing Indian Family Doctrine and Its Continued Denial of the Right to Culture for Indigenous Children," in *Facing the Future: The Indian Child Welfare Act at 30* (East Lansing: Michigan State University Press, 2009), 221–234; Phillip Lynch, "Keeping them Home:

The Best Interests of Indigenous Children and Communities in Canada and Australia," *Sydney Law Review* 23, no. 4 (2001): 501–542.

121. See notes 91, 95, 108. See also UN General Assembly, "Informe de la Relatora Especial," 6–7; UN General Assembly, "Report of the Special Rapporteur on...Her Visit to Honduras," 7; CCERD, "Concluding Observations: United States of America," 9; CERD, "Concluding Observations: Australia," 7; CERD, "Consideration of Reports Submitted by States Parties...Canada, 7.

122. See notes 92, 98, 102, 113. In the US, indigenous youth are less likely than other youth to be arrested for serious and violent offenses but are more likely to be detained and incarcerated. Rolnick, "Untangling the Web," 49–140.

123. Patrick Wolfe, "Settler Colonialism."

124. For an analysis of this phenomenon in US history see Brian W. Dippie, *The Vanishing American: White Attitudes and U.S. Indian Policy* (Lawrence: University of Kansas Press, 1991).

125. Psychologist Stephanie Fryberg has studied the effect of cultural invisibility and stereotypical representations of Native peoples on both indigenous and white youth in the United States. S. A. Fryberg and N. M. Stephens, "When the World Is Colorblind, American Indians Are Invisible: A Diversity Science Approach," *Psychological Inquiry* 21, no. 2 (2010): 115–119.

126. CRC Committee, *General Comment No. 11*, 7.

127. CRC Committee, "Day of General Discussion on the Rights of Indigenous Children," 7.

128. Graham, "Reconciling Collective and Individual Rights," 104.

129. Buck, *International Child Law*, 328; Terri Libesman, "Can International Law Imagine the World of Indigenous Children?," *International Journal of Children's Rights*, 15, no. 2 (June 2007): 283–309. Buck also points out that the Committee's interpretation frames indigenous rights as solely cultural and does not recognize or consider other types of rights, such as political or jurisdictional rights. Buck, *International Child Law*, 328.

130. In a case upholding tribal jurisdiction over an adoption covered by the Indian Child Welfare Act, the US Supreme Court held that the law protects a relationship between child and tribe that is equally important to the group and the individual child and cannot be undermined by the decision of an individual parent. "The protection of this tribal interest is at the core of the ICWA, which recognizes that the tribe has an interest in the child which is distinct from, but on a parity with, the interest of the parents. This relationship between Indian tribes and Indian children domiciled on the reservation finds no parallel in other ethnic cultures found in the United States. It is a relationship that many non-Indians find difficult to understand, and that non-Indian courts are slow to recognize." Mississippi Band of Choctaw Indians v. Holyfield, 490 U.S. 30, 52 (1989) (quoting *In re Adoption of Halloway*, 732 P.2d 962, 969–970 (1986)).

131. In a case holding that a Six Nations parent had a constitutionally protected right to pursue traditional medicine in lieu of chemotherapy for her daughter, the judge reasoned, "One of these core tenets [of aboriginal culture], and something this court is reminded of regularly in dealing with child protection cases involving the Haudenosaunee, is the ultimate respect accorded to their children. They are considered gifts from the Creator. So it is then that, in considering both the facts of this case as expressed by the mother and the history as it relates to aboriginal peoples, it does no mischief to my decision to recognize that the best interests of the child remains paramount." Hamilton Health Sciences Corp. v. D.H., 2015 ONCJ 229 (endorsement of April 24, 2014).

132. Libesman, "Can International Law Imagine?," 307; Jini Roby, "Understanding Sending Country's Traditions and Policies in International Adoption: Avoiding Legal and Cultural Pitfalls," *Journal of Law and Family Studies* 6, no. 2 (2004): 303–451.

133. Thornberry, *Indigenous Peoples and Human Rights*, 234, 241. In his view, "The end problem for the Convention is not that this or that specific concept or principle may be difficult to fit into an indigenous or other world-view, but that the essential principle of the Convention—the child as the subject of rights—may not" (241). The CRC Committee appears to anticipate conflicts between individual and collective rights in this regard and finds the answer in prioritizing the individual child's human rights.

134. Anaya, "Indigenous Peoples and Their Mark on the International Legal System," 257.

135. Borrows, "Revitalizing Canada's Indigenous Constitution," 21.

CHAPTER 28

....

CHILDREN WITH DISABILITIES: ACHIEVEMENTS, PROSPECTS, AND CHALLENGES AHEAD

....

MAYA SABATELLO AND MARY FRANCES LAYDEN

1 INTRODUCTION

....

WORLDWIDE, it is estimated that fifteen to twenty percent of all children under age eighteen have physical, mental/psychosocial, intellectual, or sensory disabilities.[1] However, throughout history and to the present day, the rights of children with disabilities have been neglected. There are multiple reasons that could account for this result. These include the relatively late understanding of children as subjects of the law, which only emerged in the mid- to late-twentieth century, primarily in Western countries; the traditional conceptualization of disability through a medical binocular, which often focuses on measures to fix one's disabling conditions and devalues those with physical and mental differences; the ongoing stigma about the seeming incapacities of children and adults with disabilities; and the view of disability as a life of misery and thus as unworthy of social investment. The result nonetheless is that, far more than their non-disabled peers, children with disabilities are commonly victims of abuse, discrimination, and marginalization.[2]

The past few decades have seen tremendous efforts to develop and implement a human rights agenda that would address the injustices experienced by children, including children with disabilities. These efforts have evolved over time—moving from non–legally binding international declarations in the late 1950s to hard law and dedicated conventions since the 1980s to promote the rights of children and, significantly, of people—including children—with disabilities. There has been subsequent progress toward securing the rights of children and persons with disabilities, at least on the level of national and international awareness and policy change. Yet much more needs to be done.

This chapter explores the state of affairs and legal protections for upholding the rights of children with disabilities. The next section introduces the population at stake and provides a snapshot of the status of children with disabilities worldwide. We then examine major developments in the international framework that pertain to the rights of children with disabilities and consider some of the prime achievements—and challenges— that arise in the implementation of a child-friendly disability rights agenda. Next, we explore two particularly salient issues for children with disabilities, namely, inclusive education and deinstitutionalization, and highlight the successes and challenges ahead. The final section provides some concluding thoughts about the present and prospects of upholding human rights for children with disabilities.

2 Children with Disabilities: The Population at Stake

There are no comprehensive and universally accepted measures to assess the global prevalence of disabilities.[3] However, it is estimated that, out of the approximately one billion people with disabilities worldwide, 93 to 150 million are children and that 80 percent of people with disabilities reside in developing countries.[4] Studies further indicate that the prevalence of disability is associated with sex: boys are 1.3–1.4 times more likely than girls to have a disability.[5] Although some impairments are congenital (e.g., intellectual disability associated with Down Syndrome), several other reasons might account for this high prevalence.

First, disability among children is bi-directionally and strongly related to poverty and malnutrition. While poverty and malnutrition are known factors leading to poorer health conditions and developmental delay and disability, one's disability (e.g., difficulty with taking in nutrients due to motor impairments) can lead to malnutrition.[6]

Second, humanitarian crises, including internal and international wars, environmental disasters, and large-scale displacements are known causes of disabilities among children. Such crises have both immediate and long-term impact on children's health and disabilities, especially when access to proper care in their aftermath is unavailable.[7] Car accidents are another major reason for childhood disabilities, especially in developing countries where the infrastructure is poor and where 90 percent of all cases of disability, including traumatic brain injuries—the leading cause of death and disability among children and adolescents throughout the world—are believed to be caused by road accidents.[8]

Regardless of the causes of impairments, their presence has tremendous and long-lasting impact on the lives of children (and future adults) with disabilities.

Studies indicate that children with disabilities, especially girls, are two to four times more likely than their non-disabled peers to be victims of violence, maltreatment, and sexual abuse.[9] Rates of abuse are especially high among children with disabilities in residential facilities, a pandemic that recent studies found to persist across all European countries, from Bulgaria, Hungary, and Greece to Austria, Sweden, and the United Kingdom,[10] and to exist also in East African countries where systematic reviews of evidence are still unavailable.[11] Although vulnerability from impairment makes children with disabilities "easier targets" and provides a partial explanation for these abuses,[12] the underlying reason is likely traditional views of children with disabilities as being unworthy and undeserving of respect.[13]

Social stigma further leads to discrimination and exclusion in less conspicuous ways. Studies indicate that environmental and attitudinal barriers often result in children with disabilities reporting lower rates of participation and involvement in school, social, and community activities[14] and that transportation barriers, costs, and lack of accessible information further reduce participation levels among children with disabilities.[15] This exclusion is especially notable in low-income countries, where the difference in school attendance among children with and without disabilities ranges from 10 percent in India to 60 percent in Indonesia.[16] Children with disabilities are also more likely to be placed in group and nursing homes as the stigma, combined with lack of community resources, diverts attention from the importance of keeping children in family environments.[17] Because such children are largely invisible in their communities, their outright exclusion also remains out of public view, notwithstanding efforts in recent decades to implement deinstitutionalization programs.

Thus, the discussion of children with disabilities highlights the challenges in, but also the importance of, claiming children's rights. Abuse and exclusion of children with disabilities often occurs in the private rather than the public sphere, the former of which has historically been beyond governmental action. And although efforts to remedy these realities through discourses on children's interests or through obligations that adults, especially parents, have toward children[18] are important, these lesser forms of claims are not enough. They are key for promoting children's development in general, but it is the rights discourse that assures positive action, by holding states responsible and by requiring their intervention when the ideal of parents/adults protecting children's interests fails.[19]

3 CHILDREN'S RIGHTS: LEGAL FRAMEWORK

Until the mid-twentieth century, children worldwide were viewed as "property" of their parents, especially their father. As such, children could not make claims on their own, and also when children were abused and mistreated, states refrained from intervening in what was deemed to be a family's private affairs. However, the technological and socioeconomic changes of the early twentieth century, combined with the growing body of human rights law post–World War II, led to a shift in attitude: children (particularly in the Global North) began to be viewed not only as meriting societal protection but, significantly, as subjects deserving of recognition, self-determination, and their own rights.[20]

The 1989 Convention on the Rights of the Child (CRC) marks the most comprehensive step toward the recognition of children's rights, including for children with disabilities. Although not the first international instrument to address children's rights issues, previous efforts have largely served as important, though insufficient stepping stones. They primarily endorsed a welfare approach to children, highlighting children's vulnerability, physical and mental immaturity, and dependence on parents (especially mothers) but did not view them as subjects of rights.[21] The CRC, in contrast, offered a revolutionary perspective, recognizing children's vulnerability and agency and as members of society deserving of both certain protections and rights.[22]

The importance of the CRC in advancing children's rights worldwide cannot be understated.[23] It was the first international treaty to include civil and political rights as well as social, economic, and cultural rights in addition to other protections that were historically included only in international humanitarian law (e.g., regulations of warfare). It integrated in its provisions contemporary understandings of human rights law—for example, expanding the child's right to life to include "survival and development."[24] And it explicitly recognized children as rights-holders and as active agents, stipulating that, in all matters that affect them, the child's best interests is to be a primary consideration and, furthermore, that children who are capable of forming their own views have a right to express freely these views and to have them taken seriously, taking into account children's evolving capacities.[25] The rapid universal endorsement of the CRC further reflects the wide support for the new global order. It entered into force only six months after its formal signing ceremony in January 1990, and by 2001, all 191 states, except the United States and Somalia, had ratified the CRC.[26] Today, the United States is the only country in the world that has yet to ratify the CRC.

In addition to its general applicability to children with disabilities, the CRC further includes explicit language conferring rights to this population. The CRC—Article 2—is the first treaty to mention disability as a prohibited ground for discrimination, which potentially expands the protections of the rights of children with disabilities in a range of areas.[27] Innovatively, Article 23 focuses solely on the needs of children with disabilities. It recognizes "that a mentally or physically disabled child should enjoy a full and decent life, in conditions which ensure dignity, promote self-reliance and facilitate the child's active participation in the community." Article 23 also stipulates a right to special care and assurance of assistance, specifically referencing education, training, health care, rehabilitation services, and preparation for employment and recreation opportunities that promote the child's social integration and individual development.

While the CRC was critical in promoting children's rights, its implementation with regard to children with disabilities faced several challenges. First, the CRC does not provide clear guidelines as to how to achieve the treaty's objectives. Article 23, for example, calls for states parties to extend accommodations and services to children with disabilities; however, it does not specify what services are required or how to ensure that such services are provided.[28] Implementing the rights of children with disabilities has thus lagged behind. One key example of this is education of children with disabilities. Although Article 28 of the CRC recognizes the right to education for all children, its reading in conjunction with Article 23, which lacks a clear need-based entitlement or right to benefit from relevant services, has resulted in half of the world's school-age children with disabilities (girls are overrepresented in this population) being out of school and in many more receiving no early childhood development and education services.[29] Similarly, in developed countries (e.g., the United States), dropout rates have been higher and graduation rates lower for adolescents with disabilities as compared to their non-disabled peers, especially for those who do not receive accommodations and services.[30]

Second, and related, the CRC failed to acknowledge that equality and non-discrimination provisions are often insufficient for upholding the rights of children with disabilities. Indeed, although accommodations are often necessary for children with disabilities to exercise their rights, denial of relevant services was not historically understood as unequal and discriminatory.[31] Moreover, the principle of non-discrimination commonly allows for different treatment if the distinction is based on reasonable and objective criteria and if it is to achieve a legislative purpose. This may be particularly impactful on children with disabilities: their different appearance or behavior may be viewed as a justification for different treatment and segregation (as is common, e.g., in the context of special education).[32]

Third, CRC's focus on special care and assistance in designated areas has, in essence, replicated the welfare- rather than the rights-based approach to children with disabilities by subjecting Article 23's implementation to the availability of resources and thus to charitable decisions about distribution of services. Furthermore, this CRC focus has diverted attention from other rights stipulated in the treaty that should have applied to this population. As a comprehensive study of states' reports found, the rights of children with disabilities have largely been confined to the services mentioned in Article 23.[33]

Finally, the CRC does not stipulate sanctions for state failure to comply with their international commitments. Although a 2011 optional protocol aimed to rectify this issue by allowing individuals, including children, to submit communications to the CRC committee, this challenge remains relevant for children, particularly those with disabilities.[34] Their minority status, combined with the common connotation of disability with lack of capacity, make the filing of such complaints difficult; furthermore, their testimonies about violation of their rights are often dismissed[35] (and, as of 2018, no complaints about non-humanitarian rights of children with disabilities had been submitted; only one complaint about a denial of an asylum request and the deportation of a child with autism and his family from Sweden has been submitted[36]). Thus, although the CRC has increased awareness of the rights of children—or the violation of their rights—worldwide, its success with regard to children with disabilities has been particularly limited.[37]

It is against this backdrop that the need for a disability treaty emerged, culminating in the 2006 Convention on the Rights of Persons with Disabilities (CRPD). The CRPD is the first UN convention dedicated to the protection of the rights of adults and children with disabilities, and it was drafted with the most extensive input of stakeholders to date. In addition to the large number of self-advocates, disabled persons organizations (DPOs), and other nongovernmental organizations that attended the meetings alongside states and intergovernmental organizations, people with disabilities and their representative organizations have played a key role in the development and negotiations of the CRPD's provisions.[38] Save the Children further involved children with disabilities in the drafting process, including securing the participation of a group of children with disabilities at a session of the ad hoc committee that drafted the convention.[39]

Following the lead of the CRC, the CRPD adopted a comprehensive—and tailored—approach to disability rights. Its so called "non-definition" of disability in Article 1 aims to be as inclusive as possible, stating a non-comprehensive list of the targeted population as "those who have long-term physical, mental, intellectual or sensory impairments which in interaction with various barriers may hinder their full and effective participation in society on an equal basis with others." Significantly, the CRPD marks a shift in the conceptualization of disability rights. It replaces the traditional medical model that focuses on inabilities, prevention, and treatment with a social model that centers on environmental, attitudinal, and other barriers imposed on people with impairments that deprive them of full participation.[40] Other hallmarks of the CRPD are the requirement that states provide reasonable accommodations—indeed, failure to do so amounts to discrimination on the basis of disability[41]—and preference for universal design, calling for products, environments, programs, and services to be usable by all people without the need for adaptation. Along with the general principles guiding the CRPD's implementation—equality, non-discrimination, and, significantly, respect for dignity and autonomy and for difference and acceptance of persons with disabilities as part of human diversity and humanity[42]—the CRPD establishes inclusion as a human right.

The CRPD also further cements the various rights of children with disabilities in a number of ways. First, the prominence of references to children with disabilities is apparent, including the obligation on states to "closely consult with and actively involve" children with disabilities, through their representative organizations in legislative and other processes to implement the CRPD.[43] Second, the CRPD adopted a twin-track approach in its address of children with disabilities. Thus, in addition to a dedicated article on children,[44] the interests, needs, and rights of children with disabilities were mainstreamed throughout the treaty.[45] This approach is commonly used for populations that face double discrimination, ensuring that the rights of individuals belonging to these groups are considered more holistically, inter alia, by avoiding the trap of a single dedicated provision, as has occurred with Article 23 of the CRC. Indeed, this approach holds particular value for children with disabilities. It recognizes them as separate subjects of rights who are in a transient phase and, building on the work of feminists and social scientists, brings to the fore relational autonomy and its underpinning of interdependence and the strong belief that individuals, and children in particular, develop within a matrix of relationships.[46]

Accordingly, Article 7 of the CRPD, which focuses on children with disabilities, stipulates the general requirement on states parties to assure children with disabilities the full enjoyment of freedoms and rights equal to all children. Article 7 further reinforces two of the CRC's key principles, namely, the child's best interests as a primary consideration and the right of children with disabilities to express their views freely—and be heard.[47] Indeed, respect for the evolving capacities of children with disabilities, along with a right to preserve their identities, are also explicitly included among the CRPD's general principles and explicit obligations on states parties in developing and implementing laws and policies related to disability rights.[48] Other important CRPD provisions relating to children with disabilities aim to rectify the lingering effects of exclusion and discrimination described above. These include: Article 16, states parties' obligations to provide protection from abuse, neglect, maltreatment, and injury as well as supports to address the needs of those experiencing such maltreatment;[49] Article 24, the first international instrument to provide binding protections for the right of children with disabilities to inclusive education;[50] and Article 19, reiterating the right to live and be included in the community. However, although the implementation of the CRPD and the CRC are key for upholding the rights of children with disabilities, successful implementation of children's rights can occur only when political will—and commitment—are present. The next sections consider the persisting challenges in two important contexts—inclusive education and de-institutionalization—to highlight the stumbling blocks that limit the children's rights revolution from reaching children with disabilities.

4 INCLUSIVE EDUCATION: CAN SEPARATE BE EQUAL?

Since Article 24 of the CRPD intended to remedy the dire state of education of children with disabilities worldwide, it was drafted to be revolutionary in several ways.

First, Article 24 explicitly recognizes the *right* of persons and children with disabilities to education. By so doing, the CRPD departs from the CRC's weaker requirement of mere governmental *intention* (as may have been connoted by the word "shall" in the CRC[51]), affirms the entitlement (nothing less!) of children and people with disabilities to education, and cements this right as a fundamental principle and obligation on states. Second, Article 24 provides guidelines for the realization of this right by stipulating negative and positive obligations on states. Thus, it prohibits exclusion of children with disabilities from general primary, secondary, higher, and vocational education systems, alongside requirements that reasonable accommodations and supports be provided to facilitate effective education and to maximize academic and social development. Third, Article 24 links education to broader participation of persons with disabilities in the community. While the chapeau of Article 24(3) requires states parties to enable persons with disabilities to learn life and social development skills, subsequent subsections recognize the key role of languages and alternative modes of communication (e.g., Braille, sign language) as well as peer support and mentoring as necessary measures to building appropriate educational environments and to maximizing academic and social development. Fourth, the need for training of educational professionals about disability rights, accessibility, and accommodation, and the employment of teachers with disabilities, are stated among the necessary measures for the right to education to be realized by people with disabilities. Finally, and most innovatively, Article 24 introduces inclusive education as "the principle and special education the exception"[52] and further connects it with the implementation of well-established principles of non-discrimination and equal opportunity.[53] By so doing, the provision also demonstrates the fallacy of the historical distinction between negative liberties and positive rights and highlights the inseparable connection among them.

The shift to inclusive education is paramount. Rather than segregated education, or efforts at integration, which have commonly resulted in attendance in mainstream schools but without the necessary support, inclusive education requires that services and accommodations are provided to children with disabilities.[54] As recognized by international authorities, including in Sustainable Development Goal 4 and by the CRPD Committee, inclusive education requires systematic changes and modifications in content, teaching methods, approaches, structures, and strategies in education to overcome barriers that discourage participation, including revising policies, culture, and practices to accommodate the needs of students with disabilities.[55] Concurrently, understanding the right to education in a holistic manner requires moving away from a one-size-fits-all approach to the provision of services that are tailored to an individual's needs. Students who are deaf, blind, and deaf-blind, for example, may need a space to learn communication skills before they can participate in inclusive education with non-disabled peers.[56] The CRPD acknowledges these needs; indeed, beyond the immediate goal of inclusive settings, education is viewed as a key equalizer for participation in the community and as a public good. As studies in Australia, Canada, the United States, and Ireland demonstrate, the social and academic beneficiaries of inclusive education are not only children with disabilities but also their non-disabled peers, not least because of the de-stigmatizing and fear-reducing effects of interaction with students with disabilities.[57]

Although recognition of the importance of inclusive education has gained traction over the past thirty years, its explicit negotiation during the drafting process and ultimate statement in the CRPD has given impetus to important changes, especially among countries that, pre-CRPD negotiations, lacked resources and a disability-focus perspective for implementing it. Thus, for example, in India the reported number of children with disabilities enrolled in regular schools increased sharply, from 566,921 in 2002–2003 to 2.35 million in 2012–2013, and the proportion of schools with ramps increased from 1.49 percent in 2004 to 55.09 percent in 2012–2013.[58] Brazil has similarly significantly enhanced its inclusive education program: 47 percent of children with disabilities attended mainstream education in 2006 compared with 21 percent in 2000.[59] In other countries, such as Tanzania, collaborations between governmental and nongovernmental organizations increased, allowing for national education legislation to better reflect the principles of the CRPD and for international funding to support inclusive educational programs.[60] Although deducing a direct causal relationship between the CRPD and these developments may be impossible, their timing and increasing international pressure promoting inclusive education are suggestive. Indeed, these trends are further promising given that since the CRPD's negotiations, its vision and provisions have become integral to states' reporting requirements under the CRPD and also have entered national and, significantly, regional courts. Thus, while in the 2003 *Autism Europe v. France* case[61] the European Court of Human Rights emphasized states' obligation to demonstrate a basic level of positive educational provision that is also compatible with the principle of progressive realization, post-CRPD cases required states to ensure accessibility, accommodation, and inclusion in college- and university-level education (e.g., *Şahin v. Turkey*[62]).

Notwithstanding these achievements, barriers to inclusive education remain. First, translating policies into practice is complicated. Some countries have a strong dual education system, with special and mainstream schools being handled by different public institutions and associations (e.g., France).[63] Closing down one system is thus impractical in the short run. In some developing countries, inclusive education remains a domain of primarily nongovernmental organizations, which inherently limits the number of children with disabilities being served.[64] Patterns of inclusion in educational settings also vary across subgroups of children with disabilities. Data in India show that children with autism and blind girls are the least represented in school of any subgroups.[65] Similarly, although 95 percent of children with disabilities in the US are served in mainstream schools, almost half of children with intellectual disabilities spend less than 40 percent of the school day in regular classes and roughly 19 percent of blind and deaf children—far more than children with other disabilities—are placed in separate education.[66] Moreover, studies indicate that children with disabilities from racial/ethnic minorities in the US are overrepresented in special education settings,[67] raising concerns about the process for identifying disability and placement decisions. The presence of such disparities has long been studied, along with different theories about socioeconomic and political forces as well as the role of genetics and environments in educational settings. However, further research is needed to better understand the reasons for these differences and, importantly, the intersectionalities of certain types of impairments, sociopolitical status, and biases (e.g., sexism, racism, ableism) that may interact with educational environments to produce, or hinder, social and educational achievements. Given the range of impairments children have, their individualized needs for accommodations, and pragmatic limitations (e.g., available resources), evidence-based research is key for assessing the practicality of, and possible steps toward, implementing the right to inclusive education.[68]

Attitudinal and economic barriers are other challenges. Studies indicate that general education teachers often hold negative perspectives about inclusive education[69] and that they lack support, knowledge, and assistance to enable them to teach students with disabilities in what are often already overcrowded classrooms.[70] While the work of NGOs and community-based initiatives may be helpful in providing innovative educational strategies,[71] such an approach is geographically limited and resource-dependent. Also, the implementation of new national training policies is often slow. Part of the challenge is that the right to education is generally subordinated to the principle of progressive realization, which only obligates states to implement their international commitments progressively, to the maximum extent of their available resources.[72] And while the provision of "reasonable accommodation" is part of the CRPD's non-discrimination clause, and thus requires immediate implementation, there are often disagreements about what it entails.[73] These challenges are further compounded in developing countries. The lack of resources and high rates of poverty commonly translate into poorer training for teachers, especially in rural areas, a lack of accommodations, and overall exclusion of children with disabilities;[74] meanwhile, monitoring and accountability are impeded due to the lack of comprehensive data about the education of children with disabilities in these countries.[75]

In addition, legal challenges persist. Although the concept of inclusive education is now enshrined in the CRPD, there is no universally agreed upon definition of it. Some countries (e.g., Sweden) suggest that inclusive education may require the homogenization of the curriculum in mainstream and special education settings, rather than the desegregation of students, to provide adaptations of material and teaching styles to meet the needs of certain children (e.g., children with intellectual disabilities).[76] Other countries (e.g., Malaysia) have established new education policies but retain the integrative, not inclusive, approach.[77] This interpretation gap may have caused confusion and negatively impacted implementation, and as suggested above, pragmatic and evidence-based research is needed to resolve this trap. Another question concerns who is the rights holder. In general, the right to education—as other rights—is an individual right. However, some countries (e.g., the Netherlands, Scotland) have adopted policies that allow parents to choose whether their child will attend inclusive or special education.[78] Although parents are commonly entrusted to make decisions on behalf of their children—indeed, several articles in the CRC also acknowledge parental rights, responsibilities, and duties in this regard[79]—the context of inclusive education is complicated. Parents may prefer educational programs that reflect their aspirations for their child but that are different from the child's own desires.[80] Moreover, if the general education system does not adequately provide services and accommodations (for whatever reason), parental choice can hardly be regarded as such.[81] Whether the CRPD Committee's emphasis in its General Comment No. 4 that the right of education belongs to the child—and therefore, that parental responsibilities in this context must be subordinated to the child's rights—will be respected and enforced is yet to be seen. Finally, some countries have entered reservations to Article 24. The United Kingdom has conditioned its commitment on possible placement of students with disabilities in schools outside of their community, if more appropriate services are available; Mauritius declared its continued practice of a parallel separate education system; and Suriname flatly declared that its education system cannot implement inclusive education for students within their communities.[82] This challenge is further complicated because some countries, such as Germany and Belgium, have not entered formal reservations but, in practice, maintain a strong focus on specialized, separate schools.[83]

Ultimately, inclusive and quality education for children with disabilities hinges on political will, resources, and sociocultural motivation. While the push toward inclusive education is a promising way for inclusion and participation of children (and adults) with disabilities in society, further research is needed to better understand how to ensure that the spirit of Article 24—the goal of achieving the full development of human potential, talents, and creativity—is best implemented.

5 FROM INSTITUTIONALIZATION TO COMMUNITY LIVING

The institutionalization of children (and adults) with disabilities has been—and remains—among the most challenging issues in disability rights. Notwithstanding significant shifts towards deinstitutionalization and community living that have taken root in the past few decades, many children with disabilities still reside in institutions. Indeed, a 2007 study has reported that across thirty European countries, one million children with disabilities live in institutions.[84] Children with intellectual, sensory (e.g., deafness), or behavioral conditions are especially vulnerable to such placements.

The definition of institutionalization varies by country and encompasses a range of institutions—from orphanages and nursing homes to residential school settings. However, such living arrangements generally share key features, in particular: overcrowding; separation from natural caregivers (parents/family relatives); extended, sometime lifelong segregation from the local community; and highly regulated restrictive environments.[85] Studies consistently show the negative, long-lasting effects of institutionalization on children's intellectual, physical, behavioral, and social emotional development,[86] not least because of overcrowding, poor hygiene, extensive inactivity, insufficient staff-to-child ratios, and "unresponsive staff."[87] Institutionalized children with disabilities, especially those with sensory, communicational, and intellectual impairments, are also at a significantly increased risk of experiencing physical, sexual, emotional, and verbal abuse as compared to other children with and without disabilities who live with their families.[88]

Article 19 of the CRPD was drafted in response to these dire consequences of institutionalization. It also aimed to address the underlying issues that have led to many unsuccessful deinstitutionalization programs from the 1960s into the 1980s in North America and other parts of the Global North—that is, the often abrupt release of people with disabilities into communities without providing them nets of support necessary for their genuine inclusion or the tying of support to particular, predetermined living arrangements, which were not always suitable to or desired by the individuals involved.[89] Accordingly, Article 19 explicitly recognizes the equal right—not mere interest or any other lesser entitlement—of all persons with disabilities, including children, to live in the community, with residential choices equal to others. It requires states parties to take "effective and appropriate measures to facilitate full enjoyment by persons with disabilities of this right" and specifies some measures for doing so. These include ensuring that people with disabilities are provided with the equal opportunity to make residential choices (e.g., place of residence, type of living arrangement, with whom they live) and, significantly, that they are provided with a range of residential options, personal assistance, and other community services that are necessary to support living and full inclusion in the community.

As emphasized by the CRPD Committee's General Comment No. 5, Article 19's right to live in the community has deep roots in international human rights law. It is inherent in various rights, including the right to personal development and societal inclusion, the right to liberty of movement and to choose one's residence, and the right to an adequate standard of living.[90] It is also intimately linked to several articles in the CRC, including the right to family, limitations on the separation of children from their parents against their will, family reunification, special protection and assistance, and the prohibition of discrimination, including on the basis of disability.[91] However, the importance of Article 19 of the CRPD cannot be understated, not only because of its direct application for adults and children with disabilities but also because of its notable embodiment of the social model of disability and commitment to upholding the right to inclusion within the community.

Implementing a global policy to deinstitutionalize children with disabilities has been uneven. Some countries (e.g., Norway, Italy, Sweden) have completely eliminated institutionalization and have developed a range of alternative community-based options.[92] Others have drastically diminished placing children in institutional care. Romania closed 70 percent of its institutions for children between 2001 and 2007.[93] The emergence of community-based rehabilitation (CBR) programs has played a key role in this achievement.[94] Developed by the World Health Organization in the 1970s and 1980s as a way to provide medically oriented rehabilitative services to countries lacking resources, CBR programs have undergone significant transformation. In addition to expanding their scope of activities to include, for example, rights-based approaches to services, poverty reduction, and inclusion of people with disabilities within society,[95] they have also aligned their mission with the CRPD's values and the social model of inclusion.[96] In the disability context, CBR programs have had a unique momentum: their trademark of collaboration with multiple governmental, nongovernmental, self-advocates, family, and community stakeholders in the development and evaluation of programs conjoined the new international investment in disability rights. Thus, the number of CBR programs demoting institutionalization and promoting inclusion of children with disabilities in the community has spiked since the CRPD's adoption, encompassing more than ninety countries worldwide.[97]

Nonetheless, work to achieve full implementation of Article 19 is still critically needed, even in countries that have adopted a policy of deinstitutionalization.

In Serbia, for example, children with disabilities have moved out of institutional care at a far lower rate than have those without disabilities (around 37 percent compared to roughly 63 percent between 2000 and 2011).[98] The factors for this vary but include the following: increased poverty rates among families with a child with disabilities; inadequate services, such as education, health care, and community-based options to care for a child with disabilities; and stigma associated with disabilities, including among both foster and biological families.[99] In addition, although there is some data indicating that CBR programs are effective in promoting disability inclusion in communities in developing countries (e.g., in South Africa),[100] there are ongoing challenges in implementing community-based alternatives. These include insufficient training of personnel leading disability CBR programs, which has resulted in tensions about equal participation and a focus on the medical rather than social model of disability; questions about the long-term sustainability of CBR programs once funding from international donors ends; and a great diversity of programs in terms of goals, structures, and activities, which complicates the monitoring and evaluation of program success.[101] Concurrently, the lack of accessibility to CBR programs for children with disabilities, the belief that community alternatives are expensive, and, importantly, the lack of political will continue to hamper the right of children with disabilities to live and be included within the community.[102] Rethinking societal priorities and working to develop consistent and evidence-based frameworks for CBR programs[103] and assistance for families of children with disabilities is urgently needed.

6 Conclusion

Great efforts have been made over the past few decades to uphold the rights of children with disabilities, but further progress is urgently needed. The CRPD is a hallmark framework that promotes inclusivity, community living, and full participation in society, recognizing that impairments alone are not the sine qua non of inabilities. However, challenges in the CRPD's implementation remain, and these challenges affect the everyday experiences of children with disabilities and their transition into adulthood. A children's rights approach to children with disabilities is key for advancing inclusion: its ideology and values of equality and justice are paramount. But data collection and evidence-based research are essential for implementing a disability rights approach, as they make the target population visible and can facilitate initiatives that hold governments responsible for their commitments under international law. Such reliable data, however, are critically lacking, especially in developing, low-income countries, where issues of implementation are already more difficult to pursue.

Inclusive education and deinstutionalization are two key contexts in which the legal regime of the CRPD aimed to translate historical wrongs into actionable rights, requiring significant transformations in practices and attitudes toward children with disabilities. These contexts also put to the test the commitment of states and the international community to making the necessary changes in society and their organizational structures. Existing data are indicative of the extensive violations of rights of children with disabilities worldwide, but comprehensive data about children with disabilities in these (and other) contexts are essential to allow for evaluating emerging programs and for monitoring and accountability. Including children with disabilities in these conversations will be important, as is research with this population to better understand their needs and the challenges involved with this human rights endeavor. These steps will hopefully get us closer to children with disabilities participating fully in society as children and then as adults.

NOTES

1. United Nations Children's Fund (UNICEF), "The State of the World's Children 2013: Children with Disabilities," report (May 2013), https://www.unicef.org/sowc2013/files/SWCR2013_ENG_Lo_res_24_Apr_2013.pdf.
2. UNICEF, "Children and Young People with Disabilities," fact sheet (May 2013), https://www.unicef.org/disabilities/files/Fact_Sheet_Children_and_Young_People_with_Disabilities_-_2013.pdf.
3. World Health Organization and the World Bank, "World Report on Disability" (2011), https://www.who.int/disabilities/world_report/2011/en (2011).
4. Hannah Kuper, Adrienne Monteath-van Dok, Kevin Wing, Lisa Danquah, Jenny Evans, Maria Zuurmond, and Jaqueline Gallinetti, "The Impact of Disability on the Lives of Children; Cross-Sectional Data Including 8,900 Children with Disabilities and 898,834 Children without Disabilities across 30 Countries," *PLoS ONE* 9, no. 9 (September 2014): 1–11.
5. Kuper et al., "Impact of Disability," 1, 3, 6.
6. Sophie Mitra, Aleksandra Posarac, and Brandon Vick, "Disability and Poverty in Developing Countries: A Multidimensional Study," *World Development* 41, no. 1 (January 2013): 1–18; Nora Groce, Eleanor Challenger, Rosangela Berman-Bieler, Amy Farkas, Nurten Yilmaz, Werner Schultink, David Clark, Cindy Kaplan, and Marco Kerac, "Malnutrition and Disability: Unexplored Opportunities for Collaboration," *Paediatrics and International Child Health* 34, no. 4 (March 2014): 308–314.
7. Rachael Reilly, "Disabilities among Refugees and Conflict-Affected Populations," *Forced Migration Review* (2010): 8–10, http://www.fmreview.org/sites/fmr/files/FMRdownloads/en/disability/FMR35/08-10.pdf.
8. Aruna Chandran, Adnan A. Hyder, and Corinne Peek-Asa, "The Global Burden of Unintentional Injuries and an Agenda for Progress," *Epidemiologic Reviews* 32, no. 1 (April 2010): 110–120; Adnan A. Hyder, Collen A. Wunderlich, Prasanthi Puvanachandra, Gopalkrishna Gururaj, and Olive C. Kobusingye, "The Impact of Traumatic Brain Injuries: A Global Perspective," *NeuroRehabilitation* 22, no. 5 (2007): 341–353.
9. Karen M. Devries, Nambusi Kyegombe, Maria Zuurmond, Jenny Parkes, Jennifer C. Child, Eddy J. Walakira, and Dipak Naker, "Violence against Primary School Children with Disabilities in Uganda: A Cross-Sectional Study," *BMC Public Health* 14, no. 1017 (September 2014): 1–9.
10. European Union Agency for Fundamental Rights (FRA), "Violence against Children with Disabilities: Legislation, Policies and Programmes in the EU," http://fra.europa.eu/en/publication/2015/children-disabilities-violence (accessed Sept. 3, 2019).

11. Niall Winters, Laurenz Langer, and Anne Geniets, "Physical, Psychological, Sexual, and Systemic Abuse of Children with Disabilities in East Africa: Mapping the Evidence," *PLoS ONE* 12, no. 9 (2017): e0184541.

12. Lisa Jones, Mark A. Bellis, Sara Wood, Karen Hughes, Ellie McCoy, Lindsay Eckley, Geoff Bates, Christopher Mikton, Tom Shakespeare, and Alana Officer, "Prevalence and Risk of Violence against Children with Disabilities: A Systematic Review and Meta-Analysis of Observational Studies," *Lancet* 380, no. 9845 (2012): 899–907.

13. UNICEF, "State of the World's Children," 11.

14. Gary Bedell, Wendy Coster, Mary Law, Kendra Liljenquist, Ying-Chia Kao, Rachel Teplicky, Dana Anaby, and Mary Alunkal Khetani, "Community Participation, Supports, and Barriers of School-Age Children with and without Disabilities," *Archives of Physical Medicine and Rehabilitation* 94, no. 2 (February 2013): 315–323.

15. Robert J. Palisano, Margo Orlin, Lisa Chiarello, Donna Oeffinger, Marcy Polansky, Jill Maggs, George Gorton, Anita Bagley, Chester Tylkowski, Lawrence Vogel, Mark Abel, and Richard Stevenson, "Determinants of Intensity of Participation in Leisure and Recreational Activities by Youth with Cerebral Palsy," *Archives of Physical Medicine and Rehabilitation* 92, no. 9 (September 2011): 1468–1476.

16. World Health Organization and the World Bank, "World Report on Disability," 207.

17. UNICEF, "Children and Young People with Disabilities," 24.

18. Onora O'Neill, "Children's Rights and Children's Lives," in *Children, Rights and the Law*, ed. Philip Alston, Stephen Parker, and John Seymour (New York: Oxford University Press, 1995), 24–42.

19. Tom D. Campbell, "The Rights of the Minor: As Person, as Child, as Juvenile, as Future Adult," in Alston, Parker, and Seymour, *Children, Rights and the Law*, 1–23.

20. Hanita Kosher, Asher Ben-Arieh, and Yael Hendelsman, "The History of Children's Rights," in *Children's Rights and Social Work* (Cham, CH: Springer International, 2016), 9–18.

21. Kosher et al., "History of Children's Rights," 23.

22. Soo J. Lee, "A Child's Voice vs. A Parent's Control: Resolving a Tension between the Convention on the Rights of the Child and U.S. Law," *Columbia Law Review* 117, no. 3 (2017): 687–727.

23. Maya Sabatello, *Children's Bioethics* (Leiden: Martinus Nijhoff/Brill, 2009).

24. UN Convention on the Rights of the Child (CRC), G.A. Res. 44/25, annex, 44 UN GAOR Supp. (No. 49), UN Doc. A/44/49 (1989; entered into force Sept. 2, 1990), 167.

25. CRC, art. 3, 12.

26. Sonia Harris-Short, "Listening to 'the Other'? The Convention on the Rights of the Child," *Melbourne International Law Journal* 2 (2001): 305.

27. Rangita S. de Alwis, "Mining the Intersections: Advancing the Rights of Women and Children with Disabilities within an Interrelated Web of Human Rights," *Pacific Rim Law and Policy Journal* 18, no. 1 (2009): 293–322.

28. Ursula Kilkelly, "Disability and Children: The Convention on the Rights of the Child," in *Human Rights and Disability*, ed. Gerard Quinn and Theresia Degener (New York: United Nations, 2002).

29. International Disability and Development Consortium, "Costing Equity: The Case for Disability-Responsive Education Financing," report (2016), http://disabilityrightsfund.org/wp-content/uploads/2016/10/iddc-report-short_16-10-17.pdf (accessed Sept. 3, 2019).

30. Chris Chapman, Jennifer Laird, Nicole Ifill, and Angelina KewalRamani, "Trends in High School Dropout and Completion Rates in the U.S.: 1972–2009," National Center for

Educational Statistics report (NCES 2012-006) (October, 2011), https://nces.ed.gov/pub-search/pubsinfo.asp?pubid=2012006.

31. Kilkelly, "Disability and Children," 192.

32. Sabatello, Maya. 2013. "Children with Disabilities: A Critical Appraisal." In *International Journal of Children's Rights*. 21, no. 3: 464–487.

33. Kilkelly, "Disability and Children," 192–193.

34. Optional Protocol to the Convention on the Rights of the Child on a Communications Procedure, U.N. Doc. A/RES/66/138 (2011; entered into force April 14, 2014).

35. Mental Disability Advocacy Center, "Access to Justice for Children with Mental Disabilities: International Standards and Findings from Ten EU Member States" (January 2015), http://www.mdac.org/sites/mdac.info/files/access_to_justice_children_ws2_standards_and_findings_english.pdf.

36. O.O.J. v. Sweden, CRPD Communication No. 28/2015 CRPD/C/18/D/28/2015 (Aug. 18, 2017).

37. Gerison Lansdown, "Children with Disabilities," in *Human Rights and Disability Advocacy*, ed. Maya Sabatello and Marianne Schulze (Philadelphia: University of Pennsylvania Press, 2014), 97–113.

38. Maya Sabatello and Marianne Schulze, "Introduction," in Sabatello and Schulze *Human Rights and Disability Advocacy*, 1–12.

39. Lansdown, "Children with Disabilities," 107.

40. Sabatello, "A Short History of the Disability Rights Movement," in Sabatello and Schulze, *Human Rights and Disability Advocacy*, 13–24, 22–23.

41. Convention on the Rights of Persons with Disabilities (CRPD), G.A. Res. 61/106, UN Doc. A/RES/61/106 (Jan. 24, 2007), art. 2

42. CRPD, art. 3.

43. CRPD, art. 4(3).

44. CRPD, art. 7.

45. Lansdown, "Children with Disabilities," 105.

46. Jennifer Nedelsky, "Re-conceiving Autonomy: Sources, Thoughts and Possibilities," *Yale Journal of Law and Feminism* 1 (1989): 7–36; Tom Cockburn, "Children and the Feminist Ethic of Care," *Childhood* 12, no. 1 (February 1989): 71–89; John O'Manique, *The Origins of Justice: The Evolution of Morality, Human Rights and Law* (Philadelphia: University Pennsylvania Press, 2003).

47. Sabatello, *Children's Bioethics*, 29–33.

48. CRPD, art. 4.

49. CRPD, art. 19.

50. Gauthier de Beco, "The Right to Inclusive Education according to Article 24 of the UN Convention on the Rights of Persons with Disabilities: Background, Requirements and (Remaining) Questions," *Netherlands Quarterly of Human Rights* 32, no. 2 (September 2014): 263–287.

51. Germana D'acquisto and Stefania D'avanzo, "The Role of Shall and Should in Two International Treaties," *Critical Approaches to Discourse Analysis across Disciplines* 3, no. 1 (2009): 36–45.

52. de Beco, "Right to Inclusive Education," 274.

53. Kelley Loper, "Equality and Inclusion in Education for Persons with Disabilities: Article 24 of the Convention on the Rights of Persons with Disabilities and its Implementation in Hong Kong," *Hong Kong Law Journal* 40, no. 2 (November 2010): 419–447.

54. de Beco, "Right to Inclusive Education," 275.

55. UN Department of Economic and Social Affairs: Disability, "Sustainable Development Goals (SDGs) and Disability," https://www.un.org/development/desa/disabilities/about-us/sustainable-development-goals-sdgs-and-disability.html (accessed Sept. 3, 2019); UN Committee on the Rights of Persons with Disabilities, *General Comment No. 4: Article 24: Right to Inclusive Education*, UN Doc. CRPD/C/G/C/4 (2016).

56. Lex Grandia, "Imagine: To Be a Part of This," in Sabatello and Schulze, *Human Rights and Disability Advocacy*, 146–156.

57. Thomas Hehir, Todd Grindal, Brian Freeman, Renee Lamoreau, Yolanda Borquaye, and Samantha Burke, "A Summary of the Evidence on Inclusive Education," Abt Associates Report prepared for Instituto Alana (August 2016), https://alana.org.br/wp-content/uploads/2016/12/A_Summary_of_the_evidence_on_inclusive_education.pdf, 1–34.

58. Nidhi Singal, "Education of Children with Disabilities in India and Pakistan: Critical Analysis of Developments in the Last 15 Years," *Prospects* 46, no. 1 (March 2016): 171–183.

59. Richard Rieser, *Implementing Inclusive Education: A Commonwealth Guide to Implementing Article 24 of the UN Convention on the Rights of Persons with Disabilities*, 2nd ed. (London: Commonwealth Secretariat, 2012).

60. Rieser, *Implementing Inclusive Education*, 175.

61. International Association Autism Europe v. France, Complaint No. 13/2002, Eur. Comm. S.R. (Sept. 29, 2003).

62. Enver Şahin v. Turkey, Application no. 23065/12, Eur. Ct. H.R. (Jan. 30, 2018).

63. Cornelia Schneider and Mary J. Harkins, "Transatlantic Conversations about Inclusive Education: France and Nova Scotia," *Research in Comparative and International Education* 4, no. 3 (2009): 276–288.

64. James Urwick and Julian Elliott, "International Orthodoxy versus National Realities: Inclusive Schooling and the Education of Children with Disabilities in Lesotho," *Comparative Education* 46, no. 2 (2010): 137–150.

65. Rieser, *Implementing Inclusive Education*, 22; Singal, "Education of Children with Disabilities," 177.

66. National Center for Educational Statistics (NCES), "Fast Facts: Students with Disabilities, Inclusion of" (2016), https://nces.ed.gov/fastfacts/display.asp?id=59 .(accessed Sept. 3, 2019).

67. Susan Aud, Mary A. Fox, and Angelina KewlRamani, "Status and Trends in the Education of Racial and Ethnic Groups," NCES report 2010-015 (July 2010), http://nces.ed.gov/pubs2010/2010015.pdf

68. Urwick and Elliott, "International Orthodoxy versus National Realities," 138–141.

69. Anke de Boer, Sip J. Pijl, and Alexander Minnaert, "Regular Primary Schoolteachers' Attitudes towards Inclusive Education: A Review of Literature," *International Journal of Inclusive Education* 15, no. 3 (2011): 331–353.

70. Singal, "Education of Children with Disabilities," 177–178.

71. Rieser, *Implementing Inclusive Education*, 294.

72. See, for example, CRC, art. 4.

73. de Beco, "Right to Inclusive Education," 279.

74. Ann C. Armstrong, Derrick Armstrong, and Ilektra Spandagou, *Inclusive Education: International Policy & Practice* (London: SAGE Publications, 2010).

75. Rieser, *Implementing Inclusive Education*, 19.

76. Dimitris Michailakis and Wendelin Reich, "Dilemmas of Inclusive Education," *European Journal of Disability Research* 3, no. 1 (2009): 24–44.

77. Rieser, *Implementing Inclusive Education*, 111.

78. Henk Blok, Thea T. D. Peetsma, and Ewoud Roede, "Increasing the Involvement of Parents in the Education of Special-Needs Children," *British Journal of Developmental Disabilities* 53, no. 104 (2007): 3–16; Sheila Riddell, "Inclusion and Choice: Mutually Exclusive Principles in Special Education Needs?," in *Special Educational Needs and Inclusive Education: Major Themes in Education*, ed. David R. Mitchell (Abingdon, UK: RoutledgeFalmer), 120–139.

79. CRC, arts. 3, 5, 18.

80. Cammie McGovern, "Looking into the Future for a Child with Autism," *New York Times*, August 31, 2017, https://www.nytimes.com/2017/08/31/well/family/looking-into-the-future-for-a-child-with-autism.html.

81. Riddell, "Inclusion and Choice," 124.

82. Convention on the Rights of Persons with Disabilities. "Ratifications and Reservations." United Nations, *Treaty Series* 2515, p. 3., *entered into force* 3, May 2008.

83. World Health Organization and the World Bank, "World Report on Disability," 210.

84. European Network for Independent Living for JBS International, Inc. (European Network), "Study on Deinstitutionalization of Children and Adults with Disabilities in Europe and Eurasia: Final Report" (December 2013), 1–67, http://bettercarenetwork.org/sites/default/files/Study%20on%20Deinstitutionalization%20of%20Children%20and%20Adults%20with%20Disabilities%20in%20Europe%20and%20Eurasia.pdf.

85. Agnes Kozma, Jim Mansell, and Julie Beadle-Brown, "Outcomes in Different Residential Settings for People with Intellectual Disability: A Systematic Review," *American Journal on Intellectual and Developmental Disabilities* 114, no. 3 (2009): 193–222; Kevin Browne, "The Risk of Harm to Young Children in Institutional Care," report for Save the Children UK (2009), 1–22, http://bettercarenetwork.org/sites/default/files/The%20Risk%20of%20Harm%20to%20Young%20Children%20in%20Institutional%20Care_0.pdf.

86. Robert B. McCall, "Review: The Consequences of Early Institutionalization: Can Institutions Be Improved?—Should They?," *Child and Adolescent Mental Health* 18, no. 4 (2013): 193–201.

87. Browne, "Risk of Harm," 9; European Network, "Study on Deinstitutionalization," 11–12.

88. Patricia M. Sullivan, "Violence Exposure among Children with Disabilities," *Clinical Child and Family Psychology Review* 12, no. 2 (2009): 196–216.

89. World Health Organization: Regional Office of Europe, "The Case for Change: Background Paper for the Conference," EUR/51298/17/5, prepared for the Better Health, Better Lives: Children and Young People with Intellectual Disabilities and Their Families Conference, November 26–27 2010, Bucharest (Sept. 6, 2010); World Health Organization and the World Bank, "World Report on Disability," 148.

90. Universal Declaration of Human Rights G.A. Res. 217 (III) A, UN Doc. A/RES/217(III) (Dec. 10, 1948), art. 29(1); International Covenant on Civil and Political Rights, 999 UNTS 171 (1966; entered into force March 23, 1976), art. 12; International Covenant on Economic, Social and Cultural Rights, 993 UNTS 3 (1966; entered into force Jan. 3, 1976), art. 11.

91. CRC, arts. 2, 9, 10, 16, 18, 20, 23.

92. World Health Organization: Regional Office of Europe, "The Case for Change," 9.

93. World Health Organization and the World Bank, "World Report on Disability," 148.

94. World Health Organization: Regional Office of Europe, "The Case for Change," 8–9

95. World Health Organization and the World Bank, "World Report on Disability," 13.

96. International Disability and Development Consortium (IDDC), "Community Based Rehabilitation and the Convention on the Rights of Persons with Disabilities," (2012), https://www.iddcconsortium.net/sites/default/files/resources-tools/files/brochure_guidance_bat_final.pdf.

97. Sue Sally Hartley Lukersmith, Pim Kuipers, Ros Madden, Gwynnyth Llewellyn, and Tinashe Dune, "Community-Based Rehabilitation (CBR) Monitoring and Evaluation Methods and Tools: A Literature Review," *Disability and Rehabilitation* 35, no. 23 (2013): 1941–1953.

98. UNICEF, "State of the World's Children," 43.

99. European Network, "Study on Deinstitutionalization," 8–10.

100. Sarah Rule, Theresa Lorenzo, and Milani Wolmarans, "Community-Based Rehabilitation: New Challenges," in *Disability and Social Change: A South African Agenda*, ed. Brian Watermeyer and Leslie Swartz (Cape Town, ZA: HSRC Press, 2006), 273–290.

101. Rieser, *Implementing Inclusive Education*, 61; Sally Hartley, Harry Finkenflugel, Pim Kuipers, and Maya Thomas, "Community-Based Rehabilitation: Opportunity and Challenge." *Lancet* 374, no. 9704 (2009): 1803–1804; Lukersmith et al., "Community-Based Rehabilitation," 5.

102. European Network, "Study on Deinstitutionalization," 26, 33, 34.

103. Lukersmith et al., "Community-Based Rehabilitation," 7.

CHAPTER 29

INDEPENDENT CHILDREN

JULIA SLOTH-NIELSEN AND KATRIEN KLEP

1 INTRODUCTION

> "Article 1 of the CRC states: 'For the purposes of the present Convention, a child means every human being below the age of eighteen years, unless under the law applicable to the child, majority is attained earlier.' The provision explains how the child is to be understood *for the purpose of that treaty*. It does not state that every person below 18 years equals a child *as such*. This is nonetheless how the concept of 'children' has been commonly defined, namely all persons below eighteen, leading to an invisibility and even infantalisation of adolescents."[1]

THERE is renewed interest in understanding the lived experiences of children "from below" or as a counter to the top-down approach to children's rights that characterizes much child rights scholarship.[2] This chapter stands in direct contrast to the conception of children as *becomings* and, instead, focuses on several groups of children whose interaction with the adult world per se could be said to render them independent children.

Here we explore the notion of *independent children*, a concept that goes against the grain of prevailing constructions of childhood that underpin legal frameworks across the globe. Furthermore, independent children find themselves in a specific unfavorable relationship to such legal frameworks, which fail to protect them—and, in some instances, even criminalize them.[3]

This chapter focuses on children who find themselves by force, choice, or both in a situation in which they have to fend for themselves without adult caregivers, adopt adult roles, and make many decisions on their own without the involvement of a regular adult caregiver. It also looks at the notion of independent children from a child rights perspective.

"The UNCRC is simultaneously a framework for recognizing the agency and status of individual children and a framework for universalizing a particular image and experience of childhood."[4] This statement reflects a crucial field of tension in the UN Convention on the Rights of the Child (CRC), for we know that what constitutes "children" and "childhood" is deeply embedded in local cultural, social, economic, and legal understandings.

Another field of tension that is relevant for the issue of independent children is the tension between conceptualizing children as rights holders and agents in their own lives as well as objects of adult protection. The Committee on the Rights of the Child's (CRC Committee) General Comment No. 20 on implementation of the rights of the child during adolescence is a case in point:

> The Committee defines evolving capacities as an enabling principle that addresses the process of maturation and learning through which children progressively acquire competencies, understanding and *increasing levels of agency* to take responsibility and exercise their rights.... In seeking to provide an appropriate balance between respect for the evolving capacities of adolescents and *appropriate levels of protection*, consideration should be given to a range of factors affecting decision-making, including the level of risk involved, the potential for exploitation, understanding of adolescent development, recognition that competence and understanding do not necessarily develop equally across all fields at the same pace and recognition of individual experience and capacity (emphasis added).[5]

Moreover, the CRC firmly roots children in a family environment (for example, the preamble and Articles 7(1), 9(3), 20(1))[6] with a crucial role for the parents or adult primary caregivers. In addition, children and adolescents live in highly diverse arrangements across the globe. What constitutes a family is again deeply embedded in local cultural, social, economic, and legal understandings and may take on another form for independent children than for other children.

Also relevant to a discussion of independent children, of course, the CRC addresses the triangular relation between the state, parents, and the child. The CRC "requires a macro-level re-orientation of the relationship between state, family, and child, with a newly established role and set of responsibilities for the state in relation to the construction of childhood and its socio-political organization.... Thus, while articles 5 and 18 recognize the primacy of the role played by families in child rearing, a subsidiary role for states to support them in these endeavors is carved out.... This underlying orientation, [which] views childhood as a matter of public, and not merely private concern."[7]

All of this prompts the question, how can we understand the experiences of children who adopt adult roles and can be considered to be independent children from a child-rights perspective?

As we shall see, from a child rights perspective, the push is generally toward protection. The situations of independent children (children in street situations, unaccompanied migrant minors,[8] child-headed households, married children) are often conceptualized as situations in which protection is warranted, and this is undoubtedly so. However, we should be wary of situating agency and protection as opposites. We need to know more about the social realities on the ground, about the ways independent children understand and cope with their situation day to day. Moreover, we will argue here that the principle of non-discrimination, economic, social, and cultural rights, and the right to be heard in tandem with the right to information are crucial elements for legal frameworks that support independent children in shaping their lives and exercising their rights.

In the first section we explore the notion of independent children by considering how the notions of *independent* and *child* can be interpreted. Next, the theoretical issues pertinent to a children's rights approach to independence are canvassed. Thereafter, a brief consideration of children in street situations, child-headed households, and married children is undertaken. The focus will be on how to look at these groups of children through the lens of children's rights.

2 Definitional and Conceptual Issues

Defining a child is a complex undertaking. Childhood is a diverse, shifting category that is shaped by cultural, social, and economic contexts. But invariably the conception of childhood envisions children first and foremost as part of a family (or at least a kinship circle).[9] In fact, millions of children around the globe live independently of adult caregivers and manage their day-to-day living on their own, often having to make mature decisions under difficult circumstances.[10]

The starting point in defining childhood in general, or "who is a child" in international human rights law, is the CRC definition of a person below the age of eighteen. However, this is just a starting point, as there are many points before that age upon which children are awarded or bestowed capacity: such as the age at which they may open a bank account, perform non-hazardous work, acquire a driver's license or learner's permit, or consent independently to medical treatment, for example. This is indeed in accordance with their evolving capacity, as recognized in Article 5 of the CRC.[11] The idea of children's evolving capacities is intended to promote and recognize children's increasing competence to act independently, and according to Karl Hanson and Laura Lundy, this concept serves as one of the "cross cutting" provisions in the CRC.[12]

Gerison Lansdown identifies three conceptual frameworks underpinning evolving capacity: First, it is a developmental concept, recognizing the extent to which children's development, competence, and emerging personal autonomy are promoted through the realization of the Convention rights. In this sense it imposes obligations on states parties to fulfill these rights. Second, it is a participatory or emancipatory concept emphasizing the rights of children to respect for their capacities and transferring the responsibility for the exercise of rights from adults to the child in accordance with their level of competence. Third, it serves as a protective concept, which acknowledges that because children's capacities are still evolving, they have rights to protection on the part of both parents and the state from participation in, or exposure to, activities likely to cause them harm, though the levels of protection they require will diminish in accordance with their evolving capacities.[13]

Conceptually, at least, the rights enjoyment of independent children can be seen to conflict with this third protective conceptual framework, as independent living may occur without any regular adult support, material or otherwise. However, increasingly, children's agency (even if forced by adverse circumstances) in choosing independent lifestyles is being recognized in children's rights annals, as will be seen in the substantive sections below. The exercise by children of their autonomy through independent living threatens traditional notions of dependence and immaturity usually ascribed to childhood. Further, such children may very well be perceived as representing a deviation from what is considered the norm, and therefore they may be demonized (as often happens with children in street situations), neglected, and overlooked (as in child-headed households) or excluded from services and programs.

The notion of independent children is far from clear-cut. It also raises questions as to what the opposite of independent children is: dependent children or just children? Must *independent* be understood as legally being without parents or caretakers or de facto being without parents or caretakers? Is there a temporal dimension involved? Or does independence point to a certain capacity in making decisions? Children may very well act independently *within* a nuclear family. Children may be profoundly neglected by their parents or may take care of their parents, for example, children of parents who are severely ill or who have psychiatric problems. It is not uncommon that children become like parents to their parents.[14]

Populations of children that may be conceptualized as independent children typically involve street children, unaccompanied migrant children, and orphaned children. Indeed, these children may be without nuclear families, though much research into the social realities of these children show that often times both nuclear and extended family do appear in the lives of these children, as do other caregivers (e.g., peers, social workers, nongovermental organizations (NGOs), schoolteachers). It is important to be aware of the fields of relatedness these children find themselves in and within which they negotiate their position and take daily decisions.[15] Some of these relations may very well be detrimental to the child, but that does not negate the fact that these constitute the reality of the child and determine their space to act.

Independent children need to survive, and therefore they make decisions within their daily reality and shape their daily lives in relation to many other actors, who may or may not be members of their (nuclear) families. It is not only the idealized image of childhood and family that is being challenged here but precisely the notion of the child, however young, that consciously acts to shape the child's daily life and that of those close to him or her.

The traditional orthodoxy of children rights is that children grow up in traditional families,[16] and law is structured accordingly.[17] It is this idealization of childhood that causes laws in many jurisdictions to fail to properly account for independent children.

For the most part, insufficient attention is paid to the complex interplay between vulnerability and maturity in independent adolescents.[18] Many have exercised a choice to leave home—whether due to violence and abuse, economic necessity, a decision to migrate, or to work. That does not mean, however, that they should be regarded as being adult equivalents. Moreover, the factors or root causes that drive children and adolescents to independent living situations should be addressed. The *independent* in *independent children* refers to the social realities of children and young people, which are often not taken into account in legal systems of many jurisdictions.

3 Children in Street Situations

Children in street situations became an object of international concern among donor agencies and international NGOs in the 1980s.[19] For the next decade and a half, the focus was on service provision relating to the direct needs of children in street situations. The numbers of children on the street continued to grow quite markedly, especially in South America, Africa, and South and South East Asia, a consequence of rapid urbanization in these regions. Although the issue of children in street situations is an urban phenomenon, the factors exacerbating the issue have their roots in rural settings.[20] Rural poverty, natural disasters, and violence push children from hinterlands, where economic and other shocks are less likely to be withstood, to the fringes of urban society, where more opportunities exist.

Around the turn of the millennium, the focus of donor communities and aid organizations shifted away from service provision toward social intervention and prevention aimed at halting the entry of children onto the street in the first place.[21] Children in street situations declined in prominence on the child rights agenda.[22]

Still the issue is of significant import; there are varied estimates of around one hundred million children in street situations globally.[23] For a variety of reasons (such as mobility and elusiveness) these numbers cannot be verified in any meaningful way, nor can it be established whether these numbers are in fact growing (as is often alleged)—though this is a likely consequence of the ongoing rapid urbanization in many parts of the world, including in Africa.

An enduring debate about the definition of street children persists in the literature, with researchers attempting to define categories of street children and their varied connectedness with the street (including those living with parents or families in street situations and children working on the street but returning home periodically). Although children in street situations may go without a regular adult caregiver for long stretches of time, this is not a fixed and necessarily final situation. Children negotiate their lives on the street by relating themselves to many actors and places, such as peers, adults connected to the streets, marketers and stall holders, public authorities, NGO workers, and so forth.

The debate about definitions spawned a plethora of city- or ward-level mapping studies that attempt to count the numbers of children concerned, to depict the ways in which their rights are compromised or violated (e.g., access to health, nutrition, exposure to violence and so forth), to explain how they negotiate their daily lives, and to highlight their agency in choosing to escape worse circumstances in their home settings.

Children on the streets are often thought of as a public nuisance, treated poorly, and in some cases even killed for petty crimes. But research indicates that the numbers of crimes or other violations committed by street children are overstated[24] and that their behavior is often characterized as much more deviant and criminal than it actually is. Children in street situations cannot be understood outside the history, social reality, and culture of their countries of origins, nor can the effects of social class be dismissed in how they are received by the society they live in. Reactions to them vary: violence from public and private actors (including police and security personnel), indifference, or, in some cases, assistance and charity.[25] Only recently have researchers begun to pay attention to girls in street situations and their experiences; the vast majority of children in street situations are boys.[26]

Children who depend on the streets for their survival lack full access to their rights. In 2011 the UN Human Rights Council strongly condemned "the violations and abuses of the rights of children living and/or working on the street, including discrimination and stigmatization and lack of access to basic services, including education and basic health care, and all forms of violence, abuse, maltreatment, neglect or negligent treatment experienced by them, such as exploitation, gender-based violence, trafficking, forced begging and hazardous work, forced recruitment by armed forces and armed groups, forced disappearances and extrajudicial killings."[27]

International law on street children has recently been augmented with the release of the CRC Committee's General Comment No. 21 on Children in Street Situations.[28] According to the General Comment, the term "children in street situations" is used to comprise "children who depend on the streets to live and/or work, whether alone, with peers or with family; and...a wider population of children who have formed strong connections with public spaces and for whom the street plays a vital role in their everyday lives and identities. This wider population includes children who periodically, but not always, live and/or work on the streets and children who do not live or work on the streets but who regularly accompany their peers, siblings or family in the streets."[29] It is important to consider, as the General Comment explains, that children in street situations are not a homogenous group.[30] Yet some—maybe most—of such children can be regarded as independent children insofar as they are separated from families and without stable and consistent adult supervision and caregiving.

A child rights approach emphasizes full respect for their autonomy, including supporting them to find alternatives to depending on the streets. It promotes their resilience and capabilities, increasing their agency in decision-making and empowering them as socioeconomic, political, and cultural actors.[31] It abhors heavy-handed tactics (often underpinned by public nuisance laws), such as round ups and arbitrary removal of children from public spaces.[32]

State obligations include taking action to secure the ability of children in street situations to gain access to such basic services as health and education, to access justice (such as remedies for violence meted out against them), to benefit from cultural activities and sport, and to have access to necessary information (such as on health promotion, substance abuse, and reproductive health). States should ensure that their child protection systems provide for specialized services on the street, involving trained social workers with good knowledge of local street connections who can help children reconnect with family—where appropriate and possible—to local community services and to wider society at large.[33] As the preambular paragraph of the General Comment explains, street children do not want to be objects of charity; they want the chance to "change their story." States therefore have an obligation to respect the dignity of children in street situations and to support them in ensuring their rights to life, survival, and development.[34]

The CRC committee underscores the necessity of a holistic approach to children in street situations. It recognizes that "the realities in which children in street situations live do not fit traditional definitions or conceptualizations of childhood"[35] and that children who find themselves in street situations are victims of direct and indirect discrimination. Inequalities based on economic status, race, and gender are among the structural causes of the emergence and exclusion of children in street situations.[36]

The General Comment advocates for the adoption of strategies that address multiple causes, ranging from structural inequalities to family violence. They also need to take into account measures for immediate implementation, such as stopping roundups and the arbitrary removal of children from public spaces, abolishing offenses that criminalize and disproportionately affect children in street situations (such as begging, breach of curfews, loitering, vagrancy, and running away from home), and adopting measures to be implemented progressively, such as comprehensive social protection.[37] The Committee signals that for those children in street situations without primary or proxy caregivers, the state is the de facto caregiver and is obliged, under CRC Article 20, to ensure alternative care to a child temporarily or permanently deprived of his or her family environment. This care should not coerce children to renounce their street connections and/or move into alternative accommodation.[38] Moreover, the Committee observes that the interpretation of CRC Article 27(3) is not limited to measures to assist parents and others responsible for the child, but also extends to assistance—material assistance and support programs—provided *directly to children*. It underlines that this is particularly relevant for children in street situations with nonexistent or abusive family connections.[39]

Although the General Comment has a clear protection-oriented focus, it also emphasizes that care does not necessarily imply taking a child completely off the street and out of its network. The General Comment recognizes the street-connected child's autonomy thus:

> Children in street situations are often distrustful of adult intervention in their lives. Their abusive treatment by adults in society has led them to be unwilling to relinquish their hard-won, albeit limited, autonomy. This approach emphasizes full respect for their autonomy, including supporting them to find alternatives to depending on the streets. It promotes their resilience and capabilities, increasing their agency in

decision-making and empowering them as socioeconomic, political and cultural actors. It builds on their existing strengths and the positive contributions they make to their own survival and development and that of their peers, families and communities. Applying this approach is not only a moral and legal imperative but also the most sustainable approach for identifying and implementing long-term solutions with children in street situations.[40]

The General Comment seems to underscore that initiatives to ensure the fulfillment of the rights of children connected with the streets must take place at the local or municipal level,[41] having first argued that characteristics, incidence, and experiences of street-connected children is a phenomenon that can vary widely within states and even from town to town.[42] This is supported by research: Rebecca Sorber and colleagues report that a "trend by local governments to deter or prevent NGOs and community-based organizations from supporting street-connecting youth is likely to have a detrimental impact on youth given that half of the population in our study reported that their primary source of support was from these agencies."[43] Indeed, their research points to more investment in child protection systems and local government–level investigations of the adverse home circumstances impeding successful reintegration. Given the heterogeneity of the group of street-connected youth in their sample, these researchers advocate for close connections being forged with NGOs (and academics) to pinpoint the best rehabilitation and reintegration strategies.

The image of a child or adolescent living on the street is at odds with the traditional image of the sheltered child as member of a family. The portrayal of street children as deviant and criminal is related to the fact that these children live in public spaces. But recognizing street children as independent children is possibly the most testing for all societies, given the extent to which these children are routinely demonized and feared, given their marginalization and exclusion, the perception that they participate regularly in illegal activities (pickpocketing, theft, prostitution, drug taking and selling), and the difficulties in integrating them into mainstream community life.[44] The tension between respect for children's autonomy and the need for protective measures presents a heightened challenge for this category of independent children.

4   CHILD-HEADED HOUSEHOLDS

The current international law environment pertaining to child-headed households dates to the early years of the millennium, when the impact of HIV/AIDS on families resulted in heightened attention being paid to orphans. Given the reality that HIV/AIDS predominantly impacted sexually active persons between the ages of twenty and forty-five, many of whom were also parents, the pandemic targeted parents and caregivers. There are multiple reasons why children chose to stay in child-headed households after the death of one or both of their parents, including that they did not want to be separated from their siblings, wanted to protect their late parents' property, were afraid of being exploited or ill-treated by their potential caregivers, and because they had promised a dying parent to keep the family together.[45] While child-headed households can emerge from events other than HIV/AIDS (such as parental migration or death from other causes), it is in the context of HIV/AIDS that the term *child-headed households* entered the children's rights lexicon.

The first soft law reference to child-headed households is to be found in the CRC Committee's General Comment No. 3 on HIV/AIDS and the rights of the child.[46] Referring directly to orphans and child-headed households, the Committee underlined the necessity of providing legal, economic, and social protection to affected children to ensure their access to education, inheritance, shelter, and health and social services,[47] protection of their property rights, and the need for adequate identificatory documentation. The CRC Committee noted that orphans are best protected and cared for when efforts are made to enable siblings to remain together and encouraged states to provide "support, financial and otherwise, when necessary, to child-headed households."[48]

In the more recent General Comment No. 20 on the rights of the child during adolescence, the CRC Committee observes that a significant number of adolescents are the primary caregivers of their families, either because they are parents or because their parents have died or disappeared or are absent.[49] It underlines that these caregivers should be provided with basic knowledge of child health and appropriate support to assist them, including material assistance, with regard to nutrition, clothing, and housing. Adolescent caregivers themselves need extra support in education, play, and participation,[50] as their own needs for recreation and leisure can be crowded out by the demands of caring for younger siblings.

At the domestic level, South Africa was first to accord a degree of autonomy to child-headed households. Children in certain child-headed households have been provided with a different legal status from that of other children, as a household headed by a child of at least sixteen years of age can be recognized as a distinct household.[51] The Children's Act 38 of 2005 requires that the state approve the child-headed household following a best-interests determination and identify an adult who is willing to provide some supervision, but it also empowers the children in unique ways, including by requiring that the child head of household sign off on expenditures and by allowing the child head of household to collect social assistance grants directly.[52] The regulations to the Act prescribe in considerable detail the functions and responsibilities of a supervising adult.

Children orphaned by AIDS are constructed as the most vulnerable on the one hand, but on the other hand, the legal recognition of child-headed households focuses on their resilience and strength. Researchers Thembelihle Lobi and Jubilani Kheswa found that the plethora of adult roles that the heads of child-headed households undertake entail caregiving, leadership, conflict management, economic provision, decision-making, and housekeeping.[53] Nevertheless, these roles should not be romanticized, as the same researchers report high levels of depression, susceptibility to intergenerational relationships with a wide gap in age so as to reduce financial stress, neglect, financial insecurity, and a high risk of dropping out of school among the adolescent heads of households.[54]

Research on the ground shows how different discourses play out in the social realities of children. "UNICEF's definition of an orphan as any child whose mother or father has died puts the emphasis on static, biological definitions of kinship and orphan hood where, traditionally, orphans are socially defined.... In efforts to raise their visibility, international NGOs highlight the plight of Africa's AIDS orphans, lifting them out of the family context that—rather than emphasizing their social resilience—creates an orphan identity that is both pathologized and made a site for benevolent humanitarian intervention. While children's rights are often used to appeal for assistance, these constructions of orphans tend to emphasize protectionist aspects of children's rights discourse rather than children's empowerment through rights."[55]

In her research quoted here, Kristen Cheney calls for deepening our understanding of AIDS-affected children's own perceptions of their circumstances, which brings out their agency.[56] Clearly their options may be extremely limited; however, they do act and deal with their situation within their possibilities. Cheney argues that a rights-based approach will work only if "social and economic rights to alleviate poverty and children's capacity to act, legally and socially on their behalf to secure resources for their survival" are emphasized and recognized.[57] In community settings, however, it might be near impossible for such children to exercise their participation rights: in the eyes of communities they may continue to be seen as children and excluded from participation.

The image of child-headed households sits uneasily with the image of the child sheltered in his or her nuclear family. These children may be considered independent children in the sense that they find themselves in a situation where they must make adult decisions and lack care from a regular adult caregiver. From a child-rights perspective, following what the CRC Committee has said on the matter, states have a role in supporting these children.

Do the legal recognition of child-headed households and the support provided empower these children and adolescents and the children they have in their care? The research points rather to extreme adversity they encounter in navigating daily life, such that support for their independence masks the reality of neglect and policy shortcomings. These may be independent children, but their reality is deeply entrenched poverty and exposure to all kinds of risks.

Child-headed households are a way of coping with the root causes of illness, poverty, and violence affecting families. When it comes to state obligations under the CRC, it is clear that children should be protected against the impact of these root causes, by their families, communities, and eventually by the state. What are the alternatives for the state? Take all these adolescents and children into alternative care or support child-headed households? Given the social reality of child-headed households, they should probably be supported in every way possible as the less disadvantageous policy choice. Access to services, social and economic rights, and some form of psychosocial support are particularly critical. On the other hand, states cannot turn away from the root causes of illness, poverty, and violence and should address these root causes as well. Children take up an adult role (being the head of a household), yet they have no adult status and therefore no access to all kinds of rights and services that require majority age, for example, access to housing and to social assistance, where available. The independence of children heading households should prompt some recognition of the autonomy that these youth exercise, while at the same time the state must also acknowledge the constrained choices and lack of alternatives options, in many cases, that these independent children have.

5 MARRIED CHILDREN

It is important to recognize that "child marriage" is a broad term that covers many different legal and social realities, traditions, and rituals. It may involve very young children, especially girls wedded to men many years their senior; it may also involve marriages between adolescent peers.

When thinking about married children in the light of independent children, a few issues must be considered. First of all, the decision to get married. How does the child reach the point of consenting to marriage? We know from research that often there is very little independence in that decision, a decision that may be heavily influenced (if not imposed) by family, community, judges, and others. In the social realities of poverty, marriage may be a way of alleviating the economic pressure on a household. Second, marriage may be a way of gaining adult status. The married child becomes, before the law or in the eyes of the community, an adult who carries specific duties and responsibilities but also privileges and rights. That said, the girl or young woman may very well come to depend entirely on her husband. Third, the impact of early sexual activity and pregnancy on the incidence of child marriage cannot be ignored; child marriage is frequently driven by parents' and communities' desire to limit out-of-marriage pregnancy as well as fear of community opprobrium for out-of-marriage sexual relations, especially concerning girls. Adolescents may very well have extremely little relational and sexual independence.

We argue that a married child could be considered independent in the sense of being legally and/or de facto independent from parents or caregivers. However, the range of options or choices that a child realistically has—in particular cultural contexts and given the social realities of poverty—to either choose marriage or refuse it may be extremely limited: what are her or his realistic options?; can she or he make (informed) choices on education, sexuality, marriage, parenthood, and so on?

Child marriage has ascended to prominence on the international child rights and women's empowerment agenda, as seen by the powerful coalition of members that have coalesced in the advocacy organization Girls not Brides. UNICEF estimates that globally twelve million girls marry each year before they turn eighteen; this is a drop from their previous estimate of fifteen million per year. The number of women alive today who were married as children has also declined from an estimated 720 to 650 million. The proportion of women worldwide aged twenty to twenty-four who were first married or in union before age eighteen has dropped from about 25 percent to 21 percent.[58]

At the African Union level, a four-year campaign to end child marriage was launched in 2014 and then extended into 2018. The African Committee of Experts on the Rights and Welfare of the Child appointed the Special Rapporteur on Child Marriage in 2014 and recently released a joint General Comment on ending child marriage with the African Commission on Human and Peoples' Rights.[59] The General Comment is firmly rooted in the understanding that African regional law completely prohibits marriage of persons below age eighteen (the African Charter on the Rights and Welfare of the Child as well as the Maputo Protocol specify this);[60] nevertheless, paragraph 42 of the General Comment carves out a role for the state in relation to already married children as follows: "States Parties should also provide support to girls and boys already married. Children who have already been affected by child marriages should: (i) be provided with comprehensive social protection and health services, (ii) appraised of their legal rights and options for redress, (iii) assisted to continue with their education, (iv) encouraged to seek advice and assistance for the violation of any other rights, especially in circumstances of domestic violence, and (v) supported in fulfilling their parenting roles in respect of children born of the union."[61]

The negative effects of child marriage on the enjoyment of other rights has been exhaustively documented: early marriage leads to early childbirth, with its attendant health risks to both mother and child; infant mortality among young mothers is higher; premature exit from education is the norm, along with decreased economic and livelihood prospects for the remainder of the soon-to-be adult's life; the risk of violence within marriage is heightened; where girls are married to much older men, they may have limited decision-making capacity in their own lives, and so forth.[62] The payment of dowries and bride prices may increase the vulnerability of women and girls to violence and to other harmful practices. The husband or his family members may engage in acts of physical or psychological violence for failure to fulfill expectations regarding the payment of a dowry or its size.[63]

Legally, a fair degree of ambivalence still prevails with respect to child marriage.[64] In many countries the legal age for marriage remains below age eighteen,[65] often something of a colonial relic dating back to when secondary school education for girls was not the norm, let alone membership of girls within the formal workforce. In places as diverse as New Zealand, South Africa, and Indonesia, the age of marriage for girls is below eighteen. The age of marriage was only raised to eighteen in the Netherlands in late 2015, and the ban extends to marriages concluded abroad before the age of eighteen.[66] In the international law sphere, a contradictory position exists. Child marriage is strictly prohibited under the regional African Charter on the Rights and Welfare of the Child.[67] In contrast, the CRC is silent on the issue, though in its Joint General Comment on Harmful Traditional Practices (with the CEDAW Committee),[68] the CRC Committee allowed marriage at a minimum age of sixteen in exceptional circumstances—the grounds for obtaining permission must be legitimate and strictly defined by law, and the marriage can only be permitted by a court of law upon the full, free, and informed consent of the child or both children.

The lower age of marriage in the General Comment has been criticized as opening the door to thinly disguised exceptions to the age of eighteen.[69] However, it does set the absolute ceiling for minimum ages (in exceptional circumstances) at sixteen, meaning that a lower age under any form of law—statutory, civil, common or customary or religious—will not be justified. Only one year later, however, the CRC Committee stated unequivocally that "the minimum age limit should be 18 years for marriage."[70]

A recent study in Zambia of six sites with a high prevalence of child marriage[71] (including both boys and girls) pointed to the agency of children deciding themselves to found a family as a primary reason for marriage; they report wishing to set up their own household to mark their independence. But the findings further suggested that many of these marriages are now considered to be born of necessity, either an individual or collective need to address adversity, such as to alleviate poverty, to prevent stigma from pregnancy, or to escape intolerable living arrangements.[72] In their study, Gillian Mann, Padraig Quigley, and Rosal Fischer note that many of these marriages are not (as elsewhere) between older men and younger girls, but between peers. Poverty is a key driver. The research revealed that the decision to marry is often influenced by peers who are married (including sisters, brothers, cousins, and friends). Unmarried children may think their married friends are in a better position than they are—enjoying a home, a sense of independence, a caring relationship, and some sense of security.[73] However, the findings also included the fact that many child marriages do not last, with a high proportion of single mothers resulting from breakups. This in turn raises the specter that cyclical poverty, lack of education and employment, and teenage pregnancy will continue into future generations.

The implications of the study's findings are numerous and far-reaching. These include that in the vast majority of cases child marriage is less a cultural practice than a reflection of social and economic inequality; that children's agency needs to be factored into understandings of child marriage; that child marriage is a gendered phenomenon that involves boys as well as girls; that understanding child marriage means understanding what adulthood has to offer children; and that child marriage is a protective strategy employed by parents as well as boys and girls.[74]

Recent ethnographic research in Indonesia[75] unravels the different layers of child marriage by studying international discourse, national laws, local administrative practices, and cultural and social dynamics on the community level.[76] The research analyzes local practices, such as covering the shame of extramarital sexual relations, marriage dispensation, and handling teenage pregnancy through arranged marriage. The researchers conclude,

> "The question is whether law is effective in supporting the government's developmental policy that aims to end child marriage. On the one hand, formal law can create an 'enabling environment' and strengthen those who seek the elimination of child marriage. But, for those who are against a fixed marriage age (whether it is 16 or 18), it will only stimulate underground practices of child marriage.... To protect

women's and children's rights, the government could focus more on supporting laws and policies on gender equality, on education, and on sexual and reproductive health rights. But, in the end, it is unavoidable for the government, to achieve its human rights and development goals, to also deal with cultural and religious concerns on adolescent sexuality."[77]

To conclude, the image of the married child is certainly at odds with the image of childhood that pervades the CRC. One could argue that married children could be considered independent children in the sense that, once they are married, their families and communities and/or the law can no longer consider them as children, but considers them as adults. In the case of married children, then, the notion of independence refers to the fact that they no longer fall under a parent or adult caregiver in the role of parent. On the other hand, their options either in favor of marriage or against it may be limited, or greatly limited, by their economic, social, and cultural realities. It is important to stress that from a child-rights perspective, all married children under the age of eighteen should still be considered as children under the CRC and endowed with all the rights laid down in it. Under the CRC, married boys and girls are equally entitled to (for example) the right to education.

We argue it is crucial that we understand the cultural, social, and economic context of children who become legally or culturally independent through marriage. It is crucial, first, in order to devise strategies for persuading children—and their communities—to resist the practice. It has been widely shown that, in particular, supporting girls' access to secondary and vocational education plays a crucial role in reducing the incidence of child marriage, with access to sexual and reproductive health services being a necessary corollary. Poverty as a root cause for child marriage also should be addressed. Second, we need to understand the social realities of married children to understand their particular needs, including those related to health, education, and work. These children are, under the CRC, equally entitled to and in need of education, health services, and social security (if at all available).

6 FINAL REFLECTIONS

The notion of independent children is not straightforward. It touches on core debates of children's rights. Within the context of the CRC, anyone below the age of eighteen is recognized to have evolving capacities (including the capacity for self-determination) together with a right to appropriate protection. In children's rights literature, *evolving capacities* is often understood as *agency* and explained through insights from developmental psychology. In social reality, the space for children to act and shape their lives and express their agency on a daily basis is not determined only by their evolving capacities but also by the options they have or can negotiate within the social, economic, cultural, and religious realities of their families, communities, and societies. In almost all situations, children are related to others, and these relations also shape their possibilities. Social realities and relations are not linear and progressive, but more like dynamic networks that change over time. This is what truly shapes children's agency.

In the child rights debate, agency is often understood too narrowly because of the focus on evolving capacities in a context that is often shaped by the so-called normal child growing up in a, quote, normal family. Hence, debates abound about consent to medical treatment and participation in health care decisions, about child preferences in situations of divorce or relocation, and about participation in educational systems, debates that often are rooted in rather Western understandings of childhood and children's capacities. For the independent children we have discussed in this chapter, these settings may have little or no relevance. On-the-ground research that looks into the lives of children, why they made the choices they did, and how they navigate their independent lives thereafter is much needed to complement our understanding of children's agency.

We have looked at three groups of children who may be considered independent: children in street situations, child-headed households, and married children. From a child rights perspective, the CRC Committee has underscored a certain level of autonomy of children and adolescents in all these situations. The Committee has also emphasized state obligations to offer specific support to these children and adolescents.

The CRC looks to the relations between the state, family, and community, and the child and in that sense perceives childhood also as a matter of public, and not merely private, concern. These relations operate very differently in each of the three situations. One could argue that especially in the case of married children and to a lesser extent in the case of child-headed households, the family and the community play an important role. In the case of children in street situations, family and community (of origin) may be (temporarily) out of view. From a state perspective, marriage and child-headed households are both private and public matters; however, it is street children for whom the state's role takes on a particularly public (safety) view with its corollary of criminalization and lack of support. The child-rights perspective counters this view by emphasizing the obligations states have toward children in these situations.

In this chapter we have tried to unpack the notion of independent children by looking at it through a child-rights perspective. We have argued that *independence* does indeed refer to a legal or de facto situation of children without parents or adult caregivers, and we have taken a closer look at how these children got to where they are. Mostly, there is little independence in their choices and options, which led us turn to the question of social realities and root causes. Once in this independent situation, children are entitled to both protection and recognition of their independent situation, which should translate to support, especially in terms of social and economic rights. These are state obligations under the CRC. Moreover, states should address the root causes (especially poverty, violence, and discrimination) which, again, engage economic, social, and cultural rights. In this way, in an ideal world, children and adolescents would be less hampered by the root causes, be more empowered through, for example, education and access to health, and thus be in a better position to make informed decisions on how to shape their own realities and those of their families and communities.

However, the crucial question remains: Who are the children most likely to become independent children, whether by marriage as a child or adolescent, as a head of a household without adult caregivers, or as street children? These are most likely the children of those families and communities that bear the brunt of socioeconomic inequalities and ethnic and racial discrimination. A child-rights approach is aware of these power inequalities in societies and how the (use of the) law may maintain or exacerbate them. Moreover, it departs from a child's perspective of social reality. Non-discrimination; social, economic, and cultural rights; and the right to be heard in tandem with the right to information are crucial elements for a legal framework that supports "independent children" in shaping their lives and exercising their rights.

Notes

1. Didier Reynaert, Ellen Desmet, Sara Lembrechts, and Wouter Vanderhole, "Introduction: A Critical Approach to Children's Rights," in *Routledge International Handbook of Children's Rights Studies*, ed. Wouter Vandenhole, Didier Reynaert, Ellen Desmet, and Sara Lembrechts (New York: Routledge, 2015), 1–24; see also Nigel Cantwell, "Are Children's Rights Still Human?," in *The Human Rights of Children: From Visions to Implementation*, ed. Antonella Invernizzi and Jane Williams (Farnham, UK: Ashgate, 2011), 37–59.
2. Reynaert et al., "Introduction: A Critical Approach," 1.
3. Jonathan Todres, "Independent Children and the Legal Construction of Childhood," *Southern California Interdisciplinary Law Journal* 23, no. 2 (2014): 261–304.
4. Stuart C. Aitken and Thomas Herman, "Literature Review on Qualitative Methods and Standards for Engaging and Studying Independent Children in the Developing World," *Innocenti Working Paper* No. 2009-05 (May 2009); Pamela Reynolds, Olga Nieuwenhuys, and Karl Hanson, "Refractions of Children's Rights in Development Practice A View from Anthropology–Introduction," *Childhood* 13, no. 3 (August 2006): 291–302.
5. UN Committee on the Rights of the Child, *General Comment No. 4: Adolescent Health and Development in the Context of the Convention on the Rights of the Child*, CRC/GC/2003/4 (2003), paras. 18 and 20.
6. Cantwell, "Are Children's Rights Still Human?," 48.
7. Julia Sloth-Nielsen, "Modern African Childhoods: Does Law Matter?," in *Law and Childhood Studies*, ed. Michael Freeman (Oxford: Oxford University Press, 2011), 117–132.
8. This chapter addresses married children, child-headed households, and children in street situations. Chapter 32, "Working Toward Recognition of the Rights of Migrant and Refugee Children," addresses the topic of unaccompanied migrant minors.
9. Todres, "Independent Children," 261–304.
10. Todres, "Independent Children," 262.
11. Article 5 of the CRC provides as follows: "States Parties shall respect the responsibilities, rights and duties of parents, or where applicable members of the extended family or community as provided for by local custom, legal guardians and other persons legally responsible for the child to provide, in manner consistent with the evolving capacities of the child, appropriate direction and guidance in the exercise by the child of the rights recognised in the present Convention."
12. Karl Hanson and Laura Lundy, "Does Exactly What It Says on the Tin? A Critical Analysis and Alternative Conceptualisation of the So-Called 'General Principles' of the Convention

on the Rights of the Child," *International Journal of Children's Rights* 25, no. 2 (August 2017): 285–306.

13. Gerison Lansdown, "The Evolving Capacities of the Child," *Innocenti Insight*, 11.

14. See, for example, the definition of a child-headed household in the Republic of South Africa Children's Act, which includes children living in a home where there is still an adult but one who is no longer able to take care of the children.

15. The concept of "field of relatedness" refers to the dynamic interplay of relations with family, peers, institutions, NGOs, and other actors that a child, as an active participant, simultaneously creates, engages in, and is shaped by. Guiseppe Bolotta and Silvia Vignato underline how the children's field of relatedness is informed by such conditions as marginality and poverty. Guiseppe Bolotta and Silvia Vignato, "Introduction: Independent Children and Their Fields of Relatedness," *Antropologia* 4, no. 2 (2017): 7–23.

16. Barbara Woodhouse, "The Family-Supportive Nature of the U.N. Convention on the Rights of the Child," in *The U.N. Convention on the Rights of the Child: An Analysis of Treaty Provisions and Implications of U.S. Ratification*, ed Jonathan Todres, Mark E. Wojcik, and Cris R. Revaz (Leiden: Brill-Nijhoff, 2006). "[T]he CRC is not a charter of children's rights to be free of parental authority and control. It is foremost a charter of children's rights to be free of abuse, neglect, and oppression by the state.... [T]he CRC recognizes parents' central role as guardians of their children's rights."

17. Todres, "Independent Children," 272.

18. Todres, "Independent Children," 294.

19. Neela Dabir, "Street-Connected Children," *Encyclopaedia of Social Work* (September 2014), http://oxfordre.com/socialwork/view/10.1093/acrefore/9780199975839.001.0001/acrefore-9780199975839-e-1044.

20. Dabir, "Street-Connected Children."

21. Habtamu Wandimu Alem and Arindam Laha, "Livelihood of Street Children and the Role of Social Intervention: Insights from Literature Using Meta-Analysis," *Child Development Research* article no. 3582101 (August 2016),http://dx.doi.org/10.1155/2016/3582101.

22. This was in part due to an increased emphasis on strengthening childprotection systems, which ought to diminish focus on specific compartmentalized sectors of vulnerable groups, including children living on the street.

23. Wikipedia, "Street Children," https://en.wikipedia.org/wiki/Street_children#Statistics_and_distribution (accessed Sept. 4, 2019); see also Sarah Thomas de Benítez, "State of the World's Street Children: Research," Consortium for Street Children, Street Children Series 2, https://www.streetchildren.org/wp-content/uploads/2013/02/State_of_the_Worlds_Street_Children_Research_final_PDF_online.pdf (which decisively argues that the numbers lack any research basis).

24. There appears to be ongoing debates about the numbers of street children (which are consistently far fewer than estimated). It seems impossible to achieve any accuracy on numbers inter alia because of the definition problems as to who is living on the street and because of the fluidity and mobility of their situations. According to Neela Dabir, overall, street children constitute a small proportion of the world's children. Dabir, "Street-Connected Children."

25. Dabir, "Street-Connected Children."

26. Thomas de Benítez, "State of the World's Street Children," 13.

27. UN Human Rights Council, "Rights of the Child: A Holistic Approach to the Protection and Promotion of the Rights of Children Working and/or Living on the Street," A/HRC/RES/16/12 (2011).

28. UN Committee on the Rights of the Child (CRC Committee), *General Comment No. 21: On Children in Street Situations*, CRC/C/GC/21 (2017).
29. CRC Committee, *General Comment No. 21*, para. 4.
30. CRC Committee, *General Comment No. 21*, para. 6.
31. CRC Committee, *General Comment No. 21*, para. 12.
32. CRC Committee, *General Comment No. 21*, para. 16.
33. CRC Committee, *General Comment No. 21*, para. 19.
34. CRC Committee, *General Comment No. 21*, para. 32.
35. CRC Committee, *General Comment No. 21*, para. 36.
36. CRC Committee, *General Comment No. 21*, paras. 8 and 14.
37. CRC Committee, *General Comment No. 21*, para. 16.
38. CRC Committee, *General Comment No. 21*, para. 44.
39. CRC Committee, *General Comment No. 21*, para. 49.
40. CRC Committee, *General Comment No. 21*, para. 12.
41. "States should encourage and support local-level, partnership-based, specialized interventions on the basis of a child rights approach, small and flexible, with adequate budgets, often led by civil society organizations with local expertise." CRC Committee, *General Comment No. 21*, para. 20.
42. CRC Committee, *General Comment No. 21*, para. 8.
43. Rebecca Sorber, Susanna Winston, Julius Koech, David Ayuku, Liangyuan Hu, Joseph Hogan, and Paula Braitstein, "Social and Economic Characteristics of Street Youth by Gender and Level of Street Involvement in Eldoret, Kenya," *PLoS ONE* 9, no. 5 (May 2014), https://doi.org/10.1371/journal.pone.0097587.
44. Many children in street situations are addicted to abusive substances.
45. Charlotte Phillips, "Child-Headed Households: A Feasible Way Forward, or an Infringement of Children's Right to Alternative Care?," (2011). https://www.researchgate.net/publication/295920616_Child-headed_households_a_feasible_way_forward_or_an_infringement_of_children's_right_to_alternative_care (accessed Sept. 4, 2019).
46. CRC Committee, *General Comment No. 3: HIV/AIDS and the Rights of the Child*, CRC/GC/2003/3 (2003); see generally Julia Sloth-Nielsen, "Of Newborns and Nubiles: Challenges in Children's Rights in the Era of HIV/Aids," *International Journal on Children's Rights* 13, nos. 1–2 (January 2005): 73–85.
47. CRC Committee, *General Comment No. 3*, para. 31.
48. CRC Committee, *General Comment No. 3*, para. 34.
49. CRC Committee, *General Comment No. 20: On the Implementation of the Rights of the Child during Adolescence*, CRC/C/GC/20 (2016).
50. CRC Committee, *General Comment No. 20*, para. 55.
51. Parliament of South Africa, Children's Act 38 of 2005 (assented to June 8, 2006), § 137 and the accompanying regulations.
52. South African Children's Act 38 of 2005, § 137.
53. Thembelihle Lobi and Jubilani G. Kheswa, "Exploring Challenges of Adolescent Females in Child-headed Households in South Africa," *Journal of Human Ecology* 58, nos. 1–2 (June 2017): 98–107.
54. Lobi and Kheswa, "Exploring Challenges," 98–107.
55. Kristen Cheney, "Malik and His Three Mothers: AIDS Orphans' Survival Strategies and How Children's Rights Translations Hinder Them," in *Reconceptualising Children's Rights in International Development: Living Rights, Social Justice, Translations*, ed. Karl Hanson and Olga Nieuwenhuys (Cambridge: Cambridge University Press, 2012), 152–172.

56. Cheney, "Malik and His Three Mothers," 169–170.

57. Cheney, "Malik and His Three Mothers," 169–170.

58. Girls Not Brides, "Girls Not Brides Welcomes Historic Drop in Global Number of Child Marriages but Warns Complacency Is Not an Option" (March 6, 2018), https://www.girlsnotbrides.org/girls-not-brides-welcomes-historic-drop-in-global-number-of-child-marriages-but-warns-complacency-is-not-an-option/.

59. African Commission on Human and Peoples' Rights (ACHPR) and the African Committee of Experts on the Rights and Welfare of the Child (ACERWC), "Joint General Comment of the African Commission on Human and Peoples' Rights (ACHPR) and the African Committee of Experts on the Rights and Welfare of the Child (ACERWC) on Ending Child Marriage" (2017), https://acerwc.africa/wp-content/uploads/2018/04/ENGLISH_Joint_GC_ACERWC-ACHPR_Ending_Child_Marriage_14_March_2018.pdf.

60. African Union Maputo Protocol (Protocol to the African Charter on Human and People's Rights on the Rights of Women in Africa), art. 6 (2003; entered into force Nov. 25, 2005); African Charter on the Rights and Welfare of the Child, art. 21(1) (1990; entered into force 1999).

61. ACHPR and ACERWC, "Joint General Comment," para. 42.

62. Convention on the Elimination of All Forms of Discrimination against Women Committee (CEDAW Committee) and the UN Committee on the Rights of the Child (CRC Committee), "Joint General Recommendation No. 31 of the Committee on the Elimination of Discrimination against Women/General Comment No. 18 of the Committee on the Rights of the Child on Harmful Practices," CEDAW/C/GC/31-CRC/C/GC/18 (2014), para. 22.

63. CEDAW Committee and CRC Committee, "Joint General Recommendation No. 31 and No. 18," para. 24.

64. According to a 2013 mapping of minimum-age-of-marriage laws by the World Policy Analysis Centre, ninety-three countries legally allow girls to marry before the age of eighteen with parental consent. Girls Not Brides, "Child Marriage and the Law," https://www.girlsnotbrides.org/child-marriage-law/#do-all-countries-have-a-minimum-age-of-marriage (accessed Sept. 4, 2019).

65. CEDAW Committee and the CRC Committee, "Joint General Recommendation No. 31 and No. 18," paras. 42–43.

66. Girls Not Brides, "The Netherlands," https://www.girlsnotbrides.org/child-marriage/the-netherlands (accessed Sept. 4, 2013).

67. African Charter on the Rights and Welfare of the Child, art. 21(2).

68. CEDAW Committee and CRC Committee, "Joint General Recommendation No. 31 and No. 18."

69. PLAN International, "In-Depth Review of Legal and Regulatory Frameworks on Child Marriage in Zimbabwe," (2016) https://www.girlsnotbrides.org/wp-content/uploads/2016/11/PLAN_18_country_report_zimbabwe_final.pdf.

70. CRC Committee, *General Comment No. 20*, para. 40.

71. Gillian Mann, Padraig Quigley, and Rosal Fischer, "Qualitative Study of Child Marriage in Six Districts of Zambia," Child Frontiers report for the Government of the Republic of Zambia (July 2015), https://www.gender.gov.zm/wp-content/uploads/2018/01/Qualitative-Research-Report.pdf. Zambia has one of the highest rates of female child marriage in Africa, with a reported national prevalence of 42 percent.

72. Mann, Quigley, and Fischer, "Qualitative Study," 24; see also CRC Committee, *General Comment No. 20*, para. 19.

73. Mann, Quigley, and Fischer, "Qualitative Study," 32.

74. Mann, Quigley, and Fischer, "Qualitative Study," 4.

75. Indonesia ranks seventh in the global top ten with the highest absolute numbers of child marriage. UNICEF Indonesia reports that, in 2012, roughly 1,349,000 girls married before the age of eighteen. Some 300,000 of them married before turning sixteen. UNICEF Indonesia, "Child Marriage in Indonesia: Progress on Pause," UNICEF Indonesia Research Brief(2016),https://www.girlsnotbrides.org/wp-content/uploads/2016/11/UNICEF-Indonesia-Child-Marriage-Research-Brief-1.pdf.

76. Mies Grijns and Hoko Horii, "Child Marriage in a Village in West Java (Indonesia): Compromises between Legal Obligations and Religious Concerns," *Asian Journal of Law and Society* (March 2018): 1–14.

77. Grijns and Horii, "Child Marriage," 14.

CHAPTER 30

....

TRAFFICKED CHILDREN

....

MIKE DOTTRIDGE

1 INTRODUCTION

CHILDREN have been moved from place to place to be exploited in diverse ways for centuries or even millennia. However, it was only in 2000 that the United Nations (UN) adopted a definition of what constitutes the crime of trafficking of children (and adults).[1] Since then traffickers of children have been convicted in many countries, though the numbers have been tiny in comparison to the estimates of how many children are trafficked. There has also been some progress in identifying how the rights of trafficked children should be protected and promoted. However, the priority for the authorities in most countries where trafficked children have been identified has been to prosecute suspected traffickers rather than to develop methods for protecting and assisting children (or trafficked adults) in line with international standards. Consequently, despite legislative developments at the national level in many countries and prosecutions of traffickers, there is less information about the implementation of other methods to end patterns of child trafficking and little data about protection and assistance methods that have been found effective, let alone the views of the children who were the subject of these methods.[2]

2 WHO ARE TRAFFICKED CHILDREN?

Article 35 of the UN Convention on the Rights of the Child (CRC)[3] requires states parties to "take all appropriate national, bilateral and multilateral measures to prevent the abduction of, the sale of or traffic in children for any purpose or in any form." However, the scope of what activities constitute child trafficking (traffic in children) only became clearer in 2000 when the UN General Assembly adopted the Protocol to Prevent, Suppress and Punish Trafficking in Persons, Especially Women and Children

---

Box 1   Definition of Trafficking in Persons in the UN Trafficking Protocol

For the purposes of this Protocol:

(a) "Trafficking in persons" shall mean the recruitment, transportation, transfer, harbouring or receipt of persons, by means of the threat or use of force or other forms of coercion, of abduction, of fraud, of deception, of the abuse of power or of a position of vulnerability or of the giving or receiving of payments or benefits to achieve the consent of a person having control over another person, for the purpose of exploitation. Exploitation shall include, at a minimum, the exploitation of the prostitution of others or other forms of sexual exploitation, forced labour or services, slavery or practices similar to slavery, servitude or the removal of organs;

(b) The consent of a victim of trafficking in persons to the intended exploitation set forth in subparagraph (a) of this article shall be irrelevant where any of the means set forth in subparagraph (a) have been used;

(c) The recruitment, transportation, transfer, harbouring or receipt of a child for the purpose of exploitation shall be considered "trafficking in persons" even if this does not involve any of the means set forth in subparagraph (a) of this article;

(d) "Child" shall mean any person under eighteen years of age."[4]

(the Trafficking Protocol, also referred to as the "Palermo Protocol"),[5] supplementing the UN Convention against Transnational Organized Crime (adopted at the same time). Its intention was to define a crime (trafficking in persons) in such a way that the authorities in different countries would share a common understanding of the offense and the ways to respond to it and would consequently cooperate more effectively in bringing traffickers to justice.

The crime of child trafficking was defined in the Trafficking Protocol to refer to the recruitment, transport, transfer, harboring or receipt of a child by another person with the intention of exploiting the child in specific ways, including prostitution, forced labor, or taking part of their body (an organ or skin, for example) to use for commercial benefit.[6]

While the crime of trafficking an adult is defined in terms of three elements—an action, an abusive means, and an exploitative purpose—the Trafficking Protocol establishes that, if the victim is a child, it is irrelevant whether abusive means are involved or not. Therefore, when a child is suspected of being trafficked, a prosecutor need only prove that the accused engaged in one of the covered acts for the purpose of exploitation of the child, whether or not abusive means were used.

The most widely publicized way in which trafficked children are exploited is via commercial sex. This used to be known as "child prostitution" and, since the 1990s, has been referred to as the "commercial sexual exploitation of children." This includes all cases in which money or anything of value is exchanged for sex with a child, including when that money is paid or passed onto a third person (known as "exploitation of the prostitution of others"[7]). However, the labor and services of trafficked children are exploited for profit in a range of other sectors as well. The following three examples are not exhaustive, but illustrate the range of experiences of trafficked children.

- A sixteen-year-old girl left Moldova with a man who promised her a job selling fruit plants, but instead she was forced into prostitution in Moscow. She was obliged to live and work in an apartment with some twenty other girls and young women, under close supervision. She was subjected to beatings and witnessed another girl being severely beaten after she tried to escape. She planned her own escape to avoid the traffickers' web of contacts (which reportedly included officials in the railway station from which trains departed toward Moldova). She managed to leave after persuading a male client to give her some money, cutting and dying her hair, and using a different station from the one for Moldova. She did not go to the police and was not identified as a victim of crime in Russia. However, once she arrived back in Moldova, she received assistance there. No one involved in recruiting, transporting, or exploiting her was prosecuted.[8]
- An eight-year-old boy from Nepal was taken to Mumbai (India), where he worked extremely long hours (up to eighteen hours a day) in an embroidery factory for seven months without being paid. His only remuneration took the form of two meals a day and an occasional glass of tea. After six months, he asked for wages and was told that he was bonded to the factory owner by the advance given to his parents, as the broker who recruited him had already been paid his wages for the first two-and-a-half years. He was tortured by his employer for working too slowly (he had salt and chili powder put in his eyes when he fell asleep at work).[9] Again, his trafficker went unpunished.
- A nine-year-old boy was abducted in Tirana (Albania) and taken to Greece, where he was made to beg and steal. He was arrested on three occasions and referred each time to a care center run by the Greek authorities. On the first two occasions, his traffickers collected him and put him back to work. On the third occasion they did not come for him, and he opted to remain in residential accommodation in Greece, fearful of what might happen to him if he returned to Albania. The traffickers were not investigated for the way they treated him.[10]

Beyond these examples, girls are also trafficked for the purpose of marriage; for example, girls are recruited in Cambodia, Myanmar, and Vietnam, taken to China, and married without any opportunity to object.[11] Some children are forced to beg and to hand some or all their takings to their "beggar master." Other children are forced to work, including taking part in criminal activities or supporting a military unit.

It is sometimes difficult to distinguish between children who have agreed to a particular form of employment and those engaged in forced work who may be regarded as trafficked. Most forced labor cases can be distinguished from more routine child labor by the nature of the coercion used to stop a child from leaving his or her job or employer. However, the extreme dependency of younger children (below the age of puberty) means that the degree of coercion required to make such children accompany a trafficker or do what they are told is generally less than the coercion required to control adults or older children. All of this can make it difficult to identify child trafficking victims, particularly labor trafficking victims.

3 Numbers of Children Who Are Trafficked

In 2007 a senior UNICEF official noted, "Even after a decade of intensive and growing global attention to trafficking, the real nature and extent of child trafficking is still unknown. There is no real way to compare the magnitude or frequency of child trafficking relative to other child protection concerns."[12] A decade later, the situation has not changed significantly. It is still not possible to estimate accurately the total numbers of trafficking victims or to determine whether prevalence has increased or decreased. The International Labour Organization (ILO) has published estimates of the number of children subjected to forced labor[13] and the number in the so-called worst forms of child labor who are thought to have been trafficked,[14] but its methods of data collection have varied over the years, as has the ILO's own criteria for considering which particular children have been trafficked. A nongovernmental organization (NGO), the Australia-based Walk Free Foundation, has also estimated how many adults and children are in—what it calls—"modern slavery" (suggesting 40.3 million in 2018, which includes 15.4 million adults and children in forced marriages) but has not disaggregated its estimates to indicate how many of these are children who have been trafficked.[15]

As far as the children identified at a national level by law enforcement or other government officials as trafficking victims, the UN Office on Drugs and Crime (UNODC) collects statistics on trafficked children and adults from governments and commented that, in 2014, "children comprised 28 per cent of detected victims"[16] (20 percent of the total were girls; 8 percent, boys). The total number of victims detected in 2014 was reported by the UNODC to be 17,752, implying that just under five thousand trafficked children were identified in that year, a tiny percentage of the total estimated by the ILO to be involved in forced labor. UN officials, along with law enforcement agencies in the United States and Europe, have argued that the numbers of prosecutions and convictions of traffickers are not proportionate to the number of adult and children being trafficked. This is probably true as far as trafficking cases are concerned, even though accurate estimates of the number of children involved remain elusive. The UNODC reported that approximately sixty-eight hundred traffickers were convicted in the years 2012 to 2014, noting that the response of criminal justice systems to trafficking offenses appeared "to be stagnating at a low level."[17]

4 The International Law Framework

4.1 The Three "Ps"

In addition to defining an offense, the Trafficking Protocol also creates a framework and corresponding state obligations to address human trafficking in a more comprehensive manner than in the past. It requires states parties to criminalize and prosecute trafficking of adults and children, protect and assist victims, and take steps to prevent human trafficking. Soon after the Trafficking Protocol was adopted, scholars and practitioners started describing its provisions in terms of the "three Ps," referring to prevention, protection, and prosecution.[18]

To prevent human trafficking, the Trafficking Protocol requires states to exchange information and train law enforcement and other relevant officials (Article 10) and to strengthen border controls (Article 11) and the "integrity and security" of travel/ identity documents (Articles 12 and 13). At the national level, it requires states to take somewhat vaguely worded measures, such as "research, information and mass media campaigns and social and economic initiatives" (Article 9.2). It also requires them to take action "to discourage the demand that fosters all forms of exploitation of persons, especially women and children, that leads to trafficking" (Article 9.5). This was a novel use of the term *demand* in the context of an international agreement to stop crime and was pushed in particular by delegates at drafting sessions who considered that the demand for commercial sex was a major causal factor responsible for human trafficking.[19]

Three articles of the Trafficking Protocol concern the protection of individuals who have been trafficked (Articles 6–8). Two of these concern the status of individuals trafficked from one country to another, suggesting that foreign victims with no right to be in a country may be allowed to remain there temporarily (Article 7) and that states should facilitate the repatriation of victims (Article 8). One article focuses on types of assistance that should be provided to victims, but the language in its provisions is not mandatory; states parties are instead invited "to consider" implementing measures to provide for the physical, psychological, and social recovery of victims of trafficking (Article 6.3). However, the CRC already made it mandatory for states to provide protection and assistance to trafficked children and other children who have been exploited (Article 39). Both the process for protecting trafficked children and some specific methods for preventing trafficking are addressed below.

On prosecution, the Trafficking Protocol not only provides a definition of "trafficking in persons," but it also requires states to criminalize and prosecute acts of trafficking (Article 5).

4.2 Related Treaties and Terminology

Although the Trafficking Protocol was the first international agreement to define the crime of trafficking in persons, a series of previous international treaties (both human rights law and labor law) had focused on and defined forms of exploitation that are covered in the Trafficking Protocol. Further, while discussions were occurring in Vienna about the provisions of the Trafficking Protocol, a new ILO Convention on the Worst Forms of Child Labour (ILO Convention No. 182) was adopted in 1999,[20] and two optional protocols to the CRC on specific forms of exploitation were agreed upon in 2000. There is some overlap between the Trafficking Protocol, the ILO Convention

No. 182, and the two optional protocols to the CRC, particularly the Optional Protocol to the CRC on the Sale of Children, Child Prostitution and Child Pornography.

Although the Trafficking Protocol is the first international instrument to define "trafficking in persons," trafficking, including child trafficking, was the subject of numerous international instruments adopted in the first half of the twentieth century, all of which focused on prostitution and were aimed either at stopping women from one country being recruited to earn money from sexual activities in another or, in the last in the series, the UN Convention for the Suppression of the Traffic in Persons and of the Exploitation of the Prostitution of Others (1949), to make it an offense to profit from the prostitution of another person in any way (i.e., whether they were women or men or girls or boys).

However, by the 1980s "trafficking in persons" was being interpreted to refer to other types of exploitation in addition to prostitution. Thus, the CRC requires states parties to "take all appropriate national, bilateral and multilateral measures to prevent ... traffic in children for any purpose or in any form" (Article 35; emphasis added) in addition to committing states parties in Article 34 "to protect the child from all forms of sexual exploitation and sexual abuse" and to take measures to prevent "the exploitative use of children in prostitution or other unlawful sexual practices" and "in pornographic performances and materials." The CRC also stipulates states' responsibilities when a child is found to have been exploited, abused, neglected, or tortured, requiring them to "take all appropriate measures to promote physical and psychological recovery and social reintegration of a child victim" and specifying that this should be in "an environment which fosters the health, self-respect and dignity of the child" (Article 39). A few years later, the Organization of American States adopted the Inter-American Convention on International Traffic in Minors (1994), specifying that "'International traffic in minors' signifies the actual or attempted abduction, removal or retention of a minor for unlawful purposes or by unlawful means."[21]

Although the Trafficking Protocol's definition of trafficking in persons lists a number of forms of exploitation covered by the definition, it does not define these other terms, resulting in law enforcement officials at the national level often being unsure of their meaning or scope. For example, *sexual exploitation* was not defined in international law at the time the Trafficking Protocol was adopted. In 2003, the UN secretary-general issued a bulletin saying the term refers to "Any actual or attempted abuse of a position of vulnerability, differential power, or trust, for sexual purposes, including, but not limited to, profiting monetarily, socially or politically from the sexual exploitation of another."[22] Subsequently, the Council of Europe Convention on the Protection of Children against Sexual Exploitation and Sexual Abuse, adopted in 2007, provides additional parameters on the term.[23]

Some of the terms used in the definition had been defined in previous international conventions. The term *slavery* is defined by the Slavery Convention (1926) as "the status or condition of a person over whom any or all of the powers attaching to the right of ownership are exercised." Four "practices similar to slavery" are defined by the UN Supplementary Convention on the Abolition of Slavery, the Slave Trade, and Institutions and Practices Similar to Slavery (1956).[24] One of the four explicitly concerns children: "Any institution or practice whereby a child or young person under the age of 18 years is delivered by either or both of his natural parents or by his guardian to another person, whether for reward or not, with a view to the exploitation of the child or young person or of his labour" (UN Supplementary Convention, Article 1(d)). This practice was subsequently labeled by the UN as the "sale of children." However, children are also subjected to the other three practices mentioned by the supplementary convention: debt bondage, serfdom, and the sale of wives. The last practice in particular involves substantial numbers of girls.

The term *forced labor* is defined by the ILO's Forced Labour Convention (Convention No. 29 (1930)) as "all work or service which is exacted from any person under the menace of any penalty and for which the said person has not offered himself voluntarily."

The transfer of the organs (or body parts) of a child for profit is addressed by the Optional Protocol to the Convention on the Rights of the Child on the Sale of Children, Child Prostitution and Child Pornography (which specifies that it should be made a crime), while the Trafficking Protocol focuses specifically on the trafficking of adults or children (i.e., their recruitment, transportation, transfer, harboring, or receipt) for the *removal* of organs.

ILO Convention No. 182 mentions "sale and trafficking of children" in its list of worst forms of child labor that should be immediately prohibited and eliminated but without defining either term. The first of the two CRC optional protocols (adopted in May 2000), the Sale of Children Protocol,[25] contains provisions overlapping with those of the Trafficking Protocol but only refers to trafficking in its preamble. Its focus is on stopping children from being subjected to sexual exploitation, notably prostitution, though it also refers to children subjected to forced labor. Like the Trafficking Protocol, it follows the 3 P's framework of prosecution, protection, and prevention, with stronger obligations on the prosecution prong.[26] However, while many countries have adopted legislation to prohibit trafficking, fewer have adopted laws making the sale of children an offense.[27]

The second Optional Protocol to the CRC (on the involvement of children in armed conflicts) was adopted at the same time as the Sale of Children Protocol.[28] Among other requirements, this optional protocol condemns the recruitment, training, and use of children in hostilities by armed groups distinct from the armed forces of a state, asserting that such armed groups should not recruit children under eighteen or use them in hostilities (Article 4). This has resulted in the authorities in some countries, notably the US, interpreting cases of recruitment that transgressed these standards to constitute child trafficking.[29]

Most regional conventions adopted since 2000 have copied the Trafficking Protocol's definition of trafficking in persons, notably the Council of Europe's Convention on Action against Trafficking in Human Beings (2005) and the Association of South East Asian Nations Convention against Trafficking in Persons, especially Women and Children (2015). The exception is the South Asian Association for Regional Cooperation (SAARC) Convention on Preventing and Combatting Trafficking in Persons for Prostitution (2002), which is concerned exclusively with trafficking in persons for the purpose of prostitution. The Council of Europe has also adopted the Convention on the Protection of Children against Sexual Exploitation and Sexual Abuse (2007), which refers to trafficking in children in its preamble but does not elaborate further on what constitutes the crime of trafficking.

5 Different Interpretations of What Constitutes Child Trafficking

5.1 Varying Interpretations of Key Terminology

Terms associated with child trafficking are open to interpretation in multiple ways, so there has been some disagreement among international organizations, governments, and academics about precisely which children should be categorized as trafficked. This section reviews some of the reasons behind the disagreements.

In the first decade after the Trafficking Protocol, several UN agencies assumed that the crime of trafficking required an element of movement. For example, in 2008 the ILO issued a resource kit asserting that "[c]hild trafficking involves movement,"[30] and the following year a UNICEF handbook suggested that "The sale of a child can take place without physical movement of the child, while the concept of child trafficking always involves an element of movement. *Moving a person* out of his or her social environment is a key element of the trafficking concept, as it enhances the vulnerability of the trafficked person" (emphasis added).[31] However, this interpretation was apparently criticized by some governments[32] on the grounds that the Trafficking Protocol definition implies that "recruiting" a child for the purpose of exploitation (whether sexual exploitation or forced labor) while still living at home also constituted an act of trafficking.

When enacting legislation against trafficking, some countries, such as the United Kingdom,[33] chose to distinguish between cases of sexual exploitation in which the child concerned continued to reside with her or his family, which were regarded as criminal acts but not as trafficking, and cases in which the child's recruitment involved a move to a different place, which were categorized as trafficking offenses. Other countries, such as the United States, do not require movement to establish the crime of human trafficking.[34]

The nature of forced labor and the distinction between cases of forced labor and other worst forms of child labor have also been contentious. For example, around the world, millions of girls work away from home as live-in domestic servants (adolescents and also younger children). Many work long hours, and some are mistreated by their employers.[35] When is it appropriate (and in the interest of the children concerned) to categorize the people who recruit them as criminals and traffickers rather than as brokers providing a potentially useful service to adolescents in search of work?

A further difference affecting the way cases are categorized depends on whether a third party—the trafficker or exploiter—is involved: relatively few countries categorize cases in which a child agrees to have sex in return for a financial or other material benefit, without the involvement of a pimp or other third party, as trafficking.

In 2016 the Interagency Working Group on Sexual Exploitation of Children lamented that the "absence of consensus at international level on several terms ... has had an impact on global efforts at data collection and identification of different modalities of sexual exploitation and sexual abuse of children."[36] The Interagency Working Group published a set of "Terminology Guidelines for the Protection of Children from Sexual Exploitation and Sexual Abuse."[37] Alongside its aim of standardizing the use of terms, it also set out to discourage the use of terms that disparaged or stigmatized children or in any way suggested that their exploitation was not abusive.

Some of the terms referring to purposes of exploitation have been interpreted to refer to criminal practices considered relevant in particular countries. For example, "the removal of organs" has been interpreted in Southern Africa to refer to taking a body part for a ritual purpose.[38]

The extent to which particular terms, such as child trafficking, have been engraved on the public's imagination since 2000 has been affected to a great extent by the relationships and competition among UN agencies, each of which has a stake in a particular term referring to the exploitation of children and in promoting a particular response by the government ministry with which the UN agency habitually works. It also has been affected by the attitude of certain governments and their promotion of particular terms. The UN's crime prevention agency, UNODC, acts as secretariat of the UN Trafficking Protocol and has promoted the term "trafficking in persons." It has been supported in this by successive US administrations, since the US adopted its own anti-trafficking law shortly before the UN adopted the Trafficking Protocol. The ILO has concentrated on "forced labor" and "child labor." It is only in the UN Human Rights Council that the term "sale of children" has been promoted, mainly as a result of the establishment of a Special Rapporteur on the Sale of Children, Child Prostitution and Child Pornography in 1990, a decade before the Optional Protocol was adopted.

5.2 Inappropriate or Imprecise Labeling of Cases as Child Trafficking

The term *child trafficking* continues to be applied to various situations that do not constitute trafficking as defined by the Trafficking Protocol. In some instances this is because a definition adopted in national law is inconsistent with the one in the Trafficking Protocol. More commonly, however, it is because of misunderstandings of the term or because someone uses it for emotive effect. Examples of imprecise use include the following:

- *Illicit adoption.* Illicit adoption can cover, broadly speaking, two types of situations. First, when an adopted child is intended to be exploited, for example, to work as a servant in the adoptive household and adoption is used as a vehicle to exploit the child, such cases typically will meet the definition of trafficking. Second, if the adopted child is treated in the same way as other adopted children, but the adoption process did not conform to law, such illicit adoptions—while problematic in other ways—would not constitute trafficking.

- *Independent child migration.* Millions of children around the world opt to leave home to earn a living, many before reaching the minimum age for entry into full-time employment and some before reaching the minimum age for leaving school. Migrant children, like adults, frequently require the services of brokers—some of those who find jobs for them have been denounced as traffickers. However, the term is only accurate if the brokers intend the child to be subjected to one of the forms of exploitation listed in the Trafficking Protocol. In the first decade of the twenty-first century, there was a move to define people in West Africa who provided assistance to the region's vast numbers of child migrants as traffickers. However, a group of intergovernmental and nongovernmental organizations worked together to explain the difference, distinguishing migrants from children who genuinely were trafficked and focusing attention in 2010 on the rights of independent child migrants.[39] In other words, while some children who migrate can end up trafficked, the mere act of migrating does not equate to trafficking.

- *Foster children.* In various parts of the world, such as the Republic of Benin in West Africa and Bolivia in Latin America, the parents of children born in villages routinely "place" them with richer relatives or acquaintances in towns, with the expectation that they will get a better education and encounter better opportunities than if they stay at home but aware that the children will help with household chores. This practice is easily abused and can become an onerous form of exploitation in which children work fourteen hours a day without attending school. In Benin, some cases involving *vidomegon* (fostered children also acting as domestic workers) are labeled as forced labor and trafficking, while others are not.[40] Although some of these situations can meet the definition of trafficking, many are not carried out for the purpose of exploitation of the child and thus, while violating other rights of the child, would not constitute trafficking.

5.3 Interpretations by Particular States of What Needs to Be Done to Combat Trafficking

Despite the broad scope of the definition of trafficking in the Trafficking Protocol, various states have opted to focus only on some types of exploitation in practice. In South Asia, for example, the authorities in Bangladesh, India, and other countries use trafficking to refer almost exclusively to cases involving commercial sexual exploitation, while trafficking of boys into forced labor in factories, for example, tends to be regarded as a much less serious offense (of employing child labor). In West Africa, the term trafficking is used to refer to a few selected sectors of the economy, such as the fishing industry, cocoa cultivation, and (in some countries only) the employment of child domestic workers, but the situation of children working in similar circumstances in other sectors (such as agriculture or mining) has not been addressed, and cases of girls trafficked into commercial sexual exploitation have been overlooked in some places. In most cases, the sectors concerned are those where cases of exploitation have received publicity outside West Africa.

For example, the Republic of Benin—which experienced a child trafficking scandal in 2001 when children were detected on a ship transporting them to Gabon—adopted a law in 2006 that prohibited anyone under eighteen from moving away from home without an official permit, ostensibly to stop them from being trafficked. Benin's Ministry of Family and Children, in a national study published in 2007, estimated that over forty thousand children were "victims of trafficking" in the country and that each year almost fifteen thousand were trafficked.[41] However, the criteria used for assessing which children had been trafficked were imprecise (any child working away from home was regarded as trafficked). The study itself noted that only 2,066 children out of 40,000 had been "moved by a broker."[42] The other 37,934 children had migrated to find work but were categorized as exploited because they were working away from home rather than on the basis of any evidence that they were being forced to work. Although some children who initially chose to migrate can end up trafficked, this study did not appear to assess individual cases. During the preparation of the 2006 law and the 2007 national study, working children were not given an opportunity to voice their views on which forms of recruitment or employment they found abusive, nor on the circumstances in which they had actually benefited from working away from home.

The country whose anti-trafficking laws have had the greatest impact on other countries is the United States. In 2001, the US government started publishing an annual report—the Trafficking in Persons Report—that assesses measures taken by other countries to prevent trafficking, prosecute traffickers, and protect victims (it now includes an evaluation of the United States, though its early editions did not).[43] The attention given to the topic of trafficking in persons by successive US administrations, through this annual report and related activities, has helped spur action, and most countries now have laws punishing human trafficking. However, the provisions of laws punishing trafficking offenses vary widely, reflecting the different meanings attributed to the term, with some regarding it as an umbrella term to refer to illegal forms of exploitation while others define it more narrowly as the process for recruiting, transporting, and harboring people for the purpose of exploiting them.

6 TRAFFICKED CHILDREN'S RIGHTS TO PROTECTION AND ASSISTANCE

Protecting and assisting trafficked children is challenging in practice, as many trafficked children are not identified while being exploited or subsequently. Identification might be by officials in government agencies, such as those responsible for child protection, but also by civil society activists. Consequently, establishing effective mechanisms to identify children who have been trafficked is a vital first step toward protecting them. Some countries in Europe have tried to achieve this by establishing what is called the National Referral Mechanism (NRM). While the name suggests this framework is concerned principally with the referral of trafficking victims to relevant services, in practice NRMs are also responsible for formally confirming whether, in the eyes of the authorities, particular individuals have been trafficked (in part to determine whether they will be authorized to remain in the country concerned and also if a government agency will pay for the costs of assistance). This has made the process of identification contentious, linked, as it often is, to immigration control rather than to child protection. Some NRMs have developed a specific set of procedures for identifying and referring trafficked children,[44] while in other countries the NRM is only responsible for the cases of adult trafficking victims, and the protection of child victims is left largely to the institutions responsible for child protection. Some NRMs specify what should be done proactively to find and identify trafficking victims. However, their ability to do so depends on there being specialized law enforcement bodies and others aware of how to distinguish trafficked children from others, and these organizations require adequate resources if they are to perform their role.

As both trafficked children and adults typically evidence signs of trauma and other harms when first removed from the control of criminals, and may be unsure whom they can trust, some countries guarantee everyone provisionally identified as a trafficking victim (adults and children) a "reflection period," during which they receive assistance and may remain in the country (if a foreign national with no legal right of residence) before they are asked to give evidence to law enforcement officials about the individuals who trafficked or exploited them. The Council of Europe Convention on Action against Trafficking in Human Beings requires states parties to give at least a thirty-day reflection period "when there are reasonable grounds to believe that the person concerned is a victim" (Article 13). In theory this means that anyone who may have been trafficked is provided with immediate assistance, without feeling that this is conditional on their providing evidence against their traffickers (a process that could re-traumatize).

Statutory agencies and courts routinely make decisions that affect children who are identified as trafficking victims. The CRC specifies that in such cases the best interests of the child are to be a primary consideration in all actions concerning children (Article 3) and that such children have a right to express their views freely in all matters affecting them and to have their views taken into consideration in accordance with their age, maturity, and understanding of the options available (Article 12).[45] Nevertheless, trafficked children who have been in contact with law enforcement or other officials have routinely reported that little or no attention was paid to their views.[46] Children who have had the experience of being trafficked have also routinely been ignored by policymakers preparing new legislation on human trafficking or on protection procedures. Indeed, the only country known to have organized an official consultation with such children about the terms of a proposed new policy is the Philippines, where girls who had been trafficked for sexual purposes were consulted at the time that the country was preparing a set of guidelines on measures to protect trafficked children (adopted in 2008).[47]

Although not legally binding, a set of UNICEF guidelines specify in detail what steps should be taken to identify, protect, and assist children who have been trafficked as well as how decisions on those identified outside their country of origin should be taken and what steps should be taken to ensure the full recovery of any trafficked child.[48] The guidelines were initially drafted in 2003 for Southeastern Europe, where, in the aftermath of armed conflicts in Bosnia and Herzegovina and in Kosovo, international peacekeeping forces had been deployed and patterns of trafficking in girls and young women were reported on a large scale. In 2006 UNICEF reviewed the guidelines and issued them as "Technical notes" for worldwide use.[49] The guidelines summarize the child rights principles that govern the protection of children who have been trafficked and go into detail on nine steps to protect and assist such children. The nine steps are:

1. identification of children as victims of trafficking;
2. appointment of a guardian for each trafficked child;
3. registration and documentation (including interviews by law enforcement officials);
4. regularization of a child's immigration status in a country other than their own;
5. interim care and protection;
6. individual case assessment and identification of what is called a "durable solution";
7. implementation of a durable solution, including possible return to a child's country of origin;
8. access for children to justice (including protection of children during legal proceedings);
9. managing the cost of proceedings, financial assistance, reparation, and compensation.

Finally, the guidelines also emphasize the importance of research and data collection, outlining a set of ethical principles for researchers to apply when collecting information about child trafficking.

6.1 Protection and the Non-Punishment Principle

The Trafficking Protocol is silent on whether trafficking victims (adult or children) may be prosecuted for offenses committed in the course of being trafficked, such as immigration offenses (entering or staying in a country without authorization) or criminal offenses (such as prostitution or theft). The UN High Commissioner for Human Rights noticed this shortcoming and in 2002 recommended that, in principle, "Trafficked persons shall not be detained, charged or prosecuted for the illegality of their entry into or residence in countries of transit and destination, or for their involvement in unlawful activities to the extent that such involvement is a direct consequence of their situation as trafficked persons."[50]

The reaction to this in criminal justice systems has been slow and inconsistent, with a gradual increase in the jurisdictions wherein the principle of not treating trafficking victims as criminals is respected. For example, since early in the twenty-first century, Vietnamese adolescents and young adults have been brought illicitly to the United Kingdom to act as cannabis gardeners in empty houses where the windows are covered over (so the cultivation of plants inside under artificial light is not visible to passersby).[51] The gardeners reportedly remain inside for long periods, being brought food so that they rarely leave the premises and have no contact with surrounding British society. When the police raided such houses in the past, the gardeners (children as well as adults) were arrested and prosecuted for drug offenses (cultivation or possession of cannabis is illegal in the UK). For example, in 2010 a fourteen-year-old boy was arrested and placed in local authority residential care. He walked out to rejoin other Vietnamese but was rearrested four months later at another cannabis farm in the company of three adults. On this occasion, he was convicted and placed under a three-year supervision order.[52] It was not until 2013 that the Court of Appeal for England and Wales overturned such convictions. The chief justice observed that, "Whether trafficked from home or overseas, they are all victims of crime. That is how they must be treated and, in the vast majority of cases they are: but not always."[53] Commenting on the principles involved, the Court noted that, "The criminality, or putting it another way, the culpability, of any victim of trafficking may be significantly diminished, and in some cases effectively extinguished, not merely because of age (always a relevant factor in the case of a child defendant) but because no realistic alternative was available to the exploited victim but to comply with the dominant force of another individual, or group of individuals."[54]

6.2 Access to Justice and Remedies via Courts

International standards require states to provide anyone who claims to be a victim of a human rights or a humanitarian law violation with equal and effective access to justice, irrespective of who may ultimately be the bearer of responsibility for the violation.[55] Although the intention of much funding of anti-trafficking efforts by governments has been to strengthen law enforcement responses to trafficking (i.e., to increase the number of successful prosecutions), it is far from clear that these efforts have been successful in addressing the prevalence or harmful consequences of child trafficking. Children (and adults) who have been trafficked, sold, or subjected to forced labor (or other worst forms of child labor) are known to experience tremendous difficulties in getting access to justice and are only rarely paid damages or compensation.

Several international and regional courts have considered cases involving children who have been subjected to forms of exploitation specified in the UN Trafficking Protocol's definition as purposes of trafficking.[56] However, while the European Court of

Human Rights has considered one specific case involving trafficking,[57] cases involving children have typically referred to slavery, servitude, and forced labor rather than to trafficking.[58] In 2005 the European Court issued a judgment about a young migrant live-in domestic worker from Togo, whom the court found had been subjected to servitude as a child of sixteen and seventeen and also as a young adult by her employers in France during the 1990s (before the adoption of the UN Trafficking Protocol). The court concluded that France's laws on servitude were too vague and the penalties imposed on the child's employers were too lenient.[59] France's law was finally amended in 2013.[60]

7 Preventing Child Trafficking

Although the provisions of the Trafficking Protocol that are intended to prevent human trafficking are vague, states have overlapping obligations under other international treaties. For example, although there has been a lack of international consensus on what measures are needed to reduce the demand related to trafficking,[61] particularly in relation to the sex industry, with respect to children the CRC Sale of Children Protocol is clear that states parties are required to "prohibit the sale of children, child prostitution and child pornography" (Article 1). To achieve this, they are required to "adopt or strengthen, implement and disseminate laws, administrative measures, social policies and programmes to prevent the offences referred to in the present Protocol" (Article 9.1).

Over the past century, numerous patterns of transporting and exploiting children, which would nowadays be categorized as child trafficking, have been brought to an end. In most cases the change was not attributable exclusively to law enforcement. The trafficking of boys to ride as jockeys in camel races in Persian Gulf countries was criticized by child rights defenders for several decades before UNICEF and other groups launched an initiative to end the practice in the United Arab Emirates (UAE) in 2005. This was described by UNICEF as "the first programme in the Gulf region to publicly acknowledge the issues of child trafficking and exploitation, and take practical steps to protect children,"[62] though the practice had already been criticized in Qatar. The UAE imposed a ban in 2002 on boys under fifteen or weighing less than 45 kilograms acting as camel jockeys, but this apparently had little effect. However, change got under way in 2005 when race organizers started using robot jockeys instead of real children, effectively removing the demand for boys as jockeys. In 2005 the UAE hosted a conference with representatives from the boys' countries of origin (Bangladesh, Mauritania, Pakistan, and Sudan). Supported by UNICEF and the International Organization for Migration, the participating governments agreed to repatriate all the boys employed as jockeys in the UAE, and the UAE authorities agreed to provide US$2.7 million to UNICEF to finance the boys' return and reintegration. The repatriation operations reportedly went well, though some children subsequently found they could hardly communicate with their relatives (they had only spoken Arabic while in the UAE) or were left at home without a livelihood and without wanting to return to school.

A quite different pattern of trafficking of adolescent girls and young women from the Republic of Moldova was reported in the late 1990s, with many trafficked to countries in the former Yugoslavia to provide commercial sex to both local men and international peacekeepers.[63] Yet others were trafficked into the sex industry in Western Europe, Turkey, and the Russian Federation. Just as the post-conflict situations provided the circumstances and demand that increased rates of trafficking in both young adult women and girls, so the reduction in the numbers of peacekeepers coincided with a gradual drop in the number of Moldovan girls reported to be trafficked out of their country during the first decade of the twenty-first century. However, administrative measures that were eventually introduced in Kosovo to restrict male peacekeepers from frequenting brothels probably also contributed to the decline.[64]

Reductions in the numbers of children trafficked for commercial sexual exploitation in another country, Cambodia, have been attributed to different factors, including law enforcement efforts. Although the political circumstances were different, again, the arrival of a UN mission in the early 1990s, along with the establishment of a new tourist industry, coincided with an increase in reports of children in brothels, both Cambodians and girls from neighboring Vietnam. The number of children involved at any one time was not established with any certainty, but NGOs suggested tens of thousands, and one estimated that around one-third of the women and girls earning money from commercial sex were between the ages of twelve and seventeen.[65] Many projects were initiated to reduce the numbers, mostly aimed at removing children from the sex industry. The government also took action, adopting in 2008 the Law on Suppression of Human Trafficking and Sexual Exploitation and ordering the closure of brothels in 2010.[66] Consequently, it is difficult to assess which interventions had the greatest impact. The International Justice Mission, an NGO that supported Cambodian law enforcement operations from 2003 onward, noted what it called a "dramatic reduction" in the prevalence of children involved during the subsequent decade, observing that by 2016, in three locations known for commercial sex, the proportion of children involved was down to 2.2 percent, with hardly any child aged under fifteen still present.[67] Others thought that NGO estimates had been exaggerated but concurred that by 2008 the numbers of children involved were much fewer than had been suggested in the 1990s.[68]

8 CONCLUSION

The concept of child trafficking has had much wider influence than the sale of children and has been recognized as a criminal offense much more widely than any of the other "worst forms of child labor" condemned by ILO Convention No. 182 adopted at much the same time. However, differing interpretations of what constitutes child trafficking, of terminology, and about the most appropriate way of estimating the total number of children involved have hampered efforts to stop child trafficking, as have ongoing difficulties in ensuring effective coordination between law enforcement agencies in separate countries. In some places, concerted efforts have been made to stop girls from being recruited to earn money through commercial sex (while efforts focused on boys have been less noticeable) and to prosecute some of the traffickers involved. Efforts to stop children from being trafficked for the purpose of forced labor or what is sometimes called labor exploitation seem to have had less impact, possibly because relevant law enforcement officials have not been provided with sufficient guidance or technical tools to distinguish such cases from more conventional forms of child labor, most of which are not considered serious enough to merit the involvement of law enforcement officials but are instead left to labor inspectors or other administrative officials to detect and handle.

It is possible that more trafficked children would be identified (and extricated from the control of traffickers and exploiters) if they were to be provided with adequate protection and assistance once they come to the attention of child protection or law enforcement officials. As long as protection and assistance remain inadequate (or, worse, result in the child victim being detained by the authorities), trafficked and exploited children may be discouraged from seeking the assistance of officials to escape their predicament. The authorities in many countries could probably do more to reduce the numbers of children being trafficked if they were to implement policies that made trafficking less profitable and assistance easier for children to obtain (both children who have been trafficked and those at high risk of being trafficked, many of whom are affected by problems in their communities or at home before being trafficked) rather than focus narrowly on the implementation of criminal law.

In recent years, the concept of human trafficking and the laws and priorities associated with it have been challenged by several states (Australia and the United Kingdom) and prominent NGOs, which prefer to use the term *modern slavery* to refer to patterns of extreme exploitation defined in the various international conventions and protocols mentioned in this chapter.[69] These and other perspectives on the harm inflicted by child trafficking, along with growing interest among governments and the public to respond to trafficking, have the potential to spur positive developments. However, it remains to be seen whether and how these emerging efforts will impact patterns of child trafficking or enhance action to stop the forms of exploitation that continue to blight children's lives around the world.

Notes

1. It bears noting that under both international law and the law of most countries, trafficking does not require movement across borders and, in many cases, does not require movement at all.
2. Some research has referred to *promising practices*—a somewhat vague term that allows organizations to promote methods they have developed but without subjecting such methods to peer review and sometimes without even noting the specific circumstances in which the proposed methods are replicable.
3. UN Convention on the Rights of the Child (CRC), G.A. Res. 44/25, 44th Sess., UN Doc. A/RES/44/25 (1989).

4. Trafficking Protocol, art. 3(a).

5. UN Protocol to Prevent, Suppress and Punish Trafficking in Persons Especially Women and Children, Supplementing the United Nations Convention against Transnational Organized Crime (Trafficking Protocol), G.A. Res. 55/25, 55th Sess., UN Doc. A/45/49 (2001).

6. See Trafficking Protocol, art. 3(a).

7. The term "exploitation of the prostitution of others" is the subject of the UN Convention for the Suppression of the Traffic in Persons and of the Exploitation of the Prostitution of Others, 96 UNTS 271 (1949; entered into force July 25, 1951). It requires states parties to make it a crime to recruit an adult or child "for purposes of prostitution" (including with the consent of the person involved) or to make money from the prostitution of another person, including running a brothel or renting a flat for the purpose of the prostitution of others, as well as pimping and pandering.

8. Mike Dottridge, "Young People's Voices on Child Trafficking: Experiences from South Eastern Europe," UNICEF Innocenti Research Centre Working Paper 2008-05 (December 2008), https://www.unicef-irc.org/publications/518-young-peoples-voices-on-childtrafficking-experiences-from-south-eastern-europe.html.

9. International Labour Organization (ILO) International Programme on the Elimination of Child Labour (IPEC), "Cross Border Trafficking of Boys" (March 2002), 34, http://www.ilo.org/public/libdoc/ilo/2002/102B09_152_engl.pdf.

10. Terre des Hommes Foundation, "The Trafficking of Albanian Children in Greece" (January 2003), 12, http://www.childtrafficking.org/pdf/user/the_trafficking_of_albanian_children_in_greece.pdf.

11. See, for example, UN Action for Cooperation against Trafficking in Persons (UN-ACT), "Human Trafficking Vulnerabilities in Asia: A Study on Forced Marriage between Cambodia and China" (2016), http://un-act.org/wp-content/uploads/2016/08/Final_UN-ACT_Forced_Marriage_Report.pdf. Such cases are easily confused with marriage migration that does not involve coercion or deception.

12. Daja Wenke, "A Broader Perspective to Protect the Human Rights of Children on the Move—Applying Lessons Learnt from Child Trafficking Research," in *Conference Report: Focus on Children in Migration—From a European Research and Method Perspective* ed. Susann Swärd and Lise Bruun (Stockholm: Save the Children, 2007).

13. ILO Special Action Programme to Combat Forced Labour (SAP-FL), "ILO Global Estimate of Forced Labour: Results and Methodology," (2012), http://www.ilo.org/wcmsp5/groups/public/---ed_norm/---declaration/documents/publication/wcms_182004.pdf. This estimated that 5.5 million children were in forced labor: almost one million children in "private sexual exploitation" and approximately 3.8 million in what the ILO called "labor exploitation." The report did not suggest what proportion had been trafficked. The ILO published new estimates of child labor in 2017 but without estimating how many were in forced labor or how many had been trafficked. See ILO, "Global Estimates of Child Labour: Results and Trends, 2012–2016" (Sept. 19, 2017), http://www.ilo.org/wcmsp5/groups/public/---dgreports/---dcomm/documents/publication/wcms_575499.pdf.

14. See ILO, "A Future without Child Labour: Global Report under the Follow-Up to the ILO Declaration on Fundamental Principles and Rights at Work" (May 6, 2002), 18, http://www.ilo.org/global/publications/ilo-bookstore/order-online/books/WCMS_PUBL_9221124169_EN/lang--en/index.htm.

15. Walk Free Foundation, "2018 Global Slavery Index," (July 19, 2018), https://www.globalslaveryindex.org/2018/findings/highlights. This suggests that 24.9 million people were in forced labor and 15.4 million were living in a forced marriage.

16. UN Office on Drugs and Crime (UNODC), "Global Report on Trafficking in Persons 2016" (2016), 6, https://www.unodc.org/documents/data-and-analysis/glotip/2016_Global_Report_on_Trafficking_in_Persons.pdf.

17. UNODC, "Global Report on Trafficking in Persons 2016," 34, 50.

18. See American Bar Association, "Human Trafficking Glossary of Terms," https://www.americanbar.org/content/dam/aba/multimedia/trafficking_task_force/FAQ/ABA_TF_HT_GLOSSARY.authcheckdam.pdf (accessed Sept. 5, 2019).

19. See Human Rights Council, "Report of the Special Rapporteur on Trafficking in Persons, Especially Women and Children," UN Doc. A/HRC/2013/23/48 (March 18, 2013).

20. ILO Convention No. 182: Concerning the Prohibition and Immediate Elimination of the Worst Forms of Child Labour (Worst Forms of Child Labour Convention), 38 ILM. 1207 (1999; entered into force Nov. 10, 2000). In its Article 3, the convention identifies four categories of "worst forms of child labour," the first of which concerns all forms of slavery and practices similar to slavery (such as the sale and trafficking of children, debt bondage, and forced or compulsory labor) and the second of which involves the use and procuring or offering of a child for prostitution for the production of pornography or for pornographic performances.

21. Inter-American Convention on International Traffic in Minors, 33 ILM. 721 (1994; entered into force Aug. 15, 1997), art. 2(b). The Convention specified a set of "unlawful purposes" (prostitution, sexual exploitation or servitude, and any other purpose that was unlawful in either the state of the child's habitual residence or the state party where the child was located) and "unlawful means" (including "kidnapping, fraudulent or coerced consent, the giving or receipt of unlawful payments or benefits to achieve the consent of the parents, persons or institutions having care of the child").

22. UN Secretary-General, "Special Measures for Protection from Sexual Exploitation and Sexual Abuse," Secretary-General's Bulletin, ST/SGB/2003/13 (Oct. 9, 2003), Section 1: Definitions.

23. Council of Europe Convention on the Protection of Children against Sexual Exploitation and Sexual Abuse, CETS No. 201 (2007; entered into force Jan. 7, 2010), arts. 18–23.

24. UN Supplementary Convention on the Abolition of Slavery, the Slave Trade, and Institutions and Practices Similar to Slavery, 18 UST 3201, 266 UNTS 3 (1956; entered into force April 30, 1957).

25. The Optional Protocol to the Convention on the Rights of the Child on Sale of Children, Child Prostitution and Child Pornography (CRC Optional Protocol 1), G.A. Res. A/RES/54/263 (May 25, 2000). The optional protocol states that children should never be involved in prostitution, whether they keep their earnings or hand them over to someone else (art. 3).

26. CRC Optional Protocol 1.

27. Article 2(a) of CRC Optional Protocol 1 states that the "[s]ale of children means any act or transaction whereby a child is transferred by any person or group of persons to another for remuneration or any other consideration." This covers many cases of child trafficking. The UN Special Rapporteur on the Sale of Children has noted specific examples that involve the sale of children but not trafficking: "[S]ituations of debt bondage where the child remains in the family home, the sale of a child for domestic work, or servile marriage

following a transaction with the child's family, may not involve trafficking. Similarly, children sold for forced begging or to perform illicit acts may not move from one place to another and may be coerced into such activities while living in their homes and usual environment." Special Rapporteur on the Sale of Children, Child Prostitution and Child Pornography, "Report of the Special Rapporteur on the Sale of Children, Child Prostitution and Child Pornography" UN Doc. A/71/261 (Aug. 1, 2016), para. 23, fn 10. Nevertheless, cases of this type would be regarded by the authorities in some countries as trafficking.

28. The Optional Protocol to the Convention on the Rights of the Child on the Involvement of Children in Armed Conflicts, G.A. Res. A/RES/54/263 (May 25, 2000).

29. See US Department of State, "Trafficking in Persons Report" (June 2007), 24, https://2009–2017.state.gov/documents/organization/82902.pdf.

30. ILO, "Combating Trafficking in Children for Labour Exploitation: A Resource Kit for Policy-Makers and Practitioners" (Nov. 1, 2008), Book 1: Understanding What Child Trafficking Is," 15. In 2007 the ILO's Committee of Experts on the Application of Conventions and Recommendations had commented that "trafficking in persons for the purpose of exploitation" was "encompassed by the definition of forced or compulsory labour." ILO Committee of Experts on the Application of Conventions and Recommendations, "General Survey concerning the Forced Labour Convention, 1930 (No. 29), and the Abolition of Forced Labour Convention, 1957 (No. 105)," ILC96-III(1B)-2007-02-0014-1-En (Feb. 14, 2007), paras. 77 and 78.

31. UNICEF Innocenti Research Centre, "Handbook on the Optional Protocol on the Sale of Children, Child Prostitution, and Child Pornography" (February 2009), 10, https://www.unicef.org/protection/optional_protocol_eng.pdf.

32. Notably the United States. See US Department of State, "Trafficking in Persons Report" (June 2010), 7, and "Trafficking in Persons Report" (June 2011)," 7.

33. The United Kingdom's Sexual Offences Act 2003 defines a series of sexual offenses against children. Section 58 focuses on "Trafficking within the UK for sexual exploitation," stating that "A person commits an offence if he intentionally arranges or facilitates travel within the United Kingdom by another person" and intends something to be done to the child or adult "during or after the journey and in any part of the world," which would involve one of the offenses specified in the Act.

34. See US Department of State, 2007 "Trafficking in Persons Report," 30.

35. In 2013 the ILO estimated that there were 17.2 million children worldwide in paid or unpaid domestic work in households other than their own, over 11 million of whom were fourteen or younger. See ILO, "Child Domestic Work: Global Estimates 2012," fact sheet (Oct. 4, 2013), https://www.ilo.org/ipec/Informationresources/WCMS_IPEC_PUB_23235/lang--en/index.htm.

36. The Interagency Working Group on Sexual Exploitation of Children consisted of both intergovernmental organizations (such as the ILO, Interpol, and UNICEF) and international nongovernmental organizations (the main one was ECPAT: End Child Prostitution, Child Pornography and the Trafficking of Children for Sexual Purposes). See Interagency Working Group on Sexual Exploitation of Children, "Terminology Guidelines for the Protection of Children from Sexual Exploitation and Sexual Abuse," http://luxembourgguidelines.org/about (accessed Sept. 6, 2019).

37. Interagency Working Group on Sexual Exploitation of Children, "Terminology Guidelines."

38. See Simon Fellows, "Trafficking Body Parts in Mozambique and South Africa," report by Liga Moçambicana dos Direitos Humanos (Human Rights League of Mozambique) (2008),

https://www.reddit.com/r/Missing411/comments/5gab2z/trafficking_body_parts_in_
mozambique_and_south.

39. ENDA Jeunesse Action, ILO, IOM, PLAN West Africa Regional Office, Save the Children,
    Terre des Hommes Foundation, and UNICEF West and Central Africa Regional Office,
    "Quelle protection pour les enfants concernés par la mobilité en Afrique de l'ouest? Nos
    positions et recommandations," Projet régional commun d'étude sur les mobilités des
    enfants et des jeunes en Afrique de l'Ouest et du Centre, https://www.unicef.org/wcaro/
    french/Rapport_FR-web.pdf (accessed Sept. 6, 2019).

40. See Bureau of International Labor Affairs, US Department of Labor, "2012 Findings on the
    Worst Forms of Child Labor," (2013), https://digitalcommons.ilr.cornell.edu/cgi/viewcontent.
    cgi?article=2808&context=key_workplace.

41. Centre de Formation et de Recherche en matière de Population (CEFORP), "Etude natio-
    nale sur la traite des enfants. Rapport d'analyse"(Cotonou, Benin: Ministry of the Family
    and Child and UNICEF, 2007).

42. CEFORP, "Etude nationale sur la traite des enfants," 19.

43. These annual trafficking in persons reports have been published by the US State
    Department every year since 2001.

44. For example, in Kosovo. See UNICEF, "Reference Guide on Protecting the Rights of Child
    Victims of Trafficking in Europe" (2006), https://resourcecentre.savethechildren.net/
    node/8257/pdf/unicef_child_trafficking_low.pdf, annex 3.

45. See Article 12 of the CRC. See also Committee on the Rights of the Child, *General
    Comment No. 12: The Right of the Child to Be Heard*, UN Doc. CRC/C/GC/12 (2009) (in
    particular, Section C.9: "In immigration and asylum proceedings," paras. 123 and 124).

46. Dottridge, "Young People's Voices on Child Trafficking."

47. Government of the Philippines, "Philippines Guidelines for the Protection of Trafficked
    Children" (2008), http://site.clkss.org.ph/resources/policies/guidelines/philippine-guidelines
    -for-the-protection-of-trafficked-children/at_download/policy_file.

48. UNICEF, "Guidelines for Protection of the Rights of Children Victims Trafficking in
    Southeastern Europe" (March 24, 2003), https://www.udiregelverk.no/en/documents/
    international-conventions-and-agreements/2003-03-24. See also UNICEF, "Reference
    Guide on Protecting the Rights of Child Victims of Trafficking in Europe".

49. UNICEF, "Guidelines on the Protection of Child Victims of Trafficking," UNICEF
    Technical Notes (September 2006), https://www.unicef.org/protection/Unicef_Victims_
    Guidelines_en.pdf.

50. UN Office of the High Commissioner for Human Rights, "Recommended Principles and
    Guidelines on Human Rights and Human Trafficking," UN Doc. E/2002/68/Add.1 (May
    20, 2002) (addendum to a report of the United Nations High Commissioner for Human
    Rights to the Economic and Social Council).

51. See Daniel Silverstone and Claire Bracknell, "Combating Modern Slavery Experienced by
    Vietnamese Nationals En Route to, and within, the UK," report ID CCS0717666636-2 of
    the Independent Anti-Slavery Commissioner (2017), http://www.antislaverycommissioner.
    co.uk/media/1159/iasc-report-combating-modern-slavery-experience-by-vietname
    -nationals-en-route-to-and-within-the-uk.pdf.

52. "Fugitive, 14, Ran £1m Drugs Farm," *Sentinel* (Staffordshire UK) (2010).

53. L., H.V.N., T.H.N., and T. v. R, [2013] EWCA Crim 991 (June 21, 2013), para. 2.

54. L., H.V.N., T.H.N., and T. v. R, para. 13.

55. See UN Office of the High Commissioner for Human Rights, "UN Basic Principles and
    Guidelines on the Right to a Remedy and Reparation for Victims of Gross Violations of

International Human Rights Law and Serious Violations of International Humanitarian Law," G.A. Res. 60/147, UN Doc. A/RES/60/147 (Dec. 16, 2005).

56. For example, a trial in the Special Court for Sierra Leone resulted in three men being convicted of forcibly recruiting (into armed units) children below the age of fifteen. See Prosecutor v. Sesay, Kallon and Gbao [2009] SCSL-04-15-T ("[C]hildren as young as 8 or 9 years old were forcibly taken for military training, some barely able to lift the guns they were to shoot.").

57. Rantsev v. Cyprus and Russia, Application No. 25965/04, Eur. Ct. H.R. (Oct. 10, 2010).

58. Trabajadores de la Hacienda Brasil Verde v. Brasil (Workers of the Green Brazil Ranch v. Brazil), Inter-Am. Ct. H.R. (Oct. 20, 2016).

59. Siliadin v. France, Application No. 73316/01, Eur. Ct. H.R. (Oct. 26, 2005).

60. The amendment came in a law dated August 5, 2018, amending the penal code (Article 225-14-2) to specify that the offense of "reducing someone to servitude" was similar to subjecting someone to forced labor but doing so on a regular basis. It was made punishable by ten years of imprisonment and a fine of €300,000. See "Loi n° 2013-711 du 5 août 2013 portant diverses dispositions d'adaptation dans le domaine de la justice en application du droit de l'Union européenne et des engagements internationaux de la France," *Journal officiel de la République française*, n° 0181 (Aug. 6, 2013): 13338.

61. See Human Rights Council, "Report of the Special Rapporteur on Trafficking in Persons, Especially Women and Children."

62. UNICEF, "Starting Over: Children Return Home from Camel Racing" (2006), 1, https://www.unicef.org/infobycountry/files/StartingOver.pdf.

63. UNICEF and Terre des Hommes, "Action to Prevent Child Trafficking in Southeastern Europe. A Preliminary Assessment" (June 2006), http://www.childtrafficking.org/eng/publication.html.

64. UNICEF and Terre des Hommes, "Action to Prevent Child Trafficking in Southeastern Europe."

65. ECPAT, "Good Practices. Law Enforcement in Cambodia." http://www.ecpat.net/eng/CSEC/good_practices/enforcement_cambodia.asp (last accessed on April 4, 2019).

66. Thomas M. Steinfatt and Simon Baker, "Measuring the Extent of Sex Trafficking in Cambodia—2008," UNIAP Trafficking Estimates (January 2011), 56, http://un-act.org/publication/view/measuring-the-extent-of-sex-trafficking-in-cambodia-2008-uniap-trafficking-estimates-competition/.

67. International Justice Mission (IJM), "IJM Celebrates Progress in Cambodia," https://www.ijm.org/news/ijm-celebrates-progress-in-cambodia (accessed Sept. 6, 2019).

68. Steinfatt and Baker, "Measuring the Extent of Sex Trafficking in Cambodia—2008."

69. The first of the Walk Free Foundation's global slavery indexes was published in 2013.

CHAPTER 31

CHILDREN IN ARMED CONFLICT

MARK A. DRUMBL

1 INTRODUCTION

CHILDREN have been enmeshed in armed conflict throughout history.[1] At times, and for multiplicities of causes both emancipatory and baleful, such children have been seen as heroes. I live in Lexington, Virginia, home to the Virginia Military Institute, whose cadets—many aged fifteen to eighteen—fiercely fought for the Confederacy in the 1864 Battle of New Market. These cadets were credited with the victory over Union forces. The Stonewall Jackson Memorial Hall, situated in the heart of the campus, displays a sprawling mural by Benjamin Clinedinst which lionizes the youthful cadets' battle charge. Among Colombia's national heroes, commemorated in a dynamic monument to *los valerosos e insobornables niños*, is twelve-year-old Pedro Pascasio Martínez, fabled for preventing the escape of a Spanish commander who sought to flee following the Battle of Boyacá—a pivotal event in the country's independence in 1819. These are just two of many examples of memorials, commemorations, and elegies for children that salute them for their martial pride, service to their *patrie*, and political engagement.

The emergence of international human rights law, international criminal law, and international humanitarian law has, however, shifted public perceptions of children entangled in armed conflict. So, too, have a series of powerful autobiographies and documentaries that have disseminated to global audiences the horrors of the child soldier experience.[2] Such children are increasingly being seen as victims, and the involvement of children in armed conflict is emerging not as untoward and undesirable or a desperate last stand but, instead, as flatly unlawful. The relationship of the child with armed conflict has shifted from one regulated by ethics and morality to one constructed by law and public policy. Many activist and humanitarian groups gravitate to the cause of ending child soldiering. Considerable funds have been deployed in this struggle. The United Nations Security Council, generally fractured, has succeeded in issuing eleven resolutions over the past two decades on children in armed conflict. UNICEF and other UN organs also have been deeply invested in the cause of ending child soldiering.[3]

The child soldier therefore suffuses the international legal imagination. Mostly, this figure evokes imagery of a poor, kidnapped, prepubescent African boy, in dilapidated sandals, barely able to hold his AK-47. This essentialized image nonetheless belies the far greater complexity of *where* children become implicated in armed conflict, *when* (as a matter of age) children become soldiers, as well as *how* and *why* they become implicated. Readers may be surprised to learn: many child soldiers are found outside of Africa; many children fulfill functions that do not involve carrying weapons; most child soldiers world wide are adolescents rather than young children; the most common path to militarized life is not abduction and kidnapping, but for children to come forward with varying degrees of volition and become enlisted; and children may face greater threats from their side than from the enemy. What is more, it is estimated that 40 percent of child soldiers world wide are girls. The invisibility of the girl soldier from the imagery of child soldiering and hence from rehabilitative and reintegrative programming remains deeply disappointing.

Accordingly, in recent decades the well-worn phrase *child soldier* has become disfavored. The 2007 Paris Commitments and Paris Principles,[4] two connected nonbinding instruments endorsed by 108 states,[5] instead normalize different language: "a child associated with an armed force or armed group." The Paris Principles did so to underscore the diversity of roles children may play in armed conflict. An armed force refers to the national militaries of a state, whereas an armed group refers to a fighting force that is separate from a state, for example, rebel groups such as the northern Uganda's Lord's Resistance Army (LRA) and Sri Lanka's Liberation Tigers of Tamil Eelam (LTTE). According to the Paris Principles:

> "A child associated with an armed force or armed group" refers to any person below 18 years of age who is or who has been recruited or used by an armed force or armed group in any capacity, including but not limited to children, boys, and girls used as fighters, cooks, porters, messengers, spies or for sexual purposes. It does not only refer to a child who is taking or has taken a direct part in hostilities.

The Paris Principles map onto international child rights law by affirming the chronological divide of eighteen as the transition point between childhood and adulthood. Assuredly, the phrase "children associated with armed forces and armed groups" is somewhat tongue-tying, so UN agencies and international activists have turned to the acronym CAAFAG instead. Yet this, too, is phonetically awkward and creates a bit of an alphabet soup. Hence, in this chapter I tend to deploy the term *child soldier* but always understand the meaning of the term to reflect the definition as provided by the Paris Principles. Although terminology matters, it might also be helpful to revisit the term *soldiering* instead of abandoning it and to recognize that in contemporary conflict it is the act of soldiering itself that could be rendered more definitionally capacious. On this note, it is striking that the most recent set of political commitments on the topic, fostered by the Canadian government in 2017, are expressly titled the Vancouver Principles on

Peacekeeping and the Prevention of the Recruitment and Use of Child Soldiers.[6] These Principles strive to prevent child recruitment in the context of peacekeeping operations and mandate peacekeepers to receive clear guidance regarding children associated with armed forces or armed groups.

To be sure, children intersect with armed conflict even if they are not part of an armed group or an armed force. Children suffer terribly from conflict-related violence. Hence, this chapter also will discuss children not at all associated with an armed force or armed group as well as children associated with groups, for example, terrorist organizations, when debate arises whether or not that group has the capacity to engage in armed conflict and hence would qualify as an armed group. On a more general note, it has been estimated that 246 million children live in areas riven with armed conflict, of which 125 million are directly affected by conflict worldwide.[7]

This chapter intends to accomplish several goals. First, so as to situate the reader, it offers a concise global survey of children associated with armed forces and armed groups. It then sets out the content of international law when it comes to the regulation of child soldiering. It does so through two steps: assessing the responsibility for child soldiering (i.e., when recruitment of children into armed groups or armed forces is unlawful) and then the responsibility of child soldiers (i.e., the consequences that arise when child soldiers commit criminal atrocities). This chapter explores challenges that inhere in reintegrating these vulnerable populations into civilian life. In conclusion, it posits that an important path forward is to ensure that the best interests of the child principle, situated in Article 3 of the United Nations Convention on the Rights of the Child (CRC), be fully actuated. Respecting best interests means foregrounding the voices of the children themselves. On this note, the protective impulse that envisions militarized youth as faultless, passive victims may not always reflect how youthful fighters see themselves nor necessarily support an emancipatory and empowering vision of how international law should promote the rights of children.

2 PRACTICES OF CHILD SOLDIERING

It is generically estimated that, in recent decades, from two hundred and fifty to three hundred thousand children worldwide are associated with armed forces or armed groups. Child soldiers—as with former child soldiers—exist in each of the world's regions. States recruit, to be sure, but in 2016 the Office of the Special Representative of the Secretary-General on Children and Armed Conflict found that non-state armed groups constitute fifty-four out of sixty-three parties listed for grave violations against children.[8] Overall, the Special Representative found that in 2016 concerns lingered but progress was made in the Philippines, the Democratic Republic of the Congo (DRC), Colombia, Sudan, Mali, Nigeria, and the Central African Republic; significant challenges were identified in Afghanistan, Somalia (where the number of militarily recruited children doubled in 2016), South Sudan, Yemen, Nigeria, Iraq, and Syria.

Child soldiering is a *global* phenomenon that is much more nuanced than might appear at first blush.

Child soldiers have been recruited into the Bolivian armed forces. Children have participated in armed violence in Guatemala and Peru. In Colombia, child soldiers were voluntarily enlisted and were forcibly recruited into armed opposition groups (the FARC and the ELN), where they laid mines and undertook support tasks. The largest pro-government paramilitary group, the AUC, also recruited child soldiers. Peace negotiations in Colombia have demobilized many FARC child soldiers and former child soldiers. Questions persist as to how such former child fighters should be reintegrated and whether they ought to face restorative processes or some element of retributive justice for crimes they may have committed during the armed conflict.

UNICEF estimates more than six thousand cases of child recruitment between 2003 and 2008 by rebels in Sri Lanka. The LTTE—a group of violent secessionists who fought the Sri Lankan government until its defeat in 2009—turned extensively to child soldiers. The Khmer Rouge used youthful cadres in the Cambodian killing fields between 1975 and 1979. Myanmar's government recruits children through harsh methods. One quarter of its national armed forces (the Tatmadaw) is estimated to be composed of persons under the age of eighteen. Child soldiers also are found within the many non-state armed groups in Myanmar. In Nepal, child soldiers—three thousand of whom were released in early 2010 as part of peace negotiations—participated in Maoist rebel groups. Child soldiers served in pro-Indonesian militia forces in Timor-Leste. Children have furthermore been associated with armed forces or armed groups in Bangladesh, Laos, Pakistan, Thailand, the Philippines, and Jammu and Kashmir.

Children have fought in Iraq and in Iran. Child soldiers have fought, killed, and died in Afghanistan through successive conflicts; children also are recruited into Afghan police forces.[9] In Palestine, the face of the first intifada was youthful: among those arrested, the average age was seventeen.[10] Israel has imprisoned Palestinian children for security offenses and for being associated with an armed group. Conflict in Yemen and Syria enmeshes children as participants. This entire region is seeing an escalation in the numbers of children associated with armed forces and armed groups. ISIS now presents one of the most visible cases of child soldiering. Circulated through social media, haunting imagery of beheadings and murders committed by the "cubs of the caliphate" shock the conscience. ISIS also succeeds in recruiting minors, frequently through abductions and brainwashing, but also because youths come forth on their own initiative and wish to enroll. Influenced by social networking and web-interfaces, adolescents have traveled long distances to join ISIS, often but not always under false pretenses. Children have carried out numerous terroristic attacks, including suicide bombings, throughout Iraq.[11] These children tend to be seen less as passive victims by the international community and more as threats to be disabled in counterterrorism programs, in part because of political impulses that treat these children differently from others associated with armed groups. Children associated with groups labeled as terroristic and extremist are therefore among the most vulnerable and poorly served by current policies. Throughout 2017 authorities in Iraq, Kurdistan, and Syria routinely detained and abused children suspected of association with ISIS. The Office of the Special Representative specifically criticizes the detention by states of children for alleged association with such armed groups and, as well, the use by these armed groups of children as human bombs.[12] On this note, Principle 9 of the 2017 Vancouver Principles requires:

> To ensure that all children apprehended and/or temporarily detained in accordance with mission-specific military rules of engagement are treated in a manner consistent with international norms and standards, as well as the special status, needs, and rights of children and to ensure that detention is used as a measure of last resort, for the shortest possible period of time, and with the best interests of the child as a primary consideration, and that they are handed over expeditiously to child protection actors and civilian authorities in line with the established policies and guidance.

Virtually all of the multiple sides to endemic conflict in the DRC conscripted, enlisted, or actively used child soldiers. Although the involvement of children in armed conflict in the DRC has attenuated over time, it has not disappeared. Armed conflict in Angola and Mozambique—now quiescent—had directly implicated thousands of children, often forcibly, but also through self-enlistment for ideological or material aspirations.[13] Children actively serve as combatants in conflicts in the Central African Republic (CAR), Chad, and Côte d'Ivoire. The use of child soldiers also is reported in Burundi and Zimbabwe. Evidence of child soldiering among national armed forces recently has emerged in Somalia. Charles Taylor, the former Liberian head of state now jailed by the Special Court for Sierra Leone (SCSL), had initially built an army around child soldiers. Government forces and rebel groups in the Sudan turned to child soldiers throughout internecine conflict, most extensively in the 1990s, though recourse to children still persists. In South Sudan, child soldiering is on the rise. Boko Haram, a group in Nigeria, viciously kidnaps and abuses children. In response, the Nigerian government is currently thought to be detaining thousands of children (as well as adults) who it fears are associated with Boko Haram. Many of the detained have been encountered during military operations, but others—including large numbers of children—appear to have been arrested arbitrarily as they fled from Boko Haram.

Children suffered terribly in the 1994 Rwandan genocide. Hutu extremists targeted Tutsi children, even infants, for elimination. Many children witnessed graphic violence. Minors also became perpetrators. Some manned the barricades that identified the Tutsi "cockroaches" to be eliminated. Youths—many of them teenagers—also became central to the effort to oust the genocidal government. These youths staffed the ranks of the Rwandese Patriotic Army (RPA), the only military force actually to intercede to halt the genocide.

In Northern Uganda, a recurrent estimate puts the number of children abducted by the rebel Lord's Resistance Army (LRA) at between twenty-five and thirty-eight thousand.[14] At some points, minors constitute 90 percent of LRA forces. Nearly all have escaped or surrendered, and the LRA has been massively weakened. Notwithstanding having been indicted by the International Criminal Court (ICC) in The Hague, LRA leader Joseph Kony remains at large, though a lower-level commander, Dominic Ongwen (himself a former child soldier brutally kidnapped into the LRA at the age of nine), is currently on trial there. Ongwen faces seventy-one counts of crimes against humanity and war crimes (the largest number of charges ever brought against anyone by an international court or tribunal).

Thousands of children were associated with all sides of the conflict that raged in Sierra Leone from 1991 to 2002. Although children were recruited by force, significant numbers willingly joined. Among Sierra Leone's child soldiers, commission of atrocities (including amputations of the hands and feet of civilian populations), resocialization into violence, and compelled drug use all were widespread. Most child soldiers remained low-level auxiliaries, but some over the age of fifteen became generals.[15]

Children have served as fighters in recent conflicts in Chechnya, Croatia, Bosnia and Herzegovina, and Serbia. Many states—including the United Kingdom, the United States, China, India, the Netherlands, Canada, France, New Zealand, Germany, and Australia—permit voluntary recruitment of minors into national armed forces, albeit largely under strict conditions.

3 LEGAL RESPONSIBILITY FOR CHILD SOLDIERING

The CRC affirms that states "shall take all feasible measures to ensure that persons who have not attained the age of fifteen years do not take a direct part in hostilities."[16] CRC Article 38(3) provides that "States Parties shall refrain from recruiting any person who has not attained the age of fifteen years into their armed forces...." The Optional Protocol to the CRC on the Involvement of Children in Armed Conflict, which was adopted in 2000, entered into force in 2002.[17] As of 2017, 167 states are parties thereto. The Optional Protocol aims to remedy some of the CRC's perceived inadequacies. It specifies that states "shall take all feasible measures to ensure that members of their armed forces who have not attained the age of 18 years do not take a direct part in hostilities."[18] On the one hand, the Optional Protocol reflects an incremental move, in that the language "all feasible measures" does not plainly read as imperative. On the other hand, the Optional Protocol has been interpreted as "elevating the minimum age for combat participation to 18."[19] A firmer ban emerges in Article 2, which provides that states "shall ensure that persons who have not attained the age of 18 years are not compulsorily recruited into their armed forces." Optional Protocol Article 3(1) then somewhat nebulously adds:

> States Parties shall raise the minimum age for the voluntary recruitment of persons into their national armed forces from that set out in article 38, paragraph 3, of the [CRC], taking account of the principles contained in that article and recognizing that under the [CRC] persons under the age of 18 years are entitled to special protection.

Article 3(1) mandates that states increase the threshold age for the voluntary recruitment of persons into their national armed forces beyond fifteen—ostensibly, then, at the very least to sixteen. The Optional Protocol *stricto sensu* permits recruitment of sixteen- and seventeen-year-olds into national armed forces. Their recruitment, however, is to be genuinely voluntary and carried out with the informed consent of the recruit's parents or legal guardians; in addition, such recruits are to be fully informed of the duties involved in service and must provide reliable proof of age.[20]

The Optional Protocol requires each state party to deposit a binding declaration upon ratification or accession that sets forth its minimum age of voluntary recruitment as determined under national law. Among states that have filed declarations, approximately three-quarters list minimum ages of voluntary recruitment of eighteen or older (a large majority within this group declare eighteen).[21] A generalized practice, therefore, is emerging (at least if the metric is to undertake a head count of states). Examples of states that, as of August 2018 declare ages lower than eighteen, include: seventeen-and-a-half years (Malaysia); seventeen years (Australia, Austria, Azerbaijan, Cabo Verde, China, Cuba, France, Germany, Guinea-Bissau, Israel, Netherlands (as military personnel on probation), New Zealand, Saudi Arabia, and United States); the "1st January of the year they become 17 years old" (Brazil, for military service); sixteen-and-a-half years (Singapore); and sixteen years (Bangladesh, Belize, Canada, Egypt, El Salvador, Guyana,[22] India, and the United Kingdom). It is noteworthy that certain of these states have large armed forces.

The Optional Protocol is more restrictive in cases of armed groups. These groups "should not, under any circumstances, recruit or use in hostilities persons under the age of 18 years."[23] What is more, pursuant to Article 4(2), states agree to take "all feasible measures" to criminalize such practices. State responsibility therefore arises, at least in theory.

Other international and regional instruments also address recruitment of children into armed forces or armed groups. The International Labor Organization's Convention No. 182 on the Prohibition and Immediate Action for the Elimination of the Worst Forms of Child Labor defines a child as a person under the age of eighteen.[24] This convention explicitly links "forced or compulsory recruitment of children for use in armed conflict" to "slavery or practices similar to slavery" and obliges ratifying member states to "take immediate and effective measures to secure the prohibition and elimination" thereof.[25] The African Charter on the Rights and Welfare of the Child, which came into force in November 1999, defines a child as "every human being below the age of 18 years" and requires parties to "take all necessary measures to ensure that no child shall take a direct part in hostilities and refrain, in particular, from recruiting any child."[26]

Article 38(1) of the CRC requires that states "undertake to respect and to ensure respect for rules of international humanitarian law applicable to them in armed conflicts which are relevant to the child." How does international humanitarian law approach children? The Fourth Geneva Convention, which concerns civilian persons, grants a number of special protections to children.[27] These protections, which may begin at different ages (twelve, fifteen, or eighteen), include barring the occupying power from compelling persons under the age of eighteen to work. In 1977 two Additional Protocols were added to the Geneva Conventions (one for international armed conflict (I), the other (II) for non-international armed conflict). Article 77(1) of Additional Protocol I mandates for parties to a conflict that "[c]hildren shall be the object of special respect and shall be protected against any form of indecent assault."[28] Article 77(2) states that "Parties to the conflict shall take all feasible measures in order that children who have not attained the age of fifteen years do not take a direct part in hostilities and, in particular, they shall refrain from recruiting them into their armed forces" while also specifying that "[i]n recruiting among those persons who have attained the age of fifteen years but who have not attained the age of eighteen years the Parties to the conflict shall endeavor to give priority to those who are oldest." Article 77(3) addresses what a party is to do when it captures enemy fighters who, despite the requirements of Article 77(2), are under the age of fifteen. In such situations, such captured persons "continue to benefit from the special protection accorded...., whether or not they are prisoners of war." Furthermore, pursuant to Article 77(4), "If arrested, detained or interned for reasons related to the armed conflict, children shall be held in quarters separate from the quarters of adults, except where families are accommodated as family units." Additional Protocol I also accords children priority in the distribution of relief consignments and restricts the ability of a party to the conflict to evacuate children other than its nationals to a foreign country.[29]

Additional Protocol II, which covers non-international armed conflict, asserts in Article 4(3)(c) that "children who have not attained the age of fifteen years shall neither be recruited in the armed forces or groups nor allowed to take part in hostilities."[30] This prohibition is firmer than its counterpart for international armed conflict in Additional Protocol I. Article 4(3) of Additional Protocol II, which generally requires that "children shall be provided with the care and aid they require," makes specific (though not exclusive) reference to education, family reunification, and the temporary removal of children from areas plagued by hostilities to safer areas. Similarly to Additional Protocol I, in Article 4(3)(d) Additional Protocol II extends special protection to children below the age of fifteen even "if they take a direct part in hostilities despite the provisions of subparagraph (c) and are captured."

In international and non-international armed conflict, the conscription, enlistment, or use of children under the age of fifteen to participate actively in hostilities is a war crime to which individual criminal responsibility attaches. The unlawfulness of illicit recruitment thereby expands to include both state responsibility as well as individual penal culpability in the case of children under the age of fifteen. This proscription is both conventional and customary. A fundamental precept underpinning this war crime is that "[r]esponsibility is placed on the adult who permits participation and never on the child."[31] Prosecutions have occurred at the SCSL and ICC.

In fact, the ICC issued its very first conviction solely on three counts of child soldier crimes, precluded in non-international armed conflict by Rome Statute Article 8(2)(b)(xxvi) (a different but identically worded provision, Article 8(2)(e)(vii), addresses international armed conflict).[32] In *Prosecutor v. Lubanga*, a rebel leader in the DRC was sentenced to fourteen years' imprisonment. Jurisprudence from these two institutions has clarified important aspects of this war crime. For example, in *Prosecutor v. Brima, Kamara, and Kanu* (the *AFRC* case), a SCSL Trial Chamber defined conscription as implying "compulsion" and as encompassing "acts of coercion, such as abductions and forced recruitment."[33] It defined enlistment as "accepting and enrolling individuals when they volunteer to join an armed force or group," which it immediately qualified by adding: "Enlistment is a voluntary act, and the child's consent is therefore not a valid defence."[34] The bottom line is that enlistment of children under the age of fifteen is impermissible regardless of circumstances. Consent of the child is no defense. In another case, the SCSL Appeals Chamber assessed the required nexus between a defendant and the moment at which a child had actually been enlisted into the CDF. This court understood enlistment to mean "any conduct accepting the child as part of the militia" but added that "there must be a nexus between the act of the accused and the child joining the armed force or group"; "knowledge on the part of the accused that the child is under the age of 15"; and knowledge that the child "may be trained for combat."[35] In *Prosecutor v. Sesay, Kallon, and Gbao*, the SCSL found that active participation in hostilities included committing crimes against civilians, engaging in arson, guarding military objectives and mines, and serving as spies and bodyguards.[36] In *Prosecutor v. Lubanga*, the ICC judges followed similar understandings to those of the SCSL. Enlistment was understood to mean "to enroll on the list of a military body," while conscription means to "enlist compulsorily."[37] In terms of using children to participate actively, the *Lubanga* judgment underscored the need for a case-by-case approach to establish the link between the activity for which the child is used and the combat in which the armed group or armed force is engaged. Another accused, Katanga, was acquitted in a subsequent case of child soldiering charges because of a lack of nexus between him and the illicit practices of child soldiering in the DRC. In terms of sentencing, it has been noted that crimes against or affecting children should be regarded as particularly grave given that children enjoy special recognition and protection under international law.

The SCSL also has addressed crimes against humanity that may disproportionately affect children. SCSL Statute Article 2(i) proscribes "other inhumane acts," which the *AFRC* appeals judgment interpreted as including acts of forced marriage perpetrated against girls. Certain other Rome Statute proscriptions bear on violence that may disproportionately, though certainly not exclusively, harm children. In terms of war crimes, one example is intentionally attacking buildings dedicated to education provided they are not military objectives; the crimes against humanity of enslavement, sexual slavery, and enforced prostitution also come to mind; as do the crimes of forcible transfer of children and child trafficking.[38] Furthermore, Rome Statute Article 6(e) includes, within the definition of *genocide*, the forcible transfer of children of one enumerated group to another enumerated group.

The Rome Statute also permits reparations to victims, including children under the age of eighteen. The ICC may make a reparative order directly against a convicted person, though such individuals are generally impecunious; it also can order the reparative award to be made through a separate trust fund for victims.[39] To date, this trust fund has allocated funds derived from voluntary grants by states to inter alia a number of projects in Uganda and the DRC. Beneficiary projects include programs for child soldiers and abductees as well as programs geared to communities, war victims, victims of sexual violence, teenage mothers, orphans, and also programs to support services, agricultural initiatives, and communications. The *Lubanga* case has established principles and practices for the distribution of reparations.

Individual penal responsibility for illicit recruitment of children is also entering national criminal jurisdictions. As the age of unlawful recruitment inches towards eighteen, it may also be that the scope of individual criminal responsibility for such recruitment moves upward to eighteen.

How far can a handful of criminal trials for adult recruiters go in terms of prevention? Cause for skepticism arises in terms of the deterrent value of such trials.[40] One major gap in the enforcement network is state responsibility for the use of children in armed forces. The conduct of the United States is a telling example. In 2008, the US passed the Child Soldiers Protection Act. This legislation forbids the US from giving military aid to any foreign government that systematically uses children in its armed forces. Yet the law also permits a waiver even for delinquent countries. Beginning in 2010 and for six years thereafter, then-President Barack Obama allocated over $1.2 billion in military assistance and arms to governments that use child soldiers while only withholding $61 million.[41] He did so, he said, in the US "national interest."

One tough issue remains. May child fighters be targeted during armed conflict? If so, how and under which circumstances? International law affirms a duty to respect and protect children in armed conflicts along with a duty to promote the best interests of children. Overcoming the presumption of civilian status might therefore require more than would be the case for an adult. In addition, even if a child is deemed targetable, the allowable means and methods must reflect the protected status of children in international law.[42] Provisions establishing a special duty to respect and protect children may tip the balance in favor of a duty to capture, where feasible. A new doctrine—described as the first of its kind—adopted by the Canadian Armed Forces in 2017 reflects a balance between security concerns and human and child rights concerns in the specific context of underage fighters.[43] On the one hand, this document accords armed forces personnel the right to use force to protect themselves from the threat of serious injury or death. It recognizes that children may pose as grave a threat as adults. On the other hand, this doctrine states that Canadian troops should "seek to de-escalate confrontations with child soldiers." If forced to engage child soldiers, the doctrine states that armed forces personnel "seek to engage adults within the group first," under the assumption that if the adult leader is eliminated or removed, then the armed group might dissolve. The doctrine adds that, if captured, underage fighters should be confined separately from adult detainees and that consideration should be given to grouping the children themselves according to their ages. Child detainees must then be turned over to nongovernmental organizations as soon as possible for purposes of counseling, rehabilitation, and family reunification.

4 PENAL RESPONSIBILITY OF CHILD SOLDIERS

Child soldiers suffer crimes, and child soldiering is a crime, but child soldiers also may commit crimes—including grievous atrocities. The victims of violent acts by child soldiers may include children as well as adults.

Although criminally prosecuting child soldiers for their alleged involvement in acts of atrocity is technically permissible under international law, such a move increasingly is viewed as inappropriate and undesirable.

The CRC nonetheless permits the "arrest, detention or imprisonment of a child" but requires that these measures "shall be used only as a...last resort and for the shortest appropriate period of time."[44] The CRC precludes the death penalty and life imprisonment without parole as sentences for children who are convicted of offenses. The CRC requires that "every child deprived of liberty shall be separated from adults unless it is considered in the child's best interest not to do so."[45] It specifies a minimum level of due process protection for children subject to criminal proceedings but also encourages the development of enhanced frameworks attuned to their specific needs. The CRC does not favor incarceration, preferring instead rehabilitation and reintegration. That said, the CRC does not bar incarceration. Article 40(3)(a) of the CRC requires parties to seek to promote the establishment of "a minimum age below which children shall be presumed not to have the capacity to infringe the penal law" but sets no such age. That said, the Committee on the Rights of the Child, which helps monitor state compliance with the CRC, has considered fourteen as a low age for criminal responsibility and "has welcomed...proposals to set the age of criminal responsibility at eighteen."[46]

What is the general practice within national jurisdictions when it comes to minors who commit ordinary common crimes? A sampling of baseline ages of criminal responsibility over the past decade include: seven (Switzerland, Nigeria, South Africa); ten (Australia, New Zealand); twelve (Canada, Netherlands, Uganda); thirteen (France); fourteen (Japan, Germany, Austria, Italy, Russian Federation, Sierra Leone); fifteen (Sweden, Norway, Denmark); sixteen (Spain, Portugal), and eighteen (Belgium, Brazil, Peru).[47] It is not uncommon for states to adjust these ages, and the trajectory of such moves is upward. National ages of criminal responsibility may be gradated. This means that jurisdictions establish an age of criminal responsibility and a separate age of adult criminal responsibility.

Turning to international humanitarian law, Article 68 of the 1949 Fourth Geneva Convention precludes imposing the death penalty on "a protected person who was under eighteen years of age at the time of the offence," as do both of the 1977 Additional Protocols. Consequently, the Fourth Geneva Convention and both Additional Protocols contemplate that minors can incur responsibility for war crimes. These instruments bar only the harshest punishments.

In 1996, pursuant to a UN General Assembly resolution, Graça Machel of Mozambique submitted a ground-breaking report entitled "Impact of Armed Conflict on Children" (widely known as the Machel Report).[48] The Machel Report was a front runner in sensitizing the international community to the hazardous effects of violent conflict on children, including child soldiers. It has had tremendous social constructivist influence. In light of the Machel Report's recommendation, for example, the Office of the Special Representative on Children and Armed Conflict was established within the UN system.

The Machel Report identifies child soldiers as victims and targets and, also, "even" as perpetrators.[49] That said, it didactically presents acts of atrocity perpetrated by child soldiers as the product of coercion or manipulation by adults. The Machel Report recognizes the complexities of "balancing culpability, a community's sense of justice and the 'best interests of the child'."[50] It does not explicitly disclaim the penal responsibility of child soldiers, but neither does it encourage child soldiers to become subjects of criminal prosecutions. Paris Principle 8.6 flatly states that "[c]hildren should not be prosecuted by an international court or tribunal." The Paris Principles also address truth-seeking and reconciliation mechanisms:

> 8.15 All children who take part in these mechanisms, including those who have been associated with armed forces or armed groups should be treated equally as witnesses or as victims.

> 8.16 Children's participation in these mechanisms must be voluntary. No provision of services or support should be dependent on their participation in these mechanisms.

The approach of the Paris Principles to preclude international criminal trials and dissuade national criminal trials is to be welcomed. So, too, is the Paris Principles' commendation of truth-seeking and reconciliation mechanisms and support (albeit quite cursory) of traditional rituals. That said, the Paris Principles shrink the ability of such mechanisms to explore fully the multidimensionality of child soldier returnees, notably their roles as perpetrators. Accordingly, the application of such mechanisms thins and becomes superficial.

In the aftermath of the Second World War, the International Military Tribunal (IMT) and a variety of other institutions, including the Nuremberg Military Tribunals (NMTs), concerned themselves with the crimes of Nazi Germany. No mention was made in the Nuremberg Statute, Control Council Law No. 10, or Control Council Ordinance No. 7 of the age at which criminal responsibility began; in any event, no minor was charged under any of these instruments. Although the IMT prosecuted Baldur von Schirach for inter alia his use of the Hitler Youth, it did not address crimes committed by the youth themselves. The constitutive statutes of the International Criminal Tribunal for the former Yugoslavia (ICTY, 1993) and the International Criminal Tribunal for Rwanda (ICTR, 1994) similarly offer no guidance regarding the age of criminal responsibility. The Rome Statute of the International Criminal court has no jurisdiction over any person who is under the age of eighteen at the time of the alleged commission of the crime.[51]

The SCSL Statute limited the SCSL's jurisdiction to defendants who were fifteen years of age or older at the time of the alleged offense.[52] The SCSL Statute gave special considerations to "juvenile offenders," that is, defendants under the age of eighteen at the time of the alleged offense and exempted them from incarceration.[53] Instead, the SCSL "shall order any of the following: care guidance and supervision orders, community service orders, counselling, foster care, correctional, educational and vocational training programmes, approved schools and, as appropriate, any programmes of disarmament, demobilization and reintegration or programmes of child protection agencies."[54] The SCSL's first chief prosecutor promptly and unequivocally stated that he would never prosecute children under the age of eighteen, including child soldiers, inter alia, because they do not bear the greatest responsibility.[55] Indeed, none were prosecuted.

But these international institutions can prosecute and incarcerate former child soldiers who committed crimes as adults. Currently, as noted above, Dominic Ongwen faces prosecution in The Hague on many counts of horrific crimes.[56] Ongwen himself was a violently abducted and abused child soldier. Ongwen came of age in the LRA. He rose through the ranks from nothing to a brigadier commander. He fled the LRA in his early forties, surrendered to US Special Forces, and was transferred to the ICC. Questions persist as to whether, and if so to what extent, his background as an abducted child matter in terms of penal liability. Indications thus far are that this background matters little, though it could, perhaps, emerge as a mitigating factor in sentencing in the event Ongwen is convicted.

5 Reintegration and Homecoming

> I did step on the egg, it broke beneath my foot and I moved into the compound. She was crying all this time. As if that wasn't enough, she had to carry me on her back as if I was a two year old kid. She took me to the house, never asked me anything about the bush.[57]

This is how Alex Olango, a formerly abducted child soldier, discusses his return home from years of brutalities in the LRA. He describes the process of *mato oput*, practiced in northern Uganda, to welcome those from afar who are filled with bad spirits, *cen*, spirits of war. Extensive deployment of *mato oput* has facilitated a significant depletion of the LRA's ranks. On a general note, many child soldiers return to their communities of origin through disarmament, demobilization, and reintegration programs. Principle 12 of the Vancouver Principles, in fact, calls for child soldiers to be included as a priority in such programs. Disarmament involves the collection of weapons. Demobilization means the discharge of individuals from fighting forces. Reintegration is the step through which the former fighter transitions to a civilian role. Of considerable concern is the sidelining of transitional justice initiatives from post-conflict programming to reintegrate former child soldiers. The phrase *transitional justice* designates the range of processes by which societies come to terms with histories of widespread violence, how they reckon with terrible human rights abuses, and how people within afflicted constituencies come to live together again. Processes commonly associated with transitional justice include criminal trials, civil liability (for example, private tort actions, restitutionary claims, and public reparations), lustration, community service programs, truth and reconciliation commissions, ceremonies, rites, rituals, public inquiries, and restorative initiatives. These processes vary considerably inter se regarding how, to whom, and to what degree they allocate responsibility for acts of atrocity. They nevertheless share the pursuit of social repair through a framework that recognizes the pain wrought by the violence. This does not necessarily mean that perpetrators have to confess or atone. Many ceremonies, for example, do not contemplate such methods. *Mato oput* in Uganda, referenced above, is such an example—once the egg is stepped on, the time in the bush is no longer discussed—as evidenced by Alex Olango's mother.

I believe these processes can promote the reintegration of child soldiers. I have argued elsewhere, however, that atrophying the three-dimensionality of child soldiers (victims, witnesses, and actors) into a safer two-dimensionality (only victims and witnesses) weakens the place of transitional justice in DDR (disarmament, demobilization, and reintegration) frameworks and hence hinders reintegration, notably for two of the most vulnerable groups of former child soldiers, namely, (1) children associated with acts of serial atrocity and (2) girl soldiers who have endured crimes (including endemic sexual assault) committed by other child soldiers.[58]

Another challenge for child soldiers is epistemological. From where do we *know* what we know about child soldiers? In terms of the development of the law, best practices, and policy, two sources of knowledge have exerted considerable influence. These are child psychology and trauma studies, on the one hand, and reports published by transnational pressure groups, NGOs, activists, and UN agencies, on the other.

Other disciplines and their literatures have not resonated with the international legal imagination. Thus, contributions from other fields remain untapped, which is unfortunate since many hail from the Global South. Examples of undervalued contributions include ethnographic participant observation, anthropological studies, qualitative research, survey data, and feminist theory. Another is adolescent developmental neurobiology, which focuses on the social category of adolescents as distinct from young children. Although not monolithic, these literatures tend to perceive child soldiers neither as crushed nor as succumbing, but rather as traversing, surviving, coping, and making what they can out of bad circumstances not of their own doing. These literatures voice a more dynamic account of child soldiers as interacting with, instead of being overwhelmed by, their environments. These literatures also tend to place children, adolescents, youth, and adults along a broader continuum that is less rigidly stratified by chronological age demarcations.

On this note, persons under the age of eighteen associated with armed forces or armed groups largely get there in one of three ways: (1) they are abducted or conscripted through force or serious threats; (2) they present themselves, whether independently or through recruitment programs, and become enlisted/enrolled; or (3) they are born into forces or groups. The first two paths, which are the most common, are not always capable of firm demarcation. However, they are distinguishable and, moreover, should be distinguished.

Readers may find it surprising, but most child soldiers are neither abducted nor forcibly recruited.[59] The international legal imagination, nevertheless, heavily emphasizes this path to militarization. Doing so exposes this horrific aspect of the phenomenon of child soldiering. This emphasis, however, also leads to the under-theorization and under-exploration of youth volunteerism. The international legal imagination cannot just wish away the fact that significant numbers of children join armed forces or armed groups in the absence of evident coercion and, in fact, exercise some—and at times considerable—initiative and maturity in this regard.

The international legal imagination is remiss to neglect the prevalence and relevance of children who volunteer for military service. To be sure, cases arise where determinations of volunteerism would be specious. Children may be offered up—like chattel—by family members or local leaders. They may be tricked into joining. They may come forward to serve as a cook, only to be given an automatic weapon and placed on the front lines. Some children may rashly present themselves for service because of excessive impulsivity. That said, many children, notably older adolescents, come forward intentionally to join armed forces or groups. Environmental factors and situational constraints—which include poverty, insecurity, lack of education, socialization into violence, and broken families—certainly inform their decisions to enlist. Children's engagement with these factors can be more usefully understood as interactive and negotiated processes of negative push and affirmative pull. In joining armed forces or groups, children may simply be pursuing paths of economic advancement, inclusion in occupational networks, pursuit of political or ideological reform, and professional development. Although assertions of volunteer service made by child soldiers should not be immunized from contextual analysis, I believe it is wrong to dismiss them summarily. Young people may understand volunteerism within the context of their lives and apply it fairly to themselves.

Dismissing what adolescents have to say contrasts sharply with assumptions of juvenile capacity and autonomy that animate other areas of law and policy. For example, when it comes to bioethical debates regarding consent to medical treatment and access to reproductive rights and technologies, in many jurisdictions adolescents tend to be presumed competent. International human rights law highlights that adolescents can exercise rights of freedom of association and expression. So, too, does international family law. This chapter argues that protective policies predicated upon children being constructed as enfeebled before and during conflict may counterproductively result in children persistently being treated as enfeebled after conflict.

6 Conclusion

This chapter argues that a more nuanced, and less didactic, account of child soldiering is a more accurate one. As the late British historian Eric Hobsbawn famously intoned, sometimes the point "really is not so much to change the world as to understand it."[60] In this instance, understanding the scourge of child soldiering, and understanding it accurately, is in fact key to changing the world in that such an understanding better helps to deter the practice and to reintegrate those children caught up in it.

Notes

1. This chapter draws from, and materially updates and expands, sections of my book *Reimagining Child Soldiers in International Law and Policy* (New York: Oxford University Press, 2012).

2. See, e.g., Faith J. H. McDonnell and Grace Akallo, *Girl Soldier: A Story of Hope for Northern Uganda's Children* (Grand Rapids, MI: Chosen Books, 2007); Ishmael Beah, *A Long Way Gone: Memoirs of a Boy Soldier* (New York: Farrar, Straus and Giroux, 2008); Alex Olango *Scars of a Boy Soldier: A Boy Soldier's Story in His Own Words* (London: New Generation Publishing, 2016); Dave Eggers, *What Is the What: The Autobiography of Valentino Achak Deng* (New York: Random House, 2007); *War Child* (2008, documentary film, dir./prod. Karim Chrobog).

3. For example, the Children, Not Soldiers campaign, launched in 2014 with UNICEF, to end and prevent the recruitment of children by government security forces. This campaign ended in 2016.

4. Paris Principles and Guidelines on Children Associated with Armed Forces or Armed Groups (February 2007), https://www.unicef.org/emerg/files/ParisPrinciples310107English. pdf, adopted together with the Paris Commitments to Protect Children from Unlawful Recruitment or Use by Armed Forces or Armed Groups. These principles and commitments build upon the 1997 Cape Town Principles and Best Practices on the Recruitment of Children into the Armed Forces and on Demobilization and Social Reintegration of Child Soldiers in Africa.

5. Watchlist on Children and Armed Conflict, " 'Protect Children from War'— 10th Anniversary of the Paris Commitments and the Paris Principles on Children Associated With Armed Forces and Armed Groups," http://watchlist.org/protect-children-war-10th-anniversary-paris-commitmentsparis-principles-children-associated-armed-forces-armed-groups (accessed Sept. 6, 2019).

6. Government of Canada, "Principles of Vancouver" (launched Nov. 15, 2017), http://international.gc.ca/world-monde/issues_development-enjeux_developpement/human _rights-droits_homme/principles-vancouver-principes.aspx?lang=eng. As of January 18, 2018, fifty-nine states had endorsed the Vancouver Principles as founders.

7. See Embassy of France in Singapore, " 'Protecting Children from War,' Conference 21, February 2017," https://sg.ambafrance.org/Protecting-Children-from-War-Conference-21-February-2017-Paris (accessed Sept. 6, 2019).

8. UN General Assembly, "Children and Armed Conflict: Report of the Secretary-General," A/72/361–S/2017/821 (2017), annual report summary, https://reliefweb.int/sites/reliefweb. int/files/resources/N1726811.pdf.

9. Josh Rogin, "Obama's Failed Legacy on Child Soldiers," *Washington Post*, September 25, 2016.

10. Ilsa M. Glazer, "Book Review," *Anthropological Quarterly* 79, no. 2 (2006): 373–384, 382.

11. Morris Loveday, "Islamic State, Losing Fighters and Territory, Increasingly Turns to Child Bombers," *Washington Post*, August 22, 2016.

12. UN General Assembly, "Children and Armed Conflict."

13. Alcinda Honwana, *Child Soldiers in Africa* (Philadelphia: University of Pennsylvania Press, 2006), 7, 29, 54.

14. Phuong N. Pham, Patrick Vinck, and Eric Stover, "The Lord's Resistance Army and Forced Conscription in Northern Uganda," *Human Rights Quarterly* 30, no. 2 (2008): 404–411.

15. Pacifique Manirakiza, "Les Enfants Face au Système International de Justice: à la Recherche d'un Modèle de Justice Pénale Internationale pour les Délinquants Mineurs," *Queen's Law Journal* 34 (2009): 719–768, 761.

16. UN Convention on the Rights of the Child (CRC), G.A. Res. 44/25, Annex, UN Doc. A/RES/44/25 (1989), art. 38(2).

17. Optional Protocol to the CRC on the Involvement of Children in Armed Conflict, G.A. Res. 54/263, U.N. Doc. A/RES/54/263 (2000).

18. Optional Protocol, art. 1.

19. Michael Wessells, *Child Soldiers* (Cambridge, MA: Harvard University Press, 2009), 234.

20. Optional Protocol, art. 3(3).

21. Some states parties do not have armed forces and, hence, have nothing to declare (although they may make declarations regarding national police, customs, gendarmerie, etc). Some states, to be clear, set higher ages. Afghanistan, for example, permits voluntary recruitment of persons aged twenty-two to twenty-eight; several states list the age of nineteen. Chile (in 2008), Paraguay (in 2006), Poland (in 2013), and Luxembourg (in 2013) adopted the minimum age of eighteen for voluntary recruitment, thereby amending their earlier declarations.

22. On November 18, 2010, Guyana raised its declared minimum age to sixteen from the previous benchmark of fourteen.

23. Optional Protocol, art. 4(1).

24. ILO Convention No. 182: Concerning the Prohibition and Immediate Elimination of the Worst Forms of Child Labour, 38 ILM. 1207 (1999; entered into the force June 17, 1999). Recommendation 190 accompanying this convention encourages the criminalization of forced or compulsory recruitment.

25. ILO Convention No. 182, arts. 1, 3(a).

26. African Charter on the Rights and Welfare of the Child, OAU Doc. CAB/LEG/24.9/49 (1990; entered into force Nov. 29, 1999) arts. 2, 22(2).

27. Convention (IV) Relative to the Protection of Civilian Persons in Time of War 75 UNTS 287 (Aug. 12, 1949), arts. 14, 17, 23, 24, 38, 50, 51, 68, 82, 89, 94, and 132.

28. Protocol Additional to the Geneva Conventions of 12 August 1949, and Relating to the Protection of Victims of International Armed Conflicts (Protocol I), 1125 UNTS 3 (June 8, 1977).

29. Protocol I, arts. 70(1), 78.

30. Protocol Additional to the Geneva Conventions of 12 August 1949, and relating to the Protection of Victims of Non-International Armed Conflicts (Protocol II), 1125 UNTS 609 (June 8, 1977).

31. Chen Reis, "Trying the Future, Avenging the Past: The Implications of Prosecuting Children for Participation in Internal Armed Conflict," *Columbia Human Rights Law Review* 28 (1997): 629–655, 654.

32. Rome Statute of the International Criminal Court (Rome Statute), 2187 UNTS 90 (1998; entered into force July 1, 2002).

33. Prosecutor v. Brima, Kamara, and Kanu, Case No. SCSL-04-16-T, SCSL Trial Chamber (June 20, 2007) ¶ 734 (hereinafter AFRC Trial Judgment).

34. AFRC Trial Judgment, ¶ 735.

35. Prosecutor v. Fofana and Kondewa, Case No. SCSL-04-14-A, SCSL Appeals Chamber (May 28, 2008) ¶¶ 141, 144. If the child "is allowed to voluntarily join . . . , his or her consent is not a valid defence" (¶ 140).

36. Prosecutor v. Sesay, Kallon, and Gbao, Case No. SCSL-04-15-T, SCSL Trial Chamber (March 2, 2009), ¶¶ 1712–1731. Domestic chores, farm work, and conducting food finding missions were however found not to constitute active participation in hostilities (¶¶ 1739, 1743).

37. Prosecutor v. Lubanga, Case No. ICC-01/04–01/06, ICC Trial Chamber I (March 14, 2012) ¶ 608.

38. Rome Statute, arts.7(1)(c), 7(1)(g), 7(1)(k), 7(2)(c), 8(2)(b)(ix), 8(2)(b)(ix), 8(2)(e)(iv), and 8(2)(e)(iv). The Office of the Special Representative has identified attacks on schools and hospitals as "one of the most disturbing trends documented in 2016." UN General Assembly, "Children and Armed Conflict," 3.

39. Rome Statute, art. 75(2).

40. Mark Drumbl, *Reimagining Child Soldiers in International Law and Policy*. (Oxford: Oxford University Press, 2012), 162–166.

41. Rogin, "Obama's Failed Legacy on Child Soldiers."

42. René Prevost, "Targeting Child Soldiers," *EJIL: Talk!*, January 12, 2016, www.ejiltalk.org/targeting-child-soldiers.

43. Stephen J. Thorne, "Doctrine on Child Soldiers Is First of Its Kind," *Legion: Canada's Military History Magazine*, March 15, 2017, https://legionmagazine.com/en/2017/03/doctrine-on-child-soldiers-is-first-of-its-kind.

44. CRC, art. 37(b) (also requiring that "[n]o child shall be deprived of his or her liberty unlawfully or arbitrarily").

45. CRC, art. 37(c).

46. Amnesty International, *Child Soldiers: Criminals or Victims?*, AI Index No. IOR 50/02/00 (Dec. 22, 2000), 15.

47. Drumbl, *Reimagining Child Soldiers*, 104 (for detailed sources of these compilations).

48. Report of the Expert of the Secretary-General, "Impact of Armed Conflict on Children," UN Doc. A/51/306 (Aug. 26, 1996), http://www.unicef.org/graca/a51-306_en.pdf (hereinafter Machel Report).

49. Machel Report, para. 24.

50. Machel Report, para. 250.

51. Rome Statute, art. 26.

52. Statute of the Special Court for Sierra Leone, 2178 UNTS 145 (2002), art. 7(1) (hereinafter SCSL Statute).

53. SCSL Statute, arts. 7(2), 19(1).

54. SCSL Statute, art. 7(2).

55. Special Court for Sierra Leone, Public Affairs Office, "Special Court Prosecutor Says He Will Not Prosecute Children," press release (Nov. 2, 2002).

56. The International Crimes Division of the Ugandan High Court, sitting in Gulu, also is prosecuting another former child soldier, Thomas Kwoyelo, who also became a commander in the Lord's Resistance Army.

57. Olango, *Scars of a Boy Soldier*, 67.

58. Drumbl, *Reimagining Child Soldiers*, 192–206.

59. Drumbl, *Reimagining Child Soldiers*, 13.

60. Tony Judt with Timothy Snyder, *Thinking the Twentieth Century* (New York: Penguin, 2013), 79. (Hobsbawn inverted a well-known saying by Karl Marx).

CHAPTER 32

WORKING TOWARD RECOGNITION OF THE RIGHTS OF MIGRANT AND REFUGEE CHILDREN

SARAH PAOLETTI

1 INTRODUCTION

A three-year-old Syrian boy washed ashore in Turkey after drowning in transit with his family fleeing a brutal and prolonged conflict. Rohingya children, some alone and some with their parents, seemingly frozen in a state of fear and expectation, having fled to Bangladesh after their communities in Myanmar were attacked. A malnourished child walking to find water in South Sudan, whose eyes communicate both skepticism and hope that the future will bring something other than persistent hunger and struggle. A roomful of Central American children sleeping on a concrete floor, covered by thin mylar sheets, in a detention center on the southern border of the United States, having fled gang violence in their communities, and sometimes extreme violence within their own home. A Honduran child looking up in tears as her mother is interrogated and detained by US immigration authorities. These are among the iconic images that have captured the plight of children displaced from their homes. But these images only tell part of the story of child migration.

In 2017 an estimated thirty-six million children and persons under the age of twenty were migrants, constituting nearly 14 percent of the total migrant population.[1] Of those children, nearly twelve million were refugees or asylum seekers.[2] An additional sixteen million children had been internally displaced due to conflict and violence.[3] Nonetheless, as Jacqueline Bhabha admonished in her seminal book *Child Migration and Human Rights in a Global Age*, "Children do not feature in [the] large-scale picture [of migration], except as occasional appendages to adults.... The failure to attend to child migration coincides with the diffusion of confused, unsatisfactory, and frequently oppressive policies that should not stand up to careful public scrutiny."[4]

This chapter is part of a growing effort among members of the international community, advocates, researchers, and academics to remedy the historical failure that Bhabha highlights.[5] It focuses on those migrant children for whom the decision to migrate is not purely voluntary. The factors contributing to human migration are multiple and often defy the binary notion that there are those who are forced migrants versus those who are voluntary migrants. This is no less true for children than it is for adults, as it is for families who migrate for one or more of the following reasons: persecution, violence, economic deprivation, lack of educational and other opportunities for personal development, environmental degradation, family reunification, and other related factors.[6] For the majority of children migrating for any combination of the above identified reasons, there are no regular pathways toward either temporary or permanent resettlement in a third country. Children are therefore often exposed to heightened vulnerabilities arising from their irregular or undocumented status.[7] In addressing the rights and obligations that apply to migrant children, this chapter seeks to dispel notions as to who is a so-called worthy migrant and who is not, notions that often evolve from the false forced versus voluntary dichotomy and the legal versus illegal label that attaches based on migration status. The worthy label most often attaches to the young and innocent child, a refugee or victim of trafficking, who has been taken from or forced from his or her home, and who needs to be saved from the harsh consequences of war and the illicit acts of elders; those children who voluntarily left their home country, particularly those who are in an irregular or undocumented status, and whose parents or who themselves are deemed complicit in and even responsible for the harms that may befall them, are deemed less worthy or unworthy.

Section 2 of this chapter begins with an overview of how laws and policies treat migrant children and reviews the key provisions of the Convention of the Rights of the Child[8] and other key international and regional human rights instruments that apply to migrant children and how those rights are often implemented, depending on how governments categorize the children. Section 3 examines tensions that arise between the rights and realities of children subject to the jurisdiction of a country that is not their country of origin. It looks first at migrant children's interactions with a government exercising its sovereign right to regulate migration across its borders. It then looks at what rights are or should be afforded to those children who have taken up residence in a new country, whether temporarily or on a more permanent basis.[9]

The chapter concludes by examining the current gaps in the rights protection regime as applied to child migrants and highlighting the need for continued thought and expertise to ensure the full engagement of children themselves not just in terms of the immediate decisions impacting their individual lives, but the lives of all children today and in the future.

2 RIGHTS VERSUS REALITIES: APPLYING THE CONVENTION ON THE RIGHTS OF THE CHILD AND CORE HUMAN RIGHTS PRINCIPLES TO ALL CATEGORIES OF MIGRANT CHILDREN

The Convention on the Rights of the Child (CRC) provides a guiding set of norms under international law for addressing the rights of all children throughout all stages of migration, norms consistent with and reiterated in other international human rights instruments and jurisprudence.[10] And international law is clear: States must treat migrant children as children first,[11] ensuring all children are provided special protections as warranted based on their physical and emotional development.[12] The best interests of the child standard must guide all legislative, administrative, and other actions that impact the lives of migrant children.[13] And states should ensure that processes are in place to enable children to exercise their voice and share their views with regard to decisions that have a direct impact on their lives.[14] Furthermore, the principle of non-discrimination as set forth in the CRC and other international and regional human rights instruments guarantees that all children, regardless of their migration status and regardless of the migration status of their parents, are entitled to equal enjoyment of all fundamental rights set forth in both the international treaties and domestic law alike, without discrimination.[15] In this way, international law serves as an important check on states as they seek to enforce immigration laws and limit non-nationals' access to socioeconomic and other rights in ways that interfere with the child's survival and development.[16]

In fulfilling their obligations vis-à-vis migrant children, states must conduct multiple preliminary assessments. As a preliminary matter, a state must determine whether a migrant is a child under international law. International law generally recognizes as a child any person under the age of eighteen, unless the applicable law sets a younger age of majority.[17] But determining a person's age is not always straightforward, particularly for migrants who: may have lost their identity documents evidencing their age; may be in possession of fraudulent identity documents obtained to facilitate migration; or whose birth was never officially registered and for whom there are, therefore, no attainable records evidencing actual age. Whether the state's interaction with the migrant is initiated in the context of its efforts to regulate a migrant's entry and stay in country, or in the context of providing a migrant with basic services, such as education and health care, the state is obligated to carry out an age assessment conducted in a safe and scientific manner that protects the dignity of the purported child, is gender-specific and culturally appropriate, and grants the benefit of the doubt to the child.[18]

In addition to identifying the age of the child, states must also assess the specific circumstances related to the child's migration and the impact those circumstances may have on a child. While the lines delineating the different categories of migrant children are often blurred, and at times overlap, or fail to account for the particular circumstances of the migrant child altogether, understanding the implications of the categories that are applied to migrant children—in accordance with different complementary and sometimes overlapping international and domestic legal regimes—is central to a state's ability to develop effective policies and practices that fulfill the rights of the child. As such, states encountering migrant children must first make an individualized assessment as to: whether a child is accompanied by parents, unaccompanied by any parent or legal guardian, or separated from said parents or legal guardians but accompanied by other family members; whether the child has been subjected to trafficking or other forms of exploitation and abuse at the hands of smugglers during the course of migration; and whether the child qualifies for refugee status or similar protection.

Until the twenty-first century, children historically had migrated predominantly with their parents and were viewed as having rights derivative of those afforded to their parents, with little attention given to the migrant children as rights-bearers themselves.[19] The rise in the number of unaccompanied children, though, has coincided with the development of international children's rights law, resulting in greater attention to the rights of migrant children as children and a recognition of the need for individualized assessments of the best interests of the child and related rights and obligations, independent of and together with those granted to the family.[20] States can no longer turn a blind eye to the children in the midst of their migrant populations, and in determining their obligations to migrant children, they must first determine the familial status of the children. A determination as to whether a child is accompanied, unaccompanied, or separated carries with it different obligations as to the child—the first predominated by respect for and preservation of familial rights, so long as those rights are carried out in light of the child's best interests, while the latter are predominated by the state's obligation to assume *in locus parentis* obligations toward that child, either until the child reaches the age of majority, is reunited with his or her parents, or is permanently placed into the care of another legal guardian. As with the dynamism that accompanies all aspects of human migration, a child's familial status is often not permanent: children may become separated from their parents while in transit; or on arrival in the host country, they may begin the journey unaccompanied in pursuit of family reunification; and other guardian relationships may evolve in the course of migration and over the course of their childhoods.

For those children who migrate out of necessity—whether accompanied or unaccompanied—access to official and documented means of migration may be limited, forcing them into irregular channels of migration, often aided by smugglers and exploited by traffickers.[21] Parents, relatives, or sometimes older children themselves may pay smugglers to assist with their migration. Others, taken by force, fraud, or coercion, who are then subjected to forced labor, prostitution, or child pornography are deemed to be trafficked; they present unique vulnerabilities that are often responded to with differing degrees of sympathy and protections than are afforded to those who are smuggled. But migrant children who supposedly entered into a relationship with a smuggler voluntarily may subsequently find themselves in a situation of trafficking or subjected to other extreme forms of abuse and exploitation. For example, a study conducted by the International Organization of Migration in Italy revealed that as many as 78 percent of child migrants had experienced trafficking or other exploitative practices in the course of their journeys.[22] Unaccompanied children are at a heightened risk of severe forms of exploitation and trafficking simply because there is no parent present to protect the child, and extra care is required to ensure the well-being of a child of any age who suffered at the hands of smugglers and traffickers alike.[23]

As with migrant children who are victims of trafficking and other forms of exploitation and abuse, refugee children and children fleeing violence and others forms of persecution warrant additional protections and are entitled to such protections under international law.[24] For children accompanied by their parents, the refugee determination is most often made as to the parent(s); the child is granted derivative refugee status. For unaccompanied or separated children, though, ensuring their rights are adequately protected in the making of a refugee status determination can be particularly challenging, especially for those who for reasons of age, development, or trauma are unable to articulate the reasons for their migration and the harms that may befall them if returned home.[25] Furthermore, the grant of refugee status alone does not in practice ensure the protection of the rights of the child. As seen in protracted refugee crises across the globe, for example, children who are granted refugee status but are not provided with a clear path toward full integration into the host community or resettlement to a third country are left in a state of limbo, without full access to education, health care, and other basic services aimed at their development, giving rise to additional vulnerabilities and rights abuses.[26]

The final category of children included among those classified herein as *migrant* are those rendered stateless, those who have been denied a nationality.[27] Stateless children lack documented status in any country, including the country in which they were born, due either to intentional government action or inaction or to the circumstances under which they were born. They may reside in the country in which they were born, though their status in that country may be deemed unlawful, or they themselves migrate, leaving the country that rendered them stateless to seek protection and opportunity from another country. Stateless children, who have no country willing to claim them, cannot prove their country of birth, most often do not have documentation evidencing their age, and are denied access to basic rights and services. Migrant children are themselves at a heightened risk of statelessness because their parents may be afraid to register their birth because they risk deportation if they make their presence known or because of other legal or logistical barriers within the country of birth. At the same time, legal and logistical barriers to obtaining citizenship status from the parents' country of origin are often too great to overcome, particularly when those parents are in flight.

For all categories of migrant and stateless children,[28] the child's family rights must remain a predominant consideration. The state's regulation of both the child's entry and stay in another country, as well as the child's parent's entry and stay in that country, impacts those relationships that often form the foundation for a child's best interests, survival, and development. It is therefore incumbent on the state to take all necessary measures to ensure that accompanied children are not separated from their parents and that reunification is facilitated where possible and where in service of the child's interests for those who are unaccompanied or have been separated from their families.

3 Children's Rights in the Context of Immigration Enforcement and Status Determinations

International law recognizes the sovereign right of a country to regulate and restrict the entry of non-nationals into and departure from its territory, but that right is not unbounded: a country cannot act in a way that is contrary to its obligation under international law to respect, protect and fulfill the human rights of all persons—adults and children alike—subject to its jurisdiction, regardless of that person's migration status.[29] This section addresses the intersection of these—sometimes competing—interests of immigration enforcement and human rights protection and the ways in which a migrant child's human rights may be subsumed by a government's regulation of who is permitted entry and stay within its borders. It looks at a state's obligations to take affirmative measures to ensure that a child's best interests are met and to contribute to the child's survival and development without discrimination. This section also highlights the procedural and substantive rights protections mandated by international human rights law to restore or ensure the primacy of the rights of the child.[30] In doing so, it looks at the child's right to be heard and to have his or her views taken into consideration as well as the challenges associated with the realization of those rights due to the age of the child and the developmental, linguistic, culturally based, and psychological or trauma-induced barriers to communication.

3.1 A State's Obligations to Child Migrants When Implementing and Enforcing Policies, Procedures, and Practices Designed to Regulate (and Restrict) Entry and Stay in Country

Children transiting through a country or seeking entry and permission to stay in a country often find themselves lost in a frightening system designed for the enforcement of immigration laws against adult migrants. In the face of increased attention on child migration, and particularly the migration of unaccompanied children, international human rights law is increasingly a source of important guidance for ensuring that the needs and vulnerabilities of children are recognized and that governments do not act in a manner that perpetuates or compounds the trauma experienced by migrant children but instead act to further the child's best interests, survival, and development. Rights most often implicated and violated by a state's policies to regulate migrants' admission and stay in the country—both as it relates to children traveling with their families and those who are unaccompanied or separated—are their rights to liberty and security of person and their right to participation in decisions that impact their lives, the right to seek asylum, and related due process considerations.

3.1.1 *Liberty Interests of the Child*

International law is clear: detention of children should be carried out only as a matter of last resort and for the shortest time possible,[31] as the best interests of the child are almost never served through deprivation of liberty. As clearly stated by UN Special Rapporteur on torture and other cruel, inhuman or degrading treatment or punishment Juan E. Méndez:

> Within the context of administrative immigration enforcement, it is now clear that the deprivation of liberty of children based on their or their parents' migration status is never in the best interests of the child, exceeds the requirement of necessity, becomes grossly disproportionate and may constitute cruel, inhuman or degrading treatment of migrant children. Therefore, States should, expeditiously and completely, cease the detention of children, with or without their parents, on the basis of their immigration status.[32]

Similarly, the UN Committee on the Rights of All Migrant Workers and Members of Their Families (CMW) and the UN Committee on the Rights of the Child (CRC Committee) have both reiterated that "children should never be detained for reasons related to their or their parents' migration status and States should expeditiously and completely cease or eradicate the immigration detention of children."[33]

Nonetheless, nearly one hundred countries across the globe continue to detain children for migration-related reasons.[34] Children are held in immigration detention facilities with their families, in mixed prison populations, and in holding centers that are intended for detaining unaccompanied and separated children. Regardless of the circumstances of detention, the long-term physical and psychological harm to children is indisputable.[35] In addition, the detention of migrant children often directly interferes with their ability to pursue their asylum claims and to exercise their voice in the administrative or judicial proceedings, both of which are key if migrant children are to determine their right to remain in the country of detention.[36]

The United States is among those countries that persist in detaining migrant children. Despite a 1997 nationwide settlement agreement in *Flores v. Reno* limiting the terms and conditions under which children could be detained, the number of detained migrant children rose to more than fifty thousand in 2014 following a US policy shift responding to the purported surge in individuals arriving in the United States from Central America to seek asylum.[37] This prompted advocates to return to court to compel the US government to release the children from detention and to ensure the release of their parents alongside them, consistent with the *Flores* settlement.[38] The Inter-American Commission on Human Rights has similarly urged the United States to ensure the prompt and safe release of migrant children from detention consistent with international law. In a 2015 report the Commission emphasized established principles of international law regarding the best interests of the child in the context of immigrant detention; quoting from the Inter-American Court on Human Rights, the Inter-American Commission urged the US to ensure the safe and prompt release of children from detention, further noting that "when the child's best interest requires keeping the family together, the imperative requirement not to deprive the child of liberty extends to her or his parents and obliges the authorities to choose alternative measures to detention for the family, which are appropriate to the needs of the children."[39]

3.1.2 *A Child's Right to Seek Asylum*

Ensuring the right to seek asylum is central to protecting the rights of children by guarding against their return to a country where they will face persecution. States must exercise extra care in refugee status determinations for children and in protecting the additional rights afforded to those children deemed to be refugees. In doing so, states must be attentive to the unique forms of persecution children may encounter, including but not limited to: forced or underage marriage, female genital circumcision, bonded or hazardous labor, forced prostitution, child pornography, forced recruitment or conscription, forced prostitution, and other forms of persecution that "encompass violations of survival and development rights as well as severe discrimination of children born outside strict family planning rules and of stateless children as a result of loss of nationality and attendant rights."[40]

Of particular relevance to today's migrant children who may be able to demonstrate risk of persecution, yet do not meet the UN Refugee Convention's requirement that such persecution be on account of race, religion, membership in particular social group or political opinion, the African Union has also sought to recognize as a refugee any person who, "owing to external aggression, occupation, foreign domination or events seriously disturbing public order in either part or the whole of his country of origin or nationality, is compelled to leave his place of habitual residence in order to seek refuge in another place outside his country of origin or nationality."[41] Similarly, the Organization of American States has called on countries within the Americas to recognize as refugees "persons who have fled their countries because their life, safety or freedom have been threatened by generalized violence, foreign aggression, internal conflicts, massive violation of human rights or other circumstances which have seriously disturbed public order."[42] These more expansive definitions are particularly relevant to children who face forced conscription or recruitment into armed conflict or violent gangs.

A determination that a child does not qualify for refugee protection, however, does not end the inquiry into whether a state ought to provide lawful status and attendant rights to the child. In addition to the Convention against Torture's prohibition on returning individuals to countries where they will face torture,[43] the CRC obligates states to ensure the well-being, "survival and development" of all children subject to its jurisdiction without discrimination.[44] A further inquiry into a specific child's situation may reveal that the provision of lawful status and attendant rights is necessary to ensuring the child's security and development, particularly in the case of a child who is stateless, has fled environmental or related humanitarian disasters, or who has been orphaned, abandoned, or subjected to human trafficking and for whom deportation or return to the country of birth or nationality is not in child's best interest and would work against the complementary obligations of the state to ensure the child's survival and development.

The ability of a child to seek these protections, though, is incumbent on the due process guarantees, access to justice rights and rights to participation that are granted a child on arrival in a country and throughout any administrative or judicial proceedings to determine the child's status and rights of entry and stay.

3.1.3 A Child's Right to Participation and Accompanying Rights to Due Process and Access to Justice

A migrant child's right to "be heard in any judicial and administrative proceedings affecting the child"[45] is often overlooked in the context of immigration enforcement and proceedings. The CRC is explicit that not only must a child be granted the opportunity to be heard, but the child's views must be assessed in light of the child's age and maturity and granted "due weight."[46] Establishing clear protocols for accompanied migrant children is particularly important to combat the perception and resulting procedures that treat the child's claims—in the context of immigration—as derivative of or subservient to the rights of the parents. For unaccompanied or separated children, ensuring the child's right to participate is important in combatting the risks associated with migration-related policy responses—both at the governmental and nongovernmental level—that are premised on the "rescue" of the child, which is often followed by "return,"[47] or—in some cases—involuntary adoptions, where a family in the host country adopts a child separated from his or her parents or guardians, without first conducting a full inquiry into whether family reunification is possible.[48]

What does the right to be heard entail, and how is that right enhanced by the due process and access to justice rights contained in international human rights law? The UN Committee on the Protection of the Rights of All Migrant Workers and Members of Their Families and the Committee on the Rights of the Child have set forth clear guidelines, many of which have been reiterated by the UN High Commissioner for Refugees (UNHCR), UNICEF, and the regional human rights systems within Africa and the Americas.[49] The host or destination country must admit all children who present themselves, regardless of available documentation, and refer those children to a person qualified to make an initial assessment of his or her need for protection in a manner that is child-sensitive and focuses on the best interests of the child.[50] The host or destination country should also provide children with information regarding procedures, rights, and responsibilities, available services, and other information that may play a role in children's ability to assess options or solutions and to fully participate in decisions as to their future.[51] In recognition of the role that age and development status, mental health, education, and familiarity with the legal systems of the host country play in determining and serving a child's ultimate rights, particularly where children are unable to effectively communicate their own interests directly, states are urged to appoint a guardian whose sole job is to ensure that the child has the necessary information to assess and identify his or her options moving forward, to assess the best interests of the child, and to communicate those interests in the course of proceedings.[52] In addition, states are called on to provide legal representation to assist children in navigating the legal process as well as an interpreter to ensure the children's understanding and ability to communicate to all parties throughout the proceedings.[53]

Both the CMW and the CRC Committee have noted "the negative impacts on children's well-being of having an insecure and precarious migration status," and they therefore recommend that states provide "clear and accessible status determination procedures for children to regularize their status on various grounds (such as length of residence)."[54] The experiences of those who have lived in protracted refugee crises—who have been born in a refugee camp or who arrived at a refugee camp in their childhood, who have not been resettled or fully integrated into the host community, and for whom the option of repatriation is foreclosed for a prolonged period of time—acutely demonstrate the harm that befalls those who are forced to spend their youth in limbo. One Liberian refugee living in a refugee camp in Ghana that was open for just over two decades reported that "sometimes she loses hope and wants to commit suicide. She has no education and no parents."[55] The loss of hope comes from seeing one's childhood and opportunities for education and development pass by while the refugee remains in a state of limbo, waiting to be accepted into a country that will become home.

3.1.4 *Rights vis-à-vis the Family*

Family unity and preservation of the family is a core principle under the CRC, the presumption being that family unity is in the best interests of the child.[56] For migrant children who are accompanied by one or both parents, therefore, the goal is often to keep that family together. For migrant children who have been separated from their parents, the goal may be to facilitate reunification where possible or to at least ensure that the child remains with the other family members in the child's company. When the child is unaccompanied and the UNHCR or the state steps into the role of *in locus parentis*, it is incumbent on that entity to take the necessary care to preserve and protect the rights of the child. In all cases, the right to family unity must be prioritized in balance with the child's best interests and participation rights.[57]

The right to family unity as assessed through the lens of the best interests of the child requires a shift in the historical paradigm for addressing child migration, through which children are viewed as the appendages to their parents, often invisible to the decision maker, or at least silent in the course of present or future decision-making; the children's rights were, and often are still, deemed as derivative of those of the parents. A child-centric approach, in contrast, requires first examining the best interests of the child and assessing, through that determination, the role that parents and family play in serving those interests. As a state then seeks to regulate migration, the child is part of the decision-making process, even where the actions are as to the parent. For example, where a parent and child are seeking asylum, and the parent cannot meet the heightened threshold required for establishing that she qualifies as a refugee but the obligations of the state vis-à-vis the child in ensuring that child's security and development dictates the granting of lawful status to the child, the state must then assess the parents' right of entry based on whether family unity is in the child's best interest.[58] Where a state detains migrants upon entry, the right to family unity dictates that the family stays together. But international law also dictates that the child not be subject to immigration detention. The result: an alternative to detention must be sought for the entire family.[59]

3.2 Meeting the Best Interests and Full Development of the Migrant Child Residing in Host Country

While children and their family members migrate in search of safety and carry with them hopes for their future in the destination country, the realities they confront in the host country often challenge their optimism. The experiences may vary based on the child's migration status, whether that child is undocumented, is in the process of seeking status, has temporary status as a refugee or a related humanitarian status, or is on a path to citizenship. Each child's needs and assets can be assessed based on that child's physical and psychological health, the level of education attained, and the level of resources—including familial support—available to the child. Furthermore, a state's obligations to ensure non-discrimination in the enjoyment of rights requires recognition of the discrimination, harassment, and other forms of abuse that migrant children may experience based on gender, gender identity, sexual orientation, race, ethnicity, and familial or other social status.

While demographic knowledge specific to the population(s) of migrant children contributes to the international community's ability and the ability of states to develop policies responsive to their needs, vulnerabilities and strengths, there persists a dearth of disaggregated data for migrants. Developing that resource will facilitate the international community's ability to respond on a more proactive basis to the needs of migrant children.

3.2.1 *The Right to Education: Dreams Deferred*

Migrant children often experience disruption in education and are ultimately denied their right to an education, even though it is often a significant motivator in migrants' decisions to leave their home countries. Many migrant children are denied access to education in their host country because they are in transit or otherwise in a state of limbo and lack a place to call home; are detained in a facility where education is not provided to them; lack the necessary documentation evidencing residency status or academic history; face language barriers; or the gap between their age and the academic grade level is seen as too great. UNICEF reports that only half of age-eligible refugee children are enrolled in primary school and that less than one quarter of age-eligible children are enrolled in secondary school.[60] This is true despite the recognition under international law that all children are entitled to an education without discrimination and regardless of immigration status.[61] Those children who are enrolled may struggle to succeed because of language barriers, difficulties adapting to a different academic system, untreated trauma, discrimination, and significant disruptions in their academic development. For these migrant youth, their dreams are deferred until they can access education freely and without discrimination. Once children reach the age of majority, they may lose their educational rights, and the opportunities feel lost to them forever.

The right to education is particularly challenged in cases of protracted refugee crises, where children find themselves in a prolonged state of limbo without the benefits associated with legal and social integration into the host community and waiting on the hopes of possible third country resettlement.[62] The situation of Liberians living in the Buduburam Refugee Camp in Ghana exemplifies this. One mother reported: "Our children who are here are not in school because we don't have money to send them. We're depending on them to rebuild. My children are just sitting there with nothing to eat or drink. I want them to go to school anywhere—they have nothing to do here."[63] But the children confronted challenges accessing the Ghanaian school system, and the educational programming available to them within Buduburam was extremely limited. As one young Liberian woman told me in 2008, "If the war hadn't come, I would be a doctor by now." She fled Liberia during the civil war as she was about to enter into high school. Despite having refugee status, she had been unable to access schooling in Ghana and instead—more than a decade later—was sitting in the only educational and vocational training available to her—classes offered by other Liberians lingering at Buduburam, learning how to braid hair, sew and make jewelry, in the hopes of developing skills that would allow her to feed herself and her family.

3.2.2 *The Right to Health: Barriers to Access*

Migrant children and their family members often have mental and physical health issues that require access to care. These issues may have existed before the circumstances that gave rise to their departure from home; may be the cause for or be directly related to the reason for departing from home; may be the result of injuries, illness, or trauma suffered in transit; or may be health issues that befell the migrant child after arrival in the host country. Regardless as to the origination of the health need mandating access to care, the CRC obligates host countries to ensure the survival and development of, and access to health care by, all children without discrimination based on migration status.[64]

A September 2016 data-driven report by UNICEF, "Uprooted: The Growing Crisis for Refugee and Migrant Children," noted that the number of child migrants and refugees with disabilities is not tracked globally but reported on a study of refugees in Jordan and Lebanon that found one in four refugees surveyed had some form of impairment.[65] The study's findings are likely not unique to the refugee populations in Jordan and Lebanon and indicate the real need to develop policies and programs that account for those impairments.[66] Furthermore, it is incumbent upon a host state to guard against measures that will cause harm to a child's health, which has particular relevance in the context of enforcement measures that result in a child's detention: as noted above, detention has a lasting deleterious effect on the mental and physical health of a child and can serve to compound the trauma that child has already experienced.

The right to health care also implicates decisions made as to the migrant child's rights in the context of the regulation of a child's entry and presence in a country. For a child who has HIV or AIDS, a move to deport that child to a country where he or she will be ostracized and denied access to medical care is a decision that runs contrary to the country's obligations to ensure the health of all children within its jurisdiction. Similarly, a state may be abrogating its obligations under international law if it moves to deport a child who has fled domestic violence or female genital circumcision.[67] Thus states must not only ensure equal access to health care for all children regardless of migration status; they also must refrain from taking steps in the course of regulating migration that may have a deleterious impact on the health of the child.

3.2.3 *Rights in Work: Hazards, Abuses, and Justice Denied*

Migrant children's age and migration status make them particularly vulnerable to exploitation, and that vulnerability is often compounded by economic desperation on the part of the unaccompanied migrant child and migrant families alike.[68] Migrant children, as with many migrant workers and particularly those who are undocumented, are employed in informal job sectors, for example, as domestic servants, where they are often hidden from or otherwise excluded from protection. They attend school at a much lower rate than non-migrant children and face hazardous working conditions.[69] Migrant children routinely experience negative health and developmental consequences resulting from labor exploitation.

A state's obligations to ensure the best interests of the child as well as the child's survival and development require the state to take measures to ensure that children are protected from economic exploitation, hazardous work, or work that interferes with the child's education or is otherwise harmful to the child's health or development[70] and to ensure that no child is engaged in bonded labor or is providing labor under circumstances of force or coercion.[71] But it is not enough to rescue a child from a situation of child labor. Rescuing a child from an exploitative work situation could result in separating the child from his or her family. Furthermore, that child is likely to end up back in that working relationship, or perhaps an even more harmful working situation, if there is not a plan to address the underlying reasons for the child's labor in the first place: most often, the economic desperation of the child and the child's family.[72] States seeking to combat child labor must also be attentive to the concern that their efforts not serve to criminalize the child. In this sense, it is critical that enforcement of labor laws be segregated from enforcement of immigration laws. Ensuring the participatory rights of migrant children in decisions specific to labor will help to ensure the development of responses that better facilitate a child's freedom from hazardous and exploitative work rather than the enactment of provisions that may result in further exploitation or harm to children.

4 CONCLUSION: LOOKING FORWARD TO DEVELOPING GLOBAL, REGIONAL, AND LOCAL PRACTICES THAT SERVE THE BEST INTERESTS OF THE CHILD

Throughout their migration journey, children cross multiple jurisdictions, contested boundaries, and international waters with an intended destination country in mind—a country they may or may not ever reach, depending on the persons into whose hands their journey has been entrusted, the physical hazards presented by the journey, and any interception and enforcement initiatives undertaken by the governments of the countries through which they transit. A constant for children throughout their transit is the risk of all forms of violence, abuse, harassment and aggression, and vulnerability to trafficking as well as a lack of access to adequate food, potable water, health services and sanitation, and restrictions on liberty and freedom of movement. This is equally true for children traveling across the Central Mediterranean seeking entry into Europe,[73] children crossing the open waters from Southeast Asia to Australia, children crossing the vast deserts of Africa, and children transiting through Central America seeking entry into the United States as well as children crossing boundaries within their region (e.g., South-South or North-North migration). When the perpetrators of violence and other rights violations are government agents, the obligations of the state are clear; those obligations are not diminished, though, when the violations are committed by private actors or when the reasons for migration are not attributable to identifiable actors, as it is the responsibility of the state to take all measures necessary to not only respect but also to protect and fulfill the rights of all children subject to its jurisdiction.

While addressing the rights and obligations set forth in the CRC and other international and regional human rights instruments, this chapter seeks to bring attention to the complexity and fluidity of migration and the motives that spurn migration; the role of family in serving the child's best interests; and the scope of considerations that must be accounted for in seeking to ensure that the next generation of immigrants is positioned to thrive. Perhaps obvious, but rarely explicitly addressed, is the reality that while children may age out of the child category, the challenges and risks confronting migrants in childhood and adolescence do not magically cease to exist when that child turns eighteen, and the experiences endured by children before their eighteenth birthday have a lasting impact.[74] What measures can and should be taken to facilitate the transition for a child migrant from the legal age of majority and adulthood, particularly for those migrants whose childhoods have been interrupted, their education deferred, and their development delayed?

In developing responses to the above questions, as with developing responses to the multitude of challenges migrant children confront, it is critical that the children and those who experienced migration as a child be part of the discussion.[75] As Jacqueline

Bhabha has reported: "This population of child migrants requires non-paternalistic support and advice to enable them to realize the rights guaranteed to them by international law, including the rights to freedom from inhumane or degrading treatment; to basic education; to adequate health care, welfare support, and shelter. Above all, young migrants need to be listened to, and given a voice with which to articulate their concerns and hopes. Legal protections related to migration status need to be coupled with child welfare investments related to social and economic rights."[76]

NOTES

1. In 1990 that number was nearly 29 million or 18.8 percent of the total migrant population globally. UN Department of Economic and Social Affairs, Population Division, "Trends in International Migrant Stock," UN database POP/DB/MIG/Stock/Rev. (2017).

2. UNICEF, "Children on the Move: Key Facts and Figures" (February2018) https://data.unicef.org/resources/children-move-key-facts-figures.

3. UNICEF, "Children on the Move." Notably, children who are internally displaced are not included among the total migrant population, which accounts only for those persons living outside their country of origin.

4. Jacqueline Bhabha, *Child Migration and Human Rights in a Global Age* (Princeton: Princeton University Press, 2014), 2.

5. The Committee on the Protection of the Rights of All Migrant Workers and Members of their Family and the Committee on the Rights of the Child, issued its first set of detailed guidelines in 2017 on protecting the rights of child migrants. Committee on the Protection of the Rights of All Migrant Workers and Members of Their Families, *General Comment No. 3*, Committee on the Rights of the Child, *General Comment No. 22: General Principles Regarding the Human Rights of Children in the Context of International Migration*, U.N. Doc. CMW/C/GC/3-CRC/C/GC/22 (2017); Committee on the Protection of the Rights of All Migrant Workers and Members of Their Families, *Joint General Comment No. 4*, and Committee on the Rights of the Child, *Joint General Comment No. 23: State Obligations Regarding the Human Rights of Children in the Context of International Migration in Countries of Origin, Transit, Destination and Return*, UN Doc. CMW/C/GC/4-CRC/C/GC/23 (2017).

Academics have also joined in the growing international call for recognition of the child's best interests in the context of international migration, refugee protection, and domestic immigration enforcement. Jacqueline Bhabha, " 'More Than Their Share of Sorrows': International Migration Law and the Rights of Children," *Saint Louis University Public Law Review* 22 (2003): 253–274; Jacqueline Bhabha, "Arendt's Children: Do Today's Migrant Children Have a Right to Have Rights?," *Human Rights Quarterly* 31 (May 2009): 410–451; Bhabha, *Child Migration and Human Rights in a Global Age*; Mary Crock, "Of Relative Rights and Putative Children: Rethinking the Critical Framework for the Protection of Refugee Children and Youth," *Australia International Law Journal* 20, no. 13/95 (December 2013): 33–53; Samantha Arnold, *Children's Rights and Refugee Law: Conceptualizing Children within the Refugee Convention* (London: Routledge, 2018); Emily A. Benfer, "In the Best Interests of the Child? An International Human Rights Analysis of the Treatment of Unaccompanied Minors in Australia and the United States," *Indiana University International & Comparative Law Review* 14 (2004): 729–770;

David B. Thronson, "Children's Rights and U.S. Immigration Law," in *Protecting Migrant Children: In Search of Best Practice*, ed. Mary Crock and Lenni Benson (Cheltenham, UK: Edward Elgar Publishing, 2018), 259–273.

6. In their request for an advisory opinion from the Inter-American Court on "Human Rights on the Rights and Guarantees of Children in the Context of Migration and/or in Need of International Protection," the petitioning States of Argentina, Brazil, Paraguay, and Uruguay noted that "boys and girls migrate due to different reasons, such as family reunification; migration in search of better economic, social or cultural conditions; migration in order to reduce extreme poverty, environmental degradation; or to escape from violence or other forms of abuse and persecution." IACtHR, Advisory Opinion OC-21/14 (2014), para. 2.

7. This chapter does not address children within the international adoption scheme to whom The Hague Convention on the Civil Aspects of International Child Abduction applies, nor does it address those children who remain behind in countries of origin when their parents or other caregivers migrate, most often for work.

8. The Convention on the Rights of the Child (CRC) has been ratified by all UN member countries, with the notable and regrettable exception of the United States. Given its near uniform acceptance, and the implementation of many of its norms within domestic legal regimes, the CRC is the preeminent rights document pertaining to children, including child migrants, and therefore serves as the principle rights document for discussion of the rights of child migrants within this chapter and before the international community.

9. This chapter does not address the rights of stateless children specifically, though there are many overlapping rights and experienced rights violations. For an in-depth discussion on the rights of stateless children see Institute on Statelessness and Inclusion (ISI), "The World's Stateless Children" (January 2017), http://children.worldsstateless.org/assets/files/worlds-stateless-full-report.pdf.

10. The UN Convention on the Rights of the Child (CRC), G.A. Res. 44/25, 44th Sess., UN Doc. A/RES/44/25 (1989), has been ratified by all UN member countries with the one significant exception of the United States. Also applicable to child migrants are: the International Covenant on Civil and Political Rights, 999 UNTS 171 (1966; entered into force March 23, 1976); the International Covenant on Economic, Social and Cultural Rights, 993 UNTS 3 (1966; entered into force Jan. 3, 1976); the International Convention on the Rights of All Migrant Workers and their Family Members, 2220 UNTS 3 (1990; entered into force July 1, 2003); and the regional international human rights instruments, such as the African Charter on Human and Peoples' Rights, OAU Doc. CAB/LEG/67/3 (1981; entered into force Oct. 21, 1986), the American Declaration on the Rights and Duties of Man, OAS Res. XXX (1948), the American Convention on Human Rights, OAS TS No. 36, OEA/Ser. L/V/II.23 doc. Rev. 2 (entered into force July 18, 1978), and the European Convention for the Protection of Human Rights and Fundamental Freedoms, 213 UNTS 222 (entered into force Sept. 3, 1953) as well as other regional human rights protocols.

11. EuCtHR, Mubilsanza Mayeka and Kaniki Mitunga v. Belgium, Judgment (2007), para. 55.

12. CRC, preamble; American Declaration on the Rights and Duties of Man, art. 19; African Charter on the Rights and Welfare of the Child, preamble.

13. CRC, art. 3.

14. CRC, art. 12.

15. CRC, art. 2 ("States Parties shall respect and ensure the rights set forth in the present Convention to each child within their jurisdiction without discrimination of any kind.");

Advisory Opinion on the Juridical Condition and Rights of Undocumented Migrants, OC-18/03, Inter-Am. Ct. H.R. (2003).

16. Convention on the Rights of the Child, art. 6(2).

17. Convention on the Rights of the Child, art. 1.

18. U.N. Committee on the Rights of the Child, *General Comment No. 6: Treatment of Unaccompanied and Separated Children Outside their Country of Origin*, CRC/GC/2005/6 (2005), para. 31; IACtHR, OC-21/14, para. 88.

19. Bhabha, *Child Migration and Human Rights in a Global Age*, 1–4.

20. Bhabha, *Child Migration and Human Rights in a Global Age*, 1–4.

21. International Organization for Migration and UNICEF, Harrowing Journeys: Children and Youth on the Move Across the Mediterranean Sea, at Risk of Trafficking and Exploitation. New York: UNICEF and Geneva: IOM, 2017https://www.unicef.org/publications/index_100621.html.

22. International Organization for Migration and UNICEF, Harrowing Journeys, 25.

23. International Organization for Migration and UNICEF, "Harrowing Journeys," 31.

24. To qualify for refugee status, a child must be residing outside of his or her country of origin due to a well-founded fear of persecution on account of race, religion, nationality, membership in a particular social group, or political opinion. 1951 Convention Related to the Status of Refugees, art. I.A(2).

25. See section 3.1 of this chapter.

26. According to UNHCR, out of the 17.2 million refugees of concern in 2016, less than one percent were resettled into third countries. UNHCR, "Resettlement," http://www.unhcr.org/en-us/resettlement.html (accessed Sept. 7, 2019). Within West Africa, a limited number of individuals may be able to obtain permission to reside and work in neighboring countries under the ECOWAS Protocol Relating to Free Movement of Persons, Residence and Establishment, but those opportunities are limited and fail to fully respond to the long-term needs of refugees in a protracted crisis. Naohiko Omata, "Forgotten People: Former Liberian Refugees in Ghana," *Forced Migration Review* 52 (May 2016): 10–12.

27. For a thorough examination on stateless children see ISI, "World's Stateless Children."

28. The term *migrant child* is used throughout this chapter to include those who are stateless as well as those with a recognized nationality.

29. IACtHR, OC-21/14, Inter-Am. Ct. H.R., paras. 39 and 62 ("The respective State must, in all circumstances, respect the said [human] rights, because they are based, precisely, on the attributes of human personality; in other words, regardless of whether the person is a national or resident of its territory or whether the person is there temporarily, in transit, legally, or in an irregular migratory situation.").

30. As the Inter-American Court on Human Rights has held: "any immigration policy that respects human rights, as well as any administrative or judicial decision concerning the entry, stay or expulsion of a child, or the detention, expulsion or deportation of her or his parents associated with their own migratory status, must give priority to the assessment, determination, consideration and protection of the best interest of the child concerned." Advisory Opinion OC-21/14, Inter-Am. Ct. H.R, para. 70.

31. Article 37 of the CRC provides: "No child shall be deprived of his or her liberty unlawfully or arbitrarily" and "only as a measure of last resort and for the shortest appropriate period of time."

32. UN Human Rights Council, "Report of the Special Rapporteur on torture and other cruel, inhuman or degrading treatment or punishment, Juan E. Méndez," A/HRC/28/68 (2015),

para. 80; see also Inter-American Commission on Human Rights, "Refugees and Migrants in the United States: Families and Unaccompanied Children" (2015), paras. 77–80.

33. Committee on the Protection of the Rights of All Migrant Workers and Members of Their Families, "*Joint General Comment 4*" and Committee on the Rights of the Child "*Joint General Comment 23*", para. 5.

34. UNICEF, "Uprooted: The Growing Crisis for Refugee and Migrant Children" (September 2016), 39, https://www.unicef.org/videoaudio/PDFs/Uprooted.pdf.

35. American Immigration Council, "Children in Danger: A Guide to the Humanitarian Challenge at the Border," special report (June 26, 2015), http://www.immigrationpolicy.org/special-reports/children-danger-guide-humanitarian-challenge-border. See also Alice Farmer, "The Impact of Immigration Detention on Children," *Forced Migration Review* 44 (September 2013): 14; International Detention Coalition, "Impacts of Detention on Children," in *Captured Childhood* (2012), chap 5, https://idcoalition.org/wp-content/uploads/2016/01/Captured-Childhood.pdf.

36. In the US, for example, the data show that those who are detained are significantly less likely to obtain representation. TRAC Immigration, "Who Is Represented in Immigration Court?," http://trac.syr.edu/immigration/reports/485 (accessed Sept. 7, 2019). As is discussed in greater detail below, an individual's ability to find legal representation in removal proceedings has a dramatic impact on that individual's likelihood of success. As is discussed below, this is particularly acute for children who do not understand the complex procedures and legal rules being applied to them and who do not speak the language. One study revealed that in 47 percent of the cases where the child was represented by an attorney, that child was granted immigration relief, whereas only 10 percent of children unrepresented by counsel were granted relief. TRAC Immigration, "New Data on Unaccompanied Children in Immigration Court," http://trac.syr.edu/immigration/reports/359 (accessed Sept. 7, 2019).

37. Global Detention Project, "U.S. Immigration Detention," note 59, https://www.globaldetentionproject.org/countries/americas/united-states#_ftnref59 (accessed Sept. 7, 2019). This number does not reflect, however, the length of detention or how many children are detained on average each day.

38. Flores v. Johnson, Memorandum in Support of Motion to Enforce Settlement of Class Action (CD Cal. filed Feb. 2, 2015), https://www.aila.org/File/Related/14111359g.pdf. See, generally, American Immigration Lawyers Association (AILA), "Documents Relating to *Flores v. Reno* Settlement Agreement on Minors in Immigration Custody," AILA Doc. No. 14111359 (Aug. 15, 2019), https://www.aila.org/infonet/flores-v-reno-settlement-agreement.

39. Inter-American Commission on Human Rights (Inter-American Commission), "Human Rights Situation of Refugee and Migrant Families and Unaccompanied Children in the United States of America," OAS/Ser.L/V/II. 155, Doc. 16 (July 24, 2015), 40¶74. See section 3.1.4 for further discussion on the intersection of family rights and the rights of migrant children.

40. UNHCR, "Guidelines on International Protection: Child Asylum Claims under Articles 1(A)2 and 1(F) of the 1951 Convention and/or 1967 Protocol relating to the Status of Refugees," UN Doc. CHR/GIP/09/08 (2009), para. 18; "[T]he elements of the [refugee] definition should be interpreted taking into account the specific forms that child persecution may adopt, such as recruitment, trafficking, and female genital mutilation, as well as the way in which [children] may experience these situations." IACtHR OC-21/14, para. 80.

41. OAU Convention Governing the Specific Aspects of Refugee Problems in Africa (1969; entered into force June 20, 1974), art. 1.2.

42. Cartagena Declaration on Refugees, adopted by the Colloquium on the International Protection of Refugees in Central America, Mexico, and Panama (Nov. 22, 1984), art. 3.

43. UN Convention against Torture and Other Cruel, Inhuman or Degrading Treatment of Punishment, G.A. Res. 39/46, 39th Sess., UN Doc. A/39/51 (1984), art. 3(1).

44. CRC, art. 6. This obligation is more expansive than that under CRC, Article 19, obligating states to protect children from harm or violence at the hands of their parents or guardians, though this too has obligations.

45. CRC, art. 12(2).

46. CRC, art. 12(1).

47. UN Office of the High Commissioner for Human Rights, "Situation of Migrants in Transit," UN Doc. A/HRC/31/35 (2016), para. 17.

48. Moussa Harouna Sambo and Fabrizio Terenzio, "Children on the Move: A Different Voice," in *Children on the Move*, International Organization for Migration (IOM) report (June 2, 2013), 23, https://issuu.com/unpublications/docs/children_on_the_move_1.

49. U.N. Committee on the Protection of the Rights of All Migrant Workers and Members of their Families, *Joint General Comment No. 4* and U.N. Committee on the Rights of the Child, *Joint General Comment No. 23*, paras. 14–19; Inter-American Court of Human Rights, Advisory Opinion OC-21/14 *on the Rights and Guarantees of Children in the Context of Migration and/or in Need of International Protection*, paras. 85–93.

50. U.N. Committee on the Protection of the Rights of All Migrant Workers and Members of their Families, *Joint General Comment No. 4* and U.N. Committee on the Rights of the Child, *Joint General Comment No. 23*, paras. 14–19.

51. UNHCR, UNICEF, and IRC, "The Way Forward to Strengthened Policies and Practices for Unaccompanied and Separated Children in Europe" (July 2017), 5, 8, https://www.refworld.org/docid/59633afc4.html.

52. U.N. Committee on the Protection of the Rights of All Migrant Workers and Members of their Families, *Joint General Comment No. 4* and U.N. Committee on the Rights of the Child, *Joint General Comment No. 23*, para. 17–19.

53. U.N. Committee on the Protection of the Rights of All Migrant Workers and Members of their Families, *Joint General Comment No. 4* and U.N. Committee on the Rights of the Child, *Joint General Comment No. 23*, paras. 14–19; IACtHR OC-21/14, paras. 83–85.

54. U.N. Committee on the Protection of the Rights of All Migrant Workers and Members of their Families, *Joint General Comment No. 4* and U.N. Committee on the Rights of the Child, *Joint General Comment No. 23*, para. 14.

55. Advocates for Human Rights, *A House with Two Rooms: Final Report of the Truth and Reconciliation Commission of Liberia Diaspora Project* (St. Paul, MN: DRI Press, 2009), 329.

56. U.N. Committee on the Protection of the Rights of All Migrant Workers and Members of their Families, *Joint General Comment No. 4* and U.N. Committee on the Rights of the Child, *Joint General Comment No. 23*, paras. 27–38. UNHCR, UNICEF, and IRC. The Way Forward *to Strengthened Policies and Practices for Unaccompanied and Separated Children in Europe*.

57. U.N. Committee on the Protection of the Rights of All Migrant Workers and Members of their Families, *Joint General Comment No. 4* and U.N. Committee on the Rights of the Child, *Joint General Comment No. 23*, para. 27. In 2010 the Human Rights Committee

ruled in Communication No. 1554/2007 that the right to family life protection under Articles 23 and 24 of the ICCPR mandated the grant of lawful status to a minor child who had moved to Denmark to be reunified with his father. UN Doc. CCPR/C/00/D/1554/2007.

58. Mubilanzila Mayeka and Kaniki Mitunga v. Belgium, ECtHR, Application No. 13178/03 (December 1, 2007); ZH (Tanzania) v. Secretary of State for the Home Department, EWCA 691 (Feb. 1, 2011).

59. Inter-American Commission, "Human Rights Situation of Refugee and Migrant Families," para. 74.

60. UNICEF, "Uprooted," 39.

61. 1951 UN Convention on the Status Related to Refugees and 1967 Protocol; CRC; CERD.

62. For general information on the human rights implications of protracted refugee crises see, generally, UNHCR, "Protracted Refugee Situations," UN Doc. EC/54/SC/CRP.14 (June 10, 2004); UNHCR, "Protracted Refugee Situations: The Search for Practical Solutions," in *The State of the World's Refugees 2006: Human Displacement in the New Millennium* (Oxford: Oxford University Press, 2006), chap. 5.

63. Advocates for Human Rights, *House with Two Rooms*, 332–333.

64. Convention on the Rights of the Child, arts. 23, 24, and 39.

65. UNICEF, "Uprooted," 39.

66. UNICEF, "Uprooted," 39.

67. In its first decision on the merits in a case brought under the Third Optional Protocol to the CRC communications procedures, the UN Committee on the Rights of the Child concluded Denmark violated its obligations under CRC Articles 3 and 19 in failing to consider the best interests of the child under Articles 3 and 19 when it ordered the deportation to Somalia of a girl who faced being subjected to female genital mutilation upon her turn to Somalia. K.Y.M. v. Denmark, CRC, Communication No. 3/2016, UN Doc. CRC/C/77/D/3/2016 (2018).

68. Hans van de Glind and Anne Kou, "Migrant Children in Child Labour: A Vulnerable Group in Need of Attention," in IOM, *Children on the Move*. IOM. https://issuu.com/unpublications/docs/children_on_the_move_1.

69. UNICEF, "Uprooted," 83.

70. Convention on the Rights of the Child, art. 32(1).

71. Migrant children engaged in work can be categorized into those children who migrate with their families, and whose labor contributions are essential to the family's economic survival, and those who are traveling independent of their families, and who therefore are at a greater risk of dependency and vulnerability on adults who may seek to exploit their labor. Hans van de Glind, "Migration and Child Labour: Exploring Child Migrant Vulnerabilities and Those of Children Left-Behind," ILO Working Paper(2010), 3–11. For a further discussion on child trafficking, see chapter 30.

72. van de Glind, "Migration and Child Labour."

73. UNICEF, "A Deadly Journey for Children: The Central Mediterranean Migration Route," UNICEF Child Alert (February 2017), https://www.unicef.org/publications/files/EN_UNICEF_Central_Mediterranean_Migration.pdf.

74. According to 2015 data collected by UN Department of Economic and Social Affairs, there were thirty-seven international migrants between the ages of ten and twenty-four. UNICEF, "Uprooted," 43.

75. In addressing key considerations pertaining to unaccompanied and separated migrant children in Europe, UNHCR, UNICEF, and IRC recognized the children themselves as "agents of change," noting: "The children and youth themselves, as they are most eager to improve their situation and have knowledge and expertise to contribute. It has long been recognized that children and youth and and want to effectively participate in issues affecting themselves, and that their perspectives often lead to significant and positive policy changes." UNHCR, UNICEF, and IRC, "Way Forward," 5.

76. Bhabha, *Child Migration and Human Rights in a Global Age*, 7.

PART VI

CONCLUSION

CHAPTER 33

HUMAN RIGHTS EDUCATION

Education about Children's Rights

R. BRIAN HOWE AND KATHERINE COVELL

1 INTRODUCTION

NELSON Mandela once said, "Education is the most powerful weapon we can use to change the world."[1] This might be an overstatement, but there is no question of the power of education in advancing the rights of children. The purpose of this chapter is to show the need for and the value of children's human rights education (HRE). Despite the call for children's HRE in the UN Convention on the Rights of the Child and related international human rights instruments, it has not been widely implemented. Although governments across the globe express symbolic support for children's HRE, commitment to its realization has been lacking. However, studies of the initiatives that have been introduced show the value of children's HRE in empowering children to act in support of human rights. It may take considerable time, but with pressure from a growing international movement for HRE, there is reason to believe that momentum will continue to build and the implementation of children's HRE will be more widespread.

HRE is described by the United Nations as education about, through, and for human rights that is directed at "the building and promotion of a universal culture of human rights."[2] It is to be achieved through not only the spread of knowledge but also the imparting of skills and the development of attitudes and values in support of human rights. We define children's HRE as a subset of HRE, where education is directed at the development of knowledge, skills, attitudes, and values in support of children's human rights, as described in the UN Convention on the Rights of the Child (CRC). Children's HRE can be part of a broader HRE, or it can be more narrowly focused on children's rights, serving as a basis for later and broader HRE. Regardless of the approach, children's HRE is important because it highlights that children's rights are not identical to adult rights and that children have rights in the here and now, not only when they become adults. Human rights education without children's HRE is incomplete. It is important to note also that children's HRE applies to different target audiences and settings. Children obviously are a primary audience because they are the subject of children's rights. But adults working with and for children—for example, teachers, social workers, lawyers, and doctors—are important audiences, too, because of their responsibilities in guiding and supporting children. Schools obviously are a primary setting. This is where the majority of children can be reached and where education can take place on a systematic basis. But non-formal education and community settings also are important, especially in developing countries, where formal education is not always available. In some countries, such as India, programs operated by nongovernmental organizations (NGOs) play a major role in HRE.

Our analysis develops as follows. First, in reference to the CRC, we describe the need for children's HRE; second, the global movement for HRE; and third, models of HRE and research showing the beneficial impact of children learning about their rights. Finally, we examine lack of commitment as an overarching challenge for children's HRE.

2 The Need for Children's Human Rights Education

The unanimous adoption of the CRC by the United Nations General Assembly in 1989 was a major step forward for children's rights. Providing a systematic statement on the human rights of children that did not exist before, the CRC was subsequently signed and ratified by virtually all countries in the world. Only the United States—because of concerns about conflict with parental authority and US sovereignty—has yet to ratify the CRC.[3] The significance of the CRC is that it is a legally binding international treaty—not simply a declaration—obligating states parties to ensure the progressive implementation of the rights of children as described in it.[4] Although countries may stall or try to evade their obligations, they cannot deny that they have officially agreed to the substance of the CRC and to their responsibility for putting children's rights into effect. This agreement is an important resource for NGOs and child advocates in prodding governments to ensure the progressive implementation of the rights of children.

Providing for children's HRE is an essential part of implementing the CRC. It is one of the requirements of the CRC. It is true that HRE is not an explicitly stated right of the CRC, and it is probably not a justiciable right capable of enforcement by the courts. However, it is logical to assume that the right is implicit in the child's right to education.[5] Under Article 28 of the CRC, children have the right to education. And under Article 29, states parties agree that education "shall be directed to the development of respect for human rights." Such development of respect presupposes that the child has knowledge and understanding of human rights, including the human rights of children. A prerequisite to this knowledge and understanding is education.[6] More generally, the CRC would lack coherence without the understanding that children have the right to HRE. If children are to enjoy and exercise their basic rights, they should know what these rights are. It is illogical that in recognizing and agreeing to implement the rights of the child, states parties would be allowed to keep children in the dark about their rights.

Apart from HRE as an implicit right, there are three fundamental reasons why education about children's rights is important. First, the CRC requires education as a matter of duty. Under Article 42, states parties agree "to undertake to make the principles and provisions of the [CRC] widely known, by appropriate and active means, to adults and children alike." Article 42 is unique in international law in that it asserts a duty of dissemination not found in previous treaties.[7] There is an explicit obligation here for states parties to ensure the spread of knowledge of children's rights. Usage of the phrase "appropriate and active means" signifies that it is not enough merely to construct websites, celebrate national child's day, or provide informational brochures or copies of the CRC.[8] Such initiatives may be important, but they are inadequate and limited in their capacity to provide a real understanding of the nature of rights. Article 42 calls not for sporadic and patchy informational programs, but for "appropriate and active" measures that will reach and educate children and adults in a systematic way. To ensure appropriate and systematic rights education, the Committee on the Rights of the Child (CRC Committee) repeatedly has pointed to the need to fully integrate children's rights into all levels of the education system, including policies, practices, teaching materials, and curricula.[9]

A second reason for children's HRE is that it is an essential part of the process of implementing the CRC. Although the CRC has spurred legislative changes in some countries, it is largely enforced and put into effect through moral and political pressure rather than a legal and court process.[10] Pressure is applied through a system of monitoring and reporting in which states parties submit reports to the CRC Committee, the Committee reviews these reports together with shadow reports from NGOs, and the Committee then submits its own reports (Concluding Observations) back to the states parties, providing feedback and making recommendations for improvement when necessary. Pressure comes from the input and criticisms of NGOs, from public opinion in support of children's rights, from the Committee's recommendations, and from the fear of public criticism and embarrassment by governments for failure to act. But the degree of pressure depends on the degree of public awareness and education. Without education, the prospects for progress are greatly lessened. With education, pressure and the implementation of children's rights are more likely.

A third reason for children's HRE is that it facilitates a broader implementation of HRE, as called for under international human rights law. Children's rights education in the early school years functions to make children more receptive to human rights education later and to increase their support for human rights in general.[11] Studies of HRE have reported on the importance of relevancy in reaching target audiences and implementing programs.[12] The logic is simple. Audiences are more engaged when the subject matter for education is relevant to them and connected to their daily lives, and so they are more receptive to learning. Thus, it is no surprise that HRE has more success when the concepts and issues highlighted are ones that audiences can relate to. Conversely, implementation is more difficult when the messages are more remote and abstract. The same logic applies to children. They are more engaged with HRE when it is related to their current realities.[13] The CRC is of particular interest to them because it is about them. They learn that they have value as bearers of rights and that their rights ought to be respected and put into effect. This is a powerful message that affects children's developing sense of self.

It is important to take into account the child's developing identity in education.[14] This includes human rights education. Identity formation results from the experiences and values to which children are exposed.[15] It is, therefore, particularly valuable to provide children experience with the values and practice of human rights. This is most likely to occur when children are taught and experience their own rights because the relevance to self and peers evokes engagement in learning.[16] Lessons that focus on adults' rights are less engaging, since they leave no room for self-interest. Self-interest not only engages children; it also promotes support and empathy for the rights of other children, democratic ideals, and human rights in general.[17] Children come to see themselves as rights-respecting and rights-supporting individuals.[18] Thus, a solid foundation is provided for children to learn about, respect, and promote human rights more broadly.

Following ratification of the CRC, in line with the need for children's HRE, the CRC Committee urged states parties during the 1990s to take measures to ensure that education about human rights was systematically and comprehensively provided.[19] First, in its general guideline to states parties in preparing their initial reports, the CRC Committee instructed countries to describe the specific measures they were taking to educate children, professionals, and the general public about the rights of children.[20] Second, in response to the initial reports and to the CRC Committee's discovery that little action had been taken beyond constructing websites and distributing informational material, the Committee expressed concern about the failure and urged countries to intensify their efforts and get serious about children's HRE.[21] In 2003 the CRC Committee consolidated its advice to states parties in its General Comment No. 5.[22] It recommended that states parties develop a comprehensive strategy for delivering children's HRE, a strategy that was to include three basic elements: the general dissemination of knowledge in society, the establishment of training programs for professionals and teachers working with and for children, and the incorporation of children's rights into the school curriculum. In reaching children, providing HRE in schools was of particular importance.

It was the hope of the CRC Committee that countries would take its prescriptions seriously. The proof would be their track records in the years to come.

3 THE MOVEMENT FOR HUMAN RIGHTS EDUCATION

During the 1990s and early 2000s an international movement for HRE (including children's HRE) gathered in strength. Advocacy for HRE had existed previously, but it now intensified.[23] This was due to a renewed appreciation of HRE as a vehicle for promoting human rights, an interest in HRE as a means of strengthening newly emerging democracies, such as those in Eastern Europe, and a growing awareness of the inadequacy of the implementation of HRE under human rights treaties, such as the CRC.[24] The aims of the movement were to strengthen international commitment to HRE and apply pressure for more serious action among governments.

A major advance came in 1993 at the UN World Conference on Human Rights held in Vienna. A key outcome of the Conference was the Vienna Declaration and Programme for Action (Vienna Declaration). It stated that "human rights education, training and public information is essential for the promotion and achievement of stable and harmonious relations among communities and for fostering mutual understanding, tolerance and peace."[25] The statement was important in affirming the need for and value of HRE. The Vienna Declaration also called for the UN Decade for Human Rights Education, which lasted from 1995 to 2004, bringing together activists, officials, and educators for consultation, the sharing of knowledge, and the development of strategies to advance HRE. Of particular importance here was the call by the UN for governments to prepare and implement national plans of action for HRE and to incorporate HRE into school curricula.[26] There was international agreement that schools were the logical and ideal places for effective HRE. In 2005, with the conclusion of the HRE Decade, the UN World Programme for Human Rights Education was established, directed by the Office of the UN High Commissioner for Human Rights. The high commissioner's work involved developing specific tools for HRE, such as national action plans and handbooks to help implement them. The Programme proceeded in three phases: the first (2005–2009) focused on HRE in primary and secondary schools, the second (2010–2014) on higher education and professional training, and the third (2015–2019) on training for journalists and media professionals.

Similarly, in 2011 the UN adopted the Declaration on Human Rights Education and Training. Article 1 stated "Everyone has the right to know, seek and receive information about all human rights and fundamental freedoms and should have access to human right education and training."[27] The Declaration also affirmed the duty of countries to spread awareness and ensure HRE. Although the Declaration was an important step forward, there were limitations. The announced right to HRE was not a justiciable right capable of enforcement through the courts. Access to HRE was not assured due to the language that everyone "should" have access to HRE. And as with other declarations, the Declaration was aspirational, not a legally binding convention. A future challenge of the United Nations is to build support and adopt a convention on HRE, preferably one with a complaints mechanism to hold governments accountable for failure to comply. The mechanism would allow children (or their representatives), as well as adults, to bring complaints to an international body about the failure of a government to provide effective human rights education. Nonetheless, the Declaration was an important step forward and an additional resource for advocacy. For example, in the wake of the Declaration, HRE 2020: Global Coalition for Human Rights Education was formed—comprising such group members as Equitas (Canada), Human Rights Educators (USA), and People's Watch (India)—to monitor educational efforts among countries and apply pressure for wider implementation of HRE, as called for by the Declaration, the CRC, and other international treaties.[28]

Alongside these developments, the proliferation of educational efforts of NGOs and advocacy groups strengthened the movement for HRE.[29] International organizations, such as Amnesty International, UNICEF, and Save the Children, became involved in campaigns to pressure governments to fulfill their international educational responsibilities. They also began developing resources for teachers and working with schools and local communities to deliver HRE programs. Regional and grassroots organizations also became active. In Latin America, for example, after the time of the military dictatorships, and building on efforts dating back to the 1970s, local groups championed HRE as a means of building democracy and preventing a return to authoritarian government.[30] In Eastern Europe, after the collapse of communism, similar pressures were applied for HRE as a means of fostering democracy. In addition, efforts were made by numerous human rights organizations to expand knowledge and publicize HRE. Particularly important was the creation of the US-based online group Human Rights Education Associates.[31] Established in 1994, it has served as a major forum for information exchange among practitioners and officials in the HRE community and as an important global educator through its online courses and distance learning program.

So in 2003, when the CRC Committee urged countries to develop comprehensive strategies to implement children's HRE, there was a growing movement in place to give support to the cause, and some progress has been made. But disappointingly, and contrary to the hope of the Committee, the pressures have failed to produce comprehensive HRE and make headway in building a universal culture of human rights. Instead, there have been scattered initiatives, patchy developments, and major variations by country.[32] There has been significant variation, for example, in the inclusion of human rights in school text books. Inclusion is much less in non-democratic, non-Western, and conflict-affected states.[33]

On the positive side, national plans of action have been developed in a number of countries.[34] The government of India, for example, has initiated a plan of action to integrate HRE into schools nationwide, which has facilitated progress at state and local levels.[35] Furthermore, in many countries there has been growing usage of human rights concepts and language in school textbooks and curricula.[36] However, more plans of action and more human rights language do not mean more actual education on a significant scale. Studies of HRE in different countries have shown that despite announced plans and intentions, there frequently has been a lack of implementation at the level of classrooms and schools.[37] Factors, which can vary from country to country, include lack of political will, lack of teacher training, resource constraints, political sensitivities, and ideological opposition.

Studies also have shown a lack of children's HRE, specifically. For example, in a comparative study of children's rights in twenty-six developed countries, it was found that in the majority of countries, children were not entitled to learn about their rights as part of the official school curriculum or education legislation.[38] In some countries—for example, Finland, France, Norway, Poland, and Sweden—this entitlement did exist. But in most countries it did not exist or, as in Ireland, children's HRE was provided only as an option or, as in countries such as Belgium, Austria, and Germany, it was provided only in some parts of the country. And importantly, in only a few countries was there provision for teacher training in children's HRE and for monitoring the quality of the education. So even where children's HRE was required, effective implementation was not assured. According to the study, in some cases, to the extent that children learned about their rights, they were not provided with full and accurate education. For example, contrary to the CRC, some children learned that their rights were dependent on fulfilling certain responsibilities not related to the rights of the child.[39] In summary, children's HRE has not been widely put into effect.

Although children's HRE has not been comprehensive, there have been important developments. In classrooms, schools, and school districts initiatives have been undertaken by committed teachers and education administrators. An example of a school district taking the lead is the Rights, Respect and Responsibility (RRR) initiative in Hampshire, England.[40] As detailed later in this chapter, the Hampshire initiative was evaluated over a decade, through which evidence indicated increasingly positive academic and social outcomes. Initiatives also have been taken by international NGOs, providing resources and teacher training to schools. Well-known examples include Amnesty International's Human Rights Friendly Schools program and UNICEF's Rights-Respecting School Award program, a program that built on the Hampshire initiative by awarding schools that successfully implemented the RRR with certificates.[41] UNICEF reports that its program has been implemented primarily in the United Kingdom (and to a lesser extent in European countries, such as France, Spain, and Slovakia), and Amnesty International reports that its program is in twenty-two countries across the globe. Although introduced in a minority of schools in different countries, growth over time reflects increasing interest in HRE.

Local NGOs have also played an important role. In India, for example, the Indian Institute of Human Rights Education has developed curricula, provided teacher training, and initiated HRE and children's HRE on a large scale.[42] Finally, in the non-formal education sector, NGOs have provided HRE in community settings for adults and for marginalized children who do not have regular access to schools. Examples include initiatives by the League of Displaced Women in Colombia, the Rights and Rice Foundation in Liberia, and the Project Melel in Chiapas, Mexico, where children are provided with children's HRE while they are working on the streets to help support their families.[43]

4 MODELS OF CHILDREN'S
HUMAN RIGHTS EDUCATION

Felisa Tibbitts has identified three pedagogical models of HRE: the Values and Awareness/Socialization Model, the Accountability/Professional Development Model, and the Activism/Transformation Model.[44] The Values and Awareness/Socialization Model is the most common one in schools. Didactic pedagogies are used to teach children facts about human rights. The focus is on lecturing, rote learning, and memorization for tests. To the extent that violations of rights are brought to attention, they typically are in reference to other countries or to the distant past. Little attention is given to children's rights in the here and now.

The Accountability/Professional Development Model is found in professional training programs. Professionals learn about children's rights as part of their occupational responsibilities. They are provided with knowledge, skills, and the motivation to respect and promote children's rights in their given field. As the learners are largely adults, pedagogies are typically participatory and interactive, aiming to engage learners, foster motivation, and promote accountability for ensuring children's rights. This may involve cultivating a critical perspective on the practice of rights, but it is usually limited to criticism within a profession.

The Activism/Transformation Model is the most comprehensive and progressive approach to human rights education. In this model, learners are equipped with knowledge, skills, and motivation to promote and protect human rights and to maintain a rights-respecting culture. According to Tibbitts, to the extent that the transformation model is applied, it is most often applied in the non-formal education sector, particularly in such settings as refugee camps or rural villages. Programs typically are delivered by NGOs or local community groups to learners who typically are adults or youth experiencing marginalization, oppression, and violations of their rights. A program's success means that learners become transformed into human rights activists seeking to change their society into one based on human rights.

The three models are, to a greater or lesser extent, in accord with the goals of HRE, as described in the UN Declaration on Human Rights Education and Training. In the Declaration, HRE should include education *about* human rights (knowledge and understanding), education *through* human rights (learning and teaching in ways that respect rights), and education *for* human rights (empowering persons to enjoy their rights and uphold the rights of others).[45] But it is only the Activism/Transformational Model—one rarely found in schools—that comprises education about human rights standards and values, provides the skills needed to promote and protect those rights, and inculcates the motivation to do so. Transformational HRE in schools, as pointed out by the CRC Committee, requires extensive teacher training about rights and participatory pedagogies, reworking school curricula to integrate rights, and re-culturing school environments to be rights-respecting.[46] The Committee has emphasized that pedagogy focused on knowledge accumulation and competition compromises the development of children's talents and abilities.[47] States parties repeatedly have been criticized for the priority given to rote learning,[48] the competitive nature of schooling,[49] and the lack of human rights education in schools.[50] Individual teacher or school initiatives, while of some impact, are considered insufficient.[51]

Human rights education only in the non-formal sector is also inadequate. Community and NGO programs are important, especially in impoverished or conflict-affected parts of the world where formal education is not available or accessible. However, if the ultimate aim of HRE, as stated by the UN, is to build "a universal culture of human rights," it is essential that children's HRE is established in schools. This is where the vast majority of children can be reached and where transformative learning can take place on a large scale. Even in the developing world, over 90 percent of children are now enrolled in primary schools.[52] If the project of cultivating a culture of human rights is to gain traction, it is imperative that children in schools are educated and empowered to stand up for the rights of others as well as their own rights. Not all children need to be transformed into activists. But through HRE they can be all be transformed into uphold-ers of children's rights and human rights, empowered not only with knowledge and values but also with the motivation to act on behalf of the rights of others. Over time, as these children grow into adults with similar values and commitments, an important foundation is laid for the building of a culture of human rights.

That transformational HRE can be successfully implemented in schools is demonstrated by the RRR initiative (now called Rights Respecting Education) launched, as noted above, by Hampshire educators in the early 2000s. It provides a model of children's human rights education that is consistent with education about, through, and for human rights. RRR remains an exemplar initiative in children's rights education for which there are independent longitudinal evaluation data on its implementation and effects.[53]

The RRR was designed to transform school cultures by building a shared values framework based on the CRC and by implementing educational practices consistent with the CRC. In line with comments by the CRC Committee, the rights of the child were not superimposed on existing curricula. In RRR-based schools, teachers were trained in the CRC and appropriate pedagogies. All teaching materials were revised to integrate rights, and only participatory pedagogies were used. A rights-respecting school environment was established in which all school policies, classroom practices, codes of conduct, mission statements, and school regulations were consistent with the rights of the CRC. Systematic opportunities for children's participation in their learning and in all school policies and practices were provided. The implementation of the RRR and its subsequent effects on teachers and children was evaluated over a decade. Overall, the evaluation data provided compelling evidence that the initiative, when fully imple-mented, was successful in promoting a culture of human rights by teaching about rights, through rights, and for rights.

That education *about* human rights was successful was evidenced in children's under-standing of the nature of rights, the importance of rights, and their corresponding responsibilities to respect the rights of others. It is noteworthy that the RRR was implemented initially with children aged four through twelve and that there were no age differences in children's ability to understand the fundamental nature and importance of rights. Differences by age were evident only in children's verbal descriptions of rights. The younger children did not explain rights in such abstract terms as equality or injustice, but their explanations reflected a fundamentally correct understanding of them. For example, rights, they explained, mean "you have clean water and healthy food," "play nicely," "stay safe," and "get treated properly." Rights are important because "it allows children to have a good life and not be hurt"; "if [children] don't have water they will dehydrate."[54] Such understanding is consistent with previous findings that children as young as ages three to five have the capacity to understand abstract concepts, such as fairness and rights,[55] and to differentiate between unjust and socially beneficial laws.[56] Children's understanding of rights was evident also in their spontaneous use of rights discourse with their peers, the staff, and teachers. They complained of rights violations, they used rights to explain behavior, and they appealed to teachers for fair treatment based on rights.

The sense of connectedness to others that was evoked by rights education was evident in children's descriptions of what it means to have a responsibility. Whereas most children who were not in RRR schools explained responsibilities in terms of objects (for example, being careful with books and picking up toys), those experienced with the RRR focused on responsibilities to other children and the environment. Examples include: "the most important responsibility is to make sure everyone has their rights"; "you have a responsibility not to hurt others and if someone is hurt to help them"; and "if there is a dead rat don't leave it."[57]

Attitudinal and behavioral changes of the students in the RRR schools demonstrated that education *through* human rights had been successful in developing the skills needed for effective democratic citizenship. Engagement in school and participation rates increased significantly and exponentially. Teachers reported more effective problem-solving, use of persuasive argument, decision-making, collaborative learning, and critical thinking over time. They commented also on increased levels of self-regulation, confidence, effort, and motivation. Underpinning these improvements was the children's use of rights as a values framework for their critical thinking and decision-making. Interestingly, these improvements were reflected in marked and steady increases in children's achievement scores on the standardized assessment tests since implementation of the RRR.

The evaluation data also demonstrated that the RRR had raised the children's social consciousness: they successfully had been educated *for* human rights. Likely as a result of the use of rights as a values framework, the children were reported to be more cooperative with each other, more inclusive, more sensitive to the needs of children with learning difficulties, and more respectful of others in general.[58] Incidents of teasing, bullying, and other inappropriate behaviors decreased significantly and were fully eliminated in some schools, and children reported a respectful, fair, and safe school climate. In essence, the children in the RRR schools increasingly displayed moral and socially responsible behaviors, and they appeared confident in their ability to act to promote and support the rights of others. Such rights-supportive behaviors were not restricted to their classmates and friends. Many wrote letters to their members of parliament to advocate for greater respect for the rights of all children; others invited politicians into their schools to be interviewed; and others made rights-based presentations at city council meetings and to school boards of governors.

Although apparent in all schools that fully implemented the RRR, its positive outcomes were disproportionately seen in schools in urban areas characterized by poverty and associated family challenges. When the RRR was introduced, absentee rates in these schools were high, behavior problems were endemic, and school failure was common. Over time, behavioral incidents and absentee rates decreased significantly, and the children's aggregate scores on national standardized tests almost doubled.[59] During this time period there was stability of school staff and family characteristics. The changes are likely because the relevant curricula, together with the respect and value the children experienced—particularly through their participation—increased the children's enjoyment in learning, their confidence, academic effort, sense of belonging, and overall positive perception of the school.[60] In essence, the data indicated that children's human rights education has the potential to promote educational resilience—the likelihood of success in school among children who are at risk of failure due to challenging family circumstances, such as poverty.

The positive effects of the RRR were not limited to children. Of particular interest was that student participation reduced teacher burnout. Teacher burnout is important because it has negative effects on teaching quality and is strongly associated with student disengagement and misbehavior. The more the children participated, the more the teachers showed gains in their sense of personal achievement as well as decreases in emotional exhaustion and depersonalization. These improvements in teacher satisfaction, which were sustained and strengthened over time, resulted in an increasingly positive school climate. When teachers are empathetic and consistent, and they encourage self-management and meaningful participation, classroom climate improves.[61] Improved school climates mean more effective HRE.

The RRR model of children's rights education also had a major effect on at least one local community, the town of Andover. Empowered by the experience of RRR, staff and students (with support of parents and the board of governors) organized a well-publicized movement to create a rights-respecting community. Having seen the improvements in the children's social behavior and respect for others, officials readily agreed to establish a charter declaring their town to be a rights-respecting community—one in which children's rights, including participation in matters that affect them, would be supported.[62] The movement gained endorsements from churches, other schools, newspapers, councils, police, a nearby university and college, and the Children's Commissioner for England.[63] The shared belief among the supporters was that bullying, racism, and vandalism would diminish significantly if all children were educated in rights-based schools.

The RRR initiative provides evidence that teachers and schools can be agents of important change and that effective HRE can be systematically implemented in schools.

Schools that were successful in so doing were ones characterized by the principal's leadership, commitment, and planning and by an appreciation that rights must be at the core of the school culture—the overarching framework into which all school functioning, teaching practices, school programs, and policies fit.[64] Consistent with the suggestions of Charles Helwig and his colleagues, and with identity formation as described earlier, there is an increased probability that children in such human rights–based schools will develop a conception of themselves as rights-respecting citizens—as autonomous persons with rights and responsibilities who can and will make rights-respecting and rights-promoting choices. Such a conception of self becomes the foundation of a developed democratic society.[65] It suggests also the possibility of advancing a universal culture of human rights where, in the words of Article 4 of the UN Declaration of Human Rights Education and Training, "everyone is aware of their own rights and responsibilities in respect of the rights of others, and promoting the development of the individual as a responsible member of a free, peaceful, pluralist and inclusive society."

5 The Challenge for Children's Human Rights Education

Despite the promise of such initiatives as the RRR, and contrary to calls by the CRC Committee, children's HRE has not been widely implemented. Most governments have not developed national strategies or plans of action for HRE, few have incorporated it into education legislation and the school curriculum, and few have required HRE and the CRC as part of teacher training. In the absence of national plans of action, the sustainability of initiatives like the RRR is not likely over the long term. Staff changes may bring new approaches, and new initiatives may compete for resources. What results is a jumble of limited and scattered efforts in classrooms, schools, and school districts.

An overarching problem is that political and educational authorities have been lacking in commitment. Wanting to be seen as part of a progressive global movement for human rights, governments may give symbolic support to HRE. This leads them to approve international agreements, such as the CRC and the Declaration on Human Rights Education and Training. But they lack genuine commitment. And because they lack commitment, they have been unwilling to move forward with serious implementation.

A number of factors account for this lack of commitment. One is the interests of governments.[66] Authoritarian governments, for example, have an obvious interest in maintaining their power. They may feel threatened by education where children learn about their rights to participation and freedom of expression rather than their duties to obey and submit to authority.[67] But the problem is not limited to authoritarian governments. Although HRE is more likely to develop in democracies, commitment is an issue there also. Democratic governments have an interest in maintaining popularity, managing expectations, and avoiding challenges to their priorities and resources. As in the United Kingdom, they may not want attention brought to more costly social and economic rights, such as in the areas of economic welfare, child care, and health care. Or as in Japan, they may want more attention on responsibilities and less on the assertion of rights.[68] So for different reasons, governments of all types have an interest in not putting HRE into full effect. Addressing such government resistance to HRE requires that child advocates provide education to, and continuous pressure on, government authorities, reminding them of the benefits of HRE and the importance of fulfilling their obligations under the international treaties they have ratified.

Another factor is the influence of ideologies that are in real or perceived conflict with children's HRE. One example is the ideology of parental rights.[69] Subscribers to this ideology, believing children's rights to be a danger to parental rights, resist any introduction of children's HRE into schools. Such ideology has had considerable sway on political and educational authorities, especially in North America. A major reason, for instance, that the United States refused to ratify the CRC was concern that the rights of children would override the rights of parents.[70] Another example is neoliberalism as it relates to education.[71] It seeks market-based approaches to education that focus on school performance, school competition, and high standards and test scores. Because of the perceived linkage between school performance and student behavior, neoliberals seek strong behavioral management policies in school. Strict discipline and control of behavior are seen as necessary to higher student achievement. Initiatives such as HRE are to be rejected because they are perceived to undermine or distract from realizing these goals. Such thinking has had influence on the decisions of governments and educators not to implement HRE or even to halt HRE programs in progress.[72] A third example is populism, xenophobia, and related hostility to refugees, immigrants, and minorities. This is demonstrated in the United Kingdom's vote to leave the European Union (Brexit), the victory of Trump in the United States, and the rising tide of populism in parts of Europe. In such an environment of intolerance, HRE is unwelcome. Addressing these anti-HRE ideologies requires extensive publicity and systematic public education explaining the meaning and value of human rights and HRE. A more accurate understanding of human rights has been shown to be linked with greater support for HRE.[73]

Finally, another factor is the general lack of enthusiasm for HRE in schools and education systems. If they decided to do so, governments could initiate comprehensive and serious HRE through changes in legislation, policies, and curricula. But they are hesitant to proceed without the interest, support, and cooperation of educational and school authorities, especially in the many decentralized education systems of the world. The fact is there has not been widespread interest. Research shows that many teachers in many countries are ambivalent about or opposed to HRE in schools.[74] Whether influenced by traditional or authoritarian thinking or by neoliberalism, some teachers express concern that the outcome of HRE would be disruption and loss of their authority and ability to control students in their classroom. Teachers in many countries also have significant discretion in the development and implementation of school curricula. So even where children's HRE has been introduced, some teachers give priority to the teaching of responsibilities rather than rights.[75] These views could be altered through teacher training about HRE, but such training has not been made widely available. Another reason for teacher disinterest is the perceived lack of need. In response to a possible introduction of HRE in schools, educators often reply, "We're already doing that!"[76] They see HRE as much the same as what they are already doing in education on social justice, citizenship, anti-bullying, or anti-racism. They fail to see HRE as anchored in international human rights principles and as a foundation for these other types of social education and for overall school functioning. Again, teacher training could correct this misconception, but it has not been widely implemented.

This lack of commitment by political and educational authorities is a formidable challenge. Change is unlikely to occur in the short term. In the long term, the prospects for progress are better. At the end of the Second World War, there was no international requirement for HRE, no global movement for HRE, and virtually no HRE in formal or non-formal education settings. But over time, educational obligations have been incorporated into international human rights treaties, including the CRC and the Declaration on Human Rights Education and Training. A significant movement for HRE has gathered, and pressure for its implementation has steadily grown. And numerous initiatives provide models and hope for HRE on a wider scale. Another reason for optimism is that a growing number of states have ratified the third optional protocol to the CRC, which allows children, groups of children, or their representatives to bring a complaint to the CRC Committee, including the complaint that their right to HRE (under CRC Articles 29 and 42) is being violated.[77]

It is true that developments have been sporadic, imperfect, and sometimes disappointing. But it also is true that education about, through, and for the human rights of children is much greater now than it was a few decades ago. The Committee on the Rights of the Child has reported the strengthening of children's HRE in countries as diverse as Denmark, Malawi, Slovenia, and Armenia.[78] Comprehensive children's HRE will take considerable time. But momentum continues to build.

Notes

1. Nelson Mandela, "Lighting Your Way to a Better Future," speech delivered at the launch of the Mindset Network, Johannesburg, July 16, 2003, http://db.nelsonmandela.org/speeches/pub_view.asp?pg=item&ItemID=NMS909.
2. UN Declaration on Human Rights Education and Training, G.A. Res 66/137, UN Doc. A/RES/66/137 (Dec. 19, 2011; entered into force Feb. 21, 2012).
3. Jonathan Todres, "Analyzing the Opposition to U.S. Ratification of the U.N. Convention on the Rights of the Child," in *The United Nations Convention on the Rights of the Child: An Analysis of Treaty Provisions and Implications of U.S. Ratification*, ed. Jonathan Todres, Mark E. Wojcik, and Cris R. Revaz (Ardsley, NY: Transnational, 2006), 19–32. The United States is nonetheless obliged to comply with other human rights treaties it has ratified that apply to the rights of children.
4. Sharon Detrick, *A Commentary on the United Nations Convention the Rights of the Child* (The Hague: Martinus Nijhoff, 1999).

5. R. Brian Howe and Katherine Covell, *Empowering Children: Children's Rights Education as a Pathway to Citizenship* (Toronto: University of Toronto Press, 2007), 29–31.

6. The right to HRE also can be inferred from previous international human rights documents that refer to the right to education, for example, the International Covenant on Economic, Social and Cultural Rights, 993 UNTS 3 (1966; entered into force Jan. 3, 1976), art. 13; and the Universal Declaration of Human Rights, G.A. Res. 217 (III) A, UN Doc. A/RES/217(III) (Dec. 10, 1948), art. 26.

7. Johan Vande Lanotte and Geert Goedertier, "Monitoring Human Rights: Formal and Procedural Aspects," in *Monitoring Children's Rights*, ed. Eugene Verhellen (The Hague: Martinus Nijhoff, 1996), 73–111.

8. Howe and Covell, *Empowering Children*, 30–31.

9. See, for example, UN Committee on the Rights of the Child (CRC Committee), "Concluding Observations on the Combined Third and Fourth Periodic Report of Canada," CRC/C/CAN/CO/3–4 (2012), para 24; CRC Committee, "Concluding Observations on the Combined Second to Fourth Periodic Reports of Antigua and Barbuda," CRC/C/ATG/CO/2–4 (2017), para. 17(b); CRC Committee, "Concluding Observations on the Combined Second to Fourth Periodic Reports of the Congo," CRC/C/COG/CO/2–4 (2014), para. 23; CRC Committee, "Concluding Observations on the Combined Second to Fourth Periodic Reports of Benin," CRC/C/CO/3–5 (2016), para. 21; CRC Committee, *General Comment No. 1: Article 29(1): The Aims of Education*, CRC/GC/2001/1 (2001).

10. Jaap Doek, "The Current Status of the United Nations Convention on the Rights of the Child," in *The United Nations CRC on the Rights of the Child*, ed. Sharon Detrick (Dordrecht, NL: Martinus Nijhoff, 1992), 632–640.

11. Katherine Covell, "Children's Human Rights Education as a Means to Social Justice: A Case Study from England," *International Journal of Education for Social Justice* 2, no. 1 (2013): 35–48 (special issue: Education for Citizenship: Challenges and Perspectives from a Social Justice Approach), http://www.rinace.net/riejs/numeros/vol2-num1/art2.pdf.

12. For example, Beniamino Cislaghi, Diane Gillespie, and Gerry Mackie, "Expanding the Aspirational Map: Interactive Learning and Human Rights in Tostan's Community Empowerment Program," in *Human Rights Education: Theory, Research, Praxis*, ed. Monisha Bajaj and Nancy Flowers (Philadelphia: University of Pennsylvania Press, 2017), 251–266, 256–262; Tracey Holland and J. Paul Martin, "Human Rights Education's Role in Peacebuilding: Lessons from the Field," in Bajaj and Flowers, *Human Rights Education*, 267–290, 276–285; Carol Anne Spreen and Chrissie Monaghan, "Leveraging Diversity to Become a Global Citizen: Lessons for Human Rights Education," in Bajaj and Flowers, *Human Rights Education*, 291–316, 299–306.

13. Howe and Covell, *Empowering Children*, 111–112, 116–117.

14. Phillip Payne, "Identity and Environmental Education," *Environmental Education* 7, no. 1 (2000): 67–88; Felisa Tibbets, "Understanding What We Do: Emerging Models for Human Rights Education," *International Review of Education* 48, nos. 3–4 (2002): 159–171 (special Issue on education and human rights).

15. Eric Erikson, *Identity: Youth and Crisis* (New York: W.W. Norton, 1968); Mordecai Nisan, "Personal Identity and Education for the Desirable," *Journal of Moral Education* 25 (July 1996): 75–84.

16. Howe and Covell, *Empowering Children*, 110–113.

17. Diane Goodman, "Motivating People from Privileged Groups to Support Social Justice," *Teachers College Record* 102 (2000): 1061–1086.

18. R. Brian Howe and Katherine Covell *Education in the Best Interests of the Child: A Children's Rights Perspective on Closing the Achievement Gap* (Toronto: University of Toronto Press, 2013), 168–181.

19. Rachel Hodgkin and Peter Newell, *Implementation Handbook for the Convention on the Rights of the Child* (New York: UNICEF, 2007), 627–633; Howe and Covell, *Empowering Children*, 37–40.

20. Hodgkin and Newell, *Implementation Handbook*, 628–630.

21. Howe and Covell, *Empowering Children*, 37–38.

22. CRC Committee, *General Comment No. 5: General Measures of Implementation of the Convention on the Rights of the Child (arts. 4, 42 and 44, para. 6)*, CRC/GC/2003/5 (2003).

23. Monisha Bajaj, "Introduction," in Bajaj and Flowers, *Human Rights Education*, 1–18, 3–6; Susan Garnett Russell and David Suarez, "Symbol and Substance: Human Rights Education as an Emergent Global Institution," in Bajaj and Flowers, *Human Rights Education*, 19–31.

24. Nancy Flowers, "Afterword," in Bajaj and Flowers, *Human Rights Education*, 317–320; Nancy Flowers, "The Global Movement for Human Rights Education," *Radical Teacher* 103 (2015): 5–11.

25. Quoted by Bajaj, "Introduction," 3.

26. Katherine Covell, "Awareness, Learning and Education in Human Rights," in *The SAGE Handbook of Human Rights*, ed. (London: SAGE Publications, 2014), 821–839.

27. Declaration on Human Rights Education and Training, art. 1.

28. Flowers, "Afterword," 319.

29. Bajaj, "Introduction," 4–6; Russell and Suarez, "Symbol and Substance," 24–27.

30. Abraham Magendzo, "Problems in Planning Human Rights Education for Reemerging Latin American Democracies," in *Human Rights Education for the Twenty-First Century*, ed. George Andreopoulos and Richard P. Claude (Philadelphia: University of Pennsylvania Press, 1997), 469–483.

31. Flowers, "Afterword," 324.

32. Katherine Covell, R. Brian Howe, and Anne McGillivray, "Implementing Children's Education Rights in Schools," in *Handbook of Children's Rights: Global and Multidisciplinary Perspectives*, ed. Martin Ruck, Michele Peterson-Badali, and Michael Freeman (New York: Routledge, 2016), 296–311, 298–299; Laura Lundy, Karen Orr, and Harry Shier, "Children's Education Rights: Global Perspectives," in Ruck, Peterson-Badali, and Freeman, *Handbook of Children's Rights*, 364–380, 373–375; Russell and Suarez, "Symbol and Substance," 35–39.

33. Russell and Suarez, "Symbol and Substance," 31–34.

34. By early 2018, 20 of 193 member states of the United Nations had specific plans for HRE. Office of the UN High Commissioner for Human Rights, "National Action Plans for Human Rights Education," http://www.ohchr.org/EN/Issues/Education/Training/Pages/NationalActionPlansHumanRightsEducation.aspx (accessed Sept. 8, 2019).

35. Monisha Bajaj and Rachel Wahl, "Human Rights Education in Postcolonial India," in Bajaj and Flowers, *Human Rights Education*, 147–169, 150–154.

36. Russell and Suarez, "Symbol and Substance," 31–36.

37. Russell and Suarez, "Symbol and Substance," 35–36; Allison E. C. Struthers, "Human Rights Education: Educating *about*, *through* and *for* Human Rights," *International Journal of Human Rights* 19, no. 1 (2015): 53–73.

38. Lee Jerome, Lesley Emerson, Laura Lundy, and Karen Orr, "Teaching and Learning about Child Rights: A Study of Implementation in 26 Countries," child rights education report

by Queen's University Belfast and UNICEF (March 2015), https://eprints.mdx.ac.uk/18078/1/Filetoupload%2C515480%2Cen.pdf.

39. Jerome et al., "Teaching and Learning," 8, 17, 25, 63.

40. Covell, Howe, and McGillivray, "Implementing Children's Education Rights," 298–299.

41. Amnesty International, "Becoming a Human Rights Friendly School: A Guide for Schools around the World," AI Index no. POL 32/001/2012 (Sept. 14, 2012), https://www.amnesty.org/en/documents/document/?indexNumber=POL32%2f001%2f2012&language=en; UNICEF UK, "Rights Respecting School Award," http://www.unicef.org.uk/rights-respecting-schools (accessed Sept. 8, 2019). For a discussion on the certificate program see Howe and Covell, *Education in the Best Interests of the Child*, 188–189.

42. Bajaj and Wahl, "Human Rights Education in Postcolonial India," 156–158.

43. Holland and Martin, "Human Rights Education's Role in Peacebuilding," 272–275.

44. Felisa Tibbitts, "Evolution of Human Rights Education Models," in Bajaj and Flowers, *Human Rights Education*, 69–95. The models presented here are revised from Tibbitts's earlier work.

45. Declaration on Human Rights Education and Training, art. 2.

46. CRC Committee, *General Comment No. 1*.

47. CRC Committee, *General Comment No. 1*.

48. See, for example, CRC Committee, "Concluding Observations: Syrian Arab Republic," CRC/C/15/ADD.212 (2003), para. 46.

49. See, for example, CRC Committee, "Concluding Observations: Japan," CRC/C/15/Add.231 (2004), para. 49; CRC Committee, "Concluding Observations: Thailand," CRC/C/THA/CO/2 (March 17, 2006), para. 63.

50. See, for example, CRC Committee, "Concluding Observations: Benin," para. 21; CRC Committee, "Concluding Observations Canada," paras. 24, 25; CRC Committee, "Concluding Observations Congo," para. 23; CRC Committee, "Concluding Observations on the Fifth Periodic Report of Denmark," CRC/C/DNK/CO/5 (2017), para. 37.

51. Flowers, "Afterword," 324–325; Lundy, Orr, and Shier, "Children's Education Rights," 374–375; Sam Mejias, "Politics, Power, and Protest: Rights-Based Education Policy and the Limits of Human Rights Education," in Bajaj and Flowers, *Human Rights Education*, 170–194, 172–174.

52. UN Sustainable Development Agenda, "Millennium Development Goals and Beyond 2015," Goal 2: Achieve Universal Primary Education, http://www.un.org/millennium-goals/education.shtml (accessed Sept. 8, 2019).

53. The ensuing discussion of the RRR is presented in detail in Howe and Covell, *Education in the Best Interests of the Child*, 172–184.

54. Howe and Covell, *Education in the Best Interests of the Child*, 178.

55. Don Rowe, "Taking Responsibility: School Behaviour Policies in England, Moral Development and Implications for Citizenship Education," *Journal of Moral Education* 35, no. 4 (2006): 519–531.

56. Charles C. Helwig and Urszula Jasiobedzka, "The Relation between Law and Morality: Children's Reasoning about Socially Beneficial and Unjust Laws," *Child Development* 72, no. 5 (2001): 1382–1393.

57. Howe and Covell, *Education in the Best Interests of the Child*, 178.

58. Howe and Covell, *Education in the Best Interests of the Child*, 177–180.

59. Howe and Covell, *Education in the Best Interests of the Child*, 179.

60. James Appleton, Sandra L. Christenson, Dongjin Kim, and Amy L. Reschly, "Measuring Cognitive and Psychological Engagement," *Journal of School Psychology* 44, no. 5 (2006): 427–445; Michael J. Furlong, Angela D. Whipple, Grace St. Jean, Jenne Simental, Alicia Soliz, and Sandy Punthuna, "Multiple Contexts of School Engagement: Moving Toward a Unifying Framework for Educational Research and Practice," *California School Psychologist* 8, no. 1 (2003): 99–113; Shane R. Jimerson, Emily Campos, and Jennifer L. Greif, "Toward an Understanding of Definitions and Measures of School Engagement," *California School Psychologist* 8, no. 1 (2003): 43–52.

61. Clea A. McNeely, James Nonnemaker, and Robert W. Blum, "Promoting School Connectedness: Evidence from the National Longitudinal Study of Adolescent Health," *Journal of School Health* 72, no. 4 (2002): 138–146.

62. Covell, "Awareness, Learning and Education," 835.

63. Joe Faretra, "Historic Day for Charter," *Andover Advertiser*, March 18, 2011, www.andoveradvertiser.co.uk/news/8918720.print.

64. Katherine Covell, R. Brian Howe, and Justin K. McNeil, "Implementing Children's Human Rights Education in Schools," *Improving Schools* 13, no. 2 (2010): 1–16.

65. Erikson, *Identity*; Charles Helwig, Mary Louise Arnold, Dingliang Tan, and Dwight Boyd, "Chinese Adolescents Reasoning about Democratic and Authority-Based Decision Making in Peer, Family, and School Contexts," *Child Development* 74, no. 3 (2003): 783–800; Charles Helwig, "The Development of Personal Autonomy though Cultures," *Cognitive Development* 21, no. 4 (2006): 458–473, http://doi.org/10.1016/j.cogdev.2006.06.009.

66. Covell, "Awareness, Learning and Education," 825–826.

67. See, for example, Bai Guimei, "Human Rights Education in Universities," in *Global Standards—Local Actions: 15 Years Vienna World Conference on Human Rights*, ed. Wolfgang Benedek, Clare Gregory, Julia Kozma, Manfred Nowak, Christian Strohal, and Engelbert Theuermann (Vienna: Wissenschaftlicher Verlag, 2009), 355–358; Mark F. Massoud, "Do Victims of War Need International Law? Human Rights Education Programs in Authoritarian Sudan," *Law and Society Review* 45, no. 1 (2011): 1–32.

68. Covell, "Awareness, Learning and Education," 826.

69. Covell, Howe, and McGillivray, "Implementing Children's Education Rights," 305–306.

70. Todres, "Analyzing the Opposition."

71. Mejias, "Politics, Power, and Protest," 174–176.

72. Mejias, "Politics, Power, and Protest," 188–190.

73. Kelly Campbell and Katherine Covell, "Children's Rights Education at the University Level: An Effective Means of Promoting Rights Knowledge and Rights-Based Attitudes," *International Journal of Children's Rights* 9, no. 2 (2001): 123–135; Katherine Covell, Johnna O'Leary, and R. Brian Howe, "Introducing a New Grade 8 Curriculum in Children's Rights," *Alberta Journal of Educational Research* 48, no. 4 (2002): 302–313.

74. Covell, "Awareness, Learning and Education," 827–828.

75. R. Brian Howe and Katherine Covell, "Miseducating Children about Their Rights," *Education, Citizenship, and Social Justice* 5 (2010): 91–102.

76. Flowers, "Afterword," 328.

77. The protocol was opened for signatures in February 2012. By the end of 2013, a total of nine states had approved it; by early 2018 there were thirty-nine. UN Optional Protocol to the Convention on the Rights of the Child on a Communications Procedure, G.A. Res. 66/138, UN Doc. A/RES/66/138 (2011; entered into force April 14, 2014).

78. CRC Committee, "Concluding Observations: Denmark," para. 37; CRC Committee, "Concluding Observations on the Combined Third to Fifth Periodic Reports of Malawi," CRC/C/MWI/CO/3–5 (2017), para. 11; CRC Committee, "Consideration of Reports Submitted by States Parties under Article 44 of the Convention: Concluding Observations: Slovenia," CRC/C/15/ADD.230 (2004), para. 52; CRC Committee, "Consideration of Reports Submitted by States Parties under Article 44 of the Convention: Armenia," CRC/C/15/Add.225 (2004), para. 53.

CHAPTER 34

....

CHILDREN'S RIGHTS IN THE TWENTY-FIRST CENTURY

Challenges and Opportunities

....

JONATHAN TODRES AND SHANI M. KING

1 INTRODUCTION

....

THIS volume has sought both to advance scholarly inquiry in the field of children's rights and to give further shape to children's rights as discipline. The foregoing chapters have mapped law, policy, and practices across a breadth of areas within the field of children's rights. Contributing authors have identified the complexities in the issues confronting children as well as critical challenges for children's rights. The issues they have identified and the ones we discuss here are essential to address if children's rights are to be meaningful in the lives of all children. Yet before we detail current and future challenges, it is worth briefly reflecting on where we are today.

When discussing children's rights, or human rights more generally, it is easy to focus on the shortcomings. We are a long way from ensuring all rights of all children. Yet it is also important to recognize that the era of children's rights, launched with the adoption of the Convention on the Rights of the Child (CRC) in 1989, has witnessed dramatic progress on a breadth of children's rights issues. Not only is the CRC the most widely accepted human rights treaty in history, but the Convention and other international children's rights instruments have helped spur positive changes in law, policies, and attitudes toward children in numerous countries.[1] Dozens of countries have incorporated provisions of the CRC, its optional protocols, and other international children's rights law directly into national law, and a number of countries have enshrined children's rights in their constitutions.[2] States have strengthened national law related to children's health and education rights; their rights to live free from trafficking, abusive labor practices, and other forms of exploitation; the administration of juvenile justice; adoption proceedings; and many other issues concerning children.[3] This progress has contributed to improvements in the lives and well-being of children over the past thirty years.[4]

Although causation might be difficult to establish (economic development and a host of other factors have contributed to the progress made), the CRC's mandate helped put children's issues on the agenda in numerous countries and on the global stage. It spurred recognition of the child as a rights holder and not merely an object subsumed within the family. That shift in our understanding and perception of children is itself significant. In addition, since the CRC's adoption, the world has become a better place for millions of children, suggesting that the children's rights movement, guided in some respects by the CRC, is making a difference. Infant mortality has declined by approximately six million children annually since 1990, the year the CRC entered into force.[5] The number of school-aged children out of school has been reduced significantly.[6] And the prevalence of child labor has declined.[7] Although substantial work remains to ensure the rights and well-being of every child, the progress achieved since the introduction of the CRC reinforces the value of children's rights and advocacy efforts to realize the rights of all children.

In this concluding chapter, rather than attempt to bring together all of the critically important insights from contributing authors, we instead look forward and discuss some of the key issues for children's rights in the near to longer term. We begin by discussing cross-cutting themes relevant to all issues affecting children's rights and child well-being. After that, we turn to a selected list of current issues that we believe demand greater focus—at research, advocacy, and policy levels. And we conclude by returning to where this chapter started—on a positive note—by offering our view on why the field of children's rights is a hopeful one.

2   CROSS-CUTTING THEMES

2.1   The Time-Sensitive Nature of Children's Rights

Children, due to the developmental nature of childhood, are more vulnerable than adults.[8] Short-term deprivations of rights can have lifelong consequences in ways that may not occur when adults experience similar deprivations. For example, children who are out of school for relatively short periods of time, as often occurs with refugee or displaced children, may face significant barriers when attempting to return to school.[9] Even relatively short disruptions in the realization of education rights can have long-term adverse consequences. The same is true of other rights deprivations. Yet the international system is not set up to mobilize quickly to respond to crises—such as have occurred in Rwanda, Syria, and elsewhere. National governments also frequently take too long to draft, deliberate, and ultimately adopt new laws or policies in response to crises that children confront. And implementation takes even longer and frequently does not reach all children. Too often we confront the prospect of a "lost generation" of children.[10] The time-sensitive nature of children's rights makes the rights of children unique and challenges governments, scholars, and advocates to explore ways to respond more quickly and efficiently to threats to children's rights wherever they may occur. And equally important, it demands that we explore and better understand the structures that need to be in place to prevent such threats from occurring in the first place.

2.2 The Interrelated Nature of Rights

Although already discussed in chapter 4, the interrelated nature of rights is so relevant to the lives of children that it merits recognition as a cross-cutting theme. Children's rights have both horizontal relationships and vertical relationships. Health and education rights offer an example of horizontal relationships, as poor health and obstacles to health rights have adverse consequences for school attendance and education rights. Vertical relationships among rights are seen frequently in the interplay between women's and children's rights.[11] For example, as women continue to bear de facto primary responsibility for child care in many countries, investing in their educational and employment opportunities can positively affect their children's rights and well-being. Consequently, when parents' rights are denied, it heightens the vulnerability of their children. Children, especially young children, are inherently dependent. Vertical rights relationships are therefore critical and merit much greater attention. Although there are potential pitfalls to connecting children's rights and women's rights advocacy,[12] there are also significant potential benefits that can accrue from taking a holistic approach to the lives and rights of children and their families. Similarly, horizontal relationships among rights matter, particularly for the most marginalized children. As the international community makes progress toward key goals—such as universal primary education—the most marginalized children often are missed, in part because they are confronting multiple rights violations simultaneously (whereas aid and interventions are often focused on a single sector). Integrated, multisector responses are critical to accounting for horizontal and vertical relationships among rights so that all children can reap the full benefits of children's rights.

2.3 Autonomy

The liberal tradition of rights is built on the idea of the autonomous individual. That traditional construct is an awkward fit for children, especially young children. Whether we speak of fifteen-year-olds, five-year-olds, or five-month-olds, children are a developmentally diverse group with more limited autonomy than adults. Indeed, infants and young children cannot survive without a caregiver. And even the most mature adolescents typically have incomplete autonomy (both individually and as a result of their status as a minor under the law). Children's rights scholars and advocates need to develop a more nuanced approach to children's rights that accounts in a meaningful way for children's autonomy or lack thereof. All children have rights, due to the fact that they are human. To suggest otherwise is to imply that rights are not inherent but rather entitlements granted by the government at a certain age (and thus equally subject to withdrawal). That children are rights holders is accepted by the vast majority of people. But critical questions remain as to how we operationalize rights when the rights holder is, for example, a one-year-old or an eight-year-old.

2.4 Participation

Today, no government or civil society effort to address racism would be taken seriously if it consulted and involved only white individuals. Similarly, no women's rights initiative would be deemed acceptable if women were not invited to participate in its development and implementation. Yet we still regularly see children's rights meetings, programs, and policies undertaken without any input from children. Of course, children are different. They are developmentally different. But arguing that children do not know enough to contribute at all undermines the entire idea of recognizing children as rights holders. Similarly, arguing that it is too difficult or cumbersome is not acceptable.[13] Implementation of rights cannot be based on convenience. Involving children in a meaningful way is challenging. Not all adults are adept at listening to, engaging, and partnering with young people. But we must do better. We must find ways to mainstream children and children's rights. That means that children must have opportunities to participate at the design, implementation, monitoring, and evaluation stages of every law, policy, and program that affects the lives of children.[14]

2.5 Taking Children's Rights Seriously

Not only must we do a better job taking children seriously, but we must ensure that all stakeholders take children's rights seriously. It is easy to spot the resistance to children's rights among certain political groups. But there also have been failings within spaces and fields that should be supportive of children's rights. Too often children and children's rights are marginalized, even in so-called rights-friendly or child-friendly fields. On many human rights agendas, for example, children's rights receive little, if any, mention. This is despite the fact that children constitute one-third of the world's population and almost half the population of certain countries. Similarly, in family law discourses, children are often addressed only tangentially or seen as the object of outcomes (e.g., in custody cases or reproductive rights issues). And in the child welfare context, there are many instances when children's rights are not even mentioned. Too often children's rights are not recognized as integral to these and other spaces where they have a natural home. Children's rights scholars and advocates must engage other human rights and family law partners, as well as child welfare professionals and others, to understand the resistance to children's rights, to raise awareness about the value of children's rights, and to encourage these partners to incorporate children's rights in their work and on their agendas.

3 CURRENT AND EMERGING CRITICAL TOPICS

Contributors to this volume have identified numerous pressing children's rights issues. Rather than summarize all of those issues, we highlight here a selected group of issues that we believe will likely be significant issues for the foreseeable future and deserve greater attention among both researchers and policymakers.

3.1 Large-Scale Human Rights Crises

Massive human rights crises, like the ongoing one in Syria, have devastating consequences for children. In Syria, 5.6 million children have been adversely affected, and more than 2.5 million Syrian children are now living as refugees outside of their home country.[15] Not only do these large-scale crises have millions of victims, but they also typically leave infrastructure devastated, complicating any response. Children's rights, and human rights more generally, have yet to figure out a way to prevent such humanitarian disasters. Political will is obviously a critical piece, but the reality for many Syrian children—like those in Rwanda and other locales where massive atrocities occur—is that they are at great risk of becoming part of a lost generation. The international community must find a better way to respond that secures the rights of children when confronted with these huge crises.

3.2 The Role of Private Sector Actors

The private sector, with its huge influence on the global agenda and far-reaching impact on the lives of people in all countries, has a major role to play in the human rights arena. That role has been debated and documented by policymakers, scholars, and others, leading to selected initiatives to outline the human rights obligations of corporations (e.g., the UN Guiding Principles on Business and Human Rights).[16] Much more is needed. Businesses have been—and continue to be—the site of significant violations of children's rights (e.g., some businesses continue to use trafficked children and child labor in their supply chains). But it is also the case that businesses have contributed to efforts to reduce violations of children's rights (e.g., a Swiss company helped develop a robot jockey for camel racing, reducing the demand for trafficked children to be used as camel jockeys in the United Arab Emirates).[17] Child rights scholars, professionals, and advocates need to continue to explore ways to more constructively engage private sector entities so that their business practices respect and ensure the rights of all children and their core capabilities can be utilized to help secure children's rights.

3.3 Technology

Technology continues to grow in influence beyond even the boldest predictions. Developments in artificial intelligence prompt questions about what the world will look like when children reach majority and throughout their lives. Social media has created spaces where young people spend significant portions of their childhood. Evidence shows that technology and social media can both expose children to risk—trafficking, bullying, and other harms—and be a vehicle for enhancing protections of children's rights and accessing assistance to remedy rights violations.[18] Understanding the role of technology, mitigating its risks, and realizing its potential to support children's rights requires engaging with young people to understand how they use technology and what challenges and opportunities they see and confront in the digital world.[19] Although in many ways the digital world acts as simply another locale where typical interactions occur—from supportive friendships to bullying—in other ways it is also having a profound impact on interpersonal interactions. Children today spend more of their time interacting with technology as compared to other human beings than in any prior generation. This phenomenon prompts questions about the impact of technology on children's development, social skills, and sense of community. And that, in turn, raises questions about the responsibility of government, the private sector, and parents in addressing technology's impact on children. In short, technology's impact is far-reaching and likely only to increase, and thus it merits greater, proactive responses.

3.4 Genetics, Epigenetics, and Scientific Advances

Advances in scientific research on genetics, epigenetics, and related topics raise questions about how best to secure the rights and well-being of all children. If there are intergenerational causes of child well-being, what implications does this have for their rights, such as the right to the highest attainable standard of health? Conversely, what are the implications for privacy rights of children and their families? The issues raised have obvious implications for how we implement and secure children's rights, but they also prompt important questions about the content of children's rights law. If the right to health has intergenerational roots, then does the content of Article 24 of the CRC (on the right to the highest attainable standard of health) mean that the state obligation extends back to parental well-being or even beyond? Scientific research has the potential to help us understand the underlying determinants of child well-being and the inputs needed to ensure each child can reach his or her potential. But that panoply of causes and inputs may not map so neatly on specific rights. These issues are connected to similar questions about how we best account for the interrelated nature of rights and require further inquiry.

3.5 Populism and the Attack on Rights and on Children

The recent rise in populism and its attendant rhetoric and acts of hate represent a significant challenge for children's rights and human rights more broadly. The apparent rise in intolerance, or at least the more public expression of such intolerance, has spurred policy developments that result in both children's rights violations and short- and long-term adverse consequences for children's well-being. For example, harsh immigration policies—such as the Trump administration's separation of children from their families at the US southern border in 2018—have inflicted trauma on children and contravened children's rights law.[20] The rise in incendiary rhetoric among political leaders and increase in hate incidents is also trickling down to children, as studies show an increase in bullying and peer aggression toward certain children based on their religion race, gender, sexual orientation, or national origin.[21] These developments present immediate challenges in terms of figuring out how to end such children's rights abuses and stop the rollback of human rights protections. And they also prompt important longer-term questions about how to build rights-respecting communities and ensure sustained progress in the implementation and realization of children's rights.[22]

3.6 Violence against Children

Violence against children is addressed in chapter 15, but it merits special attention in this section on pressing current issues. Violence strikes children in their homes, schools, and their communities. Not only is the prevalence of physical, sexual, and emotional violence against children still unacceptably high, but the persistence of violence against children and the tolerance in many circles—such as with acceptance of corporal punishment—strikes at the core of the children's rights idea. As recognized in Article 1 of Universal Declaration of Human Rights—the foundational document of the modern human rights movement—children, like all human beings, are "born free and equal in dignity and rights." Inflicting violence on children therefore is counter to the foundational values of children's rights and human rights. Yet violence against children is entrenched in community and cultural beliefs and practices in both the Global North and Global South. Prevention of violence against children, therefore, requires a commitment both to address this pervasive harm and to confront the complexities of implementing children's rights law in diverse communities with varied cultural beliefs and practices. The harm inflicted and the profound challenge it presents make it a critical issue.

3.7 Climate Change

All of the work of children's rights scholars and advocates to improve the effectiveness of children's rights law and secure the rights and well-being of children is occurring against the backdrop of the looming threat of climate change. Scientific models point to the likelihood of a radically changed planet that will present threats to a breadth of rights, including the right to life, survival, and development.[23] The overwhelming majority view is that the issue of dramatic change is not if, but when. The consequences of climate change will hit children harder than any other population. Although Chapter 22 examines climate change in depth, we would be remiss in not highlighting it as a major threat to children's rights for the foreseeable future.

The above issues are critical issues to address, in research, advocacy, and policy. They also are illustrative of the breadth of issues that shape the lives, well-being, and rights of children. Many other issues could be highlighted here, and the contributing authors to this volume have done well to identify other vital issues for children's rights in their respective areas.

4 Conclusion: A Vision of Hope

Despite the breadth and severity of challenges confronting children and children's rights, there is reason for optimism. We have witnessed significant progress in the past thirty years. Millions of children today are thriving in ways they would not have a generation ago. That progress is encouraging, but the greatest reason for hope is children themselves. Children across the globe demonstrate strength, courage, resilience, inquisitive minds, and a capacity to imagine a better world. When young people participate and are supported, they can transform their schools, neighborhoods, communities, and countries.

As we reach the thirtieth anniversary of the CRC, we—researchers, advocates, and policymakers—must begin to forge the next phase of children's rights. This means demanding greater academic rigor in the field, addressing gaps in the law, improving implementation and enforcement, and ensuring that the dream of children's rights reaches all children and their families. And all of our work must be done in partnership with and for the benefit of children.

Notes

1. See UNICEF, "25 Years of the Convention on the Rights of the Child: Is the World a Better Place for Children?" (Sept. 14, 2014), https://www.unicef.org/publications/index_76027. html; UNICEF Innocenti Research Centre, "Law Reform and the Implementation of the Convention on the Rights of the Child" (2008), www.unicef-irc.org/publications/493-law -reform-and-the-implementation-of-the-convention-on-the-rights-of-the-child.html; UNICEF Innocenti Research Centre, "The General Measures of the Convention on the

Rights of the Child: The Process in Europe and Central Asia" (2006), https://www.unicef-irc.org/publications/415-the-general-measures-of-the-convention-on-the-rights-of-the-child-the-process-in.html.

2. UNICEF Innocenti Research Centre, "Law Reform," 13–31; UNICEF Innocenti Research Centre, "General Measures,"1–14.

3. UNICEF Innocenti Research Centre, *Law Reform*, 39–90; UNICEF Innocenti Research Centre, *General Measures*, 4–13.

4. UNICEF, "25 Years of the Convention," 10–49.

5. UNICEF, "25 Years of the Convention," 11–19.

6. See UNESCO, *"Youth and Skills: Putting Education to Work*, EFA Global Monitoring Report 2012 (Paris: UNESCO, 2013). The latest data show that number further declined to 58 million as of 2012. UNESCO Institute of Statistics and UNICEF, "Fixing the Broken Promise of Education for All: Findings from the Global Initiative on Out-of-School Children" (2015), https://files.eric.ed.gov/fulltext/ED560017.pdf.

7. International Labour Office (ILO), *Marking Progress against Child Labor—Global Estimates and Trends 2000–2012* Geneva: ILO, 2013).

8. Geraldine Van Bueren, *The International Law on the Rights of the Child* (The Hague: Martinus Nijoff, 1995).

9. See, for example, Brendan O'Malley, "The Longer-Term Impact of Attacks on Education on Education Systems, Development and Fragility and the Implications for Policy Responses," background paper for the EFA Global Monitoring Report 2011 (2010), http://www.protectingeducation.org/sites/default/files/documents/efa_unesco_-_the_longer_term_impact_of_attacks.pdf; Xin Meng and R. G. Gregory, "The Impact of Interrupted Education on Subsequent Educational Attainment: A Cost of the Chinese Cultural Revolution," *Economic Development and Cultural Change* 50, no. 4 (2002): 935–959.

10. See, for example, Human Rights Watch, " 'Without Education They Lose Their Future': Denial of Education to Child Asylum Seekers on the Greek Islands" (July 18, 2018), https://www.hrw.org/sites/default/files/report_pdf/greece0718_web.pdf.

11. Jonathan Todres, "Children's Rights and Women's Rights: Interrelated and Interdependent," in *Handbook of Children's Rights: Global and Multidisciplinary Perspectives*, ed. Martin Ruck, Michele Peterson-Badali, and Michael Freeman (New York: Routledge, 2017).

12. Savitri Goonesekere, "Women's Rights and Children's Rights: The United Nations Conventions as Compatible and Complementary International Treaties," Innocenti Occasional Papers (1992), https://www.unicef-irc.org/publications/127-womens-rights-and-childrens-rights-the-united-nations-conventions-as-compatible-and.html; Linda Malone, "Protecting the Least Respected: The Girl Child and the Gender Bias of the Vienna Convention's Adoption and Reservation Regime," *William & Mary Journal of Women and the Law* 3 (1997): 1–6.

13. Laura Lundy, " 'Voice' Is Not Enough: Conceptualising Article 12 of the United Nations Convention on the Rights of the Child," *British Educational Research Journal* 33, no. 6 (2007): 927–942.

14. Jonathan Todres, "Mainstreaming Children's Rights in Post-Disaster Settings," *Emory International Law Review* 25 (2011): 1233–1261.

15. UNICEF, "Syria Crisis October 2018: Humanitarian Results," https://www.unicef.org/appeals/files/UNICEF_Syria_Crisis_Humanitarian_Situation_Report_____October_2018.pdf (accessed Sept. 9, 2019).

16. Office of the UN High Commissioner for Human Rights, "Guiding Principles on Business and Human Rights: Implementing the United Nations 'Protect, Respect and Remedy'

Framework," HR/PUB/11/04 (2011), https://www.ohchr.org/Documents/Publications/GuidingPrinciplesBusinessHR_EN.pdf.

17. Jonathan Todres, "The Private Sector's Pivotal Role in Combating Human Trafficking," *California Law Review Circuit* 3 (2012): 80–98.

18. Mark Latonero, Bronwyn Wex, and Meredith Dank, "Technology and Labor Trafficking in a Network Society: General Overview, Emerging Innovations, and Philippines Case Study" (February 2015), https://communicationleadership.usc.edu/files/2015/09/USC_Tech-and-Labor-Trafficking_Feb2015.pdf.

19. Amanda Third, Delphine Bellerose, Urszula Dawkins, Emma Keltie, and Kari Pihl, "Children's Rights in the Digital Age: A Download from Children around the World" (September 2014), http://www.uws.edu.au/__data/assets/pdf_file/0003/753447/Childrens-rights-in-the-digital-age.pdf.

20. Jonathan Todres and Daniela Villamizar Fink, "The Trauma of Trump's Family Separation and Child Detention Actions: A Children's Rights Perspective," *Washington Law Review* 95 no. 1 (forthcoming March 2020).

21. Jonathan Todres, "The Trump Effect, Children, and the Value of Human Rights Education," *Family Court Review* 56, no. 2 (2018): 331–343.

22. Todres, "Trump Effect."

23. For relevant reports and research see the Intergovernmental Panel on Climate Change (IPCC) website, https://www.ipcc.ch (accessed Sept. 9, 2019).

INDEX

....

Note: Figures and boxes are indicated by an italic "*f*" and "*b*", respectively, following the page number.